HUDSON'S

Historic Houses & Gardens

Castles and Heritage Sites

Broughton Castle, Oxfordshire

NORMAN HUDSON & COMPANY
High Wardington House, Upper Wardington,
Banbury, Oxfordshire OX17 1SP

Tel: 01295 750750 • Fax: 01295 750800
e-mail: enquiries@hudsons.co.uk
website: www.hudsons.co.uk

2000 EDITION

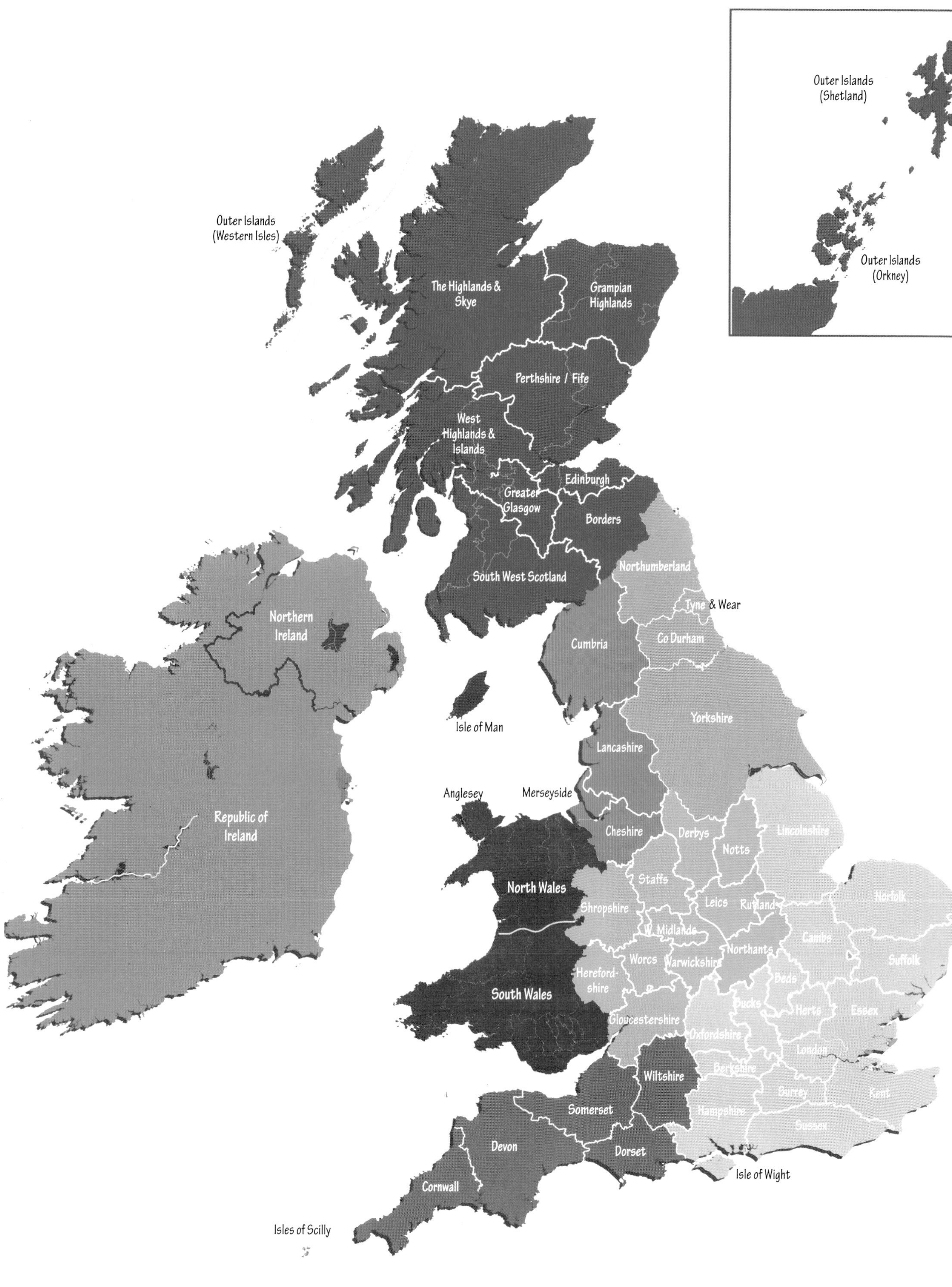

Outer Islands
(Shetland)
Outer Islands
(Orkney)
Outer Islands
(Western Isles)
The Highlands &
Skye
Grampian
Highlands
Perthshire / Fife
West
Highlands &
Islands
Edinburgh
Greater
Glasgow
Borders
South West Scotland
Northumberland
Tyne & Wear
Northern
Ireland
Cumbria
Co Durham
Isle of Man
Yorkshire
Lancashire
Anglesey
Merseyside
Republic of
Ireland
Cheshire
Derbys
Notts
Lincolnshire
North Wales
Staffs
Shropshire
Leics
Rutland
Norfolk
W. Midlands
Cambs
Worcs
Warwickshire
Northants
Suffolk
Hereford-
shire
Beds
South Wales
Bucks
Herts
Essex
Gloucestershire
Oxfordshire
London
Wiltshire
Berkshire
Surrey
Kent
Somerset
Hampshire
Sussex
Devon
Dorset
Isle of Wight
Cornwall
Isles of Scilly

Accommodation

These are not hotels, but historic properties in which accommodation can be arranged.
The standard ranges from basic comfort to ultimate luxury.

Castle Ashby

See page 35

Civil Weddings

Places with a marriage licence where the ceremony itself can take place. Many will also be able to provide facilities for receptions.

Bickleigh Castle

See page 37

Corporate Hospitality

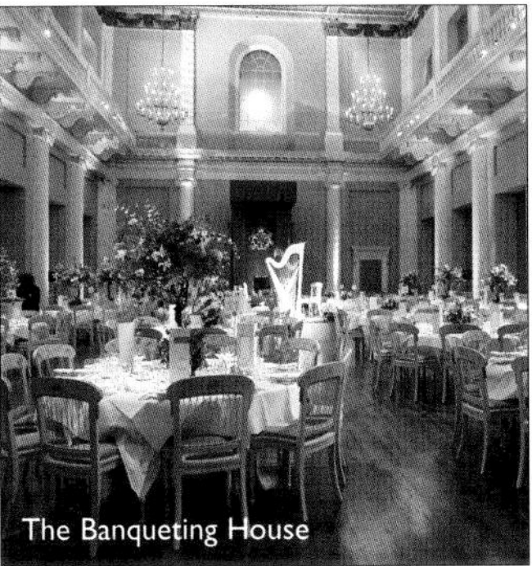
The Banqueting House

Properties which are able to accommodate corporate functions, wedding receptions and events. Individual entries will give greater detail.

See pages 38 & 39

Special Events

Don't miss our movie map on page 30

Special Events, historical re-enactments, gardening festivals, country and craft fairs, concerts and fireworks, car and steam rallies are now an established part of the summer season and throughout the year.

See pages 40 - 45

Websites

Many properties have their own website with more extensive information.
If you want to make life easy, without having to type in each address all you have to do is go to www.hudsons.co.uk and click on the direct link to any of these sites.

make your first stop

www.hudsons.co..uk

See pages 46 - 49

Plant Sales

Many historic properties and gardens offer collections of rare and unusual plants not generally available.

Hestercombe House Gardens

See page 51

Open All Year

Properties and/or their grounds included in this list are open all or most of the year.

Pollock House

National Trust for Scotland

See pages 52 - 55

English Heritage Grant Aided Properties

As well as managing and opening properties in its care, English Heritage has other equally important roles.

One of these is to provide grant aid to repair outstanding buildings. Grants are subject to appropriate public access being given.

This list, published here for the first time, gives details of those access arrangements. See pages 503 - 523

HUDSON'S

The year 2000 edition of *Hudson's*, the most comprehensive annual publication covering heritage property open to the public, is even more extensive than previous editions. It has more pages, more entries, and more illustrations.

New this year is a section devoted to the access arrangements to properties that have received repair grants from English Heritage. Some of these are open on a regular basis and therefore also feature in the main regional sections. But others (where, for conservation reasons, access has to be limited) can only be seen on a small number of days or by appointment.

In addition to being open to day visitors, ever more properties have special events or are available for functions and weddings. Not only is this indicated in individual entries, but for ease of reference is incorporated in special indexes in the front section.

In my experience most owners of historic properties are keen to maintain and improve on the quality of the experience afforded to visitors. That is why I am pleased to give coverage, within *Hudson's*, to the NPI National Heritage Awards. These are made on the basis of votes that **you** give. They reward owners and managers who have the satisfaction that their endeavours to provide an enjoyable visit have been recognised. Enjoy your visits to properties this year and don't forget to submit your vote for those that you have enjoyed most.

Norman Hudson

Editor .... Norman Hudson

Editorial/Production .... Edwina Brash

Consultant/Maps .... Patrick Lane

Administration .... Jennie Carwithen

Printed by .... Cooper Clegg, Tewkesbury

DTP & Maps .... Taurus Graphics

Graphic Design .... KC Graphics

Scanning & Pre-press .... Spot-On Reprographics

Sales .... Fiona Rolt

Distribution - UK & Europe: ... Portfolio, tel: 020 8579 7748

Cover picture:

The Topiary Walk, Parnham, Dorset © John Makepeace

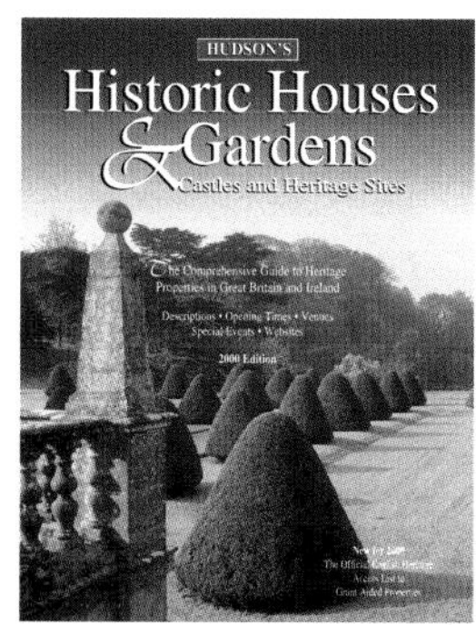

Published by: Norman Hudson & Company,
High Wardington House, Upper Wardington, Banbury,
Oxfordshire OX17 1SP

Tel: 01295 750750 **Fax:** 01295 750800
e-mail: enquiries@hudsons.co.uk **website:** http://www.hudsons.co.uk

ISBN: 0 9531426 4 7

Foreword

by the Rt Hon Chris Smith, MP
Secretary of State for Culture, Media and Sport

2-4 Cockspur Street, London SW1Y 5DH

It was a pleasure to be invited to provide the foreword for this, the Millennial edition of *Hudson's*. Britain's heritage and, in particular, its historic houses, gardens, castles and heritage sites, make a significant contribution to our tourism industry. Indeed, heritage and cultural attractions are often an important consideration when overseas visitors make the decision to visit Britain. These places are also a source of inspiration, education and delight for those of us who choose to explore and discover the many facets of interest they provide. *Hudson's* directory points the way to what there is to be seen and where, and it therefore represents a valuable contribution towards fulfilling one of my Department's key aims: providing greater access to our country's rich historic environment.

This edition has special significance at this time when we are looking to the future. This future must include the preservation of our great inheritance of historic buildings, their associated parks and gardens and especially the unparalleled associated collections which, in their quantity and quality, rival those in any part of the world. The National Trusts, English Heritage, Historic Scotland and Cadw have done a masterful job at both conserving buildings and presenting them for public view, but the majority of houses open to the public are still in private ownership. Private owners have proved to be the most cost-effective guardians of this part of our heritage. Moreover they keep it as a living heritage that continues to evolve. We can enjoy the innovation and individuality they bring to their castles, houses and gardens.

Historic houses have become part of more people's lives than ever before. We do more than visit them: we get married in them, we use them as venues for special occasions and the series of events at properties across the country have now become an established part of the British summer season. We frequently see them on television and at the cinema, for many provide locations for our most successful films. *Hudson's* gives information on all these aspects.

I am very pleased to support this valuable guide to industry and visitor alike.

CHRIS SMITH

The 1999 NPI National Heritage Awards

To recognise the hard work and dedication behind the scenes at properties throughout the country, retirement and pensions specialist NPI first introduced the NPI National Heritage Awards in 1995. Now, these prestigious Awards are gaining even more support from visitors, with voting numbers increasing each year.

Every visitor to a heritage property, and readers of BBC *Homes & Antiques* had the opportunity in 1999 to vote for a property, which in their opinion provided an enjoyable and informative day out. Voters are asked to judge on the presentation of the property, garden and grounds. In addition, they also vote on specific categories including: appeal for the whole family, the enthusiasm of the staff and the quality of the gift shops.

Uniquely these Awards really do endeavour to seek out the nation's favourite history property.

The 1999 NPI National Heritage Award winners

The 1999 Area Winners are featured below. All are nominees for the prestigious:-

Gold Award for the Best Overall Property

and for the other specialist awards

Best Property for Families • **Most Enthusiastic and Informative Staff** • **Best Gift Shop**

Results will be announced in the Spring of the year 2000, in the press, in BBC *Homes & Antiques* and on *Hudson's* Website: www.hudsons.co.uk

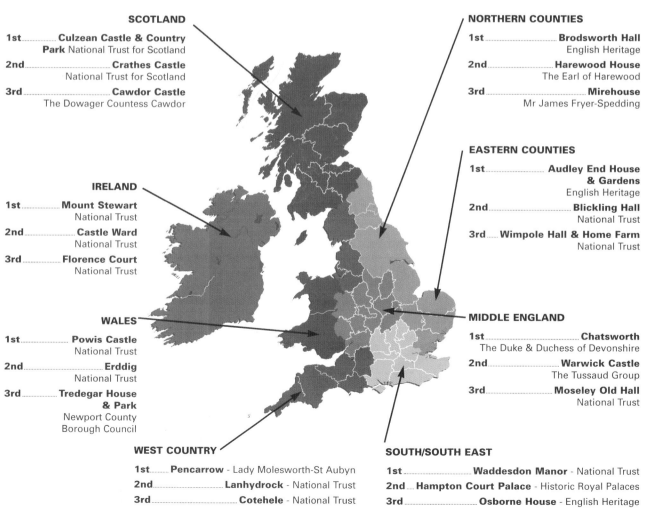

SCOTLAND

1st .... **Culzean Castle & Country Park** National Trust for Scotland

2nd .... **Crathes Castle** National Trust for Scotland

3rd .... **Cawdor Castle** The Dowager Countess Cawdor

IRELAND

1st .... **Mount Stewart** National Trust

2nd .... **Castle Ward** National Trust

3rd .... **Florence Court** National Trust

WALES

1st .... **Powis Castle** National Trust

2nd .... **Erddig** National Trust

3rd .... **Tredegar House & Park** Newport County Borough Council

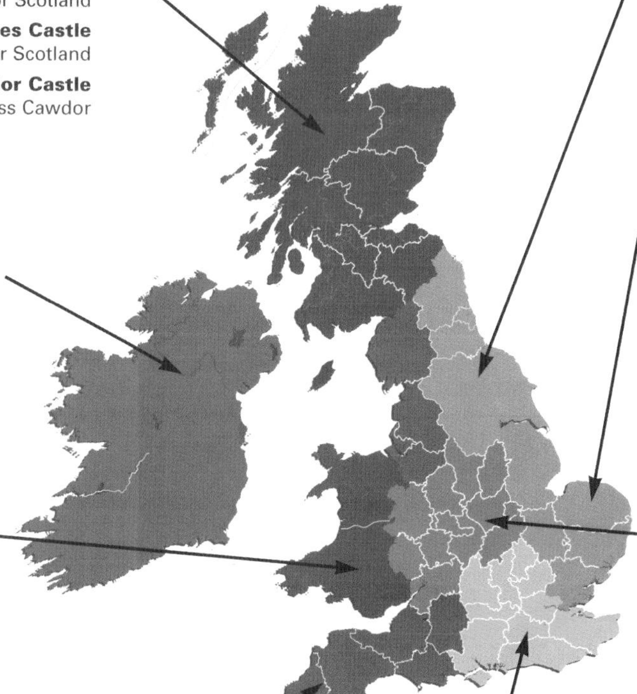

WEST COUNTRY

1st .... **Pencarrow** - Lady Molesworth-St Aubyn

2nd .... **Lanhydrock** - National Trust

3rd .... **Cotehele** - National Trust

NORTHERN COUNTIES

1st .... **Brodsworth Hall** English Heritage

2nd .... **Harewood House** The Earl of Harewood

3rd .... **Mirehouse** Mr James Fryer-Spedding

EASTERN COUNTIES

1st .... **Audley End House & Gardens** English Heritage

2nd .... **Blickling Hall** National Trust

3rd .... **Wimpole Hall & Home Farm** National Trust

MIDDLE ENGLAND

1st .... **Chatsworth** The Duke & Duchess of Devonshire

2nd .... **Warwick Castle** The Tussaud Group

3rd .... **Moseley Old Hall** National Trust

SOUTH/SOUTH EAST

1st .... **Waddesdon Manor** - National Trust

2nd .... **Hampton Court Palace** - Historic Royal Palaces

3rd .... **Osborne House** - English Heritage

1999 Area Winners

Scotland

Culzean Castle & Country Park ~ National Trust for Scotland

Robert Adam's 18th century masterpiece perched on a cliff high above the sea. Elegant interior with spectacular oval staircase. The grounds encompass Scotland's first country park. (for full details of this property see p415).

Ireland

Mount Stewart ~ National Trust

A most interesting 18th century house with 19th century additions. The garden, created largely in the 1920s, has an unrivalled collection of plants, colourful parterres and magnificent vistas (for full details of this property see p397).

Wales

Powis Castle ~ National Trust

A medieval castle with one of the finest collections of paintings and furniture in Wales. Italian and French influenced gardens with enormous clipped yews and colourful herbaceous borders (for full details of this property see p484).

West Country

Pencarrow ~ Lady Molesworth-St Aubyn

Still owned and lived-in by the family. Georgian house and listed gardens. Superb collection of pictures, furniture and porcelain. Marked walk through 50 acres of formal and woodland gardens. Victorian rockery, Italian garden, over 700 different varieties of rhododendrons, lake and ice house (for full details of this property see p182).

Northern Counties

Brodsworth Hall ~ English Heritage

A rare example of a Victorian country house that has survived largely unaltered, with much of its original furnishings and decorations intact. Set within beautifully restored Victorian gardens. (for full details of this property see p340).

Eastern Counties

Audley End House & Gardens ~ English Heritage

A palace in all but name. Over 30 rooms to see, each with period furnishings. The house and its gardens, including a 19th century parterre and rose garden, surrounded by an 18th century landscape park laid out by "Capability" Brown (for full details of this property see p231).

Middle England

Chatsworth ~ The Duke and Duchess of Devonshire

A great treasure house and winner of the 1st National Heritage Gold Award. An outstanding historic collection with contemporary works of art still being added. 105 acres of garden incorporating a 200 metre cascade and the tallest gravity-fed fountain in the world. One of the best shops at any historic property (for full details of this property see p258).

South/South East

Waddesdon Manor – National Trust

A French Renaissance-style chateau with a world-class collection, superbly presented. The 19th century garden is famous for its landscape of specimen trees and parterre. The gift shop and restaurant set a standard for others (for full details of this property see p70).

NPI National Heritage Awards
Roll of Honour

NPI is celebrating its 5th year of rewarding historic properties. With the new Millennium upon us and the launch of voting season for the 2000 NPI National Heritage Awards, it seems timely to record those properties that have previously received one of these prestigious Awards.

The Nation's Favourites

1995

Chatsworth	NPI Gold Award
Warwick Castle	NPI Family Award

Runners-up
Audley End
Blickling Hall
Bolsover Castle
Brodsworth Hall
Chartwell
Cotehele
Culzean Castle
Dover Castle
Forde Abbey
Fountains Abbey
Hampton Court Palace
Harewood House
Hever Castle
Stokesay Castle

Warwick Castle

Chatsworth

Arlington Court

1996

Arlington Court	NPI Gold Award
Beningbrough Hall	NPI Family Award
Lanhydrock	Merit

Runners-up
Beaulieu
Bolsover Castle
Brodie Castle
Brodsworth Hall
Castell Coch
Conwy Castle
Crathes Castle
Fountains Abbey & Studley Royal
Hampton Court Palace
Highclere Castle
Leeds Castle
Muncaster Castle
Osborne House
Quarry Bank & Styal
Speke Hall
Tintern Abbey
Uppark
Warwick Castle

Brodie Castle

1997

Brodsworth Hall	NPI Gold Award
Brodie Castle	NPI Family Award
Albert Memorial	Merit

Runners-up

Arlington Court
Audley End
Bolsover Castle
Caernarfon Castle
Caerphilly Castle
Castell Coch
Chatsworth
Hampton Court Palace
Levens Hall
Moseley Old Hall
Pencarrow
Waddesdon Manor

Moseley Old Hall

1998

Pencarrow	NPI Gold Award NPI Family Award NPI Staff Award
Moseley Old Hall	NPI Silver Award
Boscobel House	NPI Gift Shop Award NPI Bronze Award

Runners-up

Audley End
Brodie Castle
Brodsworth Hall
Mount Stewart
Powis Castle
Waddesdon Manor

Boscobel House

Hodnet Hall Gardens, Shropshire.

Cottesbrooke Hall Gardens, Northamptonshire.

"The HHA Friends scheme provides amazing value for the interested house and gardens visitor..."

Eyam Hall, Derbyshire.

The HHA is a group of highly individualistic and diverse properties most of which are still lived-in family houses. They range from the great palaces to small manor houses.

Many HHA member properties are open to the public and offer free admission to Friends of the HHA.

St Mary's, Bramber, Sussex.

Somerleyton Hall, Suffolk.

Prideaux Place, Cornwall.

Eastnor Castle, Herefordshire.

Broughton Castle, Oxfordshire.

Deene Park, Northamptonshire.

Dunvegan Castle, The Highlands & Skye.

Castle Howard, Yorkshire.

Bamburgh Castle, Northumberland.

Loseley Park, Surrey.

The Heritage Education Trust recognises quality education access with The Sandford Awards

The Sandford Awards for Heritage Education are made annually by the Heritage Education Trust. They recognise the provision of quality education in and about historic buildings, artefacts and landscapes. The Awards are non-competitive, recognising quality and excellence. There is no stipulation for entry on the size of the property, or the extent of the educational services provided.

Any historic property, artefact or historic landscape is eligible. As an illustration, previous Sandford Award winners include Holdenby House, Chester Cathedral, the Clipper Ship "Cutty Sark" and Wigan Pier.

Entry is, in the first place, by the completion of a pro forma application, which shows eligibility for qualification. A pair of judges will be allocated to visit, assess and report back to the main Judges' Panel, whose recommendations are passed to the Directors for their final decision. All properties receive a copy of their judges' report, which may include recommendations and advice.

On successfully achieving the status of a Sandford Award holder, properties are encouraged to use the Heritage Education Trust's logo in their educational and general publicity, to show schools and families that they have achieved this recognition and offer a quality, educational service.

Schools visiting historic properties, for whatever reason, must be able to justify on educational grounds the experience that the children will receive. Whilst many historic sites offer some degree of educational access, the Sandford Award for Heritage Education has become recognised as an industry standard for the independent assessment of the quality of service being offered.

To ensure that standards are maintained, all Sandford Award holding properties are invited to submit themselves for a reappraisal every five years. This Quinquennial Review is undertaken by a different set of judges than those who undertook the primary inspection and looks not only at the continuing adherence to the expected standard, but also to see what developments and evolution have taken place in the intervening time. Successful properties are then awarded a Quinquennial Review certificate and are continued to be listed as an award holder. They may use the Heritage Education Trust symbol to show this continuing quality.

1999 recipients of the Sandford Award for Heritage Education stretch from the Clyde Valley in Scotland to the Combes of Somerset; from the rugged tip of Pembroke to former industrial sites in Yorkshire; between is a range of historical settings which reflect the diversity of the wealth of heritage educational experiences available throughout Great Britain. The diversity is seen from Iron Age forts, through Viking sites, Roman remains, stately homes, former industrial sites, to a restored hospital workhouse; yet each gives children of all ages a unique insight into the heritage of this country and the opportunity to learn in a stimulating and practical way.

The Heritage Education Trust is an independent educational charity under the Chairmanship of the Countess of Dalkeith. It is supported by donations from charitable trusts, including the National Trust and commercial sponsorship.

The Heritage Education Trust is pleased to offer advice to potential applicants and provides a consultative service to all properties, as recommended by the Historic Houses Association.

The Trust can be contacted through:
Gareth Fitzpatrick
Chief Executive
The Heritage Education Trust
Boughton House
Kettering
Northamptonshire NN14 1BJ
(tel: 01536 515731)

A full list of past winners of the Sandford Awards is available on request.

THE CHURCHES CONSERVATION TRUST

Caring for historic churches no longer needed for regular worship

Christopher Dalton.

ST MICHAEL'S & ST MARTIN'S, EASTLEACH

If you think this church looks wonderfully inviting, why not make a trip to Gloucestershire to look round its mediaeval interior with its exquisite stone carving and attractive woodwork. Set beside the clear stream of the River Leach, its setting alone is an inspiration. But it is just *one* of the 317 churches in the care of The Churches Conservation Trust which repairs and preserves churches of outstanding architectural and historical interest when they are no longer needed for regular worship.

We try to keep the churches in our trust as accessible to visitors as possible with many usually open all year round – a selection of these are shown on the map on page 14. We have also attempted the impossible and singled out some 13 gems to describe and illustrate in more detail to give an idea of the range of glorious churches large and small in our care.

Entry to our churches is always free so why not explore our sometimes hidden but always fascinating heritage spanning the last thousand years?

Registered Charity no. 258612

Christopher Dalton.

ST PETROCK, PARRACOMBE, DEVON

John Ruskin saved this magical church from demolition in 1879. It is one of England's best examples of a humble mediaeval church with unrestored Georgian fittings which has retained the irregularity of the ages in its undulating floors and leaning arcade. Above a mediaeval wooden screen there is a painted wooden tympanum of 1758 and by its side a three-decker pulpit. Box pews rise at the west end where the band of musicians once sat. St Petrock's has an unaffected simplicity and charm.

11m NE of Barnstaple off A39, SS675 449.

Christopher Dalton.

ST CUTHBERT, HOLME LACY, HEREFORDSHIRE

The two major restorations, one in the 17th and the other during the 19th century, have added much of interest and beauty to this 13th century church, the burial place of the Scudamore family. Among their monuments are two alabaster effigies of the 16th century and one which has been attributed to Grinling Gibbons. There is much else to see and enjoy, a rare series of hatchments, a 17th century font, carved with garlands and cherubs and an extraordinary east window of the 20th century depicting St Michael weighing the souls.

5m SE of Hereford off B4399, SO569 348

ST PETER & ST PAUL OLD CHURCH, ALBURY, SURREY

The church stands in a beautiful parkland in one of the most attractive stretches of the Tillingbourne valley. Its tower is Saxon with a curious shingled dome added in the 18th century. Inside wonderfully light and airy, there is a 15th century wall painting of a doe-eyed St Christopher and a 14th century brass of a military figure. The 13th century south transept was remodelled by Augustus Welby Pugin in the 19th century. Using the best craftsmen of his time he created a magnificently opulent work, the ceiling, floor, walls, windows ablaze with colour. There are interesting tombs in the churchyard which, in January, is a carpet of many different varieties of snowdrops.

5m SE of Guildford off A248, TQ063 479

ST NICHOLAS, OZLEWORTH, GLOUCESTERSHIRE

The church stands in an ancient circular churchyard spectacularly approached down a remote valley. Its centrally placed irregular hexagonal tower of 1110-1120 is an unusual survival in this position. Succeeding generations have introduced many changes but none more remarkable than the elaborately carved arch into the nave. The arch is decorated with an intricate and exuberant pattern of chevrons and a rope motif unique in this country, testimony to the imagination and skills of its 13th century carver.

2m E of Wotton-under-Edge, ST794 933

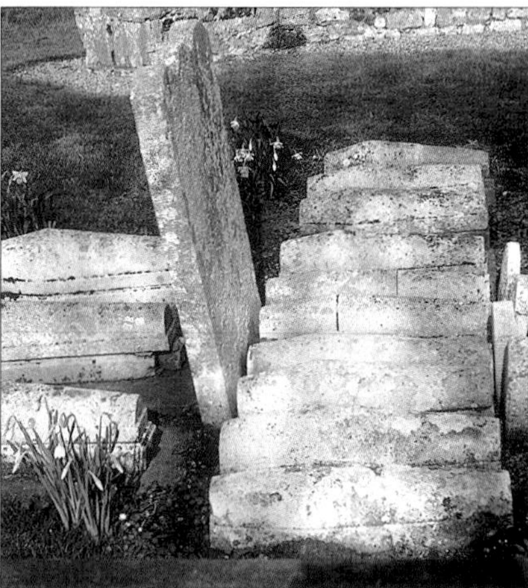

ST JAMES, COOLING, KENT

Situated on the edge of the marshes and eerily impressive on a cold winter's day it is said that the 10 bodystones of the Comport children suggested to Charles Dickens the opening pages of "Great Expectations" when Pip is surprised by the convict, Magwich. Inside the 13th and 14th century church is a striking and richly carved series of arches, sedilia and piscina. The 19th century vestry may well be unique, with its ceiling and walls covered with cockle shells, the symbol of St James.

6m N of Rochester off B2000, TQ756 759

ST LAWRENCE, SNARFORD, LINCOLNSHIRE

From outside there is nothing in this tiny remote church to suggest the magnificence of the mausoleum within. Their mansion long since gone, the greatness of the Rich and Saintpaule families are recorded in sepulchral splendour. Frances, Lady Rich, appears in two monuments, first recumbent with her husband Sir George Saintpaule and again in a beautiful and poignant double portrait with Robert, Lord Rich, Earl of Warwick, a work by one of the outstanding sculptors of the early 17th century, Epiphanius Evesham. A three tier monument to earlier Saintpaules dominates the sanctuary with its enchanting figures of cherubic praying children.

6m SW of Market Rasen off A46, TF051 825

ST MICHAEL THE ARCHANGEL, BOOTON, NORFOLK

One of the most extravagant, idiosyncratic and eccentric churches in the country, Booton was designed in 1890 by its Rector, the Reverend Whitwell Elwin to console himself after the death of three of his children. His genius was to take accurate copies of mediaeval features and arrange them in the most extraordinary, daring relationships. The crazy twin west towers are undaunted by their mediaeval neighbours at Salle and Cawston. The interior fittings are contemporary with huge, outstretched angels supporting the roof and shimmering angel musicians in the stained glass. A unique building, it is the product of one man's imagination. Lutyens' verdict was "very naughty but in the right spirit".

12m NW of Norwich and W of B1149, TG123 224

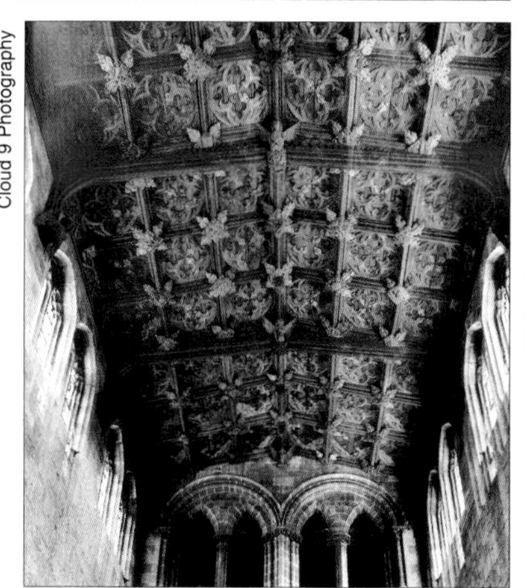

Cloud 9 Photography

ST MARY, SHREWSBURY, SHROPSHIRE

Described as the cathedral of the Trust, St Mary's spire soars to a height of 222 feet. The architecture has representative examples from the 12th-19th centuries and is as inspirational as the fittings. Not least is the Transitional north arcade with graceful piers and excellent carved capitals. St Mary's is rightly famed for its collection of stained glass, the best in a parish church in this country. There are 16th century Flemish roundels and, most lovely of all, the great Jesse east window of the 15th century. Other delights include a monument to Admiral Benbow, and the 15th century carved nave roof.

Central Shrewsbury, SJ494 126

ST JAMES, CAMELEY, SOMERSET

One of the most enchanting of Trust churches, John Betjeman called St James "Rip Van Winkle's church". An unassuming exterior conceals a sturdy Norman chancel arch and a marvellous collection of fittings, mediaeval benches, 17th and 18th century box pews, pulpit and reading desk, rows of hatpegs, a musicians' gallery at the west end and a laudian altar table, all excellent examples of their craftsmen's art. The walls are covered with layers of paintings, fragments from each century from 12th-17th. Close to the pulpit a jester is depicted. All combine to make this an unforgettable interior.

10m NE of Wells off A37, ST610 576

ST JOHN THE BAPTIST, INGLESHAM, WILTSHIRE

Saved from Victorian restoration by William Morris when he lived nearby at Kelmscott, the church has as unspoilt and mellow an interior as any in England. This is a building which takes time to reveal its gentle harmonies and singular beauty. Of the Saxon period, quoins and a powerful sculpture of the Virgin and Child survive. A Norman tympanum shelters the south doorway and inside are finely carved arcades, 15th century painted wooden screens, box pews and pulpit, uneven stone floors and, adding to the mystery and beauty, layer upon layer of wall paintings from the 13th-19th centuries, eloquent in their incompleteness.

1m S of Lechlade off A361, SU205 984

Christopher Dalton.

ST MICHAEL'S AND ST MARTIN'S, EASTLEACH, GLOUCESTERSHIRE

The twin churches at Eastleach, separated only by their river, have always been two distinct parishes held by different lords of the manor. St Michael's, illustrated at the head of this article, is a happy stone building roofed with local slates dating from the 12th century. Especially fine are the Decorated windows of the transept and Perpendicular window of the tower. In this quiet and untroubled village, John Keble, author of many hymns and a giant in the history of the Church of England in the 19th century, served his first curacy.

4m N of Lechlade off A361, SP202 052

ALL SAINTS, ICKLINGHAM, SUFFOLK

A charming thatched church on a Roman site, All Saints is one of the few Suffolk churches to have escaped restoration. Norman in origin, the building now appears to date from the 13th and 14th centuries. An intensely atmospheric and light church, the elegant architecture of the south arcade and canopied niches are complemented by a wealth of early fittings: mediaeval benches, a Jacobean pulpit, 14th century stained glass and, in the chancel, a rare collection of mediaeval floor tiles, each different in shape, colour and design.

8m NW of Bury St Edmunds on A1101, TL770 730

Mr Glen Wilson.

HOLY TRINITY, GOODRAMGATE, YORK

Mostly 15th century work, the outside is a delicious mixture of colours and textures, the interior an unrestored gem. Early 18th century rails protect the communion table and a sea of box pews swells around the 17th century pulpit. Of outstanding quality is the stained glass. That in the east window, which was given in 1471 by the Rector, includes a rare depiction of the Trinity with the Holy Ghost in bodily form.

Goodramgate, Central York, SE605 522

Christopher Dalton.

CHURCHES IN THE CARE OF THE CHURCHES CONSERVATION TRUST

Churches marked on the map are always open*. However, there are many other wonderful churches in the care of The Churches Conservation Trust, some of which have limited opening, and others of which can be visited by getting the key from a nearby keyholder. Complete the coupon (or send us the equivalent information) below for more information.

*At the time of publication, all churches on this map are open throughout the year, but emergency building work may mean that we need to close a church temporarily for safety reasons.

Complete and send to The Churches Conservation Trust, 89 Fleet Street, London, EC4Y 1DH

Name .... Title ....

Address .... Postcode ....

Please send me the following county leaflets (please specify)

....

Please send me *An Inspiration of Churches* (brochure describing 40 churches countrywide) ☐

HHH

ELTHAM PALACE

An Odyssey of Re-discovery

by Mr Treve Rosoman, Curator

The Entrance Hall

For those who work with historic houses, an ultimate dream would be the opportunity to open an important house for the first time; an emotion heightened when the house in question is almost unknown to the general public

Imagine my delight when such an opportunity arose with Eltham Palace in south east London. The secluded, moated site has been occupied continuously for over 800 years, but until 16th June 1999 has been a virtual secret, even to local people. The building has an illustrious medieval past for which there is insufficient space to detail now: suffice to say that the only roofed building to survive was a Great Hall, c1475, spanned by England. To this Hall was built on, in 1935, a country house with a stunning collection of art – including paintings by Turner and other old masters, fine antique carpets, continental ceramics, rare books etc – but a house fitted with the latest labour-saving devices and fashionable interiors. The commissioners of the new addition, Stephen and Virginia Courtauld, only lived in the house for 8 years; it was then almost stripped of its contents and Army Education Corps. In 1992 the officers moved out, leaving behind an empty but well-cared for building. What the Palace looked like in its '30s hey-day became a memory in black and white derived from a series of interior photographs from *Country Life* and an Inventory of 1939.

The chance to 're-create' such a stunning interior was a 'lottery win' – a curator's dream.

In 1995 English Heritage took on the

English Heritage Photographic Library / Jonathan Bailey

View across the South Bridge and Dry Moat.

and its gardens. It was decided to open the house to the public as an unrivalled example of an inter-war period house, built at a time when many country houses were being pulled down due, in part, to the economic depression after the 1914-18 War. Despite the fact that most of the original contents had gone, the interiors were so well recorded that the decision was taken to make replicas of the principal furnishings. Thus began a voyage of recovery and discovery. From the existing black and white photographs it was known what the furniture looked like but the most important, and ephemeral, aspect was missing: what colours were used; how colourful were the interiors?

Stephen Courtauld, the youngest scion of the Courtauld textile family, and his wife, a half-Italian, half-Hungarian divorced Countess, Virginia Peirano, often called Ginie, were a striking couple. They were married in 1923, having met while Stephen was touring the Italian Alps in 1919, as part of his recuperation from the War. They lived in 47 Grosvenor Square [now demolished] with Ginie's two nephews (who came in 1926 to live with the childless couple) and their pets, the chief of which was a ring-tailed lemur called Mah-Jongg. In 1933 the Courtaulds had to give up the Grosvenor Square house, as the Grosvenor Estate wished to re-develop the site, and they started to look for somewhere close to London but with space to create a garden. They heard of the largely ruined medieval Palace at Eltham and a deal was struck with the Crown Commissioners whereby some early 19th century buildings could be demolished and the magnificent Great Hall restored in return for being allowed to build a new house and developing the grounds. The architects were two young men starting out on their careers but socially well connected; John Seeley, son of Lord Mottistone and Paul Paget, son of the then Bishop of Chester. The principal interior designer was the Marchese Peter Malacrida, a personal friend and close neighbour of the Courtaulds in Grosvenor Square. He had decorated many interiors in and around Mayfair and had worked on at least two houses for Stephen Courtauld's brothers, Sam, founder of the Courtauld Institute, and Jack, an MP and businessman. Malacrida was, at the time, working for White Allom & Co (now Holloway White Allom) who were and still are, major interior decoration contractors. Malacrida, a name almost completely forgotten today, was well known in the '20s for his Florentine-inspired Renaissance interiors; but the interiors that he decorated elsewhere in Britain have mostly disappeared either through war damage or subsequent post-war redevelopment. Christopher Hussey, a well-known contemporary writer on design and architecture, wrote a major article on Eltham for *Country Life* in May 1937. The accompanying photographs were taken a year earlier, soon after the Courtaulds moved into the newly finished house. The article is full of names of artists/craftsmen who worked at Eltham but are virtually unknown today: the lacquer doors were by Narini, the leather needlework map by Mrs Classen Smith, the lemur cage mural by Miss G E Whinfield; and there are sculptures by makers whose works are famous if not their names – such as Charles Sargeant Jagger known for the Royal Artillery Monument, Hyde Park Corner and Gilbert Ledward, better known for The Fountain, Sloane Square, Chelsea. Possibly the one 'name' still known today was the textile designer Marion Dorn. She designed the round carpet in the Entrance Hall but, again, people are more likely to know her products than her name – she designed many of London Transport's check fabrics used for tube and bus seats. Yet another shadowy figure was the artist Winifred Knights Monnington who appears to have been an artistic adviser to the Courtaulds, but exactly what she did is still unclear. However two of her rare, finished oil paintings hung in Virginia's Boudoir. Of all the designers involved in building Eltham only one left any quantity of surviving drawings. He was the Swede Rolf Engströmer, who designed the domed Entrance Hall and all its furniture. Hussey wrote that he considered the room to be the first Swedish interior in England; a significant predecessor of a style that became so popular after the 1939-45 War. Engströmer's designs of furniture, plans for their layout and a water-colour elevation survive in the collections of the Swedish Architectural Museum, Stockholm.

Together these people created an extraordinary home for the Courtaulds and their nephews.

Fortunately an Inventory has survived, drawn up in December 1939 for possible claims as a result of War damage, along with a *Country Life* article and photographs. The principal task, therefore, for English Heritage in presenting the house lay in carrying out a thorough research project into the history and development of the house, a process undertaken by my colleague Dr Michael Turner, supported by a team of skilled consultants. Patrick Baty for paint colours, Mary Schoeser for textiles and David Luckham for carpets. A key aspect was in establishing a true and believable colour palette for the interiors. Shades of colour are as much subject to fashion as anything else so this was both vitally important and hard to establish and it was in this area that the use of genuine pre-war colour charts and colour illustrations in books such as *Colour Schemes for the Modern Home* by Derek Patmore, 1936, were useful. Paint analysis was used to determine the colours of the metal windows – a dark green – and all the interior walls and ceilings. Some walls, such as in the Italian Drawing Room and part of Virginia's Bedroom had quite complex stippled paint finishes. The stair-case walls and Great Hall Corridor were painted in imitation of the exterior dressed stone walls with a patent mix called Stic B, a precursor of modern Sandtex-type finish. As the imitation stone jointing remained, as well as the gritty texture, it was decided just to match the colour.

After the paint colours, the fabrics and carpets are most important in creating a feeling of 'period'. By good fortune the great round rug by Marion Dorn, the centrepiece of the Entrance Hall, survives today. Left behind by the Courtaulds in 1944 the Army had used it until 1970 when replacement was long overdue. With immense foresight, the Army realised that it was worth saving and gave it to the Victoria & Albert Museum where the 19ft diameter carpet is now in store. English Heritage was allowed to examine the carpet a number of times for colour and construction. Fortunately the last hand-knotting manufacturer in western Europe, Donegal Carpets in Eire, was still in business, and able to create a replica carpet. The fawns, browns and buffs of the original carpet were integral to establishing the colour palette used elsewhere in the house, notably the plain carpets of the stair-cases, landings and adjoining corridors and the large seamless carpet in the Dining Room.

It was known from the Inventory that silk sun curtains hung in most south facing rooms but the colour was not stated. From various contemporary sources it was decided to use a yellow silk, and this was duly purchased. Some months later a 1938 painting of Eltham Palace by Ethelbert White was acquired and quite clearly shows yellow sun curtains, proving our choice of yellow to have been correct. The fabric used was from the range produced by Mulberry Home. Our consultant Mary Schoeser knew that Mulberry made a number of fabrics that had the right feel and colour for the period.

The paint and textiles established, next came the furniture. The Inventory underlined its importance by stating clearly the type of woods used, for example bird's-eye maple, crossbanded with walnut and ebony on the dining table; sizes were also given. It is not easy to make copies of 3-dimensional furniture from flat photographs, however two differing views of the Dining Room and its 14 chairs gave a number of varying angles to recreate the design. The table took up much discussion time in trying to work out how it extended and the leaves fitted. Neil Stevenson and his team at N E J Stevenson Ltd carefully worked out the complex shapes of the chair legs and the table construction.

The house has many original features that we take for granted today but were rare in 1935: all electric power for lighting, cooking and supplementary heating, electric clocks in all rooms, recessed lighting, underfloor lighting, spot-lights for paintings. A sound system with speakers in each room on the ground floor – the Servants' Hall had a very early example of a radio-gram. There was a central vacuum system, and a complex internal telephone exchange. This interest in new technology spread to the decorative

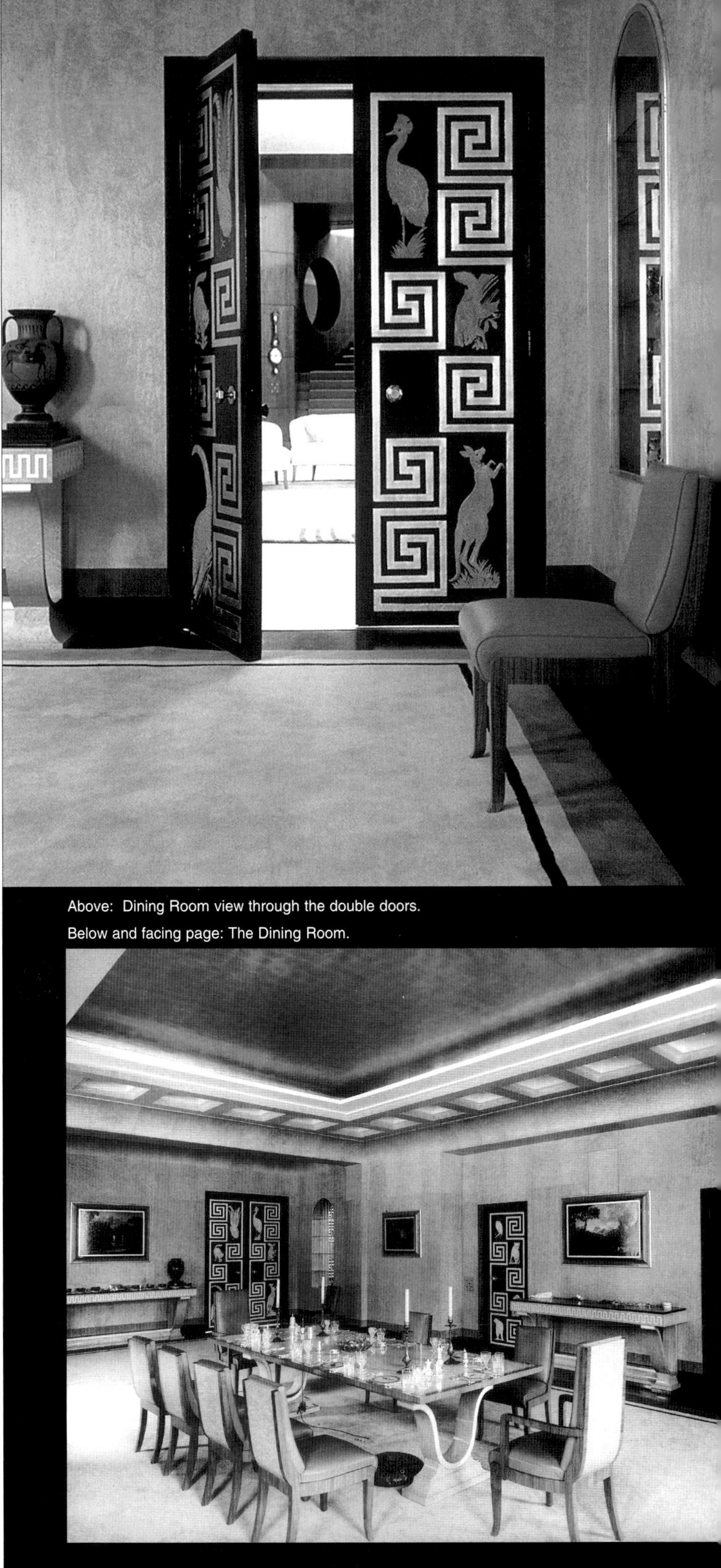

Above: Dining Room view through the double doors.

Below and facing page: The Dining Room.

surfaces as well: for example the Dining Room walls were covered in bird's-eye maple Flexwood; this was an extremely thin veneer of wood glued to an equally thin linen backing and was hung like wallpaper. This material had been removed some time in the past and presented an enormous potential problem in re-creation. By good fortune the American company is still in existence and they have an office in North London, enabling us to recreate the original 'look'.

One of the final details in completing the house but probably the most challenging was associated closely with the personality of Stephen Courtauld himself. Stephen Courtauld was of the generation that fought in the Great War. He joined up with the Artists' Rifles in October 1914 and was out in France by December that year. He was commissioned as a 'temporary gentleman', as volunteer officers were then called, into the Worcestershire Regiment and transferred into the Machine Gun Corps. He finished the War as a Major and was awarded the Military Cross in 1918, having been twice Mentioned in Despatches.

Although he had survived the War Stephen is often described as taciturn, indeed his friend the film producer Michael Balcon said of him that "He never used two words where one would do.". This may well have been, in part, a result of the War. What was certain was that in 1924 he commissioned a two foot high bronze statue of a sentry wearing a cape over his uniform, waterproof leggings and holding a bayoneted rifle. The sculptor was Charles Sargeant Jagger, an artist well known to Stephen. It is quite possible that they had met during the War for they both joined the Artists' Rifles and were commissioned into the Worcestershire Regiment, although different battalions. Another point of contact was that Jagger was a pre-war Rome Scholar and Stephen was a benefactor of the British School in Rome after the War. This stark, uncompromising bronze stood in a niche above the fireplace, directly opposite the desk in his Study. Every time he sat in his desk he could not fail to be reminded of the War.

It was not unusual for rooms to be left as memorials to sons killed on active service, for example Lanhydrock, Cornwall, or the chapel below Castle Drogo where the original wooden grave marker to the eldest Drewe is kept. But this statue at Eltham appears to be the only war memorial in a domestic setting where no close relative had died. Called *The Sentry* it is a smaller variant of an original monument by Jagger to the factory worker from Watts Warehouse, Manchester [now the Britannia Hotel]. This bronze was not included in the *Country Life* photograph of the study and neither was it mentioned in the article. The figure is recorded, but not prominently, in the Inventory and one is rather forced to conclude

Bronze cast copy of *The Sentry* by Charles Sargeant Jagger, replicated by English Heritage.

that this was a very personal memorial, made at a time when very few men spoke about their experiences in the trenches or elsewhere. So important was this bronze considered to be to the social history of the house that the family allowed us to make a copy so that today Stephen's Study is once more dominated by this lone Sentry flanked by copies of the Turner water-colours that Stephen also collected.

Eltham is a truly special house and garden; one of only a small handful of inter-war houses. It is always a privilege to work on something special and this has been the briefest of surveys, revealing some particular highlights on the path of rediscovering a rather different, and not very distant time in history.

WORDSWORTH'S LAKE DISTRICT

Derwentwater and Skiddaw — *Photo: National Trust Photographic Library/Joe Cornish*

"Here the rainbow comes - the cloud - And mists that spread the flying shroud..."

WORDSWORTH HOUSE

Cockermouth

Birthplace of William Wordsworth in 1770

Open April to October, Monday to Friday and selected Saturdays. Closed remaining Saturdays and all Sundays. Vegetarian Restaurant. Shop. Events during season. Parking in town centre car parks. National Trust.

TEL: 01900 824805

DOVE COTTAGE

Grasmere

Dove Cottage & Wordsworth Museum, Grasmere

Open Daily 9.30 to 5.30pm.
Closed 24th - 26th December

Parking next to Dove Cottage Tearoom & Restaurant immediately south of Grasmere village.

TEL: 015394 35544/35547

RYDAL MOUNT

Near Ambleside

Rydal Mount Home of William Wordsworth from 1813 - 1850

Open:
Summer: Mar - Oct 9.30 - 5.00pm
Winter: Nov - Feb 10.00 - 4.00pm

(Closed Tuesdays in Winter)

FREE PARKING

TEL: 015394 33002

RECIPROCAL DISCOUNT OFFER - DETAILS FROM ANY OF THE ABOVE ATTRACTIONS

29 Thurloe Street, London SW7 2LQ

Telephone: 020 7584 6072 Fax: 020 7225 0607

CHAIRMAN
Sir Hugh Rossi

DIRECTOR
Dr Jennifer M Freeman

The Historic Chapels Trust has been established to take into ownership redundant chapels and other places of worship in England of outstanding architectural and historic interest. Our object is to secure for public benefit the preservation, repair and maintenance of our buildings including their contents, burial grounds and curtilages.

The trust now has eleven chapels in its care which can be visited on application to the keyholder:-

Biddlestone RC Chapel, Northumberland	**01665 574420**
Coanwood Friends Meeting House, Northumberland	**01434 320256**
Cote Baptist Chapel, Oxfordshire	**01993 850421**
Farfield Friends Meeting House, West Yorkshire	**01756 710225**
The Dissenters' Chapel, Kensal Green Cemetery, London	**020 7402 2749**
Salem Chapel, East Budleigh, Devon	**01395 445236**
St Benet's Chapel and Presbytery, Netherton, Merseyside	**0151 520 2600**
St George's German Lutheran Church, Tower Hamlets, London	**020 8302 3437**
Todmorden Unitarian Church, West Yorkshire	**01706 815648**
Wallasey Unitarian Church, Merseyside	**0151 639 5137**
Walpole Old Chapel, Suffolk	**01986 798308**

For further information please ring the Director at the office address.

Walpole Old Chapel
Suffolk

Dissenters' Chapel
Kensal Green Cemetery

Farfield Friends Meeting House
West Yorkshire

Can we afford Conservation?

by Jenny Band MVO

Head of the Textile Conservation Studio for the Historic Royal Palaces

King William III's Bed

Hampton Court Palace, Windsor Castle and Uppark, rising like phoenixes from the ashes, have caused public and media interest in conservation to take off. However, ironically, at the same time conservation jobs in museums and other organisations are being cut at an alarming rate.

Conservation seems to be regarded with particular suspicion by accountants. They apparently perceive it as purely an outgoing rather than an investment. It is logical, of course, that people should be wary. After all, anyone considering having a possession conserved will naturally have attributed some value to it, monetary or otherwise. The request, therefore, to part with a significant sum for what can often be invisible work on it is, quite rightly, one to challenge.

Why conserve?

Many analogies have been drawn between conservation and medicine. Both rely on the identification and removal of the cause of damage, observation of symptoms and monitoring changes, on examination by a specialist, on diagnosis, possibly a biopsy and eventually a treatment. In both cases, the earlier a problem is dealt with, the more successful and less drastic (and less expensive) the treatment. And in both instances the specialist is mediating between the very complex processes of organic chemistry and the inevitable ravages of time. The choices of options are governed by different pressures but the rescue procedures are very similar. Yet the complexity and skill involved in conservation is rarely recognised and even its principal aims are often misunderstood.

Conservation is about continuity. Continuity underpins culture. It actively maintains the bridge between past and future by preserving those elements of high quality or significance from our present or our past that we deem valuable for our successors. Unfortunately, conservation does not slot tidily into the short-term perception which has characterised management and accountancy in the 1990s. Funding for preventative conservation has fallen away dramatically over the past decade, creating instead a need for urgent high cost conservation or the risk of complete loss. This cannot be an intentional policy. Aren't we killing the goose that lays the golden egg?

It would be unfair to imply that all conservators are eccentrics, but they often have unique and specialist skills learned through a passionate and long standing involvement in their subject. Expertise of this type however, does not carry the same cachet as that of the economist, financier or information technology buff (although many conservators use computers in their work). But economists occupy the highly paid positions in heritage organisations, museums and the management structures of historic houses, and make the decisions. The lone curators and conservators whose expertise effectively creates and sustains the 'product' are often regarded as either academic or dilettante working for the bliss of it in dusty old ivory towers, their heads swathed in clouds.

Whilst it is hardly shameful to enjoy one's work, this supposed state of financial oblivion couldn't be further from the truth. Historians and conservators usually work from primary evidence; either records, old bills and accounts or from physical evidence in the objects themselves, to build a truer picture of our past. In the furnishings of Hampton Court Palace, where the Textile Conservation Studio is based, it is abundantly clear where the original budgetary constraints lay when the details of fine finishing, exact matching and best fabric gave way to faster cruder work to save time and money wherever they would not be seen by the monarch or his court. We see it too in buildings where economies were made on materials. Lisa Jardine, in her book 'Worldly Goods' cites a catalogue of Renaissance masterpieces produced under the most constrictive contractual terms.

Rarely, it seems, is the return on an investment in conservation ever weighed up. Rarely, in fact, is conservation even regarded as an investment. Yet, properly planned, investment in conservation can bring a return that no insurance policy, gambling on the possibility of accident or damage, could ever guarantee. Conservation actively prevents the damage. Our forebears had even quantified the risk and knew that a stitch in time saved nine.

After all, conservation is about preserving the long term value of objects or buildings. Value can take many forms, cultural, aesthetic and financial, all of which can be conserved. Add into the cost–benefit equation savings on future maintenance, or on higher conservation costs if the object continues to deteriorate and even the bonus of an accrued rarity value as other peoples' (unconserved) objects bite the dust. The value of conservation is obvious in the long term.

Does conservation cost an arm and a leg?

Funding for conservation has been so lean in recent years that several large organisations have carried out surveys of their collections to assess the real extent of conservation they need. In every case the amount of conservation needed right now far exceeds what is achievable even in the medium term, and the organisations have had to face the hard reality of losing parts of their collection for ever. In this sense not conserving the collections has cost them many arms and legs.

The challenges of the ever increasing fragility of our cultural heritage also mean that the skills of those caring for it need to be continually refined. Country houses used to rely on the services of restorers who were often local artisans brought in to patch up, replace and make good. Their skills were quaint and their prices affordable. But restoration has largely passed out of favour now because it tended to remove weakened original features in order to replace them with serviceable replicas producing the cumulative effect of the famous axe which despite having a new handle and a new head was still the 'same old original axe'. Restoration serves a purpose for items where the decision is to use them now rather than to preserve them for the future. If the real aim is to preserve the object for future generations, the scientifically based ethos and the skills of conservation are essential. The fact the rest of Europe refers to its conservators as restorers, only adds to this confusion.

How can a good conservator be found?

Organisations now require transparent and accountable methods of quality assurance for conservation. The introduction of the Conservation Register by the MGS and SCB marked the start of a process whereby the professional bodies acting for conservation have worked to establish a common standard for professional practice. In future the achievement, through formal assessment, of this standard will be recognised by the title Accredited Conservator Restorer (ACR). Lists of accredited conservators will be available from such professional bodies as the UKIC (address at the end of this article).

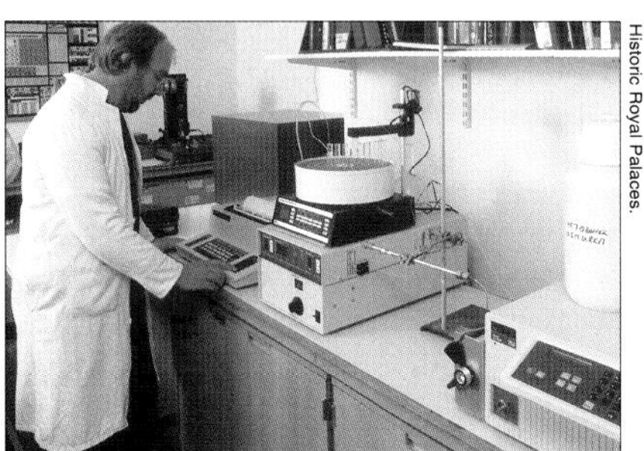

Historic Royal Palaces.

Historic Royal Palaces.

The Tapestry Conservation Section.

Historic Royal Palaces.

David Howell, Conservation Scientist in the Textile Conservation Studios.

Despite the apparent public interest in conservation, many people every year fall foul of the charlatans. The media do not help. In responding to the public appetite for information on the subject, they increasingly dish out half baked DIY tips on repairing antiques with ingenious cocktails such as brown sauce, PVA and boot polish, under the banner of conservation. While such imaginative recipes can undoubtedly produce very interesting effects, the potions are often potentially lethal to the object. Just as it is inadvisable to try out surgery at home (despite having seen the operation done on TV), conservation is best left to those trained to understand the risks and complexities of treating material whose original qualities have undergone many chemical and physical changes through the ravages of use, pollutants and time. Just as conservation is about continuity, deterioration is about change and the relationship is a dynamic one; physics and chemistry playing a key role.

Sadly for the conservator, the high point of success is often that the subtlety of their work makes it only recognisable to a trained eye. It is inordinately difficult to market and sell an invisible product and neither party wants to find themselves cheated. For this reason it is important that conservation is better understood and that red herrings become more obvious to all.

The processes of conservation range from the preventive (or 'passive') to the extremely specialist lab or studio-based treatments. Much practical conservation work can be achieved by good housekeeping. Trained conservators are often employed as housekeepers in historic houses because the risk of damaging a collection through inappropriate or inefficient action makes this a sensible measure.

What conservation do historic houses need?

Most collections have programmes to ensure that the climate in areas containing sensitive objects is monitored and maintained at as stable a level as possible, that dust is kept under control, that strong daylight is kept off sensitive objects which could fade, that heat and humidity levels in the rooms are controlled and that the rooms are kept free of insect pests. Conservation housekeepers are usually responsible for handling the furniture and objects, since handling is one of the primary risks. Conservators will also be involved where new displays are being designed. They set the standards for lighting, protection and many aspects of putting objects safely on display, working usually with curators, designers, architects and others.

Conservators are specialists and usually work in one or more main types of materials, such as metals, stone, textiles, gilding, glass, paper, paintings, frescoes, scrolls, ceramic, furniture and so on. If a piece demands knowledge of several materials the conservator who doesn't have that specialisation will often call on the expertise of a colleague in that discipline.

Historic Royal Palaces.

The Conservation Wash Facilities.

What is good conservation practice?

Whatever the discipline, conservation will involve close examination, documentation and assessment of the condition of the piece and the causes of its damage. Tests will probably be carried out. A method or options will be proposed by which the chemical and physical condition of the object can be stabilised. The proposed treatment will address the future demands on or requirements for the piece and will advise on its future care. A clear guide to the costs will be given and a record of all treatment is usually presented to the client on completion of the work, usually with good photographs for future reference. The conservator should be able to explain the rationale behind the treatment clearly and ensure that the client knows exactly what to expect from conservation.

Conservation aims to preserve extant original material, sometimes involving the removal of old repairs but missing parts will rarely be replaced unless there is a strong case to do so. The object will not look brand new but it will be well preserved for the future in its present condition. Conservation cleaning may produce a visual improvement but equally, if the object is not dirty, cleaning may be carried out only as a means of chemically removing accumulated acid products and producing a more neutral pH to slow the rate of deterioration.

The specially designed wash table at the Textile Conservation Studios, Hampton Court Palace (illustrated) has also been designed to minimise handling of large textiles when wet and at their most vulnerable. The table maximises the efficiency of the detergent's own chemical actions to preserve the textile's remaining strength and minimise its rate of decay. Faded dyes and pigments cannot be revivified despite what some dealers may say. However, the conservator will do whatever is possible to retain the aesthetic and historical sense in an object which may mean suggesting the continuation of pattern or imagery in a way that is satisfying to the viewer but would not deceive an expert. After conservation, the object will be structurally, aesthetically and chemically more stable and its life expectancy maximised.

Conservation should also be reversible and a responsible practitioner will try to minimise the amount of intervention (and labour intensive work) to meet this ethical tenet. This is more achievable in some media than others.

The UKIC list of accredited conservators is therefore the recommended path to take for anyone considering having an object conserved for the future (see end of article).

Historic Royal Palaces.

Silk Tapestry that has deteriorated.

One of the most remarkable things about Great Britain is its wealth of original material housed in a great variety of historic buildings and offering an irreplaceable insight into the values and skills of our ancestors. We still have both the goose and golden egg within our grasp but both are now very elderly indeed. Our ancestors have bequeathed a wonderful dowry to us but will we be doing the same for our offspring's offspring?

Jenny Band MVO is Head of the Textile Conservation Studio for the Historic Royal Palaces.
She is on the Council of the UKIC and is Chair of its Public Relations Committee.

Historic Royal Palaces,
Apt 37, Lord Chamberlain's Court,
Hampton Court Palace, Surrey KT8 9AU
Tel: 020 8781 9812 Fax: 020 8781 9813

UKIC Office,
109 The Chandlery,
50 Westminster Bridge Road, London SE1 7QY
Tel: 020 7721 8721 Fax: 020 7721 8722

How can visitors to historic buildings help?

While the entrance fee from visitors helps fund conservation, it is a double edged sword if conservation cannot keep pace with the wear and tear. Visitors can help the places they visit by taking measures themselves to reduce such wear and tear:

- Avoid wearing trainers, and other shoes which carry gravel and mud into a building in their incised tracks. This will minimise damage to floors. Additionally, even moderately high heeled shoes are damaging.
- Take off wet clothes before entering. This helps to minimise the effects of rainy days on the humidity levels in the rooms. Some materials can be damaged by large fluctuations in relative humidity.
- Leave behind bags and other unnecessary items. They can abrade surfaces they touch without the owner being aware. Flaking paint is a common casualty of the rogue bag.
- Do not touch or handle historic objects. The acids in skin together with movement or pressure can cumulatively cause the rapid destruction of even the most apparently robust objects. Objects touched repeatedly need more frequent cleaning which in itself is damaging. Some objects, such as state beds, seem to exert a fatal tactile attraction on visitors and the urge to test their comfort proves insurmountable.
- Textiles such as tapestries and curtains often appear much stronger than they are. Although textiles can retain their apparent structural stability for many years if left undisturbed, they have a feeble sense of self preservation. At a molecular level their strength is quietly and exponentially failing. Damage caused by touching quickly spreads as extra strain is put on surrounding parts. The stresses and strains set up can pull the textile apart in a matter of months. Once they reach that state, conservation is costly.
- Make children aware of the rarity of objects and the reasons why they must not touch them. Sticky weapons such as sweets should be vetoed before entry. It takes no time to turn a piece of white silk or marble black in days just through the glancing, affectionate touch of a hundred small, moist hands.

"A still-life drama"

The house at 18 Folegate Street in Spitalfields in the East End of London is a time capsule – sometimes opened up. In 1980 it was bought by Dennis Severs, a remarkable young American. He furnished and decorated it to tell the story of the Jervis family, Huguenot silk weavers from 1725–1919 who settled in Spitalfields following the Edict of Nantes when French dissenters were no longer welcome in their own country. Dennis Severs has since lived in the house in much the same way as its original occupants might have done in the early 18th century.

18 Folegate Street, exterior.

To enter Folegate Street is like passing through the frame of an Old Master painting: it is an extraordinary experience. Its level is poetic and, like anything so, works best on those who are endowed, willing and able to meet it half way. The house's motto is "you either see it or you don't". Post-materialist, it seeks to remind a visitor of a scientific thing: that "what we cannot see – is essential to what we do".

The game is that you interrupt the Jervis family who, though they can sometimes be heard, seem always to be just out of sight. You walk through the 10 rooms in silence – each, at night, illuminated by fire or candlelight. All senses are sharpened – to smell, to touch, to hear, and see. The floorboards creak, the fire crackles, the clocks chime, and the candles smoke and gutter with any slight draught – a half-eaten meal sits abandoned on the dining room table. Your tour begins in the Kitchen – a kettle boils on the hob and a flat-iron waits to be heated.

The Kitchen.

The Dining Room.

Above the Kitchen is the Eating Parlour or Dining Room, decorated in the early 18th century style, with dark olive painted panelling – in 1725 master weavers were comparatively well-to-do and the Dining Room reflects the Jervis' success. The high-backed chairs with slim finials, around the dining table, are the perfect place for placing the gentlemen's wigs after the ladies had retired ..... is Mr Jervis' wig not the very same as the one that hangs over the back of his chair? Everything is silent, except the 'clink-clank' of the brass clock in the corner of the room.

Spitalfields houses are distinguished by the extra dormer storey at the top of the building. Here, at the top of the house, stripped of prettiness, sparsely furnished, and filled with lodgers

The Parlour.

The Drawing Room.

– is one of the most intriguing rooms. This was the shop where the journeymen worked at their looms. There is no joy here – only poverty, toil and grinding hard work, the only solace being that God was with them – a Methodist book lies open on the bed. Wesley looked sympathetically on the labouring classes and his school rules of no holidays and long days of work and prayer would not have seemed harsh to them.

Every crevice in the room has been blocked up so that the fresh air does not dry out the silk thread. The walls are painted with distemper to counteract disease. At the centre of the room hangs a birdcage with a goldfinch in it, which twitters as the shuttles work. The space below the floor is filled with silk waste and birdseed to deaden the sound of the loom from the family below.

The Drawing Room downstairs is obviously Mrs Jervis' domain. Here she would have entertained her friends to tea. Everything about the room demonstrates her aspirations to make her house look as grand as possible. The pine panelling is stained to look like mahogany and the chimneybreast is decorated with Grinling Gibbons-style decorations made out of walnut shells.

The tour of the 10 rooms finally ends in the Morning Room brought into the 19th century and comfortably furnished in mid-Victorian style. Here, for the first time, the visitor can speak and ask questions. David Hockney once rated the visit to Folegate Street as "standing amongst one of the world's five great 'opera' experiences".

The Bedroom.

Be warned: it is a mistake to trivialise or pigeonhole the experience into any of the traditional mothball camps: 'heritage', 'local history', 'antiques', 'lifestyle museum' – or as ideal for visiting tourists or bored company directors' wives. A visit requires the same style of concentration as does an Old Masters exhibition and a most absurd – but commonly made error – is to assume that it might be either amusing or appropriate for children.

18 Folegate Street is open the first Sunday in each month between 2–5pm. The non-negotiable contribution is for the house's upkeep, and is £7.00.

Then, on the evening of the first Monday following the first Sunday, by candlelight: "Silent Night". Times vary with the light of the seasons and booking is necessary. The contribution is £10.00.

For information and bookings, telephone 020 7247 4013.

WHERE IS THAT PLACE?

Discover the house locations used for some of your favourite films and TV programmes.

Some people treat it as a game – trying to recognise the houses and places they see in films and on television. Looking at *Hudson's* can help. Many of the houses featured have been used as film and photographic locations but that is hardly surprising. Film location managers, seeking historic houses, invariably turn to *Hudson's* as one of their first sources of reference.

Filming on location provides an authenticity that cannot be achieved with studio sets. Actors often find it easier. They can imbibe the atmosphere of a place which not only helps them to be totally natural, but is also conducive to their performance. They don't have to imagine that a building actually extends beyond the studio flat wall. That is why stately homes, manor houses, historic interiors, their landscaped parks and gardens, are regularly in demand by commercial film-makers for use as locations.

But for the house owner it can be alarming. Some have likened the arrival of a film crew to that of a circus coming to town. Space has to be found for mobile canteens, make-up and hairdressing caravans, props, generators, wardrobes and artists' trailers and a production office. Those who are unfamiliar with the filming of a full-scale drama for the cinema or TV will have no idea of how demanding and destructive to normal life location work can be. Nevertheless there is a financial incentive and it can be fun. Moreover, if the house is open and the film is a success, it adds further interest for the visitor.

Some properties are found to be particularly convenient as locations because they are close to London or major television studios such as at Bristol. **Knebworth House**, Hertfordshire (see p85), is used a great deal (*Canterval Ghost*, 1997; *Wilde*, 1997) while nearby **Luton Hoo** (no longer open to the public) is also used a great deal (*Four Weddings and a Funeral*; *Mrs Brown*, 1997; *A Dance to the Music of Time*, 1997). The warm brick-and-timber façade of **Dorney Court** near Windsor (see p67), with its splendid Great Hall, is sufficiently close to London to feature in a wide variety of film and television productions. **Chavenage** (see p265) which is not far from Bristol, is regularly used, including for BBC's *Casualty* and *Cider with Rosie*, 1998.

Dunnottar Castle
Glencoe
Castle Stalker
Drummond Castle
Megginch Castle
Doune Castle
Blackness Castle
Duns Castle
Manderston
Blairquhan Castle
Alnwick Castle
Warkworth Castle
Aydon Castle
Castle Howard
Hoghton Tower
Lyme Park
Tatton Park
Haddon Hall
Little Moreton Hall
Sudbury Hall
Belton Hse
Portmeirion
Grimsthorpe Castle
Holkham
Burghley
Wingfield Old College
Peckover House
Somerleyton Hall
Helmingham
Honington Hall
Broughton Castle
Belchamp Hall
Waddesdon Manor
Chavenage
Knebworth
Luton Hoo
Hatfield Hse
Dyrham
Corsham
Dorney Court
Wilton
Old Wardour Castle
Mompesson House
Montacute House
Houghton Lodge
Arundel Castle
Mapperton
Osborne Hse
Prideaux Place
Cothele
Powderham Castle
Lanhydrock
Trerice
Saltram
St Michael's Mount

Hampton Court
Marble Hill House
Somerset House
Syon House
Tower of London

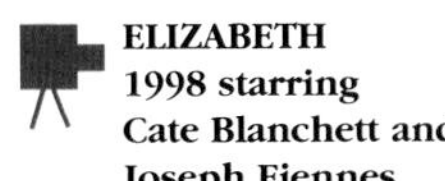

ELIZABETH
1998 starring Cate Blanchett and Joseph Fiennes

Alnwick Castle.

The young Queen Elizabeth inherits a country wracked by internal religious conflict through the rule of her father, Henry VIII and the intervention of her Catholic half-sister, Mary. In a few short years she overcomes all odds to become a powerful monarch. Shot around the UK at locations which included **Alnwick Castle** (see p332) and Bamburgh beach, **Aydon Castle** (see p335) and **Warkworth Castle** in Northumberland (see p338); **Haddon Hall,** Derbyshire (see p259) and the **Tower of London** (see p127).

HAMLET
1990 starring Mel Gibson and Glenn Close

Impressive version of Shakespeare's dark tale of Hamlet's vengeance for the murder of his father with the setting of the menacing Castle Elsinore as much a character in the story as the rest of the cast. Shot on location in Scotland using the imposing medieval **Blackness Castle** in Falkirk (see p425) and **Dunnottar Castle** near Stonehaven, Grampian (see p461).

THE MADNESS OF KING GEORGE
1994 starring Nigel Hawthorne and Helen Mirren

Wilton House.

In the late 18th century the kindly King George is taken ill and his mental instability makes room for intrigue in the Court as his son and Parliament tussle to see who will take control. The Windsor Castle interiors were shot at **Wilton House** near Salisbury (see p217) while also used were **Syon House** at Brentford (see p126), **Arundel Castle** in Sussex (see p155) and the impressive moated **Broughton Castle** near Banbury in Oxfordshire (see p142). Further scenes were shot in the Painted Hall of the Royal Naval College Greenwich and St Paul's Cathedral.

MRS BROWN (aka Her Majesty Mrs Brown),
1997 starring Judi Dench, Billy Connolly and Geoffrey Palmer

Much acclaimed and meticulously crafted drama about the extraordinary relationship between Queen Victoria, then the world's most powerful woman and John Brown, a simple but loyal Scottish Highlander. Filmed in **Osborne House**, Isle of Wight (see p88) (Victoria's elaborate holiday home), **Wilton House** near Salisbury (see p217) (doubling as Windsor Castle), **Duns Castle** west of Berwick-upon-Tweed in the Scottish Borders (see p406), and Lincoln's Inn Fields, London.

THE REMAINS OF THE DAY
1993 starring Anthony Hopkins and Emma Thompson

Dyrham Park.

Anthony Hopkins plays Mr Stephens the perfectionist butler at Darlington Hall, who watches over the ruling and serving classes during the 1930s and 40s but refuses to be emotionally drawn to events or even people. Four historic houses were used to create Darlington Hall. **Dyrham Park** near Bath (see p268) was used for exterior shots; **Corsham Court** near Chippenham (see p214) was used for the Library and Dining Room scenes; the Staircase Hall scenes were filmed at **Powderham Castle** near Exeter (see p188) and Badminton House, Gloucestershire (not open) was used for scenes of the servants' quarters.

ROB ROY
1995 starring Liam Neeson and Jessica Lange

Stirring adventure and fine retelling of the legend of the 18th century Scottish Highlander Rob Roy and his battles with the English. Shot around the west coast of Scotland and in Perthshire at **Megginch Castle** (see p446) and at **Drummond Castle** (see p444).

ROBIN HOOD PRINCE OF THIEVES
1991 starring Kevin Costner, Morgan Freeman and Alan Rickman

Shot almost everywhere except Sherwood Forest. Robin finds Marian at Hulme Priory, in the Park at **Alnwick Castle** in Northumberland (see p332); Locksley Castle is actually **Old Wardour Castle,** Wiltshire (see p220).

SENSE AND SENSIBILITY
1995 starring Emma Thompson, Kate Winslet and Alan Rickman

An Oscar winning adaptation of Jane Austen's classic novel about two sisters, one with good sense and the other with a wonderful excess of romantic sensibility. An elegant and witty film. Shot in part at **Montacute House,** Somerset (see p211); at **Saltram House** near Plymouth (see p195); at **Wilton** in Wiltshire (see p217) and at **Mompesson House** in Cathedral Close, Salisbury, Wiltshire (see p219).

SHAKESPEARE IN LOVE
1998 starring Gwyneth Paltrow, Joseph Fiennes, Judi Dench and Geoffrey Rush

Broughton Castle.

Winner of 7 Oscars including Best Picture, this is a thoroughly enjoyable tale of a young Shakespeare (Fiennes) suffering from writer's block while setting out to write his new play, "Romeo and Ethel, the pirate's daughter". He falls for the beautiful Viola De Lesseps (Paltrow) who, in turn, disguises herself as a man to take part in his new play. Many sites were used including **Broughton Castle**, Oxfordshire (see p142) (stand-in for Viola's stately home); **Hatfield House**, Hertfordshire (see p84) doubled as Greenwich Palace, and the Great Hall at Middle Temple acted as the Banqueting Hall at Whitehall Palace (see p118). Other locations in London included **Marble Hill House** (see p134) and Spitalfields. The final scenes were shot at **Holkham** beach in Norfolk (see p241).

WILDE
1997 starring Stephen Fry and Jude Law

Impressive drama about the life of the playwright and *bon vivant* Oscar Wilde (wonderfully played by Fry), tracing his fame, family life and then fall from grace through his affair with Lord Alfred "Bosie" Douglas (Law). The film-makers made elegant use of locations which included Magdalen College, Oxford; Lulworth and Studland beaches and Swanage Pier in Dorset; **Houghton Lodge**, Hampshire (see p80); Luton Hoo near Luton; and **Somerset House** in London (see p121).

A MAN FOR ALL SEASONS
1966 starring Paul Schofield, Robert Shaw and Orson Welles

This Oscar winning adaptation of Robert Bolt's play about the politico-religious conflict between adulterous King Henry VIII and fervent Catholic Sir Thomas More, is an all-time classic. It was shot on location at **Hampton Court**, Surrey (see p148), the stunning 16th century Tudor Palace on the banks of the Thames.

MONTY PYTHON AND THE HOLY GRAIL
1975 starring John Cleese, Graham Chapman, Terry Jones, Terry Gilliam, Eric Idle and Michael Palin

This hilarious Python team send-up of Arthurian legend, the team of bungling knights encounter characters such as the Knights who say "Ni", flying cows, exploding rabbits, and a Knight who fights with all his limbs cut off. Though dealing with English legend, most of the film was shot in Scotland, including **Doune Castle** near Stirling (see p453), **Glencoe** (see p454) (where the knights must answer questions to cross the stunning 'Bridge of Death' at the Meeting of Three Waters) and **Castle Stalker** near Oban (see p453) (where the Grail is found).

TWELFTH NIGHT
1996 starring Nigel Hawthorne, Helena Bonham-Carter, Ben Kingsley, Imelda Staunton and Richard E Grant

Prideaux Place.

Shot primarily in Cornwall including at **Prideaux Place**, Padstow (see p183); **Lanhydrock** (see p180) (Olivia's house, garden and estate), **Cotehele** (see p179) (quayside tavern and interior of Orsini's castle), **St Michael's Mount** (see p184) (Orsini's castle) and **Trerice** (see p186) (Olivia's estate – orchard). **Prideaux Place**, which was used extensively, was much altered for the film, but possibly the *piece de resistance* was one of the least expensive in terms of materials: an intricate ornamental grotto to form part of the Italian Garden contained thousands of shells coming from nearby beaches, local fisherman and Rick Stein's restaurant in Padstow.

The Buccaneers.

Dr Finlay shot at Blairquhan Castle, p 412.

Elizabeth.

Mrs Brown.

Sense and Sensibility.

Shakespeare in Love.

The Aristocrats,see Goodwood, p 157.

BRIDESHEAD REVISITED
1982 starring Jeremy Irons and Anthony Andrews

An epic ITV adaptation of Evelyn Waugh's novel has been a hit around the world, with a story of love, loyalty and passion amongst the upper classes during the inter-war years. **Castle Howard** near York (see p341) played the home of the Marchmain family but some interiors were also shot at **Tatton Park** in Cheshire (see p370).

Castle Howard.

MIDDLEMARCH
1994 starring Juliet Aubrey, Patrick Malahide, Douglas Hodge and Rufus Sewell

This acclaimed and popular television version of George Eliot's classic novel tells of love and disillusionment against a backdrop of the 19th century Industrial Revolution. Filmed mainly in the historical Lincolnshire town of Stamford, using also nearby **Grimsthorpe Castle** (see p239) and **Burghley House** (see p236).

Grimsthorpe Castle.

PRIDE AND PREJUDICE
1995 starring Jennifer Ehle, Colin Firth and Alison Steadman

This very popular adaptation of Jane Austen's wonderful love story is about a young woman, Elizabeth Bennet (Ehle), her feminist views and her relationship with the dashing Mr Darcy (Firth). Shot at various locations including the National Trust village of Lacock in Wiltshire; the exteriors of Pemberley are **Lyme Park** in Cheshire (see p373); **Sudbury Hall,** Derbyshire (see p263); **Belton Hall** near Grantham (see p237); and the Cathedral Close in Salisbury.

Lyme Park.

THE PRISONER
1966-68 starring Patrick McGoohan

A cult series from the 60s. Patrick McGoohan, as a former secret service agent, is kidnapped and transplanted to a surreal village from which he constantly tries to escape. Filmed at the privately owned Mediterranean-style village of **Portmeirion** in North Wales (see p483). The village was the inspiration of architect Sir Clough Williams-Ellis who fell in love with the Italian fishing village of Portofino and was determined to recreate it in Britain.

AN IDEAL HUSBAND
1999 starring Rupert Everett and Cate Blanchett

Part of the exterior scenes featuring characters and horse riders used in this filmed version of Wilde's play, were filmed at **Waddesdon Manor**, Buckinghamshire (see p70) and were supposed to portray Rotten Row in Hyde Park.

MARTIN CHUZZLEWIT
1994

The BBC version of this Dickens novel starring Paul Schofield, John Mills and Peter Postlethwaite, used as locations **Honington Hall**, Warwickshire (see p316) and **Peckover House**, Cambridgeshire (see p230).

LOVEJOY
1980s

This popular television series about a roguish antiques dealer was shot primarily in East Anglia, where one of the principal locations was **Belchamp Hall**, Suffolk (see p248) as Lady Jane's house. Other house locations for this series were **Helmingham Hall** (see p249), **Wingfield Old College** (see p252) and **Somerleyton Hall** (see p252).

MOLL FLANDERS
1996 starring Alex Kingston, Daniel Craig and Diana Rigg

Wonderful adaptation of Daniel Defoe's widely-read novel with the story romping through the bedrooms and boudoirs of 18th century England. Filmed at **Hoghton Tower**, Preston (see p387); **Grimsthorpe Castle**, Lincolnshire (see p239) and **Little Moreton Hall**, Cheshire (see p373).

TOM JONES
1997

BBC1 television version of Fielding's novel. **Mapperton** in Dorset (see p200) and **Belton**, Lincolnshire (see p237).

CHARLES AND DIANA – UNHAPPY EVER AFTER
1994. A production for ABC starring Catherine Oxenburg

Shot primarily at **Manderston**, Berwickshire (see p404) where different aspects of the house could be portrayed variously as Buckingham Palace, Kensington Palace, Highgrove and Sandringham.

THE BUCCANEERS
1994.

The television adaptation of Edith Wharton's novel "The Buccaneers" included locations at **Castle Howard**, Yorkshire (see p341) and at **Houghton Lodge**, Hampshire (see p80).

Houghton Lodge.

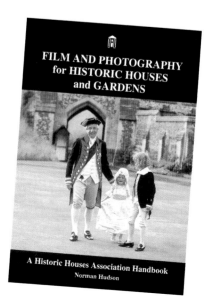

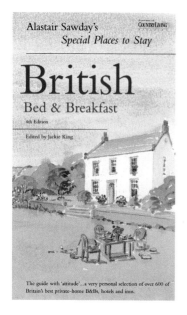

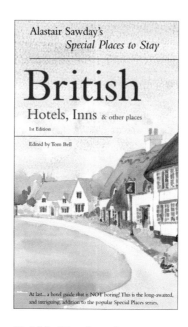

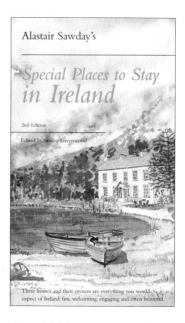

Accommodation Index

The historic properties listed below are not hotels. Their inclusion indicates that accommodation can be arranged, often for groups only. The type and standard of rooms offered vary widely from the luxurious to the utilitarian. Full details can be obtained from each individual property.

ENGLAND

SOUTH & SOUTH EAST

WEST COUNTRY

EASTERN COUNTIES

MIDLANDS

Castle Ashby, Northamptonshire (p.287).

NORTH EAST

NORTH WEST

SCOTLAND

WALES

NORTH WALES

SOUTH WALES

IRELAND

Harburn House, Edinburgh (p.423).

Alastair Sawday's 'Special Places to Stay' See opposite for more accommodation information

Weston Park, Shropshire (p.296).

"Darling, I do..."

the new trend for country house weddings

There can be few better settings for a reception than a country house. Now, thanks to a change in legislation enabling the actual marriage itself to take place in houses, the popularity of country houses as the setting for weddings has soared.

Shugborough, Staffordshire (p.303).

To become a venue for weddings, historic properties need to apply for a Civil Marriage Licence for one or more of their rooms which have no religious connections; libraries are particularly popular. Regulations are strict about food and drink, so separate rooms are set aside for receptions. Many properties included in *Hudson's* have a Licence and these are shown in the Index opposite and indicated by 🔔 in their entry.

Generally, country houses can cater for up to 100 people; more if a marquee is erected outside. Sir Thomas Ingilby at Ripley Castle, Yorkshire, once hosted a wedding for 800.

Some country houses, such as Eastnor Castle in Herefordshire, provide rooms for the bride and groom and their immediate family to stay in, but much depends on the arrangement of houses. The majority expect their clients to find alternative accommodation.

Entertainment at country house weddings can be lavish. "Couples are limited only by their imagination and budget" explains the public relations manager at Goodwood in Sussex. Fireworks, jazz bands and string quartets are popular, but there is an increasing trend for more unusual ways to amuse guests: weddings generally start during the early afternoon and last until midnight which means that more than a dinner is required to prevent guests from falling asleep!

At one Goodwood wedding a belly-dancer performed; at Longleat, Wiltshire one bride took out a safari boat while Rory Bremner impersonated David Attenborough on board; at Highclere Castle, Hampshire a bride and groom had a Scottish themed wedding – pipers manned the turrets and a football match took place between kilted competitors.

Oakham Castle, Leics. & Rutland (p.281).

Sir Thomas Ingilby of Ripley has had some of the most bizarre examples: "We had a gothic punk wedding where most of the guests (male and female) wore heavy purple and black make-up. The cake was black, semi-circular and had spikes sticking out of it like an old-fashioned landmine. At another wedding all the guests wore the brightest clothing they could find and all 22 of them went on the honeymoon".

The new Marriage legislation has changed nothing in Scotland. There, as before, you can get married at a Registry Office or have a religious ceremony anywhere, provided a Minister is willing.

This new enthusiasm for country house weddings has shown up some interesting trends...

- Those getting married tend to be in their mid to late 20s and early 30s – never in their teens – reflecting a countrywide trend for couples to get married later
- The bride and groom, rather than their parents, usually pay for the ceremony
- Classic cars are the most favoured form of transport, followed by horses and carriages, although one bride arrived on an elephant
- The most common number at a wedding is 100 people; the smallest recorded was for 2 people, the largest for 800
- Most country house weddings last from 3pm – midnight
- The most popular form of entertainment is a disco, jazz band or string quartet, but the demand for different diversions is increasing: one wedding party descended on the races for the reception; other request outdoor activities such as clay-pigeon shooting or off-road driving
- The majority of country houses do not allow confetti at weddings unless it is biodegradable
- Brides are becoming more outspoken: 57% at country house weddings make a speech
- Country house owners have noticed nothing unusual about the choice of flowers, although one American bride asked for goldfish bowls as centrepieces

(This is an extract from an article by Melanie Cable-Alexander that originally appeared in Country Life – 17 June 1999.)

Stowe School, Buckinghamshire (p.69).

This index refers to places at which the marriage ceremony itself can take place although many will also be able to provide facilities for wedding receptions.

Full details about each property are available in the regional listings. There are numerous other properties included within *Hudson's* which do not have a Civil Wedding Licence but which can accommodate wedding receptions. The Marriage Act 1995, which has resulted in many more wedding venues in England, has not changed the situation in Scotland. In Scotland religious wedding ceremonies can take place anywhere subject to the Minister being prepared to perform them. Civil Weddings, however, are still confined to Registry Offices.

ENGLAND

SOUTH & SOUTH EAST

WEST COUNTRY

EASTERN COUNTIES

MIDLANDS

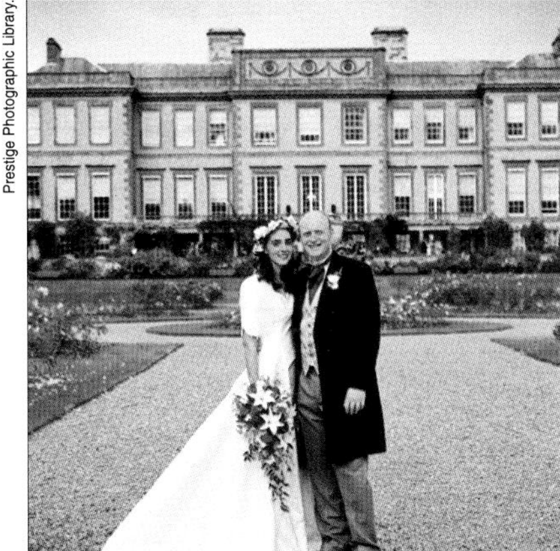

Prestige Photographic Library.

Ragley Hall, Warwickshire (p.310).

NORTH EAST COUNTIES

NORTH WEST COUNTIES

WALES

NORTH WALES

SOUTH WALES

IRELAND

This list is merely intended to draw attention to some properties which can host Civil Weddings, it is only a guide.

Properties which are able to accommodate corporate functions, wedding receptions and events.

ENGLAND

SOUTH & SOUTH EAST

Dorney Court (p.67).

Some properties specialise in this and are open only rarely, if ever, to day visitors. Others do both.

See entry for details

WEST COUNTRY

EASTERN COUNTIES

MIDLANDS

Weston Park, Shropshire (p.296).

NORTH EAST

Fairfax House, Yorkshire (p.342).

NORTH WEST

Adlington Hall, Cheshire (p.368).

SCOTLAND

Blairquhan Castle, SW Scotland (p.412).

WALES

NORTH WALES

Bodelwyddan Castle, North Wales (p.478).

SOUTH WALES

IRELAND

Malahide Castle, Ireland (p.499).

This is not an exclusive list. It is intended to draw attention to some of these properties where functions or coprorate hospitality is a major part of their business.

JANUARY

• 1 – 3
Leeds Castle, Kent
Millennium Treasure Trails.

• 1 – 31
Soho House, West Midlands
An exhibition commemorating the 1999 Vaisakhi Celebrations of 300 years of Sikhism.

• 2
Lanhydrock, Cornwall
Millennium Sunday Lunch (tel: 01208 74331 for information/booking).

• 5
Anglesey Abbey, Cambridgeshire
Trust Day – Garden History & Design Course, 10.30am-4pm (all ticket applications should be addressed to The Property Manager and include sae; please enquire for separate leaflet on this course which will run on four separate days in September, October, January and February).

• 12
Wimpole Hall & Home Farm, Cambridgeshire
Trust Day – The Making of a Landscape, 10am-3.45pm (tickets from the property either by post with sae or tel: 01223 207001. Cost £37 inc morning coffee, lunch and afternoon tea. Booking essential.)

• 17
Buckland Abbey, Devon
Wassailing in quarry orchard (free). Wear something old and warm, bring something noisy. Help to wassail the new season's apple crop in the old orchard. This is seriously light-hearted tradition!

• 22
Flatford Bridge Cottage, Suffolk
Winter Wonderland Walks – The back door to Dedham, 10.45am. After a delicious brunch, a 4 mile guided walk to the south slopes of Dedham Vale. £8.50 – booking essential (01206 289260).

• 26
Wimpole Hall & Home Farm, Cambridgeshire
Trust Day – The Architecture of a Great House, 10am-3.45pm (tickets from the property either by post with sae or tel: 01223 207001. Cost £37 inc morning coffee, lunch and afternoon tea. Booking essential.)

• 29 – 30
Chirk Castle, Wales
Snowdrop Day, 12 noon-4pm.
(£1 adults, children free.)

FEBRUARY

• 2
Anglesey Abbey, Cambridgeshire
Trust Day – Garden History & Design Course, 10.30am-4pm (all ticket applications should be addressed to The Property Manager and include sae; please enquire for separate leaflet on this course which will run on four separate days in September, October, January and February).

• 2
Nymans Gardens, Sussex
Lecture Lunch, 11.30am-3pm (£14.95 including two course lunch and coffee).

• 2
Wimpole Hall & Home Farm, Cambridgeshire
Trust Day – A Farm and its Rare Breeds, 10am-3.45pm (tickets from the property either by post with sae or tel: 01223 207001. Cost £37 inc morning coffee, lunch and afternoon tea. Booking essential.)

• 3
Nymans Gardens, Sussex
Lecture Lunch, 11am for 11.30am-3pm (£14.95 including two course lunch and coffee).

• 4
Nymans Gardens, Sussex
Lecture Lunch, 11am for 11.30am-3pm (£14.95 including two course lunch and coffee).

• 5
Sulgrave Manor, Northamptonshire
Chamber Concert with buffet supper and wine, 7.30pm. Musica Domini Dei "Bach and the Italian Temperament".

• 5 – 6
Lanhydrock, Cornwall
Snowdrop Day, 12 noon-4pm
(£1 adults, children free).

• 5 – 6
Penrhyn Castle, North Wales
Snowdrop Day, 12 noon-4pm
(£1 adults, children free).

• 9
Nymans Gardens, Sussex
Lecture Lunch, 11.30am-3pm (£14.95 including two course lunch and coffee).

• 9
Wimpole Hall & Home Farm, Cambridgeshire
Chocolate Heaven. Chocolatier Gerard Ronay will help guests create their own chocolate masterpieces and a gourmet lunch will be served. (To reserve please contact The Old Rectory Restaurant on 01223 208670. £60 per person.)

FEBRUARY

• 10
Nymans Gardens, Sussex
Lecture Lunch, 11am for 11.30am-3pm (£14.95 including two course lunch and coffee).

• 11
Nymans Gardens, Sussex
Lecture Lunch, 11am for 11.30am-3pm (£14.95 including two course lunch and coffee).

• 13 – 14
Lanhydrock, Cornwall
Snowdrop Day, 12 noon-4pm
(£1 adults, children free).

• 13 – 14
Penrhyn Castle, North Wales
Snowdrop Day, 12 noon-4pm
(£1 adults, children free).

• 16
Nymans Gardens, Sussex
Lecture Lunch, 11.30am-3pm (£14.95 including two course lunch and coffee).

• 16
Wimpole Hall & Home Farm, Cambridgeshire
Trust Day – Managing a Great House, 10am-3.45pm (tickets from the property either by post with sae or tel: 01223 207001.
Cost £37 inc morning coffee, lunch and afternoon tea. Booking essential.)

NT Photographic Library/Chris King

• 17
Nymans Gardens, Sussex
Lecture Lunch, 11am for 11.30am-3pm (£14.95 including two course lunch and coffee).

• 18
Nymans Gardens, Sussex
Lecture Lunch, 11am for 11.30am-3pm (£14.95 including two course lunch and coffee).

• 21 – 25
Leeds Castle, Kent
Half Term Story-Telling.

• 23
Nymans Gardens, Sussex
Lecture Lunch, 11.30am-3pm (£14.95 including two course lunch and coffee).

• 24
Nymans Gardens, Sussex
Lecture Lunch, 11am for 11.30am-3pm (£14.95 including two course lunch and coffee).

• 25
Nymans Gardens, Sussex
Lecture Lunch, 11am for 11.30am-3pm (£14.95 including two course lunch and coffee).

FEBRUARY

• 25 – 27
Loseley Park, Surrey
Home Design Exhibition.

• 26
Buckland Abbey, Devon
Aromatherapy – a professional aromatherapist from 'Well Oiled', Plymouth guides you through the uses of various oils. Booking required.

• 26
Flatford Bridge Cottage, Suffolk
Winter Wonderland Walks – The Stour Valley its glorious side, 10.45am. After brunch, a 5 mile guided walk to Lawford Church, Vale and Hall. £8.50 – booking essential (01206 289260).

• 26 – 29
Fairfax House, Yorkshire
"Eat Drink and Be Merry – The British at Table 1600-2000".

MARCH

• 1 – 31
Fairfax House, Yorkshire
"Eat Drink and Be Merry – The British at Table 1600-2000".

• 3 – 5
Wilton House, Wiltshire
23rd Annual Antiques Fair.

• 4
Sulgrave Manor, Northamptonshire
Chamber Concert with buffet supper and wine, 7.30pm. The Cherwell Orchestra play Handel, Mozart and Schubert.

• 5
Penrhyn Castle, North Wales
Daffodil Day to celebrate St David's Day, 12 noon-4pm (free admission, grounds and tearoom).

• 11 – 12
Powderham Castle, Devon
Torbay Motor Rally.

• 17
Flatford Bridge Cottage, Suffolk
Winter Wonderland Walks: 10.45am. After brunch, a 5 mile guided walk £8.50 – booking essential.

• 17 – 19
Ragley Hall, Warwickshire
Antiques Fair.

• 18
Penrhyn Castle, North Wales
Dèsigner Clothes Sale, 11am-4pm (ladies' day wear, jewellery, leather goods, children's clothes & toys. Grounds & tearoom open, £1 entry).

MARCH

• 18 – 31
Borde Hill Garden, Sussex
Special Camellia Days.

• 24 – 28
Naworth Castle, Cumbria
Galloway Antiques Fair.

• 28 – 30
Powderham Castle, Devon
Phillips Fine Art Sale.

• 29 – 31
Claverton Manor, Somerset
Amish Quilts from Indiana.

APRIL

• 1
Soho House, West Midlands
"Invent an Alien" children's event.

• 1
Sulgrave Manor, Northamptonshire
Chamber Concert with buffet supper and wine, 7.30pm. Cherwell Chamber Players play Mozart and Schubert's "Trout".

• 1 – 30
Claverton Manor, Somerset
Amish Quilts from Indiana.

• 1 – 30
Fairfax House, Yorkshire
"Eat Drink and Be Merry – The British at Table 1600-2000".

• 2
Cobham Hall, Kent
National Gardens Scheme.

• 2
Lanhydrock, Cornwall
Mothering Sunday, 12 noon-4pm (£1 adults, children free).

• 2
Paxton House & Country Park, Scotland
Spring Craft Fair.

• 8 – 9
Capesthorne Hall, Cheshire
Rainbow Craft Fair.

• 8 – 9
Kentwell Hall, Suffolk
Mini Re-creation event: Land Girls, 11am-6pm.

• 8 – 9
Leeds Castle, Kent
Greenhouse Weekend.

• 8 – 9
Sulgrave Manor, Northamptonshire
"Herbs, Hives and History", 10.30am-5pm. The house and grounds will feature the historic and modern use of herbs and honey. Demonstrations, stands, displays and stalls.

• 9
Haddon Hall, Derbyshire
Elizabethan Dancers.

• 9
Spencer House, London (provisional)
Craftsman Day, 11am-5pm. Opportunity to meet the skilled people involved in the 10 year restoration of this important building and the methods and techniques employed will be explained and demonstrated.

• 14 – 16
Ripley Castle, Yorkshire
Galloway Antiques Fair.

• 14 – 30
Aston Hall/Soho House/Museum of the Jewellery Quarter/Sarehole Mill, West Midlands
Connecting Threads Exhibition.
A multi-site exhibition of costume
(tel: 0121 327 0062 for details).

• 15 – 16
Borde Hill Garden, Sussex
Garden Festival.

• 15 – 16
Ragley Hall, Warwickshire
Gardeners' Weekend.

• 15 – 16
Shugborough, Staffordshire
Gamekeepers' Fair.

• 16
Beaulieu, Hampshire
Boat Jumble.

• 16
Birmingham Botanical Gardens and Glasshouses
West Midlands Orchids Show.

• 21
Plas Newydd, North Wales
National Garden Scheme Open Day, 11am-5pm (the house will not be open today). Guided Walk with the Gardener (admission + £2.50).

• 21 – 24
Blair Castle, Scotland
Spring Needlework and Lace Exhibition. One of the finest exhibitions in the country, most of which is attributed to Lady Evelyn Stewart Murray (1868-1940), over 120 pieces.

APRIL

• 21 – 24
Cobham Hall, Kent
Medway Craft Show.

• 21 – 24
Duncombe Park, Yorkshire
Easter Craft Festival.

• 21 – 24
Hedingham Castle, Essex
Life in Tudor England.

• 21 – 24
Hever Castle, Kent
Royal Tudor Easter Egg Trail.

• 21 – 24
Sulgrave Manor, Northamptonshire
Easter Customs and Attractions, 10.30am-5pm. See the house beautifully decorated with spring flowers. Hear of the Easter customs throughout the ages.

• 21 – 31
Kentwell Hall, Suffolk
Mini Re-creation event: Easter/May Day, 11am-6pm.

• 22 – 24
Leeds Castle, Kent
A Celebration of Easter.

• 23
Lulworth Castle, Dorset
Easter Bunny Hunt.

• 23
Paxton House & Country Park, Scotland
5th Great 1000 Easter Egg Eggstravaganza.

• 23
Plas Newydd, North Wales
Easter Eggstravaganza – Chocolate filled Family Fun Day, 12 noon-4pm.

• 23
Traquair, Scotland
Easter Egg Extravaganza.

• 23 – 24
Borde Hill Garden, Sussex
Easter Special for Children.

• 24
Ludlow Castle, Shropshire
Easter Egg Hunt.

• 27 – 30
Pashley Manor Gardens, Sussex
Tulip Festival.

• 29 – 30
Hever Castle, Kent
May Day Music and Dance.

• 29 – 30
Kentwell Hall, Suffolk
Mini Re-creation event: May Day, 11am-6pm.

• 30
Auckland Castle, Co Durham
Auckland Castle 10km Road Race.

• 30
Eastnor Castle, Herefordshire
Spring Country Craft Festival.

• 30
Hedingham Castle, Essex
Jousting Tournament.

• 30
Plas Newydd, North Wales
Stepping into Spring Family Fun Day, 12 noon-4pm. Woodland & Marine Wildlife Walk with the North Wales Wildlife Trust, 2-4pm.

• 30
Shugborough, Staffordshire
Classic Car Show.

MAY

• 1
Capesthorne Hall, Cheshire
Church of England Children's Society Garden Party.

• 1
Eastnor Castle, Herefordshire
Spring Country Craft Festival.

• 1
Hedingham Castle, Essex
Jousting Tournament.

• 1
Hergest Croft Gardens, Herefordshire
Flower Fair.

• 1
Hever Castle, Kent
May Day Music and Dance.

• 1
Kentwell Hall, Suffolk
Mini Re-creation event: Easter/May Day, 11am-6pm.

• 1
Pashley Manor Gardens, Sussex
Tulip Festival.

• 1
Shugborough, Staffordshire
Classic Car Show.

• 1
Sulgrave Manor, Northamptonshire
May Day Festival, 10.30am-5pm. Traditional May Day dancing, mumming, games and activities from times gone by.

• 1 – 31
Aston Hall/Soho House/Museum of the Jewellery Quarter/Sarehole Mill, West Midlands
Connecting Threads Exhibition.
A multi-site exhibition of costume (tel: 0121 327 0062 for details).

• 1 – 31
Claverton Manor, Somerset
Amish Quilts from Indiana.

• 1 – 31
Fairfax House, Yorkshire
"Eat Drink and Be Merry – The British at Table 1600-2000".

• 4 – 7
Hatfield House, Hertfordshire
Living Crafts (£6.80, group £5.80, child £3.40).

• 5 – 7
Elton Hall, Cambridgeshire
Home Design and Interiors Exhibition.

• 6
Dalemain, Cumbria
Fell Pony Society Stallion Show.

• 6
Hatch Court, Somerset
NCCPG Rare Plant Sale.

• 6 – 7
Beaulieu, Hampshire
Spring Autojumble.

• 6 – 7
Borde Hill Garden, Sussex
Children's Animal Fair.

• 6 – 7
Chatsworth, Derbyshire
Chatsworth Angling Fair.

• 6 – 7
Leonardslee Gardens, Sussex
Bonsai Weekend.

• 6 – 7
Loseley Park, Surrey
Surrey Advertiser Motor Show.

MAY

• 7
Birmingham Botanical Gardens and Glasshouses, West Midlands
Plant Market.

• 7
Dalemain, Cumbria
NWCD Carriage Driving.

• 7
Newby Hall, Yorkshire
Spring Plant Fair.

• 9
Plas Newydd, North Wales
A Walk with the Gardener, 2pm (admission + £2.50).

• 11 – 13
Sudeley Castle, Gloucestershire
Homes & Gardens Magazine Grand Sale.

• 11 – 14
Arbury Hall, Warwickshire
Birmingham National Dog Show (not open to the public, dog exhibitors only).

• 13 – 14
Chatsworth, Derbyshire
Horse Trials.

• 13 – 14
Leeds Castle, Kent
Festival of English Food & Wine.

• 13 – 14
Ludlow Castle, Shropshire
Vintage Vehicle Display.

• 13 – 14
Lulworth Castle, Dorset
Country Gardening Festival.

• 13 – 19
Pashley Manor Gardens, Sussex
Sculpture Week.

• 13 – 28
Borde Hill Garden, Sussex
Rhododendron & Azalea Time.

• 14
Plas Newydd, North Wales
Spring Plant Fair, 11am-4pm. A Walk with the Gardener, 2pm (admission + £2.50).

• 19 – 21
Deene Park, Northamptonshire
Antiques Fair (revised date).

• 21
Capesthorne Hall, Cheshire
Kit Car Show.

MAY

• 21
Pashley Manor Gardens, Sussex
Spring Plant Fair.

• 22 – 26
Chelsea Physic Garden, London
Chelsea Show Week, 12 noon – 5pm, with lunches.

• 23 – 25
Goodwood House, Sussex
Goodwood Horse Race Meetings.

• 25 – 28
Loseley Park, Surrey
Craft Fair.

• 25 – 29
Charleston, Sussex
Charleston Festival.

• 27
Blair Castle, Scotland
Atholl Highlanders' Parade, 2.40pm.

• 27
Kedleston Hall, Derbyshire
Flower Festival.

• 27 – 29
Harewood House, Yorkshire
Craft Festival.

• 27 – 29
Hever Castle, Kent
Merrie England Weekend.

• 27 – 29
Kentwell Hall, Suffolk
Mini Re-creation event: Whitsun, 11am-6pm.

• 27 – 29
Ludlow Castle, Shropshire
Festival of Crafts.

• 27 – 29
Shugborough, Staffordshire
Spring Craft Fair.

• 27 – 29
Skipton Castle, Yorkshire
Red Wyvern Society re-enactment of life in Skipton Castle in the 15th century.

• 27 – 29
Sulgrave Manor, Northamptonshire
American Memorial Day Weekend, 10.30am-5pm. Three day festival celebrating American military history with Living History display & demonstrations.

• 27 – 30
Leeds Castle, Kent
Amazing Mazes Week.

NT Photographic Library/David Levenson

MAY

• 28
Blair Castle, Scotland
Atholl Gathering and Highland Games, 1.15pm (adults £4, children £1, conc £2).

• 28
Plas Newydd, North Wales
Pirates Ahoy! Family Fun Day, 12 noon-4pm.

• 28 – 29
Finchcocks, Kent
Finchcocks Spring Garden Fair & Flower Festival.

• 28 – 29
Hedingham Castle, Essex
Medieval Festival.

• 28 – 29
Ragley Hall, Warwickshire
Transport Show.

• 29
Duncombe Park, Yorkshire
Country Fair.

• 29
Eastnor Castle, Herefordshire
Steam Fair & Country Show.

• 29
Paxton House & Country Park, Scotland
Georgian Costumed Day.

JUNE

• 1
Goodwood House, Sussex
Goodwood Horse Race Meeting.

• 1 – 3
Chichester Cathedral, Sussex
"Tidings of Great Joy", Festival of Flowers.

• 1 – 4
Fairfax House, Yorkshire
"Eat Drink and Be Merry – The British at Table 1600-2000".

• 1 – 4
Leeds Castle, Kent
Amazing Mazes Week.

• 1 – 30
Aston Hall/Soho House/Museum of the Jewellery Quarter/Sarehole Mill, West Midlands
Connecting Threads Exhibition.
A multi-site exhibition of costume (tel: 0121 327 0062 for details).

• 1 – 30
Claverton Manor, Somerset
Amish Quilts from Indiana.

• 2 – 4
Holker Hall & Gardens, Cumbria
Holker Garden Festival. Magnificent horticultural displays and floral art combined with countryside displays and Festival Gardens. Family and children entertainment. Craft demonstrations. (Show office 015395 58838).

• 3
Harewood House, Yorkshire
Phoenix Dance Festival.

• 3
Highcliffe Castle, Dorset
VCC Rally.

JUNE

• 3 – 4
Auckland Castle, Co Durham
Northumbria Quality Craft Exhibition and Fair.

• 3 – 4
Cawdor Castle, Scotland
Special Gardens Weekend: guided tours of gardens and Cawdor Big Wood.

• 4
Mellerstain House, Scotland
Borders Vintage Automobile Rally.

• 8 – 11
Bramham Park, Yorkshire
Bramham International Horse Trials & Yorkshire Country Fair.

• 8 – 11
Ripley Castle, Yorkshire
Grand Summer Sale.

• 9
Goodwood House, Sussex
Goodwood Horse Race Meeting (evening).

• 9 – 11
Duncombe Park, Yorkshire
Antiques Fair.

• 10 – 11
Capesthorne Hall, Cheshire
Cheshire Home & Garden Show.

• 10 – 11
Newby Hall, Yorkshire
Rainbow Craft Fair.

• 10 – 11
Parham House & Gardens, Sussex
Steam Rally.

• 11
Burton Constable Hall, Yorkshire
Burton Constable Country Fair.

• 11
Dalemain, Cumbria
National Gardens Scheme Open Day.

• 11
Highcliffe Castle, Dorset
Churches Together – outdoors service.

• 13
Plas Newydd, North Wales
A Walk with the Gardener, 2pm (admission + £2.50).

• 14 – 15
Painswick Rococo Garden, Gloucestershire
"The Tempest" performed by the Festival Players Theatre Company (tickets must be booked in advance).

• 15 – 18
Pashley Manor Gardens, Sussex
Summer Flower Festival.

• 16
Goodwood House, Sussex
Goodwood Horse Race Meeting (evening).

• 16 – 18
Holy Trinity, Goodramgate, York
(see Churches Conservation Trust article, p11)
Annual Flower Festival.

• 17
Chartwell, Kent
"Music, Memories & Moonlight".

JUNE

• 17
Harewood House, Yorkshire
"Pure Puccini" – Open Air Opera.

• 17
Gilbert White's House & Oates Museum, Hampshire
Picnic to "Jazz in June".

• 17 – 18
Gilbert White's House & Oates Museum, Hampshire
Unusual Plants Fair.

• 17 – 30
Borde Hill Garden, Sussex
Rosey Days.

• 18
Birmingham Botanical Gardens and Glasshouses, West Midlands
Bonsai Show.

• 18
Kentwell Hall, Suffolk
Great Annual Re-creation, 11am-5pm.

• 18
Plas Newydd, North Wales
Fathers' Day Frolics! 11am-5pm.

• 18
St Mary's, Shrewsbury, Shropshire
(see Churches Conservation Trust article, p11)
Friends' High Mass.

JUNE

• 20 – 21
Tabley House, Cheshire
Cheshire Show (please ring Cheshire Agricultural Society Secretary on 01829 760020 for details).

• 20 – 25
Gawsworth Hall, Cheshire
Open Air Theatre Festival: "Midsummer Night's Dream".

• 21
St Michael & St Martin, Eastleach, Glos
(see Churches Conservation Trust article, p11)
John Keble Commemorative Evensong (former curate of the church) 6pm.

• 21 – 24
Coventry Cathedral, West Midlands
International Church Music Festival.

• 22
Naworth Castle, Cumbria
Thomson Roddick & Laurie Fine Pictures & Furniture Auction (viewing day 21 June).

• 23
Goodwood House, Sussex
Goodwood Horse Race Meeting (evening).

• 23
Loseley Park, Surrey
Outdoor Opera.

• 23 – 25
Goodwood House, Sussex
Goodwood Festival of Speed.

• 24
Leeds Castle, Kent
Open Air Concert.

• 24 – 25
Arbury Hall, Warwickshire
Warwickshire Homes, Gardens & Leisure Show.

• 24 – 25
Hatfield House, Hertfordshire
Festival of Gardening (£6.80, group £5.80).

• 24 – 25
Hedingham Castle, Essex
Tudor History Event.

• 24 – 25
Hever Castle, Kent
Gardening Event.

• 24 – 25
Kentwell Hall, Suffolk
Great Annual Re-creation, 11am-5pm.

• 24 – 25
Leonardslee Gardens, Sussex
West Sussex Country Craft Fair.

• 24 – 30
Haddon Hall, Derbyshire
Flower Festival.

• 24 – 30
Ludlow Castle, Shropshire
Ludlow Festival.

• 25
Eastnor Castle, Herefordshire
Wood Fair.

• 27 – 28
Loseley Park, Surrey
WI Flower Show.

• 27 – 29
Powderham Castle, Devon
Phillips Fine Art Sale.

• 28
Leeds Castle, Kent
Kent Children's Prom.

• 30
Goodwood House, Sussex
Goodwood Horse Race Meeting (evening).

• 30
Leighton Hall, Lancashire
Concert & Fireworks, "Last Night of the Proms".

JULY

• 1
Leeds Castle, Kent
Open Air Concert.

• 1 – 2
Borde Hill Garden, Sussex
7th Borde Hill Horse Trials.

• 1 – 2
Duncombe Park, Yorkshire
Steam Fair.

• 1 – 2
Highcliffe Castle, Dorset
Horticultural Show.

• 1 – 2
Kentwell Hall, Suffolk
Great Annual Re-creation, 11am-5pm.

• 1 – 2
Powderham Castle, Devon
Powderham Horse Trials.

• 1 – 2
Scone Palace, Scotland
Game Conservancy Scottish Fair.

• 1 – 2
Shugborough, Staffordshire
Gardeners' Weekend.

Historic Scotland

JULY

• 1 – 9
Ludlow Castle, Shropshire
Ludlow Festival.

• 1 – 9
Sulgrave Manor, Northamptonshire
Tudor Living History, 10.30am-5pm. See the house and grounds peopled and run exactly as it was in Elizabethan times.

• 1 – 31
Aston Hall/Soho House/Museum of the Jewellery Quarter/Sarehole Mill, West Midlands
Connecting Threads Exhibition.
A multi-site exhibition of costume
(tel: 0121 327 0062 for details).

• 1 – 31
Claverton Manor, Somerset
Amish Quilts from Indiana.

• 2
Goodwood House, Sussex
Goodwood Horse Race Meeting.

• 4
Plas Newydd, North Wales
Traditional Pole-lathe turning, Greenwood working and Charcoal burning, 11am-3pm.

• 5 – 8
Parham House & Gardens, Sussex
Open Air Theatre: "Romeo and Juliet".

• 5 – 9
Gawsworth Hall, Cheshire
Open Air Theatre Festival: "The Gondoliers".

• 7 – 8
Dyrham Park, Gloucestershire
"Music in the Park"
(details from Box Office 01985 843601).

• 7 – 9
Kentwell Hall, Suffolk
Great Annual Re-creation, 11am-5pm.

• 7 – 16
Paxton House & Country Park, Scotland
3rd Summer Music at Paxton House – 10 concert Classical Music Festival.

• 8 – 9
Glamis Castle, Scotland
Strathmore Vintage Vehicle Extravaganza.

• 8 – 9
Powderham Castle, Devon
Historic Vehicle Gathering.

• 9
Haddon Hall, Derbyshire
Elizabethan Dancers.

• 9 – 31
Chelsea Physic Garden, London
Summer Exhibition "Timely Cures".

• 11
Plas Newydd, North Wales
An Evening Walk with the Gardener, 7pm (£3.50 inc NT members).

• 14
Holy Trinity, Goodramgate, York
(see Churches Conservation Trust article, p11)
Classical Concert for York Early Music Festival.

• 14 – 16
Ripley Castle, Yorkshire
Galloway Antiques Fair.

• 15
Arbury Hall, Warwickshire
Theatre in the Garden.

• 15
Wilton House, Wiltshire
Open Air Musical Evening with Fireworks.

• 15 – 16
Dalemain, Cumbria
Dalemain Rainbow Craft Fair.

JULY

• 15 – 16
Newby Hall, Yorkshire
Yorkshire Craft Pavilion.

• 15 – 16
Parham House & Gardens, Sussex
Garden Weekend.

• 16
Capesthorne Hall, Cheshire
Gordon Setter Championship Show.

• 16
Cobham Hall, Kent
National Gardens Scheme.

• 16
Eastnor Castle, Herefordshire
Performing Arts Concert (Deer Park).

• 16
Hever Castle, Kent
Longbow Warfare.

• 16
Newby Hall, Yorkshire
Historic Vehicle Rally.

• 16
Plas Newydd, North Wales
Fun Day for Teddies and their Families,
12 noon-4pm.

• 16
Shugborough, Staffordshire
Goose Fair.

• 17 – 31
Coventry Cathedral, West Midlands
Coventry Mystery Plays, performed in the ruins of the old cathedral.

JULY

• 19 – 23
Tatton Park, Cheshire
RHS Flower Show.

• 20 – 23
Leeds Castle, Kent
A Festival of Summer Floral Art.

• 21
Sand, Devon
Shakespeare in the Garden: "The Tempest", 7.30pm (gates open 6.15pm, bring your own seating and refreshment).

• 21 – 23
Loseley Park, Surrey
Great Gardening Show.

• 21 – 23
Ludlow Castle, Shropshire
Pentabus Children's Theatre.

• 22
Glamis Castle, Scotland
Grand Scottish Prom.

• 22
Hever Castle, Kent
Jousting Tournament.

• 22
Shugborough, Staffordshire
Firework & Laser Symphony Concert.

• 22 – 24
Harewood House, Yorkshire
Leeds Championship Dog Show.

• 22 – 31
Doddington Hall, Lincolnshire
Exhibition Cushions 2000.

• 23
Hever Castle, Kent
Longbow Warfare.

• 23
Plas Newydd, North Wales
Grenadier à Cheval de la Guard, 11am-4pm.

• 25
Plas Newydd, North Wales
Traditional Pole-lathe turning, Greenwood working and Charcoal burning, 11am-3pm.
All the Fun of the Annual Summer Fair, 11am-4pm.

• 25 – 30
Painswick Rococo Garden, Gloucestershire
"Twelfth Night" performed by the Gloucestershire Drama Association
(tickets must be booked in advance).

• 28 – 30
Sulgrave Manor, Northamptonshire
Outdoor Theatre Productions, 7pm on Friday and Saturday, 3pm matinee on Sunday
(play to be confirmed).

• 29
Hever Castle, Kent
Jousting Tournament.

• 29
Tatton Park, Cheshire
Hallé Concert & Fireworks.

JULY

• 29 – 30
Eastnor Castle, Herefordshire
West Midlands Balloon Club Meet (Deer Park).

• 29 – 30
Lulworth Castle, Dorset
Lulworth Horse Trials.

• 30
Capesthorne Hall, Cheshire
Sports Car Show.

• 30
Hedingham Castle, Essex
Jousting Tournament.

• 30
Hever Castle, Kent
Longbow Warfare.

• 30
Plas Newydd, North Wales
Seaside Family Fun Day with Mr Bimbamboozle,
12 noon-4pm.

AUGUST

• 1 – 5
Coventry Cathedral, West Midlands
Coventry Mystery Plays, performed in the ruins of the old cathedral

• 1 – 5
Goodwood House, Sussex
Goodwood Horse Race Festival Meeting.

• 1 – 31
Aston Hall/Soho House/Museum of the Jewellery Quarter/Sarehole Mill, West Midlands
Connecting Threads Exhibition.
A multi-site exhibition of costume
(tel: 0121 327 0062 for details).

• 1 – 31
Chelsea Physic Garden, London
Summer Exhibition "Timely Cures".

• 1 – 31
Claverton Manor, Somerset
Amish Quilts from Indiana.

• 1 – 31
Doddington Hall, Lincolnshire
Exhibition Cushions 2000.

• 2
Plas Newydd, North Wales
Traditional Pole-lathe turning, Greenwood working and Charcoal burning, 11am-3pm.

• 2 – 5
Gawsworth Hall, Cheshire
Open Air Theatre Festival:
"Blithe Spirit" (Noël Coward).

• 4
Powderham Castle, Devon
Open Air Concert.

• 4 – 5
Leighton Hall, Lancashire
Shakespeare in the Garden, "The Tempest".

NT Photographic Library/Ian Shaw

AUGUST

• 4 – 5
Scone Palace, Scotland
Perth Agricultural Show.

• 4 – 6
Broughton Castle, Oxfordshire
Celebration of the Millennium – a production of "Merrie England".

• 4 – 6
Hatfield House, Hertfordshire
Art in Clay – Pottery & Ceramics Festival (£5.00).

• 5
Ragley Hall, Warwickshire
"Close Encounters of the Classical Kind" Concert.

NT Photographic Library/Ian Shaw

• 5 – 6
Hever Castle, Kent
Jousting Tournament.

• 5 – 6
Kentwell Hall, Suffolk
Mini Re-creation event: Lammas, 11am-6pm.

• 5 – 6
Loseley Park, Surrey
QEF Classic Car Show.

• 5 – 6
Powderham Castle, Devon
Food & Drink Festival.

• 5 – 6
Traquair, Scotland
Traquair Fair.

• 6
Borde Hill Garden, Sussex
Fuchsia Show.

• 6
Drummond Castle Gardens, Scotland
Open Day.

• 6
Eastnor Castle, Herefordshire
Herefordshire Country Fair (Deer Park).

• 6
Plas Newydd, North Wales
Clown Around with James the Juggler, 12 noon-4pm.

• 6
Shugborough, Staffordshire
Victorian Street Market.

• 8
Plas Newydd, North Wales
An Evening Walk with the Gardener.

• 11 – 12
Dyrham Park, Gloucestershire
Opera in the West Garden (details from Box Office 01985 843601).

• 12
Borde Hill Garden, Sussex
"L'Elisir d'Amore"
(The Love Potion) - Garden Opera.

• 12
Parham House & Gardens, Sussex
Open Air Theatre: Sheridan's "The Rivals".

• 12 – 13
Cobham Hall, Kent
Medway Craft & Flower Show.

• 12 – 13
Hever Castle, Kent
Jousting Tournament.

• 12 – 13
Kirby Hall, Northamptonshire
"History in Action". The biggest festival of re-enactment in Europe.

• 12 – 13
Sudeley Castle, Gloucestershire
Open Air Shakespeare.

AUGUST

• 12 – 20 (except 16)
Sulgrave Manor, Northamptonshire
"Stars, Stripes and Stitches", 10.30am-5pm. Sulgrave's superb annual Needlework Festival. Exhibitions, displays and workshops.

• 13
Capesthorne Hall, Cheshire
Fireworks & Laser Concert.

• 13
Loseley Park, Surrey
Open Air Concert & Fireworks.

• 13
Pashley Manor Gardens, Sussex
Summer Plant Fair.

• 16 – 19
Gawsworth Hall, Cheshire
Open Air Theatre Festival:
"Rebecca" (Daphne du Maurier).

• 18 – 20
Parham House & Gardens, Sussex
Live Crafts.

• 19
Glenfinnan, Scotland
Glenfinnan Games.

• 19
Plas Newydd, North Wales
Open Air Jazz Concert with Firework Finale – featuring the Chris Barber Jazz and Blues Band, supported by Dr Jazz (garden open 5pm, performance 7pm). Adult £15 (£12.50 in advance), Child £7.50 (£6.50 in advance). Bring a picnic and seating (bar and food available on site). Sponsored by National Power Hydro.

• 19 – 20
Hever Castle, Kent
Jousting Tournament.

• 19 – 20
Ragley Hall, Warwickshire
Game Fair.

• 19 – 20
Skipton Castle, Yorkshire
Feudal Archers – demonstration of arms, armour and domestic life (1135-1216).

• 20
Arbury Hall, Warwickshire
Motor Transport Spectacular.

• 20
Eastnor Castle, Herefordshire
The Berkeley Household:
Living History in the 16th Century.

• 20
Shugborough, Staffordshire
Last Night of the Shugborough Proms.

• 21 – 25
Eastnor Castle, Herefordshire
Children's Fun Week.

• 24 – 27
Blair Castle, Scotland
Bowmore Blair Castle International Horse Trials & Country Fair.

• 25 – 26
Paxton House & Country Park, Scotland
250th Anniversary Costume Mask Celebration.

• 25 – 28
Kentwell Hall, Suffolk
Mini Re-creation event: High Summer, 11am-6pm.

• 25 – 28
Naworth Castle, Cumbria
Galloway Antiques Fair.

• 26
Hever Castle, Kent
Jousting Tournament.

AUGUST

• 26 – 27
Goodwood House, Sussex
Goodwood Horse Race Meeting.

• 26 – 27
Plas Newydd, North Wales
Knights of Longshanks –
combat displays between the Welsh soldiers and Anglo-Norman knights, 11am.

• 26 – 28
Auckland Castle, Co Durham
Flower Festival in aid of St John's Ambulance.

• 26 – 28
Shugborough, Staffordshire
Shugborough Summer Craft Show.

• 26 – 28
Sulgrave Manor, Northamptonshire
Seven Years War 1756-63, 10.30am-5pm. Re-enactment of George Washington's first major experience as a soldier fighting in the French-Indian Wars. Living History Camp.

• 27
Dalemain, Cumbria
Cumbrian Classic Car Show.

• 27
Floors Castle, Scotland
Family Day with Massed Pipe Bands.

• 27
Holker Hall & Gardens, Cumbria
MG Rally. Post and pre-1955 MGs in Concours and Driving Trials. Discounted admission to MG drivers. Competition entries on the day.

• 27
Leighton Hall, Lancashire
"Close Encounters of the Classical Kind" Concert & Fireworks.

• 27 – 28
Cobham Hall, Kent
Kent Country Show.

• 27 – 28
Hedingham Castle, Essex
Jousting Tournament.

• 27 – 28
Hever Castle, Kent
Longbow Warfare.

• 28
Highcliffe Castle, Dorset
Scottish Country Dancing.

• 29
Plas Newydd, North Wales
Traditional Pole-lathe turning, Greenwood working and Charcoal burning, 11am-3pm.

SEPTEMBER

• 1 – 3
Chelsea Physic Garden, London
Summer Exhibition "Timely Cures".

• 1 – 10
Doddington Hall, Lincolnshire
Exhibition Cushions 2000.

• 1 – 17
Aston Hall/Soho House/Museum of the Jewellery Quarter/Sarehole Mill, West Midlands
Connecting Threads Exhibition.
A multi-site exhibition of costume (tel: 0121 327 0062 for details).

• 1 – 30
Claverton Manor, Somerset
Amish Quilts from Indiana.

• 2
Arbury Hall, Warwickshire
Fireworks Festival in the Park.

• 2
Sulgrave Manor, Northamptonshire
Chamber Concert
with buffet supper and wine, 7.30pm.

• 2 – 3
Chatsworth, Derbyshire
Chatsworth Country Fair.

• 2 – 3
Gawsworth Hall, Cheshire
Antique Collectors Fair.

• 2 – 3
Hever Castle, Kent
Longbow Warfare.

• 2 – 3
Newby Hall, Yorkshire
Rainbow Craft Fair.

• 3
Borde Hill Garden, Sussex
Rare Plants Fair.

• 3
Plas Newydd, North Wales
Guided Fungus Foray and Family Fun Day – for all ages, 12 noon-4pm.

• 8 – 9
Goodwood House, Sussex
Goodwood Horse Race Meeting.

• 8 – 10
Hatfield House, Hertfordshire
Country Homes & Gardens Show (£5.00).

• 8 – 10
Hever Castle, Kent
Patchwork & Quilting.

• 9 – 10
Beaulieu, Hampshire
Autojumble.

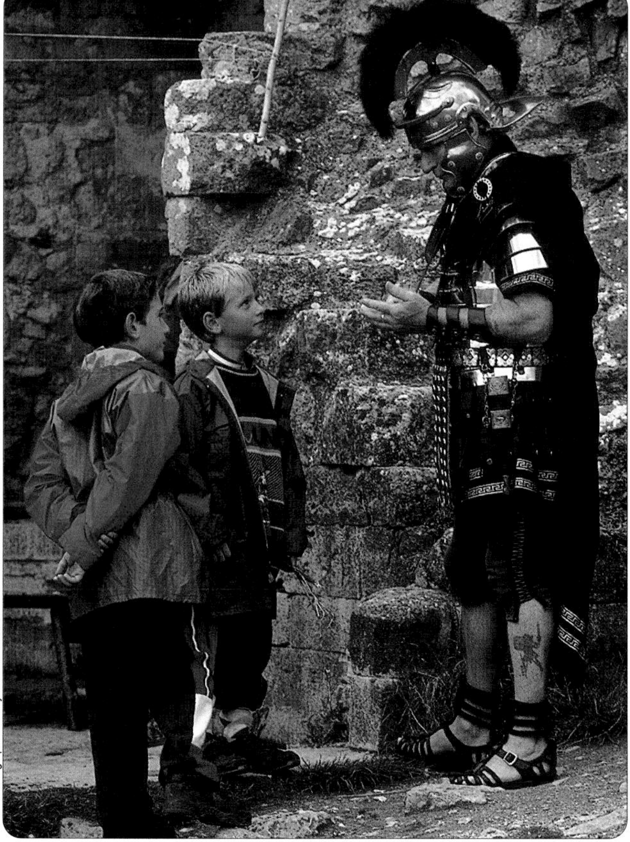

NT Photographic Library/David Levenson

SEPTEMBER

- 9 – 10
Leeds Castle, Kent
Balloon & Vintage Car Weekend.
- 9 – 10
Leighton Hall, Lancashire
Rainbow Craft Fair.
- 9 – 10
Parham House & Gardens, Sussex
Country Show.
- 10
Haddon Hall, Derbyshire
Elizabethan Dancers.
- 12
Plas Newydd, North Wales
A Walk with the Gardener, 2pm (admission + £2.50).
- 15 – 17
Goodwood House, Sussex
Goodwood Motor Circuit Event.
- 16 – 17
Aston Hall/Soho House/Museum of the Jewellery Quarter/Sarehole Mill, West Midlands
Heritage Open Days (tel: 0121 327 0062 for details).
- 16 – 17
Capesthorne Hall, Cheshire
Rainbow Craft Fair.
- 16 – 17
Sulgrave Manor, Northamptonshire
The Siege of Sulgrave 1644, 10.30am-5pm. Re-enactment of an actual event that took place at Sulgrave during the English Civil War by the "Siege Group".
- 17
Newby Hall, Yorkshire
Autumn Plant Fair.
- 20 – 21
Goodwood House, Sussex
Goodwood Horse Race Meeting.
- 23 – 24
Kentwell Hall, Suffolk
Mini Re-creation event: Michaelmas, 11am-5pm.
- 30
Sulgrave Manor, Northamptonshire
Tudor LIving History, 10.30am-5pm. Melford-hys-Companie take the house and grounds back to Tudor times with much in the way of traditional entertainment. Chamber Concert with buffet supper and wine, 7.30pm.

OCTOBER

- 1
Leighton Hall, Lancashire
Teddy Bear Fair.
- 1 – 8
Sulgrave Manor, Northamptonshire
Tudor Living History, 10.30am-5pm. Melford-hys-Companie take the house and grounds back to Tudor times with much in the way of traditional entertainment.
- 1 – 29
Claverton Manor, Somerset
Amish Quilts from Indiana.
- 6 – 8
Blair Castle, Scotland
Autumn Needlework and Lace Exhibition. One of the finest exhibitions in the country, most of which is attributed to Lady Evelyn Stewart Murray (1868-1940), over 120 pieces.
- 7 – 8
Capesthorne Hall, Cheshire
Cheshire Home & Garden Show.
- 7 – 8
Eastnor Castle, Herefordshire
Festival of Fine Food & Drink from the Heart of England.
- 8
Paxton House & Country Park, Scotland
Autumn Craft Fair.
- 10
Plas Newydd, North Wales
Trusty's October Half-term Holiday Fun, 12 noon-4pm (small extra charge for some activities).A Walk with the Gardener, 2pm (admission + £2.50).
- 13 – 15
Deene Park, Northamptonshire
Antiques Fair (revised date).
- 13 – 15
Finchcocks, Kent
Finchcocks Autumn Fair.
- 14 – 15
1066 Battle of Hastings Battlefield & Abbey, Sussex
"The Battle of Hastings". See hundreds of authentically armoured warriors re-enacting the events of 1066.
- 14 – 15
Kentwell Hall, Suffolk
Mini Re-creation event: World War II Event, 11am-5pm.
- 15
Leighton Hall, Lancashire
Dolls' House & Miniaturist Fair.

OCTOBER

- 18 – 22
Leeds Castle, Kent
Autumn Gold – A Celebration of Flowers & Produce.
- 20 – 22
Ragley Hall, Warwickshire
Antiques Fair.
- 21 – 22
Sulgrave Manor, Northamptonshire
Apple Day, 10.30am-5pm. The Manor's major event of the year – a country show featuring the Apple: displays, demonstrations, stalls, food, drink etc.
- 22
Plas Newydd, North Wales
"A Masquerade" – mask making workshop, quiz trail, face-painting and activities.
- 23 – 27
Borde Hill Garden, Sussex
Children's Fun Days.
- 23 – 27
Leeds Castle, Kent
Half Term Halloween Event.
- 24
Plas Newydd, North Wales
Kite Workshop.
- 24 – 26
Powderham Castle, Devon
Phillips Fine Art Sale.
- 26
Naworth Castle, Cumbria
Thomson Roddick & Laurie Fine Art & Furniture Sale (viewing day 25 October).
- 28
Blair Castle, Scotland
Glenfiddich Piping Championships.
- 28 – 29
Stowe School, Buckinghamshire
Craft Fair.
- 29
Birmingham Botanical Gardens and Glasshouses, West Midlands
Christmas Markets.
- 29
Blair Castle, Scotland
Glenfiddich Fiddling Championships.
- 29
Plas Newydd, North Wales
Bonkers for Conkers and Potty for Pumpkins – spooky fun for everyone!

NOVEMBER

- 3 – 5
Duncombe Park, Yorkshire
Antiques Fair.
- 4
Leeds Castle, Kent
Grand Firework Spectacular.
- 4
Sulgrave Manor, Northamptonshire
Chamber Concert with buffet supper and wine, 7.30pm.
- 4 – 5
Plas Newydd, North Wales
Annual Book Fair, 10am-4pm (£1.00 inc NT members). The House will not be open.
- 5
Soho House, West Midlands
"Boosters, Bangs and Moonbeams" Guy Fawkes children's event.
- 11 – 12
Sulgrave Manor, Northamptonshire
"Embroiderer's Casket", 10.30am-4.30pm. Inspired by the needlework in the Manor House, a weekend festival based on historic embroidery – stalls etc.
- 11 – 16
Auckland Castle, Co Durham
Northumbria Quality Craft Christmas Exhibition.
- 14
Coventry Cathedral, West Midlands
Performance of Britten's War Requiem, on the 60th anniversary of the bombing of Coventry Cathedral.
- 18 – 30
Claverton Manor, Somerset
Amish Quilts from Indiana.
- 19
Plas Newydd, North Wales
Workshop: Make a dried Seasonal Swag to keep, 2-4pm, £7.50 inc tuition and materials (booking essential).
- 25
Plas Newydd, North Wales
Children's Workshop: Make an Advent Calendar, 12 noon-4pm.
- 25 – 26
Ludlow Castle, Shropshire
Medieval Christmas Fayre.
- 25 – 26
Ragley Hall, Warwickshire
Yuletide Craft Fair.

NOVEMBER

- 26
Birmingham Botanical Gardens and Glasshouses, West Midlands
Craft Fair.
- 26
Plas Newydd, North Wales
Workshop: Make a Festive Fireplace Decoration, 2-4pm, £7.50 inc materials and tuition (bring florists' scissors or a sharp knife).
- 26
Gilbert White's House & Oates Museum, Hampshire
Mulled Wine & Christmas Shopping Day.

DECEMBER

- 1 – 10
Claverton Manor, Somerset
Amish Quilts from Indiana.
- 1 – 31
Duncombe Park, Yorkshire
Estate grown Christmas Trees on sale.

NT Photographic Library/David Levenson

- 1 – 31
Ford Green Hall, Staffordshire
Hall dressed in traditional seasonal decorations.
- 1 – 31
Lydiard Park, Wiltshire
Victorian Christmas decorations.
- 1 – 31
Tatton Park, Cheshire
"Christmas at Tatton".
- 2
Sulgrave Manor, Northamptonshire
Chamber Concert with buffet supper and wine, 7.30pm.
- 2 – 3
Duncombe Park, Yorkshire
Christmas Craft Festival.
- 2 – 3
Sulgrave Manor, Northamptonshire
A Tudor Christmas, 10.30am-1pm and 2pm-4.30pm. The Great Hall of the Manor is splendidly bedecked with seasonal greenery. Hear of the customs and traditions of Christmas past, and of food and feasting.
- 2 – 10
Aston Hall, West Midlands
Aston Hall by Candlelight (closed 5 December).
- 3
Plas Newydd, North Wales
Workshop: Make a Pot-et-Fleur, 2-4pm, £7.50 inc materials and tuition (bring florists' scissors or a sharp knife).
- 3 – 4
Soho House, West Midlands
Book and Print Fair.

DECEMBER

- 3 – 31
Fairfax House, Yorkshire
Exhibition on "The Keeping of Christmas 1760-1840".
- 5 – 8
Shugborough, Staffordshire
Christmas at Shugborough (8 Dec tickets only).
- 9 – 10
Sulgrave Manor, Northamptonshire
A Tudor Christmas, 10.30am-1pm and 2pm-4.30pm. The Great Hall of the Manor is splendidly bedecked with seasonal greenery, with the log fire burning and beeswax candles glowing. Hear of the customs and traditions of Christmas past, and of food and feasting.
- 10
Plas Newydd, North Wales
Workshop: Make a Table Centrepiece in a terracotta pot with candles, 2-4pm, £7.50 inc materials and tuition (bring florists' scissors or a sharp knife).
- 11
Plas Newydd, North Wales
Christmas Concert in the Music Room, 7.30pm. Tickets: Adult £6, Child £4 (booking essential).
- 11 – 24
Leeds Castle, Kent
Christmas at the Castle.
- 16 – 17
Sulgrave Manor, Northamptonshire
A Tudor Christmas, 10.30am-1pm and 2pm-4.30pm. The Great Hall of the Manor is splendidly bedecked with seasonal greenery. Hear of the customs and traditions of Christmas past, and of food and feasting.
- 24 – 26
Dickens House Museum, London
Christmas Festivities: House decorated as it would have been for Dickens' first Christmas there in 1837. Admission £10, Child £5, includes guidebook, mince pies & punch. 10.30am-6pm.
- 27 – 30
Sulgrave Manor, Northamptonshire
A Tudor Christmas, 10.30am-1pm and 2pm-4.30pm. The Great Hall of the Manor is splendidly bedecked with seasonal greenery. Hear of the customs and traditions of Christmas past, and of food and feasting.

The Special Events listed in this index are only a selection of those taking place. You are advised to contact the property direct for exact details, times etc. before making a special journey.

www.hudsons.co.uk – your gateway to numerous heritage sites.

Sites shown in ☛red represent those sites with a live link from the *Hudson's* web site. If you want to make life easy without having to type in each address all you have to do is go to **www.hudsons.co.uk** and click on the direct link to any of these sites. More are being added all the time – keep looking.

	ORGANISATION	WEB ADDRESS
	Hudson's	www.hudsons.co.uk
	Dúchas	www.heritageireland.ie
☛	English Heritage	www.english-heritage.org.uk
	Heritage Education Trust	www.heritageontheweb.co.uk
☛	Historic Houses Association	www.hha.org.uk
☛	Historic Royal Palaces	www.hrp.org.uk
☛	Historic Scotland	www.historic-scotland.gov.uk
	Landmark Trust	www.landmarktrust.co.uk
	National Gardens Scheme	www.ngs.org.uk
☛	National Trust Virtual tours	www.nt-education.org/virtualviews/index
☛	Alastair Sawday Publishing	www.sawdays.co.uk
☛	The Virtual Tour of Great Britain and Ireland	www.bestloved.com

	PROPERTY	COUNTY	WEB ADDRESS
	1 Royal Crescent	Somerset	www.bath-preservation-trust.org.uk
	Alnwick Castle	Northumberland	www.alnwickcastle.com
	Althorp	Northants	www.althorp.com
	Ancient House	Suffolk	www.landmarktrust.co.uk
☛	Angus Folk Museum	Scotland	www.nts.org.uk
	Apsley House	London	www.vam.ac.uk/collections/apsley/index.html
	Ardington House	Oxfordshire	www.ardingtonhouse.com
	Ardkinglas Estate	Scotland	www.ardkinglas.com
☛	Arduaine Garden	Scotland	www.nts.org.uk
	Athelhampton House & Gardens	Dorset	www.athelhampton.co.uk
	Auckland Castle	Co Durham	www.auckland-castle.co.uk
	Avington Park	Hampshire	www.avingtonpark.co.uk
☛	Bachelors' Club	Scotland	www.nts.org.uk
☛	Baddesley Clinton	Warwickshire	www.ntrustsevern.org.uk
	Ballywalter Park	Ireland	www.dunleath-estates.co.uk
☛	Bannockburn Heritage Centre	Scotland	www.nts.org.uk
☛	Banqueting House	London	www.hrp.org.uk
	Bantry House & Garden	Ireland	www.cork-guide.ie/bnry_hse.htm
☛	Barrie's Birthplace	Scotland	www.nts.org.uk
☛	Barry Mill	Scotland	www.nts.org.uk
	Beaulieu	Hampshire	www.beaulieu.co.uk
☛	Belchamp Hall	Suffolk	www.belchamphall.com
	Belmont	Kent	www.swale.gov.uk
	Belvoir Castle	Leics. & Rutland	www.country-focus.co.uk/belvoir/castle/
	Benington Lordship	Hertfordshire	http://www.beningtonlordship.co.uk
☛	Berrington Hall	Herefordshire	www.ntrustsevern.org.uk
☛	Birmingham Botanical Gardens	W Midlands	www.bham-bot-gdns.demon.co.uk
	Birr CastleDemesne	Ireland	www.birrcastle.com
	Blairquhan Castle	Scotland	www.blairquhan.co.uk
	Blenheim Palace	Oxfordshire	www.blenheimpalace.com
	Bodnant Garden	Wales	www.sissons.demon.co.uk/bodnant.htm
	Bolton Abbey	Yorkshire	www.yorkshirenet.co.uk/boltonabbey
	Bolton Castle	Yorkshire	www.boltoncastle.co.uk
	Borde Hill Garden	Sussex	www.bordehill.co.uk
☛	Boughton House	Northants	www.boughtonhouse.org.uk
	Bowood House	Wiltshire	www.bowood-estate.co.uk
☛	Branklyn Garden	Scotland	www.nts.org.uk
☛	Brodick Castle & Country Park	Scotland	www.nts.org.uk
☛	Brodie Castle	Scotland	www.nts.org.uk
	Broughton Castle	Oxfordshire	www.broughtoncastle.demon.co.uk
☛	Broughton House & Garden	Scotland	www.nts.org.uk
☛	Buckingham Palace	London	www.royal.gov.uk
	Buckfast Abbey	Devon	www.buckfast.org.uk
	Burghley House	Lincolnshire	www.stamford.co.uk/burghley/

Burncoose Nurseries & Garden	Cornwall	www.eclipse.co.uk/burncoose
Buscot Park	Oxfordshire	www.faringdon-coll.com
Caerhays Castle & Garden	Cornwall	www.eclipse.co.uk/caerhays
☛ Carlyle's Birthplace	Scotland	www.nts.org.uk
☛ Castle Bromwich Hall Gardens	West Midlands	www.cbhgt.swinternet.co.uk
☛ Castle Fraser & Garden	Scotland	www.nts.org.uk
☛ Cathedral & Abbey Church of St Alban	Hertfordshire	www.stalbansdioc.org.uk/cathedral/
☛ Charlecote Park	Warwickshire	www.ntrustsevern.org.uk
☛ Charleston	Sussex	www.charleston.org.uk
Chatsworth	Derbyshire	www.chatsworth-house.co.uk
☛ Chedworth Roman Villa	Gloucestershire	www.ntrustsevern.org.uk
☛ Claverton Manor	Somerset	www.americanmuseum.org
Clifton Park Museum	Yorkshire	www.rma.org.uk
☛ Combermere Abbey	Shropshire	www.combermereabbey.co.uk
Compton Acres Gardens	Dorset	www.comptonacres.co.uk
Coughton Court	Warwickshire	www.coughtoncourt.co.uk
Courtauld Gallery	London	www.courtauld.ac.uk
Coventry Cathedral	W Midlands	www.coventrycathedral.org
Cranborne Manor Garden	Dorset	www.cranborne.co.uk
☛ Crathes Castle	Scotland	www.nts.org.uk
☛ Croft Castle	Herefordshire	www.ntrustsevern.org.uk
☛ Culloden	Scotland	www.nts.org.uk
☛ Culross Palace	Scotland	www.nts.org.uk
☛ Culzean Castle & Country Park	Scotland	www.nts.org.uk
☛ Dalemain	Cumbria	www.dalemain.com
Dalmeny House	Scotland	www.edinburgh.org
Dimbola Lodge	Isle of Wight	*(site under construction)*
Dorset County Museum	Dorset	www.dorset.museum.clara.net
☛ Drum Castle	Scotland	www.nts.org.uk
Duart Castle	Scotland	www.holidaymull.org/members/duart.html
☛ Duncombe Park	Yorkshire	www.duncombepark.com
Dunvegan Castle	Scotland	www.dunvegancastle.com
Elsham Hall Country & Wildlife Park and Barn Theatre	Lincolnshire	www.brigg.com/elsham.htm
Ely Cathedral	Cambridgeshire	www.cathedral.ely.anglican.org
Englefield House	Berkshire	www.englefield-est.demon.co.uk
Essex Secret Bunker	Essex	http://members.tripod.co.uk/EssexSecretBunker
Exbury Gardens	Hampshire	www.exbury.co.uk
Eyam Hall	Derbyshire	www.eyamhall.co.uk
☛ Falkland Palace	Scotland	www.nts.org.uk
Finchcocks	Kent	www.argonet.co.uk/finchcocks
Finlaystone	Scotland	www.finlaystone.co.uk
☛ Ford Green Hall	Staffordshire	www.stoke.gov.uk/fordgreenhall
☛ Fountains Abbey	Yorkshire	www.fountainsabbey.org.uk
Freud Museum	London	www.freud.org.uk
☛ Fursdon	Devon	www.eclipse.co.uk/fursdon
☛ Fyvie Castle	Scotland	www.nts.org.uk
Gainsborough's House	Suffolk	www.gainsborough.org
Gardens of Easton Lodge	Essex	www.goel.mcmail.com
Gardens of the Rose	Hertfordshire	www.roses.co.uk/harkness/rnrs/garden/garden.htm
Gawsworth Hall	Cheshire	http://ourworld.compuserve.com/homepages/gawsworth
Geffrye Museum	London	www.geffrye-museum.org.uk
☛ Georgian House	Scotland	www.nts.org.uk
Gilbert Collection	London	www.gilbert-collection.org.uk
☛ Gladstone's Land	Scotland	www.nts.org.uk
☛ Glamis Castle	Scotland	www.great-houses-scotland.co.uk/glamis
☛ Glencoe	Scotland	www.nts.org.uk
☛ Glenfinnan	Scotland	www.nts.org.uk
☛ Goddards	Surrey	www.landmarktrust.co.uk
☛ Goodwood House	Sussex	ww.goodwood.co.uk
Great Dixter House & Gardens	Sussex	www.entertainnet.co.uk/attractions/htm
☛ Greenbank	Scotland	www.nts.org.uk
☛ The Greyfriars	Worcestershire	www.ntrustsevern.org.uk
Grimsthorpe Castle	Lincolnshire	www.grimsthorpe.co.uk
☛ Groombridge Place	Kent	www.groombridge.co.uk
Haddo House	Scotland	www.nts.org.uk
Haddonstone Show Garden	Northants	www.businessconnections.com/haddonstone
☛ Hall Place	Kent	www.bexley.gov.uk
☛ Ham House	London	www.nationaltrust.org.uk/southern
Hammerwood Park	Sussex	www.name.is/hammerwood
☛ Hampton Court Palace	Surrey	www.hrp.org.uk
☛ Hanbury Hall	Worcestershire	www.ntrustsevern.org.uk
Harburn House	Scotland	www.harburnhouse.com
Harewood House	Yorkshire	www.harewood.org

☛ Harmony Garden	Scotland	www.nts.org.uk
Hartham Park	Wiltshire	www.harthampark.plc.uk
Hartland Abbey	Devon	www.northdevon.co.uk/hartland.htm
Harwich Maritime & Lifeboat Museums	Essex	www.micrologic-ltd.co.uk.harwich/http
Harwich Redoubt Fort	Essex	www.micrologic-ltd.co.uk.harwich/http
☛ Hatchlands/Clandon Park	Surrey	www.nationaltrust.org.uk
Hawkstone Historic Park & Follies	Shropshire	www.hawkstone.co.uk
Hergest Croft Gardens	Herefordshire	www.hergest.co.uk
Hever Castle	Kent	www.hevercastle.co.uk
☛ Hidcote Manor Garden	Gloucestershire	www.ntrustsevern.org.uk
☛ Higham Park	Kent	www.higham-park.co.uk
☛ Highclere Castle	Hampshire	www.highclerecastle.co.uk
☛ Highcliffe Castle	Dorset	www.christchurch.gov.uk/highcliffecastle
☛ Hill House	Scotland	www.nts.org.uk
☛ Hill of Tarvit Mansionhouse	Scotland	www.nts.org.uk
☛ Sir Harold Hillier Gardens& Arboretum	Hampshire	www.hillier.hants.gov.uk/
Holme Pierrepont Hall	Nottinghamshire	http.//members.aol.com/holmepierrepont
Holkham Hall	Norfolk	www.holkham.co.uk
☛ Holmwood House	Scotland	www.nts.org.uk
☛ House of Dun	Scotland	www.nts.org.uk
☛ House of the Binns	Scotland	www.nts.org.uk
☛ Hugh Miller's Cottage	Scotland	www.nts.org.uk
☛ Hutchesons' Hall	Scotland	www.nts.org.uk
Hylands House	Essex	www.chlemsfordbc.gov.uk
☛ Inveresk Lodge Garden	Scotland	www.nts.org.uk
☛ Inverewe Garden	Scotland	www.nts.org.uk
Ironbridge Gorge Museums	Shropshire	www.ironbridge.org.uk
Kelburn	Scotland	www.kelburncastle.com
☛ Kellie Castle & Garden	Scotland	www.nts.org.uk
☛ Kensington Palace	London	www.hrp.org.uk
Kentwell Hall	Suffolk	www.kentwell.co.uk
King's College	Cambridge	www.kings.cam.ac.uk
Kinnersley Castle	Herefordshire	www.kinnersley.com/castle
Knebworth House	Hertfordshire	www.knebworthhouse.com
Kylemore Abbey	Ireland	www.kylemoreabbey.com
Leeds Castle	Kent	www.leeds-castle.co.uk
Leighton House Art Gallery & Museum	London	www.rbkc.gov.uk/kcservices/libraries/leighton.htm
☛ Leith Hall	Scotland	www.nts.org.uk
Lennoxlove House	Scotland	www.lennoxlove.org
Leonardslee Gardens	Sussex	www.leonardslee.com
Levens Hall	Cumbria	*(site under construction)*
Lodge Park Walled Gardens & Steam Museum	Ireland	http://indigo.ie/~rguinn/
Longleat House	Wiltshire	www.longleat.co.uk
Lost Gardens of Heligan	Cornwall	www.heligan.com
Lydiard Park	Wiltshire	www.swindon.gov.uk
☛ Macclesfield Museums	Cheshire	www.silk-macclesfield.org
Manderston	Scotland	www.manderston.demon.co.uk
Mapledurham House & Watermill	Oxfordshire	www.mapledurham.co.uk
Maunsel House	Somerset	www.sirbenslade.co.uk
Mellerstain House	Scotland	http://muses.calligrafix.co.uk/mellerstain
Merriments Gardens	Sussex	www.merriments.co.uk
☛ Mill Dene Garden	Glos	www.smoothhound.co.uk/hotels/milldene.html
Milton's Cottage, John	Bucks	http:/home.clara.net/pbirger
Mount Stuart House & Gardens	Scotland	www.mountstuart.com
Muncaster Castle	Cumbria	www.muncastercastle.co.uk
☛ Museum of Costume & Assembly Rooms	Somerset	www.museumofcostume.co.uk
☛ Museum of Garden History	London	www.museumgardenhistory.org
National Botanic Garden of Wales	South Wales	www.gardenofwales.org.uk
New Lanark	S Lanarkshire	www.newlanark.org
Newbury Manor	Berkshire	www.newbury-manor-hotel.co.uk
Newby Hall	Yorkshire	www.newbyhall.co.uk
☛ Nymans Garden	Sussex	www.nationaltrust.org.uk/southern
Otley Hall	Suffolk	www.otleyhall.co.uk
Owlpen Manor	Glos	www.owlpen.com
☛ Packwood House	Warwickshire	www.ntrustsevern.org.uk
☛ Painswick Rococo Gdns	Glos	www.beta.co.uk/painswick
☛ Palace of Holyroodhouse	Scotland	www.royal.gov.uk
☛ Parham	Sussex	www.parhaminsussex.co.uk
Paxton House & Country Park	Scotland	www.paxtonhouse.com
Pencarrow	Cornwall	www.chycor.co.uk/pencarrow
Penhow Castle	South Wales	www.penhowcastle.com
☛ Penshurst Place	Kent	www.seetb.org.uk/penshurst/
☛ Petworth House	Sussex	www.nationaltrust.org.uk/southern
☛ Pitmedden Garden	Scotland	www.nts.org.uk

☛ Polesden Lacey	Surrey	www.nationaltrust.org.uk/southern
☛ Pollok House	Scotland	www.nts.org.uk
Portmeirion	Wales	www.portmeirion.wales.com
Powderham Castle	Devon	www.powderham.co.uk
Powerscourt Estate	Ireland	www.powerscourt.ie
Prebendal Manor House	Northants	www.prebendal-manor.demon.co.uk
Preston Manor	Sussex	www.brighton.co.uk/tourist
Preston Mill	Scotland	www.nts.org.uk
Priorwood Garden & Dried Flower Shop	Scotland	www.nts.org.uk
Provost Skene's House	Scotland	www.aberdeen.net.uk
Quaker Tapestry Exhibition Centre	Cumbria	www.quaker-tapestry.co.uk
Queen's House	London	www.nmm.ac.uk
☛ Raby Castle	Co Durham	www.rabycastle.com
Renishaw Hall	Derbyshire	www.sitwell.co.uk
Ripley Castle	Yorkshire	www.ripleycastle.co.uk
Rochester Cathedral	Kent	www.net-west.co.uk/webs/rochester-cathedral
☛ Rockingham Castle	Northants	www.northants-uk.com/roc-cas
☛ Roman Baths & Pump Room	Somerset	www.romanbaths.co.uk
Rosslyn Chapel	Scotland	www.rosslynchapel.org.uk
Rousham House	Oxfordshire	www.information-britain.co.uk
Royal Observatory	London	www.rog.nmm.ac.uk
Royal Pavilion	Sussex	www.brighton.co.uk/tourist
☛ Royal Society of Arts	London	www.rsa.org.uk
Ryton Organic Gardens	West Midlands	www.hdra.org.uk
St Edmundsbury Cathedral	Suffolk	www.stedmundsbury.anglican.org
Salisbury Cathedral	Wiltshire	www.salisburycathedral.org.uk
Sand	Devon	www.eastdevon.net/sand
☛ Sandham MemorialChapel	Hampshire	www.nationaltrust.org.uk/southern
☛ Scampston Hall	N Yorkshire	www.scampston.co.uk
☛ Scone Palace	Scotland	www.scone-palace.co.uk
Shakespeare Houses	Warwickshire	www.shakespeare.org.uk
Shugborough	Staffordshire	www.staffordshire.gov.uk
☛ Skipton Castle	Yorkshire	www.skiptoncastle.co.uk
☛ Robert Smail's Printing Works	Scotland	www.nts.org.uk
☛ Snowshill Manor	Gloucestershire	www.ntrustsevern.org.uk
Somerley	Hampshire	www.somerley.com
☛ Somerleyton Hall	Suffolk	www.somerleyton.co.uk
Somerset House	London	www.somerset-house.org.uk
South Elmham Hall	Suffolk	www.btinternet.com/~jo.sanderson
Southwark Cathedral	London	www.dswark.org
Spencer House	London	www.spencerhouse.co.uk
☛ Standen	Sussex	www.nationaltrust.org.uk/southern
Stoneleigh Abbey	Warwickshire	www.stoneleighabbey.org
Sudeley Castle	Gloucestershire	www.stratford.co.uk/sudeley
☛ Sulgrave Manor	Northants	www.stratford.co.uk/sulgrave
Sutton Park	Yorkshire	www.statelyhome.co.uk
☛ Tenement House	Scotland	www.nts.org.uk
Thirlestane Castle	Scotland	www.great-houses-scotland.co.uk/thirlestane
☛ Threave Garden	Scotland	www.nts.org.uk
Tissington Hall	Derbyshire	www.tisshall.dircon.co.uk/
Torosay Castle & Gardens	Scotland	www.zynet.co.uk/mull/members/torosay
☛ Tower of London	London	www.hrp.org.uk
Towneley Hall Art Gallery & Museums	Lancashire	www.burnley.gov.uk/towneley
Traquair	Scotland	www.traquair.co.uk
Trebah Garden	Cornwall	www.trebah-garden.co.uk
☛ Uppark	Sussex	www.nationaltrust.org.uk/southern
☛ Upton House	Warwickshire	www.ntrustsevern.org.uk
Usk Castle	South Wales	www.usktc.force9.co.uk
☛ The Vyne	Hampshire	www.nationaltrust.org.uk/southern
Waddesdon Manor	Bucks	www.waddesdon.org.uk
Wallace Collection	London	www.the-wallace-collection.org.uk
Weald & Downland Open Air Museum	Sussex	www.wealddown.co.uk
☛ Weaver's Cottage	Scotland	www.nts.org.uk
West Dean Gardens	Sussex	www. westdean.org.uk/
☛ Westbury Court Garden	Gloucestershire	www.ntrustsevern.org.uk
Westminster Cathedral	London	www.westmintercathedral.org.uk
White Scar Cave	Yorkshire	www.wscave.co.uk
Wilmington Priory	Sussex	www.landmarktrust.co.uk
Wilton House	Wiltshire	www.wiltonhouse.com
Wimpole Hall & Wimpole Home Farm	Cambridgeshire	www.wimpole.org
Winchester Cathedral	Hampshire	www.win.diocese.org.uk/cathedral.html
☛ Windsor Castle	Berkshire	www.royal.gov.uk
Winkworth Arboretum	Surrey	www.cornuswwweb.co.uk
Wycombe Museum	Bucks	www.wycombe.gov.uk/museum

This list is merely intended to draw attention to properties which have websites, it is intended only as a guide and we take no responsiblity for the availability or content of these sites.

The National Gardens Scheme

Gardens Open For Charity

For over 70 years owners of the finest gardens throughout England and Wales have generously opened their gardens for the nursing and caring charities supported by the National Gardens Scheme.

Gardens of England and Wales Open For Charity, the best-selling annual garden visiting guide published by the Scheme, is available at all major booksellers, and is now also available on the internet at **www.ngs.org.uk.**

Garden Finder, the Scheme's unique website search and mapping facility helps garden visitors plan their itineraries by providing information on gardens which open for charity by county, date, feature or by garden name.

If you would like more information, or are interested in finding out about opening your garden for the Scheme please contact:

The National Gardens Scheme
Hatchlands Park
East Clandon
Surrey GU4 7RT

T 01483 211535
F 01483 211537
E ngs@ngs.org.uk

This index refers to properties where plants are offered for sale.

ENGLAND

SOUTH & SOUTH EAST

WEST COUNTRY

EASTERN COUNTIES

MIDLANDS

NORTH EAST COUNTIES

NORTH WEST COUNTIES

SCOTLAND

WALES

NORTH WALES

SOUTH WALES

IRELAND

This list is merely intended to draw attention to properties which have plant sales, it is intended only as a guide.

Properties included in this list are open to some extent for all or most of the year. See entry for details.

ENGLAND

SOUTH & SOUTH EAST

Dover Castle, Kent. (p.97).

Kingston Bagpuize House, Oxfordshire. (p.145).

WEST COUNTRY

The Royal Pavilion, Sussex. (p.160).

St Mawes Castle, Cornwall. (p.184).

EASTERN COUNTIES

Ely Cathedral, Cambridgeshire. (p.228).

MIDLANDS

English Heritage

Birmingham Botanical Gardens & Glasshouses, West Midlands (p.319).

This list is merely intended to draw attention to properties which are open for most of the year, it is intended only as a guide.

Warwick Castle, Warwickshire (p.314).

NORTH EAST

NORTH WEST

Adlington Hall, Cheshire. (p.368).

SCOTLAND

Argyll's Lodging (p.450).

Caerlaverock Castle (p.414).

Pollok House, Glasgow (p.435).

Kellie Castle & Garden, Perthshire. (p. 446).

WALES

NORTH WALES

Beaumaris Castle, North Wales. (p. 478).

SOUTH WALES

Castell Coch, Wales (p.487).

Fonmon Castle, South Wales. (p.488).

IRELAND

Gardens at Ardgillan Castle, Ireland. (p.494).

This list is merely intended to draw attention to properties which are open for most of the year, it is intended only as a guide.

Kenwood House, London, *see page 124.*

The Counties of

ENGLAND

National Trust Photographic Library/Jerry Harpur

Emmetts Garden, Kent

The South East

The River Test, Hampshire

Southern Tourist Board

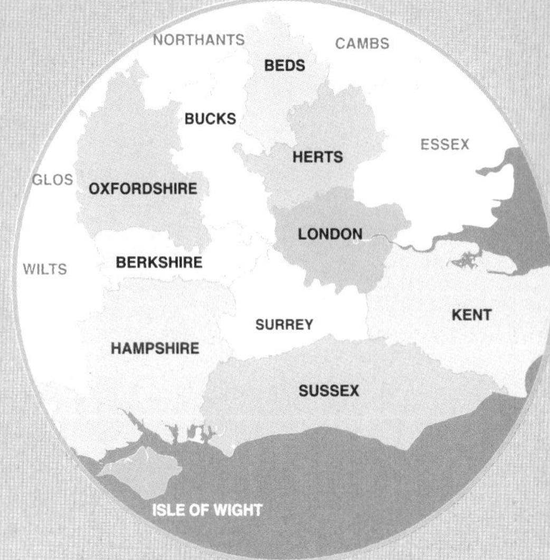

Featuring…

Broughton Castle

Broughton Castle, near Banbury, Oxfordshire, the family home of Lord and Lady Saye and Sele, has enormous charm and character.

Often used as a film location, it was seen by millions of filmgoers who watched the Oscar-winning 'Shakespeare in Love'. An island-house surrounded by a 3 acre moat, it is still approachable only across a bridge and embattled gatehouse. The weathered buildings have changed little in appearance since 1600.

Broughton came to the Fiennes family by marriage in 1451, four years after the family had acquired the barony of Saye and Sele. It was between 1550 and 1600 that the family turned the original moated, medieval manor into a fine Elizabethan mansion.

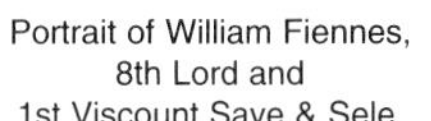

Portrait of William Fiennes, 8th Lord and 1st Viscount Saye & Sele.

Like so many of our great historic houses, it is extremely lucky to have survived the vagaries of time. Broughton was called the 'house that almost died'. But, unlike those country houses which were brought close to destruction by civil war, death duties or the aftermath of the World Wars, Broughton's brush with death came about through the flirtation of William Thomas, the 15th Baron Saye & Seles with Regency frivolity and decadence. Favouring his Kent home, Belvedere, he abandoned Broughton. The house quickly fell into total disrepair – there are many descriptions of it being completely overgrown with ivy. By 1837 he had brought the family fortunes to such a low ebb that the contents of Broughton were auctioned in an eight day sale, the final lot being the swans in the moat.

Ironically, the 5th Baron's lifestyle, whilst nearly destroying Broughton, may have protected the Castle's interiors from the architectural excesses of the Victorian age, at which time it was financially possible only to carry out repairs and minor alterations under the architect, George Gilbert Scott.

In 1956 generous financial aid received through the Historic Buildings Council, precursor of English Heritage, enabled the present and 21st Lord Saye & Sele to embark on a twenty year programme of major repairs to the fabric and internal restoration. The rooms in Broughton are a wonderfully rich amalgam of elements drawn from different periods. The present Great Hall incorporates the original medieval hall of 1300, whilst the pendant ceiling dates from the 1760s. In 1900 the plaster was removed from the walls leaving the bare stone of the fourteenth century to make a strange contrast with the sixteenth-century windows and the eighteenth-century ceiling. Yet none of this matters when standing in the Hall today, surrounded by the arms and armour of the Civil War – one can easily conjure up scenes of William, 8th Lord Saye and Sele, an active Parliamentarian, preparing with his four sons to fight at the nearby Battle of Edgehill.

Col The Hon Nathaniel Fiennes.

The character of the house changes in other rooms. The charming Queen Anne room, named to commemorate a visit by Queen Anne and James I in 1604 is a light and sunny room with a splendid fireplace and pretty 18th century four poster bed. The bed in the King's Chamber, with its remarkable 16th century chimney piece and 18th century chinese hand painted wallpapers by contrast of an interesting but entirely modern design, testament to the fact that Broughton is no museum but a continually evolving family home. The Oak Room, pure Tudor with its floor-to-ceiling oak panelling and unusual interior porch has an interesting mixture of furniture up to the present day. The garden at Broughton is no less of a delight.

For full details of this property see page 142.

WOBURN ABBEY
Woburn

Set in a beautiful 3,000 acre deer park, Woburn Abbey has been the home of the Dukes of Bedford for nearly 400 years. It is now lived in by the present Duke's heir, the Marquess of Tavistock and his family. One of the most important private art collections in the world can be seen here, including paintings by Van Dyck, Cuyp, Gainsborough, Reynolds and Velazquez. In the Venetian Room there are 21 views of Venice by Canaletto. The collection also features French and English 18th century furniture and silver. The tour of the Abbey covers three floors, including vaults, where the fabulous Sèvres dinner service presented to the 4th Duke by Louis XV of France is on display.

The deer park has nine species of deer roaming freely. One of these, the Père David, descended from the Imperial Herd of China, was saved from extinction at Woburn and is now the largest breeding herd of this species in the world. In 1985 22 Père David were given by the Family to the People's Republic of China and these are now successfully re-established in their natural habitat and number several hundred.

All catering is carried out by ourselves with banqueting, conferences, receptions and company days out our specialities in the beautiful setting of the Sculpture Gallery, overlooking the Private Gardens. It is also a popular choice for wedding receptions and a Civil Wedding Licence is held.

There are extensive picnic areas. Events are held in the Park throughout the summer including the Woburn Garden Show, Craft Fairs and the annual fly-in of the de Havilland Moth Club. The 40-shop Antique Centre is probably the most unusual such centre outside London.

Suitable for fashion shows, product launches, filming & company 'days out'. Use of parkland and garden. No photography in House.

Two shops.

Conferences, exhibitions, banqueting, luncheons, dinners in the Sculpture Gallery, Lantern & Long Harness rooms.

Wheelchairs in the Abbey by prior arrangement (max. 8 per group).

Group bookings in Sculpture Gallery. Flying Duchess Pavilion Coffee Shop.

By arrangement, max 15. Tours in French, German & Dutch at an additional charge of £10.00 per guide. Audio tape tour available – £1pp. Lectures on the property, its contents, gardens and history can be arranged.

Ample. Free.

Welcome. Special programme on request. Cost: £2.50pp (group rate).

In park on leads, and guide dogs in house.

Civil Wedding Licence. 

CONTACT

William Lash
Woburn Abbey
Woburn
Bedfordshire
MK43 0TP

Tel: 01525 290666

Fax: 01525 290271

e-mail: Woburnabbey@aol.com

LOCATION

OS Ref. SP965 325

On A4012, midway between M1/J13, 3m, J14, 6m and the A5 (turn off at Hockliffe). London approx. 1hr by road 43m. Then 4m to Woburn Village Gate in both cases.

Rail: London Euston to Leighton Buzzard, Bletchley/Milton Keynes. Kings Cross Thameslink to Flitwick.

Air: Luton 14m. Heathrow 39m.

Woburn Abbey and Safari Park ~ The 1998 Good Guide to Britain Family Attraction of the Year.

CONFERENCE/FUNCTION		
ROOM	SIZE	MAX CAPACITY
Sculpture Gallery	130' x 25'	400 220 (sit-down)
Lantern Rm	24' x 21'	100

OPENING TIMES

2 January - 25 March
Abbey: weekends only
11am - 4pm*
Deer Park: Daily
10.30am - 3.45pm

26 March - 1 October
Abbey:
Mon - Sat: 11am - 4pm*
Sun & BHs: 11am - 5pm
Deer Park:
Mon - Sat: 10am - 4.30pm
Sun & BHs: 10am - 4.45pm

2 Oct - 29 Oct
Abbey: weekends only
11am - 5pm*
Deer Park:
10.30am - 4.45pm

Abbey closed:
30 Oct - end Dec

Antiques Centre:
All year, daily
(except 24 - 26, 31 Dec 1999 & 1 Jan, 24 - 26 Dec 2000).

*last entry time

ADMISSION

Woburn Abbey
(Prices incl. Private Apts - these can be excluded for a reduction)

Adult	£7.50
Child (12 - 16yrs)	£3.00
OAP	£6.50
Groups (15+)	
Adult	£6.25
Child (7 - 16yrs)	£2.50
OAP	£5.40
Antiques Centre	Free
Grounds & Deer Park only	
Car	£5.00
Motorcycle	£2.00
Coaches	Free
Other	£0.50
Visitors from Safari Park	Free

Reduced rates apply when Private Apartments are in use by the family.

BROMHAM WATERMILL & ART GALLERY

Tel: 01234 824330

Bromham, Bedfordshire MK43 8LP

Owner: Bedfordshire County Council **Contact:** Sally Wileman

Working water mill on River Ouse. Flour milling.

Location: OS Ref. TL010 506. Location beside the River Ouse bridge on N side of the former A428, 2$^1/_2$ m W of Bedford.

Opening Times: Wed - Sat, 12 noon - 4pm. Suns, 10.30am - 5pm. Last entry 30 mins before closing.

Admission: Please telephone for admission prices.

BUSHMEAD PRIORY ⌗

Tel: 01234 376614

Colmworth, Bedford, Bedfordshire MK44 2LD **Regional Office:** 01604 730320

Owner: English Heritage **Contact:** The Custodian

A rare survival of the medieval refectory of an Augustinian priory, with its original timber-framed roof almost intact and containing interesting wall paintings and stained glass.

Location: OS Ref. TL115 607. On unclassified road near Colmworth, 2 m E of B660. 5m W of St. Neots (A1).

Opening Times: Jul - Aug weekends & BHs only: 10am - 6pm. Closed 1 - 2pm.

Admission: Adult £1.95, Child £1, Conc. £1.50.

CECIL HIGGINS ART GALLERY

CASTLE CLOSE, CASTLE LANE, BEDFORD MK40 3RP

Owner: *Bedford Borough Council & Trustees of Gallery* ***Contact:*** *The Gallery*

Tel: 01234 211222 **Fax:** 01234 327149

An unusual combination of recreated Victorian Mansion (originally the home of the Higgins family, wealthy Bedford brewers) and adjoining modern gallery housing internationally renowned collection of watercolours, prints and drawings, ceramics and glass. Room settings include many items from the Handley-Read Collection and furniture by Victorian architect William Burges. Situated in pleasant gardens near the river embankment.

Location: OS Ref. TL052 497. Centre of Bedford, just off The Embankment. E of High St.

Opening Times: Tue - Sat, 11am - 5pm (last admission 4.45pm). Sun & BH Mons, 2 - 5pm. Closed Mons, Good Fri & 20 - 28 & 31 Dec 1999.

Admission: Please telephone for admission information.

Photography in house by arrangement. By arrangement.

House & garden suitable. WC. By arrangement. By arrangement.

No parking. Guide dogs only. Telephone for details.

DE GREY MAUSOLEUM ⌗

Tel: 01525 860094 (Key-keeper)

Flitton, Bedford, Bedfordshire

Owner: English Heritage **Contact:** Mr Stimson

A remarkable treasure-house of sculpted tombs and monuments from the 16th to 19th centuries dedicated to the de Grey family of nearby Wrest Park.

Location: OS Ref. TL059 359. Attached to the church on unclassified road 1$^1/_2$ m W of A6 at Silsoe.

Opening Times: Weekends only. Key: Mr Stimson, 3 Highfield Rd, Flitton.

Admission: Free.

HOUGHTON HOUSE ⌗

Tel: 01604 730320

Ampthill, Bedford, Bedfordshire

Owner: English Heritage **Contact:** The Midlands Regional Office

Reputedly the inspiration for "House Beautiful" in Bunyan's "Pilgrim's Progress", the remains of this early 17th century mansion still convey elements which justify the description, including work attributed to Inigo Jones.

Location: OS Ref. TL039 394. 1m NE of Ampthill off A421, 8m S of Bedford, then by footpath to NE.

Opening Times: Any reasonable time.

Admission: Free.

LUTON MUSEUM & ART GALLERY

Tel: 01582 546739

Wardown Park, Luton, Bedfordshire

Owner: Luton Borough Council **Contact:** Lynette Burgess

Lively and varied collections housed in an impressive Victorian Mansion set in Wardown Park.

Location: OS Ref. TL089 230. 1$^1/_4$ m N of town centre between New and Old Bedford Rd.

Opening Times: Tue - Sat, 10am - 5pm, Suns, 1 - 5pm. Closed 25/26 Dec & New Year's Day.

Admission: Free.

MOOT HALL

Tel: 01234 266889

Elstow Green, Church View, Elstow, Bedford

Owner: Bedfordshire County Council

Timber framed market hall.

Location: OS Ref. TL048 475. 1m from Bedford, signposted from A6.

Opening Times: Apr - Oct: Tue, Wed, Thur, Sat, Sun & BHs: 2 - 5pm.

Admission: Adult £1, Conc. 50p.

STOCKWOOD PERIOD GARDENS

Tel: 01582 546739

Farley Hill, Luton, Bedfordshire

Owner: Luton Borough Council **Contact:** Lynette Burgess

Includes Knot, Medieval, Victorian and Italian gardens.

Location: OS Ref. TL085 200. 1$^1/_4$ m SW of Luton town centre by Farley Road B4546.

Opening Times: Apr - Oct: Tue - Sun & BHs, 10am - 5pm. Nov - Mar: Sat - Sun, 10am - 4pm.

Admission: Free.

SWISS GARDEN

Tel: 01767 627666 **Fax:** 01767 627443

Biggleswade Road, Old Warden, Bedfordshire

Owner: Bedfordshire County Council

Laid out in the early 1800s and steeped in the indulgent romanticism of the time, Swiss Garden combines all the elements of high fashion: formal walks and vistas, classical proportions, tiny thatched buildings, woodland glades and, hidden away, a fairytale grotto with a brilliant glazed fernery, magnificent trees and a network of ponds and bridges. Shuttleworth Mansion, home of the family that owned Swiss Garden, is open on a number of days during the year. Cream teas are served during the summer on the lawn beside the house.

Location: OS Ref. TL150 447. 1$^1/_2$ m W of Biggleswade A1 roundabout, signposted from A1 and A600. Approached from Shuttleworth Mansion, Old Warden Park.

Opening Times: Mar - Sept: Sun & BHs, 10am - 6pm. Weekdays & Sat: 1 - 6pm. Jan, Feb & Oct: Suns & New Year's Day, 11am - 3pm. Last admission $^3/_4$ hr before closing. Groups at any time on request.

Admission: Adult £3, Conc. £2, Family £7.50. Season ticket available. Special rates for groups and guided tours.

Catering. Cream teas during summer. Woodland only.

WOBURN ABBEY

See page 62 for full page entry.

Patrick Lane.

Swiss Garden, Bedfordshire.

Woburn Abbey Grotto, Bedfordshire

WREST PARK GARDENS 

English Heritage Photographic Library

English Heritage Photographic Library

SILSOE, LUTON, BEDFORDSHIRE MK45 4HS

Owner: *English Heritage* ***Contact:*** *The Custodian*

Tel: 01525 860152

Over 90 acres of wonderful gardens originally laid out in the early 18th century, including the Great Garden. During the 18th and 19th centuries the formal parterre was introduced together with marble fountains, the Bath House and the vast Orangery, built by the Earl de Grey. The gardens form a delightful backdrop to the house, built in the style of an 18th century French chateau.

Location: OS153, Ref. TL093 356. 3/4 m E of Silsoe off A6, 10m S of Bedford.

Opening Times: 1 Apr - 31 Oct: Weekends and BHs only, 10am - 6pm (5pm in Oct).

Admission: Adult £3.40, Child £1.70, Conc. £2.60. 15% discount for groups (11+).

 Telephone for details.

NEWBURY MANOR
Newbury

NEWBURY MANOR is a Grade II listed, privately owned Country House Hotel located in the centre of Newbury, off the London Road, overlooking eight acres of beautiful water meadows and the River Lambourn and the Kennet and Avon canal.

At Newbury Manor they appreciate that every conference, like every business, is different. They specialise in meetings of up to 50 people and aim to provide a personal and professional level of service in order to produce a meeting tailored to your design. They also specialise in functions from 8 - 100 people.

Newbury Manor's Executive Chef is award-winning David Sharland who was formerly the Head Chef at the Savoy Grill and the Vineyard, Stockcross before joining Newbury Manor to open 'Sharlands', Newbury Manor's restaurant.

The hotel is ideally located some five miles away from the centre of Newbury. It has recently undergone a complete refurbishment and now offers 34 bedrooms including 6 suites and 5 syndicate rooms.

CONTACT

Newbury Manor Hotel
London Road
Newbury
Berkshire
RG14 2BY

Tel: 01635 528838

Fax: 01635 523406

e-mail: enquiries@newbury-manor-hotel.co.uk

LOCATION

½m from the centre of Newbury.

Rail: Newbury Station 1m.

Air: London Airport (Heathrow).

CONFERENCE/FUNCTION		
ROOM	SIZE	MAX CAPACITY
Highclere		50

OPENING TIMES

All year

ADMISSION

Please telephone for details.

Telephone for details.

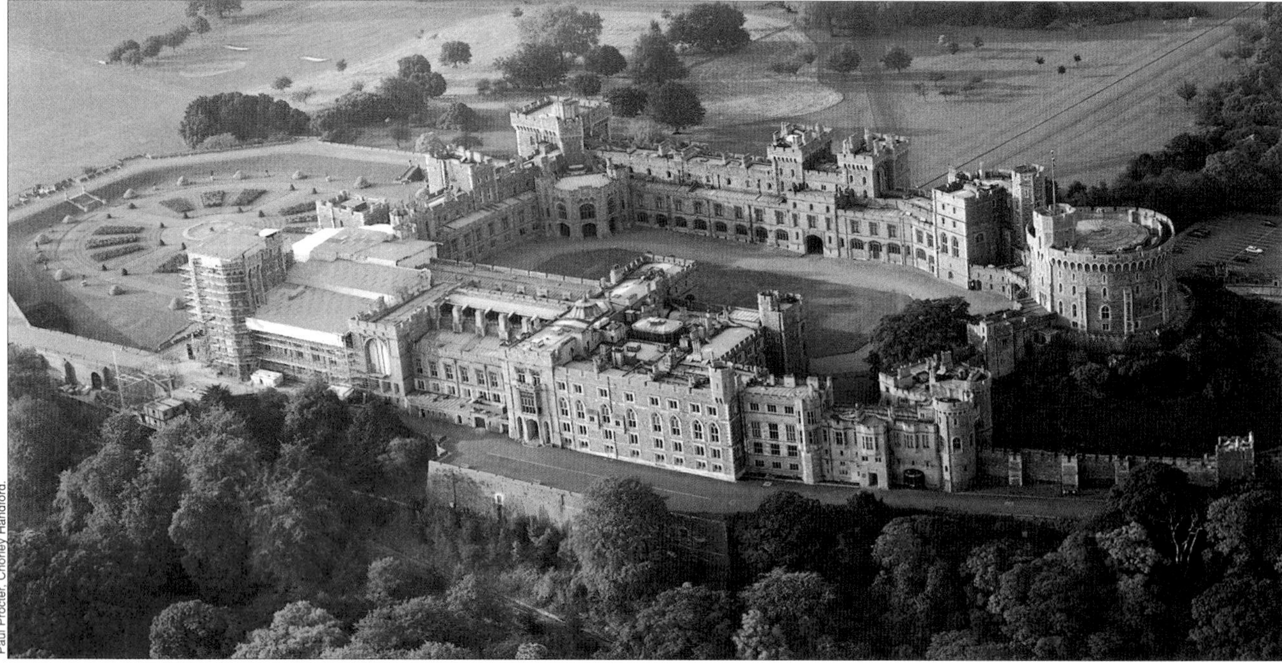

Paul Procter, Chorley Handford.

WINDSOR CASTLE
Windsor

Owner: HM The Queen

CONTACT

The Visitor Office
Windsor Castle
Windsor
Berkshire
SL4 1NJ

Tel: 01753 869898
01753 831118

Fax: 01753 832290

e-mail: information@royalcollection.org.uk

LOCATION

OS Ref. SU969 770

M4/J6, M3/J3.
20m from central London.

Rail: Regular service from London Waterloo.

Air: London Airport (Heathrow) 15m.

Coach: Victoria Coach Station - regular service.

Sightseeing tours: Tour companies operate a daily service with collection from many London Hotels. Ask your hotel concierge or porter for information.

WINDSOR CASTLE, Buckingham Palace, and the Palace of Holyroodhouse are the Official residences of the Sovereign and are used by The Queen as both a home and office. The Queen's personal standard flies when Her Majesty is in residence. Furnished with works of art from the Royal Collection, these buildings are used extensively by The Queen for State ceremonies and Official entertaining. They are opened to the public as much as these commitments will allow.

A significant proportion of Windsor Castle is opened to visitors on a regular basis including the Upper and Lower Wards, the North Terrace with its famous views towards Eton, Queen Mary's Dolls House, the State Apartments including St. George's Hall, the Crimson Drawing Room and other newly restored rooms.

HM Queen Elizabeth II

No photography.

No parking.

Guide dogs only.

OPENING TIMES

March - October:
Daily except 16 February, 21 April & 19 June
9.45am - 5.15pm
(last admission 4pm).

November - February:
Daily except 25/26 & 31 December 1999 & 1 January 2000,
9.45am - 4.15pm
(last admission 3pm).

St George's Chapel is closed to visitors on Sundays as services are held throughout the day. Worshippers are welcome.

The State Rooms are closed during Royal and State visits.

Opening arrangements may change at short notice.

ADMISSION

Adult	£10.50
Child (up to 17yrs)	£5.00
OAP	£8.00
Family (2+2)	£25.50

Groups (15+)
10% discount

SPECIAL EVENTS

With the exception of Sundays, the Changing of the Guard takes place at 11am daily from April to the end of June and on alternate days at other times of the year.

BASILDON PARK

Vera Collingwood.

LOWER BASILDON, READING RG8 9NR

Owner: *The National Trust* **Contact:** *The Property Manager*

Tel: 0118 984 3040 **Fax:** 0118 984 1267 **e-mail:** tbdgen@smtp.ntrust.org.uk

An elegant, classical house designed in the 18th century by Carr of York and set in rolling parkland in the Thames Valley. The house has rich interiors with fine plasterwork, pictures and furniture, and includes an unusual Octagon Room and a decorative Shell Room. Basildon Park has connections with the East through its builder and was the home of a wealthy industrialist in the 19th century. It was rescued from dereliction in the mid 20th century. Small flower garden, pleasure grounds and woodland walk.

Location: OS Ref. SU611 782. 2¹/₂ m NW of Pangbourne on the west side of the A329, 7m from M4/J12.

Opening Times: House: 1 Apr - 31 Oct: daily except Mon & Tue (closed Good Fri, open BH Mons), 1 - 5.30. Park, Garden & Woodland Walk: as house 12 noon - 5.30pm. Property closes at 5pm on 11/12 Aug for concerts.

Admission: House, Park & Garden: Adult £4.20, Child £2.10, Family £10.50. Park & Garden only: Adult £1.80, Child 90p. Family £4.50. Groups of 15+ by appointment.

P In grounds. On leads, in grounds only.

DONNINGTON CASTLE

Tel: 01732 778000

Newbury, Berkshire

Owner: English Heritage **Contact:** The South East Regional Office

Built in the late 14th century, the twin towered gatehouse of this heroic castle survives amidst some impressive earthworks.

Location: OS Ref. SU463 691. 1m NW of Newbury off B4494.

Opening Times: Any reasonable time.

Admission: Free.

Eton, Berkshire.

DORNEY COURT

WINDSOR, BERKSHIRE SL4 6QP

Owner/Contact: *Mrs Peregrine Palmer*

Tel: 01628 604638 **Fax:** 01628 665772

"One of the finest Tudor Manor Houses in England." Dorney Court is an enchanting, many gabled pink brick and timbered manor house with more than just a taste of history.

Grade I listed Dorney Court offers a most welcome, refreshing and fascinating experience. Built about 1440 and lived in by the present family for over 400 years. The rooms are full of the atmosphere of history: early 15th and 16th century oak, beautiful 17th century lacquer furniture, 18th and 19th century tables, 400 years of family portraits, stained glass and needlework. Here Charles II once came to seek the charms of Barbara Palmer, Countess of Castlemaine, the most intelligent, beautiful and influential of ladies. St James' Church next door, is a lovely, cool, cheerful and very English village church.

"The approach to the house is through ancient Buckinghamshire woodland which transports the visitor into a dreamland. Suddenly the early Tudor house, a ravishing half timbered vision in gabled pinkish brick, comes into view, prettily grouped with a church. This is Dorney Court, a surprisingly little known manor house … happily genuine … an idyllic image." *Daily Telegraph.*

Location: 25m W of London. W of B3026, 2¹/₂ m SW of Slough, 2m SE of Maidenhead.

Opening Times: May BHs: 2, 3, 30/ 31 May. Jul/Aug: Mon - Thur, 1 - 4.30pm. Last admission 4pm. Rest of Year: Pre-booked tours only.

Admission: House & Garden: Adult: £5, Child (10 - 16yrs) £3. Groups: (10)+ on open days Adult £4.50, Child £3. Private Visits £6. Child £3.

i No photography in house. Film & photographic shoots. Garden centre.

Garden centre suitable. Tour time 1¹/₂hrs P

Accompanying adults free, £16 for each guide required. Guide dogs only.

ENGLEFIELD HOUSE

Tel: 01189 302221 **Fax:** 01189 303226

Englefield, Theale, Reading, Berkshire RG7 5EN

Owner: Sir William & Lady Benyon **Contact:** Mrs Gloria Sleep

Seven acres of woodland and water garden. Stone balustrades and staircases descending to terraces, herbaceous and rose borders. All set in a deer park. Elizabethan house is open by appointment.

Location: OS Ref. SU622 720. 6m W of Reading on A340. Theale 1m.

Opening Times: Garden only: All year: Mons, 10am - 6pm. Apr - Oct: Mon - Thur incl. 10am - 6pm.

Admission: £2.

No photography in house. Partially suitable.WC.

By arrangement. Ample for cars, limited for coaches. 

ETON COLLEGE

Tel: 01753 671177 **Fax:** 01753 671265

Windsor, Berkshire SL4 6DW

Owner: Eton College **Contact:** Rebecca Hunkin

Eton College, founded in 1440 by Henry VI, is one of the oldest and best known schools in the country. The original and subsequent historic buildings of the Foundation are a part of the heritage of the British Isles and visitors are invited to experience and share the beauty of the ancient precinct which includes the magnificent College Chapel, a masterpiece of the perpendicular style.

Location: OS Ref. SU967 779. Off M4/J5. Access from Windsor by footbridge only. Vehicle access from Slough 2m N.

Opening Times: Mar - early Oct: Times vary, best to check with the Visits Office.

Admission: Ordinary admissions and daily guided tours. Groups by appointment only. Rates vary according to type of tour.

Suitable for conferences. Ground floor suitable. WC.

Limited. Guide dogs only.

NEWBURY MANOR

See page 65 for full page entry.

ST GEORGE'S CHAPEL WINDSOR

Tel: 01753 868286

Fine example of perpendicular architecture. Open only in conjunction with Windsor Castle.

Location: OS Ref. SU968 770.

Opening Times: As Windsor Castle, but opening times subject to change at short notice.

Admission: Admission as part of Windsor Castle ticket.

THE SAVILL GARDEN

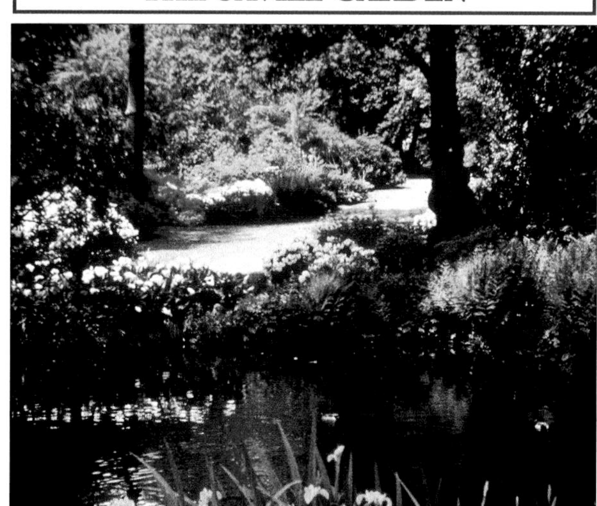

WINDSOR GREAT PARK, BERKSHIRE SL4 2HT

Owner: *Crown Property* ***Contact:*** *Jan Bartholomew*

Tel: 01753 847518 **Fax:** 01753 847536

World-renowned 35 acre woodland garden, providing a wealth of beauty and interest in all seasons. Spring is heralded by hosts of daffodils, masses of rhododendrons, azaleas, camellias, magnolias and much more. Roses, herbaceous borders and countless alpines are the great features of summer, and the leaf colours and fruits of autumn rival the other seasons with a great display.

Location: OS Ref. SU977 706. Wick Lane, Englefield Green. Clearly signposted from Ascot, Bagshot, Egham and Windsor. Nearest station: Egham.

Opening Times: Mar - Oct: 10am - 6pm. Nov - Feb: 10am - 4pm.

Admission: Apr - May: Adult £5, Child (6-16) £2, Conc. £4.50. Jun - Oct: Adult £4, Child (6-16) £1, Conc. £3.50. Nov - Mar: Adult £3, Child (6-16) £1, Conc. £2.50. Child under 6 Free. Prices valid from 1 Apr 2000.

Plant centre. Grounds suitable. WC. Licensed.

Guide dogs only.

TAPLOW COURT

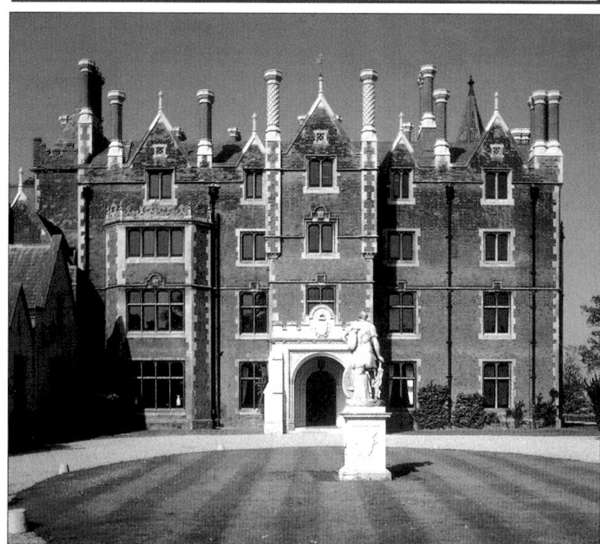

BERRY HILL, TAPLOW, Nr MAIDENHEAD, BERKS SL6 0ER

Owner: *SGI-UK* ***Contact:*** *Robert Samuels*

Tel: 01628 591215 **Fax:** 01628 773055

Set high above the Thames, affording spectacular views. Remodelled mid-19th century by William Burn. Earlier neo-Norman Hall. 18th century home of Earls of Orkney and more recently of Lord and Lady Desborough who entertained 'The Souls' here. Tranquil gardens & grounds. Anglo-Saxon burial mound. Permanent and temporary exhibitions.

Location: OS Ref. SU907 822. M4/J7 off Bath Road towards Maidenhead. 6m off M40/J2.

Opening Times: House & Grounds: Easter Sun & Mon, Suns & BH Mons up to the end of Jul: 2 - 6pm. Ring to confirm 30 July.

Admission: No charge. Free parking.

Guide dogs only.

WELFORD PARK

Tel: 01488 608203

Newbury, Berkshire RG20 8HU

Owner/Contact: Mr J Puxley

A Queen Anne house, with attractive gardens and grounds. Riverside walks.

Location: OS Ref. SU409 731. On Lambourn Valley Road. 6m NW of Newbury.

Opening Times: 29 May, 1 - 26 Jun, 28 Aug: 2.30 - 5pm.

Admission: House by prior arrangement. Adult £3.50, Child Free, Conc. £2. Grounds Free.

Grounds suitable. On leads, in grounds.

Welford Park, Berkshire.

WINDSOR CASTLE

See page 66 for full page entry.

STOWE SCHOOL

Buckingham

STOWE owes its pre-eminence to the vision and wealth of two owners. From 1715 to 1749 Viscount Cobham, one of Marlborough's Generals, continuously improved his estate, calling in the leading designers of the day to lay out the gardens, and commissioning several leading architects – Vanbrugh, Gibbs, Kent and Leoni – to decorate them with garden temples. From 1750 to 1779 Earl Temple, his nephew and successor continued to expand and embellish both Gardens and House. The House is now a major public school.

Around the mansion is one of Britain's most magnificent landscape gardens now in the ownership of the National Trust. Covering 325 acres and containing no fewer than 6 lakes and 32 garden temples, it is of the greatest historic importance. During the 1730s William Kent laid out in the Elysian Fields at Stowe, one of the first 'natural' landscapes and initiated the style known as 'the English Garden'. 'Capability' Brown worked there for 10 years, not as a consultant but as head gardener, and in 1744 was married in the little church hidden between the trees.

Owner: Stowe School

CONTACT

The Commercial Director
Stowe School
Buckingham
MK18 5EH

Tel: 01280 813650 House only
or 01280 822850 Gardens

Fax: 01280 816070

LOCATION

OS Ref. SP666 366

From London, M1 to Milton Keynes, $1^1/_2$ hrs or Banbury $1^1/_4$ hrs, 3m NW of Buckingham.

Bus: from Buckingham 3m.

Rail: Milton Keynes 15m.

Air: Heathrow 50m.

CONFERENCE/FUNCTION		
ROOM	SIZE	MAX CAPACITY
Roxburgh Hall	–	460
Music Room	–	120
Marble Hall	–	150
State Dining Rm	–	160
Garter Room	–	180
Memorial Theatre	–	120

Indoor swimming pool, sports hall, tennis court, squash courts, parkland, cricket pitches and golf course. No photography in house.

Call for opening times.

International conferences, private functions, weddings, and prestige exhibitions. Catering on request.

Visitors may alight at entrance. Allocated parking areas. WC in garden area. 'Batricars' available.

Morning coffee, lunch and afternoon tea available by pre-arrangement only, for up to 100.

For parties of 30 at additional cost. Tour time: house and garden $2^1/_2$ hrs, house only 45 mins.

Ample.

In grounds on leads.

Civil Wedding Licence.

Available.

OPENING TIMES

SUMMER

House

20 March - 11 April &
5 July - 5 September
Daily: 2 - 5pm
Suns: 12 noon - 5pm.

NB: It may be necessary to close the house at times when it is being used for private functions. Please telephone first to check.

Gardens

20 March - 11 April &
5 July - 5 September
Daily: 10am - 5pm.

14 April - 4 July &
5 Sept - 31 Oct
Mon, Wed, Fri & Sun.
Daily: 10am - 5pm.

WINTER

Closed.
(Suns by appointment only.)

ADMISSION

SUMMER

House only

Adult	£2.00
Child	£1.00
OAP	£2.00
Student	£2.00

10% discount for groups of 30+ visiting the house.

Gardens only

Adult	£4.50
Child	£2.25
OAP	£4.50
Family	£11.50

SPECIAL EVENTS

- **Oct 28/29:** Craft Fair

National Trust Photographic Library: ANdrew Peppard

WADDESDON MANOR

Nr Aylesbury

WADDESDON MANOR was built at the end of the last century for Baron Ferdinand de Rothschild to entertain his guests and display his vast collection of art treasures. It has won many awards including Museum of the Year, Best National Trust Property 1997 and the Silver Award for England for Excellence Visitor Attraction of the Year 1998.

This French Renaissance-style château houses one of the finest collection of French 18th century decorative arts in the world: Savonnerie carpets, Sèvres porcelain, Beauvais tapestries and furniture by the best French cabinet makers, as well as important portraits by Gainsborough and Reynolds and works by Dutch and Flemish Masters of the 17th century.

Other displays include collections of gold boxes, buttons and drawings, plus the Choiseul Sèvres dessert service in the Dining Room. The refurbished Bachelors' Wing is also now open.

Waddesdon has one of the finest Victorian gardens in Britain, famous for its landscape of specimen trees and parterre. The Rococo-style aviary houses a splendid collection of exotic birds and thousands of bottles of vintage Rothschild wines are found in the wine cellars.

There are gift and wine shops and a licensed restaurant. Many events are organised throughout the year including Collection study days, floodlit openings, wine tastings, and garden workshops.

CONTACT

Waddesdon
Nr Aylesbury
Buckinghamshire
HP18 0JH

Tel: 01296 653211

Booking: 01296 653226

Fax: 01296 653208

e-mail: twmsep@smtp.ntrust.org.uk

LOCATION

OS Ref. SP740 169

Between Aylesbury & Bicester, off A41.

Rail: Aylesbury 6m.

National Trust Photographic Library: Flying Pictures

No photography in house.

Conferences, corporate hospitality.

Suitable. WCs.

Licensed.

By arrangement.

Ample for coaches and cars.

Guide dogs only.

Civil Wedding Licence.

OPENING TIMES

Grounds
(including garden, aviary, restaurant and shops)
1 Mar - 24 Dec: Wed - Sun & BH Mons, 10am - 5pm.

House
(including wine cellars)
30 Mar - 29 Oct, Thur - Sun, also BH Mons & Weds in Jul & Aug, 11am - 4pm. Last recommended admission 2.30pm.

Bachelors' Wing open 30 Mar - 29 Oct: Wed, Thur - Fri in Jul & Aug, 11am - 4pm (access cannot be guaranteed).

ADMISSION

House & Grounds

Adult	£10.00
Child (5-16 yrs)	£7.50
Groups (15+)	
Adult	£8.00
Child	£6.00

Grounds only

Adult	£3.00
Child (5-16 yrs)	£1.50
1 Nov - 24 Dec	Free
Groups (15+)	
Adult	£2.40
Child	£1.20
Bachelors' Wing	£1.00

NT members free.HHA Members free entry to grounds.

Timed tickets to the house can be purchased on site or reserved in advance by phoning 01296 653226 Mon - Fri, 10am - 4pm. Advance booking fee: £3 per transaction.

Children under 5yrs are not allowed in the house. Babies must be carried in a front-sling carrier.

SPECIAL EVENTS

Wine Tasting, Study Days, Garden Workshops and tours, Family Events, Floodlit Evenings: please telephone for details.

ASCOTT

Tel: 01296 688242 **Fax:** 01296 681904

Wing, Leighton Buzzard, Bucks LU7 0PS **e-mail:** tacgen@smtp.ntrust.org.uk

Owner: The National Trust **Contact:** The Administrator

Originally a Jacobean farmhouse. The garden contains unusual trees, flower borders, naturalised bulbs, water-lilies and a topiary sundial.

Location: OS Ref. SP891 230. $^{1}/_{2}$ m E of Wing, 2m SW of Leighton Buzzard, on A418.

Opening Times: House & Garden: 1 - 30 Apr, 29 Aug - 4 Oct daily except Mons, 2 - 6pm, last admission 5pm. Garden only: 1 May - 28 Aug: every Wed & last Sun in each month, 2 - 6pm.

Admission: House & Garden: £5.60. Garden: £4. Child half price. Groups must book.

Grounds, limited access. 3 wheelchairs available. WCs. In car park only.

BOARSTALL TOWER

Boarstall, Aylesbury, Buckinghamshire HP18 9UX

Owner: The National Trust **Contact:** The Administrator

The stone gatehouse of a fortified house long since demolished. It dates from the 14th century, and was altered in the 16th and 17th centuries, but retains its crossloops for bows. The tower is almost entirely surrounded by a moat.

Location: OS Ref. SP624 141. Midway between Bicester and Thame, 2m W of Brill.

Opening Times: 1 Apr - 31 Oct: Wed & BH Mons, 2 - 6pm. Also Sats by prior arrangement with tenant.

Admission: £1.20.

Ground floor & garden. In car park only.

BUCKINGHAM CHANTRY CHAPEL

Market Hill, Buckingham, Buckinghamshire

Owner: The National Trust **Contact:** The Administrator

Rebuilt in 1475 and retaining a fine Norman doorway. The chapel was restored by Gilbert Scott in 1875, at which time it was used as a Latin or Grammar School.

Location: OS Ref. SP693 340. In narrow lane, NW of Market Hill.

Opening Times: Daily by written appointment with the Buckingham Heritage Trust, c/o Old Gaol Museum, Market Hill, Buckingham MK18 1JX.

Admission: Free.

CHICHELEY HALL

Tel: 01234 391252 **Fax:** 01234 391388

Newport Pagnell, Buckinghamshire MK16 9JJ

Owner: The Hon Nicholas Beatty **Contact:** Mrs V Child

Fine 18th century house. Naval museum, English sea paintings and furniture. Suitable for residential conferences up to 15 delegates.

Location: OS Ref. SP906 458. 2m from Milton Keynes, 5 mins from M1/J14. 10m W of Bedford.

Opening Times: All year: By appointment only

Admission: Groups (20+): Adult £5. Groups under 20: Adult £6, Child £2.

Conferences. By arrangement. Not suitable. Obligatory. 

Patrick Lane.

Chicheley Hall, Buckinghamshire.

CHILTERN OPEN AIR MUSEUM

Tel: 01494 871117 **Fax:** 01494 872774

Newland Park, Gorelands Lane, Chalfont St Giles, Buckinghamshire HP8 4AD

Owner: Chiltern Open Air Museum Ltd. **Contact:** Dr J Moir

A museum of historic buildings showing their original uses including a blacksmith's forge, stables, barns etc.

Location: OS Ref. TQ011 938. At Newland Park $1^{1}/_{2}$ m E of Chalfont St Giles, $4^{1}/_{2}$ m from Amersham. 3m from M25/J17.

Opening Times: All Year: Tues - Sun, 10am - 5pm. Daily in August and every BH Mon from 1 April - 31 Oct.

Admission: Adult £5.50, Child under 5yrs Free, Child (5-16yrs) £3, Over 60s £4.50, Family £15. 10% discount for groups (10+).

CHENIES MANOR HOUSE

CHENIES, RICKMANSWORTH, HERTS WD3 6ER

Owner: *Lt Col & Mrs MacLeod Matthews* **Contact:** *Lt Col & Mrs MacLeod Matthews or Sue Brock*

Tel/Fax: 01494 762888

15th & 16th century Manor House with fortified tower. Original home of the Earls of Bedford, visited by Henry VIII and Elizabeth I. Home of the MacLeod Matthews family. Contains contemporary tapestries and furniture, hiding places, collection of antique dolls, medieval undercroft and well. Surrounded by beautiful gardens which have featured in many publications and on TV, a Tudor sunken garden, a white garden, herbaceous borders, a fountain court, a physic garden containing a very wide selection of medicinal and culinary herbs, a parterre and two mazes. The kitchen garden is in the Victorian style with unusual vegetables and fruit. Special exhibitions, flower drying and arrangements.

Location: OS Ref. TQ016 984. N of A404 between Amersham & Rickmansworth. M25/J18, 3m.

Opening Times: 1 Apr - 28 Oct: Wed & Thur & BH Mons, 2 - 5pm. Last entry to house 4.15pm. Groups by arrangement at other times.

Admission: House & Garden: Adult £4.75, Child £2.20. Garden only: Adult £2.50, Child £1.

Unusual plants for sale. Grounds suitable. Telephone for details.

CLAYDON HOUSE 

National Trust Photographic Library: Andreas Von Einsiedel

MIDDLE CLAYDON, Nr BUCKINGHAM MK18 2EY

Owner: *The National Trust* **Contact:** *The Custodian*

Tel: 01296 730349 **Fax:** 01296 738511 **e-mail:** cdgen@smtp.ntrust.org.uk

A fine 18th century house with some of the most perfect rococo decoration in England. A series of great rooms have wood carvings in Chinese and Gothic styles, and tall windows look out over parkland and a lake. The house has relics of the exploits of the Verney family in the English Civil War and also on show is the bedroom of Florence Nightingale, a relative of the Verneys and a regular visitor to this tranquil place.

Location: OS Ref. SP720 253. In Middle Claydon, 13m NW of Aylesbury, signposted from A413, A421 and A41. $3^{1}/_{2}$ m SW of Winslow.

Opening Times: 1 Apr - 31 Oct: daily except Thur & Fri, 1 - 5pm. House closes 1hr early on event days.

Admission: Adult £4.20, Family £10.50. Groups 15+ (must book): Mon - Wed & Sat. £3.60. Garden only: £1.

Ground floor & grounds. Braille guide. WC. In park, on leads. Telephone for details.

CLIVEDEN 

NT Thames & Chiltern Photographic Library: Vera Collingwood

TAPLOW, MAIDENHEAD SL6 0JA

Owner: *The National Trust* Contact: *The Property Manager*

Tel: 01628 605069 **Fax:** 01628 669461 **e-mail:** tclest@smtp.ntrust.org.uk

152 hectares of gardens and woodland. A water garden, 'secret' rose garden, herbaceous borders, topiary, a great formal parterre, and informal vistas provide endless variety. The garden statuary is one of the most important collections in the care of The National Trust and includes many Roman antiquities collected by 1st Viscount Astor. The Octagonal Temple (Chapel) with its rich mosaic interior is open on the same days as are three of the Mansion's principal rooms.

Location: OS Ref. SU915 851. 3m N of Maidenhead, M4/J7 onto A4 or M40/J4 onto A404 to Marlow and follow signs.

Opening Times: Estate & Garden: 15 Mar - 31 Dec: daily, 11am - 6pm (closes at 4pm from 1 Nov). Mansion (3 rooms): Apr - Oct: Thurs & Suns, 3 - 6pm. Entry by timed ticket from information kiosk. Octagonal Temple: as mansion. Woodlands car park: All year: daily, 11am - 6pm (closes at 4pm from Nov - Mar).

Admission: Grounds: Adult £5, Child £2.50, Family £12.50. Mansion: £1 extra, Child 50p. Groups (must book): Adult £4.50, Child £2.25. Woodlands car park: Adult £3, Child £1.50, Family £7.50. Note: Mooring charge on Cliveden Reach.

Limited suitability. WC. Licensed. Specified woodlands only. Telephone for details.

HUGHENDEN MANOR 

National Trust Photographic Library: Matthew Antrobus.

HIGH WYCOMBE HP14 4LA

Owner: *The National Trust* Contact: *The Property Manager*

Tel: 01494 755573

Home of Prime Minister Benjamin Disraeli from 1847 - 1881, Hughenden has a red brick, 'gothic' exterior. The interior is a comfortable Victorian home and still holds many of Disraeli's pictures, books and furniture, as well as other fascinating mementoes of the life of the great statesman and writer. The surrounding park and woodland have lovely walks, and the formal garden has been recreated in the spirit of Mary Anne Disraeli's colourful designs.

Location: OS165 Ref. SU866 955. $1\frac{1}{2}$ m N of High Wycombe on the W side of the A4128.

Opening Times: House: 1 - 30 Mar: Sats & Suns. 1 Apr - 31 Oct: Wed - Sun & BH Mons, 1 - 5pm (last admission 4.30pm). Closed Good Fri. On BHs and busy days entry is by timed ticket. Gardens open same days as house, 12 noon - 5pm. Park & Woodland: All year.

Admission: House & Garden: £4.20, Family £10.50 Garden only: £1.50, Child 75p. Park & woodland Free. Groups must book, no groups on Sat, Sun or BH Mons.

Exhibition area. Limited. WC. In grounds, on leads. Guide dogs in house & formal gardens. Telephone for details.

COWPER & NEWTON MUSEUM

Tel: 01234 711516 **e-mail:** museum@olney.co.uk

Home of Olney's Heritage, Orchard Side, Market Place, Olney MK46 4AJ

Owner: Board of Trustees **Contact:** Mrs J McKillop

Once the home of 18th century poet and letter writer William Cowper and now containing furniture, paintings and belongings of both Cowper and his ex-slave trader friend, Rev John Newton (author of "Amazing Grace"). Attractions include re-creations of a Victorian country kitchen and wash-house, two peaceful gardens and Cowper's restored summerhouse. Costume gallery, important collections of dinosaur bones and bobbin lace, and local history displays.

Location: OS Ref. SP890 512. On A509, 6m N of Newport Pagnell, M1/J14.

Opening Times: 1 Mar - 23 Dec: Tue - Sat & BH Mons, 10am - 1pm & 2 - 5pm. Closed on Good Fri. Open on Sundays in June, July & August, 2 - 5pm.

Admission: Adult £2, Conc. £1.50, Child & Students (with card) £1, Family £5.

No photography. Gardens suitable. By arrangement. Guide dogs only.

DORNEYWOOD GARDEN

Tel: 01494 52805 (NT Regional Office)

Dorneywood, Burnham, Buckinghamshire SL1 8PY

Owner: The National Trust **Contact:** The Administrator

The house was given to the National Trust as an official residence for either a Secretary of State or Minister of the Crown. Garden only open.

Location: OS Ref. SU938 848. SW of Burnham Beeches. 2m E of Cliveden.

Opening Times: By written appointment only: 28 Jun, 19 Jul & 5 Aug: 2 - 5pm. Write to The Secretary, Dorneywood Trust at above address.

Admission: £2.80.

FORD END WATERMILL

Tel: 01582 600391

Station Road, Ivinghoe, Buckinghamshire **Contact:** David Lindsey

The Watermill, a listed building, was recorded in 1767 but is probably much older.

Location: OS Ref. SP941 166. 600 metres from Ivinghoe Church along B488 (Station Road) to Leighton Buzzard.

Opening Times: Easter Mon, then 30 Apr - 24 Sept: Suns & BHs, 2.30 - 5.30pm. To pre-book school parties, contact 01296 668083. Please phone for milling dates.

Admission: Adult £1, Child 30p. School Groups: 50p each adult and child.

MENTMORE TOWERS

Tel/Fax: 01296 662183

Nr Leighton Buzzard, Bedfordshire LU7 0QH

Mentmore Towers is an example of the Victorian 'Jacobethan' revival at its best.

Location: OS Ref. SP902 197. M1, M25 then A41 to Tring, follow signs to Pitstone, Cheddington and Mentmore.

Opening Times: Mentmore Towers is presently closed to the public.

JOHN MILTON'S COTTAGE

Tel: 01494 872313 **e-mail:** pbirger@clara.net

21 Deanway, Chalfont St. Giles, Buckinghamshire HP8 4JH

Owner: Milton Cottage Trust **Contact:** Mr E A Dawson

Grade I listed 16th century cottage where John Milton lived and completed 'Paradise Lost' and started 'Paradise Regained'. Three ground floor museum rooms contain important 1st editions of John Milton's 17th century poetry and prose works. Amongst many unique items on display is the portrait of John Milton by Sir Godfrey Kneller. Well stocked, attractive cottage garden, Grade II listed.

Location: OS Ref. SU987 933. $\frac{1}{2}$ m W of A413. 3m N of M40/J2. S side of street.

Opening Times: 1 Mar - 31 Oct: Tue - Sun, 10am - 1pm & 2 - 6pm. Closed Mons (open BH Mons). Coach parking by prior arrangement only.

Admission: Adult £2 entry, under 15s £1, Groups (20+) £1.50.

Ground floor suitable. Talk followed by free tour.  

NETHER WINCHENDON HOUSE

Tel: 01844 290199

Aylesbury, Buckinghamshire HP18 ODY

Owner/Contact: Mr Robert Spencer Bernard

Medieval and Tudor manor house. There is a fine 16th century frieze, ceiling and original linenfold panelling. Altered in late 18th Century in the Strawberry Hill Gothick style. Fine furniture and family portraits. Continuous family occupation since mid-16th century. Home of the last British Governor of Massachussetts Bay, 1760. Interesting garden and specimen trees.

Location: OS Ref. SP734 121. 2m N of A418 equidistant between Thame & Aylesbury.

Opening Times: 1 - 29 May & 27/28 Aug: 2.30 - 5.30pm (last party at about 4.45pm).

Admission: Adult £4 (HHA members free), Child (under 12) & OAP £2 (not weekends or BHs). Groups: any time by written appointment, min charge £40.

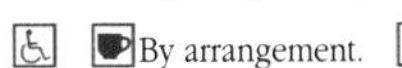
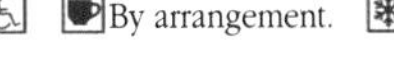
By arrangement.

PITSTONE WINDMILL

Ivinghoe, Buckinghamshire

Owner: The National Trust • **Contact:** The Administrator

One of the oldest post mills in Britain; in view from Ivinghoe Beacon.

Location: OS Ref. SP946 158. 1/2 m S of Ivinghoe, 3m NE of Tring. Just W of B488.

Opening Times: Jun - end Aug: Sun & BHs, 2.30 - 6pm.

Admission: Adult £1, Child 30p.

PRINCES RISBOROUGH MANOR HOUSE

Princes Risborough, Aylesbury, Buckinghamshire HP17 9AW

Owner: The National Trust **Contact:** The Administrator

A 17th century red-brick house with Jacobean oak staircase.

Location: OS Ref. SP806 035. Opposite church, off market square.

Opening Times: House (hall, drawing room & staircase) and front garden by written appointment only with tenant. Apr - Oct: Weds, 2.30 - 4.30pm.

Admission: £1.20.

STOWE GARDENS

English Heritage Photographic Library.

Nr BUCKINGHAM MK18 5EH

Owner: *The National Trust* Contact: *The Property Manager*

Tel: 01280 822850 **Fax:** 01280 822437 **e-mail:** tstmca@smtp.ntrust.org.uk

One of the first and finest landscape gardens in Europe, a supreme creation of the Georgian era. Its green valleys and vistas are set with lakes, monuments and temples, created and developed throughout the 18th century by some of our greatest designers and architects including Vanbrugh, Kent, Gibbs and 'Capability' Brown, who began his career here. Finest of all the garden buildings is the great Temple of Concord and Victory which celebrates Britain's success in the Seven Years War.

Location: OS Ref. SP665 366. Off A422 Buckingham - Banbury Rd. 3m NW of Buckingham.

Opening Times: Gardens: 29 Mar - 2 Jul (closed Sat, 27 May) & 10 Sept - 29 Oct: Wed - Sun. 4 Jul - 10 Sept: daily except Mons but open BH Mons, 2 - 23 Dec: Wed - Sun. Times: Mar - Oct: 10am - 5.30pm or dusk if earlier, last admission 4pm. 10 Dec - 4 Jan: last admission 3pm.

Admission: Gardens: £4.60. Family £11.50. House: Adult £2. Groups by arrangement.

Self-drive powered chairs available. WC.

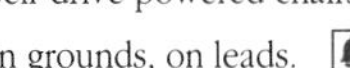
In grounds, on leads.

STOWE SCHOOL

See page 69 for full page entry.

WADDESDON MANOR

See page 70 for full page entry.

WEST WYCOMBE PARK

Tel: 01494 513569

West Wycombe, High Wycombe, Buckinghamshire HP14 3AJ

Owner: The National Trust **Contact:** The Administrator

The house will be closed in 1999 due to a major building project. The landscape garden and lake were laid out at the same time as the house with various classical temples including some by Nicholas Revett.

Location: OS Ref. SU828 947. At W end of West Wycombe S of the A40.

Opening Times: Grounds only: 1 Apr - end May: Suns, Weds & BHs, 2 - 6pm. House & Grounds: Jun, Jul & Aug: daily except Fris & Sats, 2 - 6pm. Weekday entry by timed ticket. last admission 5.15pm. Due to restoration work the house may not be open fully at the beginning of Jun, telephone 01494 513569 for details.

Admission: House & Grounds: Adult £4.60, Child £2.30, Family £11.50. Grounds only: £2.60. Note: The West Wycombe Caves and adjacent café are privately owned and NT members are liable to admission fees. Grounds only £2.60. Groups must book.

Grounds partly suitable. In car park only, on leads.

WINSLOW HALL

Tel: 01296 712323

Winslow, Buckinghamshire MK18 3HL

Owner/Contact: Sir Edward Tomkins

William and Mary house generally attributed to Wren. Virtually unchanged structurally and mostly original interiors. Good period furniture, pictures and Chinese *objets d'art*. Attractive garden with unusual trees and shrubs.

Location: OS Ref. SP772 275. In the town of Winslow on N side of the A413.

Opening Times: BH weekends, 2.30 - 5.30pm - Sat/Sun/Mon (except Christmas). Any other time by appointment.

Admission: £5. Children under 12 Free.

WYCOMBE MUSEUM

Tel: 01494 421895 **Fax:** 01494 421897
e-mail: enquiries@wycombemuseum.demon.co.uk

Priory Avenue, High Wycombe, Buckinghamshire HP13 6PX

Owner: Wycombe District Council **Contact:** Vicki Wood (Museums Officer)

Set in historic Castle Hill House and surrounded by peaceful and attractive gardens, the newly refurbished Wycombe Museum explores the history of the Wycombe district, with interactive displays, changing exhibitions, a shop and more. Discover the renowned collection of Windsor chairs.

Location: OS Ref. SU867 933. Signposted off the A404 High Wycombe/Amersham road. The Museum is about 5mins walk from the town centre and railway station.

Opening Times: Mon - Sat, 10am - 5pm. Open Suns, 2-5pm, for special events only.

Admission: Free.

WCs suitable. By arrangement. Limited.
Guide dogs only.

Cliveden, Buckinghamshire.

Owner: Lord Montagu

CONTACT

Special Visits Department
John Montagu Building
Beaulieu
Brockenhurst
Hampshire
SO42 7ZN

Tel: 01590 612345

Fax: 01590 612624

e-mail: info@beaulieu.co.uk

LOCATION

OS Ref. SU387 025

From London, M3, M27 W to J2, A326, B3054 follow brown signs.

Bus: Bus stops within complex.

Rail: Stations at Brockenhurst and Beaulieu Rd both 7m away.

CONFERENCE/FUNCTION		
ROOM	SIZE	MAX CAPACITY
Brabazon (x3)	40'x40'	120 (x3)
Domus	69'x27'	170
Theatre		200
Hartford Suite	39'x17'	50
Palace House		60
Motor Museum		300

BEAULIEU

Beaulieu

BEAULIEU is set in the heart of the New Forest and is a place that gives enormous pleasure to people with an interest in seeing history of all kinds.

Overlooking the Beaulieu River, Palace House has been the ancestral home of the Montagus since 1538. The House was once the Great Gatehouse of Beaulieu Abbey and its monastic origins are reflected in such features as the fan vaulted ceilings. Many treasures, which are reminders of travels all round the world by past generations of the Montagu family, can also be seen. Walks amongst the gardens and by the Beaulieu River can also be enjoyed.

Beaulieu Abbey was founded in 1204 and although most of the buildings have now been destroyed, much of the beauty and interest remains. The former Monks' Refectory is now the local Parish Church. The Domus, which houses an exhibition of monastic life, is home to beautiful wall hangings and 15th century beamed ceilings.

Beaulieu also houses the world famous National Motor Museum which traces the story of motoring from 1894 to the present day. 250 vehicles are on display including legendary world record breakers plus veteran, vintage and classic cars and motorcycles.

The modern Beaulieu is very much a family destination where there are various free and unlimited rides and drives on a transportation theme to be enjoyed by everyone, including a mile long monorail and replica 1912 London open-topped bus.

OPENING TIMES

SUMMER
May - September
Daily, 10am - 6pm.

WINTER
October - April
Daily, 10am - 5pm.

Closed Christmas Day and 1st January 2000.

ADMISSION

ALL YEAR

Individual rates upon application.

Groups (15+)
Rates upon application.

SPECIAL EVENTS

- **APR 16:** Boat Jumble.
- **MAY 6/7:** Spring Autojumble.
- **SEPT 9/10:** Autojumble.

All enquiries should be made to our Special Events Booking Office where advance tickets can be purchased. The contact telephone is 01590 612345.

Other Event dates yet to be confirmed to include Motorcycle World, Palace House Prom, Fireworks Fair.

BEAULIEU

Catering and Functions

Beaulieu also offers a comprehensive range of facilities for conferences, company days out, product launches, management training, corporate hospitality, promotions, film locations, exhibitions and outdoor events.

The National Motor Museum is a unique venue for drinks receptions and dinners or the perfect complement to a conference as a relaxing visit.

The charming 13th century Domus banqueting hall with its beautiful wooden beams, stone walls and magnificent wall hangings, is the perfect setting for dinners, buffets or themed evenings – 17th century Royal Feasts with period entertainment are a speciality.

Palace House, the ancestral home of Lord Montagu is an exclusive setting for smaller dinners, buffets and receptions. With a welcoming log fire in the winter and the coolness of the courtyard fountain in the summer, it offers a relaxing yet truly 'stately' atmosphere to ensure a memorable experience for your guests whatever the time of year

A purpose-built theatre, with tiered seating, can accommodate 220 people whilst additional meeting and syndicate rooms can accommodate from 5 to 200 delegates. With the nearby Beaulieu River offering waterborne activities and the Beaulieu Estate giving you the opportunity of indulging in a variety of country pursuits and outdoor management training, Beaulieu provides a unique venue for your conference and corporate hospitality needs.

i Allow 3 hrs or more for visits. Last adm. 40 mins before closing. Helicopter landing point. When visiting Beaulieu arrangements can be made to view the Estate's vineyards. Visits, which can be arranged between Apr - Oct, must be pre-booked at least one week in advance with Beaulieu Estate Office.

Palace House Shop and Kitchen Shop plus Main Reception Shop.

Disabled visitors may be dropped off outside Visitor Reception before parking. WC. Wheelchairs can be provided free of charge in Visitor Reception by prior booking.

The self-service Brabazon restaurant seats 300. Prices range to £7 for lunch. Groups can book in advance. Further details and menus from Catering Manager 01590 612345.

Attendants on duty. Guided tours by prior arrangement for groups.

P 1,500 cars and 30 coaches. During the season the busy period is from 11.30am to 1.30pm. Coach drivers should sign in at Information Desk. Free admission for coach drivers plus voucher which can be exchanged for food, drink and souvenirs.

Professional staff available to assist in planning of visits. Services include introductory talks, films, guided tours, rôle play and extended projects. In general, educational services incur no additional charges and publications are sold at cost. Starter sets available free of charge to pre-booked parties. Information pack available from Education at Beaulieu, John Montagu Building, Beaulieu, Hants SO42 7ZN.

In grounds, on leads only.

HIGHCLERE CASTLE & GARDENS

Newbury

Owner:
The Earl of Carnarvon

CONTACT

Adrian Wiley
Highclere Castle
Newbury
Berkshire
RG20 9RN

Tel: 01635 253210

Fax: 01635 255315

e-mail: theoffice@highclerecastle.co.uk

LOCATION

OS Ref. SU445 587

Approx 7m out of Newbury on A34 towards Winchester. From London: M4/J13, A34 Bypass Newbury-Winchester 20 mins. M3/J5 approx 15m.

Air: Heathrow M4 45 mins.

Rail: Paddington - Newbury 45 mins.

Taxi: $4^1/_2$ m 01635 40829.

CONFERENCE/FUNCTION		
ROOM	SIZE	MAX CAPACITY
Library	43' x 21'	120
Saloon	42' x 29'	150
Dining Rm	37' x 18'	70
Library, Saloon, Drawing Rm, Music Rm, Smoking Rm		400

Designed by Charles Barry in the 1830s at the same time as he was building the Houses of Parliament, this soaring pinnacled mansion provided a perfect setting for the 3rd Earl of Carnarvon, one of the great hosts of Queen Victoria's reign. The extravagant interiors range from church Gothic through Moorish flamboyance and rococo revival to the solid masculinity in the long Library. Old master paintings mix with portraits by Van Dyck and 18th century painters. Napoleon's desk and chair rescued from St. Helena sits with other 18th and 19th century furniture.

The 5th Earl of Carnarvon discovered the Tomb of Tutankhamun with Howard Carter. The castle houses a unique exhibition of some of his discoveries which were only rediscovered in the castle in 1988. The current Earl is the Queen's Horseracing Manager. In 1993 to celebrate his 50th year as a leading owner and breeder 'The Lord Carnarvon Racing Exhibition' was opened to the public, and offers a fascinating insight into a racing history that dates back three generations.

GARDENS

The magnificent parkland with its massive cedars was designed by 'Capability' Brown. The walled gardens also date from an earlier house at Highclere but the dark yew walks are entirely Victorian in character. The glass Orangery and Fernery add an exotic flavour. The Secret Garden has a romance of its own with a beautiful curving lawn surrounded by densely planted herbaceous gardens. A place for poets and romantics.

Conferences, exhibitions, filming, fairs, and concerts (cap. 8000). No photography in the house.

Receptions, dinners, corporate hospitality.

Visitors may alight at the entrance. WC.

Tearooms, licensed. Lunches for 20+ can be booked.

Ample.

Egyptian Exhibition: £3 per child. 1 adult free per every 10 children – includes playgroups, Brownie packs, Guides etc. Nature walks, beautiful old follies, Secret Garden.

In grounds, on leads. Civil Wedding Licence.

OPENING TIMES

1 July - 3 September

Castle
Daily: 11am - 5pm.
Last adm. 4pm, Sat 2.30pm.

Castle closed 22 & 23 July.

Tearooms
Daily: 11am - 5pm.

6 September - 30 June
By appointment only.

ADMISSION

Adult £6.50
Child (5-14yrs) £3.00
Student/OAP £5.00

Gardens only
Adult £3.00
Child (5-14yrs) £1.50

Disabled Visitors
Adult £5.00
Child £3.00
Wheelchair Pusher .. FOC

VIP Season Ticket *
(2+3) £25.00

Groups (20+)
Adult/OAP £5.00
Child (5-14yrs) £3.00
Private visit by arrangement £10pp (min. £500).

*Runs for one year from date of joining, 10% off shop, tearooms, free admission to daytime events. Discounted rate for evening concerts. £3 off Watermill Theatre in Bangor, Newbury (Tue - Fri), £2 off Newbury Racecourse Members' Enclosure badges when pre-booked, Newbury Hilton - Fri, Sat, Sun evenings - dinner for two for the price of one from chef's hot or cold table.

SPECIAL EVENTS

Please telephone for details.

Owner:
The Earl of Normanton

CONTACT

Richard Horridge
Somerley
Ringwood
Hampshire
BH24 3PL

Tel: 01425 480819

Fax: 01425 478613

e-mail: info@somerley.com

LOCATION

OS Ref. SU134 080

Off the A31 to Bournemouth 2m. London $1^3/_4$ hrs via M3, M27, A31. 2m NW of Ringwood.

Air: Bournemouth International Airport 5m.

Rail: Bournemouth Station 12m.

Taxi: A car can be arranged from the House if applicable.

CONFERENCE/FUNCTION		
ROOM	SIZE	MAX CAPACITY
Picture Gall.	80' x 30'	200
Drawing Rm	38' x 30'	50
Dining Rm	39' x 19'	50
East Library	26' x 21'	30

SOMERLEY
Ringwood

Sitting on the edge of the New Forest in the heart of Hampshire, Somerley, home of the sixth Earl and Countess of Normanton and their three children, is situated in 7,000 acres of meadows, woods and rolling parkland. Designed by Samuel Wyatt in the mid 1700s, the house became the property of the Normanton family in 1825 and has remained in the same family through the years. Housing a magnificent art and porcelain collection, the house itself, albeit impressively splendid, still retains the warmth and character of a family home.

Although never open to the public, Somerley is available for corporate events and its location, along with its seclusion and privacy, provide the perfect environment for conferences and meetings, product launches, lunches and dinners, activity and team building days (the estate boasts a hugely challenging off-road driving course) and film and photographic work.

Somerley only ever hosts one event at a time so exclusivity in an outstanding setting is always guaranteed. From groups as small as eight to perhaps a large dinner for 120, the style of attention and personal service go hand in hand with the splendour of the house and the estate itself.

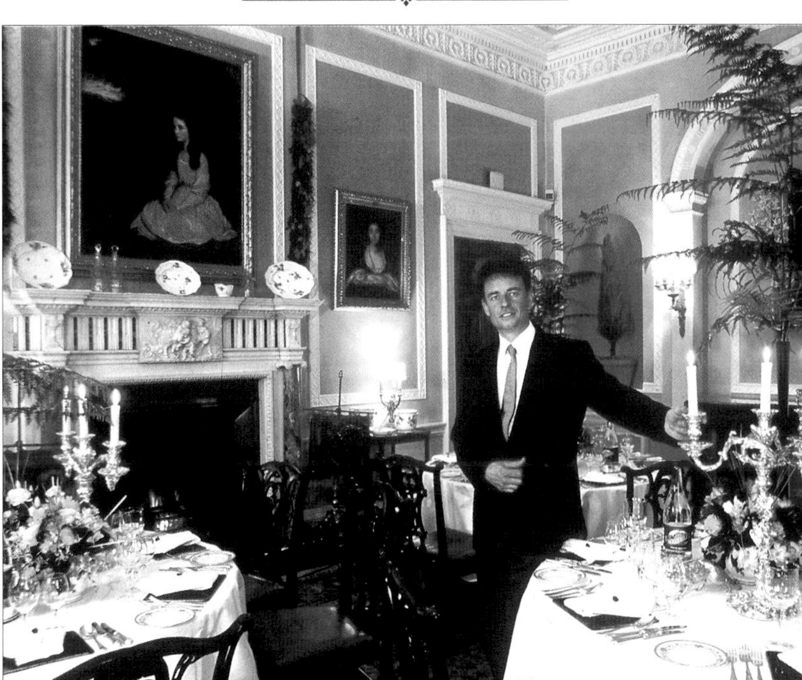

OPENING TIMES

Privately booked functions only.

ADMISSION

Privately booked functions only.

No individual visits, ideal for all corporate events, activity days and filmwork.

Dining Room and picture gallery available for private parties.

Unlimited.

4 twin & 4 double rooms.

South East England

JANE AUSTEN'S HOUSE

CHAWTON, ALTON, HAMPSHIRE GU34 1SD

Owner: *Jane Austen Memorial Trust* ***Contact:*** *The Curator*

Tel/Fax: 01420 83262

17th century house where Jane Austen wrote or revised her six great novels. Contains many items associated with her and her family, documents and letters, first editions of the novels, pictures, portraits and furniture. Pleasant garden, suitable for picnics, bakehouse with brick oven and wash tub, houses Jane's donkey carriage.

Location: OS Ref. SU708 376. Just S of A31, 1m SW of Alton, signposted Chawton.

Opening times: 1 Mar - 1 Jan: daily, 11am - 4.30pm. Jan & Feb: Sats & Suns and half term in Feb (ring for dates). Closed 25 & 26 Dec.

Admission: Adult £3, Conc. £2.50. Groups (15+) £2.50, Child (8-18yrs) 50p.

Bookshop. Ground floor & grounds suitable. WC.
Guide dogs only.

BASING HOUSE

Tel: 01256 467294

Redbridge Lane, Basing, Basingstoke RG24 7HB

Owner: Hampshire County Council **Contact:** Alan Turton

Ruins, covering 10 acres, of huge Tudor palace. Recent recreation of Tudor formal garden.

Location: OS Ref. SU665 526. 2m E from Basingstoke town centre. Signposted car parks are about 5 or 10 mins walk from entrance.

Opening Times: 1 Apr - 1 Oct: Wed - Sun & BHs, 2 - 6pm.

Admission: Adult £1.50, Child 70p.

BEAULIEU

See pages 74/75 for double page entry.

BISHOP'S WALTHAM PALACE

Tel: 01489 892460

Bishop's Waltham, Hampshire SO32 1DH

Owner: English Heritage **Contact:** The Custodian

This medieval seat of the Bishops of Winchester once stood in an enormous park. There are still wooded grounds and the remains of the Great Hall and the three storey tower can still be seen. Dower House furnished as a 19th century farmhouse.

Location: OS Ref. SU552 173. In Bishop's Waltham, 5m NE from M27/J8.

Opening Times: 1 Apr - 30 Sept: daily, 10am - 6pm. 1 Oct - 31 Oct: 10am - 5pm.

Admission: Adult £2, Child £1, Conc. £1.50.

Exhibition. Grounds suitable. Grounds only, on leads.
Tel. for details.

BOHUNT MANOR GARDENS

Tel: 01428 722208 **Fax:** 01428 727936

Liphook, Hampshire GU30 7DL

Owner: Worldwide Fund for Nature **Contact:** Lady Holman

Woodland gardens with lakeside walk, collection of ornamental waterfowl, herbaceous borders and unusual trees and shrubs.

Location: OS Ref. SU839 310. W side of B2070 at S end of village.

Opening Times: All year: daily, 10am - 6pm.

Admission: Adult £1.50, Child under 14 Free, Conc. £1. Group: 10% off.

AVINGTON PARK

WINCHESTER, HAMPSHIRE SO21 1DB

Owner/Contact: *Mrs S L Bullen*

Tel: 01962 779260 **Fax:** 01962 779864 **e-mail:** sarah@avingtonpark.co.uk

Avington Park, where Charles II and George IV both stayed at various times, dates back to the 11th century. The house was enlarged in 1670 by the addition of two wings and a classical Portico surmounted by three statues. The State rooms are magnificently painted and lead onto the unique pair of conservatories flanking the South Lawn. The Georgian church, St. Mary's, is in the grounds.

Location: OS Ref. SU534 324. 4m NE of Winchester 1/2 m S of the B3047 in Itchen Abbas.

Opening Times: May - Sept: Suns & BH Mons, 2.30 - 5.30pm. Last tour 5pm. Other times by arrangement, coach parties welcome by appointment all year.

Admission: Adult £3.50, Child £2.

Conferences. Partially suitable. WC. Obligatory. P
In grounds, on leads. Guide dogs only in house. 

BREAMORE HOUSE & MUSEUM

BREAMORE, FORDINGBRIDGE, HAMPSHIRE SP6 2DF

Owner/Contact: *Sir Edward Hulse Bt*

Tel: 01725 512233 **Fax:** 01725 512858

Elizabethan manor with fine collections of pictures and furniture. Countryside Museum takes visitors back to the time when a village was self-sufficient.

Location: OS Ref. SU152 191. W Off the A338, between Salisbury and Ringwood.

Opening Times: Apr: Easter Holiday, Tue, Wed & Sun. May, Jun, Jul & Sept: Tue, Wed, Thur, Sat & Sun & all hols. Aug: daily. House: 2 - 5.30pm. Countryside Museum: 1 - 5.30pm.

Admission: Combined ticket for house and museum: Adult £5, Child £3.50.

Ground floor & grounds suitable. WC.

BROADLANDS

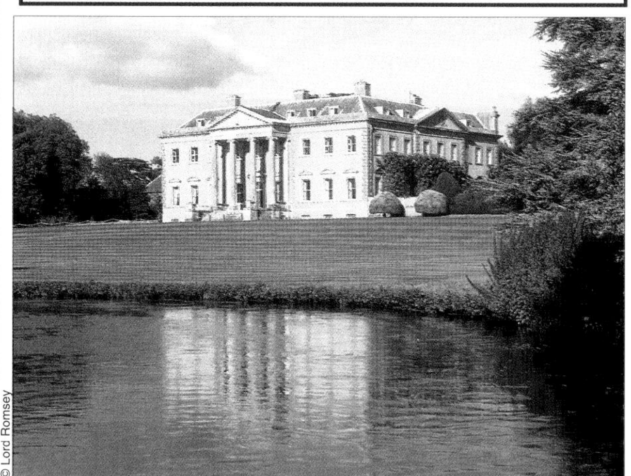
© Lord Romsey

ROMSEY, HAMPSHIRE SO51 9ZD

***Owner:** Lord & Lady Romsey* ***Contact:** Mrs S J Tyrrell*

Tel: 01794 505010 **Event Enquiry Line:** 01794 505020

Famous as the home of the late Lord Mountbatten, and equally well known as the country residence of Lord Palmerston, the Great Victorian Prime Minister. Broadlands is an elegant Palladian mansion in a beautiful landscaped setting on the banks of the River Test. Visitors may view the House with its art treasures and mementoes of the famous, enjoy the superb views from the Riverside Lawns or relive Lord Mountbatten's life and times in the Mountbatten Exhibition and spectacular Mountbatten audio-visual presentation.

Location: OS Ref. SU355 204. On A31 at Romsey.

Opening Times: 12 Jun - 1 Sept: daily, 12 noon - 5.30pm. Last admission 4pm.

Admission: Adult £5.50, Child (12-16) £3.85, Conc. £4.70. Groups (10+): Adult £4.70, Child (12-16) £3.60, Conc. £4.40. All inclusive admission charges. Accompanied child under 12, Free.

Ground floor & grounds suitable.WC.  Obligatory. Guide dogs only.

FORT BROCKHURST

Tel: 023 9258 1059

Gunner's Way, Gosport, Hampshire PO12 4DS

Owner: English Heritage **Contact:** The Head Custodian

This 19th century fort was built to protect Portsmouth, today its parade ground, moated keep and sergeants' mess are available to hire as an exciting setting for functions and events of all types. The fort is also open to visitors at weekends when tours will explain the exciting history of the site and the legend behind the ghostly activity in cell no. 3.

Location: OS196, Ref. SU596 020. Off A32, in Gunner's Way, Elson on N side of Gosport.

Opening Times: 1 Apr - 30 Sept: 10am - 6pm. 1 Oct - 31 Oct: 10am - 5pm. Weekends only.

Admission: Adult £2, Child £1, Conc. £1.50.

Fort Brockhurst, Hampshire.

CALSHOT CASTLE

Tel: 023 8089 2023

Calshot, Fawley, Hampshire SO45 1BR

Owner: English Heritage **Contact:** Hampshire County Council

Henry VIII built this coastal fort in an excellent position, commanding the sea passage to Southampton. The fort houses an exhibition and recreated pre-World War I barrack room.

Location: OS Ref. SU488 025. On spit 2m SE of Fawley off B3053.

Opening Times: 1 Apr - 30 Sept: daily, 10am - 6pm. 1 Oct - 31 Oct: 10am - 5pm.

Admission: Adult £1.80, Child 90p, Conc. £1.40.

ELING TIDE MILL

Tel: 023 8086 9575

The Toll Bridge, Eling, Totton, Southampton, Hampshire SO40 9HF

Contact: Mr David Blackwell-Eaton **e-mail:** eling.tidemill@argonet.co.uk

Owner: Eling Tide Mill Trust Ltd & New Forest District Council

Location: OS Ref. SU365 126. 4m W of Southampton. 1/2 m S of the A35.

Opening Times: Wed - Sun and BH Mons, 10am - 4pm.

Admission: Adult £1.60, Child 85p, OAP £1.20, Family £4.40. Discounts for groups and joint entry with Totton and Eling Heritage Centre. (Prices will probably change 1 Jan 2000, phone to confirm details).

EXBURY GARDENS

Tel: 023 8089 1203 **Fax:** 023 8089 9940

Exbury, Southampton, Hampshire SO45 1AZ

Owner: Edmund de Rothschild Esq **Contact:** Sebastian Green

Extensive landscaped woodland gardens overlooking the Beaulieu River. World famous Rothschild plant collection (rhododendrons, azaleas etc.) as well as many rare and wonderful trees: Rock Garden, Cascades, Ponds, River Walk, Rose Garden, Water Garden, Heather Gardens, seasonal trails and themed walks. Ample seating throughout. Gardens spectacular in Spring and Autumn.

Location: OS Ref. SU425 005. 11m SE of Totton (A35) via A326 & B3054 & minor road.

Opening Times: 26 Feb - 5 Nov: daily, 10am - 5.30pm or dusk if earlier.

Admission: Please telephone for details.

 Grounds suitable. WC. 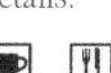  In grounds, on leads. Telephone for details.

FURZEY GARDENS

Tel: 023 8081 2464 **Fax:** 023 8081 2297

Minstead, Lyndhurst, Hampshire SO43 7GL

Owner: Furzey Gardens Charitable Trust **Contact:** Maureen Cole

Location: OS Ref. SU273 114. Minstead village 1/2 m N of M27/A31 junction off A337 to Lyndhurst.

Opening Times: Please contact property for details.

GREAT HALL & QUEEN ELEANOR'S GARDEN

Tel: 01962 846476

Winchester Castle, Winchester, Hampshire SO23 8PJ

Owner: Hampshire County Council **Contact:** Mrs Harris

The only surviving part of Henry III's medieval castle at Winchester, this 13th century hall was the centre of court and government life. The Round Table closely associated with the legend of King Arthur has hung here for over 700 years. Queen Eleanor's garden is a faithful representation of the medieval garden visited by Kings and Queens of England.

Location: OS Ref. SU477 295. Central Winchester. SE of Westgate archway.

Opening Times: All year: daily, 10am - 5pm (except weekends Nov - Feb, 10am - 4pm). Closed Christmas Day and Boxing Day.

Admission: Free .

 By arrangement.

GUILDHALL GALLERY

Tel: 01962 848289 (gallery) 01962 848269 (office)

The Broadway, Winchester SO23 9LJ **Fax:** 01962 848299

e-mail: museums@winchester.gov.uk

Owner: Winchester City Council **Contact:** Mr C Wardman Bradbury

A constantly changing programme of contemporary exhibitions including painting, sculpture, craft, photography and ceramics.

Location: OS Ref. SU485 293. Winchester - city centre. Situated above the Tourist Office in Winchester's 19th century Guildhall.

Opening Times: Tue - Sat: 10am - 5pm, Suns & Mons: 2 - 5pm. Closed Mons Oct - Mar.

Admission: Free.

HIGHCLERE CASTLE & GARDENS

See page 76 for full page entry.

South East England

THE SIR HAROLD HILLIER GARDENS & ARBORETUM

Justyn Willsmore

JERMYNS LANE, AMPFIELD, ROMSEY SO51 0QA

Owner: *Hampshire County Council* ***Contact:*** *Judith Drysdale / Tim Brooks*

Tel: 01794 368787 **Fax:** 01794 368027

Set in the rolling Hampshire countryside between Winchester and the market town of Romsey, The Sir Harold Hillier Gardens & Arboretum comprises the greatest collection of wild and cultivated woody plants in the world. Established in 1953, by the late Sir Harold Hillier, the 180 acre garden provides a stunning range of seasonal colour and interest and features 11 National Plant Collections, Champion Trees and the largest Winter Garden in Europe. A garden for all seasons.

Location: OS Ref. SU380 236. 3m NE of Romsey. Follow brown tourist signs from the town centre on A3090 (formerly A31) towards Winchester.

Opening times: Apr - Oct: Mon - Fri, 10.30am - 6pm. Sats, Suns & BHs, 9.30am - 6pm. Nov - Mar: daily, 10.30am - dusk. Closed 25 - 28 Dec, Christmas BH.

Admission: Apr - Oct: Adult £4.25, Child (5-16yrs) £1, Under 5s Free, OAP £3.75; Nov - Mar: Adult £3.25, Child (5-16) £1, Under 5s Free, OAP £2.75.

Partially suitable. WC. Licensed. By arrangement. Guide dogs only. Tel for details.

HOUGHTON LODGE

STOCKBRIDGE, HAMPSHIRE, SO20 6LQ

Owner: *Captain M W Busk* ***Contact:*** *M W Busk or Terry Grimshaw*

Tel: 01264 810177/810502 **Fax:** 01264 810177

e-mail: TGrimshaw@aol.com

'A garden of the future in a garden of the past'. An enchanting and rare 18th century 'Cottage Ornée' in a spacious and tranquil setting overlooking the River Test. Often featured in films and TV programmes. Topiary, traditional walled kitchen garden and ancient fruit trees contrast with the **Hydroponicum** where you can learn how to garden at home without soil and toil and how to control insect pests without chemicals. Hydroponic kits for sale. Refreshments and visitor centre.

Location: OS Ref. SU344 332. 1½ m S of Stockbridge (A30) on minor road to Houghton village.

Opening times: Garden: 1 Mar - 30 Sept: Sat, Sun & BHs, 10am - 5pm also Mon, Tue, Thur & Fri, 2 - 5pm. Other times by appointment. House: Groups welcome by arrangement. Hydroponicum: Weekdays in winter.

Admission: Adult £5 (Child Free), includes Garden, Hydroponicum, tour & tea or coffee. Group discount.

By arrangement. In grounds, on leads.

HINTON AMPNER GARDEN

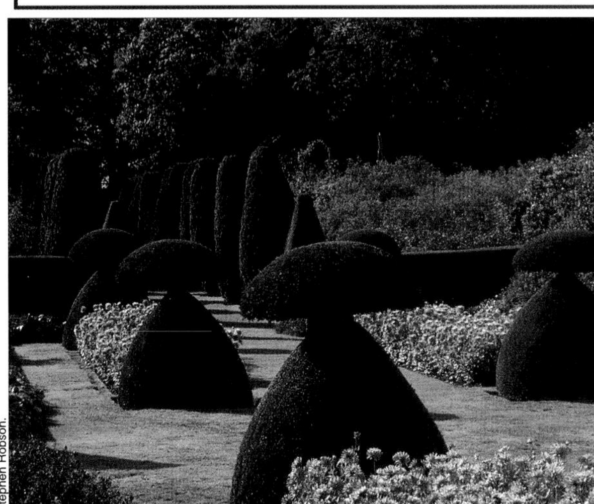
Stephen Robson.

BRAMDEAN, Nr ALRESFORD, HAMPSHIRE SO24 0LA

Owner: *The National Trust* ***Contact:*** *The Administrator*

Tel: 01962 771305 **Fax:** 01962 793101

The garden is set in superb countryside and combines formal design with informal planting, producing delightful walks with many unexpected vistas. There is colour and scent throughout the season and highlights include a dell and a sunken garden. The house, restored after a fire in 1960, has a fine collection of Regency furniture and Italian paintings. It is privately tenanted and is open by arrangement with the tenant.

Location: OS Ref. SU597 275. On A272, 1m W of Bramdean village, 8m E of Winchester.

Opening times: Garden: 21 & 28 Mar, 3rd Apr - end Sept: Tues, Weds, Sats, Suns & BH Mons. House: 6 Apr - end Sept: Tues & Weds, also Sats & Suns in Aug.

Admission: House & Garden: Adult £4. Garden only: Adult £3.20. Please phone for group rates. Child (5-16) half price. Under 5s and NT members Free.

Garden suitable.

HURST CASTLE

Tel: 01590 642344

Keyhaven, Lymington, Hampshire PO41 0PB

Owner: English Heritage **Contact:** (Managed by) Hurst Castle Services

This was one of the most sophisticated fortresses built by Henry VIII, and later strengthened in the 19th and 20th centuries, to command the narrow entrance to the Solent. There is an exhibition in the Castle, and two huge 38-ton guns form the fort's armaments.

Location: OS196 Ref. SZ319 898. On Pebble Spit S of Keyhaven. Best approach by ferry from Keyhaven. 4m SW of Lymington.

Opening times: 1 Apr - 31 Oct: daily, 10am - 5.30pm. Café: open Apr - May weekends & Jun - Sept: daily.

Admission: Adult £2.50, Child £1.50, Conc. £2.

Not suitable.

MEDIEVAL MERCHANTS HOUSE

Tel: 023 8022 1503

58 French Street, Southampton, Hampshire SO1 0AT

Owner: English Heritage **Contact:** The Custodian

The life of the prosperous merchant in the Middle Ages is vividly evoked in this recreated, faithfully restored 13th century townhouse.

Location: OS Ref. SU419 112. 58 French Street. ¼ m S of Bargate off Castle Way. 150yds SE of Tudor House.

Opening Times: 1 Apr - 30 Sept: daily, 10am - 6pm. 1 - 31 Oct: daily, 10am - 5pm.

Admission: Adult £2.10, Child £1.10, Conc. £1.60.

Patrick Lane.

Houghton Lodge Knot Garden, Hampshire.

MOTTISFONT ABBEY GARDEN, HOUSE & ESTATE

National Trust Photographic Library.

MOTTISFONT, Nr ROMSEY, HAMPSHIRE SO51 0LP

Owner: *The National Trust* **Contact:** *The Property Manager*

Tel: 01794 340757 **Fax:** 01794 341492 **Recorded Message:** 01794 341220

The Abbey and Garden form the central point of an 809 ha estate including most of the village of Mottisfont, farmland and woods. A tributary of the River Test flows through the garden forming a superb and tranquil setting for a 12th century Augustinian priory which, after the Dissolution, became a house. It contains the spring or "font" from which the place name is derived. The magnificent trees, walled gardens and the National Collection of Old-fashioned Roses combine to provide interest throughout the seasons. The Abbey contains a drawing room decorated by Rex Whistler and the cellarium of the old Priory. In 1996 the Trust acquired Derek Hill's 20th century picture collection.

Location: OS Ref. SU327 270. 4½ m NW of Romsey, ¾ m W of A3057.

Opening times: Garden & Grounds: 18 Mar - 1 Nov: Sat - Wed (open Good Fri), 12 noon - 6pm (or dusk if earlier). During peak rose season 10 - 25 Jun: (check recorded message for state of roses) open daily, 11am - 8.30pm. Last admission to grounds 1 hr before closing. House: 1 - 5pm. (Whistler Room & Cellarium: as garden). Also open at other times, telephone for details.

Admission: Garden, Grounds & Whistler Room: Adult £5, Child (5-18yrs) £2.50, Family £12.50. No reduction for groups. Coaches must book.

 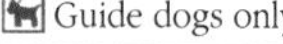 Guide dogs only.  Tel. 01372 451596 for details.

NORTH FORELAND LODGE

SHERFIELD MANOR, SHERFIELD-ON-LODDON, Nr BASINGSTOKE, HOOK RG27 0HT

Owner: *Charitable Trust* **Contact:** *Miss S Cameron*

Tel: 01256 884800 **Fax:** 01256 884803 **e-mail:** nflodge@rmplc.co.uk

North Foreland Lodge is a beautiful Victorian manor house set in 90 acres of parkland with a lake and woodland. An ideal venue for outside events, concerts, weddings or as a film location. The magnificent period rooms offer excellent banqueting facilities. A large sports hall and practical cookery room with 14 individual kitchens makes it ideal for corporate team-building activities.

Location: OS Ref. SU684 573. Between Basingstoke M3/J6 and Reading M4/J11, adjacent to the A33, 45mins from London.

Opening times: By arrangement.

Admission: Please contact for details.

Not suitable. In grounds, on leads.

NETLEY ABBEY

Tel: 01732 778000

Netley, Southampton, Hampshire

Owner: English Heritage **Contact:** The South East Regional Office

A peaceful and beautiful setting for the extensive ruins of this 13th century Cistercian abbey converted in Tudor times for use as a house.

Location: OS Ref. SU453 089. In Netley, 4m SE of Southampton, facing Southampton Water.

Opening Times: Any reasonable time.

Admission: Free.

Mottisfont Abbey Garden, Hampshire.

PORTCHESTER CASTLE

Tel: 023 9237 8291 **Fax:** 023 9237 8291

Portsmouth, Hampshire PO16 9QW

Owner: English Heritage **Contact:** The Custodian

The rallying point of Henry V's expedition to Agincourt and the ruined palace of King Richard II. This grand castle has a history going back nearly 2,000 years including the most complete Roman walls in Europe. Don't miss the interactive exhibition telling the story of the castle and see the newly conserved wallpaintings from the Viewing Gallery in the Keep.

Location: OS196, Ref. SU625 046. On S side of Portchester off A27, M27/J11.

Open: 1 Apr - 30 Sept: daily, 10am - 6pm. 1 - 31 Oct: 10am - 5pm. 1 Nov - 31 Mar: daily, 10am - 4pm. Closed 24 - 26 Dec.

Admission: Adult £2.70, Child £1.40, Conc. £2. 15% discount for groups (11+). One extra place free for every additional 20.

Exhibition. Grounds & lower levels suitable.
In grounds, on leads. Telephone for details.

PORTSMOUTH CATHEDRAL

Tel: 023 9282 3300 **Fax:** 023 9229 5480

Portsmouth, Hampshire PO1 2HH **Contact:** Rosemary Fairfax

Maritime Cathedral founded in 12th century and finally completed in 1991. A member of the ship's crew of Henry VIII's flagship *Mary Rose* is buried in Navy Aisle.

Location: OS Ref. SZ633 994. 1½ m from end of M275. Follow signs to Historic Ship and Old Portsmouth.

Opening Times: 7.45am - 6pm all year. Sun service: 8am, 9.30am, 11am, 6pm. Weekday: 6pm (Choral on Tues and Fris in term time).

Admission: Donation appreciated.

Special Events Index PAGE 40

South East England

SANDHAM MEMORIAL CHAPEL

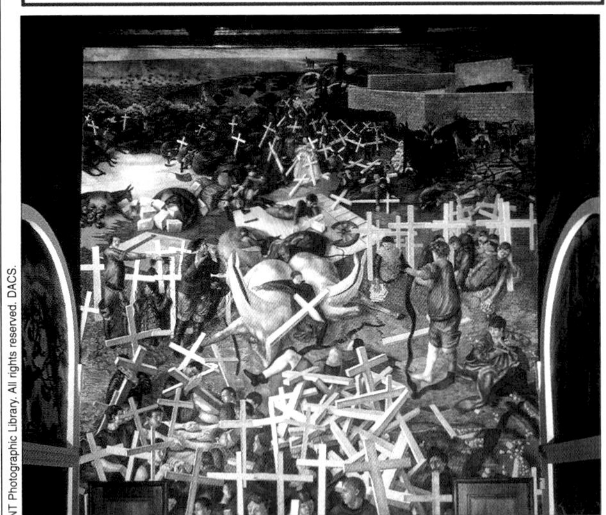

BURGHCLERE, Nr NEWBURY, HAMPSHIRE RG20 9JT

Owner: *The National Trust* ***Contact:*** *Sarah Hook*

Tel/Fax: 01635 278394

Stanley Spencer's murals, which entirely cover the interior walls of this 1920s chapel, commemorate the First World War and constitute one of the greatest achievements of 20th century painting. The murals chronicle with minute accuracy the every day life of the soldier. Inspired by Giotto's Arena Chapel in Padua, this impressive project took Spencer five years to complete.

Location: OS Ref. SU463 608. 4m S of Newbury, 1/2 m E of A34, W end of Burghclere.

Opening times: Mar & Nov: Sats & Suns, Apr - end Oct: daily except Mons & Tues (open BH Mons): Dec - Feb 2001: by appointment only. Times: Mar & Nov: 11.30am - 4pm, Apr - end Oct: 11.30am - 5pm.

Admission: Adult £2.50, Child £1. Groups by prior arrangement, no reduction.

Ramped steps.  In grounds, on leads.

STRATFIELD SAYE HOUSE

Tel: 01256 882882

Stratfield Saye, Basingstoke RG7 0AS

Owner: The Duke of Wellington **Contact:** The Administrator

Stratfield Saye was presented to the Great Duke of Wellington by a grateful nation after the battle of Waterloo in 1815, and is still the home of the present Duke and Duchess.

Location: OS Ref. SU700 615. Equidistant from Reading (M4/J11) & Basingstoke (M3/J6) 1 1/2 m W of the A33.

Opening times: Daily except Mons & Tues, Jun, Jul & Aug. Groups by arrangement – Mons & Tues in Jun, Jul & Aug. and Mon - Fri in Sept. Grounds & Exhibition: 11.30am - 5pm. House 12 noon - 3pm (last admission).

Admission: Adult £5.50, Child £2.50, OAP £5.

SOMERLEY

See page 77 for full page entry.

TITCHFIELD ABBEY

Tel: 01329 842133

Titchfield, Southampton, Hampshire

Owner: English Heritage **Contact:** Mr K E Groves

Remains of a 13th century abbey overshadowed by the grand Tudor gatehouse. Reputedly some of Shakespeare's plays were performed here for the first time. Under local management of Titchfield Abbey Society.

Location: OS Ref. SU544 067. 1/2 m N of Titchfield off A27.

Opening Times: 1 Apr - 30 Sept: daily, 10am - 6pm. 1 - 31 Oct: daily, 10am - 5pm. 1 Nov - 31 Mar: daily, 10am - 4pm.

Admission: Free.

TUDOR HOUSE MUSEUM

Tel: 023 8063 5904 **Fax:** 023 8033 9601

Bugle Street, Southampton, Hampshire

Owner: Southampton City Council **Contact:** Sian Jones

Late 15th century half timbered house. Unique Tudor knot garden.

Location: OS Ref. SU418 113. Follow signs to Old Town and waterfront from M27/M3. 150yds NW of Merchants House.

Opening Times: Tue - Fri, 10am - 12 noon, 1 - 5pm. Sats, 10am - 12 noon, 1- 4pm. Suns, 2 - 5pm. Closed Mons.

Admission: Free.

Sandham Memorial Chapel, Hampshire.

THE VYNE

SHERBORNE ST JOHN, BASINGSTOKE RG24 9HL

Owner: *The National Trust* ***Contact:*** *The Property Manager*

Tel: 01256 881337 **Fax:** 01256 881720 **e-mail:** svygen@smtp.ntrust.org.uk

Built in the early 16th century for Lord Sandys, Henry VIII's Lord Chamberlain, the house acquired a classical portico in the mid-17th century (the first of its kind in England) and contains a fascinating Tudor chapel with Renaissance glass, a Palladian staircase and a wealth of old panelling and fine furniture. The attractive grounds feature herbaceous borders and a wild garden, with lawns, lakes and woodland walks.

Location: OS Ref. SU637 566. 4m N of Basingstoke between Bramley and Sherborne St John.

Opening times: House: 1 Apr - 29 Oct: daily except Mons & Fris, 1 - 5 (open Good Fri & BH Mons). Grounds: weekends in Feb & Mar, 11am - 4pm. 1 Apr - 29 Oct: daily except Mons & Fris, 11am - 6pm (open Good Fri & BH Mons).

Admission: House & Grounds: Adult £5, Child £2.50, Family £12.50. Grounds only: Adult £3, Child £1.50. Groups: £4 (Tue - Thur only).

   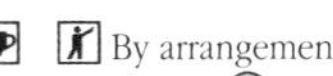

No photography in house. By arrangement.

Limited for coaches. Telephone for details.

GILBERT WHITE'S HOUSE & OATES MUSEUM

THE WAKES, HIGH STREET, SELBORNE, ALTON GU34 3JH

Owner: *Oates Memorial Trust* ***Contact:*** *Mrs Anna Jackson*

Tel: 01420 511275

Charming 18th century house in heart of old Selborne, home of Rev Gilbert White, author of *The Natural History of Selborne*. Lovely garden with many plants of the 18th century. Museum devoted to Captain Oates of Antarctic fame. Tea parlour with 18th century fare.

Location: OS Ref. SU741 336. On W side of B3006, in village of Selborne 4m NW of the A3.

Opening Times: 1 Jan - 24 Dec: daily, 11am - 5pm. Evenings also for groups.

Admission: Adult £4, Child £1, OAP £3.50.

No photography in house. Partially suitable. By arrangement. Guide dogs only.

SPECIAL EVENTS

JUN 17: Picnic to 'Jazz in June'. **JUN 17/18:** Unusual Plants Fair.
NOV 26: Mulled wine & Christmas shopping day.

WINCHESTER CATHEDRAL

Tel: 01962 857200 **Fax:** 01962 857201

Winchester, Hants SO23 9LS **e-mail:** judy.george@winchester-cathedral.org.uk

Contact: Mrs J George

The Cathedral was founded in 1079 on a site where Christian worship had already been offered for over 400 years. Special facilities for school visits. Guided tours available.

Location: OS Ref. SU483 293. Winchester city centre.

Opening Times: 8.30am - 5pm. East end closes 5pm. Access may be restricted during services. Weekday services:7.40am, 8am, 5.30pm. Sun services: 8am, 10am, 11.15am, 3.30pm.

Admission: Recommended donations: Adult £3, Child 50p, Conc. £2, Family £6, charges apply for Triforium gallery & Library - £1. Tower & Roof Tours £1.50. Group tours £3.50 should be booked through the Education centre. (Tel: 01962 857225 between 9am - 1pm).

Licensed. Guide dogs only. 

WINCHESTER COLLEGE

Tel: 01962 621209 **Fax:** 01962 621215

College Street, Winchester, Hampshire SO23 9NA **e-mail:** icds@bursary.wincoll.ac.uk

Owner: Winchester College **Contact:** Ian Stuart

One of the oldest public schools, founded by Bishop William of Wykeham in 1382.

Location: OS Ref. SU483 290. S of the Cathedral.

Opening Times: College: Apr - Sept: Mon - Sat, 10am - 1pm & 2 - 5pm. Oct - Mar: Mon - Sat, 10am - 1pm & 2 - 4pm. Open Suns pm all year. Guided tours leave Porters' Lodge: Apr - Sept: 11am, 2pm & 3.15pm except Suns when no am tour. Booked tours available all year.

Admission: Adult £2.50, Child/Conc. £2. Guided tours may be booked for groups (10+).

Ground floor & grounds suitable. Guide dogs only.

WOLVESEY CASTLE

Tel: 01962 854766

College Street, Wolvesey, Winchester, Hampshire SO23 8NB

Owner: English Heritage **Contact:** The Custodian

The fortified palace of Wolvesey was the chief residence of the Bishops of Winchester and one of the greatest of all medieval buildings in England. Its extensive ruins still reflect the importance and immense wealth of the Bishops of Winchester, occupants of the richest seat in medieval England. Wolvesey was frequently visited by medieval and Tudor monarchs and was the scene of the wedding feast of Philip of Spain and Mary Tudor in 1554.

Location: OS Ref. SU484 291. 3/4 m SE of Winchester Cathedral, next to the Bishop's Palace; access from College Street.

Opening Times: 1 Apr - 30 Sept: 10am - 6pm. 1 - 31 Oct: 10am - 5pm.

Admission: Adult £1.80, Child 90p, Conc. £1.40.

Grounds suitable. In grounds, on leads.

Portsmouth Cathedral, Hampshire.

Jerry Harpur

Owner: The Marquess of Salisbury

CONTACT

The Curator
Hatfield House
Hatfield
Hertfordshire
AL9 5NQ

Tel: 01707 262823

Fax: 01707 275719

HATFIELD HOUSE & GARDENS

Hatfield

This celebrated Jacobean house, which stands in its own great park, was built between 1607 and 1611 by Robert Cecil, 1st Earl of Salisbury and Chief Minister to King James I. It has been the family home of the Cecils ever since.

The main designer was Robert Lyminge helped, it is thought, by the young Inigo Jones. The interior decoration was the work of English, Flemish and French craftsmen, notably Maximilian Colt.

The State Rooms are rich in world-famous paintings including *The Rainbow Portrait of Queen Elizabeth I* and *The Ermine Portrait* by Nicholas Hilliard. Other paintings include works by Hoefnagel, Mytens, John de Critz the Elder and Sir Joshua Reynolds. Fine furniture from the 16th, 17th and 18th centuries, rare tapestries and historic armour can be found in the State Rooms.

Within the delightful gardens stands the surviving wing of The Royal Palace of Hatfield (1497) where Elizabeth I spent much of her girlhood and held her first Council of State in November 1558. Some of her possessions can be seen in the House.

GARDENS

John Tradescant the Elder, the celebrated plant hunter, was employed to plant and lay out the gardens after the completion of the house in 1611. During the 18th century, when landscape gardening became more fashionable, much of his work was neglected or swept away. The present Marchioness has continued with the work of restoration and redevelopment, started in the mid 19th century, so that the 42 acres of gardens now include formal, knot, scented and wilderness areas which reflects their Jacobean history. The gardens are managed entirely organically.

Jerry Harpur

No photography in house. National Collection of model soldiers, 5m of marked trails, children's play area.

Wedding receptions, functions. Elizabethan Banquets held in Old Palace throughout year: 01707 262055.

Visitors may alight at entrance. WCs & lift.

Seats 120. Pre-booked lunch and tea for groups 10+. Tel: 01707 262030.

Tue - Thur, no extra charge. Available in French, German, Italian, Spanish or Japanese by prior arrangement. Garden tour £15.

Ample. Hardstanding for coaches.

1:10 ratio. Teacher free. Guide provided. Model soldier collection, adventure playground and marked trails.

In grounds, on leads.

LOCATION

OS Ref. TL 237 084

21m N of London, M25/J23 7m, A1(M)/J4, 2m.

Bus: Local bus services from St Albans, Hertford.

Rail: From Kings Cross every 30 mins. Hatfield Station is immediately opposite entrance to Park.

Air: Luton (30 mins)

CONFERENCE/FUNCTION		
ROOM	SIZE	MAX CAPACITY
The Old Palace	112' x 33'	280

OPENING TIMES

25 March - 24 September (Closed Good Friday but open BH Mons).

House
Tue - Thur, guided tours only, Friday (Connoisseurs' Day), booked parties only (20+), 12 noon - 4pm.
Sat & Sun (no guided tours) 1 - 4.30pm.
BHs (no guided tours), 11am - 4.30pm.

Park
Daily: 10.30am - 8pm, on Fridays, 11am - 6pm.

Gardens
West: Tue - Sun.
East: Fridays only (Connoisseurs' Day), 11am - 6pm.

Restaurant: Tue - Sun, 10.30am - 5.30pm.

Shop: Tue - Sat, 11am - 5.30pm & Suns, 1 - 5.30pm.

ADMISSION

House, Park & West Garden
Adult £6.20
Child (5 - 15yrs)........£3.10
Groups (20+)*
Adult £5.20

Park only
Adult £1.80
Child (5 - 15yrs) 90p

Connoisseurs' Day (Fri)
House Tour, Park & Gardens (20+) £9.20
(Booked party only)

Park & Gardens......£5.20

SPECIAL EVENTS

- **MAY 4 - 7:** Living Crafts.
- **JUN 24/25:** Festival of Gardening.

KNEBWORTH

Nr Stevenage

Owner: Lord Cobbold

CONTACT

The Estate Office
Knebworth House
Knebworth
Hertfordshire
SG3 6PY

Tel: 01438 812661

Fax: 01438 811908

e-mail: info@knebworthhouse.com

LOCATION

OS Ref. TL230 208

Direct access off the A1(M) J7 (Stevenage South A602). 28m N of London. 15m N of M25 J23.

Rail: Stevenage Station 2m (from Kings Cross).

Air: Luton Airport 15m Landing facilities.

Taxi: 01438 811122.

CONFERENCE/FUNCTION		
ROOM	SIZE	MAX CAPACITY
Banqueting Hall	26 'x 41'	80
Dining Parlour	21' x 38'	50
Library	32' x 21'	40
Manor Barn	70' x 25'	250
Lodge Barn	75' x 30'	150

Home of the Lytton family since 1490, and still a lived-in family house. Transformed in early Victorian times by Edward Bulwer-Lytton, the author, poet, dramatist and statesman, into the unique high gothic fantasy house of today, complete with turrets, griffins and gargoyles.

Historically home to Constance Lytton, the Suffragette, and her father, Robert Lytton, the Viceroy of India who proclaimed Queen Victoria Empress of India at the Great Delhi Durbar of 1877. Visited by Queen Elizabeth I, Charles Dickens and Sir Winston Churchill.

The interior contains various styles including the magnificent Jacobean Banqueting Hall, a unique example of the 17th century change in fashion from traditional English to Italian Palladian. The high gothic State Drawing Room by John Crace contrasts with the Regency elegance of Mrs Bulwer-Lytton's bedroom and the 20th century designs of Sir Edwin Lutyens in the Entrance Hall, Dining Parlour and Library.

25 acres of beautiful gardens, simplified by Lutyens, including pollarded lime avenues, formal rose garden, maze and Gertrude Jekyll herb garden. 250 acres of gracious parkland, with herds of red and sika deer, includes children's giant adventure playground and miniature railway. World famous for its huge open-air rock concerts, and used as a film location for *Batman*, *The Shooting Party*, *Wilde*, *Jane Eyre* and *The Canterville Ghost*, amongst others.

Suitable for fashion shows, air displays, archery, shooting, equestrian events, cricket pitch, garden parties, shows, rallies, filming, helicopter landing. No pushchairs, photography, smoking or drinking in House.

Indian Raj Evenings and Elizabethan Banquets with jousting. Full catering service.

Visitors may alight at entrance. Ground floor accessible to wheelchairs.

Refreshments in 400 year old tithe barn. Special rates for advance bookings, menus on request.

Unlimited parking. Group visits must be booked in advance with Estate Office.

Mon - Fri at 30 min intervals or at booked times including evenings. Tour time 1hr. Shorter tours by arrangement. Room Wardens on duty at weekends. 'Gothick Visions' tour.

National Curriculum based worksheets & children's guide.

Guide dogs only in House. In Park, on leads.

OPENING TIMES

Park, Gardens, Fort Knebworth Adventure Playground & Miniature Railway

15 Apr - 1 May: daily.

6 - 21 May: weekends & BHs.

27 May - 4 Jun: daily.

10 Jun - 2 Jul: weekends (except 18 June).

8 Jul - 3 Sept: daily.

9 Sept - 1 Oct: weekends.

Park, Gardens, Playground & Railway

11am - 5.30pm.

House & Indian Raj Exhibition:

12 noon - 5pm (last adm. 4.30pm)

Closed at other times, but pre-booked groups (20+) welcome all year (subject to special events).

ADMISSION

House, Gardens, Park, Playground & Railway

Adult	£6.00
Child*/OAP	£5.50
Groups (20+)	
Adult	£5.00
Child*/OAP	£4.50

(subject to special events)

Gardens, Park, Playground & Railway

All persons	£5.00
Family (2+2)	£17.50
Groups (20+)	
All persons	£4.25

(subject to special events)

* Age 5 - 16yrs. Under 5s Free.
Season Tickets available.

South East England

ASHRIDGE

Tel: 01442 851227 Fax: 01442 842062 e-mail: tasalb@smtp.ntrust.org.uk

Ringshall, Berkhamsted, Hertfordshire HP4 1LT

Owner: The National Trust **Contact:** The Property Manager

The Ashridge Estate comprises over 1619ha of woodlands, commons and downland. At the northerly end of the Estate the Ivinghoe Hills are an outstanding area of chalk downland which supports a rich variety of plants and insects. The Ivinghoe Beacon itself offers splendid views. This area may be reached from a car park at Steps Hill. The rest of Ashridge is an almost level plateau with many fine walks through woods and open commons.

Location: OS Ref. SP970 131. Between Northchurch & Ringshall, just off B4506.

Opening Times: Estate: All year. Monument, Shop & Visitor Centre: 1 Apr - 29 Oct: daily except Fri but open Good Fri. Times: Mon - Thur & Good Fri: 2 - 5pm. Sat, Sun & BH Mons, 2 - 5.30pm.

Admission: Monument: £1, Child 50p.

Visitor Centre.

BENINGTON LORDSHIP GARDENS

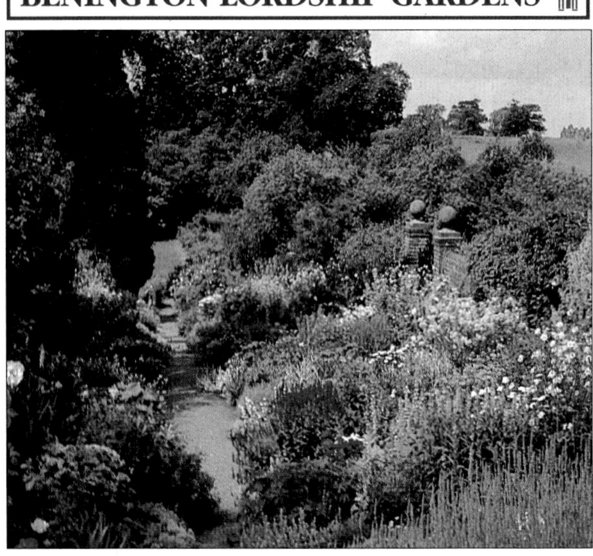

STEVENAGE, HERTFORDSHIRE SG2 7BS

Owner: *Mr C H A Bott* ***Contact:*** *Mr or Mrs C H A Bott*

Tel: 01438 869668 **Fax:** 01438 869622 **e-mail:** enquire@rhbott.u-net.com

A hilltop garden which appeals to everyone with its intimate atmosphere, ruins, Queen Anne Manor, herbaceous borders, old roses, lakes, vegetable garden, nursery and verandah teas. For films, fashion shoots etc. the gardens and estate offer excellent facilities. Mediaeval barns, cottages and other unique countryside features.

Location: OS Ref. TL296 236. In village of Benington next to the church. 4m E of Stevenage.

Opening times: Gardens only: Apr - Aug, Wed & BH Mons, 12 noon - 5pm, Sun 2 - 5pm. Sept: Weds only. Groups any time by arrangement.

Admission: Adult £2.80, Child Free.

Air-strip. Suitable for filming & fashion shoots. Unsuitable.

BERKHAMSTED CASTLE

Tel: 01442 871737

Berkhamsted, St Albans, Hertfordshire

Owner: English Heritage **Contact:** Mr Stevens - The Key Keeper

The extensive remains of a large 11th century motte and bailey castle which held a strategic position on the road to London.

Location: OS165 Ref. SP996 083. Adjacent to Berkhamsted rail station.

Opening Times: All year: daily, 10am - 4pm.

Admission: Free.

CATHEDRAL & ABBEY CHURCH OF ST ALBAN

St Albans, Hertfordshire AL1 1BY **Tel:** 01727 860780 **Fax:** 01727 850944

e-mail: cathedra@alban.u-net.com **Contact:** Deputy Administrator

Abbey church of Benedictine Monastery founded 793AD commemorating Britain's first martyr. Rebuilt 1077 became Cathedral in 1877. Many 13th century wall paintings, ecumenical shrine of St Alban (1308).

Location: OS Ref. TL145 071. Centre of St Albans.

Opening Times: All year: 9am - 5.45pm. Tel for details of services, concerts and special events Mon - Sat, 11am - 4pm.

Admission: Free of charge. (AV show, Adult £1.50, Child £1).

Audio visual show. Ground floor & grounds suitable. WC.

Licensed. By arrangement. 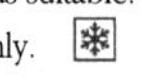 Guide dogs only.

CROMER WINDMILL

Tel: 01279 843301

Ardeley, Stevenage, Hertfordshire SG2 7QA

Owner: Hertfordshire Building Preservation Trust **Contact:** Cristina Harrison

17th century Post Windmill restored to working order.

Location: OS165, Ref. TL305 286. 4m NE of Stevenage on B1037. 1m SW of Cottered.

Opening Times: Mid-May - mid-Sept: Sun, 2nd & 4th Sat & BHs, 2.30 - 5pm.

Admission: Adult £1.50, Child 25p. Groups by arrangement.

FORGE MUSEUM & VICTORIAN COTTAGE GARDEN

Tel/Fax: 01279 843301

High Street, Much Hadham, Hertfordshire SG10 6BS

Owner: The Hertfordshire Building Preservation Trust **Contact:** The Curator

The garden reflects plants that would have been grown in 19th century, also houses an unusual 19th century bee shelter. The buildings are Grade II* listed housing a working blacksmith's forge and a museum about blacksmithing.

Location: OS Ref. TL428 195. Village centre.

Opening Times: Fri, Sat, Sun & BHs, 11am - 5pm (dusk in winter).

Admission: Adult £1, Child/Conc. 50p.

THE GARDENS OF THE ROSE

CHISWELL GREEN, ST ALBANS, HERTFORDSHIRE AL2 3NR

Owner: *The Royal National Rose Society* ***Contact:*** *Lt Col K J Grapes*

Tel: 01727 850461 **Fax:** 01727 850360 **e-mail:** mail@rnrs.org.uk

The Royal National Rose Society Gardens provide a wonderful display of one of the best and most important collections of roses in the world. There are some 30,000 roses in 1800 different varieties. The Society has introduced many companion plants which harmonise well with roses including over 100 varieties of clematis. The garden named for the Society's Patron Her Majesty The Queen Mother contains a fascinating collection of old garden roses. Various cultivation trials show just how easy roses are to grow and new varieties can be seen in the International Trial Ground. There are excellent facilities for films and fashion photography.

Location: OS Ref. TL124 045. 2m S of St Albans, M1/J6, M25/J21A. 1/2 m W of B4630.

Opening times: 27 May - 24 Sept: Mon - Sat, 9am - 5pm, Sun & Aug BHs: 10am - 6pm.

Admission: Adult £4, Child (6-16)/Student £1.50, OAP £3.50. Pre-arranged groups (min 20, max 100): Adult £3.50, Child £1.50.

Licensed.  In grounds, on leads.

GORHAMBURY HOUSE

Tel: 01727 854051 **Fax:** 01727 843675

St Albans, Hertfordshire AL3 6AH

Owner: The Earl Of Verulam **Contact:** The Administrator

Late 18th century house by Sir Robert Taylor. Family portraits from 15th - 20th centuries. Grand tour collection. Sir Francis Bacon connection.

Location: OS Ref. TL114 078. 2m W of St Albans. Accessible via private drive from A4147 at St Albans.

Opening Times: May - Sept: Thur, 2 - 5pm. Last tour of house 4.15pm.

Admission: House & Gardens: Adult £6, Child £3, OAP £4. Guided tour only. Groups by arrangement: Thursdays £5, other days £6.

HATFIELD HOUSE

See page 84 for full page entry.

HERTFORD MUSEUM

Tel: 01992 582686 **Fax:** 01992 534797

18 Bull Plain, Hertford

Owner: Hertford Museums Trust **Contact:** Andrea George

Local museum in 17th century house, altered by 18th century façade, with recreated Jacobean knot garden.

Location: OS Ref. TL326 126. Town centre.

Opening Times: Tue - Sat, 10am - 5pm.

Admission: Free.

HITCHIN BRITISH SCHOOLS

Tel: 01462 420144 **Fax:** 01462 440120

41 - 42 Queen Street, Hitchin, Hertfordshire SG4 9TS

Owner: Hitchin British Schools Trust **Contact:** Mrs Judy Lee

Unique complex of school buildings dating from 1837 to 1905. Incorporates 1837 Lancasterian Schoolroom, believed to be the only surviving example, a now rare 1853 galleried classroom (both Grade II*), Girls and Infants School from 1857 as well as two Edwardian classrooms. Related displays and small museum.

Location: OS Ref. TL186 289. Hitchin town centre.

Opening Times: Feb - Nov: Tue, 10am - 4pm. Apr - Oct: Sun, 2.30 - 5pm. Feb - Nov: School visits, Wed & Thur, 9.45am - 12.45pm.

Admission: £1. Education programme with teaching session £2.75 plus VAT per child.

 Partially suitable. WC.  Obligatory. 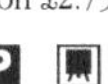 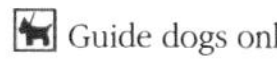 Guide dogs only.

Patrick Lane.

Hitchin British Schools, Hertfordshire.

KNEBWORTH

See page 85 for full page entry.

OLD GORHAMBURY HOUSE

Tel: 01604 730320 (Regional Office)

St Albans, Hertfordshire

Owner: English Heritage **Contact:** The Midlands Regional Office

The remains of this Elizabethan mansion, particularly the porch of the Great Hall, illustrate the impact of the Renaissance on English architecture.

Location: OS166, Ref. TL110 077. 1/4 m W of Gorhambury House and accessible only through private drive from A4147 at St Albans (2m).

Opening Times: Any reasonable time.

Admission: Free.

ST PAULS WALDEN BURY

Tel/Fax: 01438 871218/871229

Hitchin, Hertfordshire SG4 8BP

Owner: S Bowes Lyon **Contact:** S or C Bowes Lyon

A formal landscape garden, laid out in 1730, covering 40 acres. The childhood home of Queen Elizabeth, The Queen Mother. Long rides lined with beech hedges fan out to temples, statues, lake and ponds. Also more recent flower gardens. Grade I listed. Described in *Gardens of the Mind*.

Location: OS Ref. TL186 216. 5m S of Hitchin on B651.

Opening Times: Sundays 16 April, 14 May, 18 June, 2 - 7pm. Other times by appointment.

Admission: Adult £2.50, Child 50p. Other times £5.

SCOTT'S GROTTO

Tel: 01920 464131

Ware, Hertfordshire

Owner: East Hertfordshire District Council **Contact:** J Watson

One of the finest grottos in England built in the 1760s by Quaker Poet John Scott.

Location: OS Ref. TL355 137. In Scotts Rd, S of the A119 Hertford Road.

Opening Times: 1 Apr - 30 Sept: Sat & BH Mon, 2 - 4.30pm. Also by appointment.

Admission: Suggested donation of £1 for adults. Children Free. Please bring a torch.

SHAW'S CORNER

National Trust Photographic Library.

AYOT ST LAWRENCE, WELWYN, HERTFORDSHIRE AL6 9BX

Owner: *The National Trust* ***Contact:*** *The Custodian*

Tel / Fax: 01438 820307 **email:** tscgen@smtp.ntrust.org.uk

The fascinating home of playwright George Bernard Shaw until his death in 1950. The modest Edwardian villa contains many literary and personal relics, and the interior is still set out as it was in Shaw's lifetime. The garden, with its richly planted borders and views over the Hertfordshire countryside, contains the revolving summerhouse where Shaw retreated to write.

Location: OS Ref. TL194 167. At SW end of village, 2m NE of Wheathampstead, approximately 2m N from B653.

Opening times: 1 Apr - 29 Oct: Wed - Sun & BH Mons, 1 - 5pm (closed Good Fri). Parties by written appointment, Mar - Nov. Last admission 4.30pm. On busy days admission by timed ticket. On event days closes at 3.30pm. No large hand luggage inside property.

Admission: Adult £3.50, Family £8.75.

House & garden but some steps. Car park only. Tel. for details.

WALTER ROTHSCHILD ZOOLOGICAL MUSEUM

Tel: 020 7942 6171

Akeman Street, Tring, Hertfordshire HP23 6AP **Fax:** 020 7942 6150

Owner: The Natural History Museum **Contact:** Ms Teresa Wild

The museum was opened to the public by Lord Rothschild in 1892. It houses his private natural history collection. More than 4,000 species of animal in a unique Victorian setting.

Location: OS Ref. SP924 111. S end of Akeman Street, 1/4 m S of High Street.

Opening Times: Mon - Sat, 10am - 5pm, Suns, 2 - 5pm.

Admission: Adult £3, Child (0-16yrs) Free, Conc. £1.50, School groups Free.

Patrick Lane.

Benington Lordship Gardens, Hertfordshire.

English Heritage Photographic Library

Owner: English Heritage

CONTACT

The House Administrator
Osborne House
Royal Apartments
East Cowes
Isle of Wight
PO32 6JY

Tel: 01983 200022

Fax: 01983 297281

LOCATION

OS Ref. SZ516 948

1m SE of East Cowes.

Ferry: Isle of Wight ferry terminals .

East Cowes $1^1/_2$ m
Tel: 01703 334010.

Fishbourne 4m
Tel: 01705 827744.

OSBORNE HOUSE

East Cowes

OSBORNE HOUSE was the peaceful, rural retreat of Queen Victoria, Prince Albert and their family; they spent some of their happiest times here.

The Prince personally supervised the building, landscaping and alterations of this beautiful Italianate villa and its gardens which command a stunning view of the Solent.

Many of the apartments have a very intimate association with the Queen who died here in 1901 and have been preserved almost unaltered ever since. The nursery bedroom remains just as it was in the 1870s when Queen Victoria's first grandchildren came to stay. Children were a constant feature of life at Osborne (Victoria and Albert had nine). Don't miss the Swiss Cottage, a charming chalet in the grounds built for the Royal children to play and entertain their parents in.

New for Summer 2000, find out about 'life below stairs' in the newly opened 'Table Deckers' rooms.

Suitable for filming, concerts, drama. No photography in the House. Children's play area.

Durbar Room available for functions.

Wheelchairs available, access to house via ramp, ground floor access only. WC.

Teas, coffees and light snacks. Waitress service in Swiss Cottage tearoom.

Ample. Coach drivers and tour leaders free, one extra place for every additional 20. Group rates.

Visits free, please book. Education room available.

English Heritage Photographic Library

OPENING TIMES

House
1 April - 30 September
Daily: 10am - 6pm.

1 Oct - 31 Oct
Daily: 10am - 5pm
Last admission 4pm.

House Tours:
1 Nov - 12 Dec &
6 Feb - 19 Mar
Daily: 10am - 2.30pm
Sun, Mon, Wed & Thur.
Guided tours only, through booking system please call 01983 200022.

Grounds
1 April - 31 October
Daily, 10am - 6pm.

Last admission 5pm.

ADMISSION

Adult	£6.90
Child* (5-15yrs)	£3.50
Conc.	£5.20
Family	£17.30
Grounds only	
Adult	£3.50
Child* (5-15yrs)	£1.80
Conc.	£2.60
Winter & Spring	
Adult	£4.50
Child	£2.50
Conc.	£3.50

Plus normal 15% discount for groups.

* Under 5yrs Free.

APPULDURCOMBE HOUSE

Tel: 01983 852484

Wroxall, Shanklin, Isle of Wight

Owner: English Heritage **Contact:** Mr & Mrs Owen

The bleached shell of a fine 18th century Baroque style house standing in grounds landscaped by 'Capability' Brown. New Falconry Centre.

Location: OS Ref. SZ543 800. 1/2 m W of Wroxall off B3327.

Opening Times: 1 Mar - 31 Mar: Sat & Sun, 10am - 4pm. 1 Apr - 30 Sept, daily, 10am - 6pm (last entry 5pm). 1 Oct - 31 Oct, daily, 10am - 4pm. 1 Nov - 19 Dec, Sat & Sun, 10am - 4pm.

Admission: Adult £2, Child £1, Conc. £1.50.

Limited. In grounds, on leads. Tel. for details.

Patrick Lane.

Appuldurcombe House, Isle of Wight.

BEMBRIDGE WINDMILL 

Tel: 01983 873945

Enquiries to: NT Office, Strawberry Lane, Mottistone, Isle of Wight PO35 5NT

Owner: The National Trust **Contact:** The Custodian

Dating from around 1700, this is the only windmill to survive on the Island. Much of its original wooden machinery is still intact and there are spectacular views from the top.

Location: OS Ref. SZ639 874. 1/2 m W of Bembridge off B3395.

Opening Times: 27 Mar - end Jun, Sept - 27 Oct: Sun - Fri, but open Easter Sat. Jul & Aug: daily, 10am - 5pm (last admission 4.30pm).

Admission: Adult £1.50, Child 75p. Special charge for guided tours.

Not suitable. By arrangement.

CARISBROOKE CASTLE

English Heritage Photographic Library

NEWPORT, ISLE OF WIGHT PO30 1XY

***Owner:** English Heritage* ***Contact:** The Custodian*

Tel: 01983 522107 **Fax:** 01983 528632

The Island's Royal fortress and prison of King Charles I before his execution in London in 1648. See the famous Carisbrooke donkeys treading the wheel in the Well House or meet them in the donkey centre. Don't miss the castle story in the gatehouse, the museum in the great hall and the interactive coach house museum. Costumed guided tours available in summer.

Location: OS196 Ref. SZ486 877. Off the B3401, 1 1/4 m SW of Newport.

Opening times: 1 Apr - 30 Sept: daily, 10am - 6pm. 1 - 31 Oct: 10am - 5pm. 1 Nov - 31 Mar: daily, 10am - 4pm. Closed 24 - 26 Dec.

Admission: Adult £4.50, Child £2.30, Conc. £3.40, Family (2+3) £11.30. 15% discount for groups (11+), extra place for additional groups of 20.

   In grounds, on leads.  Tel. for details.

DIMBOLA LODGE

TERRACE LANE, FRESHWATER BAY PO40 9QE

***Owner:** Julia Margaret Cameron Trust* ***Contact:** Jill Wilkinson*

Tel: 01983 756814 **Fax:** 01983 755578

e-mail: administrator@dimbola.freeserve.co.uk

Historic house, former home of internationally known 19th century photographer Julia Margaret Cameron, with museum and galleries. Permanent display of Cameron images. Contemporary revolving photographic exhibitions, lectures, photographic courses, and musical performances. Available for hire, book launches, etc.

Location: OS Ref. SZ348 858. From Lymington to Yarmouth and Portsmouth to Fishbourne, Wight Link Ferries. Then A3054 to Totland and then A3055. From Southampton, Red Funnel Ferries to Cowes then A3021 to A3054.

Opening Times: All year: Tue - Sun inclusive, 10am - 5pm. Closed for 5 days at Christmas.

Admission: Adult £2.50, Child (under 16yrs) Free, Student £2.50, Disabled £1. Groups (5 - 45) 10% discount.

No photography in house. By arrangement. Limited.

HASELEY MANOR & CHILDREN'S FARM

Tel: 01983 865420 **Fax:** 01983 867547

Arreton, Isle of Wight PO30 3AN **Contact:** Mr R J Young

Location: OS Ref. SZ535 867. Main Sandown to Newport Road.

Opening Times: Apr - 31 Oct: Mon - Fri, 10am - 5.30pm. Last admission 4pm.

Admission: Adult £4.85, Child £3.55, Conc. £4, Groups £4, Family (2+2) £14.60.

MORTON MANOR

Tel: 01983 406168

Brading, Isle of Wight PO36 0EP

Owner/Contact: Mr J B Trzebski

Refurbished in the Georgian period. Magnificent gardens and vineyard.

Location: OS Ref. SZ603 863 (approx.). 1/4 m W of A3055 in Brading.

Opening Times: 5 Apr - 31 Oct: daily except Sats, 10am - 5.30pm.

Admission: Adult £4, Child £1.75, Conc. £3.50, Group £3.

MOTTISTONE MANOR GARDEN

Tel: 01983 741302

Mottistone, Isle of Wight

Owner: The National Trust **Contact:** The Gardener

A haven of peace and tranquillity with colourful herbaceous borders and a backdrop of the sea making a perfect setting for the historic Manor House. An annual open air Jazz Concert is held in the grounds during July/August.

Location: OS Ref. SZ406 838. 2m W of Brightstone on B3399.

Opening Times: 26 Mar - 29 Oct: Suns, Tues & BH Mons, 2 - 5.30pm. House: Aug BH Mon only, 2 - 5.30pm.

Admission: Adult £2.10, Child £1.05.

 Not suitable. In grounds, on leads.

Special Events Index PAGE 40

NEEDLES OLD BATTERY

Tel: 01983 754772

West High Down, Isle of Wight PO39 0JH

Owner: The National Trust **Contact:** The Administrator

High above the sea, the Old Battery was built in the 1860s against the threat of French invasion. Original gun barrels, cartoon information panels and a tea-room with one of the finest views in Britain. A 200ft tunnel leads to a restored searchlight position from which dramatic views of the Needles rocks can be seen.

Location: OS Ref. SZ300 848. Needles Headland W of Freshwater Bay & Alum Bay (B3322).

Opening Times: 26 Mar - 29 Jun, 3 Sept - 26 Oct: Sun - Thur (open Easter weekend) & Jul & Aug: daily, 10.30am - 5pm (last admission 4.30pm).

Admission: Adult £2.50, Child £1.25, Family £6. Special charge for guided tours.

Grounds suitable.  In grounds, on leads.

NUNWELL HOUSE & GARDENS

Tel: 01983 407240

Brading, Isle of Wight PO36 0JQ

Owner: Col & Mrs J A Aylmer **Contact:** Mrs J A Aylmer

A lived in family home with fine furniture, attractive gardens and historic connections with Charles I.

Location: OS Ref. SZ595 874. 1m NW of Brading. 3m S of Ryde signed off A3055.

Opening Times: 28/29 May, then Mon - Wed, 3 Jul - 6 Sept: 1 - 5pm.

Admission: Adult £4, Pair of Adults £7.50 (inc guide book), OAP/Student £3, Child (up to 10yrs) £1. Garden only: Adult £2.50.

OLD TOWN HALL

Tel: 01983 531785

Newtown, Isle of Wight

Owner: The National Trust **Contact:** The Custodian

A charming small 18th century building that was once the focal point of the 'rotten borough' of Newtown. There is also an exhibition depicting the history of the famous 'Ferguson's gang'.

Location: OS Ref. SZ424 905. Between Newport and Yarmouth, 1m N of A3054.

Opening Times: 27 Mar - end Jun, Sept - 25 Oct: Mons, Weds & Suns (open Good Fri & Easter Sat) & Jul & Aug: daily except Fri & Sat, 2 - 5pm last admission 4.45pm.

Admission: Adult £1.40, Child 70p. Special charge for guided tours (written application).

Not suitable. Limited. Guide dogs only.

OSBORNE HOUSE

See page 88 for full page entry.

YARMOUTH CASTLE

Tel: 01983 760678

Quay Street, Yarmouth, Isle of Wight PO41 0PB

Owner: English Heritage **Contact:** The Custodian

This last addition to Henry VIII's coastal defences was completed in 1547 and is, unusually for its kind, square with a fine example of an angle bastion. It was garrisoned well into the 19th century. It houses exhibitions of paintings of the Isle of Wight and photographs of old Yarmouth.

Location: OS Ref. SZ354 898. In Yarmouth adjacent to car ferry terminal.

Opening Times: 1 Apr - 30 Sept: daily, 10am - 6pm. 1 - 31 Oct: 10am - 5pm.

Admission: Adult £2.10, Child £1.10, Conc. £1.60.

Ground floor suitable. No parking. In grounds, on leads.

Osborne House, Isle of Wight.

South East England

Owner:
Mr & Mrs D Kendrick

CONTACT

Mrs M Kendrick
Boughton
Monchelsea Place
Boughton Monchelsea
Nr Maidstone
Kent
ME17 4BU

Tel: 01622 743120

LOCATION

OS Ref. TQ772 499

On B2163, 5½ m from M20/J8 or 4½ m from Maidstone via A229.

CONFERENCE/FUNCTION		
ROOM	SIZE	MAX CAPACITY
Entrance Hall	25' x 19'	50 Theatre
Dining Room	31' x 19'	50 Dining
Drawing Room	28' x 19'	40 Reception
Courtyard Room	37' x 13'	70 Theatre

BOUGHTON MONCHELSEA PLACE
Nr Maidstone

BOUGHTON MONCHELSEA PLACE is a beautiful manor house dating from 1567, set in its own country estate just outside Maidstone and only 45 miles from central London. From the front lawn there are spectacular views over the private deer park and unspoilt Kent countryside; the same views are enjoyed by the 20 acre activity site adjacent to the house. To the rear of the house is a pretty courtyard overlooked by a 17th century turret clock while steps lead up to charming walled gardens.

The interior is pleasantly furnished with mainly Victorian furniture and paintings. Boughton Monchelsea Place is lived in as a family home by Mr and Mrs Kendrick and their three children.

We are licensed for Civil marriage ceremonies and welcome corporate events, marquee receptions, product launches, exhibitions, fairs, team-building and activity days, seminars, lunches, filming, group visits, etc, but please note times of availability. Use outside these times is sometimes possible but subject to negotiation. All clients are guaranteed exclusive use of this prestige venue.

OPENING TIMES

House & Garden
Mon - Fri, 9am - 8pm
by prior arrangement only.

Event Fields
Available any time.

ADMISSION

On application

Groups (15-50)
Gardens & House Tour
Adult £4.50
Child £2.50

Gardens only
Adult £2.75
Child £1.50
(Pre-arranged only)

By arrangement.

 By arrangement.

 By arrangement.

South East England

National Trust Photographic Library: Ian Shaw

Owner: The National Trust

CONTACT

The Property Manager
Chartwell
Westerham
Kent
TN16 1PS

Tel: 01732 866368
01732 868381

Fax: 01732 868193

e-mail: kchxxx@smtp.ntrust.org.uk

LOCATION

OS Ref. TQ455 515

2m S of Westerham, forking left off B2026.

Bus: Chartwell Explorer 'green transport' bus link with Sevenoaks & Westerham. For more information contact: 01732 866368

CHARTWELL
Westerham

The family home of Sir Winston Churchill from 1924 until the end of his life. He said of Chartwell, simply *'I love the place - a day away from Chartwell is a day wasted'.* With magnificent views over the Weald of Kent it is not difficult to see why.

The rooms are left as they were in Sir Winston & Lady Churchill's lifetime with daily papers, fresh flowers grown from the garden and his famous cigars. Photographs and books evoke his career and interests, as well as happy family life. Museum and exhibition rooms contain displays and sound recordings, superb collections of memorabilia from his political career, including uniforms and a 'siren-suit'.

The garden studio contains Sir Winston's easel and paintbox, as well as many of his paintings. Terraced and water gardens descend to the lake, the gardens also include a golden rose walk, planted by Sir Winston and Lady Churchill's children on the occasion of their golden wedding anniversary, and the Marlborough Pavilion decorated with frescoes depicting the battle of Blenheim. Visitors can see the garden walls that Churchill built with his own hands, the pond stocked with the golden orfe he loved.

The Mulberry Room can be booked for meetings, conferences, dinners. Please telephone for details.

National Trust Photographic Library.

Conference facilities. Partially suitable. WC. Please telephone before visit. Licensed.

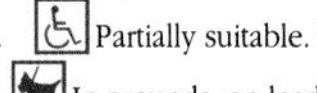
By arrangement. P In grounds, on leads.

OPENING TIMES

1 Apr - 29 Oct
Wed - Sun & BH Mons
11am - 5pm.

July & August only
Tue - Sun & BH Mon
11am - 5pm.

Last admission 4.15pm.

ADMISSION

Adult	£5.50
Child	£2.75
Family	£13.75

SPECIAL EVENTS

- **JUN 17**
  Music, Memories and Moonlight.

Scotney Castle, Kent.

Owner: Denys Eyre Bower Bequest Reg. Charity Trust

CONTACT

Mrs R Vernon
Chiddingstone Castle
Edenbridge
Kent
TN8 7AD

Tel: 01892 870347

LOCATION

OS Ref. TQ497 452

B2027, turn to Chiddingstone at Bough Beech, 1m further on to crossroads, then straight to castle.

10m from Tonbridge, Tunbridge Wells and Sevenoaks.

4m Edenbridge.

Accessible from A21 and M25/J5.

London 35m.

Bus: Enquiries: Tunbridge Wells TIC 01892 515675.

Rail: Tonbridge, Tunbridge Wells, Edenbridge then taxi. Penshurst then 2m walk.

Air: Gatwick 15m.

CONFERENCE/FUNCTION		
ROOM	SIZE	MAX CAPACITY
Assembly Rm	14' x 35'	50
Seminar Rms	15' x 15'	
Stable Block	36' x 29'	

CHIDDINGSTONE CASTLE
Edenbridge

CHIDDINGSTONE CASTLE was the dream-child of two romantics – Squire Henry Streatfeild, who rebuilt his ancestral home c1805 in the fashionable 'Castle Style'; and Denys Bower, the distinguished art connoisseur, who bought it in 1955 as a home for himself and his collections. In both cases the dream became a nightmare. The Streatfeilds could not afford this miniature version of a nobleman's residence, and eventually let it.

Denys Bower lacked means to restore it, battered by military and then scholastic occupation, though he kept at bay the destruction that engulfed countless country houses. He died in 1977 leaving everything to the National Trust. The gift was refused. Subsequently a private Charitable Trust was set up to run the Castle. Restoration was to the highest standard, helped by English Heritage. Ruth Eldridge, Managing Trustee, was awarded the MBE in 1993 for her services. Now the place is again an enchanting home: you may wander at leisure, enjoying the fine furniture and pictures, incomparable Japanese lacquer and swords, Egyptian antiquities and Royal Stuart mementoes.

The romantic 35 acre park has been fully restored. Spectacular views of the Weald combine with vistas of the Castle.

Great Hall

Conferences, receptions, concerts.
No photography in house, no smoking, no prams.

Available for special events. Wedding receptions

Partially suitable. WC.

Café. Licensed. By arrangement.

By arrangement.

Ample hardcore parking. Coaches, please book.

Teachers' pack. Educational programme.

In grounds, on leads. 

OPENING TIMES

SUMMER
Easter Hol, Spring BH.

June - September
Wed - Fri & Sun
Weekdays: 2 - 5.30pm
Sun & BHs
11.30am - 5.30pm
Last admission 5pm.

WINTER
Open only for specially booked groups (20+).

ADMISSION

Adult £4.00
Child* £2.00
Groups** (pre-booked 20+)
Adult £3.50
Child* £2.00

Fishing .... £8.00 per day
Onlooker £3.50
(1 onlooker per fisherman, no children.)

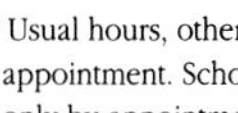

* Child under 16yrs accompanied by adult. Under 5 yrs Free.

** Usual hours, other times by appointment. School groups only by appointment.

Chiddingstone may be closed without notice for Special Events.

CHIDDINGSTONE CASTLE

Grounds (above), The restored Stable Block (below) & The Assembly Room, Conference Centre (bottom right).

SMALL CONFERENCES AND FUNCTIONS: the old domestic quarters, grouped around the courtyard, have been converted into a unique and elegant centre for various events. The self-contained Goodhugh Wing offers Assembly Room (capacity 50), three seminar rooms, and tea-kitchen. Meals can be provided in the refectory by our approved caterers. Additional lecture/meeting accommodation in the adjoining stable block, recently restored.

CIVIL MARRIAGES: The Great Hall is licensed by Kent County Council, and is specially attractive to those who desire the dignity of a church ceremony without the religious aspect. We offer all features of wedding celebrations, including reception of guests and refreshments.

EDUCATION: We welcome visits from schools who wish to use the collections in connection with classroom work. No anxiety for the teachers (admitted free). The children are safe here, can picnic and play in the grounds. We may have some exciting developments with adult education in the restored stable block. Please enquire.

Jarrold Publishing

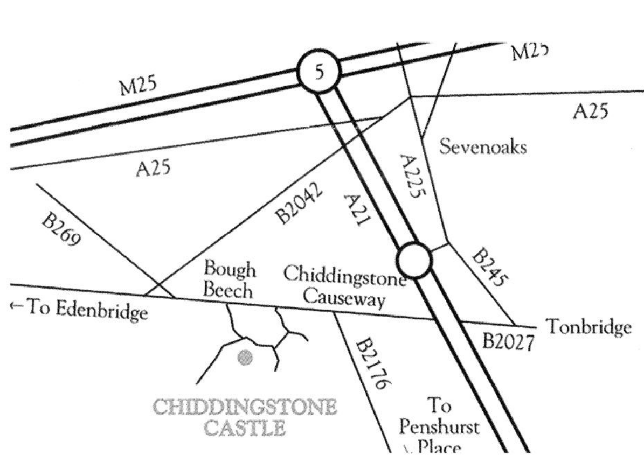

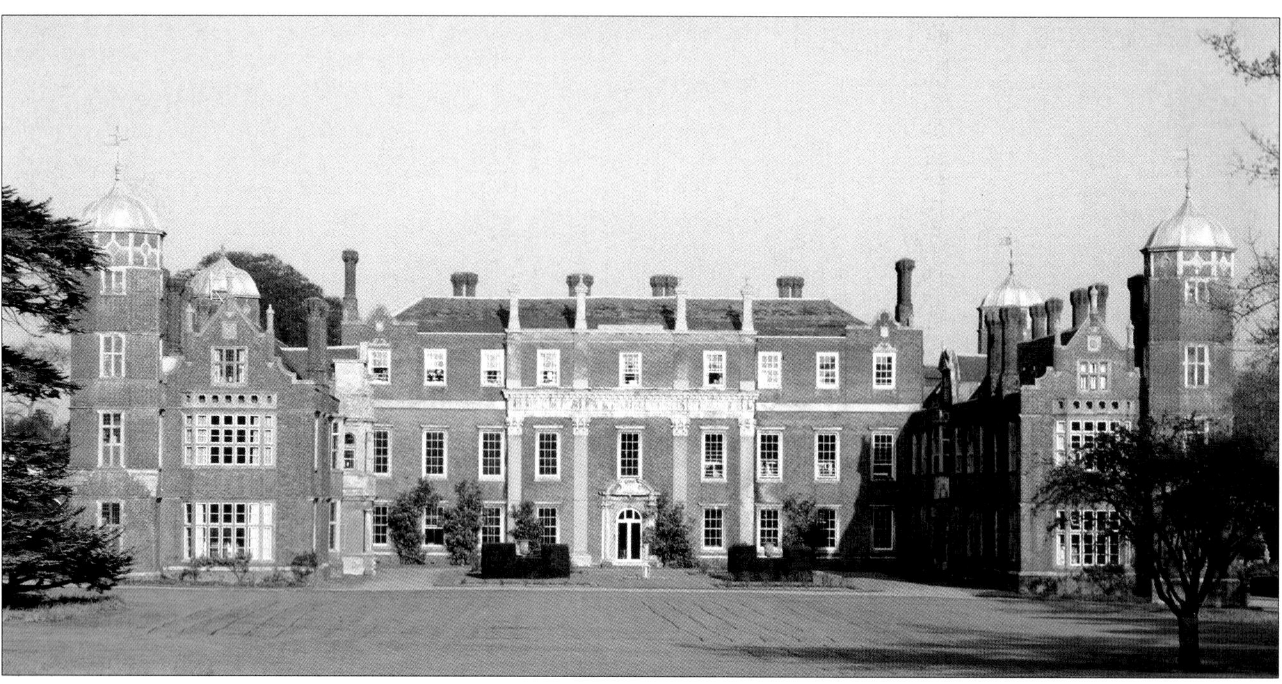

Owner: Cobham Hall Heritage Trust

CONTACT

Mr N Powell
Bursar
Cobham Hall, Cobham
Kent DA12 3BL

Tel: 01474 823371

Fax: 01474 822995
or 01474 824171

e-mail: cobhamhall@aol.com

LOCATION

OS Ref. TQ683 689

Situated adjacent to the A2/M2. 1/2 m S of A2 4m W of Strood. 8m E of M25/J2 between Gravesend & Rochester.

London 25m
Rochester 5m
Canterbury 30m

Rail: Meopham 3m
Gravesend 5m
Taxis at both stations.

Air: Gatwick 45 mins.
Heathrow 60 mins,
Stansted 50 mins.

CONFERENCE/FUNCTION		
ROOM	SIZE	MAX CAPACITY
Gilt Hall	41' x 34'	180
Wyatt Dining Rm	49' x 23'	135
Clifton Dining Rm	24' x 23'	75
Activities Centre	119' x 106'	300

COBHAM HALL
Cobham

'One of the largest, finest and most important houses in Kent', Cobham Hall is an outstandingly beautiful, red brick mansion in Elizabethan, Jacobean, Carolean and 18th century styles.

It yields much of interest to the student of art, architecture and history. The Elizabethan wings were begun in 1584 whilst the central section contains the Gilt Hall, wonderfully decorated by John Webb, Inigo Jones' most celebrated pupil, 1654. Further rooms were decorated by James Wyatt in the 18th century.

Cobham Hall, now a girls' school, has been visited by several of the English monarchs from Elizabeth I to Edward VIII, later Duke of Windsor. Charles Dickens used to walk through the grounds from his house in Higham to the Leather Bottle pub in Cobham Village. In 1883, the Hon Ivo Bligh, later the 8th Earl of Darnley, led the victorious English cricket team against Australia bringing home the 'Ashes' to Cobham.

GARDENS

The gardens, landscaped for the 4th Earl by Humphry Repton, are gradually being restored by the Cobham Hall Heritage Trust. Extensive tree planting and clearing have taken place since the hurricanes of the 1980s. The Gothic Dairy and some of the classical garden buildings are being renovated. The gardens are particularly delightful in Spring, when they are resplendent with daffodils and a myriad of rare bulbs.

Conferences, business or social functions, 150 acres of parkland for sports, corporate events, open air concerts, sports centre, indoor swimming pool, art studios, music wing, tennis courts, helicopter landing area. Filming and photography. No smoking.

In-house catering team for private, corporate hospitality and wedding receptions. (cap. 200).

House tour involves 2 staircases, ground floor access for w/chairs.

Afternoon teas, other meals by arrangement.

Obligatory guided tours; tour time 1 1/2 hrs. Garden tours arranged outside standard opening times.

Ample. Pre-booked coach groups are welcome any time.

Guide provided, Adult £3.50, Child / OAP £2.50.

In grounds, on leads.

18 single and 18 double with bathroom. 22 single and 22 double without bathroom. Dormitory. Groups only.

OPENING TIMES

SUMMER

March:
29.

April:
2, 5, 9, 12, 16, 21, 22, 23.

July:
12, 16, 19, 23, 26, 30.

August:
6, 9, 12, 13, 16, 20, 23, 28, 30.

ADMISSION

Adult £3.50
Child (4-14yrs.)........£2.50
OAP..........................£2.50

Gardens & Parkland

Self-guided tour and booklet................£1.50

Historical/Conservation tour of Grounds (by arrangement)

Per person..................£3.50

SPECIAL EVENTS

- **APR 2:** National Gardens Scheme.
- **APR 21 - 24** Medway Craft Show.
- **JUL 16:** National Gardens Scheme.
- **AUG 12 - 13:** Medway Craft & Flower Show.
- **AUG 27 - 28:** Kent Country Show.

English Heritage Photographic Library

Owner: English Heritage

CONTACT

Mr K Scott
Dover Castle
Dover
Kent
CT16 1HU

Tel: 01304 211067

Info Line: 01304 201628

LOCATION

OS Ref. TR326 416

Easy access from A2 and M20. Well signed from Dover centre and east side of Dover. 2 hrs from central London.

Rail: London Charing Cross or Victoria $1^1/_2$ hrs.

Bus: Freephone 0800 696996.

DOVER CASTLE & THE SECRET WARTIME TUNNELS

Dover

Journey deep into the White Cliffs of Dover and discover the top secret World War II tunnels. Through sight, sound and smells relive the wartime drama of the underground hospital as a wounded Battle of Britain pilot is taken to the operating theatre in a bid to save his life. Discover how life would have been during the planning days of the Dunkirk evacuation and Operation Dynamo as you are led around the network of tunnels and casements housing the communications centre.

Above ground you can explore the magnificent mediaeval keep and inner bailey of King Henry II. Visit the evocative Princess of Wales' Royal Regiment Museum. There is also the Roman Lighthouse and Anglo-Saxon church to see or take an audio tour of the intriguing 13th century underground fortifications and medieval battlements. Enjoy magnificent views of the White Cliffs from Admiralty lookout.

See the exciting 'Life Under Siege' exhibition, and discover, through a dramatic light and sound presentation, how it must have felt to be a garrison soldier defending Dover Castle against the French King in 1216. In the Keep, see a reconstruction of the Castle in preparation for a visit from Henry VIII and visit the hands-on exhibition explaining the travelling Tudor court. The land train will help you around this huge site.

Throughout the summer there are many fun events taking place, bringing the Castle alive through colourful enactments and living history.

Two.

Functions catered for including themed evenings within the Keep. For private functions tel: 01304 205830.

Lift for access to tunnels. Courtyard and grounds, some very steep slopes.

2 restaurants, hot and cold food and drinks.

Tour of tunnels approx. every 20 mins, more at peak times when a 30 min. wait can occur.

Ample. Groups welcome, discounts available. Free entry for drivers. One extra place for each additional group of 20.

Free visits available for schools. Education centre. Pre-booking essential.

English Heritage Photographic Library

OPENING TIMES

SUMMER
1 Apr - 30 Sept
Daily: 9.30am - 6pm.

1 - 31 Oct:
Daily: 10am - 5pm.

WINTER
1 November - 31 March
Daily: 10am - 4pm.

ADMISSION

Adult	£6.90
Child	£3.50
OAP	£5.20
Family (2+3)	£17.30

Groups
15% discount for groups (11+).

SPECIAL EVENTS

Please telephone for details.

English Heritage/Jonathan Bailey

Owner: English Heritage

CONTACT

The House Manager
Down House
Luxted Road
Downe
Kent
BR6 7JT

Tel: 01689 859119

DOWN HOUSE

Downe

A visit to Down House is a fascinating journey of discovery for all the family. This was the family home of Charles Darwin for over 40 years and now you can explore it to the full.

See the actual armchair in which Darwin wrote 'On the Origin of Species', which shocked and then revolutionised the way we think about the origins of mankind. His study is much the same as it was in his lifetime and is filled with belongings that give you an intimate glimpse into both his studies and everyday life.

At Down House you will discover both sides of Darwin - the great thinker and the family man.

Explore the family rooms where the furnishings have been painstakingly restored. An audio tour narrated by Sir David Attenborough will bring the house to life and increase your understanding of Darwin's revolutionary theory. Upstairs you will find state-of-the-art interpretation of the scientific significance of the house - especially designed to inspire a younger audience.

Outside, take the Sandwalk which he paced daily in search of inspiration, then stroll in lovely gardens. Complete your day by sampling the delicious selection of home-made cakes in the tea room.

English Heritage/Jonathan Bailey

OPENING TIMES

10 Apr - 31 Oct:
Wed - Sun, 10am - 6pm.

1 Nov - 31 Jan:
Wed - Sun, 10am - 4pm.

1 Mar - 31 Mar:
Wed - Sun, 10am - 4pm.

Closed 24 - 26 Dec & Feb.

On BHs and throughout August visits to Down House must be booked in advance. It is not necessary to book if you travel by public transport.

ADMISSION

Timed ticketing: available on day or pre-booked on 0870 6030145

LOCATION

OS Ref, TQ431 611

In Luxted Road, off A21 near Biggin Hill.

Rail: From London Victoria or Charing Cross.

Bus: Orpington (& Bus R2) or Bromley South (& Bus 146). Buses R2 & 146 do not run on Sunday.

Inclusive.

Limited for coaches.

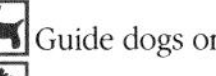

Guide dogs only.

FINCHCOCKS
Goudhurst

Owner:
Mr Richard Burnett

CONTACT

Mrs Katrina Burnett
Finchcocks
Goudhurst
Kent
TN17 1HH

Tel: 01580 211702

Fax: 01580 211007

e-mail: finchcocks@argonet.co.uk

In 1970 Finchcocks was acquired by Richard Burnett, leading exponent of the early piano, and it now contains his magnificent collection of some eighty historical keyboard instruments: chamber organs, harpsichords, virginals, spinets and early pianos. About half of these are restored to full concert condition and are played whenever the house is open to the public. The house, with its high ceilings and oak panelling, provides the perfect setting for music performed on period instruments, and Finchcocks is now a music centre of international repute. Many musical events take place here.

There is also a fascinating collection of pictures and prints, mainly on musical themes, and there is a special exhibition on display on the theme of the 18th century pleasure gardens, such as Vauxhall and Ranelagh, which includes costumes and tableaux.

Finchcocks is a fine Georgian baroque manor noted for its outstanding brickwork, with a dramatic front elevation attributed to Thomas Archer. Named after the family who lived on the site in the 13th century, the present house was built in 1725 for barrister Edward Bathurst, kinsman to Earl Bathurst. Despite having changed hands many times, it has undergone remarkably little alteration and retains most of its original features. The beautiful grounds, with their extensive views over parkland and hop gardens, include the newly restored walled garden, which provides a dramatic setting for special events.

LOCATION

OS Ref. TQ700 365

1m S of A262, 2m W of village of Goudhurst. 5m from Cranbrook, 10m from Tunbridge Wells, 45m from London (1½ hrs)

Rail: Marden 6m (no taxi), Paddock Wood 8m (taxi), Tunbridge Wells 10m (taxi).

Air: Gatwick 1 hr.

Music events, conferences, seminars, promotions, archery, ballooning, filming, television. Keyboard instruments and musical furniture for hire, marquees erected for large functions. No videos in house, photography by permission only.

Private and corporate entertaining, weddings. Full catering by arrangement. Fully licensed.

Limited. WC. Suitable for visually handicapped.

Licensed. Teas and light refreshments. Picnics permitted in grounds.

Musical tours / recitals on instruments whenever required. Tour time: 2½ - 4 hrs.

P Ample. Pre-booked groups (25 - 100) welcome from Apr - Oct. Free meals for couriers and drivers.

Opportunity to play instruments. Can be linked to special projects and National Curriculum syllabus.

Music a speciality, and musicians can be provided.

OPENING TIMES

SUMMER

Easter Sun - end Sept
Sun & BH Mons, plus Wed & Thur in August, 2 - 6pm.

Pre-booked groups and individuals welcome most days April to October mornings, afternoons and evenings and in some circumstances up to Christmas.

WINTER

Closed
January - mid-March
Available for private functions October, November & December.

ADMISSION

Open Days
House, Garden & Music

Adult	£6.50
Child	£4.00
Student	£5.00
OAP	£6.50

Garden Only

Adult	£2.00
Child	£0.50

Groups*

Adult	£6.50
Child	£4.50
Student	£5.00
OAP	£6.50

* Min. of 25 to open house.

SPECIAL EVENTS

- **MAY 28/29:** Spring Garden Fair & Flower Festival
- **SEPT WEEKENDS:** Music Festival
- **OCT 13 - 15:** Autum Fair

South East England

Owner:
Blenheim Asset Management Ltd.

CONTACT

The Estate Office
Groombridge Place
Groombridge
Tunbridge Wells
Kent
TN3 9QG

Tel: 01892 863999

Fax: 01892 863996

LOCATION

OS Ref. TQ534 375

Groombridge Place Gardens are located on the B2110 just off the A264. 4m SW of Tunbridge Wells and 9m E of East Grinstead.

Rail: London Charing Cross to Tunbridge Wells 55 mins.

Air: Gatwick.

GROOMBRIDGE PLACE GARDENS

Tunbridge Wells

Surrounded by acres of breathtaking parkland, Groombridge Place has an intriguing history stretching back to medieval times. Flanked by a medieval moat, with a classical 17th century manor as its backdrop, the beautiful formal gardens boast a rich variety of 'rooms', together with extensive herbaceous borders. High above the walled gardens and estate vineyard, hidden from view, lies The Enchanted Forest, where magic and fantasy await discovery. Here are secret mysterious gardens to challenge and delight your imagination and reward your mind's ingenuity.

Winner of 3 major awards in 2 years.

Suitable for concerts, filming and fairs.

Available for weddings.

Partially suitable. Some access to formal gardens. WC.

Tearoom.

Must book, additional charge. Tour time: 1hr.

Ample for cars. Free admittance for coach drivers.

Civil Wedding Licence.

OPENING TIMES

SUMMER
Gardens

April - October
Daily, 9am - 6pm.

The house is not open to visitors.

ADMISSION

Adult	£7.50
Child (under 17yrs)	£6.50
Student/OAP	£6.50
Family Ticket	£25.00
Groups	
Per person	£6.25
Child	£5.25
OAP	£5.25

SPECIAL EVENTS

Please telephone for details.

Andrew Butler.

Ightham Mote, Kent.

South East England

HEVER CASTLE
Edenbridge

Owner:
Hever Castle Estate

CONTACT

Anne-Marie Critchley-Salmonson
Hever Castle
Hever, Edenbridge
Kent TN8 7NG

Infoline: 01732 865224
Fax: 01732 866796
e-mail: mail@HeverCastle.co.uk

LOCATION

OS Ref. TQ476 450

Exit M25/J5 & J6 M23/J10, 1½ m S of B2027 at Bough Beech, 3m SE of Edenbridge.

Rail: Hever Station 1m (no taxis), Edenbridge Town 3m (taxis).

CONFERENCE/FUNCTION		
ROOM	SIZE	MAX CAPACITY
Dining Hall	35' x 20'	70
Breakfast Rm	22' x 15'	12
Sitting Rm	24' x 20'	20
Pavilion	96' x 40'	250
Moat Restaurant	25 'x 60'	75

HEVER CASTLE dates back to 1270, when the gatehouse, outer walls and the inner moat were first built. 200 years later the Bullen (or Boleyn) family added the comfortable Tudor manor house constructed within the walls. This was the childhood home of Anne Boleyn, Henry VIII's second wife and mother of Elizabeth I. There are many items relating to the Tudors, including two books of hours (prayer books) signed and inscribed by Anne Boleyn. The Castle was later given to Henry VIII's fourth wife, Anne of Cleves.

In 1903, the estate was bought by the American millionaire William Waldorf Astor, who became a British subject and the first Lord Astor of Hever. He invested an immense amount of time, money and imagination in restoring the castle and grounds. Master craftsmen were employed and the castle was filled with a magnificent collection of furniture, tapestries and other works of art. The Miniature Model Houses exhibition, a collection of 1/12 scale model houses, room views and gardens, depicts life in English Country Houses.

GARDENS

Between 1904-8 over 30 acres of formal gardens were laid out and planted, these have now matured into one of the most beautiful gardens in England. The unique Italian garden is a four acre walled garden containing a superb collection of statuary and sculpture. The award-winning gardens include the Rose garden and Tudor garden, a traditional yew maze and a 110 metre herbaceous border. A water maze has been added to the other water features in the gardens.

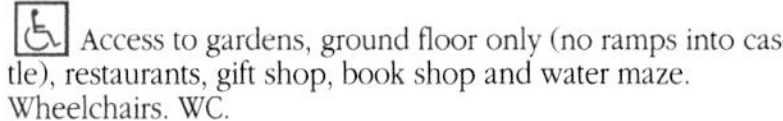

Suitable for filming, conferences, corporate hospitality, product launches. Outdoor heated pool, tennis court and billiard room. No photography in house.

Gift, garden and book.

250 seat restaurant available for functions wedding receptions, etc.

Access to gardens, ground floor only (no ramps into castle), restaurants, gift shop, book shop and water maze. Wheelchairs. WC.

Two licensed restaurants. Supper provided during open air theatre season. Pre-booked lunches and teas for groups.

Pre-booked tours in mornings. 1 Mar - 30 Nov. Tour time 1 hr. Tours in French, German, Dutch, Italian and Spanish (min 20). Garden tours in English only (min 15).

Miniature Model Houses exhibition only.

Free admission and refreshment voucher for driver and courier. Please book, group rates for 15+.

Welcome (min 5). Guide provided for groups of 20. 1:10 ratio. Free preparatory visits for teachers during opening hours. Please book.

In grounds, on leads. 

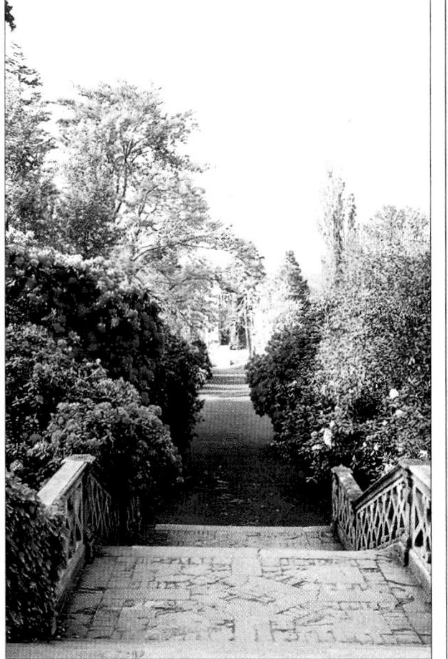

OPENING TIMES

SUMMER
1 March - 30 November
Daily:
Grounds: 11am - 6pm.
Castle: 12 noon - 6pm.
Last admission 5pm.

WINTER
March & November
Grounds: 11am - 4pm.
Castle: 12 noon - 4pm.

ADMISSION

Castle & Garden

Adult	£7.80
Child (5-16 yrs)	£4.20
OAP	£6.60
Family (2+2)	£19.80

Please ring for group prices.

Garden only

Adult	£6.10
Child (5-16 yrs)	£4.00
OAP	£5.20
Family (2+2)	£16.20

Please ring for group prices.

Pre-booked private guided tours are available between 10am & 12 noon during season.

HEVER CASTLE

Hever Castle Tudor Village was built in 1903 for William Waldorf Astor in the style of the Tudor period, to include every modern day comfort.

There are twenty individually designed rooms all with private bathroom, direct dial telephone, colour television, hair dryer, and tea and coffee making facilities. The billiard room, outdoor heated swimming pool, tennis court and croquet lawn are all available for guests to use. Hever Castle Estate includes Stables House, an imposing property with five bedrooms, overlooking the river Eden, providing additional accommodation.

The Tudor Village is a unique and unusual venue available only on an 'exclusive use' basis all year round for groups of 10 or more requiring the very highest standards of accommodation, dining and meeting facilities. There are three interconnecting reception rooms all available for private dining, receptions, product launches, private meetings or corporate hospitality.

The magnificent private dining rooms are able to seat up to 70 people for Tudor Banquets, lunches and dinners. Guests are able to enjoy a private guided tour of the Castle followed by a Tudor Banquet with Minstrels playing Tudor Music.

The Dining Hall, Sitting Room and Breakfast Room (which together form the Tudor Suite) provide formal meeting facilities for up to 30 people and 70 people 'theatre style'. Overhead projector, screen and flip charts can be provided and specialist audiovisual equipment hired. Additional arrangements can be made for laser clay pigeon shooting, archery, fishing, riding, golf and other pursuits on or near by the estate.

Hever Castle Tudor Village offers the following accommodation

- 4 Single bedded rooms
- 8 Twin bedded rooms
- 8 Double bedded rooms
- 4 Twin and 1 Double bedded rooms (in the Stables House)

SPECIAL EVENTS

- **APR 21-24**
  Royal Tudor Easter Egg Trail
- **APR 29/30, MAY 1**
  May Day Music and Dance
- **MAY 27 - 29**
  Merrie England Weekend
- **JUNE 24/25**
  Gardening Event
- **JUL 22, 29**
  AUG 5/6, 12/13, 19/20, 26
  Jousting Tournaments
- **JUL 16, 23, 30**
  AUG 27/28
  SEPT 2/3
  Longbow Warfare
- **SEPT 8-10**
  Patchwork & Quilting

Tulip Bedroom in Tudor Village.

Tudor Suite Dining Room in Tudor Village.

The Music Room in Tudor Village.

South East England

Rupert Truman

Andreas Von Einsiedel.

KNOLE
Sevenoaks

Set in an extensive deer park owned by Lord Sackville, Knole is one of the great 'treasure houses' of England. It has been the home of the Sackville family since 1603, including four Dukes of Dorset, and houses an extensive collection of furnishings and paintings, many in the house since the 17th century.

The largest private house in England, Knole is a spectacular example of late medieval architecture overlaid with extensive Jacobean embellishments, including remarkable carving and plasterwork. The Sackville family crest of the leopard rampant recurs throughout.

An internationally renowned collection of Royal Stuart furnishings, including three state beds, celebrated silver furniture, and the prototype of the 'Knole' settee. Thirteen years were spent restoring the fabrics on the bed in the Kings' room.

The 6th Earl of Dorset played host to poets Pope and Dryden. Knole was the birthplace of the writer, Vita Sackville-West, and the setting for Virginia Woolf's novel *Orlando*.

Important collection of paintings, including works by Van Dyck, Lely, Kneller,Gainsborough, Hoppner, Wootton, and a room devoted to the works of Sir Joshua Reynolds, commissioned for the house by the 3rd Duke of Dorset, including portraits of Dr Johnson, David Garrick and Oliver Goldsmith.

The experience of visiting the house, which has been little altered since the 18th century, is like stepping back in time.

Owner:
The National Trust

CONTACT

Jane Sedge
Property Manager
Knole
Sevenoaks
Kent TN15 0RP

Tel: 01732 462100

Info: 01732 450608

Fax: 01732 465528

e-mail: kknkmw@smtp.ntrust.org.uk

LOCATION

OS Ref. TQ532 543

25m SE of London. Just off A225 at S end of High Street, Sevenoaks.

Rail: 1/2 hr from London Charing Cross to Sevenoaks.

Bus: Call Knole direct for bus information

National Trust Photographic Library.

Andreas Von Einsiedel.

Concerts and other events in Great Hall and Stone Court. Full range of NT goods and souvenirs of Knole.

Wheelchair access to Green Court, Stone Court and Great Hall.

Brewhouse Restaurant serving morning coffee, lunch and teas. Also ice-creams and snacks in courtyard.

Guided tours for pre-booked groups: Thur mornings.

Ample.

Welcome. Special reduction for booked groups.

OPENING TIMES

House & Garden

1 Apr - 29 Oct:
Wed - Sat, 12 noon - 4pm.

Last admission 3.30pm.

Sun, BH Mon & Good Fri
11am - 5pm.

Last admission 4pm.

Garden

May - September
1st Wed of month only
12 noon - 4pm.

Last admission 3pm.

ADMISSION

House & Garden

Adult £5.00
Child £2.50
Family £12.50

Groups (pre-booked)
Adult £4.25

Parking.......................£2.50

Garden only £1.00

NT members Free.

Knole, Kent.

LEEDS CASTLE & GARDENS
Maidstone

This much-loved palace and home, surrounded by 500 acres of magnificent parkland and gardens and set in the middle of a natural lake, is one of the country's finest historic properties. Leeds is also proud to be one of the Treasure Houses of England.

The site of a Saxon royal manor, a Norman fortress and a royal palace to the Kings and Queens of England, the chequered history of Leeds Castle continues well into the 20th century. The last private owner, the Honourable Olive, Lady Baillie, purchased the Castle in 1926. Her inheritance helped to restore the Castle and, prior to her death, she established the Leeds Castle Foundation which now preserves the Castle for the nation, hosts important international conferences and supports the arts.

The Castle has a fine collection of paintings, tapestries and furnishings and is also home to a unique collection of antique dog collars. The Park and Grounds include the colourful and quintessentially English Culpeper Garden, the delightful Wood Garden, and the new terraced Lady Baillie Garden with its views over the tranquil Great Water. An Aviary houses rare and endangered species from around the world and, next to the Victorian Greenhouses can be found a traditional Maze with its secret underground grotto.

A highly popular and successful programme of Special Events is arranged throughout the year, details of which can be found opposite.

Culpeper Garden

Residential conferences, exhibitions, sporting days, clay shooting, falconry, field archery, golf, croquet and heli-pad. Talks can be arranged for horticultural, viticultural, historical and cultural groups. No radios.

Corporate hospitality, large scale marquee events, wedding receptions, buffets and dinners.

Shuttle for elderly/disabled, wheelchairs, wheelchair lift, special rates. WC.

Two restaurants, group lunch menus. Refreshment kiosks.

Guides in rooms. French, Spanish, Dutch, German, Italian and Russian speaking guides.

Free parking.

Welcome, outside normal opening hours, private tours. Teacher's resource pack.

Owner:
Leeds Castle Foundation

CONTACT

Sandra Barrett
Leeds Castle
Maidstone
Kent
ME17 1PL

Tel: 01622 765400

Fax: 01622 735616

LOCATION

OS Ref. TQ835 533

From London to A20/M20/J8, 40m, 1 hr. 6m E of Maidstone, 1/4 m S of A20.

Rail: BR Connex train and admission. London - Bearsted.

Coach: Nat Express/ Invictaway coach and admission from Victoria.

Air: Gatwick 45m. Heathrow 65m.

Channel Tunnel: 25m.

Channel ports: 38m.

CONFERENCE/FUNCTION		
ROOM	SIZE	MAX CAPACITY
Fairfax Hall	19.8 x 1m	200
Gate Tower	9.8 x 5.2m	50
Culpeper	7.65 x 7.34m	40
Terrace	8.9 x 15.4m	80

OPENING TIMES

OPEN ALL YEAR

SUMMER
1 March - 31 October
Daily:
10am - 5pm (last adm).

WINTER
1 November - 29 February
Daily:
10am - 3pm (last adm.).
(closed Christmas Day).

Also special private tours for pre-booked groups at any other time by appointment.

Castle & Grounds closed 24 Jun & 1 July prior to the Open Air Concerts.

ADMISSION

Rates from 1 March 2000.

Castle, Park & Gardens
Adult £9.50
Child (5 -15yrs) £6.00
OAP/Student £7.50
Family (2+3) £26.00
Disabled Visitors
Adult £4.50
Child (5 -15yrs) £3.30
Groups (15+)
Adult £7.20
Child (5 -15yrs) £5.20
OAP/Student £6.20

Park & Gardens
Adult £7.50
Child (5 -15yrs) £4.50
OAP/Student £6.00
Family (2+3) £21.00
Disabled Visitors
Adult £3.50
Child (5 -15yrs) £2.30
Groups (15+)
Adult £6.20
Child (5 -15yrs) £4.20
OAP/Student £5.00

A guidebook is published in English, French, German, Dutch, Spanish, Italian, Japanese, Mandarin and Russian.

LEEDS CASTLE

Open Air Concerts.

Half Term Story Telling

Festival of Floral Art

Autumn Gold.

Grand Firework Spectacular.

Festival of English Food & Wine.

Christmas at the Castle.

Balloon & Vintage Car Weekend.

SPECIAL EVENTS

- **JAN 1/2/3:** Millennium Treasure Trails
- **FEB 21 - 25:** Half Term Story-Telling
- **APR 8/9:** Greenhouse Weekend
- **APR 22/23/24:** A Celebration of Easter
- **MAY 13/14** Festival of English Food & Wine
- **MAY 27 - JUN 4** Amazing Mazes Week
- **JUN 24 & JUL 1:** Open Air Concerts
- **JUN 28:** Kent Children's Prom
- **JUL 20 - 23:** A Festival of Summer Floral Art
- **SEPT 9/10:** Balloon & Vintage Car Weekend
- **OCT 18 - 22:** Autumn Gold - A Celebration of Flowers and Produce
- **OCT 23 - 27:** Half Term Halloween Event
- **NOV 4:** Grand Firework Spectacular
- **DEC 11 - 24:** Christmas at the Castle

Greenhouse Weekend.

A Celebration of Easter.

Amazing Mazes Week

South East England

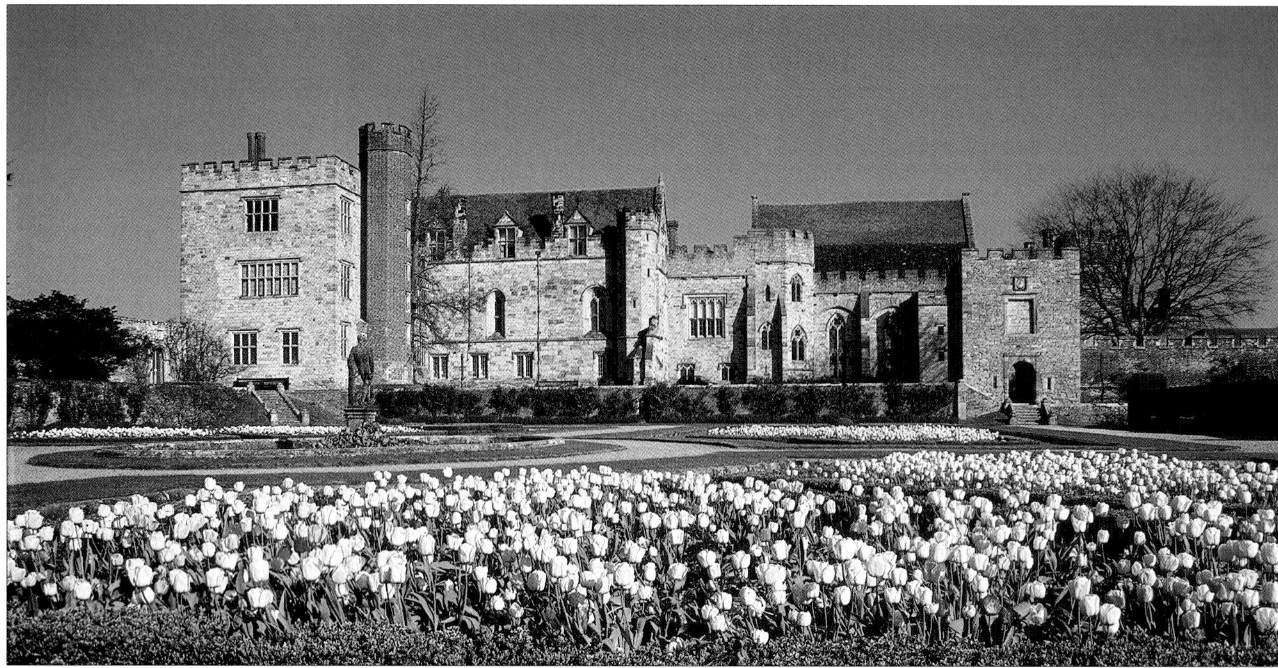

Owner:
Viscount De L'Isle

CONTACT

Bonnie Vernon
Penshurst Place
Penshurst
Nr Tonbridge
Kent
TN11 8DG

Tel: 01892 870307
Fax: 01892 870866

e-mail:penshurst@pavilion.co.uk

LOCATION

OS Ref. TQ527 438

From London M25/J5 then A21 to Tonbridge North, B2027 via Leigh; from Tunbridge Wells A26, B2176.

Visitors entrance at SE end of village, S of the church.

Bus: Maidstone & District 231, 232, 233 from Tunbridge Wells.

Rail: Charing Cross/ Waterloo - Hildenborough, Tonbridge or Tunbridge Wells; then taxi.

CONFERENCE/FUNCTION		
ROOM	SIZE	MAX CAPACITY
Sunderland Room	45' x 18'	100
Barons' Hall	64' x 39'	250
Buttery	20' x 23'	50

PENSHURST PLACE & GDNS

Nr Tonbridge

PENSHURST PLACE is one of England's greatest family-owned stately homes with a history going back six and a half centuries.

In some ways time has stood still at Penshurst; the great House is still very much a medieval building with improvements and additions made over the centuries but without any substantial rebuilding. Its highlight is undoubtedly the medieval Barons' Hall, built in 1341, with its impressive 60ft-high chestnut-beamed roof.

A marvellous mix of paintings, tapestries and furniture from the 15th, 16th and 17th centuries can be seen throughout the House, including the helm carried in the state funeral procession to St. Paul's Cathedral for the Elizabethan courtier and poet, Sir Philip Sidney, in 1587. This is now the family crest.

GARDENS

The Gardens, first laid out in the 14th century, have been developed over successive years by the Sidney family who first came to Penshurst in 1552. A twenty-year restoration and re-planting programme undertaken by the late Viscount De L'Isle has ensured that they retain their historic splendour. He is commemorated with a new Arboretum, planted in 1991. The gardens are divided by a mile of yew hedges into "rooms", each planted to give a succession of colour as the seasons change. There is also an Adventure Playground, Nature Trail and Toy Museum for children.

Product launches, garden parties, photography, filming, fashion shows, receptions, archery, clay pigeon shooting, falconry, parkland for hire, lectures on property, its contents and history. Conference facilities. Adventure playground & parkland & riverside walks. No photography in house.

Private banqueting, wedding receptions.

Limited, disabled and elderly may alight at entrance. WC.

Licensed restaurant (waitress service can be booked by groups of 20+).

Mornings only by arrangement, lunch/dinner can be arranged. Out of season tours by appointment. Guided tours of the gardens.

Ample. Double decker buses to park from village.

All year by appointment, discount rates, education room and packs.

Guide dogs only

OPENING TIMES

SUMMER
From 4 March weekends only.

1 April - 31 October

House
Daily, 12 noon - 5.30pm
Last entry 5pm.

Grounds
Daily, 10.30am - 6pm.

Shop & Plant Centre
10.30am - 6pm.

WINTER
Open to Groups by appointment only (see Guided Tours).

ADMISSION

House & Grounds
- Adult £6.00
- Child* £4.00
- OAP.........................£5.50
- Family (2+2) £16.00

Groups**
- Adult £5.30
- Child £2.80

Garden only
- Adult £4.50
- Child* £3.50
- OAP.........................£4.00
- Family (2+2) £13.00

Garden Season Ticket
..............................£22.00

House Tours (pre-booked)
- Adult.........................£6.00
- Child.........................£3.20

Garden Tours (pre-booked)
- Adult..........................£6.50
- Child..........................£4.00

House & Garden.........£7.00

* Aged 5-15yrs; under 5s Free.
** Min 20 people, afternoons only. Special rates for morning Guided Tours.

South East England

Owner:
John St A Warde Esq

CONTACT

Mrs Vale or Mrs Warde
Squerryes Court
Westerham
Kent
TN16 1SJ

Tel: 01959 562345
or 01959 563118

Fax: 01959 565949

LOCATION

OS Ref. TQ440 535

Off the M25/J6, 6m, E along A25 $^1/_2$ m SW of Westerham

London 1-1$^1/_2$ hrs.

Rail: Oxted Station 4m. Sevenoaks 6m.

Air: Gatwick, 30 mins.

CONFERENCE/FUNCTION		
ROOM	SIZE	MAX CAPACITY
Hall	32' x 32'	60
Old Library	20' x 25' 6"	40

SQUERRYES COURT & GDNS

Westerham

SQUERRYES COURT has been the home of the Wardes since 1731 and is still lived in by the family today. Although it was built in Charles II's reign in 1681 it is a typical William and Mary manor house. Squerryes is 22 miles from London and easily accessible from the M25. Surrounded by parkland, there are fine views over the lake to the hills beyond.

The house has an important collection of Italian, 18th century English and 17th century Dutch paintings acquired and commissioned by the family in the 18th century. John Warde who inherited in 1746 purchased 93 paintings in the space of 25 years. He did not go on the Grand Tour but bought from auction houses, dealers and private sales in England. This gives an insight into the taste of a man of his time and also what was available on the art market in England in the mid 18th century.

The furniture and porcelain have been in the house since the 18th century and the Tapestry Room contains a fine set of Soho tapestries made c1720. General Wolfe of Quebec was a friend of the family and there are items connected with him in the Wolfe Room.

GARDENS
These were laid out in the formal style but were re-landscaped in the mid 18th century. Some of the original features in the 1719 Badeslade print survive. The family have restored the formal garden using this print as a guide. The garden is lovely all year round with bulbs, wild flowers and woodland walks, azaleas, summer flowering herbaceous borders and roses.

Suitable for conferences, product launches, filming, photography, archery, clay pigeon shooting, garden parties. No photography in house.

Exclusive entertaining & wedding receptions (marquee).

Limited garden access, house unsuitable, tearoom access. WC.

Home-made teas on open days. Groups must book for lunch or tea. Menus upon request.

For groups (max 55), small additional charge. Owner will meet groups by prior arrangement. Tour time $^3/_4$ hr.

Ample. Free teas for drivers and couriers.

Welcome, cost £1.50 per child, guide provided. Areas of interest: nature walk, ducks and geese.

On leads, in grounds.

OPENING TIMES

SUMMER
1 April - 30 September
Wed, Sat, Sun & BH Mon.

Closed: Mon (except BH Mon), Tue, Thur & Fri.

Grounds: 12 noon - 5.30pm
House: 1.30 - 5.30pm
Last admission 5pm.

NB. Pre-booked groups welcome any day.

WINTER
October - 1 April
Closed.

ADMISSION

House & Garden
Adult £4.20
Child (under 14) £2.50
OAP £3.80
Groups (20+)
Adult £3.60
Child (under 14) £1.80
OAP £3.60

House only
Adult £4.20
Child (under 14) £2.50
OAP £3.80
Groups (20+)
Adult £3.60
Child (under 14) £1.80
OAP £3.60

Garden only
Adult £2.50
Child (under 14) £1.50
OAP £2.20
Groups (20+, booked)
Adult £2.20
Child (under 14) £1.10
OAP £2.20

THE ARCHBISHOPS' PALACE

Tel: 01622 663006 **Fax:** 01622 682451

Mill Street, Maidstone, Kent ME15 6YE

Owner: Maidstone Borough Council **Contact:** Operations Manager

Recently refurbished 14th century Palace used as a resting place for Archbishops travelling from London to Canterbury.

Location: OS Ref. TQ760 555. On the banks of River Medway SW of the centre of Maidstone.

Opening Times: Daily: 10am - 4.30pm.

Admission: Entrance to 1st floor rooms is free.

BEDGEBURY NATIONAL PINETUM

Tel: 01580 211044 **Fax:** 01580 212423

Goudhurst, Cranbrook, Kent TN17 2SL

Owner: Forestry Commission **Contact:** Mr Colin Morgan

Location: OS Ref. TQ714 337 (gate on B2079). 7m E of Tunbridge Wells on A21, turn N on B2079 for 1m.

Opening Times: Weekends Jan & Feb. 1 Mar - Christmas: daily, 10am - dusk or 7pm.

Admission: Adult £3, Child £1.50, OAP £2.50.

BEECH COURT GARDENS

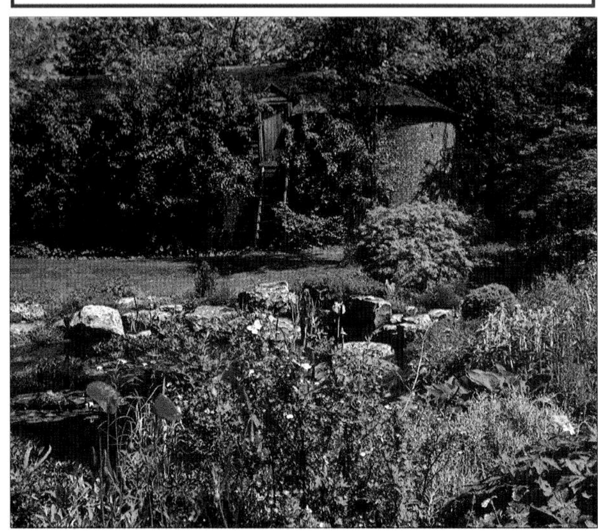

CANTERBURY ROAD, CHALLOCK, Nr ASHFORD, KENT TN25 4DJ

Owner: *Mr V Harmsworth* ***Contact:*** *Mrs Miller-Thomas*

Tel: 01233 740735 **Fax:** 01233 740842

The woodland garden with its tranquil atmosphere and surprising vistas surrounds a medieval farmhouse. Rhododendrons, azaleas and viburnums give superb spring colour. Roses, philadelphus and summer borders follow on and the vivid blue hydrangeas and autumn colours makes this a garden for all seasons.

Location: OS Ref. TQ999 501. Off A252 Charing side of Challock roundabout.

Opening Times: 25 Mar - 15 Nov: (Closed Good Fri) Mon - Thur, 10am - 5.30pm, Fri - Sun, 12 noon - 6pm.

Admission: Adult £3, Child £1, OAP/Student £2.50. Groups (12+): Adult £2, Child 50p, OAP/Student £2.

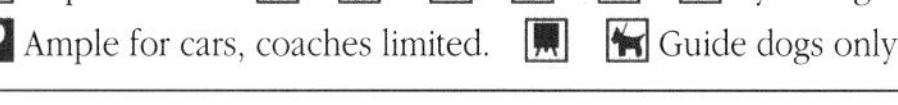

Map available. By arrangement.

Ample for cars, coaches limited. Guide dogs only.

BELMONT

BELMONT PARK, THROWLEY, FAVERSHAM ME13 0HH

Owner: *Harris (Belmont) Charity* ***Contact:*** *Lt Col F E Grant*

Tel: 01795 890202 **Fax:** 01795 890042

Belmont is a charming late 18th century country mansion by Samuel Wyatt, set in delightful grounds. The seat of the Harris family since 1801 it is beautifully furnished and contains interesting items from India and Trinidad as well as the unique clock collection formed by the 5th Lord.

Location: OS Ref. TQ986 564. 4½m SSW of Faversham, off A251.

Opening Times: 23 Apr - 30 Sept: Sats, Suns & BHs, 2 - 5pm. Last admission to house 4.30pm. Groups (20+) on other days by appointment.

Admission: House & Garden: Adult £5.25, Child £2.50, Conc. £4.75. Groups (20+): Adult £4.75, Child £2.50. Garden: Adult £2.75, Child £1. No discount for groups.

No photography in house. Partially suitable. WC. 

Obligatory.

BOUGHTON MONCHELSEA PLACE

See page 91 for full page entry.

CANTERBURY CATHEDRAL

Tel: 01227 762862 **Fax:** 01227 865222

Canterbury, Kent CT1 2EH **Contact:** Visits Office

Founded in 597AD, Mother Church of the Anglican Communion, Romanesque Crypt, 14 - 15th century Nave. Site of Becket's martyrdom and Shrine. Notable stained glass.

Location: OS Ref. TR151 579. Canterbury city centre.

Opening Times: All year: Mon - Sat, 9am - 5pm (Easter - Sept: 9am - 7pm). Suns, 12 30 - 2.30pm & 4.30 - 5.30pm.

Admission: £3, Conc. £2.

By arrangement.

CHARTWELL

See page 92 for full page entry.

CHIDDINGSTONE CASTLE

See pages 94/95 for double page entry.

COBHAM HALL

See page 96 for full page entry.

Patrick Lane.

Ladham House Gardens, Kent.

DEAL CASTLE 

VICTORIA ROAD, DEAL, KENT CT14 7BA

Owner: *English Heritage* ***Contact:*** *The Custodian*

Tel: 01304 372762

Crouching low and menacing, the huge, rounded bastions of this austere fort, built by Henry VIII, once carried 119 guns. A fascinating castle to explore, with long, dark passages, battlements and a huge basement. The interactive displays and exhibition give a fascinating insight into the Castle's history.

Location: OS Ref. TR378 521. SE of Deal town centre.

Opening Times: 1 Apr - 30 Sept: daily, 10am - 6pm. 1 - 31 Oct: 10am - 5pm. 1 Nov - 31 Mar: Wed - Sun only, 10am - 4pm. Closed 24 - 26 Dec.

Admission: Adult £3, Child £1.50, Conc. £2.30.

Restricted. Coach parking on main road.
Guide dogs only. Tel. for details.

DICKENS CENTRE - EASTGATE HOUSE

Tel: 01634 844176

High Street, Rochester, Kent ME1 1EW

Owner: Medway Council **Contact:** John Loudwell

Much altered late 16th century brick house, now containing the Dickens Centre, with exhibits of his life and works, including his best known characters. At the rear is Dickens' prefabricated chalet, brought from Switzerland.

Location: OS Ref. TQ746 683. N side of Rochester High Street, close to the Eastern Road. 400yds SE of the Cathedral.

Opening Times: Daily, 10am - 4.45pm (last admission).

Admission: Adult £3.50, Child £2.50, Family £9.50 (1999 prices).

DODDINGTON PLACE GARDENS

Tel: 01795 886101

Doddington, Sittingbourne, Kent ME9 0BB

Owner: Mr & Mrs Richard Oldfield **Contact:** Mrs Richard Oldfield

10 acres of landscaped gardens in an area of outstanding natural beauty.

Location: OS Ref. TQ944 575. 4m N from A20 at Lenham or 5m SW from A2 at Ospringe, W of Faversham. Signposted.

Opening Times: May - Sept: Sun 2 - 6pm. Wed & BHs 11am - 6pm. Groups at other times by appointment.

Admission: Adult £3, Child 50p. Groups: £2.50. Coaches by prior arrangement.

DOVER CASTLE & THE SECRET WARTIME TUNNELS

See page 97 for full page entry.

DOWN HOUSE

See page 98 for full page entry.

DYMCHURCH MARTELLO TOWER

Tel: 01304 211067

Dymchurch, Kent

Owner: English Heritage **Contact:** Area Manager

Built as one of 74 such towers to counter the threat of invasion by Napoleon, Dymchurch is perhaps the best example in the country. Fully restored. You can climb to the roof which is dominated by an original 24-pounder gun complete with traversing carriage.

Location: OS189, Ref. TR102 294. In Dymchurch, access from High Street.

Opening Times: 2 - 5 Apr, 1 - 3 May: 2 - 5.30pm. 8 May - 10 Jul: weekends & BHs, 2 - 5.30pm. 17 Jul - 30 Aug: daily, 2 - 5.30pm. 1 - 30 Sept: Sat & Sun, 2 - 5.30pm.

Admission: Adult £1, Child 50p, Conc. 80p.

EASTBRIDGE HOSPITAL OF ST THOMAS

Tel: 01227 471688

High Street, Canterbury, Kent CT1 2BD

Contact: Mrs Elizabeth Newby

Medieval pilgrims' hospital with 12th century undercroft, refectory and chapel.

Location: OS189, Ref. TR148 579. S side of Canterbury High Street.

Opening Times: Mon - Sat, 10am - 4.45pm.

Admission: Adult £1, Child 50p, Conc. 75p (1999 prices).

EMMETTS GARDEN 

NT Photographic Library: Jenny Harpur

IDE HILL, SEVENOAKS, KENT TN14 6AY

Owner: *The National Trust* ***Contact:*** *The Head Gardener*

Tel: 01732 750367/868381 (office) **e-mail:** kchxxx@smtp.ntrust.org.uk

An informal, hillside garden boasts the highest tree top in Kent. Noted for its rare trees and shrubs, bluebells and rose and rock gardens. Wonderful views across The Weald. 18 acres open to the public.

Location: OS Ref. TQ477 524. 1½m N of Ide Hill off B2042. M25/J5, then 4m.

Opening Times: 1 Apr - 31 May : Wed - Sun, Good Fri & BH Mons. 3 Jun - 29 Oct: Sats, Suns & Weds, 11am - 5.30pm. Last adm. 1 hr before close.

Admission: Adult £3.20, Child £1.50, Family £8.

Steep in places. WC. In grounds, on leads.

FINCHCOCKS

See page 99 for full page entry.

THE FRIARS - RETREAT HOUSE

Tel: 01622 717272 **Fax:** 01622 715575

Aylesford Priory, Aylesford, Kent ME20 7BX

Owner: Carmelite Friars **Contact:** Margaret Larcombe

A peaceful, tranquil retreat, set in 42 acres of lovingly tended grounds. Outstanding ceramic works of art by Adam Kossowski. Visitors are invited to picnic in the grounds, visit our tearooms situated in the restored 17th century Barn, which also houses the gift and bookshops. While you are here do call into the pottery and the upholsterers' workshops.

Location: OS Ref. TQ724 588. W end of Aylesford village. 3m NW of Maidstone.

Opening Times: Grounds open Summer & Winter, 24 hrs, 365 days.

Admission: No charge.

Partially suitable. 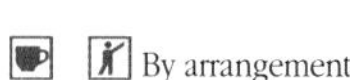 By arrangement. 
Guide dogs only.

South East England

GAD'S HILL PLACE

Tel: 01474 822366 **Fax:** 01474 822977

Gad's Hill School, Higham-by-Rochester, Kent ME3 7PA

Owner: Gad's Hill School **Contact:** Miss Anne Carter

This Grade I listed building dates from 1780. Charles Dickens lived here with his family from 1857 until his death in 1870, and wrote his last four novels here. Visitors can see his study, the newly restored conservatory, other rooms, the gardens and the grounds. Rooms can be hired for parties and weddings etc.

Location: OS Ref. TQ710 708. On A226, 3m from Rochester, 4m from Gravesend.

Opening Times: Apr - Oct: 1st Sun in month and BH Suns (inc Easter), 2 - 5pm. During Rochester Dickens Festivals (May/June & Dec), 11am - 4pm. At other times by appointment. Groups welcome.

Admission: Adult £2.50, Child £1.50, OAP £2.50, Student £1.50. Groups by arrangement.

Partially suitable. Obligatory. Guide dogs only.

GODINTON HOUSE & GARDENS

GODINTON PARK, ASHFORD, KENT TN23 3BP

Owner: *Godinton House Preservation Trust* **Contact:** *Mr D Bickle*

Tel: 01233 620773 **Fax:** 01233 632652

A hidden gem on the edge of Ashford. Set in extensive parkland, the Jacobean House incorporates a medieval hall, Tudor staircase, magnificent carving, panelling and contrasting decorative styles. Housing a fine collection of furniture and porcelain. The famous yew hedge encloses Blomfield's formal garden with Italian, walled and wild gardens beyond.

Location: OS Ref. TQ981 438. Godinton Lane, 2m NW of Ashford, off A20 (opposite Hare & Hounds public house).

Opening Times: 14 Apr - 15 Oct: Fri - Sun, 2 - 5.30pm, last tour of house 4.30pm. Groups (max. 60) on other days by appointment, groups must book.

Admission: House & Gardens: Adult £4, Child £2.

No photography in house. Partially suitable. WC.
Obligatory (house only). Limited for coaches. 

Goodnestone Park Gardens, Kent.

GOODNESTONE PARK GARDENS

GOODNESTONE PARK, Nr WINGHAM, CANTERBURY, KENT CT3 1PL

Owner: *The Lord & Lady FitzWalter* **Contact:** *Lady FitzWalter*

Tel/Fax: 01304 840107

The garden is approximately 14 acres, set in 18th century parkland. There are many fine trees, a woodland area and a large walled garden with a collection of old-fashioned roses, clematis and herbaceous plants. Jane Austen was a frequent visitor, her brother Edward having married a daughter of the house.

Location: OS Ref. TR254 544. 8m ESE of Canterbury, $1^1/2$ m E of B2046, at S end of village. The B2046 runs from the A2 to Wingham, the gardens are signposted from this road.

Opening Times: 29 Mar - 29 Oct: Suns, 12 noon - 6pm. Mons, Wed - Fri, 11am - 5pm. Closed Tues & Sats. House open by appointment to groups of 20 at £1.50.

Admission: Adult £3, Child (under 12yrs) 30p, OAP £2.50, Student £1.50. Groups (20+): Adult £2.50. Wheelchair users £1, Guided groups (20+) £3.50. House by appointment £1.80.

GREAT COMP GARDEN

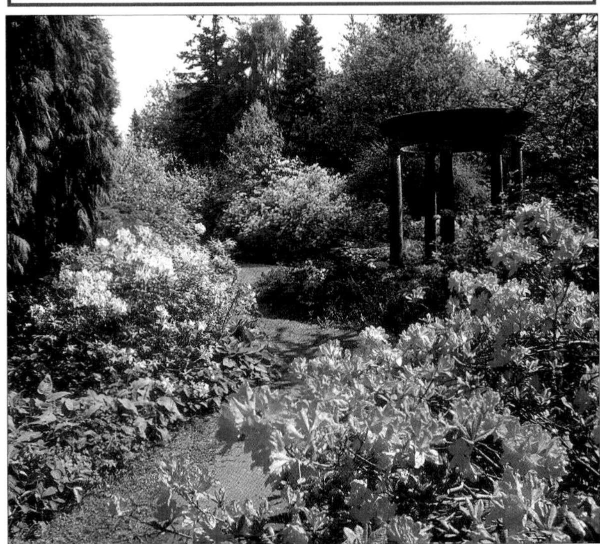

COMP LANE, PLATT, BOROUGH GREEN, KENT TN15 8QS

Owner: *R Cameron Esq* **Contact:** *Mr W Dyson*

Tel: 01732 886154

One of the finest gardens in the country, comprising ruins, terraces, tranquil woodland walks and sweeping lawns with a breathtaking collection of trees, shrubs, heathers and perennials, many rarely seen elsewhere. The truly unique atmosphere of Great Comp is further complemented by its Festival of Chamber Music held in July/September.

Location: OS Ref. TQ635 567. 2m E of Borough Green, B2016 off A20. First right at Comp crossroads. $^1/2$ m on left.

Opening Times: 1 Apr - 31 Oct: daily, 11am - 6pm.

Admission: Adult £3.50, Child £1. Groups (20+) £3, Annual ticket: Adult £10, OAP £7.

Suns, BHs & by arrangement. Guide dogs only.

GROOMBRIDGE PLACE GARDENS

See page 100 for full page entry.

HALL PLACE

Tel: 01322 526574 Fax: 01322 522921

Bourne Road, Bexley, Kent DA5 1PQ

Owner: Bexley Council **Contact:** Rosemary Evans

A fine Grade I listed country house built in 1540 for Sir John Champnels, a Lord Mayor of London. The house is set in beautiful formal gardens on the banks of the River Cray. Some rooms are open to the public, including the magnificent great hall.

Location: OS Ref. TQ502 743. Near the A2 less than 5m (London bound) from the M25/J2.

Opening Times: Mon - Sat, 10am - 5pm (4.15pm in winter), Sun & BHs, 2 - 6pm (BST only). Opening times will change from April 2000, please phone to confirm times.

Admission: Free. Pre-arranged groups: £1.

House suitable, lift & WC. Licensed. By arrangement. Ample for cars, limited for coaches. Guide dogs only.

HEVER CASTLE

See pages 102/103 for double page entry.

HIGHAM PARK & GARDENS

BRIDGE, CANTERBURY, KENT CT4 5BE

Owner/Contact: *Patricia P Gibb*

Tel/Fax: 01227 830830 **e-mail:** higham-park@talk21.com

Just opened, Higham Park is an elegant Palladian mansion (1320) with rich interiors and fine plasterwork. Visitors include Mozart, Jane Austen and General de Gaulle. Beautiful Edwardian gardens, spectacular Gardino D'Italiano. Sunken Rose, 'Secret Gardens', mixed borders, specimen trees. Massed spring bulbs. Magnificent corporate venue, wedding receptions, films, exhibitions and outdoor events.

Location: OS Ref. TR183 541. On the A2 at Bridge between Canterbury and the channel ports.

Opening Times: Apr - end Sept: Sun - Thur. Garden: 11am - 6pm. House: 12 noon - 6pm.

Admission: Garden: Adult £2.50, Child 50p, Conc. £2. House: Adult £1.50. Groups by arrangement at other times.

Partially suitable. WC. Licensed. Obligatory. In grounds, on leads. Tel. for details.

HOLE PARK

Tel: 01580 241251 Fax: 01580 241882

Rolvenden, Cranbrook, Kent TN17 4JB

Owner/Contact: D G W Barham

A 15 acre garden with all year round interest, set in beautiful parkland with fine views.

Location: OS Ref. TQ830 325. 1m W of Rolvenden on B2086 Cranbrook road.

Opening Times: 2, 9, 23 & 30 Apr. 7, 21 & 28 May. 8 & 15 Oct (Suns), for NGS. Also Weds, April, May, Jun & Oct. All 2 - 6pm. Groups and individuals by arrangement.

Admission: Adult £3, Child 50p.

IGHTHAM MOTE

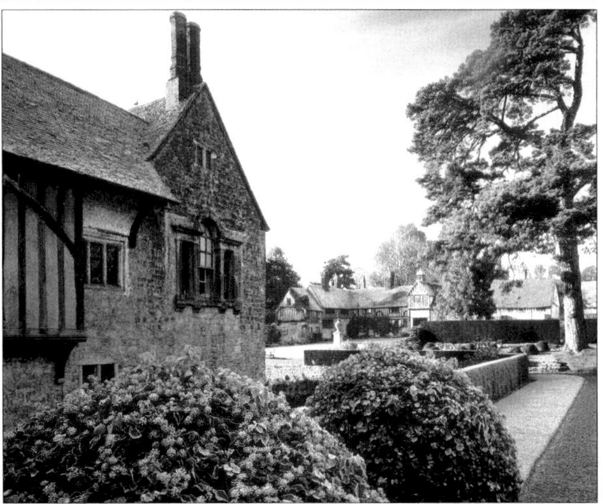

Andrew Butler

IVY HATCH, SEVENOAKS, KENT TN15 0NT

Owner: *The National Trust* ***Contact:*** *The Property Manager*

Info Line: 01732 811145 **Tel:** 01732 810378 **Fax:** 01732 811029

e-mail: kimxxx@smtp.ntrust.org.uk

Beautiful moated manor house covering 650 years of history from the Medieval Great Hall to the 1960s Library. North-west quarter re-opened in 1998 after major repair; see the Tudor chapel, billiard room and drawing room. Ongoing conservation programme which does not affect the visitor route. Exhibition details the traditional skills used. Lovely garden with lakes and woodland. Surrounding estate provides many country walks.

Location: OS Ref. TQ584 535. 6m E of Sevenoaks off A25. 2½ m S of Ightham off A227.

Opening Times: 2 Apr - 30 Oct: daily except Tues & Sats, 11am - 5.30pm. Last admission 1 hr before close.

Admission: Adult £5, Child £2.50, Family £12.50. Groups (pre-booked) £4.25.

Ground floor suitable. WC. Tea pavilion. On leads.

KNOLE

See page 104 for full page entry.

LADHAM HOUSE GARDENS

Tel: 01580 211203/212674 Fax: 01580 212596

Ladham Lane, Goudhurst, Kent TN17 1DB

Owner: Mr & Mrs Alastair Jessel **Contact:** Mrs Jessel

This Georgian house with additional French features has been in the family for over 120 years and the garden developed over that period. Mixed shrub borders with famous magnolias. Interesting bog garden replacing a leaking pond and arboretum replacing old kitchen garden. Rare trees and shrubs including cornus cousa, embothriums, American oaks, carpenteria californica and others. 10 acres of gardens set in magnificent Wealden countryside. Superb site for wedding receptions, ceremonies and private parties.

Location: OS Ref. TQ732 384. ¾ NE of Goudhurst off A262. 5m NW of Cranbrook.

Opening Times: Sun 30 April, & Sun 21 May, 1 - 5.30pm, Thurs 6 July, 6 - 9pm for NGS. Other times by appointment. Coach parties welcome.

Admission: Adult £3, Child (under 12yrs) 50p.

In grounds, on leads.

LEEDS CASTLE

See pages 106/107 for double page entry.

Special Events Index PAGE 40

LESNES ABBEY

Tel: 020 8303 9052

Abbey Road, Abbey Wood, London DA17 5DL

Owner: Bexley Council **Contact:** TIC Manager

The Abbey was founded in 1178 by Richard de Lucy as penance for his involvement in events leading to the murder of Thomas à Becket. Today only the ruins remain.

Location: OS Ref. TQ479 788. In public park on S side of Abbey Road (B213), 500yds E of Abbey Wood Station, 3/4 m N of A206 Woolwich - Erith Road.

Opening Times: Any reasonable time.

Admission: Free.

LULLINGSTONE CASTLE

Tel: 01322 862114 **Fax:** 01322 862115

Lullingstone Castle, Eynsford, Kent DA4 0JA

Owner/Contact: Guy Hart Dyke Esq

Fine state rooms, family portraits and armour in beautiful grounds. The 15th century gatehouse was one of the first ever to be made of bricks.

Location: OS Ref. TQ530 644. 1m S Eynsford W side of A225. 600yds S of Roman Villa.

Opening Times: May - Aug: Sats, Suns & BHs, 2 - 6pm. Booked groups by arrangement.

Admission: Adult £4, Child £1.50, Conc. £3, Family £10. Midweek groups (25+) 10% discount.

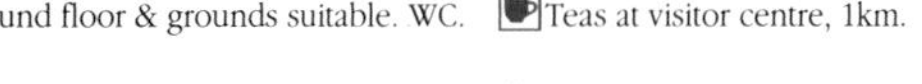

Ground floor & grounds suitable. WC. Teas at visitor centre, 1km.

LULLINGSTONE ROMAN VILLA

English Heritage Photographic Library

LULLINGSTONE LANE, EYNSFORD, KENT DA4 0JA

Owner: *English Heritage* ***Contact:*** *The Custodian*

Tel: 01322 863467

Recognised as one of the most exciting archaeological finds of the century, the villa has splendid mosaic floors and one of the earliest private Christian chapels. Take the free audio tour and discover how the middle-class owners lived, worked and entertained themselves.

Location: OS Ref. TQ529 651. 1/2 m SW of Eynsford off A225, M25/J3. Follow A20 towards Brands Hatch. 600yds N of Castle.

Opening Times: 1 Apr - 30 Sept: daily, 10am - 6pm. 1 - 31 Oct: 10am - 5pm. 1 Nov - 31 Mar: 10am - 4pm. Closed 24 - 26 Dec.

Admission: Adult £2.50, Child £1.30, Conc. £1.90.

Ground floor & grounds suitable. WC.  Tel. for details.

MAISON DIEU

Tel: 01795 534542

Ospringe, Faversham, Kent

Owner: English Heritage **Contact:** The Faversham Society

This forerunner of today's hospitals remains largely as it was in the 16th century with exposed beams and an overhanging upper storey.

Location: OS Ref. TR002 608. In Ospringe on A2, 1/2 m W of Faversham.

Opening Times: 3 Apr - 31 Oct: Weekends & BHs, 2 - 5pm. Keykeeper in Winter.

Admission: Adult £1, Child/OAP 80p.

Special Events Index PAGE 40

MILTON CHANTRY

Tel: 01474 321520

New Tavern Fort Gardens, Gravesend, Kent

Owner: English Heritage **Contact:** Gravesend Borough Council

A small 14th century building which housed the chapel of the leper hospital and the chantry of the de Valence and Montechais families and later became a tavern and in 1780 part of a fort.

Location: OS Ref.TQ652 743. In New Tavern Fort Gardens 1/4 m E of Gravesend off A226.

Opening Times: 1 Mar - 23 Dec: Wed - Sun & BH Mons, 10am - 4pm. Closed Jan & Feb.

Admission: Adult £1.50, Child 75p, Conc. 75p.

MOUNT EPHRAIM GARDENS

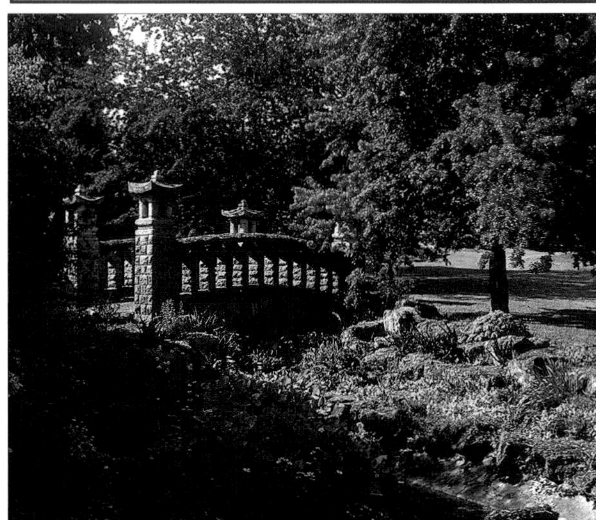

HERNHILL, FAVERSHAM, KENT ME13 9TX

Owner: *Mr & Mrs E S Dawes & Mrs M N Dawes* ***Contact:*** *Mrs L Dawes*

Tel: 01227 751496 **Fax:** 01227 750940

8 acres of superb gardens set in the heart of family run orchards. Gardens offer an attractive balance of formal and informal with an herbaceous border, topiary, a Japanese style rock garden, water garden, rose terraces and a lake, vineyard and orchard trails.

Location: OS Ref.TR065 598. In Hernhill village, 1m from end of M2. Signed from A2 & A299.

Opening Times: Easter - end Sept: Mons, Weds, Thurs, Sats & Suns, 1 - 6pm. Groups at all times by arrangement.

Admission: Adult £3, Child £1. Groups: £2.50

Conferences. Partially suitable. Licensed. By arrangement. In grounds on leads.

OLD SOAR MANOR

Tel: 01732 810378

Plaxtol, Borough Green, Kent TN15 0QX

Owner: The National Trust **Contact:** Ightham Mote

The solar block of a late 13th century knight's dwelling.

Location: OS Ref. TQ619 541. 1m E of Plaxtol. By narrow lane. 2m S of A25 at Borough Green.

Opening Times: 1 Apr - 30 Sept: daily except Fri, 10am - 6pm.

Admission: Free.

OWL HOUSE GARDENS

Tel: 01892 890230

Lamberhurst, Kent TN3 8LY **Contact:** James & Angela Kelso

16.5 acres of romantic gardens surrounding a 16th century timber framed wool smuggler's cottage (not open to the public). Woodland walks with oaks, elm, birch and beech trees. Rhododendrons, azaleas and camellias surround sunken water gardens.

Location: OS Ref. TQ665 372. 8m SE of Tunbridge Wells; 1m from Lamberhurst of A1.

Opening Times: Gardens only: All year, daily, 11am - 6pm, except 25 Dec & 1 Jan.

Admission: Adult £4, Child £1. Coach parties welcome.

Free. On leads.

PATTYNDENNE MANOR

Tel: 01580 211361

Goudhurst, Kent TN17 2QU

Owner: Mr & Mrs D C Spearing **Contact:** Mr D C Spearing

One of the great timber houses of England, built of oak trees felled from the surrounding forest twenty years before Columbus discovered America. Special architectural details include the jettying, dragon beams, king post and tie beam, corner posts of upturned oaks, and an amazing wealth of timbering only to be seen in a house built before the modern iron industry destroyed England's forests. 13th century prison. Associated with Henry VIII as a hunting lodge. Ghosts (now and then).

Location: OS Ref. TQ720 366. 10m E of Tunbridge Wells, W side of B2079, 1m S of Goudhurst (A262).

Opening Times: By prior appointment only. Groups 20 - 55 people.

Admission: Groups only. Adult £4.50.

Lecture tour by owner.

PENSHURST PLACE & GARDENS

See page 108 for full page entry.

QUEBEC HOUSE

Tel: 01892 890651

Westerham, Kent TN16 1TD

Owner: The National Trust **Contact:** Regional Office

General Wolfe spent his early years in this gabled, red-brick 17th century house. Four rooms containing portraits, prints and memorabilia relating to Wolfe's family and career are on view. In the Tudor stable block is an exhibition about the Battle of Quebec (1759) and the parts played by Wolfe and his adversary, the Marquis de Montcalm.

Location: OS Ref. TQ449 541. At E end of village, on N side of A25, facing junction with B2026, Edenbridge Road.

Opening Times: 2 Apr - 31 Oct: Suns & Tues, 2 - 6pm, last admission 5.30pm.

Admission: Adult £2.50, Child £1.25, Family (2+3) £6.25. Groups £2.10.

QUEX HOUSE & GARDEN & POWELL COTTON MUSEUM

Quex Park, Birchington, Kent CT7 0BH **Tel:** 01843 842168

e-mail: powell-cotton-museum@virgin.net

Owner: Trustees of Powell Cotton Museum **Contact:** John Harrison

Regency/Victorian country residence, walled gardens and Victorian explorers' museum.

Location: OS Ref. TR308 683. 1/2 m from Birchington Church via Park Lane.

Opening Times: Please contact Museum for details.

Admission: Summer: Adult £3.50, Child, OAP, Disabled & Carer £2.80, Student £2, Family (2+3) £11. Winter: Adult £2.50, Child, OAP, Disabled & Carer £1.80, Family (2+3) £7.50.

RECULVER TOWERS & ROMAN FORT

Tel: 01227 740676

Reculver, Herne Bay, Kent

Owner: English Heritage **Contact:** Reculver Country Park

This 12th century landmark of twin towers has guided sailors into the Thames estuary for seven centuries. Walls of a Roman fort, which were erected nearly 2,000 years ago.

Location: OS Ref. TR228 694. At Reculver 3m E of Herne Bay by the seashore.

Opening Times: Any reasonable time. External viewing only.

Admission: Free.

RICHBOROUGH ROMAN FORT

Tel: 01304 612013

Richborough, Sandwich, Kent CT13 9JW

Owner: English Heritage **Contact:** The Custodian

This fort and township date back to the Roman landing in AD43. The fortified walls and the massive foundations of a triumphal arch which stood 80 feet high still survive. The inclusive audio tour and the museum give an insight into life in Richborough's heyday as a busy township.

Location: OS Ref. TR324 602. 1 1/2 m NW of Sandwich off A257.

Opening Times: 1 Apr - 30 Sept: daily, 10am - 6pm. 1 - 31 Oct: 10am - 5pm. 1 - 31 Nov: Wed - Sun only, 10am - 4pm. Weekends only in Dec, Jan & Feb, 10am - 4pm. 1 - 31 Mar: Wed - Sun, 10am - 4pm. Closed 24 - 26 Dec.

Admission: Adult £2.50, Child £1.30, Conc. £1.90.

Museum. Ground floor suitable. Guide dogs only. Tel. for details.

RIVERHILL HOUSE

Tel: 01732 458802/452557 **Fax:** 01732 458802

Sevenoaks, Kent TN15 0RR

Owner: The Rogers Family **Contact:** Mrs Rogers

Small country house built in 1714, home of the Rogers family since 1840. Panelled rooms, portraits and interesting memorabilia. Historic hillside garden with extensive views, rare trees and shrubs. Sheltered terraces and rhododendrons and azaleas in a woodland setting. Bluebells, ancient trackway known as Harold's Road.

Location: OS Ref. TQ541 522. 2m S of Sevenoaks on E side of A225.

Opening Times: Garden: Apr, May & Jun: Weds, Suns & BH weekends, 12 noon - 6pm. House & Garden: open only to pre-booked groups of adults (20+) on any day: Apr, May & Jun.

Admission: Adult £2.50, Child 50p. Pre-booked groups: £3.50.

Conferences.    By arrangement. 

ROCHESTER CASTLE

Tel: 01634 402276

The Lodge, Rochester-upon-Medway, Medway ME1 1SX

Owner: English Heritage **Contact:** Head Custodian

(Managed by Rochester-upon-Medway City Council)

Built in the 11th century. The keep is over 100 feet high and with walls 12 feet thick. At the top you will be able to enjoy fine views over the river and surrounding city of Rochester.

Location: OS Ref. TQ743 685. By Rochester Bridge (A2), M2/J1 & M25/J2.

Opening Times: 1 Apr - 30 Sept: daily, 10am - 6pm. 1 - 31 Oct: daily, 10am - 5pm. 1 Nov - 31 Mar: daily, 10am - 4pm.

Admission: Please telephone for details.

ROCHESTER CATHEDRAL

Tel: 01634 401301 **Fax:** 01634 401410

c/o 70a High Street, Rochester, Kent ME1 1JY **Contact:** Mr P Nickless

e-mail: rochester_cathedral_ed@yahoo.co.uk

Founded in 604AD, Rochester Cathedral has been a place of Christian worship for nearly 1,400 years. The present building is a blend of Norman and gothic architecture with a fine medieval crypt. In the cloister are the remains of the 12th century chapter house and priory. A focal point is the Doubleday statue.

Location: OS Ref. TQ742 686. Signposted from M20/J6 and on the A2/M2/J3. Best access from M2/J3.

Opening Times: All year: 8.30am - 5pm. Visiting may be restricted during services.

Admission: £2 donation. Groups: £2.50 guided, £1.50 unguided. Groups must book on above number. Separate prices for schools.

Photography permit £1. By arrangement. 

ROMAN PAINTED HOUSE

Tel: 01304 203279

New Street, Dover, Kent CT17 9AJ

Owner: Dover Roman Painted House Trust **Contact:** Mr B Philp

Discovered in 1970. Built around 200AD as a hotel for official travellers. Impressive wall paintings, central heating systems and the Roman fort wall built through the house.

Location: OS Ref. TR318 414. Dover town centre. E of York St.

Opening Times: Apr - Sept: 10am - 5pm, except Mons.

Admission: Adult £2, Child/OAP 80p.

ROYDON HALL

Tel: 01622 812121 **Fax:** 01622 813959

Nr Tonbridge, Kent TN12 5NH **e-mail:** roydonhall@btinternet.com

Owner: Maharishi Foundation **Contact:** The Events Manager

Roydon Hall is a very fine Tudor manor house which was 'modified' by the Victorians. Large wood panelled rooms. Beautiful grounds overlooking the Weald. Interesting outbuildings. Church nearby.

Location: OS Ref. TQ664 518. M25 then M40 towards Paddock Wood. Follow signs for Paddock Wood into Seven Mile Lane. Sign for Roydon on right indicating turn to left on brow of hill about 4m down lane.

Opening Times: Available for film location work and corporate events. Bed and breakfast accommodation also.

Admission: Free.

ST AUGUSTINE'S ABBEY

Tel: 01227 767345

Longport, Canterbury, Kent CT1 1TF

Owner: English Heritage **Contact:** The Custodian

The Abbey, founded by St Augustine in 598, is a World Heritage Site. Take the free interactive audio tour which gives a fascinating insight into the Abbey's history and visit the museum displaying artifacts uncovered during archaeological excavations of the site.

Location: OS Ref. TR154 578. In Canterbury 1/2 m E of Cathedral Close.

Opening Times: 1 Apr - 30 Sept: daily, 10am - 6pm. 1 - 31 Oct: 10am - 5pm. 1 Nov - 31 Mar: daily, 10am - 4pm. Closed 24 - 26 Dec.

Admission: Adult £2.50, Child £1.30, Conc. £1.90. 15% discount for groups (11+). One extra place for every additional 20.

Grounds suitable. WC. Free. Guide dogs only. Tel. for details.

ST JOHN'S COMMANDERY

Tel: 01304 211067

Densole, Swingfield, Kent

Owner: English Heritage **Contact:** The South East Regional Office

A medieval chapel built by the Knights Hospitallers. It has a moulded plaster ceiling and a remarkable timber roof and was converted into a farmhouse in the 16th century.

Location: OS Ref. TR232 440. 2m NE of Densole on minor road off A260.

Opening Times: Any reasonable time for exterior viewing. Internal viewing by appointment only.

Admission: Free.

South East England

SCOTNEY CASTLE GARDEN

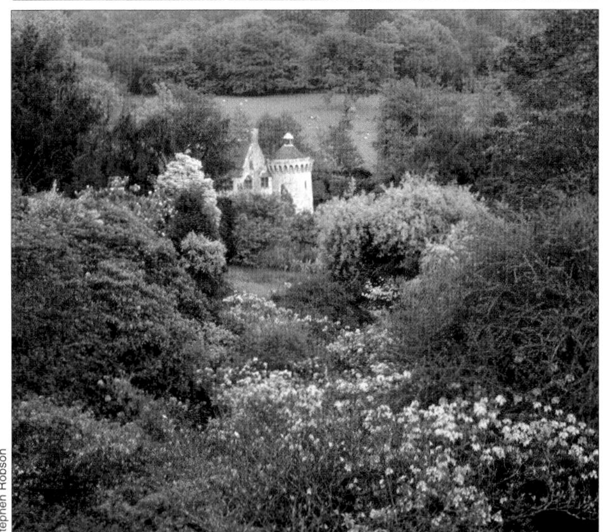

Stephen Robson

LAMBERHURST, TUNBRIDGE WELLS, KENT TN3 8JN

Owner: *The National Trust* ***Contact:*** *Administrative Assistant*

Tel: 01892 891081 **Fax:** 01892 890110 **e-mail:** kscxxx@smtp.ntrust.org.uk

One of England's most romantic gardens, surrounding the ruins of a 14th century moated castle. Rhododendrons, azaleas, water-lilies and wisteria flower in profusion. Renowned for its autumn colour. The ruined old castle with its priest hole is open for the summer. The surrounding estate has many country walks.

Location: OS Ref. TQ688 353. Signed off A21 1m S of Lamberhurst village.

Opening Times: 4 - 26 Mar: Sats & Suns, 12 noon - 4pm. 1 Apr - 29 Oct: Wed - Fri, 11am - 6pm, Sats & Suns, 2 - 6pm, BH Sun & Mons 12 noon - 6pm (closed Good Fri). Last adm. 1 hr before close. Car park: All year for estate walks.

Admission: Adult £4.20, Child £2.10, Family (2+3) £10.50. Pre-booked groups weekdays £3.50.

Grounds (but steep parts). Outside garden only, on leads.

SOUTH FORELAND LIGHTHOUSE & GATEWAY TO THE WHITE CLIFFS

© National Trust Photographic Library: David Sellham

LANGDON CLIFFS, Nr DOVER, KENT CT16 1HJ

Owner: *The National Trust* ***Contact:*** *Countryside Manager*

Tel: 01304 202756 **Fax:** 01304 205295 **e-mail:** kwcxxx@smtp.ntrust.org.uk

The Gateway to the White Cliffs is a new visitor centre with spectacular views across the English Channel. It introduces the visitor to its coast and countryside through imaginative displays and interpretation. High up on the cliffs is South Foreland Lighthouse, used by Marconi for his first ship-to-shore radio experiments.

Location: OS138 Ref. TR336 422. Follow White Cliffs brown signs from roundabout 1m NE of Dover at junction of A2/A258.

Opening Times: Gateway: 1 Mar - 31 Oct: 10am - 5pm. 1 Nov - 28 Feb: 11am - 4pm. Lighthouse: 1 Mar - 31 Oct: daily except Tues & Weds, 11am - 5.30pm (last admission 5pm).

Admission: Adult £1.80, Child 90p. Car Park £1.50, Conc. 75p.

Limited range. Partially suitable. WC. By arrangement. In grounds, on leads. Holiday cottage, 1dbl & 2 single.

SMALLHYTHE PLACE

© National Trust Photographic Library: David Sellham

TENTERDEN, KENT TN30 7NG

Owner: *The National Trust* ***Contact:*** *The Custodian*

Tel: 01580 762334 **Fax:** 01580 762334 **e-mail:** ksmxxx@smtp.ntrust.org.uk

This early 16th century half-timbered house was home to Shakespearean actress Ellen Terry from 1899 to 1928. The house contains many personal and theatrical mementoes including many of her lavish costumes. The charming cottage grounds include her rose garden and the Barn Theatre, which is open most days by courtesy of the Barn Theatre Society.

Location: OS Ref. TQ893 300. 2m S of Tenterden on E side of the Rye road B2082.

Opening Times: 1 Apr - 31 Oct: daily except Thurs & Fris (open Good Fri), 1.30 - 6pm or dusk if earlier. Groups (max. 25) Tues morning only.

Admission: Adult £3.10, Child £1.55, Family £7.55.

No photography in house. Not suitable. Limited.

SQUERRYES COURT & GARDENS **See page 109 for full page entry.**

STONEACRE **Tel:** 01622 862871 **Fax:** 01622 862157

Otham, Maidstone, Kent ME15 8RS

Owner: The National Trust **Contact:** The Tenant

A half-timbered mainly late 15th century yeoman's house, with great hall and crownpost, and newly restored cottage-style garden.

Location: OS Ref. TQ800 535. In narrow lane at N end of Otham village, 3m SE of Maidstone, 1m S of A20.

Opening Times: 1 Apr - 28 Oct: Weds & Sats, 2 - 6pm. Last admission 1hr before close.

Admission: Adult £2.50, Child £1.25, Family (2+3) £6.25. Groups £2.10.

Patrick Lane.

Stoneacre, Kent.

South East England

TEMPLE MANOR

Tel: 01634 827980

Strood, Rochester, Kent

Owner: English Heritage **Contact:** Rochester-upon-Medway City Council

The 13th century manor house of the Knights Templar which mainly provided accommodation for members of the order travelling between London and the Continent.

Location: OS Ref. TQ733 686. In Strood (Rochester) off A228.

Opening Times: 1 Apr - 30 Sept: weekends & BHs, 10am - 6pm.

Admission: Free.

THE THEATRE ROYAL, CHATHAM

Tel: 01634 306367 **Fax:** 01634 328304

102 High Street, Chatham, Kent ME4 4BY

Owner: Chatham Theatre Royal Trust Ltd **Contact:** The Administrator

Built in 1899, it is Kent's finest surviving Victorian Theatre.

Location: OS Ref. TQ755 679. In Chatham High Street.

Opening Times: Mon - Sat, 10am - 3pm. Guided tours most weekdays. Groups welcome by appointment.

Admission: Donation.

TONBRIDGE CASTLE

Tel: 01732 770929

Castle Street, Tonbridge, Kent TN9 1BG

Owner: Tonbridge & Malling Borough Council **Contact:** Sheila Kostyrka

Location: OS Ref. TQ588 466. 300 yds NW of the Medway Bridge at town centre.

Opening Times: Castle closed for repair work and upgrading. Re-opening planned for September 2000.

TURKEY MILL

TURKEY COURT, ASHFORD ROAD, MAIDSTONE ME14 5PP

Owner: *Turkey Mill Investments* ***Contact:*** *Maureen Camp*

Tel: 01622 765511 **Fax:** 01622 765522

Turkey Court, a Queen Anne house, offers the elegant Whatman Room, or pretty Pergola in the garden (summer only) for marriage ceremonies. Their own marquee, in 9 acres of parkland grounds, set amongst huge Wellingtonia Pines, Blue Cedars, a waterfall and Mill Leat, will accommodate up to 180 guests for a reception. Seymour, in 1776 said '*A pretty rural scene, perpetual verdure and clearest streams*', this is reflected today.

Location: OS Ref. TQ772 555. M20/J7, on A20 (Ashford Road) 1m E of Maidstone town centre.

Opening Times: Corporate hospitality and receptions only. Gardens open for NGS 18 June and 3 Sept.

No tied caterer. Coaches limited.

UPNOR CASTLE

Tel: 01634 718742

Upnor, Kent

Owner: English Heritage **Contact:** Rochester-upon-Medway City Council

Well-preserved 16th century gun fort built to protect Queen Elizabeth I's warships. However in 1667 it failed to prevent the Dutch Navy which stormed up the Medway destroying half the English fleet.

Location: OS Ref. TQ758 706. At Upnor, on unclassified road off A228. 2m NE of Strood.

Opening Times: 1 Apr - 30 Sept: daily, 12 noon - 5pm.

Admission: Please telephone for details.

WALMER CASTLE & GARDENS

English Heritage Photographic Library

WALMER, DEAL, KENT CT14 7LJ

Owner: *English Heritage* ***Contact:*** *The Custodian*

Tel: 01304 364288

A Tudor fort transformed into an elegant stately home. The residence of the Lords Warden of the Cinque Ports and still used by HM The Queen Mother today. Take the new free audio tour and see the Duke of Wellington's rooms and even his famous boots. Beautiful gardens including the Queen Mother's Garden. Lunches and cream teas available in the delightful Lord Warden's tearooms.

Location: OS Ref. TR378 501. S of Walmer on A258, M20/J13 or M2 to Deal.

Opening Times: 1 Apr - 30 Sept: daily, 10am - 6pm. 1 - 31 Oct: 10am - 5pm. 1 Nov - Dec: Wed - Sun only. Closed 24 - 26 Dec, Jan & Feb 2000. Mar: Wed - Sun only. Closed when Lord Warden in residence.

Admission: Adult £4.50, Child £2.30, OAP/Student £3.40. 15% discount for groups (11+). One extra place for each additional 20. EH members free.

Grounds suitable. Guide dogs only. Tel. for details.

WILLESBOROUGH WINDMILL

Tel: 01233 661866

Mill Lane, Willesborough, Ashford, Kent

125 year old restored smock mill.

Location: OS Ref. TR031 421. Off A292 close to M20/J10. At E end of Ashford.

Opening Times: Apr - Sept; Sats, Suns and BH Mons, 2 - 5pm or dusk if earlier.

Admission: Adult £1, Child/Conc. 50p. Groups 10% reduction by arrangement only.

YALDING ORGANIC GARDENS

Tel: 01622 814650 **Fax:** 01622 814 650

Benover Road, Yalding, Maidstone, Kent ME18 6EX

Owner: Henry Doubleday Research Association **Contact:** Visitors Centre Manager

Fourteen newly created gardens reflecting mankind's experience of gardening over the centuries. A series of individual gardens from medieval times through to the present day illustrating themes such as stewardship of resources, respect for wildlife and the importance of genetic diversity. Tudor garden, Victorian garden, children's garden, wildlife gardens. Tours and party bookings welcome.

Location: OS Ref. TQ698 492. 6m SW of Maidstone, 1/2 m S of village at Yalding on B2162.

Opening Times: Apr: w/ends only, 10am - 5pm. May - Sept: Wed - Sun, 10am - 5pm. Oct: w/ends only.

Admission: Adult £3 (no concessions), accompanied Child (up to 16yrs) Free. Groups (14+) £2.50 plus 50p for guided tour.

South East England Tourist Board.

Tonbridge in the Winter, Kent.

South East England

Owner:
Historic Royal Palaces

CONTACT

Irma Hay (day visitors)
Fiona Thompson (functions)
The Banqueting Hall
Whitehall
London
SW1A 2ER

Tel: 020 7930 4179
or 020 7839 7569

Fax: 020 7930 8268

LOCATION

OS Ref. TQ302 801

Tube Stations: Westminster, Embankment and Charing Cross.

Rail: Charing Cross.

CONFERENCE/FUNCTION		
ROOM	SIZE	MAX CAPACITY
Main Hall	110' x 55'	500
Undercroft	64' x 55'	350

THE BANQUETING HOUSE
Whitehall

The magnificent Banqueting House is all that survives of the great Palace of Whitehall which was destroyed by fire in 1698. It was completed in 1622, commissioned by King James I, and designed by Inigo Jones, the noted classical architect. In 1635 the main hall was further enhanced with the installation of 9 magnificent ceiling paintings by Sir Peter Paul Rubens, which survive to this day. The Banqueting House was also the site of the only royal execution in England's history, with the beheading of Charles I in 1649.

The Banqueting House is open to visitors, as well as playing host to many of society's most glittering occasions.

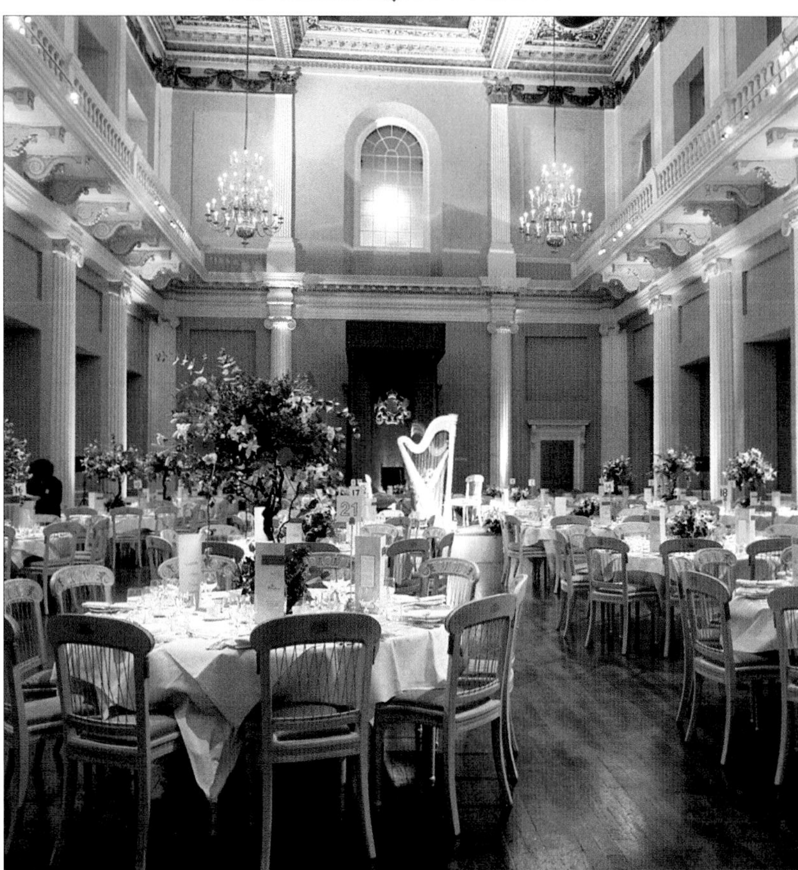

OPENING TIMES

All year
Mon - Sat
10am - 5pm
Last admission 4.30pm.

Closed
24 December - 1 January, Good Friday and other public holidays.

NB. Liable to close at short notice for Government functions.

ADMISSION

Adult £3.60
Child (5-15yrs).......... £2.30
Student..................... £2.80
OAP/Conc.................. £2.80
Under 5s .... Free

Groups...please telephone: 020 7839 7569 for details.

Concerts. No photography in house.

Banquets.

Undercroft suitable.

Video and audio guide.

No parking.

Welcome.

© HM Queen Elizabeth II

© HM Queen Elizabeth II

Owner:
HM The Queen

CONTACT

The Visitor Office
Buckingham Palace
London
SW1A 1AA

Tel: 020 7839 1377

Fax: 020 7930 9625

e-mail: information@royalcollection.org.uk

LOCATION

OS Ref. TQ291 796

Nearest underground stations: Green Park, Victoria, St James's Park.

Rail: Victoria.

Air: Heathrow.

Sightseeing tours

A number of tour companies include a visit to the State Rooms in their sightseeing tours. Ask your concierge or hotel porter for details.

BUCKINGHAM PALACE
London

BUCKINGHAM PALACE, Windsor Castle and the Palace of Holyroodhouse are the Official residences of the Sovereign and are used by The Queen as both a home and office. The Queen's personal standard flies when Her Majesty is in residence. Furnished with works of art from the Royal Collection, these buildings are used extensively by The Queen for State ceremonies and Official entertaining. They are opened to the public as much as these commitments allow.

The Royal Mews is one of the finest working stables in existence. It provides a unique opportunity for visitors to see a working department of the Royal Household. The Monarch's magnificent Carriages and Coaches including the Gold State Coach are housed here, together with their horses and State liveries.

© HM Queen Elizabeth II

No photography inside.

Wheelchair users are required to pre-book for the summer opening. The Royal Mews is fully accessible.

No guided tours.

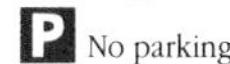 No parking.

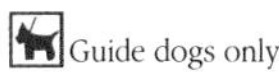 Guide dogs only.

OPENING TIMES

Opening arrangements may change at short notice.

The State Rooms
6 August - 1 October
Daily: 9.30am - 4.30pm.

Tickets available during Aug & Sept from the Ticket Office in Green Park.
To pre-book your tickets telephone the Visitor Office 020 7321 2233.

The Queen's Gallery
The Queen's Gallery is closed for refurbishment and will reopen in 2002, the year of the Queen's Golden Jubilee.

The Royal Mews
All year: Monday - Thursday
12 noon - 4pm
Last adm. 3.30pm.
Extra hours are added during the summer months.

ADMISSION

The State Rooms

Adult	£10.50
Child (up to 17yrs)	£5.00
OAP	£8.00

All pre-booked tickets are £10.50 plus £1 transaction fee.

Groups (15+)

Per person	£9.50

South East England

English Heritage Photographic Library

Owner:
English Heritage

CONTACT

Visits:
The Head Custodian
Chiswick House
Burlington Lane
London
W4 2RP

Tel: 020 8995 0508

English Heritage Hospitality:
Events Manager
23 Savile Row
London
W1X 1AB

Tel: 020 8742 1978

LOCATION

OS Ref: TQ210 775

Burlington Lane
London W4.

Rail: 1/4m NE of Chiswick Station.

Bus: LT190, 290 (Hammersmith - Richmond).

CHISWICK HOUSE

Chiswick

CHISWICK HOUSE is internationally renowned as one of the first and finest English Palladian villas. Lord Burlington, who built the villa from 1725 - 1729, was inspired by the architecture and gardens of ancient Rome and this house is his masterpiece. His aim was to create a fit setting to show his friends his fine collection of art and his library. The opulent interior features gilded decoration, velvet walls and painted ceilings. The important 18th century gardens surrounding Chiswick House have, at every turn, something to surprise and delight the visitor from the magnificent cedar trees to the beautiful Italianate gardens with their cascade, statues, temples, urns and obelisks.

English Heritage Hospitality

English Heritage Hospitality offers exclusive use of Chiswick House in the evenings for dinners, concerts, receptions and weddings.

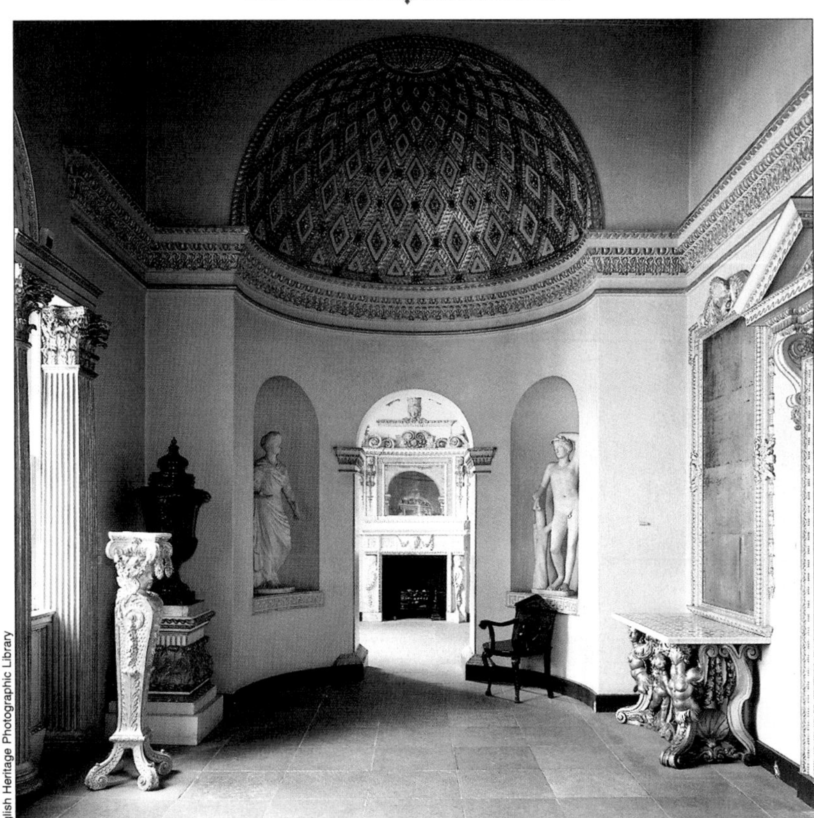

English Heritage Photographic Library

OPENING TIMES

SUMMER
1 April - 30 September
Daily, 10am - 6pm.

AUTUMN
1 - 31 October
Daily, 10am - 5pm.

WINTER
1 Nov - 31 March
Wed - Sun, 10am - 4pm.

ADMISSION

Adult	£3.00
Child (5-15yrs)	£1.50
Conc	£2.30
Groups (11+)	15% discount

Tour leader and coach driver have free entry. 1 extra place for every 20 additional people.

Filming, plays, photographic shoots.

Exclusive private & corporate hospitality.

Access to ground floor.

Homemade refreshments during the summer season.

Personal guided tours must be booked in advance. Colour guide book £2.25.

Free audio tours in English, French & German.

Free if booked in advance. Tel: 020 7973 3485.

Guide dogs in grounds.

Civil Wedding Licence.

Telephone for details.

THE COURTAULD GALLERY AND THE GILBERT COLLECTION AT SOMERSET HOUSE

London

SOMERSET HOUSE, Sir William Chambers' 18th century architectural masterpiece, is open to the public for the first time. Situated between Covent Garden and the South Bank, it takes its place as one of Europe's great centres for art and culture, and the enjoyment of long-hidden classical interiors and architectural vistas. An annual season of performing arts and events is held in the Great Court. *Opens May 2000.*

THE GILBERT COLLECTION is London's newest museum of the decorative arts. Given to the nation by Sir Arthur Gilbert, the magnificent collections of European silver, gold snuffboxes and Italian mosaics are pre-eminent in the world. Other displays include furniture, Russian Church art and portrait miniatures. The vaulted spaces of Somerset House provide an inspirational setting for these works of great historical and artistic importance. *Opens May 2000.*

THE COURTAULD GALLERY has one of the most important collections of Impressionist paintings in the world. It re-opened in 1998 restored to its full splendour and with more of the collections from the Renaissance to the 20th century on display than ever before. *'The finest small collection of its kind in the country, with masterpieces by Bellini, Tintoretto, Rubens and all the major Impressionists.'* The Sunday Telegraph. *Now open.*

 Apply at desk for permission for photography/filming.

Licensed.

By arrangement.

Gilbert Collection only.

 No parking.

Guide dogs only.

CONTACT

Somerset House
Owner: Somerset House Trust
Strand, London
WC2R 0RN
Contact: Vicky Parr

Tel: 020 7836 8686
Fax: 020 7836 7613
e-mail: info@somerset-house.org.uk

The Gilbert Collection
Owner: Heather Trust for the Arts
Contact: Suzy Denbigh

Tel: 020 7240 5782
Fax: 020 7240 8704
e-mail: info@gilbert-collection.org.uk

Courtauld Gallery
Courtauld Institute of Art
Contact: Public Affairs Administrator

Tel: 020 7848 2526
Fax: 020 7848 2589
e-mail: galleryinfo@courtauld.ac.uk

LOCATION

OS Ref. TQ308 809

Entrances Victoria Embankment or Strand.

Rail: Underground: Temple or Covent Garden.

Air: London airports.

OPENING TIMES

The Gilbert Collection & Courtauld Gallery
Mon - Sat except BHs, 10am - 6pm.
Suns & BHs, 12 noon - 6pm.
Closed 1 Jan & 24 - 26 Dec.

Somerset House
Daily except 25 Dec.

ADMISSION

The Gilbert Collection & Courtauld Gallery
Adult £4.00
Child (under 18).......Free
Student (UK full)......Free
OAP.........................£3.00
Joint Ticket £7.00

Pre-booked Groups
Adult £3.00

Mons, 10am - 2pm
Everyone ....Free

Disabled & Helper.............
...........................£2.00pp

Somerset House
Free except special exhibitions.

FUNCTION/RECEPTION

ROOM	MAX CAPACITY
Silver Gallery	300
Fine Rooms	250
Great Room	200
Fine & Gt Rm.	400
Seamen's Hall	70
Restaurant	75
River Terrace	800
Great Court	3000

English Heritage Photographic Library/Jonathan Bailey

ELTHAM PALACE

Eltham

The epitome of 1930s chic, Eltham Palace dramatically demonstrates the glamour and allure of the period.

Bathe in the light flooding from a spectacular glazed dome in the Entrance Hall as it highlights beautiful blackbean veneer and figurative marquetry. It is a *tour de force* only rivalled by the adjacent Dining Room - where an Art Deco aluminium-leafed ceiling is a perfect complement to the bird's-eye maple walls. Step into Virginia's magnificent gold-leaf and onyx bathroom and throughout the house discover lacquered, 'ocean liner' style veneered walls and built-in furniture. A Chinese sliding screen is all that separates chic '30s Art Deco from the medieval Great Hall. You will find concealed electric lighting, centralised vacuum cleaning and a loud-speaker system that allowed music to waft around the house. Authentic interiors have been recreated by the finest contemporary craftsmen. Their appearance was painstakingly researched from archive photographs, documents and interviews with friends and relatives of the Courtaulds.

Outside you will find a delightful mixture of formal and informal gardens including a rose garden, pergola and loggia, all nestled around the extensive remains of the medieval palace.

English Heritage Photographic Library/Jonathan Bailey

Owner: English Heritage

CONTACT

Events Manager
Eltham Palace
Court Yard
Eltham
SE9 5QE

Tel: 020 8294 2548

LOCATION

OS Ref. TQ425 740

M25/J3, then A20 towards Eltham. The Palace is signposted from A20 and from Eltham High Street.

Rail: Eltham or Mottingham.

CONFERENCE/FUNCTION		
ROOM	SIZE	MAX CAPACITY

OPENING TIMES

16 June - 30 September: Wed - Fri & Sun 10am - 6pm.
1 - 31 October: Wed - Fri & Suns, 10am - 5pm.
1 November - 31 March: Wed - Fri & Suns, 10am - 4pm.

Open BH Mons throughout the year.

Closed 24 - 26 December.

Groups visits must be booked in advance.

English Heritage Hospitality
The new corporate and private events service from English Heritage offers exclusive use of the Palace on Mons, Tues or Sats for conferences, meetings, dinners, concerts, receptions and weddings. Please contact Amanda Dadd on 020 8294 2577

ADMISSION

House and Grounds

Adult	£5.90
Child	£3.00
OAP	£4.40

Grounds only

Adult	£3.50
Child	£1.80
OAP	£2.60

Filming, plays and photographic shoots.

Exclusive private and corporate hospitality.

Free.

Coaches must book.

KENSINGTON PALACE STATE APARTMENTS

Kensington

Owner:
Historic Royal Palaces

CONTACT

Kensington Palace
State Apartments
London
W8 4PX

Tel: 020 7937 9561

LOCATION

OS Ref. TQ258 801

In Kensington Gardens.

Tube Station: Queensway on Central Line, High Street Kensington on Circle & District Line.

FUNCTIONS		
ROOM	SIZE	MAX CAPACITY
Orangery	7.1 x 34m	250 receptions
		150 dinners

The history of Kensington Palace dates back to 1689 when the newly crowned William III and Mary II commissioned Sir Christopher Wren to convert the then Nottingham House into a Royal Palace. The Palace was again altered when George I had the artist William Kent paint the magnificent *trompe l'oeil* ceilings and staircases which can still be enjoyed at this most private of Palaces.

This beautiful historic building has seen such momentous events as the death of George II and the birth of Queen Victoria who began her long reign as Queen in 1837, with a meeting of her Privy Council in the Red Saloon.

Multi-language sound guides are available to lead visitors round the magnificent State Apartments. Highlights include the splendid Cupola Room, the most lavishly decorated state room in the Palace and where Queen Victoria was baptised, and the beautifully restored King's Gallery which is home to several Old Masters from the collection of HM the Queen.

Kensington Palace is also home to 'Dressing for Royalty' – a stunning presentation of Royal Court and Ceremonial Dress dating from the 18th century, which allows visitors to participate in the excitement of dressing for Court – from invitation to presentation. There is also a dazzling selection of 16 dresses owned and worn by HM Queen Elizabeth II.

OPENING TIMES

1999/2000
Mid-October - mid-March:
Daily, 10am,
last entry at 4pm.

(Closed 24 - 26 December & 1 January.)

Mid-March - mid-October:
Daily, 10am -
last entry at 5pm.

ADMISSION

Adult £8.50
Child* (5-15yrs) £6.10
Conc.........................£6.70
Family £26.10

* Under 5yrs Free.

Groups:
Tel: 020 7937 7079

No photography indoors.

The Orangery serves light refreshments.

Partially suitable.

Sound guides for Dress Collection and State Apartments.

Nearby.

Welcome, please book.

In grounds, on leads. Guide dogs only in Palace.

South East England

English Heritage Photographic Library

KENWOOD HOUSE
Hampstead

Owner: English Heritage

CONTACT

The House Manager
Kenwood House
Hampstead Lane
London
NW3 7JR

Tel: 020 8348 1286

KENWOOD, one of the treasures of London, is an idyllic country retreat close to the popular villages of Hampstead and Highgate.

The house was remodelled in the 1760s by Robert Adam, the fashionable neo-classical architect. The breathtaking library or 'Great Room' is one of his finest achievements.

Kenwood is famous for the internationally important collection of paintings bequeathed to the nation by Edward Guinness, 1st Earl of Iveagh. Some of the world's finest artists are represented by works such as a Rembrandt *Self Portrait*, Vermeer's *The Guitar Player*; *Mary, Countess Howe* by Gainsborough and paintings by Turner, Reynolds and many others.

As if the house and its contents were not riches enough, Kenwood stands in 112 acres of landscaped grounds on the edge of Hampstead Heath, commanding a fine prospect towards central London. The meadow walks and ornamental lake of the park, designed by Humphry Repton, contrast with the wilder Heath below. The open air concerts held in the summer at Kenwood have become part of London life, combining the charms of music with the serenity of the lakeside setting.

English Heritage Photographic Library

English Heritage Photographic Library

Concerts, exhibitions, filming. No photography in house.

The Old Kitchen is available for wedding receptions and corporate entertainment.

Ground floor access.

Available in the Brew House.

Foreign language tours by prior arrangement.

Personal stereo tours.

West Lodge car park on Hampstead Lane. Parking for the disabled.

Free when booked in advance on 020 7973 3485.

LOCATION

OS Ref. TQ271 874

Hampstead Lane, NW3.

Bus: London Transport 210.

Rail: Hampstead Heath.

Underground: Archway or Golders Green Northern Line then bus 210.

OPENING TIMES

SUMMER
1 April - 30 September
Daily: 10am - 6pm
(10am - 8pm Sundays in Aug).

October
Daily: 10am - 5pm.

WINTER
1 November - 31 March
Daily: 10am - 4pm.

ADMISSION

House & Grounds:
Free. Donations welcome.

The 45 minute tour must be booked in advance. Please ask for details on tours available in different languages.

South East England

Mark Fiennes

Mark Fiennes

SPENCER HOUSE
St James's Place

SPENCER HOUSE, built 1756 - 66 for the 1st Earl Spencer, an ancestor of Diana, Princess of Wales (1961-97), is London's finest surviving 18th century town house. The magnificent private palace has regained the full splendour of its late 18th century appearance, after a painstaking ten-year restoration programme.

Designed by John Vardy and James 'Athenian' Stuart, the nine state rooms are amongst the first neo-classical interiors in Europe. Vardy's Palm Room, with its spectacular screen of gilded palm trees and arched fronds, is a unique Palladian setpiece, while the elegant mural decorations of Stuart's Painted Room reflect the 18th century passion for classical Greece and Rome. Stuart's superb gilded furniture has been returned to its original location in the Painted Room by courtesy of the V&A and English Heritage. Visitors can also see a fine collection of 18th century paintings and furniture, specially assembled for the house, including five major Benjamin West paintings, graciously lent by Her Majesty The Queen.

The state rooms are open to the public for viewing on Sundays. They are also available on a limited number of occasions each year for private and corporate entertaining during the rest of the week.

Mark Fiennes

CONTACT

Jane Rick
Director
Spencer House
27 St James's Place
London
SW1A 1NR

Tel: 020 7514 1964

Fax: 020 7409 2952

Info Line: 020 7499 8620

LOCATION

OS Ref. TQ293 803

Central London: off St James's Street, overlooking Green Park.

Underground: Green Park.

CONFERENCE/FUNCTION		
ROOM	SIZE	MAX CAPACITY
Receptions		500
Lunches & Dinners		130
Board Meetings		40
Theatre Style meetings		100

OPENING TIMES

ALL YEAR
All year
(except January & August)
Suns, 10.30am - 5.30pm.

Last tour 4.45pm.

Tours begin approximately every 20 mins and last 1hr 10mins. Maximum number on each tour is 20.

Open for corporate hospitality except during January & August.

ADMISSION

Adult £6.00
Conc.* £5.00

* Students, Friends of V&A, Tate Gallery and Royal Academy (all with cards), children under 16 (no under 10s admitted).

Prices include guided tour.

No photography inside House.

Ramps and lifts. WC.

Obligatory. Comprehensive colour guide-book £3.50.

No parking facilities. Coaches can drop off at door.

SPECIAL EVENTS

- **APR 9 (provisional):** Craftsman Day: Opportunity to meet the skilled people involved in the ten year restoration of this important building and the methods and techniques employed will be explained and demonstrated. 11am - 5pm.

SYON PARK
Brentford

Described by John Betjeman as 'the Grand Architectural Walk', Syon House and its 200 acre park is the London home of the Duke of Northumberland, whose family, the Percys, have lived here since the late 16th century.

Originally the site of a late medieval monastery, Syon Park has a fascinating history. The present house has Tudor origins but contains some of Robert Adam's finest interiors, which were commissioned by the 1st Duke in the 1760s.

Within the 'Capability' Brown landscaped park are 30 acres of gardens which contain the spectacular Great Conservatory designed by Charles Fowler in the 1820s. The House and Great Conservatory are available for corporate and private hire.

Syon House is an excellent venue for small meetings, lunches and dinners in the Duke's private dining room (max. 25). The State Apartments make a sumptuous setting for dinners, concerts, receptions, launches and wedding ceremonies (max. 120). Marquees can be erected on the lawn adjacent to the house for balls and corporate events. The Great Conservatory is available for summer parties, launches and wedding receptions.

Owner: The Duke of Northumberland

CONTACT

Richard Pailthorpe
Syon Park
Brentford
TW8 8JF

Tel: 020 8560 0883

Fax: 020 8568 0936

LOCATION

OS Ref. TQ173 767

Between Brentford and Twickenham, off the A4, A310 in SW London.

Rail: Kew Bridge or Gunnersbury Underground then Bus 237 or 267.

Air: Heathrow 8m.

CONFERENCE/FUNCTION		
ROOM	SIZE	MAX CAPACITY
Great Hall	50' x 20'	120
Great Conservatory	60' x 40'	160
Marquee		800

OPENING TIMES

House
15 March - 29 October only
Weds, Thurs, Suns & BHs
11am - 5pm
(open Good Fri & Easter Sat).
Other times by appointment for groups.

Gardens
daily (except 25 & 26 Dec)
10am - 5.30pm or dusk if earlier.

ADMISSION

House and Gardens
Adult £6.00
Child/Conc. £4.50
Family (2+2) £15.00

Gardens only
Adult £3.00
Child/Conc. £2.50
Family (2+2) £7.00

GROUPS (min 15, max 50)
House and Gardens
Adult £5.50
Child/Conc. £4.00

Gardens only
Adult £3.00
Child/Conc. £2.50

No photography in house. Indoor adventure playground.

Garden centre.

Partially suitable.

Licensed.

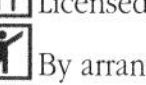

By arrangement.

Guide dogs only.

Crown Copyright: Historic Royal Palaces 2000

Crown Copyright: Historic Royal Palaces 2000

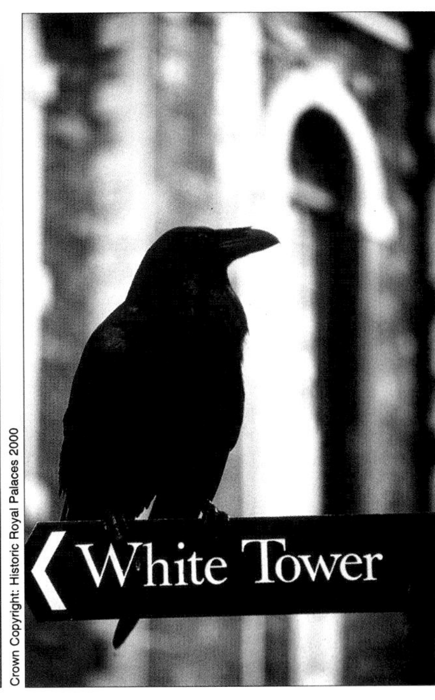

Crown Copyright: Historic Royal Palaces 2000

Managed by: Historic Royal Palaces

CONTACT

The Tower of London
London
EC3N 4AB

Tel: 020 7709 0765

LOCATION

OS Ref. TQ336 806

Tube Station: Tower Hill on Circle/District Line. Monument on Northern Line.

Docklands Light Railway: Tower Gateway Station.

Rail: Fenchurch Street Station and London Bridge Station.

Bus: 15, 25, 42, 78, 100, D1, D9, D11.

Riverboat: From Charing Cross, Westminster or Greenwich to Tower Pier.

THE TOWER OF LONDON

London

William the Conqueror began building the Tower of London in 1078 as a royal residence and to control the volatile City of London. Over the ensuing 900 years the Tower has served as a royal fortress, mint, armoury and more infamously as a prison and place of execution.

The Tower of London has been home to the Crown Jewels for the last 600 years and today visitors can see them in all their glory in the magnificent new Jewel House. They are still used by HM The Queen for ceremonies such as the State Opening of Parliament and the 'Crowns and Diamonds' exhibition details the jewels' history, alongside a pile of 2,314 diamonds lent by De Beers.

Visit the White Tower, the original Tower of London, which features new displays by the Royal Armouries including the Block and Axe, Tudor arms and armour and the Instruments of Torture.

Once inside, the Yeoman Warder 'Beefeaters' give free guided tours providing an unrivalled insight into the darker secrets of over 900 years of royal history. Above the notorious Traitors' Gate, costumed guides evoke life at the court of King Edward I in the recently restored rooms of his Medieval Palace.

See the execution site where many famous prisoners such as two of Henry VIII's wives were put to death and visit the Chapel Royal where they are buried. The Tower will be celebrating 2000 years of history with a series of special events and exhibitions throughout the year including from April 2000, the first ever public display of the Domesday Book. There are also special events every school holiday.

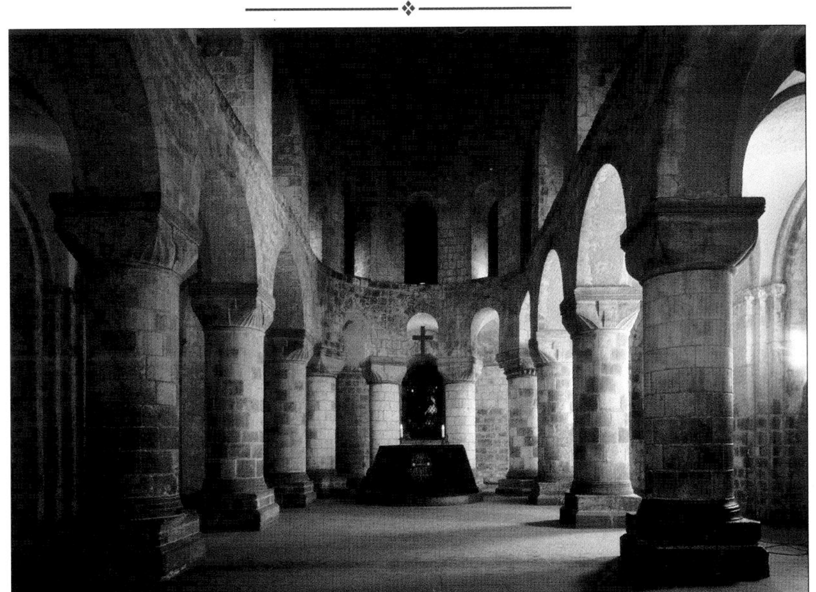

OPENING TIMES

SUMMER
1 March - 31 October
Daily
Mon - Sat: 9am - 5pm
Suns: 10am - 5pm.

WINTER
1 November - 28 February
Tues - Sat: 9am - 4pm
Mons & Suns: 10am - 4pm.

Closed 24 - 26 December and 1 January.

Last admission one hour before closing.

ADMISSION

Telephone Info Line for admission prices: 020 7709 0765.

Groups are advised to book, telephone: 020 7488 5681.

No photography in Jewel House.

020 7488 5762.

Partially suitable. WC.

Available on the wharf.

Yeoman Warder tours are free and leave front entrance every 1/2 hr.

No parking.

Welcome. Group rates on request.

Telephone for details.

South East England

THE WALLACE COLLECTION
Manchester Square

THE WALLACE COLLECTION is a national museum holding a superb range of fine and decorative arts from the 16th - 19th centuries. Formed largely between 1802 and 1875, by three generations of the Marquesses of Hertford and by the 4th Marquess' son, Sir Richard Wallace, the collection is displayed in Hertford House, an historic London town house.

Although it is probably best known for its magnificent 18th century French paintings, furniture and porcelain, the Wallace Collection also displays many other treasures such as paintings by Titian, Rembrandt, Rubens and Frans Hals (*The Laughing Cavalier*). There is also the finest collection of princely armour and arms in Britain, as well as choice and opulent displays of gold boxes, miniatures, sculpture and medieval and Renaissance works of art.

In June 2000 the Wallace Collection celebrates its centenary as a national museum with the opening of its 'Centenary Project'. Designed by Rick Mather Architects and funded by the Heritage Lottery Fund and private donors, the project provides an entire new floor of visitor space, comprising: a Lecture Theatre; Schools Room; Seminar Room; drop-in Library and four new galleries, including a Temporary Exhibition Gallery. The courtyard of Hertford House will be transformed into a Sculpture Garden Restaurant, covered by a 'floating' glass roof.

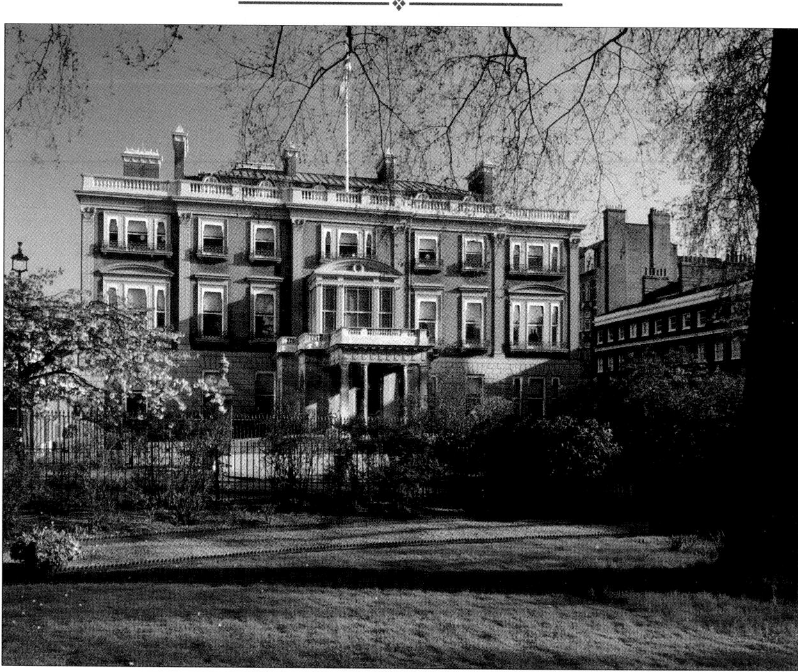

CONTACT

Jo Charlton
The Wallace Collection
Hertford House
Manchester Square
London
W1M 6BN

Tel: 020 7563 9516

Fax: 020 7224 2155

e-mail: admin@the-wallace-collection.org.uk

LOCATION

OS Ref. TQ283 813

Central London behind Selfridges department store off Duke Street.

Tube Station: Baker Street, Marble Arch and Bond Street.

CONFERENCE/FUNCTION		
ROOM	SIZE	MAX CAPACITY
Receptions		300
Dinners		150

OPENING TIMES

ALL YEAR
Weekdays: 10am - 5pm
Sunday: 2 - 5pm

Closed
Good Friday, May Day, 24 - 26 December and New Year's Day.

ADMISSION

Free.

Currently undergoing a Heritage Lottery Fund building project (completion date June 2000). Galleries remain unaffected.
No photography in house.

For information on corporate hospitality and the new lecture theatre and seminar room facilities, please contact the Development Manager on 020 7563 9545.

The entrance has ramped access. A wheelchair can be loaned upon request and a stairclimber is available for wheelchair access to the first floor galleries.

Free lectures on the collection are given every day. Private tours can also be arranged. Please contact Adult Education on 020 7563 9515.

Coaches may set down at Hertford House, parking is at Bayswater Road, W8. Meters in Manchester Square.

Please contact the Education Department on 020 7563 7551 for information on teaching sessions and activities.

Open all year.

2 WILLOW ROAD

Tel: 020 7435 6166

Hampstead, London NW3 1TH **e-mail:** twlgen@smtp.ntrust.org.uk

Owner: The National Trust **Contact:** The Custodian

The former home of Erno Goldfinger, designed and built by him in 1939. A three-storey brick and concrete rectangle, it is one of Britain's most important examples of modernist architecture and is filled with furniture also designed by Goldfinger. The interesting art collection includes works by Henry Moore and Max Ernst.

Location: OS Ref. TQ270 858. Hampstead, London.

Opening Times: 30 Mar - 25 Oct: Thur - Sat, 12 noon - 5pm. (Closed Good Fri & BH Mons). Last admission 4pm. Guided tours every 45 mins.

Admission: Adult £4.20.

Ground floor suitable, filmed tour of whole house available. Obligatory.

ALBERT MEMORIAL

Tel: 020 7495 0916 (Booking Agency)

Visitor Centre, Princes Gate, Kensington Gore SW7

Owner: English Heritage. **Contact:** The Royal Parks Agency (management agency).

An elaborate memorial by George Gilbert Scott to commemorate the Prince Consort.

Location: OS Ref. TQ266 798. Victoria Station 1½ m, South Kensington Tube ½ m.

Opening Times: All visits by booked guided tours.

Admission: Adult £3, Child £2.50.

APSLEY HOUSE

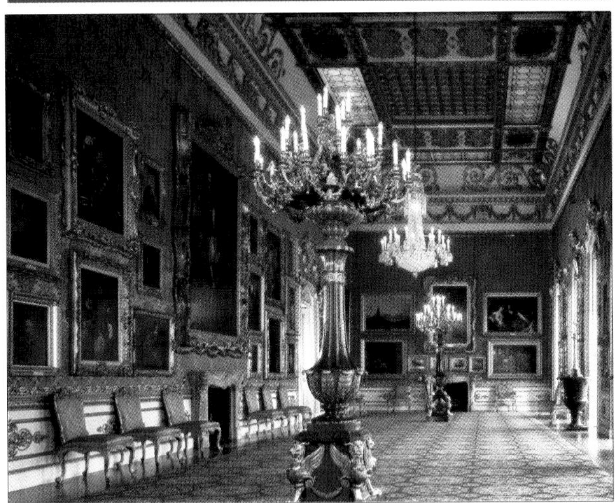

149 PICCADILLY, HYDE PARK CORNER, LONDON W1V 9FA

Owner: *V & A Museum & Dept. for Culture, Media & Sport* ***Contact:*** *The Administrator*

Tel: 020 7499 5676/495 8525 **Fax:** 020 7493 6576

Apsley House (No. 1, London) was originally designed by Robert Adam in 1771-8. In 1817 it was bought by the Duke of Wellington and enlarged. His London 'Palace' houses his magnificent collection: paintings by Velazquez, Goya, Rubens, Lawrence, Wilkie, Steen, de Hooch and other masters; sculpture, silver, porcelain, furniture, caricatures, medals and memorabilia.

Location: OS Ref. TQ284 799. N side of Hyde Park Corner. Nearest tube station: Hyde Park Corner exit 1 Piccadilly Line.

Opening Times: Tue - Sun, 11am - 5pm, last admission 4.30pm. Closed Mons, except BHs, Good Fri, May Day BH, 24 - 26 Dec and New Year's Day.

Admission: Adult £4.50, Conc. £3 (both include Soundguide), Child (under 18yrs) Free. Pre-arranged groups (10+): £2.50.

No photography in house. Partially suitable.

By arrangement. In Park Lane. Guide dogs only. 

THE BANQUETING HOUSE

See page 118 for full page entry.

BLEWCOAT SCHOOL

Tel: 020 7222 2877

23 Caxton Street, Westminster, London SW1H 0PY

Owner: The National Trust **Contact:** The Administrator

Built in 1709 at the expense of William Green, a local brewer, to provide an education for poor children. The building was used as a school until 1926, and is now the NT London Information Centre and shop.

Location: OS Ref. TQ295 794. Near the junction with Buckingham Gate.

Opening Times: All year: Mon - Fri, 10am - 5.30pm. Also 27 Nov & 4 & 11 & 18 Dec, 11am - 4.30pm. Closed BH Mon, Good Fri, 25 Dec - 1 Jan inclusive.

BOSTON MANOR HOUSE

BOSTON MANOR ROAD, BRENTFORD TW8 9JX

Owner: *Hounslow Cultural & Community Services* ***Contact:*** *Andrea Cameron*

Tel: 020 8560 5441 **Fax:** 020 8862 7602

A fine Jacobean house built in 1623. The rooms that can be viewed include the State Drawing Room with a magnificent ceiling and fireplace designed in 1623. The ceiling is divided into panels representing the senses and the elements. It is a rare example of a Jacobean house in the London area. The ground floor is available for hire and when not in use can be viewed. The rooms contain part of the local collection of paintings, and represent views of the locality from the 18th century to today.

Location: OS Ref. TQ168 784. 10 mins walk S of Boston Manor Station (Piccadilly Line) and 250yds N of Boston Manor Road junction with A4 - Great West Road, Brentford.

Opening Times: 1 Apr - 29 Oct: Sats, Suns & BHs, 2.30 - 5pm. Park open daily.

Admission: Free.

Ground floor & grounds suitable. WC. 

BRUCE CASTLE

Tel: 020 8808 8772

Haringey Museum & Archive Service, Lordship Lane, London N17 8NU

Owner: London Borough of Haringey

A Tudor building. Sir Rowland Hill (inventor of the Penny Post) ran a progressive school at Bruce Castle from 1827.

Location: OS Ref. TQ335 906. Corner of Bruce Grove (A10) and Lordship Lane, 600yds NW of Bruce Grove Station.

Opening Times: All year: Wed - Sun & Summer BHs, 1 - 5pm. Organised groups by appointment.

Admission: Free.

BUCKINGHAM PALACE

See page 119 for full page entry.

BURGH HOUSE

Tel: 020 7431 0144 Buttery: 020 7431 2516 **Fax:** 020 7435 8817

New End Square, Hampstead, London NW3 1LT

Owner: London Borough of Camden **Contact:** Ms Helen Wilton

A Grade I listed building of 1703 in the heart of old Hampstead with original panelled rooms, "barley sugar" staircase bannisters and a music room. Home of the Hampstead Museum, permanent and changing exhibitions. Prize-winning terraced garden. Regular programme of concerts, art exhibitions, and meetings. Receptions, seminars and conferences. Rooms for hire. Special facilities for schools visits. Wedding receptions.

Location: OS Ref. TQ266 859. New End Square, E of Hampstead underground station.

Opening Times: All year: Wed - Sun, 12 noon - 5pm. Sats (1 Apr - 31 Oct) by appointment only. BH Mons, 2 - 5pm. Closed Christmas fortnight, Good Fri & Easter Mon. Groups by arrangement. Buttery: Wed - Sun, 11am - 5.30pm. BHs, 1 - 5.00pm.

Admission: Free.

Ground floor & grounds suitable. WC. Licensed buttery.

No parking. Guide dogs only.

South East England

CAPEL MANOR GARDENS

BULLSMOOR LANE, ENFIELD EN1 4RQ

Owner: *Capel Manor Charitable Organisation* ***Contact:*** *Miss Julie Ryan*

Tel: 020 8366 4442 **Fax:** 01992 717544

These extensive, richly planted gardens are delightful throughout the year offering inspiration, information and relaxation. The gardens include various themes - historical, modern, walled, rock, water, sensory and disabled and an Italianate Maze, Japanese Garden and 'Gardening Which?' demonstration and model gardens. Capel Manor is a College of Horticulture and runs a training scheme for professional gardeners originally devised in conjunction with the Historic Houses Association. Special events throughout the year.

Location: OS Ref. TQ344 997. Minutes from M25/J25. Tourist Board signs posted (yellow signs in Summer).

Opening Times: Daily in summer: 10am - 5.30pm. Last ticket 4.30pm. Check for winter times.

Admission: Adult £4, Conc. £3.50, Child £2, Family £10. Charges alter for special show weekends and winter months.

Grounds suitable. WC.  In grounds, on leads.

CARLYLE'S HOUSE

24 CHEYNE ROW, CHELSEA, LONDON SW3 5HL

Owner: *The National Trust* ***Contact:*** *The Custodian*

Tel: 020 7352 7087

This Queen Anne town house was the home of the 'Sage of Chelsea', Victorian writer and historian Thomas Carlyle and his wife Jane. The atmospheric interior has the Carlyles' original furniture and decoration, together with the books, portraits and personal mementoes acquired during their 30 years here. Dickens, Chopin, Tennyson, George Eliot and Emerson were among the illustrious visitors to the house. Carlyle used to sit and enjoy the small, tranquil walled garden.

Location: OS Ref. TQ272 777. Off Cheyne Walk, between Battersea and Albert Bridges on Chelsea Embankment, or off the Kings Road and Oakley Street.

Opening Times: 1 Apr - 31 Oct: Wed - Sun & BH Mons, 11am - 5pm. Last admission 4.30pm. Closed Good Fri.

Admission: Adult £3.50, Child £1.75.

CHAPTER HOUSE, PYX CHAMBER & ABBEY MUSEUM

East Cloisters, Westminster Abbey, London SW1P 3PE **Tel:** 020 7222 5897

Owner: English Heritage **Contact:** Head Custodian

The Chapter House, built by the Royal masons in 1250 and faithfully restored in the 19th century, contains some of the finest examples of medieval English sculpture to be seen. The building is octagonal, with a central column, and still has its original floor of glazed tiles, which have been newly conserved. Its uses have varied and in the 14th century it was used as a meeting place for the Benedictine monks of the Abbey and as well as for Members of Parliament. The 11th century Pyx Chamber now houses the Abbey treasures, reflecting its use as the strongroom of the exchequer from the 14th to 19th centuries. The Abbey museum contains medieval Royal effigies.

Location: OS Ref. TQ301 795. Approach either through the Abbey or through Dean's Yard and the cloister.

Opening Times: 1 Apr - 30 Sept: daily, 9.30am - 5.30pm. 1 Oct - 31 Oct: daily 10am - 5pm. 1 Nov - 31 Mar: daily, 10am - 4pm. Liable to be closed at short notice on State Occasions.

Admission: Adult £2.50, Child £1.30, Conc. £1.90.

Inclusive. Tel. for details.

CHELSEA PHYSIC GARDEN

66 ROYAL HOSPITAL ROAD, LONDON SW3 4HS

Owner: *Chelsea Physic Garden Company* ***Contact:*** *Sue Minter*

Tel: 020 7352 5646 **Fax:** 020 7376 3910

The second oldest botanic garden in Britain, founded in 1673. For many years these 4 acres of peace and quiet with many rare and unusual plants were known only to a few. Specialists in medicinal plants, tender species and the history of plant introductions.

Location: OS Ref. TQ277 778. Off Embankment, between Chelsea & Albert Bridges. Entrance - Swan Walk.

Opening Times: 2 Apr - 29 Oct: Weds, 12 noon - 5pm & Suns, 2 - 6pm. Snowdrop opening & winter festival: 6 & 13 Feb: 11am - 3pm.

Admission: Adult £4, Child £2, Conc. £2. Carers for disabled: Free.

SPECIAL EVENTS

MAY 22 - 26: Chelsea Show Week., 12 noon - 5pm with lunches.

JUL 9 - SEPT 3: Summer Exhibition: 'Timely Cures'.

CHISWICK HOUSE

See page 120 for full page entry.

COLLEGE OF ARMS

Tel: 020 7248 2762 **Fax:** 020 7248 6448

Queen Victoria Street, London EC4V 4BT

Owner: Corp. of the Kings, Heralds & Pursuivants of Arms **Contact:** The Officer in Waiting

Mansion built in 1670s to house the English Officers of Arms and their records.

Location: OS Ref. TQ320 810. On N side of Queen Victoria Street, S of St Paul's Cathedral.

Opening Times: Earl Marshal's Court only; open all year (except BHs, State and special occasions) Mon - Fri, 10am - 4pm. Group visits (up to 10) by arrangement only. Record Room: open for tours (groups of up to 20) by special arrangement in advance with the Officer in Waiting.

Admission: Free (parties by negotiation).

THE COURTAULD GALLERY & THE GILBERT COLLECTION AT SOMERSET HOUSE

See page 121 for full page entry.

THE DE MORGAN FOUNDATION

OLD BATTERSEA HOUSE, 30 VICARAGE CRESCENT, LONDON SW11 3LD

Contact: *Susan Seagrave*

Tel: 020 7371 8385

A substantial part of the De Morgan Foundation collection of ceramics by William De Morgan, and paintings by Evelyn De Morgan (née Pickering) are displayed on the ground floor of elegantly restored Old Battersea House - a Wren period building which is privately occupied.

Location: OS Ref. TQ267 767. Close to S shore of River Thames, 1/2 m SW of S end of Battersea Bridge, via Battersea Church Road and Vicarage Crescent.

Opening Times: Weds by appointment.

Admission: Groups (4-15 persons) £2.

No photography in house. Partially suitable. Obligatory. Cars limited, no coach parking.

FENTON HOUSE

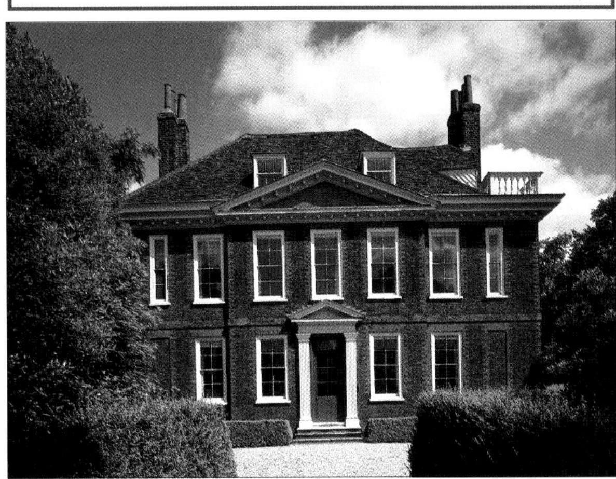

WINDMILL HILL, HAMPSTEAD, LONDON NW3 6RT

Owner: *The National Trust* ***Contact:*** *The Custodian*

Tel: 020 7435 3471 **e-mail:** tfehse@smtp.ntrust.org.uk

A delightful late 17th century merchant's house, set among the winding streets of Old Hampstead. The charming interior contains an outstanding collection of Oriental and European porcelain, needlework and furniture. The Benton Fletcher Collection of beautiful early keyboard instruments is also housed at Fenton and the instruments are sometimes played by music scholars during opening hours. The walled garden has a formal lawn and walks, an orchard and vegetable garden and fine wrought-iron gates.

Location: OS Ref. TQ262 862. Visitors' entrance on W side of Hampstead Grove. Hampstead underground station 300 yds.

Opening Times: 1 Apr - 31 Oct: daily except Mons & Tues (open BH Mons). Times: weekdays, 2 - 5pm. Weekends & BH Mons, 11am - 5pm. Groups at other times by appointment.

Admission: Adult £4.20, Child £2.10, Family £10.50. No reduction for pre-booked groups. No picnics in grounds.

Ground floor suitable. No parking.

THE DICKENS HOUSE MUSEUM

Tel: 020 7405 2127 **Fax:** 020 7831 5175

48 Doughty Street, London WC1N 2LF **e-mail:** cdickens@rmplc.co.uk

Owner: The Trustees **Contact:** Mr Andrew Xavier – Curator

House occupied by Charles Dickens and his family from 1837 - 1839 where he produced *Pickwick Papers, Oliver Twist, Nicholas Nickleby* and *Barnaby Rudge.* Contains the most comprehensive Dickens library in the world as well as portraits, illustrations and rooms laid out exactly as they were in Dickens' time. The house is one of the few venues open over Christmas itself.

Location: OS Ref. TQ308 822. W of Grays Inn Road.

Opening Times: All year: Mon - Sat, 10am - 5pm (last admission 4.30pm).

Admission: Adult £4, Child £2, Conc. £3, Family £9.

By arrangement. In grounds, on leads.

EASTBURY MANOR HOUSE

Tel: 020 8507 0119 **Fax:** 020 8507 0118

Barking IG11 9SN

Owner: The National Trust **Contact:** The Administrator

Eastbury is a rare example of a medium-sized Elizabethan manor house. Leased to the Borough of Barking and Dagenham and used for a variety of arts and heritage activities.

Location: OS177, Ref. TQ457 838. In Eastbury Square, 10 mins walk S from Upney Station.

Opening Times: Mar - Dec: first Sat every month (except Aug), 10am - 4pm. Telephone for details.

Admission: Adult £1.80, Child 60p, Conc. £1, Family £4.20. Group visits by arrangement. Rates on application. Evening tours also available.

Ground floor suitable. Visitor days. No parking. Garden only.

ELTHAM PALACE

See page 122 for full page entry.

FREUD MUSEUM

Peter Aprahamian

20 MARESFIELD GARDENS, LONDON NW3 5SX

Contact: *Ms E Davies*

Tel: 020 7435 2002 **Fax:** 020 7431 5452 **e-mail:** freud@gn.apc.org

The Freud Museum was the home of Sigmund Freud after he escaped the Nazi annexation of Austria. The house retains its domestic atmosphere and has the character of turn of the century Vienna. The centrepiece is Freud's study which has been preserved intact, containing his remarkable collection of antiquities: Egyptian, Greek, Roman, Oriental and his large library. The Freuds brought all their furniture and household effects to London; fine Biedermeier and 19th century Austrian painted furniture. The most famous item is Freud's psychoanalytic couch, where his patients reclined. Fine Oriental rugs cover the floor and tables. Videos are shown of the Freud family in Vienna, Paris and London.

Location: OS Ref. TQ265 850. Between Swiss Cottage and Hampstead.

Opening Times: Wed - Sun (inc) 12 noon - 5pm.

Admission: Adult £4, Child under 12 free, Conc. £2. Coach parties by appointment.

Ground floor suitable. Limited. Guide dogs only.

South East England

FULHAM PALACE & MUSEUM

BISHOPS AVENUE, FULHAM, LONDON SW6 6EA

Owner: *London Borough of Hammersmith & Fulham & Fulham Palace Trust*

Tel: 020 7736 5821 **Museum:** 020 7736 3233

Former home of the Bishops of London (Tudor with Georgian additions and Victorian Chapel). The gardens, famous in the 17th century, now contain specimen trees and a knot garden of herbs. The museum tells the story of this nationally important site. Education service available. Rooms and grounds are available for private functions.

Location: OS Ref. TQ240 761.

Opening Times: Gardens: open daylight hours. Museum: Mar - Oct: Wed - Sun, 2 - 5pm. Nov - Feb: Thur - Sun, 1 - 4pm. Tours of principal rooms and gardens every 2nd Sun - contact Museum; selected other Suns contact Fulham Archaeological Rescue Group 020 7385 3723, £2. Private tours £5 each by arrangement with either organisation. Private tours with teas (50 max.).

Admission: Gardens: Free. Museum: Adult £1, Conc. 50p.

Private & wedding receptions. Partially suitable. Obligatory.
No parking. Guide dogs only.

Reg. Charity No. 1020063

HAM HOUSE

HAM, RICHMOND, SURREY TW10 7RS

Owner: *The National Trust* ***Contact:*** *Mrs J Graffius*

Tel: 020 8940 1950 **Fax:** 020 8332 6903 **e-mail:** shhgen@smtp.ntrust.org.uk

Ham House, on the banks of the River Thames, is perhaps the most remarkable Stuart house in the country. Apart from the fact that its architectural fabric has survived virtually unchanged since the 1670s, it still retains many of the furnishings from that period. Ham is presented today principally as the late 17th century Lauderdale residence with overlays of the 18th and 19th centuries. Visitors view the rooms in the sequence intended at the time, progressing through a hierarchy of apartments towards the Queen's Closet - the culmination of the sequence. The gardens are being restored using plans and images which were found in the house and were laid out in compartments, reflecting the ordered symmetry of the house and together they present the modern visitor with a complete picture of 17th century aristocratic life.

Location: OS Ref. TQ172 732. 1½ m from Richmond and 2m from Kingston. On the S bank of the River Thames, W of A307 at Petersham.

Opening times: 1 Apr - 29 Oct: daily except Thurs & Fris. House: 1 - 5pm, last adm. 4.30pm. Gardens: 10.30am - 6pm/dusk if earlier. Closed 25 - 26 Dec & 1 Jan.

Admission: House & Garden: Adult £5, Child £2.50, Family £12.50. Garden only: Adult £1.50, Child 75p. Pre-booked groups (min 15): Adult £4, Child £2.

Partially suitable. WC.     

THE GEFFRYE MUSEUM

Tel: 020 7739 9893 **Fax:** 020 7729 5647

Kingsland Road, London E2 8EA **e-mail:** info@geffrye-museum.org.uk

Owner: Independent Charitable Trust **Contact:** Ms Nancy Loader

The Geffrye is one of London's most friendly and enjoyable museums, set in elegant Grade I listed 18th century almshouses with attractive gardens, just north of the city. It presents the quintessential style of English urban middle class interiors from 1600 to 2000 through a series of period rooms. Walled herb garden and series of period garden rooms.

Location: OS Ref. TQ335 833. 1m N of Liverpool St. Buses: 242, 149, 243, 67. Underground: Liverpool St. or Old St.

Opening Times: Museum: Tue - Sat, 10am - 5pm. Suns & BH Mons, 12 noon - 5pm. Closed Mons (except BHs) Good Fri, Christmas Eve, Christmas Day, Boxing Day & New Year's Day. Gardens: Apr - Oct.

Admission: Free.

 Limited meter parking. 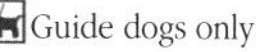 Guide dogs only. 

GEORGE INN

Tel: 020 7407 2056

77 Borough High Street, Southwark, London SE1

Owner: The National Trust

The only remaining galleried inn in London, famous as a coaching inn in the 18th and 19th centuries, and mentioned by Dickens in *Little Dorrit*. The George Inn is leased to and run by Whitbread plc as a public house.

Location: OS Ref. TQ326 799. On E side of Borough High Street, near London Bridge station.

Opening Times: During licensing hours.

GUNNERSBURY PARK MUSEUM

Tel: 020 8992 1612 **Fax:** 020 8752 0686

Gunnersbury Park, London W3 8LQ **e-mail:** gp-museum@cip.org.uk

Owner: Hounslow and Ealing Councils **Contact:** Mr Séan Sherman

Built in 1802 and refurbished by Sydney Smirke for the Rothschild family.

Location: OS Ref. TQ190 792. Acton Town underground station. ¼ m N of the junction of A4, M4 North Circular.

Opening Times: Apr - Oct: daily: 1 - 5pm. (6pm weekends & BHs). Nov - Mar: daily: 1 - 4pm. Victorian kitchens summer weekends only. Closed Christmas Day and Boxing Day. Park: open dawn - dusk.

Admission: Free. Donations welcome.

Patrick Lane.

The Geffrye Museum, London.

Open all Year Index
PAGE 52

HOGARTH'S HOUSE

HOGARTH LANE, GREAT WEST ROAD, CHISWICK W4 2QN

Owner: *Hogarth House Foundation* ***Contact:*** *Andrea Cameron*

Tel: 020 8994 6757 **Fax:** 020 8862 7602

This late 17th century house was the country home of William Hogarth, the famous painter, engraver, satirist and social reformer between 1749 and his death in 1764. It contains a collection of his engravings and prints, and the house is surrounded by an extensive garden which is in the process of restoration. The house is now a gallery, which describes Hogarth's life and work and also his wide range of interests, together with a display of his prints.

Location: OS Ref. TQ213 778. 100 yds W of Hogarth roundabout on the Great West Road - junction of Burlington Lane. Car park in named spaces in Axis Business Centre behind house and Chiswick House grounds.

Opening Times: Apr - Oct: Tue - Fri, 1 - 5pm, Sats & Suns, 1 - 6pm. Nov - Mar: Tue - Fri, 1 - 4pm, Sats & Suns, 1 - 5pm. Closed Jan, Good Fri, 25 & 26 Dec. Closed Mons except BHs.

Admission: Free.

Ground floor suitable.

JEWEL TOWER

Tel: 020 7222 2219

Abingdon Street, Westminster, London SW1P 3JY

Owner: English Heritage **Contact:** Head Custodian

Built c1365 to house the personal treasure of Edward III and one of two surviving parts of the Palace of Westminster.

Location: OS Ref. TQ302 794. Opposite S end of Houses of Parliament (Victoria Tower).

Opening Times: 1 Apr - 31 Mar: daily, 10am - 6pm (closes 5pm in Oct, & 4pm Nov - Mar).

Admission: Adult £1.50, Child 80p, Conc. £1.10.

DR JOHNSON'S HOUSE

Tel: 020 7353 3745

17 Gough Square, London EC4A 3DE **e-mail:** curator@drjh.dircon.co.uk

Owner: The Trustees

Fine 18th century house, once home to Dr Samuel Johnson, the celebrated literary figure, famous for his English dictionary.

Location: OS Ref. TQ314 813. N of Fleet Street.

Opening Times: Oct - Apr: Mon - Sat, 11am - 5pm. May - Sept: Mon - Sat, 11am - 5.30pm.

Admission: Adult £3, Child over 10 £1, Child under 10 free, Conc. £2.

KEATS HOUSE

Tel: 020 7435 2062 **Fax:** 020 7431 9293

Keats Grove, Hampstead, London NW3 2RR

Owner: Corporation of London **Contact:** Miss R Davis

Regency home of the poet John Keats (1795 - 1821).

Location: OS Ref. TQ272 856. Hampstead, NW3. Nearest underground: Belsize Park & Hampstead.

Opening Times: Summer: Apr - end Oct: weekdays, 10am - 1pm, 2 - 6pm, Sats, 10am - 1pm, 2 - 5pm, Suns, 2 - 5pm. Winter: Nov - end Mar: weekdays, 1 - 5pm, Sats, 10am - 1pm, 2 - 5pm, Suns, 2 - 5pm. Please confirm times by telephone, due to building repairs.

Admission: Free.

Ground floor & garden accessible  No parking. Guide dogs only.

KENSINGTON PALACE STATE APARTMENTS

See page 123 for full page entry.

KENWOOD HOUSE

See page 124 for full page entry.

Patrick Lane.

Keats House, London.

South East England

LEIGHTON HOUSE ART GALLERY & MUSEUM

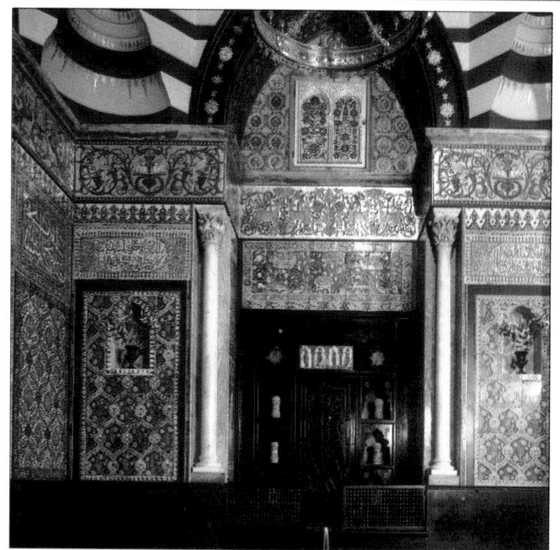

12 HOLLAND PARK ROAD, KENSINGTON, LONDON W14 8LZ

Owner: *Royal Borough of Kensington & Chelsea* ***Contact:*** *Curator*

Tel: 020 7602 3316 **Fax:** 020 7371 2467

Leighton House was the home of Frederic, Lord Leighton 1830 - 1896, painter and President of the Royal Academy, built between 1864 - 1879. It was a palace of art designed for entertaining and to provide a magnificent working space in the studio, with great north windows and a gilded apse. The Arab Hall is the centrepiece of the house, containing Leighton's collection of Persian tiles, a gilt mosaic frieze and a fountain. Victorian paintings by Leighton, Millais and Burne-Jones are on display.

Location: OS Ref. TQ247 793. N of High Street Kensington, off Melbury Rd, close to Commonwealth Institute.

Opening Times: Daily, except Suns & BHs, 11am - 5.30pm.

Admission: Free. £2.50 per head for pre-booked tours.

Please telephone for details.

LINLEY SAMBOURNE HOUSE

18 STAFFORD TERRACE, LONDON W8 7BH

Owner: *The Royal Borough of Kensington & Chelsea* ***Contact:*** *Assistant Curator*

Recorded Message: 020 8937 0663 **Info:** 020 7602 3316 **Fax:** 020 7371 2467

The home of Linley Sambourne (1844 - 1910) chief political cartoonist at Punch. A unique example of a late Victorian town house. The original decoration and furnishings have been largely preserved together with many of Sambourne's own cartoons and photographs, as well as works by other artists of the period.

Location: OS Ref. TQ252 794. Bus: 9, 10, 27, 28, 31, 49, 52, 70 & C1. Tube: Kensington High Street. Parking on Sun in nearby streets.

Opening Times: Mar - Oct: Weds, 10am - 4pm (last admission 3.30pm) & Suns, guided tours only, at 2.15pm, 3.15pm & 4.15pm, tours last approximately 45 mins. Groups at other times by appointment. Closed Nov - Feb.

Admission: Adult £3.50, Child (under 16), £2, Conc. £2.50, Family (2+2) £10.

 Not suitable. By arrangement.

LINDSEY HOUSE

Tel: 01494 528051

99 -100 Cheyne Walk, London SW10 0DQ

Owner: The National Trust **Contact:** NT Regional Office

Part of Lindsey House was built in 1674 on the site of Sir Thomas More's garden, overlooking the River Thames. It has one of the finest 17th century exteriors in London.

Location: OS Ref. TQ268 775. On Cheyne Walk, W of Battersea Bridge near junction with Milman's Street on Chelsea Embankment.

Opening Times: By written appointment only. 17 May, 14 Jun, 13 Sept & 11 Oct: 2 - 4pm. Please write to (enc. SAE): R Bourne, 100 Cheyne Walk, London SW10 0DQ.

Linley Sambourne House, London.

MARBLE HILL HOUSE

Tel: 020 892 5115

Richmond Road, Twickenham TW1 2NL

Owner: English Heritage **Contact:** House Manager

This beautiful villa beside the Thames was built in 1724 - 29 for Henrietta Howard, mistress of George II. Here she entertained many of the poets and wits of the Augustan age including Alexander Pope and later Horace Walpole. The perfect proportions of the villa were inspired by the work of the 16th century Italian architect, Palladio. Today this beautifully presented house contains an important collection of paintings and furniture, including some pieces commissioned for the villa when it was built.

Location: OS Ref. TQ174 736. A305, 600yds E of Orleans House.

Opening Times: 1 Apr - 30 Sept: daily, 10am - 6pm. 1 Oct - 31 Oct: daily, 10am - 5pm. 1 Nov - 31 Mar, Wed - Sun, 10am - 4pm.

Admission: Adult £3.30, Child £1.70, Conc. £2.50.

Ground floor & grounds suitable. WC.   Tel. for details.

WILLIAM MORRIS GALLERY

Tel: 020 8527 3782 **Fax:** 020 8527 7070

Lloyd Park, Forest Road, Walthamstow, London E17 4PP

Owner: London Borough of Waltham Forest **Contact:** Ms Nora Gillow

Location: OS Ref. SQ372 899. 15 mins walk from Walthamstow tube (Victoria line). 5 - 10 mins from M11/A406.

Opening Times: Tue - Sat and first Sun each month, 10am - 1pm and 2 - 5pm.

Admission: Free for all visitors but a charge is made for guided tours which must be booked in advance.

South East England

MUSEUM OF GARDEN HISTORY

LAMBETH PALACE ROAD, LONDON SE1 7LB

Owner: *The Tradescant Trust* ***Contact:*** *Mrs J Nicholson*

Tel: 020 7401 8865 **Fax:** 020 7401 8869

Fascinating permanent exhibition of the history of gardens, collection of ancient tools and recreated 17th century garden displaying flowers and shrubs of the period – seeds of which may be purchased in the garden shop. Visit the tombs of the Tradescants and Captain Bligh of the Bounty. They have knowledgeable staff and lectures, concerts, courses and art exhibitions are held regularly. The Knot Garden, part of the churchyard, is shown above.

Location: OS Ref. TQ306 791. At Lambeth Parish Church, next to Lambeth Palace, at E end of Lambeth Bridge.

Opening Times: Mon - Fri, 10.30am - 4pm. Suns, 10.30am - 5pm. Closed Sats. Closed 2nd Sun Dec - 1st Sun in Mar.

Admission: Free - donations appreciated.

Groups must book.   Partially suitable.  No parking.

OSTERLEY PARK

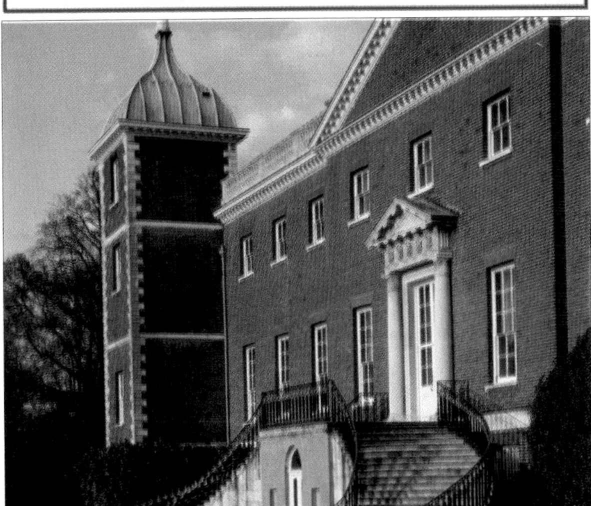

ISLEWORTH TW7 4RB

Owner: *The National Trust* ***Contact:*** *The Property Manager*

Tel/Fax: 020 8568 7714

Osterley's four turrets look out across one of the last great landscaped parks in suburban London, its trees and lakes an unexpected haven of green. Originally built in 1575, the mansion was transformed in the 18th century into an elegant villa by architect Robert Adam. The classical interior, designed for entertaining on a grand scale, still impresses with its specially made tapestries, furniture and plasterwork.

Location: OS Ref. TQ146 780. Access via Thornbury Road on N side of A4.

Opening Times: 1 Apr - 29 Oct: daily except Mons & Tues, 1 - 4.30pm. Closed Good Fri, open BH Mons. Last admission: 4pm. Grand Stable: Sun afternoon in summer. Park & Pleasure Grounds: All year, 9am - 7.30pm or sunset if earlier. Park will be closed early during major events. Car park closed Good Fri, 25 & 26 Dec.

Admission: £4.20, Family £10.50. Group: Wed - Sat £3.50, pre-booking required. £1 off adult tickets for holders of valid LT travelcard. Car Park: £2.50.

 Suitable, phone for details.  On leads in park. 

MYDDELTON HOUSE GARDENS

Tel: 01992 702200 **Fax:** 01992 702280

Bulls Cross, Enfield, Middlesex EN2 9HG

Owner: Lee Valley Regional Park Authority

Created by the famous plantsman E A Bowles.

Location: OS Ref. TQ342 992. 1/4 m W of A10 via Turkey St. 3/4 m S M25/J25.

Opening Times: Mon - Fri (except Christmas), 10am - 4.30pm. Easter - Oct: Suns & BHs, 2 - 5pm.

Admission: Adult £1.80, Conc. £1.20.

THE OCTAGON, ORLEANS HOUSE GALLERY

Tel: 020 8892 0221 **Fax:** 020 8744 0501

Riverside, Twickenham, Middlesex TW1 3DJ

Owner: London Borough of Richmond-upon-Thames **Contact:** Rachel Tranter

Outstanding example of baroque architecture built by James Gibbs c1720. Adjacent wing now converted to an art gallery.

Location: OS Ref. TQ168 734. On N side of Riverside, 700yds E of Twickenham town centre, 400yds S of Richmond Road, A305 via Lebanon Park Road and 500yds W of Marble Hill House.

Opening Times: Tue - Sat, 1 - 5.30pm (Oct - Mar closes 4.30pm). Sun & BHs, 2 - 5.30pm. Closed Mons. Garden: open daily, 9am - sunset.

Admission: Free.

WWW Website Index PAGE 46

PITSHANGER MANOR MUSEUM

Tel: 020 8567 1227 **Fax:** 020 8567 0595

Mattock Lane, Ealing, London W5 5EQ **e-mail:** pitshanger@ealing.gov.uk

Owner: London Borough of Ealing **Contact:** Mrs N Sohal

Set in Walpole Park, once owned by the architect Sir John Soane (1753 - 1837). He rebuilt most of the house to create a Regency villa. The later addition of a Victorian wing now houses a collection of Martinware pottery.

Location: OS Ref. TQ176 805. Ealing, London.

Opening Times: Tue - Sat, 10am - 5pm. Closed Suns & Mons. Also closed Christmas, Easter and New Year.

Admission: Free. Groups by arrangement.

THE QUEEN'S GALLERY

Tel: 020 7839 1377

Buckingham Palace, London SW1A 1AA

Owner: HM The Queen **Contact:** The Visitor Office

Location: OS Ref. TQ290 795. Buckingham Palace.

Opening Times: The Queen's Gallery is closed for major remodelling and extension and will re-open in 2002, the year of the Queen's Golden Jubilee.

English Heritage Photographic Library

The Ranger's House, London.

THE QUEEN'S HOUSE

© NMM

ROMNEY ROAD, GREENWICH, LONDON SE10 9NF

Owner: *National Maritime Museum* ***Contact:*** *Robin Scates*

Tel: 020 8858 4422 **Fax:** 020 8312 6632

24-hour info: 020 8312 6565 **e-mail:** bookings@nmm.ac.uk

The Story of Time, is the prestigious Millennium exhibition (until September 2000) that focuses on man's fascination with time illustrated with fine artefacts from around the world. See how artists and craftsmen throughout the ages have measured and interpreted the phenomena of time. Study notions of how the world began, how man charted and named the patterns and movements of the stars and planets, mythological concepts of the Ages of Man, Father Time and Destiny. The mechanisation of time and an examination of an instant-in-time contrasts with ideas of eternity, end times, the Apocalypse and immortality.

Location: OS Ref. TQ386 776. On the South Bank of the Thames at Greenwich.

Opening Times: Closed 24 - 26 & 31 Dec and 1 Jan 2000.

Admission: Story of Time: Adult 7.50, Child £3.75, Conc. £6.

THE RANGER'S HOUSE

Tel: 020 8853 0035

Chesterfield Walk, Blackheath, London SE10 8QX

Owner: English Heritage **Contact:** House Manager

A handsome, red-brick house which lies between two of London's great open spaces, Greenwich Park and Blackheath. The house was built for a successful seafarer, Admiral Francis Hosier around 1700 who sited the house within view of the Thames estuary. A later owner Lord Chesterfield, used to boast that the grand bow-windowed gallery commanded the three finest views in the world. Today Ranger's House is home to the Suffolk collection of paintings including elegant full-length Jacobean portraits. The first floor of the house contains an exhibition space. There is also an Architectural Study Collection, with features from 17th, 18th and 19th century dwellings. The first floor houses an exciting programme of contemporary exhibitions.

Location: OS Ref. TQ388 768. N of Shooters Hill Road.

Opening Times: 1 Apr - 30 Sept: daily, 10am - 6pm. 1 - 31 Oct: daily 10am - 5pm. 1 Nov - 31 Mar: Wed - Sun, 10am - 4pm.

Admission: Adult £2.80, Child £1.40, Conc. £2.10.

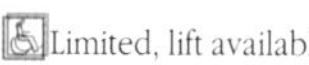 Limited, lift available.   Guide dogs only.   Tel. for details.

THE ROYAL MEWS

Tel: 020 7839 1377

Buckingham Palace, London SW1A 1AA

Owner: HM The Queen **Contact:** The Visitor Officer

Location: OS Ref. TQ289 794. Entrance in Buckingham Palace Road, W of The Queen's Gallery.

Opening Times: Oct - Jul: Mon - Thur, 12 noon - 4pm. Aug & Sept: Mon - Thur, 10.30am - 4.30pm. Last admission 30mins before closing.

Admission: Adult £4.30, Child (under 17yrs) £2.10, OAP £3.30.

ROYAL OBSERVATORY GREENWICH

Tel: 020 8312 6565 (24hr recorded info)

Greenwich Park, London SE10 9NF

Tel: 020 8858 4422 **Fax:** 020 8312 6632

e-mail: bookings@nmm.ac.uk

Owner: c/o National Maritime Museum **Contact:** Bookings Unit

Built by Wren in 1675. Famous for 'Greenwich Mean Time' and the Meridian Line (Longitude 0°), datum point for world time and the Millennium. See the timeball drop at 1 o' clock, the Astronomer Royal's apartments, famous Harrison timekeepers (1735-60) and the largest refracting telescope in Britain. Astronomy days during school holidays.

Location: OS Ref. TQ388 773. In Greenwich Park, off A2, 1/2 m S of town centre.

Opening Times: All year: daily 10am - 5pm. (not 24 - 26 & 31 Dec).

Admission: Adult £6, Child Free, Conc. £4.80. Pre-arranged groups (10+) 20% discount.

No photography.  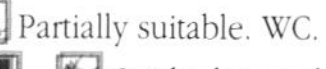 Partially suitable. WC.  By arrangement.

Coach park 625 metres.  Guide dogs only.

English Heritage

Marble Hill House, London.

ROYAL SOCIETY OF ARTS

8 JOHN ADAM STREET, LONDON WC2N 6EZ

Owner: *RSA* ***Contact:*** *Ms Y Chenaux-Smith*

Tel: 020 7839 5049 **Fax:** 020 7321 0271 **e-mail:** conference@rsa-u/z.demon.co.uk

The house of the Royal Society of Arts was designed by Robert Adam specially for the Society in the early 1770s. One of the few remaining buildings from the original Adelphi development, its Georgian façade conceals many unexpected delights of both traditional and contemporary architecture. Designed as one of London's earliest debating chambers, the Great Room is one of the most spectacular theatres in the city. The Benjamin Franklin Room is spacious and elegant, featuring an antique chandelier and two Adam fireplaces. The Vaults were originally designed as river front warehouses. Now fully restored they offer a striking contrast to the splendour of the rooms above. All rooms may be hired for meetings, receptions and weddings.

Location: OS Ref. TQ305 806. Near to Charing Cross and Waterloo.

Opening Times: All year: 8am - 8pm. Closed last 2 weeks of Aug, 24 Dec & 2 Jan.

Admission: For room hire prices, contact the RSA Conference Officer.

Product launches, themed parties, corporate announcements, film previews, dinner dances, private concerts, exhibitions, lectures on history of the house. All visits are by prior arrangement.

Private catering, lunches, dinners and receptions.

Wheelchair access to all main rooms via a lift.

Tours for groups of up to 25 may be arranged in advance. Must pre-book.

Parking at Vauxhall, meters in John Adam Street, car parks in Savoy Place & St Martin's Lane. Coaches may only set down & pick up on John Adam Street or the Strand.

Civil Wedding Licence. Open all year.

ST GEORGE'S CATHEDRAL

Tel: 020 7928 5256 **Fax:** 020 7787 8923

Westminster Bridge Road, London SE1 7HY **Contact:** The Rev James Cronin

Neo-Gothic rebuilt Pugin Cathedral bombed during the last war and rebuilt by Romily Craze in 1958.

Location: OS Ref. TQ315 794. Near Imperial War Museum. 1/2 m SE of Waterloo Stn.

Opening Times: 8am - 8pm, every day, except BHs.

Admission: Free.

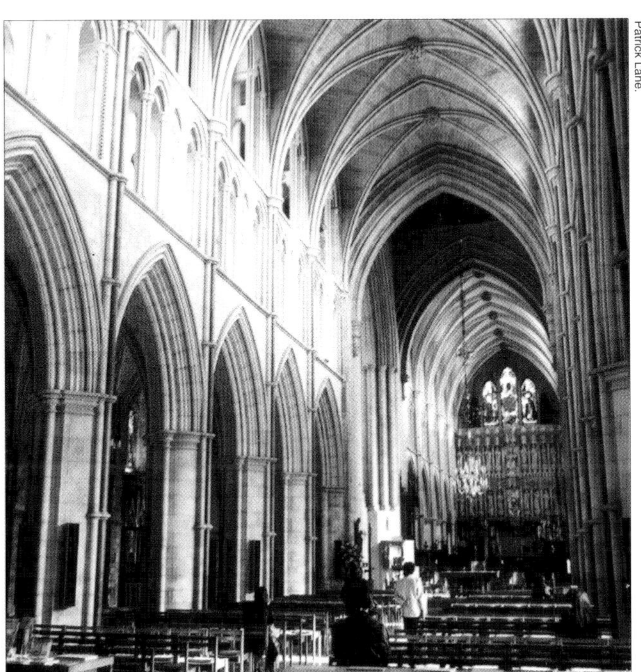

Patrick Lane.

Southwark Cathedral, London.

ST JOHN'S GATE
THE MUSEUM OF THE ORDER OF ST JOHN

ST. JOHN'S GATE, LONDON EC1M 4DA

Owner: *The Order of St. John* ***Contact:*** *Pamela Willis*

Tel: 020 7253 6644 **Fax:** 020 7336 0587

Tudor Gatehouse entrance to 12th century Priory of Clerkenwell, English home of Crusading Knights Hospitaller and St John Ambulance. Grand Priory Church, and 12th century crypt survive (despite Wat Tyler and Peasants' Revolt). Also Hogarth's home and Dr Johnson's workplace. Museum collections represent the Order from Crusade to First-Aid, including arms & armour, furniture, paintings, Maltese silver, pharmacy jars and historic First-Aid collections. New multi-media interactive St John's Ambulance exhibition now open.

Location: OS Ref. TQ317 821. St. John's Lane, Clerkenwell. Nearest underground: Farringdon, Barbican.

Opening Times: Mon - Fri: 10am - 5pm. Sats: 10am - 4pm. Closed BHs & Sat of BH weekend. Tours: Tues, Fris & Sats at 11am & 2.30pm. Reference Library: Open by appointment.

Admission: Museum Free. Tours of the building: £4, OAP £3 (donation).

Ground floor suitable. WC. Guide dogs only. 

SIR JOHN SOANE'S MUSEUM

Tel: 020 7405 2107 Fax: 020 7831 3957

13 Lincoln's Inn Fields, London WC2A 3BP

Owner: Trustees of Sir John Soane's Museum **Contact:** Ms S Palmer

The celebrated architect Sir John Soane built this in 1812 as his own house. It now contains his collection of antiquities, sculpture and paintings. included among which are *The Rake's Progress* paintings by William Hogarth.

Location: OS Ref. TQ308 816. E of Kingsway, S of High Holborn.

Opening Times: Tue - Sat, 10am - 5pm. 6 - 9pm, first Tue of the month. Closed BHs & 24 Dec.

Admission: Free. Groups must book.

SOUTHSIDE HOUSE

Tel: 020 8946 7643

Wimbledon Common, London SW19 4RJ

Owner: The Pennington-Mellor-Munthe Charity Trust **Contact:** Desmond Sanford

Late C17th and C18th house with intriguing contents and collections.

Location: OS Ref. TQ234 706. Near King's College School on Wimbledon Common.

Opening Times: 3 Jan - 21 Jun: BH Mons, Weds, Sats & Suns, 2 - 4pm. Guided tours at 2pm, 3pm & 4pm lasting approx $1^1/_2$ hrs. Groups upon written application.

Admission: Adult £5, Child (11 - 16 yrs) £3.

SOUTHWARK CATHEDRAL

Tel: 020 7367 6700 Fax: 020 7367 6725

Montague Close, Southwark, London SE1 9DA **Contact:** Mrs R Harding

London's oldest gothic building and a place of worship for over 1,000 years, St Mary Overie Priory became St Saviour's Parish Church at the Dissolution. In 1905 it became an Anglican Cathedral. It has literary connections: Gower, Chaucer, Shakespeare and Dickens, and associations with Harvard, founder of the American university. Interesting links with the Royal family over the centuries.

Location: OS Ref. TQ327 803. South side of London Bridge.

Opening Times: Daily: 8.30am - 6pm. Sun services: 9am, 11am and 3pm. Weekday services: 8am, 12.30pm and 5.30pm. Sat services, 9am and 4pm.

Admission: Recommended donation of £2.50 per person.

Indoor photography with permit.  Partially suitable. By arrangement. No parking. Guide dogs only.

STRAWBERRY HILL

ST MARY'S, STRAWBERRY HILL, WALDEGRAVE ROAD, TWICKENHAM TW1 4SX

Contact: *The Conference Office*

Tel: 020 8240 4114/020 8240 4311/020 8240 4044

Horace Walpole converted a modest house at Strawberry Hill into his own version of a gothic fantasy. It is widely regarded as the first substantial building of the Gothic Revival and as such is internationally known and admired. A century later Lady Frances Waldegrave added a magnificent wing to Walpole's original structure. Lady Waldegrave's suite of rooms can be hired for weddings, corporate functions and conferences. Please telephone for details.

Location: OS Ref. TQ158 722. Off A310 between Twickenham & Teddington.

Opening Times: Easter - Oct: Suns. Please tel: 020 8240 4224 for opening times or to make an appointment 020 8240 4114.

Admission: Adult £4.75, OAP £4.25. Group bookings: £4.25.

Conferences.  

SPENCER HOUSE

See page 125 for full page entry.

SUTTON HOUSE

Tel: 020 8986 2264

2 & 4 Homerton High Street, Hackney, London E9 6JQ

Owner: The National Trust **Contact:** The Property Manager

A rare example of a Tudor red-brick house, built in 1535 by Sir Rafe Sadleir, Principal Secretary of State for Henry VIII, with 18th century alterations and later additions. Recent restoration has revealed many 16th century details, even in rooms of later periods. Notable features include original linenfold panelling and 17th century wall paintings.

Location: OS Ref. TQ352 851. At the corner of Isabella Road and Homerton High St.

Opening Times: 2 Feb - 22 Nov & from 7 Feb (2001): Weds, Suns & BH Mons 11.30am - 5.30pm. Café Bar: All year: Wed - Sun & BH Mons, 11.30am - 5pm (closed 23 Dec - 9 Jan 2001).

Admission: £2.10, Child 60p, Family £4.80. Group visits by prior arrangement.

Ground floor only. WC. No parking. Tel. for details.

SYON PARK

See page 126 for full page entry.

THE TOWER BRIDGE EXPERIENCE

Tel: 020 7378 1928 Fax: 020 7357 7935

Tower Bridge, London SE1 2UP

Owner: Corporation of London **Contact:** Jo Murray

One of London's most unusual and exciting exhibitions is situated inside Tower Bridge. Animatronic characters from the Bridge's past guide you through a series of audio-visual presentations.

Location: OS Ref. TQ337 804. Adjacent to Tower of London, nearest Tube: Tower Hill.

Opening Times: Nov - Mar: 9.30am - 6pm. Apr - Oct: 10am - 6.30pm (last entry $1^1/_4$ hrs before closing). Closed 24 - 25 Dec and 19 Jan 2000.

Admission: Adult £6.15, Child (5-15)/ Conc. £4.15, Family (2+2) £15.50 (subject to a small increase in Apr).

THE TOWER OF LONDON

See page 127 for full page entry.

THE WALLACE COLLECTION

See page 128 for full page entry.

WESTMINSTER ABBEY

Tel: 020 7222 5152 Fax: 020 7233 2072

London SW1P 3PA **e-mail:** press@westminster-abbey.org **Contact:** Press Officer

Westminster Abbey is a living church that enshrines the History of the British nation.

Location: OS Ref. TQ301 795. Westminster.

Opening Times: Mon - Fri, 9am - 4.45pm (last admission 3.45pm), Sats, 9am - 2.45pm (last admission 1.45pm).

Admission: Adult £5, Child (11-16yrs) £2, Child under 11yrs Free, Student/OAP £3, Family (2+2) £10.

WESTMINSTER CATHEDRAL

Tel: 020 7798 9055 Fax: 020 7798 9090

Victoria, London SW1P 1QW

Owner: Diocese of Westminster **Contact:** Rev Mgr George Stack

The Roman Catholic Cathedral of the Archbishop of Westminster. Spectacular building in the Byzantine style, designed by J F Bentley, opened in 1903, famous for its mosaics, marble and music. Westminster Cathedral celebrated the Centenary of its foundation in 1995.

Location: OS Ref. TQ293 791. On Victoria Street, between Victoria Station and Westminster Abbey.

Opening Times: All year: 7am - 7pm. Please telephone for times at Easter & Christmas.

Admission: Free. Lift charge: Adult £2. Child £1. Family (2+4) £5.

Ground floor suitable. Prior booking required. No parking. Worksheets & tours. Guide dogs only.

Owner: The Baring Family

CONTACT

Ardington House
Wantage
Oxfordshire
OX12 8QA

Tel: 01235 821566

Fax: 01235 821151

LOCATION

OS Ref. SU432 883

12m S of Oxford,
12m N of Newbury,
$2^1/_2$ m E of Wantage.

CONFERENCE/FUNCTION		
ROOM	SIZE	MAX CAPACITY
Music Room		45

ARDINGTON HOUSE
Wantage

Just a few miles south of Oxford stands the hauntingly beautiful, gracefully symmetric Ardington House. Surrounded by well-kept lawns, terraced gardens and peaceful paddocks this baroque house is still the private home of the Baring family. You'll find it in the village of Ardington in the lee of the Berkshire Downs close to the Ridgeway, the historic path that runs along the top of the Downs linking the Thames Valley to the Kennet.

Its rooms to the south look across the garden and grazing horses to the river, well known to enthusiastic fly fisherman. To the front is an immaculately tended lawn, ideal for croquet and enjoyed by different generations of the Baring family as they grew up in this beautiful setting. Sir John Betjeman, one of the best loved poets of recent times, thought highly of this gracious home. But it doesn't end there because one of the greatest joys in this impressive home is the wood panelled dining room with its large oil painting of the father of the founder of this famous banking family.

The astonishing mixture of history, warmth and style you'll find at Ardington truly does place it in a class of its own.

OPENING TIMES

1 - 5 & 8 - 12 May

1 - 4, 7 - 11 &
14 - 17 August

Also BH Mons

2.30 - 4.30pm.

ADMISSION

House and Gardens
Adult £3.50

 By arrangement.

 By members of the family.

Guide dogs only.

SPECIAL EVENTS

Please telephone for details.

South East England

Owner:
The Duke of Marlborough

CONTACT

Nicholas Day
Blenheim Palace
Woodstock
OX20 1PX

Tel: 01993 811091

Fax: 01993 813527

e-mail: administration @blenheimpalace.com

LOCATION

OS Ref. SP441 161

From London, M40, A44 ($1^1/_2$ hrs), 8m NW of Oxford. London 63m Birmingham 54.

Air: Heathrow 60m. Birmingham 54m.

Coach: From London (Victoria) to Oxford.

Rail: Oxford Station.

Bus: Oxford (Cornmarket) - Woodstock.

CONFERENCE/FUNCTION		
ROOM	SIZE	MAX CAPACITY
Orangery		200
Great Hall	70' x 40'	150
Saloon	50' x 30'	72
with Great Hall		450
with Great Hall & Library		750
Library	180' x 30'	300

BLENHEIM PALACE

Woodstock

BLENHEIM PALACE, home of the 11th Duke of Marlborough and birthplace of Sir Winston Churchill, was built between 1705-1722 for John Churchill, 1st Duke of Marlborough, in grateful recognition of his magnificent victory at the Battle of Blenheim in 1704. One of England's largest private houses, it was built in the baroque style by Sir John Vanbrugh and is considered his masterpiece. The land and £240,000 were given by Queen Anne and a grateful nation.

Blenheim's wonderful interior reveals striking contrasts – from the lofty Great Hall to gilded state rooms and the majestic Long Library. The superb collection includes fine paintings, furniture, bronzes and the famous Marlborough Victories tapestries. The five-room Churchill Exhibition includes his birth room.

GARDENS

The Palace grounds reflect the evolution of grand garden design. Of the original work by Queen Anne's gardener, Henry Wise, only the Walled Garden remains; but dominating all is the superb landscaping of 'Capability' Brown. Dating from 1764, his work includes the lake, park and gardens. Achille Duchêne, employed by the 9th Duke, subsequently recreated the Great Court and built the Italian Garden on the east and the Water Terraces on the west of the Palace. Recently the Pleasure Gardens complex has been developed. This includes the Marlborough Maze, Herb Garden, Adventure Playground, Butterfly House and Putting Greens.

OPENING TIMES

SUMMER

Palace

Mid March - 31 October
Daily: 10.30am-5.30pm
Last admission 4.45pm.

WINTER

Park only

1 November - Mid March
The Duke of Marlborough reserves the right to close the Palace or Park or to amend admission prices without notice.

ADMISSION

(Prices: 13.3.00 - 31.10.00)

- Palace Tour and Churchill Exhibition
- Park
- Garden
- Butterfly House
- Herb & Lavender Garden
- Motor Launch
- Train
- Car or coach parking
- Maze & Adventure Play Area and rowing boat hire optional extras

Adult	£9.00
Child (5 - 15 yrs.)	£4.50
Child (16 & 17 yrs.)	£7.00
OAP	£7.00
Family	£22.50

Groups

Adult	£7.50
OAP/Student	£6.50
Child (5 - 15 yrs.)	£4.00
Child (16 & 17 yrs.)	£6.50

- Blenheim Park, Butterfly House, Train, Parking, (Maze & Adventure Play Area and rowing boat hire optional extras).

Coaches*	£30.00
Cars*	£6.00
Adult**	£2.00
Child**	£1.00

- Private visits† £15.00

* Including occupants.
** Pedestrians.
† By appointment only. Min. charge of £375 (mornings and £525 (evenings).

BLENHEIM PALACE

The second State Room.

The Mermaid Fountain in the Italian Garden.

Five Shops. Filming, Equestrian Events, Craft Fairs. Will consider any proposals (contact Admin Office). Lake (Rowing Boats for hire), Motor Launch trips, Train rides. Photography outside only.

Corporate hospitality, including dinners and receptions. The Orangery seats 200 for luncheon or dinner, throughout the year together with the Spencer Churchill Conference Room. For the Palace contact the Administrator, & for the Orangery contact Town and County Catering tel: 01993 813874/811274.

Visitors may alight at the Palace entrance then park in allocated area. WCs.

2 Restaurants, 2 Cafeterias. Group capacity 150. Groups can book for afternoon tea, buffets and luncheon. Menus on request. Contact Town and County Catering for further info: 01993 813874/811274.

Included in the cost of entry. Private and language tours may be pre-booked.

Unlimited for cars and coaches. Advise Administrator's office for groups of over 100. Coaches/groups welcome without pre-booking. 'Notes for Party Organisers' available by post.

Blenheim has held the Sandford Award for an outstanding contribution to Heritage Education since 1982. Operated by a very experienced headmaster, education groups may study virtually all subjects at all four stages of the National Curriculum as well as have general interest or leisure visits. Tourism Studies (all levels) available.

Dogs on leads in Park. Guide dogs for the blind & hearing dogs for the deaf only in house and garden.

South East England

Owner:
Lord Saye & Sele

CONTACT

Mrs G M Cozens
Broughton Castle
Banbury
Oxfordshire
OX15 5EB

Tel/Fax: 01295 276070

Tel/Fax: 01869 337126

e-mail: admin@broughtoncastle.demon.co.uk

LOCATION

OS Ref. SP418 382

Broughton Castle is 2 1/2m SW of Banbury Cross on the B4035, Shipston-on-Stour - Banbury Road. Easily accessible from Stratford-on-Avon, Warwick, Oxford, Burford and the Cotswolds. M40/J11.

Rail: From London/ Birmingham to Banbury.

BROUGHTON CASTLE
Banbury

BROUGHTON CASTLE is essentially a family home lived in by Lord and Lady Saye and Sele and their family.

The original medieval Manor House, of which much remains today, was built in about 1300 by Sir John de Broughton. It stands on an island site surrounded by a 3-acre moat. The Castle was greatly enlarged between 1550 and 1600, at which time it was embellished with magnificent plaster ceilings, splendid panelling and fine fireplaces.

In the 17th century William, 8th Lord Saye and Sele, played a leading role in national affairs. He opposed Charles I's efforts to rule without Parliament and Broughton became a secret meeting place for the King's opponents.

During the Civil War William raised a regiment and he and his four sons all fought at the nearby Battle of Edgehill. After the battle the Castle was besieged and captured.

Arms and armour for the Civil War and from other periods are displayed in the Great Hall. Visitors may also see the gatehouse, gardens and park together with the nearby 14th century Church of St Mary, in which there are many family tombs, memorials and hatchments.

GARDENS

The garden area consists of mixed herbaceous and shrub borders containing many old roses. In addition, there is a formal walled garden with beds of roses surrounded by box hedging and lined by more mixed borders.

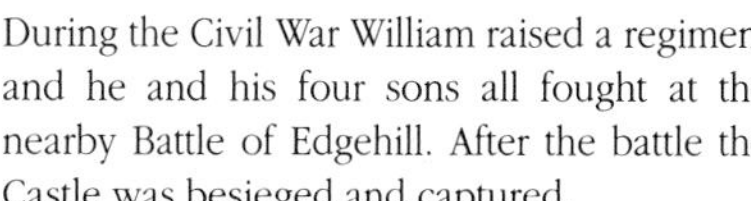

OPENING TIMES

SUMMER

21 May - 13 September
Weds & Suns
2 - 5pm.

Also Thurs in July and August and all Bank Holiday Suns and Bank Holiday Mons (including Easter)
2 - 5pm.

Groups welcome on any day and at any time throughout the year by appointment.

ADMISSION

Adult	£4.00
Child (5-15yrs)	£2.00
OAP	£3.50
Groups*	
Adult	£3.50
Child (5-15yrs)	£1.75
OAP	£3.50

* Min payment: adults £70, children £50.

Filming, product launches, advertising features, corporate events in park. Photography permitted for personal use. Brief guidance notes available in French, Spanish, Dutch, Italian, Japanese, German, Polish, Greek & Russian.

Visitors allowed vehicle access to main entrance.

Tea/coffee for guided groups if pre-booked. Other meals by arrangement.

Available to pre-booked groups at no extra charge. Not available on open days.

300 yards from the castle.

Welcome.

No dogs inside House.

Owner:
Lord & Lady Camoys

CONTACT

Lisa Severn
The Administrator
Stonor Park
Henley-on-Thames
Oxfordshire
RG9 6HF

Tel/Fax: 01491 638587

LOCATION

OS Ref. SU743 893

1 hr from London, M4/J8/9. A4130 to Henley-on-Thames. On B480 NW of Henley. A4130/B480 to Stonor.

Bus: 3m along the Oxford - London route.

Rail: Henley-on-Thames Station 5m.

STONOR
Henley-on-Thames

STONOR, family home of Lord and Lady Camoys and the Stonor family for over 800 years, is set in a valley in the beautiful woods of the Chiltern Hills and surrounded by an extensive deer park.

The earliest part of the house dates from the 12th century, whilst most of the house was built in the 14th century. Early use of brick in Tudor times resulted in a more uniform façade concealing the earlier buildings, and changes to the windows and the roof in the 18th century reflect the Georgian appearance still apparent today.

Inside, the house shows strong Gothic decoration, also from the 18th century, and contains many items of rare furniture, sculptures, bronzes, tapestries, paintings and portraits of the family from Britain, Europe and America.

The Catholic Chapel used continuously through the Reformation is sited close by a pagan stone circle. In 1581 Stonor served as a sanctuary for St Edmund Campion, and an exhibition at the house features his life and work.

John Steane says of Stonor – *'If I had to suggest to a visitor who had only one day to sample the beauties of Oxfordshire I would suggest a visit to Stonor and a walk through its delectable park'.*

GARDENS

Extensive gardens enclosed at the rear of the house face south and have fine views over the park. The springtime display of daffodils is particularly outstanding. Fine irises and roses.

Filming, craft fairs, photo shoots, car displays, product promotion, clay pigeon shooting. Evening tours and buffet suppers by prior arrangement. Lectures can be given on the property, its contents and history. No smoking and no photography in house.

Available.

Visitors may alight at the entrance before parking. Ramp access to gardens, tearoom & shop.

Open as house. Lunches, teas & suppers by arrangement for groups (20+). Licensed.

Outside normal hours for 20 - 60 people per tour. Tour time: $1^1/_4$ hrs. Single payments for group bookings.

100 yds away.

Welcome. Lectures and guided tours by arrangement.

In grounds, on leads.

OPENING TIMES

Suns: April - September 2 - 5.30pm.

Mons: (Bank Holiday Mondays only): 2 - 5.30pm

Weds: July & August only: 2 - 5.30pm.

Sats: 27 May & 26 Aug only: 2 - 5.30pm.

Groups by appointment April - September.

ADMISSION

House, Garden & Chapel
Adult £4.50
Child (under 14yrs).....Free
Groups* (12+)............£4.00

Garden and Chapel
Adult £2.50

* Min. 12 persons by a single payment. Private guided tours £5pp, min. 20 persons and by a single payment.

School groups £2.50 per head, 1 teacher for every 10 children admitted free.

ARDINGTON HOUSE

See page 139 for full page entry.

BLENHEIM PALACE

See pages 140/141 for double page entry.

BROOK COTTAGE

Tel: 01295 670303 / 670590

Well Lane, Alkerton, Nr Banbury OX15 6NL

Owner/Contact: Mrs David Hodges

4 acre hillside garden. Wide variety of trees, shrubs and herbaceous plants.

Location: OS Ref. SP378 428. 6m NW of Banbury, 1/2 m SW of A422 Banbury to Stratford-upon-Avon road.

Opening Times: 24 Apr - 27 Oct: Mon - Fri, 9am - 6pm. Evenings, weekends and all group visits by appointment.

Admission: Adult £2.50, OAP £2, Child Free. In aid of National Gardens Scheme.

BROUGHTON CASTLE

See page 142 for full page entry.

BUSCOT OLD PARSONAGE

Tel: 01793 762209

Buscot, Faringdon, Oxfordshire SN7 8DQ **e-mail:** tbcjaw@smtp.ntrust.org.uk

Owner: The National Trust **Contact:** Estate Office

An early 18th century house of Cotswold stone on the bank of the Thames with a small garden.

Location: OS Ref. SU231 973. 2m from Lechlade, 4m N of Faringdon on A417.

Opening Times: Apr - end Oct, Weds, 2 - 6pm by written appointment with tenant.

Admission: £1.20. Not suitable for groups.

BUSCOT PARK

Tel: 01367 240786 **e-mail:** estbuscot@aol.com

Buscot, Faringdon, Oxfordshire SN7 8BU

Owner: The National Trust **Contact:** Lord Faringdon

A late 18th century house with pleasure gardens, set within a park.

Location: OS Ref. SU239 973. Between Lechlade and Faringdon on A417.

Opening Times: House:1 Apr - 29 Sept: Wed - Fri. Easter Sat & Sun, plus weekends of 8 - 9 Apr, 13 - 14 & 27 - 28 May, 10 - 11 & 24 - 25 Jun, 8 - 9 & 22 - 23 Jul, 12 - 13 & 26 - 27 Aug, 9 - 10 & 23 - 24 Sept: 2 - 6pm, last admission to house 5.30pm. Grounds: 1 Apr - 29 Sept: Mon - Fri (closed BH Mons) and same weekends as house, 2 - 6pm.

Admission: House & Grounds £4.40, Grounds only £3.30. Children half price. Groups must book in writing, or by fax or e-mail.

 Not suitable.

CHASTLETON HOUSE

Infoline/Fax: 01608 674355

e-mail: tchgen@smtp.ntrust.org.uk

Chastleton, Moreton-in-Marsh, Gloucestershire GL56 0SU

Owner: The National Trust **Contact:** The Custodian

One of England's finest and most complete Jacobean houses, dating from 1612. It is filled with a mixture of rare and everyday objects and the atmosphere of four hundred years of continuous occupation by one family. The gardens have a Jacobean layout and the rules of modern croquet were codified here.

Location: OS Ref. SP248 291. 6m ENE of Stow-on-the-Wold. 1 1/2 m NW of A436. Approach only from A436 between the A44 (W of Chipping Norton) and Stow.

Opening Times: 1 Apr - 28 Oct: Wed - Sat. Apr - Sept: 1 - 5pm, last admission 4pm. Oct: 1 - 4pm, last admission 3pm. Admission for all visitors (including NT members) by timed tickets booked in advance. Bookings can be made by letter to the ticket office or tel: 01494 755572. Tue - Fri, 1.30 - 4.30pm from 1 Feb 2000.

Admission: Adult £5.10, Child £2.55. Family £12.75. Groups (11-25) by written appointment.

Not suitable. 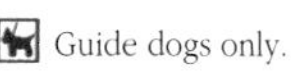 Coaches limited to 25 seat minibuses. Guide dogs only.

CHRIST CHURCH CATHEDRAL

Tel: 01865 276154

The Sacristy, The Cathedral, Oxford OX1 1DP **Contact:** Mr Jim Godfrey

12th century Norman Church, formerly an Augustinian monastery, given Cathedral status in 16th century by Henry VIII.

Location: OS Ref. SP515 059. Just S of city centre, off St Aldates. Entry via Meadow Gate visitors' entrance on S side of college.

Opening Times: Mon - Sat: 9am - 5pm. Suns: 1 - 5pm, closed Christmas Day. Services: weekdays 7.20am, 6pm. Suns: 8am, 10am, 11.15am & 6pm.

Admission: Adult £3, Child under 5 Free, Conc. £2, Family £6.

WWW Website Index PAGE 46

COGGES MANOR FARM MUSEUM

Tel: 01993 772602 **Fax:** 01993 703056

Church Lane, Witney, Oxfordshire OX8 6LA

Administered by: West Oxfordshire District Council **Contact:** Ms Catherine Mason

The Manor House dates from the 13th century, rooms are furnished to show life at the end of the 19th century. Daily cooking on the Victorian range. On the first floor, samples of original wallpapers and finds from under the floorboards accompany the story of the history of the house. In one of the rooms, rare 17th century painted panelling survives. Farm buildings including two 18th century barns, stables and a thatched ox byre, display farm implements. Traditional breeds of farm animals, hand-milking demonstration each day. Seasonal produce from the walled kitchen garden sold in the museum shop.

Location: OS Ref. SP362 097. Just off A40 Oxford - Burford Road. Access by footbridge from centre of Witney, 600 yds. Vehicle access from S side of B4022 near E end of Witney.

Opening Times: 28 Mar - 29 Oct: Tue - Fri & BH Mons, 10.30am - 5.30pm; Sat & Sun, 12 - 5.30pm. Closed Good Fri. Early closing in Oct.

Admission: Adult £4, Child £2, Conc. £2.50 Family (2+2) £11.00

Ground floor suitable. WCs. In grounds, on leads.

DEDDINGTON CASTLE

Tel: 01732 778000

Deddington, Oxfordshire

Owner: English Heritage **Contact:** The South East Regional Office

Extensive earthworks concealing the remains of a 12th century castle which was ruined as early as the 14th century.

Location: OS Ref. SP471 316. S of B4031 on E side of Deddington, 17m N of Oxford on A423. 5m S of Banbury.

Opening Times: Any reasonable time.

Admission: Free.

DITCHLEY PARK

Tel: 01608 677346

Enstone, Oxfordshire OX7 4ER

Owner: Ditchley Foundation **Contact:** Brigadier Christopher Galloway

The most important house by James Gibbs with most distinguished interiors by Henry Flitcroft and William Kent.

Location: OS Ref. SP391 214. 2m NE from Charlbury. 13m NW of Oxford.

Opening Times: Visits only by prior arrangement with the Bursar.

Admission: Groups: £5 (minimum charge £40).

Nadia MacKenzie.

Chastleton House, Oxfordshire.

FAWLEY COURT

HISTORIC HOUSE & MUSEUM, HENLEY-ON-THAMES RG9 3AE

Owner: *Marian Fathers* ***Contact:*** *The Secretary*

Tel: 01491 574917 **Fax:** 01491 411587

Designed by Christopher Wren, built in 1684 for Col W Freeman, decorated by Grinling Gibbons and by James Wyatt. The Museum consists of a library, various documents of the Polish Kings, a very well-preserved collection of historical sabres and many memorable military objects of the Polish army. Paintings, early books, numismatic collections, arms and armour.

Location: OS Ref. SU765 842. 1m N of Henley-on-Thames E to A4155 to Marlow.

Opening Times: Mar - Oct: Weds, Thurs & Suns, 2 - 5pm. Other dates by arrangement. Closed Easter and Whitsuntide weeks and Nov - Feb.

Admission: House, Museum & Gardens: Adult £4, Child £1.50, Conc. £3. Groups (15+) £3.

Ground floor & grounds suitable. WC.  Guide dogs only.

GREAT COXWELL BARN

Tel: 01793 762209

Great Coxwell, Faringdon, Oxfordshire **e-mail:** tbcjaw@smtp.ntrust.org.uk

Owner: The National Trust **Contact:** The Administrator

A 13th century monastic barn, stone built with stone tiled roof, which has an interesting timber construction.

Location: OS Ref. SU269 940. 2m SW of Faringdon between A420 and B4019.

Opening Times: All year: daily at reasonable hours.

Admission: 50p.

GREYS COURT

Infoline: 01494 755564 **Tel:** 01491 628529

Rotherfield Greys, Henley-on-Thames, Oxfordshire RG9 4PG

e-mail: tgrgen@smtp.ntrust.org.uk

Owner: The National Trust **Contact:** The Custodian

Rebuilt in the 16th century and added to in the 17th, 18th and 19th centuries, the house is set amid the remains of the courtyard walls and towers of a 14th century fortified house. A Tudor donkey wheel, well-house and an ice house are still intact, and the garden contains Archbishop's Maze, inspired by Archbishop Runcie's enthronement speech in 1980.

Location: OS Ref. SU725 834. 3m W of Henley-on-Thames, E of B481.

Opening Times: 1 Apr - end Sept: House; Wed - Fri & BH Mons, 2 - 6pm (closed Good Fri) Garden: daily Tue - Sat & BH Mons 2 - 6pm (closed Good Fri) Last admission 5.30pm.

Admission: House & Garden: Adult £4.60, Child £2.30, Family £11.50. Garden only: £3.20, Family £8. Coach parties must book in advance.

Grounds partly suitable. WCs.  In car park only, on leads.

Open all Year Index

PAGE 52

KINGSTON BAGPUIZE HOUSE

ABINGDON, OXFORDSHIRE OX13 5AX

Owner: *Mr & Mrs Francis Grant* ***Contact:*** *Mrs Francis Grant*

Tel: 01865 820259 **Fax:** 01865 821659

Beautiful manor house and family home. It has a cantilevered staircase and panelled rooms with some good furniture and pictures. Set in mature parkland, the gardens, including shrub border and woodland garden, contain a notable collection of trees, shrubs, perennials and bulbs. Available for special events, wedding receptions and filming. Facilities for small conferences.

Location: OS Ref. SU408 981. In Kingston Bagpuize village, off A415 Abingdon to Witney road S of A415/A420 intersection. Abingdon 5m, Oxford 9m.

Opening Times: 12, 26 Mar; 8, 9, 22, 23, 24, 29, 30 Apr; 1, 13, 14, 27, 28, 29 May; 10, 11, 25 Jun; 8, 9, 22, 23 Jul; 9, 12, 13, 26, 27, 28 Aug; 6, 9, 10, 23, 24 Sept; 8, 22 Oct. Times: 2 - 5.30pm (tours of house 2.30 - 4.45pm). House: guided tour only. Last entry to garden 5pm.

Admission: House & Garden: Adult £3.50, Child £2.50, (children under 5yrs not admitted to house), OAP £3. Gardens: £1.50. (child under 5yrs Free). Groups (20-100) by appointment throughout the year, prices on request.

No photography. Grounds suitable. WCs. Obligatory.

KINGSTONE LISLE PARK

Norman Hudson

KINGSTONE LISLE PARK, WANTAGE, OXON OX12 9QG

Owner: *Mr James Lonsdale* ***Contact:*** *The Secretary*

Tel: 01367 820599 **Fax:** 01367 820749

A sensational Palladian house, set in 140 acres of parkland. Superb views up to the Lambourn Downs. Three lakes beside the house complete this very attractive landscape. The hall, in the style of Sir John Soane, gives a strong impression of entering an Italian palazzo with beautiful ornate plaster ceilings, columns and figurines. In complete contrast the inner hall becomes the classical English country house, the most exciting feature being the Flying Staircase winding its way up, totally unsupported. A fine collection of art, furniture, clocks, glass and needlework, together with the architecture, evoke admiration for the craftsmanship that has existed in Britain over the centuries. 12 acres of gardens. Suitable for films, wedding receptions, functions and 'fun days'.

Location: OS Ref. SU326 876. M4/J14.

Opening Times: Coach parties only, strictly by appointment.

Admission: Telephone for details.

 In grounds, on leads. 

MAPLEDURHAM HOUSE & WATERMILL

MAPLEDURHAM, READING RG4 7TR
Owner: *The Mapledurham Trust* ***Contact:*** *Mrs Lola Andrews*

Tel: 01189 723350 **Fax:** 01189 724016 **e-mail:** mtrust1997@aol.com

Late 16th century Elizabethan home of the Blount family. Original plaster ceilings, great oak staircase, fine collection of paintings and a private chapel in Strawberry Hill Gothick added in 1797. Interesting literary connections with Alexander Pope, Galsworthy's *Forsyte Saga* and Kenneth Grahame's *Wind in the Willows*. 15th century watermill fully restored producing flour and bran which is sold in the giftshop.

Location: OS Ref. SU670 767. N of River Thames. 4m NW of Reading, 1½ m W of A4074.

Opening Times: Easter - Sept: Sats, Suns & BHs, 2 - 5.30. Last admission 5pm. Midweek parties by arrangement only (Tue - Thur).

Admission: Please call 01189 723350 for details.

Grounds suitable. WCs. Guide dogs only.

11 holiday cottages available all year.

MINSTER LOVELL HALL & DOVECOTE

Tel: 01732 778000

Witney, Oxfordshire

Owner: English Heritage **Contact:** The South East Regional Office

The ruins of Lord Lovell's 15th century manor house stand in a lovely setting on the banks of the River Windrush.

Location: OS Ref. SP324 114. Adjacent to Minster Lovell Church, ½ m NE of village. 3m W of Witney off A40.

Opening Times: Any reasonable time.

Admission: Free.

PRIORY COTTAGES 

Tel: 01793 762209 **e-mail:** tbcjaw@smtp.ntrust.org.uk

1 Mill Street, Steventon, Abingdon, Oxfordshire OX13 6SP

Owner: The National Trust **Contact:** Coleshill Office

Former monastic buildings, converted into two houses. South Cottage contains the Great Hall of the original priory.

Location: OS Ref. SU466 914. 4m S of Abingdon, on B4017 off A34 at Abingdon West or Milton interchange on corner of The Causeway and Mill Street, entrance in Mill Street.

Opening Times: The Great Hall in South Cottage only: Apr - end Sept: Weds, 2 - 6pm by written appointment.

Admission: £1.

ROUSHAM HOUSE

Tel: 01869 347110/0860 360407

Nr Steeple Aston, Bicester, Oxfordshire OX6 3QX

Owner/Contact: Charles Cottrell-Dormer Esq

Rousham represents the first stage of English landscape design and remains almost as William Kent (1685 - 1748) left it. One of the few gardens of this date to have escaped alteration. Includes Venus' Vale, Townesend's Building, seven-arched Praeneste, the Temple of the Mill and a sham ruin known as the 'Eyecatcher'. The house was built in 1635 by Sir Robert Dormer.

Location: OS Ref. SP477 242. E of A4260, 12m N of Oxford, S of B4030, 7m W of Bicester.

Opening Times: House: Apr - Sept: Wed, Sun and BH Mon 2 - 4.30pm. Garden: All year: daily, 10am - 4.30pm.

Admission: House: £3. Garden: Adult £3. No children under 15yrs.

Compulsory.

MILTON MANOR HOUSE

MILTON, ABINGDON, OXFORDSHIRE OX14 4EN
Owner: *Anthony Mockler-Barrett Esq* ***Contact:*** *Gwendoline Marsh*

Tel: 01235 862321 **Fax:** 01235 831287

Extraordinarily beautiful family house traditionally designed by Inigo Jones, with a celebrated Gothick library (pictured on right) and a beautiful Catholic chapel. Pleasant and relaxed atmosphere. Park with fine old trees, attractive walled garden, two lakes, stables (pony rides available), Shire horse cart-rides, rare-breed pigs, tame lambs and pygmy goats, other animals. Woodland walk. Plenty to see and enjoy for all ages. Also wedding receptions, filming, select conferences, etc.

Location: OS Ref. SU485 924. Just off A34, village and house signposted, 9m S of Oxford, 15m N of Newbury. 3m from Abingdon and Didcot.

Opening Times: Every Saturday and Sunday from Easter to the end of August plus all Bank Holiday Mondays, 12 noon - 5pm. Guided tours of the house at 2, 3 & 4pm.

Admission: House & Gardens: Adult £4, Child £2. House: Guided tours only. Grounds only: Adult £2.50, Child £1. Free parking. Groups by arrangement throughout the year. For group bookings only please write or phone 01235 831871.

   Guide dogs only. 

RYCOTE CHAPEL

Tel: 01732 778000 (regional office)

Rycote, Oxfordshire

Owner: English Heritage **Contact:** South East Regional Office

A 15th century chapel with exquisitely carved and painted woodwork. It has many intriguing features, including two roofed pews and a musicians' gallery.

Location: OS165 Ref. SP667 046. 3m SW of Thame, off A329. 1½ m NE of M40/J7.

Opening Times: 1 Apr - 30 Sept: Fri - Sun & BHs, 2 - 6pm.

Admission: Adult £1.60, Child 80p, Conc. £1.20. 15% discount for groups (11+).

STANTON HARCOURT MANOR

STANTON HARCOURT, Nr WITNEY, OXFORDSHIRE OX8 1RJ

Owner/Contact: *The Hon Mrs Gascoigne*

Tel: 01865 881928 **Answerphone / Fax:** 01865 880117

12 acres of garden with Great Fish Pond and Stew Ponds provide tranquil surroundings for the unique mediaeval buildings, Old Kitchen (Alexander) Pope's Tower and Domestic Chapel. The house, a fine example of a very early unfortified Manor House built to house the Harcourt family and its retainers, is still maintained as the family home.

Location: OS Ref. SP416 056. 9m W of Oxford, 5m SE of Witney off B4449 between Eynsham and Standlake.

Opening Times: 23, 24 & 30 Apr; 1, 11, 14, 25, 28 & 29 May; 8, 11, 22 & 25 Jun; 6, 9, 20 & 23 Jul; 3, 6, 17, 20, 24, 27 & 28 Aug; 7, 10, 21 & 24 Sept, 2 - 6pm.

Admission: House & Garden: Adult £5, Child (under 12yrs)/OAP £3. Garden: Adult £3, Child (under 12yrs) /OAP £2. Group visits by prior arrangement.

Limited. Guide dogs in grounds.

STONOR

See page 143 for full page entry.

SWALCLIFFE BARN

Tel: 01295 788278

Swalcliffe Village, Banbury, Oxfordshire **Contact:** Jeffrey Demmar

15th century half cruck barn, houses agricultural and trade vehicles.

Location: OS Ref. SP378 378. 6m W of Banbury Cross on B4035.

Opening Times: Easter - end Oct: Suns & BHs, 2 - 5pm.

Admission: Free.

The Kitchen at Cogges Manor Farm Museum, Oxfordshire.

UNIVERSITY OF OXFORD BOTANIC GARDEN

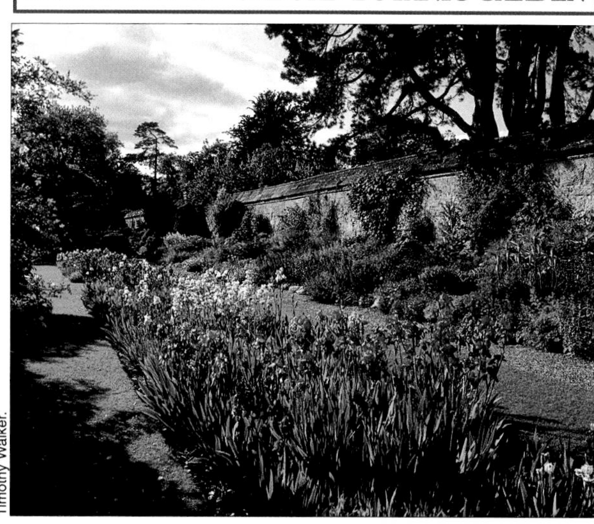

Timothy Walker.

ROSE LANE, OXFORD OX1 4AX

Owner: *University of Oxford* ***Contact:*** *Timothy Walker*

Tel/Fax: 01865 276920 **e-mail:** postmaster@botanic-garden.ox.ac.uk

Founded in 1621; oldest botanic garden in Britain; 8,000 plants from all over the world; original walled garden; many trees over 200 years old; herbaceous borders, recently renovated rock and bog gardens; national collection of euphorbias, tropical glasshouses including a 100 year old cacti and waterlillies; a peaceful oasis in the city centre.

Location: OS Ref. SP520 061. E end of High Street, on the banks of the River Cherwell.

Opening Times: Apr - Sept: 9am - 5pm (glasshouses: 10am - 4.30pm). Oct - Mar: 9am - 4.30pm (glasshouses: 10am - 4pm). Closed 25 Dec & Good Fri. Last admission 4.15pm.

Admission: Adult £2, Child (under 12ys) Free, Student £2. (Apr - Aug).

WCs for disabled only. By arrangement. No parking. Guide dogs only.

WATERPERRY GARDENS

Tel: 01844 339226 **Fax:** 01844 339883

Nr Wheatley, Oxfordshire OX33 1JZ

Owner: School of Economic Science **Contact:** P Maxwell

The gardens at Waterperry are within easy reach of Oxford and for the experienced gardener, the novice or those who have no garden of their own – here is a chance to enjoy the order of careful cultivation.

Location: OS Ref. SP630 063. Oxford 9m, London 52m, M40 J8, Birmingham 42m, M40 J8a. Well signposted locally.

Opening Times: Daily, 9am - 5pm (except 20 - 23 Jul when open only to Art in Action visitors. Teashop closed 19 - 24 Jul.)

Admission: Adult £3.40, Child £1.90, OAP £2.90. Groups (20+) £2.90, Child £1.60.

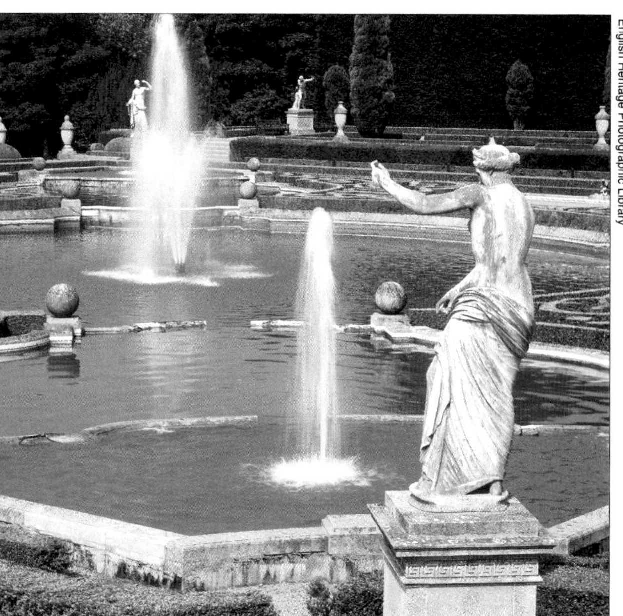

English Heritage Photographic Library

Blenheim Palace Water Garden, Oxfordshire.

South East England

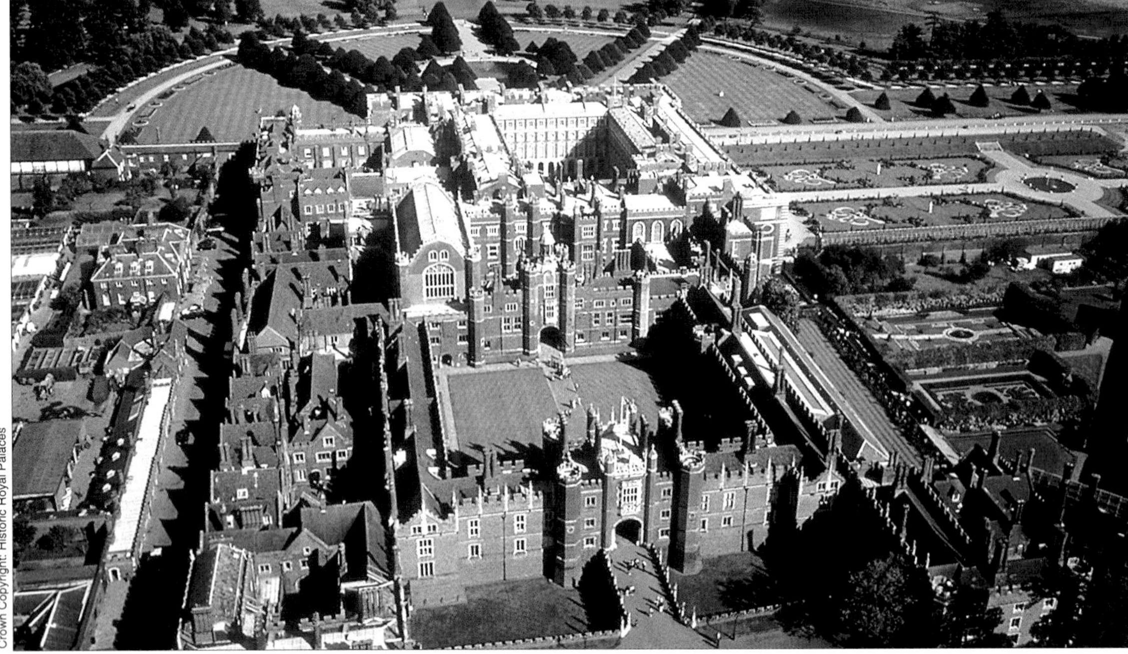

HAMPTON COURT PALACE

Surrey

Owner:

Historic Royal Palaces

CONTACT

Hampton Court Palace
Surrey
KT8 9AU

For all enquiries please telephone:

Tel: 020 8781 9500

The magnificent Hampton Court Palace has been a favoured home to some of our most famous Kings and Queens from Henry VIII to George II. Today it serves to intrigue and amaze thousands of visitors a year.

Cardinal Wolsey created it; Henry VIII, Hampton Court's most famous occupant and first royal owner, spent £62,000 enlarging it (£18 million in today's terms); Charles I was imprisoned in it; William III and Mary II commissioned Sir Christopher Wren to rebuild it; and Queen Victoria opened its doors to the public. Today the beauty of Wren's building is combined with the finest Tudor architecture in Britain.

Costumed guides bring the Palace to life, with informative tours of the sumptuous interiors of the State Apartments, giving a unique insight into the daily lives of the Kings and their courtiers, and entertaining with tales of the etiquette and gossip of court life throughout the centuries.

The Chapel Royal is a stunning example of the Palace's rich interiors, while the Great Hall is still decorated with Henry VIII's priceless Flemish tapestries. Hampton Court is also home to important Renaissance paintings from the collection of HM The Queen.

The Tudor Kitchens are the most extensive surviving 16th century kitchens in Europe. They once cooked for over a thousand people a day, and are laid out as if a feast was being prepared, with a roaring log fire and boiling cauldrons.

Hampton Court Palace is set in sixty acres of beautiful riverside Tudor, baroque and Victorian gardens, which feature the world famous maze, and the Great Vine, the oldest and largest grapevine in the world, believed to have been planted in 1768 by 'Capability' Brown.

With its five hundred years of royal history, Hampton Court Palace is a living tapestry portraying the life and times of Henry VIII to George II. It is both visually and historically interesting, and a visit here has something for everyone.

LOCATION

OS Ref. TQ155 686

From M25/J15 and A312, or M25/J12 and A308, or M25/J10 and A307.

Rail: From London Waterloo direct to Hampton Court (32 mins).

CONFERENCE/FUNCTION		
ROOM	SIZE	MAX CAPACITY
Great Hall	88'6" x 35'6"	280/400
Cartoon Gallery	22'6" x 116'	220/350
Gt Watching Chamber	66'6" x 25'	120
Painted Room	33'3" x 21'3"	60/100
Ante Room	22' x 21'6"	60/100
King's Award Chamber	60'3" x 36'4"	120/150
Public Dining Room	31'6" x 55'6"	80/150

Information Centre. No photography in house.

Available by arrangement.

Motorised buggies available at main entrance. WCs.

Licensed.

Ample for cars, coach parking nearby.

Rates on request.

In grounds, on leads. Guide dogs only in Palace.

OPENING TIMES

SUMMER

Mid March - mid October
Daily, Tue - Sun
9.30am - 6pm
Mon: 10.15am - 6pm.

WINTER

Mid October - mid March
Tue - Sun: 9.30am - 4.30pm
Mon: 10.15am - 4.30pm

Closed 24 - 26 December.

Last admission 45 mins before closing.

ADMISSION

Adult £10.00
Child (under 16yrs) ... £6.60
Child (under 5yrs) ...... Free
OAP/Conc. £7.60
Family (2+3) £29.90

SPECIAL EVENTS

For a full list of special events please telephone for details.

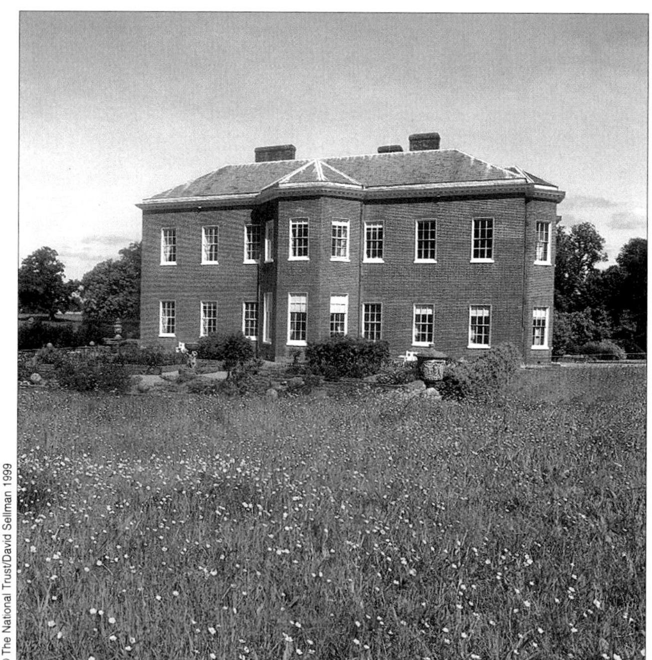

© The National Trust/David Sellman 1999

Robin Ross.

Owner: The National Trust

CONTACT

The Property Manager
Clandon Park/
Hatchlands Park
West Clandon
Guildford
Surrey
GU4 7RQ

Tel: 01483 222482

Fax: 01483 223479

e-mail: shagen@smtp.ntrust.org.uk

LOCATION

CLANDON

OS Ref. TQ042 512

At West Clandon on the A247, 3m E of Guildford.

Rail: Clandon BR 1m.

HATCHLANDS

OS Ref. TQ063 516

E of East Clandon on the A246 Guildford - Leatherhead road.

Rail: Clandon BR $2^1/_2$ m, Horsley 3m.

HATCHLANDS/CLANDON PARK

Guildford

HATCHLANDS PARK & CLANDON PARK and were built during the 18th century and are set amid beautiful parklands. They are two of the most outstanding country houses in the country and are only five minutes' drive apart.

Hatchlands Park was built in 1758 for Admiral Boscawen and is set in a beautiful Repton park offering a variety of park and woodland walks. Hatchlands contains splendid interiors by Robert Adam, decorated in appropriately nautical style. It houses the Cobbe collection, the world's largest group of early keyboard instruments associated with famous composers, eg Purcell, J C Bach, Chopin, Mahler, Elgar and Marie Antoinette. There is also a small garden by Gertrude Jekyll flowering from late May to early July.

Clandon Park is a Palladian house of dramatic contrasts; from the neo-classical marble hall to the Maori Meeting House in the garden; the opulent saloon to the old kitchen, complete with original range, below stairs. All this adds up to a fascinating insight into the different lifestyles of the ruling and serving classes in the 18th century. The house is rightly acclaimed for its remarkable collection of ceramics, textiles, furniture and its excellent restaurant. Clandon is also home to the Queen's Royal Surrey Regiment Museum.

Clive Barda, London.

The Cobbe Collection Trust holds Wednesday lunchtime and evening concerts from April to July, and from September to November in the Music Room at Hatchlands Park. Original instruments from the Cobbe Collection are played. Groups welcome. For further information and mailing list enquiries, please apply to:

The Cobbe Collection Trust
Hatchlands Park, East Clandon
Guildford GU4 7RT
Tel: 01483 211474

Harpsichord attributed to G Zenti, 1622.

Clandon Park. Tel: 01483 222482. No photography.

For wedding receptions Tel: 01483 224912.

Hatchlands suitable. Clandon partially suitable. WCs.

Licensed. Clandon: 01483 222502. H'lands: 01483 211120.

Clandon - by arrangement. Connoisseur Tours.

Hatchlands only.

Guide dogs only.

Clandon only.

OPENING TIMES

CLANDON

House
2 April - 31 October
Tue - Thur, Suns & BH Mons, Good Fri & Easter Sat
11.30am - 4.30pm.

Garden
Daily: 9am - dusk.

Museum
2 April - 31 October
Tue - Thur & Suns, BH Mons, Good Fri & Easter Sat
12 noon - 5pm.

HATCHLANDS

House
2 April - 31 October
Tue - Thur, Suns & BH Mon, Fris in August only.
2 - 5.30pm.

Park Walks
Daily (April - October)
11am - 6pm.

ADMISSION

Clandon

Adult	£4.40
Child	£2.20
Family	£11.00
Groups (Tue - Thur only)	
Adult	£3.80

Hatchlands

Adult	£4.40
Park Walks & Garden	£1.80
Child	£2.20
Park Walks & Garden	90p
Family	£11.00
Groups (Tue - Thur only)	
Adult	£3.80

Combined ticket
Clandon/Hatchlands .. £6.40

Owner:
Mr Michael More-Molyneux

CONTACT

Nicola Cheriton-Sutton
Loseley Park
Guildford
Surrey
GU3 1HS

Tel: 01483 304440

Fax: 01483 302036

LOCATION

OS Ref. SU975 471

30m S of London, leave A3 S of Guildford on to B3000. Signposted.

Bus: 1¼ m from House.

Rail: Farncombe 1½m, Guildford 2m, Godalming 3m.

Air: Heathrow 30m, Gatwick 30m.

CONFERENCE/FUNCTION		
ROOM	SIZE	MAX CAPACITY
Tithe Barn	100' x 18'	200
Marquee	sites available	
Great Hall	70' x 40'	100
Drawing Rm	40' x 30'	50
Walled Gdn	Marquee	sites

LOSELEY PARK
Guildford

LOSELEY PARK, built in 1562 by Sir William More, is a fine example of Elizabethan architecture, its mellow stone brought from the ruins of Waverley Abbey now over 850 years old. The house is set amid magnificent parkland grazed by the Loseley Jersey herd. Many visitors comment on the very friendly atmosphere of the house, it is a country house, the family home of descendants of the builder.

Furniture has been acquired by the family and includes an early 16th century Wrangelschrank beautifully inlaid with many different woods, a Queen Anne cabinet, Georgian armchairs and settee, a Hepplewhite four-poster bed and King George IV's coronation chair. The King's bedroom has Oudenarde tapestry and a carpet commemorating James I's visit.

The Christian pictures include the Henri Met de Bles triptych of the Nativity and modern mystical pictures of the living Christ, St Francis and St Bernadette. A Christian Cancer Help Centre meets twice monthly. Loseley House is available for dinners, functions and Civil weddings.

GARDEN

A magnificent Cedar of Lebanon presides over the front lawn. Parkland adjoins the lawn and a small lake adds to the beauty of Front Park. In the Walled Garden are mulberry trees, yew hedges, a grass terrace and a moat walk with herbaceous borders. Other features include an award-winning rose garden, a herb garden, flower garden, vegetable garden and idyllic fountain garden.

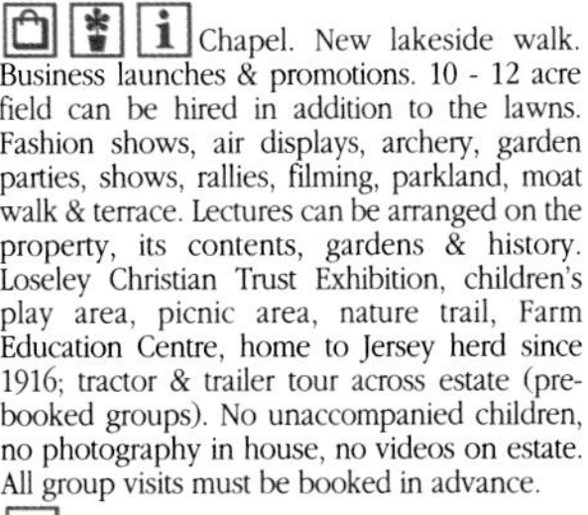

Chapel. New lakeside walk. Business launches & promotions. 10 - 12 acre field can be hired in addition to the lawns. Fashion shows, air displays, archery, garden parties, shows, rallies, filming, parkland, moat walk & terrace. Lectures can be arranged on the property, its contents, gardens & history. Loseley Christian Trust Exhibition, children's play area, picnic area, nature trail, Farm Education Centre, home to Jersey herd since 1916; tractor & trailer tour across estate (pre-booked groups). No unaccompanied children, no photography in house, no videos on estate. All group visits must be booked in advance.

Special functions, banquets & conference catering. Additional marquees for hire. Wedding receptions.

May alight at entrance to property. Access to all areas except house first floor. WCs.

Courtyard Tea Room.

Obligatory. Tour time for house, 40 mins. Trailer Tour 50 mins.

150 cars, 6 coaches. Summer overflow car park.

Loseley Park Farms Education Centre. School and group visits by prior arrangement. Holiday activity days and birthday parties.

Guide dogs only.

OPENING TIMES

SUMMER

Garden, Shop & Tea Room
1 May - 30 September
Wed - Sat & BH Mons
Also Suns in June, July & August.
11am - 5pm.

House Tours
29 May - 31 August
Wed - Sun & BH Mons
2 - 5pm. Last tour 4pm.

ALL YEAR
Tithe Barn, House and Grounds available for private/business functions, Civil weddings and receptions.

Farm Education Centre available for booked visits.

ADMISSION

House & Gardens

Adult	£5.00
Child (3-16yrs)	£3.00
Conc.	£4.00
Child (under 3yrs)	Free

Groups (15+)

Adult	£4.50
Child (3-16yrs)	£2.50
Conc.	£3.50

SPECIAL EVENTS

- **FEB 25 - 27:** Home Design Exhibition.
- **MAY 6 - 7:** Surrey Advertiser Motor Show.
- **MAY 25 - 28** Craft Fair.
- **JUN 23:** Outdoor Opera.
- **JUN 27 - 28:** WI Flower Show.
- **JULY 21 - 23:** Great Gardening Show.
- **AUG 5 - 6:** QEF Classic Car Show.
- **AUG 13:** Open Air Concert & Fireworks

CARSHALTON HOUSE

Tel: 020 8770 4781 **Fax:** 020 8770 4777

Pound Street, Carshalton, Surrey SM5 3PN

Owner: St Philomena's Catholic High School for Girls **Contact:** Ms V Murphy

A Queen Anne mansion built c1707, now in use as a school, with grounds originally laid out by Charles Bridgeman.

Location: OS Ref. TQ275 644. On A232 just S of junction with B278.

Opening Times: Please telephone for details.

Admission: Adult £3, Child under 16/Full-time students £1.50.

CLANDON/HATCHLANDS PARK

See page 149 for full page entry.

CLAREMONT LANDSCAPE GARDEN

Tel: 01372 467806

Fax: 01372 464394 **e-mail:** sclgen@smtp.ntrust.org.uk

Portsmouth Road, Esher KT10 9JG

Owner: The National Trust **Contact:** The Property Manager

One of the earliest surviving English landscape gardens, Features include a lake, island with pavilion, grotto, turf amphitheatre, viewpoints and avenues.

Location: OS Ref. TQ128 634. On S edge of Esher, on E side of A307 (no access from Esher bypass).

Opening Times: Jan - Mar, Nov - Dec: daily except Mons: 10am - 5pm or sunset if earlier. Apr - Oct: daily: Mon - Fri, 10am - 6pm, Sats, Suns & BHs, 10am - 7pm. NB: closed 11 & 12 Jul from 2pm, 13 - 16 Jul and all day 25 Dec & 1 Jan.

Admission: Adult £3.20, Child £1.60. Coach parties must book; no coach parties on Suns. Family (2+2) £8. Groups (15+), £2.70. 50p discount if using public transport.

CROYDON PALACE

Tel: 020 8688 2027

Old Palace Road, Croydon, Surrey CR0 1AX

Owner/Contact: The Whitgift Foundation

One thousand year old residence of former Archbishops of Canterbury.

Location: OS Ref. TQ320 654. 200 yds S of Croydon parish church, 400 yds W of Croydon High St.

Opening Times: 10 - 15 Apr, 29 May - 3 Jun, 10 - 15 Jul and 17 - 23 Jul.

Admission: £4.

FARNHAM CASTLE

Tel: 01252 721194 **Fax:** 01252 711283

Farnham, Surrey GU9 0AG **e-mail:** info@cibfarnham.com

Owner/Contact: The Church Commissioners

Bishop's Palace built in Norman times by Henry of Blois, with Tudor and Jacobean additions.

Location: OS Ref. SU839 474. $^1/_2$ m N of Farnham town centre on A287.

Opening Times: Please telephone for details.

Admission: Adult £2, Child, £1, Conc. £1.50 (1999 prices).

FARNHAM CASTLE KEEP

Tel: 01252 713393

Castle Hill, Farnham, Surrey GU6 0AG

Owner: English Heritage **Contact:** The Head Custodian

Used as a fortified manor by the medieval Bishops of Winchester, this motte and bailey castle has been in continuous occupation since the 12th century. You can visit the large shell-keep enclosing a mound in which are massive foundations of a Norman tower.

Location: OS Ref. SU839 474. $^1/_2$ m N of Farnham town centre on A287.

Opening Times: 1 Apr - 30 Sept: 10am - 6pm. 1 - 31 Oct, 10am - 5pm.

Admission: Adult £2, Child, £1, Conc. £1.50.

Ground floor & grounds. Free. In grounds, on leads.

GODDARDS

Tel: 01628 825920 or 01628 825925 (bookings)

Abinger Common, Dorking, Surrey RH5 6TH

Owner: The Lutyens Trust, leased to The Landmark Trust **Contact:** The Landmark Trust

Built by Sir Edwin Lutyens in 1898 - 1900 and enlarged by him in 1910. Garden by Gertrude Jekyll. Given to the Lutyens Trust in 1991 and now managed and maintained by the Landmark Trust, which let buildings for self-catering holidays. The whole house, apart from the library, is available for up to 12 people. Full details of Goddards and 167 other historic buildings available for holidays are featured in The Landmark Handbook (price £9.50 refundable against booking), from The Landmark Trust, Shottesbrooke, Maidenhead, Berkshire SL6 3SW.

Location: OS Ref. TQ120 450. $4^1/_2$ m SW of Dorking on the village green in Abinger Common. Signposted Abinger Common, Friday Street and Leith Hill from A25.

Opening Times: Strictly by appointment. Must be booked in advance, including parking, which is very limited. Visits booked for Weds afternoons from the Wed after Easter until the last Wed of Oct, between 2.30 - 5pm. Only those with pre-booked tickets will be admitted.

Admission: £3. Tickets available from Mrs Baker on 01306 730871, Mon - Fri, 9am & 6pm. Visitors will have access to part of the garden and house only.

Goddards, Surrey.

HAMPTON COURT PALACE

See page 148 for full page entry.

Historic Royal Palaces 1999.

Hampton Court Palace, Surrey.

HATCHLANDS/CLANDON PARK

See page 149 for full page entry.

HONEYWOOD HERITAGE CENTRE

Tel: 020 8770 4297 **Fax:** 020 8770 4777

Honeywood Walk, Carshalton, Surrey SM5 3NX

Owner: London Borough of Sutton **Contact:** The Curator

A 17th century listed building next to the picturesque Carshalton Ponds, containing displays on many aspects of the history of the London Borough of Sutton plus a changing programme of exhibitions and events on a wide range of subjects. Attractive garden at rear.

Location: OS Ref. TQ279 646. On A232 approximately 4m W of Croydon.

Opening Times: Wed - Fri, 10am - 5pm. Sat, Suns & BH Mons, 10am - 5.30pm. Tea rooms open Tue - Sun, 10am - 5pm.

Admission: Adult £1.10, Child 50p, under 5 Free. Groups by arrangement.

Ground floor. WC. Limited. Guide dogs only.

KEW GARDENS

Tel: 020 8940 1171 **Fax:** 020 8332 5197

Kew, Richmond, Surrey TW9 3AB **Contact:** Enquiry Unit

Kew's 300 acres offer many special attractions: including the 65ft high Palm House.

Location: OS Ref. TQ188 776. A307. Junction A305 and A205 (1m Chiswick roundabout M4).

Opening Times: 9.30am, daily except Christmas Day and New Year's Day. Closing time varies according to the season. Please telephone for further information.

Admission: Adult £5, Child £2.50, Conc. £3.50, Family £13. Groups 20% discount when pre-booked and paid.

LITTLE HOLLAND HOUSE

Tel: 020 8770 4781 **Fax:** 020 8770 4777

40 Beeches Avenue, Carshalton, Surrey SM5 3LW

Owner: London Borough of Sutton **Contact:** Ms V Murphy

The home of Frank Dickinson (1874 - 1961) artist, designer and craftsman, who dreamt of a house that would follow the philosophy and theories of William Morris and John Ruskin. Dickinson designed, built and furnished the house himself from 1902 onwards. The Grade II* listed interior features handmade furniture, metal work, carvings and paintings produced by Dickinson in the Arts and Crafts style.

Location: OS Ref. TQ275 634. On B278 1m S of junction with A232.

Opening Times: First Sun of each month and BH Suns & Mons, 1.30 - 5.30pm.

Admission: Free. Groups by arrangement, £2 per person (includes talk and guided tour).

No photography in house. Ground floor only. By arrangement. No parking. Guide dogs only.

LOSELEY PARK

See page 150 for full page entry.

OAKHURST COTTAGE

Tel: 01428 683207

Hambledon, Godalming, Surrey GU8 4HF

Owner: The National Trust **Contact:** Witley Common Information Centre

A small 16th century timber-framed cottage, painted by both Helen Allingham and Myles Birket Foster, containing furniture and artefacts reflecting two or more centuries of continuing occupation. There is a delightful cottage garden and a small barn containing agricultural implements.

Location: OS Ref. SU965 385. Hambledon, Surrey.

Opening Times: 27 Mar - end Oct: Weds, Thurs, Sats, Suns & BH Mons, 2 - 5pm. Strictly by appointment only.

Admission: Adult £2.50, Child £1.25 (including guided tour). No reduction for parties.

Not suitable. Obligatory, by arrangement. Limited.

PAINSHILL LANDSCAPE GARDEN

Jerry Harpur.

PORTSMOUTH ROAD, COBHAM, SURREY KT11 1JE

Owner: *Painshill Park Trust*
Contact: *Visitor Manager*

Tel: 01932 868113 **Fax:** 01932 868001

This is one of the finest 18th century landscape gardens, created by the Hon Charles Hamilton (1704 - 86). Situated in 158 acres, visitors can take a circuit walk through a series of emerging scenes, each one more surprising than the last. A 14-acre lake fed by a massive water wheel gives a breathtaking setting for a variety of spectacular features including a Gothic temple, ruined abbey, Turkish tent, crystal grotto, magnificent Cedars of Lebanon, replanted 18th century shrubberies and vineyard. Available for corporate and private hire, location filming, wedding receptions, etc.

Location: OS Ref. TQ099 605. M25/J10 to London. W of Cobham on A245. Entrance 200 yds E of A245/A307 roundabout.

Opening Times: Apr - Oct: Tue - Sun and BH Mons, 10.30am - 6pm (last admission 4.30pm). Gates close 6pm. Nov - Mar: daily except Mons & Fris, 11am - 4pm or dusk if earlier (last admission 3pm). Closed Christmas and Boxing Day.

Admission: Adult £3.80, Child over 5 £1.50, under 5 Free, Conc. £3.30, Groups (10+) £3.

Marquee site. Guide dogs only.

POLESDEN LACEY

GREAT BOOKHAM, Nr DORKING, SURREY RH5 6BD

Owner: *The National Trust* ***Contact:*** *The Property Manager*

Tel: 01372 452048 **Infoline:** 01372 458203
Fax: 01372 452023 **e-mail:** spljac@ smtp.ntrust.org.uk

Originally an elegant 1820s Regency villa in magnificent landscape setting. The house was remodelled after 1906 by the Hon Mrs Ronald Greville, a well-known Edwardian hostess. Her collection of fine paintings, furniture, porcelain and silver are still displayed in the reception rooms and galleries, which surround an inner courtyard. Extensive grounds, walled rose garden, lawns and landscaped walks. King George VI and Queen Elizabeth, The Queen Mother spent part of their honeymoon here.

Location: OS Ref. TQ136 522. 5m NW of Dorking, 2m S of Great Bookham, off A246.

Opening Times: House: 29 Mar - 29 Oct: Wed - Sun, 1 - 5pm also BH Mons starting with Easter, 11am - 5pm. Grounds: All year: daily, 10am - 6pm/dusk. Last admission to house 1/2 hr before closing.

Admission: Garden, grounds & landscape walks: Adult £3, Family £7.50. House: £3 extra. Family £7.50 extra. All year, booked groups £5 (house, garden & walks).

Licensed. Limited for coaches. In grounds on leads. Tel: 01372 452048 for info.

RHS GARDEN WISLEY

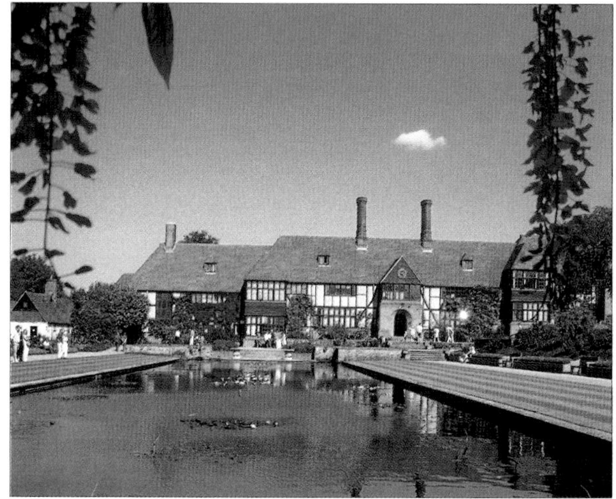

Nr WOKING, SURREY GU23 6QB

Owner/Contact: *The Royal Horticultural Society*

Tel: 01483 224234 **Fax:** 01483 211750

A world famous garden which extends to 240 acres and provides the chance to glean new ideas and inspiration. Highlights include the azaleas and rhododendrons in spring, the Glasshouses and the Model Gardens. The Giftshop and Plant Centre offer the world's finest collection of horticultural books and over 10,000 varieties of plants for sale.

Location: OS Ref. TQ066 583. NW side of A3 1/2 m SW of M25/J10.

Opening Times: All year: Mon - Fri (except Christmas Day), 10am - sunset or 6pm during the summer; Sats, 9am - sunset or 6pm during summer. RHS members only on Suns.

Admission: Adult £5, Child (up to 6) Free, Child (6-16yrs) £2. Groups (10+) £4. Companion for disabled or blind visitors, Free.

Wheelchairs available tel: 01483 211113 & special map.
Guide dogs only.

RAMSTER GARDENS

Tel: 01428 654167 **Fax:** 01428 658345

Ramster, Chiddingfold, Surrey GU8 4SN
Owner/Contact: Mrs M Gunn
20 acres of woodland and shrub garden.
Location: OS Ref. SU950 333. 1 1/2 m S of Chiddingfold on A283.
Opening Times: 16 Apr - 9 Jul: 11am - 5pm.
Admission: £3, Child Free.

SHALFORD MILL

Tel: 01483 561617

Shalford, Guildford, Surrey GU4 8BS
Owner: The National Trust
18th century watermill on the Tillingbourne, given in 1932 by "Ferguson's Gang".
Location: OS Ref. TQ000 476. 1 1/2 m S of Guildford on A281, opposite Sea Horse Inn.
Opening Times: Daily, 10am - 5pm.
Admission: Free. No unaccompanied children.

Patrick Lane.

Clandon Park, Surrey.

TITSEY PLACE

TITSEY, OXTED, SURREY RH8 0SD

Owner: *Trustees of the Titsey Foundation* ***Contact:*** *Kate Moisson*

Tel: 01273 407056 **Fax:** 01273 478995
e-mail: kate.moisson@struttandparker.co.uk

Stunning mansion house. Situated outside Limpsfield. Extensive formal and informal gardens containing Victorian walled garden, lakes, fountains and rose gardens. Outstanding features of this house include important paintings and objects d'art. Home of the Gresham and Leveson Gower family since the 15th century. Infinite capacity in this magnificent garden, numbers unavoidably restricted on house tours.

Location: OS Ref. TQ406 553. A25 Oxted - Westerham, through Limpsfield and into Bluehouse Lane and Water Lane.

Opening Times: 17 May - 27 Sept: Weds & Suns, 1 - 5pm including BH Mons. Garden only: Easter Mon.

Admission: Adult £4.50, Child £2. Groups (20+): Adult £5.

No photography in house. Not suitable. Obligatory.
Ample for cars. Limited for coaches.

WHITEHALL

Tel: 020 8643 1236 **Fax:** 020 8770 4777

1 Malden Road, Cheam, Surrey SM3 8QD

Owner: London Borough of Sutton **Contact:** The Curator

A Tudor timber-framed house, c1500 with later additions, in the heart of Cheam village conservation area. Twelve rooms open to view with displays on Nonsuch Palace, timber-framed buildings, Cheam pottery, Cheam school and William Gilpin. Changing exhibition programme and special event days throughout the year. Attractive rear garden features medieval well from c1400.

Location: OS Ref. TQ242 638. Approx. 2m S of A3 on A2043 just N of junction with A232.

Opening Times: 1 Oct - 31 Mar: Weds, Thurs, Suns, 2 - 5.30pm; Sats, 10am - 5.30pm. 1 Apr - 30 Sept: Tue - Fri, Sun, 2 - 5.30pm; Sats, 10am - 5.30pm; BH Mons, 2 - 5.30pm. Closed Christmas and New Year.

Admission: Adult £1.10, Child (under 16yrs) 50p, Child under 5yrs Free. Groups by arrangement.

Ground floor only. Guide dogs only.
Tel. for details.

Winkworth Arboretum, Surrey.

WINKWORTH ARBORETUM

Neil Campbell-Sharp

HASCOMBE ROAD, GODALMING, SURREY GU8 4AD

Owner: *The National Trust* ***Contact:*** *The Head of Arboretum*

Tel: 01483 208477 **e-mail:** swagen@smtp.ntrust.org.uk

Hillside woodland with two lakes, many rare trees and shrubs and fine views. The most impressive displays are in spring for bluebells and azaleas, autumn for colour and wildlife. Delightful 100 year old boathouse on Rowes Flashe lake. Seasonal opening.

Location: OS Ref. SU990 412. Near Hascombe, 2m SE of Godalming on E side of B2130.

Opening times: All year: daily during daylight hours. May be closed during bad weather. Boathouse: 1 Apr - 31 Oct.

Admission: Adult £3, Child (5-16yrs) £1.35, Family (2+2) £7.50, additional family member £1.50.

Limited. WC.  In grounds, on leads. 

Owner:
Arundel Castle Trustees Ltd

CONTACT

The Comptroller
Arundel Castle
Arundel
West Sussex
BN18 9AB

Tel: 01903 883136
or 01903 882173

Fax: 01903 884581

LOCATION

OS Ref. TQ018 072

1m Arundel, N of A27
Brighton 40 mins,
Worthing 15 mins,
Chichester 15 mins.
From London A3 or A24, 1½ hrs.
M25 motorway, 30m.

Bus: Bus stop 100 yds.

Rail: Station ½ m.

Air: Gatwick 25m.

ARUNDEL CASTLE
Arundel

This great castle, home of the Dukes of Norfolk, dates from the Norman Conquest. Containing a very fine collection of furniture and paintings, Arundel Castle is still a family home, reflecting the changes of nearly a thousand years.

In 1643, during the Civil War, the original castle was very badly damaged and it was later restored by the 8th, 11th and 15th Dukes in the 18th and 19th centuries. Amongst its treasures are personal possessions of Mary Queen of Scots and a selection of historical, religious and heraldic items from the Duke of Norfolk's collection.

The Duke of Norfolk is the Premier Duke, the title having been conferred on Sir John Howard in 1483 by his friend King Richard III. The Dukedom also carries with it the hereditary office of Earl Marshal of England. Among the historically famous members of the Howard family are Lord Howard of Effingham who, with Drake, repelled the Spanish Armada; the Earl of Surrey, the Tudor poet and courtier and the 3rd Duke of Norfolk, uncle of Anne Boleyn and Catherine Howard, both of whom became wives of King Henry VIII.

No unaccompanied children or photography inside the Castle.

Visitors may alight at the entrance, before parking in the allocated areas. WCs.

Restaurant seats 140. Special rates for booked groups. Self-service restaurant in Castle serves home-made food. Groups must book in advance for afternoon tea, lunch or dinner.

Pre-booked groups only, £8. Also available in French and German. Tour time 1½ hrs. Guide book translations in English, French and German.

Ample. Coaches can park opposite the Castle entrance.

Items of particular interest include a Norman Keep and Armoury. Special rates for schoolchildren (aged 5-15) and teachers.

OPENING TIMES

SUMMER
2 April - 27 October
Daily (except Sats & Good Fri)
12 noon - 5pm
Last admission 4pm.

WINTER
28 October - 31 March
Pre-booked groups only.

ADMISSION

SUMMER

Adult	£7.00
Child (5-15)	£4.50
OAP	£6.00
Family (2+2)	£19.00

Groups (20+)

Adult	£6.50
Child (5-15)	£4.00
OAP	£5.50

WINTER
Pre-booked parties

Mornings	£9.00
(Min Fee	£450.00)
Evenings, Sats & Suns	£10.00
(Min Fee	£500.00)

South East England

CHARLESTON
Lewes

Owner:
The Charleston Trust

CONTACT

Emma Whelan
Charleston
Nr Firle
Lewes
East Sussex
BN8 6LL

Tel: 01323 811265 (Visitor information)
01323 811626 (Admin)

Fax: 01323 811628

e-mail: charles @solutions-inc.co.uk

LOCATION

OS Ref. TQ490 069

6m E of Lewes on A27 between Firle and Selmeston. The lane to Charleston leads off the A27, 2m beyond the Firle turning.

London 60m. Brighton 15m. Monk's House, Rodmell (Leonard and Virginia Woolf's house) 11m.

Air: Gatwick 35m.

Rail: London (Victoria) hourly to Lewes (65 mins). Occasional train to Berwick.

Bus: Rider 125 Route on A27.

Taxi: George & Graham, Lewes 473692.

A mile or so from Firle village, near the end of a track leading to the foot of the Downs, lies Charleston. It was discovered in 1916 by Virginia and Leonard Woolf when Virginia's sister, the painter Vanessa Bell, was looking for a place in the country. Vanessa moved here with fellow artist Duncan Grant, the writer David Garnett, her two young sons and an assortment of animals. It was an unconventional and creative household which became the focal point for artists and intellectuals later to be known as the Bloomsbury set, among them Roger Fry, Lytton Strachey and Maynard Keynes.

Over the years the artists decorated the walls, furniture and ceramics with their own designs, influenced by Italian fresco painting and post-impressionist art. Creativity extended to the garden too. Mosaics were made in the piazza, sculpture was cleverly positioned to intrigue and subtle masses of colour were used in the planting.

After Duncan Grant's death in 1978, the Charleston Trust was formed to save and restore the house to its former glory. The task has been described as "one of the most difficult and imaginative feats of restoration current in Britain".

Filming and photography contact Shaun Romain: 01323 811626. Small lecture room available by special arrangement. No filming, video or photography in house.

Visitors may alight at entrance. Wheelchair visitors by prior arrangement. Ground floor only suitable. WCs.

Wed - Sun, 2 - 5pm.

Obligatory.

50 spaces. Mini coaches and cars only. Mini coaches may use the lane to the property. It is essential to arrange group visits (up to 50) in advance and out of public hours. All group visits to the house are guided. Large coaches may set down at the start of the lane, 10 mins walk.

Student pack and a teacher's guide suitable for KS I & II.

OPENING TIMES

1 April - 29 October
Wed - Sun: 2 - 5pm.

July & August
Wed - Sat: 11.30am - 5pm
Sun: 2 - 5pm.

September & October
Wed - Sun: 2 - 5pm.

November - December
Christmas shopping
Sat & Sun, 2 - 5pm.

Guided visits
Wed - Sat,
unguided on Suns.

House closed Mon & Tue except BH Mons.

Connoisseur Fridays
April - June, September and October, in-depth tour of the house, including Vanessa Bell's studio and the kitchen.

ADMISSION

House & Garden

Adult	£5.50
Child (5+)/Conc*.	£4.00
Child (under 5)	Free
Disabled	£4.00

Groups (min 10)

Adult	£5.00
Child/Student	£4.00
OAP	£5.00

Connoisseur Fridays

Adult	£6.50

* OAPs, Students & UB40 Wed & Thur only throughout season.

Organised tours should telephone for group rates.

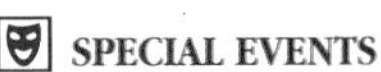

SPECIAL EVENTS

- **MAY 25 - 29:** Charleston Festival

South East England

GOODWOOD HOUSE
Chichester

Owner:
The Earl of March

CONTACT

Kathryn Bellamy
Goodwood House
Goodwood
Chichester
West Sussex
PO18 0PX

Tel: 01243 755048

Fax: 01243 755005

Recorded: 01243 755040

LOCATION

OS Ref. SU888 088

4m NE of Chichester. A3 from London then A286 or A285. M27/A27 from Portsmouth or Brighton.

Rail: Chichester 4m Arundel 9m.

Air: Heathrow $1^1/_2$ hrs Gatwick $^3/_4$ hr.

CONFERENCE/FUNCTION		
ROOM	SIZE	MAX CAPACITY
Ballroom	79' x 23'	200
11 other rooms also available		

Aristocrats, the BBC's recent real life drama, immortalised the glamorous and independent-minded daughters of the 2nd Duke of Richmond. Before their marriages the daughters lived at Goodwood, which was their father's country seat. It was here that Kildare wooed Emily, and that Sarah passed the long days during her banishment from society. Caroline and Emily left a lasting memorial of their time at Goodwood by assisting with the decoration of the exquisite Shell House, which is one of the finest surviving examples of early 18th century shell work in the country. Caroline's husband, Lord Holland, is shown at Goodwood in a painting by Stubbs. The charming Meissen snuff box, given to the Duchess as a reconciliation present four years after their elopement is also on view.

The old hunting lodge at Goodwood was first purchased by the girls' grandfather, the 1st Duke of Richmond. The natural son of King Charles II and his beautiful French mistress, Louise de Kerouaille, he was renowned for his love of life and brilliance at entertaining - a tradition which continues to this day. The French interest was pursued by the 3rd Duke who, as British Ambassador to Paris, collected wonderful French furniture and Sèvres porcelain, which can still be seen. Richly refurbished by the Earl and Countess of March, Goodwood is not only a beautiful house to visit, but has also established a worldwide reputation for excellence as the location for corporate, private and incentive entertainment requirements.

Mark Hainson

The Aristocrats

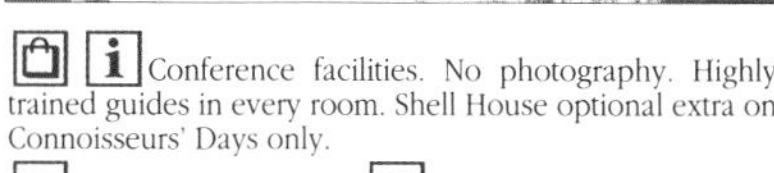

Conference facilities. No photography. Highly trained guides in every room. Shell House optional extra on Connoisseurs' Days only.

Wedding receptions.

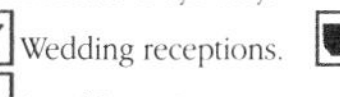

Suitable. WCs.

By appointment: open mornings & on Connoisseurs' Days.

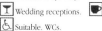

Guide dogs only in house. In grounds, on leads.

Civil Wedding Licence.

OPENING TIMES

SUMMER
2 Apr - 25 Sept:
Suns & Mons.

6 - 31 August:
Sun - Thur, 1 - 5pm.

Closed on occasional Event Days: April & May, 18, 19, 25, 26 Jun.
1 - 3 Aug (raceweek),
17 Sept. Please ring Recorded Info. line to check.

Connoisseurs' Days
Group visits with special guided tours can be booked.

ADMISSION

House
Adult £6.00
Child* £3.00

Groups (20 - 200)
Economy £5.00
Connoisseur £8.00

*12 - 18 yrs, under 12 yrs free

SPECIAL EVENTS

- **MAY - SEPT:**
Goodwood Horserace Meetings
23 - 25 May, 1, 9, 16, 23, 30 Jun, (evenings except 1 Jun), 2 Jul, 1 - 5 Aug (Festival), 26/27 Aug, 8, 9, 20, 21 Sept.
- **JUN 23 - 25:**
Goodwood Festival of Speed.
- **SEPT 15 - 17:**
Goodwood Motor Circuit Event.

South East England

Owner:
R Loder Esq

CONTACT

R Loder Esq
Leonardslee Gardens
Lower Beeding
Horsham
West Sussex
RH13 6PP

Tel: 01403 891212

Fax: 01403 891305

LOCATION

OS Ref. TQ222 260

M23 to Handcross then B2110 (signposted Cowfold) for 4m. From London: 1 hr 15 mins.

Rail: Horsham Station $4^1/_2$ m

Bus: No. 107 from Horsham and Brighton

CONFERENCE/FUNCTION		
ROOM	SIZE	MAX CAPACITY
Clock Tower		100

LEONARDSLEE GARDENS
Horsham

LEONARDSLEE GARDENS represent one of the largest and most spectacular woodland gardens in England with one of the finest collections of mature rhododendrons, azaleas, choice trees and shrubs to be seen anywhere. It is doubly fortunate in having one of the most magnificent settings, within easy reach of London, only a few miles from the M23. Laid out by Sir Edmund Loder since 1889, the gardens are still maintained by the Loder family today. The 240 acre (100 hectare) valley is world famous for its spring display of azaleas and rhododendrons around the 7 lakes, giving superb views and reflections.

The delightful Rock Garden, a photographer's paradise, is a kaleidoscope of colour in May. The superb exhibition of Bonsai in a walled courtyard shows the fascinating living art-form of Bonsai to perfection. The Alpine House has 400 different alpine plants growing in a natural rocky setting. Wallabies (used as mowing machines!) have lived wild in part of the garden for over 100 years, and deer (Sika, Fallow & Axis) may be seen in the parklands.

Many superb rhododendrons have been raised at Leonardslee. The most famous is *rhododendron loderi* raised by Sir Edmund Loder in 1901. The original plants can still be seen in the garden. In May the fragrance of their huge blooms pervades the air throughout the valley.

The Loder family collection of Victorian motorcars (1895 - 1900) provides a fascinating view of the different designs adopted on the first auto-mobile constructors.

Photography - landscape and fashion, film location.

Restaurant available for private and corporate function in the evenings and out of season.

Not suitable.

Restaurant and café. Morning coffee, lunch and teas.

Ample. Refreshments free to coach drivers. Average length of visit 2 - 4 hours.

OPENING TIMES

SUMMER
1 April - 31 October
Daily 9.30am - 6pm

May: 9.30am - 8pm

WINTER
1 November - 31 March
Closed to the general public.

Available for functions.

ADMISSION

April, June - October
Adult £4.00

May (Mon - Fri)
Adult £5.00

May (Sats, Suns & BH Mons)
Adult £6.00

Child (anytime)........£2.50

Season Ticket..........£12.00

GROUPS
April, June - October
Adult £3.50

May: (Mon - Fri).........£4.50
Sat, Sun &
BH Mons: £5.50
Child (anytime).........£2.50

SPECIAL EVENTS

- **MAY 6 - 7:** Bonsai weekend.
- **JUN 24 - 25:** West Sussex Country Craft Fair.

South East England

Oliver Benn

Owner: The National Trust

CONTACT

The Administration Office
Petworth House
Petworth
West Sussex
GU28 0AE

Tel: 01798 342207

Info Line: 01798 343929

Fax: 01798 342963

e-mail: spegen@smtp.ntrust.org.uk

LOCATION

OS Ref. SU976 218

In the centre of Petworth town (approach roads A272/A283/A285) Car park signposted.

Rail: Pulborough BR $5^1/_4$ m.

PETWORTH HOUSE
Petworth

PETWORTH HOUSE is one of the finest houses in the care of the National Trust and is home to an art collection that rivals many London galleries. Assembled by one family over 350 years, it includes works by Turner, Van Dyck, Titian, Claude, Gainsborough, Bosch, Reynolds and William Blake.

The state rooms contain sculpture, furniture and porcelain of the highest quality and are complemented by the opening of the old kitchens in the servants' block.

A continuing programme of repairs and restoration brings new interest for the visitor each year. Petworth House is also the home of Lord and Lady Egremont and extra family rooms are open on weekdays by kind permission (not Bank Holidays).

Petworth Park is a 700 acre park landscaped by 'Capability' Brown and is open to the public all year free of charge. Spring and autumn are particularly breathtaking and the summer sunsets over the lake are spectacular.

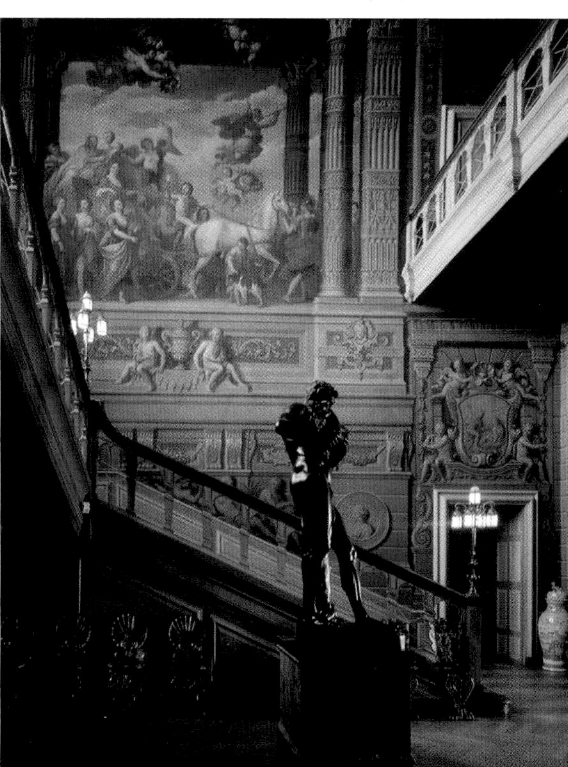

Andreas Von Einsiedel

Events throughout the year. Large musical concerts in the park. Baby feeding and changing facilities, highchairs. Pushchairs admitted in house but no prams, please. No photography in house.

Contact Retail & Catering Manager on 01798 344975.

Car park is 800 yards from house; there is a vehicle available to take less able visitors to house.

Licensed. 12-5pm.

By arrangement (Mon - Wed mornings) with the Administration Officer on variety of subjects, tailor-made to suit your group (additional charge).

800 yards from house. Coach parties alight at Church Lodge entrance, coaches then park in NT car park. Coaches must book in advance.

Welcome. Must pre-book. Teachers' pack available.

Guide dogs only in house. Dogs in park only.

OPENING TIMES

House & Servants' Quarters
1 April - 1 November
Daily except Thurs & Fris but open Good Fri and every following Fri in July & August.
1 - 5.30pm.

Last admission to house 4.30pm, servants' quarters 5pm.

Extra rooms shown on weekdays, not BH Mons.

Pleasure Ground and Car Park
18 - 19 & 25 - 26 March for spring bulbs, 12 noon - 4pm.

Dates as house 12 noon - 6pm. BH Mons, July & August, 11am - 6pm.

Park
All year: Daily, 8am - sunset.

Closed 23 - 25 June from 12 noon.

ADMISSION

House, Servants' Quarters & Pleasure Ground

Adult	£6.00
Child* (5-17yrs)	£3.00
Student	£3.00
Family (2+2)	£15.00
Park Only	Free

Groups (pre-booked 15+)

Adult	£5.50

Pleasure Ground

Adult	£1.50
Park	Free

* Under 5yrs Free

SPECIAL EVENTS

Telephone for details.

Owner:
Brighton & Hove Council

CONTACT

Visitor Services
The Royal Pavilion
Brighton
East Sussex
BN1 1EE

Tel: 01273 290900

Fax: 01273 292871

LOCATION

OS Ref. TQ313 043

The Royal Pavilion is in the centre of Brighton easily reached by road and rail. From London M25, M23, A23 - 1 hr 30 mins.

Rail: Victoria to Brighton station 50 mins. 15 mins walk from Brighton station.

Air: Gatwick 20 mins.

CONFERENCE/FUNCTION		
ROOM	SIZE	MAX CAPACITY
Banqueting Room		200
Great Kitchen		90
Music Rm		180
Queen Adelaide Suite		100
Small Adelaide		40
William IV		80

THE ROYAL PAVILION

Brighton

Universally acclaimed as one of the most exotically beautiful buildings in the British Isles, the Royal Pavilion was the famous seaside residence of King George IV.

Originally a simple farmhouse, in 1787 architect Henry Holland created a neo-classical villa on the site. It was later transformed into its current Indian style by John Nash between 1815 and 1822. With interiors decorated in the Chinese style and an astonishingly exotic exterior, this Regency Palace is quite breathtaking.

Magnificent decorations and fantastic furnishings have been re-created in the recent extensive restoration programme. From the opulence of the main state rooms to the charm of the first floor bedroom suites, the Royal Pavilion is filled with astonishing colours and superb craftsmanship.

Witness the magnificence of the Music Room with its domed ceiling of gilded scallop-shaped shells and hand-knotted carpet, and promenade through the Chinese bamboo grove of the Long Gallery.

Lavish menus were created in the Great Kitchen, with its cast iron palm trees and dazzling collection of copperware, and then served in the dramatic setting of the Banqueting Room, lit by a huge crystal chandelier held by a silvered dragon.

Set in restored Regency gardens replanted to John Nash's elegant 1820s design, the Royal Pavilion is an unforgettable experience.

The Banqueting Room ceiling will be unveiled in its full Regency splendour in January 2000 when the scaffolding comes down after a year of restoration.

Visitors will also have the opportunity to discover more about life behind the scenes at the Palace during the last 200 years with a new specially commissioned interactive multimedia presentation.

Location filming and photography, including feature films, fashion shoots and corporate videos.

Gift shop with souvenirs unique to the Royal Pavilion.

Spectacular rooms available for prestigious corporate entertaining and wedding receptions.

Access to ground floor. Free admission. Guided tours, including tactile and signed tours, are free of charge to those with disabilities but must be booked in advance with Visitor Services Tel: 01273 292820/2/3.

Tearooms with a balcony providing sweeping views across the restored Regency gardens.

Tours in English, French and German by prior arrangement. General introduction and specialist tours provided.

Close to NCP car parks, town centre voucher parking. Coach drop-off point in Church Street, parking in Madeira Drive. Free entry for coach drivers.

Specialist tours relating to all levels of National Curriculum, must be booked in advance with Visitor Services. Special winter student rates: Slide lecture presentations by arrangement.

Civil Wedding Licence.

OPENING TIMES

SUMMER

June - September
Daily: 10am - 6pm
Last admission at 6pm.

WINTER

October - May
Daily: 10am - 5pm
Last admission at 5pm.

Closed 25/26 December.

ADMISSION

Adult £4.50
Child £2.75
Conc. £3.25

Groups (20+)
Adult £3.75

Prices valid until 31.3.2000

SPECIAL EVENTS

- **SPRING & AUTUMN HALF TERM:**
  Pavilion Playtime Children's Events.
- **OCT - MAR:**
  Winter programme of events – call for details.

Owner:
Peter Thorogood Esq

CONTACT

Peter Thorogood or
Roger Linton (Curator)
St Mary's House
Bramber
West Sussex
BN44 3WE

Tel: 01903 816205

Fax: 01903 816205

LOCATION

OS Ref. TQ189 105

Bramber village off A283
From London 56m via M23/A23 or A24.

Bus: From Shoreham to Steyning, alight Bramber.

Train: To Shoreham-by-Sea with connecting bus 20 (4m).

Taxi: Southern Taxis 01273 461655.

CONFERENCE/FUNCTION		
ROOM	SIZE	MAX CAPACITY
Music Rm	60' x 30'	80
Monks' Parlour	26' x 22'	25
Painted Rm	26' x 15'	20

ST. MARY'S
Bramber

Enchanting, picturesque house in the downland village of Bramber. Built in 1470 by William Waynflete, Bishop of Winchester, founder of Magdalen College, Oxford. Classified (Grade I) as "the best example of late 15th century timber-framing in Sussex." Fine panelled rooms, including the unique *trompe l'oeil* 'Painted Room', decorated for the visit of Elizabeth I. The 'Kings Room' has connections with Charles II's escape to France in 1651. Rare 17th century painted wall leather. English furniture, ceramics, manuscripts and fine English costume-doll collection. The Library houses an important private collection of works by Victorian poet and artist Thomas Hood. Still a lived-in family home, St Mary's was awarded a 'Warmest Welcome' Commendation by the SE Tourist Board. Programme available for 14th season of concerts and events.

GARDENS

Charming gardens with amusing topiary as seen on television. Features include an exceptional example of the Living Fossil Tree, Ginkgo Biloba, a magnificently tall magnolia grandiflora and the mysterious ivy-clad Monks' Walk. Rediscover the lost Victorian walled and pleasure gardens, hidden for half a century, rescued in April 1997 and now under restoration.

Film location, lecture/demonstration facilities for up to 70, grand piano. No photography in House.

Partially suitable.

Exclusive corporate or private functions, promotional product launches, wedding receptions. Quality catering by both in-house and top London caterers.

Superb Victorian music room seats up to 70. Groups can pre-book for morning coffee or afternoon teas.

Obligatory. Larger groups (max 60) are divided into smaller groups. Tour time 1 hr.

Gravel car park, 30 cars or 2 coaches, 20 yds from house, also a village car park 50 yds. Groups must pre-book. Allow $2^1/_2$ hrs for your visit. Free tour and tea for coach driver.

Groups welcome by prior arrangement.

OPENING TIMES

General Public
Easter - end September
Sun, Thur, 2 - 6pm.

BH Mons, 2 - 6pm.

Last admission 5pm.

Groups
Easter - end September
Daily by appointment, avoiding public open afternoons. Other times by arrangement.

ADMISSION

SUMMER

House & Garden

Adult	£4.00
Child	£2.00
Student	£3.00
Groups	
Adult	
25 or more	£3.80
Less than 25	£4.00
Child	£2.00
Student	£3.00

Gardens only

Adult	£2.00
Child	£0.50

Secret Garden

Adult	£1.50
Child	£0.50

Mark Fiennes

Owner: Trustees of Stansted Park Foundation

CONTACT

The House Manager
Stansted Park
Rowlands Castle
Hampshire
PO9 6DX

Tel: 023 9241 2265

Fax: 023 92413773

e-mail: stansted@athene.co.uk

LOCATION

OS Ref. SU761 104

Follow brown heritage signs from A3 (Rowlands Castle) or A27 (Havant)

Rail: Rowlands Castle (London Waterloo $1^1/_2$ hrs.

Air: Eastleigh, Southampton.

STANSTED PARK
Rowlands Castle

STANSTED is more than an elegant house. It retains the atmosphere of a 'much loved' home with an ambience now rarely found. Set in 1750 acres of glorious park and woodland, rich in wildlife and famous for its tranquillity, it is a prime example of the Caroline revival. Not only is Stansted one of the South's most beautiful stately homes, it is also one of Sussex's best-kept secrets.

The contrast between the magnificent State Rooms and the purpose-built Servants' Quarters gives an insight into the social history of an English Country House in its heyday. The Bessborough family collection includes paintings of the famous Georgiana, Duchess of Devonshire and her sister Henrietta Frances, wife to the 3rd Earl and mother of the equally famous Lady Caroline Lamb. The visionary stained glass windows in the exquisitely decorated Ancient Chapel inspired some of Keats' finest poetry. The Gardens really are for people who love plants. With the restored Dutch Garden, Circular Garden and Ivan Hicks' well-known 'Garden in Mind', they are full of surprises. The large, well-stocked Garden Centre within the unique Walled Gardens gives regular Plant Demonstrations. The Garden Show every June is a superb exhibition, forging the links between art, design and the garden.

A unique range of facilities for conferences and business meetings. A variety of activities for Corporate Hospitality, including clay shooting, off-road driving, team-building games, action-theme days, even murder mystery evenings. Excellent film location. Childrens' play area, picnic area, woodland walk, arboretum & Garden Centre.

Partially suitable. WC.

By arrangement.

In woods, on leads.

A wide variety of facilities to suit parties of all sizes. A complete package with both ceremony and reception is just one of the options offered. Every function is tailored to individual requirements and we guarantee a special day.

Please telephone for details.

OPENING TIMES

1 March - 31 October

State Rooms & Below Stairs Experience: Jul & Aug, Sun - Wed, 1 - 5pm.

Grounds, Garden, Chapel and Ivan Hicks' Garden in Mind: daily, 1 - 5pm.

Garden Centre: All year: Mon - Sat, 9am - 5pm. Suns, 10.30am - 4.30pm.

Closed on occasional Saturdays.

Groups by appointment: May - Sept (except Sats).

ADMISSION

Grounds, Arboretum & Chapel

Adult	£1.80
Child (5-17yrs)	£1.00
OAP	£1.40
Family (2+3)	£5.50

House & Below Stairs Experience

Adult	£3.80
Child (5-17yrs)	£1.90
OAP	£2.70
Family (2+3)	£11.00

Garden in Mind (including Grounds, Arboretum & Chapel)

Adult	£2.80
Child (5-17yrs)	£1.70

(for house visitors: normal charge plus £1.70)

Groups (30-50)
House & Grounds

Adult	£3.40
Child (5-17yrs)	£1.70
OAP	£2.50

Grounds, Chapel & Arboretum

Adult	£1.60
Child (5-17yrs)	£0.90
OAP	£1.30

Ivan Hicks' Garden
In addition to either package £1.70pp

ALFRISTON CLERGY HOUSE

Andrew Butler

THE TYE, ALFRISTON, POLEGATE, EAST SUSSEX BN26 5TL

Owner: *The National Trust* ***Contact:*** *The Custodian*

Tel: 01323 870001 **Fax:** 01323 871318 **e-mail:** ksdxxx@smtp.ntrust.org.uk

This thatched Wealden Hall House was the first building bought by the National Trust in 1896. The charming garden is filled with traditional cottage favourites and set in the lovely Cuckmere Valley. Riverside walks and an intriguing variety of shops, pubs and restaurants in Alfriston village make this a wonderful day out.

Location: OS Ref. TQ521 029. 4m NE of Seaford, just E of B2108.

Opening times: 1 Apr - 30 Oct: Mons, Weds, Thurs, Sats & Suns. 10am - 5pm/ sunset if earlier, plus BH Mons & Good Fri, 10am - 5pm. Last admission 1/2 hour before closing.

Admission: Adult £2.50, Child £1.25, Family (2+3) £6.25. Pre-booked groups £2.10.

Not suitable. Parking in village car parks.

BATEMAN'S

NT Photographic Library/Rupert Truman

BURWASH, ETCHINGHAM, EAST SUSSEX TN19 7DS

Owner: *The National Trust* ***Contact:*** *The Property Manager*

Tel: 01435 882302 **Fax:** 01435 882811 **e-mail:** kbaxxx@smtp.ntrust.org.uk

Home of author Rudyard Kipling 1902-36. The house was built by a local ironmonger in 1634. Today the rooms are left as they were when the Kiplings lived here and include Kipling's study. The exhibition rooms contain memorabilia and mementos of Kipling's work and life. The garden, laid out to complement the house and surrounding countryside includes a rose, herb and wild garden. Beautiful water mill, also see Kipling's Rolls Royce.

Location: OS Ref. TQ671 238. 1/2 m S of Burwash off A265.

Opening Times: 1 Apr - 1 Nov: Sat - Wed, Good Fri & BH Mons, 11am - 5.30pm. Last admission 4.30pm.

Admission: Adult £5, Child £2.50, Family (2+3) £12.50. Pre-booked groups £4.25.

Ground floor & grounds. WC. Licensed.

ANNE OF CLEVES HOUSE

Tel: 01273 474610 **Fax:** 01273 486990

52 Southover High Street, Lewes, Sussex BN7 1JA

Owner: Sussex Archaeological Society **Contact:** Mr Stephen Watts

Anne of Cleves' house formed part of her divorce settlement from Henry VIII in 1541, although she never actually lived here. The 16th century timber-framed Wealden hall-house contains wide-ranging collections of Sussex interest. Furnished rooms give an impression of life in the 17th and 18th centuries. Artefacts from Lewes Priory, Sussex pottery and Wealden ironwork.

Location: OS198 Ref. TQ410 096. S of Lewes town centre, off A27/A275/A26.

Opening Times: 21 Feb - 5 Nov: daily, 6 Nov - 22 Dec: Tue - Sat, 4 Jan - 20 Feb: Tues, Thurs, Sats, 10am - 5.30pm (Sun, 12 noon - 5.30pm). Closed Christmas.

Admission: Adult £2.50, Child £1.20, Conc. £2.30, Family (2+2) £7. Combined ticket with Lewes Castle is also available.

Not suitable.  Guide dogs only.

ARUNDEL CASTLE

See page 155 for full page entry.

ARUNDEL CATHEDRAL

Tel: 01903 882297 **Fax:** 01903 885335

Parsons Hill, Arundel, Sussex BN18 9AY **Contact:** Rev A Whale

French Gothic Cathedral, church of the RC Diocese of Arundel and Brighton built by Henry, 15th Duke of Norfolk and opened 1873. Carpet of Flowers and Floral Festival held annually on the Feast of Corpus Christi (60 days after Easter) and day preceding.

Location: OS Ref. TQ015 072. Above junction of A27 and A284.

Opening Times: Summer: 9am - 6pm. Winter: 9am - dusk. Mass at 10am each day. Sun Masses: 8am, 9.30am & 11am, Vigil Sat evening: 6.30pm. Shop opened after services and on special occasions and otherwise at request.

Admission: Free.

1066 BATTLE OF HASTINGS BATTLEFIELD & ABBEY

English Heritage Photographic Library

BATTLE, SUSSEX TN33 0AD

Owner: *English Heritage* ***Contact:*** *The Custodian*

Tel: 01424 773792 **Fax:** 01424 775059

Visit the site of the 1066 Battle of Hastings. A free interactive audio tour will lead you around the battlefield and to the exact spot where Harold fell. Explore the magnificent Abbey ruins and see the fascinating exhibition in the gate house and '1066 Prelude to Battle' exhibition. Children's themed play area.

Location: OS Ref. TQ749 157. Top of Battle High Street. Turn off A2100 to Battle.

Opening Times: 1 Apr - 30 Sept: daily, 10am - 6pm. 1 - 31 Oct: 10am - 5pm. 1 Nov - 31 Mar: daily 10am - 4pm. Closed 24 - 26 Dec.

Admission: Adult £4, Child £2, Conc. £3, Family £10. 15% discount for groups (11+). EH members Free.

 Ground floor & grounds.  Free. In grounds, on leads.

BAYHAM OLD ABBEY

Tel/Fax: 01892 890381

Lamberhurst, Sussex

Owner: English Heritage **Contact:** The Custodian

These riverside ruins are of a house of 'White' Canons, founded c1208 and preserved in the 18th century, when its surroundings were landscaped to create its delightful setting.

Location: OS Ref. TQ651 366. 1¾ m W of Lamberhurst off B2169.

Opening Times: 1 Apr - 30 Sept: daily, 10am - 6pm. 1 - 31 Oct: 10am - 5pm. 1 Nov - 31 Mar: w/ends only 10am - 4pm.

Admission: Adult £2.10, Child £1.10, Conc. £1.60.

Grounds suitable. WC. In grounds, on leads.

BENTLEY HOUSE & MOTOR MUSEUM

Tel: 01825 840573 **Fax:** 01825 841322

Halland, Lewes, East Sussex BN8 5AF **e-mail:** barrysutherland@pavilion.co.uk

Owner: East Sussex County Council **Contact:** Mr Barry Sutherland - Manager

Early 18th century farmhouse with a large reception room of Palladian proportions added on either end in the 1960s by the architect Raymond Erith, each lit by large Venetian windows. Furnished to form a grand 20th century evocation of a mid-Georgian house.

Location: OS Ref. TQ485 160. 7m NE from Lewes, signposted off A22, A26 & B2192.

Opening Times: Estate: 20 Mar - 31 Oct: daily, 10.30am - 4.30pm (last adm.). Nov, Feb - 19 Mar: weekends only, 10.30am - 4pm (last adm.). House: 1 Apr - 31 Oct: daily 12 noon - 5pm. Estate closed Dec & Jan.

Admission: Adult £4.50 (£3.50 in winter), Child (4-15) £2.80, Conc.£3.50, Family (2+4) £13.50. Coach drivers free admission & refreshment ticket. 10% discount for groups of 11+. Special rates for the disabled. Call to verify prices (1999 rates).

Wedding receptions. Licensed. By arrangement. Guide dogs only. 

Plant Sales Index
PAGE 51

BODIAM CASTLE

Alasdair Ogilvie

BODIAM, Nr ROBERTSBRIDGE, EAST SUSSEX TN32 5UA

Owner: *The National Trust* ***Contact:*** *The Administrator*

Tel: 01580 830436 **Fax:** 01580 830398 **e-mail:** kboxxx@smtp.ntrust.org.uk

Built in 1385 against a French invasion that never came and as a comfortable dwelling for a rich nobleman, Bodiam Castle is one of the finest examples of medieval military architecture. The virtual completeness of its exterior makes it a popular filming location. Inside, although a ruin, floors have been replaced in some of the towers and visitors can climb the spiral staircase to enjoy superb views from the battlements. Audio-visual presentations of life in a castle and museum room.

Location: OS Ref. TQ782 256. 3m S of Hawkhurst, 2m E of A21 Hurst Green.

Opening Times: 1 - 4 Jan & 8 Jan - 13 Feb: Tues, Sats & Suns, 10am - 4pm. 19 Feb - 31 Oct: daily including BH Mons & Good Fri: 10am - 6pm. 4 Nov - mid Feb 2001: Sats & Suns, 10am - 4pm.

Admission: Adult £3.60, Child £1.80, Family ticket (2+3) £9. Groups £3.10. Car parking £1.50 per car.

Small museum. Ground floor & grounds suitable. Teacher and student packs and education base.

BORDE HILL GARDEN

HAYWARDS HEATH, WEST SUSSEX RH16 1XP

Owner: *Mr & Mrs A P Stephenson Clarke* ***Contact:*** *Sarah Brook*

Tel: 01444 450326 **Fax:** 01444 440427 **e-mail:** info@bordehill.co.uk

Visitor Attraction of the Year 1999 SEETB

A garden of contrast that captures the imagination and delights the senses. This truly global garden, established at the turn of the century, is set in 200 acres of spectacular Sussex parkland and contains a phenomenal range of rare trees, shrubs and perennials, where botanical interest and garden design are of equal importance. The sub-tropical Round Dell and the elegant Italian Garden lead to the tranquil Garden of Allah and on to the fragrant romantic English Rose Garden.

A Heritage Lottery Grant, awarded in 1997, has enabled a 'renaissance' to take place, with extensive replanting throughout the garden, the creation of a wildlife pond and a new Mediterranean garden, restoration of Victorian greenhouses and improvements to pathways particularly for easier disabled access.

Location: OS Ref. TQ324 265. 1½m N of Haywards Heath on Balcombe Road, 3m from A23. 45mins from Victoria Station.

Opening Times: All year: daily (including Christmas Day), 10am - 6pm.

Admission: Adult £4.50, Child £1.75, Family £11, Family season ticket £27.50. Groups (20+): Mon - Fri only, £4. Borde Hill House open to groups by prior arrangement.

By arrangement. In grounds, on leads.

Patrick Lane.

Bodiam Castle, Sussex.

BOXGROVE PRIORY ⌗

Tel: 01732 778000

Boxgrove, Chichester, Sussex

Owner: English Heritage **Contact:** The South East Regional Office

Remains of the Guest House, Chapter House and Church of this 12th century priory, which was the cell of a French abbey until Richard II confirmed its independence in 1383.

Location: OS Ref. SU909 076. N of Boxgrove, 4m E of Chichester on minor road N of A27.

Opening Times: Any reasonable time.

Admission: Free.

BRAMBER CASTLE ⌗

Tel: 01732 778000

Bramber, Sussex

Owner: English Heritage **Contact:** The South East Regional Office

The remains of a Norman castle gatehouse, walls and earthworks in a splendid setting overlooking the Adur valley.

Location: OS Ref. TQ187 107. On W side of Bramber village NE of A283.

Opening Times: Any reasonable time.

Admission: Free.

BRICKWALL HOUSE & GARDENS

Tel: 01797 253388 **Fax:** 01797 252567

Northiam, Rye, Sussex TN31 6NL

Owner: Frewen Educational Trust **Contact:** The Curator

Impressive timber-framed house. 17th century drawing room with magnificent plaster ceilings and good portraits including by Lely, Kneller and Vereist. Topiary, chess garden.

Location: OS Ref. TQ831 241. S side of Northiam village at junction of A28 and B2088.

Opening Times: By appointment only.

Admission: £3

CAMBER CASTLE ⌗

Tel: 01797 223862

Camber, Nr Rye, East Sussex

Owner: English Heritage **Contact:** Rye Harbour Nature Reserve

A fine example of one of many coastal fortresses built by Henry VIII to counter the threat of invasion during the 16th century. Monthly guided walks of Rye Nature Reserve including Camber Castle, telephone for details.

Location: OS189, Ref. TQ922 185. Across fields off A259, 1m S of Rye off harbour road.

Opening Times: 1 Jul - 30 Sept: Sats only, 2 - 5pm.

Admission: Adult £2, Child £1, Conc. £1.50.

Not suitable. By arrangement. No parking. Guide dogs only.

CHARLESTON

See page 156 for full page entry.

CHICHESTER CATHEDRAL

Tel: 01243 782595 **Fax:** 01243 536190

Chichester, Sussex PO19 1PX **Contact:** Mrs J Thom

In the heart of the city, this fine Cathedral has been a centre of Christian worship and community life for 900 years and is the site of the Shrine of St Richard of Chichester. Its treasures range from Romanesque carvings to 20th century works of art.

Location: OS Ref. SU860 047. West Street, Chichester.

Opening Times: Summer: 7.30am - 7pm, Winter: 7.30am - 5pm. Choral Evensong daily (except Weds) during term time.

Admission: Donation.

Medieval Vicars' Hall (100 max).

Loop system during services, touch & hearing centre, braille guide.

 By arrangement. Guide dogs only. 

DENMANS GARDEN

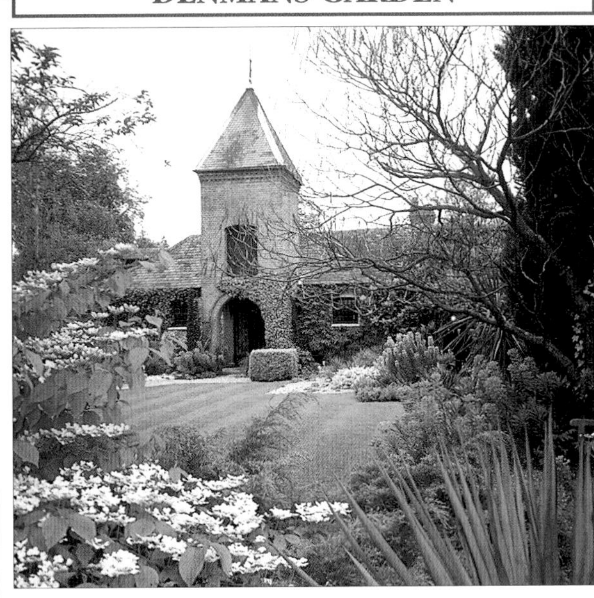

DENMANS LANE, FONTWELL, Nr ARUNDEL BS18 0SU

Owner: *Mr John Brookes* ***Contact:*** *Mr Michael J Neve*

Tel: 01243 542808 **Fax:** 01243 544064 e-mail: denmans@cwcom.net

Unique 20th century garden artistically planted forming vistas with emphasis on colours, shapes and textures for all year interest. Areas of glass, areas for tender and rare species. John Brookes school of garden design in the Clock House where seminars are available.

Location: OS Ref. SU943 065. On the S side of A27 approx. 5m W of Arundel and 5m E of Chichester.

Opening Times: 1 Mar - 31 Oct: daily, 9am - 5pm.

Admission: Adult £2.80, Child £1.50, OAP £2.50. Groups (15+): £2.20 (1999 prices).

By arrangement. 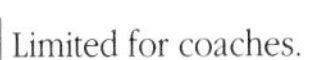 Limited for coaches.

Patrick Lane.

Batemans, Sussex.

South East England

FIRLE PLACE

Jeremy Whitaker

FIRLE, Nr LEWES, EAST SUSSEX BN8 6LP

Owner: *The Rt Hon Viscount Gage*

Tel: 01273 858335 (Info Line) **Fax:** 01273 858188 **Tel:** 01273 858307 (Restaurant)
e-mail: gage@firleplace.co.uk **Tel:** 01273 858567 (Events & other enquiries)

Firle Place is the home of the Gage family, and has been for over 500 years. It is set at the foot of the South Downs within its own parkland. This unique house contains a magnificent collection of old master paintings, fine English and European furniture and an impressive collection of Sèvres porcelain mainly collected by the 3rd Earl Cowper from Panshanger.

Restaurant: Enjoy the licensed restaurant and tea terrace with views over the gardens for luncheon and cream teas.

Events & other enquiries: The Tudor Great Hall lends itself to private dinners with drinks in the Billiard Room or on the Terrace which can incorporate a private tour of the house. The paddock area is ideal for erecting a marquee and the Park can be used for larger events using the house as a backdrop.

Location: OS Ref. TQ473 071. 5m SE of Lewes on A27 Brighton/Eastbourne Road.

Opening Times: 23, 24 & 30 Apr & 1 May. 17 May - 28 Sept: Wed - Thur, Suns & BH Mons, 2 - 4.30pm. Groups must book. Private tours by arrangement.

Admission: Adult £4, Child £2. Connoisseurs' Day (1st Wed, Jun - Sept) £4.85. Private tours: £6pp.

Car park adjacent to House. Catering for groups must be pre-arranged with Catering Manager tel: 01273 858307.

No photography in house. Ground floor & restaurant suitable. Licensed In grounds on leads.

FISHBOURNE ROMAN PALACE

SALTHILL ROAD, FISHBOURNE, CHICHESTER, SUSSEX PO19 3QR

Owner: *Sussex Archaeological Society* ***Contact:*** *David Rudkin*

Tel: 01243 785859 **Fax:** 01243 539266 **e-mail:** adminfish@sussexpast.co.uk

A Roman site built around AD75. A modern building houses part of the extensive remains including a large number of Britain's finest in-situ mosaics. The museum displays many objects discovered during excavations and an audio-visual programme tells Fishbourne's remarkable story. Roman gardens have been reconstructed. A museum of Roman gardening.

Location: OS Ref. SU837 057. $1^{1}/_{2}$ m W of Chichester in Fishbourne village off A27/A259.

Opening Times: 7 Feb - 15 Dec: Feb, Nov - Dec: 10am - 4pm. Mar - Jul & Sept - Oct: 10am - 5pm. Aug: 10am - 6pm. 16 - 31 Dec & 1 Jan - 6 Feb: Sats & Suns, 10am - 4pm. Closed Christmas.

Admission: Adult £4.40, Child £2.30, Conc. £3.70, Family (2+2): £11.50, Registered disabled £3.50. Groups: Adult £3.70, Child £2.20, Conc. £3.50.

 Guide dogs only.

GLYNDE PLACE

GLYNDE, LEWES, SUSSEX BN8 6SX

Owners: *Viscount & Viscountess Hampden* ***Contact:*** *Viscount Hampden*

Tel: 01273 858224 **Fax:** 01273 858224

Glynde Place is a magnificent example of Elizabethan architecture commanding exceptionally fine views of the South Downs. Amongst the collections of 400 years of family living can be seen a fine collection of 17th and 18th century portraits of the Trevors and a room dedicated to Sir Henry Brand, Speaker of the House of Commons 1872 - 1884 and an exhibition of 'Harbert Morley and the Great Rebellion 1638 - 1660' the story of the part played by the owner of Glynde Place in the Civil War. Plus a collection of 18th century Italian masterpieces.

Location: OS Ref. TQ457 093. In Glynde village 4m SE of Lewes on A27.

Opening Times: House: Easter & May: Suns & BHs only. Jun & Sept: Weds & Suns. Jul & Aug: Weds, Thus & Suns, 2 - 5pm. Last adm. 4.45pm.

Admission: Adult £4, Child £2.

  Free. 

GOODWOOD HOUSE See page 157 for full page entry.

GREAT DIXTER HOUSE & GARDENS

NORTHIAM, RYE, EAST SUSSEX TN31 6PH

Owner: *Christopher Lloyd* ***Contact:*** *Elaine Francis, Business Manager*

Tel: 01797 252878 **Fax:** 01797 252879 **e-mail:** greatdixter@compuserve.com

Great Dixter, birthplace and home of gardening writer Christopher Lloyd, was built in 1460 and boasts one of the largest surviving timber-framed halls in the country. Lutyens was employed to restore both the house and gardens in 1910. The gardens are now the hallmark of Christopher Lloyd with an exciting combination of meadows, ponds, topiary and the famous Long Border and Exotic Garden.

Location: OS Ref. TQ817 251. Signposted off the A28 in Northiam.

Opening Times: Apr - Oct: Tue - Sun, 2 - 5pm (last admission).

Admission: House & garden: Adult £6, Child £1.50. Garden only: Adult £4.50, Child £1. Groups (25+) by appointment. House & garden: Adult £5, Child £1.50.

No photography in House. 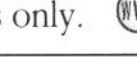 Partially suitable. WC. Obligatory. Limited for coaches. Guide dogs only.

HAMMERWOOD PARK

EAST GRINSTEAD, SUSSEX RH19 3QE

Owner/Contact: *David Pinnegar*

Tel: 01342 850594 **Fax:** 01342 850864 **e-mail:** latrobe@mistral.co.uk

Built in 1792 as an Apollo's hunting lodge by Benjamin Latrobe, architect of the Capitol and the White House, Washington DC. Owned by Led Zepplin in the 1970s, rescued from dereliction in 1982. Cream teas in the Organ Room; mural by French artists in the hall; and a derelict dining room still shocks the unwary. Guided tours (said by many to be the most interesting in Sussex) by the family.

Location: OS Ref. TQ442 390. 3½ m E of East Grinstead on A264 to Tunbridge Wells, 1m W of Holtye.

Opening Times: Easter Mon - end Sept: Wed, Sat & BH Mon, 2 - 5.30pm. Guided tour starts 2.05pm. Coaches strictly by appointment. Small groups any time throughout the year by appointment.

Admission: House & Park: Adult £5, Child £2. Private viewing by arrangement.

Conferences. Obligatory. 

In grounds. B&B. Please tel for details.

HERSTMONCEUX CASTLE GARDENS **Tel:** 01323 833816 **Fax:** 01323 834499

Hailsham, Sussex BN27 1RN **e-mail:** c_cullip@isc-queens.co.uk

Owner: Queen's University, Canada **Contact:** C Cullip

This breathtaking 15th century moated Castle is within 500 acres of parkland and gardens (including Elizabethan Garden) and is ideal for picnics and woodland walks. At Herstmonceux there is something for all the family. For information on our attractions or forthcoming events tel: 01323 833816.

Location: OS Ref. TQ646 104. 2m S of Herstmonceux village (A271) by minor road. 10m WNW of Bexhill.

Opening Times: 15 Apr - 29 Oct: daily, 10am - 6pm (last adm. 5pm) Closes 5pm from Oct.

Admission: Grounds and Gardens: Adults £3.50, Child under 5 Free, Conc. £2.75. Castle Tour: Adult £2.50, Child £1 (under 5 Free). Group rates available.

Visitor Centre. Suitable, limited for Castle Tour.

On leads. Tel. for details.

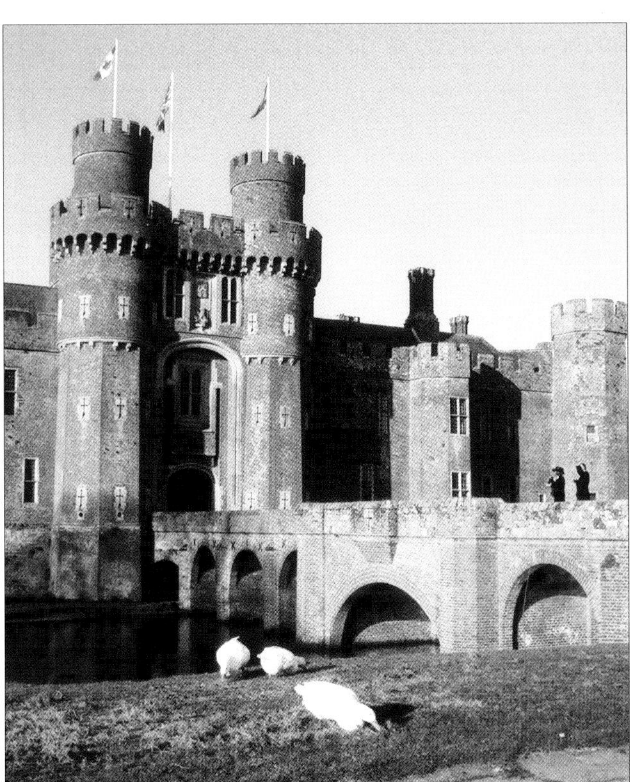

Patrick Lane.

Herstmonceux Castle Garden, Sussex.

Website Index PAGE 46

HIGH BEECHES GARDENS

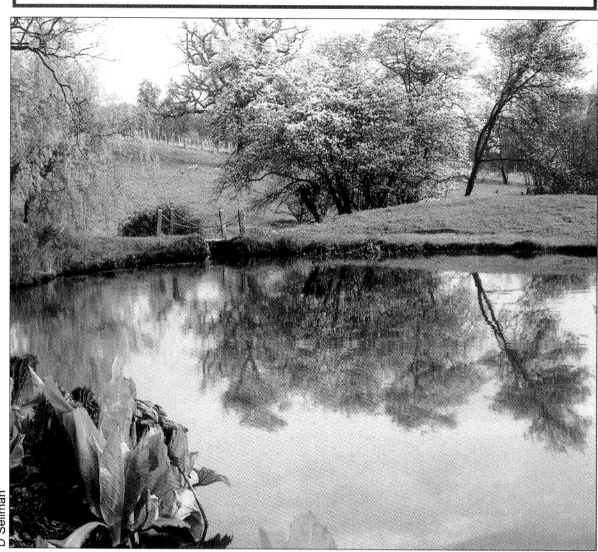

D Sellman

HIGH BEECHES, HANDCROSS, SUSSEX RH17 6HQ

Owner: *High Beeches Gardens Conservation Trust (Reg. Charity)* ***Contact:*** *Sarah Bray*

Tel: 01444 400589 **Fax:** 01444 401543

Help preserve these 20 acres of magically beautiful, peaceful woodland and water gardens. Daffodils, bluebells, azaleas, naturalised gentians, autumn colours. Rippling streams, enchanting vistas. Four acres of natural wildflower meadows. Rare plants. Tree trail. Recommended by Christopher Lloyd. Picnic area. Gardens may be booked for photographic sessions.

Location: OS Ref. TQ275 308. S side of B2110. 1m NE of Handcross.

Opening Times: Spring & Autumn: daily, 1 - 5pm. Closed Weds. Also open Jul & Aug: Mons & Tues. Enjoy our Event Days: 1 Apr, 29 May, 20 Aug, 15 Oct, 10.30am - 5pm.

Admission: Adult £4, Child Free. Groups: £4. (£15 extra outside normal opening hours). Privileged guest tour £5pp inclusive.

On Event Days. 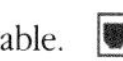 Not suitable.  Guide dogs only. 

LEWES CASTLE & BARBICAN HOUSE

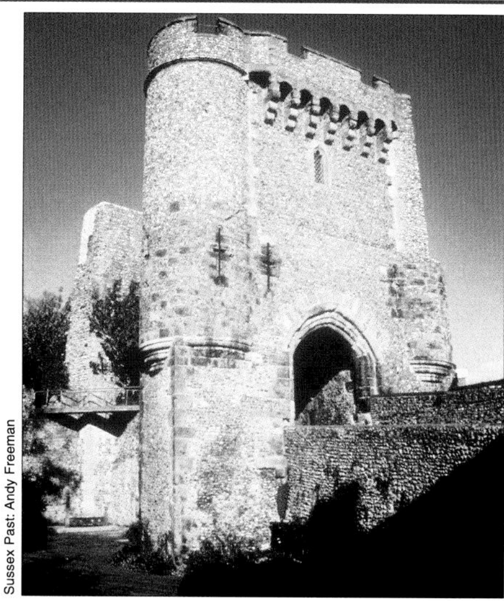

Sussex Past: Andy Freeman

169 HIGH STREET, LEWES, SUSSEX BN7 1YE

Owner: *Sussex Archaeological Society* ***Contact:*** *Mrs Jill Allen*

Tel: 01273 486290 **Fax:** 01273 486990 **e-mail:** castle@sussexpast.co.uk

Lewes's imposing Norman castle offers magnificent views across the town and surrounding downland. Barbican House towered over by the Barbican Gate is home to the Museum of Sussex Archaeology; a superb scale model of Victorian Lewes provides the centrepiece of a 25 minute audio-visual presentation telling the story of the county town of Sussex.

Location: OS198 Ref. TQ412 101. Lewes town centre off A27/A26/A275.

Opening Times: All year (except 25 - 28 Dec): Mon - Sat: 10am - 5.30pm; Suns & BHs, 11am - 5.30pm. Castle closes at dusk in winter.

Admission: Adult £3.70, Child £1.90, Conc. £3.20 Family (2+2) £10.50. Groups: Adult £3.30, Child £1.60, Conc. £2.80. Combined ticket with Anne of Cleves House available.

Not suitable. By arrangement. 

HIGHDOWN GARDENS — Tel: 01903 501054

Littlehampton Road, Goring-by-Sea, Worthing, Sussex BN12 6PE

Owner: Worthing Borough Council **Contact:** C Beardsley Esq

Unique gardens in disused chalk pit, begun in 1909.

Location: OS Ref. TQ098 040. 3m WNW of Worthing on N side of A259, just W of the Goring roundabout.

Opening Times: 1 Apr - 30 Sept: Mon - Fri, 10am - 6pm. W/ends & BHs, 10am - 6pm. 1 Oct - 30 Nov: Mon - Fri, 10am - 4.30pm. 1 Dec - 31 Jan: 10am - 4pm. 1 Feb - 31 Mar: Mon - Fri, 10am - 4.30pm.

Admission: Free.

LAMB HOUSE — Tel: 01892 890651 Fax: 01892 890110

West Street, Rye, Sussex TN31 7ES

Owner: The National Trust **Contact:** Regional Office

The home of the writer Henry James from 1898 to 1916 where he wrote the best novels of his later period.

Location: OS Ref. TQ920 202. In West Street, facing W end of church.

Opening Times: 1 Apr - 28 Oct: Weds & Sats only, 2 - 6pm. Last admission 5.30pm.

Admission: Adult £2.50, Child £1.25, Family (2+3) £6.25. Group: £2.10.

LEONARDSLEE GARDENS

See page 158 for full page entry.

MARLIPINS MUSEUM — Tel: 01273 462994

High Street, Shoreham-by-Sea, Sussex BN43 5DA

Owner: Sussex Archaeological Society **Contact:** Helen Poole

Shoreham's local and especially maritime history is explored at Marlipins, an important historic building of Norman origin. The maritime gallery contains many fine paintings and models while the museum houses exhibits dating back to man's earliest occupation of the area. Formerly an old customs house, the building has a superb chequer-work façade of knapped flint and Caen stone.

Location: OS198 Ref. TQ214 051. Shoreham town centre on A259, W of Brighton.

Opening Times: 1 May - 30 Sept: Tue - Sat, 10.30am - 4.30pm. Suns, 2.30 - 4.30pm.

Admission: Adult £1.50, Child 75p (accompanied children, free), Conc. £1.

 Not suitable. By arrangement. Guide dogs only.

Open all Year Index PAGE 52

Patrick Lane.

Lamb House, Sussex.

South East England

MERRIMENTS GARDENS

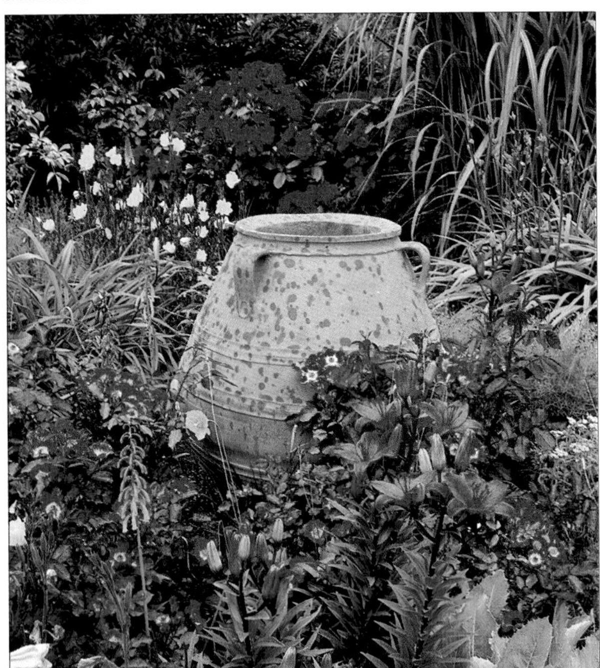

HAWKHURST ROAD, HURST GREEN, EAST SUSSEX TN19 7RA

Owner: *Family owned* ***Contact:*** *Mark Buchele*

Tel: 01580 860666 **Fax:** 01580 860324 **e-mail:** info@merriments.co.uk

'Gardened naturally, free from restriction of institute, experimenting continuously, and always permitting nature to have its say'.

Set in 4 acres of gently sloping Weald farmland, a naturalistic garden which never fails to delight. Deep curved borders richly planted and colour themed. An abundance of rare plants will startle the visitor with sheer originality.

The garden is planted according to prevailing conditions and only using plants suited for naturalising and colonising their environment. This natural approach to gardening harks back to the days of William Robinson and is growing in popularity, especially in Northern Europe. Alternatively many borders are colour themed and planted in the great tradition of English gardening. These borders use a rich mix of trees, shrubs, perennials and grasses and give an arresting display from spring to autumn.

There is a new entrance garden in the style of Monet's 'Grande Allée' at Giverny, France. Other new ventures include a rock and scree garden, a foliage border and further development of the woodland.

Location: OS198, Ref. TQ412 101. Signposted off A21 London - Hastings road, at Hurst Green.

Opening Times: Apr - Sept: Mon - Sat, 10am - 5pm, Suns, 10.30am - 5pm.

Admission: Adult £2.50, Child £1, Conc. £2.50. Groups (5+) by arrangement.

Partially suitable. Licensed. By arrangement. In grounds, on leads. 

MICHELHAM PRIORY

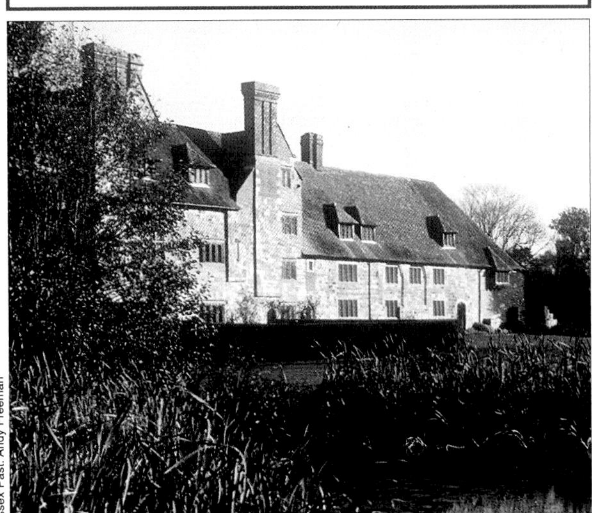
Sussex Past: Andy Freeman

UPPER DICKER, HAILSHAM, SUSSEX BN27 3QS

Owner: *Sussex Archaeological Society* ***Contact:*** *Mr Simon Turner*

Tel: 01323 844224 **Fax:** 01323 844030 **e-mail:** adminmich@sussexpast.co.uk

Set on a medieval moated island surrounded by superb gardens, the Priory was founded in 1229. The remains after the Dissolution were incorporated into a Tudor farm and country house that now contains a fascinating array of exhibits. Grounds include 14th century gatehouse, watermill, physic and cloister gardens and Elizabethan great barn.

Location: OS Ref. TQ557 093. 8m NW of Eastbourne off A22 / A27. 3m W of Hailsham.

Opening Times: 15 Mar - 31Oct: Wed - Sun & BH Mons & daily in Aug. Mar & Oct: 10.30am - 4pm. Apr - Jul & Sept: 10.30am - 5pm. Aug: 10.30am - 5.30pm.

Admission: Adult £4.40, Child £2.30, Conc. £3.80, Family (2+2) £11.40, Registered disabled and carer £2.10. Groups: Adult £3.60, Child £2.10.

Licensed. Guide dogs only.

MOORLANDS

Tel: 01892 652474

Friar's Gate, Crowborough, East Sussex TN6 1XF

Owner: Dr & Mrs Steven Smith **Contact:** Dr Steven Smith

Four acre garden set in a lush valley adjoining Ashdown Forest. Primulas, azaleas and rhododendrons flourish by streams and a small lake. New river walk with views over garden. Many unusual trees and shrubs. Good autumn colour. Featured in Meridien TV programme.

Location: OS Ref. TQ498 329. 2m NW of Crowborough. From B2188 at Friar's Gate, take left fork signposted 'Crowborough Narrow Road', entrance 100yds on left. From Crowborough crossroads take St John's Road to Friar's Gate.

Opening Times: 1 Apr - 1 Oct: Weds, 11am - 5pm. 21 May & 16 Jul: Suns, 2 - 6pm. Other times by appointment only.

Admission: Adult £2.50, Child Free.

Moorlands, Sussex.

South East England

NYMANS GARDEN

Nick Meers

HANDCROSS, HAYWARDS HEATH, SUSSEX RH17 6EB

Owners: *The National Trust* ***Contact:*** *The Property Manager*

Tel: 01444 400321/400777 **Fax:** 01444 400253 **e-mail:** snygen@smtp.ntrust.org.uk

One of the great gardens of the Sussex Weald, with rare and beautiful plants, shrubs and trees from all over the world. Wall garden, hidden sunken garden, pinetum, laurel walk and romantic ruins. Lady Rosse's library, drawing room and forecourt garden also open. Woodland walks and Wild Garden.

Location: OS Ref. TQ265 294. On B2114 at Handcross, 4½ m S of Crawley, just off London - Brighton M23 / A23.

Opening Times: 1 Mar - 29 Oct: daily except Mon & Tue but open BHs, 11am - 6pm or sunset if earlier. House: 29 Mar - 29 Oct: same days as garden, 12 noon - 4pm. Garden only: Nov - Mar: garden only, Sats & Suns, 11am - 4pm. Closed 30 & 31 Dec 2000.

Admission: Adult £5, Child £2.50, Family £12.50. Pre-booked Groups £4. Joint group ticket which includes same day entry to Standen £7 available Wed - Fri only. Winter weekends: Adult £2.50, Child £1.50, Family £6.50. Booked groups: £2.

Grounds suitable. WC. Licensed.

PASHLEY MANOR GARDENS

TICEHURST, WADHURST, EAST SUSSEX TN5 7HE

Owner: *James A Sellick* ***Contact:*** *Catherine Harbord*

Tel: 01580 200888 **Fax:** 01580 200102 **e-mail:** pashleymanor@email.msn.com

Pashley Manor Gardens offers a sumptuous blend of romantic landscaping, imaginative plantings and fine old trees, fountains, springs and large ponds. This is a quintessentially English garden of a very individual character with exceptional views to the surrounding valleyed fields. Many eras of English history are reflected here, typifying the tradition of the English Country house and its garden.

Location: OS Ref. TQ707 291. On B2099 between A21 and Ticehurst village.

Opening Times: 8 Apr - 30 Sept: Tues, Weds, Thurs, Sats and all BH Mons, 11am - 5pm. Garden only (restaurant & shop closed): 1 - 31 Oct: Mon - Fri, 11am - 4pm.

Admission: Adult £5, Child/OAP £4.50. Groups (min 10): £4.50. Coaches by appointment only.

Partially suitable. Licensed. By arrangement. P Guide dogs only.

PARHAM HOUSE & GARDENS

PARHAM PARK, Nr PULBOROUGH, WEST SUSSEX RH20 4HS

Owners: *Parham Park Trust* ***Contact:*** *Patricia Kennedy*

Tel: 01903 744888/742021 **Fax:** 01903 746557 **e-mail:** Parham@dial.pipex.com

A great favourite with all the family, this beautiful Elizabethan house with award-winning gardens is idyllically situated in an ancient deer park under the South Downs. Enjoy the important collection of paintings, furniture and needlework in panelled rooms, including Long Gallery. Light lunches and cream teas served in the 16th century Big Kitchen.

Location: OS Ref. TQ060 143. Midway between Pulborough & Storrington on A283.

Opening Times: 2 Apr - 29 Oct: Weds, Thurs, Suns & BH Mons. Picnic area, Big Kitchen and Gardens: 12 noon - 6pm. House: 2 - 6pm. Last entry 5pm. Private groups by arrangement at other times.

Admission: House & Gardens: Adult £5, OAP £4, Child £1, Family (2+2) £10. Unguided booked groups (20+) £4. Garden only: Adult/OAP £3, Child 50p (1999 prices).

i No photography in house. Partially suitable. P In grounds, on leads.

PETWORTH HOUSE See page 159 for full page entry.

PEVENSEY CASTLE **Tel:** 01323 762604

Pevensey, Sussex BN24 5LE

Owner: English Heritage **Contact:** The Custodian

Originally a 4th century Roman Fort, Pevensey was the place where William the Conqueror landed in 1066 and established his first stronghold. The Norman castle included the remains of an unusual keep within the massive walls. Free audio tour tells the story of the Castle's 2,000 year history.

Location: OS Ref. TQ645 048. In Pevensey off A259.

Opening Times: 1 Apr - 30 Sept: daily, 10am - 6pm. 1 - 31 Oct: 10am - 5pm. 1 Nov - 31 Mar: Wed - Sun only, 10am - 4pm. Closed 24 - 26 Dec.

Admission: Adult £2.50, Child £1.30, Conc. £1.90. 15% discount for groups of 11+.

Grounds suitable. Free. In grounds, on leads. Tel. for details.

Pashley Manor Gardens, Sussex.

PRESTON MANOR

PRESTON DROVE, BRIGHTON, EAST SUSSEX BN1 6SD

Owner: *Brighton & Hove Council* *Contact:* *David Beevers*

Tel: 01273 292770 **Fax:** 01273 292771

A delightful Manor House which powerfully evokes the atmosphere of an Edwardian gentry home both 'upstairs' and 'downstairs'. Explore more than twenty rooms over four floors – from the servants' quarters, kitchens and butler's pantry in the basement to the attic bedrooms and nursery on the top floor. Plus charming walled gardens, pets' cemetery and 13th century parish church.

Location: OS Ref. TQ303 064. 2m N of Brighton on the A23 London road.

Opening Times: All year: Tue - Sat 10am - 5pm, Suns 2 - 5pm, Mons 1 - 5pm (BHs 10am - 5pm). Closed Good Fri, 25/26 Dec.

Admission: Adult £3.10, Child £1.95, Conc. £2.60. Groups (20+) £2.60. Prices valid until 31 Mar 2000.

No photography. Gift kiosk. Not suitable. By arrangement. For coaches.

THE PRIEST HOUSE

Tel: 01342 810479

North Lane, West Hoathly, Sussex RH19 4PP

Owner: Sussex Archaeological Society **Contact:** Antony Smith

Standing in the beautiful surroundings of a traditional cottage garden on the edge of Ashdown Forest, the Priest House is an early 15th century timber-framed hall-house. In Elizabethan times it was modernised into a substantial yeoman's dwelling. Its furnished rooms contain 17th and 18th century furniture, kitchen equipment, needlework and household items. Formal herb garden.

Location: OS187 Ref. TQ362 325. In triangle formed by Crawley, East Grinstead and Haywards Heath, 4m off A22, 6m off M23.

Opening Times: 1 Mar - 31 Oct: Mon - Sat, 11am - 5.30pm, Suns, 2 - 5.30pm.

Admission: Adults £2.50, Child £1.20, Conc. £2.30. Groups (min 20): Adult £2.30, Child £1.10, Conc. £2.

Partially suitable. By arrangement. Limited. Guide dogs only.

THE ROYAL PAVILION

See page 160 for full page entry.

ST. MARY'S BRAMBER

See page 161 for full page entry.

SAINT HILL MANOR

SAINT HILL ROAD, EAST GRINSTEAD, WEST SUSSEX RH19 4JY

Contact: *Mrs Liz Nyegaard*

Tel: 01342 326711

Built 1792 by Gibbs Crawfurd. One of the finest Sussex sandstone buildings in existence and situated near the breathtaking Ashdown Forest. Subsequent owners included Edgar March Crookshank and the Maharajah of Jaipur. In 1959, Saint Hill Manor's final owner, acclaimed author and humanitarian L Ron Hubbard, acquired the Manor, where he lived for many years with his family. As a result of the work carried out under Mr Hubbard's direction, the Manor has been restored to its original beauty, including the uncovering of fine oak wood panelling, marble fireplaces and plasterwork ceilings. Other outstanding features of this lovely house include an impressive library of Mr Hubbard's works, elegant winter garden, and delightful Monkey Mural painted in 1945 by Winston Churchill's nephew John Spencer Churchill. This 100-foot mural depicts many famous personalities as monkeys, including Winston Churchill. Also open to the public are 59 acres of landscaped gardens, lake and woodlands. Ideal for corporate functions, wedding receptions and also available as a film location. Annual events include open-air theatre, arts festivals, classical and jazz concerts.

Location: OS Ref. TQ382 359. 2m SW of East Grinstead. At Felbridge, turn off A22, down Imberhorne Lane, and over crossroads into Saint Hill Road, 200 yds on right.

Opening Times: All year: daily, 2 - 5pm, on the hour. Groups welcome.

Admission: Free.

Ground floor suitable.  Obligatory. 

South East England

SHEFFIELD PARK GARDEN

Nr UCKFIELD, EAST SUSSEX TN22 3QX

Owner: *The National Trust* ***Contact:*** *The Property Manager*

Tel: 01825 790231 **Fax:** 01825 791264 **e-mail:** kshxxx@smtp.ntrust.org.uk

A magnificent tranquil 120 acre landscape garden, with 4 lakes linked by cascades, laid out in the 18th century by 'Capability' Brown. A garden for all seasons. Daffodils, snowdrops and bluebells in spring, its rhododendrons, azaleas and spring garden are spectacular in early summer. Cool tree-lined paths and lake reflections make it perfect for a stroll in high summer and the garden is ablaze with colour from its rare trees and shrubs in autumn. The mists and frosts in wintertime create a mystical mood and give the garden a unique atmosphere.

Location: OS Ref. TQ415 240. Midway between East Grinstead and Lewes, 5m NW of Uckfield on E side of A275.

Opening Times: Jan & Feb: Sats & Suns only, 10.30am - 4pm. Mar - end Oct: Tue - Sun, BH Mons & Good Fri, 10.30am - 6pm, last admission 5pm or sunset if earlier. Nov & Dec: Tue - Sun, 10.30am - 4pm.

Admission: Adult £4.50, Child £2.25, Family (2+3) £11.25. Pre-booked groups £3.80.

Grounds suitable. WC. Licensed (not NT).
Guide dogs only.

STANDEN

NT Photographic Library. Jonathan Gibson.

EAST GRINSTEAD, WEST SUSSEX RH19 4NE

Owner: *The National Trust* ***Contact:*** *The Property Manager*

Tel: 01342 323029 **Fax:** 01342 316424 **e-mail:** sstpro@smtp.ntrust.org.uk

Dating from the 1890s and containing original Morris & Co furnishings and decorations, Standen survives today as a remarkable testimony to the ideals of the Arts and Crafts movement. The property was built as a family home by the influential architect Phillip Webb and retains a warm, welcoming atmosphere. Details of Webb's designs can be found everywhere from the fireplaces to the original electric light fittings.

Location: OS Ref. TQ389 356. 2m S of East Grinstead, signposted from B2110.

Opening Times: 29 Mar - 5 Nov: Wed - Sun & BH Mons. House: 12.30 - 4pm (last admission). Garden: As house, 11.30am - 6pm. Garden only: 10 Nov - 17 Dec: Fri - Sun, 1 - 4pm.

Admission: House & Garden: £5, Family £12.50. Garden only: £3. Joint ticket with same day entry to Nymans Garden £7, available Wed - Fri. Groups: £4, Wed - Fri only, if booked in advance.

Partially suitable. WC. Licensed. By arrangement.
In grounds on leads, not in garden.

STANSTED PARK

See page 162 for full page entry.

UPPARK

SOUTH HARTING, PETERSFIELD GU31 5QR

Owner: *The National Trust* ***Contact:*** *The Property Manager*

Tel: 01730 825415 or 01730 825857 (Info Line) **Fax:** 01730 825873

Fine pictures, furniture and ceramics all rescued from the disastrous 1989 fire and now returned to successfully and fully restored exquisite 18th century interior. Award-winning multi-media fire/restoration exhibition. Evocative 'below stairs' rooms. H G Wells connections. Garden in the picturesque style. Wonderful setting high on the South Downs.

Location: OS Ref. SU775 177. 5m SE of Petersfield on B2146.

Opening Times: 2 Apr - 31 Oct: Sun - Thur. House: 1 - 5pm (opens 12 noon on Suns in Jul & Aug). Last admission 4 - 4.15pm. Timed tickets will be in operation on BH Suns & Mons & Suns in Jul & Aug only (inc. NT members). Car park, Woodland Walk, Exhibition, garden, shop & restaurant: 11.30am - 5.30pm.

Admission: House, Garden & Exhibition: £5.50, Family £13.75. Garden, exhibition, etc: half price. Groups by arrangement only.

Partially suitable. WC. Licensed. Coaches must pre-book.
In grounds, on leads. Please telephone for details.

Standen, Sussex.

WAKEHURST PLACE

Tel: 01444 894066

Ardingly, Haywards Heath, Sussex RH17 6TN

Owner: The National Trust (managed by Royal Botanic Gdns) **Contact:** The Administrator

A superb collection of exotic trees, shrubs and other plants, many displayed in a geographic manner. Extensive water gardens, a winter garden, a rock walk and many other features. The Loder Valley Nature Reserve can be visited by prior arrangement.

Location: OS Ref. TQ339 314. $1\frac{1}{2}$ m N of Ardingly, on B2028.

Opening Times: Daily (not 25 Dec & 1 Jan). Feb & Oct: 10am - 5pm. Mar: 10am - 6pm. Apr - end Sept: 10am - 7pm. Nov - end Jan 2000: 10am - 4pm. Mansion closed 1hr before gardens.

Admission: Adult £5, Child (5-16) £2.50, Conc. £3.50, Family (2+4) £13. Reductions for pre-paid booked groups.

 Ground floor & grounds suitable. Tel. for details.

WEALD & DOWNLAND OPEN AIR MUSEUM

Tel: 01243 811348

Singleton, Chichester, Sussex PO18 0EU

40 authentic historic buildings. Interiors and gardens through the ages.

Location: OS Ref. SU876 127. 6m N of Chichester. SE side of A286. W of Singleton.

Opening Times: 1 Mar - 31 Oct: daily, 10.30am - 6pm. Nov - Feb: Weds & w/ends only. 10.30am - 4pm. 26 Dec - 3 Jan: 10.30am - 4pm.

Admission: Adult £5.20, Child/Student £2.50, Family £14.

South East Tourist Board.

Weald & Downland Open Air Museum, Sussex.

WEST DEAN GARDENS

WEST DEAN, CHICHESTER, WEST SUSSEX PO18 0QZ

Owner: *The Edward James Foundation* ***Contact:*** *Jim Buckland, Gardens Manager*

Tel: 01243 818210 **Fax:** 01243 811342 **e-mail:** westdean@pavilion.co.uk

Visiting the Gardens you are immersed in a classic 19th century designed landscape with its $2\frac{1}{2}$ acre walled kitchen garden, 13 original glasshouses dating from the 1890s, 35 acres of ornamental grounds, 240 acre landscaped park and the 49 acre St Roche's arboretum, all linked by a scenic $2\frac{1}{4}$ mile parkland walk. Features of the grounds are a lavishly planted 300ft long Edwardian pergola terminated by a flint and stone gazebo and sunken garden. The Visitor Centre (free entry) houses a licensed restaurant and an imaginative garden shop.

Location: OS Ref. SU863 128. SE side of A286 Midhurst Road, 6m N of Chichester.

Opening Times: 1 Mar - 31 October inclusive: daily, 11am - 5pm.

Admission: Adult £4, Child £2, OAP £3.50. Groups (min 12): Adult £3.50, Child £2.

No photography in house. Licensed. Limited for coaches. By arrangement. Guide dogs only. Telephone for details.

WILMINGTON PRIORY

Tel: 01628 825920 or 825925 (bookings)

Wilmington, Nr Eastbourne, East Sussex BN26 5SW

Owner: Leased to the Landmark Trust by Sussex Archaeological Society

Contact: The Landmark Trust

Founded by the Benedictines in the 11th century, the surviving, much altered buildings date largely from the 14th century. Managed and maintained by the Landmark Trust, which lets buildings for self-catering holidays. Full details of Wilmington Priory and 167 other historic buildings available for holidays are featured in The Landmark Handbook (price £9.50 refundable against booking), from The Landmark Trust, Shottesbrooke, Maidenhead, Berkshire, SL6 3SW.

Location: OS Ref. TQ543 042. 600yds S of A27. 6m NW of Eastbourne.

Opening Times: Grounds, Ruins, Porch & Crypt: on 30 days between Apr - Oct. Whole property including interiors on 8 of these days. Telephone for details. Accommodation is available for up to 6 people for self-catering holidays.

Admission: Please contact for details.

Jim Buckland.

West Dean Gardens, Sussex.

The West Country

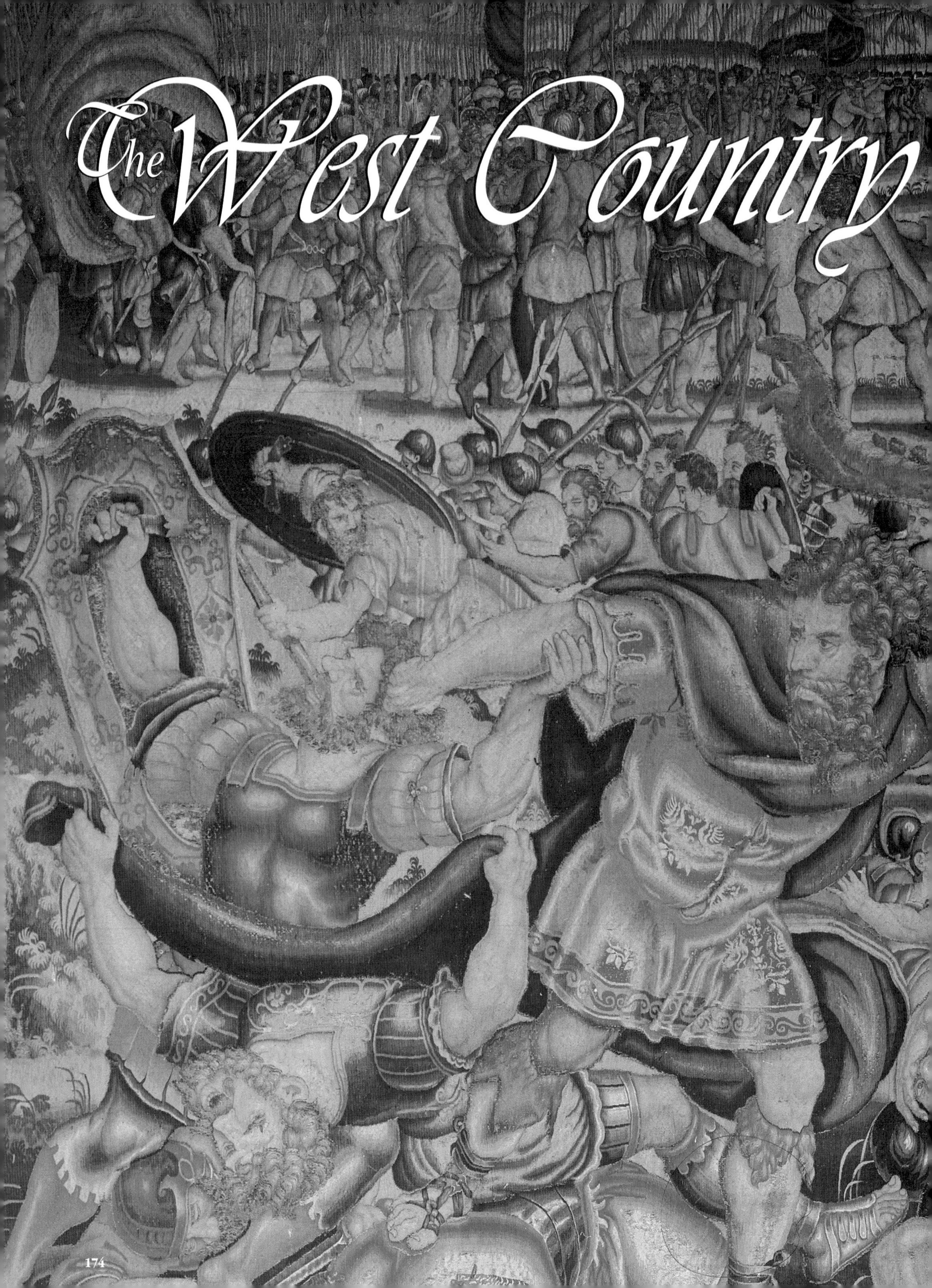

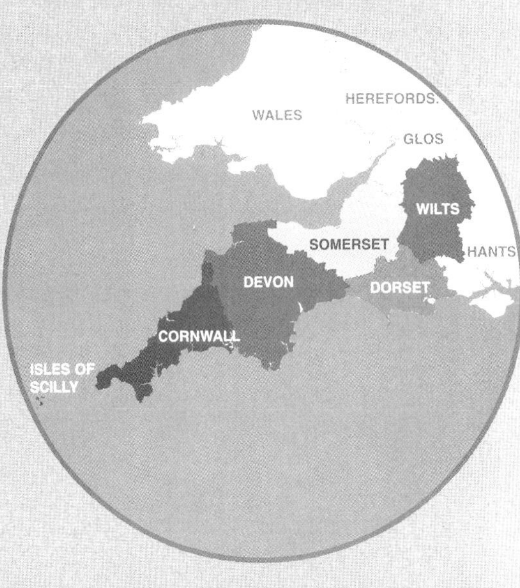

17th century Flemish Tapestry at Athelhampton.

Featuring…

Athelhampton

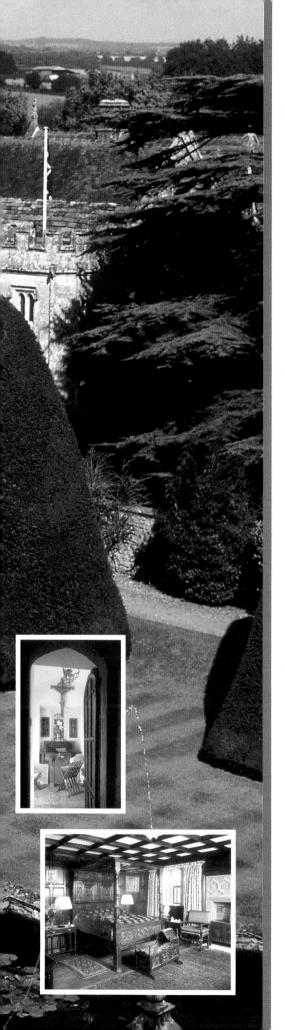

Athelhampton captured the 19th century imagination as a romantic stone manor dating back to the early Tudor period. It inspired the young Thomas Hardy who made watercolours of the property and, with the name of "Athel Hall" made it the setting for two poems: "*The Dame of Athel Hall*" and "The children and Sir Nameless". He also inscribed his signature into the lead of the Dovecote roof.

Although Athelhampton's roots are in Saxon times, dating from when Aethelhelm was Earl of Wessex, the present building dates from the end of the 15th century when Sir William Martyn, a shipowner, wealthy merchant and Lord Mayor of London, was granted a licence to enclose 160 acres of deer park and to enclose and fortify his Manor with walls of stone and lime and to build towers and crenellate them. He had backed both sides in the Wars of the Roses and felt sufficient confidence in peace to build a home that was designed for comfort rather than defence.

Athelhampton had a number of owners. In 1891 it was acquired by Alfred Cart de la Fontaine who began the most extensive works to the house and, over the following eight years, built four courts walled with Ham stone as well as the two garden pavilions. It was at this time that the yew trees were planted in the Great Court, which have since grown into topiary pyramids 25' high.

The house and garden as they are seen today owe as much to Robert V Cooke, a surgeon by profession, who had long resolved to restore an historic house for his collection of fine art and furniture. The gardens owe much to the enthusiasm of his son, Sir Robert Cooke, the politician whose son Patrick, the owner of Athelhampton, continues the work today. This has included the restoration of the house following a fire in 1992 which gutted most of the East Wing.

The Great Hall is one of the finest examples of 15th century domestic architecture in the country with a medieval roof of curved brace timbers and an oriel with fine heraldic glass.

Above all, Athelhampton captures the essence of a well loved and lived-in active family home, with wonderful panelled rooms and tapestries, fine pictures, furniture and china.

For full details of this property see page 197.

West Country England

National Trust/Peter Cade.

Antony House
Owner: The National Trust

Antony Woodland Garden
Owner:
Carew Pole Garden Trust

CONTACT

Antony House
The Administrator
Antony House & Gdn
Torpoint
Cornwall
PL11 2QA

Tel: 01752 812191

Antony Woodland Garden
Mrs Valerie Anderson
Antony
Torpoint
Cornwall
PL11 2QA

Tel: 01752 812364

LOCATION

OS Ref. SX418 564

Antony House and Antony Woodland Garden
5m W of Plymouth via Torpoint car ferry, 2m NW of Torpoint.

ANTONY HOUSE & GDN. & ANTONY WOODLAND GDN.

Torpoint

ANTONY HOUSE AND GARDEN: A superb example of an early 18th century mansion. The main block is faced in lustrous silver-grey stone, flanked by mellow brick pavilions. The ancestral home of the Carew family for nearly 600 years, the house contains a wealth of paintings, tapestries, furniture and embroideries, many linking the great families of Cornwall – set in parkland and fine gardens (including the National Collection of day lilies), overlooking the Lynher river. An 18th century Bath House can be viewed by arrangement.

ANTONY WOODLAND GARDEN: The woodland garden was established in the late 18th century with the assistance of Humphrey Repton. It features numerous varieties of camellias, together with magnolias, rhododendrons, azaleas and other flowering shrubs, interspersed with many fine species of indigenous and exotic trees. A further 50 acres of natural woods bordering the tidal waters of the Lynher provide a number of delightful walks. The Woodland Garden is at its finest in the spring and autumn months.

National Trust/ Dan Flunder

Braille guide.

OPENING TIMES

Antony House and Garden
4 Apr - 26 Oct:
Tue - Thur & BH Mons.

Jun, Jul & Aug: daily except Mons, Fris & Sats (open BH Mons).

1.30 - 5.30pm.
Last admission 4.45pm.

Bath Pond House can be seen by written application.

Guided tours at less busy times.

Antony Woodland Garden
1 March - 31 October
Daily except Mons & Fris but open BHs
11am - 5.30pm.

ADMISSION

Antony House & Garden

Adult	£4.00
Groups	£3.40
Family	£10.00

NT Garden only:
.... £2.00

Antony Woodland Garden:

Adult	£3.00

Joint Gardens-only ticket to NT-owned garden and Antony Woodland Garden

Adult	£3.50
Child	£1.50
Groups	£2.80

NB. Entrance to the Woodland Garden is free to NT members on days when the house is open.

National Trust/Andrew Besley

Owner: The National Trust

CONTACT

Lewis Eynon
Property Manager
Cotehele
St Dominick
Saltash
Cornwall
PL12 6TA

Tel: 01579 351346

Fax: 01579 351222

e-mail:
cctlce@smtp.ntrust.org.uk

LOCATION

OS Ref. SX422 685

1m SW of Calstock by foot. 8m S of Tavistock, 4m E of Callington, 15m from Plymouth via the Tamar bridge at Saltash

Trains: Limited service from Plymouth to Calstock (1¼ m uphill)

Boats: Limited (tidal) service from Plymouth to Calstock Quay (Plymouth Boat Cruises) **Tel:** 01752 822797

River taxi: Privately run from Calstock to Cotehele Quay. Tel: 01579 351346

Buses: Western National (seasonal variations) Tel: 01752 222666

COTEHELE
Saltash

COTEHELE, owned by the Edgcumbe family for nearly 600 years, is a fascinating and enchanting estate set on the steep wooded slopes of the River Tamar. Exploring Cotehele's many and various charms provides a full day out for the family and leaves everyone longing to return.

The steep valley garden contains exotic and tender plants which thrive in the mild climate. Remnants of an earlier age include a mediaeval stewpond and domed dovecote, a 15th century chapel and 18th century tower with fine views over the surrounding countryside. A series of more formal gardens, terraces, an orchard and a daffodil meadow surround Cotehele House.

One of the least altered medieval houses in the country, Cotehele is built in local granite, slate and sandstone. Inside the ancient rooms, unlit by electricity, is a fine collection of textiles, tapestries, armour and early dark oak furniture. The chapel contains the oldest working domestic clock in England, still in its original position.

A walk through the garden and along the river leads to the quay, a busy river port in Victorian times. The National Maritime Museum worked with the National Trust to set up a museum here which explains the vital role that the Tamar played in the local economy. As a living reminder, the restored Tamar sailing barge *Shamrock* (owned jointly by the Trust and the National Maritime Museum) is moored here.

A further walk through woodland along the Morden stream leads to the old estate corn mill which has been restored to working order.

This large estate with many footpaths offers a variety of woodland and countryside walks, opening up new views and hidden places. The Danescombe Valley, with its history of mining and milling, is of particular interest.

National Trust/Tymn Lintell

No photography in house. *Winner of 1996 Merit Award for Excellence, Times/NPI National Heritage Awards.*

Cotehele Quay Gallery offers a wide range of local hand-made arts and crafts.

Available for up to 90 people.

2 wheelchairs at Reception. Hall & kitchen accessible. Ramps at house, restaurant and shop. Most of garden is very steep with loose gravel. Riverside walks are flatter (from Cotehele Quay) & Edgcumbe Arms is accessible. WCs near house and at Quay. Parking near house & mill by arrangement.

In Barn restaurant (can be booked) daily (except Fri), Apr - Oct. At the Quay, Edgcumbe Arms offers lighter meals daily, Apr - Oct (plus weekends in March). Both licensed.

Near house and garden and at Cotehele Quay. No parking at Mill.

Groups (15+) must book with Property Manager and receive a coach route (limited to two per day). No groups Sun & BH weekends. Visitors to house limited to 80 at any one time. Please arrive early and be prepared to queue. Avoid dull days early and late in the season. Allow a full day to see estate.

Under control welcome only on woodland walks.

OPENING TIMES

SUMMER
1 April - 31 October.

Garden
All year: daily, 11am - dusk

House
Daily except Fri
(but open Good Fri)
11am - 5pm
(4.30pm in October)

Mill
Daily except Fri
(but open Good Fri
& Fri in July & August)
1 - 5.30pm
(6pm in July & August
4.30pm in October)

WINTER
October - March

Garden
Open daily 11am - dusk.

Shop, Gallery & Edgcumbe Arms
Open weekends in March.

ADMISSION

House, Garden & Mill

Adult	£6.00
Child (5-17yrs)	£3.00
Groups*	£5.00
Family (2+3)	£15.00

Garden & Mill only

Adult	£3.20
Child (5-17yrs)	£1.60
Family (2+3)	£8.00

*Groups must book in advance with the Property Manager. No groups Suns or BHs.

NT members free.
You may join here.

West Country England

National Trust Photographic Library. R Truman.

Owner: The National Trust

CONTACT

Property Manager
Lanhydrock
Bodmin
Cornwall
PL30 5AD

Tel: 01208 73320

Fax: 01208 74084

e-mail:
clhlan@smtp.ntrust.org.uk

LOCATION

OS Ref. SX085 636

$2^1/_2$ m SE of Bodmin, follow signposts from either A30, A38 or B3268.

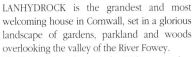

LANHYDROCK

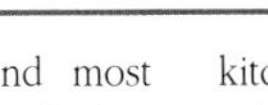

Bodmin

LANHYDROCK is the grandest and most welcoming house in Cornwall, set in a glorious landscape of gardens, parkland and woods overlooking the valley of the River Fowey.

The house dates back to the 17th century but much of it had to be rebuilt after a disastrous fire in 1881 destroyed all but the entrance porch and the north wing, which includes the magnificent Long Gallery with its extraordinary plaster ceiling depicting scenes from the Old Testament. A total of 49 rooms are on show today and together they reflect the entire spectrum of life in a rich and splendid Victorian household, from the many servants' bedrooms and the fascinating complex of kitchens, sculleries and larders to the nursery suite where the Agar-Robartes children lived, learned and played, and the grandeur of the dining room with its table laid and ready.

Surrounding the house on all sides are gardens ranging from formal Victorian parterres to the wooded higher garden where magnificent displays of magnolias, rhododendrons and camellias climb the hillside to merge with the oak and beech woods all around. A famous avenue of ancient beech and sycamore trees, the original entrance drive to the house, runs from the pinnacled 17th century gatehouse down towards the medieval bridge across the Fowey at Respryn.

National Trust Photographic Library. Andreas von Einsiedel.

National Trust/Tony Kent

No photography in house.

By arrangement.

Suitable. Braille guide. WC.

Licensed restaurant

In park, on leads. Guide dogs only in house.

Limited for coaches.

OPENING TIMES

Garden:
All year
Daily: 11am - 5.30pm
(5pm in February, March & October) open daylight hours during winter.

House:
1 Apr - 31 Oct
Daily except Mon
(but open BH Mons)
11am - 5.30pm.
Closes 5pm in Oct.

Last admission $^1/_2$ hr before closing.

ADMISSION

House, Garden & Grounds

Adult	£6.60
Child (5-17yrs)	£3.20
Family	£16.50

Pre-booked Groups (15+)

Adult	£5.50
Child	£2.75

Garden & Grounds only £3.60

SPECIAL EVENTS

Please telephone for details.

ANTONY HOUSE & GARDEN
ANTONY WOODLAND GARDEN

See page 178 for full page entry.

BURNCOOSE NURSERIES & GARDEN

Gwennap, Redruth, Cornwall TR16 6BJ **Tel:** 01209 860316 **Fax:** 01209 860011
Owner/Contact: C H Williams **e-mail:** burncoose@eclipse.co.uk

The Nurseries are set in the 30 acre woodland gardens of Burncoose.

Location: OS Ref. SW742 395. 2m SE of Redruth on main A393 Redruth to Falmouth road between the villages of Lanner and Ponsanooth.

Opening Times: Mon – Sat: 9am - 5pm, Suns, 11am - 5pm. Gardens and Tearooms open all year (except Christmas Day).

Admission: Nurseries: Free. Gardens: Adult/Conc. £2. Children Free. Group tours: £2.50 by arrangement.

Grounds suitable. WCs. In grounds, on leads.

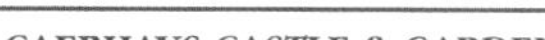

CAERHAYS CASTLE & GARDEN

Tel: 01872 501310 **Fax:** 01872 501870

Caerhays, Gorran, St Austell, Cornwall PL26 6LY **e-mail:** caerhays@eclipse.co.uk
Owner: F J Williams Esq **Contact:** Miss A B Mayes

One of the very few Nash built castles still left standing – situated within approximately 60 acres of informal woodland gardens created by J C Williams, who sponsored plant hunting expeditions to China at the turn of the century. Noted for its camellias, magnolias, rhododendrons and oaks. English Heritage listing - Grade I: Outstanding.

Location: OS Ref. SW972 415. S coast of Cornwall – between Mevagissey and Portloe. 9m SW of St Austell.

Opening Times: House: 20 Mar - 28 Apr: Mon - Fri (excluding BHs), 2 - 4pm. Gardens: 13 Mar - 19 May: Mon - Fri, 10am - 4pm. Charity openings (garden only): 2 & 23 Apr & 1 May: 10am - 4pm.

Admission: House £3.50. Gardens: £3.50, Child £1.50. House & Gardens £6. Guided group tours by Head Gardener £4 and can be arranged outside normal opening times.

  Not suitable.  In grounds, on leads. 

Caerhays Castle & Garden, Cornwall.

CHYSAUSTER ANCIENT VILLAGE

Tel: 0831 757934

Nr Newmill, Penzance, Cornwall TR20 8XA
Owner: English Heritage **Contact:** The Custodian

On a windy hillside, overlooking the wild and spectacular coast, is this deserted Romano-Cornish village with a 'street' of eight well preserved houses, each comprising a number of rooms around an open court.

Location: OS203 Ref. SW473 350. 2 1/2 m NW of Gulval off B3311.

Opening Times: 1 Apr - 31 Oct: daily, 10am - 6pm (5pm in Oct). Winter: closed.

Admission: Adult £1.60, Child 80p, Conc. £1.20. 15% discount for groups (11+).

No coaches.  On leads.  Telephone for details.

CHYVERTON

Tel: 01872 540324 **Fax:** 01872 540648

Zelah, Truro, Cornwall TR4 9HD
Owner/Contact: Nigel Holman

The garden contains one of the finest collections of woody plants in private hands originating from all the temperate regions of the world, built up over the past 75 years by the Holman family. Exceptional magnolias. All growing in the setting of a Georgian landscape garden, creating 'The Magic Jungle of Chyverton' *(Tradescant - The Garden).*

Location: OS Ref. SW797 512. A30, 20m W of Bodmin, 8m E of Redruth signed 1m W of Zelah.

Opening Times: 1 Mar - 30 Sept: by appointment.

Admission: Groups of 1-20 £4 and 21+ £3.50. Child under 16yrs Free.

Not suitable.  By arrangement.  Obligatory. Limited for coaches. 
In grounds on leads.

COTEHELE

See page 179 for full page entry.

GLENDURGAN GARDEN

National Trust/David Hastilow.

MAWNAN SMITH, FALMOUTH, CORNWALL TR11 5JZ

Owner: *The National Trust* ***Contact:*** *Reception*

Tel: 01326 250906 (opening hours) or 01872 662090 **Fax:** 01872 865808

A valley garden of great beauty with fine trees, shrubs and water gardens. The laurel maze, recently restored, is an unusual and popular feature. The garden runs down to the tiny village of Durgan and its beach on the Helford River.

Location: OS Ref. SW772 277. 4m SW of Falmouth, 1/2 m SW of Mawnan Smith, on road to Helford Passage. 1m E of Trebah Garden.

Opening Times: 22 Feb - 28 Oct: Tue - Sat & BH Mons, 10.30am - 5.30pm (closed Good Fri). Last admission 4.30pm.

Admission: £3.75, Family £8.75. Pre-arranged groups: £2.90.

  Braille guide. 

GODOLPHIN

BREAGE, HELSTON, CORNWALL TR13 9RE

Owner/Contact: *Mrs M Schofield*

Tel/Fax: 01736 763194

Godolphin is a Tudor and Stuart house with original Elizabethan stables. The recently discovered gardens show the ancient raised walks and carp ponds and are at present undergoing clearance. The most eminent Godolphins were Sidney the poet, killed in the Civil War fighting for the King, and Sidney the 1st Earl, who was Queen Anne's Lord High Treasurer. His son, the 2nd Earl, owned the famous Godolphin Arabian and a painting of the stallion by John Wootton hangs in the dining room.

Location: OS Ref. SW602 318. Breage, Helston. On minor road from Breage to Townshend.

Opening Times: Godolphin will be under repair and therefore viewing will be restricted. The property will not be open on Thurs mornings. Please contact for details.

Admission: Please contact for details.

  Guide dogs only.

THE JAPANESE GARDEN & BONSAI NURSERY

Tel: 01637 860116

St Mawgan, Nr Newquay, Cornwall TR8 4ET **Owner/Contact:** Mr & Mrs Hore

Authentic Japanese Garden set in 1 acre.

Location: OS Ref. SW873 660. Follow road signs from A3059 & B3276.

Opening Times: All year except Christmas and New Year.

Admission: Adult £2.50, Child £1. Groups (10+): £2.

KEN CARO

Tel: 01579 362446

Bicton, Liskeard PL14 5RF **Owner/Contact:** Mr and Mrs K R Willcock

4 acre plantsman's garden.

Location: OS Ref. SX313 692. 5m NE of of Liskeard.

Opening Times: 16 Apr - 28 Jun, Sun - Wed only; Jul/Aug, Tues & Weds only.

Admission: Adult £2, Child 50p.

LANHYDROCK

See page 180 for full page entry.

LAUNCESTON CASTLE

Tel: 01566 772365

Castle Lodge, Launceston, Cornwall PL15 7DR

Owner: English Heritage **Contact:** The Custodian

Set on the motte of the original Norman castle and commanding the town and surrounding countryside. The shell keep and tower survive of this medieval castle which controlled the main route into Cornwall.

Location: OS201 Ref. SX330 846. In Launceston.

Opening Times: 1 Apr - 31 Oct: daily, 10am - 6pm (5pm in Oct). Winter: Fri - Sun, 10am - 4pm. Closed 24 - 26 Dec & 1 Jan.

Admission: Adult £1.80, Child 90p, Conc. £1.40. 15% discount for groups (11+).

Grounds suitable. Limited. In grounds, on leads. Tel. for details.

MOUNT EDGCUMBE HOUSE & COUNTRY PARK

CREMYLL, TORPOINT, CORNWALL PL10 IHZ

Owner: *Cornwall County & Plymouth City Councils* ***Contact:*** *Cynthia Gaskell Brown*

Tel: 01752 822236 **Fax:** 01752 822199

Tudor home of Earls of Mount Edgcumbe, set in historic 18th century gardens on the dramatic sea-girt Rame peninsula. Wild fallow deer, follies, forts; national camellia collection. One of the Great Gardens of Cornwall.

Location: OS Ref. SX452 527. 10m W of Plymouth via Torpoint.

Opening Times: House and Earls' Garden: 1 Apr - 30 Sept: Wed - Sun & BH Mons, 11am - 4.30pm. Country Park: All year, daily 8am - dusk.

Admission: Adult £4.50, Child (5-15) £2.25, Conc. £3.50, Family (2+2 or 1+3) £10, Season Ticket £7.50. Groups: £3.50. Park: Free.

Licensed. Grounds only. 

THE LOST GARDENS OF HELIGAN

PENTEWAN, ST AUSTELL, CORNWALL PL26 6EN

Owner: *Mr T Smit* ***Contact:*** *Mr C A Howlett*

Tel: 01726 845100 **Fax:** 01726 845101 **e-mail:** info@heligan.com

These award-winning Gardens are 80 acres of superb pleasure grounds together with a magnificent complex of four walled gardens and kitchen garden, all being restored to their former glory as a living museum of 19th century horticulture. An Italian Garden, Fern Ravine, Crystal Grotto, Summerhouses, Rides, Lawns and a 20 acre sub-tropical "Jungle Garden" are just some of the delights of this "Sleeping Beauty".

Location: OS Ref. SX000 465. 5m SW of St Austell. 2m NW of Mevagissey. Take the B3273 to Mevagissey – follow tourist signs.

Opening Times: Daily except 24 & 25 Dec: 10am - 6pm. Last adm. 4.30pm.

Admission: Adult: £5.50. Child (5-15) £2.50, OAP £5. Family £15. Groups: Adult £5, OAP £4.50. Children under 5 Free. Groups and tours by prior arrangement.

  On leads only.

PENCARROW

BODMIN, CORNWALL PL30 3AG

Owner: *Molesworth-St Aubyn family* ***Contact:*** *The Administrator*

Tel/Fax: 01208 841369 **e-mail:** pencarrow@aol.com

Still owned and lived in by the family. Georgian house and listed gardens. Superb collection of pictures, furniture and porcelain. Marked walks through 50 acres of beautiful formal and woodland gardens, Victorian rockery, Italian garden, over 700 different varieties of rhododendrons, lake and ice house.

Location: OS Ref. SX040 711. Between Bodmin and Wadebridge. 4m NW of Bodmin off A389 & B3266 at Washaway.

Opening Times: 2 Apr - 15 Oct: Sun - Thur, 1.30 - 5pm. 1 Jun - 10 Sept & BH Mon opens 11am.

Admission: House & garden: Adult £4.50, Child £2. Garden only: Adult £2.50, Child Free. Groups: House & garden: £4.

Craft centre, small childrens' play area, self-pick soft fruit.

Licensed. Grounds only.

PENDENNIS CASTLE 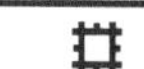

FALMOUTH, CORNWALL TR11 4LP

Owner: *English Heritage* ***Contact:*** *The Head Custodian*

Tel: 01326 316594

Pendennis and its neighbour, St Mawes Castle, face each other across the mouth of the estuary of the River Fal. Built by Henry VIII in 16th century as protection against threat of attack and invasion from France. Extended and adapted over the years to meet the changing threats to national security from the French and Spanish and continued right through to World War II. It withstood five months of siege during the Civil War before becoming the penultimate Royalist Garrison to surrender on the mainland. Pendennis today stands as a landmark, with fine sea views and excellent site facilities including exhibitions, a museum and guardhouse.

Location: OS204, Ref SW824 318. On Pendennis Head.

Opening Times: 1 Apr - 31 Oct: daily, 10am - 6pm or dusk if earlier. 1 Nov - 31 Mar: daily, 10am - 4pm. Closed 24 - 26 Dec.

Admission: Adult £3.80, Child £1.90, Conc. £2.90. 15% discount for groups of 11+.

Shop. Ground floor & grounds suitable. Tearoom. Ample. In grounds, on leads. Tel. for details.

PINE LODGE GARDENS

Tel/Fax: 01726 73500

Cuddra, St Austell, Cornwall PL25 3RQ **Owner/Contact:** Mr & Mrs R H J Clemo

30 acre estate with a wide range of 5,500 plants.

Location: OS Ref. SX044 527. Signposted on A390.

Opening Times: April - September: Wed - Sun & Bank Holidays, 2 - 5pm.

Admission: Adult £3.50, Child half price.

English Heritage Photographic Library.

Pendennis Castle, Cornwall.

PRIDEAUX PLACE

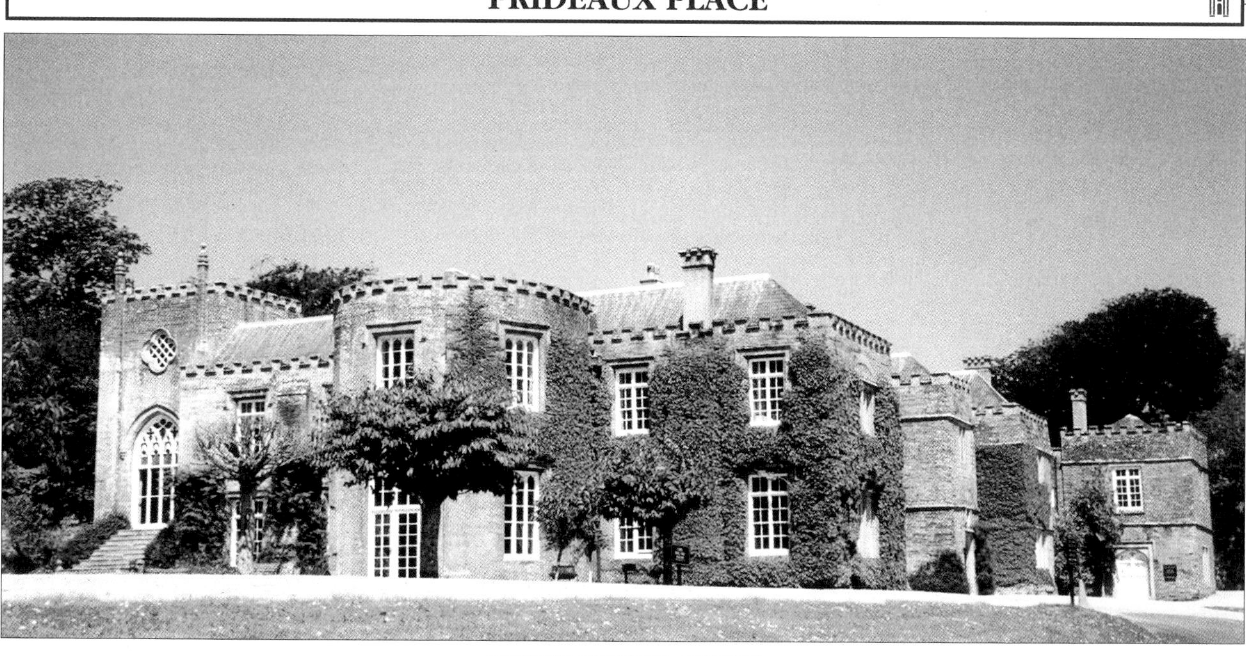

PADSTOW, CORNWALL PL28 8RP

Owner/Contact: *Peter Prideaux-Brune Esq*

Tel: 01841 532411 **Fax:** 01841 532945

Tucked away above the busy port of Padstow, the home of the Prideaux family for over 400 years, is surrounded by gardens and wooded grounds overlooking a deer park and the Camel estuary to the moors beyond. The house still retains its 'E' shape Elizabethan front and contains fine paintings and furniture as well as an exhibition reflecting its emergence as a major international film location. The impressive outbuildings have been restored in recent years and the 16th century plaster ceiling in the great chamber has been uncovered for the first time since 1760.

Location: OS Ref. SW913 756. 5m from A39 Newquay/Wadebridge link road. Signposted by Historic House signs.

Opening Times: Easter Sun - 27 Apr & 28 May - 5 Oct: Sun - Thur, 1.30 - 5pm. Open all year for groups 15+ by arrangement.

Admission: Adult £4.50, accompanied children £2. Grounds only: Adult £2 Child £1. Groups £4.

By arrangement. Ground floor & grounds suitable. By arrangement. In grounds, on leads.

RESTORMEL CASTLE

Tel: 01208 872687

Lostwithiel, Cornwall PL22 0BD

Owner: English Heritage **Contact:** The Custodian

Perched on a high mound, surrounded by a deep moat, the huge circular keep of this splendid Norman castle survives in remarkably good condition. It is still possible to make out the ruins of Restormel's Keep Gate, Great Hall and even the kitchens and private rooms.

Location: OS200 Ref. SX104 614. 1½ m N of Lostwithiel off A390.

Opening Times: 1 Apr - 31 Oct: daily, 10am - 6pm (5pm in Oct). Winter: closed.

Admission: Adult £1.60, Child 80p, Conc. £1.20. 15% discount for groups (11+).

Grounds suitable. Limited for coaches. In grounds, on leads. Telephone for details.

ST CATHERINE'S CASTLE

Tel: 0117 9750700

Fowey, Cornwall

Owner: English Heritage **Contact:** The South West Regional Office

A small fort built by Henry VIII to defend Fowey harbour, with fine views of the coastline and river estuary.

Location: OS200 Ref. SX118 508. ¾ m SW of Fowey along footpath off A3082.

Opening Times: Any reasonable time.

Admission: Free.

ST MAWES CASTLE

ST MAWES, CORNWALL TR2 3AA

Owner: *English Heritage* **Contact:** *The Head Custodian*

Tel: 01326 270526

The pretty fishing village of St Mawes is home to this castle. On the opposite headland to Pendennis Castle, St Mawes shares the task of watching over the mouth of the River Fal as it has done since Henry VIII built it as a defence against the French. With three huge circular bastions shaped like clover leaves, St Mawes was designed to cover every possible angle of approach. It is the finest example of Tudor military architecture. The castle offers views of St Mawes' little boat-filled harbour, the passenger ferry tracking across the Fal, and the splendid coastline which featured in the *Poldark* TV series. Also the start of some delightful walks along the coastal path.

Location: OS204 Ref. SW842 328. W of St Mawes on A3078.

Opening Times: 1 Apr - 31 Oct: daily, 10am - 6pm (5pm in Oct). Winter: 1 Nov - 31 Mar: Fri - Tue, 10am - 4pm. Closed 1 - 2pm & 24 - 26 Dec & 1 Jan.

Admission: Adult £2.50, Child £1.30, Conc. £1.90. 15% discount for groups (11+).

Grounds suitable. WC. Limited. Guide dogs only. Telephone for details.

Special Events Index PAGE 40

ST MICHAEL'S MOUNT

National Trust/ Peter Cade

MARAZION, Nr PENZANCE, CORNWALL TR17 0EF

Owner: *The National Trust* **Contact:** *The Manor Office*

Tel: 01736 710507 (710265 tide & ferry information) **Fax:** 01736 711544

This magical island is the jewel in Cornwall's crown. The great granite crag which rises from the waters of Mount's Bay is surmounted by an embattled medieval castle, home of the St Aubyn family for over 300 years. The Mount's flanks are softened by lush sub-tropical vegetation and on the water's edge there is a harbourside community which features shops and restaurants.

Location: OS Ref. SW515 300. At Marazion there is access on foot over causeway at low tide. In summer months there is a ferry at high tide. 4m E of Penzance.

Opening Times: 3 Apr - 31 Oct: Mon - Fri 10.30am - 5.30pm. Last admission 4.45pm. Shops & restaurants open daily. Nov - end Mar: It is essential to telephone before setting out in order to ascertain the opening arrangements for that day. The castle & grounds are open most weekends during the season. These are special charity days when National Trust members are asked to pay admission.

Admission: Adult £4.40, Family £12. Pre-arranged groups £4.

Braille and taped guides. Guide dogs only.

TATE GALLERY ST IVES

Tel: 01736 796226 **Fax:** 01736 794480

Porthmeor Beach, St Ives, Cornwall TR26 1TG

Owner: Tate Gallery **Contact:** Ina Cole

Changing displays from the Tate Gallery collection of British and modern art, focusing on the modern movement that St Ives is famous for. Also displays of new work by contemporary artists. Events programme, guided tours, gallery shop, rooftop café, with spectacular views over the beach. The Tate also manages the Barbara Hepworth Museum and Sculpture Garden in St Ives.

Location: OS Ref. SW515 407. Situated by Porthmeor Beach.

Opening Times: Tues - Sun, 10.30am - 5.30pm. Also open Mons in Jul/Aug & Bank Holidays.

Admission: Adult £3.90, Conc £2.30. Groups (10 - 30): Adult £2.50, Conc. £1.50.

Ground floor suitable. Licensed. By arrangement. Nearby. Guide dogs only. Telephone for details.

NT Photographic Library, Jerry Harpur.

Lanhydrock - Parterre, Cornwall.

TINTAGEL CASTLE

TINTAGEL, CORNWALL PL34 0HE

Owner: *English Heritage* ***Contact:*** *The Head Custodian*

Tel: 01840 770328

The spectacular setting for the legendary castle of King Arthur is the wild and windswept Cornish coast. Clinging precariously to the edge of the cliff face are the extensive ruins of a medieval royal castle, built by Richard, Earl of Cornwall, younger brother of Henry III. Also used as a Cornish stronghold by subsequent Earls of Cornwall. Despite extensive excavations since the 1930s, Tintagel Castle remains one of the most spectacular and romantic spots in the entire British Isles. Destined to remain a place of mystery and romance, Tintagel will always jealously guard its marvellous secrets.

Location: OS200 Ref. SX048 891. On Tintagel Head, 1/2 m along uneven track from Tintagel.

Opening Times: 1 Apr - 31 Oct: daily, 11am - 6pm (5pm in Oct). 1 Nov - 31 Mar: daily, 10am - 4pm. Closed 24 - 26 Dec & 1 Jan.

Admission: Adult £2.80, Child £1.40, Conc. £2.10. 15% discount for groups (11+).

No vehicles. Telephone for details.

TRELISSICK GARDEN

National Trust/Tony Kent

FEOCK, TRURO, CORNWALL TR3 6QL

Owner: *The National Trust* ***Contact:*** *The Property Manager*

Tel: 01872 862090 **Fax:** 01872 865808 **e-mail:** ctirxc@smtp.ntrust.org.uk

A garden and estate of rare tranquil beauty with glorious maritime views over Carrick Roads to Falmouth Harbour. The tender and exotic shrubs make this garden attractive in all seasons. Extensive park and woodland walks beside the river. There is an Art and Craft Gallery.

Location: OS Ref. SW837 396. 4m S of Truro by road, on both sides of B3289 above King Harry Ferry.

Opening Times: 19 Feb - 31 Oct: daily, 10.30am - 5.30pm, Sun 12.30 - 5.30pm (restaurant opens noon). Closes 5pm Feb, Mar & Oct and 5pm on Suns. Nov/Dec: Shop, Gallery & Restaurant open 10.30am - 4pm. Sun, noon - 4pm. Woodland walk open all year.

Admission: £4.30, Family £10.75. Pre-arranged group £3.60. £1.50 car park fee (refundable on admission).

By arrangement. By arrangement.

In park on leads; only guide dogs in garden.

TINTAGEL OLD POST OFFICE

Tel: 01840 770024 or 01208 74281

Tintagel, Cornwall PL34 0DB

Owner: The National Trust **Contact:** The Custodian

One of the most characterful buildings in Cornwall, and a house of great antiquity, this small 14th century manor is full of charm and interest.

Location: OS Ref. SX056 884. In the centre of Tintagel.

Opening Times: 1 Apr - 31 Oct: daily 11am - 5.30pm. Closes 4pm in October.

Admission: £2.20. Family £5.50. Pre-arranged groups £1.80.

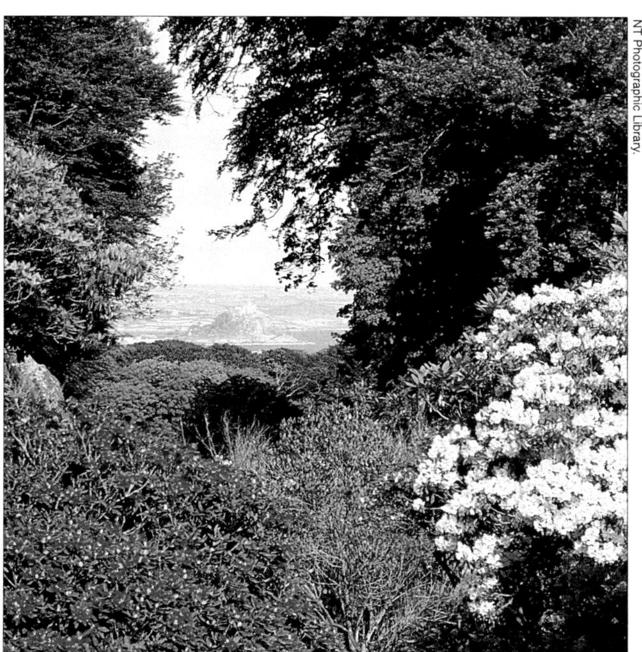

NT Photographic Library.

Trengwainton Garden, Cornwall.

TREBAH GARDEN

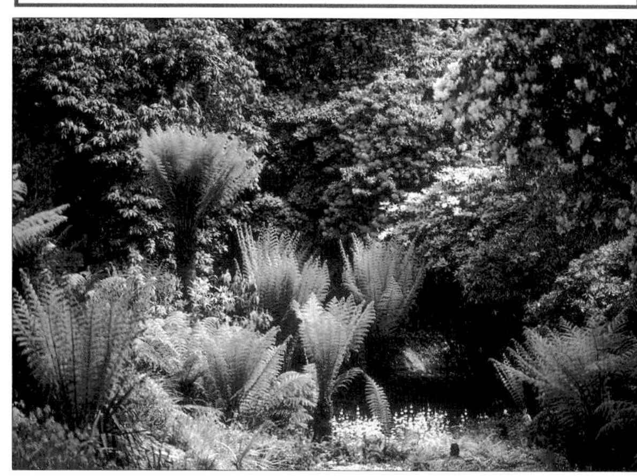

MAWNAN SMITH, Nr FALMOUTH, CORNWALL TR11 5JZ

Owner: *Trebah Garden Trust* ***Contact:*** *Vera Woodcroft*

Tel: 01326 250448 **Fax:** 01326 250781 **e-mail:** mail@trebah-garden.co.uk

Steeply wooded 25 acre sub-tropical ravine garden falls 200 feet from 18th century house to private beach on Helford River. Stream cascading over waterfalls through ponds full of Koi Carp and exotic water plants winds through 2 acres of blue and white hydrangeas and spills out over beach. Huge Australian tree ferns and palms mingle with shrubs of ever-changing colours and scent beneath over-arching canopy of 100 year old rhododendrons and magnolias. A paradise for plantsmen, artists and families.

Location: OS Ref. SW768 275. 4m SW of Falmouth, 1m SW of Mawnan Smith. Follow brown and white tourism signs from Treliever Cross roundabout at A39/A394 junction through Mawnan Smith to Trebah.

Opening Times: All year: daily, 10.30am - 5pm (last admission).

Admission: Adult £3.50, Child (5-15yrs)/Disabled £1.75, OAP £3.20. Child under 5yrs Free, Groups (12 - 50): Adult £3, Child £1. RHS members have free entry all year, NT members have free entry 1 Nov - end Feb.

Partially suitable. By arrangement. P

In grounds, on leads.

TRELOWARREN HOUSE & CHAPEL

Tel: 01326 221366

Mawgan-in-Meneage, Helston, Cornwall TR12 6AD

Owner: Sir Ferrers Vyvyan Bt **Contact:** Colin Rogers

Tudor and 17th century house. Chapel and main rooms of house are open to the public.

Location: OS Ref. SW721 238. 6m S of Helston, off B3293 to St Keverne.

Opening Times: Please telephone for details.

Admission: Please telephone for details.

TRENANCE HERITAGE COTTAGES

Tel: 01637 873922

Trenance Gardens, Newquay, Cornwall

Owner: Restormel Borough Council **Contact:** Derek James Esq

The oldest cottages in Newquay now house an exhibition of life in the early 1900s, a traditional shop and photographic exhibition.

Location: OS Ref. SW815 612. In Newquay.

Opening Times: Mar - Oct: daily, 10am - 6pm.

Admission: Adult £1, Child under 12yrs Free, Child/OAP 50p.

TRENGWAINTON GARDEN

Tel: 01736 362297 **Fax:** 01736 368142

Penzance, Cornwall TR20 8RZ

Owner: The National Trust **Contact:** The Sub-Agent

This large shrub garden, with views over Mount's Bay, is a beautiful place throughout the year and a plantsman's delight. The walled gardens have many tender plants which cannot be grown in the open anywhere else in England.

Location: OS Ref. SW445 315. 2m NW of Penzance, 1/2 m W of Heamoor on Penzance - Morvah road (B3312), 1/2 m off St. Just road (A3071).

Opening Times: 20 Feb - 31 Oct: Sun - Thur & Good Fri, 10am - 5.30pm. NB: Closes 5pm in Feb, Mar & Oct. Last admission 1/2 hr before closing.

Admission: Adult £3.50. Family £8.75. Pre-booked groups: £2.80.

  Partially suitable. Licensed. On leads.

TRESCO ABBEY GARDENS

ISLES OF SCILLY, CORNWALL TR24 0QQ

Owner: *Mr R A and Mrs L A Dorrien-Smith* ***Contact:*** *Mr M.A Nelhams*

Tel: 01720 424105 or **Tel/Fax:** 01720 422868

Tresco Abbey, built by Augustus Smith, has been the family home since 1834. The garden here flourishes on the small island. Nowhere else in the British Isles does such an exotic collection of plants grow in the open. Agaves, aloes, proteas and acacias from such places as Australia, South Africa, Mexico and the Mediterranean grow within the secure embrace of massive Holm Oak hedges. Valhalla Ships Figurehead Museum.

Location: OS Ref. SV895 143. Isles of Scilly. Isles of Scilly Steamship 0345 105555. BIH Helicopters 01736 363871. Details of day trips on application.

Opening Times: All year: 10am - 4pm.

Admission: Adult £5.50, (under 14yrs free). Weekly ticket £10. Guided group tours available.

Grounds suitable. In grounds, on leads. 

TRERICE

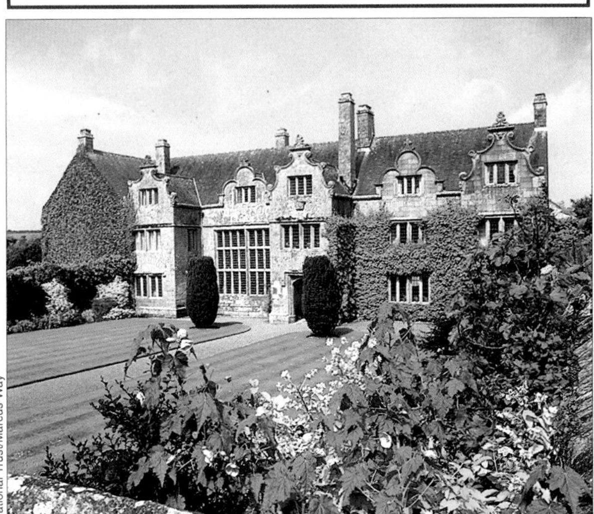

National Trust/Marcus Way

NEWQUAY, CORNWALL TR8 4PG

Owner: *The National Trust* ***Contact:*** *The Property Manager*

Tel: 01637 875404 **Fax:** 01637 879300

Trerice is an architectural gem and something of a rarity – a small Elizabethan manor house hidden away in a web of narrow lanes and still somehow caught in the spirit of its age. An old Arundell house, it contains much fine furniture, ceramics, glasses and a wonderful clock collection. A small barn museum traces the development of the lawn mower.

Location: OS Ref. SW841 585. 3m SE of Newquay via the A392 & A3058 (right at Kestle Mill).

Opening Times: 2 Apr - 23 Jul & 10 Sept - 30 Oct: daily except Tues & Sats. 24 Jul - 9 Sept: daily, 11am - 5.30pm (closes 5pm in Oct).

Admission: £4.20, Family £10.50. Pre-arranged groups £3.50.

Braille & taped guides. WC. Licensed. Guide dogs only.

TREVARNO ESTATE & GARDENS

HELSTON, CORNWALL TR13 0RU

Contact: *Yvonne Ashmore*

Tel: 01326 574274 **Fax:** 01326 574282

An historic and tranquil haven protected and unspoilt for 700 years. Experience the magical atmosphere of Trevarno, an original and fascinating Cornish Estate. Beautiful Victorian and Georgian gardens, extensive collection of rare shrubs and trees, numerous garden features and follies, fascinating Gardening Museum including an intriguing collection of tools and implements. Splendid Fountain Garden Conservatory – enjoy the plants and refreshments whatever the weather. Walled gardens, woodland walks, and abundant wildlife. Follow the progress of major restoration and conservation projects.

Location: OS Ref. SW642 302. Leave Helston on Penzance road, signed from B3302 junction and N of Crowntown village.

Opening Times: All year, 10.30am - 5pm. Groups welcome by prior arrangement.

Admission: Adult £3.50, Child (5-14yrs) £1.25, Conc. £3.20.

Partially suitable.   On leads. 

TREWITHEN

Hugh Palmer

GRAMPOUND ROAD, TRURO, CORNWALL TR2 4DD

Owner: *A M J Galsworthy* ***Contact:*** *The Estate Office*

Tel: 01726 883647 **Fax:** 01726 882301
e-mail: gardens@trewithen-estate.demon.co.uk

Trewithen means 'house of the trees' and the name truly describes this fine early Georgian House in its splendid setting of wood and parkland. *Country Life* described the house as '*one of the outstanding West Country houses of the 18th century*'.

The gardens at Trewithen are outstanding and of international fame. Created since the beginning of the century by George Johnstone, they contain a wide and rare collection of flowering shrubs. Some of the magnolias and rhododendron species in the garden are known throughout the world. They are one of two attractions in this country awarded three stars by Michelin.

Location: OS Ref. SW914 476. S of A390 between Grampound and Probus villages. 7m WSW of St Austell.

Opening Times: Gardens: 1 Mar - 30 Sept: Mon - Sat, 10am - 4.30pm. Sun in Apr & May only. Walled Garden: Mon & Tue in June & 3/4 July only. House: Apr - Jul & Aug: BH Mons, Mon & Tue, 2 - 4pm.

Admission: Adult £3.50, Child £2. Pre booked groups (20+): Adult £3.20, Child £2. Combined gardens & house £6.

No photography in house. Partially suitable. WC.
By arrangement. Limited for coaches. In grounds, on leads.

TRURO CATHEDRAL

Tel: 01872 276782 **Fax:** 01872 277788

Truro, Cornwall TR1 2AF **Contact:** The Visitors Officer

It is a perfect example of a gothic Cathedral. The architect was J L Pearson. The Victorian stained glass is considered to be the finest in England.

Location: SW826 449. Truro city centre.

Opening Times: 7.30am - 6.30pm. Sun services: 8am, 9am, 10am and 6pm. Weekday services: 7.30am, 8am and 5.30pm.

Admission: Free.

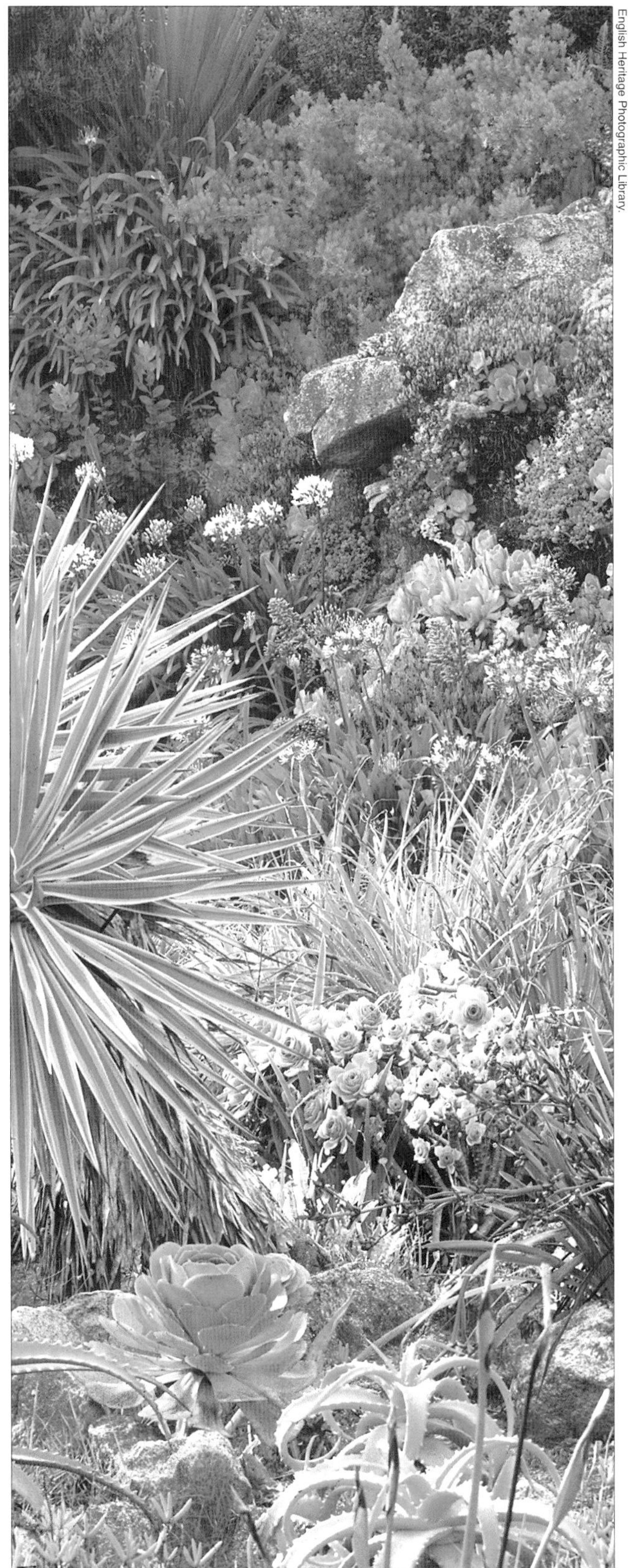

English Heritage Photographic Library.

Tresco Abbey Gardens, Cornwall.

West Country England

POWDERHAM CASTLE
Exeter

Owner: The Earl of Devon

CONTACT

Mr Tim Faulkner
The Estate Office
Powderham Castle
Kenton, Exeter
Devon
EX6 8JQ

Tel: 01626 890243

Fax: 01626 890729

e-mail: castle@powderham.co.uk

LOCATION

OS Ref. SX965 832

6m SW of Exeter, 4m S M5/J30. Access from A379 in Kenton village.

Air: Exeter Airport 9m.

Rail: Starcross Station 2m.

Bus: Devon General No: 85, 85A, 85B to Castle Gate.

CONFERENCE/FUNCTION		
ROOM	SIZE	MAX CAPACITY
Music Room	56' x 25'	170
Dining Room	42' x 22'	100
Ante Room	28' x 18'	25
Library 1	32' x 18'	85
Library 2	31'x18'	85

Historic family home of the Earl of Devon, Powderham Castle was built between 1390 and 1420 by Sir Philip Courtenay. The present Earl is his direct descendant. The Castle was extensively damaged during the Civil War and fell to the Parliamentary Forces after a protracted siege. When the family returned to the Castle seventy years later they embarked on a series of rebuilding and restoration which continued into the 19th century.

The Castle contains a large collection of portraits by many famous artists, including Cosway, Reynolds, Kneller and Hudson as well as some charming paintings by gifted members of the family. The 14ft high Stumbels Clock and the magnificent rosewood and brass inlaid bookcases by John Channon are particularly fine. One of the most spectacular rooms on view is the Music Room, designed for the 3rd Viscount by James Wyatt. It contains an exceptional Axminster carpet upon which sits recently commissioned carved gilt wood furniture.

GARDENS

The Castle is set within an ancient deer park beside the Exe Estuary and the Gardens and grounds are informally laid out. The fine Victorian Rose Garden is the home of Timothy, a 150 year old tortoise; The Children's Secret Garden houses a collection of pets and animals behind its walls to delight children and visitors of all ages; and the newly restored Woodland Garden is open in Spring and early Summer when at its best. Visit the new Farm Shop at Powderham Castle, open 364 days. Featuring high quality West Country food, a Plant Centre, Craft Shops and Restaurant, this free attraction adds another reason for visiting Powderham Castle.

Filming and car launches including 4WD vehicle rallies, open air concerts, etc. Grand piano in Music Room, 3800 acre estate, tennis court, cricket pitch, horse trials course. Deer park safari.

Conferences, dinners, corporate entertainment.

Limited facilities. Some ramps. WC.

Fully licensed restaurant and coach room access.

Fully inclusive. Tour time: 1 hr. Guide book available in French, Dutch & German.

Unlimited free parking. Commission and complimentary drinks/meals for drivers. Advance warning of group bookings preferred but not essential.

Welcome. Fascinating tour and useful insight into the life of one of England's Great Houses over the centuries. Victorian School Room and teacher pack.

In grounds, on leads.

Civil Wedding Licence.

OPENING TIMES

SUMMER
2 April - 29 October

Daily*: 10am - 5.30pm
*Except Sat: closed to public, but available for private hire.

Farm Shop: daily, 9am - 6pm, Suns, 11am - 5pm.

WINTER
Available for hire for conferences, receptions and functions, tel. for details.

ADMISSION

Adult	£5.85
OAP	£5.35
Child	£2.95
Group Rates	
Adult	£5.15
OAP	£4.65
Child	£2.45
Family	£14.65

2 adults + 2 children or 1 adult + 3 children.

SPECIAL EVENTS

- **MAR 11 - 12** Torbay Motor Rally.
- **MAR 28 - 30** Phillips Fine Art Sale.
- **JUN 27 - 29** Phillips Fine Art Sale.
- **JUL 1 - 2** Powderham Horse Trials.
- **JUL 8 - 9** Historic Vehicle Gathering.
- **AUG 4** Open Air Concert.
- **AUG 5 - 6** Food and Drink Festival.
- **OCT 24 - 26** Phillips Fine Art Sale.

A LA RONDE

Tel: 01395 265514

Summer Lane, Exmouth, Devon EX8 5BD

Owner: The National Trust **Contact:** The Custodian

A unique 16-sided house built in 1796 with fascinating interior decoration including a shell-encrusted room and a feather frieze.

Location: OS Ref. SY004 834. 2m N of Exmouth on A376.

Opening Times: 30 Mar - 31 Oct: daily except Fris & Sats, 11am - 5.30pm. Last admission 1/2 hr before closing.

Admission: Adult £3.30, Child £1.65. No reduction for groups.

BERRY POMEROY CASTLE

Tel: 01803 866618

Totnes, Devon TQ9 6NJ

Owner: The Duke of Somerset **Contact:** English Heritage

A romantic late medieval castle, dramatically sited half-way up a wooded hillside, looking out over a deep ravine and stream. It is unusual in combining the remains of a large castle with a flamboyant courtier's mansion. Reputed to be one of the most haunted castles in the country.

Location: OS202 Ref. SX839 623. 2 1/2 m E of Totnes off A385. Entrance gate 1/2 m NE of Berry Pomeroy village, then 1/2 m drive. Narrow approach, unsuitable for coaches.

Opening Times: 1 Apr - 31 Oct: daily, 10am - 6pm (5pm in Oct). Winter: closed.

Admission: Adult £2.20, Child £1.10, Conc £1.70. 15% discount for groups (11+).

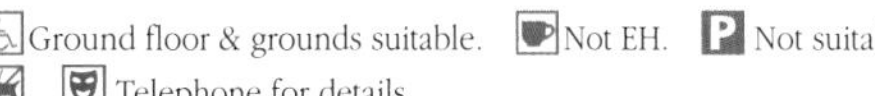

Ground floor & grounds suitable. Not EH. Not suitable for coaches. Telephone for details.

ARLINGTON COURT

Andreas Von Einsiedel

Nr BARNSTAPLE, NORTH DEVON EX31 4LP

Owner: *The National Trust* ***Contact:*** *James Stout - Property Manager*

Tel: 01271 850296 **Fax:** 01271 850711

The house, built for the Chichesters in 1822 and still with much original furniture, is full of collections for every taste, including model ships, costume, pewter, shells and many other fascinating objects. Housed in the stables is the Trust's large collection of horse drawn carriages. Carriage rides through the 30 acres of peaceful informal gardens and past the formal terraced Victorian garden, start from the front of the house. Miles of walks through woods. Parks grazed by Shetland ponies and Jacob sheep.

Location: OS180 Ref. SS611 405. 7m NE of Barnstaple on A39.

Opening Times: 1 Apr - 31 Oct: Sun - Fri (& BH Sats), 11am - 5.30pm. Paths through park and woods open during daylight hours from Nov - Mar.

Admission: House & Garden: Adult £5.30, Child £2.65, Family £13.25. Booked groups (15+) £4.50, Child £2.25. Garden & Carriage Museum only: Adult £3.30, Child £1.65.

Ground floor & grounds suitable. WC. Licensed. Teachers' pack. In grounds, on leads.

BICKLEIGH CASTLE

BICKLEIGH, Nr TIVERTON, DEVON EX16 8RP

Owner/Contact: *M J Boxall Esq*

Tel: 01884 855363

Royalist stronghold: 900 years of history and architecture. 11th century detached Chapel; 14th century Gatehouse – Armoury (Cromwellian), Guard Room – Tudor furniture and fine oil paintings, Great Hall – 52' long and 'Tudor' Bedroom, massive fourposter. 17th century Farmhouse: inglenook fireplaces, bread ovens, oak beams. The Museum, Spooky Tower, Great Hall and picturesque moated garden make Bickleigh a favoured venue for functions, particularly wedding receptions.

Location: OS Ref. SS936 068. Off the A396 Exeter-Tiverton road. Follow signs SW from Bickleigh Bridge 1m.

Opening Times: Easter Sun - Fri, then Weds, Suns & BHs until late May BH, then daily (except Sats) until 1st Sun in Oct, 2 - 5pm. Coaches & pre-booked groups welcome anytime.

Admission: Adult £4, Child (5-15yrs) £2, Family £10.

Conferences. Plant centre. Ground floor suitable. Obligatory.

AVENUE COTTAGE GARDENS

Tel/Fax: 01803 732769

Ashprington, Totnes, Devon TQ9 7UT

Owner/Contact: R J Pitts Esq & R C H Soans Esq

A completely secluded and secret garden, yet one which has been in existence for over 200 years. For the last 10 years it has been undergoing restoration and recreation by the present owners. In this lovely valley site there is a large and fascinating collection of plants which is full of interest from spring until autumn.

Location: OS Ref. SX821 574. 3m SE of Totnes, from centre of village, up hill past church for 400 yds.

Opening Times: 1 Apr - 30 Sept, Tue - Sat, 11am - 5pm. Other times by appointment.

Admission: Adult £2, Child 25p. Entrance, guided tour & tea £3.50.

Wheelchairs in grounds. By arrangement. In grounds, on leads.

BAYARD'S COVE FORT

Tel: 01803 861234

Dartmouth, Devon

Owner: English Heritage **Contact:** South Hams District Council

Set among the picturesque gabled houses of Dartmouth, on the waterfront at the end of the quay, this is a small artillery fort built 1509 - 10 to defend the harbour entrance.

Location: OS Ref. SX879 510. In Dartmouth, on riverfront 200 yds, S of S ferry.

Opening Times: Any reasonable time.

Admission: Free.

BICTON COLLEGE GARDEN & ARBORETUM

Tel: 01395 562400

East Budleigh, Budleigh Station, Devon EX9 7BY

Owner: Bicton College of Agriculture **Contact:** Paul Champion

Grade I listed parkland, lake monkey puzzle avenue, woodland garden.

Location: OS Ref. SY074 857. Off B3178 next door to Bicton Park, follow signs to plant centre.

Opening Times: Apr - Oct: daily 10am - 4.30pm. Nov - Mar: weekdays only 10am - 4.30pm.

Admission: Adult £2, Child (under 16yrs) Free.

BICTON PARK BOTANICAL GARDENS

Tel: 01395 568465

Budleigh Salterton, Devon EX9 7DP

Owner: Bicton Park Charitable Trust **Contact:** Mrs Simon Lister

Over 60 acres of Parkland and Garden, Palm House and specialist greenhouses.

Location: OS Ref. SY074 856. 2m N of Budleigh Salterton on B3178.

Opening Times: Please telephone for details.

Admission: Please telephone for details.

West Country England

BOWDEN HOUSE

Tel: 01803 863664

Totnes, Devon TQ9 7PW **Owner/Contact:** Mrs Belinda Petersen

Elizabethan mansion with Queen Anne façade.

Location: OS Ref. SX800 600. Follow signs from Totnes. 1$^1/_2$ m S of Totnes, E of A381.

Opening Times: 25 Mar - 31 Oct: Mon - Thur plus BH Suns. Museum opens 12 noon, Tours start at 2pm, or 1.30pm in high season, with ghost stories.

Admission: Adult £4.75, Child: (10-13yrs) £2.80, (6-9yrs) £1.80, under 5yrs free (1999 prices). Tickets include Photo Museum and old film shows.

BRADLEY MANOR

Tel: 01626 354513

Newton Abbot, Devon TQ12 6BN

Owner: The National Trust **Contact:** Mrs A H Woolner

A small medieval manor house set in woodland and meadows.

Location: OS Ref. SX848 709. On Totnes road A381. $^3/_4$ m SW of Newton Abbot.

Opening Times: Apr - end Sept: Weds, 2 - 5 pm: also Thurs 6 & 13 Apr, 21 & 28 Sept. Last admission 4.30pm.

Admission: £2.70, no reduction for groups.

BRANSCOMBE MANOR MILL, THE OLD BAKERY & FORGE

Tel: Manor Mill - 01392 881691 **Old Bakery** - 01297 680333 **Forge** - 01297 680481

Branscombe, Seaton, Devon EX12 3DB

Owner: The National Trust **Contact:** NT Devon Regional Office

Manor Mill, still in working order and recently restored, is a water-powered mill which probably supplied the flour for the bakery, regular working demonstrations are held. The Old Bakery was, until 1987, the last traditional working bakery in Devon. The old baking equipment has been preserved in the baking room and the rest of the building is now a tearoom. Information display in the outbuildings. The Forge is open regularly and the blacksmith sells the ironwork he produces - please telephone to check opening times (01297 680481).

Location: OS Ref. SY198 887. In Branscombe $^1/_2$ m S off A3052 by steep, narrow lane.

Opening Times: Manor Mill: 2 Apr - 25 Jun & 3 Sept - 29 Oct: Suns, 2 - 5pm. 2 Jul - 30 Aug: Suns. Weds, 2 - 5pm. The Old Bakery: Easter - Oct, daily, weekends in winter months, 11am - 5pm.

Admission: £1 Manor Mill only.

BUCKLAND ABBEY

National Trust Photographic Library

YELVERTON, DEVON PL20 6EY

Owner: *The National Trust* ***Contact:*** *Michael Coxson*

Tel: 01822 853607 **Fax:** 01822 855448

The spirit of Sir Francis Drake is rekindled at his home with exhibitions of his courageous adventures and achievements throughout the world. One of the Trust's most interesting historical buildings and originally a 13th century monastery, the abbey was transformed into a family residence before Sir Francis bought it in 1581. Fascinating new decorated plaster ceiling in Tudor Drake Chamber. Outside there are monastic farm buildings, herb garden, craft workshops and country walks. Introductory video presentation. New Elizabethan garden under construction.

Location: OS201 Ref. SX487 667. 6m S of Tavistock; 11m N of Plymouth off A386.

Opening Times: 1 Apr - 31 Oct: daily except Thur, 10.30am - 5.30pm (last adm. 4.45pm). 1 Nov - end Dec: Sat & Sun, 2 - 5pm, (last adm. 4.15pm). Other days for pre-booked groups. Closed 23/24 Dec. Special opening for Plymouth Thanksgiving Festival (23 - 26 Nov): please ring for details.

Admission: Abbey & Grounds: Adult £4.50, Child £2.20, Family £11.20. Group: £3.70. Grounds only: Adult £2.30, Child £1.10. Winter: half price Abbey admission.

Ground floor & grounds suitable. Wheelchair stairclimber may be available. WC.

Guide dogs only.

BUCKFAST ABBEY

BUCKFASTLEIGH, DEVON TQ11 0EE

Owner: *Buckfast Abbey Trust* ***Contact:*** *The Warden*

Tel: 01364 645500 **Fax:** 01364 643891 **e-mail:** enquiries@buckfast.org.uk

The monks of Buckfast welcome visitors to their medieval and modern Abbey, known for its beekeeping, tonic wine and stained glass. Magnificent Abbey Church, tranquil precinct with fascinating recreated medieval herb and pleasure gardens, exhibition, video, restaurant, bookshop, gift shop and a unique shop selling produce from other European monasteries.

Location: OS Ref. SX741 674. $^1/_2$ m from A38 Plymouth - Exeter route at Buckfastleigh turn off.

Opening Times: Church & Grounds: All year, 5.30am - 7pm. Shops/Rest/Video, Exhibition: Easter - Oct: 9am - 5pm. Nov - Easter: 10am - 4pm. Shops closed Good Fri & Christmas Day. Restaurant closed 24/25 Dec.

Admission: Free.

Licensed. By arrangement. 

Guide dogs only.  13 doubles & 4 singles. 

BURROW FARM GARDENS

Tel: 01404 831285 **Fax:** 01404 831844

Dalwood, Axminster, Devon EX13 7ET

Owner: Mr & Mrs Benger **Contact:** Mrs M Benger

Six acres of beautifully landscaped gardens, including woodland garden in Roman clay pit with ponds, moisture loving plants and wild flowers. Old roses and herbaceous plants are featured in the pergola walk. The colour themed terraced garden specialises in later summer flowering perennials. A plantsman's delight. "Good Gardens Guide" recommended. New for 2000, the Millennium garden with formal ponds, a 'rill' and 'ha ha', and a traditional summer house.

Location: OS Ref. SY242 993. $^1/_2$ m N of A35, 3m W of Axminster - 6m E of Honiton.

Opening Times: 1 Apr - 30 Sept: daily, 10am - 7pm.

Admission: Adult £3, Child 50p. Pre-arranged groups (10-100): Adult £2.50, Child 50p.

Partially suitable. By arrangement.

P Ample for cars. Limited for coaches. In grounds, on leads.

Branscombe Manor Mill, Devon.

CADHAY

OTTERY ST MARY, DEVON EX11 1QT

Owner/Contact: *Mr O N W William-Powlett*

Tel/Fax: 01404 812432

Cadhay is approached by an avenue of lime-trees, and stands in a pleasant listed garden, with herbaceous borders and yew hedges, with excellent views over the original medieval fish ponds. The main part of the house was built about 1550 by John Haydon who had married the de Cadhay heiress. He retained the Great Hall of an earlier house, of which the fine timber roof (about 1420) can be seen. An Elizabethan Long Gallery was added by John's successor at the end of the 16th century, thereby forming a unique and lovely courtyard.

Location: OS Ref. SY090 962. 3/4 m S of A30 at Fairmile. 5m W of Honiton, 9m E of Exeter.

Opening Times: Jul & Aug: Tues, Weds & Thurs, also Suns & Mons in late Spring & Summer BHs, 2 - 5.30pm. Groups by appointment only.

Admission: Adult £4, Child £2.

Ground floor & grounds suitable. By arrangement. Guide dogs only.

COLETON FISHACRE HOUSE & GDN

BROWNSTONE ROAD, KINGSWEAR, DARTMOUTH TQ6 0EQ

Owner: *The National Trust* ***Contact:*** *David Mason, Property Manager*

Tel/Fax: 01803 752466 **e-mail:** dcfdmx@smtp.ntrust.org.uk

A 9 hectare property set in a stream-fed valley within the spectacular scenery of the South Devon coast. The Lutyenesque style house with art deco interior was built in the 1920s for Rupert and Lady Dorothy D'Oyly Carte who created the delightful garden, planted with a wide range of rare and exotic plants giving year round interest.

Location: OS202 Ref. SX910 508. 3m E of Kingswear, follow brown tourist signs.

Opening Times: Garden: Mar: Suns only, 11am - 5pm. House & Garden: 1 Apr - 31 Oct: Wed - Sun & BH Mons. House: 11am - 4pm, Garden: 10.30am - 5.30pm.

Admission: Adult £4.70, Child £2.35. Family £11.75. Booked groups (15+) £4. Garden only: Adult £3.70, Child £1.85, Booked groups (15+) £3.

No photography in house. Limited access to grounds. WC. Limited. Coaches must book. Guide dogs only in garden.

CASTLE DROGO

David Cripps.

DREWSTEIGNTON, EXETER EX6 6PB

Owner: *The National Trust* ***Contact:*** *Peter Jennings, Property Manager*

Tel: 01647 433306 **Fax:** 01647 433186

Extraordinary granite and oak castle, designed by Sir Edwin Lutyens, which combines the comforts of the 20th century with the grandeur of a Baronial castle. Elegant dining and drawing rooms and fascinating kitchen and scullery. Terraced formal garden with colourful herbaceous borders and rose beds. Panoramic views over Dartmoor and delightful walks in the 300ft Teign Gorge.

Location: OS191 Ref. SX721 900. 5m S of A30 Exeter - Okehampton road.

Opening Times: Castle: 1 Apr - 31 Oct: daily except Fris (open Good Fri), 11am - 5.30pm (last admission 5pm). Sats & Suns in Mar: guided tours only (4 per day). Garden: All year: daily, 10.30am - dusk. Shop & tearoom open as Castle.

Admission: House & Garden: Adult £5.40, Child £2.70, Family £13.50. Group: £4.50. Garden only: Adult £2.60, Child £1.30.

Grounds floor & grounds suitable. WCs. Licensed. By arrangement. Guide dogs only in certain areas.

COMPTON CASTLE

Tel: 01803 872112

Marldon, Paignton TQ3 1TA

Owner: The National Trust **Contact:** The Administrator

A fortified manor house with curtain wall, built at three periods: 1340, 1450 and 1520 by the Gilbert family.

Location: OS Ref. SX865 648. At Compton, 3m W of Torquay.

Opening Times: 3 Apr - 26 Oct: Mons, Weds & Thurs, 10am - 12.15pm & 2 - 5pm. The courtyard, restored great hall, solar, chapel, rose garden and old kitchen are shown. Last admission 1/2 hr before closing.

Admission: £2.80, pre-arranged groups £2.20.

Compton Castle, Devon.

CROWNHILL FORT

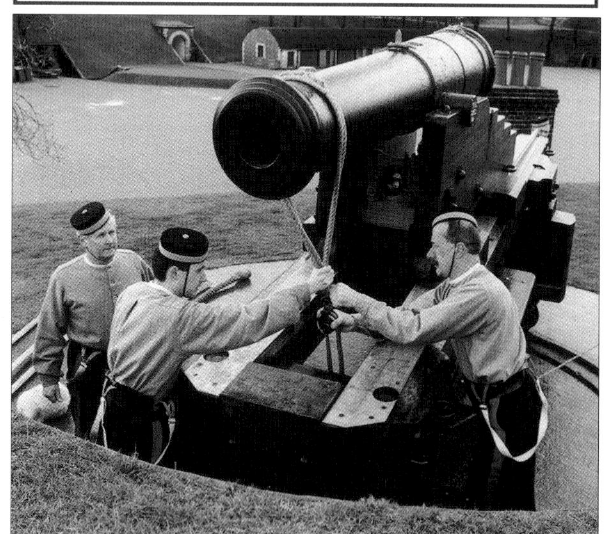

CROWNHILL FORT ROAD, PLYMOUTH, DEVON PL6 5BX

Owner: *Landmark Trust* ***Contact:*** *James Breslin*

Tel: 01752 793754 **Fax:** 01752 770065 **e-mail:** ltcfort@aol.com

At Crownhill Fort you are free to explore the 16 acre site, honeycombed with tunnels, surrounded by massive ramparts, protected by a deep dry moat and guarded by many cannon. After a long restoration the Fort now stands proud as one of the largest and best preserved of Britain's great Victorian forts, and in particular boasts the Moncrieff Disappearing Gun, the only example in the world.

Location: OS Ref. SX487 593. 4m from Plymouth City Centre and less than 1m from A38, signposted from A386 Tavistock Road.

Opening Times: 29 Mar - 31 Oct, daily, 10am - 5pm.

Admission: Adult £3.50, Child £2, OAP £3.25. Groups (15+) Adult £3.25, Child £1.75.

Partially suitable. WC. By arrangement.

Ample for cars. Limited for coaches. In grounds, on leads.

DARTMOUTH CASTLE

CASTLE ROAD, DARTMOUTH, DEVON TQ6 0JH

Owner: *English Heritage* ***Contact:*** *The Custodian*

Tel: 01803 833588

This brilliantly positioned defensive castle juts out into the narrow entrance to the Dart estuary, with the sea lapping at its foot. When begun in 1480s it was one of the most advanced fortifications in England, and was the first castle designed specifically with artillery in mind. For nearly 500 years it kept its defences up-to-date in preparation for war. Today the castle is in a remarkably good state of repair, along with excellent exhibitions, the history of the castle comes to life. A picnic spot of exceptional beauty.

Location: OS202 Ref. SX887 503. 1m SE of Dartmouth off B3205, narrow approach road.

Opening Times: 1 Apr - 31 Oct: daily, 10am - 6pm (5pm in Oct). 1 Nov - 31 Mar: Wed - Sun, 10am - 4pm. Closed 24 - 26 Dec & 1 Jan.

Admission: Adult £2.90, Child £1.50, Conc. £2.20. 15% discount for groups (11+).

Ground floor suitable. Limited.  Tel. for details.

DARTINGTON HALL GARDENS

Tel/Fax: 01803 862367

Dartington, Totnes, Devon TQ9 6EL

Owner: Dartington Hall Trust **Contact:** Mr G Gammin

28 acre gardens surrounds 14th century Hall.

Location: OS Ref. SX798 628. 30 mins from M5 at Exeter (off A38 at Buckfastleigh).

Opening Times: All year. Groups by appointment only. Guided tours by arrangement £4.

Admission: £2 donation welcome.

Christopher Dalton.

St Petrock, Parracombe, Devon.

For more information see page 11, The Churches Conservation Trust.

DOCTON MILL & GARDEN

Tel/Fax: 01237 441369

Spekes Valley, Hartland, Devon EX39 6EA

Owner/Contact: Martin G Bourcier Esq

Garden for all seasons in 8 acres of sheltered wooded valley.

Location: OS Ref. SS235 226. 3m Hartland Quay. 15m N of Bude. 3m W of A39, 3m S of Hartland.

Opening Times: Mar - Oct: 10am - 6pm. No coaches.

Admission: Adult £3.25, OAP £3.00, Child (under 14 yrs) £1.

THE ELIZABETHAN GARDENS

Tel: 01752 669982 **Fax:** 01752 222430

Plymouth Barbican Assoc. Ltd, New St, The Barbican, Plymouth

Owner: Plymouth Barbican Association **Contact:** Tony Golding Esq

Very small series of four enclosed gardens laid out in Elizabethan style in 1970.

Location: OS Ref. SX477 544. 3 mins walk from Dartington Glass (a landmark building) on the Barbican.

Opening Times: Mon - Sat, 9am - 5pm. Closed Christmas.

Admission: Free.

ESCOT COUNTRY PARK & GDNS

Tel: 01404 822188 **Fax:** 01404 822903

Escot, Ottery St Mary, Devon EX11 1LU

Owner/Contact: Mr J-M Kennaway **email:** escot@eclipse.co.uk

Otters, wild boar, birds of prey, 2 acre walled Victorian rose garden, 25 acres of shrubbery, rhododendrons and azaleas. 'Capability' Brown parkland, national award-winning pet & aquatic centre, wetlands and waterfowl park, Coach House Restaurant (all home cooking). The Kennaway family estate for over 200 years.

Location: OS Ref. SY080 977 (gate). 9m E of Exeter on A30 at Fairmile.

Opening Times: May - Sept: 10am - 6pm. Oct - Apr: 11am - 4pm. Closed Christmas Day, Boxing Day, and Mondays in January, February & March.

Admission: Adult £3.50, Child £3, Child (under 4yrs) Free, OAP £3, Family (2+2) £12.

Partially suitable. WCs.  Licensed.  By arrangement.

In grounds on leads.

EXETER CATHEDRAL

Tel: 01392 255573 **Fax:** 01392 498769

Exeter, Devon EX1 1HS **Contact:** Mrs Juliet Dymoke-Marr

Fine example of decorated gothic architecture. Longest unbroken stretch of gothic vaulting in the world.

Location: OS Ref. SX921 925. Central to the City - between High Street and Southernhay. Groups may be set down in South Street.

Opening Times: All year: Mon - Fri 7.30am - 6.30pm, Sats, 7.30am - 5pm, Suns, 8am - 7.30pm.

Admission: No formal charge – donation requested of £2.50 per person.

FURSDON HOUSE

Tel/Fax: 01392 860860 **e-mail:** fursdon@eclipse.co.uk

Cadbury, Thorverton, Exeter, Devon EX5 5JS

Owner: E D Fursdon Esq **Contact:** Mrs C Fursdon

The home of the Fursdon family is in beautiful hilly countryside above the Exe valley. The architecture reflects changes made throughout the centuries. Family memorabilia is displayed including scrap books, fine examples of 18th century costume and textiles and a letter from King Charles I during the Civil War.

Location: OS Ref. SS922 046. 1½m S of A3072 between Tiverton & Crediton, 9m N of Exeter. 2m N of Thorverton by narrow lane.

Opening Times: BHs Easter - August. Jun, Jul & Aug, Wed & Thurs.

Admission: Adult £3.75, Child (11-16yrs) £1.75, (under 10yrs Free). Groups (20+) £3.50.

Conferences.  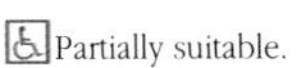 Partially suitable.  Compulsory.  Self-catering

Fursdon House, Devon.

HARTLAND ABBEY

HARTLAND, BIDEFORD, DEVON EX39 6DT

***Owner:** Sir Hugh Stucley Bt* ***Contact:** The Administrator*

Tel: 01237 441264/441234 **Fax:** 01237 441264/01884 861134

Founded as an Augustinian Monastery in 1157 in a beautiful valley only 1 mile's walk from a spectacular Atlantic Cove, the Abbey was given by Henry VIII in 1539 to the Sergeant of his Wine Cellar, whose descendants live here today. Remodelled in the 18th & 19th century, it contains spectacular architecture and murals. Important paintings, furniture, porcelain collected over generations. Documents from 1160. Victorian and Edwardian photographs. Museum. Dairy. Recently discovered Victorian fernery and paths by Jekyll. Extensive woodland gardens of camellias, rhododendrons etc. Bog Garden. 18th century walled gardens of vegetables, summer borders, tender and rare plants including echium pininana. Peacocks, donkeys and Jacob's sheep in the park. NPI Heritage Award winner 1998.

Location: OS Ref. SS240 249. 15m W of Bideford, 15m N of Bude off A39 between Hartland and Hartland Quay.

Opening Times: May - Sept (including Easter Sun/Mon): Wed, Thur, Sun & BHs, plus Tues in Jul & Aug, 2 - 5.30pm.

Admission: House, Gardens & Grounds: Adult £4.50, Child (9-15ys) £1.50. Groups (20+): Adult £4, Child £1.50. Gardens & Grounds: Adult £3, Child 50p. Groups: £2.50.

Wedding receptions. Partially suitable. WC. By arrangement. In grounds, on leads.

HEMERDON HOUSE

Tel: w/days 01752 841410 w/ends 01752 337350

Sparkwell, Plympton, Plymouth, Devon PL7 5BZ **Fax:** 01752 331477

Owner: J H G Woollcombe Esq **Contact:** Paul Williams & Partners

Late 18th century family house, rich in local history.

Location: OS Ref. SX564 575. 3m E of Plympton off A38.

Opening Times: 1 May - 30 Sept: for only 30 days including May & Aug BHs, 2 - 5.30pm. Last admission 5pm. Please contact the Administrator for opening dates.

Admission: £2.75.

Ground floor suitable. Obligatory.

HEMYOCK CASTLE

Tel: 01823 680745

Hemyock, Cullompton, Devon EX15 3RJ

Owner/Contact: Mrs Sheppard

Former medieval moated castle, displays show site's history as fortified manor house, castle and farm. Medieval, Civil war and Victorian tableaux, archaeological finds, cider press and cow parlour.

Location: OS Ref. ST135 134. M5/J26, Wellington then 5m S over the Blackdown Hills.

Opening Times: BH Mons 2 - 5pm. Other times by appointment. Groups and private parties welcome.

Admission: Adult £1, Child 50p. Group rates available.

HOUND TOR DESERTED MEDIEVAL VILLAGE

Tel: 01626 832093

Ashburton Road, Manaton, Dartmoor, Devon

Owner: English Heritage **Contact:** Dartmoor National Park Authority

The remains of the dwellings.

Location: OS191 Ref. SX746 788. 1½ m S of Manaton off Ashburton road. 6m N of Ashburton.

Opening Times: Any reasonable time.

Admission: Free.

THE GARDEN HOUSE

Tel: 01822 854769 **Fax:** 01822 855358

Buckland Monachorum, Yelverton, Devon PL20 7LQ

Owner: Fortescue Garden Trust **Contact:** Mr K Wiley

An 8 acre garden of interest throughout the year including a romantic terraced, walled garden around the ruins of a 16th century vicarage.

Location: OS Ref. SX490 682. Signposted W off A386 near Yelverton, 10m N of Plymouth.

Opening Times: 1 Mar - 31 Oct: daily, 10.30am - 5pm. Last admission 4.40pm.

Admission: Adult £4, Child £1, OAP £3.50, pre-booked groups (15+) £3 (if deposit paid).

HALDON BELVEDERE/LAWRENCE CASTLE

Tel/Fax: 01392 833668

Higher Ashton, Nr Dunchideock, Exeter, Devon EX6 7QY

Owner: Devon Historic Building Trust **Contact:** Ian Turner

18th century Grade II* listed triangular tower with circular turrets on each corner. Built in memory of Major General Stringer Lawrence, founder of the Indian Army. Recently restored to illustrate the magnificence of its fine plasterwork, gothic windows, mahogany flooring and marble fireplaces. Breathtaking views of the surrounding Devon countryside.

Location: OS Ref. SX875 861. 7m SW of Exeter. Exit A38 at Exeter racecourse for 2½m.

Opening Times: Mar - Oct: Suns, 2 - 5pm. Aug: daily except Sats, 2 - 5pm.

Admission: Adult £1.50, Child 75p. No discount for groups (20 - 50).

Not suitable. By arrangement. Limited. In grounds, on leads.

KILLERTON HOUSE & GARDEN

Chris Vile.

BROADCLYST, EXETER EX5 3LE

Owner: *The National Trust* ***Contact:*** *Denise Melhuish*

Tel: 01392 881345

The spectacular hillside garden is beautiful throughout the year with spring flowering bulbs and shrubs, colourful herbaceous borders and fine trees. The garden is surrounded by parkland and woods offering lovely walks. The house is furnished as a family home and includes a costume collection dating from the 18th century in a series of period rooms and a Victorian laundry.

Location: OS Ref. SS977 001. Off Exeter – Cullompton Rd (B3181). M5 N'bound J29, M5 S'bound J28.

Opening Times: House: 11 - 31 Mar & Oct, daily except Mons & Tues. 1 Apr - 31 Jul & Sept, daily except Tues. Aug: daily, 11am - 5.30pm (5pm during Oct) last entry 1/2 hr before closing.

Admission: House & Garden: Adult £5.10, Child £2.50, Family £12.70, Group £4.20. Garden only: Adult £3.60, Child £1.80. Reduced Nov - Feb.

Guide dogs only in house.

KNIGHTSHAYES

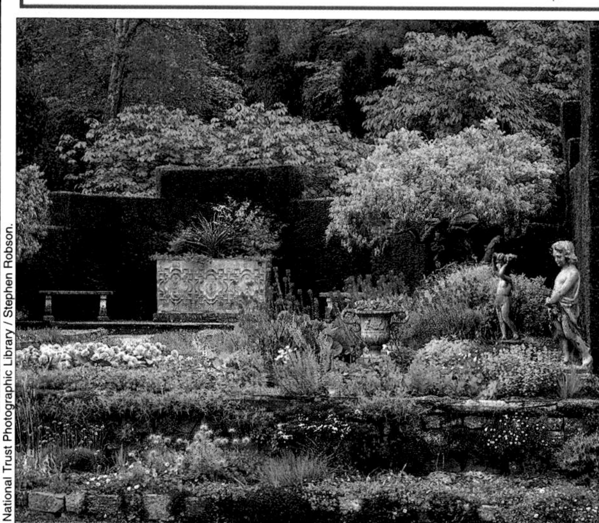

National Trust Photographic Library / Stephen Robson.

BOLHAM, TIVERTON, DEVON EX16 7RQ

Owner: *The National Trust* ***Contact:*** *Penny Woollams*

Tel: 01884 254665 **Fax:** 01884 243050

The striking Victorian gothic house is a rare survival of the work of William Burges with ornate patterns in many rooms. One of the finest gardens in Devon, mainly woodland and shrubs with something of interest throughout the seasons. Drifts of spring bulbs, summer flowering shrubs, pool garden and amusing animal topiary.

Location: OS Ref. SS960 151. 2m N of Tiverton (A396) at Bolham.

Opening Times: House: 1 Apr - 31 Oct: daily except Fris (but open Good Fri), 11am - 5.30pm (Oct: 11.30am - 4.30pm. Closed Thurs/Fris). Nov/Dec: Suns, 2 - 4pm, pre-booked groups only. Gardens: 27 Mar - 31 Oct: daily, 11am - 5.30pm.

Admission: House & Garden: Adult £5.30, Child £2.65, Family £13.25. Group £4.60. Garden only: Adult £3.70, Child £1.85.

Ground floor & grounds suitable. WC.

Guide dogs in park.

LYDFORD CASTLES & SAXON TOWN

Tel: 01822 820320

Lydford, Okehampton, Devon

Owner: English Heritage **Contact:** The National Trust

Standing above the lovely gorge of the River Lyd, this 12th century tower was notorious as a prison. The earthworks of the original Norman fort are to the south. A Saxon town once stood nearby and its layout is still discernible.

Location: OS191 Castle Ref. SX510 848, Fort Ref. SX509 847. In Lydford off A386 8m SW of Okehampton.

Opening Times: Any reasonable time.

Admission: Free.

MARKERS COTTAGE

Tel: 01392 461546

Broadclyst, Exeter, Devon EX5 3HR

Owner: The National Trust **Contact:** The Custodian

Medieval cob house containing a cross-passage screen decorated with a painting of St Andrew and his attributes.

Location: OS Ref. SX985 973. 1/4 E of B3181 in village of Broadclyst.

Opening Times: 2 Apr - 31 Oct: Sun - Tue, 2 - 5pm.

Admission: £1.

MARWOOD HILL

Tel: 01271 342528

Barnstaple, Devon EX31 4EB **Owner/Contact:** Dr J A Smart

20 acre garden with 3 small lakes. Extensive collection of camellias, bog garden. National collection of astilbes.

Location: OS Ref. SS545 375. 4m N of Barnstaple. 1/2 m W of B3230. Signs off A361 Barnstaple - Braunton road.

Opening Times: Dawn to dusk throughout the year.

Admission: Adult £3, Child (under 12yrs) Free.

MORWELLHAM QUAY

Tel: 01822 832766 **Fax:** 01822 833808

Morwellham, Tavistock, Devon PL19 8JL

Owner: The Morwellham & Tamar Valley Trust **Contact:** Anne Emerson

Award-winning visitor centre at historic river port. Train ride into old mine workings. Shire horses and stables, staff in costume, costumes to try on. Museums, workshops, cottages, woodland walks in beautiful Tamar Valley. Average visit length 5 - 6 hours.

Location: OS Ref. SX446 697. Off A390 about 15 mins drive from Tavistock, Devon. 5m SW of Tavistock. 3m S of A390 at Gulworthy.

Opening Times: Summer: daily, 10am - 5.30pm, last adm. 3.30pm. Winter: daily, 10am - 4.30pm, last adm. 2.30pm.

Admission: Adult £8.50, Child £6. Family (2+2) £28. Group rate please apply for details. Usual concessions.

Licensed. In grounds, on leads.

OKEHAMPTON CASTLE

Tel: 01837 52844

Okehampton, Devon EX20 1JB

Owner: English Heritage **Contact:** The Custodian

The ruins of the largest castle in Devon stand above a river surrounded by splendid woodland. There is still plenty to see, including the Norman motte and the jagged remains of the Keep. There is a picnic area and lovely woodland walks.

Location: OS191 Ref. SX584 942. 1m SW of Okehampton town centre off A30 bypass.

Opening Times: 1 Apr - 31 Oct: daily, 10am - 6pm (5pm in Oct). Winter: Closed.

Admission: Adult £2.30, Child £1.20, Conc. £1.70. 15% discount for groups (11+).

Grounds suitable. WC. In grounds, on leads. Tel. for details.

OLDWAY MANSION

Tel: 01803 201201

Paignton, Devon

Owner: Torbay Borough Council **Contact:** Peter Carpenter

Built by sewing machine entrepreneur I M Singer in the 1870s.

Location: OS Ref. SX888 615. Off W side of A3022.

Opening Times: All year: Mon - Fri during normal office hours. Often open on Sats for special days. Visitors should note that not all rooms will always be open, access depends on other activities.

Admission: Free.

OVERBECKS MUSEUM & GDN

SHARPITOR, SALCOMBE, SOUTH DEVON TQ8 8LW

Owner: *The National Trust* ***Contact:*** *Roy Chandler - Property Manager*

Tel: 01548 842893

A sub-tropical garden with rare and tender plants thriving in the mild climate and spectacular views over the Salcombe Estuary. In the Edwardian house are curios such as a polyphon and rejuvenating machine and displays on the maritime history and wildlife of the area. There is also a secret room for children, with dolls, tin soldiers, other toys and a ghost hunt.

Location: OS202 Ref. SX728 374. 1½ m SW of Salcombe. Signposted from Salcombe (single track lanes).

Opening Times: Museum: 1 Apr - 31 July, Sept: Sun - Fri (open Easter Sat), 11am - 5.30pm. August, daily, 11am - 5.30pm. October, Sun - Thur, 11am - 5pm. Garden: All year: daily, 10am - 8pm.

Admission: House & Garden: Adult £4, Child £2. Garden only: Adult £2.80, Child £1.40.

No photography in house. Partially suitable.

By arrangement. Limited.

SALTRAM HOUSE

PLYMPTON, PLYMOUTH, DEVON PL7 1UH

Owner: *The National Trust* ***Contact:*** *Kevin Timms, Property Manager*

Tel: 01752 336546 **Fax:** 01752 336474

A magnificent George II mansion set in beautiful gardens and surrounded by landscaped park overlooking the Plym estuary. Visitors can see the original contents including important work by Robert Adam, Chippendale, Wedgwood and Sir Joshua Reynolds. You can explore the garden follies including Fanny's Bower and the Castle, follow the tree trail in the garden and enjoy fascinating walks beside the river, through the parkland and in the woods. Saltram starred as Norland Park in the award winning film *Sense & Sensibility.*

Location: OS Ref. SX520 557. 3½ m E of Plymouth city centre. ¾ m S of A38.

Opening Times: House & Art Gallery: 1 Apr - 31 Oct: Sun - Thur & Good Fri, 12 noon - 5pm. Great Kitchen open as house but from 10.30am. Garden: Mar: Sats & Suns only, 11am - 4pm; from 1 Apr - 31 Oct as house but from 10.30am.

Admission: House & Garden: Adult £5.80, Child £2.90, Family £14.50. Groups £5.10. Garden only: Adult £2.90, Child £1.40.

Conferences. WC. Braille guide. Audio-visual tape.

Licensed. In grounds, on leads. Guide dogs in house.

POWDERHAM CASTLE

See page 188 for full page entry.

ROSEMOOR RHS GARDEN

Tel: 01805 624067 **Fax:** 01805 624717

Great Torrington, Devon **Owner/Contact:** The Royal Horticultural Society

40 acres of gardens.

Location: OS Ref. SS500 183. 1m S of Great Torrington on B3220.

Opening Times: Apr - Sept: 10am - 6pm. Oct - Mar: 10am - 5pm.

Admission: Adult £4, Child (6 - 16yrs) £1, Child (under 6yrs) Free. Groups (10+) £3.25. Companion for disabled visitor Free.

ROYAL CITADEL

Tel: 01752 775841

Plymouth Hoe, Plymouth, Devon

Owner: English Heritage **Contact:** Blue Badge Guides

A large, dramatic 17th century fortress, with walls up to 70 feet high, built to defend the coastline from the Dutch and still in use today.

Location: OS201 Ref. SX480 538. At E end of Plymouth Hoe. SE of city centre.

Opening Times: By guided tour only (1½ hrs) at 2.30pm. 1 May - 30 Sept. Tickets at Plymouth Dome below Smeaton's Tower on the Hoe.

Admission: Adult £3, Child £2, OAP £2.50.

Knightshayes, Devon.

SAND

SIDBURY, SIDMOUTH EX10 0QN

Owner/Contact: *Lt Col P Huyshe*

Tel: 01395 597230

Lived-in manor house owned by the Huyshe family since 1560 rebuilt 1592-4 lying in unspoilt valley. Mixed 4 acre garden with something for everyone. Screens passage, panelling, family documents and heraldry. Also Sand Lodge, roof structure of late 15th century hall house.

Location: OS Ref. SY146 925. ¼ m off A375, ½ m N of Sidbury. Well signed.

Opening Times: House: 23 & 24 Apr, 30 Apr & 1 May, 28 & 29 May, 2, 3, 16, 17, 30 & 31 Jul, 13, 14, 27 & 28 Aug: Suns & Mons. Garden: Apr - end Aug, Sun - Tue. 2 - 6pm, last house tour/admission 5pm.

Admission: House & Garden: Adult £4, Child/Student £1. Garden only: Adult £2.50, accompanied Child (under 16) Free.

No photography in house. Partially suitable. Obligatory.

Ample for cars. Limited for coaches. In grounds, on leads.

West Country England

SHOBROOKE PARK

Tel: 01363 775153 **Fax:** 01363 775153

Crediton, Devon EX17 1DG

Owner: Dr J R Shelley **Contact:** Clare Shelley

A classical English 180-acre park. The lime avenue dates from about 1800 and the cascade of four lakes was completed in the 1840s. The southern third of the Park is open to the public under the Countryside Commission Access Scheme. The 15 acre garden, created c1845 with Portland stone terraces, roses and rhododendrons is being restored.

Location: OS Ref. SS848 010. 1m E of Crediton. Access to park by kissing gate at SW end of park, just S of A3072. Garden access on A3072.

Opening Times: South Park: All daylight hours. Gardens: Sats, 15 Apr, 13 May & 10 Jun, 2 - 5.30pm.

Admission: Park: No charge. Gardens: NGS £2, accompanied children under 14 Free.

Limited, wheelchairs in garden only. Guide dogs only in garden.

SHUTE BARTON

Tel: 01297 34692

Shute, Axminster, Devon EX13 7PT

Owner: The National Trust

One of the most important surviving non-fortified manor houses of the Middle Ages.

Location: OS Ref. SY253 974. 3m SW of Axminster, 2m N of Colyton, 1m S of A35.

Opening Times: 1 Apr - 28 Oct: Weds & Sats, 2 - 5.30pm. Last admission 5pm.

Admission: £1.70, No group reductions.

TAPELEY PARK

Tel: 01271 342558 **Fax** 01271 342371

Instow, Bideford, Devon EX39 4NT

Owner: Tapeley Park Trust

Much altered Queen Anne building with extensive gardens and park.

Location: OS Ref. SS478 291. Between Bideford and Barnstaple near Instow. Follow brown tourist signs from the A39 onto B3233.

Opening Times: Good Fri - end Oct: daily except Sats, 10am - 5pm.

Admission: Adult £3.50, Child £2, OAP £3. House only open to pre-booked groups, extra £2 admission.

TIVERTON CASTLE 

Tel: 01884 253200/255200 **Fax:** 01884 254200

Tiverton, Devon EX16 6RP

Owner: Mr and Mrs A K Gordon **Contact:** Mrs A Gordon

After nearly 900 years few buildings evoke such an immediate feeling of history as Tiverton Castle. Many ages of architecture can be seen, from medieval to modern. With continuing conservation there is always something new and interesting to see. Old walls, new gardens. Civil War Armoury – try some on.

Location: OS Ref. SS954 130. Just N of Tiverton town centre.

Opening Times: Easter - end of Jun, Sept: Sun, Thur, BH Mon, Jul & Aug, Sun - Thur, 2.30 - 5.30pm. Open to groups (12+) by prior arrangement at any time.

Admission: Adult £3, Child (7-16yrs) £2, Child under 7 Free. Groups (12+): Adult £4, Child £2.

Plant centre. Ample for cars, limited for coaches. In grounds, on leads.

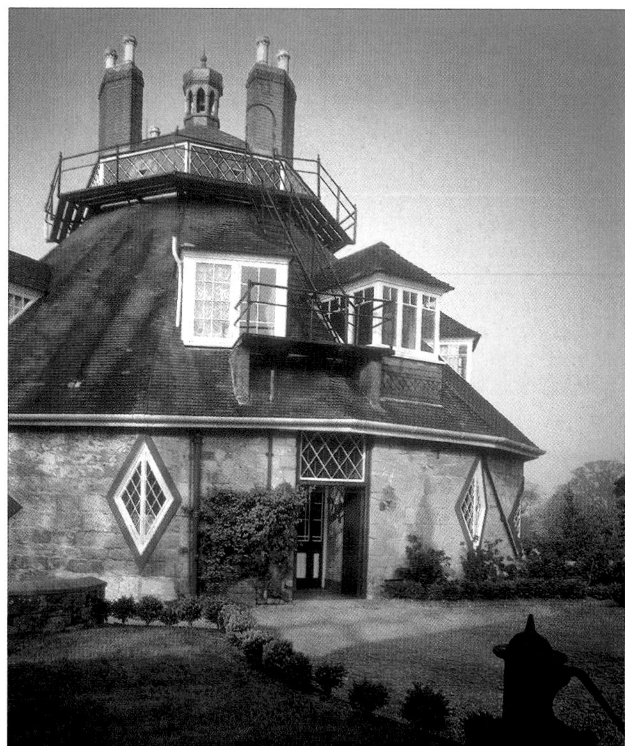

A la Ronde, Devon.

TORRE ABBEY

THE KINGS DRIVE, TORQUAY, DEVON TQ2 5JX

Owner: *Torbay Borough Council* ***Contact:*** *L Retallick*

Tel: 01803 293593 **Fax:** 01803 215948 **e-mail:** michael.rhodes@torbay.gov.uk

Torre Abbey was founded as a monastery in 1196. Later adapted as a country house and in 1741-3 remodelled by the Cary family. Bought by the Council in 1930 for an art gallery. Visitors can see monastic remains, historic rooms, family chapel, mementoes of Agatha Christie, Victorian paintings including Holman Hunt & Burne-Jones & Torquay terracotta. Torre Abbey overlooks the sea and is surrounded by parkland and gardens. Teas served in Victorian Kitchen.

Location: OS Ref. SX907 638. On Torquay sea front. Between station and town centre.

Opening Times: Apr - 1 Nov: daily, 9.30am - 6pm, last adm. 5pm. Free access to members of the National Art Collections Fund.

Admission: Adult £3, Child £1.50, Conc. £2.50, Family £7.25. Groups (pre-booked, 10+): Adult £2.25, Child £1.30.

Conferences. Not suitable. By arrangement. Schools' programme, apply for details. Guide dogs only.

TOTNES CASTLE

Tel: 01803 864406

Castle Street, Totnes, Devon TQ9 5NU

Owner: English Heritage **Contact:** The Custodian

By the North Gate of the hill town of Totnes you will find a superb motte and bailey castle, with splendid views across the roof tops and down to the River Dart. It is a symbol of lordly feudal life and a fine example of Norman fortification.

Location: OS202 Ref. SX800 605. In Totnes, on hill overlooking the town. Access in Castle St off W end of High St.

Opening Times: 1 Apr - 31 Oct: daily 10am - 6pm (5pm in Oct). 1 Nov - 31 Mar: Wed - Sun, 10am - 4 pm. Closed: 24 - 26 Dec & 1 Jan.

Admission: Adult £1.60, Child 80p, Conc. £1.20. 15% discount for groups (11+).

Not suitable. In grounds, on leads. Tel. for details.

UGBROOKE PARK

Tel: 01626 852179

Chudleigh, Devon TQ13 0AD

Owner: Captain The Lord Clifford of Chudleigh **Contact:** Mrs Martin

Location: OS Ref. SX875 000. 3/4 m NW of A380, 1m SE of Chudleigh.

Opening Times: Please contact for details.

Admission: Adult £4.50, Child (5-16yrs) £2. Groups (20+) £4. (1999 prices)

YARDE MEDIEVAL FARMHOUSE

Tel: 01548 842367

Malborough, Kingsbridge, Devon TQ7 3BY

Owner/Contact: John R Ayre Esq

Location: OS Ref. SX718 400. 5m S of Kingsbridge 1/4 m N of A381. 1/2 m E of Malborough. 1 1/2 m W of Salcombe. Coaches only by appointment.

Opening Times: Easter - 30 Sept: Suns only, 2 - 5pm.

Admission: Adult £2, Child 50p, (under 5yrs Free). Groups by appointment only.

ABBOTSBURY SUB-TROPICAL GARDENS

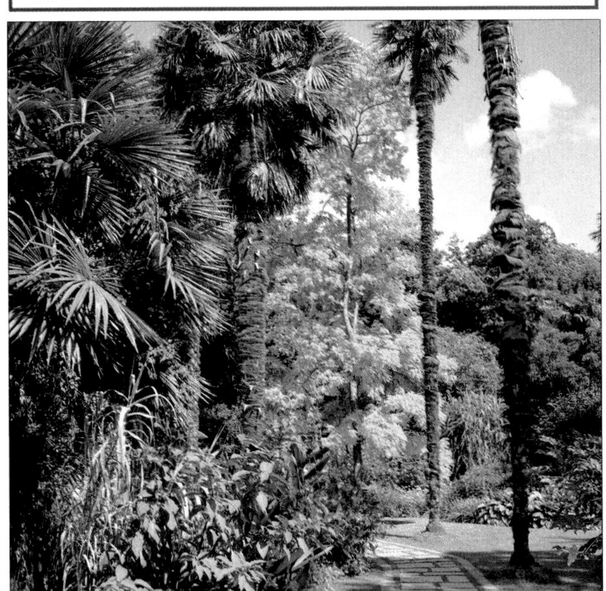

ABBOTSBURY, WEYMOUTH, DORSET DT3 4JT

Owner: *The Hon Mrs Townshend DL* ***Contact:*** *Mr A Collins*

Tel: 01305 871387

Over 20 acres of exotic and rare plants. Established in 1765. Superb colonial-style Teahouse. Extensively stocked plant centre. Quality gift shop.

Location: OS Ref. SY564 851. On B3157. Off the A35 between Weymouth & Bridport.

Opening Times: Mar - Nov, daily 10am - 6pm. Winter, daily 10am - 4pm. Last admission 1 hr before closing.

Admission: Adult £4.50, Child £3, OAP £4. Super Saver (2+2) £14.

Partially suitable. Licensed. By arrangement. Free. In grounds, on leads.

ATHELHAMPTON HOUSE & GARDENS

ATHELHAMPTON, DORCHESTER DT2 7LG

Owner/Contact: *Patrick Cooke Esq*

Tel: 01305 848363 **Fax:** 01305 848135 **e-mail:** pcooke@athelhampton.co.uk

Athelhampton is one of the finest 15th century manor houses and is surrounded by one of the great architectural gardens of England. Enjoy the Tudor Great Hall, Great Chamber, Wine Cellar and the East Wing restored after the fire in Nov 1992. Wander through 20 acres of beautiful grounds dating from 1891, including the Great Court with 12 giant yew pyramids. The walled gardens include collections of tulips, magnolias, roses, clematis and lilies in season. This glorious garden of vistas is full of surprises and gains much from the fountains and River Piddle flowing through.

Location: OS Ref. SY771 942. Off A35 (T) at Puddletown Northbrook Junction, 5m E of Dorchester.

Opening Times: Mar - Oct: daily (closed Sats). Nov - Feb: Suns only, 10.30am - 5pm.

Admission: House & Gardens: Adult £5.25, Child £1.50, OAP £4.95, Family £11. Grounds only: Adult £3.75, Child Free.

By arrangement. Ground floor & grounds only. WC. Licensed. Guide dogs only.

CHETTLE HOUSE

Tel: 01258 830209 **Fax:** 01258 830380

Chettle, Blandford Forum, Dorset DT11 8DB

Owner/Contact: Patrick Bourke Esq

A fine Queen Anne manor house designed by Thomas Archer and a fine example of English baroque architecture. The house features a basement with the typical north-south passage set just off centre with barrel-vaulted ceilings and a magnificent stone staircase. The house is set in 5 acres of peaceful gardens and there is a new rose garden.

Location: OS Ref. ST952 132. 6m NE of Blandford NW of A354.

Opening Times: Good Fri - 1 Oct: Mons, Wed - Fri & Suns, 11am - 5pm. Closed Whitsun BH. Closed 4 - 11 Jul.

Admission: Adult £2.50, Child Free (under 16yrs).

Grounds suitable.

CHRISTCHURCH CASTLE & NORMAN HOUSE

Tel: 0117 9750700

Christchurch, Dorset

Owner: English Heritage **Contact:** The South West Office

Early 12th century Norman keep and Constable's house, built c1160.

Location: OS195. Ref. SZ160 927. In Christchurch, near the Priory.

Opening Times: Any reasonable time.

Admission: Contact The South West Office.

CLOUDS HILL

Tel: 01929 405616

Wareham, Dorset BH20 7NQ

Owner: The National Trust **Contact:** The Administrator

T E Lawrence (Lawrence of Arabia) bought this cottage in 1925 as a retreat; it contains his furniture.

Location: OS Ref. SY824 909. 9m E of Dorchester, 1½ m E of Waddock crossroads B3390.

Opening Times: 2 Apr - 29 Oct: Wed - Fri, Suns & BH Mons, 12 noon - 5pm or dusk if earlier.

Admission: £2.30, no reduction for children or groups.

Braille guide. No coaches.

COMPTON ACRES GARDENS

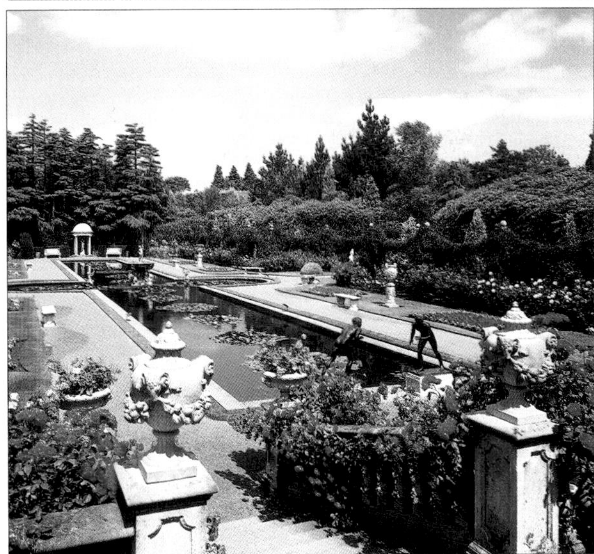

CANFORD CLIFFS ROAD, POOLE, DORSET BH13 7ES

Owner: *Mr L Green* ***Contact:*** *Mr P Willsher*

Tel: 01202 700778 **Fax:** 01202 707537

Set in a delightful area of Canford Cliffs in Poole, overlooking Poole Harbour and the Purbeck Hills beyond. Covering nearly ten acres the nice gardens include an Italian Garden, an authentic Japanese garden, a rock and water garden and woodland walk.

Location: OS Ref. SZ054 896. Off the B3065 onto Canford Cliffs Road.

Opening Times: 1 Mar - 31 Oct: daily, 10am - 5.30pm (10am - 4.30pm in early Mar & late Oct).

Admission: Adult £4.95, Child £2.95, Conc. £3.95. Groups (20+): Adult £4.45, Child £2.45, Conc. £3.45.

Suitable. Guide dogs only.

West Country England

CORFE CASTLE

Joe Cornish

WAREHAM, DORSET BH20 5EZ

Owner: *The National Trust* **Contact:** *The Property Manager*

Tel: 01929 481294

One of the most impressive medieval ruins in England, this former royal castle was besieged and slighted by parliamentary forces in 1646. Visitor centre at castle view includes interactive display and schools room, on A351 north of castle.

Location: OS Ref. SY959 824. On A351 Wareham - Swanage Rd. NW of the village.

Opening Times: 5 - 25 Mar: 10am - 4.30pm. 26 Mar - 29 Oct: 10am - 5.30pm. 30 Oct - 3 Mar 2001: 11am - 3.30pm. Closed 25 - 26 Dec and 2 days at end- Jan.

Admission: Adult £4, Child £2, Family £10/£6. Groups: Adult £3.50, Child £1.80.

 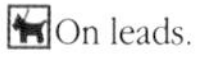 Limited. WC. On leads.

DEANS COURT

WIMBORNE, DORSET BH21 1EE

Owner: *Sir Michael & Lady Hanham* **Contact:** *Wimborne Tourist Information Centre*

Tel: 01202 886116

13 peaceful acres a few minutes walk south of the Minster. Specimen trees, lawns, borders, herb garden and kitchen garden with long serpentine wall. Chemical-free produce usually for sale, also interesting herbaceous plants. Wholefood teas in garden or in Housekeeper's room (down steps). Rose garden open from 17.6.00.

Location: OS Ref. SZ010 997. 2 mins walk S from centre of Wimborne Minster

Opening Times: 23 Apr: 2 - 6pm. 24 Apr: 10am - 6pm, 30 Apr: 2 - 6pm, 1 May: 10am - 6pm, 28 May: 2 - 6pm, 29 May: 10am - 6pm. Sun, 23 July, 2 - 6pm. Sun 27 Aug, 2 - 6pm. Mon 28 Aug 10am - 6pm. Sun 17 Sept, 2 - 6pm.
Organic Gardening Weekends: 17/18 Jun & 5/6 Aug, 2 - 6pm.

Admission: Adult £2, Child (5-15yrs) 50p, OAP £1.50. Groups by arrangement. Exhibition: Adult £3.50, Child (5-16yrs)/Student £1.50, Child (under 5yrs) Free, OAP £3. Family £6 (2 adults & children).

Garden produce sales. Guide dogs only.

CRANBORNE MANOR GARDEN

Tel: 01725 517248 **Fax:** 01725 517862

Cranborne, Wimborne, Dorset BH21 5PP

Owner: The Viscount & Viscountess Cranborne **Contact:** The Manor Garden Centre

The beautiful and historic gardens of yew hedges, walled, herb, mount and wild gardens originate from the 17th century – originally laid out by Mounten Jennings with John Tradescant supplying many of the original plants. Spring time is particularly good with displays of spring bulbs and crab apple orchard in the wild garden.

Location: OS Ref. SU054 133. On B3078 N of Bournemouth (18m), S of Salisbury (16m).

Opening Times: Mar - Sept: Weds, 9am - 5pm. Occasional weekends, phone for details. Entrance, parking and tearoom via the Garden Centre.

Admission: Adult £3, Child 50p, OAP £2.50.

Garden centre. Partially suitable. By arrangement.

Patrick Lane.

Corfe Castle, Dorset.

DORSET COUNTY MUSEUM

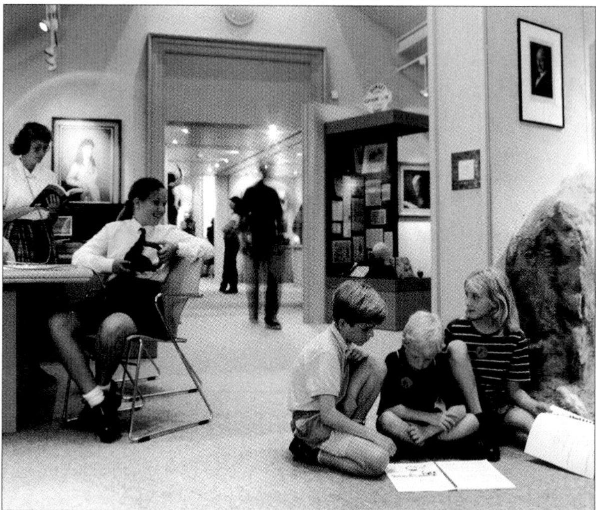

HIGH WEST STREET, DORCHESTER, DORSET DT1 1XA

Owner: *The Dorset Natural History & Archaeological Society* **Contact:** *Richard De Peyer*

Tel: 01305 262735 **Fax:** 01305 257180

Sixteen exhibition rooms in a distinguished high Victorian museum building. New 'Dorset Writer's Gallery' includes a reconstruction of Thomas Hardy's study, displays on William Barnes, author of *Lyndon Lea* and many others. Evocative Victorian Hall paved with Roman mosaics; award-winning Archaeology Gallery, Geology, Natural History and local history displays; fine temporary exhibitions gallery. Interpret Britain commendation 1997. Best Social History Museum Award 1998.

Location: OS Ref. SY688 906. In the centre of Dorchester.

Opening Times: 1 Nov '99 - 30 Apr: Mon - Sat, 10am - 5pm. Closed Good Fri & Christmas Day.

Admission: Adult £3, Child £1.50, Conc. £2. Groups (15+): Adult £2.75 (1999 prices).

Partially suitable. None - set down bay for coaches.
Guide dogs only. 

EDMONDSHAM HOUSE & GARDENS

Tel: 01725 517207

Cranborne, Wimborne, Dorset BH21 5RE

Owner/Contact: Mrs Julia E Smith

Charming blend of Tudor and Georgian architecture with interesting contents. Organic walled garden, dower house garden, 6 acre garden with unusual trees and spring bulbs. 12th century church nearby.

Location: OS Ref. SU062 116. Off B3081 between Cranborne and Verwood, NW from Ringwood 9m, Wimborne 9m.

Opening Times: House & Gardens: All BH Mons & Weds in Apr & Oct 2 - 5pm. Gardens: Apr - Oct, Suns & Weds 2 - 5pm.

Admission: House & Garden: Adult £3, Child £1 (under 5yrs Free). Garden only: Adult £1.50, Child 50p. Groups by arrangement, teas for groups.

Available if booked, max 50 persons. Obligatory.

Car park only. (max 50).

FIDDLEFORD MANOR

Tel: 0117 9750700

Sturminster Newton, Dorset

Owner: English Heritage **Contact:** The South West Regional Office

Part of a medieval manor house, with a remarkable interior. The splendid roof structures in the hall and upper living room are the best in Dorset.

Location: OS194 ST801 136. 1m E of Sturminster Newton off A357.

Opening Times: 1 Apr - 30 Sept: daily, 10am - 6pm. 1 Nov - 31 Mar: daily 10am - 4pm.

Admission: Contact South West Regional Office.

FORDE ABBEY

Nr CHARD, SOMERSET TA20 4LU

Owner/Contact: *Mark Roper Esq*

Tel: 01460 221290

Former winners of Christie's/HHA Garden of the Year Award. Founded by Cistercian monks almost 900 years ago. Today it remains a genuine family home, unchanged since the middle of the 17th century, situated in some of the most beautiful countryside in west Dorset. 30 acres of gardens with herbaceous borders, arboretum, magnificent trees and shrubs, 5 lakes, bog garden. Here you can enjoy the peace and beauty of a past age. There are no ropes or barriers in the house and no sideshows in the gardens.

Location: OS Ref. ST358 041. Just off the B3167 4m S of Chard.

Opening Times: House: 2 Apr - end Oct, Suns, Weds & BHs also Tues & Thurs, May - Sept, 1 - 4.30pm (last admission). Garden: All year: daily, 10am - 4.30pm (last admission).

Admission: House & gardens: Adult £5.20, Child Free, OAP £5, Groups (20+) £4.50, Gardens: Adult £4, Child Free, OAP £3.80, Groups (20+) £3.70.

Conferences. No photography in house. Wedding receptions.

Ground floor & gardens suitable. WC. Wheelchair available, please telephone.

Licensed. By arrangement. In grounds, on leads. 

HARDY'S COTTAGE

Tel: 01305 262366

Higher Bockhampton, Dorchester, Dorset DT2 8QJ

Owner/Contact: The National Trust

A small thatched cottage where the novelist and poet Thomas Hardy was born in 1840. It was built by his great grandfather and little altered, furnished by the Trust.

Location: OS Ref. SY728 925. 3m NE of Dorchester, ½ m S of A35.

Opening Times: 2 Apr - 31 Oct: daily except Fris & Sats (open Good Fri), 11am - 5pm or dusk if earlier.

Admission: £2.60.

Garden suitable.

HIGHCLIFFE CASTLE

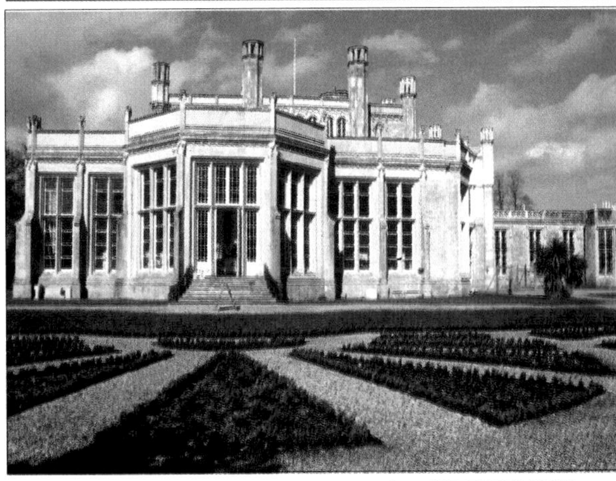

ROTHSAY DRIVE, HIGHCLIFFE-ON-SEA, CHRISTCHURCH BH23

Owner: *Christchurch Borough Council* ***Contact:*** *Mike Allen, Manager*

Tel: 01202 495131 or 01425 278807 **Fax:** 01202 474438

e-mail: m.allen@christchurch.gov.uk

Built in 1830 in the Romantic and Picturesque style of architecture for Lord Stuart de Rothesay using his unique collection of French medieval stonework and stained glass. Recently repaired externally, it remains mostly unrepaired inside. Five rooms house a visitor centre, exhibitions and events. Coastal grounds, village trail and nearby St Mark's church.

Location: OS Ref. SZ200 930. Off the A337 Lymington Road, between Christchurch and Highcliffe-on-Sea.

Opening Times: May - Sept (check exact dates): daily, 1 - 5pm. Grounds: All year.

Admission: Adult £1.50, Child Free. Group guided tour (min 12): Adult £2, Child £1. Grounds: Free.

Partially suitable. WC. By arrangement.

Limited. Parking charged. By arrangement. In grounds, on leads.

HIGHER MELCOMBE

Tel: 01258 880251

Melcombe Bingham, Dorchester, Dorset DT2 7PB

Owner: Mr M C Woodhouse **Contact:** Lt Col J M Woodhouse

Consists of the surviving wing of a 16th century house with its attached domestic chapel. A fine plaster ceiling and linenfold panelling. Conducted tours by owner.

Location: OS Ref. ST749 024. 1km W of Melcombe Bingham.

Opening Times: May - Sept by appointment.

Admission: Adult £2 (takings go to charity).

Not suitable. By written appointment only. Limited. Guide dogs only.

HORN PARK

Tel: 01308 862212

Beaminster, Dorset DT8 3HB

Owner/Contact: John Kirkpatrick Esq

Large, beautiful garden; unique position, magnificent view to sea. Plantsman's Garden, unusual trees, shrubs and plants, in rock, water garden, terraces and herbaceous borders. Woodland Garden, Bluebell Woods. Wild Flower Meadow, with over 160 species, including orchids. Plants for sale. In "Twelve Beautiful Gardens" calendar for 1998 and "Twelve Gardens to Remember" for 1999.

Location: OS Ref. ST468 030. 1m NW of Beaminster, just S of the tunnel on the A3066.

Opening Times: 1 Apr - 31 Oct: Sun - Thur, 2 - 6pm.

Admission: Adult £3.50, Child (under 16yrs) Free. Groups £3.50.

By arrangement. Dogs on leads.

THE KEEP MILITARY MUSEUM OF DEVON & DORSET

Tel: 01305 264066

Bridport Rd, Dorchester, Dorset DT1 1RN **Fax:** 01305 250373

Owner: Ministry of Defence (Museums Trustees) **Contact:** The Curator

There are four floors to explore in this Grade II listed building. Uniforms, medals and weapons reside alongside touch pad technology. Feel the experience of how it really was in the re-created world war bunker. Climb to the roof to view the county town and Hardy country. Lift available.

Location: OS Ref. SY687 906. In Dorchester at the top of High West Street.

Opening Times: All year: Mon - Sat 9.30am - 5pm (last admission 4.15pm). Suns during Jul & Aug, 10am - 4pm.

Admission: Adult £3, Conc. £2. Groups (10-100): Adult £2, Conc. £1.

No flash photography. By arrangement. Limited.

Guide dogs only. Tel. for details.

KINGSTON LACY

Rupert Truman

WIMBORNE MINSTER, DORSET BH21 4EA

Owner: *The National Trust* ***Contact:*** *The Property Manager*

Tel: 01202 883402 **Fax:** 01202 882402

A fine 17th century house designed for Sir Ralph Bankes by Sir Roger Pratt and altered by Sir Charles Barry in the 19th century. The house contains an outstanding collection of paintings, including works by Rubens, Titian,Van Dyck and Velásquez. Fascinating interiors include the fabulous gilded leather Spanish Room and the elegant grand Saloon, both with lavishly decorated ceilings. Fine collection of Egyptian artefacts from 3000BC. The house and garden are set in a wooded park, which is home to a herd of magnificent Red Devon cattle.

Location: OS Ref. ST978 013. On B3082 - Blandford / Wimborne road, 1½ m NW of Wimborne.

Opening Times: House: 1 Apr - 29 Oct: Sat - Wed, 12 noon - 5.30pm. Garden & Park: 1 Apr - 29 Oct: daily except 18 Aug, 11am - 6pm. Nov & Dec: Fri - Sun, 11am - 4pm. Special weekends openings for snowdrops, please telephone for details.

Admission: House, garden & park: Adult £6, Child £3. Park & garden only: Adult £2.50, Child £1.25, Family (2+3) £15. Pre-booked groups of 15: £5.

Garden only. Braille guide. WC.   By arrangement.

In park only. Telephone for details.

KINGSTON MAURWARD GARDENS

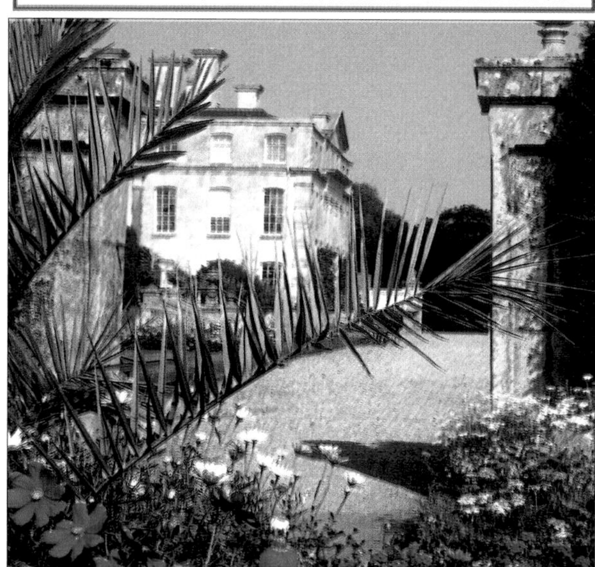

DORCHESTER, DORSET DT2 8PY

Contact: *Mike Hancock*

Tel: 01305 215003 **Fax:** 01305 215001 **e-mail:** administration@kmc.ac.uk

Classical Georgian mansion set in 35 acres of 18th century gardens including 5 acre lake. Restored Edwardian gardens with dividing hedges, stone balustrading features. Walled demonstration garden, National collections of Penstemons and Salvias. Animal park, Nature and Tree Trails. Visitors' Centre and restaurant.

Location: OS Ref. SY713 911. 1m E of Dorchester. Roundabout off A35 by-pass.

Opening Times: 11 Mar - 29 Oct: daily, 10am - 5.30pm.

Admission: Adult £3.75, Child £2.

Conferences. Wedding receptions. By arrangement.

Guide dogs only.

KNOLL GARDENS & NURSERY

Tel: 01202 873931 **Fax:** 01202 870842

Stapehill Road, Hampreston, Wimborne BH21 7ND

Owner: J & J Flude & N R Lucas **Contact:** Mr John Flude

Award-winning 6 acre gardens, with 6000+ named plants from the world over.

Location: OS Ref. SU059 001. Between Wimborne & Ferndown. Exit A31 Canford Bottom roundabout, B3073 Hampreston. Signposted 1½ m.

Opening Times: Mar: Wed - Sun, 10am - 4pm. Apr - Sept: daily 10am - 5pm. Oct: Wed - Sun, 10am - 4pm. Nov/Dec: Wed - Fris & Suns, 10am - 4pm. Closed Christmas - Feb.

Admission: Adult £3.75, Child (5-15yrs) £1.80, OAP £3.25, Student £2.75.
Groups: Adult £2.75, Child £1.50, Student £2.10. Family (2+2) £9.

LULWORTH CASTLE

See opposite for half page entry.

MAPPERTON

George Wright

BEAMINSTER, DORSET DT8 3NR

Owner/Contact: *The Earl & Countess of Sandwich*

Tel: 01308 862645 **Fax:** 01308 863348 **e-mail:** Mapperton@dial.pipex.com

Jacobean 1660s manor with Tudor features and classical north front. Italianate upper garden with orangery, topiary and formal borders descending to fish ponds and shrub gardens. All Saints Church forms south wing opening to courtyard and stables. Area of outstanding natural beauty with fine views of Dorset hills and woodlands. House and Gardens featured in *Restoration*, *Emma* and *Tom Jones*.

Location: OS Ref. SY503 997. 1m S of B3163, 2m NE of B3066, 2m SE Beaminster, 5m NE Bridport.

Opening Times: Gardens: 1 Mar - 31 Oct: daily, 2 - 6pm. House: Open only to groups by appointment (times as for gardens, but not Sat or Sun).

Admission: Gardens: £3.50, House (tour) £3.50. Child (under 18yrs) £1.50, under 5 Free.

Partially suitable.  Obligatory.

Sherborne Castle, Dorset.

West Country England

LULWORTH CASTLE

EAST LULWORTH, WAREHAM, DORSET BH20 5QS

Owner: *The Weld Estate* ***Contact:*** *Paul Pinnock*

Tel: 01929 400352 **Fax:** 01929 400563

A 17th century hunting lodge restored by English Heritage after the fire of 1929. Features include a gallery devoted to the Weld family, owners of the Castle and Estate since 1641. The kitchen and wine cellar have been furnished and the history of the building is brought to life through a video presentation. The Chapel of St Mary in the Castle grounds is reputed to be one of the finest pieces of architecture in Dorset. It is the first free standing Roman Catholic church to be built in England since the Reformation and contains an exhibition of 18th and 19th century vestments, church and recusant silver. A short walk from the Castle & Chapel is the Children's Summer Farm, Play Area and Woodland Walk. The Stables have been converted to house the licensed café. The Courtyard Shop offers a wide range of unusual gift items and selection of Dorset foods. There is a series of special events throughout the year and facilities are available for corporate hospitality, conferences, wedding receptions and private parties.

Location: OS194 SY853 822. In E Lulworth off B3070. 3m NE of Lulworth Cove.

Opening Times: All year: Sun - Fri. Summer: 10am - 6pm. Winter: 10am - 4pm. Last admission 1½ hrs before closing. Closed 24 & 25 Dec.

Admission: Adult £4.50, Child (5-16yrs) £3 under 5s Free, Conc. £3.50, Family £12. Groups (10-200): Adult £4.05. Child (5-16yrs) £2.70, Conc. £3.15. Lulworth Leisure reserve the right to close the castle without notice.

Partially suitable. WC. Licensed. By arrangement. By arrangement. On leads.

MAX GATE

Tel: 01305 262538 **Fax:** 01305 250978

Alington Avenue, Dorchester, Dorset DT1 2AA

Owner: The National Trust **Contact:** The Tenant

Poet and novelist Thomas Hardy designed and lived in the house from 1885 until his death in 1928. The house is leased to tenants and contains several pieces of Hardy's furniture.

Location: OS Ref. SY704 897. 1m E of Dorchester just N of the A352 to Wareham. From Dorchester follow A352 signs to the roundabout named Max Gate (at Jct. of A35 Dorchester bypass). Turn left and left again into cul-de-sac outside Max Gate.

Opening Times: 2 Apr - 27 Sept: Mons, Weds & Suns, 2 - 5pm.

Admission: Adult £2.10, Child £1.10.

Limited access to ground floor for wheelchairs. Limited.

MILTON ABBEY CHURCH

Tel: 01258 880484

Milton Abbas, Blandford, Dorset DT11 0BZ

Owner: Diocese of Salisbury **Contact:** Mrs D Illingworth

Abbey church dating from 14th century.

Location: OS117 ST798 024. 3½ m N of A354. Between Dorchester/Blandford Road.

Opening Times: Abbey Church: daily 10am - 6pm. Groups by arrangement please.

Admission: By donation except Easter & mid-Jul - end Aug. Adult £1.75, Child Free. (1999 prices).

MINTERNE GARDENS

Tel: 01300 341370 **Fax:** 01300 341747

Minterne Magna, Nr Dorchester, Dorset DT2 7AU

Owner/Contact: The Lord Digby

If you want to visit a formal garden, do not go to Minterne, but if you want to wander peacefully through 20 wild woodland acres, where magnolias, rhododendrons, eucryphias, hydrangeas, water plants and water lilies, provide a new vista at each turn, and where ducks enhance the small lakes and cascades, then you will be welcome at Minterne, the home of the Churchill and Digby families for 350 years.

Location: OS Ref. ST660 042. On A352 Dorchester/Sherborne Road, 2m N of Cerne Abbas.

Opening Times: 28 Mar - 10 Nov: daily, 10am - 7pm.

Admission: Adult £3, accompanied children Free.

Not suitable. In grounds on leads.

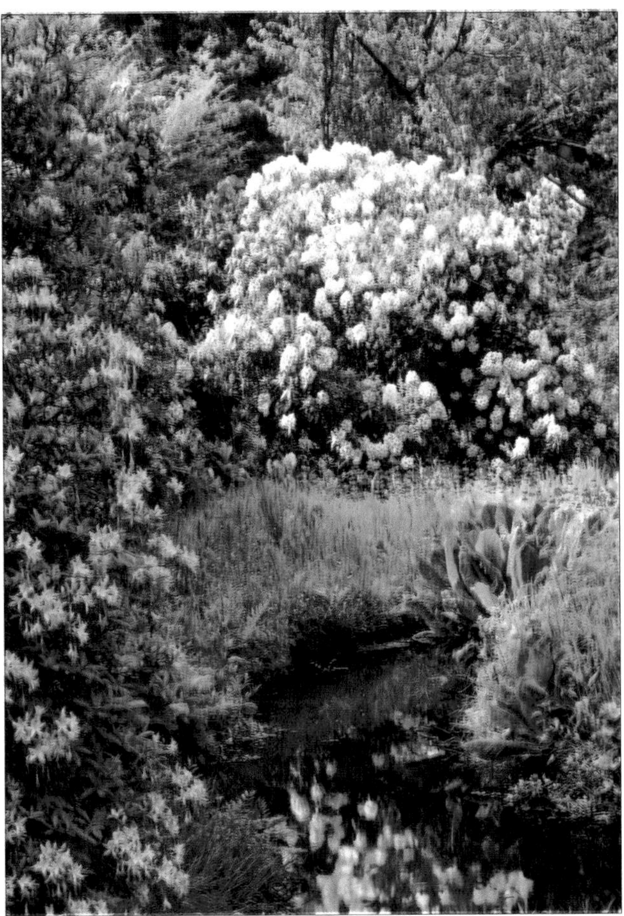

Minterne Gardens, Dorset.

PARNHAM HOUSE & GARDENS

BEAMINSTER, DORSET DT8 3NA

Owner: *John Makepeace* ***Contact:*** *The House Manager - Cdr Bruce Hunter-Inglis*

Tel: 01308 862204 **Fax:** 01308 863444

Inspiring 20th century craftsmanship displayed in the home of John and Jennie Makepeace, who have restored and enlivened this fascinating Tudor Manor House. Exhibitions of exciting contemporary work in glass, wood, textiles and ceramics. Romantic terraces and topiary in 14 acres of fine gardens and woodland walks.

Location: OS Ref. ST478 002. On A3066 5m N of Bridport, 1/2 m S of Beaminster.

Opening Times: 1 Apr - 31 Oct: Tue, Wed, Thur, Sun & BHs, 10am - 5pm.

Admission: Adult £5.50, Child (5-15yrs) £2.50, Student £2.50, Child under 5yrs Free.

Furniture workshop, seminars, wedding receptions.  Licensed.

By arrangement (max 150). In grounds, on leads.

PORTLAND CASTLE

Tel: 01305 820539

Castletown, Portland, Weymouth, Dorset DT5 1AZ

Owner: English Heritage **Contact:** The Custodian

Discover one of Henry VIII's finest coastal fortresses. Perfectly preserved in a waterfront location overlooking Portland harbour, it is a marvellous place to visit for all the family whatever the weather. You can try on armour, explore the Tudor kitchen and gun platform, see ghostly sculptured figures from the past, enjoy the superb battlement views or picnic on the lawn in front of the newly re-opened Captain's House. An excellent new audio tour, included in the admission charge, brings the castle's history and characters to life.

Location: OS194 Ref. SY684 743. Overlooking Portland harbour.

Opening Times: 1 Apr - 31 Oct: daily, 10am - 6pm (5pm in Oct). Winter: Closed.

Admission: Adult £2.50, Child £1.30, Conc. £1.90. 15% discount for groups (11+).

Ground floor suitable. WCs. Tel. for details.

PURSE CAUNDLE MANOR

Tel: 01963 250400

Purse Caundle, Sherborne, Dorset DT9 5DY

Owner/Contact: Michael de Pelet Esq

15th & 16th century manor house. Great Hall with minstrels gallery. Upstairs great chamber with barrel ceiling and oriel window. Family home.

Location: OS Ref. ST695 177. 4m E of Sherborne, just S of the A30.

Opening Times: 1 May - 30 Sept: Thurs by appointment, 2 - 5pm.

Admission: Adult £2.50, Child Free. Groups by appointment.

For groups.

ST CATHERINE'S CHAPEL

Tel: 0117 9750700

Abbotsbury, Dorset

Owner: English Heritage **Contact:** The South West Regional Office

A small stone chapel, set on a hilltop, with an unusual roof and small turret used as a lighthouse.

Location: OS194 Ref. SY572 848. 1/2 m S of Abbotsbury by pedestrian track to the hilltop.

Opening Times: Any reasonable time.

Admission: Contact the South West Regional Office.

SANDFORD ORCAS MANOR HOUSE

Tel: 01963 220206

Sandford Orcas, Sherborne, Dorset DT9 4SB

Owner/Contact: Sir Mervyn Medlycott Bt

Tudor manor house with gatehouse, fine panelling, furniture, pictures. Terraced gardens with topiary and herb garden. Personal conducted tour by owner.

Location: OS Ref. ST623 210. 2 1/2 m N of Sherborne, Dorset 4m S of A303 at Sparkford. Entrance next to church.

Opening Times: Easter Mon, 10am - 6pm. May - Sept: Suns, 2 - 6pm, Mons, 10am - 6pm.

Admission: Adult £2.50, Child £1. Groups (10+): Adult £2, Child 80p.

Not suitable. Obligatory. In grounds, on leads.

Edmondsham House & Gardens, Dorset.

SHERBORNE CASTLE

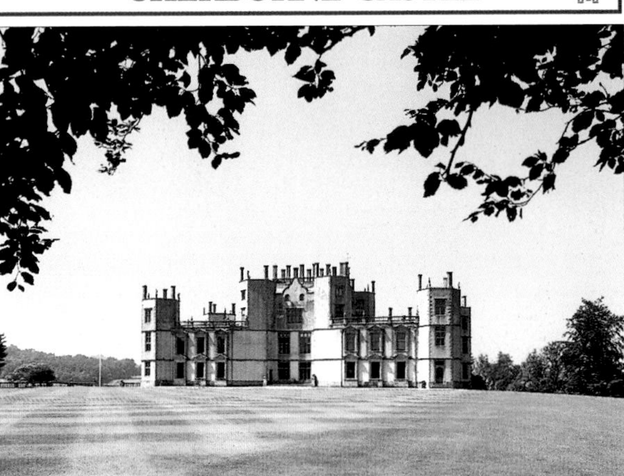

SHERBORNE, DORSET DT9 3PY

Owner: *Mr & Mrs John Wingfield Digby* ***Contact:*** *Castle & Events Manager*

Tel: 01935 813182 **Fax:** 01935 816727 **e-mail:** graham_rogers@talk21.com

Built by Sir Walter Raleigh in 1594, the Castle contains a fine collection of pictures, porcelain and furniture. Set in glorious lake lands and gardens it has been the home of the Digby family since 1617.

Location: OS Ref. ST649 164. $^{3}/_{4}$ m SE of Sherborne town centre. Follow brown signs from A30 or A352. $^{1}/_{2}$ m S of the Old Castle.

Opening Times: 1 Apr - 31 Oct: Castle: Tues, Thurs, Sats, Suns & BH Mons, 12.30 - 4.30pm (last admission). Grounds, Tearoom & Shop: daily (except Weds), 12.30 - 5pm (last admission). Groups (15+) by arrangement during normal opening hours and on other days if possible.

Admission: Grounds & Castle: Adult £5, Conc. £4.50, Child (5-16yrs) £2.50, Family (2+2) £12.50. Groups (15+): Adult £4.25, Child (5-16) £2. Private Views: £8 (min charge £120). Grounds: Adult £2.50, Child (5-16) £1.25.
Sherborne Castle Estates reserve the right to change dates, times and admission prices without prior notice.

Partially suitable. By arrangement.
In grounds, on leads. Telephone for details.

SHERBORNE OLD CASTLE

Tel: 01935 812730

Castleton, Sherborne, Dorset DT9 3SA

Owner: English Heritage **Contact:** The Custodian

The ruins of this early 12th century Castle are a testament to the 16 days it took Cromwell to capture it during the Civil War, after which it was abandoned. A gatehouse, some graceful arcading and decorative windows survive.

Location: OS183 Ref ST647 167. $^{1}/_{2}$ m E of Sherborne off B3145. $^{1}/_{2}$ m N of the 1594 Castle.

Opening Times: 1 Apr - 31 Oct: daily, 10am - 6pm (5pm in Oct). 1 Nov - 31 Mar: Wed - Sun, 10am - 4pm. Closed 24 - 26 Dec & 1 Jan.

Admission: Adult £1.60, Child 80p, Conc. £1.20. 15% discount for groups of 11+.

Grounds suitable.  Limited for cars. No coach parking.

WHITE MILL

Tel: 01258 858051

Sturminster Marshall, Nr Wimborne, Dorset

Owner: The National Trust **Contact:** The Custodian

Rebuilt in 1776 on Domesday site, this corn mill was extensively repaired in 1994 and contains much of the original and rare timber 18th century machinery (now too fragile to be operative). Peaceful setting by River Stour. Riverside picnic area nearby.

Location: OS Ref. ST958 007. On River Stour $^{1}/_{2}$ m NE of Sturminster Marshall from the B3082 Blandford to Wareham Rd, take road to SW signposted Sturminster Marshall. Mill is 1m on right. Car park nearby.

Opening Times: 25 Mar - 29 Oct: Weekends & BHs, 12 noon - 5pm.

Admission: Adult £2, Child £1.

Ground floor suitable. Large print guide. Obligatory.

WOLFETON HOUSE

Nr DORCHESTER, DORSET DT2 9QN

Owner: *Capt N T L L Thimbleby* ***Contact:*** *The Steward*

Tel: 01305 263500 or 268748 **Fax:** 01305 265090

A fine mediaeval and Elizabethan manor house lying in the water-meadows near the confluence of the rivers Cerne and Frome. It was much embellished around 1580 and has splendid plaster ceilings, fireplaces and panelling of that date. To be seen are the Great Hall, Stairs and Chamber, Parlour, Dining Room, Chapel and Cyder House. The mediaeval Gatehouse has two unmatched and older towers. There are good pictures and furniture.

Location: OS Ref. SY678 921. $1^{1}/_{2}$ m from Dorchester on the A37 towards Yeovil. Indicated by Historic House signs.

Opening Times: 15 Jul - 15 Sept: Mons & Thurs. 2 - 6pm. Groups by appointment throughout the year.

Admission: Adult £3.50, Child £1.50.

By arrangement. Ground floor suitable. By arrangement.
By arrangement.

Mapperton, Dorset.

Owner: Bath Preservation Trust

CONTACT

Mrs Ann Hollas
Administrator
1 Royal Crescent
Bath
BA1 2LR

Tel: 01225 428126

Fax: 01225 481850

LOCATION

OS Ref. ST746 653

M4/J18, then the A46 to Bath
$2^1/_2$ hrs from London
$^1/_4$ m NW of city centre.

Rail: Bath Spa Railway Station (1hr, 20 mins from London).

Taxi: Streamline.

NO. 1 ROYAL CRESCENT
Bath

NUMBER 1 was the first house to be built in the Royal Crescent, John Wood the Younger's fine example of Palladian architecture. The Crescent was begun in 1767 and completed by 1774.

The House was given to the Bath Preservation Trust in 1968 and both the exterior and interior have been accurately restored. Visitors can see a grand town-house of the late 18th century with authentic furniture, paintings and carpets.

On the ground floor are the Study and Dining Room and on the first floor a Lady's Bedroom and Drawing Room. A series of maps of Bath are on the second floor landing. In the Basement is a Kitchen and a Museum Shop.

 Not suitable. No restaurant or tearoom, but many facilities in Bath.

Guides in every room. Tours in French and Italian on request. Tour time 45 mins. Guide sheets available in French, German, Spanish, Italian, Japanese, Chinese, Danish, Dutch, Russian and Portuguese translations on request.

Be aware of restrictions in The Royal Crescent and parking regulations in the centre of Bath.

The cost per child is £2.50. School group rates on request. Guides can be provided.

OPENING TIMES

SUMMER

Mid February - End October
Daily except Mons
10.30am - 5pm
Closed Good Fri.
Open BHs and
Bath Festival Mon.

WINTER

November
Daily except Mons
10.30am - 4pm.

Last admission 30 mins before closing.

Special tours by arrangement with the administrator.

ADMISSION

ALL YEAR

Adult	£4.00
Child*	£3.00
Student	£3.00
OAP	£3.00
Family	£10.00

Groups

Adult	£2.50
School*	£2.50
Student	£2.50

* Aged 5 - 16yrs.

National Trust Photographic Library. Andreas von Einsiedel.

MUSEUM OF COSTUME & ASSEMBLY ROOMS
Bath

Owner: The National Trust

CONTACT

For Room Hire:
Mrs Ruth Warren
Sales Officer
Stall Street
Bath
BA1 1LZ

Tel: 01225 477782

Fax: 01225 477476

e-mail: ruth_warren@bathnes.gov.uk

Museum Enquiries:
Tel: 01225 477785
Fax: 01225 477743

LOCATION

OS Ref. ST750 648

Near centre of Bath, 10m from M4/J18.

Rail: Great Western from London Paddington (regular service) 1 hour 17mins duration.

Air: Bristol airport 40 mins.

CONFERENCE/FUNCTION		
ROOM	SIZE	MAX CAPACITY
Ballroom	103' x 40'	450
Octagon	47' x 47'	200
Tea Room	58' x 40'	250
Card Room	59' x 18'	70

THE ASSEMBLY ROOMS in Bath are open to the public daily (free of charge) and are also popular for dinners, dances, concerts, conferences and civil weddings.

Originally known as the Upper Rooms, they were designed by John Wood the Younger and opened in 1771. The magnificent interior consists of a splendid Ball Room, Tea Room and Card Room, connected by two fine octagonal rooms. This plan was perfect for 'assemblies', evening entertainments popular in the 18th century, which included dancing, music, card-playing and tea drinking. They are now owned by The National Trust and managed by Bath & North East Somerset Council, which runs a full conference service.

The building also houses one of the largest and most comprehensive collections of fashionable dress in the country, the Museum of Costume. Its extensive displays cover the history of fashion from the late 16th century to the present day. Hand-held audioguides allow visitors to learn about the fashions on display while the lighting is kept to levels suitable for fragile garments. The 'Dress of the Year' collection traces significant moments in modern fashion history from 1963. 'Women of Style', the special exhibition until 5 November 2000, follows the lives of six women who epitomise all that is most elegant in the fashions of their generation. For the serious student of fashion, the reference library and study facilities of the nearby Fashion Research Centre are available by appointment.

The museum shop sells publications and gifts associated with the history of costume and is open daily to all visitors.

Museum of Costume.

Museum of Costume.

OPENING TIMES

ALL YEAR
10am - 5pm

Closed 25, 26 & 31 Dec and 1 Jan 2000

Last admission 30 mins before closing.

ADMISSION

Assembly Rooms:.....Free

Museum of Costume:
Adult £4.00
Child* £2.90
OAP.........................£3.60
Groups (20+)
Adult £3.80
Child* (summer).....£2.30
Child* (winter)........£1.90

* Age 6 - 18yrs.
Child under 6yrs Free

Conference facilities.

Extensive book & gift shop.

Corporate hospitality. Function facilities.

Suitable. WC.

Garden café in August.

Hourly. Individual guided tours by arrangement.

Nearby car park.

Teachers' pack.

Guide dogs only.

Civil Weddings/Receptions.

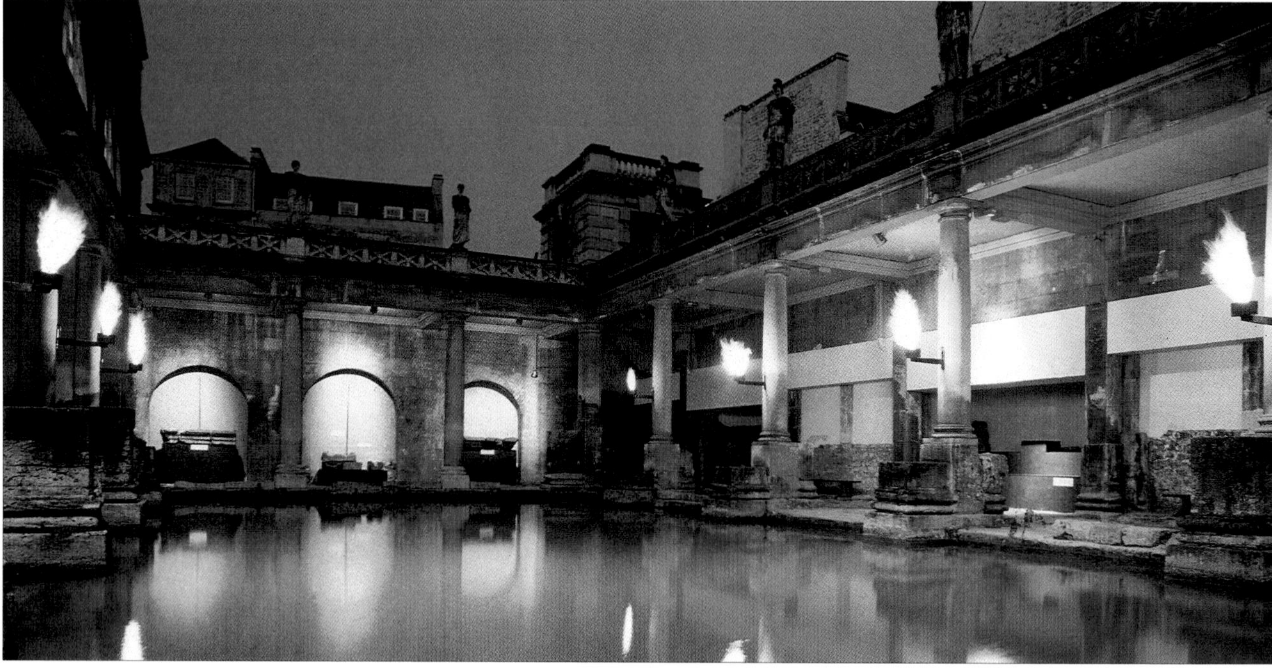
B & NES Council: Simon Mc Bride.

THE ROMAN BATHS & PUMP ROOM
Bath

Owner:
Bath & North East Somerset Council

CONTACT

For Room Hire:
Mrs Ruth Warren
Sales Officer
Stall Street
Bath BA1 1LZ
Tel: 01225 477782
Fax: 01225 477476
e-mail:
ruth_warren@bathnes.gov.uk

For visits to Roman Baths:
Tel: 01225 477785
Fax: 01225 477743

LOCATION

OS Ref. ST750 648

Centre of Bath, 10m from M4/J18

Rail: Great Western from London Paddington, half hourly service, 1 hr 17 mins duration. Good connection to other UK cities.

CONFERENCE/FUNCTION		
ROOM	SIZE	MAX CAPACITY
Great Roman Bath		400 summer 200 winter
Pump Rm.	57' x 41'	180
Terrace overlooking Great Bath	83' x 11'	70
Concert Rm	56' x 44'	100
Smoking Rm & Drawing Rm	28' x 16'	40

The first stop for any visitor to Bath is the Roman Baths surrounding the hot springs where the city began and which are still its heart. Here you'll see one of the country's finest ancient monuments – the great Roman temple and bathing complex built almost 2000 years ago. Discover the everyday life of the Roman spa and see ancient treasures from the Temple of Sulis Minerva and many other objects recovered from the Sacred Spring where they were thrown as offerings to the goddess.

The Grand Pump Room, overlooking the Spring, is the social heart of Bath. The elegant interior of 1795 is something every visitor to Bath should see. You can enjoy a glass of spa water drawn from the fountain, perhaps as an appetiser to a traditional Pump Room tea, morning coffee or lunch. The Pump Room Trio and resident pianists provide live music daily. The Roman Baths shop sells publications and gifts related to the site.

In the evening, the Pump Room is available for banquets, dances and concerts. Nothing could be more magical than a meal on the terrace which overlooks the Great Bath, or a pre-dinner drinks reception by torchlight around the Great Bath itself.

B & NES Council: Simon Mc Bride.

Extensive gift shop. Award-winning guide book in English, French and German. The Historic Buildings of Bath include the Assembly Rooms, Guildhall, and Victoria Art Gallery.

Comprehensive service for private and corporate entertainment. The Assembly Rooms, Guildhall and Pump Room are all available for private hire, contact the Pump Room.

Free access to terrace. Restricted access to the Museum, special visits for disabled groups by appointment. People with special needs welcome, teaching sessions available.

Pump Room coffees, lunches and teas, no reservation needed. Music by Pump Room Trio or pianist.

Hourly, plus personal audio guides in English, French, German, Spanish, Italian and Japanese. Private tours by appointment.

Teaching sessions available. Pre-booking necessary.

Civil Weddings in two private rooms with photographs around the Great Bath.

OPENING TIMES

SUMMER
April - September
9am - 6pm.

August
9am - 9.30pm.

WINTER
October - March
9.30am - 5pm

Last admission 1/2 hr before closing.

Closed 25/26/31 December and 1 Jan 2000.

The Pump Room Trio plays 10am - 12pm daily and 3 - 5pm in summer.

ADMISSION

Adult £6.90
Child* £4.00
Family (2+4) £17.50
OAP £6.00

Groups (20+)
Adult £5.30
Child* (summer) £2.90
Child* (winter) £2.50

Combined ticket with Museum of Costume, Bath

Adult £8.90
Child* £5.30
OAP £8.00
Family (2 + 4) £23.50

Groups (20+)
Adult £6.80
Child* (summer) £4.00
Child* (winter) £3.20

* 6 - 18 yrs.

NO. 1 ROYAL CRESCENT

See page 204 for full page entry.

BARRINGTON COURT

Tel: 01460 241938

Barrington, Ilminster, Somerset TA19 0NQ

Owner: The National Trust **Contact:** Visitor Reception Manager

A beautiful garden influenced by Gertrude Jekyll and laid out in a series of rooms, including the white garden, the rose and iris garden and the lily garden. The working kitchen garden has apple, pear and plum trees trained along high stone walls. The Tudor Manor house was restored in the 1920s by the Lyle family. It is let to Stuart Interiors and is also open to NT visitors.

Location: OS Ref. ST395 181. In Barrington village, 5m NE of Ilminster, on B3168.

Opening Times: Mar & Oct:, Fri - Sun, 11am - 4.30pm. 1 Apr - 29 Jun & Sept: daily except Fris, 11am - 5.30pm. Jul & Aug: daily, 11am - 5.30pm.

Admission: Adult £4.20, Child £2.10, Family £10.50. Groups: Adult £3.60, Child £1.75.

Grounds suitable. WC. Licensed.

Barrington Court, Somerset.

CLAVERTON MANOR

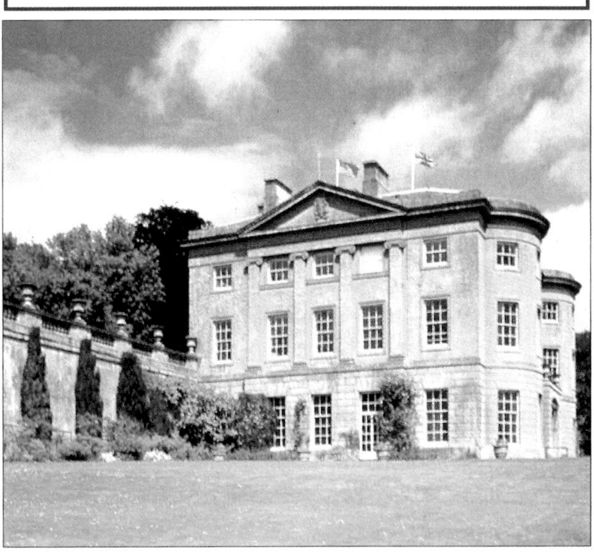

THE AMERICAN MUSEUM, BATH, SOMERSET BA2 7BD

Owner: *The Trustees of the American Museum in Britain* ***Contact:*** *Miss S Carter*

Tel: 01225 460503 **Fax:** 01225 480726 **e-mail:** amibbath@aol.com

The American Museum is housed in a Georgian mansion set in extensive grounds which include a replica of George Washington's garden and arboretum of North American trees and shrubs. The museum shows, in a series of period rooms, life from early New England Colonies to New Orleans on the eve of the Civil War. 2000 Special Exhibition: Amish quilts from Indiana.

Location: OS Ref. ST784 640 2m SE of Bath. Well-signed from city centre.

Opening Times: 25 Mar - 29 Oct: Tue - Sun. Grounds: 1 - 6pm. Museum: 2 - 5pm (closed Mons). Christmas openings: 18 Nov - 10 Dec, 1 - 4pm.

Admission: Adult £5.50, Child £3, Conc. £5. Group concessions available.

Ground floor suitable. WC. In grounds, on leads.

BECKFORD'S TOWER

Tel: 01225 460705 **Fax:** 01225 481850

Lansdown Road, Bath BA1 9BH

Owner: Bath Preservation Trust **Contact:** The Administrator

Built in 1827 for eccentric William Beckford. The tower is a striking feature of the Bath skyline.

Location: OS Ref. ST735 676. Lansdown Road, 2m NNW of city centre.

Opening Times: Closed until mid-2000 for restoration work.
Please telephone 01225 460705 for confirmation of opening dates and times.

Admission: Adult £2, Child (10-16yrs) /OAP £1. Child under 10 and Bath Preservation Trust: Free. Groups by arrangement. (1999 information)

THE BISHOP'S PALACE

Tel/Fax: 01749 678691

Wells, Somerset BA5 2PD

Owner: Church Commissioners **Contact:** Mrs K J Scarisbrick

Fortified and moated medieval palace which is today the private residence of the Bishop of Bath and Wells. Extensive grounds and arboretum. Available for functions.

Location: OS Ref. ST552 457. 20m S of Bristol and Bath on A39.

Opening Times: 1 Apr - 31 Oct: Tue - Fri & BHs & daily in Aug, 10.30am - 6pm. Suns: 2 - 6pm.

Admission: Adult £3, Child (12 - 18) £1, OAP £2, Conc. £1.50. Groups (10+) £2. Guided tour £30 plus £2 per person.

Corporate hospitality. Wedding receptions. Partially suitable.

By arrangement. In grounds on leads.

THE BUILDING OF BATH MUSEUM

Tel: 01225 333895 **Tel:** 01225 445473

The Countess of Huntingdon's Chapel, The Vineyards, The Paragon, Bath BA1 5NA

Owner: Bath Preservation Trust **Contact:** The Administrator

Discover the essence of life in Georgian Bath.

Location: OS Ref. ST751 655. 5 mins walk from city centre. Bath M4/J18.

Opening Times: 15 Feb - 30 Nov: Tue - Sun and BH Mons, 10.30am - 5pm.

Admission: Adult £3.50, Child £1.50, Conc. £2.50. Groups: Adult £2.50. Child £1.50.

CLEEVE ABBEY

Tel: 01984 640377

Washford, Nr Watchet, Somerset TA23 0PS

Owner: English Heritage **Contact:** The Custodian

There are few monastic sites where you will see such a complete set of cloister buildings, including the refectory with its magnificent timber roof. Built in the 13th century, this Cistercian abbey was saved from destruction at the Dissolution by being turned into a house and then a farm.

Location: OS181 Ref. ST047 407. In Washford, 1/4 m S of A39.

Opening Times: 1 Apr - 31 Oct: daily 10am - 6pm (5pm in Oct). 1 Nov - 31 Mar: daily 10am - 4pm (closed lunch 1 - 2pm). Closed 24 - 26 Dec & 1 Jan.

Admission: Adult £2.60, Child £1.30, Conc. £2. 15% discount for groups (11+).

Partially suitable. In grounds, on leads. Tel. for details.

CLEVEDON COURT

Tel: 01275 872257

Tickenham Road, Clevedon, North Somerset BS21 6QU

Owner: The National Trust **Contact:** The Administrator

Home of the Elton family, this 14th century manor house, once partly fortified, has a 12th century tower and 13th century hall. Collection of Nailsea glass and Eltonware. Beautiful terraced garden.

Location: OS Ref. ST423 716. 1 1/2 m E of Clevedon, on B3130, signposted from M5/J20.

Opening Times: 2 Apr - 28 Sept: Weds, Thurs, Suns & BH Mons, 2 - 5pm.

Admission: Adult £4, Child £2.

Ground floor suitable. Limited.

COLERIDGE COTTAGE

Tel: 01278 732662

35 Lime Street, Nether Stowey, Bridgwater, Somerset TA5 1NQ

Owner: The National Trust **Contact:** The Custodian

Coleridge's home for three years from 1797. It was here that he wrote the *Rhyme of the Ancient Mariner*, part of *Christabel* and *Frost at Midnight*.

Location: OS Ref. ST191 399. At W end of Nether Stowey, on S side of A39, 8m W of Bridgwater.

Opening Times: Parlour & Reading room: 2 Apr - 1 Oct: Tue - Thur & Suns, 2 - 5pm.

Admission: Adult £2.60, Child £1, no reduction for groups, which must book.

COMBE SYDENHAM COUNTRY PARK

Tel: 01984 656284

Monksilver, Taunton, Somerset TA4 4JG

Owner: Theed Estates **Contact:** Mr A Hudson

Built in 1580 on the site of a monastic settlement. Deer Park and woodland walks.

Location: OS Ref. ST075 366. Monksilver

Opening Times: Guided tours Mons, Weds, Thurs. Please telephone for details.

Admission: £3 per vehicle. Adult £5, Child £2.50 for guided tours.

COTHAY MANOR

GREENHAM, WELLINGTON, SOMERSET TA21 0JR

Owner/Contact: *Mr & Mrs Alastair Robb*

Tel: 01823 672283 **Fax:** 01823 672345 **e-mail:** cothay@aol.com

It has been said that Cothay Manor is the finest example of a small classic, medieval manor house in England. The manor has remained virtually untouched since it was built in 1480. The gardens, laid out in the 1920s have been completely re-designed and replanted within the original framework of yew hedges. A white garden, scarlet and purple garden, herbaceous borders and bog garden are but a few of the delights to be found in this magical place.

Location: OS Ref. ST721 214. From M5 W J/27, take A38 dir Wellington. $3^1/_2$ m left to Greenham. From N take A38 dir. Exeter. $3^1/_2$ m right to Greenham ($1^1/_2$ m). On LH corner at bottom of hill turn right. Cothay $1^1/_2$ m, always keeping left.

Opening Times: May - Sept: Weds, Thurs, Suns & BHs, 2 - 6pm.

Admission: Garden: Adult £3, Child (under 14yrs) Free. House: Groups (17+): by arrangement throughout the year, £4.

No photography in house. By arrangement.

CROWE HALL

Tel: 01225 310322

Widcombe Hill, Bath, Somerset BA2 6AR

Owner/Contact: John Barratt Esq

Ten acres of romantic hillside gardens. Victorian grotto, classical Bath villa with good 18th century furniture and paintings.

Location: OS Ref. ST760 640. In Bath, 1m SE of city centre.

Opening Times: Gardens only open 19 Mar, 16 Apr, 7 & 21 May, 11 Jun, 16 Jul: 2 - 6pm. House and Gardens by appointment.

Admission: House & Gardens: Adult £4. Gardens only: Adult £2, Child £1.

DUNSTER CASTLE

Tel: 01643 821314 **Fax:** 01643 823000

Dunster, Nr Minehead, Somerset TA24 6SL

Owner: The National Trust **Contact:** The Property Manager

From Norman motte-and-bailey to Jacobean mansion and Victorian eccentricity there is something for everyone. 600 years of Luttrell family residence has groomed and moulded the property from coastal fortress to a secluded country seat. The house and medieval ruins are magically framed with sub-tropical plants including the famous Dunster Lemon.

Location: OS Ref. SS992 436. In Dunster, 3m SE of Minehead.

Opening Times: Castle: 1 Apr - 27 Sept: daily except Thur/Fri, 11am - 5pm (Oct until 4pm). Garden & Park: Jan - Mar, Oct - Dec: daily, 11am - 4pm (closed 25 Dec), Apr - Sept: 10am - 5pm (open Good Friday). Last admission 30 mins before closing.

Admission: Castle: Adult £5.50, Child £3, Family £14. Garden & Park: Adult £3, Child £1.30, Family £7.30. Pre-arranged Groups: £4.80.

Guide dogs only.

DUNSTER WORKING WATERMILL

Tel: 01643 821759

Mill Lane, Dunster, Minehead, Somerset TA24 6SW

Owner: The National Trust **Contact:** The Administrator

Built on the site of a mill mentioned in the Domesday Survey of 1086, the present mill dates from the 18th century and was restored to working order in 1979.

Location: OS Ref. SS991 434. On River Avill, beneath Castle Tor, approach via Mill Lane or Castle gardens on foot.

Opening Times: 1 Apr - 29 Jun, Sept & Oct: daily except Fri (open Good Fri), 10.30am - 5pm. Jul & Aug: daily, 10.30am - 5pm.

Admission: £2.10. Family tickets available. Group rates by prior arrangement.

Ground floor suitable.

EAST LAMBROOK MANOR GARDENS

Tel: 01460 240328 **Fax:** 01460 242344

South Petherton, Somerset TA13 5HL **e-mail:** ELambrook@aol.com

Owner: Mr & Mrs Robert Williams **Contact:** Mark Stainer - Head Gardener

Grade I listed cottage-style garden, developed by the famous Margery Fish, containing many rare and unusual plants saved from extinction.

Location: OS177 Ref. ST431 189. 2m N of S Petherton off A303 (signed).

Opening Times: Gardens only: All year: Mon - Sat, 10am - 5pm.

Admission: Adult £2.50, Child/Student 50p, Conc. £2, Groups by prior arrangement £2.

Art gallery. NCCPG National Geranium collection. Not suitable. By arrangement. Limited for coaches.

ENGLISHCOMBE TITHE BARN

Tel: 01225 425073

e-mail: jennie.walker@iname.com

Rectory Farmhouse, Englishcombe, Bath BA2 9DU

Owner/Contact: Mrs Jennie Walker

An early 14th century cruck-framed Tithe Barn built by Bath Abbey.

Location: OS172 Ref. ST716 628. Adjacent to Englishcombe Village Church. 1m SW of Bath.

Opening Times: Easter - Sept: Suns & BHs, 3 - 5.30pm. Other days and times by arrangement.

Admission: Free.

FARLEIGH HUNGERFORD CASTLE

Tel: 01225 754026

Farleigh Hungerford, Bath, Somerset BA3 6RS

Owner: English Heritage **Contact:** The Custodian

Extensive ruins of 14th century castle with a splendid chapel containing wall paintings, stained glass and the fine tomb of Sir Thomas Hungerford, builder of the castle.

Location: OS173 Ref. ST801 577. In Farleigh Hungerford $3^1/_2$ m W of Trowbridge on A366.

Opening Times: Apr - Oct: daily 10am - 6pm (5pm in Oct). Nov - Mar: Wed - Sun, 10am - 4pm (closed for lunch 1 - 2 pm). Closed 24 - 26 Dec & 1 Jan.

Admission: Adult £2.30, Child £1.20, Conc. £1.70. 15% discount for groups of 11+.

Grounds suitable. Guide dogs only. Tel. for details.

GANTS MILL

Tel: 01749 812393

Bruton, Somerset BA10 0DB

Owner/Contact: Brian and Alison Shingler

4-storey working watermill with beautiful colour-themed designer garden.

Location: OS Ref. ST674 342. Off A359 $^1/_2$ m SW of Bruton.

Opening Times: Mill: Easter - end of May, Thur & BH Mons. Mill & Garden: June - end Sept, Thurs & BH Mons and 2nd & 4th Sundays in month, 2 - 5pm.

Admission: Adult £2.50, Child £1. Groups by arrangement.

GATCOMBE COURT

Tel: 01275 393141 **Fax:** 01275 394274

Flax Bourton, Somerset BS48 3QT

Owner: Mr & Mrs Charles Clarke **Contact:** Mr Charles Clarke

A Somerset manor house, dating from early 13th century, which has evolved over the centuries since. It is on the site of a large Roman village, traces of which are apparent.

Location: OS Ref. ST525 698. 5m W of Bristol, N of the A370, between the villages of Long Ashton and Flax Bourton.

Opening Times: By written appointment only.

Not suitable. By arrangement.

Gatcombe Court, Somerset.

West Country England

GAULDEN MANOR

Tel: 01984 667213

Tolland, Lydeard St. Lawrence, Nr Taunton, Somerset TA4 3PN

Owner/Contact: James Le Gendre Starkie

Small historic manor of great charm. A real lived-in family home, guided tours by owner. Past seat of the Turberville family, immortalised by Thomas Hardy. Magnificent early plasterwork, fine furniture, many examples of embroidery by owner's wife. Interesting gardens include herb garden, old fashioned roses, bog garden and secret garden beyond monks fish pond.

Location: OS Ref. ST111 314. 9m NW of Taunton off A358 and B3224.

Opening Times: Garden: 8 Jun - 28 Aug. House & Garden: 2 Jul - 28 Aug. Thurs, Suns & BH Mons, 2 - 5pm. Groups by written appointment at any time, morning, afternoon & evening.

Admission: House & Garden: Adult £4.20. Garden only: Adult £3, Child £1.

Ground floor & grounds suitable. Suns & BHs only. Obligatory.

THE GEORGIAN HOUSE

Tel: 0117 921 1262

e-mail general_museum@bristol-city.gov.uk

7 Great George Street, Bristol, Somerset BS1 5RR

Owner: City of Bristol Museums & Art Gallery **Contact:** Karin Walton

Location: OS172 ST582 730. Bristol.

Opening Times: 1 Apr - 31 Oct: Sat - Wed, 10am - 5pm. 1 Nov - 31 Mar: closed.

Admission: Free.

GLASTONBURY TRIBUNAL

Tel: 01458 832954

Glastonbury High Street, Glastonbury, Somerset

Owner: English Heritage **Contact:** The Manager

A well preserved medieval town house, reputedly once used as the courthouse of Glastonbury Abbey. Now houses Glastonbury Tourist Information Centre.

Location: OS182 Ref. ST499 390. In Glastonbury High Street.

Opening Times: 2 Apr - 30 Sept: Sun - Thur 10am - 5pm (Fri & Sat to 5.30pm). 1 Oct - 1 Apr: Sun - Thur, 10am - 4pm (Fri & Sat, 4.30pm).

Admission: TIC Free. Display areas: Adult £1.50, Child 75p, Conc £1.

Hatch Court, Somerset.

HATCH COURT

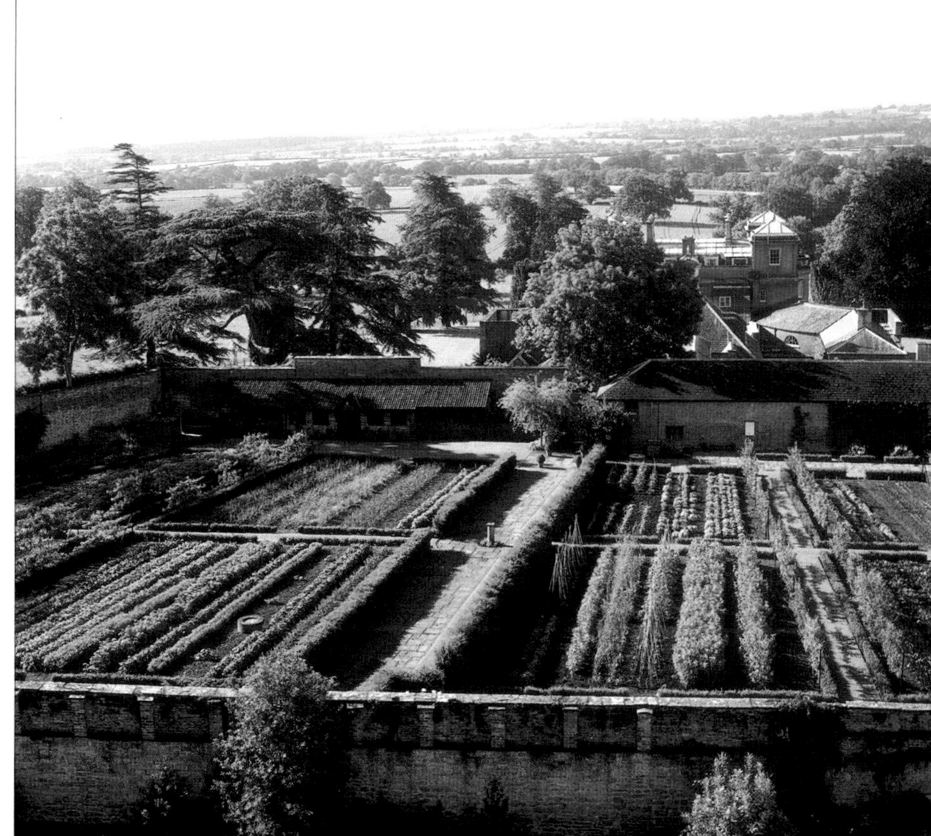

HATCH BEAUCHAMP, TAUNTON, SOMERSET TA3 6AA

Owner/Contact: *Dr & Mrs Robin Odgers*

Tel: 01823 480120 **Fax:** 01823 480058

An attractive and unusual Palladian Bath stone mansion surrounded by beautiful parkland with a herd of fallow deer. Still very much a family home, it has a good collection of pictures and furniture, a china room and military museum. The extensively restored gardens feature a spectacular working walled kitchen garden.

Location: OS193 Ref. ST306 207. Off A358 5m SE of Taunton. M5/J25.

Opening Times: House: 15 Jun - 7 Sept: Thurs, 2.30 - 5.30pm. Garden: 1 Apr - 30 Sept: daily, 10am - 5.30pm. Groups all year by appointment.

Admission: House & garden: Adult £3.50, Child £1.50. Groups (25+): £3. Garden only: Adult £2.50, Child £1, Group (25+) £2.25.

Conferences. No photography in house.

Corporate hospitality & catering.

Gardens suitable.

Homemade teas.

SPECIAL EVENTS

MAY 6: NCCPG Rare Plant Sale

West Country England

HESTERCOMBE GARDENS

CHEDDON FITZPAINE, TAUNTON, SOMERSET TA2 8LG

Owner: *Somerset County Council & Hestercombe Gardens Project*

Contact: *Mr P White*

Tel: 01823 413923 **Fax:** 01823 413747

Hestercombe's 50 acres of gardens are listed Grade I on the English Heritage Register of Parks and Gardens and encompass over three centuries of garden history.

The formal gardens, designed by Sir Edwin Lutyens and planted by Gertrude Jekyll, were completed in 1906. With terraces, pools and an orangery, they are the supreme example of their famous partnership. These gardens are now reunited with Hestercombe's secret Landscape Garden, which opened in the Spring of 1997 for the first time in 125 years. Created by Coplestone Warre Bampfylde in the 1750s, these Georgian pleasure grounds comprise 40 acres of lakes, temples and delightful woodland walks. Our tearoom, shop and plant sales area are open daily from 10am to 5pm.

Location: OS Ref. ST241 287. 4m NE from Taunton, 1m NW of Cheddon Fitzpaine.

Opening Times: All year: daily, 10am - 6pm (last admission 5pm). Groups & coach parties by arrangement.

Admission: Adult £3.60. Child (5-15yrs) £1, Child under 5 Free. Guided tour: £6.50 (min. charge £100).

  On short leads.

KENTSFORD

Tel: 01984 631307

Washford, Watchet, Somerset TA23 0JD

Owner: Wyndham Estate **Contact:** Mr R Dibble

Location: OS Ref. ST058 426.

Opening Times: House open only by written appointment with Mr R Dibble. Gardens: 14 Mar - 29 Aug: Tues & BHs.

Admission: House: £2, Gardens: Free.

Gardens only. 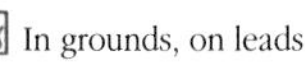Limited. In grounds, on leads.

KING JOHN'S HUNTING LODGE

Tel: 01934 732012

The Square, Axbridge, Somerset BS26 2AP

Owner: The National Trust **Contact:** The Administrator

An early Tudor merchant's house, extensively restored in 1971.

Location: OS Ref. ST431 545. In the Square, on corner of High Street, off A371.

Opening Times: Easter - end Sept: daily, 2 - 5pm.

Admission: Free. School groups by arrangement.

Ground floor suitable.

LOWER SEVERALLS

Tel: 01460 73234

Crewkerne, Somerset TA18 7NX

Owner: Mr & Mrs Howard Pring **Contact:** Mary Cooper

2 acre garden, developed over the last 25 years including herb gardens, mixed borders and island beds with innovative features, ie a giant living willow basket and a wadi.

Location: OS Ref. ST457 112. 1½ m NE of Crewkerne, between A30 & A356.

Opening Times: 1 Mar - 20 Oct: daily (except Thurs), 10am - 5pm (Suns, 2 - 5pm in May/June only).

Admission: Adult £2, Child (under 16yrs) Free.

LYTES CARY MANOR

Tel: 01985 843600

Nr Charlton Mackrell, Somerset TA11 7HU

Owner: The National Trust **Contact:** The Administrator

A manor house with a 14th century chapel, 15th century hall and 16th century great chamber. The home of Henry Lyte, translator of Niewe Herball (1578). Hedged gardens with long herbaceous border.

Location: OS Ref. ST534 265. 1m N of Ilchester bypass A303, signposted from roundabout at junction of A303. A37 take A372.

Opening Times: 1 Apr - 30 Oct: Mons, Weds & Sats, 2 - 6pm or dusk if earlier. Also Fris in Jun, Jul & Aug. Last admission 5.30pm.

Admission: £4, Child £2.

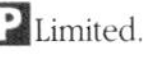Grounds suitable. Limited.

Patrick Lane.

Lower Severalls, Somerset.

MAUNSEL HOUSE

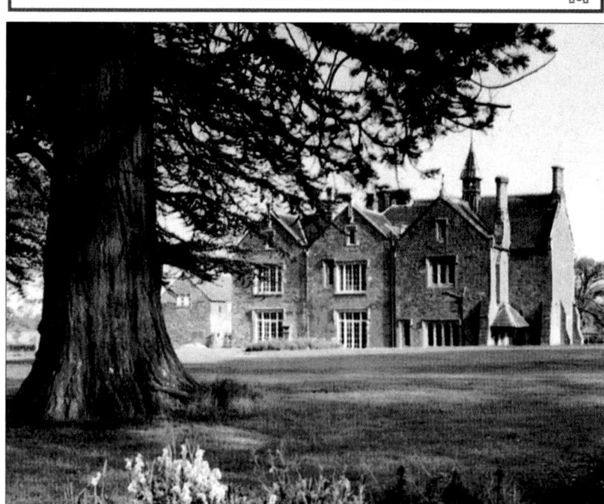

NORTH NEWTON, Nr BRIDGWATER, SOMERSET TA7 0BU

Owner: *Sir Benjamin Slade* ***Contact:*** *Olivia Boyle*

Tel: 0207 352 1132 **Fax:** 0207 352 5697

This imposing 13th century manor house offers the ideal location for wedding receptions, corporate events, private and garden parties, filming and family celebrations. The ancestral seat of the Slade family and home of the 7th baronet Sir Benjamin Slade; the house can boast such visitors as Geoffrey Chaucer, who wrote part of the *Canterbury Tales* whilst staying there. The beautiful grounds and spacious rooms provide both privacy and a unique atmosphere for any special event.

Location: OS Ref. ST302 303. Bridgwater 4m, Bristol 20m, Taunton 7m, M5/J24, turn left North Petherton. 2½ m SE of A38 at North Petherton.

Opening Times: Gardens only: 1 Apr - 1 Oct (inc Easter): Suns, 2 - 5.30pm. Coach parties and groups welcome by appointment.

Admission: £2 (honesty box).

Functions. Partially suitable. In grounds, on leads. 

MILTON LODGE GARDENS

Tel: 01749 672168

Wells, Somerset BA5 3AQ

Owner/Contact: D Tudway Quilter Esq

"The great glory of the gardens of Milton Lodge is their position high up on the slopes of the Mendip Hills to the north of Wells ... with broad panoramas of Wells Cathedral and the Vale of Avalon", (Lanning Roper). Charming, mature, Grade II listed terraced garden dating from 1909. Replanned 1962 with mixed shrubs, herbaceous plants, old fashioned roses and ground cover; numerous climbers; old established yew hedges. Fine trees in garden and in 7-acre arboretum.

Location: OS Ref. ST549 470. ½ m N of Wells from A39. N up Old Bristol Road. Free car park first gate on left.

Opening Times: Garden & Arboretum: Good Fri - 31 Oct: daily except Sats, 2 - 5pm Parties & coaches by prior arrangement.

Admission: Adult £2.50, Child (under 14yrs) Free. Open certain Suns in aid of National Gardens Scheme.

  Not suitable.

MONTACUTE HOUSE

Tel/Fax: 01935 823289

Montacute, Somerset TA15 6XP

Owner: The National Trust **Contact:** The Property Manager

A magnificent Elizabethan house, with an H-shaped ground plan and many Renaissance features, including contemporary plasterwork, chimneypieces and heraldic glass. The house contains fine 17th and 18th century furniture, an exhibition of samplers dating from the 17th century and Elizabethan and Jacobean portraits from the National Portrait Gallery displayed in the Long Gallery and adjoining rooms. The formal garden includes mixed borders and old roses, also a landscaped park.

Location: OS Ref. ST499 172. In Montacute village, 4m W of Yeovil, on S side of A3088, 3m E of A303.

Opening Times: House: 1 Apr - 30 Oct: daily except Tues, 12 noon - 5.30pm. Garden & Park: 1 Apr - 30 Oct: daily except Tues, 11am - 5.30pm or dusk if earlier. 1 Nov - Mar 2001 daily except Mons & Tues, 11.30am - 4pm.

Admission: House, Park & Garden: Adult £5.50, Child £2.80, Family £13.70. Groups: Adult £5, Child £2.50. Garden & Park: Adult £3.10, Child £1.30. Nov - Mar: £1.50.

Plant centre. Grounds suitable. WC. Licensed.

P In grounds, on leads.

MUCHELNEY ABBEY

Tel: 01458 250664

Muchelney, Langport, Somerset TA10 0DQ

Owner: English Heritage **Contact:** The Custodian

Well-preserved ruins of the cloisters, with windows carved in golden stone, and abbot's lodging of the Benedictine abbey, which survived by being used as a farmhouse after the Dissolution.

Location: OS193 Ref. ST428 248. In Muchelney 2m S of Langport.

Opening Times: 1 Apr - 31 Oct: daily 10am - 6pm (5pm in Oct). Winter: closed.

Admission: Adult £1.70, Child 90p, Conc. £1.30. 15% discount for groups (11+).

Ground floor & grounds suitable. P Tel. for details.

MUSEUM OF COSTUME & ASSEMBLY ROOMS

See page 205 for full page entry.

NUNNEY CASTLE

Tel: 0117 9750700

Nunney, Somerset

Owner: English Heritage **Contact:** The South West Regional Office

A small 14th century moated castle with a distinctly French style. Its unusual design consists of a central block with large towers at the angles.

Location: OS183 Ref. ST737 457. In Nunney 3½ m SW of Frome, 1m N of the A361.

Opening Times: Any reasonable time.

ORCHARD WYNDHAM

Tel: 01984 632309 **Fax:** 01984 633526

Williton, Taunton, Somerset TA4 4HH

Owner: Wyndham Estate **Contact:** Wyndham Estate Office

English manor house. Family home for 700 years encapsulating continuous building and alteration from the 14th to the 20th century. Limited showing space within the house. To avoid disappointment book places on tour by telephone or fax. Narrow access road suitable for light vehicles only.

Location: OS Ref. ST072 400. 1m from A39 at Williton.

Opening Times: 3 - 31 Aug: Thurs & Fris, 2 - 5pm, also BH Mons, 11am - 5pm. Last tour begins at 4pm.

Admission: Adult £4, Child (under 12) £1.

House unsuitable for wheelchairs, grounds suitable.

Obligatory & pre-booked. P In grounds, on leads.

PRIEST'S HOUSE

Tel: 01458 252621

Muchelney, Langport, Somerset TA10 0DQ

Owner: The National Trust **Contact:** The Administrator

A late medieval hall house with large gothic windows, originally the residence of priests serving the parish church across the road. Lived-in and recently repaired.

Location: OS Ref. ST429 250. 1m S of Langport.

Opening Times: 2 Apr - 25 Sept: Suns & Mons, 2.30 - 5.30pm, last admission 5.15pm.

Admission: £1.70, no reductions.

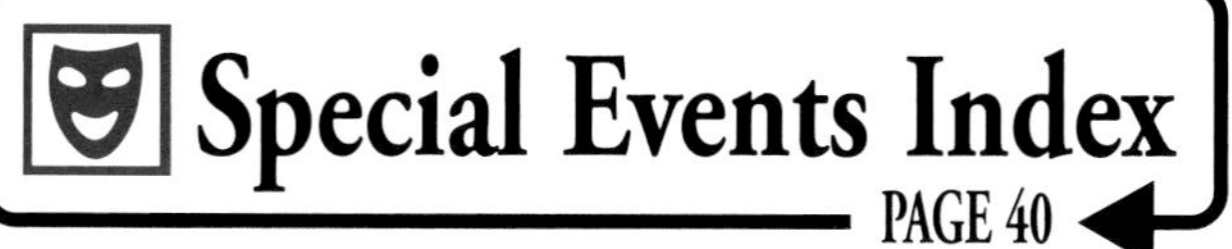

PRIOR PARK LANDSCAPE GARDEN

Tel: 01225 833422

Ralph Allen Drive, Bath BA2 5AH

Owner: The National Trust **Contact:** Gardener-in-Charge

Beautiful and intimate 18th century landscape garden created by Bath entrepreneur Ralph Allen (1693 - 1764) with advice from the poet Alexander Pope and Lancelot 'Capability' Brown. Sweeping valley with magnificent views of the City of Bath, Palladian bridge and lakes. Major restoration of the garden continues. Planning permission to open the property was granted until September 1998 only; renewal is likely to be conditional on the success of the 'green transport' scheme as no car park can be provided. For further details 01225 833422 or 24 hour information line 0891 335242 (45p per minute cheap rate, 50p per minute at all other times).

Location: OS Ref. ST760 632. Frequent bus service from City Centre. Badgerline 2 & 4.

Opening Times: Feb - 22 Apr: daily except Tues, 12 noon - 5.30pm. 22 Apr - Sept: daily except Tues, 11am - 5.30pm. Oct - Nov: daily except Tues, 12 noon - 5.30pm. Dec - Jan 2001: Fri - Sun, 12 noon - 5.30pm. Closed 25 - 26 Dec & 1 Jan 2001.

Admission: Adult: £3.80, Child £1.90. All visitors who produce a valid bus or train ticket will receive £1 off admission. NT members will receive a £1 voucher.

Grounds suitable. WC. No parking. 

THE ROMAN BATHS & PUMP ROOM

See page 206 for full page entry.

STEMBRIDGE TOWER MILL

Tel: 01985 843600

High Ham, Somerset TA10 9DJ

Owner: The National Trust **Contact:** The Administrator

The last thatched windmill in England, dating from 1822 and in use until 1910.

Location: OS Ref. ST432 305. 2m N of Langport, 1/2 m E of High Ham.

Opening Times: 2 Apr - 27 Sept: Sun - Mon & Weds, 2 - 5pm.

Admission: Adult £1.80, Child 90p. Groups by arrangement.

Limited.

STOKE-SUB-HAMDON PRIORY

Tel: 01985 843600

North Street, Stoke-sub-Hamdon Somerset TA4 6QP

Owner: The National Trust **Contact:** The Administrator

A complex of buildings, begun in the 14th century for the priests of the chantry chapel of St Nicholas, which is now destroyed.

Location: OS Ref. ST473 174. 1/2 m S of A303. 2m W of Montacute between Yeovil and Ilminster.

Opening Times: 27 Mar - 31 Oct: daily, 10am - 6pm or dusk if earlier.

Admission: Free.

Limited.

TINTINHULL GARDEN

Tel: 01935 822545

Farm Street, Tintinhull, Somerset BA22 9PZ

Owner: The National Trust **Contact:** The Head Gardener

A 20th century formal garden surrounding a 17th century house. The garden layout, divided into areas by walls and hedges, has border colour and plant themes, including shrub roses and clematis; there is also a kitchen garden.

Location: OS Ref. ST503 198. 5m NW of Yeovil, 1/2 m S of A303, on E outskirts of Tintinhull.

Opening Times: 1 Apr - 30 Sept: Wed - Sun, 12 noon - 6pm (open BH Mons).

Admission: Adult £3.80, Child £1.80. No reduction for Groups.

Grounds suitable. Limited.

TREASURER'S HOUSE

Tel: 01935 825801

Martock, Somerset TA12 6JL

Owner: The National Trust **Contact:** The Administrator

A small medieval house, recently refurbished by The Trust. The two-storey hall was completed in 1293 and the solar block is even earlier. There is also a kitchen, added later, and an interesting wall painting.

Location: OS Ref. ST462 191. 1m NW of A303 between Ilminster and Ilchester.

Opening Times: 2 Apr - 26 Sept: Sun - Tue, 2.30 - 5.30pm.

Admission: Adult £1.70 (no reductions). Groups by prior appointment.

Limited for cars. None for coaches.

WELLS CATHEDRAL

Tel: 01749 674483 **Fax:** 01749 677360

Cathedral Green, Wells, Somerset BA5 2UE

Owner: Dean & Chapter of Wells **Contact:** Mr John Roberts

Fine medieval Cathedral. The West front with its splendid array of statuary, the Quire with colourful embroideries and stained glass, Chapter House and astronomical clock should not be missed.

Location: OS Ref. ST552 458. In Wells, 20m S from both Bath & Bristol.

Opening Times: Daily: 7.15am - 8.30pm (summer), or 7.15am - 6pm (winter).

Admission: No entry charge. Donations welcomed. Photo permit £1.

WESTBURY COLLEGE GATEHOUSE

Tel: 01985 843600

College Road, Westbury-on-Trym, Bristol

Owner: The National Trust **Contact:** Rev G M Collins

The 15th century gatehouse of the College of Priests (founded in the 13th century) of which John Wyclif was a prebend.

Location: OS Ref. ST572 775. 3m N of the centre of Bristol. Just E of main street.

Opening Times: Access by key only, to be collected by prior written or telephone appointment (0117 962 1536). Rev. G M Collins, The Vicarage, 44 Eastfield Road, Westbury-on-Trym, Bristol BS9 4AG.

Admission: Adult £1.10, Child 50p.

Limited. 

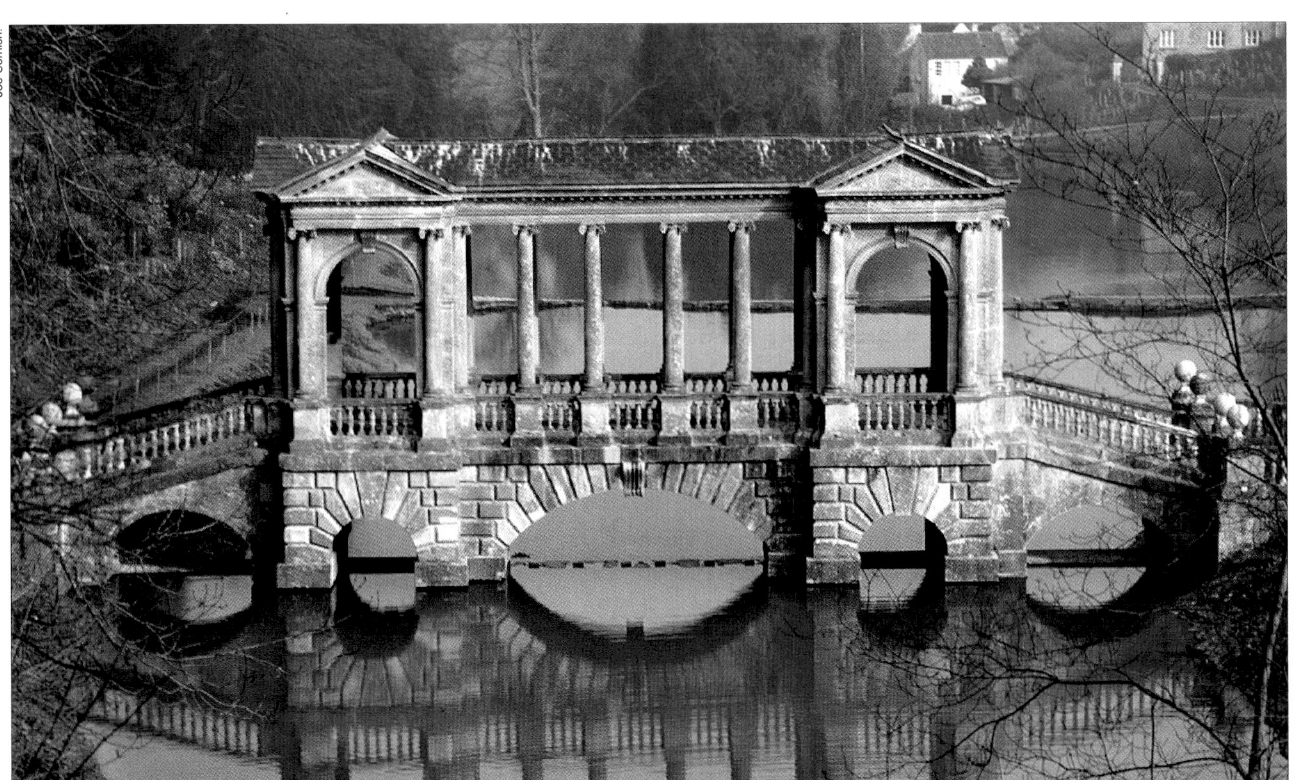

Joe Cornish.

Prior Park Landscape Garden, Somerset.

Owner:
The Marquis of Lansdowne

CONTACT

The Administrator
Bowood House and Gardens
Calne
Wiltshire
SN11 0LZ

Tel: 01249 812102

Fax: 01249 821757

e-mail: enquiries@bowood-estate.co.uk

LOCATION

OS Ref. ST974 700

From London M4/J17, off the A4 between Chippenham and Calne. Swindon 17m, Bristol 26m, Bath 16m.

Bus: to the gate, $1^{1}/_{2}$ m through park to House.

Rail: Chippenham Station 5m.

Taxi: AA Taxis, Chippenham 657777.

BOWOOD HOUSE & GARDENS

Calne

BOWOOD is the family home of the Marquis and Marchioness of Lansdowne. Begun c1720 for the Bridgeman family, the house was purchased by the 2nd Earl of Shelburne in 1754 and completed soon afterwards. Part of the house was demolished in 1955, leaving a perfectly proportioned Georgian home, over half of which is open to visitors. Robert Adam's magnificent Diocletian wing contains a splendid library, the laboratory where Joseph Priestley discovered oxygen gas in 1774, the orangery, now a picture gallery, the Chapel and a sculpture gallery in which some of the famous Lansdowne Marbles are displayed.

Among the family treasures shown in the numerous exhibition rooms are Georgian costumes, including Lord Byron's Albanian dress; Victoriana; Indiana (the 5th Marquess was Viceroy 1888-94); and superb collections of watercolours, miniatures and jewellery.

The House is set in one of the most beautiful parks in England. Over 2,000 acres of gardens and grounds were landscaped by 'Capability' Brown between 1762 and 1768, and are embellished with a Doric temple, a cascade, a pinetum and an arboretum.The Rhododendron Gardens are open for six weeks from late April to early June. All the walks have seats.

Receptions, film location, 2,000 acre park, 40 acre lake, 18-hole golf course and Country Club, open to all players holding a current handicap.

Visitors may alight at the House before parking. WCs.

The Restaurant (waitress-service, capacity 85). Parties that require lunch or tea should book in advance.

On request, groups can be given introductory talk, or for an extra charge, a guided tour. Tour time $1^{1}/_{4}$ hrs. Guide sheets in French, German, Dutch, Spanish & Japanese.

1,000 cars, unlimited for coaches, 400 yds from house. Allow 2-3 hrs to visit house, gardens and grounds.

Welcome. Special guide books. Picnic areas. Adventure playground.

OPENING TIMES

House & Garden
1 Apr - 29 Oct:
Daily
11am - 6pm or dusk if earlier.

Rhododendron Walks
Mid-April to early June for 6 weeks
11am - 6pm.

ADMISSION

House and Garden

Adult	£5.70
Child (5-15yrs)	£3.50
OAP	£4.70
Groups (20+)	
Adult	£4.80
Child (5-15yrs)	£3.00
OAP	£4.10

Rhododendron Walks

Adult	£3.00
Child (5-15yrs)	Free
OAP	£3.00

The charge for Rhododendron Walks is £2.00 if combined on same day with a visit to Bowood House & Gardens.

CORSHAM COURT
Corsham

Owner:
J Methuen-Campbell Esq

CONTACT

Corsham Court
Corsham
Wiltshire
SN13 0BZ

Tel/Fax: 01249 701610

CORSHAM COURT is an Elizabethan house of 1582 and was bought by Paul Methuen in the mid-18th century, to house a collection of 16th and 17th century Italian and Flemish master paintings and statuary. In the middle of the 19th century, the house was enlarged to receive a second collection, purchased in Florence, principally of fashionable Italian masters and stone-inlaid furniture.

Paul Methuen (1723-95) was a great-grandson of Paul Methuen of Bradford-on-Avon and cousin of John Methuen, ambassador and negotiator of the Methuen Treaty of 1703 with Portugal which permitted export of British woollens to Portugal and allowed a preferential 33¹/3 percent duty discount on Portuguese wines, bringing about a major change in British drinking habits.

The architects involved in the alterations to the house and park were Lancelot 'Capability' Brown in the 1760s, John Nash in 1800 and Thomas Bellamy in 1845-9. Brown set the style by retaining the Elizabethan Stables and Riding School, but rebuilding the Gateway, retaining the gabled Elizabethan stone front and doubling the gabled wings at either end and inside, by designing the East Wing as Stateroom Picture Galleries. Nash's work has now largely disappeared, but Bellamy's stands fast, notably in the Hall and Staircase.

The State Rooms, including the Music Room and Dining Room, provide the setting for the outstanding collection of over 150 paintings, statuary, bronzes and furniture. The collection includes work by such names as Chippendale, the Adam brothers, Van Dyck, Reni, Rosa, Rubens, Lippi, Reynolds, Romney and a pianoforte by Clementi.

GARDENS
'Capability' Brown planned to include a lake, avenues and specimen trees such as the Oriental Plane now with a 200-yard perimeter. The gardens, designed not only by Brown but also by Repton, contain a ha-ha, herbaceous borders, secluded gardens, lawns, a rose garden, a lily pool, a stone bath house and the Bradford Porch.

Souvenir desk. No umbrellas, no photography.

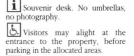

Visitors may alight at the entrance to the property, before parking in the allocated areas.

Tearooms nearby. Tel: Corsham 01249 713260.

For up to 55. If requested the owner may meet the group. Tour time 1¹/2 hrs.

400 cars, 120 yards from the house. Coaches may park at the door to the house. Coach parties must book in advance.

Available: rate negotiable. A guide will be provided.

Must be kept on leads in the garden.

LOCATION

OS Ref. ST874 706

Corsham Court is signposted from the A4, approx. 4m W of Chippenham.
From Edinburgh, A1, M62, M6, M5, M4, 8 hrs.
From London, M4, 2¹/4 hrs.
From Chester, M6, M5, M4, 4 hrs.

Motorway: M4/J17 9m.

Rail: Chippenham Station 6m.

Taxi: 01249 715959.

OPENING TIMES

SUMMER
20 March - 30 September
Daily except Mons but including BH Mons
11am - 5.30pm
Last admission 5pm.

WINTER
1 October - 19 March
Weekends only
2 - 4.30pm
Last admission 4pm.

Closed December.

NB: Open throughout the year by appointment only for groups of 15+.

ADMISSION

House & Garden

Adult	£4.50
Child (5-15yrs)	£2.50
OAP	£3.50
Groups (includes guided tour - 1 hr)	
Adult	£3.50

Garden only

Adult	£2.00
Child (5-15yrs)	£1.00
OAP	£1.50
Groups	
Per person	£3.50

Owner: Hartham Park Plc

CONTACT

Jeffrey Thomas
Hartham Park
Corsham
Wiltshire
SN13 0RP

Tel: 01249 700000

Fax: 01249 700001

e-mail: post@harthampark.plc.uk

LOCATION

OS Ref. ST861 721

Corsham, Wiltshire.

CONFERENCE/FUNCTION		
ROOM	SIZE	MAX CAPACITY
Library	43' x 19'	75
State Room	33' x 24'	75
Ballroom	62' x 23'	140
Study	37' x 18'	50
Sticke Court	82' x 30'	240

HARTHAM PARK
Corsham

Hartham Park is one of Wiltshire's best kept secrets. The estate was first recorded in the Domesday Book, while the present house, designed by James Wyatt, was built between 1790 and 1795 and is a classic example of dignified Georgian architecture. The mansion is set in acres of formal gardens surrounded by rolling parkland.

Once the home of Lord Islington, the property has recently undergone extensive restoration recreating the genteel ambience of an Edwardian country estate. Complete with one of only three remaining Sticke tennis courts in the world, Hartham Park allows the visitor to recapture the atmosphere of a bygone age.

Although Hartham Park may look like a typical stately home, behind the grandeur lies an innovative concept – an elegant venue where business and hospitality is carefully combined. An ideal setting for events, meetings and celebrations. The formal gardens and parkland are well suited to outside events such as activity days and team building.

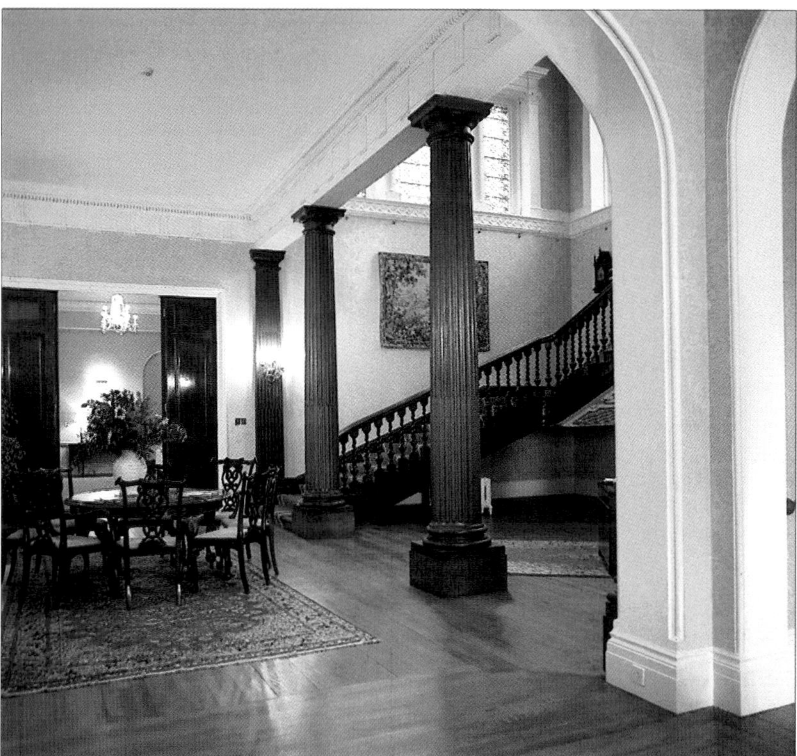

OPENING TIMES

By arrangement for groups only (10 - 40)

ADMISSION

Please telephone for details

Hartham Park produce.

Partially suitable.

Licensed.

Licensed.

Obligatory.

Limited for coaches.

In grounds, on leads.

8 doubles.

Tel. for details.

Owner:
The Marquess of Bath

CONTACT

The Estate Office
Longleat
Warminster
Wiltshire
BA12 7NW

Tel: 01985 844400

Fax: 01985 844885

e-mail:
longleat@btinternet.com

LOCATION

OS Ref. ST809 430

Off the A362 between Warminster and Frome. Just 2hrs from London following M3, A303, A36, A362 or M4/J18/A46-A36.

Rail: Mainline Paddington to Westbury 12m or Warminster station on Bristol-Salisbury line.

Air: Bristol airport 30m.

Taxi: Starline Taxis 01985 212215.

CONFERENCE/FUNCTION		
ROOM	SIZE	MAX CAPACITY
Banqueting Suite	2 x (10m x 7m)	50
Great Hall	8m x 13m	150

LONGLEAT HOUSE
Warminster

Nestling within magnificent 'Capability' Brown landscaped grounds in the heart of Wiltshire, Longleat House is widely regarded as the best example of high Elizabethan architecture in Britain and one of the most beautiful stately homes open to the public.

Built by Sir John Thynne and substantially completed by 1580, Longleat House has been the home of the same family ever since. Many treasures are included within; paintings by Tintoretto and Wootton, exquisite Flemish tapestries, fine French furniture and elaborate ceilings by John Dibblee Crace incorporating paintings from the 'School of Titian'.

The Murals in the family apartments in the West Wing were painted by Alexander Thynn, the present Marquess, and are fascinating and remarkable additions to the collections.

Apart from the ancestral home, Longleat is also renowned for its Safari Park, the first of its kind in the UK. Here, visitors have the rare opportunity to see hundreds of animals in a natural woodland and parkland setting. Amongst the most magnificent sights are the famous pride of lions, a white tiger, wolves, rhesus monkeys, elephants and zebras.

Don't miss the other attractions which make Longleat a fun day out for all the family… get lost in the 'World's Longest Hedge Maze', let off steam in the Adventure Castle, travel on the Longleat Railway, get close to the creatures in Pets Corner and marvel at the sea lions on the Safari Boats … your day at Longleat will never be long enough!

Rooms in Longleat House can be hired for conferences, gala dinners and product launches. Extensive parkland for corporate fun days, team building events, concerts, balloon festivals, equestrian events, caravan rallies and fishing. Film location.

Licensed.

Cellar Café (capacity 80). Groups pre-book for tea and other meals. Cream teas as well as lunch from £5 and sandwiches and snacks from £1.20.

Groups of up to 20. Pre-book tours, when required in French.

Ample.

Welcome with 1 teacher given free entry per 8 children. Group and education pack available on request.

In grounds, on leads.

 Tel. for details.

PASSPORT TICKETS
1 Apr - 29 Oct: includes Safari Park, Longleat House, Safari Boats, World's Longest Hedge Maze, King Arthur's Mirror Maze, Pets Corner, Adventure Castle, Longleat Railway, Simulator Ride, Butterfly Garden, Postman Pat Village, Doctor Who Exhibition, Dolls Houses, Family Bygones, Life and Times Exhibition, Grounds & Gardens.

OPENING TIMES

SUMMER
1 April - 29 October
House and Safari Park
Daily, 10am - 5pm or sunset if earlier.

Other attractions:
11am - 5.30pm.

WINTER
House & grounds only.
19 - 27 February.
1 April - 31 December (except Christmas Day).

Please tel: 01985 844400 for further details on winter opening times.

ADMISSION

SUMMER

House only
Adult £6.00
Child (4 -14yrs).........£4.00
OAP.......................£5.00

Safari Park only
Adult £6.00
Child (4 -14yrs).........£5.00
OAP.......................£5.00

Grounds only
Adult £2.00
Child (4 -14yrs) £1.00
OAP.......................£1.00

Groups of 12+ Free.

Passport Tickets
(see left under photo)
Adult £13.00
Child (4 -14yrs).......£11.00
OAP......................£11.00
Groups (25+)
Adult £8.70
Child (4 -16yrs).........£7.30
OAP.......................£7.30

Special discounted rates for groups of 12 - 24 & 25+.

West Country England

WILTON HOUSE

Nr Salisbury

Owner:
The Earl of Pembroke

CONTACT

Sally Watkins
The Estate Office
Wilton House
Wilton
Salisbury
SP2 0BJ

Tel: 01722 746720

Fax: 01722 744447

e-mail:
tourism@wiltonhouse.com

LOCATION

OS Ref. SU099 311

3m W of Salisbury on the A30.

Rail: Salisbury Station 3m.

Bus: Every 10 mins from Salisbury, Mon - Sat.

Taxi: Sarum Taxi 01722 334477.

CONFERENCE/FUNCTION		
ROOM	SIZE	MAX CAPACITY
Double cube	60' x 30'	150
Exhibition Centre	50' x 40'	140
Film Theatre	34" x 20"	67

The 17th Earl of Pembroke and his family live in Wilton House which has been their ancestral home for 450 years. In 1544 Henry VIII gave the Abbey and lands of Wilton to Sir William Herbert who had married Anne Parr, sister of Katherine, sixth wife of King Henry.

The Clock Tower, in the centre of the east front, is reminiscent of this part of the Tudor building which survived a fire in 1647. Inigo Jones and John Webb were responsible for the rebuilding of the house in the Palladian style, whilst further alterations were made by James Wyatt from 1801.

The chief architectural features are the magnificent 17th century state apartments (including the famous Single and Double Cube rooms) and the 19th century cloisters.

The house contains one of the finest art collections in Europe, with over 230 original paintings on display, including works by Van Dyck, Rubens, Joshua Reynolds and Brueghel. Also on show are Greek and Italian statuary, a lock of Queen Elizabeth I's hair, Napoleon's despatch case, and Florence Nightingale's sash.

The visitor centre houses a dynamic introductory film (narrated by Anna Massey), the reconstructed Tudor kitchen and the Estate's Victorian laundry. It provides a home for the 'Wareham Bears', an exhibition of some 200 miniature costumed teddy bears with their own house, stables and other scenes. 21 acres of landscaped parkland, water and old English rose gardens, Palladian Bridge and adventure playground.

Film location, fashion shows, product launches, equestrian events, garden parties, antiques fairs, concerts, vehicle rallies. No photography in house. French, German, Spanish, Italian, Japanese and Dutch information.

Exclusive banquets.

Excellent access. Visitors may alight at the entrance. WCs.

Licensed. Self-service restaurant open 10.30am - 5pm. Groups must book. Hot lunches 12 noon - 2pm.

By arrangement.

200 cars and 12 coaches. Free coach parking. Group rates (min 15), meal vouchers, drivers' lounge.

Teachers' handbook for National Curriculum. EFL students welcome. Free preparatory visit for group leaders.

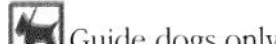

Guide dogs only.

OPENING TIMES

SUMMER
10 April - 29 October
Daily: 10.30am - 5.30pm

Last admission 4.30pm.

WINTER
Closed, except for private parties by prior arrangement.

ADMISSION

SUMMER
House, Grounds & Exhibition

Adult	£6.75
Child*	£4.00
OAP/Student	£5.75
Family (2+2)	£17.50
Groups (15+)	
Adult	£5.25
Child	£3.50

Grounds only

Adult	£3.75
Child	£2.50
Season Tickets	
Family	£39.50
Individual	£19.50

WINTER
Prices on application.

* 5 - 15 yrs - under 5s Free.

SPECIAL EVENTS

- **MAR 3 - 5:** 23rd Annual Antiques Fair.
- **JUL 15:** Musical Evening with Fireworks.

ALEXANDER KEILLER MUSEUM

Tel: 01672 539250

Avebury, Nr Marlborough, Wiltshire SN8 1RF

Owner: The National Trust **Contact:** The Custodian

The investigation of Avebury Stone Circles was largely the work of Alexander Keiller in the 1930s. He put together one of the most important prehistoric archaeological collections in Britain which can be seen at the Alexander Keiller Museum.

Location: OS Ref. SU100 699. In Avebury 6m W of Marlborough.

Opening Times: 1 Apr - 31 Oct: daily, 11am - 5pm/dusk if earlier. 1 Nov - 31 Mar: Wed - Sun, 1.30 - 4pm. Closed 18 - 26 Dec & 1 Jan.

Admission: Adult £1.80, Child 80p. English Heritage members Free.

AVEBURY MANOR & GARDEN

Tel: 01672 539250

Avebury, Nr Marlborough, Wiltshire SN8 1RF

Owner: The National Trust **Contact:** The Custodian

A regularly altered house of monastic origin, the present buildings date from the early 16th century, with notable Queen Anne alterations and Edwardian renovation by Col Jenner. The topiary and flower gardens contain medieval walls, ancient box and numerous compartments.

Location: OS Ref. SU101 701. 6m W of Marlborough, 1m N of the A4 on A4361 and B4003.

Opening Times: House: 2 Apr - 31 Oct: Tue - Wed, Suns & BH Mons, 2 - 5.30pm. Garden: 2 Apr - 31 Oct: daily except Mons & Thurs (open BH Mons), 11am - 5.30pm.

Admission: House & Garden: Adult £3.20, Child £1.50. Group: Adult £2.95, Child £1.25. Garden only: Adult £2.25, Child £1. Groups: Adult £2, Child 75p.

Partially suitable.  No dogs in house. Guide dogs only in garden.

AVEBURY STONE CIRCLES

Tel: 01672 539250

Avebury, Nr Marlborough, Wiltshire SN8 1RF

Owner: The National Trust **Contact:** The Property Manager

One of the most important Megalithic monuments in Europe, this 28½ acre site with stone circles enclosed by a ditch and external bank, is approached by an avenue of stones. The site includes the Alexander Keiller Museum and is managed and owned by the National Trust.

Location: OS Ref. SU102 699. 6m W of Marlborough, 1m N of the A4 on A4361 and B4003.

Opening Times: Stone Circle: daily.

BOWOOD HOUSE

See page 213 for full page entry.

BRADFORD-ON-AVON TITHE BARN

Tel: 0117 975 0700

Bradford-on-Avon, Wiltshire

Owner: English Heritage **Contact:** South West Regional Office

A magnificent medieval stone-built barn with a slate roof and wooden beamed interior.

Location: OS173 Ref. ST824 604. ¼ m S of town centre, off B3109.

Opening Times: Daily, 10.30am - 4pm.

Admission: Free.

BROADLEAS GARDENS

Tel: 01380 722035

Devizes, Wiltshire SN10 5JQ

Owner: Broadleas Gardens Charitable Trust **Contact:** Lady Anne Cowdray

10 acres full of interest, notably The Dell, where the sheltered site allows plantings of magnolias, camellias, rhododendrons and azaleas.

Location: OS Ref. SU001 601. Signposted SW from town centre at S end of housing estate, (coaches must use this entrance) or 1m S of Devizes on W side of A360.

Opening Times: Apr - Oct: Sun, Weds & Thurs, 2 - 6pm or by arrangement for groups.

Admission: Adult £3, Child (under 12yrs) £1, Groups (10+) £2.50.

CORSHAM COURT

See page 214 for full page entry.

THE COURTS

Tel: 01225 782340

Holt, Trowbridge, Wiltshire BA14 6RR

Owner: The National Trust **Contact:** Head Gardener

A 7 acre garden in the Hidcote tradition, full of charm and variety and set within an arboretum containing fine specimen trees. There are many interesting plants and an imaginative use of colour surrounding water features, topiary and herbaceous borders.

Location: OS Ref. ST861 618. 3m SW of Melksham, 3m N of Trowbridge, 2½ m E of Bradford-on-Avon, on S side of B3107.

Opening Times: 2 Apr - 15 Oct: daily except Sats, 1.30 - 5.30pm.

Admission: Adult £3.10, Child £1.50. Groups by arrangement.

Limited.  

GREAT CHALFIELD MANOR

Tel: 01225 782239 **Fax:** 01225 783379

Melksham, Wiltshire SN2 8NJ

Owner: The National Trust **Contact:** The Tenant

A charming manor house, encircled by a moat and defensive wall and with beautiful oriel windows and a great hall. Completed in 1480, the manor and gardens were restored earlier this century by Major R Fuller, whose family still live here and manage the property.

Location: OS Ref. ST860 633. 3m SW of Melksham via Broughton Gifford Common.

Opening Times: 4 Apr - 31 Oct: Tue - Thur, guided tours at 12.15, 2.15, 3.45 & 4.30pm. Tours limited to 25.

Admission: £3.70, no reductions.

Grounds suitable. Obligatory. Limited.

HAMPTWORTH LODGE

HAMPTWORTH, LANDFORD, SALISBURY, WILTSHIRE SP5 2EA

Owner/Contact: *Mr N J M Anderson*

Tel: 01794 390215 **Fax:** 01794 390644

Rebuilt Jacobean manor house standing in woodlands on the edge of the New Forest. Grade II* family house with period furniture including clocks. The Great Hall has an unusual roof construction. There is a collection of prentice pieces and the Moffatt collection of contemporary copies. Garden also open.

Location: OS Ref. SU227 195. 10m SE of Salisbury on road linking Downton on Salisbury/ Bournemouth Road (A338) to Landford on A36, Salisbury - Southampton.

Opening Times: 30 Mar - 30 Apr: 2.15 - 5pm except Suns. Coaches, by appointment only, 1 Apr - 30 Oct except Suns.

Admission: £3.50, Child (under 11yrs) Free. Groups by arrangement.

Ground floor & grounds suitable.

HARTHAM PARK

See page 215 for full page entry.

Sunset at Stonehenge, Wiltshire.

HEALE GARDEN

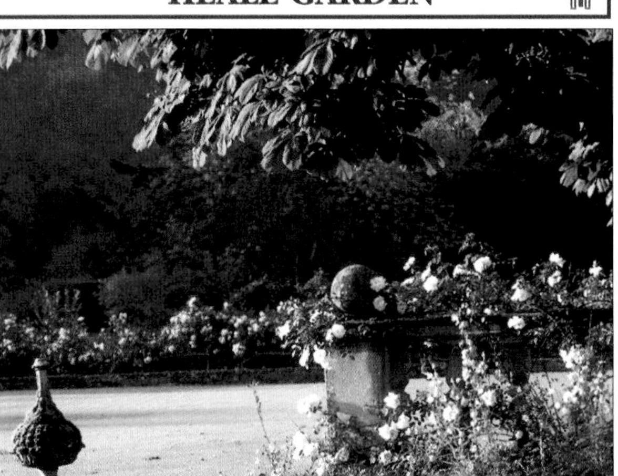

WOODFORD, SALISBURY, WILTSHIRE SP4 6NT

Owner: *Mr & Mrs Guy Rasch* ***Contact:*** *Mrs M Taylor*

Tel: 01722 782504

First winner of Christie's/HHA Garden of the Year award. Grade I Carolean Manor House where King Charles II hid during his escape in 1651. In January great drifts of snowdrops and aconites bring early colour and the promise of spring. The garden provides a wonderfully varied collection of plants, shrub, musk and other roses, growing in the formal setting of clipped hedges and mellow stonework. Particularly lovely in spring and autumn is the water garden surrounding an authentic Japanese Tea House and Nikko Bridge which create an exciting focus in this part of the garden. The specialist Plant Centre has unusual and rare plants, many propagated here, also old garden tools, old garden books, baskets,etc.

Location: OS Ref. SU125 365. 4m N of Salisbury on Woodford Valley road between A345 and A360.

Opening Times: Garden, shop & plant centre: All year, 10am - 5pm.

Admission: Adult £3, Child (under 14yrs) Free.

Grounds suitable.  In grounds, on leads.

THE KING'S HOUSE

Tel: 01722 332151 **Fax:** 01722 325611

SALISBURY & SOUTH WILTSHIRE MUSEUM

e-mail: museum@salisburymuseum.freeserve.co.uk

65 The Close, Salisbury, Wiltshire SP1 2EN

Owner: Salisbury & South Wiltshire Museum Trust **Contact:** P R Saunders

Location: OS Ref. SU141 295. In Salisbury Cathedral Close, W side, facing cathedral.

Opening Times: All year: Mon - Sat: 10am - 5pm. Suns in Jul & Aug: 2 - 5pm.

Admission: Adult £3, Child 75p, Conc. £2, Groups £2.

LACOCK ABBEY

Tel: 01249 730227/ 730459

Lacock, Chippenham, Wiltshire SN15 2LG

Owner: The National Trust **Contact:** The Property Manager

The Abbey was founded in 1232 and converted into a Tudor country house, where the pioneer of photography, William Fox Talbot, lived. Main architectural features of the Abbey are the Medieval Cloisters and Chapter House. The woodland garden boasts a fine display of spring flowers with a fine collection of rare and unusual trees. The Museum commemorates the achievements of Fox Talbot with photographic exhibitions held throughout the year.

Location: OS Ref. ST919 684. In the village of Lacock, 3m N of Melksham, 3m S of Chippenham just E of A350.

Opening Times: Museums, Cloisters & Garden: 26 Feb - 29 Oct: daily (closed Good Fri), 11am - 5.30pm. Abbey: 1 Apr - 29 Oct: daily except Tues & Good Fri, 1 - 5.30pm. Museum: Open weekends in winter. Closed 23 & 24 Dec - 7 Jan 2000.

Admission: Abbey, grounds, cloisters & museum: Adult £5.80, Child £3.20, Groups: £5.30, (Child £2.70). Grounds, cloisters & museum: Adult £3.70, Child £2.20. Museum: Winter opening, Adult £2.10.

LITTLE CLARENDON

Tel: 01985 843600

Dinton, Salisbury, Wiltshire SP3 5OZ

Owner: The National Trust **Contact:** The Administrator

A Tudor house, but greatly altered in the 17th century. Principal rooms on the ground floor are open.

Location: OS Ref. SU015 316. $^{1}/_{4}$ m E of Dinton Church. 9m W of Salisbury.

Opening Times: 1 Apr - 30 Oct:, Sats, 10am - 1pm, Mons, 1 - 5pm.

Admission: £1.50, no reductions.

 Unsuitable.

LONGLEAT HOUSE

See page 216 for full page entry.

LYDIARD PARK

LYDIARD TREGOZE, SWINDON, WILTSHIRE SN5 9PA

Owner: *Swindon Borough Council* ***Contact:*** *The Keeper*

Tel: 01793 770401 **Fax:** 01793 877909

Lydiard Park, ancestral home of the Bolingbrokes, is Swindon's treasure. Set in rolling lawns and woodland this beautifully restored Georgian mansion contains the family's furnishings and portraits, exceptional plasterwork, rare 17th century window and room devoted to 18th century society artist Lady Diana Spencer. Exceptional monuments such as the 'Golden Cavalier' in adjacent church.

Location: OS Ref. SU104 848. 4m W of Swindon, $1^{1}/_{2}$ m N of M4/J16.

Opening Times: House: Mon - Fri, 10am - 1pm, 2 - 5pm, Sat & school summer holidays, 10am - 5pm, Sun, 2 - 5pm. Nov - Feb: early closing at 4pm. Grounds: all day, closing at dusk. Victorian Christmas decorations throughout December.

Admission: Adult £1.20, Child 60p (reviewed April 2000). Groups by appointment.

No photography in house. By arrangement. Limited for coaches.  In grounds on leads.

MALMESBURY HOUSE

Tel: 01722 327027 **Fax:** 01722 334414

The Close, Salisbury, Wiltshire SP1 2EB

Owner/Contact: John Cordle Esq

Location: OS Ref. SU145 296. City of Salisbury, cathedral close, E end of North Walk, by St Ann Gate. Coaches to St John's Street.

Opening Times: Malmesbury House is now permanently closed to the public.

MOMPESSON HOUSE

Tel: 01722 335659

The Close, Salisbury, Wiltshire SP1 2EL

Owner: The National Trust **Contact:** The Property Manager

Fine Queen Anne town house containing high quality 18th century furniture, ceramics and textiles. Also the renowned Turnbull Collection of 18th century drinking glasses. Tranquil walled garden with many perfumed plants. Garden tea room serves home-made cakes. Featured in *Sense and Sensibility.*

Location: OS Ref. SU142 295. On N side of Choristers' Green in Cathedral Close, near High Street Gate.

Opening Times: 1 Apr - 31 Oct: Sat - Wed, 12 noon - 5.30pm.

Admission: Adult £3.40, Child £1.70. Groups: £2.90. Garden only: 80p.

Ground floor & grounds suitable. WC. 

Special Events Index PAGE 40

NEWHOUSE 

REDLYNCH, SALISBURY, WILTSHIRE SP5 2NX

Owner: *George & June Jeffreys* **Contact:** *Mrs Jeffreys*

Tel: 01725 510055 **Fax:** 01725 510284

A brick, Jacobean 'Trinity' House, c1609, with two Georgian wings and a basically Georgian interior. Home of the Eyre family since 1633. Contents include costume, textiles and the Hare picture.

Location: OS184 Ref. SU218 214. 9m S of Salisbury between A36 & A338.

Opening Times: 3 Apr - 12 May: Mon - Fri, 2 - 5.30pm.

Admission: Adult £3, Child £2, Conc. £3. Groups (15+): £2.50.

No photography in house. Not suitable. By arrangement. Limited. Guide dogs only.

OLD WARDOUR CASTLE

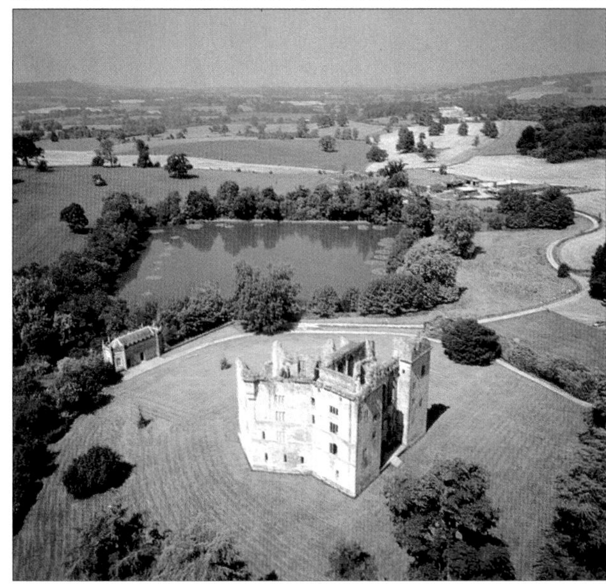

Nr TISBURY, WILTSHIRE SP3 6RR

Owner: *English Heritage* **Contact:** *The Custodian*

Tel: 01747 870487

In a picture-book setting, the unusual hexagonal ruins of this 14th century castle stand on the edge of a beautiful lake, surrounded by landscaped grounds which include an elaborate rockwork grotto.

Location: OS184 Ref. ST939 263. Off A30 2m SW of Tisbury.

Open: 1 Apr - 31 Oct: daily, 10am - 6pm (5pm in Oct). 1 Nov - 31 Mar: Wed - Sun, 10am - 4pm. Closed for lunch 1 - 2pm. Closed 24 - 26 Dec & 1 Jan.

Admission: Adult £1.90, Child £1, Conc. £1.40. 15% discount for groups (11+).

Grounds suitable. In grounds, on leads. Tel. for details.

NORRINGTON MANOR

Tel: 01722 780367 **Fax:** 01722 780667

Alvediston, Salisbury, Wiltshire SP5 5LL

Owner/Contact: T Sykes

Built in 1377 it has been altered and added to in every century since, with the exception of the 18th century. Only the hall and the 'undercroft' remain of the original. It is currently a family home and the Sykes are only the third family to own it.

Location: OS Ref. ST966 237. Signposted to N of Berwick St John and Alvediston road (half way between the two villages)

Opening Times: By appointment in writing.

Admission: A donation to the local churches is asked for.

Not suitable. By arrangement. Limited for cars, none for coaches.

OLD SARUM

Tel: 01722 335398

Castle Road, Salisbury, Wiltshire SP1 3SD

Owner: English Heritage **Contact:** The Head Custodian

Built around 500BC by the iron age peoples, Old Sarum is the former site of the first cathedral and ancient city of Salisbury. A prehistoric hillfort in origin, Old Sarum was occupied by the Romans, the Saxons, and eventually the Normans who made it into one of their major strongholds, with a motte-and-bailey castle built at its centre. Old Sarum eventually grew into one of the most dramatic settlements in medieval England as castle, cathedral, bishop's palace and thriving township. When the new city we know as Salisbury was founded in the early 13th century the settlement faded away. With fine views of the surrounding countryside, Old Sarum is an excellent picnic spot.

Location: OS184 Ref. SU138 327. 2m N of Salisbury off A345.

Opening Times: 1 Apr - 31 Oct: daily, 10am - 6pm (5pm in Oct). 1 Nov - 31 Mar: daily 10am - 4pm. Closed 24 - 26 Dec & 1 Jan.

Admission: Adult £2, Child £1, Conc. £1.50. 15% discount for groups (11+).

Grounds suitable. In grounds, on leads. Tel. for details.

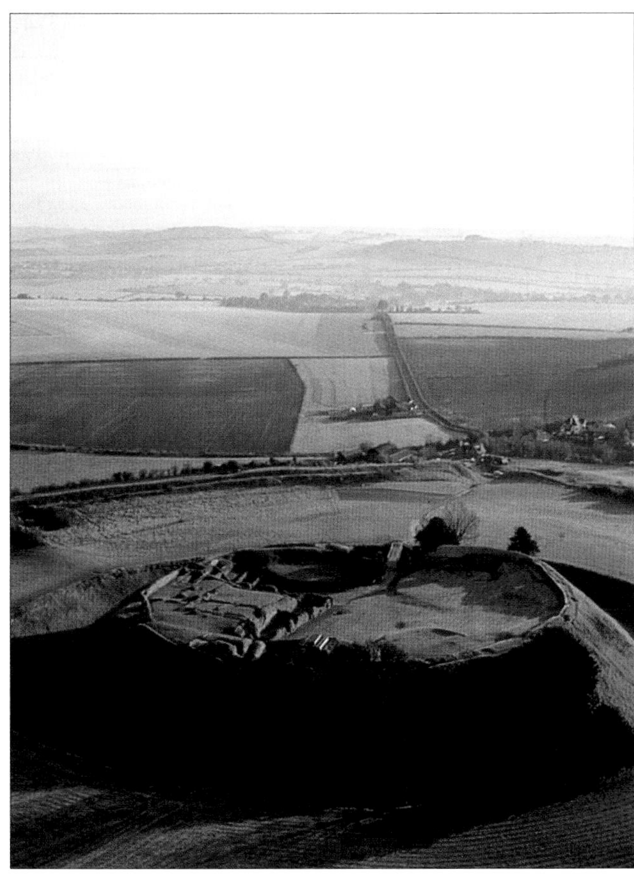

Old Sarum, Wiltshire.

THE PETO GARDEN AT IFORD MANOR

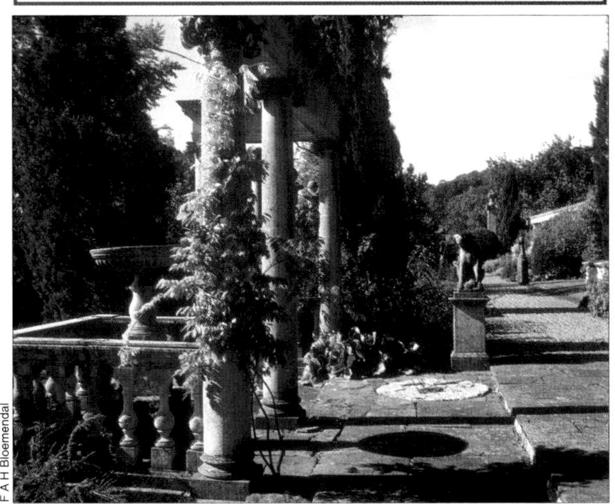
F A H Bloemendal

BRADFORD-ON-AVON, WILTSHIRE BA14 2BA

Owner/Contact: *Mrs E A J Cartwright-Hignett*

Tel: 01225 863146 **Fax:** 01225 862364

This unique Grade I Italian-style garden is set on a romantic hillside beside the River Frome. Designed by the Edwardian architect Harold A Peto, who lived at Iford Manor from 1899 - 1933, the garden has terraces, a colonnade, cloister, casita, statuary, evergreen planting and magnificent rural views. Renowned for its tranquillity and peace, the Peto Garden won the 1998 HHA/Christie's Garden of the Year Award.

Location: OS Ref. ST800 589. 7m SE of Bath via A36, signposted Iford. 2m SW of Bradford-on-Avon via Westwood.

Opening Times: Apr & Oct: Suns only & Easter Mon, 2 - 5pm. May - Sept: Tue - Thur, Sats, Suns & BH Mons, 2 - 5pm. Coaches by appointment at other times. Children under 10yrs not admitted at weekends.

Admission: Adult £3, Child (10-16yrs)/OAP £2.50. Picnic area by River Frome.

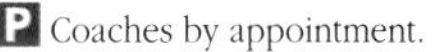 Teas (May - Aug: Sats & Suns, 2 - 5pm). Coaches by appointment. 

SALISBURY CATHEDRAL

Steve Day

33 THE CLOSE, SALISBURY SP1 2EJ

Owner: *The Dean & Chapter* ***Contact:*** *Visitor Services*

Tel: 01722 555120 **Fax:** 01722 555116 **e-mail:** headvisits@aol.com

Salisbury Cathedral is a building of world importance. Set within the elegant splendour of the Cathedral Close it is probably the finest medieval building in Britain. Built in one phase from about 1220 to 1258 the Cathedral has the highest spire, the best preserved Magna Carta, Europe's oldest working clock and a unique 13th century frieze of bible stories in the octagonal Chapter House. Boy and girl choristers sing daily services which follow a pattern of music that goes back over 750 years. Join a tower tour climbing 332 steps to the base of the spire, and marvel at the medieval craftsmanship and the magnificent views of the surrounding countryside. So much history, so much to take in, but always something new.

Location: OS Ref. SU143 295. S of City. M3, A303, A30 from London or A36.

Open: All year: Every Sunday 7am - 6.15pm. Sept - May: Daily, 7am - 6.15pm. June - August: Daily, 7am - 8.15pm.

Admission: Donation (1999 rates). Adult £3, Child £1, Conc. £2, Family (2+2) £6.

Licensed. Large groups must book. In city centre. 

PHILIPPS HOUSE **Tel:** 01985 843600

Dinton, Salisbury, Wiltshire SP3 5HJ

Owner: The National Trust **Contact:** The Administrator

A neo-Grecian house by Jeffry Wyattville, completed in 1816. Principal rooms on ground floor are open.

Location: OS Ref. SU004 319. 9m W of Salisbury, N side of B3089, 1/2 m W of Little Clarendon. Car park off St Mary's Road next to church.

Opening Times: 1 Apr - 30 Oct: Mons, 1 - 5pm, Sats, 10am - 1pm. Park: daily (closed 5 Aug for music event).

Admission: House £2.10. Dinton Park Free.

House suitable, Park limited.

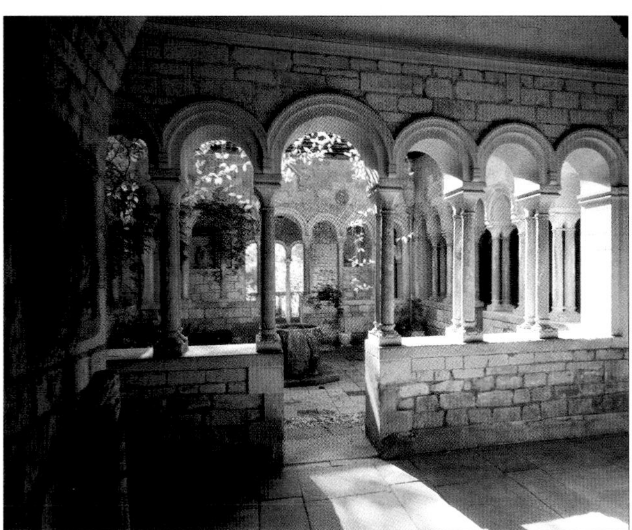

Peto Garden, Wiltshire, winner of the 1999 Christie's/HHA Garden of the Year Award.

Salisbury Cathedral Roof, Wiltshire.

STONEHENGE

English Heritage

AMESBURY, WILTSHIRE SP4 7DE

Owner: *English Heritage* ***Contact:*** *The Custodian*

Tel: 01980 624715 (Information Line)

The mystical and awe-inspiring stone circle at Stonehenge is one of the most famous prehistoric monuments in the world, designated by UNESCO as a World Heritage Site. Stonehenge's orientation on the rising and setting sun has always been one of its most remarkable features. Whether this was simply because the builders came from a sun-worshipping culture, or because – as some scholars have believed – the circle and its banks were part of a huge astronomical calendar, remains a mystery. Visitors to Stonehenge can discover the history and legends which surround this unique stone circle, which began over 5,000 years ago, with a complimentary three part audio tour available in 9 languages (subject to availability).

Location: OS Ref. SU123 422. 2m W of Amesbury on junction of A303 and A344/A360.

Opening Times: 16 - 23 Oct: 9.30am - 5pm, 24 Oct - 15 Mar: 9.30am - 4pm, 16 Mar - 31 May & 1 Sept - 15 Oct: 9.30am - 6pm. 1 Jun - 31 Aug: 9am - 7pm. Closed 24 - 26 Dec & 1 Jan. Last adm. is 1/2 hr before advertised closing times and the site will be closed promptly 20mins after the advertised closing times.

Admission: Adult £4, Child £2, Conc. £3. Family (2+3) £10. Groups (11+) 10% discount.

Tel. for details.

Fireworks on lake at Stourhead, Wiltshire.

STOURHEAD

Tel: 01747 841152

Stourton, Nr Warminster BA12 6QH

Owner: The National Trust **Contact:** The Estate Manager

An outstanding example of the English landscape style of garden. Designed by Henry Hoare II and laid out between 1741 and 1780.

Location: OS183 Ref. ST778 341. At Stourton off the B3092, 3m N of A303 (Mere). 8m S of A361 (Frome).

Opening Times: Garden: All year, daily, 9am - 7pm or sunset if earlier (except 20 - 23 July when garden will close at 5pm, last admission 4pm). House: 1 Apr - 29 Oct: daily (except Thur & Fri), 12 noon - 5.30pm or dusk if earlier, last admission 30 mins before closing. King Alfred's Tower: 1 Apr - 29 Oct: Tue - Fri, 2 - 5.30pm, Sat, Sun, Good Fri & BH Mon, 11.30am - 5.30pm or dusk if earlier.

Admission: House & Garden: Adult £8, Child £3.80, Family £20. Groups £7.70. House or Garden: Mar - Oct: Adult £4.60, Child £2.60, Family £10, Groups (by written appointment, 15+) £4.10. Garden only: Nov - end Feb: Adult £3.60, Child £1.50, Family £8. King Alfred's Tower: Adult £1.50, Child 70p.

Wheelchair accessible. 

STOURTON HOUSE FLOWER GARDEN

Tel: 01747 840417

Zeals, Warminster, Wiltshire BA12 6QF

Owner/Contact: Mrs E Bullivant

Four acres of peaceful, romantic garden where grass paths lead through unique daffodils, spring flowers, camellias, azaleas, delphiniums, hydrangeas and hedged borders. Homemade refreshments.

Location: OS Ref. ST780 340. 2m NW of Mere next to Stourhead car park, A303. Follow blue signs.

Opening Times: Apr - end Nov: Weds, Thurs, Suns, and BH Mons, 11am - 6pm. Plants & dried flowers for sale during the winter on weekdays.

Admission: Adult £2.50, Child 50p. Group guided tours by appointment.

WESTWOOD MANOR

Tel: 01225 863374

Bradford-on-Avon, Wiltshire BA15 2AF

Owner: The National Trust **Contact:** The Tenant

A 15th century stone manor house, altered in the late 16th century, with late gothic and Jacobean windows and Jacobean plasterwork. There is a modern topiary garden.

Location: OS Ref. ST813 589. 1 1/2 m SW of Bradford-on-Avon, in Westwood village, beside the church.

Opening Times: 2 Apr - 27 Sept: Suns, Tues & Weds, 2 - 5pm.

Admission: £3.70.

Not suitable. Limited. 

WILTON HOUSE

See page 217 for full page entry.

Wilton House, Wiltshire.

Window at Lydiard Park, Wiltshire.

The Eastern Counties

The Study at Doddington Hall, Lincoln.

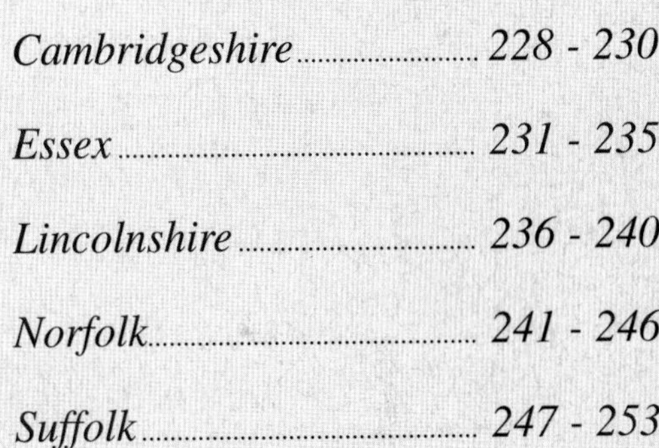

Featuring…

Doddington Hall

The Music Room.

The approach to Doddington Hall near Lincoln looks very much as it would have done when the house was first completed. Then, as now, the first view of the house standing above the flat Lincolnshire countryside, is a surprise and delight, enveloped by its Elizabethan garden walls and splendid gatehouse together with a group of Elizabethan outbuildings. With its woodlands it is a sheltered oasis in this open corner of the county.**

The designer of the house was Robert Smythson, the great Elizabethan architect, whose career began at Longleat and who was best known for his houses in the North of England – Wollaton Hall, Nottingham and Hardwick Hall, Derbyshire. Doddington is a superb example of his best late work – exhibiting all the high, proud and symmetrical lines and huge windows that symbolise the security and confidence of the Elizabethan age.

The house was completed in 1600. It was 100 years later, when it passed to the colourful Delaval family, that the interiors were transformed. Sir John Hussey Delaval was one of its more sober members and in 1760 he employed the Lumby brothers, local builders from Lincoln, on a four year campaign of radical repairs which culminated in the complete internal redecoration of the house. Most remarkably, double glazing was fitted in many of the bedrooms, in an effort to exclude the draughts. The simple and elegant 18th century plasterwork enhances the beauty of Smythson's high and light rooms. The rooms also became much lighter as Sir John removed all the small diamond paned glazing, replacing it with the beautiful Crown glass that is still seen today.

Sarah Gunman by Sir Thomas Lawrence.

Doddington is now the home of Mr and Mrs Antony Jarvis. It was after the Battle of Waterloo that ended the Napoleonic Wars in 1815, that one George Jarvis, a distinguished soldier, retired to Dover to become a banker. There he met Sarah Gunman (neé Delaval), heiress to the Doddington estate. Sarah's husband, James Gunman, was 39 years older than her and she formed a romantic attachment to George Jarvis. Tragically, she died of consumption just six months after her husband in 1825, but before doing so made an arrangement that, on her mother's death, the whole of the Doddington estate should be left to George Jarvis, who was a man of means and in a position to restore the estate from its very run-down condition.

It is by this romantic chance the Jarvis family came to Doddington. Under their ownership, over the last 150 years, Doddington has again responded to the whims of economic and social change – and, many would say luckily, passed by certain decorative trends. The house still contains the furniture and works of art acquired by the Delaval family.

Antony Jarvis trained as an architect and his skill and inspiration is evident, not only in the way in which the house is presented, but in the transformation and enhancement of the gardens. Today, the visitor can feast on the superb layout of elaborately and crisply designed gardens, with box edged parterres, rose beds and massed summer borders and beyond them, less formal areas with magnificent specimen trees and, in Spring, a stunning succession of flowering bulbs and unusual wild flowers that provide a continuing pageant from Christmas until May.

Edward Delaval.

Lord & Lady Mexborough by Sir Joshua Reynolds.

For full details of this property see page 238.

ANGLESEY ABBEY

Tel/Fax: 01223 811200 or 01223 811243 (Office)

Lode, Cambridge CB5 9EJ

Owner: The National Trust **Contact:** The Property Manager

The house, dating from 1600, is built on the site of an Augustinian priory, and contains the famous Fairhaven collection of paintings and furniture. It is surrounded by an outstanding 100 acre landscape garden and arboretum, with wonderful statues and year round floral interest.

Location: OS Ref 154. TL533 622. In Lode village, 6m NE of Cambridge on B1102, signs from A14.

Opening Times: House: 25 Mar - 22 Oct: Wed - Sun & BH Mons, 1 - 5pm. Garden: 6 Jan - 24 Mar: Thur - Sun, 10.30am - dusk. 25 Mar - 2 Jul: Wed - Sun (open BHs), 10.30am - 5.30pm. 3 Jul - 17 Sept: daily, 10.30am - 5.30pm. 20 Sept - 22 Oct: Wed - Sun, 10.30am - 5.30pm. 26 Oct - 23 Dec & 6 Jan - 23 Mar 2001: Thur - Sun, 10.30am - dusk. Lode Mill: As garden except winter when Sat & Sun only. Last admission 4.30pm and at property's discretion during winter. Closed Good Fri. Entry to house by timed tickets on Suns & BH Mons.

Admission: House & garden: £6.10 (Suns & BH Mons: £7.10). Family discounts. Groups: £5. Garden & Mill: £3.75 (Groups: £3.25). Winter: £3 (Groups: £2.50). Groups organisers send SAE for information (no reductions Suns & BHs).

Partially suitable. Licensed. In park, on leads. Tel. for details.

CAMBRIDGE UNIVERSITY BOTANIC GARDEN

Tel: 01223 336265 **Fax:** 01223 336278 **e-mail:** gardens@hermes.cam.ac.uk

Bateman Street, Cambridge CB2 1JF

Owner: University of Cambridge **Contact:** Mrs B Stacey, Administrative Secretary

40 acres of outstanding gardens with lake and glasshouses, near the centre of Cambridge, incorporating nine National collections, including Geranium and Fritillaria. Café and shop in the Gilmour building.

Location: OS Ref. TL453 573. 1m S of Cambridge city centre, off A1309 (Trumpington Rd).

Opening Times: Daily (except Christmas Day & Boxing Day), 10am - 6pm (Summer), 10am - 5pm (Spring & Autumn) 10am - 4pm (Winter). Tours by arrangement.

Admission: Admission charged weekdays Mar - Oct inclusive, plus weekends & BHs all year.

 Grounds suitable. WCs. Street/Pay & Display. Guide dogs only.

OLIVER CROMWELL'S HOUSE

Tel: 01353 662062 **Fax:** 01353 668518

29 St Mary's Street, Ely, Cambridgeshire CB7 4HF

Owner: East Cambridgeshire District Council **Contact:** Mrs A Smith

The former home of the Lord Protector.

Location: OS Ref. TL538 803. N of Cambridge, 1/4 m W of Ely Cathedral.

Opening Times: 1 Oct - 31 Mar, Mon - Sat, 10am - 5pm, Suns, 12 noon - 4pm. 1 Apr -30 Sept: daily, 10am - 5.30pm.

Admission: Adult £2.70, Conc. £2.20, Family £7. Joint Ticket (including Cathedral, Ely Museum and the Stained Glass Museum): Adult £8, Conc. £6. Group prices on application. (1999 prices - please confirm before visit).

DENNY ABBEY & THE FARMLAND MUSEUM

Ely Road, Chittering, Waterbeach, Cambridgeshire CB5 9TQ **Tel:** 01223 860489

Owner: English Heritage **Contact:** The Custodian

What at first appears to be an attractive stone-built farmhouse is actually the remains of a 12th century Benedictine abbey which, at different times, also housed the Knights Templar and Franciscan nuns. Founded by the Countess of Pembroke.

Location: OS Ref. TL495 684. 6m N of Cambridge on the E side of the A10.

Opening Times: 1 Apr - 31 Oct: 12 noon - 5pm..

Admission: Adult £3.40, Child £1.20, Conc. £2.40, Family £8.

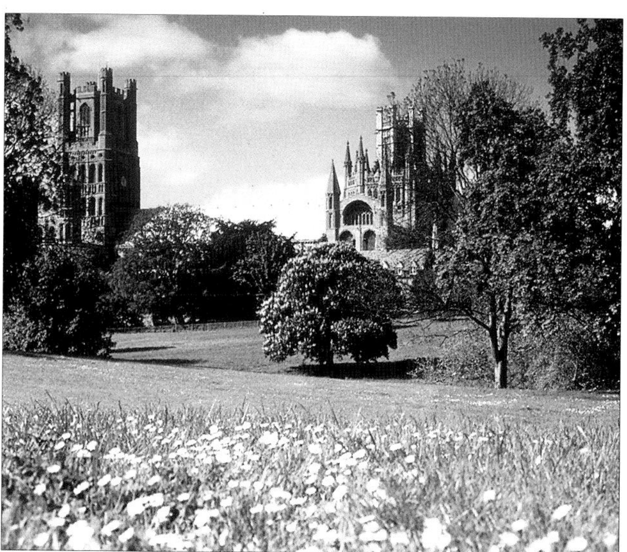

Ely Cathedral, Cambridgeshire.

DOCWRA'S MANOR GARDEN

Tel: 01763 261557 **Fax:** 01763 260677

Shepreth, Royston, Hertfordshire SG8 6PS

Owner: Mrs Faith Raven **Contact:** David Aitcheson

Extensive garden around building dating from the 18th century.

Location: OS Ref. TL393 479. In Shepreth via A10 from Royston.

Opening Times: All year: Weds & Fris, 10am - 4pm and 1st Sun in month from Apr - Oct: 2 - 5pm.

Admission: £2.

Patrick Lane.

Docwra's Manor Garden, Cambridgeshire.

ELTON HALL

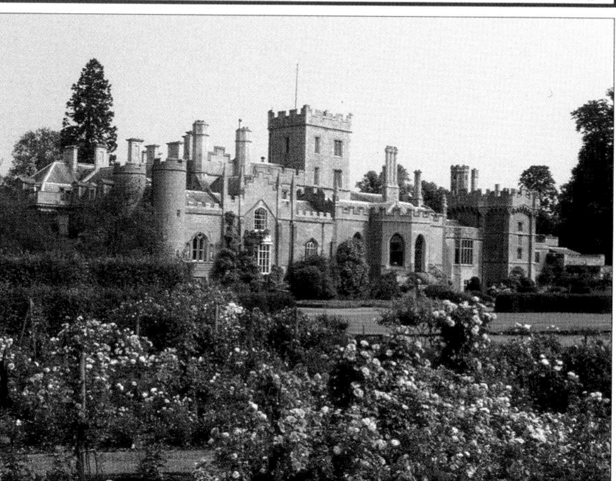

Nr PETERBOROUGH PE8 6SH

Owner: *Mr & Mrs W Proby* ***Contact:*** *The Administrator*

Tel: 01832 280468 **Fax:** 01832 280584

Elton Hall, the home of the Proby family for over 350 years is a fascinating mixture of styles. Every room contains treasures, magnificent furniture and fine paintings from the early 15th century. The library is one of the finest in private hands and includes Henry VIII's prayer book. The beautiful gardens have been carefully restored, with the addition of a new gothic Orangery to celebrate the Millennium.

Location: OS Ref. TL091 930. Close to A1 in the village of Elton, off A605 Peterborough - Oundle road.

Opening Times: 28/29 May. Jun: Weds. Jul & Aug: Wed, Thur & Sun. Plus Aug BH Mon. 2 - 5pm. Private groups by arrangement on weekdays Apr - Sept.

Admission: Hall & Gardens: Adult £5, Child (accompanied) Free. Gardens only: Adult £2.50, Child (accompanied) Free.

No photography in house. Hall not suitable. 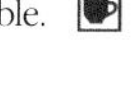 Obligatory. Guide dogs in gardens only.

ELY CATHEDRAL

Tel: 01353 667735 **Fax:** 01353 665658

The Chapter House, The College, Ely, Cambridgeshire CB7 4DL

Contact: Visitors' Manager, Heather Kilpatrick

A wonderful example of Romanesque architecture. Octagon and Lady Chapel are of special interest. Superb medieval domestic buildings surround the Cathedral. Stained Glass Museum. Brass rubbing. Octagon and West Tower tours peak season.

Location: OS Ref. TL541 803. Via A10, 15m N of Cambridge City centre.

Opening Times: Summer: 7am - 7pm. Winter: Mon - Sat, 7.30am - 6pm, Suns and week after Christmas, 7.30am - 5pm. Sun services: 8.15am, 10.30am and 3.45pm. Weekday services: 7.40am, 8am, and 5.30pm (Thurs only also 11.30am & 12.30pm).

Admission: Adult £3.50, Child Free, Conc. £3. Discounts for groups of 15+.

  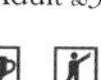   Guide dogs only. 

ISLAND HALL

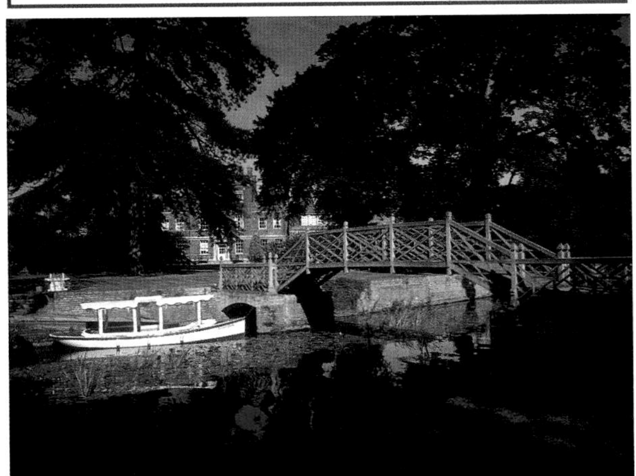

GODMANCHESTER, CAMBRIDGESHIRE PE18 8BA

Owner: *Mr Christopher & the Hon Mrs Vane Percy* **Contact:** *Mr C Vane Percy*

Tel: 020 7491 3724 **Fax:** 020 7355 4006

An important mid 18th century mansion of great charm, owned and restored by an award-winning interior designer. This family home has lovely Georgian rooms, with fine period detail, and interesting possessions relating to the owners' ancestors since their first occupation of the house in 1800. A tranquil riverside setting with formal gardens and ornamental island forming part of the grounds in an area of Best Landscape. Octavia Hill, the Victorian reformer, and a founder of the National Trust, who stayed at Island Hall at least twice in 1859 and 1865, would instantly recognise the house and grounds, and she says in a letter to her sister "*This is the loveliest, dearest old house, I never was in such a one before.*"

Location: OS Ref. TL244 706. 15m NW of Cambridge A14, 1½ m S of Huntingdon.

Opening Times: 2, 9, 16, 23, 30 Jul: 2.30 - 5pm. Last admittance 4.30pm.

Admission: Adult £3.50, Child (13-16) £2. Grounds only: Adult £2, Child (under 13yrs) £1. Group rates by arrangement for May - Sept: (except Aug) £3 (40)+. Under 15 persons, min. charge £52.50 per group.

 Not suitable. Home made teas. 

KING'S COLLEGE

KING'S PARADE, CAMBRIDGE CB2 1ST

Owner: *Provost and Fellows* **Contact:** *Mr D Buxton*

Tel/Fax: 01223 331212 **e-mail:** development.office@kings.cam.ac.uk

Visitors are welcome, but remember that this is a working college. Please respect the privacy of those who work, live and study here. The Chapel is often used for services, recordings, broadcasts, etc, and ideally visitors should check before arriving. Recorded message for services, concerts and visiting times: 01223 331155.

Location: OS Ref. TL447 584.

Opening Times: Out of term: Mon - Sat, 9.30am - 4.30pm. Sun, 10am - 5pm. In term: Mon - Fri: 9.30am - 3.30pm. Sat: 9.30am - 3.15pm. Sun: 1.15 - 2.15pm, 5 - 5.30pm.

Admission: Adult £3.50, Child (12-17yrs)/Student (ID required) £2.50, OAP £3.50 (to be confirmed). Child (under 12 & accompanied) Free.

No photography inside Chapel. Conferences. By arrangement.

By arrangement. No parking. Guide dogs only. 

KIMBOLTON CASTLE

Tel: 01480 860505 **Fax:** 01480 861763

Kimbolton, Huntingdon, Cambridgeshire PE18 0EA

Owner: Governors of Kimbolton School **Contact:** Mr J Mcleod

A late Stuart house, an adaptation of a 13th century fortified manor house, with evidence of Tudor modifications. The seat of the Earls and Dukes of Manchester 1615 - 1950, now a school. Katharine of Aragon died in the Queen's Room - the setting for a scene in Shakespeare's *Henry VIII*. A minor example of the work of Vanbrugh and Hawksmoor; Gatehouse by Robert Adam; the Pellegrini mural paintings on the Staircase, in the Chapel and in the Boudoir are the best examples in England of this gifted Venetian decorator.

Location: OS Ref. TL101 676. 7m NW of St Neots on B645.

Opening Times: 23 - 24 Apr, 28 - 29 May, 30 Jul & 6, 13, 20, 27 & 28 Aug: 2 - 6pm.

Admission: Adult £2.50, Child/Conc. £1.50. Groups by arrangement.

Not suitable. By arrangement. 

On leads in grounds only

LONGTHORPE TOWER

Tel: 01733 268482

Thorpe Rd, Longthorpe, Cambridgeshire PE1 1HA

Owner: English Heritage **Contact:** The Custodian

The finest example of 14th century domestic wall paintings in northern Europe showing a variety of secular and sacred objects. The tower, with the Great Chamber that contains the paintings, is part of a fortified manor house. Special exhibitions are held on the upper floor.

Location: OS Ref. TL163 983. 2m W of Peterborough just off A47.

Opening Times: 1 Apr - 31 Oct: weekends & BHs only: 12 noon - 5pm.

Admission: Adult £1.50, Child 80p, Conc. £1.10.

Patrick Lane.

Kimbolton Castle, Cambridgeshire.

THE MANOR, HEMINGFORD GREY

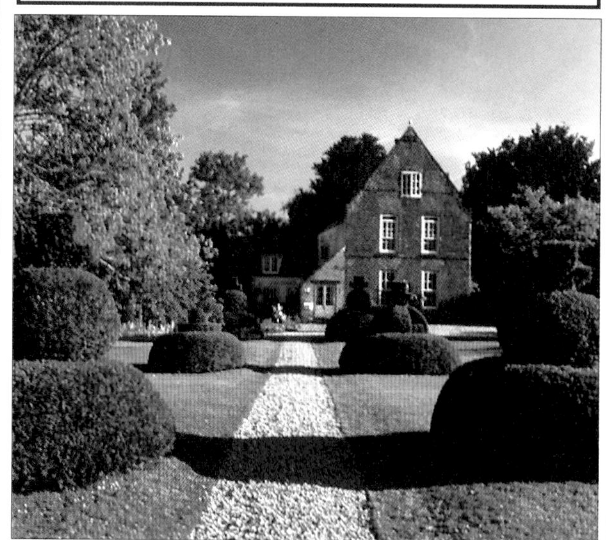

HUNTINGDON, CAMBRIDGESHIRE PE18 9BN

Owner: *Mr and Mrs P S Boston* ***Contact:*** *Diana Boston*

Tel: 01480 463134 **Fax:** 01480 465026

Built about 1130 and made famous as 'Green Knowe' by the author Lucy Boston. The Manor is reputedly the oldest continuously inhabited house in the country and much of the Norman house remains. Visitors are offered the unique chance to walk into the books and to see the Lucy Boston patchworks. The garden features topiary, old roses and herbaceous borders.

Location: OS Ref. TL290 706. Off A14, 3m SE of Huntingdon. 12m NW of Cambridge. Access is by a small gate on the riverside footpath.

Opening Times: House: All year by appointment only. Garden: All year 10am - 6pm.

Admission: Adult £4, Child £1.50, OAP £3.50. Garden only: Adult £1, Child 50p.

No photography in house. Locally, by arrangement. Obligatory. Disabled only. In garden, on leads.

Patrick Lane.

Peckover House, Cambridgeshire.

Open all Year Index PAGE 52

PECKOVER HOUSE & GARDEN

Tel/Fax: 01945 583463

North Brink, Wisbech, Cambs PE13 1JR **e-mail:** aprigjx@smtp.ntrust.org.uk

Owner: The National Trust **Contact:** The Property Manager

A town house, built c1722 and renowned for its very fine plaster and wood rococo decoration. The outstanding Victorian garden includes an orangery, summer-houses, roses, herbaceous borders, fernery, croquet lawn and reed barn.

Location: OS Ref. TF458 097. On N bank of River Nene, in Wisbech B1441.

Opening Times: House & Garden: 1 Apr - 31 Oct, Sats & Suns, Weds & BH Mons, 12.30 - 5pm. Garden only: 1 Apr - 31 Oct; Mons, Tues & Thurs, 12.30 - 5pm. Groups on house open days and at other times by appointment.

Admission: Adult £3.80. Garden only: £2.50. Groups: £3.

Partially suitable. By arrangement. Signposted.  Tel. for details.

PETERBOROUGH CATHEDRAL

Tel: 01733 343342 **Fax:** 01733 552465

Peterborough, Cambridgeshire PE1 1XS **Contact:** Visitors' Officer

West front unique in Christendom. Painted Nave ceiling (c1220) unique in England. Pure Romanesque interior. Exquisite fan vaulting (c1500) in retro-choir. Burial place of Katharine of Aragon. Former burial place of Mary Queen of Scots. Saxon sculptures. Monastic remains. Exhibition: 'Life of Peterborough Cathedral'.

Location: OS Ref. TL194 986. 4m E of A1, in City Centre.

Opening Times: Mon-Sat, 8.30am - 5.15pm. Suns, 7.30am - 5pm. Weekday services: 7.45am, 8am, 5.30pm (3.30pm Sats). Sun services: 8.15am, 9.30am, 10.30am, 3.30pm.

Admission: Donation suggested.

By arrangement. No parking. Guide dogs only. 

RAMSEY ABBEY GATEHOUSE

Tel: 01263 733471 (Regional office)

Abbey School, Ramsey, Cambridgeshire PE17 1DH

Owner: The National Trust **Contact:** The Curator (in writing)

Remains of a 15th century gatehouse of the Benedictine Abbey.

Location: OS Ref. TL291 851. At SE edge of Ramsey at point where Chatteris road leaves B1096, 10m SE of Peterborough.

Opening Times: 1 Apr - end Oct: daily, 10am - 5pm, other times by written application to curator.

Admission: Donation.

Limited. Guide dogs only.

WIMPOLE HALL & WIMPOLE HOME FARM

Tel: 01223 207257 **Fax:** 01223 207838 **e-mail:** aweusr@smtp.ntrust.org.uk

Arrington, Royston SG8 0BW

Owner: The National Trust **Contact:** The Property Manager

Wimpole is a magnificent country house built in 18th century style with a colourful history of owners. The Hall is set in recently restored formal gardens including parterres and a rose garden. Home Farm is a working farm and is the largest rare breeds centre in East Anglia.

Location: OS154 Ref. TL336 510. 8m SW of Cambridge (A603), 6m N of Royston (A1198).

Opening Times: Hall: 18 Mar - 30 Jul & 2 Sept - 22 Oct: daily except Mons & Fris (open Good Fri & BH Mons). Aug: daily except Mons (open BH Mons). 25 Oct - 5 Nov: Weds, Sats & Suns, 1 - 5pm. BH Mons, 11am - 5pm, closes 4pm after 25 Oct. Garden: As Farm. Park: daily, sunrise - sunset (closed 5pm on concert nights). Farm: 18 Mar - 2 Jul & 1 Sept - 5 Nov: daily except Mons & Fris (open Good Fri & BH Mons). Jul & Aug: daily except Mon (open BH Mons). Nov - Mar 2001: Sats & Suns (open Feb half-term week), 10.30am - 5pm. 1 Nov - Mar 2001, 11am - 4pm.

Admission: Hall: Adult £5.90, Child £2.70. Estate Ticket: Adult £8.50, Child £4.20. Garden only: £2.50. Groups (12+): Adult £4.90, Child £2.20. Family Estate Ticket £21. Farm: Adult £4.70, Child (over 3yrs) £2.70. Discounts for NT members. Groups (12+): Adult £3.70, Child £2.20. School groups: £1.50 per child.

Partially suitable. Licensed. By arrangement. Limited. In park only, on leads. Tel. for details.

Wimpole Hall and Wimpole Home Farm, Cambridgeshire.

Owner: English Heritage

CONTACT

The General Manager
Audley End House
Audley End
Saffron Walden
Essex
CB11 4JF

Tel: 01799 522399

Fax: 01799 521276

LOCATION

OS Ref. TL525 382

1m W of Saffron Walden on B1383, M11/J8 & 9 northbound only, J10 southbound.

Rail: Audley End $1^1/_4$m.

AUDLEY END HOUSE & GDNS ⌗
Saffron Walden

AUDLEY END was a palace in all but name. Built by Thomas Howard, Earl of Suffolk, to entertain King James I. The King may have had his suspicions, for he never stayed there; in 1618 Howard was imprisoned and fined for embezzlement.

Charles II bought the property in 1668 for £50,000, but within a generation the house was gradually demolished, and by the 1750s it was about the size you see today. There are still over 30 rooms to see, each with period furnishings.

The house and its gardens, including a 19th century parterre and rose garden, are surrounded by an 18th century landscaped park laid out by 'Capability' Brown.

Visitors can now also visit the working organic walled garden. Extending to nearly 10 acres it includes a 170ft long, five-bay vine house, built in 1802.

- Open air concerts and other events.
- Ground floor and grounds suitable.
- Restaurant (max 50).
- By arrangement for groups.
- Coaches to book in advance, £5 per coach. Free entry for coach drivers and tour guides. One additional place for every extra 20 people.
- School visits free if booked in advance. Contact the Administrator or tel. 01604 730325 for bookings.
- On leads only.

OPENING TIMES

1 April - 30 September
Wed - Sun and BHs
11am - 6pm.
Last admission 5pm.

1 - 31 October
Wed - Sun
10am - 3pm.

House by pre-booked guided tour only.

Guided tours only in October.

ADMISSION

House & Grounds

Adult	£6.00
Child (5 - 15yrs) *	£3.00
Conc.	£4.50
Family (2+3)	£15.00

Grounds only

Adult	£4.00
Child (5 - 15yrs) *	£2.00
Concessions	£3.00
Family (2+3)	£10.00

* Under 5yrs Free.

Groups (11+)
15% discount.

SPECIAL EVENTS

Please telephone for details of special events.

Eastern Counties England

AUDLEY END HOUSE & GARDENS

See page 231 for full page entry.

BOURNE MILL

Tel: 01206 572422

Colchester, Essex CO2 8RT

Owner: The National Trust **Contact:** The Custodian

Originally a fishing lodge built in 1591. It was later converted into a mill with a 4 acre mill pond. Much of the machinery, including the waterwheel, is intact.

Location: OS Ref. TM006 238. 1m S of Colchester centre, in Bourne Road, off the Mersea Road B1025.

Opening Times: BH Suns & Mons only; also Suns & Tues in Jun, Jul & Aug, 2 - 5.30pm.

Admission: Adult £2. No reduction for groups.

Guide dogs only.

CHELMSFORD CATHEDRAL

Tel: 01245 294480

New Street, Chelmsford, Essex CM1 1AT **Contact:** Mrs Gillian Brandon

15th century building became a Cathedral in 1914. Extended in 1920s, major refurbishment in 1980s with contemporary works of distinction and splendid new organs in 1994 and 1996.

Location: OS Ref. TL708 070. In Chelmsford.

Opening Times: Daily: 8am - 5.30pm. Sun services: 8am, 9.30am, 11.15am and 6pm. Weekday services: 8.15am and 5.15pm.

COGGESHALL GRANGE BARN

Tel: 01376 562226

Coggeshall, Colchester, Essex CO6 1RE

Owner: The National Trust **Contact:** The Custodian

The oldest surviving timber framed barn in Europe, dating from around 1140, and originally part of a Cistercian Monastery. It was restored in the 1980s by the Coggeshall Grange Barn Trust, Braintree District Council and Essex County Council. Features a small collection of farm carts and wagons.

Location: OS Ref. TQ848 223. Signposted off A120 Coggeshall bypass. West side of the road southwards to Kelvedon.

Opening Times: 2 Apr - 15 Oct: Tues, Thurs, Suns & BH Mons, 2 - 5pm.

Admission: £1.60. Groups £1, by prior arrangement. Joint ticket with Paycocke's £3.

P Coaches must book. Guide dogs only.

COLCHESTER CASTLE MUSEUM

Tel: 01206 282931/2 **Fax:** 01206 282925

14 Ryegate Road, Colchester, Essex CO1 1YG

Owner: Colchester Borough Council **Contact:** Museum Resource Centre

The largest Norman Castle Keep in Europe with fine archaeological collections on show.

Location: OS Ref. TL999 253. In Colchester town centre, off A12.

Opening Times: All year: Mon - Sat, 10am - 5pm, also Suns, 1 - 5pm during Mar - Nov.

Admission: Adult £3.70, Child/Conc. £2.40, Saver ticket £9.90. Booked groups (20+) £3.20. Prices will increase from 1 April 2000.

COPPED HALL

See opposite.

ESSEX SECRET BUNKER

Tel: 01206 392271 **Fax:** 01206 393847
e-mail: Bunker9248@aol.com

Crown Building, Shrubland Road, Mistley, Manningtree, Essex CO11 1HS

Owner: The Bunker Preservation Trust Ltd **Contact:** The Curator

The county nuclear war headquarters with its authentic contents preserved in the original vast concrete bunker. The exhibition is interpreted by films, videos and sound effects as you wind your way through the maze of passageways and rooms. Suitable for all the family to visit with an insight into the 'secrets of the Cold War'.

Location: OS Ref. TM120 315. In Mistley near Manningtree on the B1352. Follow brown tourist signs from A120.

Opening Times: 1 Apr - 31 Sept: daily, 10.30am - 4.30pm (Aug 6pm). Oct, Nov, Feb, Mar: Sats & Suns, 10.30am - 4.30pm.

Admission: Adult £4.95, Child/Student £3.65, OAP £4.35, Family £15. Groups (10+): Adult £3.95, Child/Student £2.65, OAP £3.35. Special evening tours throughout the year by appointment for groups: (10+) £6. Further discounts for groups of 30+.

Partially suitable. WC. By arrangement. P Guide dogs only.

Open all Year Index PAGE 52

COPPED HALL

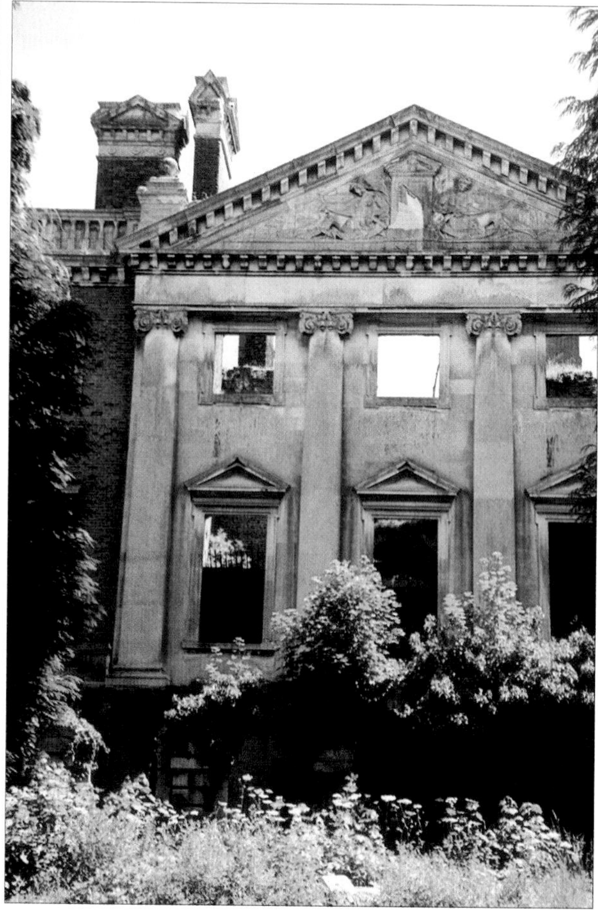

CROWN HILL, EPPING, ESSEX CM16 5HH

Owner: *Copped Hall Trust* ***Contact:*** *Alan Cox*

Tel: 020 7267 1679 **Fax:** 020 7482 0557

Burnt-out 18th century Palladian mansion situated on ridge overlooking excellent landscaped park. Built adjacent to site of 16th century mansion where *'A Midsummer's Night Dream'* was first performed. Former elaborate gardens gradually being rescued from abandonment. Victorian ancillary building including stables and small racquets court. Very large early 18th century walled garden.

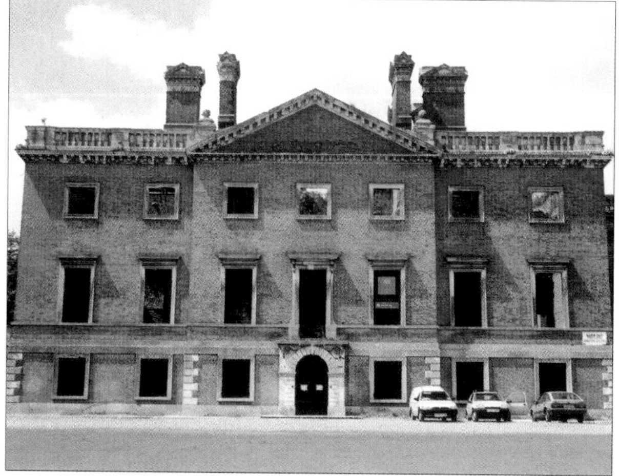

Location: OS Ref. TL433 016. 4m SW of Epping, N of M25.

Opening Times: By appointment only.

Admission: Pre-arranged groups (20+) only: Adult £3, Child £1.

  Partially suitable. Obligatory. P In grounds on leads. 

GARDENS OF EASTON LODGE

WARWICK HOUSE, EASTON LODGE, LITTLE EASTON, GT DUNMOW CM6 2BB

Owner/Contact: *Mr Brian Creasey*

Tel/Fax: 01371 876979 **e-mail:** gardens.easton@mcmail.com

Beautiful gardens set in 25 acres. Horticultural associations from the 16th century to date. Visit the Italian gardens, currently undergoing restoration, designed by Harold Peto for 'Daisy' Countess of Warwick (Edward VII's mistress). In the dovecote, study the history of the house, garden and owners over 400 years. A peaceful and atmospheric haven!

Location: OS Ref. TL593 240. 4m NW of Great Dunmow, off the B184 Dunmow to Thaxted road.

Opening Times: Feb (snowdrops). dates according to season - 31 Oct: Fri - Sun & BHs, 12 noon - 6pm or dusk if earlier. Groups at other times by appointment.

Admission: Adult £3.30, Child (3-12yrs) £1, OAP £3. Group (20+): £3. Schools (20+) £1 per child, 1 teacher free per 10 children.

Exhibition & Study Centre in Dovecote. Partially suitable. WC. Picnics. By arrangement. Limited for coaches. In grounds on leads.

HEDINGHAM CASTLE

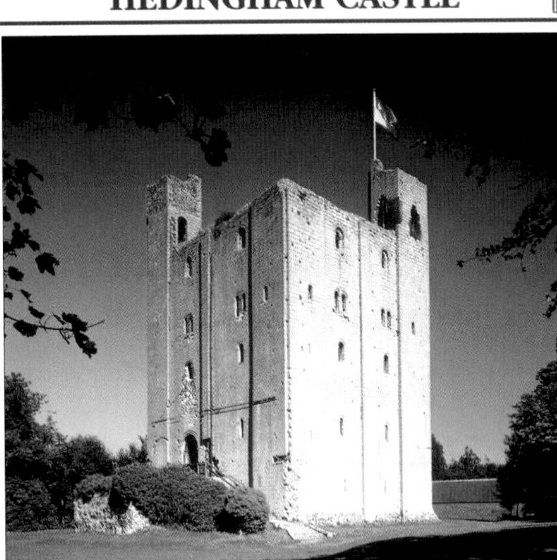

CASTLE HEDINGHAM, Nr HALSTEAD, ESSEX CO9 3DJ

Owner: *The Hon Thomas Lindsay* ***Contact:*** *Mrs Diana Donoghue*

Tel: 01787 460261 **Fax:** 01787 461473

Splendid Norman keep built in 1140 by the famous de Veres, Earls of Oxford. Visited by Kings Henry VII and VIII and Queen Elizabeth I and besieged by King John. Magnificent banqueting hall with minstrel's gallery and finest Norman arch in England. Beautiful grounds, peaceful woodland and lakeside walks. Beside medieval village with fine Norman church.

Location: OS Ref. TL787 358. On B1058, 1m off A1017 between Cambridge and Colchester.

Opening Times: 15 Apr - 31 Oct: daily, 10am - 5pm.

Admission: Adult £3.50, Child £2.50, Conc. £3. Groups (20+): £3.

Partially suitable. By arrangement. In grounds, on leads.

HARWICH MARITIME & LIFEBOAT MUSEUMS

Tel: 01255 503429

Harwich Green, Harwich

Owner: The Harwich Society **Contact:** Mr Sheard

One housed in a disused lighthouse and the other in the nearby disused Victorian Lifeboat House, complete with full size lifeboat.

Location: OS Ref. TM262 822. On Harwich Green.

Opening Times: 1 May - 31 Aug: daily, 10am - 1pm & 2 - 5pm. Groups by appointment at any time.

Admission: Adult 50p, Child Free (no unaccompanied children).

HARWICH REDOUBT FORT

Tel: 01255 503429

Main Road, Harwich, Essex

Owner: The Harwich Society **Contact:** Mr Sheard

180ft diameter circular fort built in 1808 to defend the port against Napoleonic invasion. Being restored by Harwich Society and part is a museum. Eleven guns on battlements.

Location: OS Ref. TM262 322. Rear of 29 Main Road.

Opening Times: 1 May - 31 Aug: daily, 10am - 5pm. Sept - Apr: Suns only. Groups by appointment at any time.

Admission: Adult £1, Child Free (no unaccompanied children).

Audley End House & Gardens, Essex.

HYLANDS HOUSE

HYLANDS PARK, LONDON ROAD, CHELMSFORD CM2 8WQ

Owner: *Chelmsford Borough Council* ***Contact:*** *Ceri Lowen*

Tel: 01245 606812 **Fax:** 01245 606970

This beautiful villa, with its neo-classical exterior is surrounded by over 500 acres of parkland, including formal gardens. The house re-opened at Easter 1999 after a period of restoration work. The Library, Drawing Room and Saloon have been restored to their appearance in the early Victorian period. The Entrance Hall was restored to its Georgian origins in the 1995 restoration. It is possible to view the Banqueting Room and Victorian staircase, as yet unrestored. There is an exhibition detailing the restoration work and the history of the house.

Location: OS Ref. TL681 054. 2m SW of Chelmsford. Signposted on A1016 near Chelmsford.

Opening Times: All year: Suns, Mons & BHs, 11am - 6pm, except Christmas Day.

Admission: Adults £3, Child (12-16 yrs) £2, (under 12yrs) Free, Conc. £2. Groups: £3pp or £75 (whichever greater).

No photography in house. Sun only. By arrangement. Limited for coaches. In grounds. Guide dogs only in house. Please tel. for details.

INGATESTONE HALL

HALL LANE, INGATESTONE, ESSEX CM4 9NR

Owner: *The Lord Petre* ***Contact:*** *The Administrator*

Tel: 01277 353010 **Fax:** 01245 248979

16th century mansion, set in 11 acres of grounds (formal garden and wild walk), built by Sir William Petre, Secretary of State to four Tudor monarchs, which has remained in the hands of his family ever since. The two Priests' hiding places can be seen, as well as the furniture, portraits and family memorabilia accumulated over the centuries.

Location: OS Ref. TQ653 986. Off A12 between Brentwood & Chelmsford. Take Station Lane at London end of Ingatestone High Street, cross level-crossing and continue for 1/2 m to SE.

Opening Times: 22 Apr - 1 Oct: Sats, Suns & BH Mons, plus 12 Jul - 8 Sept: Weds - Fris, 1 - 6pm.

Admission: Adult £3.50, Conc. £3, Child £2, Under 5yrs Free. 50p per head discount for groups (20+). Family Ticket (admits 5, up to 3 adults) £10.50.

No photography in house. Grounds suitable. WC.
By arrangement. Guide dogs only.

LAYER MARNEY TOWER

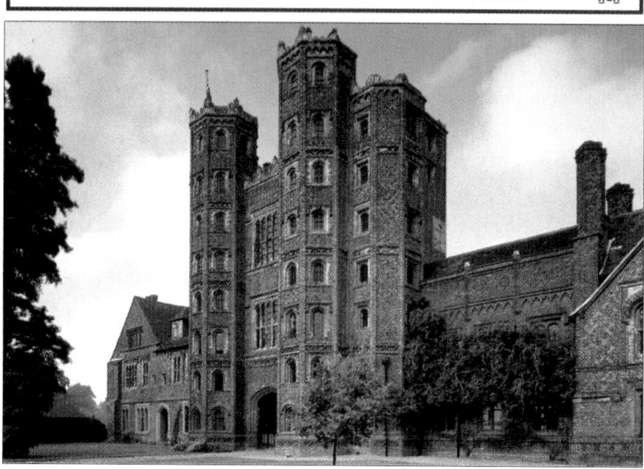

Nr COLCHESTER, ESSEX CO5 9US

Owner/Contact: *Mr Nicholas Charrington*

Tel/Fax: 01206 330784

Built in the reign of Henry VIII, the tallest Tudor gatehouse in Great Britain. Lord Henry Marney clearly intended to rival Wolsey's building at Hampton Court, but he died before his masterpiece was finished. His son John died two years later, in 1525, and building work stopped. Layer Marney Tower has some of the finest terracotta work in the country, most probably executed by Flemish craftsmen trained by Italian masters. The terracotta is used on the battlements, windows, and most lavishly of all, on the tombs of Henry and John Marney. Visitors may climb the Tower, passing through the History Room, and enjoy the marvellous views of the Essex countryside. There are fine outbuildings, including the Long Gallery with its magnificent oak roof and the medieval barn which now houses some of the Home Farm's collection of Rare Breed farm animals. Function room available for receptions, etc.

Location: OS Ref. TL929 175. 5m SW of Colchester, signed off B1022.

Opening Times: 2 Apr - 1 Oct: Sun - Fri, 12 noon - 5pm. Group visits and guided tours throughout the year by arrangement.

Admission: Adult £3.50, Child £2, Family £10. Groups (15+): Adult £3, Child £1.50. Guided tours (pre-booked) £4.75, min. charge £120. Schools by arrangement.

 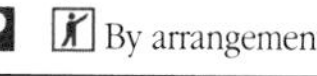 Mostly suitable. WC.  By arrangement.

LOWER DAIRY HOUSE GARDEN

Tel: 01206 262220

Water Lane, Nayland, Colchester, Essex CO6 4JS

Owner/Contact: Mr & Mrs D J Burnett

Plantsman's garden, approx 1 1/2 acres.

Location: OS Ref. TL966 330. 7m N of Colchester off A134. 1m SW of Nayland on E side of road to Little Horkesley.

Opening Times: 9, 16, 23/24, 30 Apr; 1, 7, 14, 21, 28/29 May; 4, 11, 18, 25 Jun; 2, 9 Jul, 2 - 6pm. Also by appointment for groups.

Admission: £2.

MISTLEY TOWERS

Tel: 01206 393884

Colchester, Essex

Owner: English Heritage **Contact:** The Custodian

The remains of one of only two churches designed by the great architect Robert Adam. Built in 1776. It was unusual in having towers at both the east and west ends.

Location: OS Ref. TM116 320. On B1352, 1 1/2 m E of A137 at Lawford, 9m E of Colchester.

Opening Times: Telephone for opening times.

Admission: Key available from Mistley Quay workshops - 01206 393884.

SIR ALFRED MUNNINGS ART MUSEUM

CASTLE HOUSE, DEDHAM, ESSEX CO7 6AZ

Owner: *Castle House Trust* ***Contact:*** *Mrs C Woodage*

Tel/Fax: 01206 322127

The home, studios and grounds where Sir Alfred Munnings, KCVO, 1878 – 1959 (PRA 1944 – 1949) lived and painted for 40 years. Castle House, part Tudor part Georgian, restored and with original Munnings' furniture, exhibits over 200 Munnings' works representing his life's work, is augmented by private loans each season. Special exhibition for 2000.

Location: OS Ref. TM060 328. 3/4 m from Dedham centre. 8m from Colchester, 12m from Ipswich.

Opening Times: Easter Sun - first Sun in Oct: Weds, Suns & BH Mons, 2 - 5pm. Additionally Thurs & Sats in Aug, 2 - 5pm.

Admission: Adult £3, Child 50p, Conc. £2. Groups (25+): min. price £75, larger groups per admission prices.

No photography in house. Partially suitable.
Ample for cars. Limited for coaches. In grounds, on leads.

PAYCOCKE'S

Tel: 01376 561305

West Street, Coggeshall, Colchester, Essex C06 1NS

Owner: The National Trust **Contact:** The Tenant

A merchant's house, dating from about 1500, with unusually rich panelling and wood carving. A display of lace, for which Coggeshall was famous, is on show. Delightful cottage garden leading down to small river.

Location: OS Ref. TL848 225. Signposted off A120.

Opening Times: 2 Apr - 15 Oct: Tues, Thurs, Suns & BH Mons, 2 - 5.30pm, last adm: 5pm.

Admission: £2.20, groups (10+) by prior arrangement, no reduction for groups. Joint ticket with Coggeshall Grange Barn £3.

Access to ground floor and garden. NT's at the Coggeshall Grange Barn.

PRIORS HALL BARN ⌗

Tel: 01799 522842

Widdington, Newport, Essex

Owner/Contact: Audley End House

One of the finest surviving medieval barns in south-east England and representative of the group of aisled barns centred on north-west Essex.

Location: OS Ref. TL538 319. In Widdington, on unclassified road 2m SE of Newport, off B1383.

Opening Times: 1 Apr - 30 Sept: Sats & Suns, 10am - 6pm.

Admission: Telephone for further details.

RHS GARDEN HYDE HALL

RETTENDON, Nr CHELMSFORD, ESSEX CM3 8ET

Owner: *The Royal Horticultural Society*

Tel: 01245 400256 **Fax:** 01245 402100

A charming hilltop garden. Highlights include the spring bulbs in profusion, an extensive colour themed herbaceous border, farmhouse garden and a large collection of roses of all kinds. Two ornamental ponds are home to a wide variety of bog plants and water lilies. Among a wide range of ornamental tree and shrub plantings are National Collections of viburnums and ornamental crab apples. New projects for 2000 include a rose garden and new plantings in the Malus field. Delightful hot and cold meals are available in the Essex thatched barn.

Location: OS Ref. TQ782 995. 2m E of Rettendon, 6m SE of Chelmsford. Signed off the A130.

Opening Times: 22 Mar - 29 Oct: daily, 11am - 6pm. Sept - Oct: 11am - 5pm. Last entry 1 hour before closing.

Admission: Adult £3, Child (under 6yrs) Free, Child (6 - 16yrs) 70p. Pre-booked groups (10+), £2.50. Companion for wheelchair user or blind visitors Free. (1999 prices).

    Guide dogs only.

RHS Garden Hyde Hall, Essex.

Audley End House, Essex.

English Heritage Photographic Library

SALING HALL GARDEN

Tel: 01371 850 243 **Fax:** 01371 850 274

Great Saling, Braintree, Essex CM7 5DT

Owner/Contact: Hugh Johnson Esq

Twelve acres including a walled garden dated 1698. Water gardens and landscaped arboretum.

Location: OS Ref. TL700 258. 6m NW of Braintree, 2m N of A120.

Opening Times: May, Jun & Jul: Weds, 2 - 5pm. Sun 18 June: 2 - 6pm.

Admission: Standard £2.50, Child Free.

SHALOM HALL

Tel: 01206 330338

Layer Breton, Colchester, Essex CO2 0PT

Owner/Contact: Lady Hillingdon

19th century country house containing a collection of 17th and 18th century French furniture and portraits by famous English artists including Thomas Gainsborough and Sir Joshua Reynolds.

Location: OS Ref. TL960 160. 7m SW of Colchester, on the B1026 Colchester - Tolleshunt road.

Opening Times: Aug: Mon - Fri, 10am - 1pm & 2.30 - 5.30pm.

Admission: Free.

TILBURY FORT ⌗

Tel: 01375 858489

No. 2 Office Block, The Fort, Tilbury, Essex RM18 7NR

Owner: English Heritage **Contact:** The Custodian

The best and largest example of 17th century military engineering in England, commanding the Thames. The fort shows the development of fortifications over the following 200 years. Exhibitions, the powder magazine and the bunker-like 'casemates' demonstrate how the fort protected London from seaborne attack. Elizabeth I gave a speech near here on the eve of the Spanish Armada.

Location: OS Ref. TQ651 754. 1/2 m E of Tilbury off A126.

Opening Times: 1 Apr - 31 Oct: daily, 10am - 6pm (5pm in Oct). 1 Nov - 31 Mar: Wed - Sun, 10am - 4pm. Closed 24 - 26 Dec & 1 Jan.

Admission: Adult £2.60, Child £1.30, Conc. £2.

 Tel. for details.

VALENCE HOUSE MUSEUM & ART GALLERY

Tel: 020 8227 5293

Becontree Avenue, Dagenham, Essex RM8 3HT

Owner: Barking & Dagenham Council **Contact:** Ms Susan Curtis

The only remaining manor house in Dagenham, partially surrounded by a moat. Dates from 15th century. There is an attractive herb garden to the west of the house.

Location: OS Ref. TQ481 865. S side of Becontree Ave, 1/2 m W of A1112 at Becontree Heath.

Opening Times: Tue - Fri, 9.30am - 1pm & 2 - 4.30pm. Sats, 10am - 4pm.

Admission: Free.

WALTHAM ABBEY GATEHOUSE & BRIDGE ⌗

Tel: 01604 730320

Waltham Abbey, Essex **Contact:** The Midlands Regional Office

Owner: English Heritage

The late 14th century abbey gatehouse, part of the north range of the cloister and the medieval 'Harold's Bridge' of one of the great monastic foundations of the Middle Ages.

Location: OS Ref. TL381 008. In Waltham Abbey off A112. Just NE of the Abbey church.

Opening Times: Any reasonable time.

Admission: Free.

Eastern Counties England

BURGHLEY HOUSE
Stamford

Owner:
Burghley House Preservation Trust Ltd

CONTACT

Jon Culverhouse
Burghley House
Stamford
Lincolnshire
PE9 3JY

Tel: 01780 752451

Fax: 01780 480125

e-mail: burghley@dial.pipex.com

BURGHLEY HOUSE, home of the Cecil family for over 400 years, was built as a country seat during the latter part of the 16th century by Sir William Cecil, later Lord Burghley, principal adviser and Lord Treasurer to Queen Elizabeth.

The House was completed in 1587 and there have been few alterations to the architecture since that date thus making Burghley one of the finest examples of late Elizabethan design in England. The interior was remodelled in the late 17th century by John, 5th Earl of Exeter who was a collector of fine art on a huge scale, establishing the immense collection of art treasures at Burghley. Burghley is truly a 'Treasure House', containing one of the largest private collections of Italian art, unique examples of Chinese and Japanese porcelain and superb items of 18th century furniture. The remodelling work of the 17th century means that examples of the work of the principal artists and craftsmen of the period are to be found at Burghley: Antonio Verrio, Grinling Gibbons and Louis Laguerre all made major contributions to the beautiful interiors.

PARK AND GARDENS

The house is set in a 300-acre deer park landscaped by 'Capability' Brown. A lake was created by him and delightful avenues of mature trees feature largely in his design. The park is home to a herd of fallow deer and is open to visitors at all times of the year. A Sculpture Garden has recently been created in an area that had become overgrown. New plantings of trees and shrubs have replaced brambles and exciting contemporary sculptures are being introduced. This part of the garden is open all year round. The gardens surrounding the house are only open for the display of Spring bulbs. Please telephone for details.

OPENING TIMES

SUMMER

1 April - 8 October (closed 2 September).
Daily: 11am - 4.30pm.

NB. The house is viewed by guided tour except on Sat and Sun afternoons when there are stewards throughout the house and visitors may wander.

WINTER

9 October - 1 April closed to the general public.

LOCATION

OS Ref. TF048 062

Burghley House is 1m SE of Stamford. From London, A1 2hrs.

Visitors entrance is on B1443.

Rail: Stamford Station $1^{1}/_{2}$ m.

Taxi: Direct Line: 01780 481481.

CONFERENCE/FUNCTION		
ROOM	SIZE	MAX CAPACITY
Great Hall	70' x 30'	150
Orangery	100' x 20'	120

Suitable for a variety of events, large park, golf course, helicopter landing area, cricket pitch. No photography in house.

Visitors may alight at the entrance. WC. Chair lift to Orangery Coffee Shop, house tour involves two staircases one of which has a chairlift.

Restaurant/tearoom. Groups can book in advance.

Obligatory, except Sats & Suns after 1pm. Tour time: $1^{1}/_{2}$ hrs at $^{1}/_{2}$ hr intervals. Max. 25.

Ample. Free refreshments for coach drivers.

Welcome. Guide provided; £3.

No dogs in house.

ADMISSION

Adult	£6.50
Child*	£3.20
OAP	£6.10
Groups (20+)	
Adult	£5.65
Child	£3.00

* One child (under 12yrs) admitted FREE per paying adult.

AUBOURN HALL

Tel: 01522 788270 Fax: 01522 788199

Lincoln LN5 9DZ
Owner/Contact: Lady Nevile
Late 16th century house with important staircase and panelled rooms. Garden.
Location: OS Ref. SK928 628. 6m SW of Lincoln. 2m SE of A46.
Opening Times: Weds in Jul & Aug, 2 - 5pm.
Admission: Adult £3, OAP £2.50.

AYSCOUGHFEE HALL MUSEUM & GARDENS

CHURCHGATE, SPALDING, LINCOLNSHIRE PE11 2RA
Owner: South Holland District Council Contact: Mrs S Sladen

Tel: 01775 725468 **Fax:** 01775 762715
A late Medieval wool merchant's house surrounded by five acres of walled gardens. The Hall contains the Museum of South Holland Life and has galleries on local villages, the history of Spalding, agriculture and horticulture. There is also a gallery dedicated to Matthew Flinders, the district's most famous son. Many specimens from the Ashley Maples bird collections are on display.
Location: OS Ref. TF240 230. E bank of the River Welland, 5 mins walk from Spalding town centre.
Opening Times: All year: Mon - Fri, 9am - 5pm, Sats, 10am - 5pm. Suns & BHs, 11am - 5pm. Closed weekends in Nov - Feb.
Admission: Free.

TIC located in Hall.  Partially suitable. By arrangement.
Limited for coaches.
In grounds, on leads. Guide dogs only in Hall

BELTON HOUSE

National Trust Photographic Library/Nick Meers.

GRANTHAM, LINCOLNSHIRE NG32 2LS
Owner: The National Trust Contact: The Property Manager

Tel: 01476 566116 / 592900 **Fax:** 01476 579071
The crowning achievement of Restoration country house architecture, built 1685 - 88 for Sir John Brownlow, and altered by James Wyatt in the 1770s. Plasterwork ceilings by Edward Goudge and fine wood carvings of the Grinling Gibbons school. The rooms contain portraits, furniture, tapestries, oriental porcelain, silver and silver gilt. Gardens with orangery, landscaped park with lakeside walk, woodland adventure playground, and Bellmount Tower. Fine church with family monuments.
Location: OS Ref. SK929 395. 3m NE of Grantham on A607. Signed off the A1.
Opening Times: House: 1 Apr - 31 Oct: House: Wed - Sun & BH Mons (closed Good Fri), 1 - 5.30pm. Garden & Park: 11am - 5.30pm. Last admission to house, garden & park 5pm.
Admission: Adult £5.30, Child £2.60, Family £13.20. Groups (15+): Adult £4.30, Child £2.20.

Partially suitable. Please telephone for arrangements. Licensed.

BURGHLEY HOUSE

See page 236 for full page entry

BAYSGARTH HOUSE MUSEUM

Tel: 01652 632318

Caistor Road, Barton-on-Humber, North Lincolnshire DN18 6AH
Owner: North Lincolnshire Council **Contact:** Mr D J Williams
18th century town house and park. Displays of porcelain and local history.
Location: OS Ref. TA035 215. Caistor Road, Barton-on-Humber.
Opening Times: Please contact for details.
Admission: Please contact for details.

Burghley, Lincolnshire.

Eastern Counties England

DODDINGTON HALL

LINCOLN LN6 4RU

Owner: *Mr & Mrs A Jarvis* ***Contact:*** *The Secretary*

Tel: 01522 694308 **Fax:** 01522 682584

Magnificent Smythson mansion was completed in 1600 and stands today with its contemporary walled gardens and gatehouse. The Hall is still very much the home of the Jarvis family and has an elegant Georgian interior with a fine collection of porcelain, furniture, paintings and textiles representing 400 years of unbroken family occupation. The beautiful gardens contain a superb layout of box-edged parterres, sumptuous borders that provide colour all seasons, and a wild garden with a marvellous succession of spring bulbs and flowering shrubs set among mature trees. Sandford Award winning schools project, and a nature trail into the nearby countryside.

Location: OS Ref. SK900 701. 5m W of Lincoln on the B1190, signposted off the A46 Lincoln bypass.

Opening Times: Gardens only: 20 Feb - 30 Apr: Suns, 2 - 6pm. House & Garden: May - Sept: Weds, Suns & BH Mons, 2 - 6pm.

Admission: House & Garden: Adult £4.30, Child £2.15, Family £11.75. 10% group discount on open days. Garden only half price.

No photography. No stilettos. Occasional. Gardens suitable. WC. By arrangement. Guide dogs only.

ELSHAM HALL COUNTRY & WILDLIFE PARK & BARN THEATRE

Tel: 01652 688698 **Fax:** 01652 688240

Elsham, Brigg, Lincolnshire DN20 0QZ

Owner: Elwes Trust **Contact:** Robert Elwes

Winner of ten awards for tourism. Attractions include falconry, the mini zoo, Georgian courtyard, craft workshops, arboretum, theatre and conference centre, clocktower museum, garden and pet centre and beautiful lakeside gardens with carp and trout lakes.

Location: OS Ref. TA030 120. 10 mins from M180/J5, Humber Bridge turn-off.

Opening Times: Easter - mid Sept: daily, closed Mons (except on Bank holidays and during Spring/Summer Holidays) 11am - 5pm. Theatre & Craft Centre open separately.

Admission: Adult £3.95, Child £2.50 (3+), OAP £3.50. Group rates for groups (20+).

Medieval banquets. Licensed. By arrangement. Guide dogs only.

Patrick Lane.

Gainsborough Old Hall, Lincolnshire.

FULBECK HALL

FULBECK, LINCOLNSHIRE NG32 3JW

Owner/Contact: *Mrs M Fry*

Tel: 01400 272205 **Fax:** 01400 272205

Home of the Fane family since 1632 with alterations and additions by nearly every generation. Mainly 18th century house. Arnhem Museum commemorates 1st Airborne Division for whom Fulbeck Hall was HQ during the War. Eleven acres of formal and wild garden with magnificent views over the Trent Vale. Conference facilities, private dining, corporate hospitality, wedding venue. All details on request.

Location: OS Ref. SK947 505. On A607 14m S of Lincoln. 11m N of Grantham.

Opening Times: Not open to the public in 2000 except Museum which is open by appointment.

Admission: Arnhem Museum: Adult £1.50.

Partially suitable. WC. Guide dogs only.

Max 6, only if attending conferences/functions. 

GAINSBOROUGH OLD HALL

Tel: 01427 612669

Parnell Street, Gainsborough, Lincolnshire DN21 2NB

Owner: English Heritage **Contact:** The Custodian

A large medieval house with a magnificent Great Hall and suites of rooms. A collection of historic furniture and a re-created medieval kitchen are on display.

Location: OS Ref. SK815 895. In centre of Gainsborough, opposite library.

Opening Times: Easter Sun - 31 Oct: Mon - Sat, 10am - 5pm. Suns, 2 - 5.30pm. 1 Nov - Easter Sat: Mon - Sat, 10am - 5pm (closed Good Fri, 24 - 26 Dec & 1 Jan).

Admission: Charge made.

GRIMSTHORPE CASTLE, PARK & GARDENS 

GRIMSTHORPE, BOURNE, LINCOLNSHIRE PE10 0NB

Owner: *Grimsthorpe and Drummond Castle Trust Ltd* ***Contact:*** *Ray Biggs*

Tel: 01778 591205 **Fax:** 01778 591259 **e-mail:** ray@grimsthorpe.co.uk

Home of the Willoughby de Eresby family since 1516. Examples of 13th century architecture, Tudor period and Sir John Vanbrugh's last major work. State Rooms and picture galleries contain magnificent contents and paintings. 3,000 acre landscaped park, with lakes, ancient woods, nature trail, woodland adventure playground, red deer herd, formal and woodland gardens, unusual ornamental vegetable garden, family cycle trail, events programme. Landrover tours with park ranger.

Location: OS Ref. TF040 230. 4m NW of Bourne on A151, 8m E of Colsterworth roundabout off A1.

Opening Times: Easter Sun - 24 Sept: Suns, Thurs & BHs. Aug: daily except Fris & Sats. Park & Gardens: 11am - 6pm. Castle: 1 - 4.30pm (last admission). Tearoom: open from 11am (last orders 5.15pm).

Admission: Park & Garden: Adult £3, Child £1.50, Conc. £2, Family (2+2) £7.50. Castle, Park & Garden: Adult £6.50, Child £3.25, Conc. £4.75, Family (2+2) £16.25. Special charges may be made for special events. Group rates on application.

No photography in house. Conferences (up to 70), inc catering. Partially suitable. WC. Licensed. Obligatory except Suns. Limited for coaches. In grounds, on leads. Tel. for details.

GUNBY HALL

Tel: 01909 486411 **Fax:** 01909 486377

Gunby, Spilsby, Lincolnshire PE23 5SS

Owner: The National Trust **Contact:** Regional Office

A red brick house with stone dressings, built in 1700 and extended in 1870s. Within the house, there is good early 18th century wainscoting and a fine oak staircase, also English furniture and portraits by Reynolds. Also of interest is the contemporary stable block, a walled kitchen and flower garden, sweeping lawns and borders and an exhibition of Field Marshall Sir Archibald Montgomery-Massingberd's memorabilia. Gunby was reputedly Tennyson's 'haunt of ancient peace'.

Location: OS122 Ref. TF466 672. 2 1/2 m NW of Burgh Le Marsh, 7m W of Skegness. On S side of A158 (access off roundabout).

Opening Times: Ground floor of house & garden: 5 Apr - end Sept: Weds, 2 - 6pm. Last admission 5.30pm. Closed BHs. Garden also open Thurs, 2 - 6pm. House & garden also open Tues, Thurs & Fris by written appointment to J D Wrisdale at above address.

Admission: House & Garden: Adult £3.60, Child £1.80, Family £9. Garden only: Adult £2.50, Child £1.20, Family £6.20. No reduction for groups. Access roads unsuitable for coaches which must park in layby at gates 1/2 m from Hall.

Grounds suitable. In grounds, on leads.

HARLAXTON MANOR

Tel: 01476 403000 **Fax:** 01476 403030

Harlaxton, Grantham, Lincolnshire NG32 1AG

Owner: University of Evansville **Contact:** Mrs F Watkins

Neo-Elizabethan house. Grandiose and imposing exterior by Anthony Salvin. Internally an architectural tour de force with various styles and an unparalleled Cedar Staircase.

Location: OS Ref. SK895 323. 3m W of Grantham (10 mins from A1) A607. SE of the village.

Opening Times: Garden: Apr - Sept: 11am - 5pm. House: Sun 4 Jun & Sun 2 Jul: 11am - 5pm. House open at other times for group tours by appointment only.

Admission: Garden: Adult £3, Child £1.25, OAP £2. No reduction for Groups. House open days: Adult £4.50, Child £2, OAP £4.

LEADENHAM HOUSE

Tel: 01400 273256 **Fax:** 01400 272237

Leadenham House, Lincolnshire LN5 0PU

Owner: Mr P Reeve **Contact:** Mr and Mrs P Reeve

Late eighteenth century house in park setting.

Location: OS Ref. SK949 518. Entrance on A17 Leadenham bypass (between Newark and Sleaford).

Opening Times: 1 - 7 May, 5 - 18 Jun & 1 - 7 Jul. Also Spring & Aug BH Mons: 2 - 5pm.

Admission: £3. Groups by prior arrangement only.

No photography.

LINCOLN CASTLE

Tel: 01522 511068

Castle Hill, Lincoln LN1 3AA **Contact:** The Manager

Built by William the Conqueror in 1068. Informative exhibition of the 1215 Magna Carta.

Location: OS Ref. SK975 718. Opposite west front of Lincoln Cathedral.

Opening Times: BST: Sats, 9.30am - 5.30pm, Suns, 11am - 5.30pm. GMT: Mon - Sat: 9.30am - 4pm, Suns, 11am - 4pm. Closed Christmas Day, Boxing Day & New Year's Day.

Admission: Adult £2.50, Child £1, Family (2+3) £6.50

LINCOLN CATHEDRAL

Tel: 01522 544544

Lincoln LN2 1PZ **Contact:** Communications Office

Medieval Gothic Cathedral of outstanding historical and architectural merit. Schools centre.

Location: OS Ref. SK978 718. At the centre of Uphill, Lincoln.

Opening Times: All year: May - Aug: 7.15am - 8pm, Suns, 7.15am - 6pm. Sept - May: 7.15am - 6pm, Suns, 7.15am - 5pm. Tours daily: Jan - Apr & Oct - Dec: 11am & 2pm. May - Sept: 11am, 1pm & 3pm. Roof tours available. Booked tours throughout the year.

Admission: Suggested donation of Adult £4, Conc. £1.50, Family £7. Annual passes £12.50.

Special Events Index PAGE 40

LINCOLN MEDIEVAL BISHOPS' PALACE

Tel: 01522 527468

Minster Yard, Lincoln LN2 1PU

Owner: English Heritage **Contact:** The Custodian

In the shadow of Lincoln Cathedral are the remains of this medieval palace of the Bishop of Lincoln. Climb the stairs to the Alnwick Tower, explore the undercroft and see one of the most northerly vineyards in Europe.

Location: OS121 Ref. SK981 717. S side of Lincoln Cathedral, in Lincoln.

Opening Times: 1 Apr - 31 Oct: daily, 10am - 6pm (5pm in Oct). 1 Nov - 31 Mar: weekends only, 10am - 4pm. Closed 24 - 26 Dec & 1 Jan.

Admission: Adult £1.90, Child £1, Conc. £1.40. 15% discount for groups (11+).

 Tel. for details.

NORMANBY HALL

See right.

SIBSEY TRADER WINDMILL

Tel: 01205 820065

Sibsey, Boston, Lincolnshire

Owner: English Heritage **Contact:** The Custodian

An impressive old mill built in 1877, with its machinery and six sails still intact. Flour milled on the spot can be bought here.

Location: OS Ref. TF345 511. ½ m W of village of Sibsey, off A16, 5m N of Boston.

Opening Times: Mill seen in action on: 29 Mar, 19 Apr, 10 & 31 May, 14 & 28 Jun, 12 & 26 Jul, 9 & 23 Aug, 13 Sept.

Admission: Adult £1.70, Child 90p, Conc. £1.30.

TATTERSHALL CASTLE

Tel: 01526 342543

Tattershall, Lincoln, Lincolnshire LN4 4LR

Owner: The National Trust **Contact:** The Custodian

A vast fortified tower built c1440 for Ralph Cromwell, Lord Treasurer of England. The Castle is an important example of an early brick building, with a tower containing state apartments, rescued from dereliction and restored by Lord Curzon 1911-14. Four great chambers, with ancillary rooms, contain late gothic fireplaces and brick vaulting. There are tapestries and information displays in turret rooms.

Location: OS122 Ref. TF209 575. On S side of A153, 15m NE of Sleaford, 10m SW of Horncastle.

Opening Times: 15 Apr - 2 Jul: daily except Thurs & Fris. 3 - 14 Jul: closed for conservation work (this closed period may be delayed for one or two weeks). 15 Jul - 31 Oct: daily except Thurs & Fris, 10.30am - 5.30pm. 4 Nov - 17 Dec: Sats & Suns, 12 noon - 4pm.

Admission: Adult £3, Child £1.50, Family £7.50. Child Free Jul/Aug. Discount for groups.

Ground floor. WC. Car park only. Free.

THORNTON ABBEY

Tel: 0191 269 1200

Scunthorpe, Humberside

Owner: English Heritage **Contact:** The North Regional Office

The magnificent brick gatehouse of this ruined Augustine priory stands three storeys high.

Location: OS Ref. TA115 190. 18m NE of Scunthorpe on minor road N of A180.

Opening Times: 1 Apr - 30 Sept: 1st & 3rd Suns, 12 - 6pm. 1 Oct - 31 Mar: 3rd Suns, 12 - 4pm.

Admission: Free.

WOOLSTHORPE MANOR

Tel: 01476 860338

23 Newton Way, Woolsthorpe-by-Colsterworth, Grantham NG33 5NR

Owner: The National Trust **Contact:** The Custodian

This small 17th century farmhouse was the birthplace and family home of Sir Isaac Newton. Some of his major work was formulated here, during the Plague years (1665 - 67); an early edition of the *Principia* is on display. The orchard has a descendant of the famous apple tree. Discovery Centre and exhibition of Sir Isaac Newton's work.

Location: OS130 Ref. SK924 244. 7m S of Grantham, ½ m NW of Colsterworth, 1m W of A1.

Opening Times: 1 Apr - 31 Oct: Wed - Sun & BH Mons (closed Good Fri), 1 - 5.30pm. Last admission. 5pm.

Admission: Adult £3.20, Child £1.60, Family £8, no reduction for groups which must book in advance.

Ground floor suitable. Limited. Car park only.

NORMANBY HALL

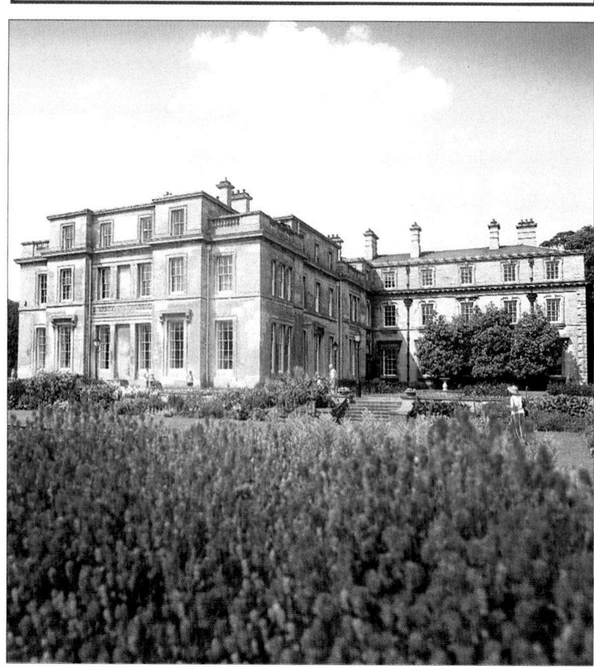

NORMANBY, SCUNTHORPE, NORTH LINCOLNSHIRE DN15 9HU

***Owner:** North Lincolnshire Council* ***Contact:** Park Manager*

Tel: 01724 720588 **Fax:** 01724 721248

The restored working Victorian Walled Kitchen Garden is growing produce for the 'big house' as it would have done 100 years ago. Victorian varieties of fruit and vegetables are grown using organic and Victorian techniques. Set in 300 acres of Park, visitors may also see the Regency Mansion, designed by Sir Robert Smirke, which the Garden was built to serve.

The ground floor rooms of the Hall are displayed in Regency style, while those upstairs reflect the changing styles of the Victorian and Edwardian eras. Costume from the Museum Service's collections is also exhibited.

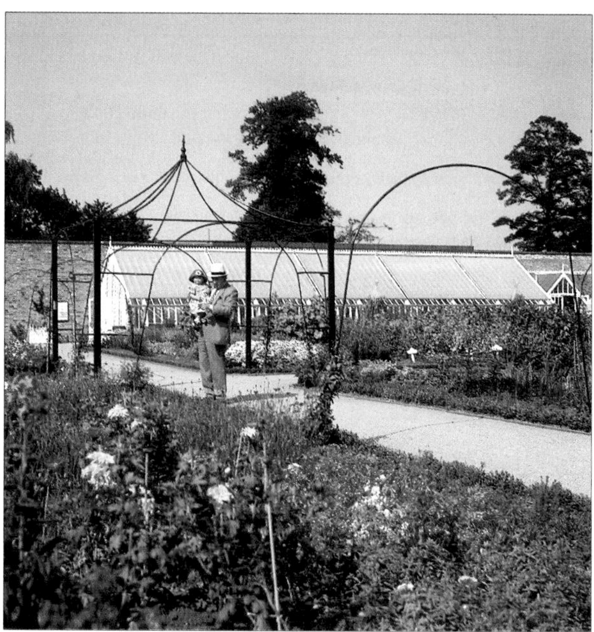

Location: OS Ref. SE886 166. 4m N of Scunthorpe off B1430. Follow signs for M181 & Humber Bridge. Tours by arrangement.

Opening Times: Hall & Farming Museum: 27 Mar - 1 Oct: 1 - 5pm. Park: daily, 9am - dusk. Walled Garden: daily, 11am - 5pm (4pm in winter). Last admission at all venues ½ hour before closing.

Admission: Summer Season: Adult £2.50, Conc. £1.50, Family (2+3) £6.50, half price for North Lincolnshire residents. Winter Season: £2 per car. (1999 rates).

All details correct at time of going to press. For up to date information, please contact Normanby Hall Country Park.

 Wedding receptions. Ground floor & grounds suitable. WC.

By arrangement.   In grounds, on leads. 

Owner:
The Earl of Leicester

CONTACT

The Administrator
Holkham Hall
Estate Office
Wells-next-the-Sea
Norfolk
NR23 1AB

Tel: 01328 710227

Fax: 01328 711707

LOCATION

OS Ref. TF885 428

From London 120m
Norwich 35m
King's Lynn 30m.

Rail: Norwich Station 35m
King's Lynn Station 30m.

Air: Norwich Airport 32m.

HOLKHAM HALL

Wells-next-the-Sea

HOLKHAM HALL has been the home of the Coke family and the Earls of Leicester for almost 250 years. Built between 1734 and 1764 by Thomas Coke, 1st Earl of Leicester and based on a design by William Kent, this fine example of 18th century Palladian style mansion reflects Thomas Coke's natural appreciation of classical art developed during the Grand Tour. It is constructed mainly of local yellow brick with a magnificent Entrance Hall of English alabaster.

The State Rooms occupy the first floor and contain Greek and Roman statuary, paintings by Rubens, Van Dyck, Claude, Poussin and Gainsborough and original furniture.

On leaving the House visitors pass Holkham Pottery and its adjacent shop, both under the supervision of the Countess of Leicester. Fine examples of local craftsmanship are for sale including the famous Holkham Florist Ware.

Beyond are the 19th century stables now housing the Holkham Bygones Collection; some 4,000 items range from working steam engines, vintage cars and tractors to craft tools and kitchenware. A History of Farming exhibition is in the former Porter's Lodge.

The House is set in a 3,000-acre park with 600 head of fallow deer. On the lake, 1 mile long, are many species of wildfowl. Two walks encircle either the lake or agricultural buildings.

Holkham Nursery Gardens occupy the 18th century walled Kitchen Garden and a large range of stock is on sale to the public.

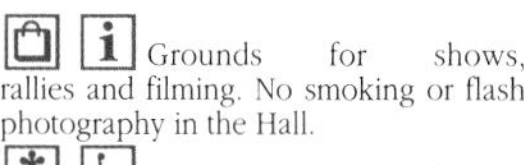

Grounds for shows, rallies and filming. No smoking or flash photography in the Hall.

Visitors may alight at entrance, stairs in the Hall. WC.

Menus for pre-booked groups on request.

Guides are posted in each room. Audio tour £2, other times guided tours by arrangement.

Unlimited for cars, 20+ coaches. Parking, admission, refreshments free to coach drivers, coach drivers' rest room.

Welcome. Areas of interest: Bygones Collection, History of Farming, two nature walks, deer park, lake and wildfowl.

No dogs in Hall, on leads in grounds.

OPENING TIMES

SUMMER
28 May - 30 September
Sun - Thur (inclusive)
1 - 5pm.

Easter, May, Spring & Summer BHs
Suns & Mons
11.30am - 5pm.

Last admission 4.45pm.

Restaurant, shop and Holkham Nursery Gardens from 10am.

WINTER
October - May
Open by appointment.

ADMISSION

SUMMER

Hall
Adult £4.00
Child (5-15yrs) £2.00

Bygones
Adult £4.00
Child (5-15yrs) £2.00

Combined Ticket
Adult £6.00
Child (5-15yrs) £3.00

GROUPS (min. 20)

Hall
Adult £3.60
Child (5-15yrs) £1.80

Bygones
Adult £3.60
Child (5-15yrs) £1.80

Combined Ticket
Adult £5.40
Child (5-15yrs) £2.70

Private guided tours by arrangement. Rates on application.

WINTER
By arrangement.

Owner: H M The Queen

CONTACT

Mrs Gill Pattinson
The Estate Office
Sandringham
Norfolk
PE35 6EN

Tel: 01553 772675

Fax: 01485 541571

LOCATION

OS Ref. TF695 287

8m NE of King's Lynn on B1440 off A148.

Rail: King's Lynn.

Air: Norwich.

CONFERENCE/FUNCTION		
ROOM	SIZE	MAX CAPACITY
Restaurant		200
Tearoom		60

SANDRINGHAM

Norfolk

SANDRINGHAM is the charming country retreat of Her Majesty The Queen, hidden in the heart of 60 acres of beautiful wooded grounds. Still maintained in the style of Edward and Alexandra, Prince and Princess of Wales (later King Edward VII and Queen Alexandra), all the main ground floor rooms used by The Royal Family, full of their treasured ornaments, portraits and furniture, are open to the public. In 2000 an exhibition of HRH The Duke of Edinburgh's collection of cartoons by Giles will be displayed in the ballroom.

More family possessions are displayed in the Museum housed in the old stable and coach houses including vehicles ranging in date from the first car owned by a British monarch, a 1900 Daimler, to a half-scale Aston Martin used by Princes William and Harry. A new display tells the mysterious tale of the Sandringham Company who fought and died at Gallipolli in 1915, recently made into a TV film 'All the King's Men'.

In the Gardens informal glades, dells, lakes and lawns are surrounded by magnificent trees and bordered by colourful shrubs and flowers. A free Land Train from within the entrance will carry passengers less able to walk through the grounds to the House and back.

No photography in house.

Visitor Centre only.

Plant centre.

Suitable.

Tearoom.

Licensed.

By arrangement. Private evening tours.

Ample.

Teachers' pack.

Guide dogs only.

OPENING TIMES

House
15 April - 18 July
3 August - 8 October
daily, 11am - 4.45pm.
Closed Good Friday.

Museum & Gardens
15 April - 22 July
3 August - 8 October
daily, 11am - 5pm.
Closed Good Friday.

ADMISSION

House and Garden

Adult	£5.50
Child (5-15yrs)	£3.50
Conc.	£4.50

Groups (20+)
10% discount for payment in full one month in advance.

BERNEY ARMS WINDMILL

Tel: 01493 700605

c/o 8 Manor Road, Southtown, Gt Yarmouth NR31 0QA

Owner: English Heritage **Contact:** The Custodian

A wonderfully situated marsh mill, one of the best and largest remaining in Norfolk, with seven floors, making it a landmark for miles around. It was in use until 1951.

Location: OS134 Ref. TG465 051. 3$^{1}/_{2}$ m NE of Reedham on N bank of River Yare, 5m from Gt. Yarmouth. Accessible by boat or by footpath, from Halvergate (3$^{1}/_{2}$ m).

Opening Times: 1 Apr - 31 Oct: daily, 9am - 5pm (closed 1 - 2pm).

Admission: Adult £1.60, Child 80p, Conc. £1.20.

BINHAM PRIORY

Tel: 01604 730320 (Regional Office)

Binham-on-Wells, Norfolk

Owner: English Heritage **Contact:** The Midlands Regional Office

Extensive remains of a Benedictine priory, of which the original nave of the church is still in use as the parish church.

Location: OS132 Ref. TF982 399. $^{1}/_{4}$ m NW of village of Binham-on-Wells, on road off B1388.

Opening Times: Any reasonable time.

Admission: Free.

BIRCHAM WINDMILL

Tel: 01485 578393

Snettisham Road, Great Bircham, Norfolk PE31 6SJ

Owner/Contact: Mr & Mrs G Wagg

One of the last remaining complete windmills.

Location: OS Ref. TF760 326. $^{1}/_{2}$ m W of Bircham. N of the road to Snettisham.

Opening Times: Please contact for details.

Admission: Adult £2.20, Child 75p, Retired £2. (1999 prices).

BLICKLING HALL

Tel: 01263 738030 **Fax:** 01263 731660

Blickling, Norwich NR11 6NF

Owner: The National Trust **Contact:** The Property Manager

Built in the early 17th century and one of England's great Jacobean houses. Blickling is famed for its spectacular long gallery, superb library and fine collections of furniture, pictures and tapestries.

Location: OS133 Ref. TG178 286. 1$^{1}/_{2}$m NW of Aylsham on B1354. Signposted off A140 Norwich (15m) to Cromer.

Opening Times: House: 8 Apr - 29 Oct:Wed - Sun (incl BH Mons); Aug: Tue - Sun, 1 - 4.30pm, last admission 4.30pm. Garden: 8 Apr - 29 Oct: Wed - Sun (incl. BH Mons), Aug: Tue - Sun, 10.30am - 5.30pm. 2 Nov - 17 Dec, Thur - Sun, 6 Jan - end Mar 2001: Sats & Suns, 11am - 4pm. Park & Woods: daily, dawn - dusk.

Admission: Adult £6.50. Garden only: £3.70. Family & group discounts. Groups must book with SAE to the Property Office.

Open as garden. Partially suitable. Licensed. By arrangement. In park, on leads. Tel for details.

BRADENHAM HALL GARDENS

Tel: 01362 687243

Bradenham, Thetford, Norfolk IP25 7QP

Owner/Contact: Mrs Jane Allhusen

A garden for all seasons with massed daffodils in arboretum of over 900 species, all labelled. Rose gardens, herbaceous and mixed borders, wall shrubs and roses, fruit and vegetable garden, glasshouses. Featured in *Country Life* and *House and Garden*. Excellent tearoom with home-made cakes, and quality plants for sale.

Location: OS Ref. TF921 099. Off A47, 6m E of Swaffham, 5m W of East Dereham.

Opening Times: Apr - Sept: 2nd, 4th & 5th Sun of each month, 2 - 5.30pm.

Admission: Adult £3, Child Free.

Cream teas.

BURGH CASTLE

Tel: 01604 730320 (Regional Office)

Breydon Water, Great Yarmouth, Norfolk

Owner: English Heritage **Contact:** The Midlands Regional Office

Impressive walls, with projecting bastions, of a Roman fort built in the late 3rd century as one of a chain to defend the coast against Saxon raiders.

Location: OS134 Ref. TG475 046. At far W end of Breydon Water, on unclassified road 3m W of Great Yarmouth. SW of the church.

Opening Times: Any reasonable time.

Admission: Free.

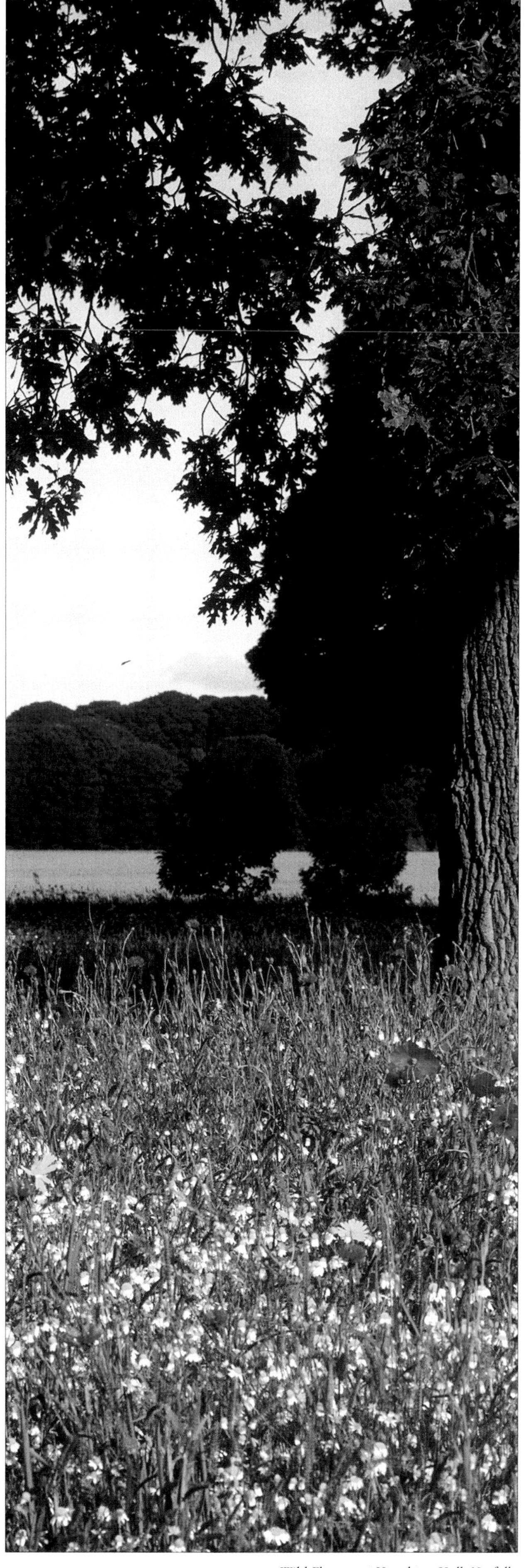

Wild Flowers at Houghton Hall, Norfolk.

CASTLE ACRE PRIORY

Tel: 01760 755394

Stocks Green, Castle Acre, King's Lynn, Norfolk PE32 2XD

Owner: English Heritage **Contact:** The Custodian

The great west front of the 12th century church of this Cluniac priory still rises to its full height and is elaborately decorated. Other substantial remains include the splendid prior's lodgings and chapel and the delightful modern herb garden should not be missed.

Location: OS Ref. TF814 148. 1/4 m W of village of Castle Acre, 5m N of Swaffham.

Opening Times: 1 Apr - 31 Oct: daily, 10am - 6pm (5pm in Oct). 1 Nov - 31 Mar: Wed - Sun, 10am - 4pm. Closed 24 - 26 Dec & 1 Jan.

Admission: Adult £3.20, Child £1.60, Conc. £2.40.

Ground floor & grounds. Tel. for details.

CASTLE RISING CASTLE

Tel: 01553 631330

Castle Rising, King's Lynn, Norfolk PE31 6AH

Owner: Greville Howard **Contact:** The Custodian

Possibly the finest mid-12th century Keep left in England: it was built as a grand and elaborate palace. It was home to Queen Isabella, grandmother of the Black Prince. Still in surprisingly good condition, the Keep is surrounded by massive ramparts up to 120 feet high.

Opening Times: 1 Apr - 31 Oct: daily, 10am - 6pm, (5pm in Oct). 1 Nov - 31 Mar: Wed - Sun, 10am - 4pm. Closed 24 - 26 Dec & 1 Jan.

Admission: Adult £3, Child £1.50, Conc. £2.50. 15% discount for groups (11+).

Grounds suitable. WC.

DRAGON HALL

Tel: 01603 663922

115 - 123 King Street, Norwich, Norfolk NR1 1QE

Owner: Norfolk & Norwich Heritage Trust Ltd **Contact:** Mr Neil Sigsworth

Magnificent medieval merchants' hall described as "one of the most exciting 15th century buildings in England". A wealth of outstanding features include living hall, screens passage, vaulted undercroft, superb timber-framed Great Hall, crown-post roof and intricately carved and painted dragon. Built by Robert Toppes, a wealthy and influential merchant. Dragon Hall is a unique legacy of medieval life, craftsmanship and trade.

Location: OS Ref. TG235 084. SE of Norwich city centre.

Opening Times: Apr - Oct: Mon - Sat, 10am - 4pm. Nov - Mar: Mon - Fri, 10am - 4pm. Closed 23 Dec - 2 Jan & BHs.

Admission: Adult £1.50, Child 50p, Conc. £1.

House suitable. Obligatory. Guide dogs only.

FELBRIGG HALL, GARDEN & PARK

Tel: 01263 837444 **Fax:** 01263 837032

Felbrigg, Norwich NR11 8PR

Owner: The National Trust **Contact:** The Property Manager

One of the finest 17th century houses in East Anglia, the hall contains its original 18th century furniture and Grand Tour paintings, as well as an outstanding library. The walled garden has been restored and features a dovecote and small orchard.

Location: OS133 Ref. TG193 394. Nr Felbrigg village, 2m SW of Cromer, entrance off B1436, signposted from A148 and A140.

Opening Times: 1 Apr - 31 Oct: daily except Thurs & Fris, 1 - 5pm; BH Suns & Mons, 11am - 5pm. Garden: As house, 11am - 5.30pm. Woodland, Lakeside Walks & Parkland: daily, dawn - dusk (closed 25 Dec).

Admission: Adult £5.70, Child £2.80, Family £14.20. Garden only: £2.20. Groups: (except BHs, £4.70. Groups must book with the Property Manager.

Tel: 01263 837040. 01263 838237. Licensed. Licensed. Partially suitable. By arrangement. In park, on leads. Tel. 01263 838297 for details.

GRIME'S GRAVES

Tel: 01842 810656

Lynford, Thetford, Norfolk IP26 5DE

Owner: English Heritage **Contact:** The Custodian

These remarkable Neolithic flint mines, unique in England, comprise over 300 pits and shafts. The visitor can descend some 30 feet by ladder into one excavated shaft, and look along the radiating galleries, from where the flint used for making axes and knives was extracted. Special flint-knapping days are advertised throughout the year.

Location: OS144 Ref. TL818 898. 7m NW of Thetford off A134.

Opening Times: 1 Apr - 31 Oct, daily, 10am - 6pm, (5pm in Oct). 1 Nov - 31 Mar: Wed - Sun, 10am - 4pm (closed 1 - 2pm) Closed 24 - 26 Dec & 1 Jan. Last visit to pit 20 mins before close. NB: Visits to pit for children under 5yrs at the discretion of the custodian.

Admission: Adult £2, Child £1, Conc. £1.50.

Tel. for details.

HOLKHAM HALL

See page 241 for full page entry.

FAIRHAVEN WOODLAND & WATER GARDEN

2 THE WOODLANDS, WYMERS LANE, SOUTH WALSHAM NR13 6EA

Owner: *The Fairhaven Garden Trust* ***Contact:*** *George Debbage, Manager*

Tel/Fax: 01603 270449

180 acre woodland & water garden with private broad in the beautiful Norfolk Broads. 900 Year Old Oak Tree. The largest collection of naturalised candelabra primulas in England. Over 90 recorded species of birds, many rare plants and shrubs. Special times to visit the gardens include, 'primrose weeks' during April, 'candelabra primula weeks' last two weeks in May, 'Autumn Colours' October. Wildlife Sanctuary, Boat Trips, Children's Nature Trail.

Location: OS Ref. TG368 134. 9m NE of Norwich just N of the B1140 at South Walsham.

Opening Times: Daily (except 25 Dec), 10am - 5pm, from May - Aug: Wed & Thurs evenings until 9pm.

Admission: Adult £3, Child £1 (under 5yrs Free), OAP £2.70. Group reductions.

Children's nature trail. Broads boat trips. Partially suitable. By arrangement. In grounds, on leads.

Castle Rising, Norfolk.

HOUGHTON HALL

HOUGHTON, KING'S LYNN, NORFOLK PE31 6UE

Owner: *The Marquess of Cholmondeley* ***Contact:*** *Susan Cleaver*

Tel: 01485 528569 **Fax:** 01485 528167

Houghton Hall was built in the 18th century by Sir Robert Walpole. Original designs were by Colen Campbell and revised by Thomas Ripley with interior decoration by William Kent. It is regarded as one of the finest examples of Palladian architecture in England. Houghton was later inherited by the 1st Marquess of Cholmondeley through his grandmother, Sir Robert's daughter. Situated in beautiful parkland, the house contains magnificent furniture, pictures and china. A private collection of 20,000 model soldiers and militaria. Newly restored walled garden.

Location: OS Ref. TF792 287. 13m E of King's Lynn, 10m W of Fakenham 1$^1/_2$m N of A148.

Opening Times: 4 Apr - 26 Sept: Suns, Thurs & BH Mons, 1 - 5.30pm. House: 2 - 5.30pm. Last adm. 5pm.

Admission: Adult £6, Child (5-16) £3, Groups (20+): Adult £5.50, Child £2.50. Excluding house: Adult £3.50, Child £2, Groups (20+) Adult £3, Child £1.50.

HOVETON HALL GARDENS

Tel: 01603 782798 **Fax:** 01603 784564

Wroxham, Norwich, Norfolk NR12 8RJ

Owner: Mr & Mrs Andrew Buxton **Contact:** Mrs Buxton

10 acres of rhododendrons, azaleas, woodland and lakeside walks, walled herbaceous and vegetable gardens. Traditional tearooms and plant sales. The Hall (which is not open to the public) was built 1809 - 1812. Designs attributed to Humphry Repton.

Location: OS Ref. TG314 202. 8m N of Norwich. 1$^1/_2$m NNE of Wroxham on A1151. Follow brown tourist signs.

Opening Times: Easter Sun - mid-Sept: Weds, Fris, Suns & BH Mons, 11am - 5.30pm.

Admission: Adult £3, Child £1, Season ticket £8. Groups: £2.50 (if booked in advance). (1999 prices).

LETHERINGSETT WATERMILL

Tel: 01263 713153 **e-mail:** watermill@ic24.net

Riverside Road, Letheringsett, Holt, Norfolk NR25 7YD

Owner/Contact: M D Thurlow

Water-powered mill producing wholewheat flour from locally grown wheat. Built in 1802.

Location: OS Ref. TG062 387. Riverside Road, Letheringsett, Holt, Norfolk.

Opening Times: Whitsun - Oct: Mon - Fri, 10am - 5pm, Sat 9am - 1pm. Working demonstration, every afternoon, 2 - 4.30pm. Viewing may take place at any other time. Oct - Whitsun: Mon - Fri, 9am - 4pm. Sat, 9am - 1pm. Working demonstration, Tue - Fri, 1.30 3.30pm. BH Suns & Mons, 2 - 5pm.

Admission: Adult £2, Child £1.50. When demonstrating: Adult £3, Child £2, OAP £2.50, Family (2+2) £9.

The Walled Garden at Houghton Hall, Norfolk.

MANNINGTON GARDENS & COUNTRYSIDE

Tel: 01263 584175
Mannington Hall, Norwich NR11 7BB **Fax:** 01263 761214
Owner: The Lord & Lady Walpole **Contact:** Lady Walpole

Gardens with lake, moat and woodland. Outstanding rose collection, heritage rose gardens.

Location: OS Ref. TG144 320. Signposted from Saxthorpe crossroads on the Norwich - Holt road B1149. 1½ m W of Wolterton Hall.

Opening Times: Gardens: May - Sept: Suns 12 - 5pm. Jun - Aug: Wed - Fri, 11am - 5pm. Walks: daily from 9am. Medieval Hall open by appointment.

Admission: Adult £3, Child (under 16yrs) Free, Conc. £2.50. Groups by arrangement.

No photography. Grounds suitable. WCs. Licensed. By arrangement. Guide dogs only.

THE MANOR HOUSE

Great Cressingham, Thetford, Norfolk IP25 6NJ
Owner/Contact: Mrs L R Chapman

Small Tudor manor house famous for its terracotta façade.

Location: OS Ref. TF852 020. 6m S of Swaffham. 1½ m E of A1065.

Opening Times: By written appointment only.

Admission: Prices on application.

NORWICH CASTLE MUSEUM

Tel: 01603 493624 **Fax:** 01603 765651
Norwich, Norfolk NR1 3JU

Norman Castle Keep, housing displays of art, archaeology and natural history.

Location: OS Ref. TG233 085. City centre.

Opening Times: Norwich Castle Museum is closed until April 2001 due to extensive refurbishment of the historic Norman Keep and redisplay of the Museum's galleries.

OXBURGH HALL, GARDEN & ESTATE

Tel: 01366 328258 **Fax:** 01366 328066
King's Lynn, Norfolk PE33 9PS **e-mail:** aohusr@smtp.ntrust.org.uk
Owner: The National Trust **Contact:** The Property Manager

A moated manor house built in 1482 by the Bedingfeld family, who still live here. The rooms show the development from medieval austerity to Victorian comfort and include an outstanding display of embroidery done by Mary Queen of Scots. The attractive gardens include a French parterre, kitchen garden and orchard.

Location: OS143 Ref. TF742 012. At Oxborough, 7m SW of Swaffham on S side of Stoke Ferry road.

Opening Times: House: 1 - 26 Apr & 1 - 29 Oct: Tues, Weds, Sats & Suns (open BH Mons). 29 Apr - 31 Jul & 1 - 30 Sept: daily except Thurs & Fris. Aug: daily, 1 - 5pm. Garden: 4 - 26 Mar: Sats & Suns, 11am - 4pm. 1 Apr - 31 Jul & 1 Sept - 29 Oct: daily except Thurs & Fris; Aug: daily, 11am - 5.30pm.

Admission: Adult £5.30, Family discounts. Garden & Estate only: Adult £2.60. Groups: £4.20. Groups must book with SAE to the Property Manager.

Licensed. Partially suitable. By arrangement. In grounds, on leads. Send SAE for details.

RAVENINGHAM HALL GARDENS

Tel: 01508 548222 **Fax:** 01508 548958
Raveningham, Norwich, Norfolk NR14 6NS **e-mail:** raveningham@freenet.co.uk
Owner: Sir Nicholas Bacon Bt **Contact:** Mrs J Woodard

Gardens laid out approximately 100 years ago around a red brick Georgian house which is not open to the public.

Location: OS Ref. TM399 965. Between Beccles and Loddon off B1136/B1140.

Opening Times: Easter Sun & Mon, April, May, Jun & Jul: Sun & BH Mon, 2 - 5pm.

Admission: Adult £2, Child Free. Groups by prior arrangement.

ROW 111 HOUSE, OLD MERCHANT'S HOUSE, & GREYFRIARS' CLOISTERS

South Quay, Great Yarmouth, Norfolk NR30 2RQ **Tel:** 01493 857900
Owner: English Heritage **Contact:** The Custodian

Two 17th century Row Houses, rows 111 and 113, a type of building unique to Great Yarmouth, containing original fixtures and displays of local architectural fittings and early wall paintings.

Location: OS134 Ref. TG525 072. In Great Yarmouth, make for South Quay, by riverside and dock, ½ m inland from beach.

Opening Times: 1 Apr - 31 Oct: daily, 10am - 5pm. Guided tours depart from Row 111 house at 10, 11am, 12 noon, 2, 3 & 4pm.

Admission: Adult £1.85, Child 90p, Conc. £1.40. 15% discount for groups of 11+.

ST GEORGE'S GUILDHALL

Tel: 01553 765565
27 Kings Street, Kings Lynn, Norfolk PE30 1HA
Owner: The National Trust **Contact:** The Administrator

The largest surviving English medieval guildhall, with adjoining medieval warehouse, now in use as an Arts Centre.

Location: OS132 Ref. TF616 202. On W side of King Street close to the Tuesday Market Place.

Opening Times: All year: Mon - Fri (closed Good Fri & Aug BH Mon) 10am - 4pm; Sats 10am - 1pm & 2 - 3.30pm. Closed 25, 26 Dec & 1 Jan.

Admission: Free.

Access to galleries. Licensed.

SANDRINGHAM

See page 242 for full page entry.

WALSINGHAM ABBEY GROUNDS & SHIREHALL MUSEUM 

Tel: 01328 820259 **Fax:** 01328 820098
Little Walsingham, Norfolk NR22 6BP
Owner: Walsingham Estate Company **Contact:** The Agent

Set in Walsingham, a picturesque medieval village, the grounds contain the remains of an Augustinian Priory founded in 1153 on a site next to the Holy House and provide pleasant river and woodland walks. Snowdrop walks during February & March. Refreshments and accommodation in the village.

Location: OS Ref. TF934 367. B1105 N from Fakenham - 5m.

Opening Times: Please contact for details.

Admission: Please telephone for details.

Pay & Display, 50 yds. In grounds, on leads.

WOLTERTON PARK

Tel: 01263 584175 **Fax:** 01263 761214
Norwich, Norfolk NR11 7BB
Owner: The Lord and Lady Walpole **Contact:** The Lady Walpole

18th century Hall. Historic park with lake.

Location: OS Ref. TG164 317. Situated near Erpingham village, signposted from Norwich - Cromer Rd A140.

Opening Times: Park: daily from 9am. Hall: Fridays Spring - Autumn, 2 - 5pm; some Sundays.

Admission: £2 car park fee only. Groups by application. Hall tours: See local press, from £4 groups, £5 individuals.

Partially suitable. WC. Obligatory for Hall. In grounds, on leads.

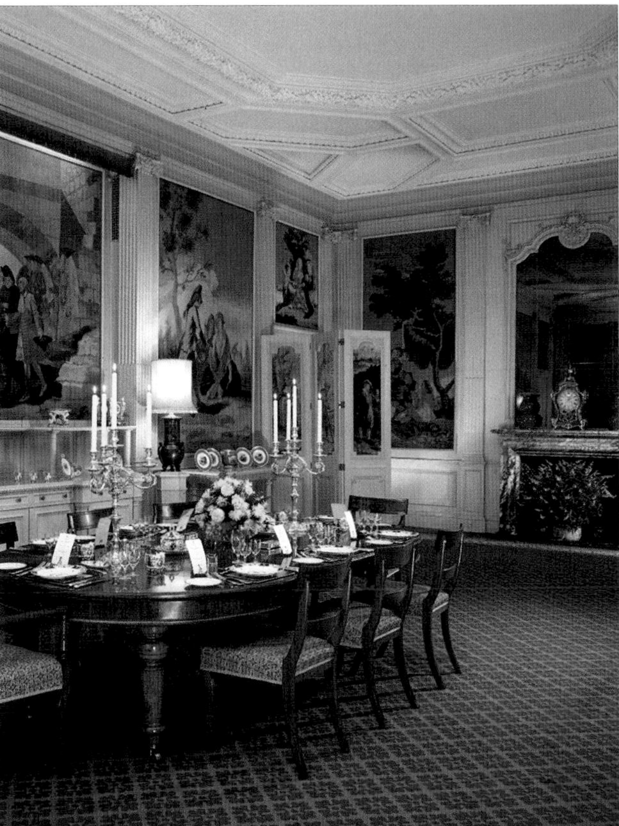

The Dining Room, Sandringham, Norfolk.

Owner:
Patrick Phillips Esq

CONTACT

Mrs J G Phillips
Kentwell Hall
Long Melford
Suffolk
CO10 9BA

Tel: 01787 310207

Fax: 01787 379318

LOCATION

OS Ref. TL864 479

Off the A134.
4m N of Sudbury, 14m S of Bury St. Edmunds
1m NNW of Long Melford off A134.

Rail: Sudbury Station 4m
Colchester Station 20m.

Air: Stansted 30m.
Airstrip at Kentwell suitable for light aircraft and microlites.

Taxi: Sudbury Town Taxis 01787 377366.

CONFERENCE/FUNCTION		
ROOM	SIZE	MAX CAPACITY
Great Hall	40' x 24'	120
Main Dining Room	24' x 24'	75
Drawing Rm	35' x 24'	75
Library	36' x 20'	20
Overcroft	120' x 22'	300

KENTWELL HALL
Long Melford

KENTWELL HALL is a beautiful redbrick Tudor Manor House surrounded by a broad moat.

Built by the Clopton Family, from wealth made in the wool trade, Kentwell has an air of timeless tranquillity. The exterior is little altered in 450 years. The interior was remodelled by Hopper in 1825 and his work has been embellished and enhanced in restoration by the present owners. Hopper's interiors, notably the Great Hall and Dining Room, emphasise their Tudor provenance, but the Drawing Room and Library are simply and restrainedly classical; all are eminently habitable.

Kentwell, as well as being a family home, conveys a deep feeling of the Tudor period with the service areas: great kitchen, bakery, dairy and forge always fully equipped in 16th century style. Kentwell's unique 16th century atmosphere and large collection of 16th century artefacts make it an ideal location for films and videos.

The gardens are part of Kentwell's delight. Intimate yet spacious, you are seldom far from a moat, clipped yews (some 30ft high) or mellow brick wall. There is a fine walled garden with original 17th century layout and a well established large Herb Garden and Potager.

The farm is run organically and is set around timber-framed buildings and stocked with rare breed farm animals.

Home to the award winning **'Re-creations of Tudor Domestic Life'** when visitors meet numerous 'Tudors' with dress, speech, activities and locations appropriate for the 16th century. These take place on selected weekends between April and September.

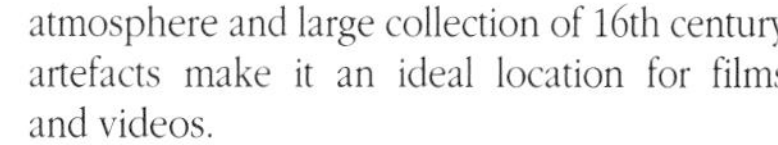

Corporate events include conferences and 'company days', specially devised one-day programme of fun, stimulation and challenges. A wide range of Tudor activities can be arranged for visitors, including longbow shooting, working bakery, dairy and still-room, spinning, etc. or even clay pigeon shooting in the Park. No photography in house.

Genuine Tudor-style banquets, wedding receptions, formal but friendly luncheons and dinners.

Visitors may alight at house, with prior notice. WC.

Home-made food. The Undercroft comfortably seats 96. Overcroft can accommodate up to 300.

Ample.

There is a highly developed schools programme dealing with 700 parties per year. Schools can visit a re-creation of Tudor life, re-create Tudor life themselves for the day or take one of the tours conducted by experienced guides on the House, Garden, Farm or aspects of each.

No dogs.

OPENING TIMES

House, Gardens & Farm

- 2 April - 11 June: Suns only, 17 - 20 April: daily and Half-term: 30 May - 2 June. 12 noon - 5pm.
- 12 July - 3 September daily 12 noon - 5pm.
- 10 Sept - 29 Oct Suns only, 12 noon - 5pm
- 23 - 27 Oct daily: 12 noon - 5pm

Gardens & Farm only

- 5 - 26 March: Suns only, 12 noon - 5pm.

The Great Annual Re-creation

- 18 June - 9 July: Sats & Suns only & Fri, 7 July, 11am - 5pm.

Other Re-creations

- 8 - 9 Apr: Land Girls
- 21 Apr - 1 May: Easter/ May Day
- 29 Apr - 1 May: May Day
- 27 - 29 May: Witsun
- 5 - 6 Aug: Lammas
- 25 - 28 Aug: High Summer
- 23 - 24 Sept: Michaelmas
- 14 - 15 Oct: World War II Event

All 11am - 6pm, sometimes 5pm.

Special Prices apply. Please see Special Events Section.

ADMISSION

House, Gardens & Farm

Adult £5.50
Child (5-15yrs) £3.30
OAP..........................£4.75

Gardens & Farm only

Adult £3.50
Child (5-15yrs) £2.25
OAP..........................£3.00

Great Annual Re-creation

Adult £11.60
Child (5-15yrs) £8.25
OAP..........................£9.95

THE ANCIENT HOUSE

Tel: 01628 825920 or 825925 (bookings)

Clare, Suffolk CO10 8NY

Owner: Leased to the Landmark Trust by Clare Parish Council

Contact: The Landmark Trust

A 14th century house extended in the 15th and 17th centuries, decorated with high relief pargetting. Half of the building is managed by the Landmark Trust, which lets buildings for self-catering holidays. The other half of the house is run as a museum. Full details of The Ancient House and 167 other historic buildings available for holidays are featured in The Landmark Handbook (price £9.50 refundable against booking), from The Landmark Trust, Shottesbrooke, Maidenhead, Berkshire SL6 3SW.

Location: OS Ref. TL769 454. Village centre, on A1092 8m WNW of Sudbury.

Opening Times: By appointment only and for Clare Arts Festival, week commencing 17 Jun (please telephone for details). Museum: Contact 01787 277662 for details.

Admission: Please contact for details.

BELCHAMP HALL

BELCHAMP WALTER, SUDBURY, SUFFOLK CO10 7AT

Owner/Contact: *Mr C F V Raymond*

Tel: 01787 881961 **Fax:** 01787 880729

Superb Queen Anne house on a site belonging to the Raymond family since 1611. Historic portraits and period furniture. Suitable for receptions and an ideal film location, often seen as Lady Jane's house in *Lovejoy*. Gardens including a cherry avenue, follies, a sunken garden, walled garden and lake. Medieval church with 15th century wall paintings.

Location: OS Ref. TL827 407. 5m SW of Sudbury, opposite Belchamp Walter Church.

Opening Times: By appointment only: May - Sept: Tues, Thurs & BHs, 2.30 - 6pm.

Admission: Adult £4, Child £1.75. No reduction for groups.

No photography in house. By arrangement. Obligatory. Guide dogs only.

CHRISTCHURCH MANSION

Tel: 01473 253246 **Fax:** 01473 281274

Christchurch Park, Ipswich, Suffolk IP4 2BD

Owner/Contact: Ipswich Borough Council

A fine Tudor house set in beautiful parkland.

Location: OS Ref. TM165 450. Christchurch Park, near centre of Ipswich.

Opening Times: All year: Tue - Sat, 10am - 5pm (dusk in winter). Suns, 2.30 - 4.30pm (dusk in winter). Also open BH Mons. Closed 24 - 26 Dec, 1/2 Jan and Good Fri.

Admission: Free.

EAST BERGHOLT PLACE GARDEN

Tel/Fax: 01206 299224

East Bergholt, Suffolk CO7 6UP

Owner: Mr & Mrs R L C Eley **Contact:** Sara Eley

Fifteen acres of garden and arboretum originally laid out at the beginning of the century by the present owner's great-grandfather. A wonderful collection of fine trees and shrubs, many of which are rarely seen growing in East Anglia and originate from the famous plant hunter George Forrest. Particularly beautiful in the spring when the rhododendrons, magnolias and camellias are in flower. There is a specialist plant centre in the Victorian walled garden.

Location: OS Ref. TM084 343. 2m E of A12 on B1070, Manningtree Rd, on the edge of East Bergholt.

Opening Times: Mar - Sept: daily, 10am - 5pm. Closed Easter Sun.

Admission: Adult £2, Child Free. (Proceeds to garden up-keep).

By arrangement.

EUSTON HALL

Tel: 01842 766366 **Fax:** 01842 766764

Estate Office, Euston, Thetford, Norfolk IP24 2QP

Owner: The Duke of Grafton **Contact:** Mrs L Campbell

18th century house contains a famous collection of paintings including works by Stubbs, Van Dyck, Lely and Kneller. The Pleasure Grounds were were laid out by John Evelyn and William Kent. 17th century parish church in Wren style. River walk, watermill and picnic area.

Location: OS Ref. TL897 786. 12m N of Bury St Edmunds, on A1088. 2m E of A134.

Opening Times: 1 Jun - 28 Sept: Thurs 2.30 - 5pm. Also Suns 25 Jun & 3 Sept: 2.30 - 5pm.

Admission: Adult £3, Child 50p, OAP £2.50. Groups (12+): Adult £2.50, Child 50p.

Grounds suitable.

FLATFORD BRIDGE COTTAGE

Tel: 01206 298260 **Fax:** 01206 299193

Flatford, East Bergholt, Colchester, Essex CO7 6OL

Owner: The National Trust **Contact:** The Property Manager

Just upstream from Flatford Mill, the restored thatched cottage houses a display about John Constable, several of whose paintings depict this property. Facilities include a tea garden, shop, boat hire, an Information Centre and countryside walks.

Location: OS Ref. TM077 332. On N bank of Stour, 1m S of East Bergholt B1070.

Opening Times: Mar & Oct - 19 Dec: Wed - Sun; Apr - end Sept: daily. Times: Mar, Apr & Oct: 11am - 5.30pm; May - Sept: 10am - 5.30pm. Nov - Feb: Sats & Suns, 11am - 3pm.

Admission: Guided walks £1.80, accompanied child Free. Car park charge (NT members included).

Ground floor suitable. WC. Guide dogs only.

FRAMLINGHAM CASTLE

FRAMLINGHAM, SUFFOLK IP8 9BT

Owner: *English Heritage* ***Contact:*** *The Custodian*

Tel: 01728 724189

A superb 12th century castle which, from the outside, looks almost the same as when it was built. From the continuous curtain wall linking 13 towers, there are excellent views of Framlingham and the charming reed-fringed mere. At different times the castle has been a fortress, an Elizabethan prison, a poor house and a school. The many alterations over the years have led to a pleasing mixture of historic styles.

Location: OS Ref. TM287 637. In Framlingham on B1116. NE of town centre.

Opening Times: 1 Apr - 31 Oct: daily 10am - 6pm (5pm in Oct). 1 Nov - 31 Mar: daily 10am - 4pm. Closed 24 - 26 Dec & 1 Jan.

Admission: Adult £3.20, Child £1.60, Conc. £2.40. 15% discount for groups (11+).

Ground floor & grounds suitable. WCs. Tel. for details.

Special Events Index

PAGE 40

GAINSBOROUGH'S HOUSE

46 GAINSBOROUGH ST, SUDBURY, SUFFOLK CO10 2EU

Owner: *Gainsborough's House Society* **Contact:** *Rosemary Woodward*

Tel: 01787 372958 **Fax:** 01787 376991 **e-mail:** mail@gainsborough.org

Birthplace of Thomas Gainsborough RA (1727-88). Georgian-fronted town house, with attractive walled garden, displays more of the artist's work than any other gallery. The collection is shown together with 18th century furniture and memorabilia. Varied programme of contemporary exhibitions organised throughout the year includes: fine art, craft, photography, printmaking, sculpture and highlights the work of East Anglian artists.

Location: OS Ref. TL872 413. 46 Gainsborough Street, Sudbury town centre.

Opening Times: All year: Tue - Sat, 10am - 5pm, Suns & BH Mons, 2 - 5pm. Closes at 4pm Nov - Mar. Closed: Mons, Good Fri and Christmas to New Year.

Admission: Adult £3, Child/Student £1.50, OAP £2.50.

No photography. Ground floor suitable. WCs.
No parking.

HELMINGHAM HALL GARDENS

STOWMARKET, SUFFOLK IP14 6EF

Owner: *The Lord & Lady Tollemache* **Contact:** *Ms Jane Tresidder*

Tel: 01473 890363 **Fax:** 01473 890776

The Tudor Hall surrounded by its wide moat is set in a 400 acre deer park. Two superb gardens, one surrounded by its own moat and walls extends to several acres and has wide herbaceous borders and an immaculate kitchen garden. The second enclosed within yew hedges, has a special rose garden with a herb and knot garden containing plants grown in England before 1750.

Location: OS Ref. TM190 578. B1077, 9m N of Ipswich, 5m S of Debenham.

Opening Times: Gardens only: 30 Apr - 10 Sept: Suns, 2 - 6pm. Groups: by appointment only on Weds, 2 - 5pm. (We can also accept individual bookings on a Wed if a group is booked.)

Admission: Adult £3.75, Child (5-15yrs) £2. Groups (30+) £3.25. Weds: £3.75pp.

Grounds suitable. WCs. By arrangement.
In grounds, on leads.

HADLEIGH GUILDHALL

Tel: 01473 827752

Hadleigh, Suffolk IP7 5DT

Owner: Hadleigh Market Feoffment Charity **Contact:** Jane Haylock

Fine timber framed guildhall, one of the least known medieval buildings in Suffolk.

Location: OS Ref. TM025 425. In centre of Hadleigh.

Opening Times: Jun - Sept: Thurs & Suns, 2 - 5pm

Admission: £1.50, Conc. £1. Garden only: Free.

HAUGHLEY PARK

Tel: 01359 240701

Stowmarket, Suffolk IP14 3JY

Owner/Contact: R J Williams Esq

Jacobean manor house, garden and woodland walks.

Location: OS Ref. TM005 618. 4m W of Stowmarket signed off A14.

Opening Times: Garden only: May - Sept: Tues & 1st two Suns in May, 2 - 5.30pm. House open by prior appointment at the same times (tel: 01359 240701).

Admission: Adult £2, Child £1.

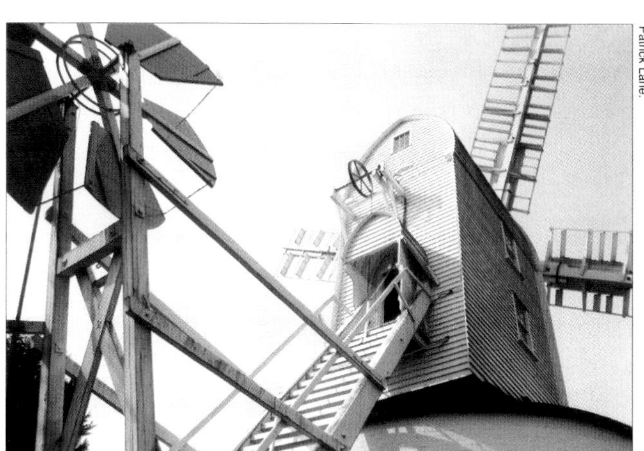

Patrick Lane.

Saxstead Green Post Mill, Suffolk.

ICKWORTH HOUSE, PARK & GARDEN

Tel: 01284 735270 **Fax:** 01284 735175 **e-mail:** arore@smtp.ntrust.org.uk

The Rotunda, Horringer, Bury St Edmunds IP29 5QE

Owner: The National Trust **Contact:** The Property Manager

One of the most unusual houses in East Anglia. The huge Rotunda of this 18th century Italianate house dominates the landscape. Inside are collections of Georgian silver, Regency furniture, Old Master paintings and family portraits.

Location: OS155 Ref. TL816 613. In Horringer, 3m SW of Bury St Edmunds on W side of A143.

Opening Times: House: 18 Mar - 29 Oct: daily except Mons & Thurs (open BH Mons), 1 - 5pm, last admission 4.30pm (closes 4.30pm in Oct). Garden: 18 Mar - 29 Oct: daily, 10am - 5pm, last admission 4.30pm. 1 Nov - end Mar 2001: daily except Sats & Suns, 10am - 4pm. Park: daily, 7am - 7pm. Garden & Park closed 25 Dec.

Admission: Adult £5.50, Child £2.40. Family discounts. Park & Garden only: Adult £2.40, Child 80p. Groups (must book):Adult £4.50, Child £1.90. No group discounts on Suns & BH Mons.

Partially suitable. Licensed. By arrangement.
In park, on leads. Tel. for details.

KENTWELL HALL

See page 247 for full page entry.

LANDGUARD FORT 

Tel: 01394 277767

Felixstowe, Suffolk

Owner: English Heritage **Contact:** The Custodian

Impressive 18th century fort with later additions built on a site originally fortified by Henry VIII and in use until after World War II. There is also a museum (not EH).

Location: OS Ref. TM284 318. 1m S of Felixstowe at extreme S end of dock area.

Opening Times: Museum: Easter, 4/5 April, 2 May - 10 Oct: Suns & BHs , 10.30am - 5pm. 15 June - 18 Sept, Tues, Weds & Sats, 1 - 5pm

Admission: Charge.

LAVENHAM: THE GUILDHALL OF CORPUS CHRISTI

Tel: 01787 247646

The Market Place, Lavenham, Sudbury CO10 9QZ **e-mail:** almjtg@smtp.ntrust.org.uk

Owner: The National Trust **Contact:** The Property Manager

This splendid 16th century timber-framed building dominates the Market Place of the picturesque town of Lavenham with its many historic houses and wonderful church. Inside are exhibitions on local history, farming and industry, as well as the story of the medieval woollen cloth trade. There is also a walled garden with dye plants.

Location: OS155 Ref. TL915 942. 6m NNE of Sudbury. Village centre. A1141 and B1071.

Opening Times: Mar & Nov: Sats & Suns, 11am - 4pm. 1 - 20 Apr: Thur - Sun (closed Good Fri), 11am - 5pm. 22 Apr - 5 Nov: daily, 11am - 5pm. The building, or parts of it, may be closed occasionally for community use.

Admission: Adult £3, accompanied child Free. Groups: £2.50. School parties (by arrangement) 60p per child.

 Partially suitable.

LEISTON ABBEY

Tel: 01604 730320 (Regional Office)

Leiston, Suffolk

Owner: English Heritage **Contact:** The Midlands Regional Office

The remains of this abbey for Premonstratensian canons, including a restored chapel, are amongst the most extensive in Suffolk.

Location: OS Ref. TM445 642. 1m N of Leiston off B1069.

Opening Times: Any reasonable time.

Admission: Free.

LITTLE HALL

Tel: 01787 247179 **Fax:** 01787 248341

Market Place, Lavenham, Suffolk CO10 9QZ

Owner: Suffolk Building Preservation Trust **Contact:** R Attew

Little Hall, a Grade II Listed Building with a Crown Post roof, reveals five centuries of change. Its history mirrors the rise and fall of Lavenham's cloth trade. Restored by the Gayer-Anderson twins in the 1930s.

Location: OS Ref. TL917 494. Market Place, Lavenham. 50yds E of Guildhall.

Opening Times: 1 Apr - end Oct: Weds, Thurs, Sats, Suns, 2 - 5pm. BHs: 11am - 5.30pm.

Admission: Adult £1.50, Child Free.

MANOR HOUSE MUSEUM

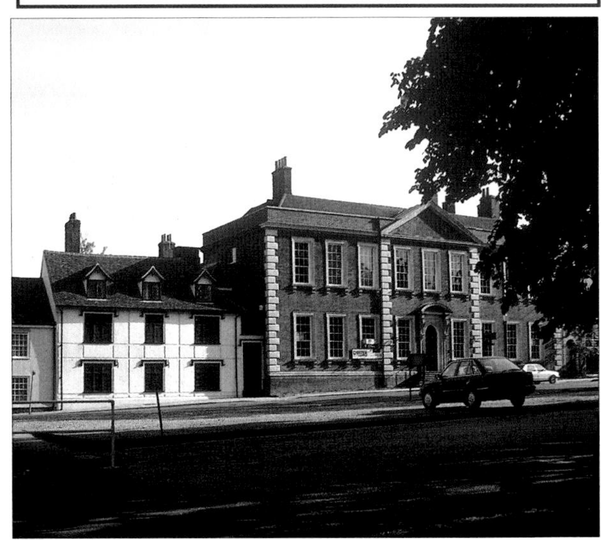

HONEY HILL, BURY ST EDMUNDS, SUFFOLK IP33 IHF

Owner: *St Edmundsbury Borough Council* ***Contact:*** *The Manager*

Tel: 01284 757076 **Fax:** 01284 757079

A Georgian town house, built by the Earl of Bristol for his wife Elizabeth between 1736 and 1737 as her town house in which she would entertain her friends during the day and into the evening, before returning to Ickworth House, the family seat. Extensive restoration in the '80s it now houses a collection of clocks, watches and wooden time pieces, a collection of costume, local and international artists. Also a friendly ghost.

Location: OS Ref. TL858 640. Bury town centre off A14. Just S of Abbey grounds.

Opening Times: 1 Feb - Sept: daily except Mons, 10am - 5pm. Oct - Mar 2001: 10am - 4pm.

Admission: Adult £3, Child £2, Family £8.

Tel. for details.

MELFORD HALL

Tel: 01787 880286

Long Melford, Sudbury, Suffolk CO10 9AH

Owner: The National Trust **Contact:** The Administrator

A turreted brick Tudor mansion, little changed since 1578 with the original panelled banqueting hall, an 18th century drawing room, a Regency library and Victorian bedrooms, showing fine furniture and Chinese porcelain.

Location: OS Ref. TL867 462. In Long Melford off A134, 14m S of Bury St Edmunds, 3m N of Sudbury.

Opening Times: Apr & Oct: Sat, Sun & BH Mon, 2 - 5.30pm. May - Sept: Wed - Sun & BH Mon, 2 - 5.30pm. Last admission 5pm.

Admission: £4.30. Groups (pre-arranged) £3.30. Wed - Sat only.

Stairlift to 1st floor. WC.

In car park & park walk only, on leads. Guide dogs only in Hall.

MOYSES HALL MUSEUM

Tel: 01284 757488 **Fax:** 01284 757079

Cornhill, Bury St Edmunds, Suffolk IP33 1DX

Owner: St Edmundsbury Borough Council **Contact:** The Gallery Supervisor

Very early 12th century flint house, now a museum of local history.

Location: OS Ref. TL853 644. Town centre off A14. 300 yds NW of Abbey grounds.

Opening Times: Daily: 10am - 5pm, except Suns: 2 - 5pm. Closed Good Fri, 25/26 Dec.

Admission: (from 1 April 2000) Adult £1.70, Child/Conc. £1.10, Family £5.20. Free for local residents of the borough.

ORFORD CASTLE

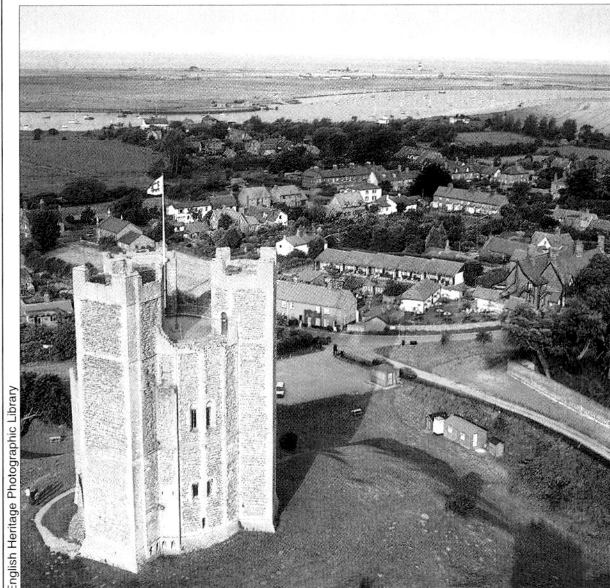

English Heritage Photographic Library

ORFORD, WOODBRIDGE, SUFFOLK IP12 2ND

Owner: *English Heritage* ***Contact:*** *The Custodian*

Tel: 01394 450472

A royal castle built by Henry II for coastal defence in the 12th century. A magnificent keep survives almost intact with three immense towers reaching to 30m (90ft). Fine views over Orford and the surrounding countryside.

Location: OS169 Ref. TM419 499. In Orford on B1084, 20m NE of Ipswich.

Opening Times: 1 Apr - 31 Oct: daily 10am - 6pm (5pm in Oct). 1 Nov - 31 Mar: Wed - Sun, 10am - 4pm. Closed 1 - 2pm. Closed 24 - 26 Dec & 1 Jan.

Admission: Adult £2.60, Child £1.30, Conc. £2. 15% discount for groups (11+).

Tel. for details.

Open all Year Index
PAGE 52

OTLEY HALL

OTLEY, IPSWICH, SUFFOLK IP6 9PA

Owner: *Mr Nicholas Hagger* ***Contact:*** *Mrs Chris Buckle (Administrator)*

Tel: 01473 890264 **Fax:** 01473 890803

A stunning 15th century Moated Hall (Grade I), set in gardens and grounds of 10 acres, frequently described as "one of England's loveliest houses". Rich in history and architectural detail. Features of particular note are richly carved beams, superb linenfold, c1559 wall paintings, herringbone brickwork and vine-leaf pargetting. From around 1401 Otley Hall was the home of the Gosnold family for some 300 years. Bartholomew Gosnold voyaged to the New World in 1602 and named Cape Cod and Martha's Vineyard. He returned in 1607 to found the Jamestown settlement, the first English-speaking settlement in the US, 13 years before the Mayflower landed. The account of the 1602 voyage is thought to have provided the geography for Shakespeare's *Tempest.* The Gardens are formal and informal, with canal, mount, nutteries, rose garden, woodland, and historically accurate Tudor features including a knot and herb garden, designed by Sylvia Landsberg (author of *The Medieval Garden*).

Location: OS Ref. TM207 563. 7m N of Ipswich, off the B1079.

Opening Times: Every BH Sun & Mon, 12.30 - 6pm. Gardens: Mons only from 10 Apr - 25 Sept, 2 - 5pm.

Admission: Adult £4.50, Child £2.50. Garden days: Adult £2.80, Child £1, OAP £2.60. Coach parties welcome all year by appointment for private guided tours.

Partially suitable. By arrangement. P

In grounds on leads.

PAKENHAM WATERMILL

Tel: 01359 270570

Mill Road, Pakenham, Bury St Edmunds, Suffolk

Owner: Suffolk Building Preservation Trust **Contact:** Roger Gillingham

Fine 18th century working watermill.

Location: OS Ref. TL937 694. Signposted from A143 Ixworth bypass.

Opening Times: 1 Apr - 30 Sept: Weds, Sats, Suns & BHs, 2 - 5.30pm.

Admission: Adult £2, Child £1.20, OAP £1.75.

ST EDMUNDSBURY CATHEDRAL

Tel: 01284 754933 **Fax:** 01284 768655

Angel Hill, Bury St Edmunds, Suffolk IP33 1LS **e-mail:** cathedral@btconnect.com

Owner: The Church of England **Contact:** Charles Borthwick

At the heart of Christian worship since Saxon times, evidence of previous churches is visible. The elegant, English Perpendicular 16th century Nave of St James' survived its patron, the once great, now ruined, Abbey of St Edmund, to become the Cathedral of Suffolk in 1914. It was skilfully extended with Quire and Crossing in the 1960s and a magnificent gothic-style lantern tower, Transept and Apostles' Chapel, will complete the Cathedral to mark the millennium. Dedication to St James, Patron Saint of Pilgrims, is subtly reflected in architectural hints of Spain.

Location: OS Ref. TL857 642. Bury St Edmunds town centre.

Opening Times: All year: daily 8.30am - 6pm, Jun - Aug: 8.30am - 8pm.

Admission: Donation invited.

Partially suitable. WC. Licensed. By arrangement.

Guide dogs only.

SAXTEAD GREEN POST MILL

Tel: 01728 685789

Post Hill Bungalow, Saxtead Green, Woodbridge, Suffolk IP13 9QQ

Owner: English Heritage **Contact:** The Custodian

The finest example of a Suffolk Post Mill. Still in working order, you can climb the wooden stairs to the various floors, full of fascinating mill machinery. Ceased production in 1947.

Location: OS Ref. TM253 645. $2^1/_2$ m NW of Framlingham on A1120.

Opening Times: 1 Apr - 31 Oct: Mon - Sat, 10am - 6pm (5pm in Oct). Closed 1 - 2pm.

Admission: Adult £2.10, Child £1.10, Conc. £1.60.

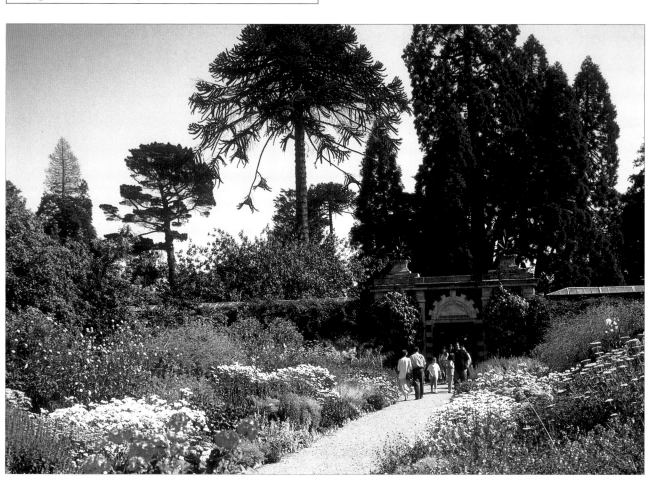

Somerleyton Hall, Suffolk.

SHRUBLAND PARK GARDENS

Tel: 01473 830221 Fax: 01473 832202

Ipswich, Suffolk IP6 9QQ

Owner/Contact: Lord de Suamarez

One of the finest examples of an Italianate garden in England, designed by Sir Charles Barry.

Location: OS Ref. TM125 525. 6m N of Ipswich to the E of A14/A140.

Opening Times: 9 Apr - 24 Sept: Suns & BH Mons, 2 - 5pm.

Admission: Adult £2.50, Child/OAP £1.50.

SOMERLEYTON HALL & GARDENS

SOMERLEYTON, LOWESTOFT, SUFFOLK NR32 5QQ

Owner/Contact: *The Rt Hon Lord Somerleyton GCVO*

Tel: 01502 730224 office or 01502 732950 (Entrance Gate) **Fax:** 01502 732143

Splendid early Victorian mansion built in Anglo-Italian style by Sir Morton Peto, with lavish architectural features, magnificent carved stonework and fine state rooms. Paintings by Landseer, Wright of Derby and Stanfield, wood carvings by Willcox of Warwick and Grinling Gibbons. Somerleyton's 12-acre gardens are justly renowned with beautiful borders, specimen trees and the 1846 yew hedge maze which ranks amongst the finest in the country. Special features include glasshouses by Paxton, 300ft pergola, walled garden, Vulliamy tower clock, Victorian ornamentation.

Location: OS134 Ref. TM493 977. 5m NW of Lowestoft on B1074, 7m SW of Great Yarmouth off A143.

Opening Times: Easter Sun - Sept: Thurs, Suns, BHs. Jul & Aug: Tue - Thur, Suns & BHs. Gardens: 12.30 - 5.30pm. Hall: 1 - 5pm. Closed all other dates except by appointment. Private group tours by arrangement.

Admission: Adult £5, Child £2.50, OAP £4.80, Family (2+2) £14.20. Groups: Adult £4.50, Child/Student £2.30. Prices and opening times subject to review.

No photography in house. Receptions/functions/conferences. By arrangement.

SOUTH ELMHAM HALL

Tel: 01986 782526 **Fax:** 01986 782203

St Cross, Harleston, Norfolk IP20 0PZ **e-mail:** jo.sanderson@btinternet.com

Owner: John Sanderson **Contact:** Jo & John Sanderson

A Grade I listed medieval manor house set inside moated enclosure. Originally built by the Bishop of Norwich around 1270. Much altered in the 16th century. Self guided trail through former deer park to South Elmham Minster, a ruined Norman chapel with Saxon origins.

Location: OS30 Ref. TM778 324. Between Harleston and Bungay from the A143 take the B1062 signposted 'Farm Walks'.

Opening Times: House: selected days, May, Jun, Jul, please contact property for details. Grounds & Minster: All year, daily except Christmas Day.

Admission: House: Adult £6, Child £2. Groups (12 - 50): Adult £4, Child £1, tours available all year except Aug, larger groups can be taken around grounds.

Not suitable. By arrangement. Limited for coaches. In grounds on leads. 3 doubles.

THE TIDE MILL

Tel: 01473 626618

Woodbridge, Ipswich, Suffolk

Owner/Contact: Geoff Gostling

First recorded in 1170, now fully restored, machinery demonstrated at low tide. Ring for wheel turning times.

Location: OS Ref. TM275 487. By riverside 1/4 m SE of Woodbridge town centre. 1 1/4 m off A12.

Opening Times: Easter, then May - Sept: daily. Apr & Oct: Sats & Suns only, 11am - 5pm.

Admission: Adult £1, Child/Student 50p, Family £2.50.

WINGFIELD OLD COLLEGE & GDNS

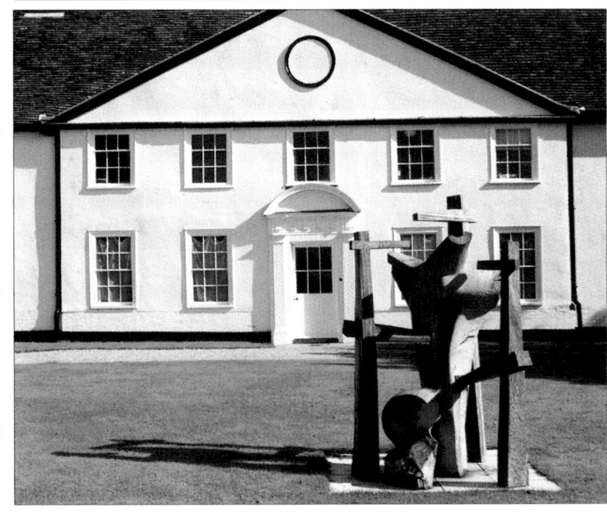

WINGFIELD, Nr STRADBROKE, SUFFOLK IP21 5RA

Owner: *Mr & Mrs Ian Chance* ***Contact:*** *Mrs H Chance*

Tel: 01379 384888 **Fax:** 01379 388082

Delightful family home with walled gardens. Lovely old Suffolk house with spectacular medieval great hall, contemporary art, garden sculpture, collections of ceramics and textiles, 4 acres of gardens with topiary, ponds and old roses, in unspoilt Suffolk countryside. Steeped in history, this "oasis of arts and heritage" offers an afternoon of discovery and relaxation. Children's play garden, teas in the new creative arts visitor centre.

Location: OS Ref. TM230 767. Signposted off B1118 (2m N of Stradbroke) and B1116 at Fressingfield.

Opening Times: 22 Apr - 30 Sept: Sats & Suns, 2 - 6pm.

Admission: Adult £3.60, Child/Student £1.50, OAP £3, Family £8.50 (1999 prices).

Wedding receptions. By arrangement for groups. Guide dogs only.

WYKEN HALL GARDENS

STANTON, BURY ST EDMUNDS, SUFFOLK IP31 2DW

Owner: *Sir Kenneth & Lady Carlisle* ***Contact:*** *Mrs Barbara Hurn*

Tel: 01359 250287 **Fax:** 01359 252256

The Elizabethan manor house is surrounded by a romantic, plant-lover's garden with maze, knot and herb garden and rose garden featuring old roses. A walk through ancient woodlands leads to Wyken Vineyards, winner of EVA Wine of the Year. In the 16th century barn, the Vineyard Restaurant now featured in the *Good Food Guide*, serves a range of Wyken wines along with a menu of fresh fish, game and vegetables from the kitchen garden.

Location: OS Ref. TL963 717. 9m NE of Bury St. Edmunds 1m E of A143. Follow brown tourist signs to Wyken Vineyards from Ixworth.

Opening Times: 14 Jan - 24 Dec: Wed - Sun & BH Mons, 10am - 6pm. Book for meals in The Leaping Hare Café at Wyken Vineyards, Fris & Sats dinner from 7pm. Garden closed on Sats. Gardens only: 1 Apr - 1 Oct.

Admission: Gardens: Adult £2.50, Child (under 12yrs) Free, Conc. £2. Groups (30+) by appointment on Weds.

 Grounds suitable. WC.  Licensed. In grounds, on leads. 

Kentwell Hall, Suffolk

The Midlands

Eastnor Castle, Herefordshire.

Featuring...

Eastnor Castle

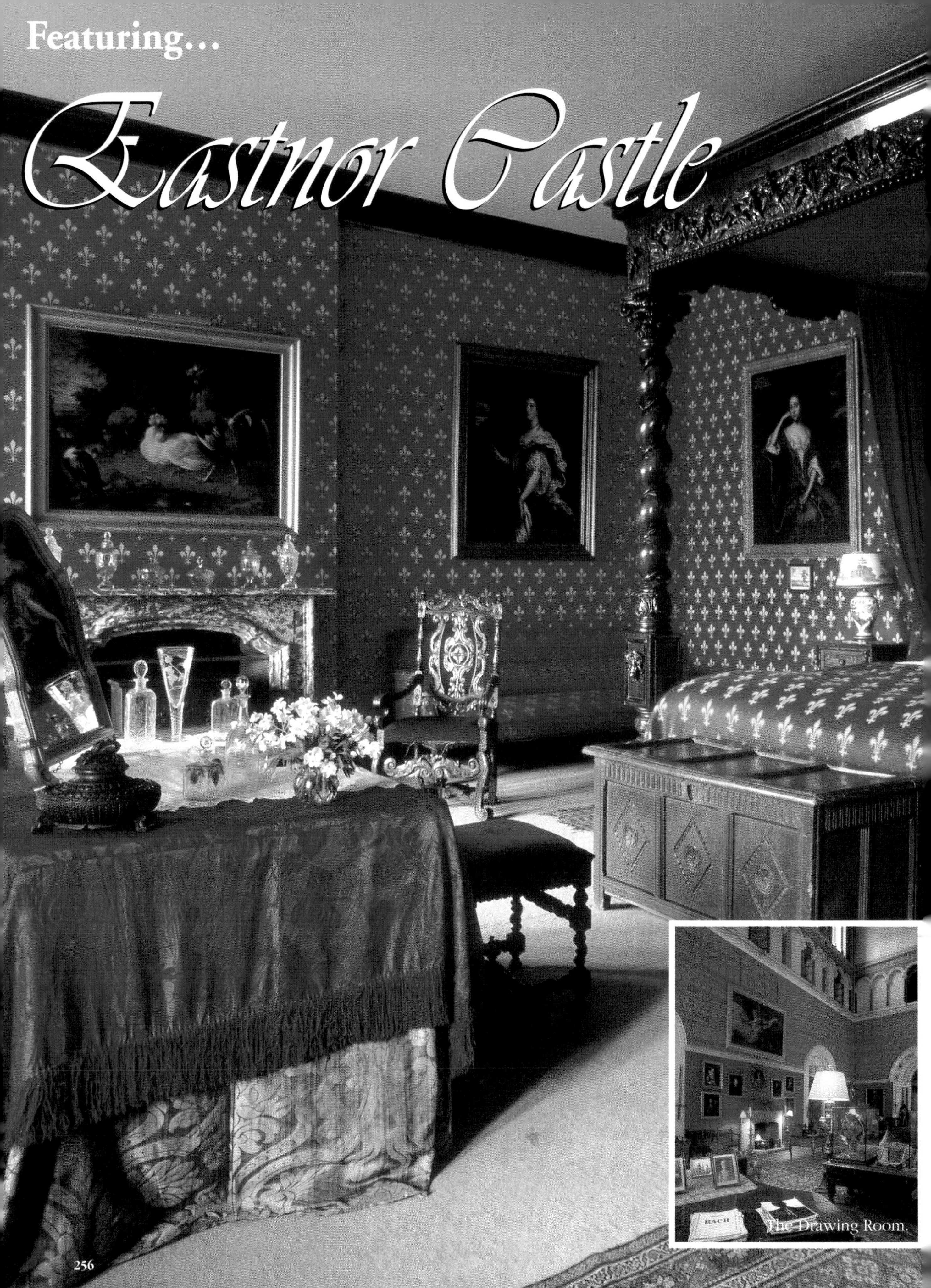

The Drawing Room.

The Red Bedroom.

The Library.

The imposing mass and enormous turreted scale of Eastnor Castle, dramatically set against the Malvern Hills near Ledbury in Herefordshire, aptly reflects the swaggering, extrovert personality of its creator, John Cocks, Lord Lieutenant of Herefordshire and the future Earl Somers. Having made the family's fortunes in banking, no expense was to be spared in reflecting what he saw to be the family's important standing in society.

Eastnor was designed and built by Robert Smirke, who was later to design the British Museum. Like so many Georgian Gothic buildings, Eastnor lies somewhere between the medieval and classical. The desire to impress is illustrated by the huge 60ft entrance hall whilst the Cloverleaf Towers, which jut out diagonally from each of the four corners of the main building, make the structure appear even more massive and flamboyant.

Robert Smirke presented his final bill for works in 1817, by which time £82,000 had been spent on the building of Eastnor. Even for this sum, many parts of the interior of the castle, remained little more than a shell. The Entrance Hall, Great Staircase and Dining Room retain Smirke's original decorative schemes – it took different members of the family a further century to make other areas of the Castle habitable and equally impressive. The Gothic Drawing Room survives largely unchanged from when it was redecorated by the Crace brothers to the designs of A W Pugin for the 2nd Earl in 1849. Apparently the extravagance of the work caused such a stir in the neighbourhood at the time, that it was believed the Queen was planning to visit.

Eastnor of the 1990s is owned James Hervey-Bathurst who, with his wife Sarah and young family, took over the running of the estate in 1988. Today the Castle lies at the centre of a 5,000 acre agricultural and sporting estate; but at its most impressive the family's lands exceeded 13,000 acres. Since the 1900s Eastnor's fortunes had gradually declined. The house was left unoccupied in the late 1920s and early 30s while James' grandparents moved to Australia when his grandfather was appointed Governor.

In 1939 on the outbreak of the Second World War, the Castle contents were removed, leaving it available for Government use if necessary. This did not happen, but at the end of the War when James' grandmother returned to the Castle, it was a shadow of its former self. Reduced to living mostly in the servants' wing, the family found themselves hard hit by death duties, which amounted to £200,000, the equivalent of £4.6 million today.

Yet Eastnor has survived – due in great part to the will and imagination of it current owners. Under James' parents tough decisions had to be made to sell part of the Castle's collection, to finance capital tax bills and to begin to reinvest in a modernisation programme for the estate.

It is, however, under the custodianship of the present owners that Eastnor's fortunes have revived. Benefiting from English Heritage grants, major external repairs have been carried out on the Castle. Sarah Hervey-Bathurst has master-minded the redecoration of many of the rooms in Eastnor to their original brilliance - new furnishings have been bought, and furniture has apparently even been borrowed from other members of the family to fill the gaps! All this to develop a successful corporate entertainment business and thereby ensure the long-term future of the house and estate. The enormity of this task for the family does not diminish, but having successfully started a wedding and conference business they have brought Eastnor back to life for all of us to enjoy.

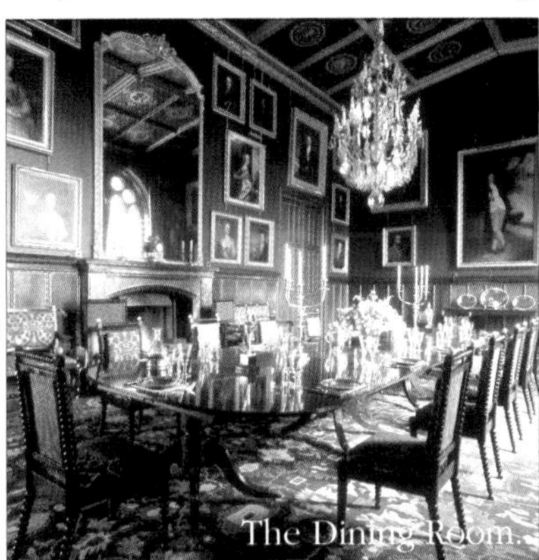

The Dining Room.

For full details of this property see page 274.

Owner: Trustees of the Chatsworth Settlement. Home of the Duke & Duchess of Devonshire

CONTACT

Mr John Oliver
Chatsworth
Bakewell
Derbyshire
DE45 1PP

Tel: 01246 582204
01246 565300

Fax: 01246 583536

LOCATION

OS Ref. SK260 703

From London 3 hrs M1/J29, signposted via Chesterfield.

3m E of Bakewell, off B6012, 10m W of Chesterfield.

Rail: Chesterfield Station, 11m.

Bus: Chesterfield - Baslow, $1^1/_2$ m.

CONFERENCE/FUNCTION		
ROOM	SIZE	MAX CAPACITY
Hartington Rm.		70
Coffee Rm.		24

CHATSWORTH
Bakewell

The great Treasure House of Chatsworth was first built by Bess of Hardwick in 1552 and has been lived in by the Cavendish family, the Dukes of Devonshire, ever since. The House today owes its appearance to the 1st Duke who remodelled the building at the end of the 17th century, while the 6th Duke added a wing 130 years later. Visitors can see 26 rooms including the run of 5 virtually unaltered 17th century State Rooms and Chapel. There are painted ceilings by Verrio, Thornhill and Laguerre, furniture by William Kent and Boulle, tapestries from Mortlake and Brussels, a library of over 17,000 volumes, sculpture by Cibber and Canova, old master paintings by Rembrandt, Hals, Van Dyck, Tintoretto, Veronese, Landseer and Sargent; the collection of neo-classical sculpture, Oriental and European porcelain and the dazzling silver collection, including an early English silver chandelier. The present Duke has added to the collection. In 2000, to celebrate their 50th year at Chatsworth, the Duke and Duchess have chosen favourite treasures from the private collection to show visitors, from illuminated manuscripts to Lucian Freud portraits. In 1996, Chatsworth was voted the public's favourite house, winning the first NPI National Heritage Gold Award.

GARDEN

The 105 acre garden was created during three great eras in garden and landscape design. The 200 metre Cascade, the Willow Tree fountain and the Canal survive from the 1st Duke's formal garden. 'Capability' Brown landscaped the garden and park in the 1760s. The 6th Duke's gardener, Sir Joseph Paxton, built rockeries and designed a series of glasshouses. He also created the Emperor fountain, the tallest gravity-fed fountain in the world. More recent additions include the Rose, Cottage and Kitchen gardens, the Serpentine Hedge and the Maze. In 1999, a new water sculpture, Revelation, was unveiled.

Farmyard and Adventure Playground. Guide book translations and audio guides in French, German, Italian, Spanish and Japanese.

No wheelchairs in house, but welcome in garden (3 electric, 7 standard available). WCs. Special leaflet.

New rooms available for conferences and private functions. Contact Head of Catering.

Restaurant (max 300); home-made food. Menus on request.

Private tours of house or Greenhouses and Behind the Scenes Days, by arrangement only (extra charges apply). Tape recorded tour may be hired at entrance. Groups please pre-book.

Cars 100 yds, Coaches 25 yds from house.

Guided tours, packs, trails and school room. Free preliminary visit recommended.

OPENING TIMES

SUMMER
15 March - 29 October

Daily: 11am - 4.30pm.

WINTER
Closed.

The Park is open free throughout the year.

ADMISSION

House & Garden

Adult	£6.75
Child	£3.00
OAP/Student	£5.50
Family	£16.75
Pre-booked groups	
Adult	£6.00
School (no tour)	£3.00
School (w/tour)	£3.50
OAP/Student	£4.75

Garden only

Adult	£3.85
Child	£1.75
OAP/Student	£3.00
Family	£9.50

Scots Suite

Adult	£1.00
Child	£0.50
Car Park	£1.00

Farmyard & Adventure Playground

All	£3.50
Groups (5+)	£3.00
OAP/School	£2.80

SPECIAL EVENTS

- **MAY 6 - 7:** Chatsworth Angling Fair.
- **MAY 13 - 14:** Horse Trials.
- **SEPT 2 - 3:** Chatsworth Country Fair.

HADDON HALL
Bakewell

Owner:
Lord Edward Manners

CONTACT

Janet O'Sullivan
Estate Office
Haddon Hall
Bakewell
Derbyshire
DE45 1LA

Tel: 01629 812855

Fax: 01629 814379

LOCATION

OS Ref. SK234 663

From London 3 hrs
Sheffield $^{1}/_{2}$ hr
Manchester 1 hr
Haddon is on the E side of A6 $1^{1}/_{2}$ m S of Bakewell.
M1/J30.

Rail: Chesterfield Station, 12m.

Bus: Chesterfield Bakewell.

William the Conqueror's illegitimate son, Peverel, and his descendants held Haddon for a hundred years before it passed into the hands of the Vernons. Over the following four centuries, the existing medieval and Tudor manor house developed from its Norman origins. In the late 16th century, the estate passed through marriage to the Manners family, later to become Dukes of Rutland, in whose possession it has remained ever since.

Little has been added since the reign of Henry VIII, whose elder brother, Arthur, was a frequent guest of the Vernons. He would have been quite familiar with the house as it stands today – the Great Hall, kitchens and Chapel all dating from the 14th century. Incredibly, despite its time worn steps, no other medieval house has so triumphantly withstood the passage of time. *Jane Eyre* (1996), *The Prince and the Pauper* (1996) and *Elizabeth* (1997) were filmed at Haddon.

GARDENS

The award-winning terraced Rose Gardens are planned for year-round colour. Over 150 varieties of rose and clematis, many over 70 years old, provide colour and scent throughout the summer.

Recent productions testify to Haddon's suitability as a film location: *Jane Eyre* (1996) Rochester Films; *Prince and the Pauper* (1996) BBC; *Elizabeth I* (1997).

Not suitable, steep approach, varying levels of house.

Self-service restaurant (max 75). Home-made food.

Special tours £25 extra for groups of 15, 7 days' notice.

Ample, 450 yds from house. 50p per car.

Tours of the house bring alive Haddon Hall of old. Costume room also available, very popular!

Guide dogs only.

OPENING TIMES

SUMMER
1 April - 30 September
(closed Sun 16 July)

Daily: 10.30am - 5.45pm
Last admission 5pm.

October: Mon - Thur
10.30am - 4.30pm
Last admission 4pm.

WINTER
November - 31 March
Closed.

ADMISSION

SUMMER

Adult	£5.75
Child (5 -15yrs)	£3.00
Conc.	£4.75
Family (2+3)	£15.00
Groups (20+)	
Adult	£4.75
Child (5 -15yrs)	£2.50
Conc.	£4.00

SPECIAL EVENTS

- **APR 9:** Elizabethan Dancers.
- **JUN 24 - 30** Flower Festival.
- **JUL 9:** Elizabethan Dancers.
- **SEP 10:** Elizabethan Dancers.

BAKEWELL OLD HOUSE MUSEUM

Tel: 01629 815294

Cunningham Place, Bakewell DE45 1DD

Owner: Bakewell District Historical Society **Contact:** The Secretary

A rare and curious Peakland house built by Ralf Gell in 1534.

Location: OS Ref. SK215 685. 100 yds W of Bakewell Parish Church.

Opening Times: Please contact for details.

Admission: Adult £2.50, Child £1, Child under 5yrs free. (1999 prices.)

BOLSOVER CASTLE

English Heritage Photographic Library

CASTLE STREET, BOLSOVER, DERBYSHIRE S44 6PR

Owner: *English Heritage* **Contact:** *The Custodian*

Tel: 01246 823349/822844

An enchanting and romantic spectacle, situated high on a wooded hilltop dominating the surrounding landscape. Built on the site of a Norman castle, this is largely an early 17th century mansion. Most delightful is the 'Little Castle', a bewitching folly with intricate carvings, panelling and wall painting. There is also an impressive 17th century indoor Riding School built by the Duke of Newcastle. A new Visitor Centre has been completed and a wedding ceremony licence applied for.

Location: OS120, Ref. SK471 707. Off M1/J29, 6m from Mansfield. In Bolsover 6m E of Chesterfield on A632.

Opening Times: 1 Apr - 31 Oct: daily, 10am - 6pm (5pm in Oct). 1 Nov - 31 Mar: Wed - Sun, 10am - 4pm. Closed 24 - 26 Dec & 1 Jan.

Admission: Adult £4.20, Child £2.10, Conc. £3.20. 15% discount for groups (11+).

Grounds suitable. WC. Tel. for details.

CALKE ABBEY

Tel: 01332 863822 **Fax:** 01332 865272

Ticknall, Derbyshire DE73 1LE

Owner: The National Trust **Contact:** The Property Manager

The house that time forgot, this baroque mansion, built 1701 - 3 for Sir John Harpur and set in a landscaped park. Little restored, Calke is preserved by a programme of conservation as a graphic illustration of the English country house in decline; it contains the family's collection of natural history, a magnificent 18th century state bed and interiors that are virtually unchanged since the 1880s. Walled garden, pleasure grounds and recently restored orangery. Early 19th century Church. Historic parkland with Portland sheep and deer. Staunton Harold Church is nearby.

Location: OS128 Ref. SK356 239. 10m S of Derby, on A514 at Ticknall between Swadlincote and Melbourne.

Opening Times: House, Garden & Church: 27 Mar - 1 Nov: Sat - Wed & BH Mons (closed 1pm Good Fri). House & Church: 1 - 5.30pm (last admission 5pm), Garden: 11am - 5.30pm (last adm. 5pm). Park: Most days until 9pm or dusk if earlier. Ticket office from 11am. Closed Sat 12 Aug for concert.

Admission: All sites: Adult £5.10, Child £2.50, Family £12.70. Garden only: £2.40. Discount for pre-booked groups.

House suitable. Braille guide. Wheelchairs. WCs. Licensed.

By arrangement. In park, on leads only.

Open all Year Index PAGE 52

CARNFIELD HALL

SOUTH NORMANTON, Nr ALFRETON, DERBYSHIRE DE55 2BE

Owner/Contact: *J B Cartland*

Tel: 01773 520084

Unspoilt Elizabethan 'Mansion House'. Panelled rooms, two 17th century staircases, great chamber. From 1502 the seat of the Revell, Wilmot and Cartland families. Atmospheric interior with three centuries of portraits, furniture, china, needlework, costumes, royal relics and manorial documents. Guided tours by the owner. Fine fan and costume collection, if booked for groups in advance, and candlelit evening visits.

Location: OS Ref. SK425 561. 1 1/2 m W of M1/J28 on B6019. Alfreton Station 5 mins walk.

Opening Times: Spring & Summer BHs including Good Fri & Mon; Easter – 30 Sept: most weekends; Jul & Aug: Most Tues & Thurs; 2 - 5pm. By appointment throughout the year (including evenings) for groups (2-22). Winter: Some weekends if fine, 2 - 4pm. NB. Times may vary. Please telephone to confirm dates and times.

Admission: Adult £3.50, Child (8 - 16yrs) £2, Conc. £2.50. Groups: Adult £3, Child (8 - 16yrs) £1.50, Conc. £2. Groups must book. No reduction for evening visits.

No photography in Hall. Grounds suitable. WCs.
Licensed. Obligatory. In grounds, on leads only.

CATTON HALL

CATTON, WALTON-ON-TRENT, SOUTH DERBYSHIRE DE12 8LN

Owner/Contact: *Robin & Katie Neilson*

Tel: 01283 716311 **Fax:** 01283 712876 **e-mail:** kncatton@aol.com

Catton, built in 1745, has been in the hands of the same family since 1405 and is still lived in by the Neilsons as their private home. This gives the house a unique, relaxed and friendly atmosphere making guests feel at home whether they are inside for a formal occasion, or outside enjoying activities from a marquee. The 100 acres of parkland are ideal for all types of outdoor events. Corporate multi-activity days, management training sessions and the more traditional country sports of shooting, fishing or falconry can be arranged. There is also a small private chapel which is ideal for special weddings.

Location: OS Ref. SK206 154. 2m E of A38 at Alrewas between Lichfield & Burton-on-Trent (8m from each). Birmingham NEC 20m.

Opening Times: By arrangement only: Corporate entertainment, management training, multi-activity days, wedding receptions, fairs, dinners, 4 x 4 course, etc.

Conference facilities. By arrangement. By arrangement.
3 x four posters, 5 twin, all en-suite.

CHATSWORTH

See page 258 for full page entry.

CROMFORD MILL (SIR RICHARD ARKWRIGHT'S) Tel/Fax: 01629 823256

Cromford, Nr Matlock, Derbyshire DE4 3RQ **Contact:** The Visitor Services Dept.

Built in 1771, Cromford Mill is the world's first successful water powered cotton spinning mill. Set in the beautiful Derwent Valley surrounded by gritstone tors and rolling hills. There is a wholefood restaurant on site with shops, free car parking and friendly staff. A tour guide will explain the story of this important historic site and describe the development plans for the future.

Location: OS Ref. SK296 569. 3m S of Matlock, 17m N of Derby just off A6.

Opening Times: All year except Christmas Day, 9am - 5pm.

Admission: Free entry. Guided tours: Adult £2, Conc. £1.50.

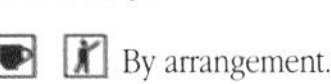 Partially suitable. WCs. 

In grounds, on leads.

ELVASTON CASTLE COUNTRY PARK Tel: 01332 571342 Fax: 01332 758751

Borrowash Road, Elvaston, Derbyshire DE72 3EP

Owner: Derbyshire County Council **Contact:** The Park Manager

200 acre park landscaped in 19th century. Walled garden. Estate museum with exhibitions of traditional crafts.

Location: OS Ref. SK407 330. 5m SE of Derby, 2m from A6 or A52.

Opening Times: Please contact park for details.

Admission: Museum: Adult £1.20, Child 60p, Family (2+2) £3. Park and Gardens free. Car park: Midweek 70p, weekends/BHs £1.30, Coaches £7.50.

Ground floor & grounds suitable. WCs. By arrangement.

In grounds, on leads.

EYAM HALL

EYAM, HOPE VALLEY, DERBYSHIRE S32 5QW

Owner: *Mr R H V Wright* ***Contact:*** *Mrs Nicola Wright*

Tel: 01433 631976 **Fax:** 01433 631603 **e-mail:** nicwri@globalnet.co.uk

This small but charming manor house in the famous plague village has been the home of the Wright family since 1671. The present family opened the house to the public in 1992, but it retains the intimate atmosphere of a much-loved private home. The Jacobean staircase, fine tapestries, family portraits and costumes and an impressive tester bed are among its interior treasures. Craft centre, buttery and shops in a historic farmyard, with crafts people at work and authentic local products for sale.

Location: OS119 Ref. SK216 765. Approx 10m from Sheffield, Chesterfield and Buxton. Eyam is off A623 between Stockport and Chesterfield. Eyam Hall is in the centre of the village, past the church.

Opening Times: Easter - Oct: Weds, Thurs, Suns & BH Mons: 11am - 4pm. Victorian Christmas Tours (booked groups only): 26 Nov - 16 Dec. Craft centre, buttery & gift shop: All year: daily except Mons, 10.30am - 5pm. Please phone for schools details.

Admission: Adult £4, Child £3, Conc. £3.50. Family (2+4) £12.50. Group rates available (must book for discount).

Craft centre. Partially suitable. WC.  Licensed.

Obligatory.

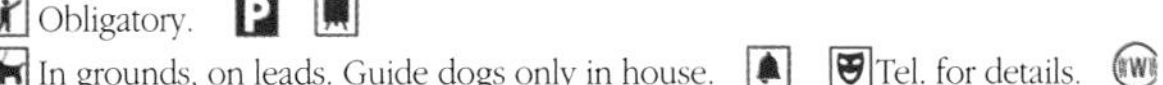

In grounds, on leads. Guide dogs only in house. Tel. for details.

HADDON HALL

See page 259 for full page entry.

HARDSTOFT HERB GARDEN Tel: 01246 854268

Hall View Cottage, Hardstoft, Chesterfield, Derbyshire S45 8AH

Owner: Mr Stephen Raynor/L M Raynor **Contact:** Mr Stephen Raynor

Consists of four display gardens with information boards and well labelled plants.

Location: OS Ref. SK438630. On B6039 between Holmewood & Tibshelf, 3m from J29 on M1.

Opening Times: 15 Mar - 15 Sept: daily (except Tues) 10am - 5pm. Closed Sunday follwing Aug BH weekend.

Admission: Adult £1, Child Free.

HARDWICK ESTATE - STAINSBY MILL Tel: 01246 850430

Stainsby, Chesterfield, Derbyshire S44 5QJ **Fax:** 01246 854200

Owner: The National Trust **Contact:** The Property Manager

18th century water-powered corn mill in working order.

Location: OS120 Ref. SK455 653. From M1/J29 take A6175, signposted to Clay Cross then first left and left again to Stainsby Mill.

Opening Times: 1 Apr - 31 Oct: Weds, Thurs, Sats, Suns & BH Mons, 11am - 4.30pm. Jun - Sept: also open Fris, 11am - 4.30pm. Last admission 4pm.

Admission: Adult £1.80, Child 90p, Family £4.50. No discounts for groups. School Groups: Weds & Thurs (plus Fri: Jun - Sept), for information send SAE to Property Manager at Hardwick Hall.

In park, on leads.

HARDWICK HALL Tel: 01246 850430 Fax: 01246 854200

Doe Lea, Chesterfield, Derbyshire S44 5QJ **Shop / Restaurant:** 01246 854088

Owner: The National Trust **Contact:** The Property Manager

A late 16th century 'prodigy house' designed by Robert Smythson for Bess of Hardwick. The house contains outstanding contemporary furniture, tapestries and needlework including pieces identified in an inventory of 1601; a needlework exhibition is on permanent display. Walled courtyards enclose fine gardens, orchards and a herb garden. The country park contains Whiteface Woodland sheep and Longhorn cattle.

Location: OS120 Ref. SK456 651. 7½ m NW of Mansfield, 9½ m SE of Chesterfield: approach from M1/J29 via A6175.

Opening Times: Hall: 1 Apr - 31 Oct: Weds, Thurs, Sats, Suns & BH Mons, 12.30 - 5pm (closed Good Fri). Last adm. to Hall 4.30pm. Garden: 1 Apr - 31 Oct: daily 12 noon - 5.30pm. Restaurant: open as per Hall: 12 noon - 2pm lunches, 2 - 4.45pm teas.

Admission: Hall & Garden: Adult £6, Child £3, Family £15. Garden only: Adult £3, Child £1.50, Family £7.50. Pre-booking for groups essential, discount for groups of 15+. Timed tickets on busy days, inc NT members. Joint ticket available (Old and New Hall).

House limited, garden suitable. Licensed. In park, on leads.

HARDWICK OLD HALL

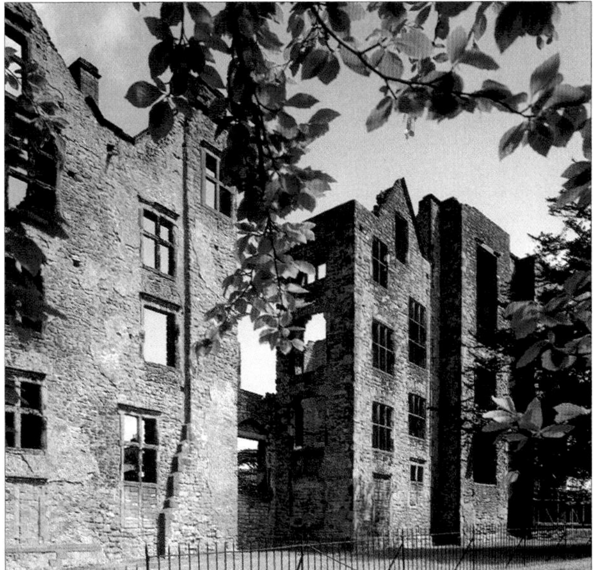

DOE LEA, Nr CHESTERFIELD, DERBYSHIRE S44 5QJ

Owner: *English Heritage* ***Contact:*** *The Custodian*

Tel: 01246 850431

This large ruined house, finished in 1591, still displays Bess of Hardwick's innovative planning and interesting decorative plasterwork. The views from the top floor over the country park and 'New' Hall are spectacular.

Location: OS120 Ref. SK463 638. 7½ m NW of Mansfield, 9½ m SE of Chesterfield, off A6175, from J29/M1.

Opening Times: 1 Apr - 31 Oct: Wed - Sun, 10am - 6pm (5pm in Oct).

Admission: Adult £2.60, Child £1.30, Conc. £2. 15% discount for groups (11+).

 On leads.

KEDLESTON HALL

Oliver Benn.

DERBY, DERBYSHIRE DE22 5JH

Owner: *The National Trust* ***Contact:*** *The Property Manager*

Tel: 01332 842191 **Fax:** 01332 841972

Experience the age of elegance in this neo-classical house built between 1759 and 1765 for the Curzon family and little altered since. Set in 800 acres of parkland with an 18th century pleasure ground, garden and woodland walks – a day at Kedleston is truly an experience to remember. The influence of the architect Robert Adam is everywhere, from the Park buildings to the decoration of the magnificent state rooms. Groups are welcome and an introductory talk can be arranged.

Location: OS Ref. SK312 403. 5m NW of Derby, signposted from roundabout where A38 crosses A52 Derby ring road.

Opening Times: House: 1 Apr - 31 Oct: Sat - Wed, 12 - 4.30pm. Last adm. 4pm. Park & Gardens: 11am - 6pm. Restaurant: 11am - 5pm. Shop: 11am - 5pm. Park only: Thur & Fri, 11am - 6pm, Vehicle charge.

Admission: Adult £5, Child £2.50, Family £12.50. Garden & Park: Adult £2.20, Child £1. Discount for groups, please telephone.

Stairclimber & Batricar. Licensed. In grounds, on leads.

SPECIAL EVENTS

MAY 27: Flower Festival. **JUL:** Outdoor Classical Concert with Fireworks.

Please telephone for a full list of Special Events at Kedleston Hall.

LEA GARDENS

Tel: 01629 534380/534260 **Fax:** 01629 534260

Lea, Matlock, Derbyshire DE4 5GH

Owner/Contact: Mr & Mrs J Tye

The gardens are sited on the remains of a medieval millstone quarry and cover 4 acres within a wooded hillside. A unique collection of rhododendrons, azaleas, kalmias.

Location: OS Ref. SK324 570. On W side of small lane 600yds SW of Lea village & 1/2 m N of Holloway. 1 1/2 m NE of A6, 2 1/2 m SE of Matlock.

Opening Times: 20 Mar - 30 Jun: 10am - 5.30pm.

Admission: Adult £3, Child 50p, Season ticket £4.

Patrick Lane.

Revolution House, Derbyshire.

MELBOURNE HALL & GARDENS

English Heritage Photographic Library

MELBOURNE, DERBYSHIRE DE73 1EN

Owner: *Lord & Lady Ralph Kerr* ***Contact:*** *Mrs Gill Weston*

Tel: 01332 862502 **Fax:** 01332 862263

This beautiful house of history, in its picturesque poolside setting, was once the home of Victorian Prime Minister William Lamb. The fine gardens, in the French formal style, contain Robert Bakewell's intricate wrought iron arbour and a fascinating yew tunnel.

Location: OS Ref. SK389 249. 8m S of Derby. From London, exit M1/J24.

Opening Times: Hall: Aug only (not first 3 Mons) 2 - 5pm. Last admission 4.15pm. Gardens: 1 Apr - 30 Sept: Weds, Sats, Suns, BH Mons, 2 - 6pm.

Admission: Hall: Adult £2.50, Child £1, OAP £2. Gardens: Adult £3, Child/OAP £2. Hall & Gardens: Adult £4.50, Child £2.50, OAP £3.50.

Crafts. No photography in house. Partially suitable. 

Obligatory. Limited. No coach parking. Guide dogs only.

Patrick Lane.

Peveril Castle, Derbyshire.

PEVERIL CASTLE

Tel: 01433 620613

Market Place, Castleton, Hope Valley S33 8WQ

Owner: English Heritage **Contact:** The Custodian

There are breathtaking views of the Peak District from this castle, perched high above the pretty village of Castleton. The great square tower stands almost to its original height. Formerly known as Peak Castle.

Location: OS110 Ref. SK150 827. S side of Castleton, 15m W of Sheffield on A6187.

Open: 1 Apr - 31 Oct: daily, 10am - 6pm (5pm in Oct). 1 Nov - 31 Mar, Wed - Sun, 10am - 4pm. Closed 24 - 26 Dec & 1 Jan.

Admission: Adult £2.20, Child £1.10, Conc. £1.70. 15% discount for groups (11+).

Tel: for details.

RENISHAW HALL

SHEFFIELD, DERBYSHIRE S31 9WB

Owner: *Sir Reresby Sitwell Bt DL* ***Contact:*** *Peter W McGilben*

Tel: 01246 432310 **Fax:** 01246 430706
e-mail: info@renishawhall.free-online.co.uk

Home of Sir Reresby and Lady Sitwell. Seven acres of Italian style formal gardens stand in 300 acres of mature parkland, encompassing statues, shaped yew hedges, a water garden and lakes. The Sitwell museum and art gallery (display of Fiori de Henriques sculptures) are located in the Georgian stables alongside craft workshops and café, furnished with contemporary art.

Location: OS Ref. SK435 786. 3m from M1/J30, equidistant from Sheffield & Chesterfield.

Opening Times: Good Fri - end Sept: Fri - Sun & BHs, 10.30am - 4.30pm.

Admission: House: by written application only. Garden only: Adult £3, Conc. £2 Museum & Art Exhib: Adult £3, Conc. £2. Garden, Museum & Art Exhib: Adult £5, Conc. £3.

Conferences.
By arrangement. In grounds, on leads. 

REVOLUTION HOUSE

Tel: 01246 345727

High Street, Old Whittington, Chesterfield, Derbyshire S41 9LA

Contact: Ms A M Knowles

Originally the Cock and Pynot ale house, now furnished in 17th century style.

Location: OS Ref. SK384 749. 3m N of Chesterfield on B6052 off A61.

Opening Times: Good Fri - end Oct: daily, 10am - 4pm. Special opening over Christmas period.

Admission: Free.

SUDBURY HALL

Tel: 01283 585305 **Fax:** 01283 585139

Ashbourne, Derbyshire DE6 5HT

Owner: The National Trust **Contact:** The Property Manager

One of the most individual of late 17th century houses, begun by George Vernon c1660. The rich decoration includes wood carvings by Gibbons and Pierce, superb plasterwork, mythological decorative paintings by Laguerre. The great staircase is one of the finest of its kind in an English house. Also National Trust Museum of Childhood in 19th century service wing of the Hall.

Location: OS128 Ref. SK160 323. 6m E of Uttoxeter at the junction of A50 Derby - Stoke & A515 Ashbourne.

Opening Times: 1 Apr - 31 Oct: Wed - Sun & BH Mons, 1 - 5.30pm. Last adm. 30 mins before closing. Grounds: 1 - 5.30pm. Museum: As house.

Admission: Hall: Adult £3.70, Child £1.80, Family £9.20. Groups by prior arrangement. Museum: As house. Hall & Museum: Adult £5.90, Child £2.80, Family £14.60.

Limited, braille guide. WC. Licensed. Car park only.

SUTTON SCARSDALE HALL

Tel: 01604 730320 (Regional Office)

Chesterfield, Derbyshire

Owner: English Heritage **Contact:** Midlands Regional Office

The dramatic hilltop shell of a great early 18th century baroque mansion.

Location: OS Ref. SK441 690. Between Chesterfield & Bolsover, 1½ m S of Arkwright Town.

Opening Times: 10am - 6pm (5pm Oct - Mar).

Admission: Free.

TISSINGTON HALL

ASHBOURNE, DERBYSHIRE DE6 1RA

Owner/Contact: *Sir Richard FitzHerbert Bt*

Tel: 01335 352200 **Fax:** 01335 352201 **e-mail:** tisshall@dircon.co.uk

Home of the FitzHerbert family for over 500 years. The Hall stands in a superbly maintained estate village, and contains wonderful panelling and fine old masters. A 10 acre garden and arboretum. Schools very welcome. Award-winning Old Coach House Tearoom, open daily 11am - 5pm for lunch and tea.

Location: OS Ref. SK175 524. 4m N of Ashbourne off A515 towards Buxton.

Opening Times: 20 Jun - 24 Aug: Tues, Weds & Thurs, 1.30 - 4.30pm. 21 & 25 Aug: 1.30 - 4.30pm. Groups & societies welcome by appointment throughout the year. Corporate days and events also available, contact: The Estate Office on 01335 352200

Admission: Adult £5, Child (10-16yrs) £2.50, Conc. £4.50, Garden only: Adult £2, Child £1.

No photography in house. Partially suitable. WCs at tearooms.
Tearoom adjacent to Hall. Obligatory. Limited.
Guide dogs only.

WINGFIELD MANOR

Tel: 01773 832060

Garner Lane, South Wingfield, Derbyshire

Owner: English Heritage **Contact:** The Custodian

Huge, ruined, country mansion built in the mid-15th century. Mary Queen of Scots was imprisoned here in 1569.

Location: OS Ref. SK374 548. S side of B5035, ½ m S of South Wingfield village. Access by 600yd drive (no vehicles). From M1 J28, W on A38, A615 (Matlock road) at Alfreton and turn onto B5035 after 1½m.

Opening Times: 1 Apr - 31 Oct: Wed - Sun, 12 - 5pm. 1 Nov - 31 Mar: weekends only, 10am - 4pm. Closed 24 - 26 Dec & 1 Jan. Closed 1 - 2pm in winter. The Manor incorporates a working farm. Visitors are requested to respect the privacy of the owners and refrain from visiting outside official opening times.

Admission: Adult £3, Child £1.50, Conc. £2.30.

Owner: Mr R J G Berkeley

CONTACT

The Custodian
Berkeley Castle
Gloucestershire
GL13 9BQ

Tel: 01453 810332

LOCATION

OS Ref. ST685 990

SE side of Berkeley village. Midway between Bristol & Gloucester, 2m W off the A38.

From motorway M5/J14 (5m) or J13 (9m).

Bus: No 308 from Bristol & Gloucester.

CONFERENCE/FUNCTION		
ROOM	SIZE	MAX CAPACITY
Great Hall		200
Long Drawing Rm		100

BERKELEY CASTLE

Berkeley

Not many can boast of having their private house celebrated by Shakespeare nor of having held it in the possession of their family for nearly 850 years, nor having a King of England murdered within its walls, nor of having welcomed at their table the local vicar and Castle Chaplain, John Trevisa (1342-1402), reputed as one of the earliest translators of the Bible, nor of having a breach battered by Oliver Cromwell, which to this day it is forbidden by law to repair even if it was wished to do so. But such is the story of Berkeley.

This beautiful and historic Castle, begun in 1117, still remains the home of the famous family who gave their name to numerous locations all over the world, notably Berkeley Square in London, Berkeley Hundred in Virginia and Berkeley University in California. Scene of the brutal murder of Edward II in 1327 (visitors can see his cell and nearby the dungeon) and besieged by Cromwell's troops in 1645, the Castle is steeped in history but twenty-four generations of Berkeleys have gradually transformed a Norman fortress into the lovely home it is today.

The State Apartments contain magnificent collections of furniture, rare paintings by primarily English and Dutch masters, and tapestries. Part of the world-famous Berkeley silver is on display in the Dining Room. Many other rooms are equally interesting including the Great Hall upon which site the Barons of the West Country met in 1215 before going to Runnymede to force King John to put his seal to the Magna Carta.

The Castle is surrounded by lovely terraced Elizabethan Gardens with a lily pond, Elizabeth I's bowling green, and sweeping lawns.

Fashion shows and filming. Butterfly farm. No photography inside the Castle.

Wedding receptions and corporate entertainment.

Visitors may alight in the Outer Bailey.

Licensed. Serving lunches and home-made teas.

Free. Max. 120 people. Tour time: One hour. Evening groups by arrangement.Group visits must be booked.

Cars 150 yds from Castle and up to 15 coaches 250 yds away.

Welcome. General and social history and architecture.

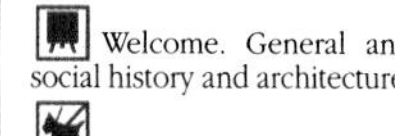

OPENING TIMES

April - May
Tue - Sun, 2 - 5pm.

June & September
Tue - Sat, 11am - 5pm,
Suns, 2 - 5pm.

July & August
Mon - Sat, 11am - 5pm
Suns, 2 - 5pm

October
Suns, 2 - 5pm

BH Mons, 11am - 5pm

NB. Groups must book.

ADMISSION

Castle and Garden
Adult £5.40
Child £2.90
OAP........£4.40

Groups (25+ pre-booked)
Adult £4.90
Child £2.60
OAP £4.10
Family (2+2) £14.50

Gardens only
Adult £2.00
Child £1.00

Butterfly Farm
Adult £2.00
Child/OAP £1.00
Family (2+2) £4.50
School Groups 80p

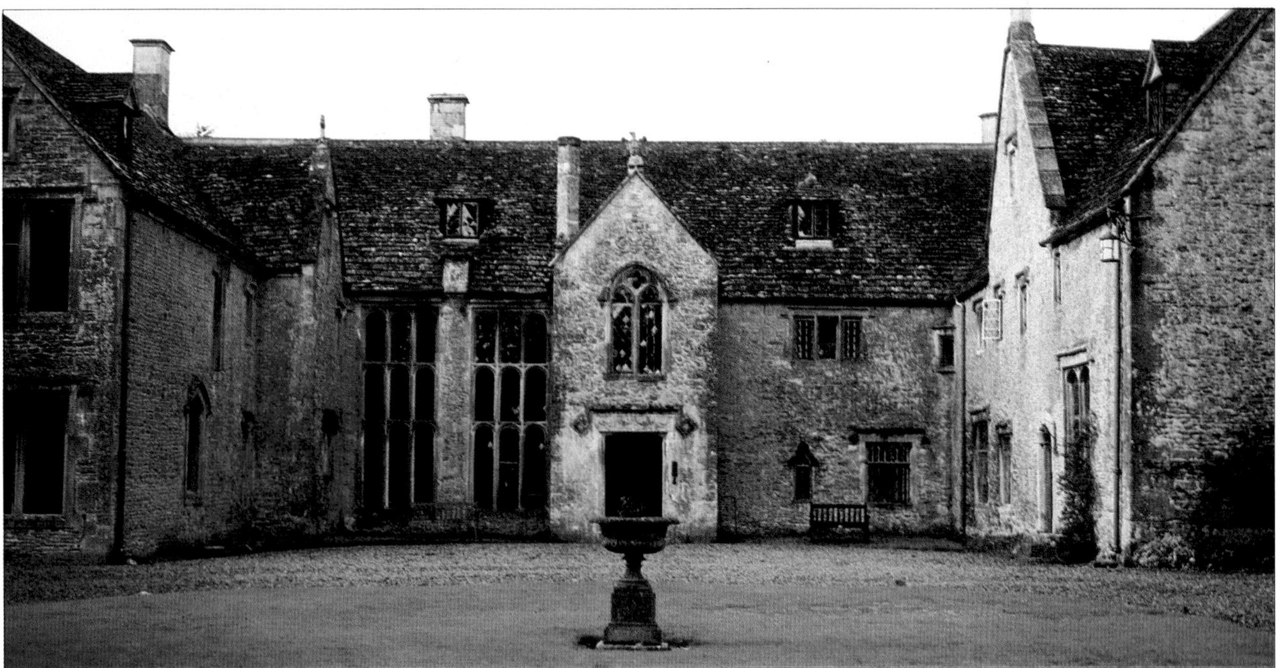

Owner:
Mr David Lowsley-Williams

CONTACT

D Lowsley-Williams
Chavenage
Tetbury
Gloucestershire
GL8 8XP

Tel: 01666 502329

Fax: 01453 836778

CHAVENAGE

Tetbury

CHAVENAGE is a wonderful Elizabethan house of mellow grey Cotswold stone and tiles which contains much of interest for the discerning visitor.

The approach aspect of Chavenage is virtually as it was left by Edward Stephens in 1576. Only two families have owned Chavenage; the present owners since 1891 and the Stephens family before them. A Colonel Nathaniel Stephens, MP for Gloucestershire during the Civil War was cursed for supporting Cromwell, giving rise to legends of weird happenings at Chavenage since that time.

Inside Chavenage there are many interesting rooms housing tapestries, fine furniture, pictures and many relics of the Cromwellian period. Of particular note are the Main Hall, where a contemporary screen forms a minstrels' gallery and two tapestry rooms where it is said Cromwell was lodged.

Recently Chavenage has been used as a location for TV and film productions including a Hercule Poirot story *The Mysterious Affair at Styles*, many episodes of the sequel to *Are you Being Served* now called *Grace & Favour*, a *Gotcha* for *The Noel Edmonds' House Party*, episodes of *The House of Elliot* and *Casualty* and in 1997/98 *Berkeley Square* and *Cider with Rosie*.

Chavenage is especially suitable for those wishing an intimate, personal tour, usually conducted by the owner, or for small groups wanting a change from large establishments. It also provides a charming venue for small conferences and functions.

OPENING TIMES

SUMMER
May - September
Easter Sun, Mons & BHs, 2 - 5pm.

Thurs & Suns
2 - 5pm.

NB. Will open at other times by prior arrangement for groups.

WINTER
October - March
By appointment only for groups.

LOCATION

OS Ref. ST872 952

Less than 20m from M4/J16/17 or 18. 1¾ m NW of Tetbury between the B4104 & A4135. Signed from Tetbury. Less than 15m from M5/J13 or 14. Signed from A46 (Stroud -Bath road)

Rail: Kemble Station 7m.

Taxi: Tetbury Cars, Tetbury 503393

Air: Bristol 35m. Birmingham 70m. Grass airstrip on farm.

CONFERENCE/FUNCTION		
ROOM	SIZE	MAX CAPACITY
Ballroom	70' x 30'	120
Oak Room	25 'x 20'	30

Clay pigeon shooting, archery, cross-bows, pistol shooting, ATV driving, small fashion shows, concerts, plays, seminars, filming, product launching, photography. No photography in house.

Corporate entertaining. In-house catering for drinks parties, dinners, wedding receptions. Telephone for details.

Partially suitable. WC.

Lunches, teas, dinners and picnics by arrangement.

By owner. Large groups given a talk prior to viewing. Couriers and group leaders should arrange tour format prior to visit.

Up to 100 cars and 2 - 3 coaches. Coaches only by appointment; stop at gates for parking instructions.

Chairs can be arranged for lecturing. Tour of working farm, modern dairy and corn facilities can be arranged.

In grounds on leads. Guide dogs only in house.

ADMISSION

Tours are inclusive in the following prices.

SUMMER
Adult £4.00
Child (5 - 16 yrs).......£2.00

CONCESSIONS
By prior arrangement, concessions may be given to groups of 20+ and also to disabled and to exceptional cases.

WINTER
Groups only:
Rates by arrangement.

Owner: Lady Ashcombe

CONTACT

The Secretary
Sudeley Castle
Winchcombe
Nr Cheltenham
Gloucestershire
GL54 5JD

Tel: 01242 602308

Fax: 01242 602959

e-mail: marketing@sudeley.ndirect.co.uk

LOCATION

OS Ref. SP032 277

8m NE of Cheltenham, at Winchcombe off B4632.

From Bristol or Birmingham M5/J9. Take A46 then B4077 towards Stow-on-the-Wold.

Bus: Castleways to Winchcombe.

Rail: Cheltenham Station 8m.

Air: Birmingham or Bristol 45m.

CONFERENCE/FUNCTION		
ROOM	SIZE	MAX CAPACITY
Chandos Hall		80
North Hall		40
Library		80
Banquet Hall & Pavilion		150

SUDELEY CASTLE
Winchcombe

SUDELEY CASTLE, home of Lord and Lady Ashcombe, is one of England's great historic houses with royal connections stretching back 1000 years. Once the property of King Ethelred the Unready, Sudeley was later the magnificent palace of Queen Katherine Parr, Henry VIII's sixth wife, who is buried in the Castle church. Henry VIII, Anne Boleyn, Lady Jane Grey and Elizabeth I all stayed at the Castle as did Charles I, whose nephew Prince Rupert made it his headquarters during the Civil War.

During the 19th century a programme of reconstruction under the aegis of Sir Giles Gilbert Scott, restored Sudeley for its new owners, the Dent brothers. The interiors were largely furnished with pieces bought by the Dents at the famous Strawberry Hill sale when the contents of Horace Walpole's house were sold.

Surrounding the castle are eight enchanting gardens which have gained international recognition. In 1996 the family was the recipient of the HHA/Christie's 'Garden of the Year' award. Famous for its topiary and its fine collection of old roses, the visitor must see the Queen's Garden, the Tudor Knot Garden, the Secret Garden designed by Rosemary Verey and the Victorian Kitchen Garden featuring vegetables grown during that era and which are cultivated under natural organic conditions.

Visitors can wander through the Tythe Barn ruins, past the carp and wildfowl ponds to the castle, which contains some interesting pieces of Civil War memorabilia as well as pictures by Turner, Van Dyck and Rubens. An excellent restaurant, gift shop and a new plant centre specialising in old-fashioned roses complete a perfect day.

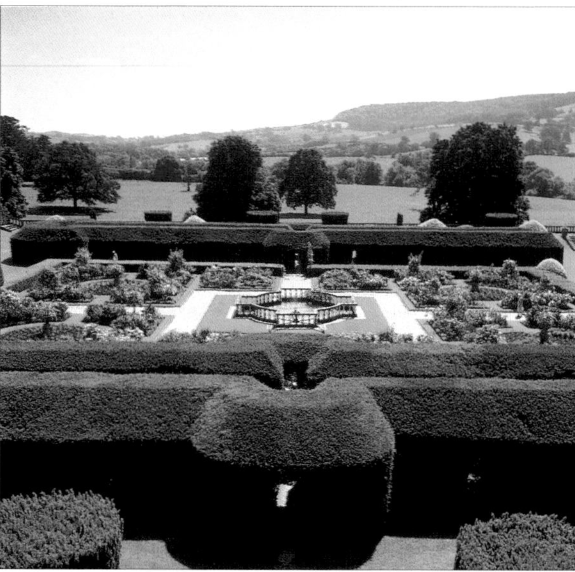

Photography and filming, concerts, corporate events and conferences. Product launches, garden parties, craft fairs and activity days. Sudeley reserves the right to close part or all of the castle, gardens and grounds and to amend information as necessary.

Private dining, banquets, and medieval dinners.

Not suitable.

Licensed restaurant and tearooms. Groups should book.

Special interest tours can be arranged.

1,000 cars. Meal vouchers, free access for coach drivers.

14 holiday cottages for 2 - 5 occupants.

OPENING TIMES

SUMMER

Gardens, Exhibition Centre, Shop & Plant Centre
4 March - 29 October
Daily: 10.30am - 5.30pm.

Castle Apartments & Church
1 April - 29 October
Daily: 11am - 5pm.

Restaurant
1 April - 29 October
Daily: 10.30am - 5pm.

WINTER
Groups (30+) by appointment.

ADMISSION

Castle & Gardens*

Adult	£6.20
Child (5-15 yrs.)	£3.20
Conc.	£5.20
Family (2+2)	£17.00
Groups* (min. 20)	
Adult	£5.20
Child (5-15 yrs.)	£3.20
Conc.	£4.20

Gardens & Exhibitions

Adult	£4.70
Child (5-15 yrs.)	£2.50
OAP	£3.70

Audio tour £2.00

Adventure Playground only (5-15 yrs.) £1.00

SPECIAL EVENTS

- **MAY 11 - 13:** Homes & Gardens Magazine Grand Sale.
- **AUG 12 - 13:** Open Air Shakespeare.

Sudeley Castle, Gloucestershire.

BARNSLEY HOUSE GARDEN

Tel: 01285 740561 **Fax:** 01285 740628

Barnsley House, Cirencester GL7 5EE

Owner: Mr & Mrs Charles Verey **Contact:** Charles Verey

Mature $4^1/_2$ acre garden designed by Rosemary Verey. Bulbs, mixed borders, autumn colours, knot of herb garden, laburnum walk (late May, early June). Decorative vegetable garden, garden furniture by Charles Verey. Fountain and statues by Simon Verity. Two 18th century summer houses. Winner of the HHA/Christie's Garden of the Year award, 1988.

Location: OS Ref. SP076 049. In Barnsley village, 4m NE of Cirencester on B4425.

Opening Times: 1 Feb - mid Dec: Mons, Weds, Thurs & Sats, 10am - 5.30pm.

Admission: Adult £3.75, Child under 16 Free, OAP £3. No charge for group tour leader.

Partially suitable. By arrangement.

Ample for cars. Limited for coaches.

BATSFORD ARBORETUM

Tel: 01386 701441 **Fax:** 01608 650290

Moreton-in-Marsh, Gloucestershire GL56 9QF

Owner: The Batsford Foundation **Contact:** Christine Dyer

50 acres of arboretum.

Location: OS Ref. SP183 324. $1^1/_2$ m NW of Moreton-in-Marsh, off A44 to Broadway.

Opening Times: 1 Mar - mid Nov.

Admission: Adult £3.50, Child Free, OAP £3.

BERKELEY CASTLE

See page 264 for full page entry.

BLACKFRIARS

Tel: 0117 9750700

Ladybellegate Street, Gloucester

Owner: English Heritage **Contact:** The South West Regional Office

A small Dominican priory church converted into a rich merchant's house at the Dissolution. Most of the original 13th century church remains, including a rare scissor-braced roof.

Location: OS Ref. SO830 186. In Ladybellegate St, Gloucester, off Southgate Street and Blackfriars Walk.

Opening Times: Please contact the South West Regional Office.

Admission: Free.

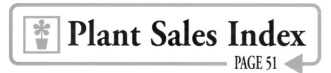

Plant Sales Index PAGE 51

BOURTON HOUSE GARDEN

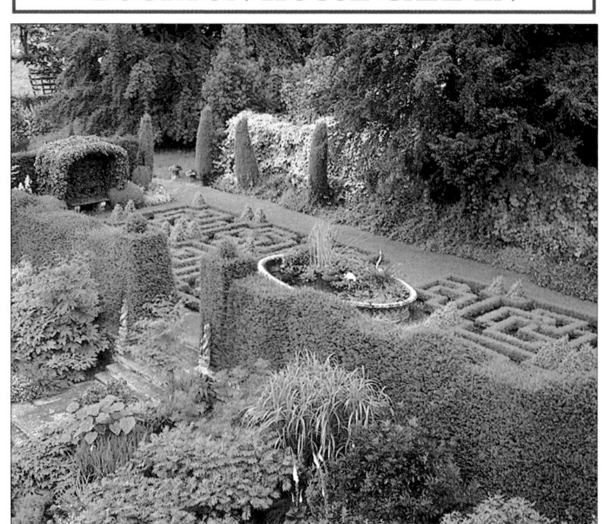

BOURTON-ON-THE-HILL GL56 9AE

Owner/Contact: *Mr & Mrs Richard Paice*

Tel: 01386 700121 **Fax:** 01386 701081

Exciting 3 acre garden surrounding a delightful 18th century Cotswold manor house and 16th century tithe barn. Featuring flamboyant borders, imaginative topiary, a unique shade house, a profusion of herbaceous and exotic plants and, not least, a myriad of magically planted pots. The mood is friendly and welcoming, the atmosphere tranquil yet inspiring. The garden... "positively fizzes with ideas".

Location: OS Ref. SP180 324. $1^3/_4$ m W of Moreton-in-Marsh on A44.

Opening Times: 25 May - 20 Oct: Thurs & Fris, 10am - 5pm. 28 - 29 May & 27 - 28 Aug.

Admission: Adult £3.50, Child Free.

Partially suitable.  By arrangement.

Ample for cars. Limited for coaches.

CHAVENAGE

See page 265 for full page entry.

CHEDWORTH ROMAN VILLA

Ian Shaw

YANWORTH, CHELTENHAM, GLOS GL54 3LJ

Owner: *The National Trust* ***Contact:*** *The Property Manager*

Tel: 01242 890256 **Fax:** 01242 890544 **e-mail:** chedworth@smtp.ntrust.org.uk

The remains of a Romano-British villa, excavated 1864. Set in beautiful wooded combe. Includes fine 4th century mosaics, two bath houses, spring with temple. A museum houses the smaller finds.

Location: OS163 Ref. SP053 135. 3m NW of Fossebridge on Cirencester - Northleach road A429. Coaches must avoid Withington.

Opening Times: 1 Mar - 30 Apr & 4 Oct - 19 Nov: daily except Mons & Tues (but open Easter Mon), 11am - 4pm. 2 May - 1 Oct: daily except Mons (but open BH Mon), 10am - 5pm.

Admission: Adult £3.60, Child £1.80, Family £9. (Increased charge on special event days, including NT members).

Grounds limited. WC. By arrangement. Limited. Tel. for details.

FRAMPTON COURT

Tel: 01452 740267 **Fax:** 01452 740698

Frampton-on-Severn, Gloucestershire GL2 7EU

Owner/Contact: Mrs Peter Clifford

Listed Grade I, by Vanburgh. 1732. Stately family home of the Cliffords who have lived at Frampton since granted land by William the Conqueror, 1066. Fine collection of original period furniture, tapestries, needlework and porcelain. Panelled throughout. The famous botanical paintings of *The Frampton Flora* are all on show. Fine views over parkland to extensive lake. A famous gothic orangery stands in the garden reflected in a Dutch ornamental canal.

Location: OS Ref. SO750 078. In Frampton, 1/4 m SW of B4071, 3m NW of M5/J13.

Opening Times: By arrangement.

Admission: House & Garden: £4.50.

No photography in house. Not suitable. Obligatory. Limited for coaches. In grounds on leads. Ensuite. Tel for details. 

FRAMPTON MANOR

Fax: 01452 740698

Frampton-on-Severn, Gloucestershire GL2 7EU

Owner: Mr & Mrs P R H Clifford **Contact:** Mrs P R H Clifford

Medieval/Elizabethan timber-framed manor house with walled garden. Reputed 12th century birthplace of 'Fair Rosamund' Clifford, mistress of King Henry II. Wool barn c1500 and c1800 granary with dovecote.

Location: OS Ref. SO748 080. 3m M5/J13.

Opening Times: House & Garden: open throughout the year by written appointment. Garden: 1 May - 17 Jul: Mons, 2 - 5pm.

Admission: House & Garden: £3.50. Garden only: £2.

HAILES ABBEY

Tel: 01242 602398

Nr Winchcombe, Cheltenham, Gloucestershire GL54 5PB

Owner: English Heritage & The National Trust **Contact:** The Custodian

Seventeen cloister arches and extensive excavated remains in lovely surroundings of an abbey founded by Richard, Earl of Cornwall, in 1246. There is a small museum and covered display area.

Location: OS150, Ref. SP050 300. 2m NE of Winchcombe off B4632. 1/2 m SE of B4632.

Opening Times: 1 Apr - 31 Oct: daily, 10am - 6pm (5pm in Oct). 1 Nov - 31 Mar: Sat - Sun, 10am - 4pm. Closed 24 - 26 Dec & 1 Jan.

Admission: Adult £2.60, Child £1.30, Conc. £2.

Partially suitable. WC. In grounds, on leads.  Tel. for details.

DYRHAM PARK

NT Photographic Library/Rupert Truman

Nr CHIPPENHAM, WILTSHIRE SN14 8ER

Owner: *The National Trust* ***Contact:*** *The Property Manager*

Tel/Fax: 0117 9372501

Built for William Blathwayt, Secretary at State and at War to William III, between 1691 - 1702. The rooms have changed little since they were furnished by Blathwayt and recorded in his housekeeper's inventories. The content of the house was much influenced by the Dutch style, including paintings, ceramics and furniture. The house is set in a 263 acre park with a herd of fallow deer, with a 3 acre garden and views across the Severn valley.

New for 2000: restored domestic rooms open for the first time, including kitchen, bells passage, bakehouse, larders, tenants' hall and Delft-tiled dairy. The car park has been relocated to the East Lodge, and a free 'easy access' shuttle bus takes visitors to the house and garden, thereby restoring the house to its original, car free setting.

Location: OS Ref. ST743 757. 8m N of Bath, 12m E of Bristol. Approached from Bath - Stroud road (A46), 2m S of Tormarton interchange with M4/J18.

Opening Times: House: 1 Apr - 29 Oct: Fri - Tue, 12 noon - 5.30pm. Garden: as house, 11am - 5.30pm. Park: daily (closed 25 Dec), 12 noon - 5.30pm (opens at 11am if house and garden open). Last admission 1/2 hr before closing or dusk if earlier. Property closed 7, 8 & 9 Jul.

Admission: Adult £7.50, Child £3.70, Family (2+3) £18.50.

HARDWICKE COURT

Tel: 01452 720212 **Fax:** 01452 724465

Gloucester GL2 4RS **Owner/Contact:** C G M Lloyd Baker Esq

Early 19th century small country house designed by Robert Smirke.

Location: OS150, Ref. SO787 118. 6m S of Gloucester on A38.

Opening Times: Easter - end Sept: Mons, 2 - 4pm.

Admission: £1.

HIDCOTE MANOR GARDEN

Stephen Robson.

CHIPPING CAMPDEN, GLOUCESTERSHIRE GL55 6LR

Owner: *The National Trust* ***Contact:*** *The Property Manager*

Tel: 01386 438333 **Fax:** 01386 438817 **e-mail:** hidcote_manor@smtp.ntrust.org.uk

One of the most delightful gardens in England, created this century by the great horticulturist Major Lawrence Johnston; a series of small gardens within the whole, separated by walls and hedges of different species; famous for rare shrubs, trees, herbaceous borders, 'old' roses and interesting plant species.

Location: OS151 Ref. SP176 429. 4m NE of Chipping Campden, 1m E of B4632 off B4081. At Mickleton 1/4 m E of Kiftsgate Court.

Opening Times: 1 Apr - end May & Aug - 5 Nov: daily except Tues & Fris (open Good Fri). Jun & Jul: daily except Fris. Times: Apr - end Sept: 11am - 7pm. Oct: 11am - 6pm, last admission 1hr before closing or dusk if earlier.

Admission: Adult £5.60, Child £2.80, Family £14.

Grounds, but limited. WC.  Licensed.

HORTON COURT

Tel: 01249 730141

Horton, Nr Chipping Sodbury B17 6QR

Owner: The National Trust **Contact:** Lacock Estate Office

A Cotswold manor house with 12th century Norman hall and early Renaissance features. Of particular interest is the late perpendicular ambulatory, detached from the house. Norman hall and ambulatory only shown.

Location: OS Ref. NT766 849. 3m NE of Chipping Sodbury, 3/4 m N of Horton, 1m W of A46.

Opening Times: 1 Apr - 28 Oct: Weds & Sats, 2 - 6pm or dusk if earlier.

Admission: Adult £1.80, Child 90p.

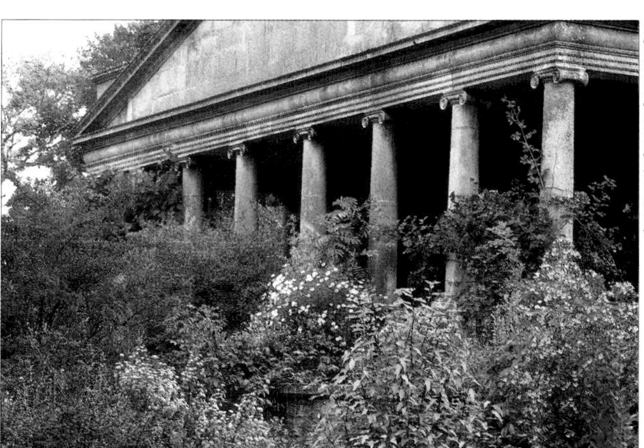

English Heritage Photographic Library.

Kiftsgate Court Gardens, Gloucestershire.

KELMSCOTT MANOR

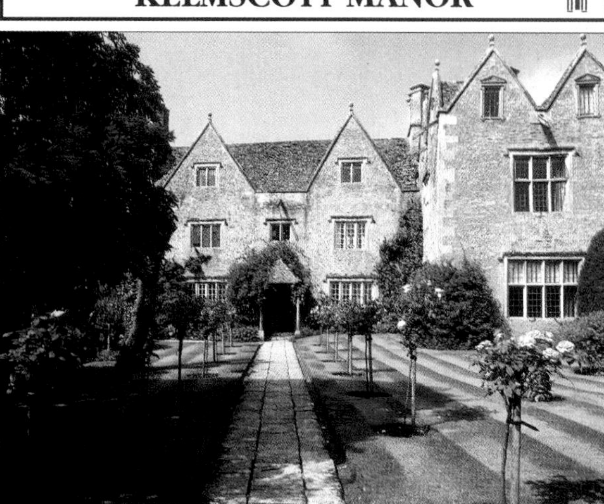

Nigel Fisher

KELMSCOTT, Nr LECHLADE, GLOUCESTERSHIRE GL7 3HJ

Owner: *Society of Antiquaries* ***Contact:*** *Helen Webb*

Tel: 01367 252486 **Fax:** 01367 253754

The home of William Morris, poet, craftsman and socialist from 1871 until his death in 1896. The house contains a collection of the possessions and works of Morris and his associates including furniture, textiles, carpets and ceramics. An exhibition of 'William Morris at Kelmscott' is being held in one of the barns during normal opening times.

Location: OS Ref. SU252 988. At SE end of the village, 2m due E of Lechlade, off the Lechlade - Faringdon Road.

Opening Times: Apr - Sept: Weds, 11am - 5pm. 3rd Sat in Apr, May, Jun & Sept, also 1st & 3rd Sat in July & Aug, 2 - 5pm. Private visits for groups on Thurs & Fris. Please note house only closed on Weds, 1 - 2pm.

Admission: Adult £6, Child/Student £3.

Grounds suitable. WCs. Licensed. By arrangement. Limited for coaches.

KIFTSGATE COURT GARDENS

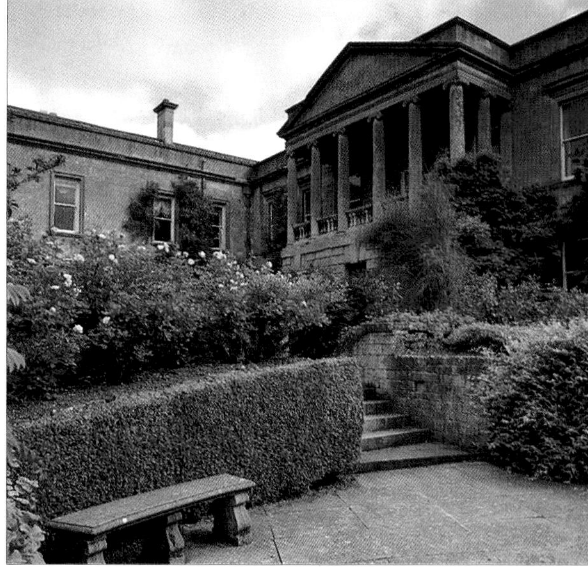

CHIPPING CAMPDEN, GLOUCESTERSHIRE GL55 6LW

Owner: *Mr and Mrs J G Chambers* ***Contact:*** *Mr J G Chambers*

Tel/Fax: 01386 438777

Magnificently situated garden on the edge of the Cotswold escarpment with views towards the Malvern Hills. Many unusual shrubs and plants including tree peonies, abutilons, specie and old-fashioned roses.

Location: OS Ref. SP173 430. 4m NE of Chipping Campden. 1/4 m W of Hidcote Garden.

Opening Times: Apr, May, Aug, Sept: Weds, Thurs & Suns, 2 - 6pm. Jun & Jul: Weds, Thurs, Sats & Suns, 12 noon - 6pm. BH Mons, 2 - 6pm. Coaches by appointment.

Admission: Adult: £4, Child £1.

LITTLEDEAN HALL

Tel: 01594 824 213

Littledean, Gloucestershire GL14 3NR

Owner/Contact: Mrs S Anthony

'*Reputedly England's oldest inhabited house*', Guinness Book of Records. Site of Roman temple.

Location: OS Ref. SO673 131. 2m E of Cinderford, 500 yds S of A4151.

Opening Times: 1 Apr - 31 Oct: daily, 11am - 5pm.

Admission: Adult £3.50, Child £1.50, OAP £2.50. Groups £2.25 (by appointment).

LYDNEY PARK GARDENS & ROMAN TEMPLE SITE

Tel/Fax: 01594 842027

Lydney, Gloucestershire GL15 6BU

Owner: The Viscount Bledisloe **Contact:** Mrs Sylvia Jones

Eight acres of extensive valley gardens with trees and lakes. Roman temple site and museum.

Location: OS Ref. SO620 022. On A48 between Lydney and Aylburton.

Opening Times: 26 Mar - 4 Jun: Suns, Weds & BHs. Easter Sun; 23 - 28 Apr; 28 May - 2 Jun: 11am - 6pm.

Admission: Adult £3 (Wed £2), Child Free. Groups of (25+) by arrangement.

MILL DENE GARDEN

OLD MILL DENE, BLOCKLEY, MORETON-IN-MARSH GL56 9HU

Owner: *Mr & Mrs B S Dare* ***Contact:*** *Mrs Wendy Dare*

Tel: 01386 700457 **Fax:** 01386 700526 **e-mail:** milldenegarden@barrydare.cix.co.uk

In a naturally beautiful situation this $2^1/_2$ acre Cotswold water-mill garden has been designed and planted by the owner. Paths along steep lawned terraces rise from the mill-pool, stream and grotto; wander through a rose-walk to the cricket lawn, then to the potager at the top. All the garden has glimpses of the church as a back-drop and views over the Cotswold Hills. Plenty of seats encourage contemplation of tranquil water and vistas.

Location: OS Ref. SP165 345. From A44 Bourton-on-the-Hill, take turn to Blockley. $1^1/_3$m down hill, turn left behind 30mph sign labelled cul-de-sac. Follow brown signs.

Opening Times: 1 Apr - 31 Oct: Mon - Fri, 10am - 6pm or by appointment.

Admission: Adult £2.50, Child 50p.

Lunches for groups (max 10).   By arrangement. Limited.
3 dble/2 ensuite bathrooms.

Misarden Park Gardens, Gloucestershire.

MISARDEN PARK GARDENS

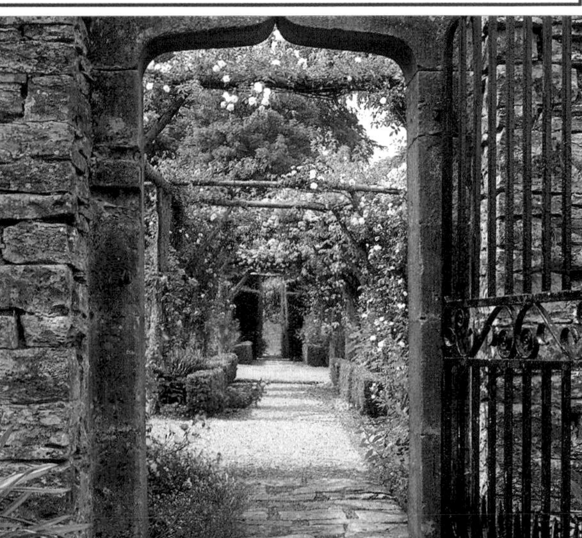

STROUD, GLOUCESTERSHIRE GL6 7JA

Owner/Contact: *Major M T N H Wills*

Tel: 01285 821303 **Fax:** 01285 821530

Noted in the spring for its bulbs and flowering trees and in mid-summer for the large double herbaceous borders. Fine topiary throughout and a traditional rose garden. Outstanding position, standing high overlooking the 'Golden Valley'. New summer house and rill.

Location: OS Ref. SO940 089. 6m NW Cirencester. Follow signs westward from A417 from Gloucester or Cirencester or B4070 from Stroud.

Opening Times: 1 Apr - 30 Sept: Tue - Thur, 10am - 5pm.

Admission: Adult £3 (guided tours extra), Child Free.
10% reduction for pre-arranged groups (20+).

Nurseries: daily except Mons. Grounds suitable. Guide dogs only.

OWLPEN MANOR

Nr ULEY, GLOUCESTERSHIRE GL11 5BZ

Owner: *Mr & Mrs Nicholas Mander* ***Contact:*** *Mrs M Keevil*

Tel: 01453 860261 **Fax:** 01453 860819 **Restaurant:** 01453 860816

e-mail: sales@owlpen.com

Romantic Tudor manor house, 1450-1616, with Cotswold Arts & Crafts associations. Remote wooded valley setting, with 16th and 17th century formal terraced gardens and magnificent yews. Contains unique painted cloth wall hangings, family and Arts & Crafts collections. Mill (1726), Court House (1620); licensed restaurant in medieval Cyder House. Victorian church. "*Owlpen - ah, what a dream is there!*" - Vita Sackville-West.

Location: OS Ref. ST801 984. 3m E of Dursley, 1m E of Uley, off B4066, by Old Crown pub, or follow brown signs.

Opening Times: 1 Apr - 15 Oct: daily, Tue - Sun & BH Mons, 2 - 5pm. Restaurant 12 noon - 5pm.

Admission: Adult £4.50, Child (5-14yrs) £2, Family (2+4) £12.50. Gardens & Grounds: Adult £3.25, Child £1. Group rates available.

 Not suitable.  Licensed. Holiday cottages, sleep 2 - 9. 

PAINSWICK ROCOCO GARDENS

PAINSWICK, GLOUCESTERSHIRE GL6 6TH

Owner: *Painswick Rococo Garden Trust* ***Contact:*** *P R Moir*

Tel: 01452 813204 **e-mail:** Painsgard@aol.com

Unique 18th century garden restoration situated in a hidden 6 acre Cotswold combe. Charming contemporary buildings are juxtaposed with winding woodland walks and formal vistas. Famous for its early spring show of snowdrops. Newly planted maze.

Location: OS Ref. SO864 106. 1/2 m NW of village of Painswick on B4073.

Opening Times: 2nd Wed in Jan - 30 Nov: Wed - Sun & BHs. Jul - Aug: daily, 11am - 5pm.

Admission: Adult £3.30, Child £1.75, OAP £3. Family (2+2) £8.75.

Licensed. In grounds, on leads.

RODMARTON MANOR

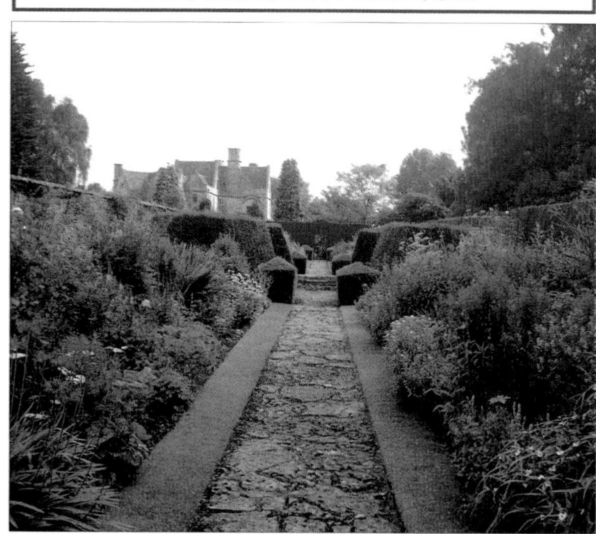

CIRENCESTER, GLOUCESTERSHIRE GL7 6PF

Owner: *Mr & Mrs Simon Biddulph* ***Contact:*** *Simon Biddulph*

Tel: 01285 841253 **Fax:** 01285 841298

One of the last great country houses to be built in the traditional way and containing beautiful furniture, ironwork, china and needlework specially made for the house. The large garden complements the house and contains many areas of great beauty and character including the magnificent herbaceous borders, topiary, roses, rockery and kitchen garden.

Location: OS Ref. ST943 977. Off A433 between Cirencester & Tetbury.

Opening Times: House & Garden: 10 May - 30 Aug: Weds, Sats & BH Mons, 2 - 5pm. Groups please book. Guided house tours, garden and garden visits can be booked at other times for groups of 20+. Guided tours of garden.

Admission: House & Garden: £6, Child (under 14yrs) £3. Min. group charge £120. Garden only: £2.50, accompanied children Free.

By arrangement.

THE PRIORY GARDENS

Tel: 01386 725258

The Priory, Kemerton, Nr Tewkesbury GL20 7JN

Owner/Contact: The Hon Mrs Healing

This 4 acre garden was replanned and planted by the present owner and her husband in 1965, though tree planting had been thoughtfully planned since they came to the garden in 1939, and some 70 new specimen trees were planted. On the south facing slopes of Bredon Hill, the garden has matured and features long herbaceous borders planted in colour groups, at their best from mid-July through September and includes a stream garden, sunken garden and sweeping lawns down to a part reserved for wild flowers. There is a well-stocked kitchen garden.

Location: OS Ref. SO950 378. In Kemerton. 2m E of B4030 at Bredon.

Opening Times: Suns: 18 Jun, 9 Jul, 6 & 27 Aug, 8 & 24 Sept and every Thur, 2 - 6pm.

Admission: Adult: Jun: £1.50, Jul - Sept: £2.

Suns only.  By arrangement. Limited for coaches. In grounds on leads.

Westbury Court Gardens, Gloucestershire.

ST MARY'S CHURCH

Tel: 0117 9750700

Kempley, Gloucestershire

Owner: English Heritage **Contact:** The South West Regional Office

A delightful Norman church with superb wall paintings from the 12th - 14th centuries which were only discovered beneath whitewash in 1871.

Location: OS149 SO670 313. On minor road. 1 1/2 m SE of Much Marcle, A449.

Opening Times: 1 Apr - 30 Sept: 10am - 6pm, 1 Oct - 31 Mar: 10am - 4pm.

Admission: Free.

SEZINCOTE

Moreton-in-Marsh, Gloucestershire GL56 9AW

Owner: Mr and Mrs D Peake **Contact:** Mrs D Peake

Exotic oriental water garden by Repton and Daniell. Large semi-circular orangery. House by S P Cockerell in Indian style was the inspiration for Brighton Pavilion.

Location: OS Ref. SP183 324. 2 1/2 m SW of Moreton-in-Marsh. Turn W along A44 to Broadway and left into gateway just before Bourton-on-the-Hill (opposite the gate to Batsford Park, then 1m drive.

Opening Times: Garden: Thurs, Fris & BH Mons, 2 - 6pm (dusk if earlier) throughout the year except Dec. House: May, Jun, Jul & Sept, Thurs & Fris, 2.30 - 6pm. Groups by appointment.

Admission: House & Garden £5 (no children in house). Garden: Adult £3.50, Child £1 (under 5yrs Free).

Not suitable.  Guide dogs only.

SNOWSHILL MANOR

Andreas Von Einsiedel.

SNOWSHILL, Nr BROADWAY WR12 7JU

Owner: *The National Trust* ***Contact:*** *The Property Manager*

Tel/Fax: 01386 852410 **e-mail:** snowshill@smtp.ntrust.org.uk

A Tudor house with a c1700 façade, 21 rooms containing Charles Paget Wade's collection of craftsmanship, including musical instruments, clocks, toys, bicycles, weavers' and spinners' tools, Japanese armour, small formal garden and Charles Wade's cottage. The Manor is a 10 minute walk (500 yds) along an undulating countryside path.

Location: OS150 Ref. SP096 339. 3m SW of Broadway, turning off the A44, by Broadway Green.

Opening Times: 1 Apr - 29 Oct: daily except Mons & Tues (open BH Mons & Mons in Jul & Aug), 12 noon - 5pm. Last admission 45mins before closing. Timed tickets issued for house. Grounds: As house, 11am - 5.30pm.

Admission: Adult £6, Child £3, Family £15. Grounds, shop & restaurant £3.

STANWAY WATER GARDEN

STANWAY, CHELTENHAM, GLOS GL54 5PQ

Owner: *Lord Neidpath* ***Contact:*** *Lorna Poulton*

Tel: 01386 584469 **Fax:** 01386 584688

"*As perfect and pretty a Cotswold manor house as anyone is likely to see*" (Fodor's '*Great Britain '98* guidebook), Stanway's peaceful Jacobethan architecture and the beauty of its surrounding villages and parkland are now complemented by its magnificent, newly restored baroque water garden, with pyramid, cascade, upper pond, waterfall, grand canal and 70 ft high fountain.

Location: OS Ref. SP061 323. N of Winchcombe, just off B4077.

Opening Times: Gardens: Aug & Sept: Tues & Thurs, 2 - 5pm. Private tours by arrangement at other times.

Admission: Adult £3, Child £1, OAP £2.50.

Film & photographic location. In village. By arrangement. In grounds on leads.

SUDELEY CASTLE See page 266 for full page entry.

WESTBURY COURT GARDEN

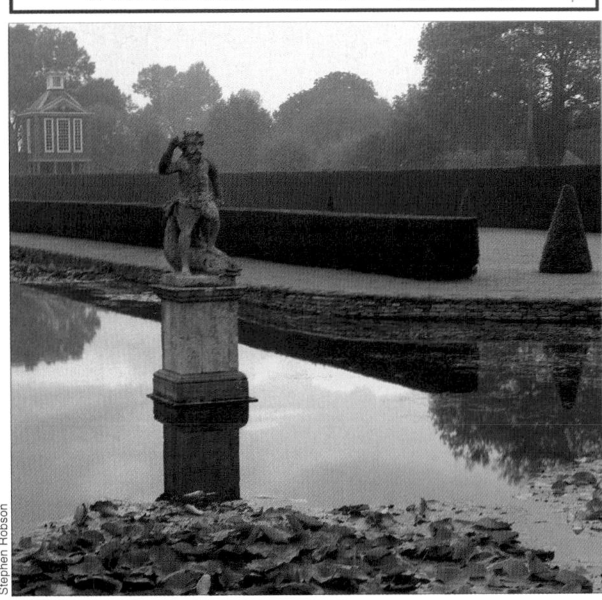

Stephen Robson

WESTBURY-ON-SEVERN, GLOUCESTERSHIRE GL14 1PD

Owner: *The National Trust* ***Contact:*** *The Head Gardener*

Tel: 01452 760461 **e-mail:** westbury@smtp.ntrust.org.uk

A formal water garden with canals and yew hedges, laid out between 1696 and 1705; the earliest of its kind remaining in England. Restored in 1971 and planted with species dating from pre-1700 including apple, pear and plum trees.

Location: OS162 SO718 138. 9m SW of Gloucester on A48.

Opening Times: 1 Apr - 29 Oct: Wed - Sun & BH Mons, 11am - 6pm (open Good Fri). Other times by appointment only.

Admission: Adult £2.80, Child £1.40.

Access to most parts of the garden. WC. Guide dogs only.

WESTONBIRT ARBORETUM **Tel:** 01666 880220 **Fax:** 01666 880559

Tetbury, Gloucestershire GL8 8QS

Owner: The Forestry Commission **Contact:** Mr A Russell

600 acres arboretum begun in 1829, now with 18,000 catalogued trees.

Location: OS Ref. ST856 896. 3m S of Tetbury on the A433.

Opening Times: 365 days a year, 10am - 8pm (or dusk if earlier).

Admission: Adult £4, Child £1, OAP £3.

WHITTINGTON COURT **Tel:** 01242 820556 **Fax:** 01242 820218

Whittington, Cheltenham, Gloucestershire GL54 4HF

Owner: Mr & Mrs Jack Stringer **Contact:** Mrs J Stringer

Elizabethan manor house. Family possessions.

Location: OS Ref. SP014 206. 4m E of Cheltenham on N side of A40.

Opening Times: 22 Apr - 7 May; 12 - 28 Aug inclusive: 2 - 5pm.

Admission: Adult £3, Child £1, OAP £2.50.

WOODCHESTER PARK MANSION **Tel:** 01453 750455 **Fax:** 01453 750457

Stroud, Gloucestershire GL5 1AP

Owner: Woodchester Mansion Trust **Contact:** Matthew Haynes

Hidden in a wooded valley near Stroud is one of the most intriguing houses in the country. Woodchester Mansion was started in 1856 but abandoned incomplete in 1870. It offers a unique insight into traditional building techniques. The Trust's repair programme includes courses in stone masonry and building conservation.

Location: OS Ref. SO795 015 (gateway on B4066). 5m S of Stroud on B4066. NW of the village of Nympsfield, then 1m path E from gate.

Opening Times: Easter - Oct: 1st weekend in each month (open every Sun during Jul & Aug) & BH weekends (Sat/Sun/Mon) 11am - 4pm. Groups and private visits by arrangement.

Admission: Adult £4, Child (under 12yrs) £2, Student £2. Groups (min 10 people or £50): Adult £5.

Not suitable.  Limited for coaches. Guide dogs only.

John Blake

BERRINGTON HALL

Nr Leominster

Owner: The National Trust

CONTACT

The Property Manager
Berrington Hall
Nr Leominster
Herefordshire
HR6 0DW

Tel: 01568 615721

Fax: 01568 613263

Restaurant: 01568 610134

e-mail: berrington@smtp.ntrust.org.uk

LOCATION

OS137 SP510 637

3m N of Leominster, 7m S of Ludlow on W side of A49.

Rail: Leominster 4m.

BERRINGTON HALL is the creation of Thomas Harley, the 3rd Earl of Oxford's remarkable son, who made a fortune from supplying pay and clothing to the British Army in America and became Lord Mayor of London in 1767 at the age of thirty-seven. The architect was the fashionable Henry Holland. The house is beautifully set above the wide valley of a tributary of the River Lugg, with views west and south to the Black Mountains and Brecon Beacons. This was the site advised by 'Capability' Brown who created the lake with its artificial island. The rather plain neo-classical exterior with a central portico gives no clue to the lavishness of the interior. Plaster ceilings now decorated in muted pastel colours adorn the principal rooms. Holland's masterpiece is the staircase hall rising to a central dome. The rooms are set off with a collection of French furniture, including pieces which belonged to the Comte de Flahault, natural son of Talleyrand, and Napoleon's step-daughter Hortense.

In the dining room, vast panoramic paintings of battles at sea, three of them by Thomas Luny, are a tribute to the distinguished Admiral Rodney.

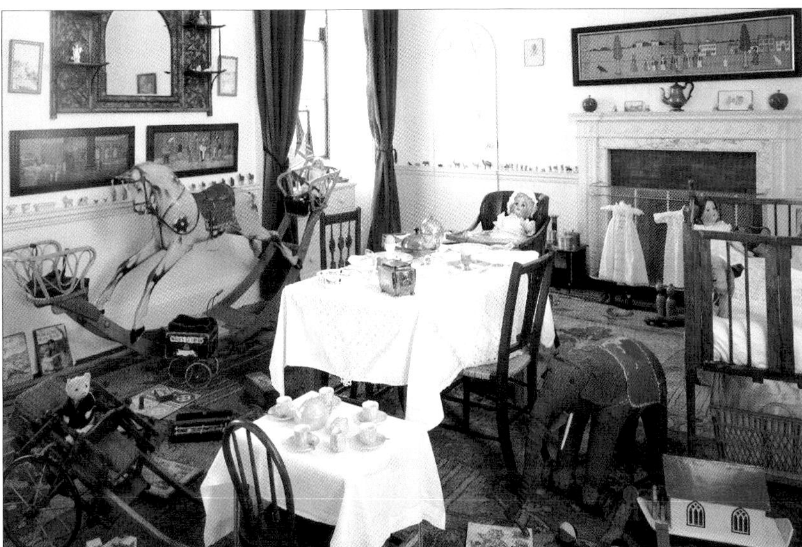

No photography in the house. Groups by arrangement only.

Single seater batricar, stairclimber; pre-booking essential. Audio tours for the visually impaired

Licensed restaurant: open as house: 12.30 - 5.30pm (4.30pm in Oct).

By arrangement only. Tour time: 1 hr.

Ample for cars. Parking for coaches limited; instructions given when booking is made.

Children's quizzes. Play area in walled garden.

Guide dogs only.

OPENING TIMES

House

1 Apr - 31 Oct:
Daily except Thurs & Fris.
(open Good Fri)
1.30 - 5.30pm.
(4.30pm in Oct).

Garden

1 Apr - 31 Oct:
Daily except Thurs & Fris.
(open Good Fri)
12.30 - 6pm.
(5pm in Oct).

Park Walk
1 Jul - 31 Oct:
Daily except Thurs & Fris.
1.30 - 5.30pm
(4.30pm in Oct).

ADMISSION

Adult	£4.20
Child (5-12yrs)	£2.10
Family (2+3)	£10.00
Groups (15-25)*	
Adult	£3.40
Garden Ticket	£2.00

Groups must pre-book. Two groups can visit at a time.

SPECIAL EVENTS

For details of other events please telephone 01568 615721.

EASTNOR CASTLE
Ledbury

Owner:
Mr J & The Hon Mrs Hervey-Bathurst

CONTACT

Simon Foster
Portcullis Office
Eastnor Castle
Nr Ledbury
Herefordshire HR8 1RL

Tel: 01531 633160

Fax: 01531 631776

e-mail: eastnorcastle@btinternet.com

LOCATION

OS Ref. SO735 368

2m SE of Ledbury on the A438 Tewkesbury road. Alternatively M50/J2 & from Ledbury take the A449/A438.

Tewkesbury 20 mins, Malvern 20 mins, Gloucester 25 mins Hereford 25 mins, Worcester 30mins, Cheltenham 30 mins B'ham 1 hr, London 2¼ hrs.

Taxi: Meredith Taxis 01531 632852
Clive Fletcher 0589 299283

CONFERENCE/FUNCTION		
ROOM	SIZE	MAX CAPACITY
Library	18 x 8m	120
Great Hall	16 x 8m	150
Dining Rm	11 x 7m	80
Gothic Rm	11 x 7m	80
Octagon Rm	9 x 9m	50

Encircled by the Malvern Hills and surrounded by a famous arboretum and lake, this fairytale castle looks as dramatic inside as it does outside.

The atmosphere Everyone is struck by it. The vitality of a young family brings the past to life and the sense of warmth and optimism is tangible. Eastnor, however grand, is a home.

'Sleeping' for the past fifty years, the Castle has undergone a triumphant renaissance – 'looking better than it probably ever has', *Country Life* 1993.

Hidden away in attics and cellars since 1939, many of the castle's treasures are now displayed for the first time – early Italian Fine Art, 17th century Venetian furniture and Flemish tapestries, mediaeval armour and paintings by Van Dyck, Romney, Wootton and Watts, photographs by Julia Margaret Cameron. Drawing Room by Pugin.

'The princely and imposing pile' as it was described in 1812 when it was being built to pitch the owner into the aristocracy, remains the home of his descendants. The castle contains letters diaries, clothes and furnishings belonging to friends and relations who include: Horace Walpole, Elizabeth Barrett Browning, Tennyson, Watts, Julia Margaret Cameron and Virginia Woolf.

Encircled by the Malvern Hills, the medieval beauty of the estate remains unchanged.

GARDENS
Castellated terraces descend to a 21 acre lake with a restored lakeside walk. The arboretum holds a famous collection of mature specimen trees. There are spectacular views of the Malvern hills across a 300 acre deer park, once part of a mediaeval chase and now designated a Site of Special Scientific Interest.

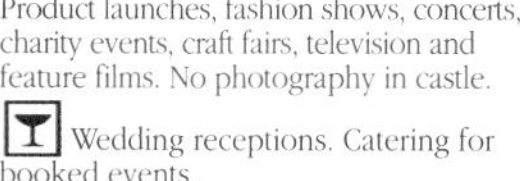

Plant Centre.

Maze, off-road driving, clay-pigeon shooting, quad bikes, archery and falconry. Survival training, team building activity days. Product launches, fashion shows, concerts, charity events, craft fairs, television and feature films. No photography in castle.

Wedding receptions. Catering for booked events.

Visitors may alight at the castle. Priority parking.

Home-made food, menus on request, groups must book.

By arrangement.

Ample 10 - 200 yds from castle. Coaches phone in advance to arrange parking & catering. Free meal for drivers.

Welcome. Guides available if required. Children's fun worksheets.

On leads in Castle and grounds.

Luxury accommodation within castle for small groups. 3 single rooms and 8 double. Ensuite available.

OPENING TIMES

SUMMER
23 April - 1 October: Suns & BH Mons.
July - August: Sun - Fri 11am - 5pm.

NB. Groups by appointment at other times when the castle is closed to casual visitors.

ADMISSION

SUMMER
Castle & Grounds

Adult £4.75
Child (5-14yrs) £2.50
Family (2+2) £12.00

Groups* (with guide)
Adult £5.75
Child £3.00

Groups* (without guide)
Adult £4.25
Child £2.00

Grounds only
Adult £2.75
Child (5-14yrs) £1.50

* Min. payment for 20 people.

Season Ticket
Adult £14.25
Child (5-14yrs) £7.50
Family £36.00

WINTER
By appointment.

SPECIAL EVENTS

Please telephone for details of special events.

ABBEYDORE COURT GARDENS

Tel/Fax: 01981 240419

Abbey Dore, Hereford HR2 0AD

Owner/Contact: Mrs C L Ward

6 acre rambling garden, intersected by the River Dore. Shrubs and herbaceous perennials, rock garden and ponds. Small nursery.

Location: OS Ref. SO387 309. 3 m W of A465 midway Hereford - Abergavenny.

Opening Times: Apr - Sept: daily except Weds & Mons, 11am - 6pm.

Admission: Adult £2.50, Child 50p.

BERRINGTON HALL

See page 273 for full page entry.

CROFT CASTLE

Rupert Truman

LEOMINSTER, HEREFORDSHIRE HR6 9PW

Owner: *The National Trust* ***Contact:*** *The House Manager*

Tel: 01568 780246 **e-mail:** croft@smtp.ntrust.org.uk

Home of the Croft family since Domesday (with a break of 170 years from 1750). Walls and corner towers date from 14th and 15th centuries, interior mainly 18th century when fine Georgian-Gothic staircase and plasterwork ceilings were added; splendid avenue of 350 year old Spanish chestnuts. Iron Age Fort (Croft Ambrey) may be reached by footpath. The walk is uphill (approx. 40 mins).

Location: OS137 Ref. SO455 655. 5m NW of Leominster, 9m SW of Ludlow, approach from B4362.

Opening times: Castle: Apr & Oct: Sats & Suns, Good Fri & BH Mons. May - end Sept: daily except Mons & Tues, 1.30 - 5.30pm (closes 4.30pm in Oct). Park & Croft Ambrey: daily.

Admission: Adult £3.80, Child £1.90. Family £9.50. Grounds only: Car park £2 per car, £10 per coach.

CWMMAU FARMHOUSE

Tel: 01497 831251

Brilley, Whitney-on-Wye, Herefordshire HR3 6JP

Owner: The National Trust **Contact:** Mr D Joyce

Early 17th century timber-framed and stone-tiled farmhouse.

Location: OS Ref. SO267 514. 4m SW of Kington between A4111 & A438, approach by a narrow lane leading S from Kington - Brilley road at Brilley Mountain.

Opening Times: May - Aug: Weds & BH Mons, 2 - 5.30pm.

Admission: £2.50.

 Obligatory.

EASTNOR CASTLE

See page 274 for full page entry.

GOODRICH CASTLE

Tel: 01600 890538

Ross-on-Wye, Herefordshire HR9 6HY

Owner: English Heritage **Contact:** The Custodian

This magnificent red sandstone castle is remarkably complete with a 12th century keep and extensive remains from 13th & 14th centuries. From the battlements there are fine views over the Wye Valley to Symonds Yat. Marvel at the maze of small rooms and the 'murder holes'.

Location: OS162, Ref. SO579 199. 5m S of Ross-on-Wye, off A40.

Opening Times: 1 Apr - 31 Oct: daily, 10am - 6pm (5pm in Oct). 1 Nov - 31 Mar: daily, 10am - 4pm. Closed 24 - 26 Dec & 1 Jan.

Admission: Adult £3.20, Child £1.60, Conc. £2.40. 15% discount for groups (11+).

Tel. for details.

HELLENS

Tel: 01531 660504

Much Marcle, Ledbury, Herefordshire HR8 2LY

Owner: Pennington-Mellor-Munthe Charity Trust **Contact:** The Custodian

Manorial house, built in the 13th century, Tudor, Jacobean and Stuart additions.

Location: OS Ref. SO661 332. 1/2 m E of Much Marcle, access from B4024, 400yds S of A449 crossroads.

Opening Times: Good Fri - end Sept: Weds, Sats, Suns & BH Mons, guided tours at 2, 3, 4pm. Pre-arranged groups at other times.

Admission: Adult £3.50, Child £1.50.

HEREFORD CATHEDRAL

Tel: 01432 359880

Hereford HR1 2NG

e-mail: office@mappa-mundi.co.uk

Contact: Mr D Harbour

Location: OS Ref. SO510 398. Hereford city centre on A49.

Opening Times: 9.15am - 5pm. Sun services: 8am, 10am, 11.30am & 3.30pm. Weekday services: 8am and 5.30pm.

Admission: Admission only for Mappa Mundi and Chained Library. Discounts for booked groups of 10+.

HERGEST COURT

Tel/Fax: 01544 230160

c/o Hergest Estate Office, Kington HR5 3EG

Owner/Contact: W L Banks

The ancient home of the Vaughans of Hergest, dating from the 13th century.

Location: OS Ref. SO283 554. 1m W of Kington on unclassified road to Brilley.

Opening Times: Strictly by appointment only through Estate Office.

Admission: Adult £4, Child £1.50. Groups: Adult £3.50, Child £1.

Not suitable. Limited. Guide dogs only. 

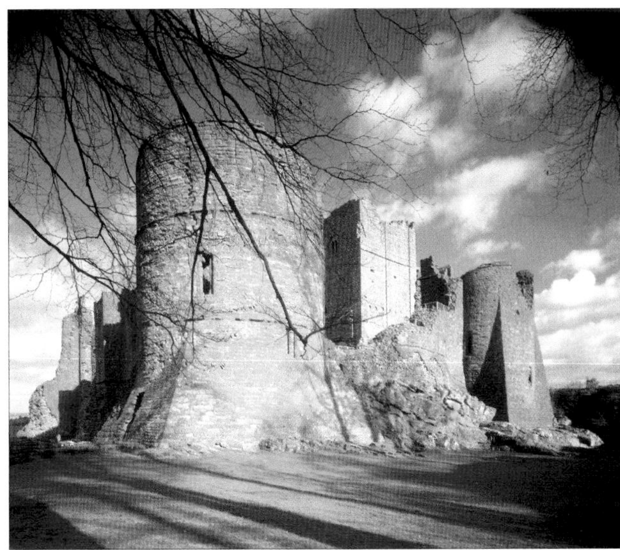

Goodrich Castle, Herefordshire.

HERGEST CROFT GARDENS 

KINGTON, HEREFORDSHIRE HR5 3EG

Owner: *W L Banks* ***Contact:*** *Elizabeth Banks*

Tel/Fax: 01544 230160 **e-mail:** banks@hergest.kc3ltd.co.uk

From spring bulbs to autumn colour, this is a garden for all seasons. An old-fashioned kitchen garden has spring and summer borders and roses. Over 59 Champion trees and shrubs grow in one of the finest collections in the British Isles. Holds National Collection of birches, maples and zelkovas. Park Wood is a hidden valley with rhododendrons up to 30 ft tall.

Location: OS Ref. SO281 565. On W side of Kington. 1/2 m off A44, left at Rhayader end of bypass. Turn right and gardens are 1/4 m on left. Signposted from bypass.

Opening Times: 1 Apr - 31 Oct: 1.30 - 6pm. Season tickets and groups by arrangement throughout the year. Winter by appointment.

Admission: Adult £3.50, Child (under 16yrs) Free. Groups (20+) £3. Guided groups (20+) £4.50 (must book). Season ticket £12.

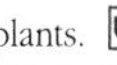   

Gift sales. Rare plants. In grounds, on leads.

KINNERSLEY CASTLE

KINNERSLEY, HEREFORDSHIRE HR3 6QF

Contact: *Caius & Kate Hawkins*

Tel: 01544 327507 **Fax:** 01544 327663 **e-mail:** castle@kinnersley.com

Welsh border castle remodelled by Roger Vaughan in the 1580s. Still a family home, it has housed among others the de Kinnardsleys, the de la Beres and parliamentary general Sir Thomas Morgan. Shows some fine plasterwork and panelling. Gardens boast one of the largest ginkgo trees in the UK. Many yew hedges and a walled kitchen garden. Will be hosting open air theatrical events this summer.

Location: OS Ref. SO346 496. 4m W of Weobley on A4112, 15m W of Hereford.

Opening Times: Castle & Gardens: 17 Jul - 20 Aug: daily except Mons, for guided tours only at 2.30 & 3.30pm. Coach parties by arrangement.

Admission: Castle & Gardens: Adult £2.50, Child £1.50, Conc. £2. Groups: £2. Groups by arrangement throughout the year.

  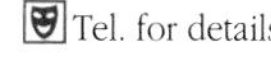 

Teas by arrangement. Tel. for details.

HOW CAPLE COURT GARDENS

Tel: 01989 740626 **Fax:** 01989 740611

How Caple, Hereford HR1 4SX

Owner: Mr & Mrs Roger Lee **Contact:** Howard Oddy

Exciting 11 acre garden overlooking River Wye.

Location: OS Ref. SO613 306. In NE end of How Caple. 1m W of the B4224 Ross-on-Wye/Fownhope Road.

Opening Times: Mar - Sept: daily, 9am - 5pm.

Admission: Adult £2.50, Child £1.25.

Hergest Croft Gardens, Herefordshire.

LONGTOWN CASTLE

Tel: 01604 730320 (Regional Office)

Abbey Dore, Herefordshire

Owner: English Heritage **Contact:** The Midlands Regional Office

An unusual cylindrical keep built c1200 with walls 15ft thick. There are magnificent views of the nearby Black Mountains.

Location: OS Ref. SO321 291. 4m WSW of Abbey Dore.

Opening Times: Any reasonable time.

Admission: Free.

LOWER BROCKHAMPTON

Tel: 01885 488099

Bringsty, Worcestershire WR6 5UH

Owner: The National Trust **Contact:** The Administrator

A late 14th century moated manor house, with an attractive detached half-timbered 15th century gatehouse, a rare example of this type of structure. Also, the ruins of a 12th century chapel. Woodland walks including sculpture trail. Easy access for all, long and short waymarked walks.

Location: OS149, Ref. SO682 546. 2m E of Bromyard N side of A44, reached by narrow road through 1 1/2 m of woods and farmland.

Opening Times: Medieval Hall, parlour, minstrel gallery, information room, gatehouse and chapel: 1 Apr - end Oct: Wed - Sun & BH Mons, 12.30 - 5pm. Closed Good Fri. Last admission 1/2 hr before closing.

Admission: Adult £2.50, Child £1.25, Family £5.50. Car park £1.50.

Partially suitable.

MOCCAS COURT

Tel: 01981 500381

Moccas, Herefordshire HR2 9LH

Owner: Trustees of the Baunton Trust **Contact:** Ivor Saunders

18th century Adam interiors, 'Capability' Brown park.

Location: OS149 Ref. SO359 434. 1m N of B4352, 3 1/2 m SE of Bredwardine.

Opening Times: Apr - Sept: Thurs, 2 - 6pm.

Admission: £2.

OLD SUFTON

Tel: 01432 870268/850328 Fax: 01432 850381

Mordiford, Hereford HR1 4EJ

Owner: Trustees of Sufton Heritage Trust **Contact:** Mr & Mrs J N Hereford

A 16th century manor house which was altered and remodelled in the 18th and 19th centuries and again in this century. The original home of the Hereford family (see Sufton Court) who have held the manor since the 12th century.

Location: OS Ref. SO575 384. Mordiford, off B4224 Mordiford - Dormington road.

Opening Times: By written appointment to Sufton Court or by fax.

Admission: Adult £2, Child 50p.

Partially suitable. Obligatory.  

ROTHERWAS CHAPEL

Tel: 01604 730320 (Regional Office)

Hereford, Herefordshire

Owner: English Heritage **Contact:** Midlands Regional Office

This Roman Catholic chapel, dating from the 14th and 16th centuries, is testament to the past grandeur of the Bodenham family and features an interesting mid-Victorian side chapel and High Altar.

Location: OS Ref. SO537 383. 1½ m SE of Hereford 500yds N of B4399.

Opening Times: Any reasonable time. Keykeeper at nearby filling station.

Admission: Free.

SUFTON COURT

Tel: 01432 870268/850328 Fax: 01432 850381

Mordiford, Hereford HR1 4LU

Owner: J N Hereford **Contact:** Mr & Mrs J N Hereford

Sufton Court is a small Palladian mansion house. Built in 1788 by James Wyatt for James Hereford. The park was laid out by Humphrey Repton whose 'red book' still survives. The house stands above the rivers Wye and Lugg giving impressive views towards the mountains of Wales.

Location: OS Ref. SO574 379. Mordiford, off B4224 on Mordiford to Dormington road.

Opening Times: 16 - 29 May & 15 - 28 Aug: 2 - 5pm.

Admission: Adult £2, Child 50p.

Partially suitable. Obligatory. Only small coaches. In grounds, on leads.

THE WEIR

Tel: 01684 855300

Swainshill, Hereford, Herefordshire

Owner: The National Trust **Contact:** Regional Office

Delightful riverside garden particularly spectacular in early spring, with fine view over the River Wye and Black Mountains.

Location: OS Ref. SO435 421. 5m W of Hereford on S side of A438.

Opening Times: 14 Feb - 31 Oct: Wed - Sun (incl. Good Fri) & BH Mons 11am - 6pm.

Admission: £2.

Not suitable. No parking.

Eastnor Castle, Herefordshire.

BELVOIR CASTLE
Grantham

BELVOIR CASTLE, home of the Duke and Duchess of Rutland, commands a magnificent view over the Vale of Belvoir. The name Belvoir, meaning beautiful view, dates back to Norman times, when Robert de Todeni, Standard Bearer to William the Conqueror, built the first castle on this superb site. Destruction caused by two Civil Wars and by a catastrophic fire in 1816 have breached the continuity of Belvoir's history. The present building owes much to the inspiration and taste of Elizabeth, 5th Duchess of Rutland and was built after the fire.

Inside the Castle are notable art treasures including works by Poussin, Holbein, Rubens, and Reynolds, Gobelin and Mortlake tapestries, Chinese silks, furniture, fine porcelain and sculpture.

The Queen's Royal Lancers' Museum at Belvoir has a fascinating exhibition of the history of the Regiment, as well as a fine collection of weapons, uniforms and medals.

GARDENS

The Statue Gardens are built into the hillside below the castle and take their name from the collection of 17th century sculptures on view. The garden is planted so that there is nearly always something in flower.

The Duchess' private Spring Gardens are available for viewing throughout the year by pre-booked groups of 20 persons or more. Details from the Estate Office.

Owner: His Grace The Duke of Rutland

CONTACT

Diana Marshall
Castle Estate Office
Belvoir Castle
Grantham
Lincolnshire
NG32 1PD

Tel: 01476 870262

Fax: 01476 870443

LOCATION

OS Ref. SK820 337

A1 from London 110m York 100m Grantham 7m. A607 Grantham-Melton Mowbray.

Air: East Midlands International.

Rail: Grantham Station 7m

Bus: Melton Mowbray - Vale of Belvoir via Castle Car Park.

Taxi: Grantham Taxis 01476 563944 / 563988.

CONFERENCE/FUNCTION		
ROOM	SIZE	MAX CAPACITY
State Dining Room	52' x 31'	130
Regents Gallery	131' x 16'	300
Old Kitchen	45' x 22'	100

Suitable for exhibitions, product launches, conferences, filming, photography welcomed (permit £2).

Banquets, private room available.

Ground floor and restaurant accessible. Please telephone for advice. WC.

Licensed restaurant. Groups catered for.

By prior arrangement Additional charge of £1pp. Tour time: $1^{1}/_{4}$ hrs.

Ample. Coaches can take passengers to entrance by arrangement but should report to the main car park and ticket office on arrival.

Guided tours. Teacher's pack. Education room. Picnic area and adventure playground.

Guide dogs only.

OPENING TIMES

SUMMER
1 April - 1 October

Tue - Thur, Sats, Suns & BHs. Suns only in Oct. 11am - 5pm.

WINTER
Groups welcome by appointment.

ADMISSION

Adult	£5.25
Child (5-16yrs)	£3.00
OAP/Student	£4.00
Family (2+2)	£14.50
Groups (20-200)	
Adult	£4.00
Child (5-16yrs)	£2.50
Student	£2.50
OAP	£3.50

SPECIAL EVENTS

Please telephone for details of special events.

Owner: The Lady Braye

CONTACT

Lt Col E H L Aubrey-Fletcher
Stanford Hall
Lutterworth
Leicestershire
LE17 6DH

Tel: 01788 860250

Fax: 01788 860870

LOCATION

OS Ref. SP587 793

M1/J18 6m, M1/J19 (from/to the N only) 2m, M6 exit/access at A14/M1(N)J 2m, A14 2m.

Follow Historic House signs.

Rail: Rugby Station $7^1/_2$ m.

Air: Birmingham Airport 27m.

Taxi: Fone-A-Car. 01788 543333.

CONFERENCE/FUNCTION		
ROOM	SIZE	MAX CAPACITY
Ballroom	39' x 26'	100
Old Dining Rm	30' x 20'	70
Crocodile Room	39' x 20'	60

STANFORD HALL
Nr Rugby

STANFORD has been the home of the Cave family, ancestors of the present owner, Lady Braye, since 1430. In the 1690s, Sir Roger Cave commissioned the Smiths of Warwick to pull down the old Manor House and build the present Hall, which is an excellent example of their work and of the William and Mary period.

As well as over 5000 books, the handsome Library contains many interesting manuscripts, the oldest dating from 1150. The splendid pink and gold Ballroom has a fine coved ceiling with four *trompe l'oeil* shell corners. Throughout the house are portraits of the family and examples of furniture and objects which they collected over the centuries. There is also a collection of Royal Stuart portraits, previously belonging to the Cardinal Duke of York, the last of the male Royal Stuarts. An unusual collection of family costumes is displayed in the Old Dining Room, which also houses some early Tudor portraits and a fine Empire chandelier.

The Hall and Stables are set in an attractive Park on the banks of Shakespeare's Avon. There is a walled Rose Garden behind the Stables. An early ha-ha separates the North Lawn from the mile-long North Avenue.

Craft centre (most Suns). No photography in house. Available for corporate days, clay pigeon shoots, filming, photography, small conferences and fashion shows. Parkland, helicopter landing area, lecture room, Blüthner piano, fishing.

Available for lunches, dinners and wedding receptions using outside caterers.

Visitors may alight at the entrance. WC.

Homemade teas, lunch, and supper. Groups (70 max.) must book.

Tour time: 3/4 hr in groups of approx 25.

1,000 cars and 6 - 8 coaches. Free meals for coach drivers, coach parking on gravel in front of house.

£1.80 per child. Guide provided by prior arrangement, nature trail with guide book & map, motorcycle museum.

 In park, on leads.

OPENING TIMES

SUMMER

Easter - end Sept:
Sats & Suns, 2.30 - 5.30pm.

Closed Mon - Fri except BH Mons & Tues following 2.30 - 5.30pm.

Last admission 5pm.

NB. On BHs & Event days, open at 12 noon (House at 2.30pm). Open any day or evening for pre-booked parties.

WINTER

October - Easter
Closed to public, except during October for corporate events.

ADMISSION

House & Grounds

Adult	£4.00
Child (4-15yrs)	£2.00
Groups (20+)	
Adult	£3.70
Child (4-15yrs)	£1.80

Grounds only

Adult	£2.30
Child (4-15yrs)	£1.00

Motorcycle Museum

Adult	£1.00
Child (4-15yrs)	£0.35
School Group	
Adult	FREE
Child (4-15yrs)	£0.20

SPECIAL EVENTS

Please telephone for details of special events.

ABBEY PUMPING STATION

Tel: 0116 2995111 **Fax:** 0116 2995125

Corporation Road, Leicester LE4 5PX

Owner: Leicester City Council **Contact:** Stuart Warburton

A Victorian sewage pumping station with four massive beam engines still working by steam. Exhibition 'Flushed with Pride' history, science and technology of public health. Exhibitions include: 'Fun at the Flicks' and 'Transport of Delight'. Series of special events and steam rallies/days throughout the year.

Location: OS Ref. SK589 067. 2m N of city centre situated on River Soar riverside walk and A6. 5 mins from Belgrave Hall.

Opening Times: Apr - Oct: Mon - Sat, 10am - 5pm, Sun, 2 - 5pm. Nov - Mar: Mon - Sat, 10am - 4.30pm, Sun, 1.30 - 4.30pm.

Admission: Free except for special events.

Partially suitable. On event days. By arrangement. Guide dogs only. Tel. for details.

ASHBY-DE-LA-ZOUCH CASTLE

Tel: 01530 413343

South Street, Ashby-de-la-Zouch, Leicestershire LE65 1BR

Owner: English Heritage **Contact:** The Custodian

The impressive ruins of this late medieval castle are dominated by a magnificent tower, over 80 feet high, which was split in two during the Civil War. Panoramic views.

Location: OS Ref. SK363 167. In Ashby de la Zouch, 12m S of Derby on A511. SE of town centre.

Opening Times: 1 Apr - 31 Oct: daily, 10am - 6pm (5pm in Oct). 1 Nov - 31 Mar: Wed - Sun, 10am - 4pm. Closed 24 - 26 Dec & 1 Jan.

Admission: Adult £2.60, Child £1.30, Conc. £2.

Grounds suitable. On leads. Tel. for details.

BELGRAVE HALL & GARDENS

Tel: 0116 2666590 **Fax:** 0116 2613063

Church Road, off Thurcaston Road, Leicester LE4 5PE

Contact: Stuart Warburton

Belgrave Hall and Gardens, famed for its ghost story, is a period house with period decoration ranging from 1750 - 1900. The three story house is open throughout, and a series of special events is organised throughout the year using themes and living interpretation. The gardens include period Victorian formal gardens. Displays include the Gimson Collection.

Location: OS Ref. SK593 072. 2m N of city centre, on riverside walk and off the A6/A46 Loughborough Road.

Opening Times: Apr - Oct: Mon - Sat, 10am - 5pm, Sun, 2 - 5pm. Nov - Mar: Mon - Sat, 10am - 4.30pm, Sun, 1.30 - 4.30pm.

Admission: Free.

Partially suitable. WC. Staff with sign language skills. By arrangement. Limited (on street). Guide dogs only. Tel. for details.

BELVOIR CASTLE

See page 278 for full page entry.

BRADGATE PARK & SWITHLAND WOOD COUNTRY PARK

Bradgate Park, Newtown Linford, Leics **Tel:** 0116 2362713 **Fax:** 0116 2341851

Owner: Bradgate Park Trust **Contact:** M H Harrison

Includes the ruins of the brick medieval home of the Grey family and childhood home of Lady Jane Grey. Also has a medieval deer park.

Location: OS Ref. SK534 102. 7m NW of Leicester, via Anstey & Newtown Linford. Country Park gates in Newtown Linford. 1¼ m walk to the ruins.

Opening Times: All year during daylight hours.

Admission: No charge. Car parking charges.

DONINGTON-LE-HEATH MANOR HOUSE

Tel: 01530 831259

Manor Road, Donington-le-Heath, Leicestershire LE67 2FW

Owner/Contact: Leicestershire County Council

Medieval manor c1280 with 16th-17th century alterations.

Location: OS Ref. SK421 126. ½ m SSW of Coalville. 4½ m W of M1/J22, by A50.

Opening Times: Apr - Sept: daily, 11am - 5pm. Oct - Mar: daily 11am - 3pm.

Admission: Free.

Special Events Index PAGE 40

THE GUILDHALL

Tel: 0116 2532569 **Fax:** 0116 2539626

Guildhall Lane, Leicester LE1 5FQ

Owner: Leicester City Council **Contact:** Nicholas Ladlow

Magnificent timber-framed medieval building c1390. First used by the Corpus Christi Guild. Became town hall until 1876, includes 17th century town library and Victorian police cells. The great hall provides a unique setting for a varied programme of music, storytelling and theatre.

Location: OS Ref. SK584 044. Adjacent to High Street, Cathedral and St Nicholas Place.

Opening Times: Apr - Oct: Mon - Sat, 10am - 5pm, Sun, 2 - 5pm. Nov - Mar: Mon - Sat, 10am - 4.30pm, Sun, 1.30 - 4.30pm.

Admission: Free.

Partially suitable. Obligatory. No parking. Guide dogs only. Tel. for details.

JEWRY WALL MUSEUM & SITE

Tel: 0116 2473021 **Fax:** 0116 2512257

St Nicholas Circle, Leicester LE1 4LB

Owner: Leicester City Council **Contact:** Bob Rutland (Curator)

Jewry Wall Museum focuses on the archaeology and history of Leicestershire from prehistoric times to 1485. Inside you can see the skeleton of the Saxon 'Glen Parva Lady' alongside fine mosaics, wall paintings and other legacies of the Roman settlement. A series of exhibitions explain key aspects of Leicestershire archaeology over the years. After visiting the museum, explore the site of the Roman baths and wonder at the massive 2nd century Jewry Wall.

Location: OS Ref. SK581 044. On St Nicholas Circle, at W end of High Street, opposite the Holiday Inn, next to St Nicholas Church.

Opening Times: Apr - Oct: Mon - Sat, 10am - 5pm, Sun, 2 - 5pm. Nov - Mar: Mon - Sat, 10am - 4.30pm, Sun, 1.30 - 4.30pm.

Admission: Free.

Partially suitable. WC. By arrangement. No parking. Guide dogs only.

KIRBY MUXLOE CASTLE

Tel: 01162 386886

Kirby Muxloe, Leicestershire

Owner: English Heritage **Contact:** Midlands Regional Office

Picturesque, moated, brick built castle begun in 1480 by William Lord Hastings. It was left unfinished after Hastings was executed in 1483.

Location: OS Ref. SK524 046. 4m W of Leicester off B5380.

Opening Times: 1 Apr - 31 Oct: weekends & BHs only, 12 noon - 5pm.

Admission: Adult £1.95, Child £1, Conc. £1.50.

LYDDINGTON BEDE HOUSE

Tel: 01572 822438

Blue Coat Lane, Lyddington, Uppingham, Rutland LE15 9LZ

Owner: English Heritage **Contact:** The Custodian

Set among golden-stone cottages, the Bede House was originally a medieval palace of the Bishops of Lincoln. It was later converted into an alms house.

Location: OS Ref. SP875 970. In Lyddington, 6m N of Corby, 1m E of A6003.

Opening Times: 1 Apr - 31 Oct: daily, 10am - 6pm (5pm in Oct). Closed 1 - 2pm.

Admission: Adult £2.60, Child £1.30, Conc. £2.

NEW WALK MUSEUM

Tel: 0116 2554100 **Fax:** 0116 2473005

New Walk, Leicester LE1 7EA

Owner: Leicester City Council **Contact:** John Martin

Leicester's first public museum, opened in 1849, houses six permanent exhibitions: The Ancient Egypt Gallery, Natural History (including dinosaurs), German Expressionist, Victorian and European Art Galleries and a Decorative Art Gallery. The Discovery Room invites younger visitors to try on replica clothes, handle real objects and explore the natural world.

Location: OS Ref. SK591 039. Museum Sq, New Walk, Leicester. Leicester Station 250metres.

Opening Times: Apr - Oct: Mon - Sat, 10am - 5pm, Sun, 2 - 5pm. Nov - Mar: Mon - Sat, 10am - 4.30pm, Sun, 1.30 - 4.30pm.

Admission: Free.

By arrangement. Limited. Guide dogs only.

NEWARKE HOUSES MUSEUM

Tel: 0116 2473222 **Fax:** 0116 2470403

The Newarke, Leicester LE2 7BY

Owner: Leicester City Council **Contact:** Yolanda Countney

Over 500 years of Leicester's social history can be traced through a visit to Newarke Houses. Everyday life at home and at work is represented in displays of domestic equipment, clocks, toys and furniture. Visit the 1940s village grocer's shop, the reconstructed Victorian street scene and workshops of various local trades. Items belonging to Daniel Lambert, Leicester's largest man, can be seen in the museum. Don't forget to visit the beautiful gardens to the rear of the museum.

Location: OS Ref. SK584 041. Just SW of city centre ring road.

Opening Times: Apr - Oct: Mon - Sat, 10am - 5pm, Sun, 2 - 5pm. Nov - Mar: Mon - Sat, 10am - 4.30pm, Sun, 1.30 - 4.30pm.

Admission: Free.

Photography in house by permission only. Not suitable. By arrangement. No parking. Guide dogs only.

OAKHAM CASTLE

Tel: 01572 723654

Rutland County Museum, Catmos St, Oakham, Rutland LE15 6HW

Owner: Rutland County Council **Contact:** Mr Clough

Exceptionally fine Norman Great Hall of a late 12th century fortified manor house, with contemporary musician sculptures. Bailey earthworks and remains of earlier motte. The hall contains over 200 unique horseshoes forfeited by royalty and peers of the realm to the Lord of the Manor from Edward IV onwards.

Location: OS Ref. SK862 088. Near town centre, E of the church.

Opening Times: Castle grounds: Apr - Oct: daily 10am - 5.30pm. Nov - Mar: daily 10am - 4pm. Great Hall: Apr - Oct: Tue - Sat & BH Mons, 10am - 1pm & 2 - 5.30pm, Suns, 2 - 5.30pm. Nov - Mar: Tue - Sat, 10am - 1pm & 2 - 4pm. Suns, 2 - 4pm. Closed Good Fri & 25/26 Dec.

Admission: Free.

Great Hall suitable. For disabled, on request.  

Oakham Castle, Leicestershire.

PRESTWOLD HALL

LOUGHBOROUGH, LEICESTERSHIRE LE12 5SQ

Owner: *E J Packe-Drury-Lowe* ***Contact:*** *Henry Weldon*

Tel: 01509 880236 **Fax:** 01509 889060 **e-mail:** henryweldon@hotmail.com

A magnificent private house, largely remodelled in 1843 by William Burn. For the past 350 years it has been the home of the Packe family and contains fine Italian plasterwork, 18th century English and European furniture and a collection of family portraits. The house is not open to the general public but offers excellent facilities as a conference centre, corporate entertainment and wedding venue. Up to 150 guests can be seated and the 20 acres of gardens provide a perfect setting for larger events using marquees. Excellent chefs provide a selection of varied menus complemented by a well stocked wine cellar. Activity days, clay pigeon shooting, motor sports and archery can also be organised on request.

Location: OS Ref. SK578 215. At the heart of the Midlands, 3m E of Loughborough on B675. 5m W of A46 via B676.

Admission: Corporate entertaining venue, conference centre and function venue by arrangement only.

Conferences. Ground floor & grounds suitable. WC.  

Stanford Hall, Leicestershire.

STANFORD HALL

See page 279 for full page entry.

STAUNTON HAROLD CHURCH

Tel: 01332 863822 **Fax:** 01332 865272

Staunton Harold Church, Ashby-de-la-Zouch, Leicestershire

One of the very few churches to be built during the Commonwealth, erected by Sir Robert Shirley, an ardent Royalist. The interior retains its original 17th century cushions and hangings, and includes fine panelling and painted ceilings.

Location: OS Ref. SK379 208. 5m NE of Ashby-de-la-Zouch, W of B587.

Opening Times: 1 Apr - 1 Oct: Wed - Sun & BH Mons (closed Good Fri), 1 - 5pm or sunset if earlier. Oct: Sats & Suns only, 1 - 5pm.

Admission: £1 donation.

Partially suitable. At hall.

WARTNABY GARDENS

Tel: 01664 822296 **Fax:** 01164 822231

Melton Mowbray, Leicestershire LE14 3HY

Owner: Lord and Lady King

This garden has delightful little gardens within it, including a white garden, a sunken garden and a purple border of shrubs and roses, and there are good herbaceous borders, climbers and old-fashioned roses. A large pool has an adjacent bog garden with primulas, ferns, astilbes and several varieties of willow. There is an arboretum with a good collection of trees and shrub roses, and alongside the drive is a beech hedge in a Grecian pattern. Greenhouses, a fruit and vegetable garden with rose arches and cordon fruit.

Location: OS Ref. SK709 228. 4m NW of Melton Mowbray. From A606 turn W in Ab Kettleby for Wartnaby.

Opening Times: 30 Apr & 25 Jun, 11am - 4pm. Groups by appointment at other times (except Weds). Plant sales only on 25 June.

Admission: Adult £2.50, Child Free.

By arrangement. Limited for coaches. In grounds on leads.

WYGSTON'S HOUSE MUSEUM OF COSTUME

Tel: 0116 2473056

12 Applegate, St Nicholas' Place, Leicester LE1 5LD

Fax: 0116 2620964

Owner: Leicester City Council **Contact:** Nicholas Ladlow

A fine late 15th century dwelling thought to be the home of Roger Wygston (1430 - 1507), one of Leicester's benefactors. Now displays 'Kaleidoscope of Crafts' and a reconstructed 1920s drapers' shop. There is also a children's dressing-up area which includes replica costumes.

Location: OS Ref. SK583 044. Off St Nicholas' Circle at the top of the High Street, 200yds W of Guildhall and Cathedral.

Opening Times: Apr - Oct: Mon - Sat, 10am - 5pm, Sun, 2 - 5pm. Nov - Mar: Mon - Sat, 10am - 4.30pm, Sun, 1.30 - 4.30pm.

Admission: Free.

Partially suitable. By arrangement. Car park adjacent. 

Guide dogs only.

Owner: The Earl Spencer

CONTACT

Visitor Manager
Althorp
Northampton
NN7 4HQ

Tel: 01604 770107

Fax: 01604 770042

Dedicated booking line: 01604 592020

LOCATION

OS Ref. SP682 652

From the M1/J16, 7m J18, 10m. Situated on A428 Northampton - Rugby. London on average 85 mins away.

Rail: 5m from Northampton station. 14m from Rugby station.

ALTHORP
Northampton

The history of Althorp is the history of a family. The Spencers have lived and died here for nearly five centuries and twenty generations.

Since the death of Diana, Princess of Wales, Althorp has become known across the world, but before that tragic event, connoisseurs had heard of this most classic of English stately homes on account of the magnificence of its contents and the beauty of its setting.

Next to the mansion at Althorp lies the honey-coloured stable block, a truly breathtaking building which at one time accommodated up to 100 horses and 40 grooms. The stables are now the setting for the Exhibition celebrating the life of Diana, Princess of Wales and honouring her memory after her death. The freshness and modernity of the facilities are a unique tribute to a woman who captivated the world in her all-too-brief existence.

All visitors are invited to view the House, Exhibition and Grounds as well as the Island in the Round Oval where Diana, Princess of Wales is laid to rest.

Please contact the dedicated booking line (24 hour service) Tel: 01604 592020

Information leaflet issued to all ticket holders who book in advance. No indoor photography with still or video cameras.

Suitable. Visitor Centre and ground floor of house accessible. WCs.

Café.

Limited for coaches.

Guide dogs only.

© John O'Brien

OPENING TIMES

SUMMER
1 July - 30 August
Daily, 9am - 5pm.

Last admission 4pm.

At the time of booking visitors will be asked to state a preference for a morning or an afternoon visit.

Pre-booking strongly recommended.

WINTER
Closed.

ADMISSION

House & Garden (Pre-booked)

Adult	£10.00
Child* (5-17yrs)	£5.00
OAP	£7.50

(Paying at gate subject to availablity)

Adult	£11.00
Child* (5-17yrs)	£5.00
OAP	£8.50

Groups (30+)

Per person	£9.50

* under 5yrs free.

Group visits by arrangement only.

All the profits from visitor activity at Althorp are donated to the **Diana, Princess of Wales Memorial Fund**.

Numbers are limited each day. Advance booking is strongly recommended.

Owner:
His Grace The Duke of Buccleuch & Queensberry KT

CONTACT

Gareth Fitzpatrick
The Living Landscape Trust
Boughton House
Kettering
Northamptonshire
NN14 1BJ

Tel: 01536 515731

Fax: 01536 417255

e-mail:
llt@boughtonhouse.org.uk

LOCATION

OS Ref. SP900 815

3m N of Kettering on A43 - junction from A14.

Signposted through Geddington.

CONFERENCE/FUNCTION		
ROOM	SIZE	MAX CAPACITY
Lecture		100
Seminar Rm		25
Conference facilities available in stable block adjacent to House		

BOUGHTON HOUSE
Kettering

BOUGHTON HOUSE is the Northamptonshire home of the Duke of Buccleuch and Queensberry KT, and his Montagu ancestors since 1528. A 500 year old Tudor monastic building gradually enlarged around seven courtyards until the French style addition of 1695, which has lead to Boughton House being described as 'England's Versailles'.

The house contains an outstanding collection of 17th and 18th century French and English furniture, tapestries, 16th century carpets, porcelain, painted ceilings and notable works by El Greco, Murillo, Caracci and 40 Van Dyck sketches. There is an incomparable Armoury and Ceremonial Coach.

Beautiful parkland with historic avenues, lakes, picnic area, gift shop, adventure woodland play area, plant centre and tearoom. Boughton House is administered by The Living Landscape Trust, which was created by the present Duke of Buccleuch to show the relationship between the historic Boughton House and its surrounding, traditional, working estate.

For information on the groups visit programme and educational services, including fine arts courses run in conjunction with Sotheby's Institute, please contact The Living Landscape Trust. Our newly developed Internet website gives information on Boughton House and The Living Landscape Trust, including a 'virtual' tour, together with full details of our schools' educational facilities (Sandford Award winner 1988, 1993 and 1998).

Silver award winner of the 1st Historic House Awards, given by AA and NPI, in co-operation with the Historic Houses Association, for the privately-owned historic house open to the public which has best preserved its integrity, character of its architecture and furniture, while remaining a lived-in family home.

Parkland available for film location and other events. Stable block contains 100 seats and lecture theatre. No inside photography. No unaccompanied children. Browse our web site for a 'virtual' tour of the house

Access and facilities, no charge for wheelchair visitors. WCs.

Tearoom seats 80, groups must book. Licensed.

By arrangement.

P

Heritage Education Trust Sandford Award winner 1988, 1993 & 1998. School groups free, teachers' pack.

No dogs in house and garden, welcome in Park on leads.

By arrangement.

OPENING TIMES

SUMMER

House
1 August - 1 September
Daily, 2 - 4.30pm.

Grounds
1 May - 1 September
Daily:
(except Fris, May - July)
1 - 5pm.

During August opening staterooms on view strictly by prior appointment which can be made by telephone.

WINTER

Daily by appointment throughout the year for educational groups - contact for details.

ADMISSION

SUMMER

House & Grounds
Adult £6.00
Child/Conc. £5.00

Grounds
Adult £1.50
Child/Conc. £1.00

Wheelchair visitors free. HHA Friends are admitted Free in August.

WINTER

Group rates available – contact for further details.

Owner:
E Brudenell Esq

CONTACT

The House Keeper
Deene Park
Corby
Northamptonshire
NN17 3EW

Tel: 01780 450278
or 01780 450223

Fax: 01780 450282

LOCATION

OS Ref. SP950 929

6m NE of Corby off A43. From London via M1/J15 then A43. or via A1, A14, A43 - 2 hrs.

From Birmingham via M6, A14, A43, 90 mins.

Rail: Kettering Station 20 mins.

CONFERENCE/FUNCTION		
ROOM	SIZE	MAX CAPACITY
Great Hall	–	150
Tapestry Rm	–	75
East Room	–	18

DEENE PARK
Corby

A very interesting house which developed over six centuries from a typical medieval manor around a courtyard into a Tudor and Georgian mansion. Many rooms of different periods are seen by visitors who enjoy the impressive yet intimate ambience of the family home of the Brudenells, seven of whom were Earls of Cardigan. The most flamboyant of them was the 7th Earl who led the Light Brigade charge at Balaklava and of whom there are some historic relics and pictures.

The present owner is Mr Edmund Brudenell who has carefully restored the house from its dilapidated condition at the end of the last war and also added considerably to the furniture and picture collection.

The gardens have been made over the last thirty years, with long, mixed borders of shrubs, old fashioned roses and flowers, a recent parterre designed by David Hicks and long walks under fine old trees by the water.

The car park beside the big lake is a good place for picnics.

Suitable for indoor and outdoor events, filming, specialist lectures on house, its contents, gardens and history. No photography in house.

Including buffets, lunches and dinners.

Partially suitable. Visitors may alight at the entrance, access to ground floor and garden. WC.

Special rates for groups, bookings can be made in advance, menus on request.

Tours inclusive of admittance, tour time 90 mins. Owner will meet groups if requested.

Unlimited for cars, space for 3 coaches 10 yards from house.

In car park only.

Residential conference facilities by arrangement.

OPENING TIMES

SUMMER
June - August
Suns, 2 - 5pm

Open Suns & Mons for Easter, early and late Spring BHs & August BH 2 - 5pm.

Open at all other times by arrangement, including pre-booked parties.

WINTER
House and Gardens closed to casual visitors. Open at all other times by arrangement for groups.

ADMISSION

SUMMER

House & Gardens

Adult	£5.00
Child (10-14yrs)	£2.50
Child (under 10)	Free*

Gardens only

Adult	£3.00
Child (10-14yrs)	£1.50
Child (under 10)	Free*

Groups (20+)

Weekdays (Min £80)	£4.00
Weekends & BHs (Min £100)	£5.00

* Child up to 10yrs free with an accompanying adult.

WINTER
Groups visits only by prior arrangement.

SPECIAL EVENTS

- **MAY 17 - 21:** Antiques Fair
- **OCT 11 - 15:** Antiques Fair

LAMPORT HALL & GARDENS

Northampton

Owner: Lamport Hall Trust

CONTACT

George Drye
Executive Director
Lamport Hall
Northampton
NN6 9HD

Tel: 01604 686272

Fax: 01604 686224

e-mail: administrator@lamport-hall.co.uk

LOCATION

OS Ref. SP759 745

From London via M1/J15, $1^1/_4$ hours. Entrance on A508, 8m N of Northampton at junction with B576. $3^1/_2$ m S of A14 (A1/M1 link).

Rail: Kettering Station 9m. Northampton 8m.

Bus: From Northampton and Market Harborough.

CONFERENCE/FUNCTION		
ROOM	SIZE	MAX CAPACITY
Dining Rm	31' x 24' 6"	70

Home of the Isham family from 1560 to 1976. The 17th and 18th century façade is by John Webb and the Smiths of Warwick and the North Wing of 1861 by William Burn.

The Hall contains a wealth of outstanding furniture, books and paintings including portraits by Van Dyck, Kneller, Lely and others. The fine rooms include the High Room of 1655 with magnificent plasterwork, the 18th century library with books from the 16th century, the early 19th century Cabinet Room containing rare Venetian cabinets with mythological paintings on glass and the Victorian Dining Room where refreshments are served.

The first floor has undergone lengthy restoration allowing further paintings and furniture to be displayed as well as a photographic record of Sir Gyles Isham, a Hollywood actor, who initiated the restoration.

The tranquil gardens were laid out in 1655 although they owe much to Sir Charles Isham, the eccentric 10th Baronet who, in the mid-19th century, created the Italian Garden and the Rockery where he introduced the first garden gnomes to England. There are also box bowers, a rose garden and lily pond and extensive walks, borders and lawns all surrounded by a spacious park.

Conferences, garden parties, activity days, clay pigeon shoots, equestrian events, fashion shows, air displays, archery, rallies, filming, parkland, grand piano, 2 exhibition rooms. Lectures on history of property and gardens. Lecture/meeting rooms. No unaccompanied children. No photography in house.

Special functions, buffets, lunches and dinners, wedding receptions.

Visitors may alight at the entrance, access to ground floor and gardens. WC.

Dining/tearoom. Groups can book in advance.

At no additional cost, by prior arrangement, max 70 people, tour time $1^1/_4$ hours.

100 cars & 3 coaches, 20 yds from property. Use main entrance only (on A508).

Work room, specialist advisory teachers, study packs. Further information contact Education Officer or the Trust Office.

In grounds, on leads.

Tel. for details.

Tel. for further information.

OPENING TIMES

SUMMER
Easter - 1 October
Suns and BH Mons
2.15 - 5.15pm.
Last admission/tour 4pm.

August: Mon - Sat
open for only one
tour at 3.30pm.

21 & 22 October
2.15 - 5.15pm.

Tours on other days by prior arrangement.

WINTER
Group visits only by arrangement.

ADMISSION

SUMMER

House & Garden

Adult	£4.00
Child (5-16yrs)	£2.00
OAP	£3.50
Group*	POA

* Min. payment £135.00 excluding refreshments

WINTER
Group visits only by prior arrangement.

ROCKINGHAM CASTLE

Nr Corby

Owner:
James Saunders Watson Esq

CONTACT

Michael Tebbutt
Rockingham Castle
Market Harborough
Leicestershire
LE16 8TH

Tel: 01536 770240

Fax: 01536 771692

e-mail:
michaeltebbutt@lineone.net

LOCATION

OS Ref. SP867 913

2m N of Corby. 9m E of Market Harborough. 14m SW of Stamford on A427. 8m from Kettering on A6003.

Vehicle entrance on A6003 just S of junction with A6116.

CONFERENCE/FUNCTION		
ROOM	SIZE	MAX CAPACITY
Great Hall	37'6" x 22'	100
Panel Room	36' x 23'	100
Long Gallery	87' x 16'6"	100
Walkers House 1	31' x 17'6"	60
Walkers House 2	24' x 18'	50

A Royal castle until 1530, since then home of the Watson family. Rockingham Castle was built by William the Conqueror on the site of an earlier fortification and was regularly used by the early Kings of England until the 16th century, when it was granted by Henry VIII to Edward Watson whose family still live there today.

The house itself is memorable not so much as representing any particular period, but rather a procession of periods. The dominant influence in the building is Tudor within the Norman walls, but practically every century since the 11th has left its mark in the form of architecture, furniture or works of art. The castle has a particularly fine collection of English 18th, 19th and 20th century paintings, and Charles Dickens, who was a frequent visitor, was so captivated by Rockingham that he used it as a model for Chesney Wold in *Bleak House.*

The castle stands in 12 acres of formal and wild garden and commands a splendid view of five counties. Particular features are the 400 year old elephant hedge and the rose garden marking the foundations of the old keep. See Special Exhibition: "450 years a royal castle, 450 years a family home".

Concerts, conferences, fashion shows, product launches, receptions, seminars, air displays, clay pigeon shoots, archery, equestrian events, fairs, garden parties, filming. Exhibition celebrating 900 years of life in the castle. Parkland and cricket pitch. Strip for light aircraft 4m. No photography in Castle.

By arrangement.

Visitors may alight at entrance, ramps provided.

Home-made cream teas and light lunches. From 12.45pm.

All pre-booked parties have guided tour, except on open-days at no additional cost. Owner may meet groups by prior arrangement. Tour time 1 hour.

Unlimited.

Winner of 3 Sandford Awards for Heritage Education, special pack designed with National Curriculum. Tours for schools. £1.50 per head (min. charge £37.50). 1 adult free/15 children.

OPENING TIMES

SUMMER

23 Apr (Easter Sun) - 15 Oct
Thurs, Suns, BH Mons & Tues following and all Tues in August: 1 - 5pm.
Grounds open 11.30am on Suns & BHs. 12.45pm on other open days.
Refreshments available from 12.45pm on open days.

WINTER

By appointment for booked parties and schools.

ADMISSION

House & Garden

Adult £4.40
Child (up to 16 yrs)...£2.90
Conc......................£3.90
Family (2+2) £12.00

Groups (Min. charge £78)
Adult £3.90
Child (up to 16 yrs)...£2.90

Grounds only

.............................£2.90

Schools (min. charge £37.50)
Each child £1.50
1 adult Free with every 15 children.

Groups and school parties can be accommodated on most days by arrangement. Children qualify 5 - 16, Under 5s Free.

Prices may vary for special events held in grounds.

Please telephone for details.

ALTHORP See page 282 for full page entry.

BOUGHTON HOUSE See page 283 for full page entry.

CANONS ASHBY **Tel:** 01327 860044 **Fax:** 01327 860168

Canons Ashby, Daventry, Northamptonshire NN11 3SD

Owner: The National Trust **Contact:** The Property Manager

Home of the Dryden family since the 16th century, this Elizabethan manor house was built c1550, added to in the 1590s, and altered in the 1630s and c1710; largely unaltered since. Within the house, Elizabethan wall paintings and outstanding Jacobean plasterwork are of particular interest. A formal garden includes terraces, walls and gate piers of 1710. There is also a medieval priory church and a 70 acre park.

Location: OS152 Ref. SP577 506. Access from M40/J11, or M1/J16. Signposted from A5 2m S of Weedon crossroads. Then 7m to SW.

Opening Times: House: 1 Apr - 31 Oct: Sat - Wed including BH Mons (closed Thurs & Fris) 1 - 5.30pm/dusk. Last admissions 5pm. Park, Gardens & Church open as house, 12 noon - 5.30pm, access through garden. Shop: 12.30 - 5pm; Tea Room 12 noon - 5pm.

Admission: Adult £4, Child £2, Family £10. Discount for booked groups, contact Property Manager.

Suitable, some steps. WC.  In grounds, on leads.

CASTLE ASHBY

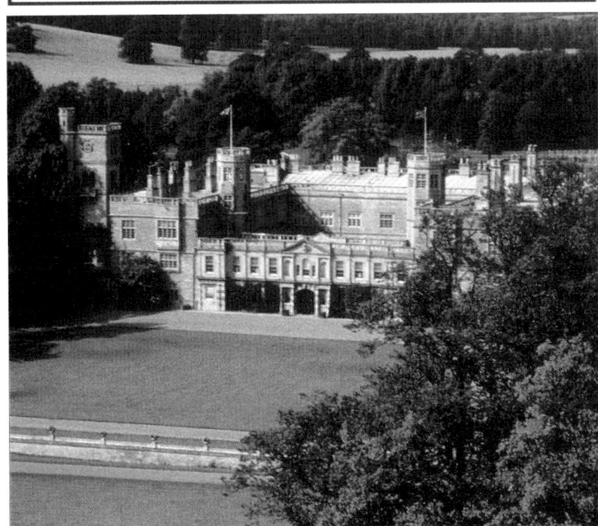

CASTLE ASHBY HOUSE, CASTLE ASHBY, NORTHAMPTON NN7 1LQ

Owner: *7th Marquess of Northampton* ***Contact:*** *General Manager*

Tel: 01604 696696 **Fax:** 01604 696516 **e-mail:** andreafowkes@castleashby.co.uk

Castle Ashby is the ancestral home of the 7th Marquess of Northampton, and was built in 1574 to entertain Queen Elizabeth. The castle itself has 26 exquisite bedrooms, including the State Suite, and is available on an exclusive basis for private events. The extensive gardens are open throughout the year and offer a combination of styles.

Location: OS Ref. SP862 582. 55m N of London, between Bedford and Northampton, off A428.

Opening Times: House not open to the public but available for private events. Gardens: All year, 10am - dusk.

Admission: Please telephone for details.

Private & corporate events.  

COTON MANOR GARDEN

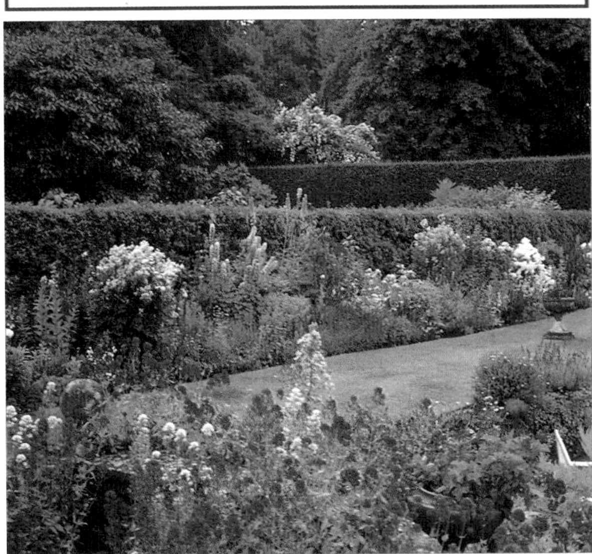

GUILSBOROUGH, NORTHAMPTONSHIRE NN6 8RQ

Owner: *Ian & Susie Pasley-Tyler* ***Contact:*** *Sarah Ball*

Tel: 01604 740219 **Fax:** 01604 740838

Traditional English garden laid out on different levels surrounding a 17th century stone manor house. Many herbaceous borders, with extensive range of plants, old yew and holly hedges, rose garden, water garden and fine lawns set in 10 acres. Also wild flower meadow and bluebell wood.

Location: OS Ref. SP675 716. 9m NW of Northampton, between A5119 (formerly A50) and A428.

Opening Times: 1 Apr - 30 Sept: Wed - Suns & BHs, 12 noon - 5.30pm.

Admission: Adult £3.50, Child £2, Conc. £3. Groups: £3.

 Grounds suitable. WC. By arrangement.

Tudor re-enactment, Sulgrave Manor, Northamptonshire.

COTTESBROOKE HALL & GDNS 

COTTESBROOKE, NORTHAMPTONSHIRE NN6 8PF

Owner: *Capt & Mrs John Macdonald-Buchanan* ***Contact:*** *The Administrator*

Tel: 01604 505808 **Fax:** 01604 505619

Architecturally magnificent house built in the reign of Queen Anne. The identity of the original architect remains a mystery but the house has stayed essentially the same since that time. Renowned picture collection, particularly of sporting and equestrian subjects. Fine English and Continental furniture and porcelain. House reputed to be the pattern for Jane Austen's *Mansfield Park*.

Celebrated gardens of great variety including herbaceous borders, water and wild gardens, fine old cedars and specimen trees. Magnolia, cherry and acer collections and several fine vistas across the Park. Notable planting of containers. A number of distinguished landscape designers have been involved including Rober Weir Schultz, the late Sir Geoffrey Jellicoe and the late Dame Sylvia Crowe.

Location: OS Ref. SP711 739. 10m N of Northampton near Creaton on A5199 (formerly A50), near Brixworth on A508 or Kelmarsh on A14.

Opening Times: House & Gardens: Easter - end Sept: Thurs & BH Mons, plus May - Sept: 1st Sun in each month, 2 - 5.30pm. Gardens only: Tue - Fri & BH Mons, plus May - Sept: 1st Sun in each month, 2 - 5.30pm.

Admission: House & Gardens: Adult £4. Gardens only: Adult £2.50, Child half price. RHS members Free. Private groups welcome (except weekends) by prior arrangement.

No photography in house. Craft Fairs & Open Air Concerts. Filming outside.

Unusual plants.

Banqueting facilities, corporate hospitality and catering for functions.

Gardens suitable. WC. Obligatory.

DEENE PARK

See page 284 for full page entry.

EDGCOTE HOUSE

Edgcote, Banbury, Oxfordshire OX17 1AG

Owner/Contact: Christopher Courage

Early Georgian house with good rococo plasterwork.

Location: OS Ref. SP505 480. 6m NE of Banbury off A361.

Opening Times: By written appointment only.

ELEANOR CROSS

Tel: 01604 730320 (Regional Office)

Geddington, Kettering, Northamptonshire

Owner: English Heritage **Contact:** The Midlands Regional Office

One of a series of famous crosses, of elegant sculpted design, erected by Edward I to mark the resting places of the body of his wife, Eleanor, when brought for burial from Harby in Nottinghamshire to Westminster Abbey in 1290.

Location: OS Ref. SP896 830. In Geddington, off A43 between Kettering and Corby.

Opening Times: Any reasonable time.

HADDONSTONE SHOW GARDEN

Tel: 01604 770711 **Fax:** 01604 770027

The Forge House, East Haddon, Northampton NN6 8DB

e-mail: info@haddonstone.co.uk

Owner: Haddonstone Ltd **Contact:** Marketing Director

See Haddonstone's classic garden ornaments in the beautiful setting of the walled manor gardens – including urns, troughs, fountains, statuary, bird baths, sundials and balustrading. The garden is on different levels with shrub roses, conifers, clematis and climbers. The newly opened Jubilee garden features a pavilion, temple and Gothic grotto.

Location: OS Ref. SP667 682. 7m NW of Northampton off A428.

Opening Times: Mon - Fri, 9am - 5.30pm. Closed weekends, BHs & Christmas period.

Admission: Free. Groups by appointment only. Not suitable for coach groups.

By arrangement. Limited. Guide dogs only. 

Patrick Lane.

Canons Ashby, Northamptonshire.

HOLDENBY HOUSE GARDENS & FALCONRY CENTRE

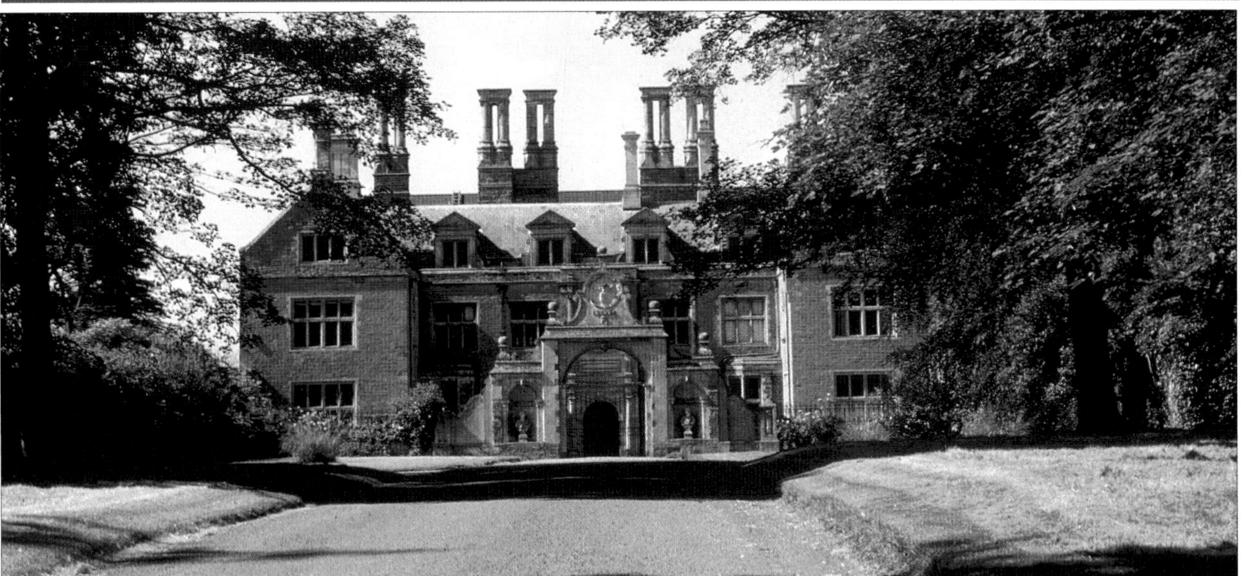

HOLDENBY, NORTHAMPTONSHIRE NN6 8DJ

Owner: *James Lowther Esq* ***Contact:*** *Mrs Sarah Maughan*

Tel: 01604 770074 **Fax:** 01604 770962

Just across the fields from Althorp lies Holdenby, a house whose royal connections go back over 400 years. Built by Sir Christopher Hatton to entertain Elizabeth I, this once largest house in England became the palace of James I and the prison of his son Charles I. Today the house is a family home and a splendid backdrop to a beautiful garden and Falconry Centre. Wander through Rosemary Verey's Elizabethan Garden and Rupert Golby's Fragrant Walk. Evoke the feeling of the 17th century by visiting the 17th century Farmstead. Then sit back to watch our magnificent birds of prey soar over this pastoral scene of so much history. Shop, teas and children's attractions.

Location: OS Ref. SP693 681. M1/J15a. 6m NW of Northampton off A428 or A5199.

Opening times: 1 Apr - end Sept. Gardens & Falconry Centre: Suns, 1 - 5pm. BH Suns & Mons, 1 - 6pm. Jul & Aug: daily except Sats, 1 - 5pm. House: 24 Apr, 29 May & 28 Aug, 1 - 6pm or by appointment.

Admission: Garden & Falconry Centre: Adult £3, Child (3-15yrs) £1.75, OAP £2.50. BH Events: Adult £4, Child £2, OAP £3.50. BH Events with house open: Adult £5, Child £3, OAP £4.50. Private tours: ring for prices.

Partially suitable. WC. Home-made teas. Groups must book. By arrangement. Sandford Award-winner. In grounds, on leads. Tel. for details.

KELMARSH HALL

Tel/Fax: 01604 686543

Kelmarsh, Northampton NN6 9LU

Owner: Kelmarsh Hall Estate Preservation Trust

Designed in the Palladian manner by James Gibbs and set in 3,500 acres of farm and woodland, Kelmarsh Hall was built between 1728 and 1732.

Location: OS Ref. SP736 795. $^1/_2$ m N of A508 / A14 (J2). 12m N of Northampton.

Opening Times: House & Gardens: 23 Apr - 28 Aug: Suns & BH Mons. Gardens only: 25 Apr -28 Sept: Tues & Thurs, 2.30 - 5pm.

KIRBY HALL

Tel: 01536 203230

Deene, Corby, Northamptonshire NN17 5EN

Owner: English Heritage **Contact:** The Custodian

Outstanding example of a large, stone-built Elizabethan mansion, begun in 1570 with 17th century alterations. There are fine gardens with topiary, home to peacocks. Jane Austen's *Mansfield Park* was filmed at Kirby Hall in 1998. A Civil wedding licence has been applied for.

Location: OS141 Ref. SP926 927. On unclassified road off A43, Corby to Stamford road, 4m NE of Corby. 2m W of Deene Park.

Opening Times: 1 Apr - 31 Oct: daily 10am - 6pm (5pm in Oct). 1 Nov - 31 Mar: Sats & Suns, 10am - 4pm. Closed 24 - 26 Dec & 1 Jan.

Admission: Adult £2.70, Child £1.40, Conc. £2.

    Tel. for details.

Special Events Index PAGE 40

LAMPORT HALL & GARDENS

See page 285 for full page entry.

LYVEDEN NEW BIELD

Tel: 01832 205358 **Fax:** 01832 205358

Nr Oundle, Peterborough PE8 5AT

Owner: The National Trust **Contact:** The Custodian

An incomplete lodge or garden house, begun in 1595 by Sir Thomas Tresham and now an intriguing and roofless shell. Designed in the shape of a cross, with interesting exterior friezework. Elizabethan water gardens.

Location: OS141 Ref. SP983 853. 4m SW of Oundle via A427, 3m E of Brigstock, off Harley Way. Access by foot along a $^1/_2$ m farm track.

Opening Times: All year: Wed - Sun, 9am - 5pm. Groups by arrangement with Custodian: Lyveden New Bield Cottage, Oundle, Peterborough PE8 5AT. Elizabethan water gardens open to groups by arrangement.

Admission: £2.

Limited. On leads.

Kirby Hall, re-enactment, Northamptonshire.

THE MENAGERIE

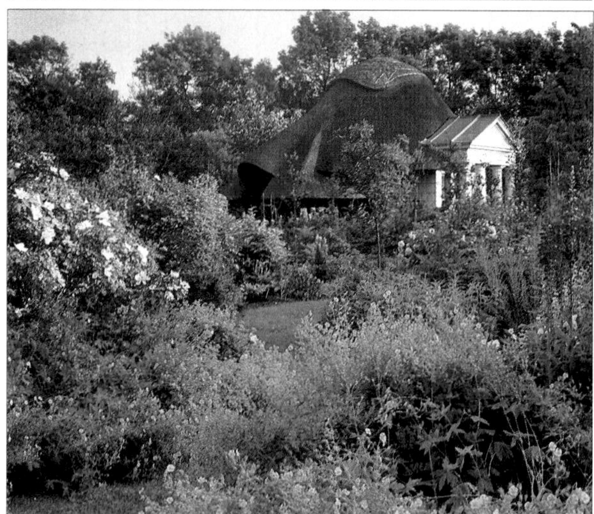

HORTON, NORTHAMPTON NN7 2BX

***Owner:** Mr A Myers* ***Contact:** Ms P Hammond*

Tel: 01604 870957

Folly built in the 1750s for the 2nd Earl of Halifax by the architect and astronomer Thomas Wright of Durham. The north front of the house has just been restored. The gardens, where Lord Halifax's animals were once kept, were created by the late Ian Kirby and include formal ponds, wetland and bog area, herbaceous border, two thatched arbours, one gothic and one circular and classical which is now a chapel. The whole grotto is covered in shells and minerals and devoted to Orpheus playing to the animals in the underworld.

Location: OS Ref. SP822 534. 5m SE of Northampton. Entry by field gate on E of A526.

Opening Times: Grotto & Gardens open to groups (20+) by arrangement £5. Gardens: Apr - Sept: Mons & Thurs, 2 - 5pm. Last Sun of each month 2 - 6pm.

Admission: Adult £3.50, Child £1.50.

Grounds suitable.

THE PREBENDAL MANOR HOUSE

NASSINGTON, PETERBOROUGH PE8 6QG

***Owner/Contact:** Mrs J Baile*

Tel: 01780 782575 **e-mail:** info@prebendal-manor.demon.co.uk

Grade I listed and dating from the early 13th century, it is the oldest manor in Northamptonshire and one of the longest continually occupied houses in the country. The manor still retains many fine original medieval features and included in the visit are the 15th century dovecote, tithe barn museum and medieval fish ponds. Designed by Michael Brown and unique to the area and encompassing 5 acres are the 14th century re-created medieval gardens.

Location: OS Ref. TL063 962. 6m N of Oundle, 9m W of Peterborough, 7m S of Stamford.

Opening times: May, Jun & Sept: Suns, Weds & BH Mons. Jul/Aug: Suns, Weds & Thurs. 1 - 5.30pm. Closed Christmas.

Admission: Adult £4, Child £1.20. Groups (20 - 50) outside normal opening times by arrangement: Adult £3.50, Child £1.

No photography. Wedding receptions. Partially suitable. Lunches & home-made teas. Limited. Free. Guide dogs only.

ROCKINGHAM CASTLE

See page 286 for full page entry.

RUSHTON TRIANGULAR LODGE

Tel: 01536 710761

Rushton, Kettering, Northamptonshire NN14 1RP

Owner: English Heritage **Contact:** The Custodian

This extraordinary building, completed in 1597, symbolises the Holy Trinity. It has three sides, 33 ft wide, three floors, trefoil windows and three triangular gables on each side.

Location: OS Ref. SP830 831. 1m W of Rushton, on unclassified road 3m from Desborough on A6.

Opening Times: 1 Apr - 31 Oct: daily, 10am - 6pm (5pm in Oct).

Admission: Adult £1.50, Child 80p, Conc. £1.10.

SOUTHWICK HALL

Tel: 01832 274064

Nr Oundle, Peterborough PE8 5BL

Owner: Christopher Capron Esq **Contact:** W J Richardson

A family home since 1300, retaining medieval building dating from 1300, with Tudor rebuilding and 18th century additions. Exhibitions: Victorian and Edwardian Life, collections of agricultural and carpentry tools and local archaeological finds.

Location: OS152 Ref. TL022 921. 3m N of Oundle, 4m E of Bulwick.

Opening Times: 23/24 Apr, 30 Apr/1 May, 28/29 May, 27/28 Aug, also Weds May - Aug: 2 - 5pm.

Admission: Adult £3.50, Child £2, OAP £3.

Partially suitable. WC. By arrangement. In grounds on leads.

STOKE PARK PAVILIONS

Tel: 01604 862172

Stoke Bruerne, Towcester, Northamptonshire NN12 7RZ.

Owner: A S Chancellor Esq **Contact:** Mrs C Cook

The two Pavilions, dated c1630 and attributed to Inigo Jones, formed part of the first Palladian country house built in England by Sir Francis Crane. The central block, to which the Pavilions were linked by quadrant colonnades, was destroyed by fire in 1886. The grounds include extensive gardens and overlook the former park, now farmland.

Location: OS Ref. SP740 488. 7m S of Northampton.

Opening Times: Aug: daily, 3 - 6pm. Other times by appointment only.

Admission: Adult £3, Child £1.

Grounds suitable. Limited. In grounds, on leads.

SULGRAVE MANOR

MANOR ROAD, SULGRAVE, BANBURY, OXON OX17 2SD

***Owner:** Sulgrave Manor Board* ***Contact:** Martin Sirot-Smith*

Tel: 01295 760205 **Fax:** 01295 768056

A delightful 16th century Manor House that was the home of George Washington's ancestors. Today it presents a typical wealthy man's home and gardens of Elizabethan times. Restored with scholarly care and attention to detail that makes a visit both a pleasure and an education. *'A perfect illustration of how a house should be shown to the public'* – Nigel Nicholson, *Great Houses of Britain*. New Courtyard development with fine visitor/education facilities.

Location: OS152 Ref. SP561 457. Off Banbury - Northampton road (B4525) 5m from M40/J11. 15m from M1/J15A.

Opening Times: 1 Apr - 31 Oct: daily except Weds. W/days 2 - 5.30pm, W/ends 10.30am - 1pm & 2 - 5.30pm. Nov, Dec & Mar: W/ends only, 10.30am - 1pm & 2 - 4.30pm. Also open 27 - 30 Dec. Closed 25 Jun, 25 - 26 & 31 Dec & Jan. Open by appointment for groups and school groups out of normal hours.

Admission: Adult £3.75, Child £2, Conc. £3.75. Groups: Adult £3.50, Child £1.75, Conc. £3.50. Special Events: Adult £4.50, Child £2.25, Family £12. Groups: Adult £4, Child £2. Gardens only: £2.

No photography in house. Partially suitable.

Obligatory.   In grounds, on leads. 

CARLTON HALL

Tel: 01636 821421 Fax: 01636 821554

Carlton-on-Trent, Nottinghamshire NG23 6LP

Owner/Contact: Lt Col & Mrs Vere-Laurie

Mid 18th century house by Joseph Pocklington of Newark. Stables attributed to Carr of York. Family home occupied by the same family since 1832.

Location: OS Ref. SK799 640. 7m N of Newark off A1. Opposite the church.

Opening Times: By appointment only.

Admission: Hall and Garden £3.50. Minimum charge for a group £35.

 Conferences.  Not suitable. 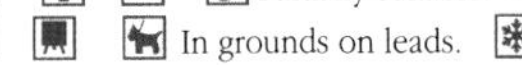 In grounds, on leads. Guide dogs in house. 

CASTLE MUSEUM & ART GALLERY

Tel: 01159 9153700 Fax: 01159 9153653

Nottingham NG1 6EL **Contact:** The Curator

17th century mansion with 13th century gateway, now a museum and art gallery.

Location: OS Ref. SK569 395. SW of the city centre on hilltop.

Opening Times: Daily (closed Fris from Nov-Feb): 10am - 5pm. Closed 24, 25 Dec & 1 Jan.

Admission: Weekdays Free. Weekends: Adult £2, Child £1 (1999 times & prices).

CLUMBER PARK

Tel: 01909 476592 Fax: 01909 500721

Clumber Park, Worksop, Nottinghamshire S80 3AZ

Owner: The National Trust **Contact:** Claire Herring, Property Manager

Historic parkland with peaceful woods, open heath and rolling farmland around a serpentine lake. Formerly home to the Dukes of Newcastle, Clumber House was demolished in 1938, but many estate features remain, including the gothic revival chapel, Hardwick village and the walled kitchen garden housing the longest glasshouses in National Trust ownership.

Location: OS120 Ref SK626 746. $4^1/_2$m SE of Worksop, $6^1/_2$m SW of Retford, just off A1/A57 via A614. 11m from M1/J30.

Opening Times: Park: All year during daylight hours, except 15 Jul & 19 Aug. Walled Kitchen Garden: Apr - end Sept: Weds & Thurs, 10.30am - 5.30pm, Sats, Suns & BH Mons, 10.30am - 6pm. Chapel: Apr - end Sept: Mon - Fri, 10.30am - 5.30pm, Sats & Suns, 10.30am - 6pm. Oct - 12 Jan 2001: daily, 10.30am - 4pm. Closed 13 Jan - end Mar for conservation cleaning.

Admission: Pedestrians: Free, NT Members: Free, Cars £3, Caravans/mini-coaches £4.30. Coaches Free weekday, £7 weekends & BH Mons. Walled kitchen garden 70p.

Partially suitable. Wheelchairs available. Licensed. In grounds on leads.

C Boyd.

Holme Pierrepont Hall, Nottinghamshire.

HODSOCK PRIORY GARDEN

Tel: 01909 591204 Fax: 01909 591578

Blyth, Nr Worksop, Nottinghamshire S81 0TY

Owner: Sir Andrew & Lady Buchanan **Contact:** Lady Buchanan

Sensational snowdrops, winter flowering plants and shrubs, woodland walk.

Location: OS Ref. SK612 853. W of B6045 Worksop/Blyth road, 1m SW of Blyth, less than 2m from A1.

Opening Times: Snowdrop period, please telephone for details.

Admission: Adult £3, accompanied Child (6-16yrs) 50p.

HOLME PIERREPONT HALL 

HOLME PIERREPONT, Nr NOTTINGHAM NG12 2LD

Owner: *Mr & Mrs Robin Brackenbury* ***Contact:*** *Robert Brackenbury*

Tel: 0115 933 2371

This charming late medieval manor house is set in thirty acres of Park and Gardens with regional furniture and family portraits. The recently restored Ball Room, Dining Room and Long Gallery which seats 100 people are available, on an exclusive basis, for business events and wedding receptions. Filming welcome.

Location: OS Ref. SK628 392. 5m ESE of central Nottingham. Follow signs to the National Water Sports Centre and continue for $1^1/_2$ m.

Opening Times: Easter, Spring & Summer BHs (Suns & Mons). Jun: Thurs, Jul: Weds & Thurs. Aug: Tue - Thurs, 2 - 5.30pm. Private functions at other times by arrangement.

Admission: Adult £3.50, Child £1.50. Gardens only £1.50.

Partially suitable. WC. Business & charity functions, wedding receptions. In grounds on leads.

NEWARK TOWN HALL

Tel: 01636 680333 Fax: 01636 680350

Market Place, Newark, Nottinghamshire NG24 1DU

Owner: Newark Town Council **Contact:** The Town Clerk

A fine Georgian town hall. Refurbished to John Carr's original concept.

Location: OS Ref. SK540 639. 12m N of Nottingham 1m W of the A60 Mansfield Rd.

Opening Times: By appointment.

Admission: Free.

NEWSTEAD ABBEY

Tel: 01623 455900 Fax: 01623 455903

Newstead Abbey Park, Nottinghamshire NG15 8GE **Contact:** Mr Brian Ayers

Historic home of the poet, Lord Byron, set in grounds of over 300 acres. Mementoes of Byron and decorated rooms from medieval to Victorian times.

Location: OS Ref. SK540 639. 12m N of Nottingham 1m W of the A60 Mansfield Rd.

Opening Times: 1 Apr - 30 Sept: 12 noon - 5pm, last adm. 4pm. Grounds: All year except last Fri in Nov. Apr - Sept: 9am - 7.30pm. Oct - Mar: 9am - 5pm.

Admission: House & Grounds: Adult £4, Child £1.50, Conc. £2. Grounds only: Adult £2, Conc. £1.50.

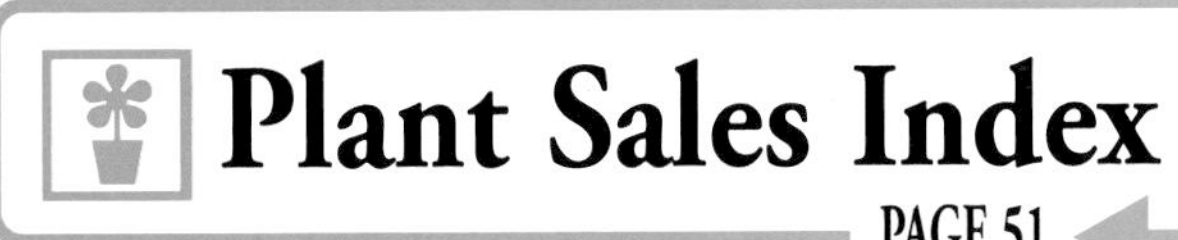

NORWOOD PARK

SOUTHWELL, NOTTINGHAMSHIRE NG25 0PF

Owner: *Sir John & Lady Starkey* ***Contact:*** *Sarah Dodd, Events Manager*

Tel: 01636 815649 **Fax:** 01636 815702 **e-mail:** starkey@farmline.com

Delightful Georgian country house and stables set in a medieval deer park, with ancient oaks, fishponds and eyecatcher Temple, overlooking apple orchards and cricket ground. Perfect venue for all manner of business or social occasion. Combination of reception/meeting/dining rooms available in the house for smaller groups. Unique Stables Gallery complex adjacent to the house, ideal for fairytale wedding receptions, corporate dances and promotions for larger groups. Idyllic and versatile grounds for activity days, promotional work and filming. USA designed 9-hole golf course and practice area in the magnificent parkland available for event days.

Location: OS Ref. SK688 545. 3/4 m W of Southwell.

Opening Times: All year by appointment only.

Admission: Please telephone for information.

Outdoor activity days. Events/weddings. Partially suitable. By arrangement. By arrangement. Limited for coaches. In grounds, on leads. Honeymoon suite only.

SUTTON BONINGTON HALL

Nr LOUGHBOROUGH, NOTTINGHAM LE12 5PF

Owner: *Lady Anne Elton* ***Contact:*** *Mr & Mrs Henry Weldon*

Tel: 01509 672355 **Fax:** 01509 889060 **e-mail:** henryweldon@hotmail.com

Sutton Bonington Hall, home of the Paget family since 1750, is a magnificent example of Queen Anne architecture, with an early conservatory (1810), and fine Queen Anne furniture. Sutton Bonington is not open to the general public, but offers excellent facilities for small conferences, corporate dinners and weddings. Extensive formally laid-out gardens can accommodate marquees for larger events. Seven luxurious bedrooms (all en-suite) can accommodate up to 14 guests in style.

Location: SK505 255. 1m E of A6, 5m N of Loughborough. In the heart of the Midlands, a short distance from Nottingham, Derby, Leicester, M1 and East Midlands airport.

Opening Times: By arrangement.

Admission: Corporate/private entertainment and wedding venue by arrangement only. Residential rooms by prior reservation only.

Partially suitable. Ample for cars. In grounds, on leads. 7 doubles.

PAPPLEWICK HALL

Tel: 0115 963 3491 **Fax:** 0115 964 2767

Papplewick, Nottinghamshire NG15 8FE

Owner: Dr R Godwin-Austen

A beautiful stone built classical house set in a park with woodland garden laid out in the 18th century. The house is notable for its very fine plasterwork and elegant staircase. Grade I listed.

Location: OS Ref. SK548 518. Halfway between Nottingham & Mansfield, 3m E of M1/J27 on B683.

Opening Times: By appointment and 1st, 3rd & 5th Wed in each month, 2 -5pm.

Admission: Adult £5. Groups (10+): £4.

No photography. Obligatory. Limited for coaches. In grounds on leads.

RUFFORD ABBEY

Tel: 01604 730320

Ollerton, Nottinghamshire NG22 9DF

Owner: English Heritage **Contact:** The Midlands Regional Office

The remains of a 17th century country house; displaying the ruins of a 12th century Cistercian Abbey. It is set in what is now Rufford Country Park.

Location: OS Ref. SK645 646. 2m S of Ollerton off A614.

Opening Times: 1 Apr - 31 Oct: Daily, 10am - 5pm. 1 Nov - 31 Mar: daily, 10am - 4pm. (Closed 24 - 26 Dec & 1 Jan).

Admission: Free.

Patrick Lane.

Wollaton Hall Natural History Museum, Nottinghamshire.

THRUMPTON HALL

THRUMPTON, NOTTINGHAM NG11 0AX

Owner/Contact: *The Hon Mrs R Seymour*

Tel: 01159 830333 **Fax:** 01159 831309

Fine Jacobean house, built in 1607 incorporating an earlier manor house. Priest's hiding hole, magnificent carved Charles II staircase, carved and panelled saloon. Other fine rooms containing beautiful 17th and 18th century furniture and many fine portraits. Large lawns separated from landscaped park by ha-ha and by lake in front of the house. The house is still lived in as a home and the owner will show parties around when possible. Dining room with capacity for 52 with silver service or buffet. Free access and meal for coach drivers.

Location: OS Ref. SK508 312. 7m S of Nottingham, 3m E M1/J24, 1m from A453.

Opening Times: By appointment. Parties of 20+ 10.30am - 7.30pm.

Admission: Adult £5, Child £2.50.

Conferences. Ground floor & grounds suitable. WC. In grounds on leads.

UPTON HALL

Tel: 01636 813795

Upton, Newark, Nottinghamshire NG23 5TE

Owner: British Horological Institute **Contact:** The Director

Location: OS Ref. SK735 544. A612 between Newark and Southwell.

Opening Times: Nov - Mar: Weekdays, 1.30 - 5pm. Apr - Oct: Daily (except Sats), 1.30 - 5pm.

Admission: Adult £2.50, Child £1, (under 11yrs free), OAP £2.

WINKBURN HALL

Tel: 01636 636465 **Fax:** 01636 636717

Winkburn, Newark, Nottinghamshire NG22 8PQ

Owner/Contact: Richard Craven-Smith-Milnes Esq

A fine William and Mary house.

Location: OS Ref. SK711 584. 8m W of Newark 1m N of A617.

Opening Times: Throughout the year by appointment only.

Admission: £4.20.

WOLLATON HALL NATURAL HISTORY MUSEUM

Tel: 0115 915 3900

Wollaton Park, Nottingham NG8 2AE

Owner: Nottingham City Council **Contact:** The Administrator

Flamboyant Elizabethan house built by Robert Smythson in a park.

Location: OS Ref. SK532 392. Wollaton Park, Nottingham. 3m W of city centre.

Opening Times: Summer: 11am - 5pm. Winter: 11am - 4pm. Closed Fridays from Nov - Mar.

Admission: Weekdays Free. Weekends & BHs Adult: £1.50, Child 80p. Joint ticket for Wollaton Hall & Industrial Museum. Grounds £1/car (free orange badge holders).(1999 times and prices).

Norwood Park, Nottinghamshire.

Owner:
Hawkstone Park Leisure Ltd

CONTACT

Kevin L Brazier
Hawkstone Historic Park
and Follies
Weston-under-Redcastle
Nr Shrewsbury
Shropshire
SY4 5UY

Tel: 01939 200611

Fax: 01939 200311

e-mail:
info@hawkstone.co.uk

LOCATION

OS Ref. SJ576 286

12m NE of Shrewsbury off A49

3m from Hodnet off A53/A442

M6 to M54 then either A49 or A41, A442.

Rail: Shrewsbury Station 12m.

Wem Station 7m.

CONFERENCE/FUNCTION		
ROOM	SIZE (M)	MAX CAPACITY
Waterloo	15.45 x 10	200
Wellington	6.1 x 7.62	50
Redcastle	12.2 x 8.8	100
Hill	8.5 x 7	50

HAWKSTONE HISTORIC PARK & FOLLIES

Nr Shrewsbury

HAWKSTONE PARK, with its well hidden pathways, concealed grottos, secret tunnels and magical collection of follies is truly unique. It is a forgotten masterpiece; originally one of the most visited landscapes in Britain and now the only Grade I landscape in Shropshire.

Sir Roland Hill started it all in the 18th century with his son Richard 'The Great Hill', arranging for some 15 miles of paths and some of the best collections of follies in the world to be constructed in the grounds of their ancestral home. At the turn of the 19th century the Hills could no longer accommodate the growing number of sightseers to the Hall. As a result an Inn, which is now Hawkstone Park Hotel, was opened and guided tours were organised. Little has changed since then. The park is full of attractions, surprises and features. You can see dramatic cliffs and rocks, towers, monuments, tunnels, passageways, precipice rocks, paths, rustic 'sofas', romantic secret valleys. It takes around three hours to complete the whole tour of the Park (bring sensible shoes). From the Green House you embark upon a unique experience. Paths, steps, walls, even the Greek Urn, were put in place during the busy period. Caves and seats, handy resting places for the weary visitor, were hewn into the rock face.

At the top of the Terrace sits a folly, the White Tower, where you meet the Duke of Wellington discussing the Battle of Waterloo. Close by is the Monument, a 112-foot column, at the top of which stands the new statue of Sir Roland Hill, the first Protestant Lord Mayor of London. The seemingly endless numbers of tracks leading from the Terrace will tempt visitors off the straight and narrow perhaps to the Swiss Bridge or to St Francis' Cave or the Fox's Nob.

The tour then continues from the bottom of the Terrace to Grotto Hill via Gingerbread Hall and the magnificent Serpentine Tunnel and cleft which leads to the longest grotto passageway in Europe where you can come face to face with King Arthur. Hawkstone Historic Park was the TV location for the *Chronicles of Narnia*.

Winner of: Europa Nostra
Award, Civil Trust Award,
Heart of England Award

Filming and TV location work, festivals, musical events and craft fairs. Golf courses (2 x 18 hole) adjacent to Park, golf tournaments, practice grounds, driving range, residential golf school, clay pigeon shooting, archery. Photography by prior arrangement.

Partially suitable. WCs.

Tearoom open all day. Terrace Restaurant within grounds serving snacks, grills and alcoholic beverages.

Ample. Bring sensible shoes.

Special rates for schools, coaches & groups. Teachers' pack.

Dogs on leads permitted.

Hotel adjacent.

OPENING TIMES

SPRING & AUTUMN
1 April - 2 July &
4 September - 29 October:
Wed - Sun (open BHs).
Weekdays: 10.30am - 4pm.
Weekends: 10am - 4pm.

SUMMER
3 Jul - 3 September: Daily
Weekdays: 10.30am- 5pm.
Weekends: 10am -5pm.

WINTER
30 October - 5 January: closed other than Santa Grotto (tel. for details).
6 January - 30 March: Sats & Suns only: 10am - 3.30pm.

Hotel: Open all year.
Tel: 01939 200611

ADMISSION

Weekdays

Adult	£4.50
Child	£2.50
OAP/Student	£3.50
Family (2+3)	£12.00
Groups**	
Coaches	
(12 -15 seats)	£30.00*
Adult (up to 25)	£50.00*
Child (up to 50)	£100.00*

* plus £3/extra occupant.
**Groups: Bookable and payable in advance. Discounts for 15+.

Weekends
BHs & Special Events

Adult	£5.00
Child	£3.00
OAP/Student	£4.00
Family (2+3)	£14.00

Winter Weekends

Adult	£3.50
Child	£2.00
OAP/Student	£2.50
Family (2+3)	£10.00

SPECIAL EVENTS

Please contact Hawkstone Historic Park for full details of events.

OAKLEY HALL
Market Drayton

Owner:
Mr & Mrs F Fisher

CONTACT

Mrs Ann E Fisher
Oakley Hall
Market Drayton
Shropshire
TF9 4AG

Tel: 01630 653472

Fax: 01630 653282

OAKLEY HALL is situated in magnificent countryside on the bôundary of Shropshire and Staffordshire. The present Hall is a fine example of a Queen Anne mansion house and was built on the site of an older dwelling mentioned in the Domesday Survey of 1085. Oakley Hall was the home of the Chetwode family until it was finally sold in 1919.

GARDENS
Set in 100 acres of rolling parkland, the Hall commands superb views over the surrounding countryside and the gardens include wild areas in addition to the more formal parts.

Oakley Hall is a privately owned family house and since it is not open to the general public it provides a perfect location for exclusive private or corporate functions. The main hall can accommodate 120 people comfortably and has excellent acoustics for concerts. The secluded location and unspoilt landscape make Oakley an ideal setting for filming and photography.

The surrounding countryside is rich in historical associations. St Mary's Church at Mucklestone, in which parish the Hall stands, was erected in the 13th century and it was from the tower of this Church that Queen Margaret of Anjou observed the Battle of Blore Heath in 1459. This was a brilliant victory for the Yorkist faction in the Wars of the Roses and the blacksmith at Mucklestone was reputed to have shod the Queen's horse back to front in order to disguise her escape.

LOCATION

OS Ref. SJ701 367

From London 3hrs: M1, M6/J14, then A5013 to Eccleshall, turn right at T-junction, 200 yards, then left onto B5026. Mucklestone is $1^3/_4$ m from Loggerheads on B5026. 3m NE of Market Drayton N of the A53, $1^1/_2$ m W of Mucklestone, off B5145.

CONFERENCE/FUNCTION		
ROOM	SIZE	MAX CAPACITY
Hall	50' x 30'	100
Dining Rm	40' x 27'	80
Ballroom	40' x 27'	80

OPENING TIMES

ALL YEAR

Not open to the public. The house is available all year round for private or corporate events.

ADMISSION

Please telephone for details.

Concerts, conferences (see left for rooms available). Slide projector, word processor, fax and secretarial assistance are all available by prior arrangement, fashion shows, product launches, seminars, clay pigeon shooting, garden parties and filming. Grand piano, hard tennis court, croquet lawn, horse riding. No stiletto heels.

Wedding receptions, buffets, lunches and dinners can be arranged for large or small groups, using high quality local caterers.

Visitors may alight at the entrance to the Hall, before parking in allocated areas. WCs.

By prior arrangement groups will be met and entertained by members of the Fisher family.

100 cars, 100/200 yds from the Hall.

 3 double with baths.

Owner:
The Weston Park Foundation

CONTACT

Alison Robbins
Weston Park
Weston-under-Lizard
Nr Shifnal
Shropshire
TF11 8LE

Tel: 01952 852100

Fax: 01952 850430

e-mail: enquiries@weston-park.com

LOCATION

OS Ref. SJ808 107

Birmingham 40 mins.
Manchester 1 hr.
Motorway access M6/J12 or M54/J3.
House situated on A5 at Weston-under-Lizard.

Rail: Nearest Railway Stations: Wolverhampton, Stafford or Telford.

Air: Birmingham.

CONFERENCE/FUNCTION		
ROOM	SIZE	MAX CAPACITY
Dining Rm	52' x 23'	120
Orangery	51' x 20'	120
Music Rm	50' x 20'	80
The Old Stables	58' x 20'	60
Conference Room	40' x 7'6"	60

WESTON PARK

Nr Shifnal

WESTON PARK is a magnificent Stately Home and Parkland situated on the Staffordshire/Shropshire border. The former home of the Earls of Bradford, the Park is now held in trust for the nation by The Weston Park Foundation.

Built in 1671 by Lady Elizabeth Wilbraham, this warm and welcoming house boasts a superb collection of paintings, including work by Van Dyck, Gainsborough and Stubbs, furniture and *objets d'art*, providing continued interest and enjoyment for all of its visitors.

Step outside to enjoy the 1,000 acres of glorious Parkland, designed by the legendary 'Capability' Brown - meander through the formal gardens, take one of a variety of woodland walks and then relax in The Stables Restaurant. Take time to browse through the Gift Shop, completing your day with a delicious ice-cream from the Ice-Cream Parlour.

With the exciting Woodland Adventure Playground, Pets Corner and Deer Park, as well as the Miniature Railway, there is so much for children to do.

Weston Park has a long-standing reputation for staging outstanding events. The exciting and varied programme of entertainment includes Balloon Festivals, Music Festivals, Opera Evenings and Battle Re-enactments.

House available on an exclusive use basis. Conferences, product launches, outdoor concerts and events, filming location. Helipad and airstrip. Sporting activities organised for private groups eg. clay pigeon shooting, archery, hovercrafts, rally driving. Interior photography by prior arrangement only.

Gift Shop.

Full event organisation service. Residential parties, special dinners, wedding receptions. Dine and stay arrangements in the house on selected dates.

House and part of the grounds. WCs.

The Stables restaurant and tearoom provide meals and snacks. Licensed.

Ample 100 yds away. Private booked groups may park vehicles at front door.

Tues, Weds and Thurs in the latter half of Jun and all Jul. Must book. Teachers' guidance notes and National Curriculum related workpacks available.

Weston Park offers 28 delightful bedrooms with bathrooms, 19 doubles, 6 twins, 3 singles. On an exclusive only basis.

In grounds, on leads.

Telephone for details.

OPENING TIMES

Easter weekend: 22 - 24 April.

29 April - 1 May

May - June: weekends (including 1 & 2 June).

24 June - 3 September (closed 15 July, 12 - 13 & 18 - 21 August)

Every weekend in September until 17 September, then closed.

House: 1 - 5pm
Last admission 4.30pm.

Park: 11am - 7pm
Last admission 5pm.

NB. Visitors are advised to telephone first to check this information.

ADMISSION

Park & Gardens

Adult	£4.00
Child (3 - 16yrs)	£2.50
OAP	£3.00

House

Adult	£1.50
Child (3 - 16yrs)	£1.00
OAP	£1.50

ACTON BURNELL CASTLE

Tel: 01604 730320 (Regional Office)

Acton Burnell, Shrewsbury, Shropshire

Owner: English Heritage **Contact:** The Midlands Regional Office

The warm red sandstone shell of a fortified 13th century manor house.

Location: OS Ref. SJ534 019. In Acton Burnell, on unclassified road 8m S of Shrewsbury.

Opening Times: Any reasonable time.

Admission: Free.

ADCOTE SCHOOL

Tel: 01939 260202 **Fax:** 01939 261300

Little Ness, Shrewsbury, Shropshire SY4 2JY

Owner: Adcote School Educational Trust Ltd **Contact:** Mrs A Read

Adcote is a Grade I listed building designed by Norman Shaw, and built to a Tudor design in 1879. Its features include a Great Hall, Minstrels' Gallery, William De Morgan tiled fireplaces and stained glass windows. Landscaped gardens include many fine trees.

Location: OS Ref. SJ420 195. 7m NW of Shrewsbury. 2m NE of A5.

Opening Times: By appointment only.

Admission: Free, but the Governors reserve the right to make a charge.

BENTHALL HALL

Tel: 01952 882159

Benthall, Nr Broseley, Shropshire TF12 5RX

Owner: The National Trust **Contact:** The Custodian

A 16th century stone house with mullioned windows and moulded brick chimneys.

Location: OS Ref. SJ658 025. 1m NW of Broseley (B4375), 4m NE of Much Wenlock, 1m SW of Ironbridge.

Opening Times: 2 Apr - 27 Sept: Weds, Suns & BH Mons 1.30 - 5.30pm. Last adm. 5pm. Groups at other times by prior arrangement.

Admission: Adult: £3, Child: £1. Garden: £2. Reduced rates for groups.

Ground floor suitable. WC. By arrangement. Limited.

ATTINGHAM PARK

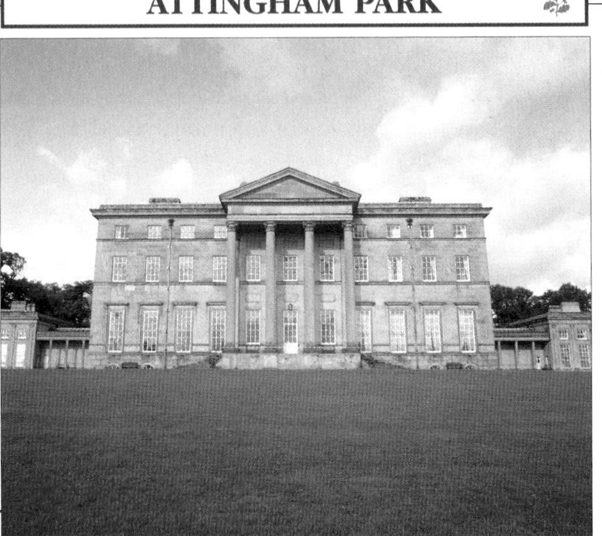

SHREWSBURY, SHROPSHIRE SY4 4TP

Owner: *The National Trust* ***Contact:*** *The Property Manager*

Infoline: 01743 708123 **Tel:** 01743 708162 **Fax:** 01743 708175

One of the great houses of the Midlands. An elegant late 18th century mansion by George Steuart, with a Picture Gallery by Nash. It has magnificent Regency interiors with exceptional collections of ambassadorial silver, Italian neo-classical furniture and Grand Tour paintings. The park was landscaped by Repton in 1797.

Location: OS127 Ref. SJ837 083. 4m SE of Shrewsbury on N side of B4380 in Atcham village.

Opening Times: 24 Mar - 31 Oct: daily (closed Wed & Thur), 1.30 - 5pm. Deer Park & Grounds: daily, closed 25 Dec. Last admission 1 hr before closing.

Admission: House & Grounds: Adult £4.20, Child £2.10. Grounds only: Adult £2, Child £1. Groups (15+): Adult £3.80, Child £1.90.

No photography in house. Licensed.
By arrangement. In grounds on leads.

BOSCOBEL HOUSE

English Heritage Photographic Library

BREWOOD, BISHOP'S WOOD, SHROPSHIRE ST19 9AR

Owner: *English Heritage* ***Contact:*** *The Custodian*

Tel: 01902 850244

This 17th century hunting lodge was destined to play a part in Charles II's escape from the Roundheads. A descendant of the Royal Oak, which sheltered the fugitive King from Cromwell's troops after the Battle of Worcester in 1651, still stands in the fields near Boscobel House. The timber-framed house where the King slept in a tiny 'sacred hole' has been fully restored and furnished in Victorian period and there are panelled rooms and secret hiding places. There is an exhibition in the house as well as the farmyard and smithy.

Location: OS127 Ref. SJ837 083. On unclassified road between A41 & A5. 8m NW of Wolverhampton.

Opening Times: 1 Apr - 31 Oct: daily: 10am - 6pm (5pm in Oct). 1 Nov - 31 Mar: Wed - Sun, 10am - 4pm. Closed 24 - 26 Dec & Jan. Last adm. 1 hr before closing.

Admission: Adult £4.30, Child £2.20, Conc. £3.20. 15% discount on groups (11+).

Grounds suitable. WC.  Obligatory.  Tel. for details.

BUILDWAS ABBEY

Tel: 01952 433274

Shropshire

Owner: English Heritage **Contact:** The Custodian

Extensive remains of a Cistercian abbey built in 1135 and set beside the River Severn. The remains include the church which is almost complete except for the roof.

Location: OS Ref. SJ642 044. On S bank of River Severn on A4169, 2m W of Ironbridge.

Opening Times: 1 Apr - 31 Oct: daily, 10am - 6pm (5pm in Oct).

Admission: Adult £1.95, Child £1, Conc. £1.50.

Open all Year Index PAGE 52

BURFORD HOUSE GARDENS

TENBURY WELLS, WORCESTERSHIRE WR15 8HQ

Owner: *Treasures of Tenbury Ltd* ***Contact:*** *Charles Chesshire*

Tel: 01584 810777 **Fax:** 01584 810673 **e-mail:** treasures@burford.co.uk

Four acre garden in beautiful riverside setting, home to the national clematis collection, with over 300 varieties, and 2,000 varieties of other plants. New designs include a wildflower garden, bamboo and grass garden. Also visit Treasures Plant Centre, Burford House Gallery, Burford Buttery, Gift Shop, Mulu Exotic Plants and Jungle Giants Bamboos.

Location: OS Ref. SO585 680. 1m W of Tenbury Wells on the A456, 8m from Ludlow.

Opening Times: All year: daily, 10am - 5pm.

Admission: Adult £3.50, Child £1. Groups (10+): £3.

Licensed. By arrangement. Guide dogs only.

DAVENPORT HOUSE

WORFIELD, Nr BRIDGNORTH, SHROPSHIRE WV15 5LE

Owner/Contact: *Roger Murphy*

Tel: 01746 716221 / 716345 **Fax:** 01746 716021

A Grade I listed country house of 1726 by the architect Francis Smith of Warwick. The house sits within an extensive estate and is a popular regional venue for wedding receptions, civil marriage ceremonies and corporate and social group entertainment. Open to the public as a restaurant Wednesday evenings, advance booking only.

Location: OS Ref. SO756 955. Worfield village, drive entrance by war memorial.

Opening Times: Available for weddings and other functions throughout the year.

Admission: Please telephone for details.

Partially suitable. Licensed.

CLUN CASTLE

Tel: 01604 730320 (Regional Office)

Clun, Ludlow, Shropshire

Owner: English Heritage **Contact:** The Midlands Regional Office

Remains of a four storey keep and other buildings of this border castle are set in outstanding countryside. Built in the 11th century.

Location: OS Ref. SO299 809. In Clun, off A488, 18m W of Ludlow. 9m W of Craven Arms.

Opening Times: Any reasonable time.

Admission: Free.

COLEHAM PUMPING STATION

Tel: 01743 362947 **Fax:** 01743 358411

Longden Coleham, Shrewsbury, Shropshire SY3 7DN

Owner: Shrewsbury & Atcham Borough Council **Contact:** Mary White

Two Renshaw beam engines of 1901 are being restored to steam by members of Shrewsbury Steam Trust. The Trust organises open days throughout the summer months to show visitors their work.

Location: OS Ref. SJ497 122. Shrewsbury town centre, near the River Severn.

Opening Times: Apr - Sept: 4th Sun in each month, 10am - 4pm. Plus occasional other days. Details: 01743 361196.

Admission: Adult £1, Child 50p, Student £1.

Partially suitable. By arrangement. No parking. Guide dogs only.

COMBERMERE ABBEY

Tel: 01948 871637 **Fax:** 01948 871293

Whitchurch, Shropshire SY13 4AJ **e-mail:** cottages@combermereabbey.co.uk

Owner: Mrs S Callander Beckett **Contact:** Mrs Carol Sheard/Mrs Sue Brookes

Combermere Abbey, originally a Cistercian Monastery, and remodelled as a Gothic house in 1820 sits in a magnificent 1000 acre private parkland setting. Host to many remarkable historical personalities, the splendid 17th century Library and elegant Porter's Hall are licensed for weddings, receptions, concerts and lectures. Excellent accommodation is available on the Estate.

Location: OS Ref. SJ590 440. 5m E of Whitchurch, off A530.

Opening Times: By arrangement for groups.

Admission: Groups: £5 per person inclusive of refreshments.

No photography. Not suitable. By arrangement. By arrangement. Limited.

DUDMASTON

Michael Caldwell

QUATT, BRIDGNORTH, SHROPSHIRE WV15 6QN

Owner: *The National Trust* ***Contact:*** *The Administrator*

Tel: 01746 780866 **Fax:** 01746 780744

Late 17th century manor house. Contains furniture and china, Dutch flower paintings, watercolours, botanical art and modern pictures and sculpture, family and natural history. 9 acres of lakeside gardens and Dingle walk. Two estate walks $5^1/_2$ m and $3^1/_2$ m starting from Hampton Loade car park.

Location: OS Ref. SO748 888. 4m SE of Bridgnorth on A442.

Opening Times: 28 Mar - 29 Sept: House; Tues, Weds, Suns & BH Mons, 2 - 5.30pm. Garden; Mon - Wed & Suns, 12 noon - 6pm. Thurs booked groups by arrangement. Tearoom: 11.30am - 5.30pm. Last admission to house 5pm.

Admission: House & Garden: Adult £3.75, Child £2.25, Family £9. Groups £2.90. Garden only: £2.75.

In grounds, on leads.

HAUGHMOND ABBEY

Tel: 01743 709661

Upton Magna, Uffington, Shrewsbury, Shropshire SY4 4RW

Owner: English Heritage **Contact:** The Custodian

Extensive remains of a 12th century Augustinian abbey, including the Chapter House which retains its late medieval timber ceiling, and including some fine medieval sculpture.

Location: OS Ref. SJ542 152. 3m NE of Shrewsbury off B5062.

Opening Times: 1 Apr - 31 Oct: daily, 10am - 6pm (5pm in Oct).

Admission: Adult £1.95, Child £1, Conc. £1.50.

 Tel. for details.

HAWKSTONE HALL & GARDENS

Tel: 01630 685242 **Fax:** 01630 685565

Marchamley, Shrewsbury SY4 5LG

Owner: The Redemptorists **Contact:** Guest Mistress

Grade I Georgian mansion and restored gardens set in spacious parkland.

Location: OS Ref. SJ581 299. Entrance 1m N of Hodnet on A442.

Opening Times: 5 - 31 Aug, daily, 2 - 5pm.

Admission: Adult £3.50, Child £1.

HAWKSTONE HISTORIC PARK & FOLLIES

See page 294 for full page entry.

HODNET HALL GARDENS

HODNET, MARKET DRAYTON, SHROPSHIRE TF9 3NN

Owner: *Mr and the Hon Mrs A Heber-Percy* ***Contact:*** *Mrs M A Taylor*

Tel: 01630 685202 **Fax:** 01630 685853

Beautiful woodland walks through trees and shrubs in 60 acres of flowering lakeside gardens. Tearooms serve light lunches and afternoon teas. Gift shop.

Location: OS Ref. SJ613 286. 12m NE of Shrewsbury on A53; M6/J15, M54/J3.

Opening Times: 1 Apr - 30 Sept: Tue - Sun & BH Mons, 12 noon - 5pm.

Admission: Adult £3.25, Child £1.20, OAP £2.75. Reduced rates for groups.

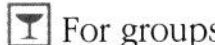 Kitchen garden sales. 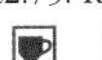 For groups. 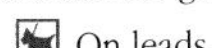 On leads.

IRON BRIDGE

Tel: 01604 730320 (Regional Office)

Ironbridge, Shropshire

Owner: English Heritage **Contact:** The Midlands Regional Office

The world's first iron bridge and Britain's best known industrial monument. Cast in Coalbrookdale by local ironmaster, Abraham Darby, it was erected across the River Severn in 1779.

Location: OS Ref. SJ672 034. In Ironbridge, adjacent to A4169.

Opening Times: Any reasonable time.

Admission: Free crossing.

IRONBRIDGE GORGE MUSEUMS

IRONBRIDGE, TELFORD, SHROPSHIRE TF8 7AW

Owner: *Independent Museum* ***Contact:*** *Visitor Information*

Tel: 01952 433522 or 432166 (7 day line) **Fax:** 01952 432204

Freephone: 0800 590258 for a **free** colour guide.

Scene of pioneering events which led to the Industrial Revolution. The Ironbridge Gorge is home to nine unique museums set in six square miles of stunning scenery. These include Jackfield Tile Museum, Coalport China Museum and a recreated Victorian Town where you can chat to locals as they go about their daily business. You'll need two days here.

Location: OS Ref. SJ666 037. Telford, Shropshire via M6/M54.

Open: All year: daily from 10am - 5pm (closed 24/25 Dec & 1 Jan). Please telephone for winter details before visit.

Admission: Passport ticket which allows admission to all museums; Adult £9.50, Child/Student £5.50, OAP £8.50, Family £29. Prices valid until Easter 2000. Group discounts available.

  Licensed.  Guide dogs only.

LANGLEY CHAPEL

Tel: 01604 730320 (Regional Office)

Acton Burnell, Shrewsbury, Shropshire

Owner: English Heritage **Contact:** The Midlands Regional Office

A delightful medieval chapel, standing alone in a field, with a complete set of early 17th century wooden fittings and furniture.

Location: OS Ref. SJ538 001. 1½ m S of Acton Burnell, on unclassified road 4m E of the A49, 9½ m S of Shrewsbury.

Opening Times: Open any reasonable time. Closed 24- 26 Dec & 1 Jan.

Admission: Free.

LILLESHALL ABBEY

Tel: 01604 730320 (Regional Office)

Oakengates, Shropshire

Owner: English Heritage **Contact:** The Midlands Regional Office

Extensive ruins of an abbey of Augustinian canons including remains of the 12th and 13th century church and the cloister buildings. Surrounded by green lawns and ancient yew trees.

Location: OS Ref. SJ738 142. On unclassified road off the A518, 4m N of Oakengates.

Opening Times: Any reasonable time.

Admission: Adult £1.30, Child 70p, Conc. £1.

LONGNER HALL

Tel: 01743 709215

Uffington, Shrewsbury, Shropshire SY4 4TG

Owner: Mr R L Burton **Contact:** Mrs R L Burton

Designed by John Nash in 1803, Longner Hall is a Tudor Gothic style house set in a park landscaped by Humphry Repton. The home of one family for over 700 years. Longner's principal rooms are adorned with plaster fan vaulting and stained glass.

Location: OS Ref. SJ529 110. 4m SE of Shrewsbury on Uffington road, ¼ m off B4380, Atcham.

Opening Times: Apr - Oct: Tues & BH Mons, 2 - 5pm. Groups any time by arrangement.

Admission: Adult £5, Child/OAP £3.

No photography in house. Partially suitable.
By arrangement for groups. Obligatory. Limited for coaches.
By arrangement. Guide dogs only.

LUDLOW CASTLE

CASTLE SQUARE, LUDLOW, SHROPSHIRE SY8 1AY

Owner: *The Earl of Powis & The Trustees of the Powis Estate* ***Contact:*** *Helen Duce*

Tel: 01584 873355

900 year old castle of the Marches, dates from 1086 and greatly extended over the centuries to a fortified Royal Palace. Ludlow Castle became a seat of government with the establishment of the Council for Wales and the Marches. Privately owned by the Earls of Powis since 1811. A magnificent ruin set in the heart of Ludlow and surrounding countryside.

Location: OS Ref. SO509 745. Shrewsbury 28m, Hereford 26m. A49 centre of Ludlow.

Opening Times: Jan: weekends only, 10am - 4pm, Feb - Apr & Oct - Dec: 10am - 4pm. May - Jul & Sept: 10am - 5pm. Aug: 10am - 7pm. Last adm. 30mins before closing. Closed 25 Dec.

Admission: Adult £3, Child £1.50, Conc. £2.50, Family £8.50. 10% reduction for groups (10+).

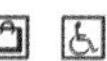 

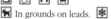

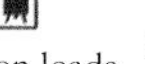 In grounds on leads.

SPECIAL EVENTS

APR 24: Easter Egg Hunt
MAY 13/14: Vintage Vehicle Display
MAY 27 - 29: Festival of Crafts
JUN 24 - JUL 9: Ludlow Festival
JUL 21-23: Pentabus Childrens' Theatre
NOV 25/26: Medieval Christmas Fayre
Weds during summer school holidays.

MORETON CORBET CASTLE

Tel: 01604 730320 (Regional Office)

Moreton Corbet, Shrewsbury, Shropshire

Owner: English Heritage **Contact:** The Midlands Regional Office

A ruined medieval castle with the substantial remains of a splendid Elizabethan mansion, captured in 1644 from Charles I's supporters by Parliamentary forces.

Location: OS Ref. SJ562 232. In Moreton Corbet off B5063, 7m NE of Shrewsbury.

Opening Times: Any reasonable time.

Admission: Free.

MORVILLE HALL

Tel: 01743 708100

Bridgnorth, Shropshire WV16 5NB

Owner: The National Trust **Contact:** Dr & Mrs C Douglas

An Elizabethan house of mellow stone, converted in the 18th century. The Hall is in a fine setting, with three attractive gardens.

Location: OS Ref. SO668 940. Morville, on A458 3m W of Bridgnorth.

Opening Times: By written appointment only with the tenants.

By arrangement.

OAKLEY HALL

See page 295 for full page entry.

PREEN MANOR GARDENS

Tel: 01694 771207

Church Preen, Church Stretton, Shropshire SY6 7LQ

Owner: Mr & Mrs P Trevor-Jones **Contact:** Mrs P Trevor-Jones

Six acre garden on site of Cluniac monastery, with walled, terraced, wild, water, kitchen and chess gardens. 12th century monastic church with a yew tree reputedly the oldest in Europe.

Location: OS Ref. SO544 981. 10m SSE of Shrewsbury. 7m NE of Church Stretton, 6m SW of Much Wenlock.

Opening Times: Refer National Gardens Scheme Yellow Book. Coach parties Jun & Jul by appointment only.

Admission: Adult £2.50, Child 50p.

ROWLEY'S HOUSE MUSEUM

Tel: 01743 361196 **Fax:** 01743 358411

Barker Street, Shrewsbury, Shropshire SY1 1QH

Owner: Shrewsbury and Atcham Borough Council **Contact:** Mrs M White

Impressive timber-framed building and attached 17th century brick mansion with costume, archaeology and natural history, geology, local history and temporary exhibitions.

Location: OS Ref. SJ490 126. Barker Street.

Opening Times: All year: Tue - Sat, 10am - 5pm. Easter - end Sept: Suns & BH Mons 10am - 4pm. Closed Christmas & New Year period (please telephone for details).

Admission: Free.

No photography. Not suitable. No parking. 

Guide dogs only.

SHIPTON HALL

Tel: 01746 785225 **Fax:** 01746 785125

Much Wenlock, Shropshire TF13 6JZ

Owner: Mr J N R Bishop **Contact:** Mrs M J Bishop

Built around 1587 by Richard Lutwyche who gave the house to his daughter Elizabeth on her marriage to Thomas Mytton. Shipton remained in the Mytton family for the next 300 years. The house has been described as 'an exquisite specimen of Elizabethan architecture set in a quaint old fashioned garden, the whole forming a picture which as regards both form and colour, satisfies the artistic sense of even the most fastidious'. The Georgian additions by Thomas F Pritchard include some elegant rococo interior decorations and some noteworthy Tudor and Jacobean panelling. Family home. In addition to the house visitors are welcome to explore the gardens, the dovecote and the parish church which dates back to Saxon times.

Location: OS Ref. SO563 918. 7m SW of Much Wenlock on B4378. 10m W of Bridgnorth.

Opening Times: Easter - end Sept: Thurs, 2.30 - 5.30pm. Also Suns and Mons of BH, 2.30 - 5.30pm. Groups of 20+ at any time of day or year by prior arrangement.

Admission: Adult £3, Child £1.50. Discount of 10% for groups (20+).

Not suitable. By arrangement for groups (20+). Obligatory. Guide dogs only.

SHREWSBURY ABBEY

Tel: 01743 232723 **Fax:** 01743 240172

Shrewsbury, Shropshire SY2 6BS **Contact:** Mr Terence Hyde

Benedictine Abbey founded in 1083, tomb of Roger de Montgomerie and remains of tomb of St Winefride, 7th century Welsh saint. The Abbey was part of the monastery and has also been a parish church since the 12th century. Now made popular by Ellis Peters author of 'Brother Cadfael' novels. Historical exhibition from Saxon times to present.

Location: OS Ref. SJ499 125. Signposted from Shrewsbury bypass (A5 and A49). 500yds E of town centre, across English Bridge.

Opening Times: Easter - 31 Oct: 9.30am - 5.30pm. Nov - Easter: 10.30am - 3pm.

Admission: Donation. Guided tours £10 per pre-arranged group.

SHREWSBURY CASTLE & SHROPSHIRE REGIMENTAL MUSEUM

Castle Street, Shrewsbury SY1 2AT **Tel:** 01743 358516 **Fax:** 01743 358411

Owner: Shrewsbury & Atcham Borough Council **Contact:** Steve Martin

Norman Castle with 18th century work by Thomas Telford. Free admission to attractive floral grounds. The main hall houses the Shropshire Regimental Museum and displays on the history of the castle.

Location: OS Ref. SJ495 128. Town centre, adjacent BR and bus stations.

Opening Times: Easter - end Sept: Tue - Sun & BH Mons, 10am - 4.30pm. Dec - Feb opening please telephone for details. Grounds also open Mons.

Admission: Free.

No photography.  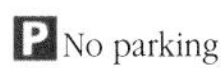  

Ironbridge Gorge Museum, Shropshire.

STOKESAY CASTLE 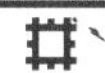

English Heritage Photographic Library

Nr CRAVEN ARMS, SHROPSHIRE SY7 9AH

Owner: *English Heritage* ***Contact:*** *The Custodian*

Tel: 01588 672544

This perfectly preserved example of a 13th century fortified manor house gives us a glimpse of the life and ambitions of a rich medieval merchant. Lawrence of Ludlow built this country house to impress the landed gentry. Lawrence built a magnificent Great Hall where servants and guests gathered on feast days, but the family's private quarters were in the bright, comfortable solar on the first floor. From the outside the castle forms a picturesque grouping of castle, parish church and timber-framed Jacobean gatehouse set in the rolling Shropshire countryside.

Location: OS137 Ref. SO436 817. 7m NW of Ludlow off A49. 1m S of Craven Arms off A49.

Opening Times: 1 Apr - 31 Oct: daily, 10am - 6pm (5pm in Oct). 1 Nov - 31 Mar (except 24 - 26 Dec & 1 Jan): Wed - Sun, 10am - 4pm. Closed 1 - 2pm in Winter.

Admission: Adult £3.50, Child £1.80, Conc. £2.60. Groups of 11+ 15% discount.

Great Hall & gardens only. WC. Tel. for details.

WALCOT HALL

LYDBURY NORTH, Nr BISHOP'S CASTLE, SHROPSHIRE SY7 8AZ

Owner/Contact: *C R W Parish*

Tel: 0171 581 2782 **Fax:** 0171 589 0195

Georgian home of Lord Clive of India who commissioned Sir William Chambers to re-design it and the stable block, in 1763. His son added the free-standing Ballroom and developed 30 acres of arboretum and pools to the rear, with mile-long lakes in the front. Suitable for film locations, balls, corporate events, receptions, parties and shows.

Location: OS Ref. SO348 850. On the edge of the Clun Forest. 3m SE of Bishop's Castle on B4385; 1/2 m outside Lydbury North. The drive is adjacent to the Powis Arms Pub.

Opening Times: House & Garden: BHs, Suns & Mons (except Christmas and New Year), 2.15 - 4.30pm. All other times by appointment.

Admission: Adult £3, Child (under 15yrs) Free. Teas by arrangement.

House suitable. WC. By arrangement. On leads. 

WENLOCK GUILDHALL

Tel: 01952 727509

Much Wenlock, Shropshire TF13 6AE

Owner/Contact: Much Wenlock Town Council

16th century half-timbered building has an open-arcade market area.

Location: OS127 Ref. SJ624 000. In centre of Much Wenlock, next to the church.

Opening Times: 1 Apr - 30 Sept: Mon - Sat, 10.30am - 1pm & 2 - 4pm. Suns: 2 - 4pm.

Admission: Adult 50p, Child 25p (1999 prices).

WENLOCK PRIORY

Tel: 01952 727466

Much Wenlock, Shropshire TA3 6HS

Owner: English Heritage **Contact:** The Custodian

A prosperous, powerful priory at its peak in the Middle Ages. A great deal of the structure still survives in the form of high, romantic ruined walls and it is the resting place of St Milburga the first Abbess. A monastery was first founded at Wenlock in the 7th century, and little more is known of the site until the time of the Norman Conquest when it became a Cluniac monastery. These majestic ruins of the priory church are set in green lawns and topiary, and there are substantial remains of the early 13th century church and Norman Chapter House.

Location: OS127 Ref. SJ625 001. In Much Wenlock.

Opening Times: 1 Apr - 31 Oct: daily: 10am - 6pm (5pm in Oct). 1 Nov - 31 Mar (except 24 - 26 Dec & 1 Jan): Wed - Sun, 10am - 4pm (closed 1 - 2pm in winter).

Admission: Adult £2.70, Child £1.40, Conc. £2 . 15% discount for groups (11+).

  Tel. for details.

WESTON PARK

See page 296 for full page entry.

WILDERHOPE MANOR

Tel: 01694 771363

Longville, Much Wenlock, Shropshire TF13 6EG

Owner: The National Trust **Contact:** The Warden

This limestone house stands on southern slope of Wenlock Edge in remote country with views down to Corvedale. Dating from 1586, it is unaltered but unfurnished. Features include remarkable wooden spiral stairs, unique bow rack and fine plaster ceilings.

Location: OS Ref. SO545 929. 7m SW of Much Wenlock. 7m E of Church Stretton, $^1/_2$ m S of B4371.

Opening Times: Apr - Sept: Weds & Sats, 2 - 4.30pm. Oct - Mar: Sats only, 2 - 4.30pm.

Admission: £1. No reduction for groups. Steep access to house.

WOLLERTON OLD HALL GARDEN

Tel: 01630 685760 **Fax:** 01630 685583

Wollerton, Market Drayton, Shropshire TF9 3NA

Owner: Mr & Mrs J D Jenkins **Contact:** Mrs Di Oakes

Three acre plantsman's garden created around a 16th century house (not open).

Location: OS Ref. SJ623 296. 14m NE of Shrewsbury off A53 between Hodnet and Market Drayton.

Opening Times: 1 May - 28 Aug: Fris, Suns & BHs, 12 noon - 5pm. Groups (25+) by appointment at other times.

Admission: Adult £3, Child £1.

WROXETER ROMAN CITY

Tel: 01743 761330

Wroxeter, Shrewsbury, Shropshire SY5 6PH

Owner: English Heritage **Contact:** The Custodian

The part-excavated centre of the fourth largest city in Roman Britain, originally home to some 6,000 men and several hundred houses. Impressive remains of the 2nd century municipal baths. There is a site museum in which many finds are displayed, including those from recent work by Birmingham Field Archaeological Unit.

Location: OS Ref. SJ568 088. At Wroxeter, 5m E of Shrewsbury, on B4380.

Opening Times: 1 Apr - 31 Oct: daily 10am - 6pm (5pm in Oct). 1 Nov - 31 Mar (except 24 - 26 Dec & 1 Jan): Wed - Sun, 10am - 4pm (closed for lunch 1 - 2pm in winter).

Admission: Adult £3.20, Child £1.60, Conc. £2.40.

  Tel. for details.

English Heritage Photographic Library.

Stokesay Castle, Shropshire.

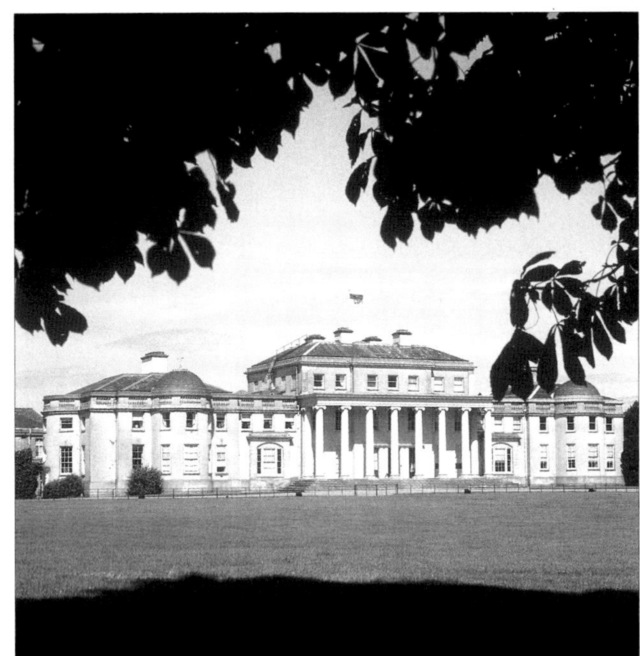

SHUGBOROUGH
Stafford

Owner:
The National Trust

CONTACT

Sales and Marketing Office
Shugborough
Milford
Stafford
ST17 0XB

Tel: 01889 881388

Fax: 01889 881323

e-mail: shugborough.promotions@staffordshire.gov.uk

LOCATION

OS Ref. SJ992 225

10mins from M6/J13 on A513 Stafford/ Lichfield Road.

Rail: Stafford 6m.

Taxi: Anthony's 01785 252255

CONFERENCE/FUNCTION		
ROOM	SIZE	MAX CAPACITY
Banqueting Hall	15 x 6.5m	65
Saloon	15 x 6m	80
Conference Suite	6 x 6m	35
Granary	5.5 x 9.5m	60
Blue Drawing Rm	6.5 x 8m	20
Tower of the Winds	6.5 x 6.5m	20

SHUGBOROUGH is the magnificent 900 acre ancestral home of the 5th Earl of Lichfield, who is known world-wide as Patrick Lichfield the leading photographer.

The 18th century mansion house contains a fine collection of ceramics, silver, paintings and French furniture. Part of the house is still lived in by the Earl and his family.

Visitors can enjoy the splendid 18 acre Grade I Historic Garden with its Edwardian Rose Garden and terraces. A unique collection of neo-classical monuments by James Stuart can be found in the parkland which also includes walks and trails.

Other attractions include the County Museum which is housed in the original servants' quarters. The working laundry, kitchens and brewhouse have all been lovingly restored and are staffed by costumed guides who show how the servants lived and worked over 100 years ago.

Shugborough Park Farm is a Georgian working farm which features an agricultural museum and restored working corn mill. It is also a rare breeds centre. In the farmhouse kitchen visitors can see bread baked in brick ovens and cheese and butter being made in the dairy.

Throughout the year a lively collection of themed tours are in operation for the coach market. There is also an award-winning educational programme for schools. From April to December an exciting events programme is in operation.

Shugborough is an ideal venue for weddings, meetings, conferences, corporate activity days and product launches.

Private and corporate entertainment, conferences, product launches and dinner parties. Filming and event location. Over 900 acres of parkland and gardens available for hire. Themed activities. No photography in house.

Catering for special functions/ conferences.

Visitors may alight at entrance before parking. WCs. Stairclimber to house. Batricars available. Disabled-friendly picnic tables available. Taped tours.

Licensed tearoom/café seating 95, also tearoom at Farm seats 30. Prior notice for large groups.

Tour time 1hr. Themed tours as required. Groups of 15+. Please telephone for details.

Ample car and coach parking. Discounted vouchers for coach drivers' meals available.

Award-winning educational packages. Curriculum-related. Contact Sales & Development Officer.

In grounds, on leads.

Civil Wedding Licence.

OPENING TIMES

25 March - 1 October
Daily: 11am - 5pm except Mondays (open Bank Holiday Mondays).

Pre-booked parties throughout the year.

ADMISSION

Each attraction

Adults	£4.00
Conc*	£3.00

Voyager Tickets (all 3 sites)

Adult	£8.00
Conc*	£6.00
Family	£18.00

Gardens and Parkland

Cars	£2.00
Coaches	Free

* Concessions for children (under 5yrs Free), OAPs, Students, registered unemployed & groups.

** NT Members free admission to Mansion House, Museum and Farm.

SPECIAL EVENTS

- **APR 15/16:** Gamekeepers' Fair
- **APR 30/MAY 1:** Classic Car Show
- **MAY 27/28/29:** Spring Craft Fair
- **JULY 1/2:** Gardeners' Weekend
- **JULY 16:** Goose Fair
- **JULY 22:** Firework & Laser Symphony Concert
- **DEC 5 - 8: (2000)** Christmas at Shugborough (8 Dec tickets only)

THE ANCIENT HIGH HOUSE

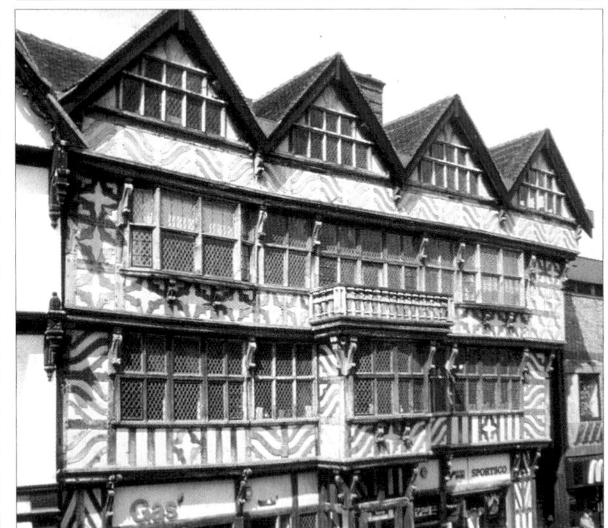

GREENGATE STREET, STAFFORD ST16 2JA

Owner: *Stafford Borough Council* ***Contact:*** *K Stringer*

Tel/Fax: 01785 619136

This building is the largest timber-framed town house in England. Built in 1595 by the Dorrington family, this house is still very impressive on Stafford's skyline. It was lived in by Richard Sneyd, a member of one of Staffordshire's greatest families when King Charles I stayed here in 1642. It is now a registered museum with displays set out as period room settings which present aspects of the house's history. The Staffordshire Yeomanry Museum is on the top floor.

Location: OS Ref. SJ922 232. Town centre.

Opening Times: Mon - Fri, 9am - 5pm, Weds, 10am - 5pm. Sats (Apr - Oct) 10am - 4pm. Sats (Nov - Mar) 10am - 3pm. Check BHs.

Admission: Adult £2, Child/Conc. £1.20. Family (2+2) £4.

TIC. Not suitable. Guide dogs only.

BIDDULPH GRANGE GARDEN

Ian Shaw

GRANGE ROAD, BIDDULPH, STOKE-ON-TRENT ST8 7SD

Owner: *The National Trust* ***Contact:*** *The Garden Office*

Tel: 01782 517999 **Fax:** 01782 510624

A rare and exciting survival of a High Victorian garden, restored by the National Trust. The garden is divided into a series of themed gardens within a garden, with a Chinese temple, Egyptian court, pinetum, dahlia walk, glen and many other settings.

Location: OS Ref. SJ891 592. E of A527, 3$^{1}/_{2}$ m SE of Congleton, 8m N of Stoke-on-Trent.

Opening Times: 25 Mar - 29 Oct: Wed - Fri, 12 noon - 6pm. Sats, Suns & BH Mons, 11am - 6pm. Also open 4 Nov - 17 Dec: Sats, Suns, 12 noon- 4pm or dusk if earlier.

Admission: Adult £4.30, Child £2.20, Family (2 +2) £10.70. Half price Nov and Dec. Joint ticket with Little Moreton Hall available during main season. Adult £6.50, Family £16.

  In car park, on leads.

BARLASTON HALL

Tel: 01782 372749 **Fax:** 01782 372391

Barlaston, Staffordshire ST12 9AT

Owner/Contact: Mr & Mrs James Hall

Barlaston Hall is a mid-18th century Palladian villa, attributed to Sir Robert Taylor. Extensively restored during the 1990s with the help of English Heritage. The four public rooms open to visitors contain some fine examples of 18th century plasterwork.

Location: OS Ref. SJ895 391. $^{1}/_{2}$ m E of A34 between Stoke and Stafford.

Opening Times: By appointment to groups of 10-30. Admission includes refreshments. Please write to the above address or fax giving details of numbers, possible dates and a contact telephone number. Recorded message with other opening times on above number.

Admission: Pre-arranged groups: £3.50.

No photography. Not suitable. Limited.

CHILLINGTON HALL

Tel: 01902 850236 **Fax:** 01902 850768

Codsall Wood, Wolverhampton, Staffordshire WV8 1RE

Owner/Contact: Mr & Mrs J W Giffard **e-mail:** mrsplod@globalnet.co.uk

Georgian red brick house with fine saloon by Soane set in 'Capability' Brown park having one of the largest lakes created by Brown. Extensive woodland walks.

Location: OS Ref. SJ864 067. 2m S of Brewood off A449. 4m NW of M54/J2.

Opening Times: Easter Sun, Suns prior to both May BHs and Thurs & Suns in Aug. Jun & Jul: Thurs, 2 - 5pm.

Admission: Adult £3, Child £1.50. Grounds only: half price.

Partially suitable. Obligatory. In grounds, on leads.

Christmas at Shugborough, Staffordshire.

THE DOROTHY CLIVE GARDEN

WILLOUGHBRIDGE, MARKET DRAYTON, SHROPSHIRE TF9 4EU

Owner: *Willoughbridge Garden Trust* ***Contact:*** *Mrs M Grime*

Tel: 01630 647237 **Fax:** 01630 647902

The Dorothy Clive Garden accommodates a wide range of choice and unusual plants providing year round interest. Features include a quarry with spectacular waterfall, flower borders, a scree and water garden. Tearoom serving home-baked hot and cold snacks throughout the day.

Location: OS Ref. SJ753 400. A51, 2m S of Woore, 3m from Bridgemere.

Opening Times: 1 Apr - 31 Oct: daily, 10am - 5.30pm.

Admission: Adult £3, Child (11-16yrs) £1, (under 11yrs free), OAP £2.50. Groups (20+) £2.50.

 In grounds on leads.

FORD GREEN HALL

Tel: 01782 233196 **Fax:** 01782 233194

Ford Green Road, Smallthorne, Stoke-on-Trent ST6 1NG

Owner: Stoke-on-Trent City Council **Contact:** Angela Graham

Ford Green Hall is a timber-framed yeoman farmer's house built for the Ford family in 1624, with brick wings added in the 18th century. A rare survival from the pre-industrial Potteries, the rooms are furnished with original and reproduction pieces according to inventories of the 17th and 18th century. A period garden is being developed around the Hall.

Location: OS Ref. SJ887 508. On B5051 Burslem – Endon road in Stoke-on-Trent (the route to Leek in the Staffordshire Moorlands).

Opening Times: All year except 25 Dec - 1 Jan: Sun - Thur, 1 - 5pm.

Admission: Adult £1.50, Conc. £1.

Partially suitable. By arrangement. Limited for coaches. Guide dogs only. Telephone for details.

SAMUEL JOHNSON BIRTHPLACE MUSEUM

Tel: 01543 264972

Breadmarket Street, Lichfield, Staffordshire WS13 6LG **Fax:** 01543 258441

Owner: Lichfield City Council **Contact:** Dr G Nicholls

The house where Samuel's father had a bookshop is now a museum with many of Johnson's personal relics.

Location: OS Ref. SK115 094. Breadmarket Street, Lichfield.

Opening Times: Daily: 10.30am - 4.30pm. Closed Suns, Nov - Jan.

Admission: Adult £2, Child/Conc. £1.10, Family £5.40. Groups: £1.10. (1999 prices).

LICHFIELD CATHEDRAL

Tel: 01543 306240 **Fax:** 01543 306109

Lichfield, Staffordshire WS13 7LD **e-mail:** lich.cath@virgin.net

Contact: Canon A Barnard

800-year old Gothic Cathedral with three spires on a 1300-year old Christian site. 8th century Gospel manuscript, 16th century Flemish glass, silver collection - a worshipping community.

Location: OS Ref. SK115 097. Approach from A38 and A51, N from M42 and M6. N of city centre.

Opening Times: All year: daily.

Admission: Suggested donation, £3 per adult.

MOSELEY OLD HALL

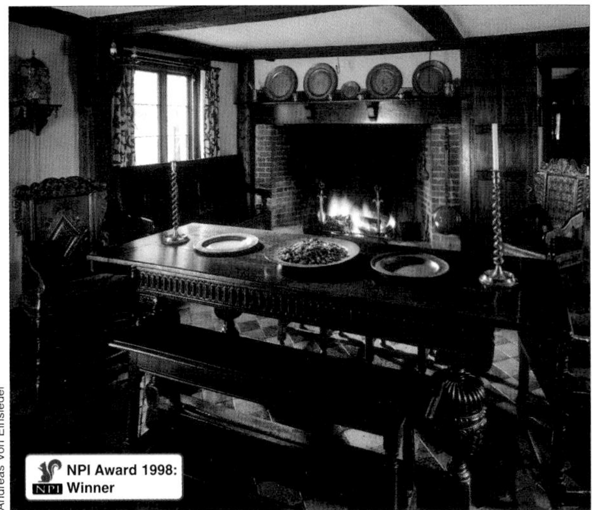

Andreas Von Einsiedel

FORDHOUSES, WOLVERHAMPTON WV10 7HY

Owner: *The National Trust* ***Contact:*** *The Property Manager*

Tel/Fax: 01902 782808

An Elizabethan house with later alterations. Charles II hid here after the Battle of Worcester and the bed in which he slept is on view, as well as the hiding place he used. The small garden has been reconstructed in 17th century style with formal box parterre; only 17th century plants are grown. The property is a Sandford Education Award Winner. Tearoom in 18th century barn. Charles II exhibition in the barn.

Location: OS Ref. SJ932 044. 4m N of Wolverhampton between A449 and A460.

Opening Times: 25 Mar - end May: Sats, Suns, BH Mons & following Tues (except 2 May). Jun, Sept & Oct: Weds, Sats, Suns. Jul & Aug: daily except Mons, Thurs & Fris (open BH Mons). 1.30 - 5.30pm (BH Mons, 11am - 5pm). Pre-booked groups at other times including evening tours.

Admission: Adult £4, Child £2, Family £10.

Ground floor & grounds suitable. WC. Guide dogs only.

WWW Website Index PAGE 46

SANDON HALL

SANDON, STAFFORDSHIRE ST18 OBZ

Owner: *The Earl of Harrowby* ***Contact:*** *Michael Bosson*

Tel/Fax: 01889 508004

Ancestral seat of the Earls of Harrowby, conveniently located in the heart of Staffordshire. The imposing neo-Jacobean house was rebuilt by William Burn in 1854. Set amidst 400 acres of glorious parkland, Sandon, for all its grandeur and elegance, is first and foremost a home. The family museum which opened in 1994 has received considerable acclaim, and incorporates several of the State Rooms. The 50 acre landscaped gardens feature magnificent trees and are especially beautiful in May and autumn.

Location: OS Ref. SJ957 287. 5m NE of Stafford on the A51, between Stone and Lichfield, easy access from M6/J14.

Opening Times: All year: for events, functions and for pre-booked visits to the museum and gardens. Evening tours by special arrangement. Closed Christmas Day, Boxing Day and New Year's Day.

Admission: Museum: Adult £4, Child £3, OAP £3.50. Gardens: Adult £1.50, Child £1, OAP £1. NB. Max group size 22 or 45 if combined Museum and Gardens.

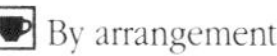 Grounds suitable.  By arrangement. In grounds, on leads. 

STAFFORD CASTLE & VISITOR CENTRE

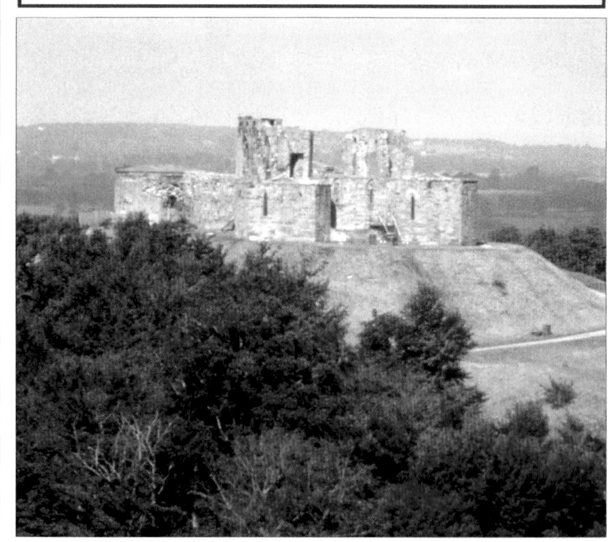

NEWPORT ROAD, STAFFORD ST16 1DJ

Owner: *Stafford Borough Council* ***Contact:*** *N Thomas*

Tel/Fax: 01785 257698

This impressive site was once a Norman motte and bailey castle. Earl Ralph, a founder member of the Order of the Garter, spent part of his fortune building a stone keep in 1348. During the Civil War, the castle was successfully defended, but eventually demolished. The current building was erected in the early 19th century and fell into ruin through this century. The Visitor Centre displays artefacts found during recent excavations. An imaginative audio-visual presentation describes the castle's mixed fortunes.

Location: OS Ref. SJ904 220. On N side of A518, $1^1/_2$ m WSW of town centre.

Opening Times: Apr - Oct: Tue - Sun, 10am - 5pm. Nov - Mar: Tue - Sun, 10am - 4pm.

Admission: Adult £2, Child/Conc. £1.20. Family (2+2) £4.

  Grounds suitable. WC. In grounds, on leads. 

SHUGBOROUGH

See pages 303 for full page entry.

Patrick Lane.

Biddulph Grange Garden, Staffordshire.

TAMWORTH CASTLE

THE HOLLOWAY, TAMWORTH, STAFFORDSHIRE B79 7LR

Owner: *Tamworth Borough Council* ***Contact:*** *Mrs Esme Ballard*

Tel: 01827 709626 Fax: 01827 709630

Dramatic Norman castle with 15 rooms open to the public, spanning 800 years of history. Attractive town centre park with floral terraces.

Location: OS Ref. SK206 038. Town centre off A51.

Opening Times: All year: Mon - Sat, 10am - 5.30pm. Suns, 2 - 5.30pm. Last adm. 4.30pm. Please check opening times after 1 Nov.

Admission: Adult £4.20, Conc. £2.10, Family £11.60. Groups: Adult £3.15, Child £1.60, OAP £1.60.

 Ground floor suitable. By arrangement. Guide dogs only.

TUTBURY CASTLE

Tel: 01283 812129

Tutbury, Staffordshire

Owner: The Duchy of Lancaster **Contact:** Barry Vallens

Remains of a large motte and bailey castle overlooking the Dove Valley.

Location: OS Ref. SK210 291. W side of Tutbury off A50 Tutbury - Barton road.

Opening Times: Apr - Oct: Wed - Suns, 10am - 6pm. Also weekends throughout winter, weather permitting.

Admission: Adult £3, Child/OAP £1.50.

WALL ROMAN SITE (Letocetum)

Tel: 01543 480768

Watling Street, Nr Lichfield, Staffordshire WS14 0AW

Owner: English Heritage **Contact:** The Custodian

The remains of a staging post alongside Watling Street. Foundations of an Inn and a Bath House can be seen and there is a display of finds in the site museum.

Location: OS139 Ref. SK099 067. Off A5 at Wall, nr Lichfield.

Opening Times: 1 Apr - 31 Oct: daily, 10am - 6pm (5pm in Oct).

Admission: Adult £2.30, Child £1.10, Conc. £1.70. 15% discount for groups (11+).

Tel. for details.

IZAAK WALTON'S COTTAGE

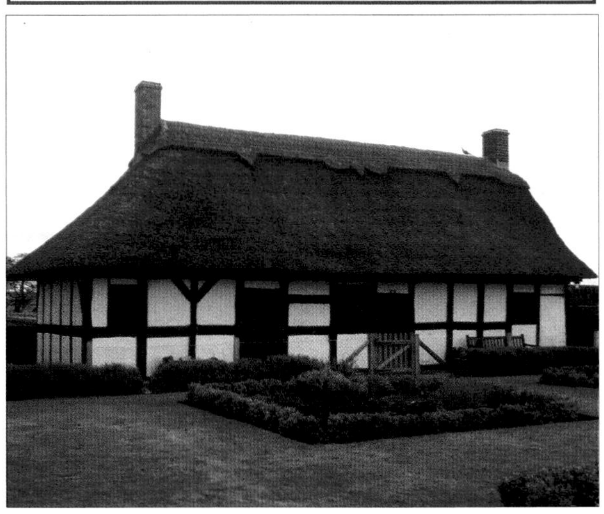

WORSTON LANE, SHALLOWFORD, Nr STAFFORD ST15 0PA

Owner: *Stafford Borough Council* ***Contact:*** *S Bailey*

Tel/Fax: 01785 760278

Thatched, timber-framed cottage in the heart of the Staffordshire countryside. Bequeathed by Izaak Walton, author of the *Compleat Angler,* it has displays on the history of angling. Ground floor rooms are set out in 17th century style.

Location: OS Ref. SJ876 293. Shallowford, nr Great Bridgeford, 6m N of Stafford.

Opening Times: Apr - Oct: Tue - Sun, 11am - 4.30pm.

Admission: Adult £2, Child/Conc. £1.20. Family (2+2) £4.

By arrangement. Guide dogs only.

SPECIAL EVENTS:

Events programme during the summer. Please telephone for details.

WHITMORE HALL

WHITMORE, NEWCASTLE-UNDER-LYME ST5 5HW

Owner: *Mr Guy Cavenagh-Mainwaring* ***Contact:*** *Mr Michael Cavenagh-Thornhill*

Tel: 01782 680478 **Fax:** 01782 680906

Whitmore Hall is a Grade I listed building, designated as a house of outstanding architectural and historical interest, and is a fine example of a small Carolinian manor house, although parts of the hall date back to a much earlier period. The hall has beautifully proportioned light rooms, curving staircase and landing. There are some good family portraits to be seen with a continuous line, from 1624 to the present day. It has been the family seat, for over 900 years, of the Cavenagh-Mainwarings who are direct descendants of the original Norman owners. The interior of the hall has recently been refurbished and is in fine condition. The grounds include a beautiful home park with a lime avenue leading to the house, as well as landscaped gardens encompassing an early Victorian summer house. One of the outstanding features of Whitmore is the extremely rare example of a late Elizabethan stable block, the ground floor is part cobbled and has nine oak-carved stalls, while the upstairs floor houses the remains of the stable boys' rooms and a ghost!

Location: OS Ref. SJ811 413. On A53 Newcastle - Market Drayton Road, 3m from M6/J15.

Opening Times: 1 May - 31 Aug: Tues, Weds & BHs, 2 - 5.30pm.

Admission: Adult £3, Child 50p.

Ground floor & grounds suitable.

Special Events Index PAGE 40

Shugborough, Staffordshire.

Owner:
The Viscount Daventry

CONTACT

Colonel CMG Hendy OBE
Arbury Hall
Nuneaton
Warwickshire CV10 7PT

Tel: 024 7638 2804

Fax: 024 7664 1147

LOCATION

OS Ref. SP335 893

London, M1, M6/J3 (A444 to Nuneaton), 2m SW of Nuneaton. 1m W of A444.

Chester A51, A34, M6 (from J14 to J3), 2½ hrs. Nuneaton 10 mins.

London 2 hrs, Birmingham ½ hr, Coventry 20 mins.

Bus: Nuneaton 3m.

Rail: Nuneaton Station 3m.

Air: Birmingham International 17m.

CONFERENCE/FUNCTION		
ROOM	SIZE	MAX CAPACITY
Dining Room	35' x 28'	120
Saloon	35' x 30'	70
Long Gallery	48' x 11'	40
Stables Tearooms	31' x 18'	80

ARBURY HALL
Nuneaton

ARBURY HALL has been the seat of the Newdegate family for over 400 years and is the ancestral home of Viscount Daventry. This Tudor/Elizabethan House was gothicised by Sir Roger Newdegate in the 18th century and is regarded as the 'Gothic Gem' of the Midlands. The Hall contains a fine collection of both oriental and Chelsea porcelain, portraits by Lely, Reynolds, Devis and Romney and furniture by Chippendale and Hepplewhite. The principal rooms, with their soaring fan vaulted ceilings and plunging pendants and filigree tracery, stand as a most breathtaking and complete example of early Gothic Revival architecture and provide a unique and fascinating venue for corporate entertaining, product launches, receptions, fashion shoots and activity days. Exclusive use of this historic Hall, its gardens and parkland is offered to clients. The Hall stands in the middle of beautiful parkland with landscaped gardens of rolling lawns, lakes and winding wooded walks. Spring flowers are profuse and in June rhododendrons, azaleas and giant wisteria provide a beautiful environment for the visitor.

George Eliot, the novelist, was born on the estate and Arbury Hall and Sir Roger Newdegate were immortalised in her book '*Scenes of Clerical Life*'.

Corporate hospitality, film location, small conferences, product launches and promotions, marquee functions, clay pigeon shooting, archery and other sporting activities, grand piano in Saloon, helicopter landing site. No cameras or video recorders.

Exclusive lunches and dinners for corporate parties in dining room, max. 50, buffets 120.

Visitors may alight at the Hall's main entrance. Parking in allocated areas. Ramp access to main hall.

By arrangement for groups.

Obligatory. Tour time: 1hr.

200 cars and 3 coaches 250 yards from house. Follow tourist signs. Approach map available for coach drivers.

Welcome, must book. School room available.

In gardens on leads. Guide dogs only in house.

OPENING TIMES

ALL YEAR

Open all year for corporate events.

Also pre-booked visits to Hall and Gardens for groups of 25+ on Tues, Weds & Thurs from Easter to the end of September.

Hall & Gardens open 2 - 5pm on BH weekends only (Suns & Mons) Easter - September.

ADMISSION

SUMMER

Hall & Gardens
Adult £4.50
Child (up to 14 yrs.)..£2.50
Family (2+2) £10.00

Gardens Only
Adult £3.00
Child (up to 14 yrs.)..£2.00

Groups (25+)
Adult £4.00
Child £2.50

Evening visits..........£5.00 (30+)

Special rates for pre-booked groups of 25+.

SPECIAL EVENTS

- **MAY 11 - 14:** Birmingham National Dog Show (not open to the public).
- **JUN 24/25:** Home, Gardens & Leisure Show.
- **JUL 15:** Theatre in the Garden.
- **AUG 20:** Motor Transport Spectacular.
- **SEPT 2:** Fireworks Festival in the Park.

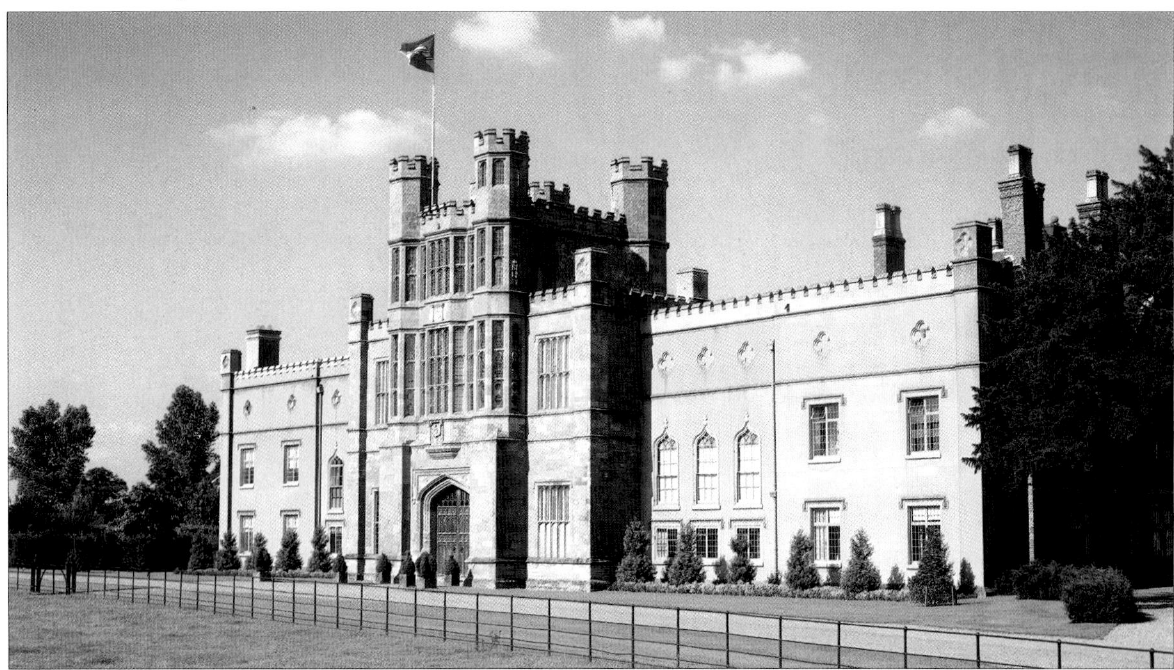

Owner:
Mrs C Throckmorton

CONTACT

Mr A McLaren
Coughton Court
Alcester
Warwickshire
B49 5JA

Tel: 01789 400777

Fax: 01789 765544

Visitor Information: 01789 762435

e-mail: information@coughtoncourt.co.uk

LOCATION

OS Ref. SP080 604

Located on A435, 2m N of Alcester, 10m NW of Stratford-on-Avon. 18m from Birmingham City Centre.

Rail: Birmingham International

Air: Birmingham International

CONFERENCE/FUNCTION		
ROOM	SIZE	MAX CAPACITY
Dining Rm	45' x 27'	60
Saloon	60' x 36'	100

The Saloon, which has particularly good acoustics, is often used for music recording.

COUGHTON COURT
Alcester

COUGHTON COURT has been the home of the Thockmortons since the 15th century and the family still live here today. The magnificent Tudor gatehouse was built around 1530 with the north and south wings completed 10 or 20 years later. The gables and the first storey of these wings are of typical mid-16th century half-timbered work.

Of particular interest to visitors is the Thockmorton family history from Tudor times to the present generation. On view are family portraits through the centuries with other family memorabilia and recent photographs. Also furniture, tapestries and porcelain.

A long-standing Roman Catholic theme runs through the family history as the Thockmortons have maintained their Catholic religion until the present day. The house has a strong connection with the Gunpowder Plot and also suffered damage during the Civil War. Exhibitions on the Gunpowder Plot as well as Children's Clothes (included in price).

Gardens

The house stands in 25 acres of gardens and grounds along with two churches and a lake. A formal garden was constructed in 1992 with designs based on an Elizabethan knot garden in the courtyard. A new $1^1/_2$ acre garden in the old walled garden opened in 1996. Visitors can also enjoy a specially created walk beside the River Arrow and a new bog garden opened in 1997.

Receptions, special dinners, filming, buffets, business meetings, fairs and garden parties. The excellent acoustics of the Saloon make it ideal for concerts, especially chamber music.Marquees can be erected on the large lawn area, grand piano. No photography or stiletto heels in house.

Buffet or sit-down meals can be provided by arrangement, in the Dining Room and Saloon. In-house catering can be arranged for other events. Wedding receptions welcome.

Ground floor of house and gardens. WC.

Licensed restaurant, 11am - 5.30pm. Capacity 100 inside and 60 outside.

By arrangement.

Unlimited for cars plus 4 coaches.

Car park only.

OPENING TIMES

House
18 - 31 March: Sats & Suns
Apr - Sept: Wed - Sun
11.30am - 5pm
(BH Mons open 11am).

Also open BH Mon & Tue plus Tues in Jul & Aug (Closed Good Fri & Sat 24 Jun).

October: Sats & Suns (closes 29 Oct for winter).

Gardens, Restaurant, Gift Shop & Plant Centre: 11am - 5.30 on house open days.

Last admission to House and Gardens including Walled Garden, 4.30pm.

Christmas: 2 - 17 Dec: Sat & Sun, 11am - 4pm. Gift shop & gardens admission free.

Grounds
As house: 11am - 5.30pm.

House may be closed on some Sats, the gardens and remainder of the property will remain open. Please check visitor information line.

ADMISSION

House & Gardens
Adult £6.40
Child* (5-15yrs) £3.20
Family (2+4)...........£19.50
Booked Groups (15+)
Adult £5.15
Child £2.50

Gardens only
Adult £4.60
Child* (5-15yrs) £2.30
Family (2+4)...........£14.40
Groups (15+)
per person £3.70

*under 5yrs Free.
NT members Free admission to house, £2 charge to walled garden.

Owner:
The Marquess of Hertford

CONTACT

Mrs Julie Timms
Ragley Hall
Alcester
Warwickshire
B49 5NJ

Tel: 01789 762090

Fax: 01789 764791

e-mail:
ragley.hall@virginnet.co.uk

LOCATION

OS Ref. SP073 555

Off A46/A435 1m SW of Alcester.
From London 100m, M40 via Oxford and Stratford-on-Avon.

Rail: Evesham Station 9m.

Air: Birmingham International 20m.

Taxi: 007 Taxi 01789 414007

CONFERENCE/FUNCTION		
ROOM	SIZE	MAX CAPACITY
Great Hall	70' x 40'	150
Red Saloon	30' x 40'	150
Green Drawing Rm	20' x 30'	150
Supper	45' x 22'	100
Seymour	25' x 23'	30

RAGLEY HALL
Alcester

RAGLEY HALL, home of the Marquess and Marchioness of Hertford and their family, was designed by Robert Hooke in 1680 and is one of the earliest and loveliest of England's great Palladian houses. The perfect symmetry of its architecture remains unchanged except for the massive portico added by Wyatt in 1780.

In 1750, when Francis Seymour owned Ragley, James Gibbs designed the magnificent baroque plasterwork of the Great Hall. On completion, Francis filled the Hall with French and English furniture and porcelain and had portraits of himself and his sons painted by Sir Joshua Reynolds. Notable also is the mural, by Graham Rust, in the south Staircase Hall which was completed in 1983.

PARK, GARDENS & GROUNDS

Ragley is a working estate with more than 6000 acres of land, the house is situated in 27 acres of gardens that were designed by 'Capability' Brown, and include the beautiful Rose Garden. Near to the hall are the working stables, housing a carriage collection dating back to 1760 and a display of assorted historical equestrian equipment. For children there is the adventure playground and maze situated by the lake.

Product launches, dinners and activity days, film and photographic location, park, lake and picnic area, marquee. No photography or camcorders in the house. Guide book translated in French and German.

Private and corporate entertainment, wedding receptions, conferences, seminars. Telephone for details.

Visitors may alight at entrance. Parking in allocated areas. WCs. Lifts.

Licensed tea rooms 11am - 5pm. Groups must pre-book.

Coach drivers admitted free and receive info pack and luncheon voucher. Please advise of group visits.

Welcome, £2.50 per head. Teachers' packs and work modules on request. Adventure Wood and Woodland Walk.

In grounds, on leads.

OPENING TIMES

13 April - 1 October
(House, Park & Gardens are closed Good Friday).

House
Thurs, Fris & Suns,
12.30 - 5pm
(last adm. 4.30pm),
Sats, 11am - 3.30pm
(last adm. 3.00pm).
BH Mons, 11am - 5pm
(last adm. 4.30pm).

Park & Gardens
Thur - Sun & BH Mons
10am - 6pm
(last adm. 4.45pm).
Also open
13 Apr - 2 May;
30 & 31 May;
24 Jul - 3 Sept: daily.

ADMISSION

House Park & Garden
Adult £5.00
Child (5-16yrs) £3.50
OAP £4.50
Orange Badge Holders £4.50
Groups* (20-100)
Adult £4.50
Schools £2.50
OAP £4.50

Park & Garden
Adult £4.00
Child (5-16yrs) £3.00
OAP £3.50
Orange Badge Holders £3.50
Groups* (20-100)
Adult £3.50
Schools £2.50
OAP £3.50

* Groups of 20+ must book and confirm in writing prior to visit.

Season tickets available.

See Special Events Index.

Shakespeare's Birthplace

Anne Hathaway's Cottage

Owner:
The Shakespeare Birthplace Trust

CONTACT

Tracey Powell
Marketing & Publicity Manager
The Shakespeare Birthplace Trust
Henley Street
Stratford-upon-Avon
CV37 6QW

Tel: 01789 204016 (General enquiries)

Tel: 01789 201806 (Group Visits)

Fax: 01789 296083

E-mail: info@shakespeare.org.uk

LOCATION

OS Refs:
Birthplace - **SP201 552**
New Place - **SP201 548**
Hall's Croft - **SP200 546**
Hathaway's - **SP185 547**
Arden's - **SP166 582**

Direct rail services from London (Paddington)

2 hrs from London
45 mins from Birmingham by car.

4m from M40/J15 and well signed from all approaches.

THE SHAKESPEARE HOUSES
Stratford-upon-Avon

Step back in time to enjoy these beautifully preserved Tudor homes connected with William Shakespeare and his family; the architectural character, period furniture, special collections, attractive gardens, grounds and walks and craft displays.

In Town: Shakespeare's Birthplace: This half timbered house where the dramatist was born was purchased as a national memorial in 1847. It has been a place of pilgrimage for nearly 300 years. Today it is approached through a Visitors' Centre, with a fine exhibition, *Shakespeare's World*, and the garden.

Nash's House and New Place: The site and grounds of Shakespeare's home from 1597 until his death, with its Elizabethan-style garden, is approached through Nash's House adjoining, which contains exceptional furnishings and displays of the history of Stratford.

Hall's Croft: A delightful Elizabethan town house, once the home of Dr Hall, Shakespeare's physician son-in-law. Exceptional furniture and paintings and exhibition on Tudor medicine. Fine walled garden. Meals and refreshments available which can also be served in the beautiful garden.

Out of Town: Anne Hathaway's Cottage: This famous, picturesque thatched cottage was Anne's home before her marriage to Shakespeare. Cottage garden and Shakespeare Tree Garden as well as a garden shop and attractive Shottery Brook and Jubilee Walks. Summer tea garden.

Mary Arden's House and The Shakespeare Countryside Museum: Tudor farmstead (home of Shakespeare's mother) with out-buildings and nearby Glebe Farm containing exhibits illustrating country life over 400 years. Gypsy caravans, dovecote, duck pond, rare breeds, field walk, and all-day displays of falconry. Refreshments and picnic area.

Shakespeare's Birthplace

Regular guided bus tour service connecting the town house with Anne Hathaway's Cottage and Mary Arden's House. No photography inside properties.

Shops at Shakespeare's Birthplace, Hall's Croft, Anne Hathaway's Cottage and Mary Arden's House.

Available, details upon request.

WCs. Naturally difficult levels everywhere but much for disabled to enjoy at Mary Arden's House.

Available on site or close by.

By special arrangement.

The Trust provides a free coach terminal for delivery and pick-up of groups, max. stay 30 mins at Shakespeare's Birthplace. Parking at Anne Hathaway's Cottage and Mary Arden's House.

Available for all properties. For information 01789 201804.

Guide dogs only.

OPENING TIMES

SUMMER
20 March - 19 October

Birthplace & Anne Hathaway's
Mon - Sat: 9am - 5pm.
Suns: 9.30am - 5pm

Nash's House/New Place, Hall's Croft & Mary Arden's House
Mon - Sat: 9.30am - 5pm.
Suns: 10am - 5pm

WINTER
20 October - 19 March

Birthplace & Anne Hathaway's
Mon - Sat: 9.30am - 4pm.
Suns: 10am - 4pm

Nash's House/New Place, Hall's Croft & Mary Arden's House
Mon - Sat: 10am - 4pm.
Suns: 10.30am - 4pm

1 Jan 2000 Houses open 12 noon. Closed 23 - 26 December. Open evenings out of hours by special arrangement.

ADMISSION

Prices valid until 30.4.2000
2000 prices on application.

Shakespeare's Birthplace
Adult ... £4.90
Child ... £2.20
Family (2+3) ... £12.00

New Place/Nash's House or Hall's Croft
Adult ... £3.30
Child ... £1.60
Family (2+3) ... £7.50

Anne Hathaway's Cottage
Adult ... £3.90
Child ... £1.60
Family (2+3) ... £9.00

Mary Arden's House
Adult ... £4.40
Child ... £2.20
Family (2+3) ... £11.00

All 3 in-town properties
Adult ... £7.50
Child ... £3.70
Conc. ... £6.50
Family (2+3) ... £18.00

All five properties
Adult ... £11.00
Child ... £5.50
Conc. ... £10.00
Family ... £26.00

Accompanied groups 20+, 10% discount.

STONELEIGH ABBEY
Kenilworth

Owner:
Stoneleigh Abbey Ltd

CONTACT

Shahab Seyfollahi
The Estate Office
Stoneleigh Abbey
Kenilworth
Warwickshire
CV8 2LF

Tel: 01926 858585

Fax: 01926 850724

e-mail: enquiries @stoneleighabbey.org

LOCATION

OS Ref. SP318 712

Off A46/B4115, 2m W of Kenilworth. From London 100m, M40 to Warwick.

Rail: Coventry station 5m, Leamington Spa station 5m.

Air: Birmingham International 20m.

Re-opening in 2000, after more than two years renovation work, Stoneleigh Abbey is one of the finest country house estates in the Midlands. The repairs have been funded by the Heritage Lottery Fund, English Heritage and the European Regional Development Fund.

The Abbey was founded in the reign of Henry II on royal land. After the Dissolution, the Abbey was granted to the Duke of Suffolk. The estate then passed into the ownership of the Leigh family who remained for 400 years. The estate is now managed by a charitable trust.

Visitors will experience a wealth of architectural styles spanning more than 600 years.

These include: the magnificent state rooms and chapel of the 18th century Baroque West Wing designed by Francis Smith of Warwick; the medieval Gatehouse, one of very few complete monastic gatehouses left, most are in ruins; the Gothic Revival style Regency Stables, the first two bays of which have been fully restored using the same methods and materials employed in their original construction; 690 acres of grounds and parkland with the River Avon flowing through, displaying the design influences of Humphry Repton and other major landscape designers.

Other attractions include a riverside conservatory serving light refreshments. A series of special events will be staged throughout the season.

OPENING TIMES

From Spring 2000, please telephone for details.

ADMISSION

Please telephone for details.

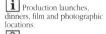

 Production launches, dinners, film and photographic locations.

Suitable.

 By arrangement.

 In grounds, on leads.

Tel. for details.

© NT Severn/R Charlton

UPTON HOUSE

Banbury

Owner:
The National Trust

CONTACT

The Property Manager
Upton House
Banbury
Oxfordshire
OX15 6HT

Tel: 01295 670266

e-mail: upton_house
@smtp.ntrust.org.uk

LOCATION

OS151 Ref. SP371 461

On A422, 7m NW of Banbury. 12m SE of Stratford-upon-Avon

Rail: Banbury Station, 7m.

UPTON HOUSE stands less than a mile to the south of the battlefield of Edgehill and there has been a house on this site since the Middle Ages. The present house was built at the end of the 17th century and remodelled 1927 - 29 for the 2nd Viscount Bearsted.

He was a great collector of paintings, china and many other valuable works of art, and adapted the building to display them. The paintings include works by El Greco, Bruegel, Bosch, Memling, Guardi, Hogarth and Stubbs. The rooms provide an admirable setting for the china collection which includes Chelsea figures and superb examples of beautifully decorated Sèvres porcelain. The set of 17th century Brussels tapestries depict the Holy Roman Emperor Maximilian I's boar and stag hunts.

New in 1999 and continuing in 2000: Artists and Shell Exhibition of Paintings and Posters commissioned by Shell for use in its publicity 1921 - 1949, while the 2nd Viscount Bearsted was chairman of the company, founded by his father.

GARDEN

The outstanding garden is of interest throughout the season with terraces descending into a deep valley from the main lawn. There are herbaceous borders, the national collection of asters, over an acre of kitchen garden, a water garden laid out in the 1930s and pools stocked with ornamental fish.

Over a mile from the house, but just visible from the west end of the terrace on the garden front, is the lower lake which was formed in the mid-18th century after the fashion of 'Capability' Brown. A small temple with Doric columns and pediment sits in the centre of the one straight edge.

© NT Severn/R Charlton

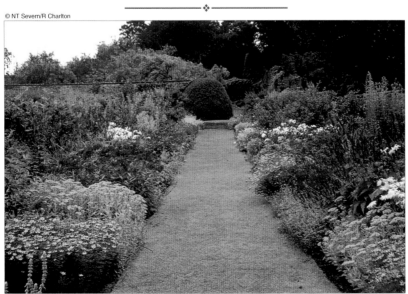

OPENING TIMES

SUMMER
1 April - 31 October
Sat - Wed including
BH Mons & Good Fri,
2 - 6pm.

Closed Thurs & Fris
Last admission 5.30pm,
5pm after 25 October.

Timed tickets: Suns in holiday periods & BH Mons (delays possible).

ADMISSION

Adult	£5.40
Child	£2.70
Family	£13.50
Garden	
Adult	£2.70

Parent & baby room. No indoor photography.

Wheelchair available. Access to all ground floor rooms. WC. Motorised buggy to /from lower garden.

Tour time $1^1/_2$ - 2hrs. Groups (15+) must pre-book. Evening tours by written appointment (no reduction).

Coaches park in the main car park.

SPECIAL EVENTS

- **ALL YEAR:**
  Fine arts study tours, jazz concerts and other events, please send SAE or telephone for details

CONTACT

Sales Office
Warwick Castle
Warwick
CV34 4QU

Tel: 01926 495421 (Admin)
01926 406600 (Info)

Fax: 01926 401692

LOCATION

OS Ref. SP284 648

2m from M40/J15.
Birmingham 35 mins
Leeds 2 hrs 5 mins
London, 1 hr 30 mins
Vehicle entrance from A429
1/2 m SW of town centre.

Rail: Intercity from London Euston to Coventry. Direct service Chiltern Line from Marylebone & Paddington to Warwick.

CONFERENCE/FUNCTION		
ROOM	SIZE	MAX CAPACITY
Great Hall	61' x 34'	130
State Dining Room	40' x 25'	32
Undercroft	46' x 26'	120
Stables Hayloft	44' x 19'	70
Marquees		2000

WARWICK CASTLE
Warwick

Along with the pomp, Warwick Castle give you the circumstance. Over a thousand years of secrets hide in the shadows of Warwick Castle. Murder, mystery, intrigue and scandal: the Castle has witnessed it all, and now reveals the secret life of England as you have never seen it before.

From the days of William the Conqueror to the reign of Queen Victoria, the Castle has provided a backdrop for many turbulent times.

Here you can join a mediaeval household in our Kingmaker attraction, watching them prepare for the final battle of the Earl of Warwick. Enter the eerie Ghost Tower, where it is said that the unquiet spirit of Sir Fulke Greville, murdered most foully by a manservant, still roams.

Descend into the gloomy depths of the Dungeon and Torture Chamber, then step forward in time and marvel at the grandeur of the State Rooms. The 14th century Great Hall lies at the heart of the Castle and here you can see the death mask of Oliver Cromwell and Bonnie Prince Charlie's shield.

Witness the perfect manners and hidden indiscretions of Daisy, Countess of Warwick and her friends at the Royal Weekend Party 1898 or stroll through the 60 acres of grounds and gardens, landscaped by 'Capability' Brown, which surround the Castle today.

Besides the secrets, there are a host of special events to enjoy throughout the year, including Birds of Prey, Jousting and a Mediaeval Festival.

Warwick Castle really is one of the best days out in history.

Corporate events, receptions and Kingmaker's Feasts. Guide books available in French, German, Japanese, Spanish and Italian.

Four shops.

Parking spaces in Stables Car Park, free admission for registered blind and visitors in wheelchairs.

Available, ranging from cream teas to three-course hot meals. During the summer there is an open air barbecue and refreshment pavilion in the grounds (weather permitting).

For groups (must be pre-booked). Guides in every room.

Limited free car parking in main car park. Free coach parking, free admission and refreshment voucher for coach driver.

Ideal location, being a superb example of military architecture dating back to the Norman Conquest and with elegant interiors up to Victorian times. Group rates apply. Education packs available.

Registered assistance dogs only.

OPENING TIMES

SUMMER
April - October
10am - 6pm
Last admission 5.30pm.

WINTER
November - March
10am - 5pm
Last admission 4.30pm.

ADMISSION

1 Mar (1999) - 31 May & 1 Sept - 29 Feb 2000

Adult	£9.50
Child (4 - 16yrs)	£5.80
Student	£7.25
OAP	£6.85
Family (2+2)	£27.00

Groups (20+)

Adult	£7.75
Child	£5.00
Student	£6.70
OAP	£6.15

Call the Warwick Castle Information Line on: 01926 406600 for the latest admission prices.

ARBURY HALL See page 308 for full page entry.

BADDESLEY CLINTON

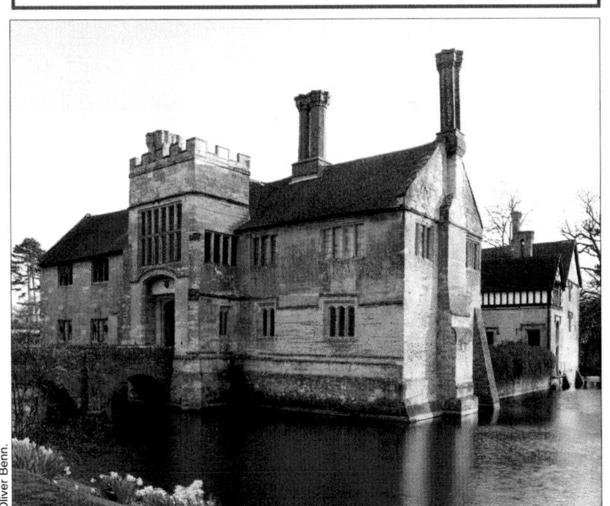

Oliver Benn.

RISING LANE, BADDESLEY CLINTON, KNOWLE, SOLIHULL B93 0DQ

Owner: *The National Trust* ***Contact:*** *The Property Manager*

Tel: 01564 783294 **Fax:** 01564 782706 **e-mail:** baddesley@smtp.ntrust.org.uk

A romantically sited medieval moated manor house, dating from 14th century; little changed since 1634; family portraits, priest holes; garden; ponds and lake walk.

Location: OS139, Ref. SP199 715. 3/4 m W of A4141 Warwick/Birmingham road at Chadwick End.

Opening Times: 1 Mar - 29 Oct: Wed - Sun & BH Mons. Mar, Apr & Oct: 1.30 - 5pm. May - Sept: 1.30 - 5.30pm. Grounds: 13 Feb - 17 Dec: Wed - Sun & BH Mons. Times: 13 - 27 Feb, Nov - 17 Dec: 12 noon - 4.30pm. Mar, Apr & Oct: 12 noon - 5pm. May - end Sept: 12 noon - 5.30pm.

Admission: Adult £5.20, Child £2.60, Family £13. Grounds, restaurant & shop only: £2.60.

Ground floor only & grounds. WC.  

Farnborough Hall, Warwickshire.

CHARLECOTE PARK

Matthew Antrobus

WELLESBOURNE, WARWICK CV35 9ER

Owner: *The National Trust* ***Contact:*** *The Property Manager*

Tel: 01789 470277 **Fax:** 01789 470544 **e-mail:** charlecote@smtp.ntrust.org.uk

Owned by the Lucy family since 1247, Sir Thomas built the house in 1558. Now, much altered, it is shown as it would have been a century ago, complete with Victorian kitchen, brewhouse and family carriages in the coach house. A video of Victorian life can be viewed. Two bedrooms, a dressing room and the main staircase will open at the end of June. Also a new garden, in the forecourt to the house and designed by Sir Edmund Fairfax-Lucy, will be completed by 21 April.

Location: OS151, Ref. SP263 564. 1m W of Wellesbourne, 5m E of Stratford-upon-Avon.

Opening Times: Park, Shop and Tea Bar only: 3 Feb - 16 Apr, Sat & Sun 1 - 4pm. 21 Apr - 5 Nov: daily except Weds & Thurs. House: 12 noon - 5pm. Grounds: 11am - 6pm. Last adm. to house 1/2 hr before closing.

Admission: Adult £5.40, Child £2.70, Family £13.50.

Licensed. By arrangement. Limited for coaches. Guide dogs only.

COUGHTON COURT See page 309 for full page entry.

FARNBOROUGH HALL **Tel:** 01295 690002

Banbury, Oxfordshire OX17 1DU

Owner: The National Trust **Contact:** Mr G Holbech

A classical mid-18th century stone house, home of the Holbech family for 300 years; notable plasterwork, the entrance hall, staircase and 2 principal rooms are shown; the grounds contain charming 18th century temples, a 2/3 mile terrace walk and an obelisk.

Location: OS151, Ref. SP430 490. 6m N of Banbury, 1/2 m W of A423.

Opening Times: House, grounds and terrace walk: Apr - end Sept: Weds & Sats also 30 Apr & 1 May, 2 - 6pm. Terrace walk only, Thurs & Fris, 2 - 6pm, closed Good Fri. Last admission to house 5.30pm.

Admission: House, grounds & terrace walk: Adult £3. Garden & terrace walk: £1.50. Terrace walk only (Thurs & Fris) £1.

House & grounds, but steep terrace walk. In grounds, on leads.

THE HILLER GARDEN **Tel:** 01789 490991 **Fax:** 01789 490439

Dunnington Heath Farm, Alcester, Warwickshire B49 5PD

Owner: Mr & Mrs R Beach **Contact:** Mr David Carvill

2 acre garden of unusual herbaceous plants and over 200 rose varieties.

Location: OS Ref. SP066 539. 1 1/2 m S of Ragley Hall on B4088 (formerly A435).

Opening Times: All year: daily 10am - 5pm.

Admission: Free.

The Midlands England

HONINGTON HALL

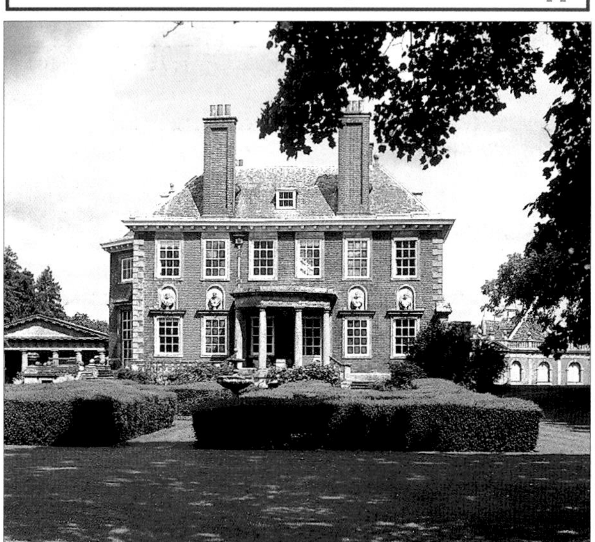

SHIPSTON-ON-STOUR, WARWICKSHIRE CV36 5AA

Owner/Contact: *Benjamin Wiggin Esq*

Tel: 01608 661434 **Fax:** 01608 663717

This fine Caroline manor house was built in the early 1680s for Henry Parker in mellow brickwork, stone quoins and window dressings. Modified in 1751 when an octagonal saloon was inserted. The interior was also lavishly restored around this time and contains exceptional mid-Georgian plasterwork. Set in 15 acres of grounds.

Location: OS Ref. SP261 427. 10m S of Stratford-upon-Avon. 1½m N of Shipston-on-Stour. Take A3400 towards Stratford, then signed right to Honington.

Opening Times: Jun - Aug: Weds only. BH Mon, 2.30 - 5pm. Groups at other times by appointment.

Admission: Adult £3, Child £1.50.

Not suitable. Obligatory.

KENILWORTH CASTLE

English Heritage Photographic Library

KENILWORTH, WARWICKSHIRE CV8 1NE

Owner: *English Heritage* ***Contact:*** *The Custodian*

Tel: 01926 852078

Kenilworth is the largest castle ruin in England, the former stronghold of great Lords and Kings. Its massive walls of warm red stone tower over the peaceful Warwickshire landscape. The Earl of Leicester entertained Queen Elizabeth I with 'Princely Pleasures' during her 19 day visit. He built a new wing for the Queen to lodge in and organised all manner of lavish and costly festivities. The Great Hall, where Gloriana dined with her courtiers, still stands and John of Gaunt's Hall is second only in width and grandeur to Westminster Hall. Climb to the top of the tower beside the hall and you will be rewarded by fine views over the rolling wooded countryside. New exhibition, interactive castle model and café in Leicester's Barn.

Location: OS140 Ref. SP278 723. In Kenilworth, off A452, W end of town.

Opening Times: 1 Apr - 31 Oct: daily, 10am - 6pm (5pm in Oct). 1 Nov - 31 Mar: daily 10am - 4pm. Closed 24 - 26 Dec & 1 Jan.

Admission: Adult £3.60, Child £1.80, Conc. £2.70. 15% discount for groups (11+).

Tel. for details.

LORD LEYCESTER HOSPITAL

Tel: 01926 491422

High Street, Warwick CV34 4BH

Owner: The Governors of Lord Leycester Hospital **Contact:** Capt D I Rhodes

Location: OS Ref. SP280 648. 1m N of M40/J15 on A429. SW side of town centre.

Opening Times: Tue - Sun: 10am - 5pm (Oct - Mar: 10am - 4pm). Closed Good Fri and Christmas Day.

Admission: Adult £2.95, Child £1.75, Conc. £2.25. 5% discount for groups (20+).

MIDDLETON HALL

Tel: 01827 283095 **Fax:** 01827 285717

Middleton, Tamworth, Staffordshire B78 2AE

Owner: Middleton Hall Trust **Contact:** Mrs B Gould

Hall (1285 - 1824). Former home of Hugh Willoughby (Tudor explorer), Francis Willughby and John Ray (17th century naturalists). Links with Elizabeth I; Lady Jane Grey; Handel; Jane Austen. Features walled gardens, Site of Special Scientific Interest, lakes, nature trail, restored smithy, award-winning craft centre, gift shop and tearoom.

Location: OS Ref. SP193 982. A4091, S of Tamworth.

Opening Times: 2 Apr - 24 Sept: 2 - 5pm, BH Mons, 11am - 5pm.

Admission: Adult £2, OAP £1.

Partially suitable. WC. By arrangement.

No parking for coaches.. Welcome, under control. 

PACKWOOD HOUSE

© SWT / D Sellman

LAPWORTH, SOLIHULL B94 6AT

Owner: *The National Trust* ***Contact:*** *The Property Manager*

Tel: 01564 783294 **e-mail:** baddesley@smtp.ntrust.org.uk

Originally a 16th century house, Packwood has been much altered over the years and today is the vision of Graham Baron Ash who recreated a Jacobean house in the 1920s and '30s. A fine collection of 16th century textiles and furniture. Important gardens with renowned herbaceous border and famous yew garden based on the Sermon on the Mount.

Location: OS139, Ref. 174 722. 2m E of Hockley Heath (on A3400), 11m SE of central Birmingham.

Opening Times: House: 29 Mar - 29 Oct: daily except Mons & Tues (open BH Mons & Good Fri). Times: Mar, Apr & Oct: 12.30 - 4.30pm. May - end Sept: 1.30 - 5.30pm. Garden: 1 Mar - 29 Oct: daily except Mons & Tues (open BH Mons). Times: Mar, Apr & Oct: 10am - 4.30pm. May - end Sept: 10am - 5.30pm. Park & Woodland Walks: All year, daily.

Admission: Adult £4.60, Child £2.30, Family £11.50, Garden only: £2.30. Timed tickets may be used at busy times.

House & parts of grounds suitable. WC. Free.  

Stephen Robson.

Packwood House, Warwickshire.

RAGLEY HALL

See page 310 for full page entry.

ST JAMES CHURCH

Tel: 01676 522020

Packington Park, Meriden, Nr Coventry CV7 7HF

Owner: Trustees of the St James Great Packington Trust **Contact:**

This red brick building has four domes topped by finules and it has been described as one of the very first truly international buildings that neo-classicism produced. The church was built to celebrate the return to sanity of King George III. The organ was designed by Handel for his librettist, Charles Jennens, who was the cousin of the 4th Earl of Aylesford who built the church.

Location: OS Ref. SP230 842. Packington Park, off the A45 at Meriden.

Opening Times: By appointment with the Estate Office.

Admission: Free. Donations to restoration fund appreciated.

THE SHAKESPEARE HOUSES

See page 311 for full page entry.

STONELEIGH ABBEY

See page 312 for full page entry.

UPTON HOUSE

See page 313 for full page entry.

WARWICK CASTLE

See page 314 for full page entry.

Honington Hall, Warwickshire.

HAGLEY HALL
Stourbridge

Owner: Viscount Cobham

CONTACT

Mrs Lesley Haynes
Hagley Hall
Stourbridge
West Midlands
DY9 9LG

Tel: 01562 882408

Fax: 01562 882632

LOCATION

OS Ref. SO920 807

Easily accessible from all areas of the country. 1/4 m S of A456 at Hagley.

Close to the M42, M40, M6 and only 5m from M5/J3/J4.

Birmingham City Centre 12m.

Rail: Railway Station and the NEC 25 mins.

Air: Birmingham International Airport 25 mins.

CONFERENCE/FUNCTION		
ROOM	SIZE	MAX CAPACITY
Gallery	85' x 17'	140
Crimson Rm	23' x 31'	60
State Dining Room	34' x 27'	80
Westcote	31' x 20'	60

HAGLEY HALL is set in a 350-acre landscaped park yet is only 25 minutes from Birmingham city centre, the NEC and ICC and close to the motorway network of M5, M6, M40 and M42.

The house is available throughout the year on an exclusive basis for conferences, product launches, presentations, lunches, dinners, country sporting days, team building activities, themed evenings, murder mysteries, concerts, filming and wedding receptions.

Hagley's high standards of catering are now available at other venues as well as at Hagley Hall.

The elegant Palladian house, completed in 1760, contains some of the finest examples of Italian plasterwork. Hagley's rich rococo decoration is a remarkable tribute to the artistic achievement of great 18th century amateurs and is the much loved home of the 11th Viscount Cobham.

Available on an exclusive basis for conferences, presentations, lunches, dinners, product launches, themed evenings, murder mysteries, concerts, wedding receptions. Extensive parkland for country sporting days, team-building activities, off-road driving and filming.

As well as in-house catering, Hagley also offers a unique catering service at the venue of your choice.

Visitors may alight at the entrance. No WC.

Teas available during opening times.

Please book parties in advance, guided tour time of house 1 hr. Colour guide - book.

Unlimited for coaches and cars.

By arrangement.

OPENING TIMES

House

3 January - 27 January
& 30 January - 27 February:
Daily except Saturdays.

21 April - 27 April;
28 May - 31 May &
27 August - 30 August:
Daily.

2 - 5pm.

ADMISSION

House

Adult	£3.50
Child (under 14 yrs)	£1.50
OAP	£2.50

ASTON HALL

TRINITY ROAD, BIRMINGHAM, WEST MIDLANDS B6 6JD

Owner: *Birmingham City Council* ***Contact:*** *Curator/Manager*

Tel: 0121 327 0062 **Fax:** 0121 327 7162

A large Jacobean mansion built 1618 - 1635 from plans by John Thorpe. The Hall is brick-built with a fairytale skyline of gables and turrets. The interior has period rooms from the 17th, 18th and 19th centuries and a splendid long gallery measuring 136ft. A large kitchen and servants' rooms are also on display.

Location: OS139, Ref. SP080 899. 3m NE of Birmingham, 1/4 m from A38(M).

Opening times: 14 Apr - 5 Nov: daily 2 - 5pm. Parkland open all year round.

Admission: Free.

Ground floor & grounds suitable.  Guide dogs only.

THE BIRMINGHAM BOTANICAL GARDENS AND GLASSHOUSES

WESTBOURNE ROAD, EDGBASTON, BIRMINGHAM B15 3TR

Owner: *Birmingham Botanical & Horticultural Society* ***Contact:*** *Mrs H Champion*

Tel: 0121 454 1860 **Fax:** 0121 454 7835
e-mail: admin@bham-bot-gdns.demon.co.uk

Tropical, Mediterranean and Desert Glasshouses contain a wide range of exotic and economic flora. 15 acres of beautiful gardens with the finest collection of plants in the Midlands. Home of the National Bonsai Collection. Children's adventure playground, aviaries and gallery.

Location: OS Ref. SP048 855. 2m W of city centre. Follow signs to Edgbaston then brown tourist signs.

Opening times: Daily: 9am - Dusk (7pm latest except pre-booked groups). Suns opening time 10am.

Admission: Adult £4.30 (£4.60 on Suns & BHs), Child (under 5) Free, Family £11.50 (£12.50 on Suns & BHs), Conc. £2.40. Reduced rates for groups (11+). Prices from April 2000.

   Licensed. Guide dogs only.   

BLAKESLEY HALL

Tel: 0121 783 2193

Blakesley Road, Yardley, Birmingham B25 8RN

Owner: Birmingham City Council **Contact:** Curator/Manager

Blakesley Hall has been awarded a grant by the Heritage Lottery Fund and will be closed during 2000 for development. The Hall will re-open in April 2001, with more rooms returned to their 17th century appearance and a new building with tearooms, shop and display gallery.

Location: OS139, Ref. SP130 862. 6m E of Birmingham city centre off A4040 from A45.

Opening times: Closed for 2000.

CASTLE BROMWICH HALL GARDENS

Tel/Fax: 0121 749 4100

Chester Road, Castle Bromwich, Birmingham B36 9BT

Owner: Castle Bromwich Hall Gardens Trust **Contact:** The Secretary

A unique example of 17th and 18th century formal garden design within a 10 acre walled area, comprising interesting and historic plants and vegetables, with a 19th century holly maze. Classical patterned parterres can be seen at the end of the holly walk, together with restored green house and summer house.

Location: OS Ref. SP142 898. On A47, 4m E of Birmingham city centre, 1m from M6/J5 (exit northbound only). Southbound M6/J6 and follow A38 & A452.

Opening Times: Easter - end Sept (Apr weekends only): Tue - Thur, 1.30 - 4.30pm. Sats, Suns & BHs 2 - 6pm. Closed Mons & Fris.

Admission: Adult £3, Child £1, OAP £2.

Daily. Limited for coaches. In grounds, on leads.

COVENTRY CATHEDRAL

Tel/Fax: 02476 227597/02476 631448

7 Priory Road, Coventry CV1 5ES **e-mail:** information@coventrycathedral.org

Owner: Provost & Canons of Coventry Cathedral **Contact:** The Visits Secretary

The remains of the medieval Cathedral, bombed in 1940, stand beside the new Cathedral by Basil Spence, consecrated in 1962. Modern works of art include a huge tapestry by Graham Sutherland, a stained glass window by John Piper and a bronze sculpture by Epstein. '*Reconciliation*' statue by Josefina de Vasconcellos.

Location: OS Ref. SP336 790. City centre.

Opening Times: Cathedral: Easter - Oct: from 8.30am - 6pm. Nov - Easter: 9.30am - 5pm. Visitors Centre: Easter - Oct: Mon - Sat, 10am - 4pm. Nov - Easter: Mon - Sat, 11am - 3pm.

Admission: Cathedral: £2 donation. Visitor Centre: Adult £2, Child/Conc. £1. Groups (10+): Adult £1, Child/Conc. 75p. Groups must book in advance.

Photo permit required. Partially suitable. WC. By arrangement. No parking. By arrangement. Guide dogs only.

HAGLEY HALL

See page 318 for full page entry.

HALESOWEN ABBEY

Tel: 01604 730320 (Regional Office)

Halesowen, Birmingham, West Midlands

Owner: English Heritage **Contact:** The Custodian

Remains of an abbey founded by King John in the 13th century, now incorporated into a 19th century farm. Parts of the church and the monks' infirmary can still be made out.

Location: OS Ref. SO975 828. Off A456 Kidderminster road, 6m W of Birmingham city centre.

Opening Times: Jul - Aug: Weekends only 10am - 6pm.

Admission: Adult £1.50, Child 80p, Conc £1.10

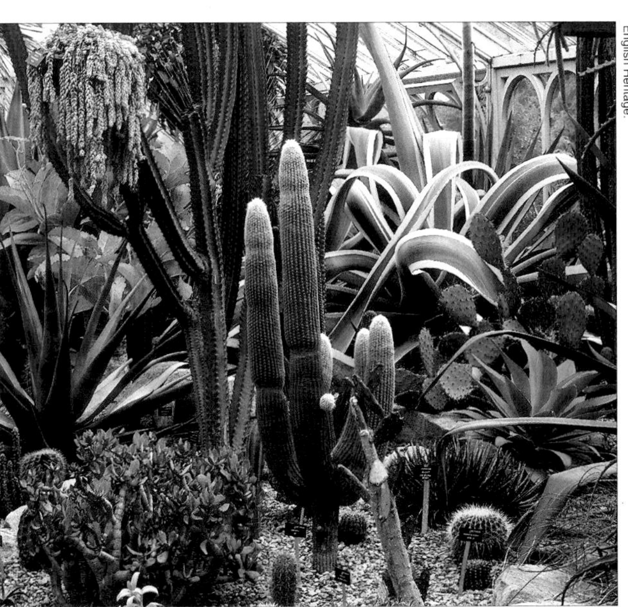

English Heritage.

The Birmingham Botanical Gardens, West Midlands.

MUSEUM OF THE JEWELLERY QUARTER

75 - 79 VYSE STREET, HOCKLEY, BIRMINGHAM B18 6HA

Owner: *Birmingham City Council* ***Contact:*** *The Curator*

Tel: 0121 554 3598 **Fax:** 0121 554 9700

Built around the preserved workshops and offices of Smith and Pepper, a Birmingham jewellery firm. This lively working Museum offers a fascinating insight into the city's historic jewellery trade. Enjoy a tour of the factory with one of our knowledgeable guides and meet skilled jewellers at work. You can also explore the displays which tell the story of the Quarter and the jeweller's craft, practiced in this distinctive part of Birmingham for over 200 years. The museum is available for private evening bookings with catering provision if required.

Location: OS Ref. SP060 880. ¾ m NW of city centre, just within A4540 (ring road).

Opening Times: Mon - Fri, 10am - 4pm. Sats, 11am - 5pm. Closed Suns.

Admission: Adult £2.50, Conc. £2, Family (2+3) £6.50. 10% discount for booked groups (10+).

Temporary exhibitions. On street parking only. Guide dogs only.

SOHO HOUSE

SOHO AVENUE, HANDSWORTH, BIRMINGHAM B18 5LB

Owner: *Birmingham City Council* ***Contact:*** *Curator / Manager*

Tel: 0121 554 9122 **Fax:** 0121 554 5929

The elegant home of the industrial pioneer Matthew Boulton from 1766 to 1809, Soho House has been carefully restored. Special features include an early 19th century hot air heating system. Period rooms and displays on Boulton's businesses, family and associates as well as the architectural development of the house.

Location: OS Ref. SP054 893. S side of Soho Avenue, just SW of Soho Hill/Soho Road (A41). 2m NW of city centre. Follow signs for Handsworth then brown tourist signs.

Opening Times: Tue - Sat, 10am - 5pm. Suns, 12 noon - 5pm. Closed Mons except BHs.

Admission: Adult £2.50, Conc. £2, Family £6.50. 10% discount for booked groups.

Meeting room. By arrangement. Limited for cars. Guide dogs only.

RYTON ORGANIC GARDENS

Tel: 024 7630 3517 **Fax:** 024 7663 9229

Ryton-on-Dunsmore, Coventry, West Midlands CV8 3LG

Owner: Henry Doubleday Research Association **Contact:** Sally Furness

Beautiful and informative gardens including herbs, shrubs, flowers, rare and unusual vegetables, all organically grown.

Location: OS Ref. SP400 745. 5m SE of Coventry off A45 on the road to Wolston.

Opening Times: Daily (closed Christmas week): 9am - 5pm (1999 prices).

Admission: Adult £3 (no concessions), accompanied child free. Groups of 14+ £2.50 plus 50p for garden tour.

SELLY MANOR

Tel: 0121 472 0199 **Fax:** 0121 471 4101

Maple Road, Bournville, West Midlands B30 1UB **e-mail:** GillianEllis@bvt.org.uk

Owner: Bournville Village Trust **Contact:** Gillian Ellis

Two half timbered buildings rescued and reassembled by George Cadbury. Now a local museum.

Location: OS Ref. SP045 814. N side of Sycamore Road, just E of Linden Road (A4040). 4m SSW of City Centre.

Opening Times: All year: Tue - Fri & BHs, 10am - 5pm. Apr - Sept: Sat & Suns, 2 - 5pm. Closed Mons.

Admission: Adult £2, Child 50p, Conc. £1.50, Family £4.50.

Partially suitable. WC. By arrangement. Limited. Guide dogs only.

WIGHTWICK MANOR

National Trust Photographic Library.

WIGHTWICK BANK, WOLVERHAMPTON, WEST MIDLANDS WV6 8EE

Owner: *The National Trust* ***Contact:*** *The Property Manager*

Tel: 01902 761108 **Fax:** 01902 764663

Begun in 1887, the house is a notable example of the influence of William Morris, with many original Morris wallpapers and fabrics. Also of interest are pre-Raphaelite pictures, Kempe glass and De Morgan ware. The 17 acre Victorian/Edwardian garden designed by Thomas Mawson has formal beds, pergola, yew hedges, topiary and terraces, woodland and two pools.

Location: OS Ref. SO869 985. 3m W of Wolverhampton, up Wightwick Bank (A454), beside the Mermaid Inn.

Opening Times: 1 Mar - 31 Dec: Thurs & Sats, 2.30 - 5.30pm (last entry 5pm). Admission by timed ticket. Guided groups through ground floor, freeflow upstairs. Min. tour time approx. 1 hr 30 mins. Also open BH Sats, Suns & Mons, 2.30 - 5.30pm (last entry 5pm) - ground floor only, no guided tours. booked groups Weds & Thurs. Garden: Weds & Thurs, 11am - 6pm; Sats, BH Mons, 1 - 6pm.

Admission: Adult £5.50, Child £2.75. Garden only: £2.50.

Ground floor & grounds suitable. In grounds, on leads.

Special Events Index PAGE 40

AVONCROFT MUSEUM OF HISTORIC BUILDINGS

Tel: 01527 831886 **Fax:** 01527 876934

Stoke Heath, Bromsgrove, Worcestershire B60 4JR

Owner: Council of Management **Contact:** Dr Simon Penn

Historic buildings rescued and restored in 15 acres of Worcestershire countryside.

Location: OS Ref. SO954 684. 2m S of Bromsgrove just SE of A38 by-pass.

Opening Times: Mar & Nov: Tue - Thur, Sats & Suns 10.30am - 4pm. Apr - Jun & Sept - Oct: daily except Mons, 10.30am - 4.30pm. Jul & Aug: daily 10.30am - 5pm. (5.30pm Sat s& Suns).

Admission: Adult £4.60, Child £2.30, OAP £3.70, Family (2+3) £12.50. Booked groups at reduced rates.

BROADWAY TOWER COUNTRY PARK

BROADWAY, WORCESTERSHIRE WR12 7LB

Owner: *Broadway Tower Country Park Ltd* ***Contact:*** *Annette Gorton*

Tel: 01386 852390 **Fax:** 01386 858038 **e-mail:** broadway-tower@clara.net

Broadway Tower is a unique historic building on top of the Cotswold ridge, having been built by the 6th Earl of Coventry in the late 1790s. Its architecture, the fascinating views as well as its exhibitions on famous owners and occupants (including William Morris) make the Tower a "must" for all visitors to the Cotswolds. The Tower is surrounded by 35 acres of parkland with animal enclosures, picnic/ BBQ facilities and adventure playground. A complete family day out.

Location: OS Ref. SP115 362. $^{1}/_{2}$ m SW of the A44 Evesham to Oxford Rd. $1^{1}/_{2}$ m E of Broadway.

Open: 27 Mar – 31 Oct: daily, 10.30am - 5pm. Nov - Mar: Sats & Suns (weather permitting), 11am - 3pm.

Admission: Adult £3.20, Child £2.20, Conc. £2.50, Family (2+3) £9.50. Group rate on request. Passport Ticket: (free adm. for 1 yr) Adult £10, Conc. £9, Family £27.

Wedding receptions. WC.   Licensed. 
In grounds, on leads.

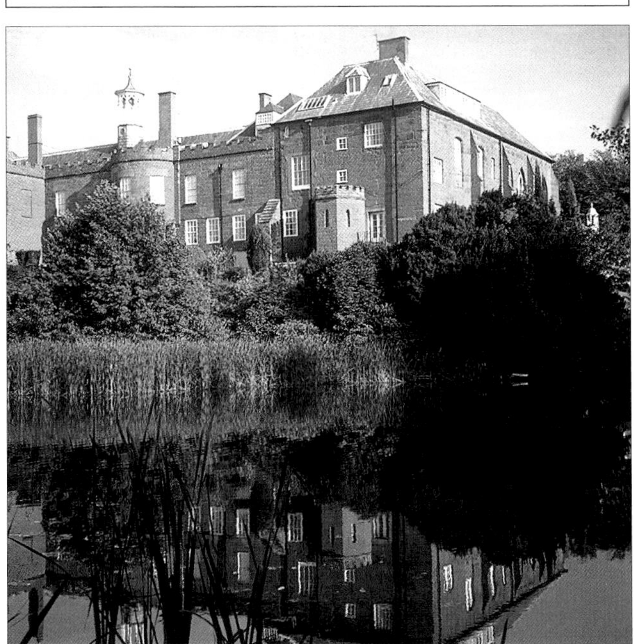

Hartlebury Castle, Worcestershire.

THE COMMANDERY

SIDBURY, WORCESTER WR1 2HU

Owner: *Worcester City Council* ***Contact:*** *Amanda Lunt*

Tel: 01905 361821 **Fax:** 01905 361822

A complex of mainly timber-framed buildings, the Commandery was originally founded as a monastic institution and served as the Royalist headquarters at the Battle of Worcester in 1651. Today it contains a museum devoted to England's Civil War, historic Stuart interiors and, new for 2000, a special Millennium Exhibition.

Location: OS Ref. SO853 544. Worcester city centre. 350 yds SE of cathedral.

Opening Times: All year: Mon - Sat, 10am - 5pm; Suns, 1.30 - 5pm.

Admission: Adult £3.60, Child/Conc. £2.50, Family £9.60. Groups (20-100): Adult £2.50, Child/Conc. £2.

Partially suitable. By arrangement. Limited.
Guide dogs only.

THE ELGAR BIRTHPLACE MUSEUM

Tel/Fax: 01905 333224

Crown East Lane, Lower Broadheath, Worcester WR2 6RH

Owner: The Elgar Foundation **Contact:** The Curator

The cottage, where the composer Sir Edward Elgar was born in 1857, now houses a unique collection of priceless manuscripts, press cuttings, photographs and personal memorabilia.

Location: OS Ref. SO805 558. 3m W of Worcester 1m NW of A44.

Opening Times: 1 May - 30 Sept: 10.30am - 6pm. 1 Oct - 15 Jan: 1.30 - 4.30pm. Closed 16 Jan - 15 Feb. 16 Feb - 30 Apr: 1.30 - 4.30pm. Closed on Weds throughout the year.

Admission: Adult £3, Child 50p, OAP £2, Conc. £1. Groups on application. (1999 times and prices).

THE GREYFRIARS

Tel: 01905 23571 **e-mail:** greyfriars@smtp.ntrust.org.uk

Worcester WR1 2LZ

Owner: The National Trust **Contact:** The Custodian

Built in 1480, with early 17th and late 18th century additions, this timber-framed house was rescued from demolition at the time of the Second World War and has been restored and refurbished; interesting textiles and furnishings add character to the panelled rooms; an archway leads through to a delightful garden.

Location: OS150, Ref. SO852 546. Friar Street, in centre of Worcester.

Opening Times: 5 Apr - end Oct: Weds, Thurs & BH Mons, 2 - 5pm. Also open: 30 Nov, 1 - 2 Dec: Street Fayre.

Admission: Adult £2.60, Child £1.30, Family £6.50.

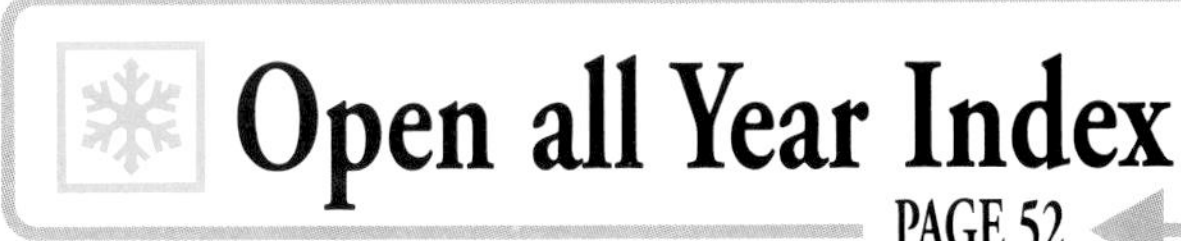

HANBURY HALL 

DROITWICH, WORCESTERSHIRE WR9 7EA

Owner: *The National Trust* ***Contact:*** *The Property Manager*

Tel: 01527 821214 **Fax:** 01527 821251 **e-mail:** hanbury@smtp.ntrust.org.uk

Set in 400 acres of parkland and gardens, this delightful William and Mary house was home to the Vernon family for three centuries. The permanent home of the Watney collection of fine porcelain and Dutch flower paintings, Hanbury Hall also boasts magnificent staircase and ceiling paintings by Sir James Thornhill. Restored 18th century garden, orangery and ice house.

Location: OS150, Ref. SO943 637. 4½ m E of Droitwich, 4m SE M5/J5.

Opening Times: 2 Apr - 29 Oct: Sun - Wed, 2- 6pm (open Good Fri). Last adm. 5.30pm or dusk if earlier. Gardens, shop & tearoom open at 12.30pm.

Admission: House & Garden: Adult £4.60, Child £2.30, Family £11.50. Garden only: Adult £2.90, Child £1.45. Special rates for groups by prior arrangement.

Ground floor & grounds suitable. WC. For pre-booked groups. Guide dogs only.  

Jerry Harpur

Little Malvern Court, Worcestershire.

HARTLEBURY CASTLE

Tel: 01299 250416 **Fax:** 01299 251890

Hartlebury, Nr Kidderminster DY11 7XZ **e-mail:** museum@worcestershire.gov.uk

Owner: The Church Commissioners **Contact:** The County Museum

Hartlebury Castle has been home to the Bishops of Worcester for over a thousand years. The three principal State Rooms - the medieval Great Hall, the Saloon and the unique Hurd library contain period furniture, fine plasterwork and episcopal portraits.

In the former servants' quarters in the Castle's North Wing, the County Museum brings to life the past inhabitants of the county, from Roman times to the twentieth century. A wide range of temporary exhibitions and events are held each year, and detailed listings are available from the Museum.

Location: OS Ref. SO389 710. N side of B4193, 2m E of Stourport, 4m S of Kidderminster.

Opening Times: 1 Feb - 30 Nov. County Museum: Mon - Thur, 10am - 5pm. Fris & Suns, 2 - 5pm. Closed Good Fri and Sats. Staterooms: Tue - Thur, 10am - 5pm.

Admission: Combined ticket (Museum & State rooms): Adult £2.20, Child/OAP £1.10. Family (2+3) £6 (1999 prices).

Ground floor & grounds. WC. By arrangement for groups. Guide dogs only.

HARVINGTON HALL

Tel: 01562 777846

Harvington, Kidderminster, Worcestershire DY10 4LR

Owner: Roman Catholic Archdiocese of Birmingham **Contact:** The Administrator

Moated medieval and Elizabethan manor, with secret hiding places and rare wall paintings.

Location: OS Ref. SO839 710. On minor road, ½ m NE of A450/A448 crossroads at Mustow Green. 3m SE of Kidderminster.

Opening Times: Mar & Oct: Sats & Suns; Apr - Sept: Wed - Sun & BH Mons (closed Good Fri), 11.30am - 5pm. Open at other times by appointment. Occasionally the Hall may be closed for a private function.

Admission: Adult £3.80, Conc. £2.50, Family £10.50. Garden: £1.

HAWFORD DOVECOTE

Tel: 01684 855300

Hawford, Worcestershire

Owner: The National Trust **Contact:** Regional Office

A 16th century half-timbered dovecote.

Location: OS Ref. SO846 607. 3m N of Worcester, ½ m E of A449.

Opening Times: Apr - 31 Oct: daily 9am - 6pm or sunset if earlier. Closed Good Fri, other times by prior appointment.

Admission: 60p.

LEIGH COURT BARN

Tel: 01604 730320 - Regional Office

Worcester

Owner: English Heritage **Contact:** The Midlands Regional Office

Magnificent 14th century timber-framed barn built for the monks of Pershore Abbey. It is the largest of its kind in Britain.

Location: OS Ref. SO784 534. 5m W of Worcester on unclassified road off A4103.

Opening Times: 1 Apr - 30 Sept: Thur - Sun, 10am - 6pm.

Admission: Free.

LITTLE MALVERN COURT

Tel: 01684 892988 **Fax:** 01684 893057

Nr Malvern, Worcestershire WR14 4JN

Owner: Trustees of the late T M Berington **Contact:** Mrs T M Berington

Prior's Hall, associated rooms and cells, c1480, of former Benedictine Monastery. Formerly attached to, and forming part of the Little Malvern Priory Church which may also be visited. It has an oak-framed roof, 5-bay double-collared roof, with two tiers of cusped windbraces. Library. Collections of religious vestments, embroideries and paintings. Gardens: 10 acres of former monastic grounds with spring bulbs, blossom, old fashioned roses and shrubs.

Location: OS130, Ref. SO769 403. 3m S of Great Malvern on Upton-on-Severn Rd (A4104).

Opening Times: 19 Apr - 20 Jul: Weds & Thurs, 2.15 - 4.30pm.

Admission: House & Garden: Adult £4.50, Child £2.50, Garden only: Adult £3.50, Child £1.50.

Garden partially suitable.

MADRESFIELD COURT

Tel: 01684 573614 **Fax:** 01684 569197

Madresfield, Malvern WR13 5AU **e-mail:** madresfield@clara.co.uk

Owner: The Trustees of Madresfield Estate **Contact:** Mr Peter Hughes

Elizabethan and Victorian house with medieval origins. Fine contents. Extensive gardens and arboretum.

Location: OS Ref. SO809 474. 6m SW of Worcester. 1½ m SE of A449. 2m NE of Malvern.

Opening Times: Guided tours between mid-Apr and Jul on specified dates which are available from the Estate Office, Madresfield, Malvern, Worcs WR13 5AH. All visitors must join a guided tour and pre-booking is advisable to avoid disappointment.

Admission: £6.

Not suitable. Obligatory. 

SPETCHLEY PARK GARDEN 

SPETCHLEY, WORCESTER WR5 1RS

Owner: *Spetchley Garden Charitable Trust* ***Contact:*** *Mr R J Berkeley*

Tel: 01905 345213/345224 **Fax:** 01453 511915

This lovely 30 acre private garden contains a large collection of trees, shrubs and plants, many rare or unusual. A garden full of secrets, every corner reveals some new vista, some treasure of the plant world. The exuberant planting and the peaceful walks make this an oasis of beauty, peace and quiet. Deer Park close by.

Location: OS Ref. SO895 540. 2m E of Worcester on A422. Leave M5/J6 or J7.

Opening Times: 1 Apr - 30 Sept: Tue - Fri & BH Mons, 11am - 5pm. Suns, 2 - 5pm. Closed all Sats and all other Mons.

Admission: Adult £3.20, Child £1.60. Groups: Adult £3, Child £1.50.

Grounds suitable.   

THE TUDOR HOUSE

Tel: 01684 592447/594522

16 Church Street, Upton-on-Severn, Worcestershire WR8 0HT

Owner: Mrs Lavender Beard **Contact:** Mrs Wilkinson

Upton past and present, exhibits of local history.

Location: OS Ref. SO852 406. Centre of Upton-on-Severn, 7m SE of Malvern by B4211.

Opening Times: Apr - Oct: daily, 2 - 5pm (Suns until 4pm). Winter Suns only, 2 - 4pm.

Admission: Adult £1, Conc. 50p, Family £2.

WICHENFORD DOVECOTE

Tel: 01684 855300

Wichenford, Worcestershire

Owner: The National Trust **Contact:** Regional Office

A 17th century half-timbered dovecote.

Location: OS Ref. SO788 598. 5½m NW of Worcester, N of B4204. Behind the barns.

Opening Times: Apr - Oct: daily, 9am - 6pm or sunset if earlier. Closed Good Fri, other times by appointment.

Admission: 60p.

WITLEY COURT 

GREAT WITLEY, WORCESTER WR6 6JT

Owner: *English Heritage* ***Contact:*** *The Custodian*

Tel: 01299 896636

The spectacular ruins of a once great house. An earlier Jacobean manor house, converted in the 19th century into an Italianate mansion, with porticos by John Nash. The adjoining church, by James Gibbs, has a remarkable 18th century baroque interior. The gardens, William Nesfield's 'Monster Work' were equally elaborate and contained immense fountains, which survive today. The largest is the Perseus and Andromeda Fountain. The landscaped grounds, fountains and woodlands are being restored to their former glory. The historic parkland will eventually contain the Jerwood Foundation Sculpture Park, consisting of 40 modern British sculptures.

Location: OS150, Ref. SO769 649. 10m NW of Worcester on A443.

Opening Times: 1 Apr - 31 Oct: daily, 10am - 6pm (5pm in Oct). 1 Nov - 31 Mar: Wed - Sun, 10am - 4pm. Closed 24 - 26 Dec & 1 Jan.

Admission: Adult £3.70, Child £1.90, Conc. £2.80. 15% discount for groups of 11+.

Visitor welcome point. Grounds suitable. WC.  Tel. for details.

National Trust Photographic Library.

Hanbury Hall, Worcestershire.

The North East

Newby Hall, Yorkshire.

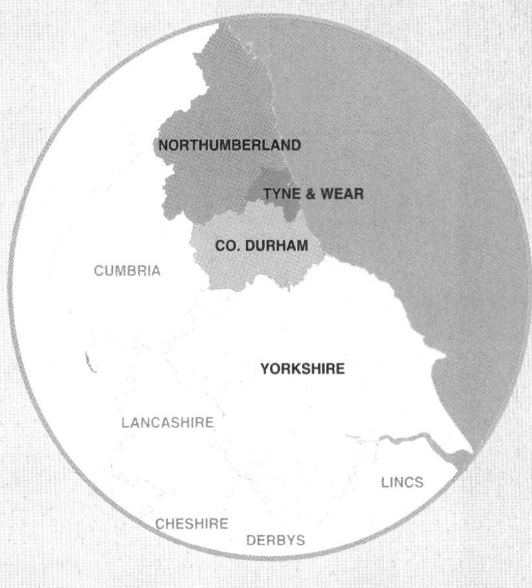

Featuring…

Newby Hall

The Rose Garden.

Armorial Shield.

Newby Hall, near Ripon, North Yorkshire epitomises all that is best about the English country house. A beautiful riverside setting in parkland, wonderful interiors exquisitely restored and a 25 acre garden which transcends its design and the rare and beautiful collection of plants within, to capture the fine 'spirit of the place'.

Newby has been owned by the same family for over 250 years. This year it starts a new chapter in its continuing life as a lived-in family home. Richard and Lucinda Compton and their children are moving in, taking on responsibility from Richard's parents, Mr and Mrs Robin Compton who, since they inherited in 1960, have been entirely responsible for the total restoration of the house and further development of its gardens.

Newby was built in 1695 for the Blackett family, who subsequently sold it to the Comptons' ancestor, William Weddell in 1748. Whilst Blackett built the main block of the house that is seen today in the 1690s in the style of Sir Christopher Wren, it was under Weddell that the house was to see great changes.

William Weddell was a man of great taste and, importantly, considerable means! Having made the Grand Tour in 1765-6, on his return to England he made contact with most of the day's leading neo- classical architects. Initially Weddell commissioned John Carr of York to add the wings to the east of the house, but in 1767 Robert Adam was approached to complete the Statue Gallery and to decorate the Tapestry room and some of the other interiors in the house.

Bust of William Weddell

By the 1770s Adam was at the height of his decorative powers – the darling of fashionable society. In 1785 the Countess of Bute on seeing Newby was to write: "You must have heard of the elegance and magnificence of Mr Weddell's house, all ornamented by Mr Adam in his highest and (indeed I think) best taste."

When Robin Compton inherited the estate from his father in 1960, it would have been hard to believe the Countess' words – the house needed total restoration and redecoration and everything was in the wrong place! Twenty years on, and the interiors of Newby today glisten with a freshness and soft vitality, that allow the visitor to appreciate fully why Adam's style was so admired by his contemporaries. This transformation must be owed in great part to Mrs Robin Compton's exacting attention to detail and referral to primary sources when restoring the interiors.

Horace Walpole dismissed Robert Adam's decorative style as "all gingerbread, filigraine and fan painting" – harsh words! But at Newby the proportions of the rooms seem to work and his style is shown at its best, none better than in the Tapestry Room, Statue Gallery and Library.

The Tapestry Room is one of the marvels of 18th century decoration in England. William Weddell was one of five other Englishmen who commissioned sets of the famous Boucher Neilson medallion tapestries from the Gobelins factory in Paris. To the English milord wishing to keep apace with fashion, Paris of the 1760s and especially a Gobelins purchase, was a must! This room is unique in that it has survived quite remarkably in its entirety, every generation having taken great care of it.

It is perhaps the Statue Gallery that captures all that is great about Newby – you can almost feel Weddell, the quintessential 18th century dilettanti collector, discussing with an excitement and pride, the best way of showing his newly-purchased antique sculptures. This gallery remains today, as do many of the rooms, the perfect example of the Age of Elegance.

Outside, the Comptons' magnificent and inspired garden planting over the last 70 years has created an exuberant, interesting and spectacular setting for this lovely house. It is hardly surprising that the family's devotion and efforts were rewarded by the British Tourist Authority in 1979, who acknowledged the outstanding contribution made by Newby Hall and Gardens to British tourism: in 1983 they also won an award for the best restored house and garden and, in 1986, the HHA/Christie's Garden of the Year Award.

The Three Graces.

Sculpture Gallery.

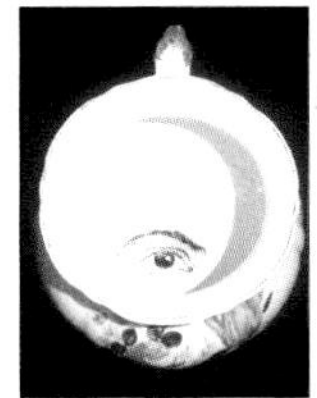

For full details of this property see page 345.

Owner: Church Commissioners

CONTACT

The Manager
Auckland Castle
Bishop Auckland
Co. Durham
DL14 7NR

Tel: 01388 601627

Fax: 01388 609323

e-mail: auckland.castle@zetnet.co.uk

LOCATION

OS Ref. NZ214 303

Bishop Auckland, N end of town centre

Rail: Bishop Auckland.

Air: Newcastle or Teesside.

CONFERENCE/FUNCTION		
ROOM	SIZE	MAX CAPACITY
Throne	59 x 30	200
Long Dining Room	52 x 22	120
King Charles	76 x 20	40

AUCKLAND CASTLE
Bishop Auckland

Principal country residence of the Bishops of Durham since Norman times and now the official residence of the present day Bishop. The Chapel, reputedly the largest private chapel in Europe, was originally the 12th century banquet hall where the Bishop of the time would entertain his hunting party guests. Converted to a chapel in the 17th century it houses fine examples of the richly carved woodwork from that period, as well as a Father Smith organ. Rooms include the Throne Room, its walls displaying a collection of portraits of past Prince Bishops and their successors, and the Long Dining Room (pictured above) with the famous set of paintings of *Jacob and his twelve sons* by Francesco Zurbaran. These were painted in Seville in the 1640s but have been at Auckland Castle since purchased by Bishop Richard Trevor in 1756. The elegant King Charles Dining Room with its delicate plaster ceiling is a prime example of 18th century craftsmanship within a 16th century section of the building. An exhibition in the site of the medieval kitchens explores the life of St Cuthbert and the different roles played by the Bishops of Durham. Adjacent to the castle is the Bishop's Park with its 18th century Deer House.

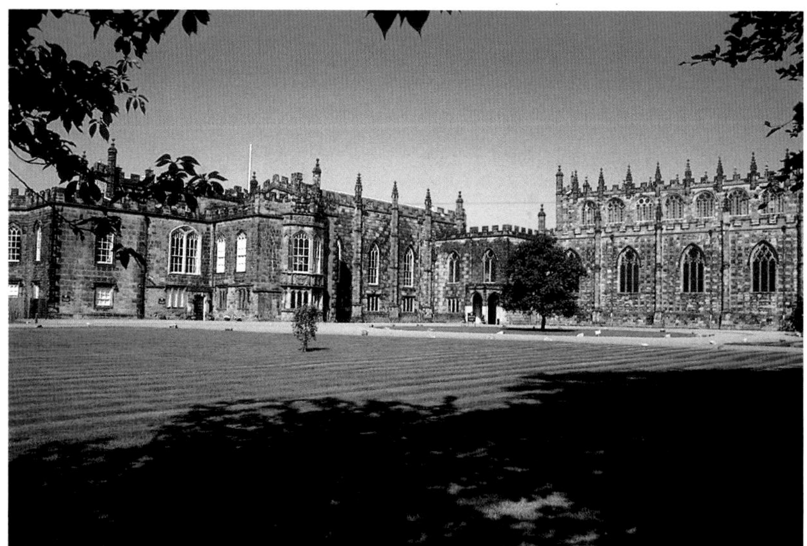

Exhibition. Photography in Chapel only.

Not suitable.

Wedding receptions, functions.

Obligatory.

Guide dogs only.

OPENING TIMES

1 May - 16 July and September
Fris & Suns, 2 - 5pm
(plus BH Mons).

17 July - 31 August: daily except Sats, 2 - 5pm
(plus special events).

ADMISSION

House and Garden

Adult £3.00
Child (12-16)..........£2.00
OAP.......................£2.00

Children under 12yrs Free.

Group (15+)
Adult £2.00
(during normal opening hours).

Groups accepted throughout the year by appointment.

Bishop's Park...............Free

SPECIAL EVENTS

- **APR 30**
  10km Road Race
- **JUN 3/4**
  Northumbria Quality Craft Exhibition & Fair
- **AUG 26 - 28**
  Flower Festival in aid of St John's Ambulance
- **NOV 11/12**
  Northumbria Quality Craft Christmas Exhibition

Lord Barnard

RABY CASTLE

Darlington

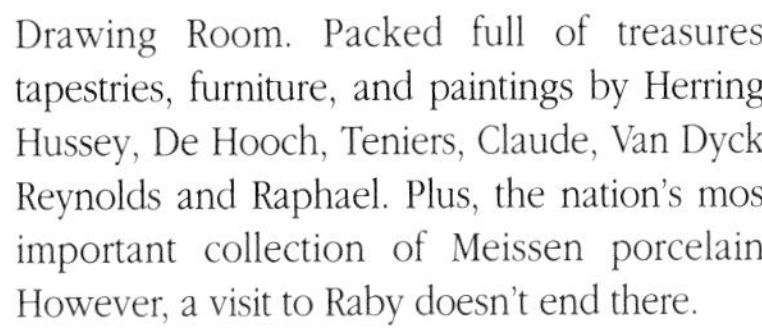

Owner: The Lord Barnard

CONTACT

Mrs V Longstaff
Administrator
Raby Castle
PO Box 50
Staindrop
Darlington
Co. Durham
DL2 3AY

Tel: 01833 660202

Fax: 01833 660169

e-mail: admin@rabycastle.com

LOCATION

OS Ref. NZ129 218

On A688, 1m N of Staindrop. 8m NE of Barnard Castle, 12m WNW of Darlington.

Rail: Darlington Station, 12m.

Air: Teesside Airport, 20m.

Celebrating nearly 1,000 years of history, Raby is without doubt one of the most impressive castles in all England. Legend has it was founded by King Cnut in the early 11th century, being built by the powerful Nevills during the 14th century and remaining in the ownership of the Lord Barnard's family, under the various titles of Dukes of Cleveland and Southampton, Earls of Darlington, Viscounts and Barons Barnard and Lords of Raby, since 1626. The Castle was the childhood home of Cicely, the Rose of Raby, mother of Kings Edward IV and Richard III. It was the scene of the Plotting of the Rising of the North, a Parliamentary stronghold during the Civil War, and according to local myth, site of the world's first cricket pitch. Raby has everything to make a fabulous day out.

Despite its rugged appearance, the Castle has some of the most sumptuous interiors imaginable, including the renowned Octagon Drawing Room. Packed full of treasures, tapestries, furniture, and paintings by Herring, Hussey, De Hooch, Teniers, Claude, Van Dyck, Reynolds and Raphael. Plus, the nation's most important collection of Meissen porcelain. However, a visit to Raby doesn't end there.

Situated amidst a 200 acre Deer Park in the foothills of the dramatic North Pennines, the gently undulating parkland, complete with two lakes and a gazebo, is home to herds of Red and Fallow Deer and ancient Longhorn Cattle. Ten acres of renowned walled gardens frame picturesque views of the Castle and the valley beyond, with the 18th century stable block containing a stunning collection of horse drawn coaches including a 19th century fire engine. With a new Adventure Playground, complete with aerial runway located near to the Castle's celebrated tea rooms and gift shop, Raby has something for everyone to enjoy.

Neil Jinkerson/Jarrold Publishing

Game and soft fruits available in season. Lectures on castle, its contents, gardens and history. No photography or video filming is permitted, slides are on sale.

Partially suitable. WC.

Licensed.

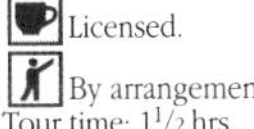

By arrangement. Tour time: 1 1/2 hrs.

Suitable for up to 60 children.

Guide dogs only in castle. On leads in park.

OPENING TIMES

SUMMER

Castle

Easter & BH weekends
Sat - Wed, 1- 5pm.

May & September:
Weds & Suns only, 1 - 5pm.

June, July & August:
Daily except Sats, 1 - 5pm.

Groups by arrangement
Easter - September:
Mon - Fri

Garden and Park

11am - 5.30pm on days shown above.

WINTER

October - Easter Closed.

ADMISSION

Castle, Park & Gardens

Adult	£5.00
Child (5-15yrs)	£2.00
OAP/Student	£4.00
Family (2+2/3)	£12.00

Park & Gardens

Adult	£3.00
Child (5-15yrs)	£2.00
Other	£2.00
Season Ticket	
Adult	£12.00
Other	£10.00

Groups (20+) welcome by arrangement.

AUCKLAND CASTLE

See page 328 for full page entry.

AUCKLAND CASTLE DEER HOUSE

Tel: 0191 2691200

Bishop Auckland, Durham

Owner: English Heritage **Contact:** The North Regional Office

A charming building erected in 1760 in the Park of the Bishops of Durham so that the deer could shelter and find food.

Location: OS Ref. NZ216 305. In Bishop Auckland Park, just N of town centre on A689. About 500 yds N of the castle.

Opening Times: Park opening times – see Auckland Castle.

Admission: Free.

Patrick Lane.

Auckland Castle Deer House, Co Durham.

BARNARD CASTLE

Tel: 01833 638212

Barnard Castle, Castle House, Durham DL12 9AT

Owner: English Heritage **Contact:** The Custodian

The substantial remains of this large castle stand on a rugged escarpment overlooking the River Tees. Parts of the 14th century Great Hall and the cylindrical 12th century tower, built by the Baliol family can still be seen.

Location: OS92 Ref. NZ049 165. In Barnard Castle.

Opening Times: 1 Apr - 30 Sept: daily, 10am - 6pm. 1 - 31 Oct: daily, 10am - 5pm. 1 Nov - 31 Mar: Wed - Sun, 10am - 4pm. Closed 24 - 26 Dec. Closed 1 - 2pm.

Admission: Adult £2.30, Child £1.20, Conc. £1.70. 15% discount for groups (11+).

Grounds suitable. Inclusive. No parking.
In grounds, on leads. Tel. for details.

BINCHESTER ROMAN FORT

Tel: 0191 3834212

Bishop Auckland, Co. Durham

Owner: Durham County Council **Contact:** Niall Hammond

Once the largest Roman fort in Co Durham, the heart of the site has been excavated.

Location: OS92 Ref. NZ210 312. 1$^1/_2$ m N of Bishop Auckland, signposted from A690 Durham - Crook and from A688 Spennymoor - Bishop Auckland roads.

Opening Times: Easter weekend & 1 May - 30 Sept: daily, 11am - 5pm.

Admission: Please contact for details.

THE BOWES MUSEUM

Tel: 01833 690606

Barnard Castle, Durham DL12 8NP

Owner: Durham County Council

A stunning French-style château containing the largest collection of French paintings in the country. Also ceramics, textiles, fine furniture, archaeology and local history.

Location: OS Ref. NZ055 164. $^1/_4$ m E of Market Place in Barnard Castle.

Opening Times: All year: Daily, 11am - 5pm.

Admission: Adult £3.90, Child/OAP £2.90, Family £12. Prices and opening times subject to review, please check with museum in advance.

CROOK HALL & GARDENS

Tel: 0191 3848028

Sidegate, Durham DH1 5SZ

Owner: Keith & Maggie Bell **Contact:** Mrs Maggie Bell

Medieval manor house set in rural landscape on the edge of Durham city.

Location: OS Ref. NZ274 432. $^1/_2$ m N of city centre.

Opening Times: 21 - 24 Apr. BHs & Suns in May. Jun, Jul & Aug: daily except Sats, 1 - 5pm.

Admission: Adult £3.75, Child/OAP £2.75, Family £9.

DERWENTCOTE STEEL FURNACE

Tel: 0191 2691200

Newcastle, Durham

Owner: English Heritage **Contact:** The Custodian

Built in the 18th century it is the earliest and most complete authentic steel making furnace to have survived.

Location: OS Ref. NZ131 566. 10m SW of Newcastle N of the A694 between Rowland's Gill and Hamsterley.

Opening Times: 1 Apr - 30 Sept: 1 - 5pm, 1st & 3rd Sun of every month.

Admission: Free.

Patrick Lane.

Derwentcote Steel Furnace, Co Durham.

DURHAM CASTLE

Tel: 0191 3743863 **Fax:** 0191 3747470

Palace Green, Durham DH1 3RW **Contact:** Mrs Julie Marshall

Durham Castle, founded in the 1070s, with the Cathedral is a World Heritage Site.

Location: OS Ref. NZ274 424. City centre, adjacent to cathedral.

Opening Times: Mar - Sept: 10am - 12 noon & 2 - 5pm. Oct - Mar: 2 - 4pm.

Admission: Adult £3, Child £2, Family £6.50. Guide book £2.50.

DURHAM CATHEDRAL

Tel: 0191 3864266 **Fax:** 0191 3864267

Durham DH1 3EH **e-mail:** enquiries@durhamcathedral.co.uk

Contact: Miss A Heywood

A World Heritage Site. Norman architecture. Burial place of St Cuthbert and the Venerable Bede. Claustral buildings including Monk's Dormitory and medieval kitchen.

Location: OS Ref. NZ274 422. Durham city centre.

Opening Times: Summer: 27 May - 30 Sept: 9.30am - 8pm. Winter: 1 Oct - 7 Apr 2001: Mon - Sat, 9.30am - 6pm, Suns, 12.30 - 5pm. Open only for worship and private prayer: All year: Mon - Sat, 7.15am - 9.30am and Suns 7.15am - 12.30pm. The Cathedral is closed to visitors during evening recitals and concerts.

Admission: Cathedral: Donation. Tower: Adult £2, Child (under 16) £1, Family £5. Monk's Dormitory: Adult 80p, Child 20p, Family £1.50. AV: Adult 80p, Child 20p, Family £1.50.

EGGLESTONE ABBEY

Tel: 0191 2691200

Durham

Owner: English Heritage **Contact:** The North Regional Office

Picturesque remains of a 12th century abbey, located in a bend of the River Tees. Substantial parts of the church and abbey buildings remain.

Location: OS Ref. NZ062 151. 1$^1/_2$ m SE of Barnard Castle on minor road off B6277.

Opening Times: Any reasonable time.

Admission: Free.

ESCOMB CHURCH

Escomb, Bishop Auckland DL14 7ST **Contact:** Mrs E Kitching (01388 662265) or The Vicar (01388 602861)

Owner: Church of England

Saxon church dating from the 7th century built of stone from Binchester Roman Fort.

Location: OS Ref. NZ189 302. 3m W of Bishop Auckland.

Opening Times: Summer: 9am - 8pm. Winter: 9am - 4pm. Key available from 22 Saxon Green, Escomb.

Admission: Free.

FINCHALE PRIORY

Tel: 0191 3863828

Finchdale Priory, Brasside, Newton Hall DH1 5SH

Owner: English Heritage **Contact:** The Custodian

These beautiful 13th century priory remains are located beside the curving River Wear.

Location: OS85 Ref. NZ297 471. 4$^1/_2$ m NE of Durham.

Opening Times: 1 Apr - 30 Sept: daily, 10am - 6pm. 1 - 31 Oct: daily, 10am - 5pm.

Admission: Adult £1.30, Child 70p, Conc. £1. 15% discount for groups (11+).

PIERCEBRIDGE ROMAN FORT

Tel: 01325 460532

Piercebridge, Co. Durham

Owner: Darlington Borough Council **Contact:** Steven Dyke

Visible Roman remains include the east gate and defences, courtyard building and Roman road. Also remains of a bridge over the Tees.

Location: OS85 Ref. NZ211 157. Through narrow stile and short walk down lane opposite car park off A67 NE of the village. Bridge via signposted footpath from George Hotel car park.

Opening Times: At all times.

Admission: Free.

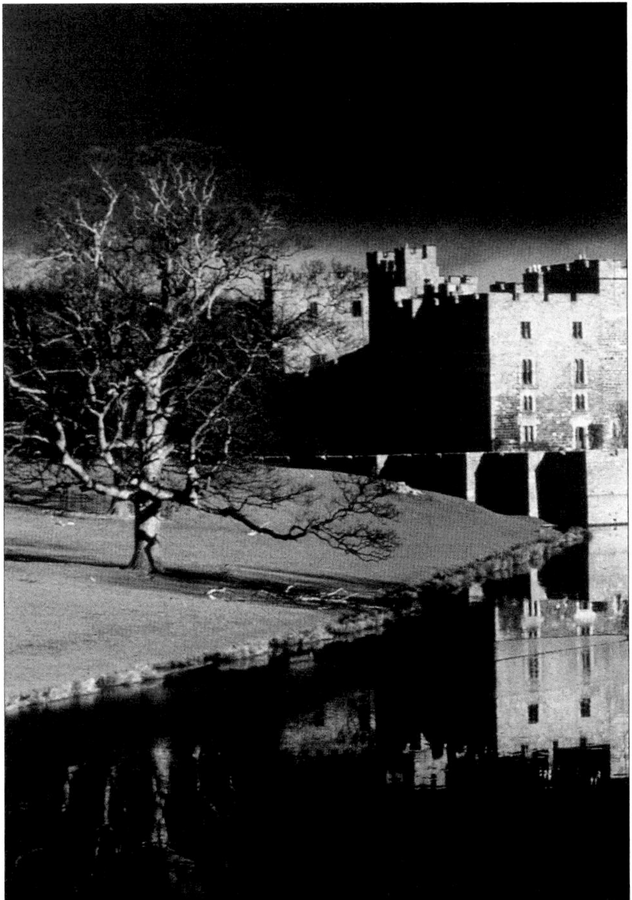

Lord Barnard.

Raby Castle, Co. Durham.

ROKEBY PARK

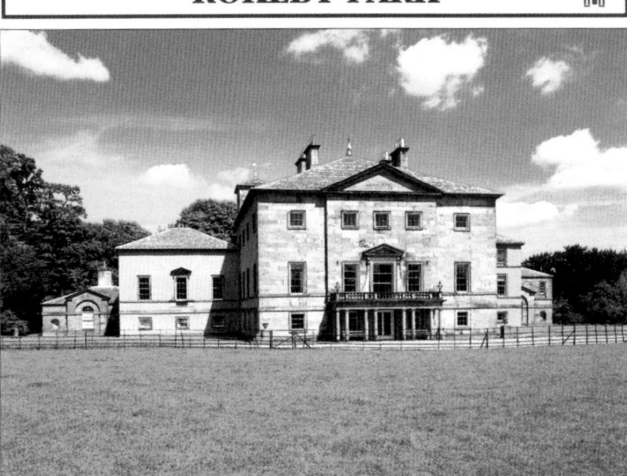

ROKEBY PARK, Nr BARNARD CASTLE, CO. DURHAM DL12 9RZ

Owner: *Trustees of Mortham Estate* ***Contact:*** *Mrs P I Yeats (Curator)*

Tel: 01833 637334

Rokeby, a fine example of a 18th century Palladian-style country house, was built by its owner Sir Thomas Robinson, a leading amateur architect of the day. The house was completed by 1735 and continued to be owned by Sir Thomas until 1769 when it was sold to J S Morritt, an ancestor of the present owner. A special feature of the house is a unique collection of needlework pictures worked in the 18th century by Anne Morritt with enormous skill. The house also has a very early 'print room'. For many years Velasquez's painting '*Toilet of Venus*', now in the National Gallery, hung in the house and a very good copy can still be seen in the original room. Sir Walter Scott was a frequent guest at Rokeby and he dedicated his epic poem '*Rokeby*' to his host.

Location: OS Ref. NZ082 142. Between A66 & Barnard Castle.

Opening Times: May BH Mon then each Mon & Tue from Spring BH until the second Tue in Sept. Groups (25+) on other days by appointment.

Admission: Adult £5, Child £1.50, OAP £4.50. Group prices on request.

Ground floor suitable. WC. By arrangement. 

RABY CASTLE

See page 329 for full page entry.

THE WEARDALE MUSEUM

Tel: 01388 517433

Ireshopeburn, Co. Durham DL13 1EY **Contact:** D T Heatherington

Small folk museum in minister's house. Includes 1870 Weardale cottage room, Wesley room and local history displays.

Location: OS Ref. NZ872 385. Adjacent to 18th century Methodist Chapel.

Opening Times: Easter & May - Sept: Wed - Sun & BH, 2 - 5pm. Aug: daily, 2 - 5pm.

Admission: Adult £1, Child 30p.

Open all Year Index PAGE 52

North East England

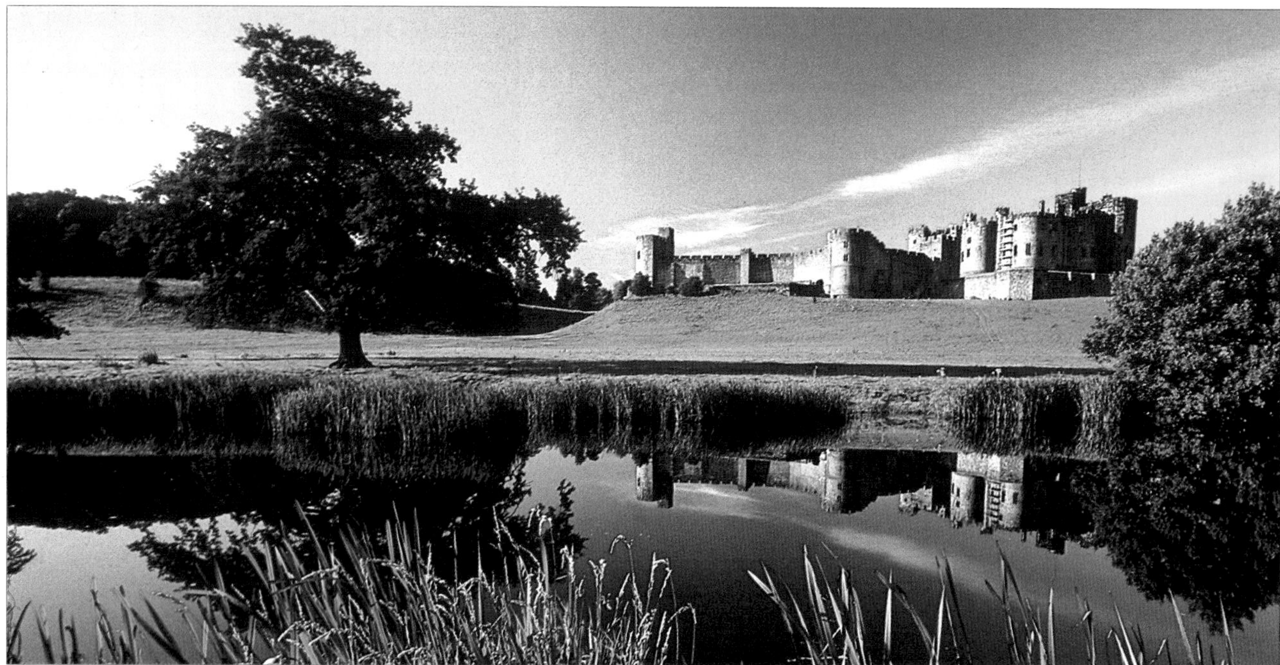

ALNWICK CASTLE
Alnwick

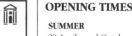

Described by the Victorians as the 'Windsor of the North', Alnwick Castle is the main seat of the Duke of Northumberland, whose family, the Percys, have lived here since 1309.

This Border stronghold has survived many battles, but now peacefully dominates the picturesque market town of Alnwick, overlooking landscape designed by 'Capability' Brown. The stern medieval exterior belies the treasure house within, furnished in palatial Renaissance style, with painting by Titian, Van Dyck and Canaletto, fine furniture and an exquisite collection of china.

The Regimental Museum of the Northumberland Fusiliers is housed in the Abbot's Tower of the Castle, while the Postern Tower contains an exhibition of the Duke's collection of archaeology. In the Constable's Tower is an exhibition of the Percy Tenantry Volunteers 1798 - 1814.

Other attractions include the Percy State Coach, dungeon, gun terrace and the grounds which offer peaceful walks and superb views over the surrounding countryside.

Alnwick Castle Guest Hall is one of the chief buildings of Anthony Salvin's 19th century restoration. Built as a magnificent coach house, it has throughout its history served as a venue for entertainment. This splendid Guest Hall is available for conferences, entertaining, wedding receptions, concerts, dinner dances and theatre productions. Please note that the Guest Hall is **not** open to Castle visitors.

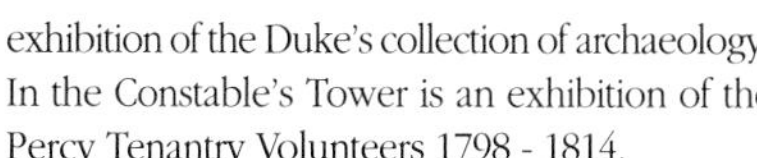

Conference facilities. Fashion shows, fairs, filming, parkland for hire. No photography inside the castle. No un-accompanied children.

Wedding receptions.

Not suitable. By arrangement.

Coffee, light lunches and teas, seats 80.

70 cars and 4 coaches.

Guidebook and worksheet, special rates for children and teachers.

Guide dogs only.

Owner:
His Grace the Duke of Northumberland

CONTACT

Alnwick Castle
Estate Office
Alnwick
Northumberland
NE66 1NQ

Tel: 01665 510777

Info: 01665 511100

Fax: 01665 510876

e-mail: enquiries@alnwickcastle.com

LOCATION

OS Ref. NU187 135

In Alnwick 1½ m W of A1.

From London 6 hrs, Edinburgh 2 hrs, Chester 4 hrs, Newcastle 40mins
North Sea ferry terminal 30mins.

Bus: From bus station in Alnwick.

Rail: Alnmouth Station 5m. Kings Cross, London 3½hrs

Air: Newcastle 40mins.

CONFERENCE/FUNCTION		
ROOM	SIZE	MAX CAPACITY
The Guest Hall	100' x 30'	300

OPENING TIMES

SUMMER

20 April - end October daily, 11am - 5pm, last admission 4.15pm.

Private tours and functions by arrangement.

WINTER

October - Easter
Pre-booked parties only.

ADMISSION

SUMMER

House & Garden

Adult	£6.25
Child (5-16yrs)	£3.50
Conc.	£5.25
Family (2+2)	£15.00

Pre-booked Groups (14+)

Adult	£5.50
Child (5-16yrs)	£3.00
Conc.	£5.00

WINTER

By arrangement only.

Jarrold Colour Publications

Owner:
Trustees Lord Armstrong decd.

CONTACT

P Bolam
R G Bolam & Son
Townfoot
Rothbury
Northumberland
NE65 7SP

Tel: 01669 620314

Fax: 01669 621236

LOCATION

OS Ref. NU184 351

42m N of Newcastle-upon-Tyne. 20m S of Berwick upon Tweed. 6m E of Belford by B1342 from A1 at Belford.

Bus: Bus service 200 yards.

Rail: Berwick-upon-Tweed 20m.

Taxi: J Swanston 01289 306124.

Air: Newcastle-upon-Tyne 45m.

BAMBURGH CASTLE
Bamburgh

BAMBURGH CASTLE is the home of Lady Armstrong and her family. The earliest reference to Bamburgh shows the craggy citadel to have been a royal centre by AD 547. Recent archaeological excavation has revealed that the site has been occupied since prehistoric times.

The Norman Keep has been the stronghold for nearly nine centuries, but the remainder has twice been extensively restored, initially by Lord Crewe in the 1750s and subsequently by the first Lord Armstrong at the end of the 19th century. This Castle was the first to succumb to artillery fire – that of Edward IV.

The public rooms contain many exhibits, including the loan collections of armour from HM Tower of London, the John George Joicey Museum, Newcastle-upon-Tyne and other private sources, which complement the castle's armour. Porcelain, china, jade, furniture from many periods, oils, water-colours and a host of interesting items are all contained within one of the most important buildings of Britain's national heritage.

VIEWS

The views from the ramparts are unsurpassed and take in Holy Island, the Farne Islands, one of Northumberland's finest beaches and, landwards, the Cheviot Hills.

OPENING TIMES

April - October
Daily, 11am - 5pm.
Last entry 4.30pm.

Tours by arrangement at any time.

ADMISSION

SUMMER

Adult	£4.00
Child (6 - 16yrs)	£1.50
OAP	£3.00
Groups *	
Adult	£3.00
Child (6 - 16yrs)	£1.00
OAP	£2.00

* Min payment £30
(1999 prices)

WINTER
Group rates only quoted.

Filming. No photography in house.

Limited access. WC.

Tearooms for light refreshments. Groups can book.

By arrangement at any time, min charge out of hours £30.

100 cars, coaches park on tarmac drive at entrance.

Welcome. Guide provided if requested, educational pack.

Guide dogs only.

CHILLINGHAM CASTLE

Nr Alnwick

Owner:
Sir Humphry Wakefield Bt

CONTACT

The Administrator
Chillingham Castle
Near Alnwick
Northumberland
NE66 5NJ

Tel: 01668 215359

Fax: 01668 215463

This remarkable castle, the home of Sir Humphry Wakefield Bt, with its alarming dungeons has, since the 1200s, been continuously owned by the family of the Earls Grey and their relations. You will see active restoration of complex masonry, metalwork and ornamental plaster as the great halls and state rooms are gradually brought back to life with antique furniture, tapestries, arms and armour as of old and even a torture chamber.

At first a 12th century stronghold, Chillingham became a fully fortified castle in the 14th century. Wrapped in the nation's history it occupied a strategic position as a fortress during Northumberland's bloody border feuds, often besieged and at many times enjoying the patronage of royal visitors. In Tudor days there were additions but the underlying medieval character has always been retained. The 18th and 19th centuries saw decorative refinements and extravagances including the lake, garden and grounds laid out by Sir Jeffrey Wyatville, fresh from his triumphs at Windsor Castle.

GARDENS

With romantic grounds, the castle commands breathtaking views of the surrounding countryside. As you walk to the lake you will see, according to the season, drifts of snowdrops, daffodils or bluebells and an astonishing display of rhododendrons. This emphasises the restrained formality of the Elizabethan topiary garden, with its intricately clipped hedges of box and yew. Lawns, the formal gardens and woodland walks are all fully open to the public.

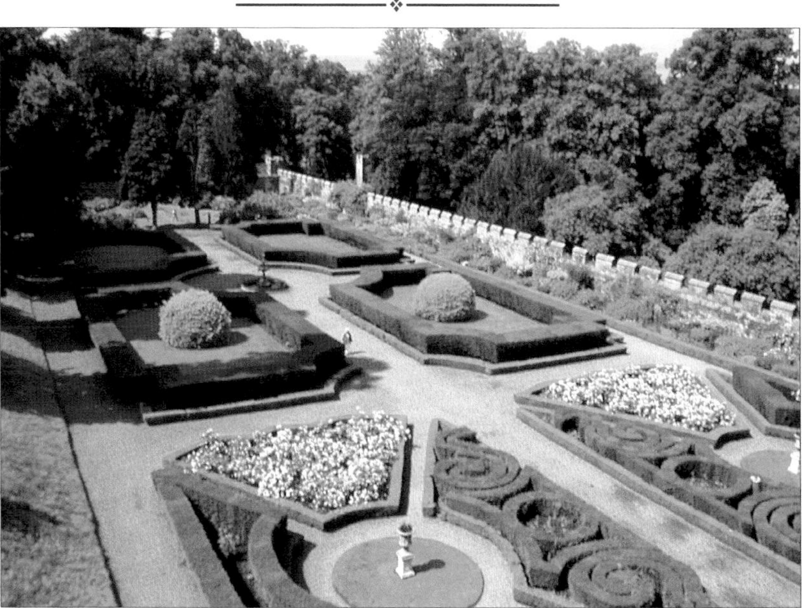

OPENING TIMES

SUMMER
1 May - 30 September
Daily except Tues
12 noon - 5pm.

July - August and BHs,
Daily: 12 noon - 5pm.

WINTER
January - December
any time by
appointment only.

ADMISSION

SUMMER

Adult £4.30
OAP.........................£3.80
Child*.......................Free

Groups (10+)
Per person £3.50
(1999 prices)

Pre-booking is essential.

* up to 5 accompanied children.

LOCATION

OS Ref. NU062 258

45m N of Newcastle between A697 & A1.
2m S of B6348 at Chatton.
6m SE of Wooler.

Rail: Alnmouth or Berwick.

CONFERENCE/FUNCTION		
ROOM	SIZE	MAX CAPACITY
King James I Room		120
Great Hall		100
Minstrels' Hall		60
2 x Drawing Room		60 each
Museum		150
Tea Room		35
Lower Gallery		30
Upper Gallery		40

Corporate entertainment, lunches, drinks, dinners, wedding ceremonies and receptions.

Booked meals for up to 100 people.

By arrangement.

Avoid Lilburn route, coach parties welcome by prior arrangement.

8 self-contained 2 bedroom apartments. For up to 30 guests.

Civil Wedding Licence.

ALNWICK CASTLE

See page 332 for full page entry.

AYDON CASTLE

Tel: 01434 632450

Corbridge, Northumberland NE45 5PJ

Owner: English Heritage **Contact:** The Custodian

One of the finest fortified manor houses in England, dating from the late 13th century. Its survival, intact, can be attributed to its conversion to a farmhouse in the 17th century.

Location: OS87 Ref. NZ002 663. 2m NE of Corbridge, on minor road off B6321 or A68.

Opening Times: 1 Apr - 30 Sept: daily, 10am - 6pm. 1- 31 Oct: daily, 10am - 5pm.

Admission: Adult £2, Child £1, Conc. £1.50. 15% discount for groups (11+).

Ground floor & grounds suitable. Limited. In grounds, on leads. Tel. for details.

BAMBURGH CASTLE

See page 333 for full page entry.

BELSAY HALL, CASTLE & GARDENS

Tel: 01661 881636 **Fax:** 01661 881043

Belsay, Nr Ponteland, Northumberland NE20 0DX

Owner: English Heritage **Contact:** The Custodian

The buildings, set amidst 30 acres of magnificent landscaped gardens, have been occupied by the same family for nearly 600 years.

Location: OS87, Ref. NZ088 785. In Belsay 14m (22.4 km) NW of Newcastle on SW of A696. 7m NW of Ponteland. Nearest airport and station is Newcastle.

Opening Times: 1 Apr - 30 Sept: daily, 10am - 6pm. 1 - 31 Oct: daily, 10am - 5pm. 1 Nov - 31 Mar: daily, 10am - 4pm.

Admission: Adult £3.90, Child £2.90, Conc. £2. 15% discount for groups (11+).

Tel. for details.

BERWICK BARRACKS

Tel: 01289 304493

The Parade, Berwick-upon-Tweed, Northumberland TD15 1DF

Owner: English Heritage **Contact:** The Custodian

Among the earliest purpose built barracks, these have changed very little since 1717. They house an exhibition '*By Beat of Drum*', which recreates scenes such as the barrack room from the life of the British infantryman, the Museum of the King's Own Scottish Borderers and the Borough Museum with fine art, local history exhibition and other collections. Guided tours available.

Location: OS75 Ref. NT994 535. On the Parade, off Church Street, Berwick town centre.

Opening Times: 1 Apr - 30 Sept: daily, 10am - 6pm. 1 - 31 Oct: daily, 10am - 5pm. 1 Nov - 31 Mar: Wed - Sun, 10am - 4pm. Closed 24 - 26 Dec.

Admission: Adult £2.60, Child £1.30, Conc. £2. 15% discount for groups (11+).

Ground floor & grounds suitable. Limited. In grounds, on leads. Tel. for details.

BERWICK RAMPARTS

Tel: 0191 269 1200

Berwick-upon-Tweed, Northumberland

Owner: English Heritage **Contact:** The Northern Regional Office

A remarkably complete system of town fortifications consisting of gateways, ramparts and projecting bastions built in the 16th century.

Location: OS Ref. NT994 535. Surrounding Berwick town centre on N bank of River Tweed.

Opening Times: Any reasonable time.

Admission: Free.

BRINKBURN PRIORY

Tel: 01665 570628

Long Framlington, Morpeth, Northumberland NE65 8AF

Owner: English Heritage **Contact:** The Custodian

This late 12th century church is a fine example of early gothic architecture, almost perfectly preserved, and is set in a lovely spot beside the River Coquet.

Location: OS81, Ref. NZ116 984. 4½ m SE of Rothbury off B6344 5m W of A1.

Opening Times: 1 Apr - 30 Sept: daily, 10am - 6pm. 1 - 31 Oct, daily, 10am - 5pm.

Admission: Adult £1.60, Child 80p, Conc. £1.20. 15% discount for groups (11+).

Not suitable. Limited. On leads. Tel. for details.

CAPHEATON HALL

Tel: 01830 530253

Newcastle-upon-Tyne NE19 2AB

Owner/Contact: J Browne-Swinburne

Built for Sir John Swinburne in 1668 by Robert Trollope, an architect of great and original talent.

Location: OS Ref. NZ038 805. 17m NW of Newcastle off A696.

Opening Times: By written appointment only.

Admission: Adult £3.

CHERRYBURN

Tel: 01661 843276

Station Bank, Mickley, Stocksfield, Northumberland NE43 7DB

Owner: The National Trust **Contact:** The Administrator

Birthplace of Northumbria's greatest artist, wood engraver and naturalist, Thomas Bewick, b.1753. The Museum explores his famous works and life with occasional demonstrations of wood block printing in the printing house. Farmyard animals, picnic area, garden.

Location: OS Ref. NZ075 627. 11m W of Newcastle on A695 (200yds signed from Mickley Square). 1½ m W of Prudhoe.

Opening Times: 1 Apr - 31 Oct: daily except Tues & Weds, 1 - 5.30pm. Last admission 5pm.

Admission: Adult £3. No group rate.

Some steps. WC. Morning coffee for booked groups

CHESTERS ROMAN FORT & MUSEUM

CHOLLERFORD, Nr HEXHAM, NORTHUMBERLAND NE46 4EP

Owner: *English Heritage* ***Contact:*** *The Custodian*

Tel: 01434 681379

The best preserved example of a Roman cavalry fort in Britain, including remains of the bath house on the banks of the River North Tyne. The museum houses a fascinating collection of Roman sculpture and inscriptions.

Location: OS87, Ref. NY913 701. 1½ m from Chollerford on B6318.

Opening Times: 1 Apr - 30 Sept: daily, 9.30am - 6pm. 1 - 31 Oct: daily, 10am - 5pm. 1 Nov - 31 Mar: daily, 10am - 4pm. Closed 24 - 26 Dec.

Admission: Adult £2.80, Child £1.40, Conc. £2.10. 15% discount for groups (11+).

Grounds suitable. WC. Summer only. In grounds, on leads. Tel. for details.

CHILLINGHAM CASTLE

See page 334 for full page entry.

CHIPCHASE CASTLE

Tel: 01434 230203 **Fax:** 01434 230740

Wark, Hexham, Northumberland NE48 3NT

Owner/Contact: Mrs P J Torday

The castle overlooks the River North Tyne and is set in formal and informal gardens. One walled garden is used as a nursery specialising in unusual perennial plants.

Location: OS Ref. NY882 758. 10m NW of Hexham via A6079 to Chollerton. 2m SE of Wark.

Opening Times: Castle: 1 - 28 Jun: daily 2 - 5pm. Tours by arrangement at other times. Castle Gardens & Nursery: Easter - 31 Jul, Thur - Sun & BH Mons, 10am - 5pm.

Admission: Castle £4, Garden £1.50, concessions available. Nursery Free.

Not suitable. Obligatory.

CORBRIDGE ROMAN SITE

Tel: 01434 632349

Corbridge, Northumberland NE45 5NT

Owner: English Heritage **Contact:** The Custodian

A fascinating series of excavated remains, including foundations of granaries with a grain ventilation system. From artefacts found, which can be seen in the site museum, we know a large settlement developed around this supply depot.

Location: OS87 Ref. NY983 649. 1/2 m NW of Corbridge on minor road, signposted for Corbridge Roman Site.

Opening Times: 1 Apr - 30 Sept: daily, 10am - 6pm. 1 - 31 Oct: daily, 10am - 5pm. 1 Nov - 31 Mar: Wed - Sun, 10am - 4pm. Closed 1 - 2pm during winter & 24 - 26 Dec.

Admission: Adult £2.80, Child £1.40, Conc. £2.10. 15% discount for groups (11+).

Partially suitable. Inclusive. Limited for coaches. In grounds, on leads. Tel. for details.

CRAGSIDE

NT Photographic Library: Rupert Truman

ROTHBURY, MORPETH, NORTHUMBERLAND NE65 7PX

Owner: *The National Trust* ***Contact:*** *Property Manager*

Tel: 01669 620150 **Fax:** 01669 620066

Enter the world of a Victorian 'magician'. Visitors to Lord Armstrong's 1000 acre Victorian estate and country house are transported into a wooded realm of lakes, streams and wildlife. Children will enjoy exploring the woodland adventure play area and Nelly's Labyrinth. One day is not sufficient to enjoy all that Cragside has to offer.

Location: OS Ref. NU073 022. 1/2 m NE of Rothbury on B6341.

Opening Times: House: 1 Apr - 29 Oct: daily except Mons (open BH Mons), 1 - 5.30pm. Last admission 4.30pm. Estate & Formal Garden: 1 Apr - 29 Oct: daily except Mons (open BH Mons), 10.30am - 7pm. Last admission 5pm. 1 Nov - 17 Dec: Estate & Formal Garden: Wed - Sun, 11am - 4pm (house closed).

Admission: House, Estate & Formal Garden: Adult £6.50, Child £3.25, Family (2+3) £16. Estate & Formal Garden: Adult £4, Child £2, Family (2+3) £10.

DUNSTANBURGH CASTLE

Tel: 01665 576231

c/o 14 Queen Street, Alnwick, Northumberland NE66 1RD

Owner: The National Trust **Guardian:** English Heritage **Contact:** The Custodian

An easy, but bracing, coastal walk leads to the eerie skeleton of this wonderful 14th century castle sited on a basalt crag, rearing up more than 100 feet from the waves crashing on the rocks below. The surviving ruins include the large gatehouse, which later became the keep, and curtain walls.

Location: OS75 Ref. NU258 220. 8m NE of Alnwick.

Opening Times: 1 Apr - 30 Sept: daily, 10am - 6pm. 1 - 31 Oct, daily, 10am - 5pm. 1 Nov - 31 Mar: Wed - Sun, 10am - 4pm. Closed 24 - 26 Dec.

Admission: Adult £1.80, Child 90p, Conc. £1.40. 15% discount for groups (11+).

Not suitable. No parking. In grounds, on leads.

EDLINGHAM CASTLE

Tel: 0191 269 1200

Edlingham, Alnwick, Northumberland

Owner: English Heritage **Contact:** The Northern Regional Office

Set beside a splendid railway viaduct this complex ruin has defensive features spanning the 13th and 15th centuries.

Location: OS Ref. NU115 092. At E end of Edlingham village, on minor road off B6341 6m SW of Alnwick.

Opening Times: Any reasonable time.

Admission: Free.

ETAL CASTLE

Tel: 01890 820332

Cornhill-on-Tweed, Northumberland

Owner: English Heritage **Contact:** The Custodian

A 14th century castle located in the picturesque village of Etal. Award-winning exhibition about the castle, Border warfare and the Battle of Flodden.

Location: OS75 Ref. NT925 394. In Etal village, 10m SW of Berwick.

Opening Times: 1 Apr - 30 Sept: daily, 10am - 6pm. 1 - 31 Oct: daily, 10am - 5pm.

Admission: Adult £2.60, Child £1.30, Conc. £2. 15% discount for groups (11+).

Partially suitable. WC. Inclusive. Limited. In grounds, on leads. Tel. for details.

HERTERTON HOUSE GARDENS

Tel: 01670 774278

Hartington, Cambo, Morpeth, Northumberland NE61 4BN

Owner/Contact: C J "Frank" Lawley

One acre of formal garden in stone walls around a 16th century farmhouse, including a small topiary garden, physic garden, flower garden, fancy garden (due to be completed by Apr 2000) and gazebo.

Location: OS Ref. NZ022 881. 2m N of Cambo, just off B6342.

Opening Times: 1 Apr - 30 Sept: Mons, Weds, Fri - Sun, 1.30 - 5.30pm.

Admission: Adult £2.20, Child (5-15yrs) £1. Groups by arrangement.

Not suitable. By arrangement. Limited for coaches. Guided tours for adult students only.

HOUSESTEADS ROMAN FORT

Tel: 01434 344363

Nr Haydon Bridge, Northumberland NE47 6NN

Owner: The National Trust **Guardian:** English Heritage **Contact:** The Custodian

Perched high on a ridge overlooking open moorland, this is the best known part of the Wall. The fort covers five acres and there are remains of many buildings, such as granaries, barrack blocks and gateways. A small exhibition displays altars, inscriptions and models.

Location: OS87 Ref. NY790 687. 2m NE of Bardon Mill.

Opening Times: 1 Apr - 30 Sept: daily, 10am - 6pm. 1 - 31 Oct: daily, 10am - 5pm. 1 Nov - 31 Mar: daily, 10am - 4pm. Closed 24 - 26 Dec.

Admission: Adult £2.80, Child £1.40, Conc. £2.10. 15% discount for groups (11+).

Not suitable. Charge. In grounds, on leads. Tel. for details.

HOWICK HALL GARDENS

Tel/Fax: 01665 577285

Howick, Alnwick, Northumberland NE66 3LB **e-mail:** howickarb@compuserve.com

Owner: Howick Trustees Ltd **Contact:** Lord Howick

Romantically landscaped grounds surrounding the house in a little valley, with rare rhododendrons and flowering shrubs and trees.

Location: OS Ref. NU249 175. 6m NE of Alnwick. 1m E of B1339.

Opening Times: Apr - Oct: daily 1 - 6pm.

Admission: Adult £2, Child/OAP £1, Student (up to 16yrs) £1. Season tickets available.

Grounds partly suitable. WC. Limited.

KIRKLEY HALL GARDENS

Tel: 01661 860808 **Fax:** 01661 860047

Ponteland, Northumberland NE20 0AQ **Contact:** Mike Swinton

Over 9 acres of beautiful gardens incorporating a Victorian walled garden, woodland walks, sunken garden and wildlife areas and ponds.

Location: OS Ref. NZ150 772. 10m from the centre of Newcastle upon Tyne. 2 1/2 m N of Ponteland on byroad to Morpeth.

Opening Times: 1 Apr - 30 Sept: daily, 10am - 5pm.

Admission: Free. Guided tours: £2.50.

Open all Year Index PAGE 52

North East England

THE LADY WATERFORD HALL & MURALS

Ford, Berwick-upon-Tweed TD15 2QA **Tel:** 01890 820524 **Fax:** 01890 820384

Owner: Ford & Etal Estates **Contact:** The Caretaker

Commissioned in 1860 by Louisa Anne, Marchioness of Waterford as the village school in Ford, the walls of this beautiful building are decorated with beautiful murals depicting well known Bible stories, painted by Lady Waterford between 1862 and 1883. Children from the school and their families were used as models for the characters making the hall a portrait gallery of people who lived and worked in Ford during the 1860s and 1870s. Louisa also included native plants and animals within the murals, thus creating a unique collection of Northumbrian art treasures. Her great friend, John Ruskin visited the gallery along with many other dignitaries of the day.

Location: OS Ref. NT945 374. On the B6354, 9m from Berwick-upon-Tweed, midway between Newcastle-upon-Tyne and Edinburgh, close to the A697.

Opening Times: 1 Apr - 29 Oct: daily, 10.30am - 12.30pm & 1.30 - 5.30pm. By arrangement with the caretaker during winter months.

Admission: Adult £1.50, Child Free (over 12yrs 50p), Conc. £1. Groups by arrangement.

Parking at door. Guide dogs only. 

LINDISFARNE CASTLE

Tel: 01289 389244

Holy Island, Berwick-upon-Tweed, Northumberland TD15 2SH

Owner: The National Trust **Contact:** The Administrator

Built in 1550 to protect Holy Island harbour from attack, the castle was restored and converted into a private house for Edward Hudson by Sir Edwin Lutyens in 1903. Small walled garden was designed by Gertrude Jekyll. 19th century lime kilns in field by the castle.

Location: OS Ref. NU136 417. On Holy Island, 3/4 m E of village, 6m E of A1 across causeway. Usable at low tide.

Opening Times: 1 Apr - 31 Oct: daily except Fris (but open Good Fri), 12 noon - 3pm, but earlier or later as the tide allows. Last admission 1/2 before close. Admission to garden only when gardener in attendance. Holy Island is cut off by the tide from 2 hours before and 3 1/2 hours after high tide. Visitors are advised to check tide times before visiting.

Admission: £4, Family £10. No group rate. Groups (15+) must pre-book.

NT Shop (in Main St.) Not suitable. No parking. In grounds, on leads.

MELDON PARK 

MORPETH, NORTHUMBERLAND NE61 3SW

Owner/Contact: *M Cookson*

Tel: 01670 772661

Isaac Cookson III purchased the Meldon land in 1832. John Dobson, the famous architect, was commissioned to build a house by Isaac Cookson and he recommended the present site. The entrance is through an Ionic porch having two rows of columns to the front door. Once inside you are in the main hall which has an enormous staircase lit by a large window to the north. Between the two World Wars Edwin Lutyens was employed to enrich the Hall, which included mahogany balustrades and 18th century decorations. The garden has a wonderful collection of rhododendrons best seen in early June, an old-fashioned kitchen garden and greenhouses.

Location: OS Ref. NZ105 856. 7m W of Morpeth on B6343. 5m N of Belsay.

Opening Times: 20 May - 17 Jun, 2 - 5pm & Aug BH weekend, 2 - 5.30pm.

Admission: Adult £3, Child £1.50, OAP £2.

No photography. Sundays only. By arrangement. Guide dogs only.

LINDISFARNE PRIORY

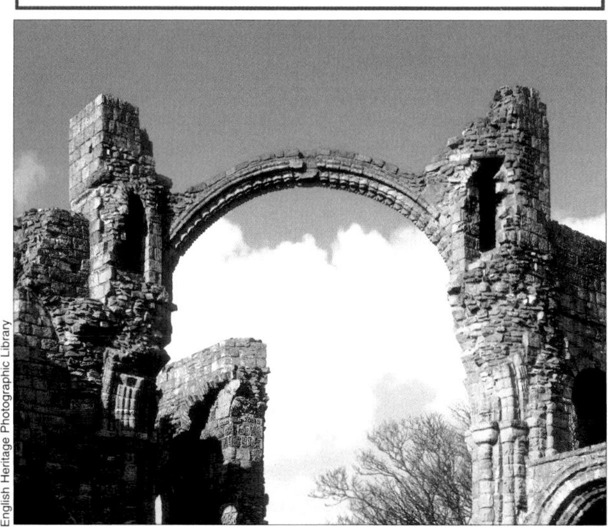

English Heritage Photographic Library

HOLY ISLAND, BERWICK-UPON-TWEED TD15 2RX

Owner: *English Heritage* ***Contact:*** *The Custodian*

Tel: 01289 389200

The site of one of the most important early centres of Christianity in Anglo-Saxon England. St Cuthbert converted pagan Northumbria, and miracles occurring at his shrine established this 11th century priory as a major pilgrimage centre. The evocative ruins, with the decorated 'rainbow' arch curving dramatically across the nave of the church, are still the destination of pilgrims today. The story of Lindisfarne is told in an exhibition which gives an impression of life for the monks, including a reconstruction of a monk's cell.

Location: OS75 Ref. NU126 418. On Holy Island, check tide times.

Opening Times: 1 Apr - 30 Sept: daily, 10am - 6pm. 1 - 31 Oct: daily, 10am - 5pm. 1 Nov - 31 Mar: daily, 10am - 4pm. Closed 24 - 26 Dec.

Admission: Adult £2.80, Child £1.40, Conc. £2.10. 15% discount for groups (11+).

Partially suitable. Charge. Restricted.  Tel. for details.

NORHAM CASTLE

Tel: 01289 382329

Norham, Northumberland

Owner: English Heritage **Contact:** The Custodian

Set on a promontory in a curve of the River Tweed, this was one of the strongest of the Border castles, built c1160.

Location: OS75 Ref. NT907 476. 6m SW of Berwick.

Opening Times: 1 Apr - 30 Sept: daily, 10am - 6pm. 1 - 31 Oct: daily, 10am - 5pm.

Admission: Adult £1.80, Child 90p, Conc. £1.40. 15% discount for groups (11+).

PRESTON TOWER

Tel: 01665 589227

Chathill, Northumberland NE67 5DH

Owner/Contact: Major T Baker Cresswell

The Tower was built by Sir Robert Harbottle in 1392 and is one of the few survivors of 78 pele towers listed in 1415. The tunnel vaulted rooms remain unaltered and provide a realistic picture of the grim way of life under the constant threat of "Border Reivers". Two rooms are furnished in contemporary style and there are displays of historic and local information. Visitors are welcome to walk in the grounds which contain a number of interesting trees and shrubs. A woodland walk to the natural spring from which water is now pumped up to the Tower for the house and cottages.

Location: OS Ref. NU185 253. Follow Historic Property signs on A1 7m N of Alnwick.

Opening Times: Daylight hours all year.

Admission: Adult £1, Child/Conc./Groups 50p.

Grounds suitable.

PRUDHOE CASTLE

Tel: 01661 833459

Prudhoe, Northumberland NE42 6NA

Owner: English Heritage **Contact:** The Custodian

Set on a wooded hillside overlooking the River Tyne are the extensive remains of this 12th century castle including a gatehouse, curtain wall and keep. Small exhibition and video presentation.

Location: OS88 Ref. NZ092 634. In Prudhoe, on minor road N from A695.

Opening Times: 1 Apr - 30 Sept: daily, 10am - 6pm. 1 - 31 Oct: daily, 10am - 5pm.

Admission: Adult £1.80, Child 90p, Conc. £1.40. 15% discount for groups (11+).

Partially suitable. Limited. In grounds, on leads. Tel. for details.

North East England

SEATON DELAVAL HALL

Tel: 0191 2373040 **Fax:** 0191 2371493

Seaton Sluice, Whitley Bay, Northumberland NE26 4QR

Owner: The Lord Hastings **Contact:** F Hetherington

A splendid English baroque house, regarded by many as Sir John Vanbrugh's masterpiece.

Location: OS Ref. NZ322 766. 1/2 m from Seaton Sluice on A190, 3m from Whitley Bay.

Opening Times: May & Aug BH; Jun - 30 Sept: Weds & Suns, 2 - 6pm.

Admission: Adult £3, Child £1, Conc. £2.50.

WALLINGTON

National Trust Photographic Library/ Marianne Majerus

CAMBO, MORPETH, NORTHUMBERLAND NE61 4AP

Owner: *The National Trust* ***Contact:*** *The House Manager*

Tel: 01670 774283 **Fax:** 01670 774420

A beautiful walled garden, Edwardian conservatory, woodland walks and ornamental ponds make a delightful setting for the Trevelyan's historic home. Wallington Hall dates from 1688 and boasts fine interiors, a superb collection of ceramics and William Bell-Scott's famous paintings of Northumbrian history but still retains the atmosphere of a much loved family home.

Location: OS Ref. NZ030 843. Near Cambo, 6m NW of Belsay (A696).

Opening Times: House: 1 Apr - 30 Sept: daily (except Tues), 1 - 5.30pm. 1 Oct - 31 Oct: daily (except Tues), 1 - 4.30pm. Gardens: daily, 10am - 7pm (summer). Grounds: all year.

Admission: House, Garden & Grounds: Adult £5.40, Child £2.70, Family £13.50, Group: £4.90. Garden & Grounds: Adult £3.90, Child £1.95, Groups £3.40.

No photography in house. By arrangement. In grounds on leads. Please telephone for details.

WARKWORTH CASTLE

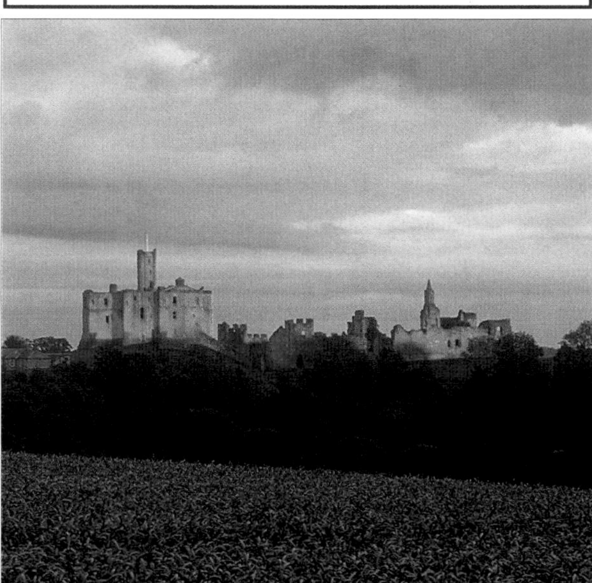

English Heritage Photographic Library

WARKWORTH, MORPETH, NORTHUMBERLAND NE66 0UJ

Owner: *English Heritage* ***Contact:*** *The Custodian*

Tel: 01665 711423

The great towering keep of this 15th century castle, once the home of the mighty Percy family, dominates the town and River Coquet. Warkworth is one of the most outstanding examples of an aristocratic fortified residence.

Location: OS81 Ref. NU247 057. 7m S of Alnwick on A1068.

Opening Times: 1 Apr - 30 Sept: daily, 10am - 6pm. 1 - 31 Oct: daily, 10am - 5pm. 1 Nov - 31 Mar: daily, 10am - 4pm (closed 1 - 2pm). Closed 24 - 26 Dec.

Admission: Adult £2.40, Child £1.20, Conc. £1.80. 15% discount for groups (11+).

Grounds suitable. On leads. Tel. for details.

WARKWORTH HERMITAGE

Tel: 01665 711423

Warkworth, Northumberland

Owner: English Heritage **Contact:** The Custodian

Upstream by boat from the castle this curious hermitage cuts into the rock of the river cliff.

Location: OS Ref. NU247 057. 7 1/2 m SE of Alnwick on A1068.

Opening Times: 1 Apr - 30 Sept: Weds, Suns & BHs, 11am - 5pm.

Admission: Adult £1.60, Child 80p, Conc. £1.20.

Northumbria Tourist Board.

Dunstanburgh Castle, Northumberland.

ARBEIA ROMAN FORT

Tel: 0191 456 1369 **Fax:** 0191 427 6862

Baring Street, South Shields, Tyne & Wear NE33 2BB

Owner: South Tyneside Metropolitan Borough Council **Contact:** The Curator

Managed by: Tyne & Wear Museums

Extensive remains of 2nd century Roman fort, including fort defences, stone granaries, gateways and latrines. Full-scale reconstruction of Roman gateway and museum featuring finds including weapons, coins, jewellery and tombstones. Watch excavations throughout the year.

Location: OS Ref. NZ365 679. Near town centre and Metro Station.

Opening Times: Easter - Oct: Mon - Sat: 10am - 5.30pm, Suns, 1 - 5pm. Open BH Mons. Winter: Mon - Sat, 10am - 4pm.

Admission: Free, except for guided tours and Timequest Gallery: Adult £1.50, Conc. 80p.

BEDE'S WORLD MUSEUM

Tel: 0191 489 2106 **Fax:** 0191 428 2361

Church Bank, Jarrow, Tyne & Wear NE32 3DY

Managed by: Jarrow 700AD Ltd **Contact:** Miss M Harte

A new museum telling the story of the Venerable Bede and Anglo-Saxon Northumbria.

Location: OS Ref. NZ339 652. Just off A19, S end of Tyne Tunnel.

Opening Times: Apr - Oct: Tue - Sat, 10am - 5.30pm, Suns, 12 noon - 5.30pm. Nov - Mar: Tue - Sat, 10am - 4.30pm, Suns, 12 noon - 4.30pm. Also open BH Mons.

Admission: Adult £3, Conc. £1.50, Family £7.20. Groups by arrangement (prices will increase from end of May 2000).

BESSIE SURTEES HOUSE

Tel: 0191 269 1200

41 - 44 Sandhill, Newcastle, Tyne & Wear

Owner: English Heritage **Contact:** The Custodian

Two 16th and 17th century merchants' houses stand on the quayside near the Tyne Bridge. One is a rare example of Jacobean domestic architecture. 3 rooms open.

Location: OS Ref. NZ252 639. 41- 44 Sandhill, Newcastle.

Opening Times: Weekdays only: 10am - 4pm. Closed BHs, 24 - 26 Dec and 1 Jan.

Admission: Free.

CATHEDRAL CHURCH OF ST NICHOLAS

Newcastle-upon-Tyne, Tyne & Wear NE1 1PF **Tel:** 0191 232 1939 **Fax:** 0191 230 0735

e-mail: stnicholas@aol.com **Contact:** Rev Canon Peter Strange

Mostly 14th century surmounted by 15th century lantern spire, one medieval window, two Renaissance memorials, one large 15th century Flemish brass.

Location: OS Ref. NZ250 640. City centre, 1/2 m from A167 signposted from Swan House roundabout.

Opening Times: Suns: 7am - 12 noon, 4 - 7pm. Mon - Fri: 7am - 6pm. Sats: 8.30am - 4pm.

By arrangement. No parking. Guide dogs only.

GIBSIDE

Tel: 01207 542255

Nr Rowlands Gill, Burnopfield, Newcastle-upon-Tyne NE16 6BG

Owner: The National Trust **Contact:** The Property Manager

Gibside is one of the finest 18th century designed landscapes in the north of England. The Chapel was built to James Paine's design soon after 1760. Outstanding example of Georgian architecture approached along a terrace with an oak avenue. Walk along the River Derwent through woodland.

Location: OS Ref. NZ172 583. 6m SW of Gateshead, 20m NW of Durham. Entrance on B6314 between Burnopfield and Rowlands Gill.

Opening Times: Grounds: 1 Apr - 31 Oct: daily except Mons (open BH Mons), 10am - 6pm. Last admission 4.30pm. 1 Nov - 31 Mar: 10am - sunset. Last admission 1 hour before sunset. Chapel: 1 Apr - 31 Oct: as grounds, otherwise by arrangement.

Admission: Chapel and Grounds: Adult £3, Child half price. Booked groups £2.60.

NEWCASTLE CASTLE GARTH

Tel: 0191 232 7938

Castle Keep, Castle Garth, Newcastle-upon-Tyne NE1 1RQ

Owner: Newcastle City Council **Contact:** Paul MacDonald

The Keep originally dominated the castle bailey. The 'new' castle was founded in 1080.

Location: OS Ref. NZ251 638. City centre between St Nicholas church and the high level bridge.

Opening Times: All year: daily, 9.30am - 5pm.

Admission: Adult £1.50, Child/Conc. 50p.

ST PAUL'S MONASTERY

Tel: 0191 489 2106

Jarrow, Tyne & Wear

Owner: English Heritage **Contact:** The Custodian

The home of the Venerable Bede in the 7th and 8th centuries, partly surviving as the chancel of the parish church. It has become one of the best understood Anglo-Saxon monastic sites.

Location: OS Ref. NZ339 652. In Jarrow, on minor road N of A185.

Opening Times: Any reasonable time.

Admission: Free.

SOUTER LIGHTHOUSE

Tel: 0191 529 3161

Coast Road, Whitburn, Tyne & Wear SR6 7NR

Owner: The National Trust **Contact:** The Property Manager

Shore-based lighthouse and associated buildings, built in 1871, the first to be powered by an alternative electric current.

Location: OS Ref. NZ408 641. 2 1/2 m S of Southshields on A183. 5m N of Sunderland.

Opening Times: 1 Apr - 31 Oct: daily except Fris (open Good Fri), 11am - 5pm. Last admission 4.30pm.

Admission: Adult £2.80, Child half price. Booked Groups: £2.30. Family £7.

Ground floor & grounds suitable. WC. By arrangement. In grounds, on leads.

TYNEMOUTH PRIORY & CASTLE

Tel: 0191 257 1090

North Pier, Tynemouth, Tyne & Wear NE30 4BZ

Owner: English Heritage **Contact:** The Custodian

The castle walls and gatehouse enclose the substantial remains of a Benedictine priory founded c1090 on a Saxon monastic site. Their strategic importance has made the castle and priory the target for attack for many centuries. In World War I, coastal batteries in the castle defended the mouth of the Tyne.

Location: OS88 Ref. NZ374 695. In Tynemouth.

Opening times: 1 Apr - 30 Sept: daily, 10am - 6pm. 1 - 31 Oct: daily, 10am - 5pm. 1 Nov - 31 Mar: Wed - Sun, 10am - 4pm (closed 1 -2 pm).

Admission: Adult £1.80, Child 90p, Conc. £1.40. 15% discount for groups (11+).

Grounds suitable. By arrangement. In grounds, on leads. Tel. for details.

English Heritage Photographic Library.

Tynemouth Priory & Castle, Tyne & Wear.

WASHINGTON OLD HALL

Tel: 0191 416 6879

The Avenue, Washington Village, Tyne & Wear NE38 7LE

Owner: The National Trust **Contact:** The Property Manager

Jacobean manor house incorporating portions of 12th century house of the Washington family.

Location: OS Ref. NZ312 566. In Washington on E side of Avenue. 5m W of Sunderland (2m from A1), S of Tyne Tunnel, follow signs for Washington New Town District 4 and then village.

Opening Times: 1 Apr - 31 Oct: daily except Thurs, Fris & Sats (open Good Fri), 11am - 5pm. Last admission 4.30pm.

Admission: Adult £2.80, Child half-price, Family £7. Groups (15+) by arrangement only: £2.30.

Conferences. Ground floor & grounds suitable. By arrangement. Limited. In grounds, on leads.

Owner: English Heritage

CONTACT

The Custodian
Brodsworth Hall
Brodsworth
Nr Doncaster
Yorkshire
DN5 7XJ

Tel/Fax: 01302 722598

LOCATION

OS Ref. SE505 070

In Brodsworth, 5m NW of Doncaster off A635. Use A1(M)/J37.

Rail: Doncaster.

BRODSWORTH HALL & GDNS ⌗

Nr Doncaster

BRODSWORTH HALL is a rare example of a Victorian country house that has survived largely unaltered with much of its original furnishings and decorations intact. Designed and built in the 1860s it remains an extraordinary time capsule. The now faded grandeur of the reception rooms speaks of an opulent past whilst the cluttered servants wing, with its great kitchen from the age of Mrs Beeton, recalls a vanished way of life. Careful conservation by English Heritage has preserved the patina of time throughout the house to produce an interior that is both fascinating and evocative. The Hall is set within beautifully restored Victorian gardens rich in features which are a delight in any season.

Exhibitions about the family, the servants and gardens.

Most of house is accessible. WCs.

Seating for 70.

Groups must book. Booked coach parties: 10am - 1pm.

220 cars and 3 coaches. Free.

Education Centre. Free if booked in advance.

No dogs in gardens.

OPENING TIMES

SUMMER

1 April - 31 October
Tue - Sun, & BHs.

House: 1 - 6pm
(last admission 1 hour before closing).

Gardens: 12 noon - 6pm.

WINTER

Gardens, Shop & Tearoom only
6 November - 26 March
Sats & Suns: 11am - 4pm.

ADMISSION

SUMMER

House

Adult	£5.00
Child* (5-15yrs)	£2.50
Conc.	£3.80

Groups (11+) 15% discount

Free admission for tour leaders and coach drivers.

Gardens

Adult	£2.60
Child* (5-15yrs)	£1.30
Conc.	£2.00

WINTER

Adult	£1.60
Child* (5-15yrs)	£0.80
Conc.	£1.20

* Under 5yrs Free

SPECIAL EVENTS

Please telephone for details.

North East England

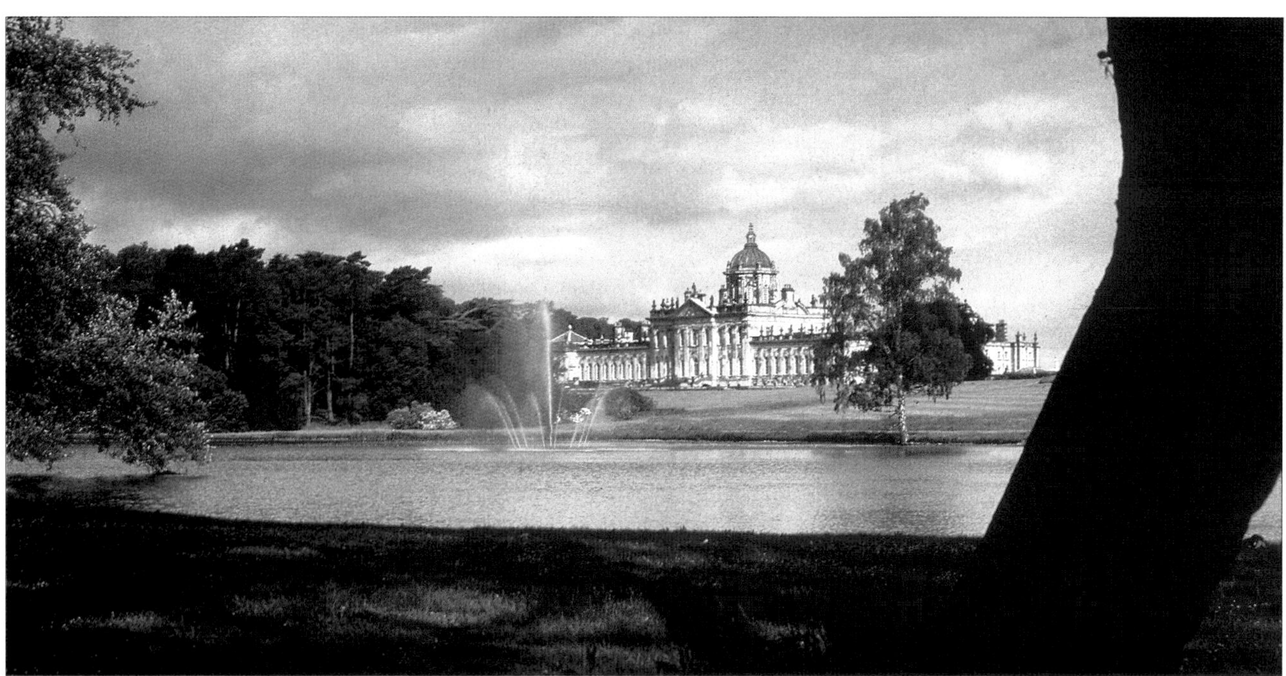

CASTLE HOWARD
York

Owner: The Hon Simon Howard

CONTACT

Mrs M E Carmichael
Castle Howard
York, North Yorks,
YO60 7DA

Tel: 01653 648444
Fax: 01653 648501
e-mail: mec@castlehoward.co.uk

LOCATION

OS Ref. SE716 701

Approaching from S, A64 to Malton, on entering Malton, take Castle Howard road via Coneysthorpe village. Or from A64 following signs to Castle Howard via the Carrmire Gate 9' wide by 10' high.

York 15m (20 mins), A64. From London: M1/J32, M18 to A1(M) to A64, York/Scarborough Road, 3½ hrs.

Train: London Kings Cross to York 1hr. 50 mins. York to Malton Station 30 mins.

Bus: Service and tour buses from York Station.

CONFERENCE/FUNCTION		
ROOM	SIZE	MAX CAPACITY
Long Gallery	197' x 24'	280
Grecian Hall	40' x 40'	160

In a dramatic setting between two lakes with extensive gardens and impressive fountains, this 18th century Palace was designed by Sir John Vanbrugh in 1699. Undoubtedly the finest private residence in Yorkshire it was built for Charles Howard, 3rd Earl of Carlisle, whose descendants still live here.

With its painted and gilded dome reaching 80ft into the Yorkshire sky, this impressive house has collections of antique furniture, porcelain and sculpture, while its fabulous collection of paintings is dominated by the famous Holbein portraits of Henry VIII and the Duke of Norfolk.

GARDENS

Designed on a heroic scale covering 1,000 acres. The gardens include memorable sights like the Temple of the Four Winds and the Mausoleum, the New River Bridge and the recently restored waterworks of the South Lake, Cascade, Waterfall and Prince of Wales Fountain. The walled garden has collections of old and modern roses.

Ray Wood, acknowledged by the Royal Botanic Collection, Kew, as a "rare botanical jewel" has a unique collection of rare trees, shrubs, rhododendrons, magnolias and azaleas.

Suitable for concerts, craft fairs, fashion shows, clay pigeon shooting, equestrian events, garden parties, filming, product launches. Helicopter landing. Firework displays.

Booked private parties and receptions, min. 25.

Transport equipped for wheelchairs. Chairlift in house to main floor. WCs.

Two cafeterias.

Guides posted throughout house. Private garden tours and lectures by arrangement covering house, history, contents and garden.

400 cars, 20 coaches.

1:10 teacher/pupil ratio required. Special interest: 18th century architecture, art, history, wildlife, horticulture.

OPENING TIMES

SUMMER

17 March - late October
Daily, 11am - 4.30pm.

Last admission 4.30pm.

NB. Grounds, Rose Gardens, Plant Centre and Stable Courtyard Complex open 10am.

WINTER

November - mid March

Grounds open most days November, December and January - telephone for confirmation.

ADMISSION

SUMMER

House & Garden

Adult	£7.50
Child (4-16yrs)	£4.50
OAP	£6.75

Groups (12+)

Adult	£6.50
Child (4-16yrs)	£4.00
OAP	£6.00

Garden only

Adult	£4.50
Child*	£2.50

WINTER

Grounds only.

FAIRFAX HOUSE

York

Owner:
York Civic Trust

CONTACT

Mr Peter Brown
Fairfax House
Castlegate
York
YO1 9RN

Tel: 01904 655543

Fax: 01904 652262

LOCATION

OS Ref. SE605 515

In centre of York between Castle Museum and Jorvik Centre.

London 4 hrs by car, 2 hrs by train.

Rail: York Station, 10 mins walk.

Taxi: Station Taxis 01904 623332.

FAIRFAX HOUSE was acquired and fully restored by the York Civic Trust in 1983/84. The house, described as a classic architectural masterpiece of its age and certainly one of the finest townhouses in England, was saved from near collapse after considerable abuse and misuse this century, having been converted into a cinema and dance hall.

The richly decorated interior with its plaster-work, wood and wrought-iron, is now the home for a unique collection of Georgian furniture, clocks, paintings and porcelain.

The Noel Terry Collection, gift of a former treasurer of the York Civic Trust, has been described by Christie's as one of the finest private collections formed this century. It enhances and complements the house and helps to create that special 'lived-in' feeling, providing the basis for a series of set-piece period exhibitions which bring the house to life in a very tangible way.

Suitable for filming. No photography in house. Liveried footmen, musical & dancing performances can be arranged.

Max. 28 seated. Groups up to 50: buffet can be provided.

Visitors may alight at entrance prior to parking. No WCs except for functions.

A guided tour can be arranged at a cost of £5. Evening and daytime guided tours, telephone for details. Available in French and German. Tour time: 1½ hrs.

300 cars, 50 yds from house. Coach park is ½ m away, parties are dropped off; drivers please telephone for details showing the nearest coach park and approach to the house.

OPENING TIMES

SUMMER

26 February - 6 January

Mon - Thur: 11am - 5pm.

Fris: Guided tours only at 11am and 2pm.

Sats: 11am - 5pm.

Suns: 1.30 - 5pm.

Last admission 4.30pm.

WINTER

Closed

7 January - 19 February & 24 - 26 December.

ADMISSION

Adult	£4.00
Child (5 -16yrs)	£1.50
Conc.	£3.50
Groups*	
Adult	£3.00
Child (5 -16yrs)	£1.00
Conc.	£3.00

* Min payment 15 persons.

SPECIAL EVENTS

- **FEB 26 - JUN 4:** Eat Drink and Be Merry - The British at Table 1600 - 2000. This major loan exhibition, sponsored by Waitrose, charts changing attitudes and patterns of behaviour between the first Elizabethan era and the present. A series of celebratory feasts are re-created in great detail, uniting once more, food, art and objects in the way they were originally intended to be enjoyed.
- **DEC 3 - JAN 6:** Exhibition on the 'Keeping of Christmas'. Information extracted from the family papers helps re-create, in a very tangible way, the ritual and decoration of Christmas celebrations in Fairfax House from 1760 -1840. Booked parties can be given mulled wine and mince pies at end of the tour.

Mike Williams

Owner:
The National Trust

CONTACT

The National Trust
Fountains Abbey
and Studley Royal
Ripon
North Yorkshire
HG4 3DY

Tel: 01765 608888

Fax: 01765 608889

LOCATION

OS Ref. SE275 700

Abbey entrance; 4m W of Ripon off B6265.

8m W of A1.

FOUNTAINS ABBEY & STUDLEY ROYAL

Ripon

One of the most remarkable sites in Europe, sheltered in a secluded valley, Fountains Abbey and Studley Royal, a World Heritage Site, encompasses the spectacular remains of a 12th century Cistercian abbey, an Elizabethan mansion, and one of the best surviving examples of a Georgian green water garden. Elegant ornamental lakes, avenues, temples and cascades provide a succession of unforgettable eye-catching vistas in an atmosphere of peace and tranquillity. St Mary's Church, built by William Burges in the 19th century, provides a dramatic focal point to the medieval deer park with over 500 deer.

Audio visual programme and exhibition at the Visitor Centre. Small museum near to the Abbey. Exhibitions in Fountains Hall and Swanley Grange.

The Abbey is maintained by English Heritage. St Mary's Church is owned by English Heritage and managed by the National Trust.

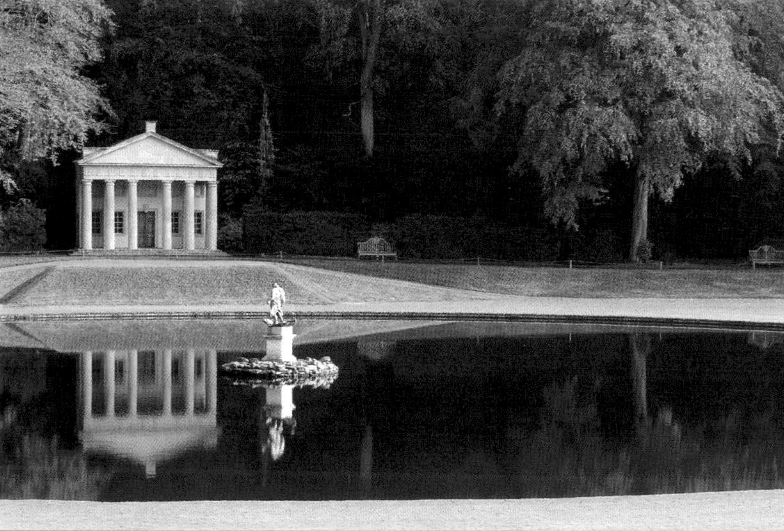

Events held throughout the year. Exhibitions. Seminar facilities. Outdoor concerts, meetings, activity days, walks.

Two shops.

Dinners and dances.

Free batricars & wheelchairs, please book, tel. 01765 601005. 3-wheel Batricars not permitted due to terrain. Tours for visually impaired, please book. WC.

Groups please book, discounted rates.

Free, but seasonal. Groups, please use Visitor Centre entrance.

Drivers must book groups.

Welcome by prior arrangement.

On leads only.

OPENING TIMES

April - September
Daily: 10am - 7pm.

January - March & October - December
Daily: 10am - 5pm.

Last admission 1 hr before closing.

Closes at 4pm on 7/8 July & 5 August.

Closed 24/25 December, and Fris in November - January.

ADMISSION

Adult	£4.30
Child	£2.10
Family	£10.50
Groups (15-30)	
Adult	£3.70
Child	£1.90
Groups (31+)	
Adult	£3.20
Child	£1.70

Group discount applicable only with prior booking.

Group visits and disabled visitors, please telephone in advance, 01765 601005.

HAREWOOD HOUSE
Leeds

Owner: The Earl of Harewood

CONTACT

Mary Stuart
Moor House
Harewood Estate
Harewood
Leeds
West Yorkshire
LS17 9LQ

Tel: 0113 2181010
Fax: 0113 2181002
e-mail: business@harewood.org

LOCATION

OS Ref. SE311 446

A1 N or S to Wetherby.

A659 via Collingham, Harewood is on A61 between Harrogate and Leeds. Easily reached from A1, M1, M62 and M18. Half an hour from York,

15 mins from centre of Leeds or Harrogate.

Rail: Leeds Station 7m.

Bus: No. 36 from Leeds or Harrogate.

CONFERENCE/FUNCTION		
ROOM	SIZE	MAX CAPACITY
State Dining Rm.		32
Gallery		96
Courtyard Suite		120
Courtyard Marquee	20' x 24'	400

HAREWOOD HOUSE, Yorkshire home of the Queen's cousin, the Earl of Harewood, is an architectural masterpiece where priceless treasures mingle with Royal memorabilia. The house is renowned for its stunning architecture, magnificent Adam interiors, Chippendale furniture, fine porcelain and outstanding art collections including Italian Renaissance masterpieces, Turner watercolours, 18th century portraits and 20th century works.

In the grounds, landscaped by 'Capability' Brown, are lakeside and woodland walks, a magnificent collection of Rhododendrons (April - June) and Sir Charles Barry's recently restored parterre Terrace, complete with box scrolls and seasonal bedding. The hugely popular Lakeside Bird Garden is home to over 120 rare and endangered species, as well as popular favourites - penguins, flamingos and owls.

Throughout the season there are a host of special events including open air concerts, craft fairs and car rallies, plus regularly changing exhibitions in the Watercolour Rooms and contemporary Terrace Art Gallery.

New for 2000, a major Chippendale exhibition featuring exquisite samples of his work, including the newly restored 'Chippendale State Bed' as the stunning centrepiece of the exhibition - unseen for over 150 years! A whole programme of talks and activities will accompany the exhibition, to present the fascinating background to Yorkshire's world-famous son, and his amazing craft skills. Telephone for further details.

Marquees can be accommodated, concerts and product launches. No photography in the house.

Ideal for corporate entertaining including drinks receptions, buffets and wedding receptions. Certain rooms available for corporate entertaining plus Courtyard Suite for conferences/product launches.

Visitors may alight at entrance. Parking in allocated areas. Most facilities accessible. Wheelchair available at house and Bird Garden. WC. Special concessions apply to disabled groups. Some steep inclines.

Licensed.

Cars 400 yds from house. 50+ coaches 500 yds from house. Drivers to verify in advance.

By arrangement. Audio tour of house £1.50. Lectures by arrangement.

Dogs on leads in grounds, guide dogs only in house.

Civil Wedding Licence.

OPENING TIMES

SUMMER

1 April - 29 October 2000 except 9 June (closed to public)

House
Daily from 11am - 4.30pm.

Bird Garden & Grounds
Daily from 10am.

Café
10.30am - 4.30pm.

WINTER

House closed: Nov - Mar.
Grounds & Gardens: Nov/Dec, open weekends (ring to confirm times).

ADMISSION

All attractions

Adult	£7.25
Child (4-15yrs)	£5.00
Student	£5.00
OAP	£6.50
Family (2+3)	£25.00
Groups (15+)	
Adult	£6.00
OAP	£5.50

Bird Garden & Grounds

Adult	£6.00
Child (4-15yrs)	£3.50
Student	£3.50
OAP	£5.00
Family (2+3)	£18.00

SPECIAL EVENTS

- **MAY 27 - 29:** Craft Festival.
- **JUNE 3:** Phoenix Dance Festival
- **JUNE 17** 'Pure Puccini' Open Air Concert
- **JULY 22 - 24** Leeds Championship Dog Show

NEWBY HALL & GARDENS

Ripon

Owner:
Mr Richard Compton

CONTACT

The Opening Administrator
Newby Hall
Ripon
North Yorkshire
HG4 5AE

Tel: 01423 322583

Fax: 01423 324452

e-mail:
info@newbyhall.co.uk

LOCATION

OS Ref. SE348 675

Midway between London and Edinburgh, 4m W of A1, towards Ripon. S of Skelton 2m NW of (A1) Boroughbridge. 4m SE of Ripon.

Taxi: Ripon Taxi Rank 01765 601283.

Bus: On Ripon - York route.

CONFERENCE/FUNCTION		
ROOM	SIZE	MAX CAPACITY
Grantham Room	90' x 20'	200

NEWBY HALL, the Yorkshire home of the Compton family, is a late 17th century house built in the style of Sir Christopher Wren. William Weddell, an ancestor of Mr Compton, made the Grand Tour in the 1760s, and amongst the treasures he acquired were magnificent classical statuary and a superb set of Gobelin Tapestries. To house these treasures, Weddell commissioned Robert Adam to create the splendid domed Sculpture Gallery and Tapestry Room that we see today. The Regency dining room and billiard room were added later. There is much fine Chippendale furniture and in recent years Mrs Robin Compton restored the decoration of the house, painstakingly researching colour and decor of the Adam period.

GARDENS

25 acres of glorious gardens contain rare and beautiful shrubs and plants. Newby's famous double herbaceous borders, flanked by great bastions of yew hedges, sweep down to the River Ure. Formal gardens such as the Autumn and Rose Gardens – each with splashing fountains – a Victorian rock garden, the tranquillity of Sylvia's Garden, pergolas and even a tropical garden, make Newby a 'Garden for all Seasons'. Newby holds the National Collection of the Genus Cornus and in 1987 won the Christie's/ HHA Garden of the Year Award. The gardens also incorporate an exciting children's adventure garden and miniature railway.

Suitable for filming and for special events, craft and country fairs, vehicle rallies etc, promotions and lectures. No indoor photography. Allow a full day for viewing house and gardens.

Wedding receptions & special functions.

5 wheelchairs available. Access to ground floor of house and key areas in gardens. WC.

Garden restaurant, teas, hot and cold meals. Booked groups in Grantham Room. Menus/rates on request.

Ample. Hard standing for coaches.

Welcome. Rates on request. Grantham Room for use as wet weather base subject to availability. Woodland discovery walk, adventure gardens and train rides on $10^1/_4$" gauge railway.

Guide dogs only.

SPECIAL EVENTS

- **MAY 7:** Spring Plant Fair.
- **JUN 10 - 11:** Rainbow Craft Fair.
- **JUL 15 - 16:** Yorkshire Craft Pavilion

See Special Events Index for full details

OPENING TIMES

SUMMER

House
1 April - end September
Daily except Mons but open BH Mons,
12 noon - 5pm
Last admission 4.30pm.

Garden
1 April - end September
Daily except Mons but open BH Mons.
11am - 5.30pm
Last admission 5pm.

WINTER
October - end March
Closed.

ADMISSION

1999 prices.
Prices due to change for 2000, please telephone to confirm.

House & Garden
Adult £6.30
Child (4-16yrs)..........£3.80
OAP......................£5.20
Disabled.................£3.80
Group (20+)
Adult £5.00
Child (4-16yrs) £3.40

Garden only
Adult £4.50
Child (4-16yrs)..........£3.00
OAP......................£3.90
Disabled.................£3.00
Group (20+)
Adult £3.70
Child (4-16yrs) £2.60

Additional charge for train.

Oakwell Hall

Owner:
Kirklees Cultural Services

CONTACT

Red House Museum
Oxford Road
Gomersal
West Yorkshire BD19 4JP

Tel: 01274 335100
Fax: 01274 335105

Oakwell Hall
Nutter Lane
Birstall
Batley
West Yorkshire WF17 9LG

Tel: 01924 326240
Fax: 01924 326249

LOCATION

OS Ref. SE210 260
Red House:
On A651 in Gomersal. M62/J27, follow A62 to wards Huddersfield to Birstall, follow brown tourist signs.

OS Ref. SE217 271
Oakwell Hall:
On A652 in Birstall. Take J27/A62 towards Huddersfield to Birstall.

OAKWELL HALL:

CONFERENCE/FUNCTION		
ROOM	SIZE	MAX CAPACITY
Barn		120
Classroom		15-25

RED HOUSE MUSEUM & OAKWELL HALL COUNTRY PARK
Gomersal / Batley

RED HOUSE MUSEUM

This delightful house was once home to the Taylor family who were merchant clothiers. Not only is the house beautifully displayed with original and reproduction 1830s furnishings, it also has an important literary connection with Charlotte Brontë, who was a close friend of the Taylors; she featured the house as *Briarmains* in *Shirley*. Charlotte's links with the area and her friendships with Mary Taylor and Ellen Nussey are explored in *The Secret's Out* exhibition in the renovated barn; and the 20th century memories of local people are brought to life in *Spen Valley Stories*. The museum shop sells period toys and gifts and the garden has been recreated in 19th century style.

OAKWELL HALL COUNTRY PARK

Set in period gardens and in over 100 acres of country park, this Elizabethan Manor House was the real setting for *Fieldhead* in Charlotte Brontë's *Shirley*. The house is now set out as the home of the Batt family in the 1690s, giving visitors valuable insight into 17th century gentry life.

The exciting and interactive *Discover Oakwell* exhibition introduces children (and adults!) to the ecology of a country park.

The site has excellent visitor facilities, a delightful period garden, a café and a well-stocked shop. The country park boasts nature trails, picnic areas, an equestrian arena and an adventure playground.

Red House Museum. Hanson.

RED HOUSE MUSEUM

Brass band concerts, etc. Various exhibitions.

Large print notes, braille info, WCs. Lower floor only.

Self-serve hot and cold drinks in exhibition room.

By arrangement for groups at an extra charge.

Turn into car park is difficult unless travelling south on A651 towards Dewsbury. Groups should book.

Booking essential. Teachers' info and staff assistance (extra charge).

Oakwell Hall Country Park. Hanson.

OAKWELL HALL COUNTRY PARK

Various events during the year, concerts, fairs, etc. Allow 1/2 day for visit. Adventure playground.

Ground floor only. RADAR WC, braille guide, large print guide.

By arrangement for groups at extra charge.

Ample. Groups should book.

Booking essential. Teachers' resource pack.

Guide dogs only.

OPENING TIMES

Both properties

All year:
Mon - Fri: 11am - 5pm.
Sat & Sun: 12 noon - 5pm.

ADMISSION

Red House Museum
Free all year.

Oakwell Hall Country Park

SUMMER
Adult £1.20
Child £0.50
Family £2.50

Discounts are available for booked groups (10+).

WINTER
Free entry.

RIPLEY CASTLE

Harrogate

RIPLEY CASTLE has been the home of the Ingilby family for twenty-six generations and Sir Thomas and Lady Ingilby together with their five children continue the tradition. The guided tours are amusing and informative, following the lives and loves of one family for over 670 years and how they have been affected by events in English history. The Old Tower dates from 1555 and houses splendid armour, books, panelling and a Priest's Secret Hiding Place, together with fine paintings, china, furnishings and chandeliers collected by the family over the centuries. The extensive Victorian Walled Gardens have been transformed and are a colourful delight through every season. In the Spring you can appreciate 150,000 flowering bulbs which create a blaze of colour through the woodland walks, and also the National Hyacinth Collection whose scent is breathtaking. The restored Hot Houses have an extensive tropical plant collection, and in the Kitchen Gardens you can see an extensive collection of rare vegetables from the Henry Doubleday Research Association.

Ripley village on the Castle's doorstep is a model estate village with individual charming shops, an art gallery, delicatessen and Farmyard Museum.

Owner:
Sir Thomas Ingilby Bt

CONTACT

Tours: Wendy McNae
Meetings/Dinners:
Chloë Evans
Ripley Castle
Ripley
Harrogate
North Yorkshire
HG3 3AY

Tel: 01423 770152

Fax: 01423 771745

e-mail: visitors@ripleycastle.co.uk

LOCATION

OS Ref. SE283 605

W edge of village. Just off A61, 3½ m N of Harrogate, 8m S of Ripon. M1 18m S, M62 20m S.

Rail: London - Leeds/York 2hrs. Leeds/York - Harrogate 30mins.

Taxi: Blueline taxis Harrogate (01423) 503037.

CONFERENCE/FUNCTION		
ROOM	SIZE	MAX CAPACITY
Morning Rm	27' x 22'	80
Large Drawing Rm	30 'x 22'	80
Library	31 x 19'	75
Tower Rm	33' x 21'	75
Map Rm	19' x 14'	20
Dining Rm	23' x 19'	30

Management training courses. No photography inside castle unless by prior written consent. Parkland for outdoor activities & concerts. Murder mystery weekends. Dry ski slope.

VIP lunches & dinners (max. 66): unlimited in marquees. Full catering service, wedding receptions, banquets and medieval banquets.

5/7 rooms accessible. Gardens accessible (not Tropical Collection). WCs. Parking 50 yds.

Cromwell's Eating House (seats 80) in Castle courtyard. Licensed. Pub lunches or dinner at hotel (100 yds). Groups must book.

Obligatory. Tour time 75 mins.

290 cars - 300 yds from castle entrance. Coach park 50 yds. Free.

Welcome by arrangement, between 10.30am - 7.30pm. Educational Fact Pack.

Guide dogs only.

Boar's Head Hotel (RAC***) 100 yds. Owned and managed by the estate.

Civil Wedding Licence.

Open all year.

OPENING TIMES

SUMMER
Castle & Gardens
January - May,
September - October:
Tues, Thurs, Sats & Suns:
10.30am - 3pm.

June - August:
Daily: 10.30am - 3pm.
Nov/Dec:
Tues, Thurs, Sats & Suns
11am - 2pm.

Gardens
Daily, 10am - 5pm.

WINTER
November - March:
Tues, Thurs, Sats & Suns.
10am - last guided tour 3pm.

ADMISSION

ALL YEAR
Castle & Gardens

Adult	£5.00
Child (5-16yrs)	£2.50
OAP	£4.00
Groups (15+)	
Adult	£4.00
Child (5-16yrs)	£2.00

Gardens only

Adult	£2.50
Child (5-16yrs)	£1.00
OAP	£2.00
Groups (15+)	
Adult	£2.00

SPECIAL EVENTS

- **APR 14 - 16:** Galloway Antiques Fair
- **JUNE 8 - 11:** Grand Summer Sale
- **JULY 14 - 16:** Galloway Antiques Fair

SKIPTON CASTLE
Skipton

CONTACT

Judith Parker
Skipton Castle
Skipton
North Yorkshire
BD23 1AQ

Tel: 01756 792442

Fax: 01756 796100

e-mail: info@skiptoncastle.co.uk

LOCATION

OS Ref. SD992 520

In the centre of Skipton, at the N end of High Street.

Skipton is 20m W of Harrogate on the A59 and 26m NW of Leeds on A65.

Rail: Regular services from Leeds & Bradford.

Guardian of the gateway to the Yorkshire Dales for over 900 years, this is one of the most complete and well-preserved medieval castles in England. From 1310 stronghold of the Cliffords, two Lords of Skipton went out from here to die on Roses battlefields. In the Civil War this was the last Royalist bastion in the North, falling after a three year siege.

Every phase of this turbulent history has left its mark, from the Norman entrance arch and gateway towers to the beautiful early Tudor courtyard built in the heart of the castle by 'The Shepherd Lord'; it was there in 1659, that Lady Anne Clifford planted a yew tree (in whose shade you can sit today) to mark the completion of her repairs after the Civil War. Thanks to her, and to Cromwell, who permitted them on condition that the roofs should not be able to support cannon – the castle is still fully roofed, making a visit well worthwhile at any time of year. A delightful picnic area has been created on the Chapel Terrace with views over the town and woods.

The gatehouse of the castle contains the Shell Room, decorated in 1620 with shells and Jamaican coral said to have been brought home by Lady Anne's father, George Clifford, 3rd Earl of Cumberland, Champion to Queen Elizabeth and one of her Admirals against the Armada; he lies beneath a splendid tomb in Skipton's parish church, a few yards from the castle gates.

On leaving the castle, the visitor is at once in the town's bustling High Street, with its four market days every week (and lots of other good shopping) and a great variety of pubs and restaurants. Close by, the Leeds and Liverpool canal presents a lively scene.

OPENING TIMES

ALL YEAR
(closed 25 December)

Mon - Sat: 10am - 6pm
Suns: 12 noon - 6pm
(October - February 4pm).

ADMISSION

Adult	£4.20
Child (0 - 4yrs)	Free
Child (5-17yrs)	£2.10
OAP	£3.60
Student (with ID)	£3.60
Family (2+3)	£11.50
Groups (15+)	
Adult	£3.40
Child (0-17yrs)	£2.10

Includes illustrated tour sheet in a choice of eight languages, plus free badge for children.

Groups welcome:
Guides available for booked groups at no extra charge.

Not suitable.

Tearoom. Indoor and outdoor picnic areas.

By arrangement.

Large public coach and car park off nearby High Street. Coach drivers' rest room at Castle.

Welcome. Guides available. Teachers free.

In grounds on leads.

SPECIAL EVENTS

- **MAY 27 - 29:** Red Wyvern Society re-enactment of life in Skipton Castle in the 15th century.
- **AUG 19 - 20:** Feudal Archers: demonstration of arms, armour & domestic life (1135 - 1216).

Owner: Antony Bagshaw

CONTACT

John Connaughton
White Scar Cave
Ingleton
North Yorkshire
LA6 3AW

Tel: 01524 241244

Fax: 01524 241700

e-mail: wsb@oyez.freeserve.co.uk

LOCATION

OS Ref. SD713 745

$1^1/_2$ m from Ingleton on B6255 road to Hawes.

WHITE SCAR CAVE
Ingleton

WHITE SCAR CAVE is the longest show cave in Britain. The guided tour covers one mile, and takes about 80 minutes. The highlight of the tour is the impressive 200,000 year old Battlefield Cavern. Over 330 feet long, with its roof soaring in places to 100 feet, this is one of the largest caverns in Britain. It contains thousands of delicate stalactites, which hang from the roof in great clusters.

The tour begins near the original entrance found by Christopher Long, the student who discovered the cave in 1923. The path winds its way past cascading waterfalls, between massive banks of flowstone, and through galleries decorated with cream- and carrot-coloured stalactites and stalagmites. Under the steel-grid walkways you can see the stream rushing and foaming on its way. Your guide will show you curious cave formations, including the Devil's Tongue, the Arum Lily and the remarkably lifelike Judge's Head.

There is electric lighting throughout, and the principal features are floodlit. White Scar Cave is part of a Site of Special Scientific Interest. It enjoys a spectacular location in the Yorkshire Dales National Park on the slopes of Ingleborough Hill (2372 ft).

OPENING TIMES

ALL YEAR
Daily: 10am
Last tour at 5.30pm.
Closed 25 December.

ADMISSION

Adult £6.20
Child.........................£3.40

Groups (min. 12)
Adult £4.95
Child £2.60

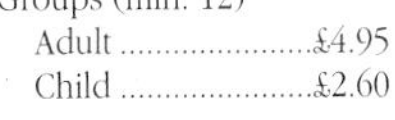

Partially suitable.

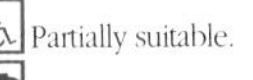
Obligatory.

Fact sheets.

In grounds on leads.

ALDBOROUGH ROMAN TOWN 

Tel: 01423 322768

High Street, Boroughbridge, North Yorkshire YO5 9ES

Owner: English Heritage **Contact:** The Custodian

The principal town of the largest Roman tribe in Britain. The delightfully located remains include Roman defences and two mosaic pavements, a small museum displays finds.

Location: OS99 Ref. SE405 661. Close to Boroughbridge off A1.

Opening Times: 1 Apr - 30 Sept: daily, 10am - 6pm. 1 - 31 Oct: daily, 10am - 5pm. Closed 1 - 2pm.

Admission: Adult £1.70, Child 90p, Conc. £1.30. 15% discount for groups (11+).

AMPLEFORTH COLLEGE JUNIOR SCHOOL

Tel: 01439 788238

The Castle, Gilling East, York, Yorkshire YO6 4HP **Fax:** 01439 788538

Owner: Ampleforth Abbey Trustees **Contact:** Fr Jeremy Sierla

The garden faces south in a delightful position bordered by woods on three sides, and the castle on the front. The land falls away to the south giving scope for terracing with formality and informality combined. The plants are traditional British garden plants but the location and pleasant views are its characteristic features.

Location: OS Ref. SE610 768. W of Gilling East village. 20m N of York on B1363.

Opening Times: House: term time, 10am - 12 noon & 2 - 4pm. Gardens - all year: dawn - dusk.

Admission: Gardens: Adult £1, House: Free (Great Hall & Entrance Hall only).

No public toilets. Not suitable. Guide dogs only.

ASKE HALL

See right.

BAGSHAW MUSEUM

Tel: 01924 326155

Wilton Park, Batley, Yorkshire WF17 0AS

Owner: Kirklees Metropolitan Council **Contact:** Catherine Hall

Travel through Asia, Africa and the Americas with an array of objects including many representing real and mythical animals.

Location: OS Ref. SE235 257. From M62/J27 follow A62 to Huddersfield. At Birstall, follow tourist signs. Bagshaw Museum is approached through a small housing estate.

Opening Times: Mon - Fri, 11am - 5pm. Sats & Suns, 12 noon - 5pm. Pre-booked groups and school parties welcome.

Admission: Free.

BENINGBROUGH HALL & GARDENS

Tel: 01904 470666

Beningbrough, North Yorkshire YO30 1DD **Fax:** 01904 470002

Owner: The National Trust **Contact:** The Visitor Services Manager

Imposing 18th century house with over 100 portraits from the National Portrait Gallery. Exciting newly restored walled garden, children's playground.

Location: OS Ref. SE516 586. 8m NW of York, 3m W of Shipton, 2m SE of Linton-on-Ouse, follow signposted route.

Opening Times: 1 Apr - 29 Oct: Sat - Wed & Good Fri also Fris in Jul & Aug. House: 12 noon - 5pm. Last admission 4.30pm.

Admission: House & Garden: Adult £5, Child £2.50, Family £12.50. Garden: Adult £3.50, Child £1.70, Family £8.70.

Partially suitable. WC.

BISHOPS' HOUSE

Tel: 0114 2557701

Meersbrook Park, Norton Lees Lane, Sheffield, Yorkshire S8 9BE

Owner: Sheffield Galleries & Museums Trust **Contact:** Ms K Streets

This beautiful 16th century timber-framed farmhouse is set in parkland and commands panoramic views over the city of Sheffield.

Location: OS Ref. SK348 843. A61, 2m S of city centre E of the Chesterfield Road.

Opening Times: Please contact for details.

Admission: Please contact for details.

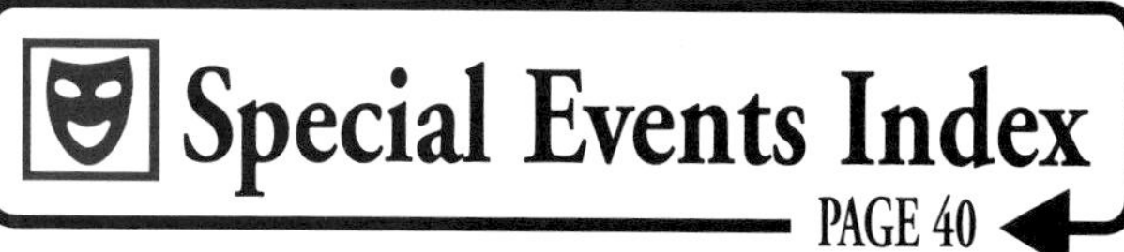

ASKE HALL

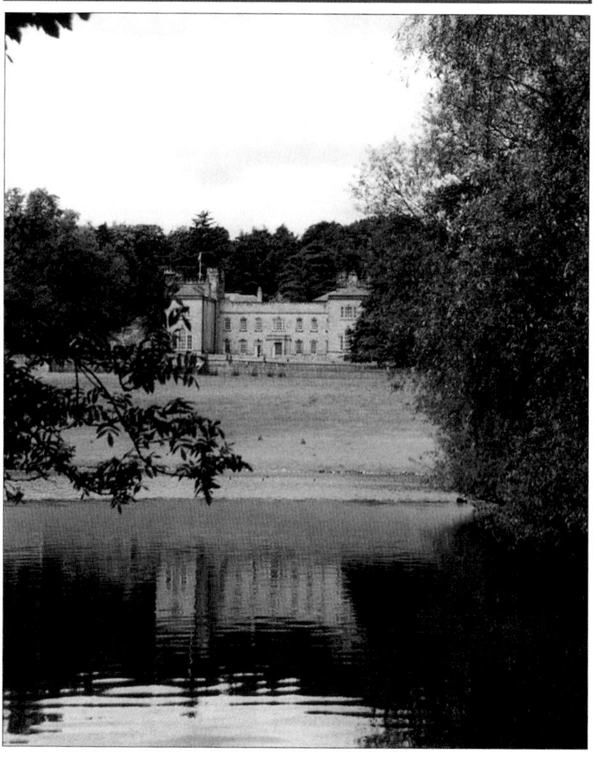

RICHMOND, NORTH YORKSHIRE DL10 5HJ

Owner: *The Marquess of Zetland* ***Contact:*** *Mbairi Mercer*

Tel: 01748 850391 **Fax:** 01748 823252

Nestling in 'Capability' Brown landscaped parkland, Aske has been the family seat of the Dundas family since 1763. This Georgian treasure house boasts exquisite 18th century furniture, paintings and porcelain, including work by Robert Adam, Chippendale, Gainsborough, Raeburn and Meissen.

Aske is an architectural kaleidoscope. There is the original 13th century pele tower and remodelled Jacobean tower. John Carr's stable block, built in 1765, was later converted into a chapel with Italianate interior. A coach house with clock tower houses the family's carriage. There are follies and a lake as well as the new three tier terraced garden.

Location: OS Ref. NZ179 035. 2m SW of A1 at Scotch Corner, 1m from the A66, on the Gilling West road (B6274).

Opening Times: All year: for groups (15+) by appointment only.

Admission: House & grounds: Adult £6, Child £3.50.

Conferences. No photography in house. Partially suitable. By arrangement. In grounds on leads.

Telephone for programme of special events.

BOLLING HALL MUSEUM

Tel: 01274 723057

Bowling Hall Road, Bradford, Yorkshire BD4 7LP

Owner: City of Bradford Metropolitan District Council **Contact:** Jane Whittaker

Medieval tower with 17th century additions.

Location: OS Ref. SE174 315. 1½ m SE of Bradford centre, ¼ m SE of A650.

Opening Times: Please telephone for details.

Admission: Free.

BOLTON ABBEY

SKIPTON, NORTH YORKSHIRE BD23 6EX

Owner: *Trustees of the Chatsworth Settlement* ***Contact:*** *Mrs B Allen*

Tel: 01756 710533 **Fax:** 01756 710535 **e-mail:** boltonabbey@dalesweb.co.uk

Wordsworth, Turner and Landseer were inspired by this romantic and varied landscape. The Estate, centred around Bolton Priory (founded 1154), is the Yorkshire home of the Duke and Duchess of Devonshire and provides 75 miles of footpaths to enjoy some of the most spectacular landscape in England.

Location: OS Ref. SE074 542. On B6160, N from the junction with A59 Skipton - Harrogate road, 23m from Leeds.

Opening Times: All year.

Admission: £3 per car, £1.50 for disabled (car park charge only).

Licensed. Licensed. In grounds, on leads. Devonshire Arms Country House Hotel nearby.

Patrick Lane.

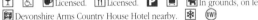

Bolling Hall Museum, Yorkshire.

BOLTON CASTLE

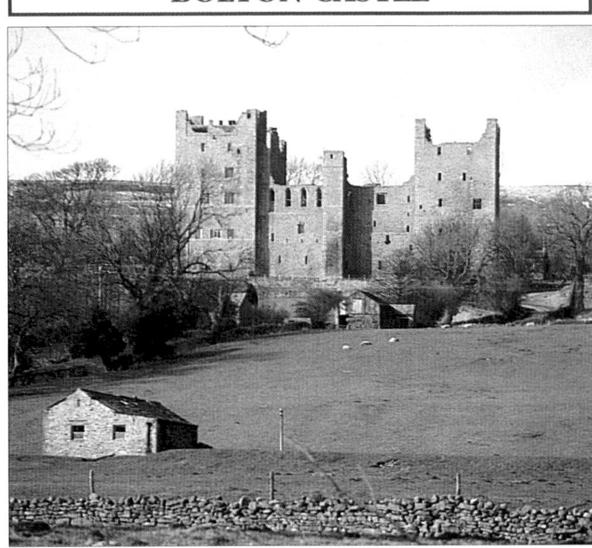

LEYBURN, NORTH YORKSHIRE DL8 4ET

Owner/Contact: *Hon Mr & Mrs Harry Orde-Powlett*

Tel: 01969 623981 **Fax:** 01969 623332 **e-mail:** harry@boltoncastle.co.uk

A fine medieval castle that overlooks beautiful Wensleydale. Bolton Castle celebrates its 600th anniversary this year. Set your imagination free as you wander round this fascinating castle, which once held Mary Queen of Scots prisoner for 6 months and succumbed to a bitter Civil War siege. Don't miss the beautiful medieval garden and vineyard.

Location: OS Ref. SE034 918. Approx 6m from Leyburn. 1m NW of Redmire.

Opening Times: Mar - Nov: daily, 10am - 5pm or dusk. Dec - 1 Mar: restricted opening, please telephone for details.

Admission: Adult £4, Conc. £3. Groups: Adult £3, Conc. £2.

Wedding receptions. Partially suitable. In grounds, on leads.

BRAMHAM PARK

WETHERBY, WEST YORKSHIRE LS23 6ND

Owner: *George Lane Fox* ***Contact:*** *Estate Office*

Tel: 01937 844265 **Fax:** 01937 845923

This Queen Anne house is 5 miles south of Wetherby on the A1, 10 miles from Leeds and 15 miles from York. The grand design of the gardens (66 acres) and pleasure grounds (100) are the only example of a formal, early 18th century landscape in the British Isles. Unexpected views and grand vistas, framed by monumental hedges and trees, delight the visitor, while temples, ornamental ponds and cascades focus the attention. The profusion of spring and summer wild flowers give a constant variety of colour and include many rare species.

Location: OS Ref. SE410 416. Half way from London to Edinburgh, 1m W of A1, 5m S of Wetherby, 10m NE of Leeds, 15m SW of York.

Opening Times: Gardens: 2 Feb - 30 Sept: daily, 10.30am - 5.30pm. Closed 5 - 11 Jun. House: by appointment for groups (6+).

Admission: Garden only: Adult £2.95, Child under 5yrs Free, Child (under 16yrs)/ OAP £1.95.

Grounds suitable. WC. In grounds, on leads.

SPECIAL EVENTS

JUN 8 - 11: Bramham International Horse Trials & Yorkshire Country Fair.

BROCKFIELD HALL

Tel: 01904 489298

Warthill, York YO19 5XJ

Owner/Contact: Lord Martin Fitzalan Howard

Late Georgian house.

Location: OS Ref. SE664 550. 5m E of York off A166 or A64.

Opening Times: Aug: daily except Mons, 1 - 4pm. Tours by arrangement.

Admission: Adult £3.50, Child £1.

BRODSWORTH HALL & GARDENS

See page 340 for full page entry.

BRONTË PARSONAGE MUSEUM

Tel: 01535 642323 **Fax:** 01535 647131
e-mail: bronte@bronte.prestel.co.uk

Church St, Haworth, Keighley, West Yorkshire BD22 8DR

Owner: The Brontë Society **Contact:** The Administrator

Georgian Parsonage, former home of the Brontë family, now a museum with rooms furnished as in the sisters' day and displays of their personal treasures.

Location: OS Ref. SE029 373. 8m W of Bradford, 3m S of Keighley.

Opening Times: Apr - Sept: 10am - 5.30pm, Oct - Mar: 11am - 5pm. Daily except 1 Jan & 10 Jan - 4 Feb, 27 Dec 2000. Last admission 1/2 hour before closing.

Admission: Adult £3.80, Child £1.20, Conc. £2.80, Family £8.80.
Discounts for booked groups.

BURTON AGNES HALL

DRIFFIELD, YORKSHIRE YO25 0ND

Owner: *Burton Agnes Hall Preservation Trust Ltd* ***Contact:*** *Mrs Susan Cunliffe-Lister*

Tel: 01262 490324 **Fax:** 01262 490513

A lovely Elizabethan Hall containing treasures collected by the family over four centuries from the original carving and plasterwork to modern and Impressionist paintings. The Hall is surrounded by lawns and topiary yew. The old walled garden contains a maze, potager, jungle garden, campanula collection and colour gardens incorporating giant game boards. Children's corner.

Location: OS Ref. TA103 633. Off A166 between Driffield and Bridlington.

Opening Times: 1 Apr - 31 Oct: daily, 11am - 5pm.

Admission: House & Gardens: Adult £4.50, Child £2.25, OAP £4. Grounds only: Adult £2.25, Child £1, OAP £2. 10% reduction for groups of 30+.

Ground floor & grounds. Café. Ice-cream parlour.

Registered Charity No. 272796.

BROUGHTON HALL

SKIPTON, YORKSHIRE BD23 3AE

Tel: 01756 799608 **Fax:** 01756 700357
e-mail: tempest@broughtonhall.co.uk **e-mail:** infor@ruralsolutions.co.uk

Owner: *The Tempest Family* ***Contact:*** *The Estate Office*

The Hall was built in 1597 by the Tempest family and it continues to be their private home which provides it with a very special atmosphere. The building is Grade I listed and set in 3000 acres of parkland and rolling countryside and is available to groups for tours by prior arrangement throughout the year and also as a prestigious venue for business promotions and functions. The grounds were designed by Nesfield in 1855 including fine Italianate gardens, gazebo, fountains and balustrades. The magnificent conservatory is a particular feature. Filming often takes place at Broughton with its wide diversity of settings and locations and the owners appreciate and understand production requirements.

Separate from the Hall is the Broughton Hall Business Park formed from listed Estate buildings housing 38 companies employing 450 people in cutting edge office accommodation.

Location: OS Ref. SD943 507. On A59, 3m W of Skipton midway between the Yorkshire and Lancashire centres. Good air and rail links.

Open: Year round tours for groups by arrangement.

Admission: £5.

   By arrangement.  Excellent local hotels. 

BURTON AGNES MANOR HOUSE

Tel: 0191 269 1200

Burton Agnes, Bridlington, Humberside
Owner: English Heritage **Contact:** The North Regional Office
A rare example of a Norman house, altered and encased in brick in the 17th & 18th centuries.
Location: OS Ref. TA103 633. Burton Agnes village, 5m SW of Bridlington on A166.
Opening Times: Please telephone for details.
Admission: Free.

Patrick Lane.

Burton Agnes Manor House, Yorkshire.

BURTON CONSTABLE HALL

SKIRLAUGH, EAST YORKSHIRE HU11 4LN

Owner: *Burton Constable Foundation* ***Contact:*** *Mrs P Connelly*

Tel: 01964 562400 **Fax:** 01964 563229
Built in the 16th century and set in 300 acres of parkland landscaped by 'Capability' Brown, Burton Constable Hall is the magnificent ancestral home of the Constable family. Superb interiors containing paintings, prints and fine English furniture. 30 rooms open to view including a unique 'Cabinet of Curiosities', a fascinating Lamp Room and servants' corridors.
Location: OS Ref. TA193 369. 14m E of Beverley via A165 Bridlington Road, follow Historic House signs. 7m NE of Hull via B1238 to Sproatley then follow Historic House signs.
Open: Easter Sun - 31 Oct: Sat - Thur. Grounds & tearoom open 12 noon. Hall: 1 - 5pm.
Admission: Adult £4, Child £1.50, OAP £3.70, Family £9. Group rates available for 30+.

No photography in house.   By arrangement. 
In grounds on leads.

Registered Charity No. 1010121

BYLAND ABBEY

Tel: 01347 868614

Coxwold, Helmsley, North Yorkshire YO6 4BD
Owner: English Heritage **Contact:** The Custodian
Hauntingly beautiful ruin, set in peaceful meadows in the shadow of the Hambleton Hills. It illustrates later development of Cistercian churches, including a beautiful floor of mosaic tiles.
Location: OS100 Ref. SE549 789. 2m S of A170 between Thirsk and Helmsley, NE of Coxwold village.
Opening Times: 1 Apr - 30 Sept: daily 10am - 6pm. 1 - 31 Oct: daily, 10am - 5pm. Closed 1 - 2pm.
Admission: Adult £1.60, Child 80p, Student £1.20. 15% discount for groups (11+).

 Limited. On leads. Tel. for details.

CANNON HALL MUSEUM

Tel: 01226 790270 **Fax:** 01226 792117

Cawthorne, Barnsley, South Yorkshire S75 4AT
Owner: Barnsley Metropolitan Borough Council **Contact:** The Keeper
Late 17th century house, remodelled in the 1760s by John Carr. Contains decorative arts collections including fine furniture and paintings. Moorcroft pottery and Glass galleries. Also the Regimental Museum of the 13th/18th Hussars. Surrounding 18th century park landscaped by Richard Woods, with Walled Garden. Events and education programme.
Location: OS Ref. SE272 084. 6m NW of Barnsley of A635.
Opening Times: 1 Nov - 31 Mar: Sats, 10.30am - 5pm. Suns, 12 noon - 5pm. 1 Apr - 31 Oct: Tue - Sat, 10.30am - 5pm. Suns, 12 noon - 5pm. Last admission 4.15pm. Closed Christmas and New Year's Day.
Admission: Adults £1, Child/Conc. 50p, (1999 prices). Group discount (10+).

Partially suitable. WC. Seasonal.
In grounds, on leads. Please telephone for details.

CASTLE HOWARD

See page 341 for full page entry.

CAWTHORNE VICTORIA JUBILEE MUSEUM

Tel: 01226 790545

Taylor Hill, Cawthorne, Barnsley, Yorkshire S75 4HQ
Owner: Cawthorne Village **Contact:** Mrs Mary Herbert
A quaint and eccentric collection with something for everyone in a half-timbered building.
Location: OS Ref. SE285 080. Just W of the church in Cawthorne village. 1/4 m N of A635.
Opening Times: Palm Sun - end Oct: Sats, Suns & BH Mons, 2 - 5pm. Groups by appointment throughout the year.
Admission: Adult 50p, Child 20p.

CLIFFE CASTLE

Tel: 01535 618231

Keighley, West Yorkshire BD20 6LH
Owner: City of Bradford Metropolitan District Council **Contact:** Jane Whittaker
Typical Victorian manufacturer's mansion of 1878 with tall tower and garden. Now a museum.
Location: OS Ref. SE057 422. 3/4 m NW of Keighley off the A629.
Opening Times: Please telephone for details.
Admission: Free.

CLIFFORD'S TOWER

Tel: 01904 646940

Clifford Street, York, Yorkshire YO1 1SA
Owner: English Heritage **Contact:** The Custodian
A 13th century tower on one of two mottes thrown up by William the Conqueror to hold York. There are panoramic views of the city from the top of the tower.
Location: OS105 Ref. SE 605 515. York city centre.
Opening Times: 1 Apr - 30 Sept: daily, 10am - 6pm (9.30am - 7pm Jul & Aug). 1 - 31 Oct: daily, 10am - 5pm. 1 Nov - 31 Mar: daily, 10am - 4pm.
Admission: Adult £1.80, Child 90p, Conc. £1.40. 15% discount available for groups (11+).

Not suitable. In grounds, on leads.

CLIFTON PARK MUSEUM

Tel: 01709 823635

Clifton Park, Rotherham, Yorkshire S65 2AA
Owner: Rotherham Metropolitan Borough Council. **Contact:** Guy Kilminster
Furnished period rooms and one of the best collections of Rockingham porcelain in the country in an 18th century house set within a delightful park.
Location: OS Ref. SK435 926.
Opening Times: Mon - Thur & Sats, 10am - 5pm. Suns, 1.30 - 5pm (Apr - Sept) & 1.30 - 4.30pm (Oct - Mar).
Admission: Free.

CONISBROUGH CASTLE

Tel: 01709 863329

Conisbrough, Yorkshire
Owner: English Heritage **Contact:** The Administrator
The oldest circular keep in England and one of the finest medieval buildings.
Location: OS111 Ref. SK515 989. 4 1/2 m SW of Doncaster.
Opening Times: 1 Apr - 30 Sept: daily 10am - 5pm (6pm at weekends & BHs). 10 Oct - 31 Mar: daily, 10am - 4pm.
Admission: Adults £2.80, Child £1, Conc. £1.80, Family £6.75.

North East England

CONSTABLE BURTON HALL GARDENS

LEYBURN, NORTH YORKSHIRE DL8 5LJ

Owner/Contact: *M C A Wyvill Esq*

Tel: 01677 450428 **Fax:** 01677 450622

A delightful terraced woodland garden of lilies, ferns, hardy shrubs, roses and wild flowers attached to a beautiful Palladian house designed by John Carr (not open). Near to the entrance drive is a stream, bog garden and rockery. Impressive spring display of daffodils, aconites and snowdrops.

Location: OS Ref. SE164 913. 3m E of Leyburn off the A684.

Opening Times: Garden only: 26 Mar - 15 Oct: daily, 9am - 6pm.

Admission: Adult £2.50, Child (under 16yrs) 50p, OAP £2.

DUNCOMBE PARK

HELMSLEY, YORK YO62 5EB

Owner/Contact: *Lord & Lady Feversham*

Tel: 01439 770213 **Fax:** 01439 771114 **e-mail:** sally@duncombepark.com

Lord and Lady Feversham's restored family home in the North York Moors National Park. Built on a virgin plateau overlooking Norman Castle and river valley, it is surrounded by 35 acres of beautiful 18th century landscaped gardens and 400 acres of parkland with national nature reserve and veteran trees.

Location: OS SE604 830. Entrance just off Helmsley Market Square, signed off A170 Thirsk - Scarborough road.

Open: 2 Apr - 29 Oct. Apr & Oct: Sun - Thur. May - Sept: Sun - Fri. House & Gardens: 10.30am - 6pm (last admission 4pm). Parkland, tearoom, shop & walks: 10.30am - 5.30pm (last orders in tearoom 5.15pm).

Admission: House & Gardens: Adult £6, Child £3, Conc. £5, Family (2+2) £13.50 Groups (15+): £4.50. Gardens & Parkland: Adult £4, Child (10-16yrs) £2. Parkland: Adult £2, Child (10-16yrs) £1. Season ticket (2+2) £35.

Country walks, nature reserve, orienteering, conferences.

Banqueting facilities. Partially suitable. Licensed.

Obligatory. In park on leads.

CRAKEHALL WATERMILL

Tel: 01677 423240

Little Crakehall, Nr Bedale, North Yorkshire DL8 1HU

Owner/Contact: Mrs Gill

Site of a mill since 1086, still milling stone-ground wholemeal flour.

Location: OS Ref. SE244 902. 1/2 m from village centre.

Opening Times: Easter - End September: Closed Mons & Tues. Please telephone for details.

Admission: Adult £1, Child/OAP 60p (1999 prices).

DANBY WATERMILL

Tel: 01287 660330

Danby, Whitby, Yorkshire YO21 2JL

Owner/Contact: Frank & Brenda Palmer

350 year old watermill restored to working order.

Location: OS Ref. NZ708 082. 1/2 m from the Moors Centre in Danby, just before the bridge over the Esk.

Opening Times: Please contact for details.

Admission: Adult £1.50, Child/OAP 75p (1999 prices).

Duncombe Park, Yorkshire.

EASBY ABBEY

Tel: 0191 269 1200

Nr Richmond, North Yorkshire

Owner: English Heritage **Contact:** The Custodian

Substantial remains of the medieval abbey buildings stand by the River Swale near Richmond.

Location: OS92 Ref. NZ185 003. 1m SE of Richmond off B6271.

Opening Times: 1 Apr - 1 Nov: daily, 10am - 6pm or dusk in Oct.

Admission: Adult £1.60, Child 80p, Conc. £1.20.

EAST RIDDLESDEN HALL

Tel: 01535 607075 **Fax:** 01535 691462

Bradford Road, Keighley, West Yorkshire BD20 5EL

Owner: The National Trust **Contact:** Assistant Property Manager

Homely 17th century merchant's house with beautiful embroideries, Yorkshire carved oak furniture, fine ceilings and stonework. Explore the magnificent Great Barn or feed the hungry ducks. Delightful flower and herb borders.

Location: OS104 SE079 421. 1m NE of Keighley on S side of A650 in Riddlesden. 50yds from Leeds/Liverpool Canal. Bus: Frequent services from Skipton, Bradford and Leeds. Railway station at Keighley 2m.

Opening Times: 1 Apr - 5 Nov: daily except Mons, Thurs & Fris (open Good Fri, BH Mons & Mons in Jul & Aug), 12 noon - 5pm, Sats, 1 - 5pm.

Admission: Adult £3.50, Child £1.80, Family £8.80.

Partially suitable. WC.

Limited for coaches, please book.  Tel. for details.

Open all Year Index
PAGE 52

EPWORTH OLD RECTORY

Tel: 01427 872268

1 Rectory Street, Epworth, Doncaster, South Yorkshire DN9 1HX

Owner: World Methodist Council **Contact:** C J Barton (Warden)

1709 Queen Anne period house, John and Charles Wesley's boyhood home. Portraits, period furniture, Methodist memorabilia. Garden, picnic facilities, cinematic presentation.

Location: OS Ref. SE785 036. Epworth lies on A161, 3m S M180/J2. 10m N of Gainsborough. When in Epworth follow the Wesley Trail information boards.

Opening Times: 1 Mar - 31 Oct. Mar, Apr & Oct: Mon - Sat, 10am - 12 noon & 2 - 4pm, Suns, 2 - 4pm. May - Sept: Mon - Sat, 10am - 4.30pm, Suns, 2 - 4.30pm.

Admission: Adult £2.50, Children in full-time education £1, OAP £2, Family £6.

Ground floor & grounds suitable. Obligatory. Limited. Guide dogs only. 2 doubles.

FAIRFAX HOUSE

See page 342 for full page entry.

FOUNTAINS ABBEY & STUDLEY ROYAL

See page 343 for entry.

HANDS ON HISTORY

Tel: 01482 613902 **Fax:** 01482 613710

Market Place, Hull HU1 1EP

Owner: Hull City Council **Contact:** S R Green

Housed in the Old Grammar School this history resource centre offers hands on activities for the public and schools alike.

Location: OS Ref. TA099 285. 50 yds SW of the Church at centre of the Old Town.

Opening Times: School holidays and weekends open to the public. Please phone for details.

Admission: Free.

HAREWOOD HOUSE

See page 344 for full page entry.

HELMSLEY CASTLE

Tel: 014397 70442

Helmsley, North Yorkshire YO6 5AB

Owner: English Heritage **Contact:** The Custodian

Close to the market square, with a view of the town, is this 12th century castle. Spectacular earthworks surround a great ruined Norman keep. Exhibition and tableau on the castle's history.

Location: OS100 SE611 836. In Helmsley town.

Opening Times: 1 Apr - 30 Sept: daily, 10am - 6pm. 1 - 31 Oct, daily, 10am - 5pm. 1 Nov - 31 Mar: Wed - Sun, 10am - 4pm (closed 1 - 2pm). Closed 24 - 26 Dec.

Admission: Adult £2.30, Child £1.20, Conc £1.70. 15% discount for groups (11+).

 Tel. for details.

HELMSLEY WALLED GARDEN

Tel/Fax: 01439 771427

Cleveland Way, Helmsley, North Yorkshire YO6 5AH

Owner: Helmsley Walled Garden Ltd **Contact:** Paul Radcliffe/Lindsay Tait

A 5 acre walled garden under restoration. Historic glasshouses rescued, awaiting repair. Pigs and small animals.

Location: OS100 SE611 836. 25m N of York, 15m from Thirsk. In Helmsley follow signs to Cleveland Way.

Open: 1 Apr - 31 Oct: daily, 10.30am - 5pm. Nov - Mar: Sats/Suns, 12 noon - 4pm.

Admission: Adult £2, Child Free, Conc. £1.

Hovingham Hall, Yorkshire.

HOVINGHAM HALL

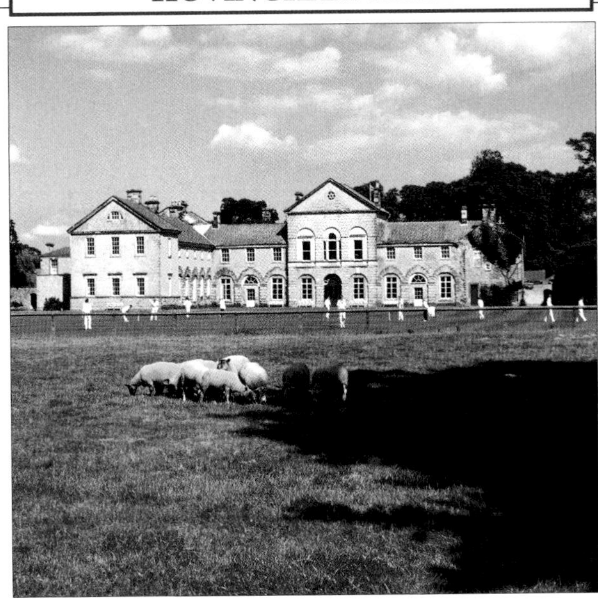

YORK, NORTH YORKSHIRE YO62 4LU

Owner: *Sir Marcus Worsley* ***Contact:*** *Mrs Lamprey*

Tel: 01653 628206 **Fax:** 01653 628668

Palladian house built c1760 by Thomas Worsley to his own design. Unique entry by huge riding school. Visitors see family portraits and rooms in everyday use; also extensive gardens with magnificent yew hedges, dovecot and private cricket ground, said to be the oldest in England.

Location: OS Ref. SE666 756. 18m N of York on Malton/Helmsley Road (B1257).

Opening Times: Apr - 30 Sept: 11am - 7pm by appointment only.

Admission: Adult £4. Groups(15+): £60 min. charge.

No photography in house. Partially suitable. Obligatory. Guide dogs only.

JERVAULX ABBEY

Tel: 01677 460391

Ripon, Yorkshire HG4 4PH

Owner/Contact: Mr I S Bourdon

Extensive ruins of a former Cistercian abbey.

Location: OS100 Ref. SE169 858. Beside the A6108 Ripon - Leyburn road, 5m SE of Leyburn and 5m NW of Masham.

Opening Times: Daily during daylight hours. Visitor centre: Mar - end Nov: daily, 10am - 5pm.

Admission: Adult £2, Child £1.50.

KIPLIN HALL

Tel: 01748 818178

Kiplin, Nr Scorton, Richmond, Yorkshire DL10 6AT

Owner: Kiplin Hall Trustees **Contact:** JW Kirby, Warden

17th century Jacobean house.

Location: OS Ref. SE274 976. Signposted from Scorton - Northallerton road (B6271).

Opening Times: Please telephone for details. Opening times are limited due to major refurbishment programme during 2000.

Admission: Please contact for details.

KIRKHAM PRIORY

Tel: 01653 618768

Kirkham, Whitwell-on-the-Hill, Yorkshire YO6 7JS

Owner: English Heritage **Contact:** The Custodian

The ruins of this Augustinian priory include a magnificent carved gatehouse.

Location: OS100 Ref. SE735 657. 5m SW of Malton on minor road off A64.

Opening Times: 1 Apr - 30 Sept: daily, 10am - 6pm. 1 - 31 Oct: daily, 10am - 5pm.

Admission: Adult £1.60, Child 80p, Conc. £1.20. 15% discount for groups (11+).

 Limited. On leads.

KNARESBOROUGH CASTLE

Tel: 01423 556188 **Fax:** 01423 556130

Knaresborough, North Yorkshire HG5 8AS **e-mail:** lg31@harrogate.gov.uk

Owner: Duchy of Lancaster **Contact:** Ms Mary Kershaw

Ruins of 14th century castle standing high above the town. Local history museum housed in Tudor Courthouse. Gallery devoted to the Civil War.

Location: OS Ref. SE349 569. 5m E of Harrogate, off A59.

Opening Times: Easter BH - 30 Sept: daily, 10.30am - 5pm.

Admission: Adult £2, Child/OAP £1.50, Family £5.50, Groups (10+) £1.50.

LEDSTON HALL

Tel: 01423 523423 **Fax:** 01423 521373

Hall Lane, Ledston, Castleford, West Yorkshire WF10 2BB

Owner/Contact: James Hare

17th century mansion with some earlier work.

Location: OS Ref. SE437 289. 2m N of Castleford, off A656.

Opening Times: Exterior only: May - Aug, Mon - Fri, 9am - 4pm. Other days by appointment.

Admission: Free.

LING BEECHES GARDEN

Tel: 0113 2892450

Ling Lane, Scarcroft, Leeds, Yorkshire LS14 3HX

Owner/Contact: Mrs A Rakusen

A 2 acre woodland garden designed by the owner.

Location: OS Ref. SE354 413. Off A58 midway between Leeds & Wetherby. At Scarcroft turn into Ling Lane, signed to Wike on brow of hill.

Opening Times: Twice a year for Northern Horticultural Society (telephone for details). Also by appointment.

Admission: Adult £2, Child Free.

LOTHERTON HALL

Tel: 0113 2813259 **Fax:** 0113 2812100

Aberford, West Yorkshire LS25 3EB

Owner: Leeds City Council **Contact:** Adam White

Late Victorian and Edwardian country house of great charm and character.

Location: OS92 Ref. SE450 360. 2$^1/_2$ m E of M1 J47 on B2177 the Towton Road.

Opening Times: 1 Apr - 31 Oct: Tue - Sat, 10am - 5pm, Suns, 1 - 5pm. 1 Nov - 31 Dec & Mar: Tue - Sat, 10am - 4pm, Suns, 12 noon - 4pm. Closed Jan & Feb.

Admission: Adult £2, Child 50p, Conc. £1. Groups: £1. Parking: £5 includes 1 yrs free admission to house. Day ticket: £2.

MARKENFIELD HALL

Tel: 01609 780306 **Fax:** 01609 777510

Hell Wath Lane, Ripon, Yorkshire HG4 3AD

Owner: The Lady Grantley **Contact:** Strutt & Parker

Fine example of a moated English Manor House (14th and 15th century).

Location: OS Ref. SE294 672. Local access from gate on W side A61, 3m S of Ripon.

Opening Times: Groups by appointment only.

Admission: Please contact for details.

Patrick Lane.

Burton Agnes Hall, Yorkshire.

MERCHANT ADVENTURERS' HALL

FOSSGATE, YORK YO1 9XD

Owner: *The Company of Merchant Adventurers* ***Contact:*** *The Clerk*

Tel/Fax: 01904 654818 **e-mail:** The.Clerk@mahall-york.demon.co.uk

The finest medieval guild hall in Europe, built in 1357/62 and substantially unaltered. In it the Merchants transacted their business, as their successors still do today. On the ground floor was their hospice, where they cared for the poor, and their private chapel, a unique survival in England. There are good collections of early portraits, furniture, silver and other objects used by the Merchants over the centuries, when their wealth and influence helped to make York the second city in England after London.

Location: OS Ref. SE606 518. Main entrance in Piccadilly, other entrance in Fossgate.

Opening Times: 3 Jan - 20 Apr, 1 Oct - 23 Dec & 3 Jan - 12 Apr 01: Mon - Sat, 9.30am - 3.30pm (closed Suns). 21 Apr - 30 Sept: Mon - Sat, 9.30am - 5pm, Suns, 12 noon - 4pm. Closed 24 Dec - 2 Jan 01.

Admission: Adult £2, Child (7-17yrs) 70p, Child under 7 Free, Conc. £1.70. Group rates available by prior arrangement.

Wedding receptions. Ground floor & grounds suitable. WCs. By arrangement. In grounds, on leads.

MIDDLEHAM CASTLE

Tel: 01969 623899

Middleham, Leyburn, Yorkshire DL8 4RJ

Owner: English Heritage **Contact:** The Custodian

This childhood home of Richard III stands controlling the river that winds through Wensleydale. There is a massive 12th century keep with splendid views of the surrounding countryside from the battlements.

Location: OS99 Ref. SE128 875. At Middleham, 2m S of Leyburn of A6108.

Opening Times: 1 Apr - 30 Sept: daily, 10am - 6pm. 1 - 31 Oct, daily, 10am - 5pm. 1 Nov - 31 Mar: Wed - Sun, 10am - 4pm (closed 1 - 2pm). Closed 24 - 26 Dec.

Admission: Adult £2.30, Child £1.20, Conc. £1.70. 15% discount for groups (11+).

Exhibition. Grounds suitable. In grounds, on leads. Tel. for details.

MOTHER SHIPTON'S CAVE & PETRIFYING WELL

Tel: 01423 864600

Prophecy House, Knaresborough, North Yorkshire HG5 8DD

Contact: Mr McBratney, General Manager

The cave and well lie at the heart of the Mother Shipton Estate - a relic of the ancient forest of Knaresborough.

Location: OS Ref. SE346 565. Access from A59 at S end of bridge then by riverside footpath.

Opening Times: 12 Feb - Sunday 3 Dec: daily 9.30am - 5pm. Also open weekends from 4 Dec - 12 Feb (2001).

Admission: Adult £4.75, Child £3.65 (under 5yrs Free), OAP £4.45, Family (2+2) £13.15.

Ripley Castle, Yorkshire.

MOUNT GRACE PRIORY

SADDLE BRIDGE, NORTH YORKSHIRE DL6 3JG

Owner: *National Trust* ***Managed by:*** *English Heritage* ***Contact:*** *The Custodian*

Tel: 01609 883494

Hidden in tranquil wooded countryside at the foot of the Cleveland Hills, one of the loveliest settings of any English priory, and the best preserved Carthusian monastery in England. Monks lived as hermits in their cells and one cell, recently restored, is furnished to give a clear picture of their austere routine of work and prayer. Visitors enter through the manor built by Thomas Lascelles in 1654 on the site of the monastery guest house. It was rebuilt at the turn of the century using traditional techniques, typical of the Arts and Crafts movement.

Location: OS Ref. SE449 985. 12m N of Thirsk, 7m NE of Northallerton on A19.

Opening Times: 1 Apr - 30 Sept: daily, 10am - 6pm. 1 - 31 Oct: daily, 10am - 5pm. 1 Nov - 31 Mar: Wed - Sun, 10am - 4pm (closed 1 - 2pm). Closed 24 - 26 Dec.

Admission: Adult £2.80, Child £1.40, Conc. £2.10. 15% discount for groups (11+).

Ground floor & grounds suitable. Tel. for details.

THE MUSEUM OF SOUTH YORKSHIRE LIFE

Tel: 01302 782342

Cusworth Hall, Cusworth Lane, Doncaster, South Yorkshire DN5 7TU

Owner: Doncaster Metropolitan Borough Council **Contact:** Mr F Carpenter, Curator

A magnificent Grade I country house set in a landscaped parkland and built in 1740, with a chapel and other rooms designed by James Paine, the house is now the home of a museum showing the changing home, work and social conditions of the region over the last 250 years.

Location: OS Ref. SE547 039. A1(M)/J37, then A635 and right into Cusworth Lane.

Opening Times: Mon - Fri, 10am - 5pm. Sats, 11am - 5pm, Suns, 1 - 5pm. Closes at 4pm Dec & Jan.

Admission: Free.

Shibden Hall, Yorkshire.

NEWBURGH PRIORY

Tel: 01347 868435

Coxwold, Yorkshire YO6 4AS

Owner/Contact: Sir George Wombwell Bt

Augustinian priory founded in 1145 converted into Tudor mansion, and again later in 18th century. Beautiful water garden.

Location: OS Ref. SE541 764. 7m SE Thirsk. 1/2 m SE of Coxwold.

Opening Times: Apr - end Jun: Weds & Suns: House: 2.30 - 4.45pm, Garden: 2 - 6pm. Guided tours approx 60 mins. (please telephone to confirm times).

Admission: Gardens only: £2. House & Grounds: £3.50. Child Free. (1999 prices).

NEWBY HALL & GARDENS

See page 345 for full page entry.

NORTON CONYERS

Tel: 01765 640333 **Fax:** 01765 692772

Nr Ripon, North Yorkshire HG4 5EQ

Owner: Sir James and Lady Graham **Contact:** Lady Graham

Visited by Charlotte Brontë in 1839, Norton Conyers is an original of the 'Thornfield Hall' in *Jane Eyre* and a family legend was an inspiration for the mad Mrs Rochester. Building is late medieval with Stuart and Georgian additions. Friendly atmosphere, resulting from 376 years of occupation by the same family. 18th century walled garden near house, with orangery and herbaceous borders. Small plant sales area specialising in unusual hardy plants. Pick your own fruit in season.

Location: OS Ref. SF319 763. 4m N of Ripon. 3 1/2m from the A1.

Opening Times: House & Garden: 23 Apr - 3 Sept: Suns & BH Mons. 3 - 8 Jul: daily, house 2 - 5pm, garden, 11.30am - 5pm.

Admission: House: Adult £3, Child (10-16yrs)/Conc. £2.50. Garden: Free, donations welcome, but charges are made at charity openings.

No photography. No stilettos in house. Partially suitable. WC. By arrangement. In grounds, on leads.

NOSTELL PRIORY

Tel: 01924 863892 **Fax:** 01924 865282

Wakefield, West Yorkshire WF4 1QE

Owner: National Trust **Contact:** The Property Manager

Location: OS Ref. SE403 175. 6m SE of Wakefield, off A638 Wakefield to Doncaster road.

Opening Times: Nostell Priory is closed in 2000 for the upgrade of services in the house but will open for occasional events in the grounds. Please telephone for further details.

Admission: Please contact for details.

NUNNINGTON HALL

Tel: 01439 748283 **Fax:** 01439 748284

Nunnington, North Yorkshire Y062 5UY

Owner: National Trust **Contact:** The Visitor Manager

17th century manor house with fine panelled hall and staircase. Carlisle collection of miniature rooms on display, walled garden with peacocks, orchard and clematis collection.

Location: OS Ref. SE670 795. In Ryedale, 4 1/2 m SE of Helmsley, 1 1/2 m N of B1257.

Opening Times: 1 Apr - 29 Oct: daily except Mons & Tues (open BH Mons). 1 Jun - 31 Aug: daily except Mons (open BH Mons). Apr - Oct: 1.30 - 4.30pm. 1 May - end Sept: 1.30 - 5pm.

Admission: House and Garden: Adult £4, Child £2. Family £10. Garden only: Adult £1.50, Child Free.

Ground floor & grounds suitable. WC. Guide dogs only.

OLD SLENINGFORD HALL

Tel: 01765 635229 **Fax:** 01765 635485

Ripon, North Yorkshire HG4 3JD

Contact: Mrs Ramsden

Unusual garden with extensive lawns, interesting trees, lake and islands watermill in walled kitchen garden and Victorian fernery.

Location: OS99 Ref. SE265 768. From Ripon on A6108. After North Stainley take 2nd left, follow signs to Mickley for 1m from main road.

Opening Times: Spring BH Mon, Whit BH Sun & Mon also all year by appointment.

Admission: Adult £2.50, Child 50p.

ORMESBY HALL

Tel: 01642 324188

Church Lane, Ormesby, Middlesbrough TS7 9AS

Owner: National Trust **Contact:** The House Manager

A mid 18th century house with opulent decoration inside, including fine plasterwork by contemporary craftsmen. A Jacobean doorway with a carved family crest survives from the earlier house on the site. The stable block, attributed to Carr of York, is a particularly fine mid 18th century building with an attractive courtyard leased to the Mounted Police; also an attractive garden with holly walk.

Location: OS Ref. NZ530 167. 3m SE of Middlesbrough.

Opening Times: 2 Apr - 29 Oct: daily except Mons, Fris & Sats (open Good Fri & BH Mons), 2 - 5pm. Garden tours, last Thur of each month (please enquire for further details).

Admission: House, garden, railway and exhibitions: Adult £3.50, Child £1.70, Family £8.50. Garden, railway and exhibitions: Adult £2.20, Child £1.

Ground floor & grounds suitable. WC.

PARCEVALL HALL GARDENS

Tel: 01756 720311

Skyreholme, Skipton, Yorkshire BD23 6DE **Contact:** Jo Makin (Administrator)

Owner: Walsingham College (Yorkshire Properties) Ltd.

Location: OS Ref. SE068 613. E side of Upper Wharfedale, $1^{1}/_{2}$ m NE of Appletreewick. 12m NNW of Ilkley by B6160 and via Burnsall.

Opening Times: 1 Apr - 31 Oct: 10am - 6pm.

Admission: £2.50, Child 50p.

PICKERING CASTLE 

Tel: 01751 474989

Pickering, Yorkshire YO18 7AX

Owner: English Heritage **Contact:** The Custodian

A splendid motte and bailey castle, once a royal ranch. It is well preserved, with much of the original walls, towers and keep, and there are spectacular views over the surrounding countryside. There is an exhibition on the castle's history.

Location: OS100 Ref. SE800 845. In Pickering, 15m SW of Scarborough.

Opening Times: 1 Apr - 30 Sept: daily, 10am - 6pm. 1 - 31 Oct: daily, 10am - 5pm. 1 Nov - 31 Mar: Wed - Sun, 10am - 4pm (closed 1 - 2pm). Closed 24 - 26 Dec.

Admission: Adult £2.30, Child £1.20, Conc. £1.70. 15% discount for groups (11+).

Partially suitable. Limited. In grounds, on leads.

RED HOUSE MUSEUM & OAKWELL HALL COUNTRY PARK

See page 346 for full page entry.

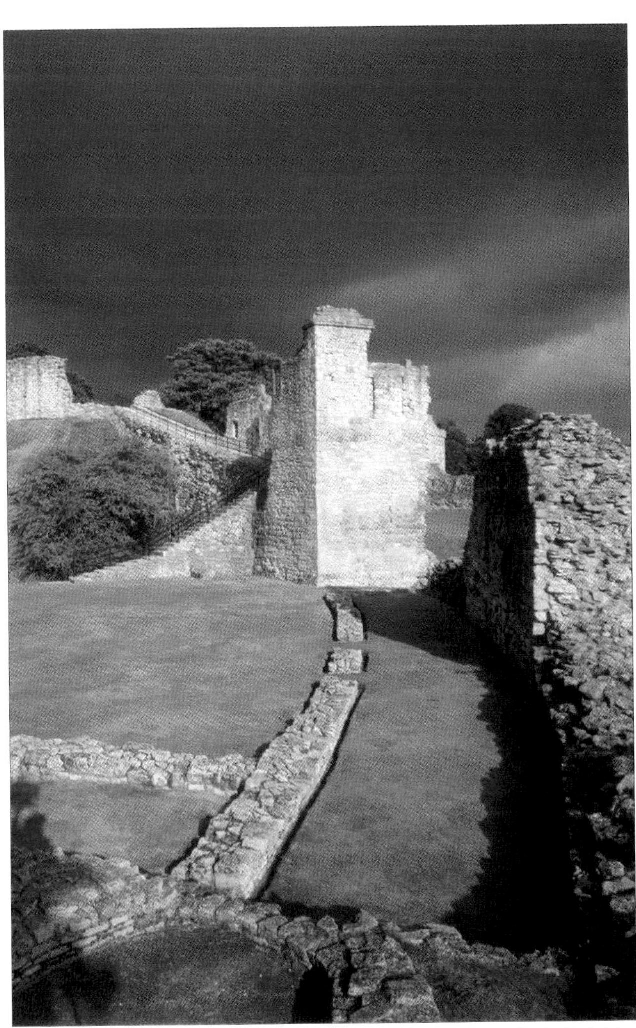

Pickering Castle, Yorkshire.

RICHMOND CASTLE

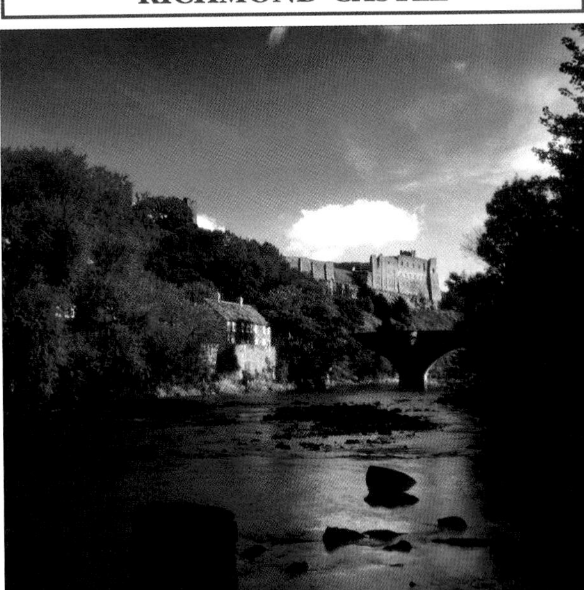

RICHMOND, NORTH YORKSHIRE DL10 4QW

Owner: *English Heritage* **Contact:** *The Custodian*

Tel: 01748 822493

A splendid medieval fortress, with a fine 12th century keep and 11th century remains of the curtain wall and domestic buildings. There are magnificent views from the 100 feet high keep.

Location: OS92 Ref. NZ174 006. In Richmond.

Opening Times: 1 Apr - 30 Sept: daily, 10am - 6pm. 1 - 31 Oct: daily, 10am - 5pm. 1 Nov - 31 Mar: daily, 10am - 4pm (closed 1 - 2pm). Closed 24- 26 Dec.

Admission: Adult £2.30, Child £1.20, Conc. £1.70. 15% discount for groups (11+).

Partially suitable. In grounds, on leads. Tel. for details.

RIEVAULX ABBEY

RIEVAULX, Nr HELMSLEY, NORTH YORKSHIRE YO6 5LB

Owner: *English Heritage* **Contact:** *The Custodian*

Tel: 01439 798228

In a deeply wooded valley by the River Rye you can see some of the most spectacular monastic ruins in England, dating from the 12th century. The church has the earliest large Cistercian nave in Britain. A fascinating exhibition shows how successfully the Cistercians at Rievaulx ran their many businesses and explains the part played by Abbot Ailred, who ruled for twenty years. New for 2000: exhibition and interactive display.

Location: OS100 Ref. SE577 849. $2^{1}/_{4}$ m W of Helmsley on minor road off B1257.

Opening Times: 1 Apr - 30 Sept: daily, 10am - 6pm (Jul & Aug: 9.30am - 7pm). 1 - 31 Oct: daily, 10am - 5pm. 1 Nov - 31 Mar: daily, 10am - 4pm. Closed 24- 26 Dec.

Admission: Adult £3.40, Child £1.70, Conc. £2.60. 15% discount for groups (11+).

Partially suitable.   On leads. Tel. for details.

RIEVAULX TERRACE AND TEMPLES

Tel: 01439 748283

Rievaulx, Helmsley, North Yorkshire YO62 5LJ

Owner: The National Trust **Contact:** The Visitor Manager

A 1/2 m long grass-covered terrace and adjoining woodlands with vistas over Rievaulx Abbey and Rye valley to Ryedale and the Hambleton Hills. There are two mid 18th century temples: the Ionic Temple has elaborate ceiling paintings and fine 18th century furniture. A permanent exhibition in the basement is on English landscape design in the 18th century. An abundance of wild flowers clothe the terrace in spring and summer.

Location: OS Ref. SE579 848. 2 1/2 m NW of Helmsley on B1257. E of the Abbey.

Opening Times: 1 Apr - 29 Oct. Apr & Oct: daily, 10.30am - 5pm (4pm in Oct). May - Sept: daily, 10.30am - 5pm.

Admission: Adult £3, Child £1.50, Family £7.50.

Grounds suitable. In grounds, on leads.

RIPLEY CASTLE

See page 347 for full page entry.

RIPON CATHEDRAL

Tel: 01765 604108 (information on tours etc.)

Ripon, Yorkshire HG4 1QR

Contact: Canon Keith Punshon

One of the oldest crypts in Europe (672). Marvellous choir stalls and misericords (500 years old). Almost every type of architecture. Treasury.

Location: OS Ref. SE314 711. 5m W signposted off A1, 12m N of Harrogate.

Opening Times: All year: 8am - 6pm.

Admission: Donations. £2 per head pre-booked guided tours.

RIPON WORKHOUSE

Tel: 01765 602142

Allhallowgate, Ripon Yorkshire

Contact: Mr D Gowling, 01765 602142

The workhouse shows restored vagrants' wards and the treatment of paupers.

Location: OS Ref. SE312 712 Close to Market Square.

Opening Times: Please telephone for details.

Admission: Adult £1, Child 50p, Conc. 60p. (1999 prices)

ROCHE ABBEY

Tel: 01709 812739

Maltby, Rotherham, South Yorkshire S66 8NW

Owner: English Heritage **Contact:** The Custodian

This Cistercian monastery, founded in 1147, lies in a secluded landscaped valley sheltered by limestone cliffs and trees. Some of the walls still stand to their full height and excavation has revealed the complete layout of the abbey.

Location: OS111 Ref. SK544 898. 1m S of Maltby off A634.

Opening Times: 1 Apr - 30 Sept: daily, 10am - 6pm. 1 - 31 Oct: daily, 10am - 5pm.

Admission: Adult £1.60, Child 80p, Conc. £1.20. 15% discount for groups (11+).

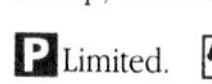  

Partially suitable. Limited. In grounds, on leads. Tel. for details.

RYDALE FOLK MUSEUM

Tel: 01751 417367

Hutton Le Hole, York, North Yorkshire YO6 6UA

Owner: The Crosland Foundation **Contact:** Martin Watts

13 historic buildings showing the lives of ordinary folk from earliest times to the present day.

Location: OS Ref. SE705 902. Follow signs from Hutton Le Hole.

Opening Times: 12 Mar - 5 Nov: 10am - 5.30pm last admission 4.30pm.

Admission: Adult £3.25, Child £1.75, Conc. £2.75 (1999 prices).

ST WILLIAM'S COLLEGE

Tel: 01904 557233 **Fax:** 01904 557234

5 College Street, York, Yorkshire YO1 2JF

Owner: The Dean and Chapter of York **Contact:** Sandie Clarke

15th century medieval home of Minster Chantry Priests. Three large medieval halls, available for functions, conferences, weddings, medieval banquets, etc. Halls open to view when not in use. Information Centre.

Location: OS Ref. SE605 522. College Street, York.

Opening Times: 10am - 5pm.

Admission: Adult 60p, Child 30p. For further details please telephone.

SCAMPSTON HALL

Tel: 01944 758224 **Fax:** 01944 758700

Scampston, Malton, North Yorkshire YO17 8NG

Owner/Contact: Sir Charles Legard Bt

Opened for the first time in 1997, this country house has remained in the same family since it was built towards the end of the 17th century. The house was extensively remodelled in 1801 by the architect Thomas Leverton and has fine Regency interiors. It houses an important collection of works of art including pictures by Gainsborough, Marlow, Scott and Wilson. The park was laid out under the guidance of 'Capability' Brown and includes 10 acres of lakes and a Palladian bridge. The garden features a recently restored 19th century walk in rock and water garden with a collection of alpines, some of which are available for sale.

Location: OS100 Ref. SE865 755. 5m E of Malton, off A64.

Opening Times: 21 May - 4 Jun & 23 Jul - 6 Aug (closed Sats), 1.30 - 5pm. Last admission 4.30pm.

Admission: House & Garden: £5, Garden £2, no concessions. Groups and coaches by appointment only. Prices for groups by arrangement.

Not suitable. Guided tours only.

SCARBOROUGH CASTLE

Tel: 01723 372451

Castle Road, Scarborough, North Yorkshire YO11 1HY

Owner: English Heritage **Contact:** The Custodian

Spectacular coastal views from the walls of this enormous 12th century castle. The buttressed castle walls stretch out along the cliff edge and remains of the great rectangular stone keep still stand to over three storeys high. There is also the site of a 4th century Roman signal station. The castle was frequently attacked, but despite being blasted by cannons of the Civil War and bombarded from the sea during World War I, it is still a spectacular place to visit.

Location: OS101, Ref. TA050 893. Castle Road, E of town centre.

Opening Times: 1 Apr - 30 Sept: daily, 10am - 6pm. 1 - 31 Oct: daily, 10am - 5pm. 1 Nov - 31 Mar: Wed - Sun, 10am - 4pm (closed 1 -2 pm). Closed 24 - 26 Dec.

Admission: Adult £2.30, Child £1.20, Conc. £1.70. 15% discount for groups (11+).

Partially suitable. Inclusive. In grounds, on leads. Tel. for details.

SEWERBY HALL & GARDENS

Tel: 01262 673769 **Fax:** 01262 673090 **e-mail:** museum@pop3.poptel.org.uk

Church Lane, Sewerby, Bridlington, East Yorkshire Y015 1EA

Owner: East Riding of Yorkshire Council **Contact:** Peter Cappleman

Sewerby Hall and Gardens, set in 50 acres of parkland, dates back to 1715. The Georigan house contains: 19th century orangery; history/archeology displays; art galleries and an Amy Johnson Room. The Grounds include: walled gardens, woodland, children's zoo and play area, golf and putting.

Location: OS Ref. TA203 690. 2m N of Bridlington in Sewerby village.

Opening Times: Hall: 19 Feb - 18 Apr, Sat - Tues, 11am - 4pm; 21 Apr - 29 Oct, Daily 10am - 6pm; 30 Oct - 17 Dec, Sat - Tues, 11am - 4pm. Gardens only: daily, dawn - dusk.

Admission: Please telephone for admission prices.

Licensed. In grounds, on leads.

SHANDY HALL

Tel/Fax: 01347 868465

Coxwold, York YO61 4AD

Owner: The Laurence Sterne Trust **Contact:** Mrs J Monkman

Built as a timber-framed hall in the 15th century.

Location: OS Ref. SE531 773. W end of Coxwold village, 4m E of A19 & 20m N of York, via Easingwold.

Opening Times: 1 May - 30 Sept: Weds, 2 - 4.30pm. Suns, 2.30 - 4.30pm. Other times by appointment. Garden: 1 May - 30 Sept: Sun - Fri, 11am - 4.30pm.

Admission: Hall & Garden: Adult £3.50, Child £1.50. Garden only: Adult £2.50, Child £1.

SHIBDEN HALL

Tel: 01422 352246 **Fax:** 01422 348440

Lister's Road, Halifax, West Yorkshire HX3 6XG

Owner: Calderdale MBC **Contact:** Valerie Stansfield

A half-timbered manor house, the home of Anne Lister set in a landscaped park. Oak furniture, carriages and an array of objects make Shibden an intriguing place to visit.

Location: OS Ref. SE106 257. 1 1/2 m E of Halifax off A58.

Opening Times: 1 Mar - 30 Nov: Mon - Sat, 10am - 5pm. Suns, 12 noon - 5pm. Last admission 4.30pm. Dec - Feb: Mon - Sat, 10am - 4pm. Suns, 12 noon - 4pm.

Admission: Adult £1.90, Child £1, Conc. £1, Family £5.

 Ground floor & grounds suitable.  Guide dogs only. 

SION HILL HALL

Tel: 01845 587206 **Fax:** 01845 587486

Kirby Wiske, Thirsk, North Yorkshire YO7 4EU

Owner: H W Mawer Trust **Contact:** R M Mallaby

Falconry Centre: 01845 587522 **Fax:** 01845 523735

Antique Centre/Tearoom: 01845 587071

Designed in 1912 by the renowned York architect Walter H Brierley, 'the Lutyens of the North'. Received an award from Royal Institute of British Architects as being of 'outstanding architectural merit'. Sion Hill contains the H W Mawer collection of fine furniture, porcelain, paintings and clocks in superb room settings.

Location: OS Ref. SE373 844. B44 Signed off A167. 6m S of Northallerton, 4m NW of Thirsk, 8m E of A1 via A61.

Opening Times: Hall: Good Fri - 30 Sept: Wed - Sun & BH Mons, 1 - 5pm, last entry 4pm. Falconry, Tearoom & Antique Centre: Mar - Oct: daily, 10.30am - 5.30pm.

Admission: Hall: Adult £4, Child under 12 Free (if accompanied by an adult), Conc. £3.50.

Partially suitable. WC. In grounds, on leads.

SKIPTON CASTLE

See page 348 for full page entry.

SLEDMERE HOUSE

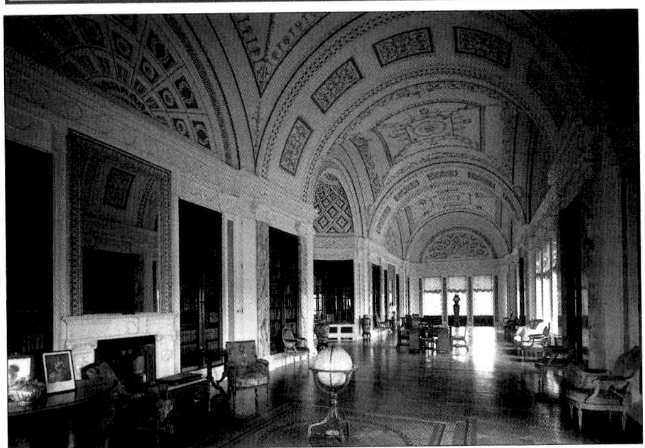

SLEDMERE, DRIFFIELD, EAST YORKSHIRE YO25 3XG

Owner: *Sir Tatton Sykes Bt* ***Contact:*** *Mrs Anne Hines*

Tel: 01377 236637 **Fax:** 01377 236500

Sledmere House is the home of Sir Tatton Sykes, 8th Baronet. There has been a manor house at Sledmere since medieval times. The present house was designed and built by Sir Christopher Sykes, 2nd Baronet, a diary date states "*June 17th, 1751 laid the first stone of the new house at Sledmere.*" Sir Christopher employed a fellow Yorkshireman, Joseph Rose, the most famous English plasterer of his day, to execute the decoration of Sledmere. Rose's magnificent work at Sledmere was unique in his career. A great feature at Sledmere is the 'Capability' Brown parkland and the beautiful 18th century walled rose gardens. Also worthy of note is the recently laid out knot-garden.

Location: OS Ref. SE931 648. Off the A166 between York & Bridlington. 1/2 m drive from York, Bridlington & Scarborough.

Opening Times: 2 Apr - 1 Oct: closed Sats & Mons but open BH Sats & Mons: 11.30am - 4.30pm.

Admission: House & Gardens: Adult £4.50, Child £2, OAP £4. Gardens & Park: Adult £1.50, Child £1.

No photography in house. Licensed. By arrangement. In grounds on leads. Guide dogs in house.

SPOFFORTH CASTLE

Tel: 0191 269 1200

Harrogate, Yorkshire

Owner: English Heritage **Contact:** The Northern Regional Office

This manor house has some fascinating features including an undercroft built into the rock. It was once owned by the Percy family.

Location: OS Ref. SE360 511. 3 1/2 m SE of Harrogate on minor road off A661 at Spofforth.

Opening Times: 1 Apr - 30 Sept: daily, 10am - 6pm. 1 - 31 Oct: daily, 10am - 6pm or dusk if earlier. 1 Nov - 31 Mar: 10am - 4pm.

Admission: Free.

STOCKELD PARK

WETHERBY, YORKSHIRE LS22 4AH

Owner: *Mr and Mrs P G F Grant* ***Contact:*** *Mrs L A Saunders*

Tel: 01937 586101 **Fax:** 01937 580084

Stockeld is a beautifully proportioned Palladian villa designed by James Paine in 1763, featuring a magnificent cantilevered staircase in the central oval hall. Stockeld is still very much a family home, with a fine collection of 18th and 19th century furniture and paintings. The house is surrounded by lovely gardens of lawns, large herbaceous and shrub borders, fringed by woodland, and set in 100 acres of fine parkland in the midst of an extensive farming estate.

Location: OS Ref. SE376 497. York 12m, Harrogate 5m, Leeds 12m.

Opening Times: 27 Apr - 12 Oct: Thurs only, 2 - 5pm. Groups please book.

Admission: Adult £3. Group prices on application.

House only. Obligatory.

STUDLEY ROYAL: ST MARY'S CHURCH

Tel: 01765 608888

Ripon, Yorkshire

Owner: English Heritage **Contact:** The Custodian

A magnificent Victorian church, designed by William Burges in the 1870s, with a highly decorated interior. Coloured marble, stained glass, gilded and painted figures and a splendid organ.

Location: OS Ref. SE278 703. 2 1/2 m W of Ripon off B6265, in grounds of Studley Royal estate.

Opening Times: 1 Apr - 30 Sept: daily, 1 - 5pm.

Admission: Free.

Scarborough Castle, Yorkshire.

SUTTON PARK

SUTTON-ON-THE-FOREST, NORTH YORKSHIRE YO61 1DP

Owner: *Sir Reginald & Lady Sheffield* ***Contact:*** *Mrs A Wilkinson*

Tel: 01347 810249/811239 **Fax:** 01347 811251 **e-mail:** suttonpark@fsbdial.co.uk

The Yorkshire home of Sir Reginald and Lady Sheffield. Charming example of early Georgian architecture. Magnificent plasterwork by Cortese. Rich collection of 18th century furniture, paintings, porcelain, needlework, beadwork. All put together with great style to make a most inviting house. Award winning gardens attract enthusiasts from home and abroad.

Location: OS Ref. SE583 646. 8m N of York on B1363 Helmsley Road.

Opening Times: House: 2 Apr - 27 Sept: Suns & Weds, also Good Fri - Easter Mon, 21 - 24 Apr & BH Mons, 1.30 - 5pm. Tearoom: as house, 12 noon - 5pm. Private Groups: Any other day of the week by appointment. House open Oct - Mar for private groups only.

Admission: House & Garden: Adult £4.50, Child £2.50, Conc. £4. Gardens only: Adult £2, Child 50p, Conc. £1.50. Coach parties: £4, gardens only £1.50. Private Groups: £5. Caravans: £4 per night.

No photography. Hosted lunches & dinners. Obligatory. 3 double with ensuite bathrooms.

TEMPLE NEWSAM HOUSE

Tel: 0113 2647321 **Fax:** 0113 2602285

Leeds LS15 0AE

Owner: Leeds City Council **Contact:** Denise Lawson

A Tudor-Jacobean mansion with over thirty rooms open to the public.

Location: OS Ref. SE358 321. 5m E of city centre, off A63 Selby Road. M1/J46.

Opening Times: 1 Apr - 31 Oct: Tue - Sat, 10am - 5pm. Suns, 1 - 5pm. 1 Nov - 31 Dec & Mar: Tue - Sat, 10am - 4pm, Suns, 12 noon - 4pm. Last admission 3/4 hr before closing time. Closed Jan & Feb.

Admission: Adult £2, Child 50p, Conc. £1. Groups (10+): Adult £1, Child 50p.

THORP PERROW ARBORETUM

Tel/Fax: 01677 425323

Bedale, North Yorkshire DL8 2PR **e-mail:** ropner.thorp@btinternet.com

Owner: Sir John Ropner Bt **Contact:** Louise Seymour

85 acres of woodland walks. One of the largest collections of trees and shrubs in the north of England, including a 16th century medieval spring wood and 19th century pinetum. The arboretum holds 3 National Collections - ash, lime and walnut. There are tree and nature trails, children's trail, playground with mini beast station, tearoom and plant centre.

Location: OS Ref. SE258 851. Bedale - Ripon road, S of Bedale., 4m from Leeming Bar on A1.

Opening Times: All year: dawn - dusk.

Admission: Adult £3.50, Child £2, OAP £2.50, Family (2+2) £10, (2+4) £14.

Picnic area. Children's playground. By arrangement. In grounds, on leads.

TREASURER'S HOUSE

MINSTER YARD, YORK, NORTH YORKSHIRE YO1 7JH

Owner: *The National Trust* ***Contact:*** *The Property Manager*

Tel: 01904 624247

An elegant townhouse situated in the tranquil surroundings of the Minster Close. A series of period rooms is the setting for a fine collection of furniture and paintings given to the National Trust by Yorkshire industrialist Frank Green, who lived here from 1897 to 1930. Introductory video and exhibition.

Location: OS Ref. SE604 523. The N side of York Minster. Entrance on Chapter House St.

Opening Times: 1 Apr - 31 Oct: daily except Fris, 10.30am - 4.30pm.

Admission: Adult £3.50, Child £1.75. Family £8.50. Groups by arrangement.

Ground floor suitable. WC. Licensed.

WAKEFIELD CATHEDRAL

Tel: 01924 373923 **Fax:** 01924 215054

Northgate, Wakefield, West Yorkshire WF1 1HG

Owner: Church of England **Contact:** Mr F Arnold, Head Verger

Built on the site of a previous Saxon church, this 14th century Parish Church became a cathedral in 1888 and was extended by Pearson and completed by his son. It also boasts, at 247ft, the highest spire in Yorkshire.

Location: OS Ref. SE333 208. Wakefield city centre. M1/ J39-41, M62/J29W, J30 E.

Opening Times: Mon - Sat: 8am - 5pm. Suns: between services only. Sunday Services: Holy Communion: 8am. Parish Eucharist: 9.15am. Solemn Eucharist: 11am. Choral Evensong (Winter): 4pm. Choral Evensong (Summer): 6.30pm. Daily Services: Holy Communion: Daily, 8am plus 10.30am on Weds & Sats and 12.30pm on Fris. Choral Evensong: Thurs, 6.30pm. Said Evensong: Mons, Tues, Fris & Sats, 5pm.Weds (girls' choir) Choral Evensong 6pm.

Admission: Free admission. Donations welcome.

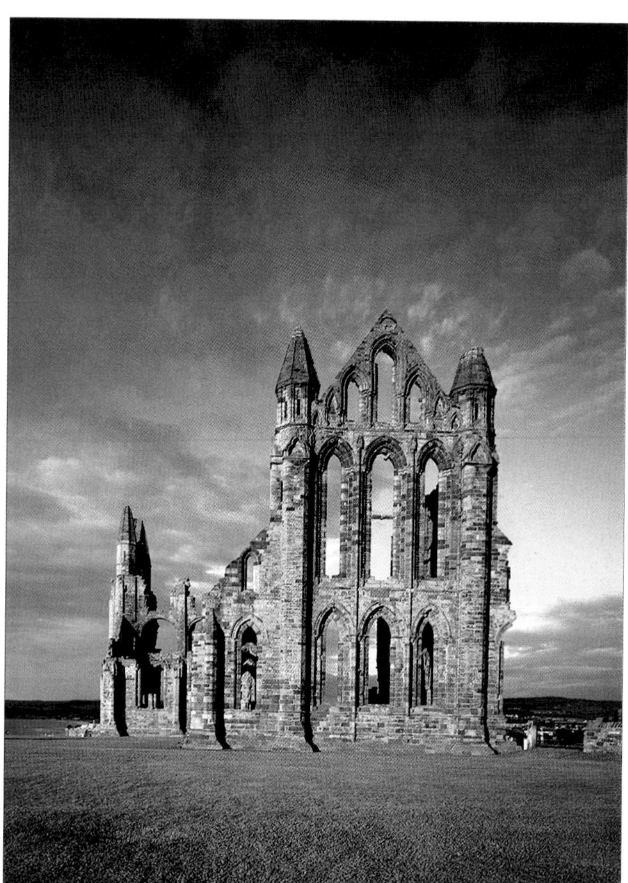

Whitby Abbey, Yorkshire.

WENTWORTH CASTLE GARDENS

Tel: 01226 731269

Lowe Lane, Stainborough, Barnsley, Yorkshire S75 3ET

Owner: Barnsley MBC **Contact:** Chris Margrave

300 years old, these gardens are the only Grade I listed gardens in South Yorkshire, 28 listed buildings and monuments and the national collection of rhododendrons, magnolias and Williamsii Camellias.

Location: OS Ref. SE320 034. 5km W of Barnsley, M1/J36 via Birdwell & Rockley Lane then Lowe Lane.

Opening Times: May & Jun: by guided tours only. Please contact C Margrave for times and dates.

Admission: £2.50, Conc. £1.50.

WHITBY ABBEY

English Heritage Photographic Library

WHITBY, NORTH YORKSHIRE YO22 4JT

Owner: *English Heritage* ***Contact:*** *The Custodian*

Tel: 01947 603568

An ancient holy place, once a burial place of kings and an inspiration for saints. A religious community was first established at Whitby in 657 by Abbess Hilda and was the home of Caedmon, the first English poet. The remains we can see today are of a Benedictine church built in the 13th and 14th centuries, and include a magnificent three-tiered choir and north transept. It is perched high above the picturesque harbour town of Whitby.

Location: OS94, Ref. NZ904 115. On cliff top E of Whitby.

Opening Times: 1 Apr - 30 Sept: daily 10am - 6pm. 1 - 31 Oct: daily, 10am - 5pm. 1 Nov - 31 Mar: daily, 10am - 4pm. Closed 24 - 26 Dec.

Admission: Adult £1.70, Child 90p, Conc. £1.30. 15% discounts for groups (11+).

Ground floor suitable. In grounds, on leads. Tel. for details.

Special Events Index PAGE 40

WHITE SCAR CAVE

See page 349 for full page entry.

WILBERFORCE HOUSE

Tel: 01482 613902 **Fax:** 01482 613710

High Street, Hull, Yorkshire HU1 1EP

Owner: Hull City Council **Contact:** S R Green

Built c1656 the house is a museum to the memory of William Wilberforce.

Location: OS Ref. TA102 286. High Street, Hull.

Opening Times: Mon - Sat, 10am - 5pm. Suns, 1.30 - 4.30pm. Closed Good Fri & Christmas Day.

Admission: Free.

WORTLEY HALL

Tel: 0114 2882100 **Fax:** 0114 2830695

Wortley, Sheffield, Yorkshire S35 7DB

Owner: Labour, Co-operative & Trade Union Movement **Contact:** John Howard

15 acres of formal Italianate gardens surrounded by 11 acres of informal pleasure grounds.

Location: OS Ref. SK313 995. 10kms S of Barnsley in Wortley on A629.

Opening Times: Gardens: All year except 7 - 14 Aug & 6 - 13 Nov.

Admission: Free. Groups must book for gardeners' tour, £1.25.

YORK MINSTER

Tel: 01904 557216 **Fax:** 01904 557218

Deangate, York YO1 7HH

Owner: Dean and Chapter of York **Contact:** Dorothy Lee, Visitors' Officer

Large gothic church housing the largest collection of medieval stained glass in England.

Location: OS Ref. SE603 522. Centre of York.

Opening Times: Nov - Mar: 7am - 6pm, Apr: 7am - 6.30pm, May: 7am - 7.30pm, Jun - Aug: 7am - 8.30pm, Sept: 7am - 8pm, Oct: 7am - 7pm, daily.

Admission: By donation. Tour companies £3 per person, Child (6-16yrs) £1.

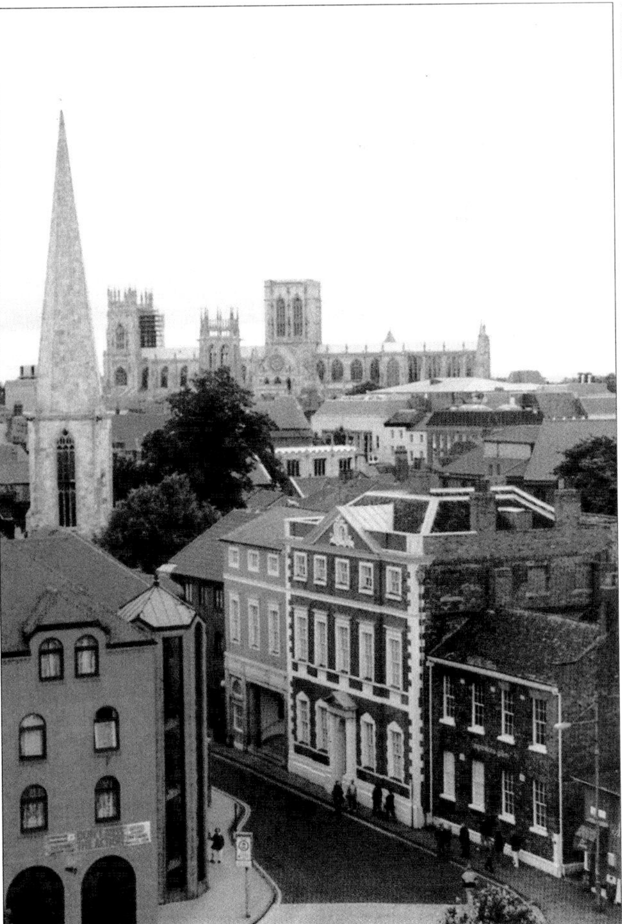

Patrick Lane.

View of York Minster (showing Fairfax House in the foreground), Yorkshire.

The North West

Village of Newton, Forest of Bowland.

North West Tourist Board

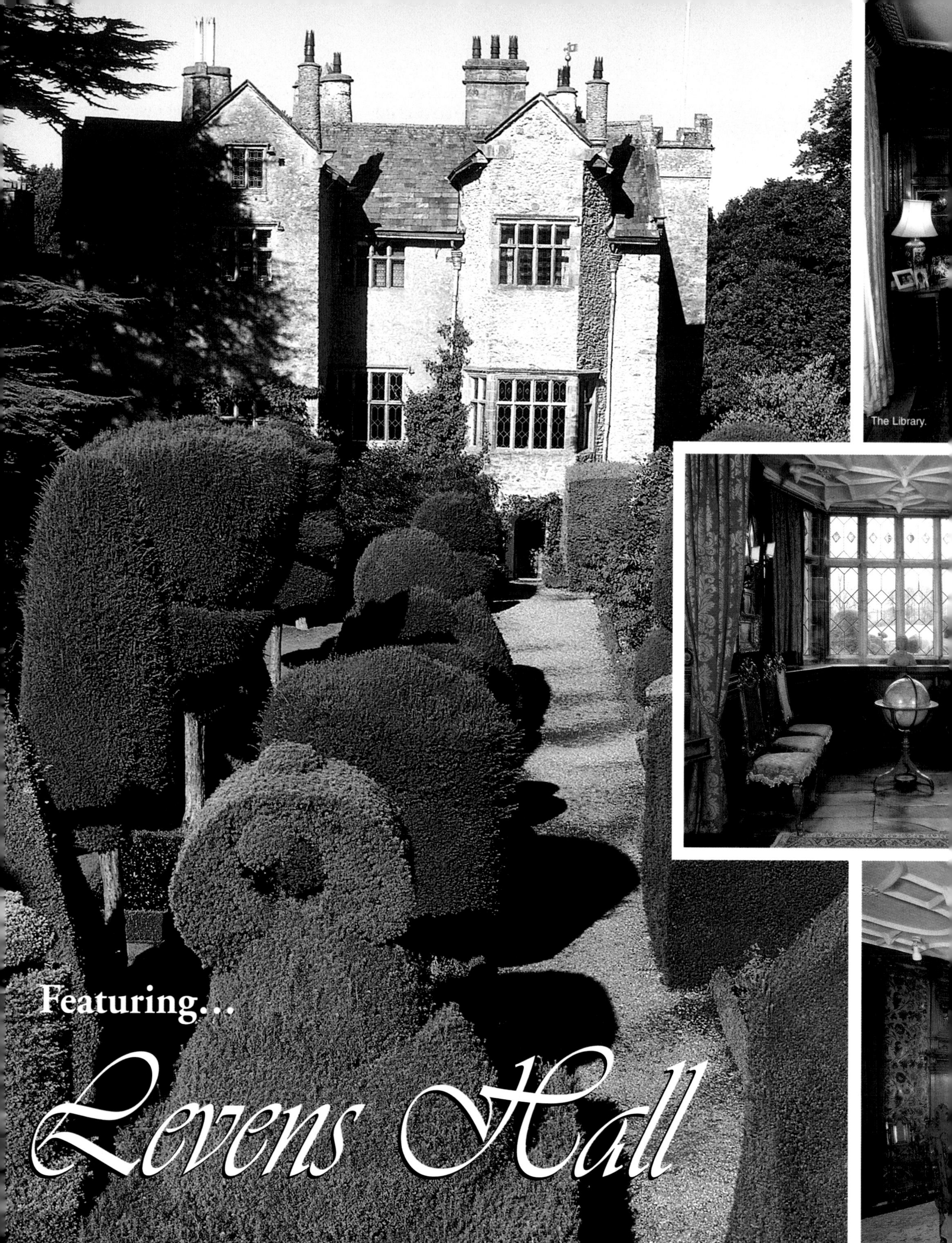

Featuring…

Levens Hall

Like many border houses, at the heart of Levens Hall in Kendal, Cumbria, is a medieval pele tower and hall. It was built by the Redman family in the late 13th century and converted into a gentleman's residence by the Bellinghams, cousins of the de Redmans, in the late 16th century. But it was Colonel James Grahme, first cousin of the last Bellingham, who furnished the house in fine taste during the latter part of the 17th century and, with the help of Monsieur Beaumont, laid out the park and the outstanding topiary garden.

Today, still in continual family ownership for over 700 years, Levens is the home of Hal and Susan Bagot. Both work hard to care for Levens, keeping it not only as a lively and bustling family home but as a place where visitors can continue to appreciate and enjoy its many charms.

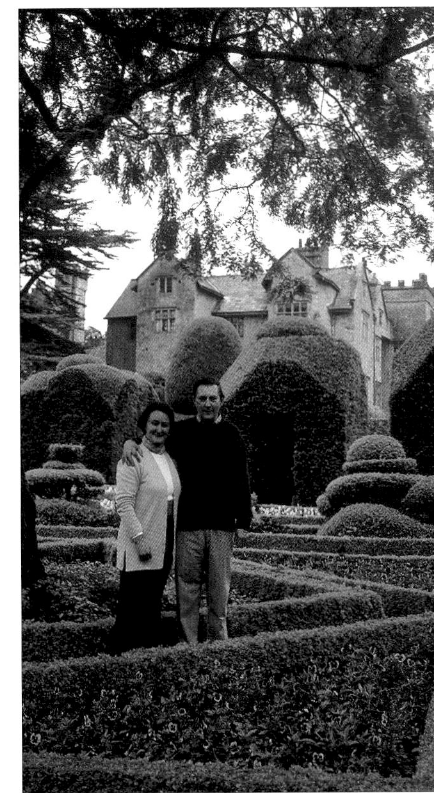

Hal and Susie Bagot.

Earliest English Patchwork.

The Drawing Room.

The interiors of Levens often seem to be eclipsed by the gardens. But they shouldn't be, for they are an equal delight. The great majority of rooms have rich, mellow Elizabethan panelling and fine, delicate ceiling plasterwork – all of which evoke a feeling of intimacy and comfort.

Many of the pieces of furniture and porcelain in the house also have interesting histories. For example, Sir Charles Bagot (1769-1825), himself a distinguished career diplomat, married Lady Mary Wellesley, a niece of the Duke of Wellington. Hence, in the Small Drawing Room you will find a chocolate service (see left) made in the Sèvres factory, originally intended as a gift for Napoleon's mother – as well as other treasures relating to Napoleon and Wellington.

Maintenance of the gardens is very labour intensive, requiring great skill, particularly in the clipping of the giant beech hedges and intricate topiary work. This is done annually and starts with the beech in mid-August and finally finishes with the clipping of yew and box hedges in December. The Bagots were, therefore, delighted to receive the prestigious HHA/Christie's Garden of the Year Award in 1994 in recognition of everyone's efforts in caring for this outstanding garden.

The Dining Room.

For full details of this property see page 379.

Sir Charles Bagot.

Owner:
Mrs C J C Legh

CONTACT

Julian Langlands-Perry
or Tessa Quayle
The Estate Office
Adlington Hall
Macclesfield
Cheshire
SK10 4LF

Tel: 01625 829206 (Corporate)
01625 820875 (Hall Tours)

Fax: 01625 828756

e-mail: info@adlington-hall.demon.co.uk

LOCATION

OS Ref. SJ905 804

5m N of Macclesfield, A523, 13m S of Manchester. London 178m.

Rail: Macclesfield and Wilmslow stations 5m.

Air: Manchester Airport 8m.

CONFERENCE/FUNCTION		
ROOM	SIZE	MAX CAPACITY
Great Hall	11 x 8m	120
Dining Rm	10.75 x 7m	90
Courtyard	27 x 17m	300

ADLINGTON HALL

Macclesfield

ADLINGTON HALL, the home of the Leghs of Adlington from 1315 to the present day, was built on the site of a Hunting Lodge which stood in the Forest of Macclesfield in 1040. Two oaks, part of the original building, remain with their roots in the ground and support the east end of the Great Hall, which was built between 1480 and 1505.

The Hall is a manor house, quadrangular in shape, and was once surrounded by a moat. Two sides of the Courtyard and the east wing were built in the typical 'Black and White' Cheshire style in 1581. The south front and west wing (containing the Drawing Room and Dining Room) were added between 1749 and 1757 and are built of red brick with a handsome stone portico with four Ionic columns on octagonal pedestals. Between the trees in the Great Hall stands an organ built by 'Father' Bernard Smith (c1670-80). Handel subsequently played on this instrument, and now fully restored, it is the largest 17th century organ in the country.

GARDENS

The gardens were landscaped in the style of 'Capability' Brown in the middle of the 18th century. Visitors may walk round the 'wilderness' area, among the follies to be seen are 'Temple to Diana', a 'Shell Cottage', Chinese bridge and T'ing house. There is a fine yew walk and a lime avenue planted in 1688. Old fashioned rose garden and yew maze recently planted.

OPENING TIMES

Open throughout the year to groups by prior arrangement only.

ADMISSION

Hall & Gardens

Groups (20+)
Adult £4.00
Child £1.50
Student £1.50
Groups of 25+ £3.50

Suitable for corporate events, product launches, business meetings, conferences, concerts, fashion shows, garden parties, rallies, clay-pigeon shooting and filming.

The Great Hall and Dining Room are available for corporate entertaining. Catering can be arranged.

Visitors may alight at entrance to Hall. WCs.

By arrangement.

For 100 cars and 4 coaches, 100 yds from Hall.

Schools welcome. Guide can be provided.

No dogs.

CAPESTHORNE HALL

Macclesfield

Owner:
Mr & Mrs Bromley-Davenport

CONTACT

Gwyneth Jones,
Hall Manager
Capesthorne Hall
Siddington
Macclesfield
Cheshire
SK11 9JY

Tel: 01625 861221

Fax: 01625 861619

LOCATION

OS Ref. SJ840 727

5m W of Macclesfield.

30 mins S of Manchester on A34.

Near M6, M63 and M62.

Airport: Manchester International 20 mins.

Rail: Macclesfield 5m (2 hrs from London).

Taxi: 01625 533464.

CONFERENCE/FUNCTION		
ROOM	SIZE	MAX CAPACITY
Theatre	45' x 19'	155
Garden Room	52' x 20'	84
Saloon	40' x 25'	80
Queen Anne Room	34' x 25'	84
Board Room		10

CAPESTHORNE HALL, set in 100 acres of picturesque Cheshire parkland, has been touched by nearly 1,000 years of English history - Roman legions passed across it, titled Norman families hunted on it and, during the Civil War, a Royalist ancestress helped Charles II to escape after the Battle of Worcester. The Jacobean-style Hall has a fascinating collection of fine art, marble sculptures, furniture and tapestries. Originally designed by the Smiths of Warwick it was built between 1719 and 1732. It was altered by Blore in 1837 and partially rebuilt by Salvin in 1861 following a disastrous fire.

The present Squire is William Bromley-Davenport, Lord Lieutenant of Cheshire, whose ancestors have owned the estate since Domesday times when they were appointed custodians of the Royal Forest of Macclesfield.

In the grounds near the family Chapel the 18th century Italian *Milanese Gates* open onto the herbaceous borders and maples which line the beautiful lakeside gardens. But amid the natural spectacle and woodland walks, Capesthorne still offers glimpses of its man-made past... the remains of the Ice House, the Old Boat House and the curious Swallow Hole.

Facilities at the Hall can be hired for corporate occasions and family celebrations including Civil wedding ceremonies.

Available for corporate functions, meetings, product launches, promotions, exhibitions, presentations, seminars, activity days, Civil weddings and receptions, family celebrations, still photography, fishing, clay shooting, car rallies, garden parties, barbecues, firework displays, concerts, antique, craft, country and game fairs. No photography in Hall.

Catering can be provided for groups (full menus on request). Function rooms available for wedding receptions, corporate hospitality, meetings and other special events. 'The Butler's Pantry' serves tea, coffee and ices.

Compacted paths, ramps. WCs.

For up to 50. Tours are by staff members or Hall Manager. Tour time 1 hr.

100 cars/20 coaches on hard-standing and unlimited in park, 50 yds from house. Rest room and free refreshment for coach drivers.

Guide dogs in Hall. Under control in Park.

Civil Wedding Licence. 

OPENING TIMES

SUMMER
April - October
BHs, Weds & Suns.

House, Gardens & Chapel
Open at 1.30pm
Last admission 3.30pm.

Gardens & Chapel
12 noon - 6pm.

Groups welcome by appointment.

Caravan Park also open Easter - end September.

Corporate enquiries welcome all year.

ADMISSION

Hall & Gardens
Adult £6.00
Child (5-18yrs) £2.50
OAP £5.50
Family £12.00

Gardens & Chapel
Adult £3.50
Child (5-18yrs) £1.50
OAP £3.00

Transfers to Hall
Adult/OAP £3.50
Child (5-18yrs) £1.50

Caravans
Up to 2 people .... £11 p.n
Over 2 people .... £13 p.n

Groups (25+) please telephone for details.

SPECIAL EVENTS

- **APR 8 - 9 & SEPT 16 - 17:** Rainbow Craft Fair
- **JUN 10 - 11 & OCT 7 - 8** Cheshire Home & Garden Show
- **JUL 16:** Gordon Setter Champ Show
- **AUG 13** Fireworks and Laser Concert

See the Special Events Section or telephone for more details and other special events.

The National Trust Photographic Library.

TATTON PARK
Knutsford

Owner:
The National Trust

CONTACT

Conferences, exhibitions, social occasions
Sheila Hetherington
Sales & Booking Officer
01625 534406

Party Visits
Janet Gidman
Tatton Park
Knutsford
Cheshire WA16 6QN
Tel: 01625 534400
or 01625 534428
Fax: 01625 534403

LOCATION

OS Ref. SJ745 815

From M56/J7 follow signs.

From M6/J19, signed on A56 & A50.

Rail: Knutsford or Altrincham Station, then taxi.

Air: Manchester Airport 6m.

CONFERENCE/FUNCTION		
ROOM	SIZE	MAX CAPACITY
Tenants' Hall	125' x 45'	330 - 400
Foyer	23' x 20'	50 - 100
Tenants' Hall Event Wing – total of 8,000 sq.ft. available		
Lord Egerton's Apartment	20' x 16'	16 - 40
	24' x 18'	19 - 40
Stable Block	31' x 20'	80

TATTON is one of the most complete historic estates in Britain. Five separate features, special events and private functions attract over 700,000 visits each year.

Man's occupation of Tatton began 10,000 years ago. The Landscape History Trail guides walkers through time. The Palladian mansion by Wyatt is the jewel in Tatton's crown. The Egerton family collection of fine paintings, porcelain and furniture is found in the splendid setting of the magnificent staterooms. In stark contrast, the Victorian kitchens and cellars give a fascinating insight into life 'downstairs'. The Home Farm is still working with traditional breeds of animal and estate workshops.

Extending to 50 acres, the gardens are amongst the most important in England. Attractions include the famous Japanese garden, restored orangery, New Zealand tree fernery, Italian terraced garden and maze.

Across the Park at the Tudor Old Hall, visitors are guided through the smoky shadows of the 16th century great hall, lit by flickering candles and through time to the home of a 1950s estate employee. The Old Hall was leased to his cousin by Thomas Egerton, Lord Chancellor of England during the reign of Queen Elizabeth I and James I.

800 red and fallow deer can be seen when walking or driving in the parkland and around the two meres. Tatton Park is maintained, managed and financed by Cheshire County Council on lease from the National Trust to whom the Mansion and Gardens were bequeathed in 1958 by the late Rt Hon Maurice, Baron Egerton of Tatton, "for the benefit of the Nation".

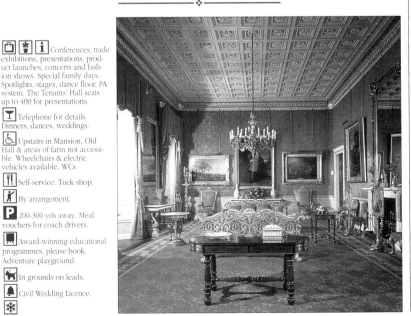

Conferences, trade exhibitions, presentations, product launches, concerts and fashion shows. Special family days. Spotlights, stages, dance floor, PA system. The Tenants' Hall seats up to 400 for presentations.

Telephone for details. Dinners, dances, weddings.

Upstairs in Mansion, Old Hall & areas of farm not accessible. Wheelchairs & electric vehicles available. WCs.

Self-service. Tuck shop.

By arrangement.

200-300 yds away. Meal vouchers for coach drivers.

Award-winning educational programmes, please book. Adventure playground.

In grounds on leads.

Civil Wedding Licence.

OPENING TIMES

SUMMER
1 April - 31 October
Park: Daily 10.30am - 6pm
Gardens: Tue - Sun 10.30am - 5pm
Mansion: Tue - Sun 12 noon - 4pm. (2 - 31 Oct: Sat & Sun only). Open on the hour at certain times only, please ring for details.
Old Hall: Guided tours, 3pm & 4pm.
Restaurant: Daily
Shops: Tue - Sun

WINTER
1 Nov - 31 Mar 2001
Park: Tue - Sun, 11am - 4pm
Gardens: Tue - Sun 11am - 4pm
Opening times for Farm and Old Hall on request.
Restaurant, Garden Shop & Housekeeper's Store: Tue - Sun

Gift Shop: W/ends only.

All attractions open w/ends in Oct. Mansion & Farm open w/ends in Dec. before Xmas.

ADMISSION

	Single	Group*
Any two attractions		
Adult	£4.50	£3.60
Child**	£2.50	£2.00
Mansion or Garden		
Adult	£3.00	£2.40
Child**	£2.00	£1.50
Family	£8.00 (NT Free)	
Farm or Old Hall		
Adult	£2.50	£2.00
Child**	£1.50	£1.20
Family	£8.00	
Parking		
Per car		£3.50
Coaches		Free

*Min. 12 ** Aged 4 - 15yrs.
OAP rate as Adult
Tours available outside normal opening times £6.

SPECIAL EVENTS

- **JUL 19 - 23:** RHS Flower Show at Tatton Park.
- **JUL 29:** Hallé Concert & Fireworks.
- **DEC:** 'Christmas at Tatton'.

ARLEY HALL & GARDENS

ARLEY, Nr NORTHWICH, CHESHIRE CW9 6NA

Owner: *Viscount Ashbrook* ***Contact:*** *Estate Manager*

Tel: 01565 777353 / 777284 **Fax:** 01565 777465 **e-mail:** arley@info-guest.com

Home of Viscount and Viscountess Ashbrook, was built c1840 by the owner's great-great-grandfather, to the design of the Nantwich architect, George Latham. An important example of the Victorian Jacobean style, it has fine plasterwork and wood panelling as well as interesting furniture, pictures and other contents. Adjoining Arley Hall is a large private Chapel designed by Anthony Salvin, who also designed Westminster Abbey. Activities can be held both in the Hall and in the grounds, from corporate conferences of any size to cocktail parties and ambassadorial receptions. Arley Hall offers all its visitors an elegant setting combined with the professional approach to top class management. Catering to the highest standards.

Overlooking beautiful parkland, the Gardens extending over 12 acres, rank among the finest in the country. The features include the Double Herbaceous Border, one of the earliest to be established in England (1846), unique avenue of clipped *Quercus Ilex*, collection of shrub roses, fine yew hedges, Herb Garden, Walled Garden, Woodland Garden with exotic trees, shrubs, azaleas and a collection of over 200 varieties of rhododendrons.

Location: OS Ref. SJ675 809. Knutsford 5m, NW Northwich 5m, N M6/J19 & 20 5m M56/J9 & 10, 5m.

Opening Times: 9 Apr - 1 Oct: Tue - Sun & BH Mons, 11am - 5pm. Hall: please telephone for open days, 12 noon - 5pm.

Admission: Gardens, Grounds & Chapel: Adult £4.40, Child £2.20, OAP £3.80, Family £11. Groups: Adult £3.75, Child £2, OAP £3.25. Season ticket £19.50, Family season ticket £50 (2+2). Hall & Gardens: Adult £6.90, Child £3.70, OAP £5.80, Family £17.50. Groups: Adult £6, Child £3.25, OAP £5.

Photography in gardens only. Licensed. By arrangement. In grounds, on leads. Tel for details.

ADLINGTON HALL See page 368 for full page entry.

BEESTON CASTLE **Tel:** 01829 260464

Beeston, Tarporley, Cheshire CW6 9TX

Owner: English Heritage **Contact:** The Custodian

Standing majestically on sheer, rocky crags which fall sharply away from the castle walls, Beeston has possibly the best views of the surrounding countryside of any castle in England.

Location: OS117, Ref. SJ537 593. 11m SE of Chester on minor road off A49, or A41. 2m SW of Tarporley.

Opening Times: 1 Apr - 30 Sept: 10am - 6pm. 1 - 31 Oct: daily, 10am - 5pm. 1 Nov - 31 Mar: daily, 10am - 4pm. Closed 24 & 25 Dec.

Admission: Adult £2.80, Child £1.40, Conc. £2.10. 15% discount for groups (11+).

Exhibition. Not suitable. In grounds on leads. Tel. for details.

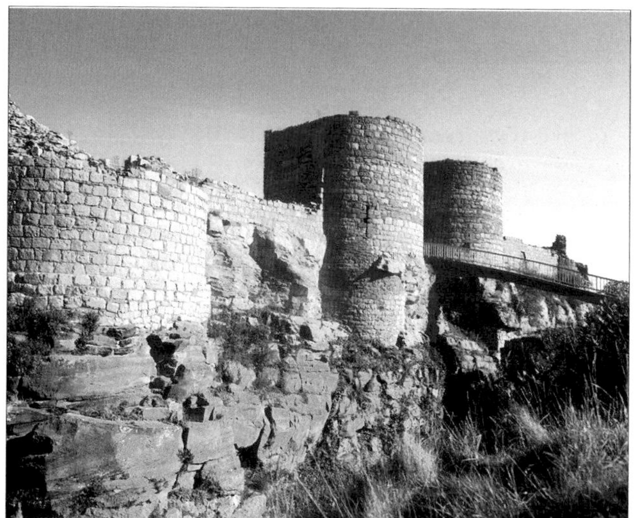

Beeston Castle, Cheshire.

BRAMALL HALL

BRAMHALL PARK, BRAMHALL, STOCKPORT SK7 3NX

Owner: *Stockport MBC* ***Contact:*** *Ruth Maddocks*

Tel: 0161 485 3708 **Fax:** 0161 486 6959

Surrounded by 70 acres of beautiful parkland, Bramall Hall is a superb example of a Cheshire black and white timber-framed manor house, dating from the 14th century. The house has beautiful Tudor rooms with splendid Victorian additions. Extensive events programme and ideal for weddings.

Location: OS117, Ref. SJ886 863. 4m S of Stockport, off A5102.

Opening Times: Good Fri - 30 Sept: Mon - Sat, 1 - 5pm, Suns & BHs, 11am - 5pm. 1 Oct - 1 Jan: Tue - Sat, 1 - 4pm, Suns & BHs, 11am - 4pm. Closed 25/26 Dec. 2 Jan - 4 Apr: Sats & Suns, 12 noon - 4pm.

Admission: Adult £3.50, Child/Conc. £2. Group prices on request.

Partially suitable. By arrangement. Limited for coaches. In grounds on leads. Tel for details.

North West England

CAPESTHORNE HALL

See page 369 for full page entry.

CHESTER CATHEDRAL

Tel: 01244 324756 **Fax:** 01244 341110

12 Abbey Square, Chester, Cheshire CH1 2HU **Contact:** Mr N Fry

Founded in 1092 as a Benedictine monastery, it became an Anglican cathedral in 1541. All styles of architecture are represented as well as spectacular medieval woodwork.

Location: OS Ref. SJ406 665. Chester city centre.

Opening Times: 7.30am - 6.30pm, daily.

Admission: Donation.

CHESTER ROMAN AMPHITHEATRE

Tel: 0191 269 1200

Vicars Lane, Chester, Cheshire

Owner: English Heritage **Contact:** The North Regional Office

The largest Roman amphitheatre in Britain, partially excavated. Used for entertainment and military training by the 20th Legion, based at the fortress of Deva.

Location: OS Ref. SJ404 660. On Vicars Lane beyond Newgate, Chester.

Opening Times: Any reasonable time.

Admission: Free.

CHOLMONDELEY CASTLE GARDEN

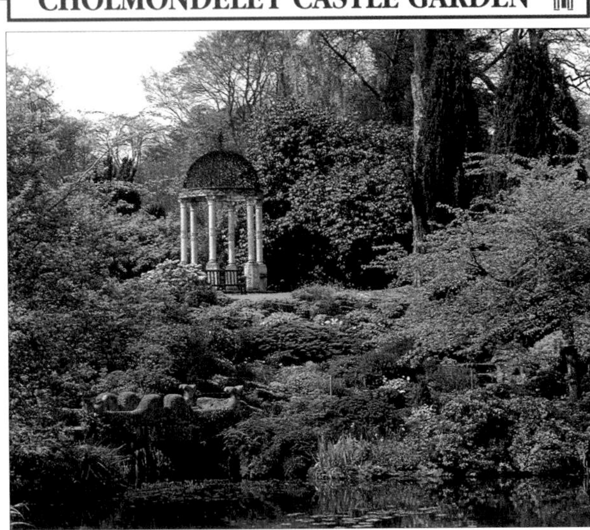

MALPAS, CHESHIRE SY14 8AH

Owner: *The Marchioness of Cholmondeley* ***Contact:*** *The Secretary*

Tel/Fax: 01829 720383

Extensive pleasure gardens dominated by romantic Gothic Castle built in 1801 of local sandstone. Imaginatively laid out with fine trees, water gardens and extensively replanted since the 1960s with rhododendrons, azaleas, magnolias, cornus, acer and many other acid-loving plants. As well as the beautiful water garden, there is a rose garden and many mixed borders. Lakeside picnic area, rare breeds of farm animals, including llamas. Ancient private chapel in park. Children's play area.

Location: OS Ref. SJ540 515. Off A41 Chester/Whitchurch Rd. & A49 Whitchurch/Tarporley Road. 7m N of Whitchurch.

Opening Times: 2 Apr - 28 Sept: Weds, Thurs, Suns & BHs (closed Good Fri), 11.30am - 5pm. Groups (25+): other days by prior arrangement at reduced rates.

Admission: Adult £3, Child £1, OAP £2.50.

 Limited suitability. WCs. In grounds on leads only.

DORFOLD HALL

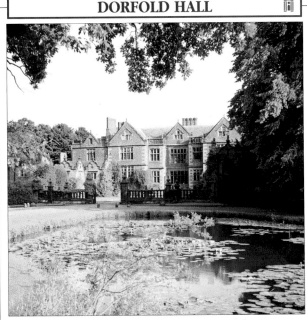

ACTON, Nr NANTWICH, CHESHIRE CW5 8LD

Owner/Contact: *Richard Roundell*

Tel: 01270 625245 **Fax:** 01270 628723

Jacobean country house built in 1616 for Ralph Wilbraham. Family home of Mr & Mrs Richard Roundell. Beautiful plaster ceilings and oak panelling. Attractive woodland gardens and summer herbaceous borders.

Location: OS Ref. SJ634 525. 1m W of Nantwich on the A534 Nantwich - Wrexham road.

Opening Times: Apr - Oct: Tues only and BH Mons, 2 - 5pm.

Admission: Adult £4.50, Child £3.

Obligatory. Limited. Narrow gates with low arch prevent coaches. In grounds on leads.

DUNHAM MASSEY

Patrick Lane

ALTRINCHAM, CHESHIRE WA14 4SJ

Owner: *The National Trust* ***Contact:*** *The Property Manager*

Tel: 0161 941 1025 **Fax:** 0161 929 7508

Originally an early Georgian house, Dunham Massey has sumptuous interiors, with collections of walnut furniture, paintings and magnificent Huguenot silver. The richly planted garden contains waterside plantings, late flowering azaleas, an orangery and Elizabethan mount. The surrounding deer park escaped the attentions of 18th century landscape gardeners and contains some notable specimen trees.

Location: OS Ref. SJ735 874. 3m SW of Altrincham off A56. M56/J7.

Opening Times: House: 1 Apr - 27 Sept: Sat - Wed, 12 noon - 5pm (11am - 5pm BH Sun & Mon), last admission 4.30pm. 30 Sept - 1 Nov: Sat - Wed, 12 noon - 4pm (access by guided tour only Mon - Wed). Garden: 1 Apr - 1 Nov: daily, 11am - 5.30pm, last admission 5pm (closes 4.30pm 30 Sept - 1 Nov). Park open daily throughout the year.

Admission: House & Garden: Adult £5, Child £2.50, Family £12.50 (2 adults + children). House or Garden only: Adult £3, Child £1.50. Car entry: £3 per car. Coach /minibus entry: £5 (free to booked parties). Motorcycle: £1. Booked Groups: £4 for 15 or more paying adults, not available Suns & BHs.

No photography in house. Partially suitable. WC. Batricars. Licensed. By arrangement.  In grounds, on leads. 

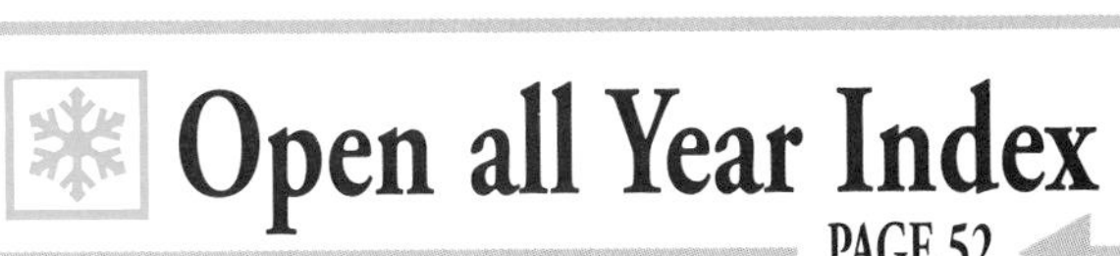
Open all Year Index
PAGE 52

GAWSWORTH HALL

MACCLESFIELD, CHESHIRE SK11 9RN

Owner: *Mr and Mrs T Richards* ***Contact:*** *Mr T Richards*

Tel: 01260 223456 **Fax:** 01260 223469 **e-mail:** gawsworth@compuserve.com

Fully lived-in Tudor half-timbered manor house with Tilting Ground. Former home of Mary Fitton, Maid of Honour at the Court of Queen Elizabeth I, and the supposed 'Dark Lady' of Shakespeare's sonnets. Pictures, sculpture and furniture. Open air theatre with covered grandstand - June, July and August, please telephone for details. Situated halfway between Macclesfield and Congleton in an idyllic setting close to the lovely medieval church.

Location: OS Ref. SJ892 697. 3m S of Macclesfield on the A536 Congleton to Macclesfield road.

Opening Times: 20 Apr - 1 Oct: daily, 2 - 5pm. Closed Sats in April, May & Sept (except BH Sats).

Admission: Adult £4.20, Child £2.10.

Guide dogs in garden only.  Telephone for details.

LITTLE MORETON HALL

National Trust Photographic Library

CONGLETON, CHESHIRE CW12 4SD

Owner: *The National Trust* ***Contact:*** *The Property Manager*

Tel: 01260 272018

Begun in 1450 and completed 130 years later, Little Moreton Hall is regarded as the finest example of a timber-framed moated manor house in the country. The drunkenly reeling South Front topped by its Elizabethan Long Gallery opens onto a cobbled courtyard and the main body of the Hall. The Chapel, Great Hall, wall paintings and Knot Garden are of particular interest. Location for many TV series and films including *Moll Flanders* and *Lady Jane.*

Location: OS Ref. SJ833 589. 4m SW of Congleton on E side of A34.

Opening Times: 25 Mar - 5 Nov: Wed - Sun & BH Mons, 11.30am - 5pm. Last admission 4.30pm. 11 Nov - 26 Nov: Sats & Suns, 11.30am - 4pm. 2 Dec - 23 Dec: Sats & Suns, 11.30am - 4pm, free access to ground floor, shop & restaurant. Christmas festivities and decorations during Dec.

Admission: Adult £4.30, Child £2.10, Family £10.70. Groups: £3.50 (must book). Joint ticket with Biddulph Grange Garden £6.50, Family £16. 2 - 23 Dec Free.

Braille guide, wheelchair & electric vehicle. WCs.

Car park only.

HARE HILL

Over Alderley, Macclesfield, Cheshire SK10 4QB

Owner: The National Trust **Contact:** The Head Gardener

A woodland garden surrounding a walled garden with pergola, rhododendrons and azaleas; parkland: link path to Alderley Edge (2m).

Location: OS Ref. SJ875 765. Between Alderley Edge and Prestbury, turn N at B5087, Greyhound Road.

Opening Times: 1 Apr - 30 Oct: Weds, Thurs, Sats, Suns & BH Mons, 10am - 5.30pm. Special opening to see rhododendrons & azaleas: 10 - 30 May: daily, 10am - 5.30pm. Closed Nov - Mar.

Admission: £2.50. Entrance per car £1.50 refundable on entry to garden. Groups by written appointment c/o Garden Lodge at address above.

Gravel paths - strong companion advisable. Not in garden, elsewhere on leads.

LYME PARK

Geoff Morgan

DISLEY, STOCKPORT, CHESHIRE SK12 2NX

Owner: *The National Trust* ***Contact:*** *The Property Manager*

Tel: 01663 762023 **Infoline:** 01663 766492 **Fax:** 01663 765035

Legh family home for 600 years. Part of the original Elizabethan house survives with 18th and 19th century additions by Giacomo Leoni and Lewis Wyatt. Four centuries of period interiors – Mortlake tapestries, Grinling Gibbons carvings, unique collection of English clocks. Historic gardens with conservatory by Wyatt, a lake and a 'Dutch' garden. A 1,400 acre park, home to red and fallow deer. Exterior featured as 'Pemberley' in BBC's *Pride and Prejudice.*

Location: OS Ref. SJ966 843. Off the A6. 6½ m SE of Stockport.

Opening Times: Park: Apr - Oct: daily, 8am - 8.30pm; Nov - Mar 8am - 6pm. Gardens: 24 Mar - 31 Oct: Fri - Tue, 11am - 5pm, Wed/Thur 1 - 5pm. House: 24 Mar - 31 Oct: Fri - Tue, 1 - 5pm, last entry 4.30pm. BHs, 11am - 5pm. Park Shop & Coffee Shop: Apr - Oct: daily, 11am - 5pm. Hall, tearoom & gift shop: 26 Mar - 31 Oct: Fri - Tue 11am - 5pm. For Nov - Mar opening times please telephone for details.

Admission: Park only £3.50/car. Garden only: Adult £2. House only: Adult £3.50, Combined House & Garden: £4.50. Family £12. All inclusive ticket (1 vehicle with 2 adults & 2 children) to House, Park & Gardens: £15.

By arrangement. WCs. By arrangement.

In park, close control. Guide dogs only in house & garden.

Special Events Index

PAGE 40

MACCLESFIELD MUSEUMS

Tel: 01625 613210 **Fax:** 01625 617880

Roe Street, Macclesfield SK11 6UT **e-mail:** postmaster@silk-macc.u-net.com

Owner: Macclesfield Museums Trust **Contact:** Louanne Collins

Silk museum housed in Georgian Sunday School. Development of the silk industry is told through an award-winning audio-visual programme, exhibitions, models and costume. Nearby Paradise Mill houses 26 hand jacquard silk looms. Tours with knowledgeable guides, demonstrations of weaving, shows life in the 1930s.

Location: OS Ref. SJ917 733. Centre of Macclesfield.

Opening Times: Silk Museum: Mon - Sat, 11am - 5pm, BHs & Suns, 1 - 5pm. Paradise Mill: Tue - Sun, 1 - 5pm, Nov - Mar, 1 - 4pm. Both closed 25 & 26 Dec, 1 Jan & Good Fri.

Admission: Adult £2.70, Child/Conc. £1.90. Joint ticket: Adult £4.75, Child/Conc. £2.70. Special evening rates. (1999 prices).

  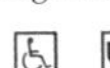 Licensed. By arrangement. Guide dogs only.

NESS BOTANIC GARDENS

Tel: 01513 530123 **Fax:** 01513 531004

Ness, Neston, Cheshire CH64 4AY

Owner: University of Liverpool **Contact:** Dr E J Sharples

Location: OS Ref. SJ302 760 (village centre). Off A540. 10m NW of Chester. 1½ m S of Neston.

Opening Times: 1 Mar - 31 Oct: 9.30am - dusk. Nov - Feb: 9.30am - 4pm.

Admission: Adult £4.50, Accompanied child (under 18yrs) Free. Conc. £4. 10% discount for groups.

NETHER ALDERLEY MILL

Tel: 01625 523012 **Fax:** 01625 527139

Congleton Road, Nether Alderley, Macclesfield, Cheshire SK10 4TW

Owner/Contact: The National Trust

A fascinating overshot tandem wheel watermill, dating from the 15th century, with a stone-tiled low pitched roof. The machinery is in full working order, and grinds flour occasionally for demonstrations.

Location: OS Ref. SJ844 763. 1½ m S of Alderley Edge, on E side of A34.

Opening Times: Apr, May & Oct: Weds, Suns & BH Mons, 1 - 4.30pm. Jun - Sept: daily (except Mons but open BH Mons), 1 - 5pm.

Admission: Adult £2, Child £1. Groups by prior arrangement (max. 20).

Not suitable. By arrangement. 

NORTON PRIORY WALLED GARDEN & MUSEUM

Tel: 01928 569895

Tudor Road, Manor Park, Runcorn, Cheshire WA7 1SX

Owner/Contact: The Norton Priory Museum Trust

Site of medieval priory set in beautiful woodland gardens.

Location: OS Ref. SJ545 835. 3m from M56/J11. 2m E of Runcorn.

Opening Times: Garden: 1 Mar - 31 Oct, every afternoon. Museum: all year.

Admission: Adult £3.30, Child/Conc. £2, Family £8.80, Groups £1.80.

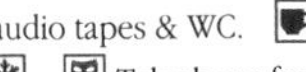W/chairs, braille guide, audio tapes & WC. By arrangement.
In grounds, on leads. Telephone for details.

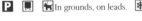

PECKFORTON CASTLE

Tel: 01829 260930 **Fax:** 01829 261230

Stonehouse Lane, Nr Tarporley CW6 9TN

Owner: Mrs Graybill **Contact:** Mrs Jones

The only intact medieval style castle in Britain. Built mid-1800s, designed by Anthony Salvin.

Location: OS Ref. SJ533 581. Access by gateway on W side of minor road ¾ m S of Beeston village, ¾ m N of Peckforton village. 12m E of Chester.

Opening Times: Private functions and weddings only. No public access.

PEOVER HALL

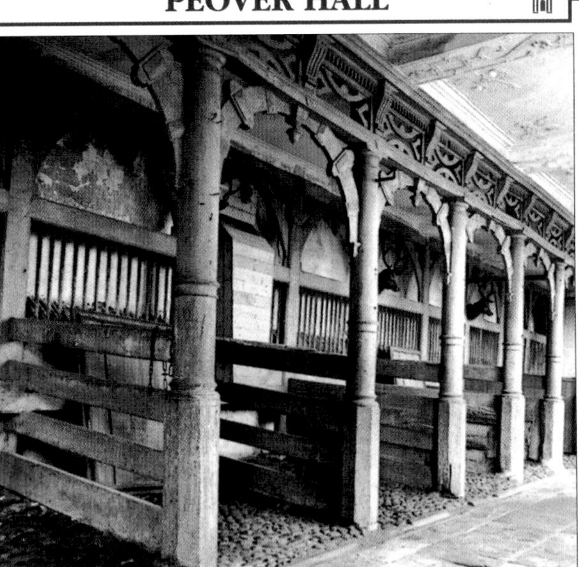

OVER PEOVER, KNUTSFORD WA16 9HN

Owner: *Randle Brooks* ***Contact:*** *I Shepherd*

Tel: 01565 632358

An Elizabethan house dating from 1585. Fine Carolean stables. Mainwaring Chapel, 18th century landscaped park. Large garden with topiary work, also walled and herb gardens.

Location: OS Ref. SJ772 734. 4m S of Knutsford off A50 at Whipping Stocks Inn.

Opening Times: Apr - Oct: House, Stables & Gardens: Mons except BHs, 2 - 5pm. Tours of the House at 2.30 & 3.30pm. Stables & Gardens only: Thurs, 2 - 5pm.

Admission: House, Stables & Gardens: Adult £3, Child £2. Stables & Gardens only: £2.

Mondays only. Obligatory. 

QUARRY BANK MILL & STYAL COUNTRY PARK

Styal, Wilmslow, Cheshire SK9 4LA **Tel:** 01625 527468 **Fax:** 01625 539267

Owner: The National Trust **Contact:** Quarry Bank Mill Trust Ltd

Location: OS Ref. SJ835 830. 1½ m N of Wilmslow off B5166. 2½ m from M56/J5.

Opening Times: Mill: Apr - end Sept: daily, 11am - 6pm, last admission 4.30pm. Oct - Mar: daily except Mons, 11am - 5pm, last admission 3.30pm. Apprentice House & garden: daily except Mons (but open BH Mons),Tue - Fri, 2 - 4.30pm, Sats, Suns & Aug: 11am - 6pm.

Admission: Adult £5.80, Child/Conc. £4.80, Family £15.50. Mill only: Adult £4.80, Child/Conc. £3.40, Family £14.00. Apprentice House & Garden: Adult £3.60, Child/Conc. £2.60. Advance bookings essential for groups (10+).

Patrick Lane.

Peover Hall, Cheshire.

RODE HALL

CHURCH LANE, SCHOLAR GREEN, CHESHIRE ST7 3QP

Owner/Contact: *Sir Richard Baker Wilbraham Bt*

Tel: 01270 873237 **Fax:** 01270 882962

The Wilbraham family have lived at Rode since 1669; the present house was constructed in two stages, the earlier two storey wing and stable block around 1705 and the main building was completed in 1752. Later alterations by Lewis Wyatt and Darcy Braddell were undertaken in 1812 and 1927 respectively. The house stands in a Repton landscape and the extensive gardens include a woodland garden, with a terraced rock garden and grotto, which has many species of rhododendrons, azaleas, hellebores and climbing roses following snowdrops and daffodils in the early spring. The formal rose garden was designed by W Nesfield in 1860 and there is a large walled kitchen garden which is at its best from the middle of June. The icehouse in the park has recently been restored.

Location: OS Ref. SJ819 573. 5m SW of Congleton between the A34 and A50. Kidsgrove railway station 2m NW of Kidsgrove.

Opening Times: 5 Apr - 27 Sept: Weds & BHs (closed Good Fri) and by appointment. Garden only: Tues & Thurs, 2 - 5pm.

Admission: House, Garden & Kitchen Garden: Adult £4, OAP £2.50. Garden & Kitchen Garden: Adult £2.50, OAP £1.50.

 Home-made teas.  On leads.

TABLEY HOUSE

KNUTSFORD, CHESHIRE WA16 0HB

Owner: *Victoria University of Manchester* ***Contact:*** *The Administrator*

Tel: 01565 750151 **Fax:** 01565 653230

The finest Palladian mansion in the North West of England, Grade I, by John Carr of York completed 1767 for the Leicester family who lived at Tabley for over 700 years. The first collection of English works of art – paintings, furniture and memorabilia, can be seen in the State Rooms. Private chapel 1678 re-erected due to brine pumping.

Location: OS Ref. SJ725 777. M6/J19, A556 S on to A5033. 2m W of Knutsford.

Opening Times: Apr - end Oct inclusive: Thurs, Fris, Sats, Suns & BHs, 2 - 5pm.

Admission: Adult £4. Child £1.50. Groups by arrangement.

Registered Charity 1047299.

TATTON PARK See page 370 for full page entry.

WOODHEY CHAPEL **Tel:** 01270 524215

Faddiley, Nr Nantwich, Cheshire CW5 8JH **Contact:** Mr Robinson, The Curator

Owner: The Trustees of Woodhey Chapel

Small private chapel that has been recently restored.

Location: OS Ref. SJ573 528. Proceeding W from Nantwich on A534, turn left 1m W of the Faddiley - Brindley villages onto narrow lane, keep ahead at next turn, at road end obtain key from farmhouse.

Opening Times: Apr - Oct: Sats & BHs, 2 - 5pm, or apply for key at Woodhey Hall.

Admission: £1.

Tabley House, Cheshire.

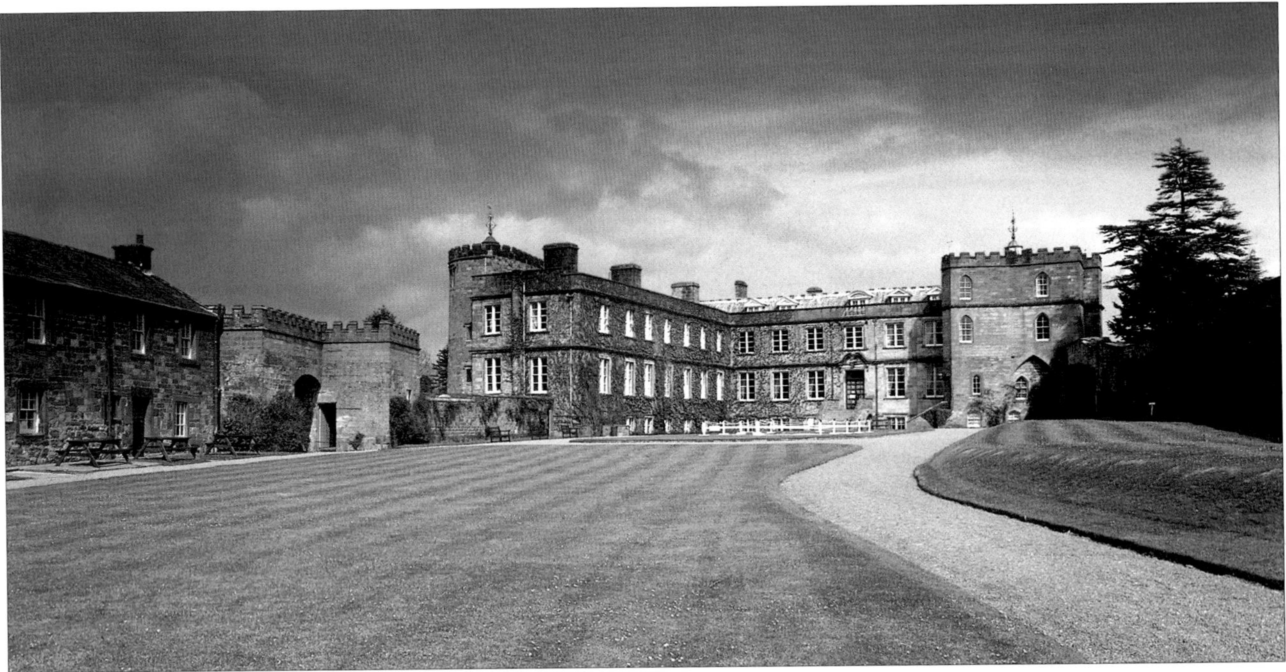

APPLEBY CASTLE
Appleby-in-Westmorland

Owner:
Christopher Nightingale

CONTACT

The Administrator
Appleby Castle
Appleby
Cumbria
CA16 6XH

Tel: 01768 351402

Fax: 01768 351082

Situated in the beautiful Eden Valley at the edge of the ancient county town of Westmorland Appleby Castle has stood for over 800 years. Dominated by its impressive Norman Keep, the castle was a major stronghold of the powerful Clifford family, who helped to hold the Northern Marches during medieval times and fought (and sometimes died) in most of the famous medieval battles, Bannockburn, Crécy, the Wars of the Roses and Flodden.

Later the castle was a favourite home of Lady Anne Clifford, the last of her line, who stubbornly held out for her heritage in the troubled years of the Civil War and left an enduring legacy at the castle, which was further enhanced by her descendants, the Tufton family.

Today visitors may enjoy a castle which has something to offer from each period of history. The Norman Keep has five floors and a dramatic view from the top. The curtain wall and defensive earthworks are amongst the most impressive in northern England. The Great Hall of the castle contains the famous Great Painting of Lady Anne and her family, together with other period pieces.

In the grounds, the castle has a variety of birds and animals, both domestic and foreign, including rare breeds, with special gentle areas for children. The castle's stable block, built in the outer bailey is also of interest as is Lady Anne's 'Beehouse', actually a small oratory.

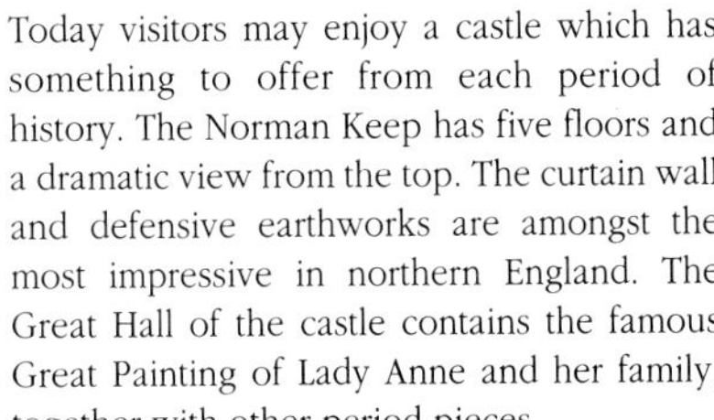

LOCATION

OS Ref. NY685 201

From M6/J38 northbound, J40 southbound. Penrith - Scotch Corner A66 Trunk Road to A1(M).

Rail: Appleby 1/2 m on scenic Settle - Carlisle line. Penrith 11m.

Air: Teesside 45m, Manchester 100m.

OPENING TIMES

Please telephone for details.

ADMISSION

Please telephone for details.

Partially suitable. WC.

Licensed.

By arrangement.

Additional parking in town. Limited for coaches.

Teachers' pack.

In grounds, on leads.

Civil Wedding Licence.

Visitors specifically wishing to attend any event are advised to telephone the Castle for further information beforehand on 01768 351402 to check details and timings.

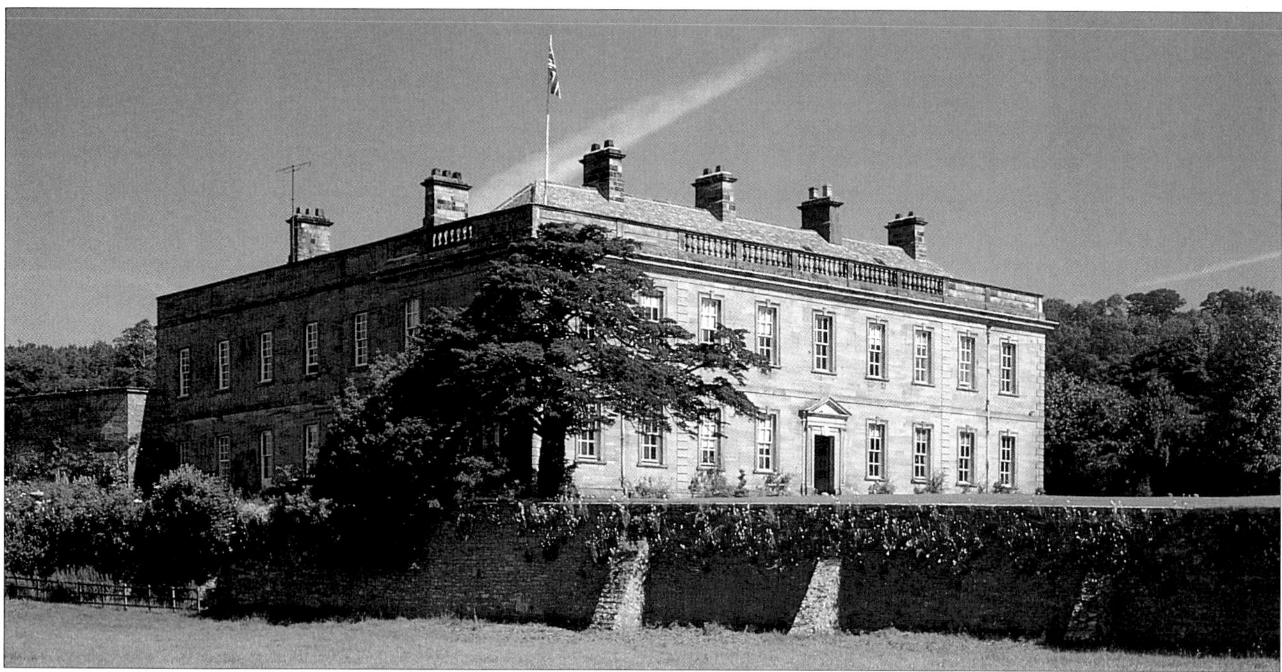

DALEMAIN
Penrith

DALEMAIN is a fine mixture of mediaeval, Tudor and early Georgian architecture. The imposing Georgian façade strikes the visitor immediately but in the cobbled courtyard the atmosphere of the north country Tudor manor is secure. The present owner's family have lived at Dalemain since 1679 and have collected china, furniture and family portraits. Visitors can see the grand Drawing Rooms with 18th century Chinese wallpaper and fine oak panelling, also the Nursery and Housekeeper's Room. The Norman pele tower contains the regimental collection of the Westmorland and Cumberland Yeomanry. The house is full of the paraphernalia of a well established family house which is still very much lived in by the family.

The 16th century Great Barn holds a collection of agricultural bygones and a Fell Pony Museum. Do not miss Mrs Mouse's house on the back stairs or the Nursery with toys from all ages. Something of interest for all the family. Location for ITV's production of *Jane Eyre*.

GARDENS

The Gardens have a long history stretching back to a mediaeval herb garden. Today a knot garden remains, with a fine early Roman fountain and box hedges enclosing herb beds. The imposing terrace wall supports a full and colourful herbaceous border during the summer months. Visitors can enjoy the fine views of the park and the woodland and riverside walks. The gardens have been featured on television's *Gardener's World* and also in *Country Life*. Deer Park.

Owner: Robert Hasell McCosh Esq

CONTACT

Bryan McDonald
Administrator
Dalemain Estate Office
Dalemain
Penrith
Cumbria
CA11 0HB

Tel: 017684 86450

Fax: 017684 86223

LOCATION

OS Ref. NY477 269

On A592 1m S of A66. 4m SW of Penrith. From London, M1, M6/J40: 4 hrs.

From Edinburgh, A73, M74, M6/J40: 2 1/2 hrs.

Rail: Penrith 4m.

Taxi: Lakeland Taxis: Penrith 01768 865722.

CONFERENCE/FUNCTION		
ROOM	SIZE	MAX CAPACITY
Dining Room		40
Old Hall		50

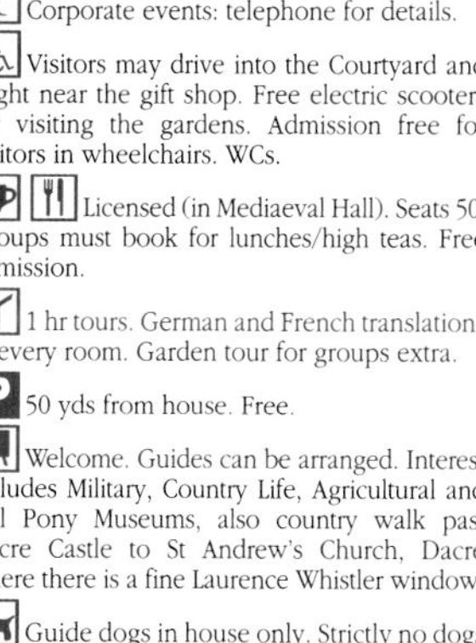

Fashion shows, archery, clay pigeon shooting, garden parties, rallies, filming, caravan rallies, antique fairs and children's camps. Business meetings and conferences. Grand piano available. Deer Park. Lectures on the house, gardens and history by arrangement (max 50). No photography in house. Moorings available on Ullswater.

Corporate events: telephone for details.

Visitors may drive into the Courtyard and alight near the gift shop. Free electric scooters for visiting the gardens. Admission free for visitors in wheelchairs. WCs.

Licensed (in Mediaeval Hall). Seats 50. Groups must book for lunches/high teas. Free admission.

1 hr tours. German and French translations in every room. Garden tour for groups extra.

50 yds from house. Free.

Welcome. Guides can be arranged. Interest includes Military, Country Life, Agricultural and Fell Pony Museums, also country walk past Dacre Castle to St Andrew's Church, Dacre where there is a fine Laurence Whistler window.

Guide dogs in house only. Strictly no dogs in garden but allowed in grounds.

OPENING TIMES

SUMMER
2 April - 8 October
Sunday - Thursday

House: 11am - 4pm.

Gardens, restaurant, tearoom, gift shop, plant sales & museums: 10.30am - 5pm.

NB. Groups (12+) please book.

WINTER
October - Easter open by special arrangement with the Administrator.

ADMISSION

House & Garden

Adult	£5.00
Child (6-16yrs)	£3.00
Family	£13.00

Gardens only

Adult	£3.00
Child (6-16yrs)	Free

Groups (12+)

Adult	£4.00
Child (6-16yrs)	£3.00

All prices include VAT.

SPECIAL EVENTS

- **JUL 15 - 16:** Dalemain Rainbow Craft Fair.
- **AUG 27:** Cumbrian Classic Car Show.

Please telephone for further details.

Jarrold Publishing

HOLKER HALL & GARDENS

Cark-in-Cartmel

Owner: Lord Cavendish of Furness

CONTACT

Mrs Jillian Rouse
Holker Hall & Gardens
Cark-in-Cartmel
Grange-over-Sands
Cumbria
LA11 7PL

Tel: 01539 558328

Fax: 01539 558776

LOCATION

OS Ref. SD359 773

Close to Morecambe Bay, 5m W of Grange-over-Sands by B5277. From Kendal, A6, A590, B5277, B5278: 16m.

Motorway: M6/J36.

Bus: From Grange-over-Sands.

Rail: Cark Station.

Taxi: Parkers Motors, Grange-over-Sands.

Air: Blackpool/ Manchester.

CONFERENCE/FUNCTION		
ROOM	SIZE	MAX CAPACITY
Burlington		100

HOLKER HALL, home of Lord and Lady Cavendish, shows the confidence, spaciousness and prosperity of Victorian style on its grandest scale. The New Wing, built by the 7th Duke of Devonshire (1871-4), replaced a previous wing totally destroyed by fire. Workmanship throughout is of the highest quality, particularly the detailed interior carving and linenfold panelling.

Despite this grand scale, Holker is very much a family home. Visitors can wander freely throughout the New Wing. Photographs, beautiful floral displays and bowls of scented pot pourri create the warm and friendly atmosphere so often remarked upon by visitors. Varying in period and style, Louis XV pieces happily mix with the Victorian. Pictures range from an early copy of the famous triple portrait of Charles I by Van Dyck to a modern painting by Douglas Anderson.

GARDENS

Christie's/HHA Garden of the Year (1991), includes formal and woodland areas covering 24 acres. Designated *"amongst the best in the world in terms of design and content"* by the *Good Gardens Guide.* This wonderful Italianate-cum-English garden includes a lime-stone cascade, a fountain, a rose garden and many rare and beautiful plants and shrubs. The gardens featured in BBC2's *Gardeners' World.* Holker is home to the Holker Garden Festival 2 - 4 June.

Jarrold Publishing

Suitable for filming and photography. Deer Park. Lakeland Motor Museum, adventure playground and exhibitions. No photography in house. Guide book translations in French, Spanish and German.

Wedding receptions.

Visitors alight at entrance. Ramps and unisex WCs.

The Coach House licensed café (max 120).

Pre-booked tours at additional cost of 50p each.

150 yds from Hall. Plus grass car parking.

Environmental study day for primary school children £2. Holker holds 2 Sandford Awards for Heritage Education and provides a wide range of educational opportunities for primary aged children to fit in with curriculum requirements, ie. Houses and Home, Technology and Design; Structures, Victorians.

In grounds on leads. No dogs in the gardens.

OPENING TIMES

SUMMER

1 April - 31 October
Daily except Sats
10am - 6pm.

Last admission 4.30pm.

WINTER

1 November - 31 March
Closed.

ADMISSION

SUMMER

House & Garden (1999)

Adult	£6.00
Child*	£3.25
Groups (20-100)	
Adult	£3.95
Child*	£2.70
OAP	£3.65

* Under 6yrs Free.

SPECIAL EVENTS

- **JUN 2 - 4:**
  Holker Garden Festival. Magnificent horticultural displays & floral art combined with countryside displays and festival gardens. Family & children entertainment, craft demonstrations etc.
  Tel: 01539 558838
  Fax: 01539 558776
- **AUG 27:**
  MG Rally. Post and Pre 1955 MGs in concours and driving trials. Discounted admission to MG drivers. Competition entries on the day.

Owner: C H Bagot

CONTACT

Peter Milner
Levens Hall
Kendal
Cumbria
LA8 0PD

Tel: 01539 560321

Fax: 01539 560669

e-mail: levens.hall@farmline.com

LOCATION

OS Ref. SD495 851

5m S of Kendal on the A6. Exit M6/J36.

Rail: Oxenholme 5m.

LEVENS HALL

Kendal

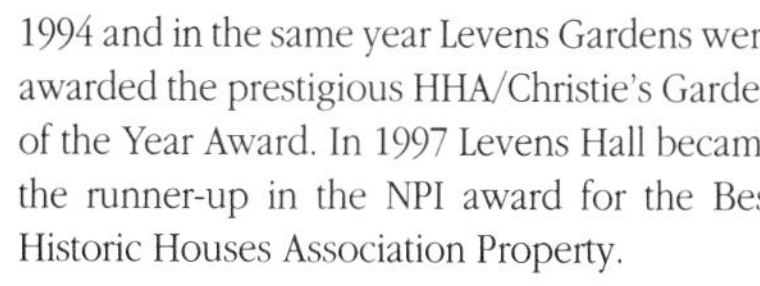

LEVENS HALL is an Elizabethan mansion built around a 13th century pele tower. The much loved home of the Bagot family, visitors comment on the warm and friendly atmosphere. Fine panelling and plasterwork, period furniture, Cordova leather wall coverings, paintings by Rubens, Lely and Cuyp, the earliest English patchwork and Wellingtoniana combine with other beautiful objects to form a fascinating collection.

The world famous Topiary Gardens were laid out by Monsieur Beaumont from 1694 and his design has remained largely unchanged to this day. Over ninety individual pieces of topiary, some over nine metres high, and massive beech hedges, provide a magnificent visual impact. A new Fountain Garden was created in 1994 and in the same year Levens Gardens were awarded the prestigious HHA/Christie's Garden of the Year Award. In 1997 Levens Hall became the runner-up in the NPI award for the Best Historic Houses Association Property.

On Sundays and Bank Holidays 'Bertha', a full size Showman's Engine, is in steam together with a scale model 'Little Gem'. The fine collection of working model steam engines runs on house Open Days from 2 - 5pm. Delicious home-made lunches and teas are available, together with the award winning Levens beer 'Morocco Ale', in the recently extended tearoom. A new gift shop opened in Spring 1999, completing a two year programme of improvements and refurbishment of visitor facilities.

No indoor photography.

Partially suitable. WC. Wheelchair loan - gardens only suitable.

Licensed.

By arrangement.

Educational programme.

Guide dogs only.

OPENING TIMES

SUMMER

2 April - 12 October
Suns - Thurs
(closed Fris & Sats).

House: 12 noon - 5pm
Last admission 4.30pm.

Group tours of Hall at 10am & 11am available by arrangement.

Gardens & Tearoom: 10am - 5pm.

WINTER

Closed.

ADMISSION

House & Gardens

Adult	£5.50
Child	£2.80
Groups (20+)	
Adult	£4.50
School	£2.60
Family (2+3)	£16.00

Gardens

Adult	£4.00
Child	£2.10
Groups (20+)	
Adult	£3.50
School*	£1.90
Family (2+3)	£11.50

Evening Tours

House & Garden for groups (20+) by arrangement £6.50

Gardens only groups (20+) by prior arrangement £4.50

Morning Tours

House tours for groups (20+/min charge £98.) by arrangement £5.00

Season Tickets

Garden (single) £15.00

No admission charge for gift shop, tearoom and plant centre

MUNCASTER CASTLE
GARDENS & OWL CENTRE, Ravenglass

Owner: Mrs Phyllida Gordon-Duff-Pennington

CONTACT

Peter Frost-Pennington
Muncaster Castle
Ravenglass
Cumbria
CA18 1RQ

Tel: 01229 717614
Fax: 01229 717010

e-mail: info@muncastercastle.co.uk

LOCATION

OS Ref. SD103 965

On the A595 1m S of Ravenglass, 19m S of Whitehaven.

From London 6 hrs, Chester 2 1/2 hrs, Edinburgh 3 1/2 hrs, M6/J36, A590, A595 (from S). M6/J40, A66, A595(from E). Carlisle, A595 (from N).

Rail: Ravenglass (on Barrow-in-Furness-Carlisle Line) 1 1/2 m.

Air: Manchester 2 1/2 hrs.

CONFERENCE/FUNCTION		
ROOM	SIZE	MAX CAPACITY
Drawing Rm	–	120
Dining Rm	–	50
Family Dining Rm	–	60
Great Hall	–	110
Old Laundry	–	120
Library	–	40

MUNCASTER CASTLE has been owned by the Pennington family since 1208. It has grown from the original pele tower built on Roman foundations to the impressive structure visible today. Outstanding features are the Great Hall and Salvin's Octagonal Library and the Drawing Room with its barrel ceiling.

The castle contains many treasures including beautiful furniture, exquisite needlework panels, tapestries and oriental rugs. The family silver is very fine and is accompanied in the Dining Room by the Ongley Service, the most ornamental set of porcelain ever created by the Derby factory, Florentine 16th century bronzes and an alabaster lady by Giambologna can be seen. All the rooms open to the public are lived in by the family who are actively involved in entertaining their many visitors, including those who now come to be married at Muncaster.

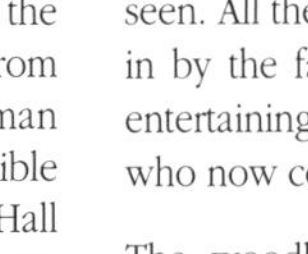

The woodland gardens cover 77 acres and command spectacular views of the Lakeland Fells, with many delightful walks. From mid-March to June the rhododendrons, azaleas, camellias and magnolias are at their best.

The Owl Centre boasts a fine collection of owls from all over the world. 'Meet the Birds' occurs daily at 2.30pm (19 Mar to 28 Oct), when a talk is given on the work of the centre. Weather permitting, the birds fly free.

Church. Suitable for fashion shoots, garden parties, film location, clay pigeon shooting. No photography inside the castle. Home of the World Owl Trust, run by TV naturalist Tony Warburton.

Wedding receptions. For catering and functions in the castle Tel: 01229 717614.

By prior arrangement visitors alight near Castle. Wheelchairs for loan. WCs. Special audio tour tapes for the partially sighted/those with learning difficulties. Allocated parking.

Creeping Kate's Kitchen (licensed) (max 80) – full menu. Groups can book: 01229 717432 to qualify for discounts.

Individual audio tour (40mins) included in price. Private tours with a personal guide (family member possible) can be arranged at additional fee. Lectures by arrangement.

500 cars 800 yds from House; coaches may park closer.

Guides available. Historical subjects, horticulture, conservation, owl tours.

In grounds, on leads.

OPENING TIMES

Castle
19 March - 5 November
Daily (closed Sats),
12 noon - 5pm.

Gardens & Owl Centre
All year: daily: 11am - 6pm or dusk if earlier.

'Meet the Birds'
19 March - 5 November
Daily at 2.30pm

Winter
Castle closed. Open by appointment for groups.

ADMISSION

Castle, Gardens & Owl Centre

Adult	£6.00
Child (5-15yrs)	£4.00
Under 5yrs	Free
Family (2+2)	£17.00
Groups	
Adult	£5.00
Child (5-15yrs)	£3.00

Season Tickets
Telephone for details.

ABBOT HALL ART GALLERY

'Two Lovers Espied by a Child' by George Romney

KENDAL, CUMBRIA LA9 5AL

***Owner:** Lake District Art Gallery & Museum Trust* ***Contact:** Mr E King*

Tel: 01539 722464 **Fax:** 01539 722494

Abbot Hall is a jewel of a building in a beautiful setting on the banks of the River Kent, surrounded by a park and overlooked by the ruins of Kendal Castle. This is one of Britain's finest small art galleries and a wonderful place in which to see and enjoy changing exhibitions in the elegantly proportioned rooms of a Grade I Listed Georgian building. The permanent collection at Abbot Hall alone is worth a visit. You can view 18th century paintings in their period setting, alongside furniture and *objets d'art* of the time. The collection of society portraits of the day includes key works by George Romney (1734-1802), who served his apprenticeship in Kendal. The adjacent Museum of Lakeland Life is a popular family attraction with a Victorian street scene, farmhouse rooms, Arthur Ransome room and displays of Arts and Crafts movement furniture and fabrics.

Location: OS Ref. SD516 922. 10mins from M6/J36. Follow brown museum signs to South Kendal. S end of town, just NE of parish church.

Opening Times: 10 Feb - 22 Dec: daily, 10.30am - 5pm. Reduced hours in winter.

Admission: Adult £3, Child/Student £1.50, OAP £2.80, Family £7.50. Concession, Family and Season tickets available.

Chairlifts in split level galleries. WCs. Licensed. By arrangement.

ACORN BANK GARDEN & WATERMILL

Tel: 017683 61893

Temple Sowerby, Penrith, Cumbria CA10 1SP

Owner: The National Trust **Contact:** The Custodian

A one hectare garden protected by fine oaks under which grow a vast display of daffodils. Inside the walls there are orchards containing a variety of fruit trees surrounded by mixed borders with shrubs, herbaceous plants and roses, while the impressive herb garden has the largest collection of culinary and medicinal plants in the north. A circular woodland walk runs beside the Crowdundle Beck to Acorn Bank Watermill, which although under restoration, is open to visitors. The house is not open.

Location: Gate: OS Ref. NY612 281. Just N of Temple Sowerby, 6m E of Penrith on A66.

Opening Times: 1 Apr - 31 Oct: daily, 10am - 5pm. Last admission 4.30pm.

Admission: Adult £2.30, Child £1.20, Family £5.80. Pre-arranged groups £1.70.

Grounds only. WCs.

APPLEBY CASTLE

See page 376 for full page entry.

BEATRIX POTTER GALLERY

Tel: 01539 436355

Main Street, Hawkshead, Cumbria LA22 0NS

Owner: The National Trust **Contact:** The Custodian

An annually changing exhibition of original sketches and watercolours painted by Beatrix Potter for her children's stories. One of many historic buildings in this picturesque village, this was once the office of the author's husband, the solicitor William Heelis. The interior remains substantially unaltered since his day.

Location: OS Ref. SD352 982. 5m SSW of Ambleside. In the Square.

Opening Times: 2 Apr - 29 Oct: Sun - Thur (closed Fris & Sats except Good Fri) 10.30am - 4.30pm. Last admission 4pm. Admission is by timed ticket (incl. NT members).

Admission: Adult £3, Child £1.50. No reduction for groups.

Guide dogs only.

BROUGH CASTLE

Tel: 0191 269 1200

Brough, Cumbria

Owner: English Heritage **Contact:** The North Regional Office

This ancient site dates back to Roman times. The 12th century keep replaced an earlier stronghold destroyed by the Scots in 1174.

Location: OS Ref. NY791 141. 8m SE of Appleby S of A66. South part of the village.

Opening Times: Any reasonable time.

Admission: Free.

BROUGHAM CASTLE

Tel: 01768 862488

Penrith, Cumbria CA10 2AA

Owner: English Heritage **Contact:** The Custodian

These impressive ruins on the banks of the River Eamont include an early 13th century keep and later buildings. You can climb to the top of the keep and survey the domain of its eccentric one-time owner Lady Anne Clifford, who restored the castle in the 17th century. There is a small exhibition of Roman tombstones from the nearby fort.

Location: OS Ref. NY537 290. 1½ m SE of Penrith, between A66 & B6262.

Opening Times: 1 Apr - 30 Sept: daily, 10am - 6pm. 1 - 31 Oct: daily, 10am - 5pm.

Admission: Adult £2, Child £1, Conc. £1.50. 15% discount for groups (11+).

Grounds suitable. Limited. In grounds, on leads. Tel. for details.

CARLISLE CASTLE

English Heritage Photographic Library

CARLISLE, CUMBRIA CA3 8UR

***Owner:** English Heritage* ***Contact:** The Custodian*

Tel: 01228 591922

This impressive medieval castle, where Mary Queen of Scots was once imprisoned, has a long and tortuous history of warfare and family feuds. A portcullis hangs menacingly over the gatehouse passage, there is a maze of passages and chambers, endless staircases to lofty towers and you can walk the high ramparts for stunning views. There is also a medieval manor house in miniature: a suite of medieval rooms furnished as they might have been when used by the castle's former constable. The castle is also the home of the Museum of the King's Own Border Regiment (included in the admission price).

Location: OS85 Ref. NY397 563. In Carlisle town, at N end of city centre.

Open: 1 Apr - 30 Sept: daily, 9.30am - 6pm. 1 - 31 Oct: daily, 10am - 5pm. 1 Nov - 31 Mar: daily, 10am - 4pm. Closed 24 - 26 Dec.

Admission: Adult £3, Child £1.50, Conc £2.30. 15% discount for groups (11+).

Partially suitable, wheelchairs available. By arrangement. No parking. Dogs on leads. Tel. for details.

CARLISLE CATHEDRAL

Tel: 01228 548151 **Fax:** 01228 547049

Carlisle, Cumbria CA3 8TZ

e-mail: office@carlislecathedral.org.uk

Contact: Ms C Baines

Fine sandstone Cathedral, founded in 1122. Medieval stained glass. Carvings and painted wall panels. Treasury with displays of silver, diocesan and cathedral treasures.

Location: OS Ref. NY399 559. Carlisle city centre, 2m from M6/J43.

Opening Times: Mon - Sat: 7.45am - 6.15pm, Suns, 7.45 - 5pm. Closes 4pm between Christmas Day & New Year. Sun services: 8am, 10.30am & 3pm. Weekday services: 8am, 5.30pm & a 12.30 service on Weds, Fris and Saints' Days.

Admission: Donation.

DALEMAIN

See page 377 for full page entry.

DOVE COTTAGE & WORDSWORTH MUSEUM

Tel: 01539 435544/435547

Grasmere, Cumbria LA22 9SH **Fax:** 01539 435748

See full page advertisement on page 21

Owner: Wordsworth Trust **Contact:** Allan Ellison

Wordsworth's home 1799 - 1808, Dove Cottage is beautifully preserved. Visitors are offered guided tours. The garden is open, weather permitting. The award-winning Wordsworth Museum displays a permanent exhibition and a programme of special exhibitions and events.

Location: OS Ref. NY342 070. Immediately S of Grasmere village on A591. Main car/coach park next to Dove Cottage Tea Rooms.

Opening Times: All year: daily, 9.30am - 5pm. Closed 10 Jan - 6 Feb (inc) & 24 - 26 Dec.

Admission: Adult £5, Child £2.40, Student £4.20, OAP £4.70. Pre-arranged groups (15-60): Adult £4.40, Child £2.20. Reciprocal discount ticket with Rydal Mount and Wordsworth House, Cockermouth.

No photography. Partially suitable. WC. Obligatory. Limited. Guide dogs only. Please telephone for details.

FURNESS ABBEY

Tel: 01229 823420

Barrow-in-Furness, Cumbria LH13 0TJ

Owner: English Heritage **Contact:** The Custodian

Hidden in a peaceful green valley are the beautiful red sandstone remains of the wealthy abbey founded in 1123 by Stephen, later King of England. This abbey first belonged to the Order of Savigny and later to the Cistercians. There is a museum and exhibition.

Location: OS96, Ref. SD218 717. 1 1/2 m NE of Barrow-in-Furness.

Opening Times: 1 Apr - 30 Sept: daily, 10am - 6pm. 1 - 31 Oct:, daily, 10am - 5pm. 1 Nov - 31 Mar: Wed - Sun, 10am - 4pm. Closed 1 - 2pm in winter. Closed 24 - 26 Dec.

Admission: Adult £2.60, Child £1.30, Conc. £2. 15% discount for groups (11+).

Grounds suitable. Inclusive. In grounds, on leads. Tel. for details.

HARDKNOTT ROMAN FORT

Tel: 0191 269 1200

Ravenglass, Cumbria

Owner: English Heritage **Contact:** The North Regional Office

This fort, built between AD120 and 138, controlled the road from Ravenglass to Ambleside.

Location: OS Ref. NY218 015. At the head of Eskdale. 9m NE of Ravenglass, at W end of Hardknott Pass.

Opening Times: Any reasonable time. Access may be hazardous in winter.

Admission: Free.

HILL TOP

Tel: 01539 436269

Near Sawrey, Ambleside, Cumbria LA22 0LF

Owner: The National Trust **Contact:** The Property Manager

Beatrix Potter wrote many *'Peter Rabbit'* books in this little 17th century house, which contains her furniture and china. There is a traditional cottage garden attached.

Location: OS Ref. SD370 955. 2m S of Hawkshead, in hamlet of Near Sawrey, behind the Tower Bank Arms.

Opening Times: Mar - May: 11am - 4.30pm. June - Aug, 10.30am - 5pm. Sept & Oct, 11am - 4.30pm. Last admission 30mins before closing.

Admission: Adult £4, Child £2, Family £9.75. No reduction for groups.

HOLEHIRD

Tel: 01539 446008

Patterdale Road, Windermere, Cumbria LA23 1NP

Owner: Lakeland Horticultural Society **Contact:** The Hon Secretary

Over 4 acres of hillside gardens overlooking Troutbeck Valley, including a walled garden and national collection of astilbes, hydrangeas and polystichum ferns. All of the work in the gardens is done by volunteers.

Location: OS Ref. NY410 008. On A592, 3/4 m N of junction with A591. 1/2 m N of Windermere. 1m from Townend.

Opening Times: All year: dawn to dusk.

Admission: Free. Donation appreciated (at least £2 suggested).

HOLKER HALL

See page 378 for full page entry.

HUTTON-IN-THE-FOREST

PENRITH, CUMBRIA CA11 9TH

Owner: *Lord Inglewood* ***Contact:*** *Edward Thompson*

Tel: 01768 484449 **Fax:** 01768 484571

The home of Lord Inglewood's family since 1605. Built around a medieval pele tower with 17th, 18th and 19th century additions. Fine collections of furniture and paintings, ceramics and tapestries. Outstanding grounds with terraces, topiary, walled garden, dovecote and woodland walk through magnificent specimen trees.

Location: OS Ref. NY460 358. 6m NW of Penrith & 2 1/2 m from M6/J41 on B5305.

Opening Times: 20 Apr - 1 Oct: Thur - Fri, Suns & BH Mons. 12.30 - 4pm (last entry). Tearoom: As house: 12 noon - 4.30pm. Grounds: daily except Sats, 11am - 5pm.

Admission: House, Gardens & Grounds: Adult £4, Child £2, Family £10. Gardens & Grounds: Adult £2.50, Child Free.

Picnic area. Gift stall. By arrangement. Partially suitable. Obligatory (except Jul/Aug & BHs).

LANERCOST PRIORY

Tel: 01697 73030

Brampton, Cumbria CA8 2HQ

Owner: English Heritage **Contact:** The Custodian

This Augustinian priory was founded c1166. The nave of the church, which is intact and in use as the local parish church, contrasts with the ruined chancel, transepts and priory buildings.

Location: OS86, Ref. NY556 637. 2m NE of Brampton. 1m N of Naworth Castle.

Opening Times: 1 Apr - 30 Sept: daily, 10am - 6pm. 1 - 31 Oct: daily, 10am - 5pm.

Admission: Adult £2, Child £1, Conc. £1.50. Groups: 15% discount for groups (11+).

 Ground floor suitable. Inclusive.  Limited.  Tel. for details.

MIREHOUSE

KESWICK, CUMBRIA CA12 4QE

Owner: *James Fryer-Spedding* ***Contact:*** *Clare Spedding*

Tel/Fax: 017687 72287 **e-mail:** info@mireho.freeserve.co.uk

1998 winner of the NPI award for 'The Warmest Family Welcome in the North'. Our visitors particularly appreciate the spectacular setting between mountain and lake, the extraordinary literary and artistic connections, varied gardens, walks, natural playgrounds, live classical music and the personal attention of members of the family. The tearoom is known for generous Cumbrian cooking.

Location: OS Ref. NY235 284. Beside A591, 3½m N of Keswick. Good bus service.

Opening Times: 1 Apr - 31 Oct: Gardens & Tearoom: daily, 10am - 5.30pm. House: Sun & Wed (also Fris in Aug), 2 - 4.30pm (last entry). At other times for groups by appointment.

Admission: House & Garden: Adult £4, Child £2, Family £11.50. Gardens & lakeside walk: Adult £1.70, Child £1.

No photography in house. By arrangement.  Limited. In grounds on leads.

LEVENS HALL

See page 379 for full page entry.

MUNCASTER CASTLE

See page 380 for full page entry.

MUNCASTER WATER MILL

Tel: 01229 717232

Ravenglass, Cumbria CA18 1ST

Owner: Lake District Estates **Contact:** E & P Priestly

Working old manorial mill with 13ft overshot wheel and all milling equipment.

Location: OS Ref. SD094 977. 1m N of Ravenglass on A595.

Opening Times: Easter - Oct: daily 10am - 5pm. Nov - Mar: weekends only, 11am - 4pm.

Admission: Adult £1.60, Child 80p, Family £4 (1999 prices).

English Heritage Photographic Library.

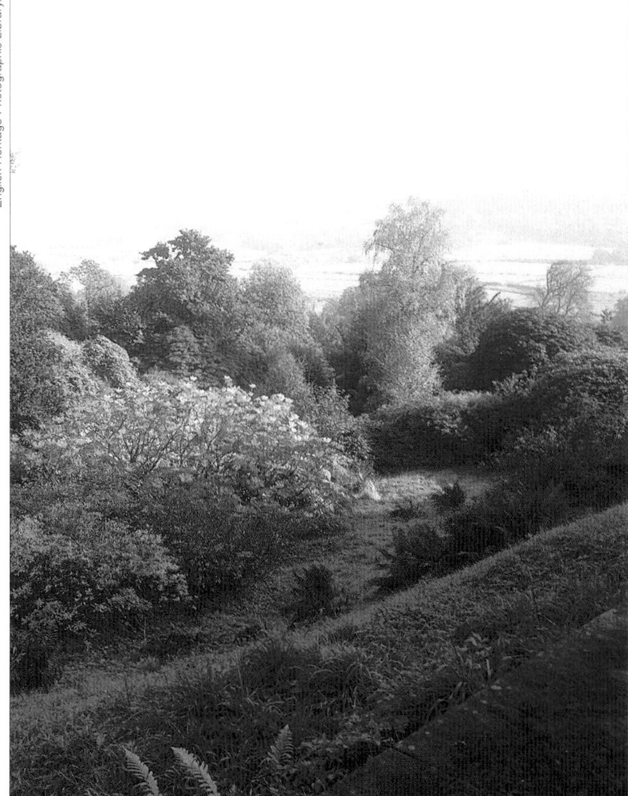

View from Muncaster Castle towards Eskdale, Cumbria.

Cumbria Tourist Board.

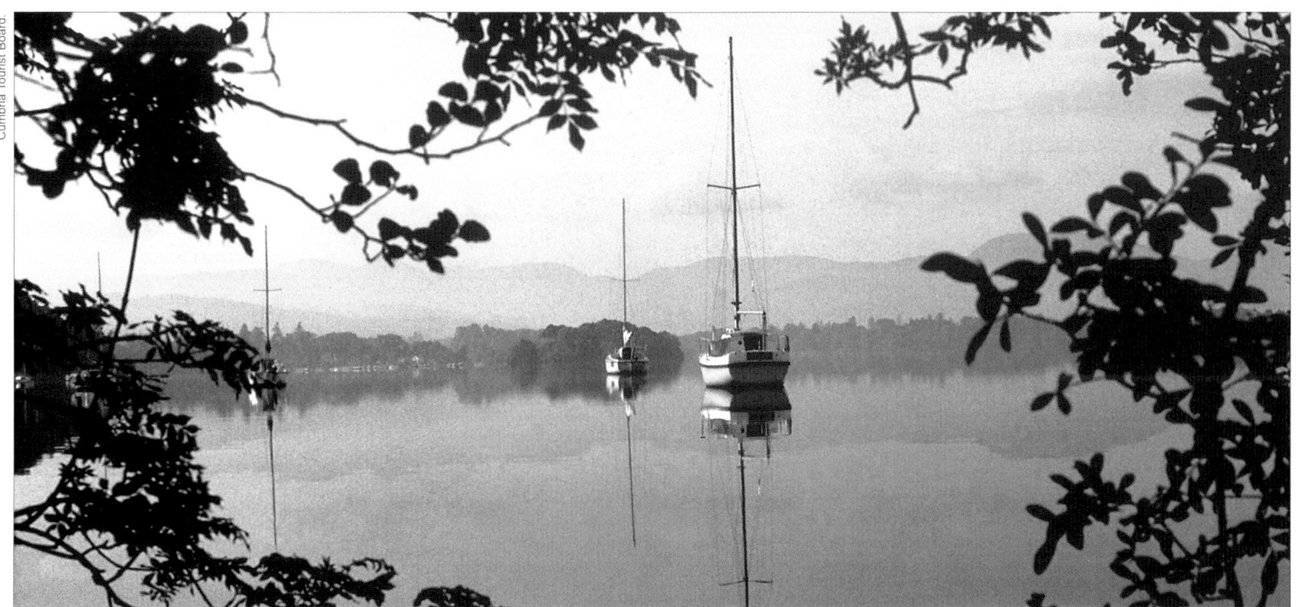

Lake Windermere, Cumbria.

NAWORTH CASTLE

BRAMPTON, CUMBRIA CA8 2HF

Owner: *Philip Howard* ***Contact:*** *Colleen Hall*

Tel: 01697 73229 **Fax:** 01697 73679 **e-mail:** pcwh@naworth.co.uk

Naworth Castle is now Cumbria's premier function venue for weddings and corporate events. The Great Hall can seat up to 200 people for a banquet. A lot of refurbishment was undertaken in 1999 including the Great Hall, the Library, the Drawing Room, the Walled Garden and all of the bedrooms. Naworth is ideal for small residential training breaks/conferences. Marquee facilities in the garden and grounds. Clients guaranteed exclusive use and outstanding personal service. Corporate clients include British Telecom, Honda, Dresdner RCM, Thorn EMI, Rover. Previous filming *Jane Eyre*, Catherine Cookson's *The Black Candle* and *The National Lottery Live*.

Location: OS Ref. NY560 626. $^1/_2$ m off main A69 Carlisle - Newcastle road. 3m E of Brampton. Carlisle 12m, Newcastle 46m, M6 9m.

Opening Times: All year by appointment only. All tours must be pre-booked: minimum 15 people. We are ideal for specialist coach parties. Most tours by owner. Lunches, teas and dinners and accommodation available upon request.

Superb clay pigeon layout, river & lake fishing, game shooting. Conference and corporate breaks, ideal for team building (2500 acre estate with 400 acres of woods and $10^1/_2$ acre flat field). Ideal for product launches, concerts, charity events, balls, banquets and exhibitions.

High quality retained caterers available for all events and overnight parties. Own wine list.

13 double/twin bedrooms with en-suite shower/bathrooms. 2 bedroomed apartment with shower/WC.

Civil Wedding Licence.

SPECIAL EVENTS

MAR 24 - 28 & AUG 25 - 28: Galloway Antiques Fair.

JUN 22: Thomson Roddick & Laurie Fine Pictures & Furniture Auction (viewing Jun 21).

OCT 26: Thomson Roddick & Laurie Fine Art & Furniture Sale (viewing Oct 25).

PENRITH CASTLE

Tel: 0191 269 1200

Penrith, Cumbria

Owner: English Heritage **Contact:** The North Regional Office

This 14th century castle, set in a park on the edge of the town, was built to defend Penrith against repeated attacks by Scottish raiders.

Location: OS Ref. NY513 299. Opposite Penrith railway station. W of the town centre. Fully visible from the street.

Opening Times: Park opening hours.

Admission: Free.

THE QUAKER TAPESTRY EXHIBITION CENTRE

Tel/Fax: 01539 722975

Friends Meeting House, Stramongate, Kendal, Cumbria LA9 4BH

e-mail: info@quaker-tapestry.co.uk

Owner: Trustees of the Quaker Tapestry **Contact:** Bridget Guest

This unique exhibition of 77 panels of community embroidery delights visitors of all ages. Explore the Quaker journey from 17th century to the present day as you uncover over 300 years of social history, beautifully illustrated by 4000 men, women and children from 15 countries.

Location: OS Ref. SD517 927. Centre of Kendal, access from either Stramongate or New Road.

Opening Times: 3 Apr - 4 Nov: Mon - Sat, 10am - 5pm, last admission 4.15pm.

Admission: Adult £3, Child £1, Conc. £2.50.

No indoor photography. Demonstrations. For group visits (20+). By arrangement. Limited. Guide dogs only.

RYDAL MOUNT & GARDENS

Tel: 01539 433002 **Fax:** 01539 431738

Ambleside, Cumbria LA22 9LU **e-mail:** Rydalmount.aol.com

Owner: Rydal Mount Trustees **Contact:** Peter & Marian Elkington

See full page advertisement on page 21

The historic house of William Wordsworth from 1813 until his death in 1850, now the family home of his descendants. It contains family portraits and his personal possessions. The extensive garden, landscaped by the poet, includes terraces, rare shrubs, trees and the poet's summerhouse which overlooks beautiful Rydal Water.

Location: OS Ref. NY364 063. $1^1/_2$ m N of Ambleside on A591 Grasmere Road.

Opening Times: Mar - Oct: Daily, 9.30am - 5pm. Nov - Feb: Daily except Tues, 10am - 4pm.

Admission: Adult £3.75, Child £1.25, Student £3, OAP £3.25. Pre-arranged groups £2.75. Garden only: £1.75. Free parking. Reciprocal discount ticket with Dove Cottage and Wordsworth House.

No inside photography. Partially suitable. By arrangement. Limited. In grounds, on leads. Guide dogs only in house.

SIZERGH CASTLE

Tel: 01539 560070 **Fax:** 01539 561621

Nr Kendal, Cumbria LA8 8AE

Owner: The National Trust **Contact:** The House Manager

The Strickland family have lived here for more than 750 years. The impressive 14th century pele tower was extended in Tudor times, with some of the finest Elizabethan carved overmantels in the country. Contents include good English and French furniture and family portraits. The castle is surrounded by gardens of beauty and interest, including the Trust's largest limestone rock garden; good autumn colour. Large estate; walks leaflet available in shop.

Location: OS Ref. SD498 878. $3^1/_2$ m S of Kendal, NW of the A590/A591 interchange.

Opening Times: Castle: 28 May - 31 Oct: Sun - Thur, 1.30 - 5.30pm.
Garden: 23 Apr - 31 Oct from 12.30pm. Last admission 5pm.

Admission: Adult £4.60, Child £2.30, Family £11.50. Garden only: £2.30. Groups (15+): £3 by arrangement (not on BHs).

STAGSHAW GARDEN

Tel / Fax: 015394 46027

Ambleside, Cumbria LA22 0HE

Owner: The National Trust **Contact:** Windermere & Troutbeck Property Office

This woodland garden was created by the late Cubby Acland, Regional Agent for the National Trust. It contains a fine collection of azaleas and rhododendrons, planted to give good blends of colour under the thinned oaks on the hillside; also many trees and shrubs, including magnolias, camellias and embothriums.

Location: OS Ref 200. NY380 029. ½ m S of Ambleside on A591.

Opening Times: 1 Apr - end Jun: daily, 10am - 6.30pm. Jul - end Oct: by appointment.

Admission: £1.50, no reduction for groups.

Not suitable. No parking. 

STEAM YACHT GONDOLA

Tel/Fax: 015394 63856

(NT Gondola Bookings) National Trust Office, The Hollens, Grasmere, LA22 9QZ

Owner: The National Trust **Contact:** The Manager

The Steam Yacht Gondola, first launched in 1859 and now completely renovated by the Trust, provides a steam-powered passenger service, carrying 86 passengers in opulently upholstered saloons. A superb way to see Coniston's scenery.

Location: OS Ref. SD305 975. Coniston (½ m to Coniston Pier).

Opening Times: Sails from Coniston Pier daily at 11am, 1 Apr - 31 Oct. The Trust reserves the right to cancel sailings in the event of high winds or lack of demand. Piers at Coniston, Park-a-Moor and Brantwood (not NT).

Admission: Ticket prices & timetable on application and published locally. Family ticket available. No reduction for NT members as Gondola is an enterprise and not held solely for preservation. Groups & private charters by prior arrangement.

Not suitable. Dogs on leads, outside saloons, 50p any journey.

STOTT PARK BOBBIN MILL

Tel: 01539 531087

Low Stott Park, Ulverston, Cumbria LA12 8AX

Owner: English Heritage **Contact:** The Custodian

When this working mill was built in 1835 it was typical of the many mills in the Lake District which grew up to supply the spinning and weaving industry in Lancashire but have since disappeared. A remarkable opportunity to see a demonstration of the machinery and techniques of the Industrial Revolution. There is a working Static Steam Engine on Tuesdays to Thursdays.

Location: OS96 Ref. SD373 883. Near Newby Bridge on A590.

Opening Times: 1 Apr - 30 Sept: daily, 10am - 6pm. 1 - 31 Oct: daily, 10am - 5pm. Last admission 1hr before closing.

Admission: Adult £3, Child £1.50, Conc. £2.30. Groups: discount for groups (11+).

Ground floor suitable. WC.  Inclusive. 

HELENA THOMPSON MUSEUM

Tel: 01900 326254

Park End Road, Workington, Cumbria CA14 4DE

Owner: Allerdale Borough Council **Contact:** Philip Crouch Esq

The museum is housed in a fine listed mid-Georgian building. Displays include pottery, silver, glass, furniture and dress collection.

Location: OS Ref. NY007 286. Corner of A66, Ramsey Brow & Park End Road.

Opening Times: Apr - Sept: Mon - Sat, 10.30am - 4pm. Nov - Mar: Mon - Sat, 11am - 3pm.

Admission: Free.

TOWNEND

Tel: 01539 432628

Troutbeck, Windermere, Cumbria LA23 1LB

Owner: The National Trust **Contact:** The Administrator

An exceptional relic of Lake District life during past centuries. Originally a 'statesman' (wealthy yeoman) farmer's house, built about 1626. Townend contains carved woodwork, books, papers, furniture and fascinating implements of the past which were accumulated by the Browne family who lived here from 1626 until 1943.

Location: OS Ref. NY407 020. 3m SE of Ambleside at S end of Troutbeck village. 1m from Holehird, 3m N of Windermere.

Opening Times: 2 Apr - 31 Oct: Tue - Fri, Suns & BH Mons, 1 - 5pm or dusk if earlier. Last admission 4.30pm.

Admission: Adult £3, Child £1.50, Family £7.50. No reduction for groups which must be pre-booked. Townend and village unsuitable for coaches; 12 - 15 seater mini-buses are acceptable; permission to take coaches to Townend must be obtained from the Transportation and Highways Dept, Cumbria CC, Carlisle, Cumbria (tel: 01228 23456).

Unsuitable for wheelchairs. Braille guide. 

WORDSWORTH HOUSE

Tel: 01900 824805

Main Street, Cockermouth, Cumbria CA13 9RX

Owner: The National Trust **Contact:** The Custodian

See full page advertisement on page 21

A Georgian town house where William Wordsworth was born in 1770 in the ancient market town of Cockermouth. Several rooms contain some of the poet's personal effects. His childhood garden, with terraced walk attractively restored, with views over the River Derwent referred to in '*The Prelude*'.

Location: OS Ref. NY118 307. Main Street, Cockermouth.

Opening Times: 27 Mar - 27 Oct: weekdays only, plus all BH Sats and Sats in Jun, Jul & Aug, 10.30am - 4.30pm. Last admission 4pm.

Admission: Adult £3, Child £1.50, Family £7.50. Pre-booked groups £2.20. Reciprocal discount ticket with Dove Cottage and Rydal Mount.

By arrangement only. No parking. 

WORKINGTON HALL

Tel: 01900 326408

Ramsey Brow, Workington, Cumbria

Owner: Allerdale Borough Council **Contact:** Allerdale Borough Council Tourism Dept.

Refuge for Mary Queen of Scots during her last night of freedom in May 1568, this was one of the finest Manor houses in the region. Now a ruin.

Location: OS Ref. NY007 288. In public park on N side of A66

Opening Times: Easter - Oct: Tue - Fri & BHs, 10am - 1pm & 2 - 5pm, Sats & Suns 2 - 5pm.

Admission: Adult 85p, Conc. 55p, Family (2+2/1+3) £2.25.

Cumbria Tourist Board.

Loweswater, Cumbria.

North West England

English Life Publication Ltd

LEIGHTON HALL

Carnforth

Owner:
Richard Reynolds Esq

CONTACT

Mrs C S Reynolds
Leighton Hall
Carnforth
Lancashire
LA5 9ST

Tel: 01524 734474

Fax: 01524 720357

e-mail: leightonhall@yahoo.co.uk

LOCATION

OS Ref. SD494 744

9m N of Lancaster, 10m S of Kendal, 3m N of Carnforth. $1^1/_2$ m W of A6. 3m from M6/A6/J35, signed from J35A.

Rail: Lancaster Station 9m.

Air: Manchester Airport 65m.

Taxi: Carnforth Radio Taxis, Carnforth 732763.

CONFERENCE/FUNCTION		
ROOM	SIZE	MAX CAPACITY
Music Room	24' x 21' 6"	80

LEIGHTON HALL is one of the most beautifully sited houses in the British Isles, situated in a bowl of parkland, with the whole panorama of the Lakeland Fells rising behind. The hall's neo-gothic façade was superimposed on an 18th century house, which, in turn, had been built on the ruins of the original medieval house. The present owner is descended from Adam d'Avranches who built the first house in 1246.

The whole house is lived in by the Reynolds family and emphasis is put on making visitors feel welcome in a family home.

Connoisseurs of furniture will be particularly interested in the 18th century pieces by Gillow of Lancaster. Mr Reynolds is directly descended from the founder of Gillow and Company, hence the strong Gillow connection with the house. Also on show are some fine pictures, clocks, silver and *objets d'art*.

GARDENS

The main garden has a continuous herbaceous border and rose covered walls, while the Walled Garden contains flowering shrubs, a herb garden, an ornamental vegetable garden and a maze. Beyond is the Woodland Walk, where wild flowers abound from early Spring.

A varied collection of Birds of Prey is on display in the Bird Garden, and flown each afternoon that the hall is open, weather permitting.

English Life Publication Ltd

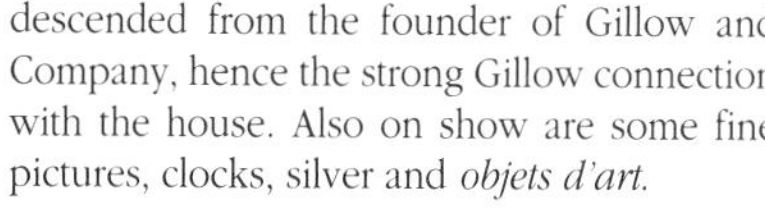

Product launches, seminars, filming, garden parties, conferences, rallies, overland driving, archery and clay pigeon shoots, grand piano. No photography in house. Large collection of birds of prey on display in the afternoon, some of which fly at 3.30pm, weather permitting.

Buffets, lunches, dinners and wedding receptions.

Partially suitable. WC. Visitors may alight at the entrance.

Groups must book, menus on request.

Obligatory. By prior arrangement owner may meet groups, tour time: 45 mins. House and flying display tour time: 2 hrs. Lectures on property, its contents, gardens and history.

Ample.

School programme 10am-2pm daily May-Sept except Mons & Sats. Birds of prey flown for schools at 12pm. Schools Visit Programme won the Sandford Award for Heritage Education in 1983 and in 1989.

Guide dogs only.

OPENING TIMES

SUMMER

1 May - 30 September
Daily except Mons & Sats
2 - 5pm. Open BH Mons.

August only:
11.30am - 5pm.

NB. Booked groups (25+) at any time by arrangement.

WINTER

1 October - 30 April
Open to booked groups (25+).

ADMISSION

SUMMER

House, Garden & Birds

Adult	£4.00
Child (up to 16yrs)	£2.75
OAP	£3.50
Groups (Min. payment £80)	
Adult	£3.25
Child (up to 16yrs)	£2.50
Family (2+3)	£12.00
School	£2.50

Grounds only
(after 4.30pm)

Per person	£1.50

WINTER

As above but groups by appointment only.

SPECIAL EVENTS

- **JUN 30:** Concert & Fireworks: 'Last Night of the Proms'.
- **AUG 4 - 5:** Shakespeare in the Garden: 'The Tempest'.
- **AUG 27:** 'Close Encounters of the Classical Kind' - Concert & Fireworks.
- **SEPT 9 - 10:** Rainbow Craft Fair.
- **OCT 1:** Teddy Bear Fair.
- **OCT 15:** Dolls House & Miniaturist Fair.

ASTLEY HALL

Tel: 01257 515555 **Fax:** 01257 515556

Astley Park, Off Hall Gate, Chorley PR7 1NP **e-mail:** astleyhall@lineone.net

Owner: Chorley Borough Council **Contact:** Dr Nigel Wright

A charming house, dating back to 1580, with additions in the 1660s and 1820s. Interiors include sumptuous plaster ceilings, fine 17th century oak furniture and tapestries, plus displays of fine and decorative art. Set in parkland.

Location: OS Ref. SD574 183. 2m W of Chorley, off A581 Chorley - Southport road. 5 mins from M61/J8.

Opening Times: Easter - end Oct: Tue - Sun, 12 noon - 5pm. Plus BH Mons. Nov - Easter: Fri - Sun, 12 noon - 4pm. Closed Christmas & New Year.

Admission: Adult £2.90, Child/Conc. £1.90. Groups: Adult £2.30, Child/Conc. £1.30.

No photography. Partially suitable. Braille guide.
Guide dogs only.

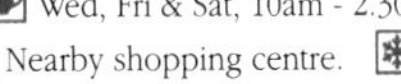

BLACKBURN CATHEDRAL

Tel: 01254 51491 **Fax:** 01254 689666

Cathedral Close, Blackburn, Lancashire BB1 5AA **Contact:** Mrs Alison Feeney

On an historic Saxon site in town centre. The 1826 Parish Church dedicated as the Cathedral in 1977 with new extensions to give a spacious and light interior. The distinctive 'crowning glory' Lantern Tower was rebuilt in 1998 with 56 panels of newly-designed symbolic stained glass to give a new and unique magnificence by day and night. Other features include a fine Walker organ, 12 peal bells and a 'corona' (crown of thorns) above the central altar.

Location: OS Ref. SD684 280. 9m E of M6/J31, via A59 and A677. City centre.

Opening Times: Daily, 9am - 5pm. Sun services: at 8am, 9.15am, 10.30am and 4pm.

Admission: Free. Donations invited.

Wheelchair access. Wed, Fri & Sat, 10am - 2.30pm or by arrangement.
By arrangement. Nearby shopping centre.

Blackburn Cathedral, Lancashire.

GAWTHORPE HALL

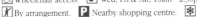

Tel: 01282 771004 **Fax:** 01282 770178

Padiham, Nr Burnley, Lancashire BB12 8UA

Owner: The National Trust **Contact:** The Property Manager

The house was built in 1600-05, and restored by Sir Charles Barry in the 1850s. Barry's designs have been re-created in the principal rooms. Gawthorpe was the home of the Shuttleworth family, and the Rachel Kay-Shuttleworth textile collections are on display in the house, private study by arrangement. Collection of portraits on loan from the National Portrait Gallery.

Location: OS Ref. SD806 340. M65/J8. On E outskirts of Padiham, 3/4 m to house on N of A671. Signed to Clitheroe, then signed from 2nd set of traffic lights.

Opening Times: Hall: 1 Apr - 31 Oct: daily except Mons & Fris, open Good Fri & BH Mons, 1 - 5pm. Last adm. 4.30pm. Garden: All year: daily, 10am - 6pm.

Admission: Hall: Adult £3, Child £1.30, Conc. £1.50, Family £8 (prices may change). Garden: Free. Groups must book.

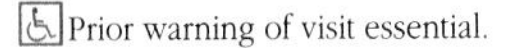 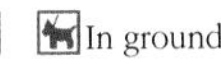 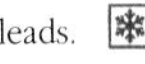

Prior warning of visit essential. In grounds on leads.

HALL I'TH'WOOD

Tel: 01204 301159

off Green Way, Tonge Moor, Bolton BL1 8UA

Owner: Bolton Metropolitan Borough Council **Contact:** W H Farrell

Late medieval manor house with 17/18th century furniture, paintings and decorative art.

Location: OS Ref. SD724 116. 2m NNE of central Bolton. 1/4 m N of A58 ring road between A666 and A676 crossroads.

Opening Times: Please contact for details.

Admission: Adult £2, Conc. £1.

HOGHTON TOWER

HOGHTON, PRESTON, LANCASHIRE PR5 0SH

Owner: *Sir Bernard de Hoghton Bt* ***Contact:*** *Office*

Tel: 01254 852986 **Fax:** 01254 852109

Hoghton Tower, home of 14th Baronet, is one of the most dramatic looking houses in northern England. Three houses have occupied the hill site since 1100 with the present house re-built by Thomas Hoghton between 1560 - 1565. Rich and varied historical events including the Knighting of the Loin 'Sirloin' by James I in 1617.

Location: OS Ref. SD622 264. M65/J3. Midway between Preston & Blackburn on A675.

Opening Times: Jul, Aug & Sept: Mon - Thur, 11am - 4pm. Suns, 1 - 5pm. BH Suns & Mons excluding Christmas & New Year. Group visits by appointment all year.

Admission: House only: Adult £2.50, Child £1.25, Conc. £2. Pre-arranged groups: Adult £3.50. House tours: Adult £3, Child/Conc. £2, Family £8. Gardens, Shop & Tearoom only: £2. Private tours by arrangement (25 min) £6, OAP £5.

Conferences, wedding receptions. Not suitable.
Obligatory.

Gawthorpe Hall, Lancashire.

North West England

LEIGHTON HALL

See page 386 for full page entry.

MANCHESTER CATHEDRAL

Tel: 0161 833 2220 **Fax:** 0161 839 6226

Manchester M3 1SX

In addition to regular worship and daily offices, there are frequent professional concerts, day schools, organ recitals, guided tours and brass-rubbing. The cathedral contains a wealth of beautiful carvings and has the widest medieval nave in Britain.

Location: OS Ref. SJ838 988. Manchester.

Opening Times: Daily.

Admission: Donations welcome.

MARTHOLME

Great Harwood, Blackburn, Lancashire BB6 7UJ

Owner: Mr & Mrs T H Codling **Contact:** Miss P M Codling

Part of medieval manor house with 17th century additions and Elizabethan gatehouse.

Location: OS Ref. SD753 338. 2m NE of Great Harwood off A680 to Whalley.

Opening Times: By written appointment only.

Admission: £3.50.

ROSSENDALE MUSEUM

Tel: 01706 217777 or 01706 226509

Whitaker Park, Rawtenstall, Rossendale, Lancashire BB4 6RE

Owner: Rossendale Borough Council **Contact:** Mrs S Cruise

Former 19th century mill owner's house set in Whitaker Park. Displays include fine and decorative arts and furniture.

Location: OS Ref. SD805 226. Off A681, 1/4 m from Rawtenstall Centre.

Opening Times: Apr - Oct: Mon - Fri, 1 - 5pm, Sats, 10am - 5pm, Suns, 12 noon - 5pm. Nov - Mar: Mon - Fri, 1 - 5pm, Sats, 10am - 4pm, Suns, 12 noon - 4pm. BHs, 1 - 5pm. Closed Christmas Day, Boxing Day and New Year's Day.

Admission: Free.

RUFFORD OLD HALL

Tel/Fax: 01704 821254

Rufford, Nr Ormskirk, Lancashire L40 1SG

Owner: The National Trust **Contact:** The Property Manager

There is a legend that William Shakespeare performed here for the owner Sir Thomas Hesketh in the Great Hall of this, one of the finest 16th century buildings in Lancashire. The playwright would have delighted in the magnificent hall with its intricately carved movable wooden screen. Built in 1530, it established the Hesketh family seat for the next 250 years. In the Carolean Wing, altered in 1821, there are fine collections of 16th and 17th century oak furniture, arms, armour and tapestries.

Location: OS Ref. SD463 160. 7m N of Ormskirk, in village of Rufford on E side of A59.

Opening Times: 1 Apr - 1 Nov: Sat - Wed, 1 - 5pm. Last admission 4.30pm. Also open 1 Jun and 3, 10, 17 & 24 Aug. Garden: same days as house, 12 noon - 5.30pm.

Admission: House & Garden: Adult £3.80, Child £1.90, Family £9.50. Garden only: £2. Reduction for pre-booked groups (no groups on Suns & BH Mons).

 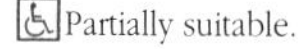Partially suitable.  In grounds, on leads.

Rufford Old Hall, Lancashire.

SAMLESBURY HALL

Tel: 01254 812010 **Fax:** 01254 812174

Preston New Road, Samlesbury, Preston PR5 0UP

Owner: Samlesbury Hall Trust **Contact:** Mr David Hornby

Built in 1325, the hall is an attractive black and white timbered manor house set in extensive grounds.

Location: OS Ref. SD623 305. N side of A677, 4m WNW of Blackburn.

Opening Times: All year: daily except Mons: 11am - 4.30pm. Closed over Christmas and New Year.

Admission: Adult £2.50, Child £1.

SMITHILLS HALL MUSEUM

Tel: 01204 841265

Smithills Dean Road, Bolton BL1 7NP

Owner: Bolton Metropolitan Borough Council **Contact:** Linda McKay

14th century fortified manor house with Tudor panelling. Stuart furniture. Stained glass.

Location: OS Ref. SD699 119. 2m NW of central Bolton, 1/2 m N of A58 ringroad.

Opening Times: Please contact for details.

Admission: Adult £2, Conc. £1.

STONYHURST COLLEGE

Tel: 01254 826345 **Fax:** 01254 826732

Stonyhurst, Clitheroe, Lancashire BB7 9PZ **Contact:** Miss F Ahearne

The original house dates from the late 16th century. Set in extensive grounds with ornamental gardens.

Location: OS Ref. SD690 391. 4m SW of Clitheroe off B6243.

Opening Times: House: 17 Jul - 28 Aug: Sat - Thur (including Aug BH Mon), 1 - 5pm. Grounds & Gardens: 1 Jul - 28 Aug: Sat - Thur (including Aug BH Mon), 1 - 5pm.

Admission: House & Grounds: Adult £4.50, Child (4-14yrs)/OAP £3.50. Grounds only £1.

TOWNELEY HALL ART GALLERY & MUSEUMS

Burnley BB11 3RQ **Tel:** 01282 424213 **Fax:** 01282 436138

Owner: Burnley Borough Council **Contact:** Miss Susan Bourne

House dates from the 14th century with 17th and 19th century modifications. Collections include oak furniture, 18th and 19th century paintings. There is a Museum of Local Crafts and Industries and a Natural History Centre with an aquarium in the grounds.

Location: OS Ref. SD854 309. 1/2 m SE of Burnley on E side of Todmorden Road (A671).

Opening Times: All year: Mon - Fri, 10am - 5pm. Suns, 12 noon - 5pm. Closed Sats throughout the year. Closed Christmas - New Year.

Admission: Free. Guided tours: Tues, Weds & Thurs afternoons or as booked for parties.

Ground floor & grounds suitable. WC. Tel. for details.

TURTON TOWER

Tel: 01204 852203 **Fax:** 01204 853759

Chapeltown Road, Turton BL7 0HG

Owner: Lancashire County Council **Contact:** Martin Robinson-Dowland

Country house based on a medieval tower, extended in the 16th, 17th and 19th centuries. Extensive collection of English wood furniture. Exhibitions and activities programme. Woodland gardens in moorland setting.

Location: OS Ref. SD733 153. On B6391, 4m N of Bolton.

Opening Times: Feb & Nov: Suns, 1 - 4pm. Mar, Apr & Oct: Sat - Wed: 1 - 4pm. May - Sept: Mon - Thur, 10am - 12 noon, 1 - 5pm. Sats & Suns 1 - 5pm.

Admission: Adult £3, Child/OAP £1.50, Family £8. Season ticket available.

WARTON OLD RECTORY

Tel: 0191 269 1200

Warton, Carnforth, Lancashire

Owner: English Heritage **Contact:** The North Regional Office

A rare medieval stone house with remains of the hall, chambers and domestic offices.

Location: OS Ref. SD499 723. At Warton, 1m N of Carnforth on minor road off A6.

Opening Times: Any reasonable time.

Admission: Free.

Plant Sales Index
PAGE 51

Rufford Old Hall, Lancashire. National Trust Photographic Library/Andreas Von Einsiedel.

CROXTETH HALL & COUNTRY PARK

Tel: 0151 228 5311 **Fax:** 0151 228 2817

Liverpool, Merseyside L12 0HB

Owner: Liverpool City Council **Contact:** Mrs Irene Vickers

Ancestral home of the Molyneux family. 500 acres country park. Special events and attractions most weekends.

Location: OS Ref. SJ408 943. 5m NE of Liverpool city centre.

Opening Times: Parkland: daily throughout the year. Hall, Farm & Garden: daily, 11am - 5pm during main season. Telephone for exact dates.

Admission: Parkland: Free. Hall, Farm & Garden: prices on application.

LIVERPOOL CATHEDRAL

Tel: 0151 709 6271 **Fax:** 0151 709 1112

Liverpool, Merseyside L1 7AZ

Owner: The Dean and Chapter **Contact:** Canon Noel Vincent

Sir Giles Gilbert Scott's greatest creation. Built this century from local sandstone with superb glass, stonework and major works of art, it is the largest cathedral in Britain and has a fine musical tradition, a tower offering panoramic views, and an award-winning refectory. There is a unique collection of church embroidery, and SPCK shop with a full range of souvenirs, cards and religious books.

Location: OS Ref. SJ354 893. Central Liverpool, 1/2 m S of Lime Street Station.

Opening Times: 8am - 6pm. Sun services: 8am, 10.30am, 3pm, 4pm. Weekdays: 8am & 5.30pm. Sats: 8am & 3pm.

Admission: Donation.

Grounds suitable. WC. Guide dogs only.

LIVERPOOL METROPOLITAN CATHEDRAL OF CHRIST THE KING

Liverpool, Merseyside L3 5TQ **Tel:** 0151 709 9222 **Fax:** 0151 708 7274

Owner: Roman Catholic Archdiocese of Liverpool **Contact:** Rt Rev P Cookson

Modern circular cathedral with spectacular glass by John Piper and numerous modern works of art. Extensive earlier crypt by Lutyens. Grade II* listed.

Location: OS Ref. SJ356 903. Central Liverpool, 1/2 m E of Lime Street Station.

Opening Times: 8am - 6pm (closes 5pm Suns in Winter). Sun services: 8.30am, 10am, 11am, 3pm & 7pm. Weekday services: 8am, 12.15pm, 5.15pm & 5.45pm. Sats, 9am & 6.30pm.

Admission: Donation.

Except crypt. WCs. By arrangement. Ample for cars. Guide dogs only.

MEOLS HALL

Tel: 01704 228326 **Fax:** 01704 507185

Churchtown, Southport, Merseyside PR9 7LZ

Owner: Robert Hesketh Esq **Contact:** Pamela Whelan

17th century house with subsequent additions. Interesting collection of pictures and furniture.

Location: OS Ref. SD365 184. 3m NE of Southport town centre in Churchtown. SE of A565.

Opening Times: 14 Aug - 14 Sept: daily, 2 - 5pm.

Admission: Adult £3, Child £1. Groups £8.50 (inclusive of afternoon tea).

PORT SUNLIGHT VILLAGE & HERITAGE CENTRE

Tel: 0151 6446466 **Fax:** 0151 6458973

95 Greendale Road, Port Sunlight CH62 4XE **Contact:** Information Officer

Port Sunlight is a picturesque 19th century garden village on the Wirral.

Location: OS Ref. SJ340 845. Follow signs from M53/J4 or 5 or follow signs on A41.

Opening Times: All year, 10am - 4pm in summer; 11am - 4pm in winter.

Admission: Adult 60p, Child 30p, Conc. 50p. Group rates on application.

SPEKE HALL

Tel: 0151 427 7231 **Fax:** 0151 427 9860

The Walk, Liverpool L24 1XD **Info Line:** 0345 585702 (local rate)

Owner: The National Trust **Contact:** The Property Manager

One of the most famous half-timbered houses in the country.

Location: OS Ref. SJ419 825. North bank of the Mersey, 6m SE of city centre. Follow signs for Liverpool airport.

Opening Times: House: 28 Mar - 29 Oct: daily except Mons (but open BH Mons), 1 - 5.30pm. 4 Nov - 10 Dec: Sats & Suns, 1 - 4.30pm. Garden: 28 Mar - 29 Oct: open as house from 12 noon. Nov - Mar 2000: daily except Mons, 12 noon - 4pm. Closed Good Fri, 24/25/26/31 Dec & 1 Jan. Last admission 30 mins before close.

Admission: House & Garden: £4.20, Garden only: £1.60. Family £10.50.

Patrick Lane.

Speke Hall, Merseyside.

The Regions of

SCOTLAND

Dumfries and Galloway Tourist Board

Fleet Oakwood (Woodland Glade)

The development of Scottish Castles

by Martin Coventry

The design of castles depended very much on the social organisation, political climate, expense and building fashions of the time – but it was always a show of the lord's wealth, prestige and power, and a symbol of his authority.

The earliest fortified sites consist of hill forts, brochs and duns, dating from before recorded history. Some of these were occupied as late as the 17th century – and the sites of many others were reused for later fortresses. Hill forts are found all over Scotland, but brochs and duns tend to be concentrated in the north and west.

After the Battle of Hastings, motte and bailey castles were introduced to Scotland along with feudalism – although they are unevenly distributed, being particularly numerous in Galloway, for example, but with few surviving examples in Lothian. This form of defence was not used for long.

By the 13th century, castles of enclosure (enceinte) were being built, where a site was surrounded by a strong stone wall encircling timber or stone buildings. These developed, in some cases, into large castles with large keeps, gatehouses and towers.

Large stone castles were expensive to build and maintain and in the late 14th and 15th centuries simple keeps were built, usually with a small enclosure or courtyard. The keep evolved into the tower house, which was not as massive or simple, and had more regard to comfort. Hundreds of these towers were built in the 16th century. During the later 16th and 17th centuries, the simple rectangular tower house developed into L- and Z-plan tower houses, which provide more accommodation, covering fire and amenity.

At the same time as nobles built and developed keeps and tower houses, the kings of Scots built or refurbished ornate royal palaces. These were often developed out of older strongholds but during the 15th and 16th centuries were remodelled in the Renaissance style to become comfortable residences.

As the need for defence decreased, many castles and tower houses were developed into mansion houses.

There is a great deal of overlap between the different types of stronghold and often a new castle was built on the site of a previous one, and reused materials from the original or simply built around, or out of, the existing building. There are also definite regional differences. In areas such as the Borders, feuds, reiving and warfare contributed to the building of a large number of simple tower houses, peel towers and bastles, although few of these survive intact; whereas in Grampian there are a large number of 17th century Z-plan tower houses. The topography of particular areas influenced the position and style of building: an island in a marsh was as good a site as a rocky promontory.

Hill forts, Brochs and Duns

Hill forts may date from as early as the Neolithic period to about 500BC, and some were used until medieval times. Ramparts of earth and stone walls, laced with timber, or wooden palisades protected hilltops or other defensible sites. Some hill forts enclosed whole villages within their ramparts.

Brochs and duns date from about 100BC, and a few were occupied into the 17th century.

Brochs are round hollow towers, built of dry-stone masonry, with very thick walls. These walls were formed from two shells of masonry with a gallery running up inside the wall. The entrance was extremely narrow, allowing only one person at a time to enter, and a small guard chamber defended the entrance. There were often many buildings around the broch, with outer ditches and ramparts to defend the settlement. Brochs appear to have been concentrated in Orkney and Shetland, Caithness and Sutherland, and the Western Isles, but there are also examples in other parts of the country, including Lothian and Dumfries and Galloway.

The best remaining examples of brochs are Mousa and Clickhimin (Shetland), Dun Carloway (Lewis), Midhowe and Gurness (Orkney), Dun

Mousa Broch.

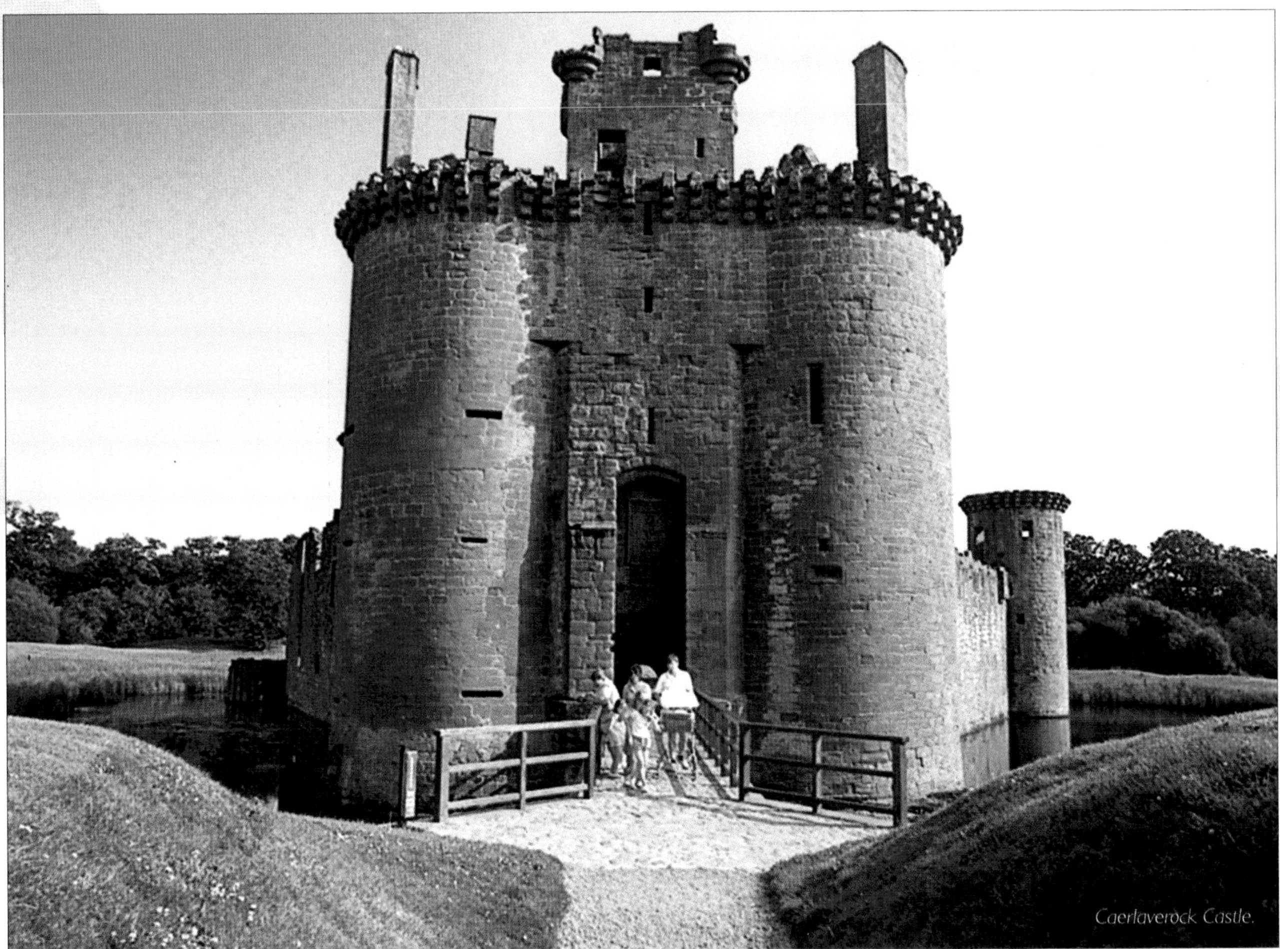
Caerlaverock Castle.

Dornigail (Sutherland), the Glen Elg brochs (Lochaber) and Dun Beag (Skye).

Duns are also most thickly concentrated in the north and west. Dun in Gaelic means fortified place and is used for both duns and brochs in Gaelic-speaking areas.

The general distribution of duns is similar to that of brochs but duns are usually irregular in plan, following the contours of a rock, and can vary in size from a small homestead to a hill fort. The building style was very similar to brochs, and they often had galleried walls and small cells within the walls. Dun an Sticar and Dun Ban on North Uist are good examples of duns, although both were occupied into medieval times.

It is hard to see how it has been possible to always distinguish the two types of structures, when existing remains of both are so fragmentary and overbuilt. It is also not clear who they were built to defend against, although it may have been Roman slave ships.

Motte and Bailey Castles
(12th century)

During the 12th century, motte and bailey castles were introduced along with feudalism into Scotland, mostly into lowland areas, where the style was adopted and adapted by native lords. Motte and bailey castles are mostly concentrated in Clydesdale, Galloway and Grampian. There appear to have been few in central Scotland, Lothians, the north-west and the Highlands.

Motte and bailey castles consisted of an earthern mound, known as a motte, and a courtyard, or bailey, enclosed by a wooden palisade and defended by a ditch. The plan of the motte was usually round, but some were also oval or rectangular and used existing defensive features such as ravines, spits of land between rivers, or cliff tops. At the base of the motte was a dry or wet ditch or moat.

A wooden tower was built on the motte, where the lord and his followers could shelter if attacked. The bailey contained many buildings, such as the hall, chapel, kitchen, bakehouse and stables. The motte and bailey were linked by a removable bridge which spanned the ditch.

Often all that remains today is evidence of the earthworks, some good examples of these being Motte of Urr (Galloway), Peel Ring of Lumphanan and Doune of Invernochty (both Gordon). Duffus Castle (Moray) and Rothesay Castle (Bute) are two of the few examples where a stone keep was added. Other mottes and their surrounding earthworks were reused by later castle builders.

Wooden castles were not used for long, as they could be set alight, but had the advantage of being easy and quick to build. Most of the castles built by Edward I of England to control Scotland were built of wood; after his costly Welsh campaigns, which included the building of such massive castles as Caernarvon, he could afford little else.

Stone Castles of Enclosure or Enceinte *(12/13th century)*

Stone began to be used as a building material because it was less vulnerable to attack by fire and because it was easily obtainable.

Stone castles of enclosure were built as early as the 12th century, but the majority appeared in the 13th century. The simplest form was a wall enclosing a two-storey hall block of wood or stone. The entrance to the hall block was on the first floor and was reached by a ladder, which could be removed easily during attack. The wall was usually surrounded by a ditch and rampart.

There are some good examples of castles of enclosure on the western side of Scotland, including Castle Sween (Argyll), Castle Tioram (Morvern) and Mingary Castle (Ardnamurchan).

By the 13th century, walls were heightened and strengthened, enclosing a courtyard which contained both the hall and lord's chamber, as well as kitchens, bakeries, brewhouses, stables and storerooms. Corner towers were added to defend the castle. The walls were pierced by slits through which crossbows could be fired.

The weakest part of these castles was the entrance through the wall and strong gatehouses were added with portcullises, drawbridges, iron-studded doors and murder-holes. The curtain walls were given battlements for archers to shelter behind.

By the 14th century, large stone castles such as Bothwell Castle (Lanarkshire), Caerlaverock Castle (Dumfries) and Kildrummy Castle (Grampian) had been built. These castles had a keep – a large strong tower separate from the rest of the castle – as well as a gatehouse. The keep had a hall and chambers for the lord. These castles also had thick curtain walls with round or square corner towers.

There are relatively few large castles left in Scotland, partly due to the expense of constructing and maintaining such large buildings, and partly because many were destroyed by the Scots, during the Wars of

Independence, so that they could not be reused by the English. However, some strong royal castles were maintained, including those at Edinburgh, Stirling, Roxburgh, Dumbarton and Dunbar, and a few of the most powerful families could also afford massive fortresses such as the Douglas strongholds of Tantallon (Lothian) and Threave (Galloway) and the Keith stronghold of Dunnottar (Grampian).

Simple Keeps *(14/15th century)*

These consisted of a simple square or rectangular tower, usually with an adjoining courtyard. The walls of the keep were thick and normally rose to at least three storeys to a flush crenellated parapet. The basement and first floor were vaulted to increase the strength of the building. The size of the keep depended on the wealth of the builder.

The basement contained a cellar, often with no connection to the floor above. The hall was on the first floor, with a private chamber for the lord on the floor above, and a garret storey above this. The thick walls contained many mural chambers, either small bedrooms or garderobes. The entrance was at first-floor level and was reached by an external timber stair, which could be removed during an attack. Stairs led up, within the walls, to each floor. The keep was roofed with stone slates, or slabs, to protect the keep against attack by fire.

The courtyard enclosed buildings such as a kitchen, stables, chapel, brewhouse, and was surrounded by a wall often with a ditch and drawbridge.

Royal Palaces

(15/16th century)

The Stewart kings spent much of their energy acquiring wealth, usually by forfeiting unpopular subjects. They built or remodelled royal palaces in the Renaissance style at Stirling, Holyrood (Edinburgh), Linlithgow (West Lothian) and Falkland (Fife).

Holyrood Royal Palace

Tower Houses *(16th century)*

In 1535 an Act of Parliament declared that every landed man that had land valued at £100 (Scots) was to build a tower or castle to defend his lands.

Although there is no clear divide, tower houses evolved from keeps. The walls became less thick and the entrance was moved to the basement. Parapets were corbelled-out so that they would overhang the

Edzell Castle (Tower House).

wall and missiles could be dropped on attackers below. The corners had open rounds and the stair was crowned by a caphouse and watch-chamber. Gunloops and shot-holes replaced arrowslits. The walls were harled and often whitewashed.

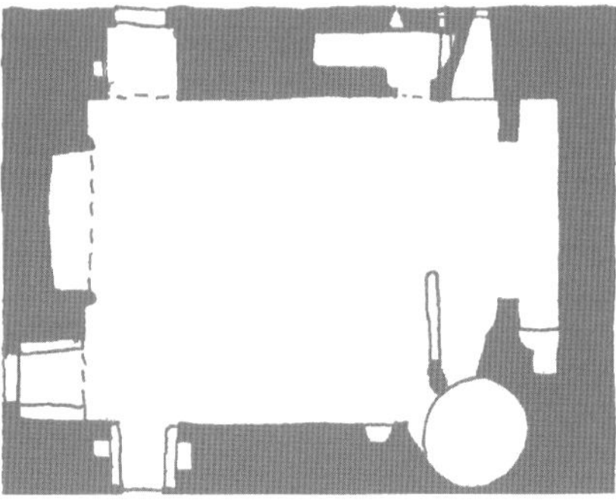

Plan of 16th century tower house.

Tower houses also underwent change and adaption in the 16th century. After the Reformation, with the increased wealth of Protestant landowners and the increased availability of land, which had previously belonged to the Church, many examples of more comfortable tower houses were built. These were mostly in the north-east, the central belt and the south, including the Borders and Galloway.

The reduction in need for defensive features meant that these later tower houses were more spacious and comfortable. The structures were still built vertically and most continued to have one room on each floor. However, wings or towers were either incorporated into or added to the design. Good examples of tower houses can be found at Smailholm Tower (Borders), Crathes Castle (Grampian) and Amisfield Tower (Dumfries & Galloway).

L-plan Tower Houses

(mid-16th century)

The L-plan tower house had a stair-wing added to the main block. The stair was usually turnpike and climbed only to the hall on the first floor. The upper floors were reached by a turnpike stair in a small stair-turret corbelled out, above first-floor level, in the re-entrant angle. This stair was crowned by a caphouse and watch-chamber. In some cases, the wing contained a stair which climbed to all floors and sometimes a separate stair-tower stood within the re-entrant angle, and the wing contained chambers. Greenknowe Tower (Borders) is a fine ruined L-plan tower house while Craigievar (Grampian) is complete.

The defensive features became less obvious. Larger windows were still protected by iron yetts or grills, and gunloops became

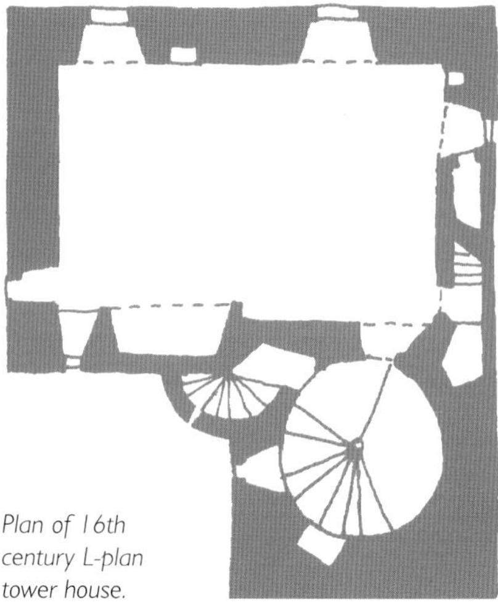

Plan of 16th century L-plan tower house.

Drum Castle

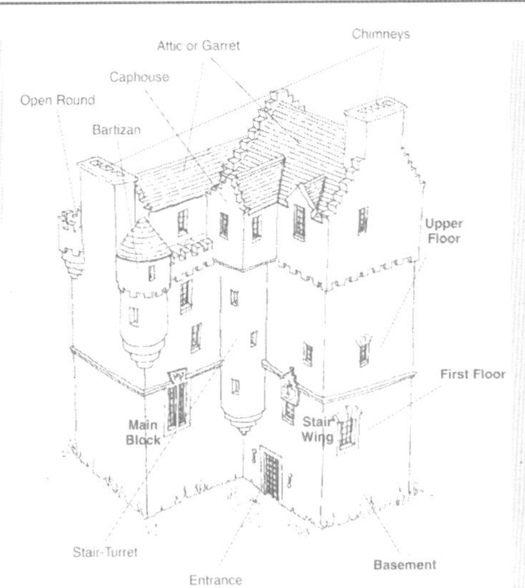

Diagram of L-plan tower house, showing the three main floors:
The basement contained the entrance, at the foot of the stair-wing, and was occupied by a kitchen, wine-cellar and food-cellar. The main turnpike stair only climbed to the first-floor hall, while the upper floors were reached by a turnpike stair in the turret in the re-entrant angle. The lord's private chamber was on the floor above the hall, although there was little privacy for the rest of the household, as each room opened from the last. The turret stair rose up to the parapet and was crowned by a caphouse and watch-chamber.
The tower would have had a walled courtyard, or barmkin, enclosing ranges of buildings, including stabling, workshops, a brewhouse and more accommodation.
The walls of the tower were usually harled and whitewashed. The heraldic panel showed the arms of the lord and his wife, who used her own family name, and the date of building or alteration.

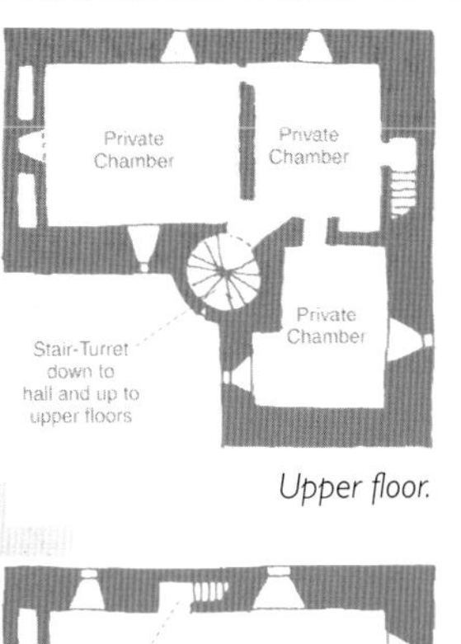

Upper floor.

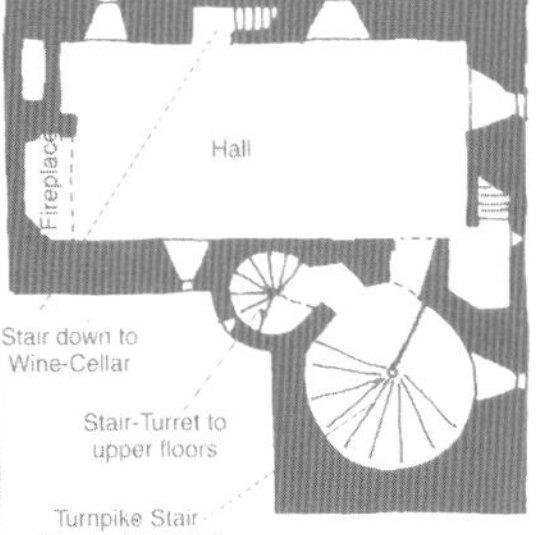

First floor.

Fireplace
Kitchen
Wine-Cellar
Food-Cellar
Passage
Entrance
Stair up to Hall
Turnpike Stair

Basement.

ornamental. Open rounds were replaced by bartizans, with conical roofs and parapets were covered. Decorative features, as well as heraldic panels, inscribed lintels, tempera painting and modelled plaster work were introduced. These design features showed French and Italian influences. The tower usually had a small courtyard with ranges of buildings, including a brewhouse, stabling and more accommodation.

The basement was vaulted and contained a kitchen with a large fireplace, a wine-cellar with a small stair to the hall above, and other cellars. The hall was on the first floor of the main block with private chambers on the floors above and within the garret or attic storey.

Z-plan Tower Houses

(late 16th century)

A variation of the L-plan, a Z-plan tower house consisted of a main block, with two towers at diagonally opposite corners. One of the towers usually housed a stair, while the other provided more accommodation. Often further wings or ranges were added to the tower, making it E-plan.

Glenbuchat Castle (Grampian) is a fine example of a ruined Z-plan tower house, as is Drochil Castle (Borders), while Claypotts Castle (Tayside) is still roofed.

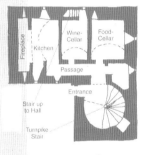

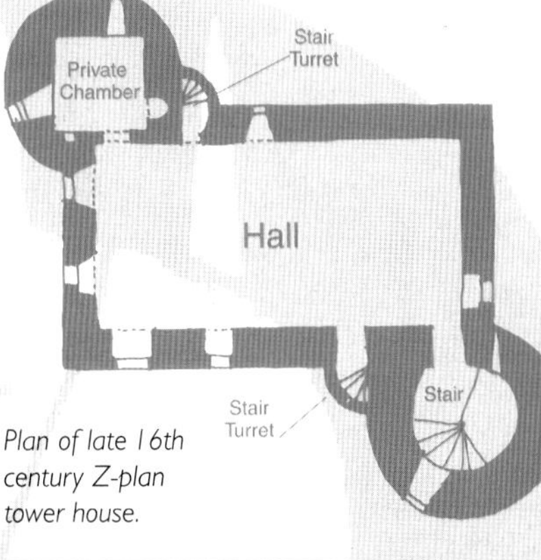

Plan of late 16th century Z-plan tower house.

Castle Fraser

Forts (16th/17th/18th century)

With the advent of more sophisticated artillery, the castle became increasingly redundant as a major defensive structure. As early as the 1540s, forts were being built to withstand attack by cannon. The English constructed forts, during the invasion of Scotland in 1547-50, including those at Roxburgh (Borders), Eyemouth (Borders) and Haddington (Lothian), which consisted of ramparts and bastions of earth rather than high walls. In the 1650s Cromwell built forts such as those at Ayr, Leith (Lothian), Perth, Inverlochy (Highland) and Aberdeen. The Hanoverian Government built forts, barracks and roads after the Jacobite Risings of 1715 and 1745, including those at Fort George, Fort William, Fort Augustus and Ruthven Barracks (all Highland). Other castles such as Corgarff and Braemar (Grampian) were given artillery bastions and were used as bases for campaigns against illicit whisky distilling in the late 18th century.

Castellated Mansion Houses

Even before the Jacobite Risings, most houses had ceased to be fortified. By the mid-18th century, most new houses were built in a classical, palladian or symmetrical style, designed by architects such as Robert Adam. Many castles were abandoned at this time, because they were uncomfortable and unfashionable as dwellings – many landowners wishing to forget their unruly and barbaric past.

In the 19th century baronial mansions came into fashion, incorporating or recreating mock castellated features such as towers and turrets, corbelling and machiolations. Castles were reused, restored and reoccupied. Architects such as William Burn and David Bryce in the 19th century, and Sir Robert Lorimer in the 20th century, designed these castellated mansions. Many of these large country houses did not survive use by the government in World War II. The fashion for restoring and living in many of the smaller towers and fortified houses has greatly increased in recent years.

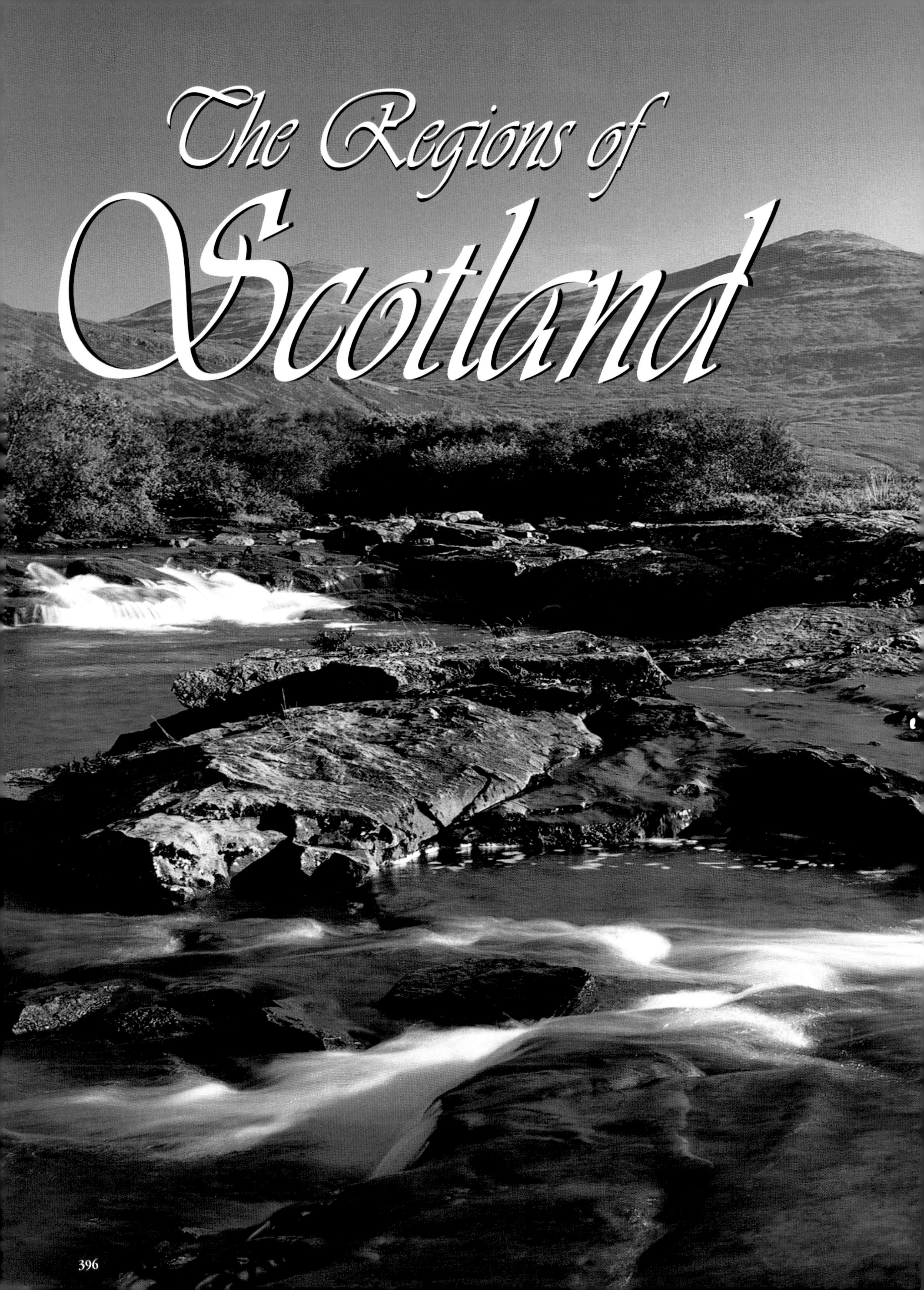

The Regions of Scotland

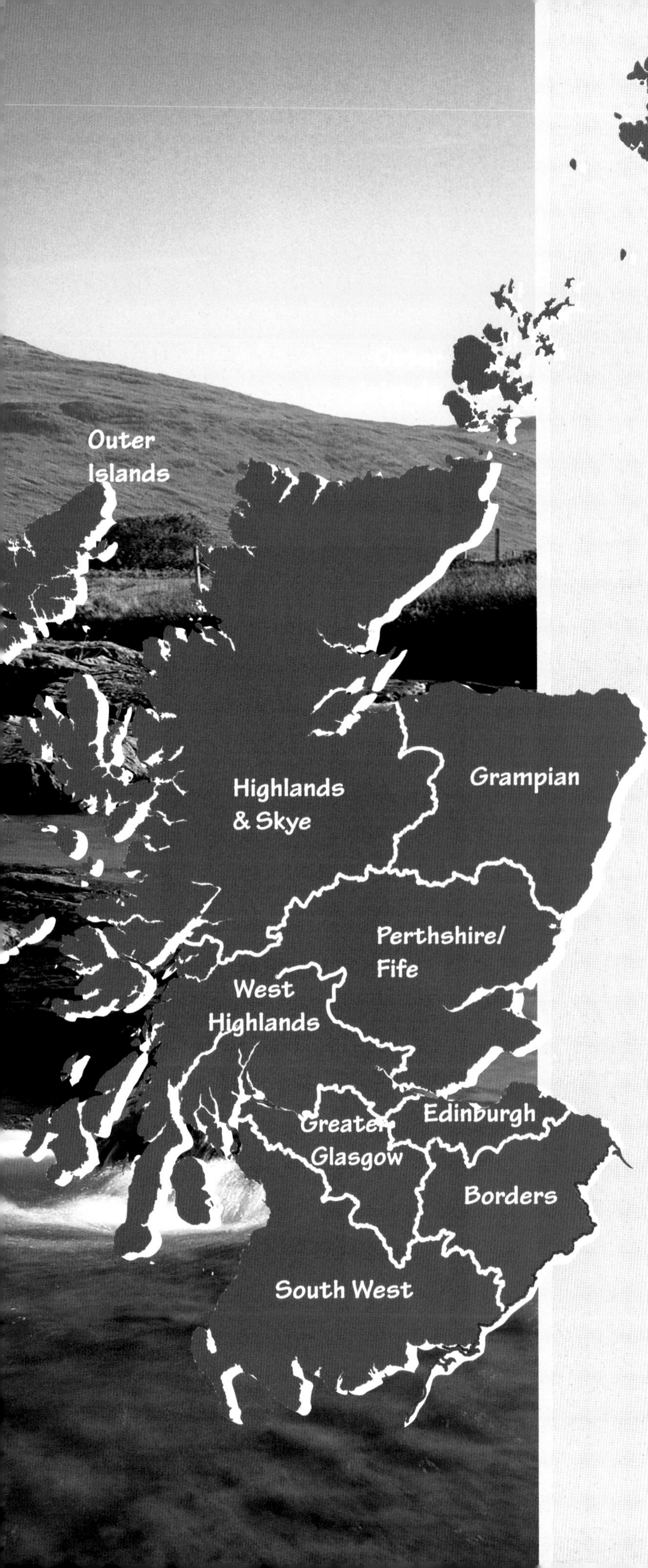

Scotland is divided into nine regions to coincide with Scotland's Area Tourist Boards.

 Historic Houses Association Member, offering access under HHA Friends Scheme.

 Property owned by The National Trust for Scotland.

 Property in the care of Historic Scotland.

River Coladoir & Ben More, Isle of Mull.

Borders of Scotland

Thirlestane Castle, Borders.

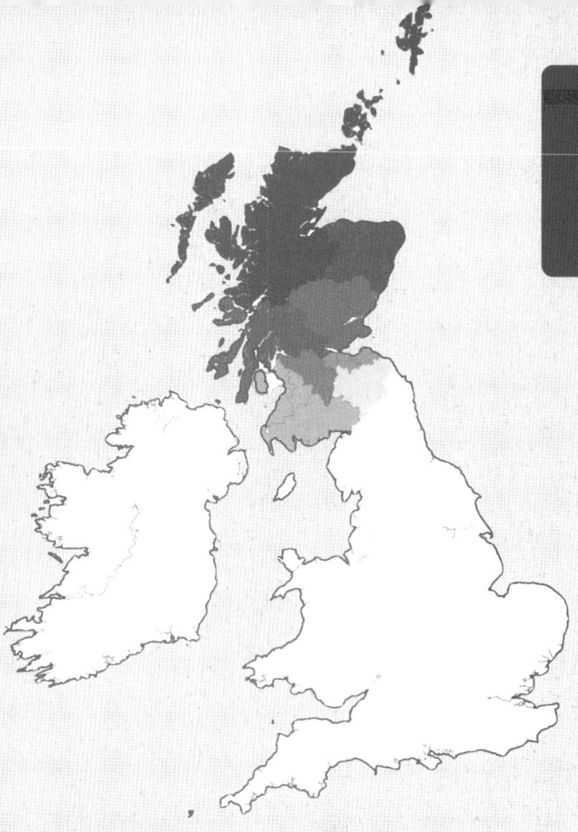

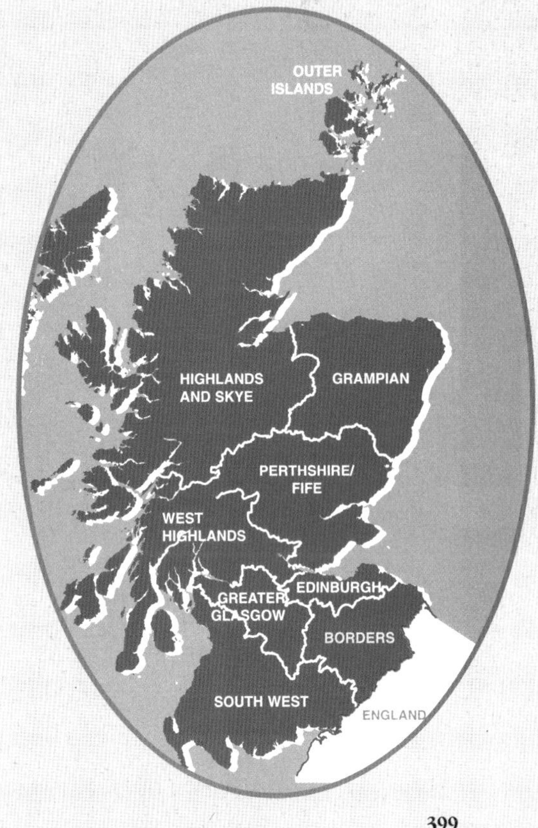

Featuring…

Thirlestane Castle

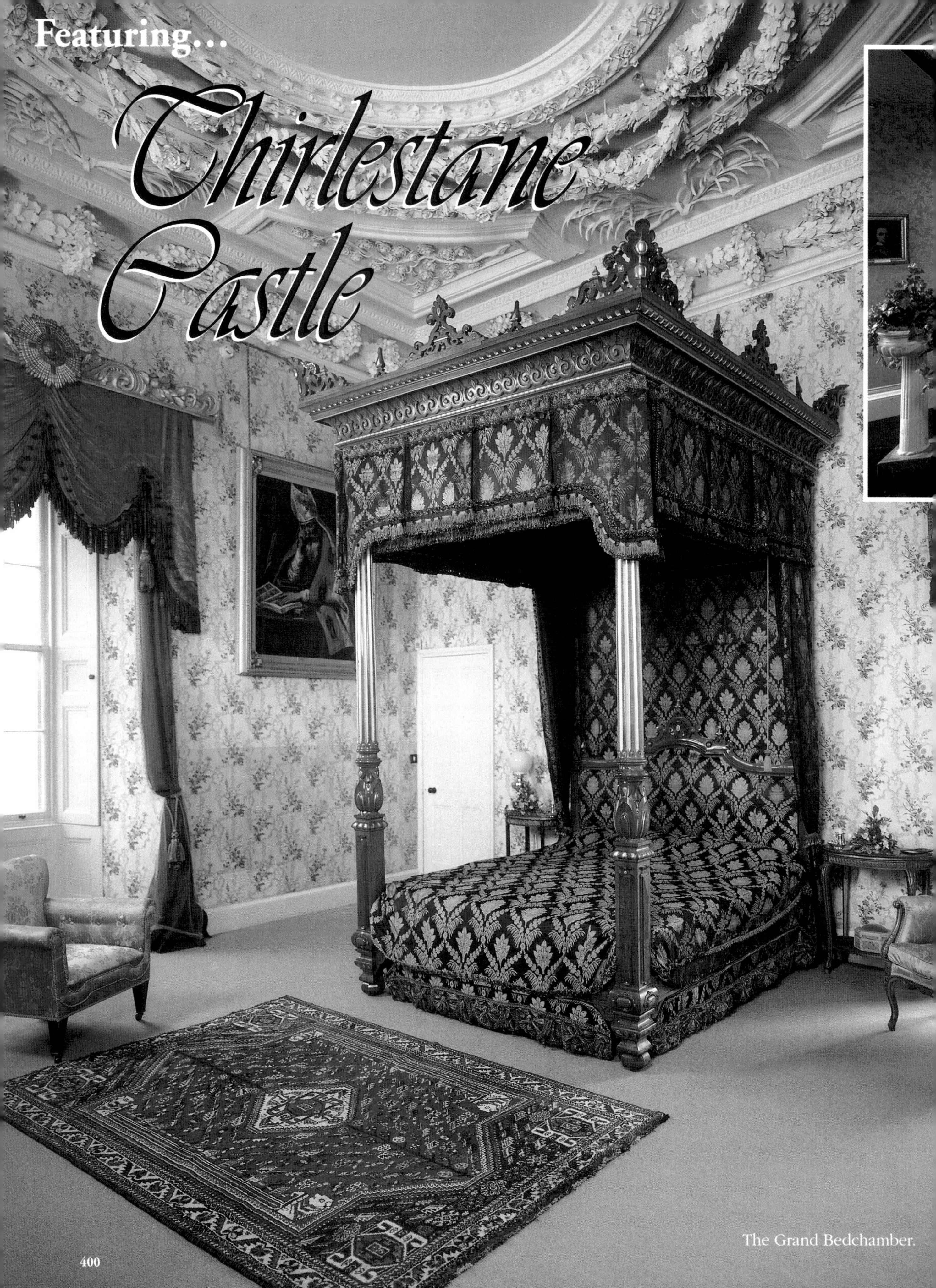

The Grand Bedchamber.

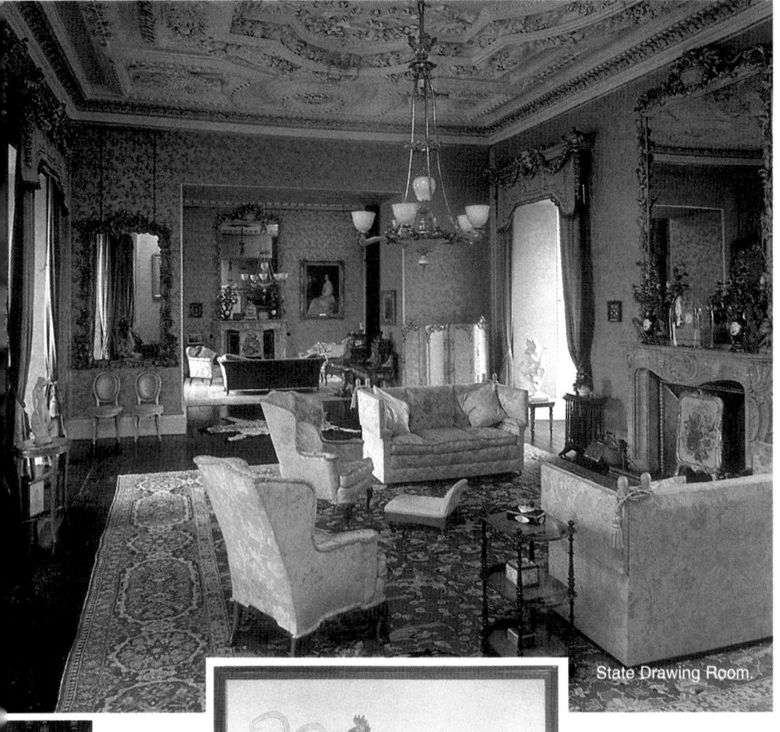

State Drawing Room.

The first view of Thirlestane Castle conveys splendour. The dramatic composition of the rose-pink sandstone façade with its turreted skyline, reflects the Restoration love of pomp and show. Only 28 miles south of Edinburgh, it occupies a strategically important position overlooking the Leader Water.

Thirlestane was a loyal stronghold and centre of military importance which, not surprisingly, changed hands more than once during the Scots' struggle for independence. As late as 1548 the 'auld enemy' in the person of Protector Somerset, strengthened the Castle to hold an English garrison. By the end of the century it was back in the hands of its rightful owners and then began the re-edification of the Castle as it is today, when the oblong part of the great stone 'T' which it forms was built by Chancellor Maitland (1545-95). It was John Maitland, 2nd Earl and 1st Duke of Lauderdale (1616-82), a powerful statesman and trusted friend of Charles II, who impressed his personality most strongly on the Castle. He built the jutting wings which flank the entrance on the west front and made the final transformation of the building from fort to mansion, bringing skilled craftsmen from royal service and from Holland to carve and model the interiors.

Chinese silk painting.

The castle has been in the Maitland family ever since and is today the home of Capt the Hon Gerald Maitland-Carew and his family, although now owned by a charitable trust which he set up to ensure its future. When he inherited Thirlestane in 1972 it was in a very sorry state. The central tower was near collapse and no fewer than 40 outbreaks of dry rot were found. The cost of these repairs was quite beyond the means of the family. While the Historic Buildings Council for Scotland provided grant aid to allow repairs to be carried out, the problems of maintaining magnificent buildings such as this do not lessen. In 1984, to help secure the future of the Castle, Capt Maitland-Carew gave the main part, together with its contents, to a charitable trust for its preservation. This enabled the National Heritage Memorial Fund to endow the charity and in this way, this remarkable building has been saved for future generations to enjoy.

Chinese cabinet.

Amongst the most memorable features of Thirlestane are the State Apartments ceilings. These are perhaps the finest Restoration period ceilings in existence. The immensely rich plasterwork of the State Rooms is the work of an English plasterer, George Dunsterfield. The main characteristic of his work is the depth of relief and extreme realism achieved. He is thought to have been inspired by the Italian Renaissance artist Andrea Mantegna (1431-1506) whose work in the ducal palace at Mantua particularly shows many features in common with the Thirlestane ceilings.

Fly Screen.

For full details of this property see page 409.

'The Pink Boy' - Sir Joshua Reynolds

BOWHILL HOUSE & COUNTRY PARK

Selkirk

Owner: His Grace the Duke of Buccleuch & Queensberry KT

CONTACT

Mrs P Gray
Buccleuch Heritage Trust
Bowhill House & Country Park
Bowhill
Selkirk
TD7 5ET

Tel/Fax: 01750 22204

e-mail: bht@buccleuch.com

Scottish Borders home of the Duke and Duchess of Buccleuch, dating mainly from 1812 and christened 'Sweet Bowhill' by Sir Walter Scott in his *Lay of the Last Minstrel.*

Many of the works of art were collected by earlier Montagus, Douglases and Scotts or given by Charles II to his natural son James, Duke of Monmouth and Buccleuch. Paintings include Canaletto's *Whitehall,* works by Guardi, Claude, Ruysdael, Gainsborough, Raeburn, Reynolds, Van Dyck and Wilkie. Superb French furniture, Meissen and Sèvres porcelain, silver and tapestries.

Historical relics include Monmouth's saddle and execution shirt, Sir Walter Scott's plaid and some proof editions, Queen Victoria's letters and gifts to successive Duchesses of Buccleuch, her Mistresses of the Robes.

There is also a completely restored Victorian Kitchen, 19th century horse-drawn fire engine, 'Bowhill Little Theatre', a lively centre for the performing arts and where, prior to touring the house, visitors can see 'The Quest for Bowhill', a 20 minute audio-visual presentation by Dr Colin Thompson.

Conference centre, arts courses, literary lunches, education service, visitor centre. Shop, tearoom, adventure playground, woodland walks, nature trails, picnic areas. Garden and landscape designed by John Gilpin.

Fashion shows, air displays, archery, clay pigeon shooting, equestrian events, charity garden parties, shows, rallies, filming, lecture theatre. House is open by appointment outside public hours to groups led by officials of a recognised museum, gallery or educational establishment. No photography inside house.

Inside caterers normally used but outside caterers considered.

Visitors may alight at entrance. WC. Wheelchair visitors free.

Groups can book in advance (special rates), menus on request.

For groups. Tour time 1¼ hrs.

60 cars and 6 coaches within 50yds of house.

Welcome. Projects in Bowhill House and Victorian kitchen, Education Officers (service provided free of charge), schoolroom, ranger-led nature walks, adventure playground. Heritage Education Trust Sandford Award winner 1993 and 1998.

On leads.

'Winter' - Sir Joshua Reynolds

LOCATION

OS Ref. NT426 278

3m W of Selkirk off A708 Moffat Road, A68 from Newcastle, A7 from Carlisle or Edinburgh.

Bus: 3m Selkirk.

Taxi: 01750 20354.

CONFERENCE/FUNCTION		
ROOM	SIZE	MAX CAPACITY
Bowhill Little Theatre		72

OPENING TIMES

SUMMER
22 April - 28 August

Country Park
Daily except Fris (open Fris in July)
12 noon - 5pm.

House
1 - 31 July
Daily: 1 - 4.30pm.

WINTER
By appointment only, for educational groups.

ADMISSION

SUMMER

House & Country Park
Adult £4.50
Child (5-16yrs) £2.00
OAP/Student £4.00
Group (20+) £4.00
Wheelchair visitors Free

Country Park only
All ages £2.00

WINTER

House & Country Park
Adult £6.00
Child (5-16yrs) £2.00

Pre-booked educational groups (20+) welcomed.

Owner: His Grace the Duke of Roxburghe

CONTACT

Philip Massey
Director of Operations
Roxburghe Estates Office
Kelso
Roxburghshire
Scotland
TD5 7SF

Tel: 01573 223333

Fax: 01573 226056

LOCATION

OS Ref. NT711 347

From South A68, A698.

From North A68, A697/9
In Kelso follow signs.

Bus: Kelso Bus Station 1m.

Rail: Berwick 20m.

CONFERENCE/FUNCTION		
ROOM	SIZE	MAX CAPACITY
Dining Rm	18m x 7m	150
Ballroom	21m x 8m	150

FLOORS CASTLE

Kelso

FLOORS CASTLE, home of the Duke and Duchess of Roxburghe, is situated in the heart of the Scottish Border Country. It is reputedly the largest inhabited castle in Scotland. Designed by William Adam, who was both masterbuilder and architect, for the first Duke of Roxburghe, building started in 1721.

It was the present Duke's great-great-grand-father James, the 6th Duke, who embellished the plain Adam features of the building. In about 1849 Playfair, letting his imagination and talent run riot, transformed the castle, creating a multitude of spires and domes.

The apartments now display the outstanding collection of French 17th and 18th century furniture, magnificent tapestries, Chinese and European porcelain and many other fine works of art. Many of the treasures in the castle today were collected by Duchess May, American wife of the 8th Duke.

The castle has been seen on cinema screens worldwide in the film *Greystoke*, as the home of Tarzan, the Earl of Greystoke.

Gardens

The extensive parkland and gardens over-looking the Tweed provide a variety of wooded walks. The walled garden contains splendid herbaceous borders and in the outer walled garden a summerhouse built for Queen Victoria's visit in 1867 can still be seen. An excellent children's playground and picnic area are very close to the castle.

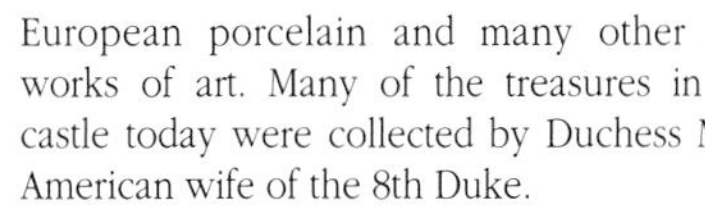

Gala dinners, conferences, product launches, 4 x 4 driving, incentive groups, highland games and other promotional events. Extensive park, helicopter pad, fishing, clay pigeon and pheasant shooting. No photography inside the castle.

Visitors may alight at the entrance. WC.

Self-service, licensed, seats 125 opens 10am.

By arrangement for up to 100. Tour time 1¼ hrs.

Unlimited for cars, 100 yds away, coach park 50 yds. Coaches can be driven to the entrance, waiting area close to restaurant exit. Lunch or tea for coach drivers.

Welcome, guide provided. Playground facilities.

Guide dogs only.

OPENING TIMES

SUMMER

21 April - 29 October
Daily: 10am - 4.30pm.

Last admission 4pm.

WINTER

November - March
Closed to the general public, available for events.

ADMISSION

SUMMER

Adult £5.00
Child (5 - 15yrs) £3.00
OAP/Student...........£4.50
Family £12.00

Groups (min 20)
Adult £4.00
Child (5 - 15yrs) £2.50
OAP/Student...........£3.75

Grounds only
...............................£3.00
Groups....................£2.50

SPECIAL EVENTS

- **AUG 27:** Family Day with Massed Pipe Bands.

MANDERSTON

Duns

MANDERSTON, together with its magnificent stables, stunning marble dairy and 56 acres of immaculate gardens, forms an ensemble which must be unique in Britain today.

The house was completely rebuilt between 1903 and 1905, with no expense spared.

Visitors are able to see not only the sumptuous State Rooms and bedrooms, decorated in the Adam manner, but also all the original domestic offices, in a truly 'upstairs downstairs' atmosphere. Manderston boasts a unique and recently restored silver staircase.

There is a special museum with a nostalgic display of valuable tins made by Huntley and Palmer from 1868 to the present day. Winner of the AA/NPI Bronze Award UK 1994.

GARDENS

Outside, the magnificence continues and the combination of formal gardens and picturesque landscapes is a major attraction: unique amongst Scottish houses.

The stables, still in use, have been described by *Horse and Hound* as "probably the finest in all the wide world."

Owner: The Lord Palmer

CONTACT

The Lord or Lady Palmer
Manderston
Duns
Berwickshire
Scotland
TD11 3PP

Tel: 01361 883450
Secretary: 01361 882636

Fax: 01361 882010

e-mail: palmer@manderston.demon.co.uk

LOCATION

OS Ref. NT810 544

From Edinburgh 47m, 1hr.
1½ m E of Duns on A6105.

Bus: 400 yds.

Rail: Berwick Station 12m.

Taxi: Chirnside 818216.

Airport: Edinburgh or Newcastle both 60m or 80 mins.

CONFERENCE/FUNCTION		
ROOM	SIZE	MAX CAPACITY
Dining Rm	22' x 35'	100
Ballroom	34' x 21'	150
Hall	22' x 38'	130
Drawing Rm	35' x 21'	150

Corporate & incentives venue. Ideal retreat: business groups, think-tank weekends. Fashion shows, air displays, archery, clay pigeon shooting, equestrian events, garden parties, shows, rallies, filming, product launches and marathons. Two airstrips for light aircraft, approx 5m, grand piano, billiard table, fox-hunting, pheasant shoots, sea angling, salmon fishing, stabling, cricket pitch, tennis court, lake. Nearby: 9-hole golf course, indoor swimming pool, squash court. No photography in house.

Available. Buffets, lunches and dinners. Wedding receptions.

Special parking available outside the House.

Tearoom (open as house) with waitress service. Can be booked in advance, menus on request.

Included. Available in French. Guides in rooms. If requested, the owner may meet groups. Tour time 1¼ hrs.

400 cars 125yds from house, 30 coaches 5yds from house. Appreciated if group fees are paid by one person.

Welcome. Guide can be provided. Biscuit Tin Museum of particular interest.

Grounds only, on leads.

5 twin, 4 double and 1 single.

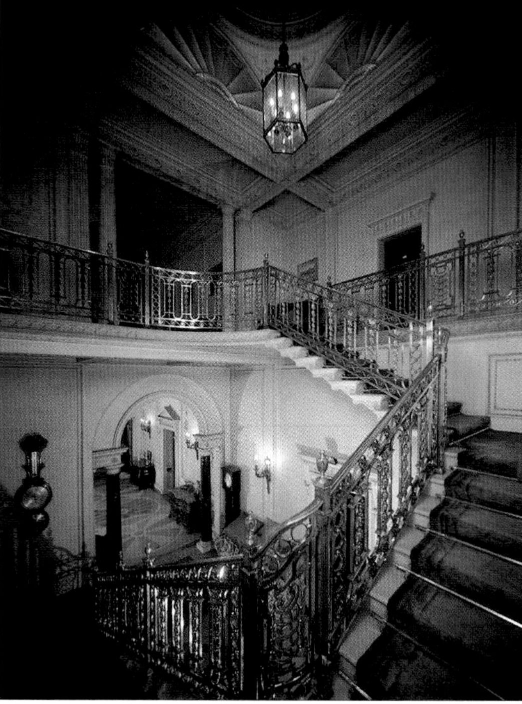

OPENING TIMES

SUMMER

Mid-May - end September
Thurs & Suns
2 - 5pm.

BH Mons, late May & August
2 - 5pm.

Groups welcome all year by appointment.

WINTER

September - May
Group visits welcome by appointment.

ADMISSION

House & Grounds

Adult	£6.00
Child	£3.00
Groups (20+ on open days)	
Per person	£5.00

Grounds only

Including Stables & Marble Dairy

Adult	£3.50
Child	£1.50

On days when the house is closed to the public, groups viewing by appointment will have personally conducted tours. The Gift Shop will be open. On these occasions reduced party rates (except for school children) will not apply. Group visits (20+) other than open days are £6 (minimum £120). Cream teas on open days only.

ABBOTSFORD HOUSE

Tel: 01896 752043 Fax: 01896 752916

Melrose, Roxburghshire TD6 9BQ

Sir Walter Scott purchased the Cartley Hall farmhouse on the banks of the Tweed in 1812. Together with his family and servants he moved into the farm which he renamed Abbotsford. Scott had the old house demolished in 1822 and replaced it with the main block of Abbotsford as it is today. Scott was a passionate collector of historic relics including an impressive collection of armour and weapons and over 9,000 rare volumes in his library.

Location: OS Ref. NT508 343. 35m S of Edinburgh. Melrose 3m, Galashiels 2m.

Opening Times: 20 Mar - 31 Oct: Mon - Sat, & Suns (Jun - Sept only) 10am - 5pm. Also Suns in Mar - May & Oct, 2 - 5pm. Other dates by arrangement.

Admission: Adult £3.80, Child £1.90. Groups: Adult £2.80, Child £1.40.

House suitable. WC. Guide dogs only.

AIKWOOD TOWER & JAMES HOGG EXHIBITION

Tel: 01750 52253

Ettrick Valley, Nr Selkirk TD7 5HJ

Fax: 01750 52261

Owner: Lord & Lady Steel of Aikwood **Contact:** Judy Steel

A fine 16 century peel tower and exhibition of James Hogg.

Location: OS Ref. NT419 260. SE side of B7009, 4m SW of Selkirk.

Opening Times: May - Sept: Tues, Thurs & Suns, 2 - 5pm.

Admission: £2.

AYTON CASTLE

AYTON, EYEMOUTH, BERWICKSHIRE TD14 5RD

Owner: *D I Liddell-Grainger of Ayton* ***Contact:*** *The Curator*

Tel: 018907 81212 or 018907 81550

Built in 1846 by the Mitchell-Innes family and designed by the architect James Gillespie Graham. Over the last ten years it has been fully restored and is now a family home. It is a unique restoration project and the quality of the original and restored workmanship is outstanding. The castle stands on an escarpment surrounded by mature woodlands containing many interesting trees and has been a film-making venue due to this magnificent setting.

Location: OS Ref. NT920 610. 7m N of Berwick-on-Tweed on Route A1.

Opening Times: 10 May - 13 Sept: Suns, 2 - 5 pm or by appointment.

Admission: Adult £3, Child (under 15yrs) Free.

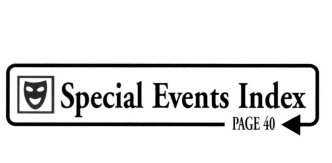

Special Events Index PAGE 40

BOWHILL HOUSE & COUNTRY PARK

See page 402 for full page entry.

BUGHTRIG GARDEN

Tel: 01890 840678 Fax: 01890 840509

Bughtrig, Coldstream, Berwickshire TD12 4JP

Owner: Major General C A & the Hon Mrs Ramsay **Contact:** The Secretary

Bughtrig is a classic Georgian family house c1785 with later additions. The formal garden is hedged and close to the house, surrounded by fine specimen trees which provide remarkable shelter. Its $2^1/_2$ acres contain an interesting combination of herbaceous plants, roses, shrubs, annuals, fruit, vegetables and a tree nursery. Small picnic area.

Location: OS Ref. NT797 447. $^1/_4$ m E of Leitholm Village on B6461.

Opening Times: Garden: Jun - Sept: daily, 11am - 5pm. House: by appointment only.

Admission: Adult £2, Child (under 18yrs) £1. Rates for House or accommodation by arrangement.

Partially suitable. Limited. Guide dogs only.
4 twin bedrooms/3 bathrooms.

DAWYCK BOTANIC GARDEN

Tel: 01721 760254 Fax: 01721 760214

Stobo, Peeblesshire EH45 9JU **Contact:** The Curator

Renowned historic arboretum. Amongst mature specimen trees – some over 40 metres tall – are a variety of flowering trees, shrubs and herbaceous plants. Explore the world's first Cryptogamic Sanctuary and Reserve for 'non-flowering' plants.

Location: NT168 352. 8m SW of Peebles on B712.

Opening Times: 1 Mar - 31 Oct: daily, 9.30am - 6pm.

Admission: Adult £3, Child £1, Family £7, Conc. £2.50, Group discounts available.

DRUMLANRIG'S TOWER

Tel: 01450 373457 Fax: 01450 378506

Tower Knowe, Hawick TD9 9EN

Owner: Scottish Borders Council **Contact:** The Curator

An 18th century town house containing the remains of a fortified tower of the 1550s.

Location: OS Ref. NT502 144. In Hawick town centre at W end of the High Street.

Opening Times: Please contact for details.

Admission: Adult £2, Conc. £1. 10% group discount. Free for local residents.

DRYBURGH ABBEY

Tel: 01835 822381

St Boswells, Melrose

Owner: Historic Scotland **Contact:** The Custodian

The ruins of Dryburgh Abbey are remarkably complete. The burial place of Sir Walter Scott and Field Marshal Earl Haig. Perhaps the most beautiful of all the Border abbeys.

Location: OS Ref. NT591 317. 5m SE of Melrose off B6356. $1^1/_2$ m N of St Boswells.

Opening Times: 1 Apr - 30 Sept: daily, 9.30am - 6.30pm. Last ticket 6pm. 1 Oct - 31 Mar: Mon - Sat, 9.30am - 4.30pm, Suns, 2 - 4.30pm, last ticket 4pm.

Admission: Adult £2.50, Child £1, Conc. £1.90.

Historic Scotland.

Dryburgh Abbey, Borders.

Borders Scotland

DUNS CASTLE

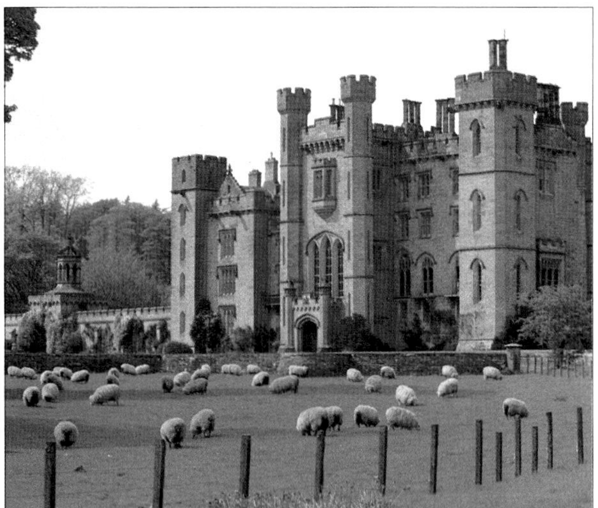

DUNS, BERWICKSHIRE TD11 3NW

Owner: *Alexander Hay of Duns* ***Contact:*** *Mrs Aline Hay*

Tel: 01361 883211 **Fax:** 01361 882015 **e-mail:** aline_hay@lineone.net

This historical 1320 pele tower has been home to the Hay family since 1696, and the current owners Alexander and Aline Hay offer it as a welcoming venue for individuals, groups and corporate guests to enjoy. They have renovated it to produce the highest standards of comfort while retaining all the character of its rich period interiors. Wonderful lakeside and parkland setting.

Location: OS Ref. NT777 544. 10m off A4. Rail: Berwick station 16m. Airports: Newcastle & Edinburgh, 1 hr.

Opening Times: Not open to the public except by arrangement and for individuals, groups and companies for day or residential stays. Available all year.

Admission: Rates for private and corporate visits, wedding receptions, filming by arrangement.

4 x 4-poster, 3 x double, 3 x twin (all with bathrooms), 2 single. 

FLOORS CASTLE See page 403 for full page entry.

HALLIWELL'S HOUSE MUSEUM **Tel:** 01750 20096 **Fax:** 01750 23282

Halliwell's Close, Market Place, High Street, Selkirk

Owner: Scottish Borders Council **Contact:** Ian Brown

Re-creation of buildings, formerly used as a house and ironmonger's shop.

Location: OS Ref. NT472 286. In Selkirk town centre.

Opening Times: Easter - 31 Oct: Mon - Sat, 10am - 5pm, Suns, 2 - 4pm. Jul & Aug: Mon - Sat, open until 6pm, Suns until 5pm.

Admission: Free.

HARMONY GARDEN  **Tel:** 01721 722502 **Fax:** 01721 724700

St Mary's Road, Melrose TD6 9LJ

Owner: The National Trust for Scotland **Contact:** Head Gardener

A tranquil garden offering herbaceous and mixed borders, lawns, vegetable and fruit areas. Fine views of Melrose Abbey and the Eildon Hills. Garden set around 19th century house (not open to visitors).

Location: OS Ref. NT549 342. In Melrose, opposite the Abbey.

Opening Times: 1 Apr - 30 Sept: Mon - Sat, 10am - 5.30pm, Suns, 1.30 - 5.30pm.

Admission: £2 (honesty box).

No parking.

HERMITAGE CASTLE **Tel:** 01387 376222

Liddesdale, Newcastleton

Owner: Historic Scotland **Contact:** The Custodian

Eerie fortress at the heart of the bloodiest events in the history of the Borders. Mary Queen of Scots made her famous ride here to visit her future husband.

Location: OS Ref. NY497 961. In Liddesdale 5½ m NE of Newcastleton, B6399.

Opening Times: 1 Apr - 30 Sept: daily, 9.30am - 6.30pm, last ticket 6pm.

Admission: Adult £1.80, Child 75p, Conc. £1.30.

FERNIEHIRST CASTLE

JEDBURGH, ROXBURGHSHIRE TD8 6NX

Owner: *The Marquess of Lothian* ***Contact:*** *Mrs J Fraser*

Tel: 01835 862201 **Fax:** 01835 863992

Ferniehirst Castle – Scotland's Frontier Fortress. Ancestral home of the Kerr family. Restored (1984/1987) by the 12th Marquess of Lothian. Unrivalled 16th century Border architecture. Grand Apartment and Turret Library. A 16th century Chamber Oratory. The Kerr Chamber – Museum of Family History. A special tribute to Jedburgh's Protector to Mary Queen of Scots – Sir Thomas Kerr. Riverside walk by Jed Water. Archery Field opposite the Chapel where sheep of Viking origin still graze as they did four centuries ago.

Location: OS Ref. NT653 181. 2m S of Jedburgh on the A68.

Opening Times: Jul: Tue - Sun (closed Mons), 11am - 4pm.

Admission: Adult £3, Child £1.50. Groups (max. 50) by prior arrangement (01835 862201).

Partially suitable. WCs.

Guided tours only, groups by arrangement.

Ample for cars and coaches.

In grounds, on leads.

THE HIRSEL GARDENS, COUNTRY PARK & HOMESTEAD MUSEUM

Coldstream, Berwickshire TD12 4LP **Tel/Fax:** 01890 882834

Owner: Lord Home of the Hirsel **Contact:** Peter Goodall, Hirsel Estate Office

Wonderful spring flowers and rhododendrons. Homestead museum and crafts centre. Displays of estate life and adaption to modern farming.

Location: OS Ref. NT838 393. Immediately W of Coldstream off A697.

Opening Times: Grounds: daily, during daylight hours. Museum & Craft Shop: weekdays, 10am - 5pm. Weekends, 12 noon - 5pm.

Admission: Parking charge only, winter £1, Easter - 31 Oct £2.

JEDBURGH ABBEY

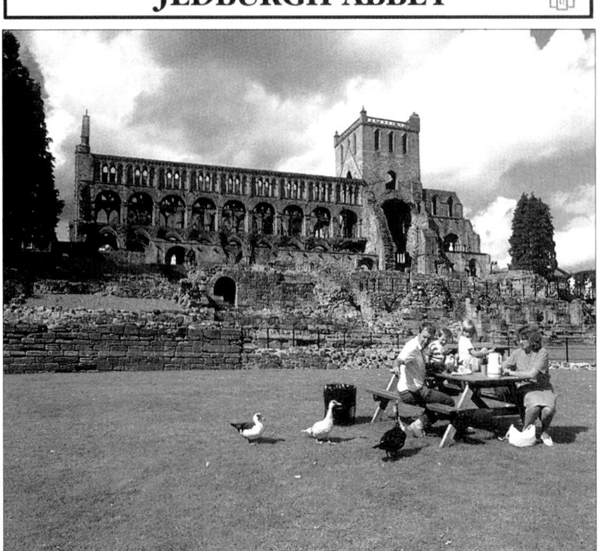

Historic Scotland

4/5 ABBEY BRIDGEND, JEDBURGH TD8 6JQ

Owner: *Historic Scotland* ***Contact:*** *The Steward*

Tel: 01835 863925

Founded by David I c1138 for Augustinian Canons. The church is mostly in the Romanesque and early Gothic styles and is remarkably complete. The award-winning visitor centre contains the priceless 12th century 'Jedburgh Comb' and other artefacts found during archaeological excavations.

Location: OS Ref. NT650 205. In Jedburgh on the A68.

Opening Times: Apr - Sept: daily, 9.30am - 6.30pm. Oct - Mar: Mon - Sat, 9.30am - 4.30pm, Suns, 2 - 4.30pm. Last ticket 30 mins before closing. 10% discount for groups (10+).

Admission: Adult £3, Child £1, Conc. £2.30.

Picnic area. Partially suitable. WC. Free when booked. Guide dogs only.

MANDERSTON

See page 404 for full page entry.

MARY QUEEN OF SCOTS' HOUSE

Tel/Fax: 01835 863331

Jedburgh, Roxburghshire

Owner: Scottish Borders Council **Contact:** The Curator

16th century fortified bastel house. Telling the story 'Scotland's tragic Queen'.

Location: OS Ref. NT652 206. In Queen Street between High Street and A68.

Opening Times: Mar - Nov: Mon - Sat, 10am - 4.30pm, Suns, 12 noon - 4.30pm. Jun - Aug: Suns, 10am - 4.30pm.

Admission: Adult £2, Conc. £1. 10% group discount. Free for local residents.

WWW **Website Index** PAGE 46

MELLERSTAIN HOUSE

MELLERSTAIN, GORDON, BERWICKSHIRE TD3 6LG

Owner: *The Earl of Haddington* ***Contact:*** *Mr A Ashby*

Tel: 01573 410225 **Fax:** 01573 410636 **e-mail:** mellerstain.house@virgin.net

One of Scotland's great Georgian houses and a unique example of the work of the Adam family; the two wings built in 1725 by William Adam, the large central block by his son, Robert 1770-78. Rooms contain fine plasterwork, colourful ceilings and marble fireplaces. The library is considered to be Robert Adam's finest creation. Many fine paintings and period furniture.

Location: OS Ref. NT648 392. From Edinburgh A68 to Earlston, turn left 5m, signed.

Opening Times: 21 Apr - 30 Sept: daily except Sats, 12.30 - 5pm. Groups at other times by appointment. Last admission 4.30pm.

Admission: Adult £4.50, Child £2, Conc. £3.50. Groups (20+) £3.50. Grounds only: £2.

No photography or video cameras. Partially suitable. Licensed. Licensed. By arrangement. In grounds, on leads, Guide dogs only in house. Tel. for details.

MELROSE ABBEY

Historic Scotland

MELROSE, ROXBURGHSHIRE TD6 9LG

Owner: *Historic Scotland* ***Contact:*** *The Steward*

Tel: 01896 822562

The Abbey was founded about 1136 by David I as a Cistercian Abbey and at one time was probably the richest in Scotland. Richard II's English army largely destroyed it in 1385 but it was rebuilt and the surviving remains are mostly 14th century. Burial place of Robert the Bruce's heart. Local history displays.

Location: OS Ref. NT549 342. In the centre of Melrose off the A68 or A7.

Opening Times: Apr - Sept: daily, 9.30am - 6.30pm. Oct - Mar: Mon - Sat, 9.30am - 4.30pm, Suns, 2 - 4.30pm. Last ticket 30 mins before closing.

Admission: Adult £3, Child £1, Conc. £2.30. 10% discount for groups (10+).

Picnic area. Tape for visitors with learning difficulties. Pre-booked visits free. Guide dogs only.

MERTOUN GARDENS

Tel: 01835 823236 **Fax:** 01835 822474

St Boswells, Melrose, Roxburghshire TD6 0EA

Owner: His Grace the Duke of Sutherland **Contact:** Mrs Barnsley

26 acres of beautiful grounds. Walled garden and well-preserved circular dovecote.

Location: OS Ref. NT617 318. Entrance off B6404 2m NE of St Boswells.

Opening Times: Apr - Sept: weekends & Public Holiday Mons only, 2 - 6pm. Last admission 5.30pm.

Admission: Adult £1.50, Child 50p. Groups by arrangement: Adult £1.35, Child 45p.

By arrangement. 

MONTEVIOT HOUSE GARDEN

Tel: 01835 830380 (mornings only)

Jedburgh, Roxburghshire TD8 6UQ **Fax:** 01835 830288

Contact: The Administrator

The river garden planted with herbaceous shrub borders, has a beautiful view of the River Teviot. A semi-enclosed rose garden with a collection of hybrid teas, floribunda and shrub roses. The pinetum is full of unusual trees and nearby a water garden of islands is linked by bridges.

Location: OS Ref. NT648 247. 3m N of Jedburgh. S side of B6400 (to Nisbet). 1m E of A68.

Opening Times: Apr - Oct: daily, 12 noon - 5pm. Coach parties by prior arrangement.

Admission: Adult £2, Child (under 14yrs) Free.

Partially suitable. Parking & WCs. By arrangement. P In grounds, on leads.

NEIDPATH CASTLE

Tel/Fax: 01721 720333

Peebles, Scottish Borders EH45 8NW

Owner: Wemyss and March Estates **Contact:** The Custodian

Authentic 14th century castle converted to tower house (17th century) home of Fraser, Hay and Douglas families. Pit prison, Laigh Hall with displays, Great Hall with 'Life of Mary Stuart - Queen of Scots' in Batik wall hangings. Wonderful setting in wooded gorge of River Tweed. Popular film location (7 to date).

Location: OS Ref. NT237 405. In Tweeddale 1m W of Peebles on A72.

Opening Times: Easter then summer months: Mon - Sat, 11am - 5pm, Suns, 1 - 5pm. Group bookings only in Oct.

Admission: Adult £3, Child £1, Conc. £2.50, Family (2+3) £7.50. 10% discount for groups (20+). School rate available, 1 teacher free for every 10 children.

Ground floor & grounds suitable. P In grounds, on leads.

OLD GALA HOUSE

Tel: 01750 20096

Scot Crescent, Galashiels TD1 3JS

Owner: Scottish Borders Council

Dating from 1583, the former house of the Lairds of Gala. Particularly memorable is the painted ceiling dated 1635.

Location: OS Ref. NT492 357. S of town centre, signed from A7.

Opening Times: Late Mar - 31 Oct: Tue - Sat, 10am - 4pm.

PAXTON HOUSE & COUNTRY PARK

BERWICK-UPON-TWEED TD15 1SZ

Owner: *The Paxton Trust* ***Contact:*** *Martin Purslow*

Tel: 01289 386291 **Fax:** 01289 386660 **e-mail:** info@paxtonhouse.com

Highly Commended by the Scottish Tourist Board 1999

Award-winning country house and country park built from 1758-62 to the design of John and James Adam for Patrick Home, Laird of Wedderburn. The house boasts the pre-eminent collection of Chippendale furniture in Scotland, the largest picture gallery in a Scottish country house built by Robert Reid in 1814, now acting as the first outstation of the National Galleries of Scotland, and a fine collection of regency furniture by William Trotter of Edinburgh. The estate has woodland trails, riverside walks, gardens, park land, red squirrel hide, highland cattle and croquet. There are shops, a stables tearoom, a function suite and a temporary exhibition programme.

Location: OS Ref. NT931 520. 3m off the A1 Berwick-upon-Tweed on B6461.

Opening Times: 1 Apr - 31 Oct: Grounds: 10am - sunset. House: 11am - 5pm. Last house tour 4.15pm. Open to groups/schools all year by appointment.

Admission: Adult £5, Child £2.50, OAP £4.75, Student £4. Groups (pre-arranged, 12+). Adult £4, Child £1.50, OAP £4. Grounds only: Adult £2.25, Child £1.

No photography. Conferences, wedding receptions. Partially suitable. Licensed. Obligatory. P In grounds, on leads.

PRIORWOOD GARDEN & DRIED FLOWER SHOP

Melrose TD6 9PX **Tel:** 01896 822493
Owner: The National Trust for Scotland **Contact:** Mrs Cathy Ross

Overlooked by the Abbey's 15th century ruins is this unique garden, where most of the plants are suitable for drying. With the aid of volunteers, Priorwood Garden markets a wide variety of dried flower arrangements through its own dried flower shop.

Location: OS Ref. NT549 341. In the Border town of Melrose, beside the Abbey.

Opening Times: 1 Apr - 30 Sept: Mon - Sat, 10am - 5.30pm, Suns, 1.30 - 5.30pm. 1 Oct - 24 Dec: Mon - Sat, 10am - 4pm, Suns, 1.30 - 4pm.

Admission: Honesty box £2.

Grounds suitable. WC. No parking. Guide dogs only.

ROBERT SMAIL'S PRINTING WORKS

Tel: 01896 830206

High Street, Innerleithen, Perthshire EH44 6HA
Owner: The National Trust for Scotland **Contact:** Edward Nicol

A printing time-capsule featuring a completely restored Victorian printing works. Visitors can experience the almost forgotten craft of hand typesetting. They will discover the secrets of the printing works from the archive-based posters and see the fully restored machines in action. The buildings also contain the Victorian office with its acid-etched windows, reconstructed waterwheel and many historic items which provide an insight into the history of the Border town of Innerleithen.

Location: OS Ref. NT333 366. In High Street, Innerleithen, 30m S of Edinburgh.

Opening Times: 21 - 24 Apr; 1 May - 30 Sept: Mon - Sat, 10am - 1pm & 2 - 5pm, Suns, 2 - 5pm. W/ends in Oct: Sats: 10am - 1pm & 2 - 5pm, Suns, 2 - 5pm. Last admission 45 mins before closing morning or afternoon.

Admission: Adult £2.50, Conc. £1.70. Groups: Adult £2, Child/School £1.

Ground floor suitable. No parking.

SMAILHOLM TOWER 

Tel: 01573 460365

Smailholm, Kelso
Owner: Historic Scotland **Contact:** The Custodian

Set on a high rocky knoll this well preserved 16th century tower houses an exhibition of tapestries and costume dolls depicting characters from Sir Walter Scott's *Minstrelsy of the Scottish Borders*.

Location: OS Ref. NT638 347. Nr Smailholm Village, 6m W of Kelso on B6937.

Opening Times: 1 Apr - 30 Sept: daily, 9.30am - 6.30pm. Last tickets 1/2 hour before closing.

Admission: Adult £2, Child 75p, Conc. £1.50.

THIRLESTANE CASTLE 

LAUDER, BERWICKSHIRE TD2 6RU

Owner: *Thirlestane Castle Trust* ***Contact:*** *Peter Jarvis*

Tel: 01578 722430 **Fax:** 01578 722761
e-mail: thirlestane@great-houses-scotland.co.uk

One of Scotland's oldest and finest castles standing in lovely Border countryside. Thirlestane was the seat of the Earls and Duke of Lauderdale and is still home to the Maitland family. Unsurpassed 17th century ceilings, fine portrait collection, large collection of historic toys, country life exhibitions. Woodland walks. STB commended. MGC Registered. State rooms available for functions.

Location: OS Ref. NT540 473. Off A68 at Lauder, 28m S of Edinburgh.

Opening Times: 21 Apr - 31 Oct: daily except Sats, 11am - 4.15pm (last admission).

Admission: Adult £5, Child £3, Family £12. Groups (30+): Adult £4, Child £3. Grounds only: £1.50.

One of the 7 Great Houses of Scotland. Not suitable. WC. By arrangement. In grounds, on leads.

TRAQUAIR

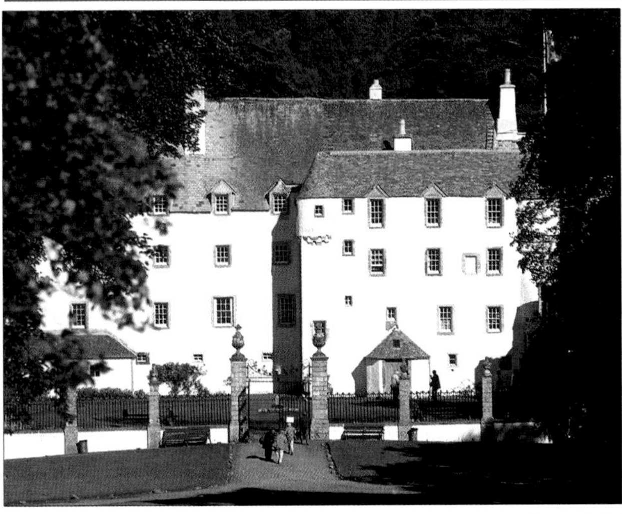

INNERLEITHEN, PEEBLESSHIRE EH44 6PW

Contact: *Ms C Maxwell Stuart*

Tel: 01896 830323 **Fax:** 01896 830639
e-mail: enquiries@traquair.co.uk

Traquair, situated amidst beautiful scenery and close by the River Tweed, is the oldest inhabited house in Scotland - visited by twenty-seven kings. Originally a Royal hunting lodge, it was owned by the Scottish Crown until 1478 when it passed to a branch of the Royal Stuart family whose descendants still live in the house today. Nearly ten centuries of Scottish political and domestic life can be traced from the collection of treasures in the house. It is particularly rich in associations with the Catholic Church in Scotland, Mary Queen of Scots and the Jacobite Risings.

70 acres of grounds with peacocks, ducks and other wildlife. In spring there is a profusion of daffodils followed by rhododendrons, wild flowers and herbaceous plants. A maze in beech/leylandii cyprus is behind the house.

Location: OS Ref. NY330 354. On B709 near junction with A72. Edinburgh 1hr, Glasgow 1 1/2 hrs, Carlisle 1 1/2 hrs, Newcastle 1 1/2 hrs.

Opening Times: 22 Apr - 31 Oct: daily, 12.30 - 5.30pm. Jun, Jul & Aug: 10.30am - 5.30pm. Last admission 5pm. Restaurant: open from 11am. Jun, Jul & Aug open from 10.30am.

Admission: House & Garden: Adult £5.20, Child (under 15yrs) £2.60. Groups: Adult £4.60, Child (under 15yrs) £2. Garden only: Adult £2, Child (under 15yrs) £1. Winter: Groups: £7, includes glass of wine/whisky/Traquair Ale and shortbread (min charge £100).

No photography in house. Licensed, self-service. Outside opening hours. Coaches please book. In grounds on leads. 2 four-poster suites, B&B.

SPECIAL EVENTS

- **APR 23:** Easter Egg Extravaganza.
- **AUG 5/6:** Traquair Fair.

South West
Scotland

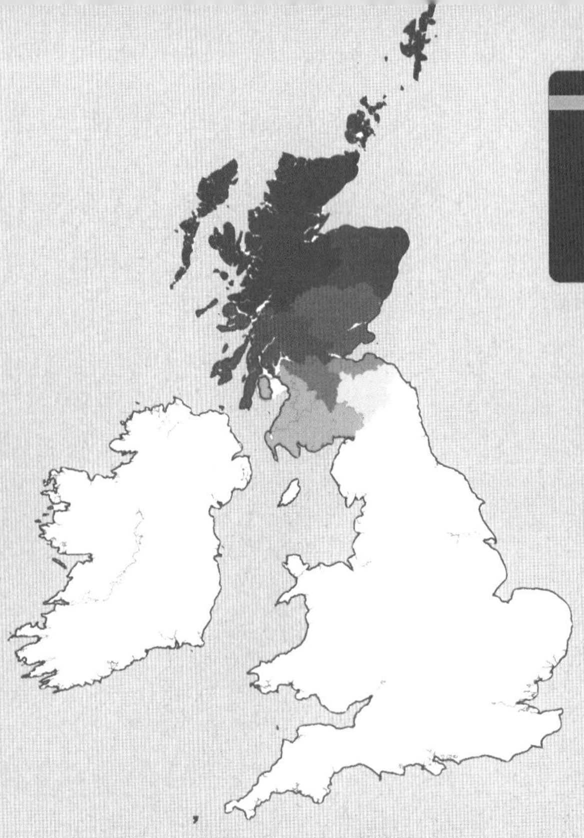

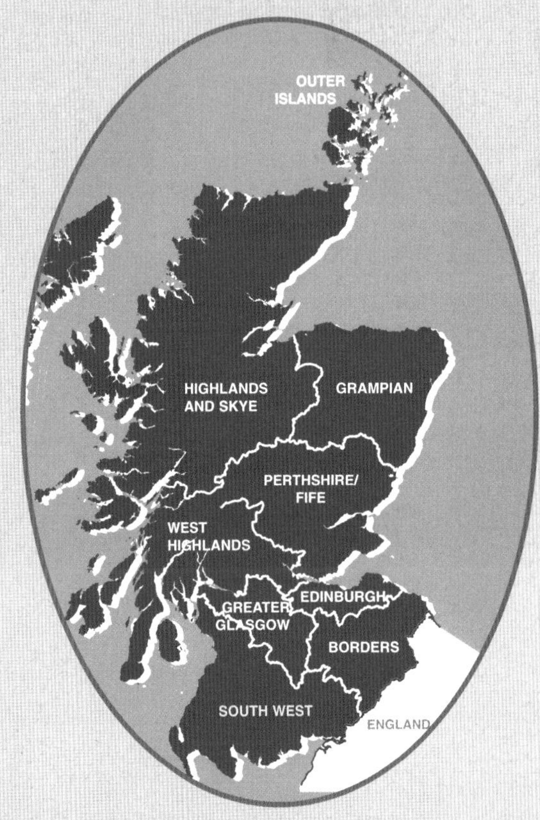

Loch Trool.

Dumfries & Galloway Tourist Board.

Christine Ottewill

Owner: James Hunter Blair

CONTACT

James Hunter Blair
Blairquhan Castle
Maybole
Ayrshire
KA19 7LZ

Tel: 01655 770239

Fax: 01655 770278

e-mail: enquiries@blairquhan.co.uk

LOCATION

OS Ref. NS366 055

From London M6 to Carlisle, A75 to Crocketford, A712 to A713 nr New Galloway, B741 to Straiton, B7045 to Ayr. Turn left 1/4 m beyond village. 6m SE of Maybole off B7045.

Rail: Maybole 7m.

Air: Prestwick Airport, 15m. Direct flights to London, Belfast & Dublin. Executive Travel: contact 01655 882666.

CONFERENCE/FUNCTION		
ROOM	SIZE	MAX CAPACITY
Drawing Rms	1200 sq ft	100
Dining Rm	750 sq ft	100
Library	400 sq ft	25
Saloon	600 sq ft	100
Meeting Rm	255 sq ft	50

BLAIRQUHAN CASTLE
Maybole

BLAIRQUHAN is the home of James Hunter Blair, the great-great-grandson of Sir David Hunter Blair, 3rd Baronet for whom it was designed by William Burn and built in 1821-24.

All the Regency furniture bought for the house remains, and the house has not been altered except discreetly to bring it up-to-date. There are ten double bedrooms including four four-poster beds, with en-suite bathrooms, five singles, and many public rooms which can be used for conferences and every sort of occasion.

The castle is approached by a 3 mile private drive along the River Girvan and is situated in one of the most charming parts of south west Scotland. There is a well-known collection of pictures. It is particularly suitable for conferences because the house is entirely at your disposal.

A five minute walk from the Castle are the walled gardens, laid out around the 1800s and recently replanned and replanted.

Blairquhan is only 50 miles from Glasgow. It is within about half an hour's drive of the world-famous golf courses of Prestwick, Troon and Turnberry, the last two of which are venues for the British Open Golf Championships.

Christine Ottewill

Tree trail, fashion shows, air displays, archery, shooting, equestrian events, garden parties, shows, rallies, filming, grand piano, snooker, fishing. Slide projector, overhead projector, screen, and secretarial assistance for meetings. No photography in castle.

Wedding receptions.

Two main floors suitable. WC.

Teas, lunches, buffets and dinners. Groups can book in advance, special rates for groups.

By arrangement. Also available in French.

Unlimited.

Guide and schoolroom provided, cost negotiable.

10 doubles (4 4-posters) with bathrooms en-suite, 5 singles. The Dower House at Milton has 10 doubles, 1 single, 6 bathrooms. 7 holiday cottages on the Estate.

In grounds on leads.

OPENING TIMES

SUMMER

15 July - 13 August
Daily (except Mons)
1.30 - 4.15pm
(Last admission).

Open at all other times by appointment.

WINTER

Open by appointment.

ADMISSION

House & Garden

Adult £5.00
Child (6-16yrs)..........£3.00
Conc........................£4.00

Groups*
Negotiable

* Minimum payment £20.

SPECIAL EVENTS

- **EVENTS EVERY WEEKEND INCLUDING:**
  Archery
  Model aeroplane flying
  Battle re-enactments.

Owner: His Grace the Duke of Buccleuch & Queensberry KT

CONTACT

A Fisher
Drumlanrig Castle
Thornhill
Dumfriesshire
DG3 4AQ

Tel: 01848 330248

Fax: 01848 331682

Countryside Service: 01848 331555

e-mail: bre@drumlanrigcastle.org.uk

LOCATION

OS Ref. NX851 992

18m N of Dumfries, 3m NW of Thornhill off A76. 16m from M74 at Elvanfoot. Approx. $1^1/2$ hrs by road from Edinburgh, Glasgow and Carlisle.

CONFERENCE/FUNCTION		
ROOM	SIZE	MAX CAPACITY
Visitors' Centre	6m x 13m	50

DRUMLANRIG CASTLE

Thornhill

DRUMLANRIG CASTLE, Gardens and Country Park, the home of the Duke of Buccleuch and Queensberry KT was built between 1679 and 1691 by William Douglas, 1st Duke of Queensberry. Drumlanrig is rightly recognised as one of the first and most important buildings in the grand manner in Scottish domestic architecture. James Smith, who made the conversion from a 15th century castle, made a comparable transformation at Dalkeith a decade later.

The castle, of local pink sandstone, offers superb views across Nithsdale. It houses a renowned art collection, including work by Leonardo, Holbein, and Rembrandt, as well as cabinets made for Louis XIV's Versailles, relics of Bonnie Prince Charlie and a 300 year old silver chandelier.

The story of Sir James Douglas, killed in Spain while carrying out the last wish of Robert Bruce, pervades the castle in the emblem of a winged heart. Douglas family historical exhibition. Working forge. The gardens, now being restored to the plan of 1738, add to the overall effect. The fascination of Drumlanrig as a centre of art, beauty and history is complemented by its role in the Queensberry Estate, a model of dynamic and enlightened land management.

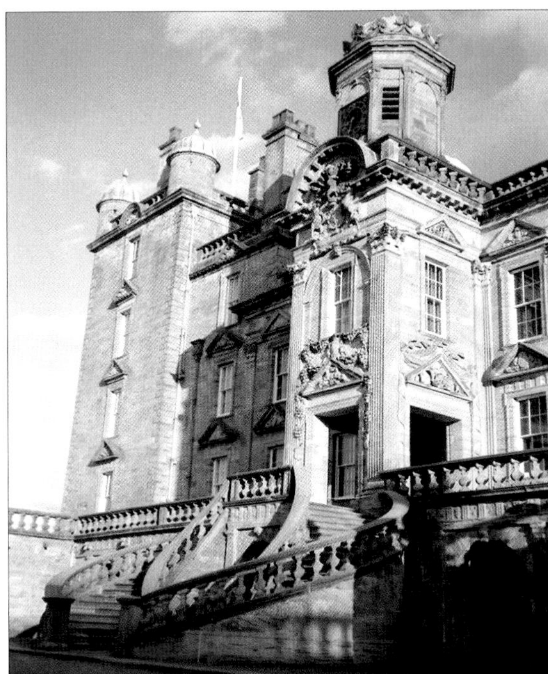

No photography inside the castle.

Suitable. WC. Please enquire about facilities before visit.

Snacks, lunches and teas during opening hours.

Adjacent to the castle.

Children's quiz and worksheets. Ranger-led activities, including woodlands and forestry. Adventure playground. School groups welcome throughout the year by arrangement.

In grounds on leads.

OPENING TIMES

SUMMER

Castle
Easter Saturday - 13 August

26 - 31 August:
Weekdays: 11am - 4pm,
Suns, 12 noon - 4pm.

1 - 30 September by appointment only.

Country Park, Gardens & Adventure Woodland

Easter Sat - 30 Sept, daily, 11am - 5pm.

WINTER

By appointment only.

ADMISSION

Castle and Country Park

Adult	£6.00
Child	£2.00
OAP/Student	£4.00
Family (2+4)	£14.00
Disabled in wheelchairs	Free
Pre-booked groups (20+)	
Adult	£4.00
Child	£2.00
Outside normal opening times	£8.00

Country Park only

Adult	£3.00
Child	£2.00

ARDWELL GARDENS

Tel: 01776 860227

Ardwell, Nr Stranraer, Dumfries and Galloway DG9 9LY

Owner: Mr Francis Brewis **Contact:** Mrs Terry Brewis

The gardens include a formal garden, wild garden and woodland.

Location: OS Ref. NX102 455. A716 10m S of Stranraer.

Opening Times: 1 Apr - 30 Sept: daily, 10am - 5pm.

Admission: Adult £1.50, Child/Conc. 75p.

BACHELORS' CLUB

Tel: 01292 541940

Sandgate Street, Tarbolton KA5 5RB

Owner: The National Trust for Scotland **Contact:** David Rodger

17th century thatched house in which poet Robert Burns and friends formed a debating society in 1780. Burns' mementos and relics, period furnishings.

Location: OS Ref. NS430 270. In Tarbolton, B744, 7½m NE of Ayr, off B743.

Opening Times: 1 Apr - 30 Sept: daily, 1.30 - 5.30pm. Weekends in Oct: 1.30 - 5.30pm. Last admission 5pm.

Admission: Adult £2.50, Conc. £1.70. Groups: Adult £2, School £1.

Ground floor suitable. 

BARGANY GARDENS

Tel: 01465 871249 **Fax:** 01465 871282

Girvan, Ayrshire KA26 9QL

Owner/Contact: Mr John Dalrymple Hamilton

Lily pond, rock garden and a fine collection of hard and softwood trees.

Location: OS Ref. NS250 001. 4m ENE of Girvan by B734. After 2½ m keep ahead on to minor road to Dailly.

Opening Times: 1 Mar - 31 Oct: 10am - 7pm.

Admission: £1 per car. Buses by arrangement.

BLAIRQUHAN CASTLE

See page 412 for full page entry.

BROUGHTON HOUSE & GARDEN

Tel/Fax: 01557 330437

High Street, Kirkcudbright DG6 4JX

Owner: The National Trust for Scotland **Contact:** Frances Scott

This fascinating 18th century house in the pleasant coastal town of Kirkcudbright was the home and studio from 1901 - 1933 of the artist E A Hornel, one of the 'Glasgow Boys'. It contains many of his works, along with paintings by other contemporary artists, and an extensive collection of rare Scottish books, including valuable editions of Burns' works.

Location: OS Ref. NX684 509. Off A711 / A755, in Kirkcudbright, at 12 High St.

Opening Times: House & Garden: 1 Apr - 31 Oct: daily, 1 - 5.30pm. Jul & Aug: 11am - 5.30pm. Last admission 4.45pm.

Admission: Adult £3.50, Conc. £2.50. Groups: Adult £2.80, Child/School £1.

Not suitable. By arrangement. Limited. 

BURNS' COTTAGE

Tel: 01292 441215

Alloway, Ayrshire KA7 4PY **Contact:** J Manson

Thatched cottage, birthplace of Robert Burns in 1759. Now a museum.

Location: OS Ref. NS335 190. 2m SW of Ayr.

Opening Times: Apr - Oct: daily, 9am - 6pm. Nov - Mar: daily, 10am - 4pm (Suns, 12 noon - 4pm).

Admission: Adult £2.80, Child/OAP £1.40, Family £8. Admission charge includes entry to Burns' Monument and Gardens.

Ayrshire & Arran Tourist Board.

Burns' Cottage, South West Scotland.

BRODICK CASTLE & COUNTRY PARK

Harvey Wood

ISLE OF ARRAN KA27 8HY

Owner: *The National Trust for Scotland* ***Contact:*** *Administrator*

Tel: 01770 302202 **Fax:** 01770 302312

This is a castle you will never forget! The tall, stately building beckons you with the glow of its warm red sandstone. The setting is staggering, fronted by the sea, bedecked with gardens and overlooked by the majestic mountain of Goatfell. The castle was built on the site of a Viking fortress and dates from the 13th century. The contents are magnificent and include superb silver, porcelain, paintings and sporting trophies. The woodland garden ranks as one of Europe's finest.

Location: OS Ref. NS010 360. Isle of Arran. Ferries from Ardrossan & Claonaig and Kintyre. Ferry enquiries: 01475 650100.

Opening Times: Castle: 1 Apr - 30 Jun & 1 Sept - 31 Oct: daily, 11am - 4.30pm, last admission 4pm. 1 Jul - 31 Aug: daily, 11am - 5pm, last admission 4.30pm. Reception Centre and shop: (dates as castle) 10am - 5pm; restaurant: 11am - 5pm. Shop & Restaurant: weekends in Nov & Dec: 11am - 3pm. Walled Garden: All year: daily, 9.30am - 5pm. Country Park: All year, daily 9.30am - sunset. Goatfell open all year.

Admission: Castle & Garden: Adult £6, Conc. £4. Groups: Adult £4.80, Child/School £1. Garden & Country Park: Adult £2.50, Conc. £1.70. Groups: Adult £2, Child/School £1.

Suitable. WC. Licensed. In grounds, on leads.

CAERLAVEROCK CASTLE

Historic Scotland

GLENCAPLE, DUMFRIES DG1 4RU

Owner: *Historic Scotland* ***Contact:*** *The Steward*

Tel: 01387 770244

One of the finest castles in Scotland on a triangular site surrounded by moats. Its most remarkable features are the twin-towered gatehouse and the Renaissance Nithsdale lodging. The site of two famous sieges. Children's park, replica siege engines and nature trail to site of earlier castle.

Location: OS84 NY025 656. 8m S of Dumfries on the B725.

Opening Times: Apr - Sept: daily, 9.30am - 6.30pm. Oct - Mar: Mon - Sat, 9.30am - 4.30pm, Suns, 2 - 4.30pm. Last ticket sold 30 mins before closing.

Admission: Adult £2.50, Child £1, Conc. £1.90. 10% discount for groups (10+).

Partially suitable. WCs. Limited for coaches. Free if pre-booked. In grounds, on leads.

CARDONESS CASTLE

Tel: 01557 814427

Gatehouse of Fleet

Owner: Historic Scotland **Contact:** The Custodian

Well preserved ruin of a four storey tower house of 15th century standing on a rocky platform above the Water of Fleet. Ancient home of the McCullochs. Very fine fireplaces.

Location: OS Ref. NX591 553. 1m SW of Gatehouse of Fleet, beside the A75.

Opening Times: 1 Apr - 30 Sept: daily, 9.30am - 6.30pm. Last ticket 6pm. 1 Oct - 31 Mar: Sats, 9.30am - 4.30pm, Suns, 2 - 4.30pm. Last ticket 4pm.

Admission: Adult £2, Child 75p, Conc. £1.50.

CARLYLE'S BIRTHPLACE

Tel: 01576 300666

Ecclefechan, Dumfriesshire DG11 3DG

Owner: The National Trust for Scotland **Contact:** The Manager

Thomas Carlyle was born here in The Arched House in 1795, the year before Burns died. Carlyle was a brilliant essayist, historian, social reformer, visionary and literary giant. When he was 14 he walked the 84 miles to Edinburgh University - taking three days. Upstairs is the bedroom in which Carlyle was born. There is also a little museum with a notable collection of photographs, manuscripts and other documents.

Location: OS Ref. NY193 745. Off M74, 6m SE of Lockerbie. In Ecclefechan village.

Opening Times: 1 Apr - 30 Sept: Fri - Mon, 1.30 - 5.30pm. Last admission 5pm.

Admission: Adult £2.50, Conc. £1.70. Groups: Adult £2, Child/School £1.

 Not suitable.  By arrangement.  Limited.

CASTLE KENNEDY GARDENS

Tel: 01776 702024 **Fax:** 01776 706248

Stair Estates, Rephad, Stranraer, Dumfries and Galloway DG9 8BX

Owner: The Earl & Countess of Stair **Contact:** The Earl of Stair

75 acres of gardens, originally laid out in 1730, includes rhododendrons, pinetum, walled garden and circular lily pond.

Location: OS Ref. NX109 610. 3m E of Stranraer on A75.

Opening Times: Apr - Sept: daily.

Admission: Adult £3, Child £1, OAP £2.

CRAIGDARROCH HOUSE

Tel: 01848 200202

Moniaive, Dumfriesshire DG3 4JB

Owner/Contact: Mr Alexander Sykes

Location: OS Ref. NX741 909. S side of B729, 2m W of Moniaive, 19m WNW of Dumfries.

Opening Times: Jul: daily, 2 - 4pm.

Admission: £2.

CRAIGIEBURN GARDEN

Tel: 01683 221250

Craigieburn House, Nr Moffat, Dumfriesshire DG10 9LF **e-mail:** ajmw1@aol.com

Owner/Contact: Janet Wheatcroft

A plantsman's garden with a huge range of rare and unusual plants surrounded by natural woodland.

Location: OS Ref. NT117 053. NW side of A708 to Yarrow & Selkirk, 2½ m E of Moffat.

Opening Times: Easter - Sept: Thur - Sun, 10am - 6pm.

Admission: Adult £2, Child Free.

CROSSRAGUEL ABBEY

Tel: 01655 883113

Maybole, Strathclyde

Owner: Historic Scotland **Contact:** The Custodian

Founded in the early 13th century by the Earl of Carrick. Remarkably complete remains include church, cloister, chapter house and much of the domestic premises.

Location: OS Ref. NS275 083. 2m S of Maybole on the A77.

Opening Times: 1 Apr - 30 Sept: daily, 9.30am - 6.30m. Last ticket 6pm.

Admission: Adult £1.80, Child 75p, Conc. £1.30.

Ayrshire & Arran Tourist Board.

Dean Castle Country Park, South West Scotland.

CULZEAN CASTLE & COUNTRY PARK

John K Wilkie

MAYBOLE KA19 8LE

Owner: *The National Trust for Scotland* ***Contact:*** *Jonathan Cardale*

Tel: 01655 884455 **Fax:** 01655 884503

Robert Adam's 18th century masterpiece, a real 'castle in the air', is perched on a cliff high above the crashing waves of the Firth of Clyde. Arrow slits and mock battlements give medieval touches to the sturdy exterior, and on the seaward-side front is the imposing drum tower. The interior is the epitome of disciplined elegance, crowned by the spectacular oval staircase ascending through ornamental pillars and ironwork balustrading. Adam also designed many interior fittings. The exterior grounds encompass Scotland's first country park.

Location: OS Ref. NS240 100. 12m SW of Ayr, on A719, 4m W of Maybole.

Opening Times: Castle, Walled Garden, Visitor Centre, Restaurants & Shop: 1 Apr - 31 Oct: daily, 10.30am - 5.30pm. Last admission 5pm. Other times by appointment. Country Park: All year: daily 9.30am - sunset.

Admission: Castle & Country Park: Adult £7, Conc. £5. Groups: Adult £6. Country Park only: Adult £3.50, Conc. £2.50. Groups: Adult £3, School coach £20.

 Suitable. WC. Licensed. In grounds, on leads. 

DALGARVEN MILL

Tel: 01294 552448

Dalry Road, Kilwinning, Ayrshire K13 6PL

Owner: Dalgarven Mill Trust **Contact:** The Administrator

Water-driven flour mill and country life museum.

Location: OS Ref. NS295 460. On A737 2m from Kilwinning.

Opening Times: All year: Easter - end Oct: Mon - Sat, 10am - 5pm. Suns, 11am - 5pm. Winter closes at 4pm, may not be open Mons/Tues - ring to check.

Admission: Adult £2.50, Family £6.

DEAN CASTLE COUNTRY PARK

Tel: 01563 574916

Dean Road, Kilmarnock, East Ayrshire KA3 1XB

Owner: East Ayrshire Council **Contact:** Andrew Scott-Martin

Set in 81 hectares of Country Park. Visits to castle by guided tour only.

Location: OS Ref. NS437 395. Off A77. 1¼ m NNE of town centre.

Opening Times: Country Park & Visitor Centre: All year. Castle: Easter - end Oct: daily, 12 noon - 5pm (last tour 4.15pm). Oct - Easter: weekends only, 12 noon - 4pm (last tour 3.15pm).

Admission: Adult £2.60, Conc. £1.30, Family (2+4) £7. East Ayrshire residents free.

DRUMLANRIG CASTLE

See page 413 for full page entry.

DUNDRENNAN ABBEY

Tel: 01557 500262

Kirkcudbright

Owner: Historic Scotland **Contact:** The Custodian

Mary Queen of Scots spent her last night on Scottish soil in this 12th century Cistercian Abbey founded by David I. The Abbey stands in a small and secluded valley.

Location: OS Ref. NX749 475. 6½ m SE of Kirkcudbright on the A711.

Opening Times: 1 Apr - 30 Sept: daily, 9.30am - 6.30pm. Last ticket 6pm. 1 Oct - 31 Mar: Sats, 9.30am - 4.30pm, Suns, 2 - 4.30pm.

Admission: Adult £1.80, Child 75p, Conc. £1.30.

GALLOWAY HOUSE GARDENS

Tel: 01988 600680

Garlieston, Newton Stewart, Wigtownshire DG8 8HF
Owner: Galloway House Gardens Trust **Contact:** D Marshall
Created in 1740 by Lord Garlies, currently under restoration.
Location: OS Ref. NX478 453. 15m S of Newton Stewart on B7004.
Opening Times: 1 Mar - 31 Oct: 9am - 5pm.
Admission: Adult £1, Child/Conc. 50p, Family £2.50.

GILNOCKIE'S TOWER

Tel: 01387 371876

Hollows, Canonbie, Dumfriesshire
Owner/Contact: Edward Armstrong
16th century tower house, occupied by the Clan Armstrong Centre.
Location: OS Ref. NY383 787. 2m N of Canonbie on minor road E of A7 just N of Hollows.
Opening Times: Summer months by guided tours: 10am & 2.30pm (closed 11.45am - 2pm).
Admission: Adult £3, Child (under 14yrs) £1.50.

GLENLUCE ABBEY

Tel: 01581 300541

Glenluce
Owner/Contact: Historic Scotland
A Cistercian Abbey founded in 1190. Remains include a 16th century Chapter House.
Location: OS Ref. NX185 587. 2m NW of Glenluce village off the A75.
Opening Times: 1 Apr - 30 Sept: daily 9.30am - 6.30pm. Last ticket 6pm. 1 Oct - 31 Mar: Sats, 9.30am - 4.30pm, Suns, 2 - 4.30pm. Last ticket 4pm.
Admission: Adult £1.80, Child 75p, Conc. £1.30.

GLENWHAN GARDENS

Tel: 01581 400222 **Fax:** 01581 400295

Dunragit, Stranraer, Wigtownshire DG9 8PH
Owner/Contact: Mrs Tessa Knott
Beautiful 12 acre garden overlooking Luce Bay and the Mull of Galloway.
Location: OS Ref. NX150 580. N side of A75, 6m E of Stranraer.
Opening Times: 1 Apr - 30 Sept: daily, 10am - 5pm or by appointment.
Admission: Adult £2.50, Child £1, Conc. £2.

LOGAN BOTANIC GARDEN

Tel: 01776 860231 **Fax:** 01776 860333

Port Logan, Stranraer, Wigtownshire DG9 9ND
Owner: Royal Botanic Garden Edinburgh **Contact:** The Curator
Scotland's most exotic garden. Take a trip to the south west of Scotland and experience the southern hemisphere!
Location: OS Ref. NX097 430. 14m S of Stranraer on B7065.
Opening Times: 1 Mar - 31 Oct: daily, 9.30am - 6pm.
Admission: Adult £3, Child £1, Conc. £2.50, Family £7. Group discount available.

MACLELLAN'S CASTLE

Tel: 01557 331856

Kirkcudbright
Owner: Historic Scotland **Contact:** The Custodian
Castellated mansion, built in 1577 using stone from an adjoining ruined monastery by the then Provost. Elaborately planned with fine architectural details, it has been a ruin since 1752.
Location: OS Ref. NX683 511. Centre of Kirkcudbright on the A711.
Opening Times: 1 Apr - 30 Sept: daily, 9.30am - 6.30pm. Last ticket 6pm.
Admission: Adult £1.80, Child 75p, Conc. £1.30.

NEW ABBEY CORN MILL

Tel: 01387 850260

New Abbey Village
Owner: Historic Scotland **Contact:** The Custodian
This carefully renovated 18th century water-powered oatmeal mill is in full working order and regular demonstrations are given for visitors in the summer.
Location: OS Ref. NX962 663. 8m S of Dumfries on the A710. Close to Sweetheart Abbey.
Opening Times: 1 Apr - 30 Sept: daily, 9.30am - 6.30pm. Last ticket 6pm. 1 Oct - 31 Mar: Mon - Wed & Sat, 9.30am - 4.30pm, Thurs, 9.30am - 12 noon, Fris closed, Suns, 2 - 4.30pm. Last ticket 4pm.
Admission: Adult £2.50, Child £1, Conc. £1.90. Joint entry ticket with Sweetheart Abbey: Adult £3, Child £1.20, Conc. £2.25.

RAMMERSCALES

Tel: 01387 810229/811988 **Fax:** 01387 810940

Lockerbie, Dumfriesshire DG11 1LD
Owner/Contact: Mr M A Bell Macdonald
Georgian house.
Location: OS Ref. NY080 780. W side of B7020, 3m S of Lochmoben.
Opening Times: Last week in Jul, 1st three weeks in Aug: daily (excluding Sats), 2 - 5pm.
Admission: £5.

SHAMBELLIE HOUSE MUSEUM OF COSTUME

Tel: 01387 850375 **Fax:** 01387 850461

New Abbey, Dumfries DG2 8HQ
Owner: National Museums of Scotland **Contact:** Sheila Watt
Shambellie House is a small country house designed by David Bryce in 1856 for William Stewart. It is set in woodland just outside the village of New Abbey. Inside, in room settings, it displays costume as worn in a country house between 1860 and 1950.
Location: OS Ref. NX960 665. On A710, 7m outside Dumfries on Solway coast road.
Opening Times: 1 Apr - 31 Oct: daily, 11am - 5pm.
Admission: Adult £2.50, Child Free, Conc. £1.50. Season ticket for all National Museums of Scotland sites: Adult £5, Conc. £3.

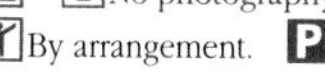 No photography in house. 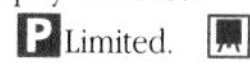 Not suitable. 
By arrangement. Limited.  In grounds, on leads.

Ayrshire & Arran Tourist Board.

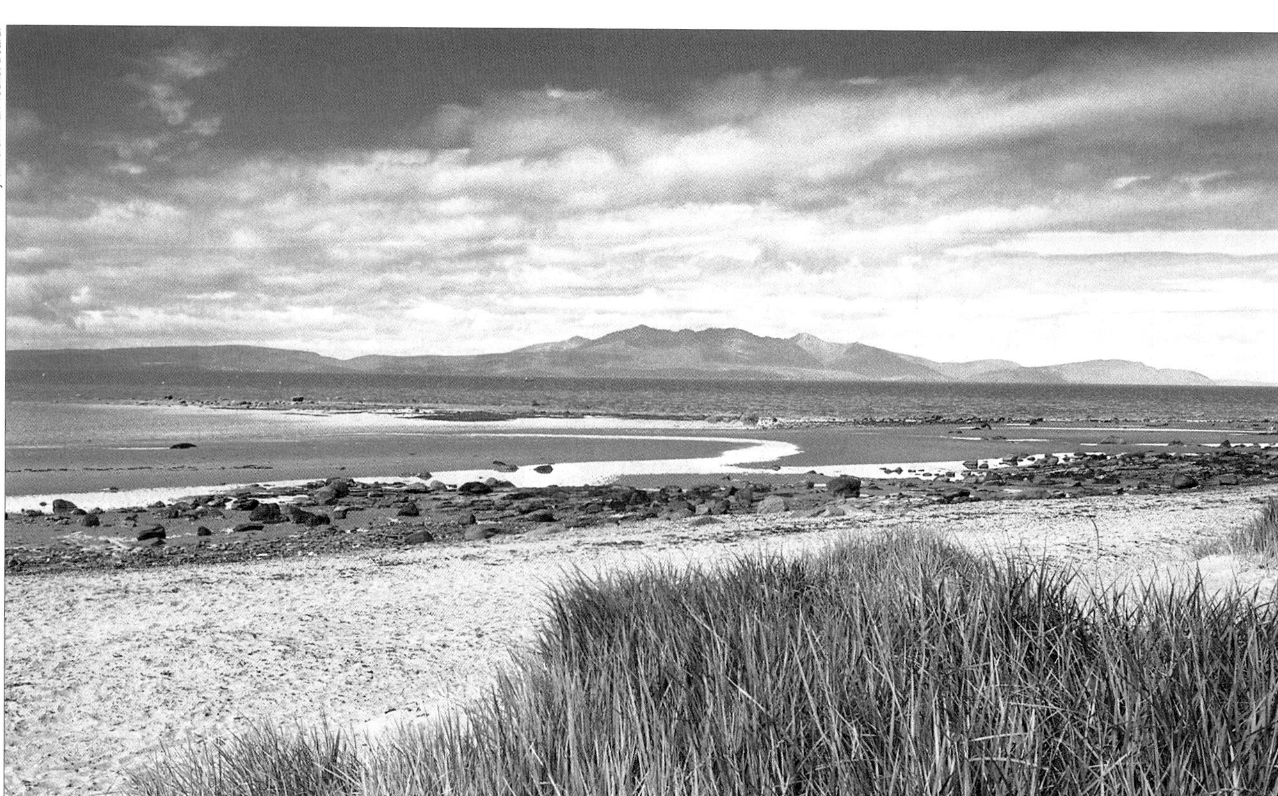

Looking to Arran.

SORN CASTLE

Tel: 01290 551555

Ayrshire KA5 6HR

Owner/Contact: Mrs R G McIntyre

14th century castle. James V visited it in 1598. Enlarged several times, most recently in 1908.

Location: OS Ref. NS555 265. 4m E of Mauchline on B743.

Opening Times: 15 Jul - 12 Aug: daily, 2 - 4pm.

SOUTER JOHNNIE'S COTTAGE

Tel: 01655 760603

Main Road, Kirkoswald KA19 8HY

Owner: The National Trust for Scotland **Contact:** Ms Jan Gibson

The home of John Davidson, original 'Souter' (cobbler) of Robert Burns' famous narrative poem *Tam O' Shanter*. Burns mementos and restored cobbler's workshop. Life-sized stone figures in adjacent 'ale-house'.

Location: OS Ref. NS240 070. On A77, in Kirkoswald village, 4m SW of Maybole.

Opening Times: 21 Apr - 30 Sept: daily, 11.30am - 5pm. Weekends in Oct: 11.30am - 5pm (last admission 4.30pm).

Admission: Adult £2.50, Conc. £1.70. Groups: Adult £2, Child/School £1.

House suitable. Limited.  

STRANRAER CASTLE

Tel: 01776 705088 **Fax:** 01776 705835

Stranraer, Galloway

Owner: Dumfries & Galloway Council **Contact:** John Pickin

Much altered 16th century L-plan tower house, now a museum telling the history of the castle.

Location: OS Ref. NX061 608. In Stranraer, short distance SW of junction between A77 & B737, 1/4 m short of the harbour.

Opening Times: Easter - mid-Sept: Mon - Sat, 10am - 1pm & 2 - 5pm.

Admission: Adult £1.20, Conc. 60p.

SWEETHEART ABBEY 

Tel: 01387 850397

New Abbey Village

Owner: Historic Scotland **Contact:** The Custodian

Cistercian abbey founded in 1273 by Devorgilla, in memory of her husband John Balliol. The principal feature is the well-preserved precinct wall enclosing 30 acres.

Location: OS Ref. NX965 663. In New Abbey Village, on A710 8m S of Dumfries.

Opening Times: 1 Apr - 30 Sept: daily, 9.30am - 6.30pm. Last ticket 6pm. 1 Oct - 31 Mar: Mon - Wed & Sat, 9.30am - 4.30pm, Thurs, 9.30am - 12 noon, Fris closed, Suns, 2 - 4.30pm. Last ticket 4pm.

Admission: Adult £1.50, Child 50p, Conc. £1.10. Joint entry ticket with New Abbey Corn Mill: Adult £3, Child £1.20, Conc. £2.25.

THREAVE CASTLE 

Tel: 01831 168512

Castle Douglas

Owner: The National Trust for Scotland **Contact:** Historic Scotland

Built by Archibald the Grim in the late 14th century, early stronghold of the Black Douglases. Around its base is an artillery fortification built before 1455 when the castle was besieged by James II. Ring the bell and the custodian will come to ferry you over. Long walk to property. Owned by The National Trust for Scotland but under the guardianship of Historic Scotland.

Location: OS Ref. NX739 623. 2m W of Castle Douglas on the A75.

Opening Times: 1 Apr - 30 Sept: daily, 9.30am - 6.30pm. Last ticket 6pm.

Admission: Adult £2, Child 75p, Conc. £1.50. Charges include ferry trip.

THREAVE GARDEN

Tel: 01556 502575 **Tel:** 01556 502683

Castle Douglas DG7 1RX

Owner: The National Trust for Scotland **Contact:** Trevor Jones

The garden has a wide range of features and a good collection of plants. There are peat and woodland garden plants and a colourful rock garden. Summer months bring a superb show from the herbaceous beds and borders. The heather gardens give a splash of colour, along with bright berries in the autumn. Truly a garden for all seasons.

Location: OS Ref. NX752 605. Off A75, 1m SW of Castle Douglas.

Opening Times: Estate & garden: All year: daily, 9.30am - sunset. Walled garden and glasshouses: all year: daily, 9.30am - 5pm. Visitor Centre, Exhibition, & Shop: 1 Apr - 31 Oct: daily, 9.30am - 5.30pm. Restaurant: 10am - 5pm.

Admission: Adult £4.50, Conc. £3. Groups: Adult £3.60, Child/School £1.

Grounds suitable. WC. 

WHITHORN PRIORY

Tel: 01988 500700

Whithorn

Owner: Historic Scotland **Contact:** The Project Manager

The site of the first Christian church in Scotland. Founded as 'Candida Casa' by St Ninian in the early 5th century it later became the cathedral church of Galloway.

Location: OS Ref. NX445 403. At Whithorn on the A746.

Opening Times: Please telephone for details.

Admission: Joint ticket gives entry to Priory, Priory Museum and archaeological dig.

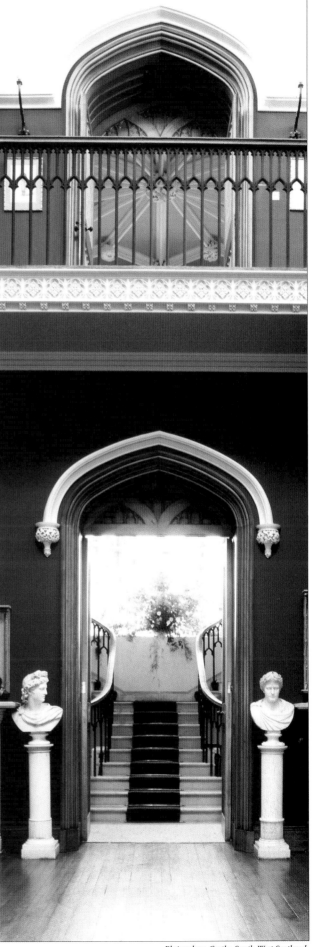

Christine Ottewill

Blairquhan Castle, South West Scotland.

Edinburgh

A Winter's Night.

Edinburgh and Lothians Tourist Board.

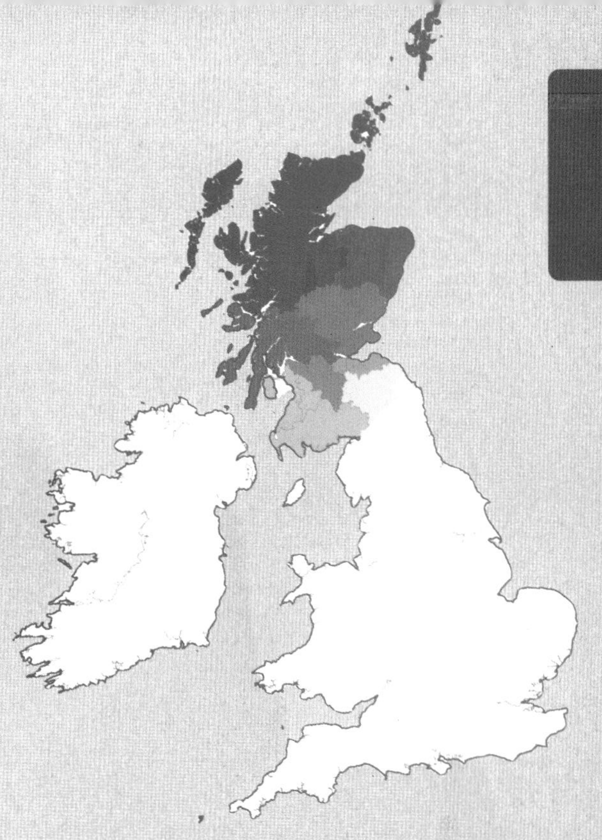

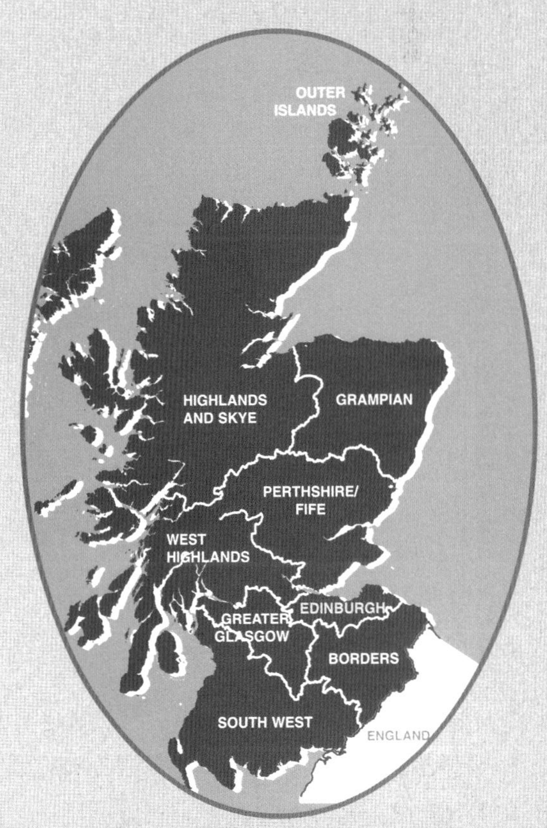

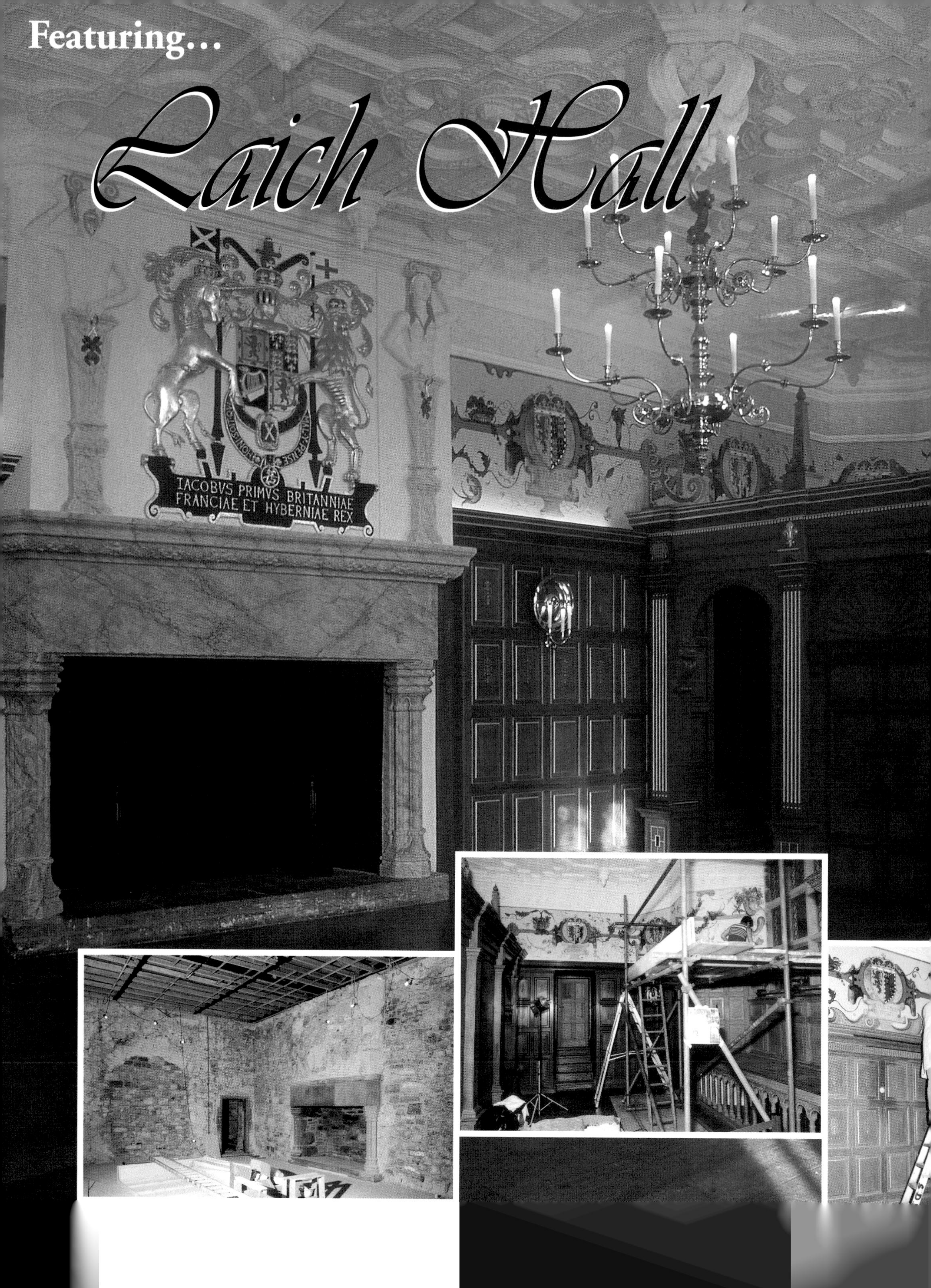
Featuring…
Laich Hall
IACOBVS PRIMVS BRITANNIAE
FRANCIAE ET HYBERNIAE REX

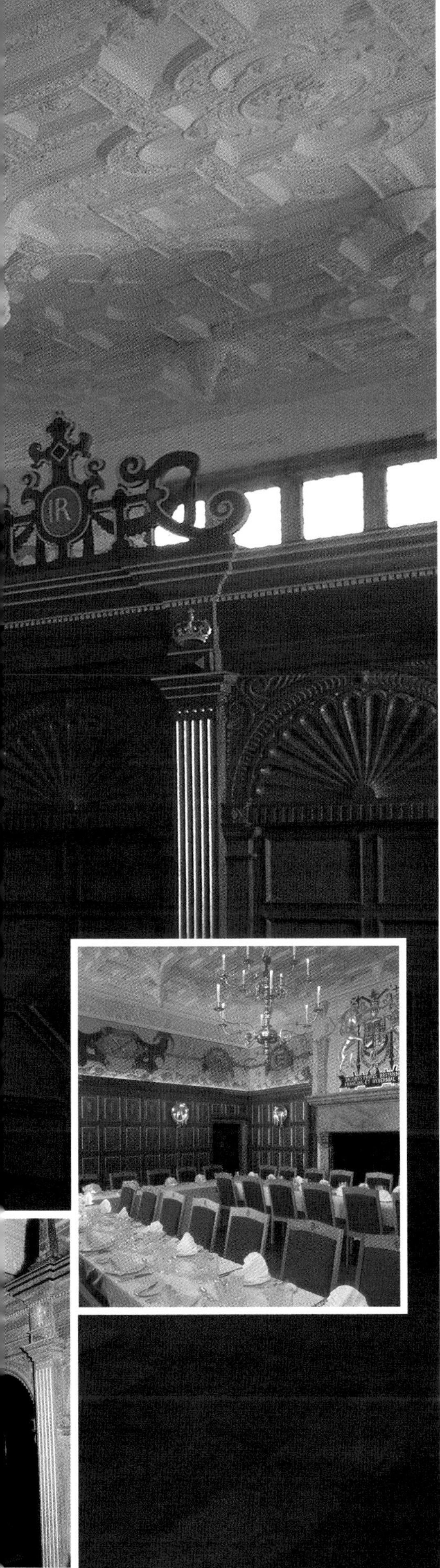

Laich Hall, Edinburgh Castle.

James VI.

The recently opened Royal Apartments, Laich Hall and Presence Chamber at Edinburgh Castle are wonderful examples of late 20th century detective work by Historic Scotland to restore and recreate the Royal Apartments as they may typically have appeared for the long-awaited 'Hamecoming' of King James VI in 1617. This was in fact to be James VI's only visit to Scotland after the Union of the Crowns. Yet less than 50 years after they were prepared for the 'Hamecoming' by Sir James Murray, Master of the King's Works, the Royal Apartments had been taken over by the army and the Laich Hall reduced to a quartermaster's store. Later still it was used by the Ministry of Works as the tearoom for visitors to the Castle!

It is hard to believe today, when looking at the wonderful Scots pine panelling and ornately gilded and exquisitely painted plasterwork, that apart from the stone fireplaces, doorcases and the small room where Mary Queen of Scots gave birth to the future king, nothing remained of the original grandeur of the Royal Apartments – that is until the painstaking research to restore the apartments began in 1993.

Led by Clare Lawrence, Historic Scotland Project Architect, the 'detective work' began and, like all great stories, it started from the smallest scrap of evidence – a single fragment of plaster frieze found in the Castle. From this the team examined and compared contemporary work at other castles and houses in Scotland and England and, bit by bit, pieced together clues and evidence as to how the rooms would have appeared. The team found that the pattern on the plaster fragment matched complete friezes at Muchalls Castle near Stonehaven and Glamis Castle in Angus. Both friezes clearly came from the same mould.

The plasterwork in these castles is known to be later than the refurbishment of Edinburgh Castle in 1617. Obviously the fashion conscious noblemen of Scotland employed the same plasterers used at Edinburgh. This is confirmed by evidence uncovered from the accounts of the Master of Works, which refers to moulds for plasterwork being loaned and borrowed.

The frieze that can be seen today depicts the Stewart succession from Robert II to James VI. The original magnificent sandstone fireplaces has been hand-marbled to produce a white/grey effect typical of the period. The wooden floor is covered with hand-plaited water reed, which would have provided warmth and comfort.

Graeme Munro, Historic Scotland Director and Chief Executive, is keen to stress that this restoration project is more than mere 'set dressing'. It has given today's craftsmen a fantastic opportunity to rediscover and research the materials and techniques originally used. Indeed Historic Scotland intends to publish this research, to assist others involved in the repair of 17th century ceilings.

This apart, for today's visitor to Edinburgh Castle these Apartments wonderfully evoke the smell, colour and texture of the pomp and splendour that would have greeted James VI on his fleeting visit to Scotland.

For full details of this property see page 426.

Owner: The Earl of Rosebery

CONTACT

The Administrator
Dalmeny House
South Queensferry
Edinburgh
EH30 9TQ

Tel: 0131 331 1888

Fax: 0131 331 1788

e-mail: events@dalmeny.co.uk

LOCATION

OS Ref. NT167 779

From Edinburgh A90, B924, 7m N, A90 $^1/_2$ m.

On south shore of Firth of Forth.

Bus: From St Andrew Square to Chapel Gate 1m from House.

Rail: Dalmeny railway station 3m.

Taxi: Hawes Landing 0131 331 1077 Caledonian Private Hire 0131 331 3321.

CONFERENCE/FUNCTION		
ROOM	SIZE	MAX CAPACITY
Library	10.4 x 7m	20
Dining Rm	11.2 x 7.4m	100
Garden Restaurant	12.7 x 9m	200
Rosebery Rooms		150

DALMENY HOUSE
South Queensferry

DALMENY HOUSE rejoices in one of the most beautiful and unspoilt settings in Great Britain, yet it is only seven miles from Scotland's capital, Edinburgh, fifteen minutes from Edinburgh airport and less than an hour's drive from Glasgow. It is an eminently suitable venue for group visits, business functions, meetings and special events, including product launches. Outdoor activities such as off-road driving, also feature strongly.

Dalmeny Estate, the family home of the Earls of Rosebery for over 300 years, boasts superb collections of porcelain and tapestries, fine paintings by Gainsborough, Raeburn, Reynolds and Lawrence, together with the exquisite Mentmore Rothschild collection of 18th century French furniture. There is also the Napoleonic collection, assembled by the 5th Earl of Rosebery, Prime Minister, historian and owner of three Derby winners.

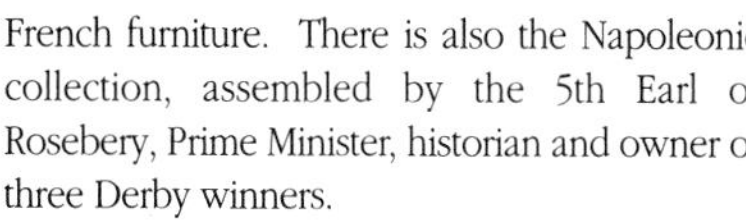

The Hall, Library and Dining Room will lend a memorable sense of occasion to corporate receptions, luncheons and dinners. Alternatively, there are the recently renovated areas of the former kitchen and servants' hall (now named the Rosebery Rooms) and the new Courtyard Restaurant, with facilities specifically designed for business meetings, small conferences, promotions, exhibitions and product launches. A wide range of entertainment can also be provided, from piano recitals to a floodlit pipe band Beating the Retreat.

Fashion shows, product launches, archery, clay pigeon shooting, equestrian events, shows, filming, background photography, small meetings and special events. Lectures on House, contents and family history. Screen and projector. Helicopter landing area. House is centre of a $4^1/_2$ m shore walk from Forth Rail Bridge to small foot passenger ferry at Cramond (ferry 9am - 1pm, 2 - 7pm in summer, 2 - 4pm winter, closed Fri). No fires, picnics or cameras.

Conferences and functions, buffets, lunches, dinners.

Visitors may alight at entrance. WC.

Teas and lunches, groups can book in advance.

Special interest tours can be arranged outside normal opening hours.

60 cars, 3 coaches. Parking for functions in front of house.

No dogs. 

OPENING TIMES

SUMMER

July and August
Sun - Tue, 2 - 5.30pm.
Last admission 4.45pm.

WINTER

Open at other times by appointment only.

ADMISSION

SUMMER

Adult	£3.80
Child (10-16yrs)	£2.00
OAP	£3.30
Student	£2.80
Groups (20+)	£3.00

HARBURN HOUSE
Nr Livingston

Owner: Humphrey & Rozi Spurway

CONTACT

Rozi Spurway
Harburn House
Harburn
West Calder
West Lothian
EH55 8RN

Tel: 01506 461818

Fax: 01506 416591

e-mail: information@harburnhouse.com

LOCATION

OS Ref. NT045 608

Off B7008, 2½ m S of A71. 2m N of A70. 20m SW of Edinburgh. Almost equidistant between Glasgow and Edinburgh, within 1hr of Perth, Stirling, Dundee and the Border country.

CONFERENCE/FUNCTION		
ROOM	SIZE	MAX CAPACITY
Conference Room	30' x 18'	20
Drawing Rm	30' x 18'	40
Dining Rm	30' x 18'	40
Library	14' x 12'	15
Morning Rm	16' x 15'	20
Whole house		80
Marquee	120' x 40'	500

HARBURN HOUSE offers its guests the perfect alternative to a first class hotel. This privately owned Georgian mansion, surrounded by its own 3000 acre sporting and leisure estate, is ideally situated offering unparalleled accessibility.

Harburn is essentially small and very personal. It is therefore frequently taken over exclusively for conferences, incentive travel, training seminars and product launches, etc. In this way guests may enjoy the luxury of a five star hotel, combined with the comfort and privacy of their own home.

The policies and lawns of Harburn are ideal for larger events and these can be complemented by our own fully lined and floored marquee.

A stay at Harburn is a very relaxed and informal affair. The staff are first class and the atmosphere is one of a private house party.

The estate provides the full range of sporting and leisure activities including, golf, game shooting, fishing, clay pigeon shooting, tennis, riding and archery to name but a few.

The complete privacy and outstanding scenery, so accessible to the major cities and beauty spots, makes Harburn the ultimate choice for the discerning event or conference organiser.

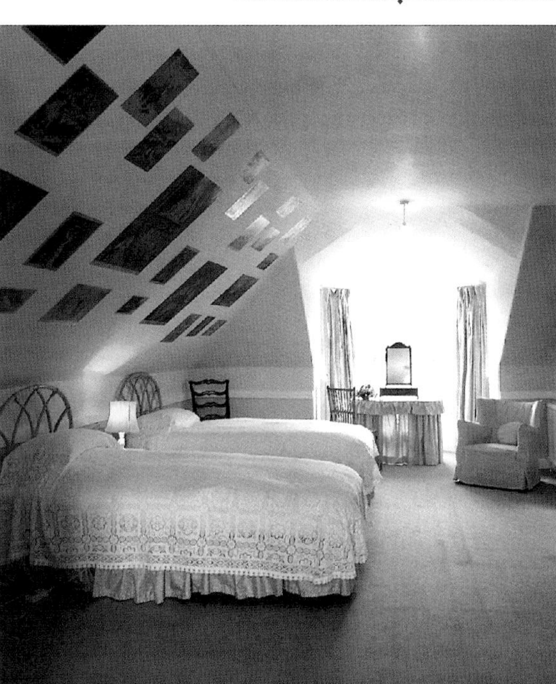

Filming, conferences, activity days, product launches, golf, riding, fishing, archery, buggies, game shooting, falconry, etc. Golf and Country Club nearby.

High quality in-house catering by our own top chef and fully trained staff. Prices and menus on request. Wedding receptions.

Ground floor bedroom, dining room and drawing room.

Parking for 300 cars and 10 coaches in summer, 100+/10 in winter. Follow one way system and 20 mph speed limit, vehicles should not park on grass verges.

On leads.

20 bedrooms, all with their own bathrooms, exclusive to one group at a time.

OPENING TIMES

All year by appointment for exclusive use of house and grounds.

ADMISSION

The exclusive use of House and Grounds for activity days (without accommodation).

Per day from £700.00

Accommodation Rates

Double with bath
Per person..............£90.00

Dinner, bed & breakfast
Per person............£110.00

Day Delegate Rate
Per person..............£42.50

24 hour rate
Per person............£125.00

VAT is not included in the above rates.

HOPETOUN HOUSE
Edinburgh

Owner: Hopetoun House Preservation Trust

CONTACT

Lois Bayne Jardine
Hopetoun House
South Queensferry
Edinburgh
West Lothian
EH30 9SL

Tel: 0131 331 2451

Fax: 0131 319 1885

LOCATION

OS Ref. NT089 790

2½ m W of Forth Road Bridge.

12m W of Edinburgh (25 mins. drive).

34m E of Glasgow (50 mins. drive).

CONFERENCE/FUNCTION		
ROOM	SIZE	MAX CAPACITY
Ballroom	92' x 35'	300
Tapestry Rm	37' x 24'	100
Red Drawing Rm	44' x 24'	100
State Dining Rm	39' x 23'	20

HOPETOUN HOUSE is a unique gem of Europe's architectural heritage and undoubtedly 'Scotland's Finest Stately Home'. Situated on the shores of the Firth of Forth, it is one of the most splendid examples of the work of Scottish architects Sir William Bruce and William Adam. The interior of the house, with opulent gilding and classical motifs, reflects the aristocratic grandeur of the early 18th century, whilst its magnificent parkland has fine views across the Forth to the hills of Fife. The house is approached from the Royal Drive, used only by members of the Royal Family, notably King George IV in 1822 and Her Majesty Queen Elizabeth II in 1988.

Hopetoun is really two houses in one, the oldest part of the house was designed by Sir William Bruce and built between 1699 and 1707. It shows some of the finest examples in Scotland of carving, wainscotting and ceiling painting. In 1721 William Adam, by now a renowned Scottish architect, started enlarging the house by adding the magnificent façade, colonnades and grand State apartments which were the focus for social life and entertainment in the 18th century.

The house is set in 100 acres of rolling parkland including fine woodland walks, the red deer park, the spring garden with a profusion of wild flowers, and numerous picturesque picnic spots.

Hopetoun has been home of the Earls of Hopetoun, later created Marquesses of Linlithgow, since it was built in 1699 and in 1974 a charitable trust was created to preserve the house with its historic contents and surrounding landscape for the benefit of the public for all time.

Private functions, special events, antiques fairs, concerts, Scottish gala evenings, conferences, grand piano, boules (petanque) piste, croquet lawn, helicopter landing. No smoking or flash photography in house.

Receptions, gala dinners.

Restaurant and exhibitions on ground floor. WC.

Licensed. Groups (up to 250) can book in advance, menus on request tel: 0131 331 4305.

By arrangement. Foreign language guides are usually available.

Close to the house for cars and coaches. Book if possible, allow 1-2hrs for visit (min).

Holders of 2 Sandford Awards for Heritage Education. Special tours of house and/or grounds for different age/interest groups. Teachers' information pack.

No dogs in house, (on leads) in grounds. 

OPENING TIMES

SUMMER

31 March - 1 October: daily, 10am - 5.30pm
Last admission 4.30pm.

WINTER

By appointment only for groups of 15+.

ADMISSION

Adult £5.30
Child (5-16yrs) £2.70
Conc........................ £4.70
Group
Adult £4.70
Child (5-16yrs) £2.20

Under 5yrs Free.

Winter prices on request.

SPECIAL EVENTS

For a full programme of special events please call on: 0131 331 2451.

AMISFIELD MAINS

Tel: 01875 870201 **Fax:** 01875 870620

Nr Haddington, East Lothian EH41 3SA

Owner: Wemyss and March Estates Management Co Ltd **Contact:** M Andrews

Georgian farmhouse with gothick barn and cottage.

Location: OS Ref. NT526 755. Between Haddington and East Linton on A1 Edinburgh-Dunbar Road.

Opening Times: Exterior only: By appointment, Wemyss and March Estates Office, Longniddry, East Lothian EH32 0PY.

Admission: Please contact for details.

ARNISTON HOUSE

GOREBRIDGE, MIDLOTHIAN EH23 4RY

Owner: *Mrs A Dundas-Bekker* ***Contact:*** *Miss H Dundas-Bekker*

Tel/Fax: 01875 830515

Magnificent William Adam mansion started in 1726. Fine plasterwork, Scottish portraiture, period furniture and other fascinating contents. Beautiful country setting beloved by Sir Walter Scott.

Location: OS Ref. NT326 595. Off B6372, 1m from A7, Temple direction.

Opening Times: Apr, May & Jun: Tues. Guided tours at 2pm & 3.30pm. 2 Jul - 14 Sept: Sun, Tue & Thur, 2 - 5pm. Guided tours at $\frac{1}{2}$ hourly intervals. Pre-arranged groups (10-50) accepted throughout the rest of the year.

Admission: Adult £3.50, Child £1.50 (under school age Free).

Obligatory. In grounds, on leads.

BEANSTON

Tel: 01875 870201 **Fax:** 01875 870620

Nr Haddington, East Lothian EH41 3SB

Owner: Wemyss and March Estates Management Co. Ltd **Contact:** M Andrews

Georgian farmhouse with Georgian orangery.

Location: OS Ref. NT546 763. Between Haddington and East Linton on A1 Edinburgh-Dunbar Road.

Opening Times: Exterior only: By appointment, Wemyss and March Estates Office, Longniddry, East Lothian EH32 0PY.

Admission: Please contact for details.

BIEL

Tel: 01620 860355

Dunbar, East Lothian EH42 1SY

Owner/Contact: C G Spence

Originally a fortified tower, considerably added to over time.

Location: OS Ref. NJ620 770. 5m from Dunbar on the A1 towards Edinburgh.

Opening Times: By appointment.

Admission: Contribution to charity.

BLACKNESS CASTLE

Tel: 01506 834807

Blackness

Owner: Historic Scotland **Contact:** The Custodian

One of Scotland's most important strongholds. Built in the 14th century and massively strengthened in the 16th century as an artillery fortress, it has been a Royal castle and a prison armaments depot and film location for *Hamlet*. It was restored by the Office of Works in the 1920s. It stands on a promontory in the Firth of Forth.

Location: OS Ref. NT055 803. 4m NE of Linlithgow on the Firth of Forth, off the A904.

Opening Times: 1 Apr - 30 Sept: daily, 9.30am - 6.30pm, last ticket 6pm. 1 Oct - 31 Mar: Mon - Sat, 9.30am - 4.30pm, last ticket 4pm. Closed Thur pm, Fri & Sun in winter.

Admission: Adult £2, Child 75p, Conc. £1.50.

CRAIGMILLAR CASTLE

Tel: 0131 661 4445

Edinburgh

Owner: Historic Scotland **Contact:** The Custodian

Mary Queen of Scots fled to Craigmillar after the murder of Rizzio and it was here that the plot was hatched for the murder of her husband Lord Darnley. This handsome structure with courtyard and gardens covers an area of one and a quarter acres. Built around an L-plan tower house of the early 15th century including a range of private rooms linked to the hall of the old tower.

Location: OS Ref. NT285 710. $2\frac{1}{2}$ m SE of Edinburgh off the A68.

Opening Times: 1 Apr - 30 Sept: daily, 9.30am - 6.30pm, last ticket 6pm. 1 Oct - 31 Mar: Mon - Sat, 9.30am - 4.30pm, Suns, 2 - 4.30pm, last ticket 4pm. Closed Thur pm & Fri in winter.

Admission: Adult £2, Child 75p, Conc. £1.50.

CRICHTON CASTLE

Tel: 01875 320017

Pathhead

Owner: Historic Scotland **Contact:** The Custodian

A large and sophisticated castle with a spectacular façade of faceted stonework in an Italian style added by the Earl of Bothwell between 1581 and 1591 following a visit to Italy. Mary Queen of Scots attended a wedding here.

Location: OS Ref. NT380 612. $2\frac{1}{2}$ m SSW of Pathhead off the A68.

Opening Times: 1 Apr - 30 Sept: daily, 9.30am - 6.30pm, last ticket 6pm.

Admission: Adult £1.80, Child 75p, Conc. £1.30.

Crichton Castle, Edinburgh.

DALKEITH COUNTRY PARK

Tel: 0131 663 5684

Dalkeith, Midlothian EH22 2NJ

Contact: J C Manson

Extensive grounds of Dalkeith Palace. 18th century bridge and orangery. Interpretation area.

Location: OS Ref. NT333 679. 7m SE of Edinburgh.

Opening Times: Mar - Oct: 10am - 6pm.

Admission: Adult/Child £2, Family £7, Groups £1.50.

DALMENY HOUSE

See page 422 for full page entry.

DIRLETON CASTLE & GARDEN

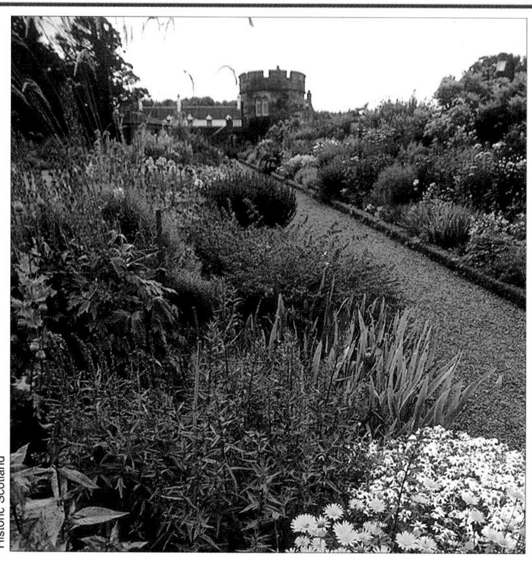

Historic Scotland

DIRLETON, EAST LOTHIAN EH39 5ER

Owner: *Historic Scotland* ***Contact:*** *The Steward*

Tel: 01620 850330

The oldest part of this romantic castle dates from the 13th century, when it was built by the De Vaux family. The renowned gardens, first laid out in the 16th century, now include a magnificent Arts and Crafts herbaceous border (the longest in the world) and a re-created Victorian Garden. In the picturesque village of Dirleton.

Location: OS Ref. NT516 839. In Dirleton, 7m W of North Berwick on the A198.

Opening Times: Apr - Sept: daily, 9.30am - 6.30pm. Oct - Mar: Mon - Sat, 9.30am - 4.30pm, Suns, 2 - 4.30pm. Last ticket 30 mins before closing.

Admission: Adult £2.50, Child £1, Conc. £1.90. 10% discount for groups (10+).

Partially suitable. Free if booked. Guide dogs only.

DUNGLASS COLLEGIATE CHURCH 

Tel: 0131 668 8800

Cockburnspath

Owner: Historic Scotland

Founded in 1450 for a college of canons by Sir Alexander Hume. A handsome cross-shaped building with vaulted nave, choir and transepts.

Location: OS Ref. 67 NT766 718. 1m NW of Cockburnspath. SW of A1.

Opening Times: All year.

Admission: Free.

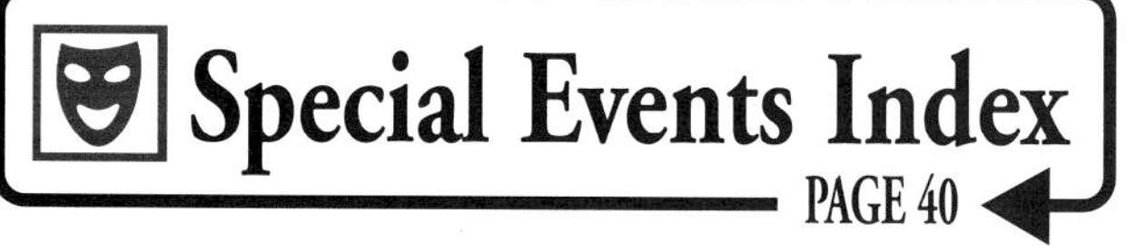

EDINBURGH CASTLE

Crown Copyright

CASTLEHILL, EDINBURGH EH1 2NG

Owner: *Historic Scotland* ***Contact:*** *Neil Young*

Tel: 0131 225 9846 **Fax:** 0131 220 4733

Scotland's most famous castle, dominating the capital's skyline and giving stunning views of the city and countryside. Home to the Scottish crown jewels, the Stone of Destiny and Mons Meg. Other highlights include St Margaret's Chapel, the Great Hall and the Scottish National War Memorial.

Location: OS Ref. NT252 736. At the top of the Royal Mile in Edinburgh.

Opening Times: Apr - Sept: daily, 9.30am - 6pm. Oct - Mar: daily, 9.30am - 5pm. Last ticket 45 mins before closing.

Admission: Adult £7, Child £2, Conc. £5. Pre-booked school visits available free, except Jun - Aug.

Private evening hire of restaurant.
Partially suitable. WCs. Courtesy vehicle. Licensed.
In 6 languages. Ample (except Jun-Oct) Guide dogs. 

THE GEORGIAN HOUSE

Douglas MacGregor

7 CHARLOTTE SQUARE, EDINBURGH EH2 4DR

Owner: *The National Trust for Scotland* ***Contact:*** *Jacqueline Wyer*

Tel/Fax: 0131 226 3318

The north side of Charlotte Square is Robert Adam's masterpiece of urban architecture - a splendid example of the neo-classical 'palace front'. The three floors of No.7, The Georgian House, are delightfully furnished as they would have been around 1796. There is a fascinating array of china and silver, pictures and furniture, gadgets and utensils from the decorative to the purely functional.

Location: OS Ref. NT247 740. In Edinburgh's city centre, NW of Princes St.

Opening Times: 1 Apr - 31 Oct: Mon - Sat, 10am - 5pm, Suns, 2 - 5pm. Last admission 4.30pm. Shop: As house, but opens at 11am.

Admission: Adult £5, Conc. £3.50. Groups: Adult £4, Child/School £1.

Inclusive in price. No parking. 

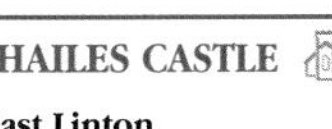

Gladstone's Land, Edinburgh.

HAILES CASTLE

Tel: 0131 668 8800

East Linton

Owner: Historic Scotland

Beautifully-sited ruin incorporating a fortified manor of the 13th century. It was extended in the 14th and 15th centuries. There are two vaulted pit prisons.

Location: OS Ref. NT575 758. 1½ m SW of East Linton. 4m E of Haddington. S of A1.

Opening Times: All year.

Admission: Free.

HARBURN HOUSE

See page 423 for full page entry.

HARELAW FARMHOUSE

Tel: 01875 870201 **Fax:** 01875 870620

Nr Longniddry, East Lothian EH32 0PH

Owner: Wemyss and March Estates Management Co Ltd **Contact:** M Andrews

Early 19th century 2-storey farmhouse built as an integral part of the steading. Dovecote over entrance arch.

Location: OS Ref. NT450 766. Between Longniddry and Drem on B1377.

Opening Times: Exteriors only: By appointment, Wemyss and March Estates Office, Longniddry, East Lothian EH32 0PY.

Admission: Please contact for details.

GLADSTONE'S LAND

Tel: 0131 226 5856 **Fax:** 0131 226 4851

477b Lawnmarket, Royal Mile, Edinburgh EH1 2NT

Owner: The National Trust for Scotland **Contact:** Pat Wigston

Gladstone's Land was the home of a prosperous Edinburgh merchant in the 17th century. On the Royal Mile, near the Castle, it is decorated and furnished with great authenticity to give visitors an impression of life in Edinburgh's Old Town some 300 years ago. Features of the 6-storey building are the painted ceilings and the reconstructed shop both complete with replicas of 17th century goods.

Location: OS Ref. NT255 736. In Edinburgh's Royal Mile, near the castle.

Opening Times: House & Shop: 1 Apr - 31 Oct: Mon - Sat, 10am - 5pm, Suns, 2 - 5pm, last admission 4.30pm.

Admission: Adult £3.50, Conc. £2.50. Groups: Adult £2.80, Child/School £1. Group visits must be booked.

Ground floor suitable. No parking.

HOPETOUN HOUSE

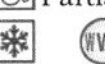

See page 424 for full page entry

HOUSE OF THE BINNS

Tel: 01506 834255

Linlithgow, West Lothian EH49 7NA

Owner: The National Trust for Scotland **Contact:** Tam & Kathleen Dalyell

A 17th century house, the home of the Dalyells, one of Scotland's great families, since 1612. Here in 1681, General Tam Dalyell raised the Royal Scots Greys Regiment, named after the colour of their uniforms. The house contains fine Italian-style plasterwork and an outstanding collection of family paintings.

Location: OS Ref. NT051 786. Off A904, 15m W of Edinburgh. 3m E of Linlithgow

Opening Times: House: 1 May - 30 Sept: daily except Fris, 1.30 - 5.30pm, last admission 5pm. Parkland: 1 Apr - 31 Oct: daily, 10am - 7pm. 1 Nov - 31 Mar: daily, 10am - 4pm, last admission 30mins before close.

Admission: House & Parkland: Adult £4, Conc. £3. Groups: Adult £3.20, Child/School £1. Group visits must be booked. Members of the Royal Scots Dragoon Guards admitted Free.

Partially suitable. WCs. Limited. Obligatory. Guide dogs only.

GOSFORD HOUSE

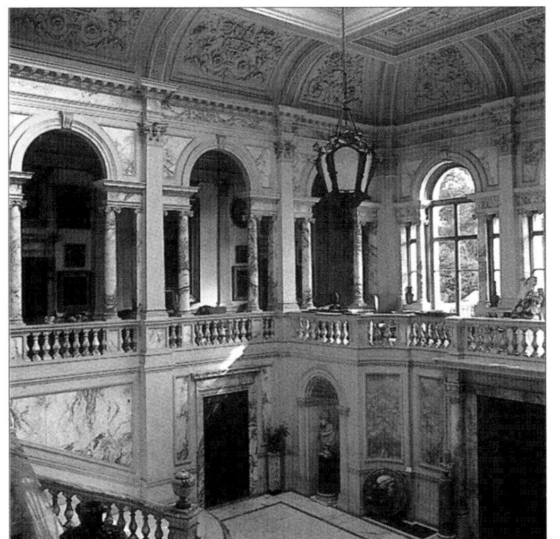

LONGNIDDRY, EAST LOTHIAN EH32 0PX

***Owner/Contact:** The Earl of Wemyss*

Tel: 01875 870201 **Fax:** 01875 870376

Robert Adam designed the central block and wings. These wings were later demolished. Two wings were rebuilt in 1890 by William Young. The Big Saloon was burnt in 1940 during military occupation and although it is unrestored, a new roof was constructed in 1987. The south wing is the family home and contains the famous Marble Hall (Staffordshire alabaster). Parts of the south wing are open. There is a fine collection of paintings and works of art. Surrounding gardens are being redeveloped, extensive policies, artificial ponds, greylag geese and other wildfowl breeding. Geese approach house closely.

Location: OS Ref. NT453 786. Off A198 2m NE of Longniddry.

Opening Times: 8 Jul - 11 Aug: Wed - Fri and Sats & Suns, 2 - 5pm.

Admission: Adult £4, Child £1.

Grounds suitable. Limited. In grounds, on leads.

House of the Binns, Edinburgh.

INVERESK LODGE GARDEN

Tel: 01721 722502 **Fax:** 01721 724700

24 Inveresk Village, Musselburgh, East Lothian EH21 7TE

Owner: The National Trust for Scotland **Contact:** Head Gardener

Small garden in grounds of 17th century house, with large selection of plants. House closed.

Location: OS Ref. NT348 718. A6124, S of Musselburgh, 6m E of Edinburgh.

Opening Times: 1 Apr - 31 Oct: Mon - Fri, 10am - 4.30pm, Sat & Sun, 2 - 5pm. 1 Nov - 31 Mar: Mon - Fri, 10am - 4.30pm, Suns, 2 - 5pm.

Admission: £2 (honesty box).

Grounds suitable. Limited. No dogs in the garden. Cars to be parked by garden wall only.

LAURISTON CASTLE

Tel: 0131 336 2060 **Fax:** 0131 312 7165

Cramond Road South, Edinburgh EH4 5QD

Owner: City of Edinburgh Council **Contact:** Robin Barnes

A beautiful house overlooking the Firth of Forth. The oldest part is a 16th century tower house.

Location: OS Ref. NT203 761. Between Davidsons Mains and Cramond, NW Edinburgh.

Opening Times: 1 Apr - 31 Oct: daily except Fris, 11am - 1pm and 2 - 5pm. 1 Nov - 31 Mar: Sats & Suns, 2 - 4pm. Admission by guided tour only.

Admission: Adult £4, Conc. £3. (1999 prices, please contact for 2000 prices).

LENNOXLOVE HOUSE

HADDINGTON, EAST LOTHIAN EH41 4NZ

Owner: *Lennoxlove House Ltd* ***Contact:*** *House Administrator*

Tel: 01620 823720 **Fax:** 01620 825112 **e-mail:** lennoxlove@compuserve.com

Home of the Duke of Hamilton. The 14th century keep houses a death mask said to be that of Mary Queen of Scots, a silver casket which once contained incriminating letters that helped send Mary to her death, and a sapphire ring given to her by Lord John Hamilton. The 17th century part of the house contains the Hamilton Palace collection of pictures, furniture and porcelain arranged in classic stately home style.

Location: OS Ref. NT515 721. 20m SE of Edinburgh, near Haddington.

Opening Times: Easter - end Oct: Wed, Thur, Sat & Sun, 2 - 4.30pm. Guided tours. Please check if house is open on a Sat before arriving.

Admission: Adult £4, Child £2. Group charges on application.

No photography in house. Weddings, gala dinners. Obligatory.

LIBERTON HOUSE

Tel: 0131 467 7777 **Fax:** 0131 467 7774

73 Liberton Drive, Edinburgh EH16 6NP **e-mail:** ngrarch@aol.com

Owner/Contact: Nicholas Groves-Raines

Built around 1600 for the Littles of Liberton, this harled L-plan house has been carefully restored by the current architect owner using original detailing and extensive restoration of the principal structure. Public access restricted to the Great Hall and Old Kitchen. The restored garden layout suggests the original and there is a late 17th century lectern doocot by the entrance drive.

Location: OS Ref. NT267 694. 73 Liberton Drive, Edinburgh.

Opening Times: 1 Mar - 31 Oct: 10am - 4.30pm, by prior appointment only.

Admission: Free.

Not suitable. Limited.

LINLITHGOW PALACE

LINLITHGOW, WEST LOTHIAN EH49 7AL

Owner: *Historic Scotland* ***Contact:*** *The Steward*

Tel: 01506 842896

The magnificent remains of a great royal palace set in its own park and beside Linlithgow Loch. A favoured residence of the Stewart monarchs, James V and his daughter Mary Queen of Scots were born here. Bonnie Prince Charlie stayed here during his bid to regain the British crown.

Location: OS Ref. NT003 774. In the centre of Linlithgow off the M9.

Opening Times: Apr - Sept: daily, 9.30am - 6.30pm. Oct - Mar: Mon - Sat, 9.30am - 4.30pm, Suns, 2 - 4.30pm. Last ticket 30 mins before closing.

Admission: Adult £2.50, Child £1, Conc. £1.90. 10% discount for groups (10+).

Picnic area. Private evening hire. Partially suitable. By arrangement. Cars only. Free if booked. In grounds, off leads.

NEWLISTON

Tel: 0131 333 3231 **Fax:** 0131 335 3596

Kirkliston, West Lothian EH29 9EB

Owner/Contact: Mrs Caroline Maclachlan

Late Robert Adam house. Costumes on display. 18th century designed landscape, rhododendrons, azaleas and water features. On Sundays tea is in the Edinburgh Cookery School in the William Adam Coach House. Also on Sundays there is a ride-on steam model railway from 2 - 5pm. An inventory of chattels not on public display can be inspected and such chattels can be viewed by request when the house is open to the public.

Location: OS Ref. NT110 735. 8m W of Edinburgh, 3m S of Forth Road Bridge, off B800.

Opening Times: 3 May - 4 Jun: Wed - Sun, 2 - 6pm. Also by appointment.

Admission: Adult £1.50, Child/OAP 50p, Student £1.

Grounds suitable. In grounds, on leads.

Newliston, Edinburgh.

THE PALACE OF HOLYROODHOUSE

Andrew Holt

HM The Queen

EDINBURGH EH8 8DX

Owner: *HM The Queen* ***Contact:*** *The Superintendent*

Tel: 0131 556 1096 **Fax:** 0131 557 5256

The Palace of Holyroodhouse, Buckingham Palace and Windsor Castle are the Official residences of the Sovereign and are used by The Queen as both a home and office. The Queen's personal standard flies when Her Majesty is in residence. Furnished with works of art from the Royal Collection, these buildings are used extensively by The Queen for State ceremonies and Official entertaining. They are opened to the public as much as the commitments allow. At the end of the Royal Mile stands the Palace of Holyroodhouse. Set against the spectacular backdrop of Arthur's Seat, Holyroodhouse has evolved from a medieval fortress into a baroque residence. The Royal Apartments, an extensive suite of rooms, epitomise the elegance and grandeur of this ancient and noble house, and contrast with the historic tower apartments of Mary Queen of Scots, which are steeped in intrigue and sorrow. These intimate rooms where she lived on her return from France in 1561, witnessed the murder of David Rizzio, her favourite secretary, by her jealous husband, Lord Darnley and his accomplices.

Location: OS Ref. NT269 739. Central Edinburgh, E end of Royal Mile.

Opening Times: Apr - Oct: daily, 9.30am - 5.15pm. Nov - Mar: daily, 9.30am - 3.45pm. Closed Good Fri, 25 - 26 & 31 Dec, 1 Jan and during Royal visits. Opening arrangements may change at short notice.

Admission: Adult £6, Child (up to 17yrs) £3, Over 60yrs £4.50, Family (2+2) £13.50.

Suitable. Guide dogs only. 

PARLIAMENT HOUSE

Tel: 0131 225 2595

Parliament Square, Royal Mile, Edinburgh **Contact:** Reception Desk at Door 11

Supreme Court for Scotland, adjacent exhibition detailing the history of Parliament House and its important features.

Location: OS Ref. NT258 736. In the centre of Edinburgh's Royal Mile.

Opening Times: All year: Mon - Fri, 9am - 5pm.

Admission: Free.

PRESTON MILL 

Tel: 01620 860426

East Linton, East Lothian EH40 3DS

Owner: The National Trust for Scotland **Contact:** Property Manager

For centuries there has been a mill on this site and the present one operated commercially until 1957. While the interior of the mill is exciting, the exterior is extremely evocative and much favoured by artists who come from near and far to paint the attractive old buildings, with their red pantile roofs, fringed by the tranquillity of the mill pond with its ever present ducks.

Location: OS Ref. NT590 770. Off the A1, in East Linton, 23m E of Edinburgh.

Opening Times: 1 Apr - 30 Sept: Mon - Sat, 11am - 1pm and 2 - 5pm, Suns, 1.30 - 5pm. Weekends in Oct: 1.30 - 4pm, last admission 20mins before closing morning and afternoon.

Admission: Adult £2.50, Conc. £1.70. Group: Adult £2, Child/School £1. Group visits must book.

Grounds suitable. WC. Limited. Guide dogs only.

Preston Mill, Edinburgh.

ROSSLYN CHAPEL

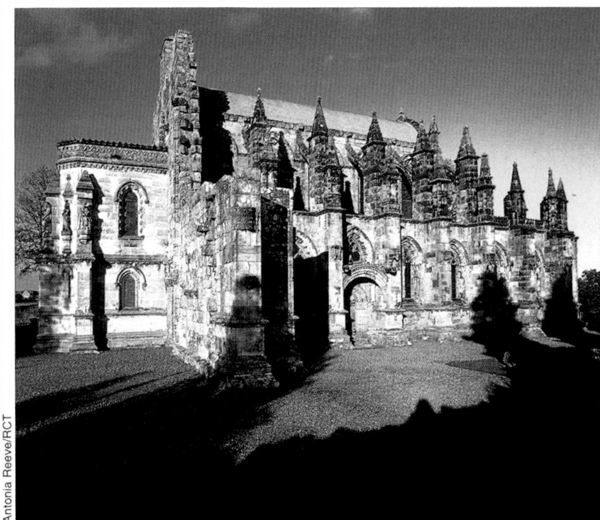

Antonia Reeve/RCT

ROSLIN, MIDLOTHIAN EH25 9PU

Owner: *The Earl of Rosslyn* ***Contact:*** *Stuart Beattie*

Tel: 0131 440 2159 **Fax:** 0131 440 1979 **e-mail:** rosslynch@aol.com

This most remarkable of churches was founded in 1446 by William St Clair, Prince of Orkney. Set in the woods of Roslin Glen and overlooking the River Esk, the Chapel is renowned for its richly carved interior and world famous apprentice pillar. Visitors to the chapel can enjoy a walk in some of Scotland's most romantic scenery. As Sir Walter Scott wrote,'*A morning of leisure can scarcely be anywhere more delightfully spent than in the woods of Rosslyn*'. The chapel is available for weddings throughout the year.

Location: OS Ref. NT275 630. 6m S of Edinburgh off A701. Follow B7006.

Opening Times: All year: Mon - Sat, 10am - 5pm, Suns, 12 noon - 4.45pm.

Admission: Adult £3.50, Child £1, Conc. £3. 10% discount for groups (20-40).

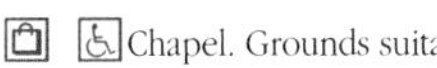  Limited for coaches. 

ROYAL BOTANIC GARDEN

Tel: 0131 552 7171 **Fax:** 0131 248 2901

20A Inverleith Row, Edinburgh EH3 5LR **Contact:** Press Office

Scotland's premier garden. Discover the wonders of the plant kingdom in over 70 acres of beautifully landscaped grounds.

Location: OS Ref. NT249 751. Off A902, 1m N of city centre.

Opening Times: Daily (except 25 Dec & 1 Jan): open from 9.30am. Closing: Feb 5pm; Mar 6pm; Apr - Aug 7pm; Sept 6pm; Oct 5pm; Nov - Jan 4pm.

Admission: Free. Donations welcome.

ST GILES' CATHEDRAL

Tel: 0131 225 9442 **Fax:** 0131 220 4763

Royal Mile, Edinburgh EH1 1RE

Owner: St Giles' Cathedral **Contact:** Jan-Andrew Henderson

St Giles' Cathedral dates from the 12th century and is central to Scotland's turbulent history. This beautiful building was the church of John Knox during the Reformation.

Location: OS Ref. NT258 736. In the centre of Edinburgh's Royal Mile.

Opening Times: Easter - Mid Sept: Mon - Fri, 9am -7pm, Sats, 9am - 5pm, Suns, 1 - 5pm. Mid Sept - Easter: Mon - Sat, 9am - 5pm, Suns, 1 - 5pm.

Admission: Admission free - donation of £1 per head suggested.

ST MARY'S CATHEDRAL

Tel: 0131 225 6293 **Fax:** 0131 225 3181

Palmerston Place, Edinburgh EH12 5AW **Contact:** Cathedral Secretary

Neo-gothic grandeur in the classical new town.

Location: OS Ref. NT241 735. 1/2 m W of west end of Princes Street.

Opening Times: 7.30am - 6pm. Sun services: 8am, 10.30am and 3.30pm. Weekday services: 7.30am, 1.05pm and 5.30pm. Sat service: 7.30am.

Admission: Free.

SCOTTISH NATIONAL PORTRAIT GALLERY

Tel: 0131 624 6200

1 Queen Street, Edinburgh EH2 1JD **Contact:** Lindsay Isaacs

Unique visual history of Scotland.

Location: OS Ref. NT256 742. At E end of Queen Street, 300yds N of Princes Street.

Opening Times: All year: Mon - Fri, 10am - 5pm. Suns, 2 - 5pm. Closed 25 & 26 Dec.

Admission: Free.

Historic Scotland

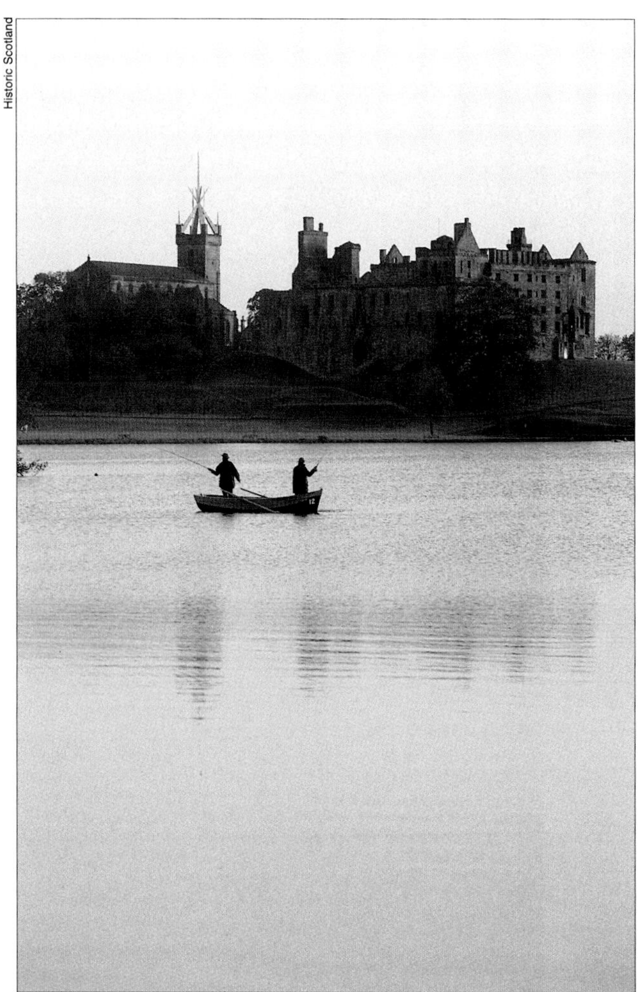

Linlithgow Palace, Edinburgh.

TANTALLON CASTLE

Crown Copyright

BY NORTH BERWICK, EAST LOTHIAN EH39 5PN

Owner: *Historic Scotland* ***Contact:*** *The Steward*

Tel: 01620 892727

Set on the edge of the cliffs, looking out to the Bass Rock, this formidable castle was a stronghold of the powerful Douglas family. The castle has earthwork defences and a massive 80-foot high 14th century curtain wall. Interpretive displays include a replica gun.

Location: OS67 Ref. NT595 850. 3m E of North Berwick off the A198.

Opening Times: Apr - Sept: daily, 9.30am - 6.30pm. Oct - Mar: Mon - Sat, 9.30am - 6.30pm (but closed Thur pm & all day Fri), Suns, 2 - 4.30pm.

Admission: Adult £2.50, Child £1, Conc. £1.90. 10% discount for groups (10+).

Picnic area. Partially suitable. Booked school visits free. In grounds, on leads.

WINTON HOUSE

PENCAITLAND, TRANENT, EAST LOTHIAN EH34 5AT

Owner: *The Winton Trust* ***Contact:*** *Francis Ogilvy*

Tel: 01620 824986 **Fax:** 01620 823961 **e-mail:** enquiries@wintonhouse.co.uk

A masterpiece of the Scottish Renaissance with famous stone twisted chimneys and magnificent plaster ceilings. A family home, still after 500 years with many treasures inside, including paintings by some of Scotland's most notable artists, fine furniture and a family exhibition of costumes and photographs. Specimen trees and terraced gardens.

Location: OS Ref. NT439 695. 14m SE of Edinburgh off the A1 at Tranent. Lodge gates S of New Winton (B6355) and in Pencaitland (A6093).

Opening Times: 2nd & 3rd weekends in April, May & Sept: 12 noon - 5pm and other times by prior arrangement.

Admission: Adult £4.20, Child £2, Conc. £3.50. Groups should pre-book (10+).

Filming, product launches. Pottery. Suitable. WCs. Obligatory. In grounds, on leads. Tel. for details.

Greater Glasgow

New Lanark.

Greater Glasgow & Clyde Valley Tourist Board.

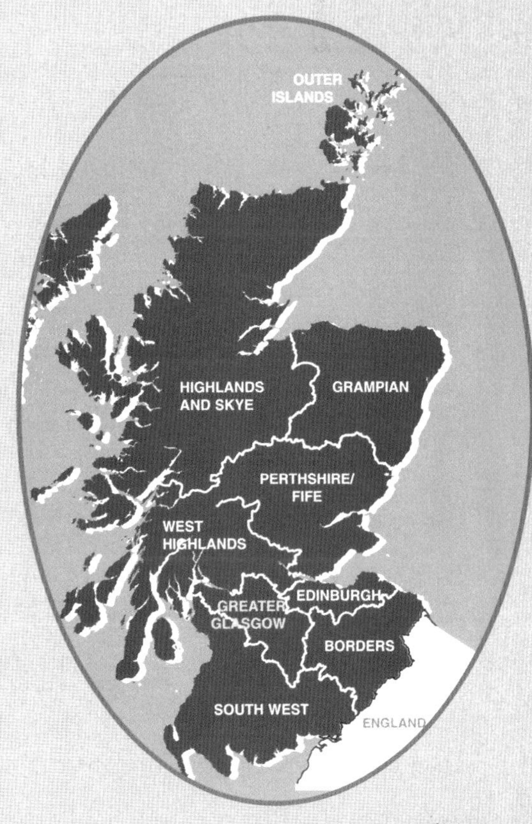

KELBURN

Largs

KELBURN has been the home of the Boyle family, later the Earls of Glasgow, since the 13th century and it continues to be used as a family home.

The original Norman Keep was extended in 1580, and the magnificent 1700 William and Mary Mansion House was added by the 1st Earl of Glasgow, whose title was bestowed as reward for his role in the Act of Union. The final addition is the Victorian wing of 1879 with its original William Morris wallpaper.

The essential charm of the Castle is its intimate lived-in atmosphere, its varied styles and stunning location.

The beautiful and extensive grounds are used for the Country Centre, and include the dramatic glen with woodland trails, waterfalls, and deep gorges. The peaceful walled garden 'The Plaisance' is dominated by two 1,000 year old yew trees and its exotic shrubs benefit from the Gulf Stream climate. Historical features include the Robert Adam Monument, 18th century Sundial and an Ice House.

For the active, there is horse riding, adventure courses, young children's stockade and soft play area.

The Secret Forest provides a series of exotic follies and fairytale features, "a unique attraction and a delight for all ages".

Owner: The Earl of Glasgow

CONTACT

The Earl of Glasgow
Kelburn Castle & Country Centre
South Offices
Fairlie, Nr Largs,
Ayrshire KA29 0BE

Tel: Country Centre: 01475 568685
Castle: 01475 568204

Fax: Country Centre: 01475 568121
Castle: 01475 568328

e-mail: info@kelburncastle.com

LOCATION

OS Ref. NS210 580

M8 Edinburgh to Glasgow, M8 Glasgow to Greenock, A78 to Largs, 2m S of Largs.

Rail: Largs Station 2m.

Air: Glasgow 25m. Prestwick Int'national 28m.

Bus: A78 main bus route to Ayr, stop adjacent to property.

Taxis: A2B taxis 01475 673976.

CONFERENCE/FUNCTION		
ROOM	SIZE	MAX CAPACITY
Drawing Rm	33' x 24'	70
Dining Rm	30' x 20'	60

Corporate events, clay pigeon shoots, exhibitions, business meetings, conferences, fashion shows, filming, product launches, nature activities and barbecues. Helicopter landing pad. Additional rooms for non-plenary sessions. No photography in house.

Full catering facilities for functions / conferences.

Partially suitable, visitors may alight at entrance. WC. Some stairs.

Licensed restaurant and a tearoom. Groups can book (special rates).

Max. 25 in Castle, tour time 45 mins. Lectures on Castle, grounds and history if booked. Ranger tour of grounds.

Coach passengers can alight at the forecourt, coach park 5-10 mins walk.

Welcome. Teachers free, ratio of 1:10. Ranger service for guided walks and nature activities. Worksheets, pets' corner, pony rides/treks, adventure play areas.

In grounds, on leads.

OPENING TIMES

SUMMER

Castle
July, August & September
Daily tours: 1.45pm, 3pm & 4.15pm. (Except when there are functions).

Tours can be arranged at other times of the year.

Country Centre & Gardens
Easter - end October
Daily: 10am - 6pm.

WINTER

Castle
By arrangement only.

Country Centre
End October - Easter
11am - 5pm
Grounds only.

ADMISSION

SUMMER

Castle tours
Per person £1.50
Student £1.20

(Does not include entry to Centre.)

Country Centre
Adult £4.50
Child £3.00
Conc. £2.50
Groups (min 12)
Adult £3.00
Child £2.00
Conc. £1.75
(1999 prices)

BOTANIC GARDENS

Tel: 0141 334 2422 **Fax:** 0141 339 6964

730 Great Western Road, Glasgow G12 0UE

Owner: Glasgow City Council **Contact:** The General Manager

Location: OS Ref. NS568 674.

Opening Times: All year: 7am - dusk. For glasshouse opening times please ring.

Admission: Free.

BOTHWELL CASTLE

Tel: 01698 816894

Uddingston, Strathclyde

Owner: Historic Scotland **Contact:** The Custodian

The largest and finest 13th century stone castle in Scotland, much fought over during the Wars of Independence. Part of the original circular keep survives, but most of the castle dates from the 14th and 15th centuries. In a beautiful setting overlooking the Clyde.

Location: OS Ref. NS688 593. 1m NW of Bothwell. At Uddingston off the B7071.

Opening Times: 1 Apr - 30 Sept: daily, 9.30am - 6.30pm, last ticket 6pm. 1 Oct - 31 Mar: Mon - Sat, 9.30am - 4.30pm, Suns, 2 - 4.30pm, last ticket 4pm. Closed Thur pm & Fri & Sun mornings in winter.

Admission: Adult £2, Child 75p, Conc £1.50.

BURRELL COLLECTION

Tel: 0141 331 1854

Pollok Country Park, 2060 Pollokshaws Road, Glasgow G2 3EH

Owner: Glasgow Museums **Contact:** Mr Mark McTee

An internationally renowned, outstanding collection of art.

Location: OS Ref. NS560 615.

Opening Times: All year: Mon - Sat, 10am - 5pm. Suns, 11am - 5pm.

Admission: Free.

CHATELHERAULT HUNTING LODGE

Tel: 01698 426213 **Fax:** 01698 421532

Ferniegair, Hamilton ML3 7UE

Owner: South Lanarkshire Council **Contact:** Morvern Anderson

Built for James, 5th Duke of Hamilton, designed by William Adam, completed around 1744. Set in 500 acre country park.

Location: OS Ref. NS737 540. W side of A72, 1½ m SE of Hamilton.

Opening Times: Mon - Sat, 10am - 5pm. Suns, 12 noon - 5pm (Easter Sun - end Sept, 5pm). Closed Christmas and New Year.

COLZIUM HOUSE & WALLED GARDEN

Tel/Fax: 01236 823281

Colzium-Lennox Estate, off Stirling Road, Kilsyth G65 0RZ

Owner: North Lanarkshire Council **Contact:** Charlie Whyte

A walled garden with an extensive collection of conifers, rare shrubs and trees. Kilsyth Heritage Museum, curling pond, tearoom, picnic tables, pitch and putt, woodland walks.

Location: OS Ref. NS762 786. Off A803 Banknock to Kirkintilloch Road. ½ m E of Kilsyth.

Opening Times: House: All year, daily, 9am - 4pm (closed 25 Dec & 1 Jan). Walled garden: Apr - Sept: daily, 12 noon - 7pm; Oct - Mar: Sats & Suns, 12 noon - 4pm.

Admission: Free.

COREHOUSE

Tel: 01555 663126 or 0131 667 1514

Lanark ML11 9TQ

Owner: The Trustees of the late Lt Col A J E Cranstoun MC **Contact:** Estate Office

Designed by Sir Edward Blore and built in the 1820s, Corehouse is a pioneering example of the Tudor Architectural Revival in Scotland.

Location: OS Ref. NS882 416. On S bank of the Clyde above the village of Kirkfieldbank.

Opening Times: 26 Jul - 27 Aug for guided tours. Weekdays: 1 & 2pm, Weekends: 1.30 & 2.30pm. Closed Mons & Tues.

Admission: Adult £4, Child (under 14yrs) £2, OAP £2.

CRAIGNETHAN CASTLE

Tel: 01555 860364

Lanark, Strathclyde

Owner: Historic Scotland **Contact:** The Custodian

In a picturesque setting overlooking the River Nethan and defended by a wide and deep ditch with an unusual caponier, a stone vaulted artillery chamber, unique in Britain.

Location: OS Ref. NS815 463. 5½ m WNW of Lanark off the A72. ½ m footpath to W.

Opening Times: 1 Apr - 30 Sept: daily, 9.30am - 6.30pm.

Admission: Adult £2, Child 75p, Conc. £1.50.

FINLAYSTONE

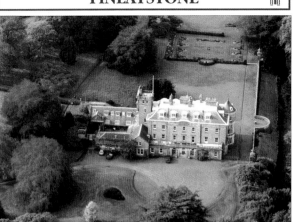

LANGBANK, RENFREWSHIRE PA14 6TJ

Owner: *Mr Arthur MacMillan* ***Contact:*** *Mrs Jane MacMillan*

Tel: 01475 540285 **Fax:** 01475 540285 **e-mail:** info@finlaystone.co.uk

Perched above the River Clyde, Finlaystone was the home of the Earls of Glencairn for 4 centuries and is now the home of the Chief of the Clan MacMillan. Visitors to this unspoilt country estate can explore delightful gardens and woodlands all year round. The Visitor Centre, with its unique doll collection, also houses natural history, celtic art and Clan MacMillan displays and information. An enjoyable day out for all the family with childrens' play areas and ranger service.

Location: OS Ref. NS390 730. On A8, 7m W of Glasgow airport.

Opening Times: Grounds; all year, 10.30am - 5pm. House: Jul: Sun pm guided tours or groups any time by appointment. Refreshments & visitor centre: Apr - Sept: daily, 11am - 4.30pm.

Admission: Grounds: Adult £2.50, Child/Conc. £1.50. Extra for House: Adult £1.50, Child/Conc. £1. 'Dolly Mixture': 50p.

Ground floor & grounds suitable. WC. By arrangement. In grounds, on leads.

GLASGOW CATHEDRAL

Tel: 0141 552 6891

Glasgow

Owner: Historic Scotland **Contact:** The Custodian

The only Scottish mainland medieval cathedral to have survived the Reformation complete. Built over the tomb of St Kentigern. Notable features in this splendid building are the elaborately vaulted crypt, the stone screen of the early 15th century and the unfinished Blackadder Aisle.

Location: OS Ref. NS603 656. E end of city centre. In central Glasgow.

Admission: Free.

GREENBANK

Tel: 0141 639 3281

Clarkston, Glasgow G76 8RB

Owner: The National Trust for Scotland **Contact:** Mr Jim May

Be allured by the beautiful bronze water nymph 'Foam' whose exquisite form complements the circular pool and surrounding greenery. There are several small gardens including a parterre layout illustrating different aspects of gardening. The larger borders contain a wide range of shrub roses and perennial and annual flowers.

Location: OS Ref. NS563 566. Flenders Road, off Mearns Road, Clarkston. Off M77 and A726, 6m S of Glasgow city centre.

Opening Times: All year: daily, 9.30am - sunset, closed 25 - 26 Dec & 1 - 2 Jan. Walled Garden: 9.30am - 5pm. Shop & tearoom: 1 Apr - 31 Oct: daily, 11am - 5pm. 1 Nov - 31 Mar: Sats & Suns, 2 - 4pm. House: 1 Apr - 31 Oct: Suns only, 2 - 4pm & during special events (subject to functions in progress).

Admission: Adult £3.50, Conc. £2.50. Groups: Adult £2.80, Child/School £1.

 Grounds suitable. WC.  In grounds, on leads. No dogs in garden.

HOLMWOOD HOUSE

The National Trust for Scotland

61 NETHERLEE ROAD, CATHCART, GLASGOW G44 3YG

Owner: *The National Trust for Scotland* ***Contact:*** *The Property Manager*

Tel: 0141 637 2129

This unique villa has been described as Alexander 'Greek' Thomson's finest domestic design. It was built in 1857-8 for James Couper who owned Millholm Paper Mills. The architectural style of the house is classical Greek and many rooms are richly ornamented in wood, plaster and marble. Conservation work continuing to reveal this decoration.

Location: OS Ref. NS580 593. Netherlee Road, off Clarkston road (off A77 and B767).

Opening Times: 1 Apr - 31 Oct: daily, 1.30 - 5.30pm. Access may be restricted at peak times and at the discretion of the property. Groups must book.

Admission: Adult £3.50, Conc. £2.50. Groups: Adult £2.80, Child/School £1.

i No photography in house. P Limited for coaches. 

HUTCHESONS' HALL

Tel: 0141 552 8391 **Fax:** 0141 552 7031

158 Ingram Street, Glasgow G1 1EJ

Owner: The National Trust for Scotland **Contact:** Carla Sparrow

Described as one of Glasgow city centre's most elegant buildings, the Hall by David Hamilton, replaced the earlier 1641 hospice founded by George and Thomas Hutcheson. Reconstructed in 1876, the building is now 'A-Listed' as being of national importance.

Location: OS Ref NS594 652. Glasgow city centre, near SE corner of George Square.

Opening Times: Information centre, shop & function hall: All year (except BHs & 24 Dec - 6 Jan): Mon - Sat, 10am - 5pm. (Hall on view subject to functions in progress).

Admission: Free.

i Conferences. Up to 120.  Stairlift. WC. By arrangement. 

KELBURN

See page 432 for full page entry.

DAVID LIVINGSTONE CENTRE

Tel: 01698 823140

165 Station Road, Blantyre, Glasgow G72 9BT

Owner: The National Trust for Scotland **Contact:** Karen Carruthers

Scotland's most famous explorer and missionary was born here in 1813 and today the Centre commemorates his life and work. Livingstone's childhood home - consisting of just one room - remains much as it would have done in his day and gives a fascinating insight into the living conditions endured by industrial workers in the 19th century. The museum contains a wide range of his personal belongings and travel aids.

Location: OS Ref NS690 575. In Blantyre town centre.

Opening Times: Mon - Sat, 10am - 5pm, Suns, 12.30 - 5pm. Closed 24 Dec 1999 - 26 May 2000 for major redevelopment.

Admission: Adult £3, Conc. £2.

MOTHERWELL HERITAGE CENTRE

Tel: 01698 251000

High Road, Motherwell ML1 3HU

Owner: North Lanarkshire Council **Contact:** The Manager

Multimedia exhibition and other displays of local history. STB Commended attraction.

Location: OS Ref. NS750 570.

Opening Times: All year: Mon - Sat, 10am - 5pm. Suns, 12 noon - 5pm. (closed 25/26 Dec & 1 Jan).

Admission: Free.

NEW LANARK

NEW LANARK MILLS, LANARK, S. LANARKSHIRE ML11 9DB

Owner: *New Lanark Conservation Trust* ***Contact:*** *Richard Evans*

Tel: 01555 661345 **Fax:** 01555 665738 **e-mail:** visit@newlanark.org

The historic village of New Lanark is a nominated World Heritage Site. Surrounded by woodlands, and the Falls of Clyde, this cotton-spinning village was founded in 1785 and made famous by social pioneer Robert Owen. Beautifully restored as both a living community and attraction, its history is interpreted in the award-winning Visitor Centre. Accommodation available in the stunning New Lanark Mill Hotel and self-catering 'Waterhouses'.

Location: OS Ref. NS880 426. 1m S of Lanark.

Opening Times: All year: daily, 11am - 5pm (closed 25 Dec & 1/2 Jan).

Admission: Visitor Centre: Adult £3.75, Child/OAP £2.50. Groups: 1 free/10 booked.

i Conference facilities.

Partially suitable. WC. Visitor Centre is wheelchair friendly.

By arrangement. P 5 min walk. In grounds, on leads.  

NEWARK CASTLE

Tel: 01475 741858

Port Glasgow, Strathclyde

Owner: Historic Scotland **Contact:** The Custodian

The oldest part of the castle is a tower built soon after 1478 with a detached gatehouse, by George Maxwell. The main part was added in 1597 - 99 in a most elegant style. Enlarged in the 16th century by his descendent, the wicked Patrick Maxwell who murdered two of his neighbours.

Location: OS Ref. NS329 744. In Port Glasgow on the A8.

Opening Times: 1 Apr - 30 Sept: daily, 9.30am - 6.30pm. Last ticket 6pm.

Admission: Adult £2, Child 75p, Conc. £1.50.

POLLOK HOUSE

The National Trust for Scotland

POLLOK COUNTRY PARK, POLLOKSHAWS ROAD, GLASGOW G43 1AT

Owner: *Glasgow City Council (Managed by The National Trust for Scotland)*
Contact: *The Property Manager*

Tel: 0141 616 6410

The Maxwell family have lived at Pollok since the 13th century. Three earlier castles here were replaced by the present house (c1740) after consultation with William Adam. The house now contains an internationally famed collection of paintings as well as porcelain and furnishings appropriate to an Edwardian house.

Location: OS Ref. NS550 616. In Pollok Country Park, off M77/J1, follow signs for Burrell Collection.

Opening Times: House, Shop & Restaurant: 1 Apr - 31 Oct: daily, 10am - 5pm. 1 Nov - 31 Mar: daily, 11am - 4pm. Closed 25, 26 Dec & 1, 2 Jan.

Admission: Adult £4, Conc. £3. Groups: Adult £3.20, Child/School £1. 1 Nov - 31 Mar: Free.

i No photography in house. Partially suitable. P

THE TENEMENT HOUSE

Tel: 0141 333 0183

145 Buccleuch Street, Glasgow G3 6QN

Owner: The National Trust for Scotland **Contact:** Miss Lorna Hepburn

A typical Victorian tenement flat of 1892, and fascinating time capsule of the first half of the 20th century. It was the home of an ordinary Glasgow shorthand typist, who lived up this 'wally close' for more than 50 years. It is exceptional as the gaslit flat retains many of its original fittings and items such as her mother's sewing machine.

Location: OS Ref. NS583 662. Garnethill (three streets N of Sauchiehall Street, near Charing Cross), Glasgow.

Opening Times: 1 Mar - 31 Oct; daily, 2 - 5pm, last admission 4.30pm. Weekday morning visits by educational and other groups (max 15) by advance booking only.

Admission: Adult £3.50, Conc. £2.50. Groups: Adult £2.80, Child/School £1.

Not suitable. P Very restricted. By appointment. 

THE TOWER OF HALLBAR

Tel: 0171 930 8030 **Fax:** 0171 930 2295

Braidwood Road, Braidwood, Lanarkshire **e-mail:** aniela@vivat.demon.co.uk

Owner: The Vivat Trust **Contact:** Miss Aniela Waitt

A 16th century defensive tower and Bothy set in ancient orchards and meadowland. Converted into self-catering holiday accommodation and furnished and decorated in keeping with its history, by The Vivat Trust. Hallbar sleeps up to seven people, including facilities for a disabled person and their carer.

Location: OS Ref. NS834 471. 45mins outsite Glasgow, on B7056 in Braidwood.

Opening Times: All year: Sats afternoon only, 2 - 3pm, by appointment. Also four open days a year.

Admission: Free.

Partially suitable. By arrangement. P Limited. In grounds, on leads. 3 single, 1 twin & 1 double.

WEAVER'S COTTAGE

Tel: 01505 705588

Shuttle Street, Kilbarchan, Renfrew PA10 2JG

Owner: The National Trust for Scotland **Contact:** Grace Murray

Typical cottage of an 18th century handloom weaver contains looms, weaving equipment and domestic utensils. Attractive cottage garden. Regular weaving demonstrations.

Location: OS Ref. NS402 633. Off A740 (off M8) and A737, at The Cross, Kilbarchan, (nr Johnstone, Paisley) 12m SW of Glasgow.

Opening Times: 21 Apr - 30 Sept: daily, 1.30 - 5.30pm. Weekends in Oct: 1.30 - 5.30pm. Last admission 5pm.

Admission: Adult £2.50, Conc. £1.70. Groups: Adult £2, Child/School £1.

ST MARY'S EPISCOPAL CATHEDRAL

Tel: 0141 339 6691 **Fax:** 0141 334 5669

300 Great Western Road, Glasgow G4 9JB **Contact:** Rev Griff Dines

Fine Gothic Revival church by Sir George Gilbert Scott, with outstanding contemporary murals by Gwyneth Leech. Regular concerts and exhibitions.

Location: OS Ref. NS578 669. $^1/_4$ m after the Dumbarton A82 exit from M8 motorway.

Opening Times: Mon - Fri, 9.30am - 5pm, Sat, 9.30am - 12 noon. Sun services: 8.30am, 10am, 12 noon & 6.30pm. Weekday services: please telephone. Bookshop: Mon - Fri, 10am - 4pm.

SUMMERLEE HERITAGE PARK

Tel: 01236 431261

Heritage Way, Coatbridge, North Lanarkshire ML5 1QD

Owner: North Lanarkshire Council **Contact:** The Manager

STB 'Commended' attraction. 22 acres of industrial heritage including Scotland's only remaining electric tramway; a re-created addit mine and mine workers' cottages.

Location: OS Ref. NS730 650.

Opening Times: All year. Summer, 10am - 5pm. Winter: 10am - 4pm (closed 25/26 Dec & 1/2 Jan).

Admission: Free. Tram ride: Adult 60p, Child 35p.

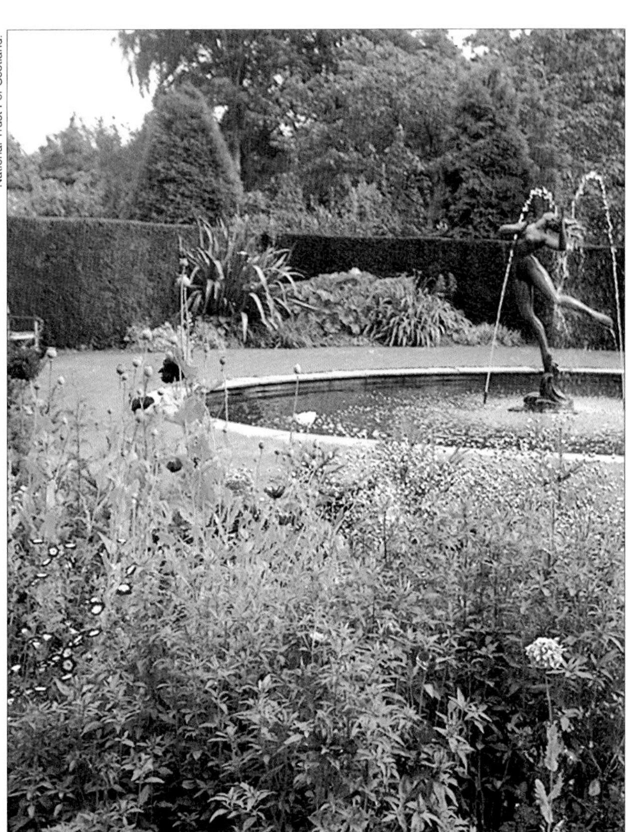

National Trust For Scotland.

Greenbank Gardens, Greater Glasgow.

Perthshire,

Angus & Dundee & The Kingdom of Fife

Rolling Fields.

Perthshire Tourist Board

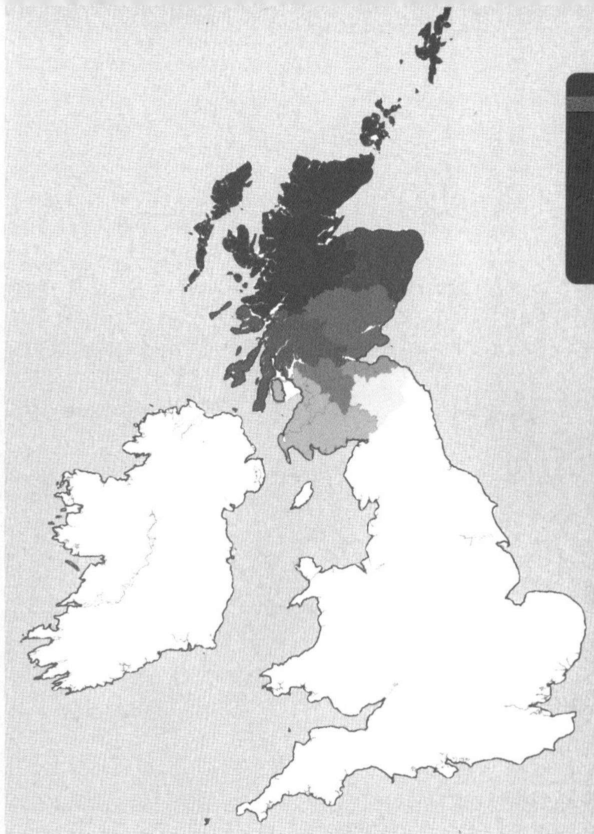

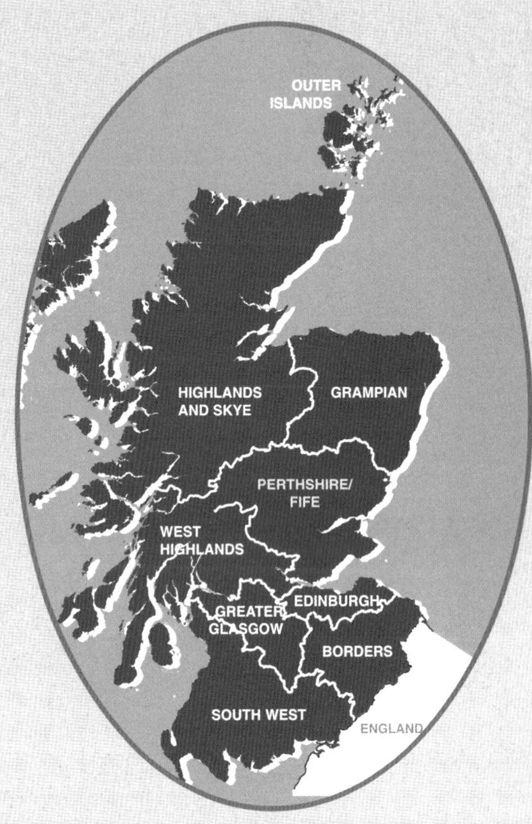

The Drawing Room.

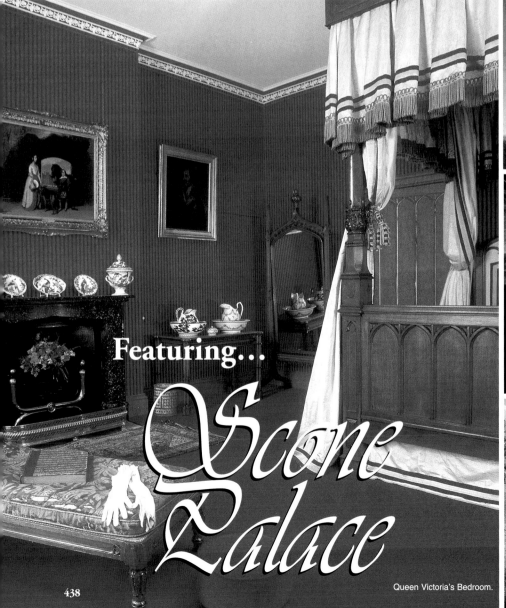

The Lady Elizabeth Murray with Dido, by Zoffany.

William Murray, 1st Earl of Mansfield, by Martin.

Featuring...

Scone Palace

Queen Victoria's Bedroom.

Portrait of the present Earl of Mansfield, with his son and grandson, by Carlos Sanchez.

Faithful unto virtue alone.

Scone Palace is the seat of the Murrays, Earls of Mansfield since 1604. It has been described as more than a building; it is also an idea, a state of mind – for a hundred yards north of this great house rises the Moot-Hill which is in a sense the heart of the Scottish kingdom; here the Pictish kings held council, here successive kings were enthroned, and it was here that on New Year's Day in 1651 Charles II was crowned before his march to Worcester.

Moot-Hill was also associated with the famous Stone of Scone, until Edward I took it to Westminster where it was placed under the chair on which the kings of the joint kingdom have been crowned since the time of James VI. The Stone was returned to Scotland in 1996 and now lies in Edinburgh Castle.

During the 6th century, followers of St Columba established a religious foundation at Scone; this was succeeded in the early 12th century by an Augustinian abbey. This abbey was destroyed in 1159 during the Scottish reformation and after 1580 the powerful Ruthven family, Earls of Gowrie, built themselves a house in the ruins of the monastic buildings. Following their treachery through the 'Gowrie Conspiracy', James VI rewarded his loyal supporter, Sir David Murray, with the lands and the House at Scone.

Victorian group on the front steps of Scone.

Murray, who was created Lord Scone in 1604, appears to have built two principal ranges of the Palace, to the south and east. However, the Palace that we see today is the creation of the 3rd Earl Mansfield, who employed William Atkinson, the talented pupil of James Wyatt, in 1802 to design and build the existing Georgian Gothic building. The interiors of this red sandstone, castellated palace are large, airy and well-lit, with gothic detailing to be found on the pelmets and chandeliers.

The halls and the Gallery, with their vaulted ceilings, make reference to Scone's monastic past. William Atkinson was later to work on Abbotsford, and by comparison Scone would have seemed conservative and restrained in style, however it still cost Lord Mansfield, by the end of 1811, more than £60,000 to remodel his home.

If the styling of Scone is somewhat 'understated', it acts as a wonderful backdrop for the richly varied collection of furniture and works of art, collected by the Murray family over successive generations.

Writing table made for Marie Antoinette of France, by Riesener.

Today the present 8th Earl of Mansfield and his wife the Countess of Mansfield, take an active interest in the running of Scone and their 25,000 acre estate. This is run on thoroughly modern lines with the aim of providing a secure livelihood for as many people as possible, together with preserving intact a beautiful piece of Scottish countryside and a unique historic palace.

Scone actually stood unoccupied for 30 years until the 7th Earl of Mansfield and his Countess moved back in the 1950s. It is now the much loved home of the Earl and Countess of Mansfield and it is through the care of the current Countess, a former chairman of the Scottish branch of the Historic Houses Association, that the house has truly come back to life – it now has over 100,000 annual visitors.

The present Earl, like his forebears, has combined his estate interests with an active role in public life. In 1979 Lord Mansfield became Minister of State for Scotland and later a Minister for Northern Ireland and latterly before his retirement he became the first Crown Estate Commissioner, running the hereditary lands of the Sovereign.

One of a pair of Chinese Porcelain Vases.

The Gothic Reading Room.

For full details of this property see page 442.

BLAIR CASTLE
Pitlochry

Owner: Blair Castle Charitable Trust

CONTACT

Geoff G Crerar
Tourism Administrator
Blair Castle
Blair Atholl
Pitlochry
Perthshire
PH18 5TL

Tel: 01796 481207

Fax: 01796 481487

LOCATION

OS Ref. NN880 660

From Edinburgh 80m, M90 to Perth, A9, follow signs for Blair Castle, $1^1/_2$ hrs.
Trunk Road A9 2m.

Bus: Bus stop 1m in Blair Atholl.

Train: 1m, Blair Atholl Euston-Inverness line.

Taxi: Elizabeth Yule, 01796 472290.

FUNCTION		
ROOM	SIZE	MAX CAPACITY
Ballroom	89' x 35'	400
State Dining Rm	36' x 25'	200
Exhibition Hall	55' x 27'	90

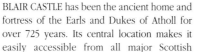

BLAIR CASTLE has been the ancient home and fortress of the Earls and Dukes of Atholl for over 725 years. Its central location makes it easily accessible from all major Scottish centres in less than two hours.

The castle has known the splendour of Royal visitations, submitted to occupation by opposing forces on no less than four occasions, suffered siege and changed its architectural appearance to suit the taste of successive generations.

Today 32 rooms of infinite variety display beautiful furniture, fine collections of paintings, arms, armour, china, costumes, lace and embroidery, Jacobite relics and other unique treasures giving a stirring picture of Scottish life from the 16th to 20th centuries.

The Duke of Atholl has the unique distinction of having the only remaining private army in Europe - The Atholl Highlanders.

GARDENS

Blair Castle is set in extensive parklands. Near the car and coach parks, there is a picnic area, a deer park and a unique two acre plantation of large trees known as 'Diana's Grove.' It has been said that "it is unlikely that any other two acres in the world contain such a number of different conifers of such heights and of such small age." A restored 18th century garden re-opened to visitors in 1996.

Fashion shows, garden parties, equestrian events, shows, rallies, filming, highland and charity balls, piping championships, grand piano, helicopter pad, cannon firing by Atholl Highlanders, resident piper, needlework displays. No smoking.

Buffets, dinners, wedding receptions and banquets.

Visitors may alight at the entrance. WC & wheelchair.

Non-smoking. Seats up to 125.

In English, German and French at no extra cost. Max group size 25, tour time $1^1/_2$ hrs (max).

200 cars, 20 coaches. Coach drivers/couriers free, plus free meal and shop voucher, information pack.

Nature walks, deer park, children's games & pony trekking.

Grounds only.

OPENING TIMES

SUMMER
1 April - 27 October
Daily, 10am - 6pm
Last admission 5pm.
(Jul & Aug: opens 9.30am).
At other times by special arrangement.

WINTER
Access by arrangement.

ADMISSION

House & Grounds

Adult	£6.00
Child (5-16yrs)	£4.00
OAP/Student	£5.00
Family	£18.00
Disabled	£2.00

Groups (12-40) (Please book)

Adult	£5.00
Child (5-16yrs)	£4.00
Primary School	£3.00
OAP	£4.50
Student	£4.00
Disabled	£2.00

Grounds only

Adult	£2.00
Child	£1.00
OAP/Student	£2.00
Family	£5.00
Disabled	Free

SPECIAL EVENTS

- **APR 21-24:** Spring Needlework & Lace Exhibition.
- **MAY 27:** Atholl Highlanders' Parade.
- **MAY 28:** Atholl Gathering & Highland Games.
- **AUG 24 - 27:** Bowmore Blair Castle International Horse Trials.
- **OCT 6 - 8:** Autumn Needlelace Exhibition.
- **OCT 28:** Glenfiddich Piping Championships.
- **OCT 29:** Glenfiddich Fiddling Championships.

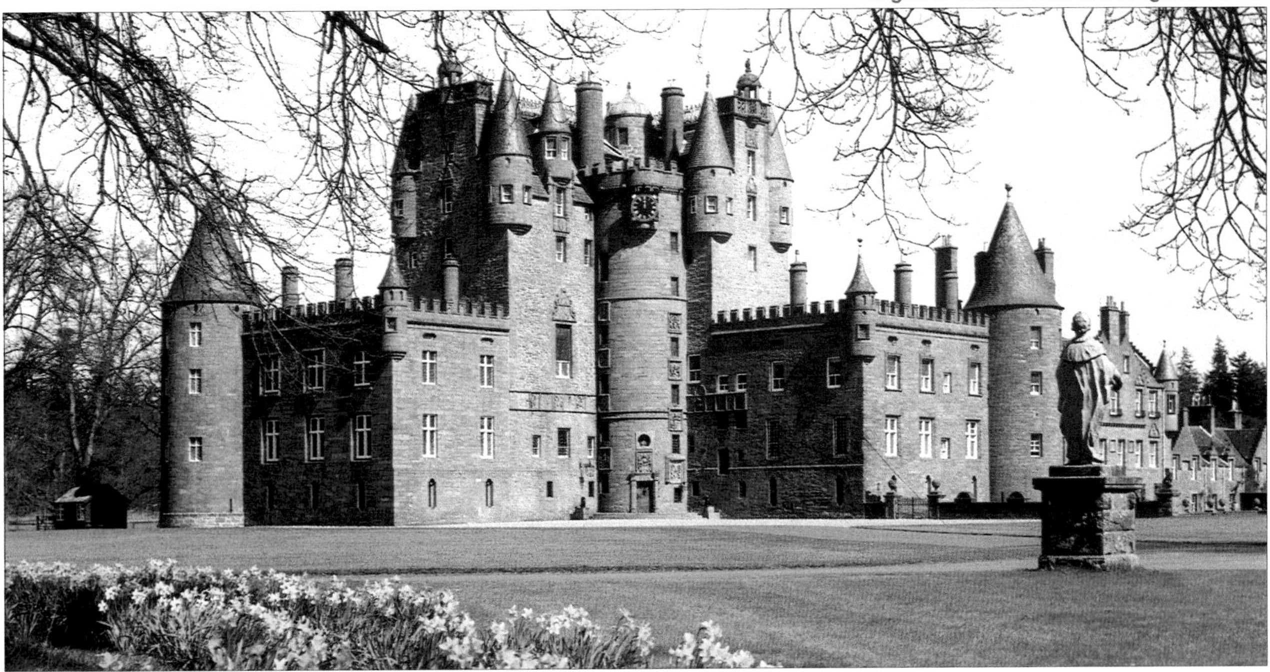

Owner: The Earl of Strathmore & Kinghorne

CONTACT

Lt Col P J Cardwell Moore
(The Administrator)
Estates Office
Glamis Castle
Glamis
by Forfar
Angus
DD8 1RJ

Tel: 01307 840393

Fax: 01307 840733

e-mail: glamis@great-houses-scotland.co.uk

LOCATION

OS Ref. NO386 480

From Edinburgh M90, A94, 81m.
From Forfar A94, 6m.
From Glasgow 93m.

Motorway: M90.

Rail: Dundee Station 12m.

Air: Dundee Airport 12m.

Taxi: K Cabs 01575 773744.

CONFERENCE/FUNCTION		
ROOM	SIZE	MAX CAPACITY
Dining Rm	84 sq.m.	120
Restaurant	140 sq.m.	100
16th century Kitchens		50

GLAMIS CASTLE
by Forfar

GLAMIS CASTLE is the family home of the Earls of Strathmore and Kinghorne and has been a royal residence since 1372. It is the childhood home of Her Majesty Queen Elizabeth The Queen Mother, the birthplace of Her Royal Highness The Princess Margaret and the legendary setting of Shakespeare's play *Macbeth*. Although the castle is open to visitors it remains a family home lived in and loved by the Strathmore family.

The castle, a five-storey 'L' shaped tower block, was originally a royal hunting lodge. It was remodelled in the 17th century and is built of pink sandstone. It contains the Great Hall, with its magnificent plasterwork ceiling dated 1621, a beautiful family Chapel constructed inside the Castle in 1688, an 18th century billiard room housing what is left of the extensive library once at Glamis, a 19th century dining room containing family portraits and the Royal Apartments which have been used by Her Majesty Queen Elizabeth The Queen Mother.

The castle stands in an extensive park, landscaped towards the end of the 18th century, and contains the beautiful Italian Garden and the Pinetum which reflect the peace and serenity of the castle and grounds.

Fashion shoots, archery, clay pigeon shooting, equestrian events, shows, rallies, filming, product launches, highland games, new cricket pavilion, grand piano. No photography in the castle.

Shopping complex.

The State Rooms are available for grand dinners, lunches and wedding receptions.

Disabled visitors may alight at entrance. Those in wheelchairs will be unable to tour the castle but may visit the two exhibitions. WC.

Morning coffees, light lunches, afternoon teas. Self-service, licensed restaurant.

All visits are guided, tour time 50 - 60 mins. Tours leave every 10 - 15 mins. Tours in French, German, Italian and Spanish by appointment at no additional cost. Three exhibitions.

500 cars and 20 coaches 200 yds from castle. Coach drivers and couriers admitted free. Beware narrow gates; they are wide enough to take buses (10ft wide).

One teacher free for every 10 children. Nature trail, family exhibition rooms, dolls' house, play park. Glamis Heritage Education Centre in Glamis village. Education pack. Winner of Sandford Award in 1997.

In grounds, on leads.

OPENING TIMES

2 April - 12 November
Daily, 10.30am - 5.30pm.

(July - August opens 10am, November 10.30am - 4pm)

Last admission 4.45pm.

Groups welcome by appointment at other times.

WINTER

By arrangement.

ADMISSION

SUMMER

House & Grounds

Adult	£6.00
Child (5-16yrs)	£3.00
OAP/Student	£4.50
Family	£16.50

Groups (20+)

Adult	£5.00
Child (5-16yrs)	£2.50
OAP/Student	£4.00

Grounds only

Adult	£3.00
Child (5 - 16yrs)	£1.50
OAP/Student	£1.50
Disabled	Free

SPECIAL EVENTS

- **JUL 8 - 9:** Strathmore Vintage Vehicle Extravaganza.
- **JUL 22:** Grand Scottish Prom.

Owner: The Earl of Mansfield

CONTACT

The Administrator
Scone Palace
Perth
PH2 6BD

Tel: 01738 552300

Fax: 01738 552588

e-mail: sconepalace@cqm.co.uk

LOCATION

OS Ref. NO114 266

From Edinburgh Forth Bridge M90, A93 1 hr.

Bus: Regular buses from Perth (including open-top tours).

Rail: Perth Station 3m.

Motorway: M90 from Edinburgh.

Taxi: 01738 636777.

CONFERENCE/FUNCTION		
ROOM	SIZE	MAX CAPACITY
Long Gallery	140' x 20'	200
Queen Victoria's Rm	20' x 20'	20
Drawing Rm	48' x 25'	80

SCONE PALACE
Perth

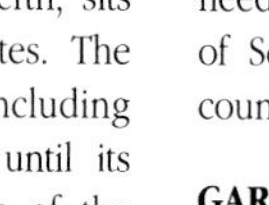

SCONE PALACE, on the outskirts of Perth, sits on one of Scotland's most historic sites. The crowning place of Scottish kings including Macbeth and Robert the Bruce, and until its infamous removal by Edward I, home of the Stone of Destiny on the Moothill.

The Palace was built on the ruins of the old Abbey and Bishop's Palace which were destroyed in the Reformation. After a brief spell under the Gowrie family, in 1600 Scone passed to the Murray family who continue to maintain it. Extensively rebuilt by the 3rd Earl around 1804, Scone now houses unique collections of Vernis Martin, French furniture, clocks, 16th century needlework (including pieces by Mary Queen of Scots), ivories, *objets d'art* and one of the country's finest porcelain collections.

GARDENS
The grounds of the Palace house magnificent collections of shrubs, with woodland walks through the pinetum containing David Douglas' original fir and are home to the new Murray Star Maze. There are Highland cattle and peacocks to admire and an adventure play area for children. Like the Palace, the grounds and wooded parklands that stretch down to the River Tay are available for a variety of events, including corporate and private entertaining.

Receptions, fashion shows, war games, archery, clay pigeon shooting, equestrian events, garden parties, shows, rallies, filming, shooting, fishing, floodlit tattoos, product launches, highland games, parkland, cricket pitch, helicopter landing, croquet, racecourse, polo field, firework displays, adventure playground.

Grand dinners in state rooms, buffets, receptions, wedding receptions, cocktail parties.

All state rooms on one level, wheelchair access to restaurants. Visitors may alight at entrance. WC.

Two restaurants. Teas, lunches & dinners, can be booked, menus upon request, special rates for groups.

By arrangement. Guides in rooms, tour time 45 mins. French and German guides available by appointment.

Welcome.

300 cars and 15 coaches, groups please book, couriers and coach drivers free meal and admittance.

In grounds on leads.

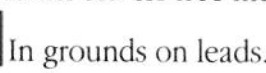

OPENING TIMES

SUMMER
2 April - 23 October
Daily: 9.30am - 5.15pm.

Last admission 4.45pm

Evening tours by appointment.

WINTER
By appointment only.

ADMISSION

SUMMER

Palace & Garden

Adult	£5.60
Child (5-16)	£3.30
Conc.	£4.80
Family	£17.00
Groups (20+)	
Adult	£5.10
Child (5-16)	£2.80
Conc.	£4.40

Grounds only

Adult	£2.70
Child (5-16)	£1.50

Private Tour £30 supplement.

WINTER
Per person £12.50
(£250 min. payment)

SPECIAL EVENTS

- **MAY - SEPT (Monthly):** Horse Trials.
- **APR - SEPT:** Perth Races (01738 551597).
- **JUL 1/2:** Game Conservancy Scottish Fair.
- **AUG 4/5:** Perth Agricultural Show.

ABERDOUR CASTLE

Tel: 01383 860519

Aberdour, Fife

Owner: Historic Scotland **Contact:** The Custodian

A 14th century castle built by the Douglas family. The gallery on the first floor gives an idea of how it was furnished at the time. The castle has a 14th century tower extended in the 16th and 17th centuries, a delightful walled garden and a circular dovecote.

Location: OS Ref. NT193 854. In Aberdour 5m E of the Forth Bridge on the A921.

Opening Times: 1 Apr - 30 Sept: daily, 9.30am - 6.30pm, last ticket 6pm. 1 Oct - 31 Mar: Mon - Sat, 9.30am - 4.30pm, Suns, 2 - 4.30pm, last ticket 4pm. Closed Thur pm & Fris in winter.

Admission: Adult £2, Child 75p, Conc. £1.50.

ALLOA TOWER

Tel: 01259 211701

Alloa Park, Alloa, Clackmannanshire FK10 1PP

Owner: The National Trust for Scotland **Contact:** Piers de Salis

Alloa Tower is a beautifully restored and furnished 14th century Tower House with an unusual 18th century interior. It contains several rare medieval features including the original oak-beamed roof, groin vaulting and interior well. Alloa Tower was the ancestral home of the Erskines, Earls of Mar, and contains a superb collection of family portraits, including works on loan from the present Earl.

Location: OS Ref. NS886 925. On A907, in Alloa.

Opening Times: 1 Apr - 30 Sept: daily, 1.30 - 5.30pm. Weekends in Oct, 1.30 - 5.30pm, last admission 5pm.

Admission: Adult £2.50, Conc. £1.70. Groups: Adult £2, Child/ School £1. 25% discount to Clackmannanshire residents.

Partially suitable. WC.

ANGUS FOLK MUSEUM

Tel: 01307 840288
Fax: 01307 840233

Kirkwynd, Glamis, Forfar, Angus DD8 1RT

Owner: The National Trust for Scotland **Contact:** Kathleen Ager

Where will you find cruisie lamps, pirn winders, cloutie rugs, bannock spades and a thrawcrook? All these fascinating items, and many more, are to be found in the Angus Folk Museum, one of Scotland's finest. The domestic section is housed in six charming 18th century cottages in Kirkwynd, and the agricultural collection is in the farmsteading opposite. The displays inside the building explain and illustrate changes in the Angus countryside in the last 200 years.

Location: OS Ref. NO385 467. Off A94, in Glamis, 5m SW of Forfar.

Opening Times: 1 Apr - 30 Sept; daily, 11am - 5pm. 1 Jul - 31 Aug: daily, 10am - 5pm. Weekends in Oct: 11am - 5pm, last admission 4.30pm.

Admission: Adult £2.50, Conc. £1.70. Groups: Adult £2, Child/School £1.

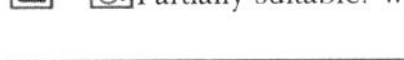
Partially suitable. WC. Limited.

ARBROATH ABBEY

Tel: 01241 878756

Arbroath, Tayside

Owner: Historic Scotland **Contact:** The Custodian

The substantial ruins of a Tironensian monastery, notably the gate house range and the abbot's house. Arbroath Abbey holds a very special place in Scottish history. It was here in 1320 that Scotland's nobles swore their independence from England in the famous 'Declaration of Arbroath'.

Location: OS Ref. NO644 414. In Arbroath town centre on the A92.

Opening Times: 1 Apr - 30 Sept: daily 9.30am - 6.30pm, last ticket 6pm. 1 Oct - 31 Mar: Mon - Sat, 9.30am - 4.30 pm, Suns, 2 - 4.30pm, last ticket 4pm.

Admission: Adult £2, Child 75p, Conc. £1.50.

BALGONIE CASTLE

Tel: 01592 750119 **Fax:** 01592 753103

Markinch, Fife KY7 6HQ

Owner/Contact: The Laird of Balgonie

14th century tower, additions to the building up to 1702. Still lived in by the family. 14th century chapel for weddings.

Location: OS Ref. NO313 006. 1/2 m S of A911 Glenrothes - Leven road at Milton of Balgonie on to B921.

Opening Times: All year: daily, 10am - 5pm.

Admission: Adult £3, Child £1.50, OAP £2.

BALHOUSIE CASTLE (BLACK WATCH MUSEUM)

Tel: 0131 310 8530

Hay Street, North Inch Park, Perth PH1 5HR

Owner: MOD **Contact:** Major Proctor

Regimental museum housed in the castle.

Location: OS Ref. NO115 244. 1/2 m N of town centre, E of A9 road to Dunkeld.

Opening Times: May - Sept: Mon - Sat, 10am - 4.30pm. Oct - Apr: Mon - Fri, 10am - 3.30pm. Closed 23 Dec - 5 Jan & last Sat in Jun.

Admission: Free.

Not suitable. By arrangement. Limited. Guide dogs only.

BARRIE'S BIRTHPLACE

Tel: 01575 572646

9 Brechin Road, Kirriemuir, Angus DD8 4BX

Owner: The National Trust for Scotland **Contact:** Karen Gilmour or Mrs Sheila Philip

'Do you believe in fairies?' The creator of the eternal magic of *Peter Pan*, J M Barrie, was born here in 1860. He was the ninth of ten children born to David Barrie, a handloom weaver and his wife Margaret Ogilvy. See the imaginative exhibition about this famous novelist and dramatist with life-size figures, miniature stage sets, dioramas, theatre posters and stage costumes, while a darting light, 'Tinkerbell', moves around the room!

Location: OS Ref. NO388 542. On A926/B957, in Kirriemuir, 6m NW of Forfar.

Opening Times: 1 Apr - 30 Sept: Mon - Sat, 11am - 5.30pm, Suns, 1.30 - 5.30pm. Weekends in Oct: Sats, 11am - 5.30pm, Suns, 1.30pm - 5.30pm, last adm. 5pm.

Admission: Adult £2.50, Conc. £1.70. Groups: Adult £2, Child/School £1.

Stairlift. No parking.

BARRY MILL

Tel: 01241 856761

Barry, Carnoustie, Angus DD7 7RJ

Owner: The National Trust for Scotland **Contact:** Peter Ellis

19th century meal mill. Demonstrations and displays. Waymarked walks. Picnic area.

Location: OS Ref. NO533 349. N of village between A92 & A930, 2m W of Carnoustie.

Opening Times: 1 Apr - 30 Sept; daily, 11am - 5pm. Weekends in Oct: 11am - 5pm.

Admission: Adult £2.50, Conc £1.70. Groups: Adult £2, Child/School £1.

BLAIR CASTLE

See page 440 for full page entry.

BOLFRACKS GARDEN

Tel: 01887 820207

Aberfeldy, Perthshire PH15 2EX

Owner/Contact: Mr J D Hutchison

A garden of approximately 4 acres with splendid views over the River Tay to the hills beyond. A walled garden contains a wide collection of trees, shrubs and perennials. Also a burn garden with rhododendrons, azaleas, meconopsis, primulas etc. with peat wall arrangements. Lots of bulbs and good autumn colour.

Location: OS Ref. NN822 481. 2m W of Aberfeldy on A827 towards Kenmore.

Opening Times: 1 Apr - 31 Oct: daily, 10am - 6pm.

Admission: Adult £2.50, Child (under 16 yrs) Free.

BRANKLYN GARDEN

Tel: 01738 625535

Dundee Road, Perth PH2 7BB

Owner: The National Trust for Scotland **Contact:** Steve McNamara

Small but magnificent garden with an impressive collection of rare and unusual plants. Among the most breathtaking is the Himalayan blue poppy, *Meconopsis x sheldonii*. There is a rock garden with purple maple and the rare golden *Cedrus*. Seasonal highlights in May and June are the alpines and rhododendrons and in autumn the fiery red *Acer palmatum*.

Location: OS Ref. NO125 225. On A85 at 116 Dundee Road, Perth.

Opening Times: 1 Mar - 31 Oct; daily, 9.30am - sunset.

Admission: Adult £2.50, Conc. £1.70. Groups: Adult £2, Child/School £1.

Grounds suitable, but limited access.

CAMBO GARDENS

Tel: 01333 450054 **Fax:** 01333 450987

Cambo Estate, Kingsbarns, St Andrews, Fife KY16 8QD

Owner: Mr & Mrs T P N Erskine **Contact:** Catherine Erskine

Enchanting Victorian walled garden designed around the Cambo Burn. Snowdrops, lilac and roses are specialities. Ornamental potager, autumn borders. Garden supplies mansion house (not open) with fruit, vegetables and flowers. Woodland walks to sandy beach.

Location: OS Ref. NO603 114. 3m N of Crail. 7m SE of St Andrews on A917.

Opening Times: All year: daily except Christmas and New Year, 10am - dusk.

Admission: Adult £2, Child Free.

Conferences. Mail order snowdrops in the green.
Limited for coaches. In grounds, on leads.
2 doubles & self-catering apartments/cottages.

CASTLE MENZIES

Tel: 01887 820982

Weem, Aberfeldy, Perth PH15 2JD

Owner: Menzies Charitable Trust **Contact:** R A Adam

Magnificent example of a 16th century 'Z' plan fortified tower house, seat of the Chiefs of Clan Menzies for over 400 years. 'Bonnie Prince Charlie' was given hospitality here in 1746. Visitors can explore the whole building, together with part of 19th century addition. Small clan museum and gift shop.

Location: OS Ref. NN838 497. 1 1/2 m from Aberfeldy on B846.

Opening Times: 1 Apr - 14 Oct: Mon - Sat, 10.30am - 5pm, Suns, 2 - 5pm, last entry 4.30pm.

Admission: Adult £3, Child £1.50, Conc. £2.50, Groups (20+): Adult £2.70.

Ground floor suitable. WC. Guide dogs only.

CHARLETON HOUSE

Tel: 01333 340249 **Fax:** 01333 340583

Colinsburgh, Leven, Fife KY9 1HG

Location: OS Ref. NO464 036. Off A917. 1m NW of Colinsburgh. 3m NW of Elie.

Opening Times: Sept: 12 noon - 3pm. Admission every 1/2 hr with guided tours only.

Admission: £6.

Obligatory.

CULROSS PALACE 

Tel: 01383 880359 **Fax:** 01383 882675

Culross, Fife KY12 8JH

Owner: The National Trust for Scotland **Contact:** Property Manager

Relive the domestic life of the 16th and 17th centuries at this Royal Burgh fringed by the River Forth. Here the old buildings and cobbled streets create a time warp for visitors as they explore the old town. Enjoy too the Palace, dating from 1597 and the medieval garden.

Location: OS Ref. NS985 860. Off A985. 12m W of Forth Road Bridge and 4m E of Kincardine Bridge, Fife.

Opening Times: Palace & Town House: 1 Apr - 31 May & 1 - 30 Sept: daily, 1.30 - 5pm; 1 Jun - 31 Aug: daily, 10am - 5pm; Weekends in Oct: 1.30 - 5pm. Last admission to Palace 4pm, to Town House 4.30pm. Study: same dates, 1.30 - 5pm. Groups at other times by appointment. Tearoom (in Bessie Bar Hall), dates as Palace, 10.30am - 4.30pm.

Admission: Combined ticket: Adult £5, Conc. £3.50. Groups: Adult £4, Child/School £1.

WC. By arrangement.

DRUMMOND CASTLE GARDENS

See below.

DUNFERMLINE ABBEY & PALACE

Tel: 01383 739026

Dunfermline, Fife

Owner: Historic Scotland **Contact:** The Custodian

The remains of the Benedictine abbey founded by Queen Margaret in the 11th century. The foundations of her church are under the 12th century Romanesque-style nave. Robert the Bruce was buried in the choir. Substantial parts of the Abbey buildings remain, including the vast refectory.

Location: OS Ref. NY090 873. In Dunfermline off the M90.

Opening Times: 1 Apr - 30 Sept: daily, 9.30am - 6.30pm, last ticket 6pm. 1 Oct - 31 Mar: Mon - Sat, 9.30am - 4.30pm, Suns, 2 - 4.30pm, last ticket 4pm. Closed Thur pm and Fris in winter.

Admission: Adult £2, Child 75p, Conc. £1.50.

DUNNINALD

Tel: 01674 674842 **Fax:** 01674 674860

Montrose, Angus DD10 9TD

Owner/Contact: J Stansfeld

This house, the third Dunninald built on the estate, was designed by James Gillespie Graham in the gothic Revival style, and was completed for Peter Arkley in 1824. It has a superb walled garden and is set in a planned landscape dating from 1740. It is a family home.

Location: OS Ref. NO705 543 2m S of Montrose, between A92 and the sea.

Opening Times: 1 - 30 Jul: Tue - Sun, 1 - 5pm. Garden: from 12 noon.

Admission: Adult £4, Child £2.50, Conc. £2.50. Garden only: £2.

No photography in house. Not suitable. Obligatory. In grounds, on leads.

EDZELL CASTLE AND GARDEN

Tel: 01356 648631

Edzell, Angus

Owner: Historic Scotland **Contact:** The Custodian

The beautiful walled garden at Edzell is one of Scotland's unique sights, created by Sir David Lindsay in 1604. The 'Pleasance' is a delightful formal garden with walls decorated with sculptured stone panels, flower boxes and niches for nesting birds. The fine tower house, now ruined, dates from the last years of the 15th century. Mary Queen of Scots held a council meeting in the castle in 1562 on her way north as her army marched against the Gordons.

Location: OS Ref. NO585 691. At Edzell, 6m N of Brechin on B966. 1m W of village.

Opening Times: 1 Apr - 30 Sept: daily, 9.30am - 6.30pm, last ticket 6pm. 1 Oct - 31 Mar: Mon - Sat, 9.30am - 4.30pm, Suns, 2 - 4.30pm, last ticket 4pm. Closed Thur pm and Fris in winter.

Admission: Adult £2.50, Child £1, Conc. £1.90.

ELCHO CASTLE

Tel: 01738 639998

Perth

Owner: Historic Scotland

This handsome and complete fortified mansion of 16th century date has four projecting towers. The original wrought-iron grilles to protect the windows are still in place.

Location: OS Ref. NO164 211. On the Tay, 3m SE of Perth.

Opening Times: 1 Apr - 30 Sept: daily, 9.30am - 6.30pm, last ticket 6pm.

Admission: Adult £1.80, Child 75p, Conc. £1.30.

DRUMMOND CASTLE GARDENS

Kathy Collins

MUTHILL, CRIEFF, PERTHSHIRE PH5 2AA

Owner: *Grimsthorpe & Drummond Castle Trust* ***Contact:*** *Irene Wyper*

Tel: 01764 681257 **Fax:** 01764 681550 **Weekends:** 01764 681433

e-mail: the gardens@drummondcastle.sol.co.uk

Scotland's most important formal gardens, among the finest in Europe. A mile of beech-lined avenue leads to a formidable ridge top tower house. Enter through the woven iron yett to the terraces and suddenly revealed is a magnificent Italianate parterre, celebrating the saltire and family heraldry, surrounding the famous multiplex sundial by John Milne, master mason to Charles I. First laid out in the early 17th century by John Drummond, the 2nd Earl of Perth and renewed in the early 1950s by Phyllis Astor, Countess of Ancaster.

Location: OS Ref. NN844 181. 2m S of Crieff off the A822.

Opening Times: Easter weekend, then 1 May - 31 Oct: 2 - 6pm, last entry 5pm.

Admission: Adult £3, Child £1.50, OAP £2.

Partially suitable. WC. By arrangement. In grounds, on leads.

SPECIAL EVENTS

AUG 6: Open Day, entertainments, teas, raffle.

FALKLAND PALACE

FALKLAND KY15 7BU

Owner: *The National Trust for Scotland* **Contact:** *Mrs Margaret Marshall*

Tel: 01337 857397 **Fax:** 01337 857980

The Royal Palace of Falkland, set in the heart of a unique medieval village, was the country residence and hunting lodge of eight Stuart monarchs, including Mary Queen of Scots. Built between 1502 and 1541, the Palace is an extremely fine example of Renaissance architecture. It includes the exceptionally beautiful Chapel Royal, and is surrounded by internationally known gardens, laid out in the 1950s. The Royal Tennis Court, reputedly the world's oldest, is still used today.

Location: OS Ref. NO253 075. A912, 11m N of Kirkcaldy.

Opening Times: Palace & Garden: 1 Apr - 31 May & 1 Sept - 31 Oct: Mon - Sat, 11am - 5.30pm, Suns, 1.30 - 5.30pm. 1 Jun - 31 Aug: Mon - Sat, 10am - 5.30pm, Suns, 1.30 - 5.30. Last admission to Palace 4.30pm, to Garden 5pm. Groups at other times by appointment. Town Hall by appointment only.

Admission: Palace & Garden: Adult £5, Conc. £3.50. Groups: Adult £4, Child/School £1. Garden only: Adult £2.50, Conc. £1.70. Groups: Adult £2, Child/School £1. Members of Scots Guards' Association admitted Free.

 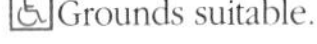Grounds suitable.  

HOUSE OF DUN

MONTROSE, ANGUS DD10 9LQ

Owner: *The National Trust for Scotland* **Contact:** *John Oatts*

Tel: 01674 810264 **Fax:** 01674 810722

This beautiful Georgian house, overlooking the Montrose Basin, was designed by William Adam and built in 1730 for David Erskine, Lord Dun. Lady Augusta Kennedy-Erskine was the natural daughter of William IV and Mrs Jordan and House of Dun contains many royal mementos. The house features superb plasterwork by Joseph Enzer.

Location: OS Ref. NO670 599. 3m W Montrose on A935.

Opening Times: House & shop: 1 Apr - 31 May & 1 - 30 Sept: daily, 1.30 - 5.30pm; 1 Jun - 31 Aug: daily, 11am - 5.30pm; weekends in Oct, 1.30 - 5.30pm (last admission 5pm). Restaurant opens at 11am. Gardens & Grounds: All year, daily, 9.30am - sunset.

Admission: House & Gardens: Adult £4, Conc. £3. Groups: Adult £3.20, Child/School £1. Gardens & grounds: Honesty box £1.

Conferences. Ground floor & basement suitable. WC. In grounds, on leads. Special dog walk.

GLAMIS CASTLE

See page 441 for full page entry.

GLENEAGLES

Tel: 01764 682388

Auchterarder, Perthshire PH3 1PJ

Owner: Gleneagles 1996 Trust **Contact:** J Martin Haldane of Gleneagles

Gleneagles has been the home of the Haldane family since the 12th century. The 18th century pavilion is open to the public by written appointment.

Location: OS Ref. NS931 088. Auchterarder.

Opening Times: By written appointment only.

HILL OF TARVIT MANSIONHOUSE

Tel/Fax: 01334 653127

Cupar, Fife KY15 5PB

Owner: The National Trust for Scotland **Contact:** Mrs June Pratt

This fine house was rebuilt in 1906 by Sir Robert Lorimer, the renowned Scottish architect, for a Dundee industrialist, Mr F B Sharp. The house still presents a perfect setting for Mr Sharp's notable collection of superb French, Chippendale and vernacular furniture. Fine paintings by Raeburn and Ramsay and a number of eminent Dutch artists are on view together with Chinese porcelain and bronzes. Don't miss the restored Edwardian laundry behind the house which is set in the midst of a delightful garden.

Location: OS Ref. NO379 118. Off A916, 2½m S of Cupar, Fife.

Opening Times: House: 1 Apr - 31 May & 1 - 30 Sept: daily, 1.30 - 5.30pm; 1 Jun - 31 Aug: daily, 11am - 5.30pm; weekends in Oct, 1.30 - 5.30pm (last admission 4.45pm). Tearoom opens at 11am. Garden & Grounds: 1 Apr - 30 Sept: daily, 9.30am - 9pm; 1 Oct - 31 Mar: daily, 9.30am - 4.30pm.

Admission: House & Garden: Adult £4, Conc. £3. Groups: Adult £3.20, Child/School £1. Garden & Grounds only: £1 (honesty box).

Ground floor & grounds suitable. WC. By arrangement. P

HUNTINGTOWER CASTLE

Tel: 01738 627231

Perth

Owner: Historic Scotland **Contact:** The Custodian

The splendid painted ceilings are especially noteworthy in this castle, once owned by the Ruthven family. Scene of a famous leap between two towers by a daughter of the house who was nearly caught in her lover's room. The two towers are still complete, one of 15th - 16th century date, the other of 16th century origin. Now linked by a 17th century range.

Location: OS Ref. NO084 252. 3m NW of Perth off the A85.

Opening Times: 1 Apr - 30 Sept: daily, 9.30am - 6.30pm, last ticket 6pm. 1 Oct - 31 Mar: Mon - Sat, 9.30am - 4.30pm, Suns, 2 - 4.30pm, last ticket 4pm. Closed Thur pm & Fris in winter.

Admission: Adult £2, Child 75p, Conc. £1.50.

INCHCOLM ABBEY

Tel: 01383 823332

Inchcolm, Fife

Owner: Historic Scotland **Contact:** The Custodian

Known as the 'Iona of the East'. This is the best preserved group of monastic buildings in Scotland, founded in 1123. Includes a 13th century octagonal chapter house.

Location: OS Ref. NT190 826. On Inchcolm in the Firth of Forth. Reached by ferry from South Queensferry (30 mins) tel. 0131 331 4857, and from North Queensferry (weather permitting).

Opening Times: 1 Apr - 30 Sept: daily, 9.30am - 6.30pm, last ticket 6pm.

Admission: Adult £2.50, Child £1, Conc. £1.90. Additional charge for ferries.

INCHMAHOME PRIORY

Tel: 01877 385294

Port of Menteith

Owner: Historic Scotland **Contact:** The Custodian

A beautifully situated Augustinian priory on an island in the Lake of Menteith founded in 1238 with much of the building surviving. The five year old Mary Queen of Scots was sent here for safety in 1547.

Location: OS Ref. NN574 005. On an island in Lake of Menteith. Reached by ferry from Port of Menteith, 4m E of Aberfoyle off A81.

Opening Times: 1 Apr - 30 Sept: daily, 9.30am - 6.30pm, last ticket 6pm.

Admission: Adult £3, Child £1, Conc. £2.30. Charge includes ferry trip.

KELLIE CASTLE & GARDEN

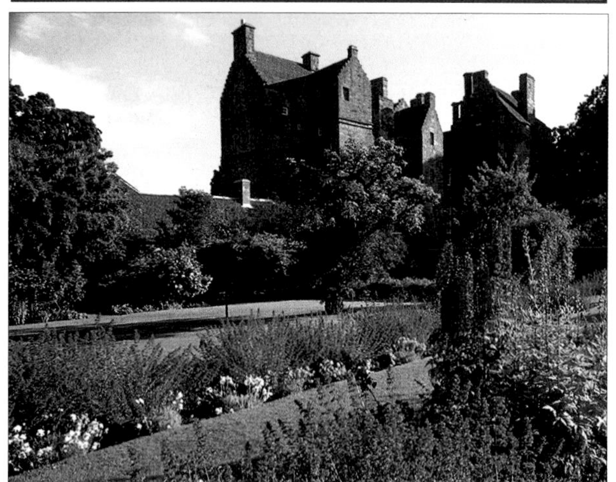

PITTENWEEM, FIFE KY10 2RF

Owner: *The National Trust for Scotland* ***Contact:*** *The Property Manager*

Tel: 01333 720271 **Fax:** 01333 720326

This very fine example of domestic architecture in Lowland Scotland dates from the 14th century and was sympathetically restored by the Lorimer family in the late 19th century. The castle contains magnificent plaster ceilings and painted panelling as well as fine furniture designed by Sir Robert Lorimer. Of particular interest are the Victorian nursery and the old kitchen. The late Victorian garden features a fine collection of old-fashioned roses and herbaceous plants which are cultivated organically.

Location: OS Ref. NO519 051. On B9171, 3m NW of Pittenweem, Fife.

Opening Times: Castle: 1 Apr - 30 Sept: daily, 1.30 - 5.30pm, weekends in Oct, 1.30 - 5.30pm (last admission 4.45pm). Garden & Grounds: All year, daily, 9.30 - sunset.

Admission: House & Grounds: Adult £4, Conc. £3. Groups: Adult £3.20, Child/School £1. Garden & Grounds: £1 (honesty box).

 Ground floor & grounds suitable. 

LOCH LEVEN CASTLE

Tel: 0388 040483

Loch Leven, Kinross

Owner: Historic Scotland **Contact:** The Regional Custodian

Mary Queen of Scots endured nearly a year of imprisonment in this 14th century tower before her dramatic escape in May 1568. During the First War of Independence it was held by the English, stormed by Wallace and visited by Bruce.

Location: OS Ref. NO138 018. On island in Loch Leven reached by ferry from Kinross off the M90.

Opening Times: 1 Apr - 30 Sept: daily, 9.30am - 6.30pm, last ticket 6pm.

Admission: Adult £3, Child £1, Conc. £2.30. Prices include ferry trip.

MEGGINCH CASTLE GARDENS

Tel: 01821 642222 **Fax:** 01821 642708

Errol, Perthshire PH2 7SW

Owner: Captain Drummond of Megginch and Lady Strange

15th century castle, 1,000 year old yews, flowered parterre, double walled kitchen garden, topiary, astrological garden, pagoda dovecote in courtyard. Part used as a location for the film *Rob Roy*.

Location: OS Ref. NO241 245. 8m E of Perth on A90.

Opening Times: Apr - Oct: Weds. Aug: daily, 2.30 - 6pm.

Admission: Adult £2.50, Child £1.

Partially suitable. By arrangement. Limited for coaches. In grounds, on leads.

MEIGLE SCULPTURED STONE MUSEUM 

Tel: 01828 640612

Meigle

Owner: Historic Scotland

A remarkable collection of 25 sculptured monuments of the Celtic Christian period. This is one of the finest collections of Dark Age sculpture in Western Europe.

Location: OS Ref. NO287 446. In Meigle on the A94.

Opening Times: 1 Apr - 30 Sept: daily, 9.30am - 6.30pm, last ticket 6pm.

Admission: Adult £1.80, Child 75p, Conc. £1.30.

MONZIE CASTLE

Tel: 01764 653110

Crieff, Perthshire PH7 4HD

Owner/Contact: Mrs C M M Crichton

Built in 1791. Destroyed by fire in 1908 and rebuilt and furnished by Sir Robert Lorimer.

Location: OS Ref. NN873 244. 2m NE of Crieff.

Opening Times: 13 May - 11 Jun: daily, 2 - 5pm. By appointment at other times.

Admission: Adult £3, Child £1. Groups: Adult £2.50.

PITTENCRIEFF HOUSE

Tel: 01383 313838/722935

Dunfermline, Fife

Owner: Fife Council **Contact:** Ms Lin Collis

17th century T-plan house now housing a collection of costumes, displays on the history of the house and park. Art gallery.

Location: OS Ref. NN087 873. In Dunfermline, S of A994 in Pittencrieff Park.

Opening Times: All year. May - Sept: 11am - 5pm. Oct - Apr: 11am - 4pm.

Admission: Free.

ST ANDREWS CASTLE 

THE SCORES, ST ANDREWS, KY16 9AR

Owner: *Historic Scotland* ***Contact:*** *The Steward*

Tel: 01334 477196

This was the castle of the Bishops of St Andrews and has a fascinating mine and counter-mine, rare examples of medieval siege techniques. There is also a bottle dungeon hollowed out of solid rock. Cardinal Beaton was murdered here and John Knox was sent to the galleys when the ensuing siege was lifted.

Location: OS Ref. NO513 169. In St Andrews on the A91.

Opening Times: Apr - Sept: daily, 9.30am - 6.30pm. Oct - Mar: Mon - Sat, 9.30am - 4.30pm; Suns, 2 - 4.30pm. Last ticket 30 mins before closing. Joint ticket with St Andrews Cathedral available.

Admission: Adult £2.50, Child £1, OAP/Student £1.90. 10% discount for groups (10+). Free pre-booked school visits.

Visitor centre. Private evening hire. Partially suitable. WCs. By arrangement. On street. Free if booked. Guide dogs.

SCONE PALACE

See page 442 for full page entry.

STOBHALL GARDENS & CHAPEL

Tel: 01821 640332

Stobhall, Guildtown, Perthshire PH2 6DR

Owner: The Earl of Perth **Contact:** J Stormonth-Darling

Dramatic shrub gardens surround this unusual and charming cluster of historic buildings in a magnificent situation overlooking the River Tay. Access to 14th century chapel with its unique painted ceiling (1630).

Location: OS Ref. NO132 343. 8m N of Perth on A93.

Opening Times: 27 May - 24 Jun: 1 - 5pm. Also 29 Oct & 5 Nov, 2 - 5pm.

Admission: Adult £2, Child £1.

Partially suitable. WC. Limited.
Schools welcome if suitably accompanied. No education programme.
Guide dogs only.

West Highlands & Islands

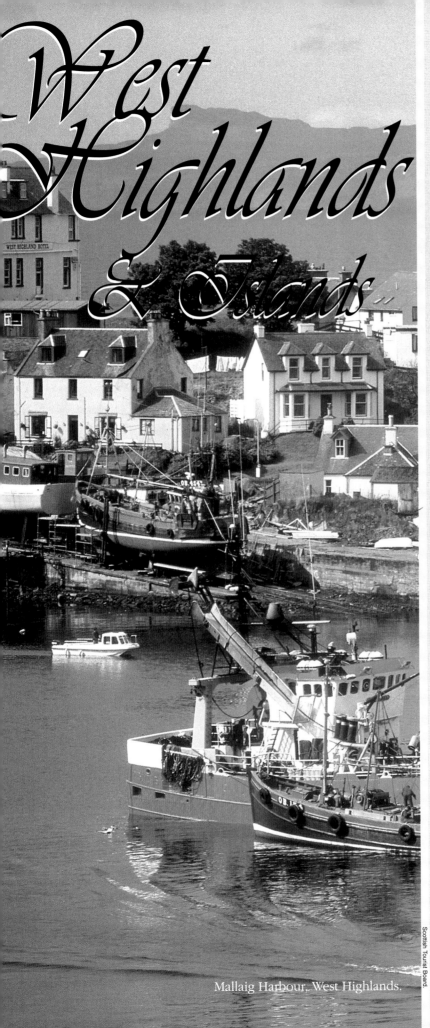

Mallaig Harbour, West Highlands.

Scottish Tourist Board.

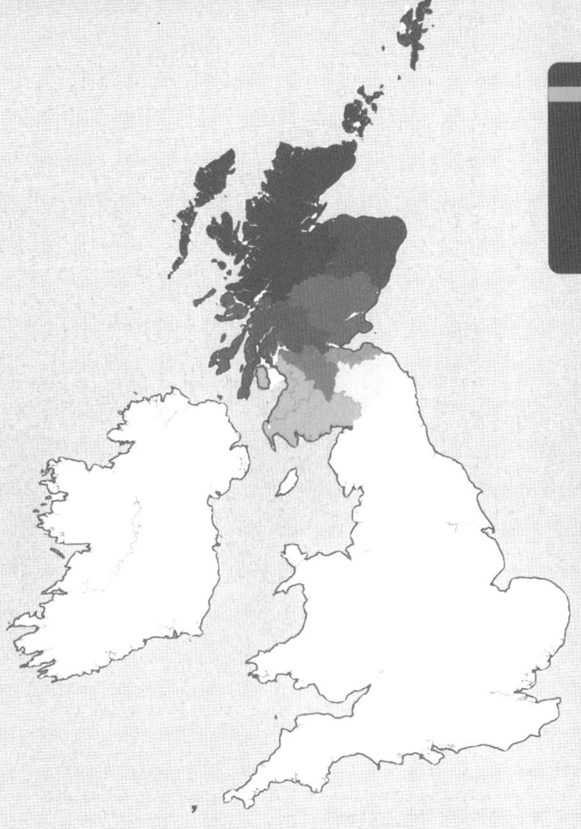

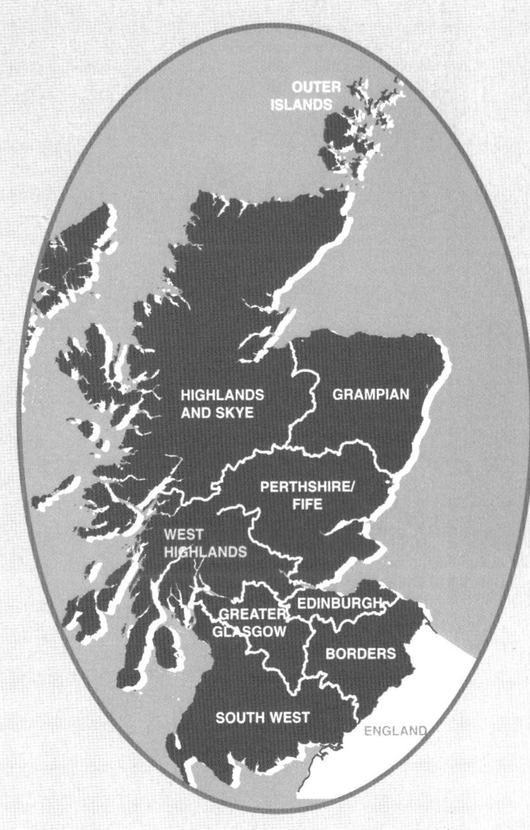

Featuring...

The Great Hall
Stirling Castle

Circular Stonework & Sca

Roof Timbers.

The stunning restoration of Stirling Castle's Great Hall – the largest medieval banqueting hall in Scotland – is the jewel in the crown of the £22 million Stirling Castle restoration project undertaken by Historic Scotland. This project, conceived in the early 1900s, has brilliantly achieved its two main aims: to enhance the Castle as a visitor attraction and conserve it as a monument of international importance.

In the year 2000 the visitor to the Castle will be able to visit the Great Hall, as well as enjoying the Chapel Royal built by James VI for the baptism of his son, Prince Henry, which has been refurbished in a £1.5 million conservation project. The Castle's medieval kitchens have also been recreated with life-size models portraying life 'below stairs' and a lively exhibition on life in the medieval court has been installed in the vaults of the Renaissance Palace built by James V.

With such wonderful changes the 400,000 visitors who flock annually to the Castle could be forgiven for forgetting that Stirling was a military depot for more than 350 years. Indeed, it was in the late 18th century, when the threat from Napoleon created the need for an urgent military build-up, that the Great Hall was hurriedly converted into a three-storey barrack. The medieval windows were blocked-up and sash and case windows inserted. The hammer-beam roof was removed to accommodate the third level of barrack rooms.

The first step in the £8.5 million restoration project was to dismantle the labyrinth of internal walls and floors within the Great Hall that had been put in by the army. It was only then that the original scale of the Hall – 38 metres long, 11 metres wide and 17 metres high, started to emerge. The Great Hall as it stands in all its glory today, is a wonderful tribute to the skills of 20th century craftsmen in reviving and copying the skills of their medieval counterparts. Historic Scotland's masons painstakingly carved the new sandstone blocks using chisel, mell and square, just as their forebears would have done. Where possible original masonry was retained but over the course of a year, these highly skilled masons built 1,000 tonnes of new masonry.

It is though the hammer-beam roof, built without a single nail – handmade wooden pegs lock the structure together – which is the great marvel of the Hall. Nearly 400 oak trees were supplied by the Forestry Commission for the roof, and specialist carpenters cut and jointed these timbers.

The roof was built in only 10 weeks. Finally on 2 September 1999, carved stone and gilded beasts, two lions and two unicorns, were winched into their crown shaped bases along the ridge of the Great Hall, the final touch to returning the Hall to its breathtaking and awesome Renaissance splendour.

For full details of this property see page 455.

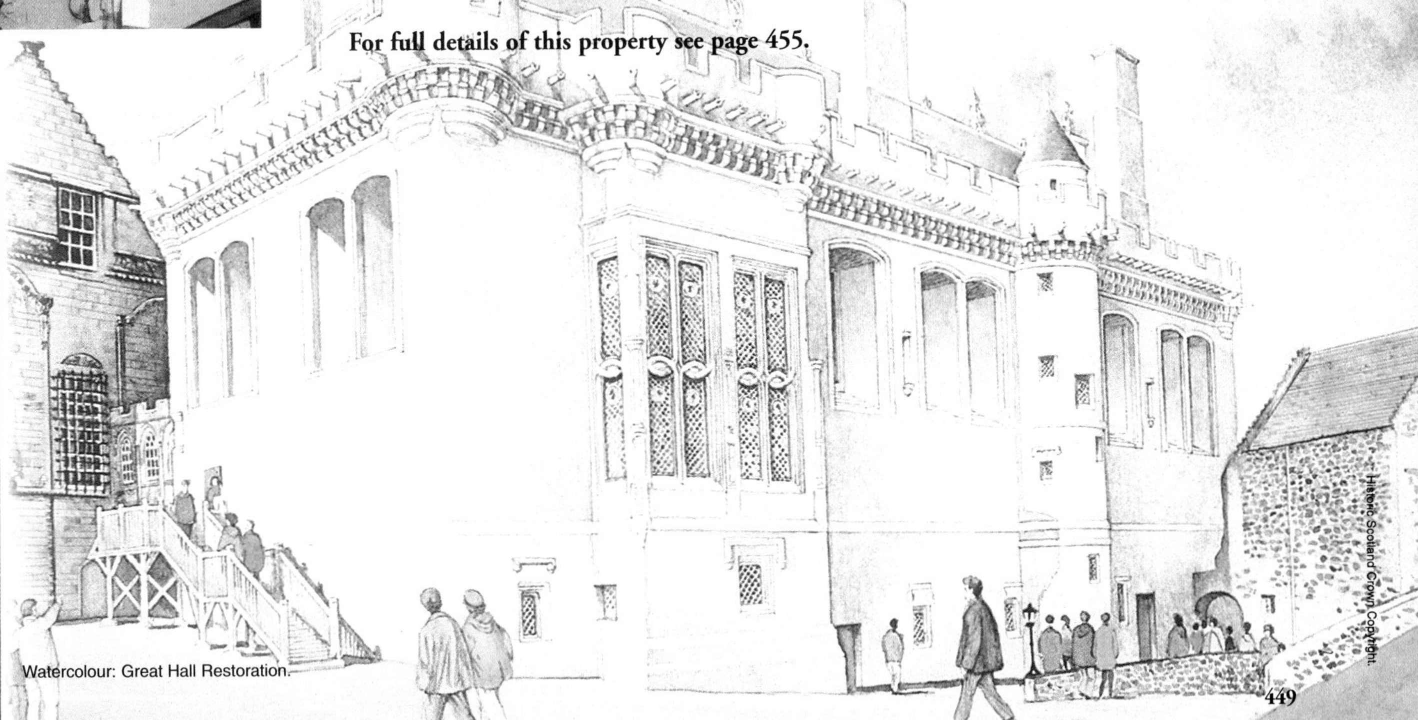

Watercolour: Great Hall Restoration.

Historic Scotland

ARGYLL'S LODGING
Stirling

ARGYLL'S LODGING, the residence of the Earls of Argyll in Stirling, is the finest and most complete surviving example in Scotland of a 17th century town residence. Set back behind a screen wall on the upper approaches to Stirling Castle, its fine architecture marks it out as a town house intended for the household of a great nobleman serving the Royal Stewart Court within the Castle. The principal rooms within the lodging – including the Laigh Hall, Dining Room, Drawing Room and Bedchamber – have recently been restored and furnished as they would have been when the 9th Earl of Argyll lived there in 1680. The Earl was executed for treason in 1685.

Interpretation scheme includes computer animations; joint ticket with Stirling Castle available.

Evening receptions/dinners.

Partially suitable. No wheelchair access to upper floor.

Ample parking for coaches and cars on Stirling Castle Esplanade.

Free pre-booked school visits scheme.

Guide dogs only.

Owner: Historic Scotland

CONTACT

Jon MacNeil
Argyll's Lodging
Castle Wynd
Stirling
FK8 1EJ

Tel: 01786 431319

Fax: 01786 448194

LOCATION

OS Ref. NS793 938

At the top and on E side of Castle Wynd in Stirling.

Train: Stirling.

Air: Edinburgh or Glasgow.

FUNCTION

ROOM	SIZE	MAX CAPACITY
Laigh Hall	11 x 6m	60 for reception
High Dining Room	11 x 6m	26 for dinner
Both rooms: 120 for receptions		

OPENING TIMES

April - September:
Daily: 9.30am - 6pm.

October - March:
Daily: 9.30am - 5pm.

ADMISSION

Adult	£2.80
Child*	£1.20
Conc.	£2.00

*up to 16 years

Owner: Trustees of the 10th Duke of Argyll

CONTACT

The Factor
Dept HHD
Argyll Estates Office
Cherry Park
Inveraray
Argyll
PA32 8XE

Tel: 01499 302203

Fax: 01499 302421

LOCATION

OS Ref. NN100 090

From Edinburgh $2^1/_2$ - 3 hrs via Glasgow.

Just NE of Inveraray on A83. W shore of Loch Fyne.

Bus: Bus route stopping point within $^1/_2$ m.

INVERARAY CASTLE
Inveraray

The Duke of Argyll's family have lived in Inveraray since the early 15th century. The present Castle was built between 1745 and 1790.

The ancient Royal Burgh of Inveraray lies about 60 miles north west of Glasgow by Loch Fyne in an area of spectacular natural beauty combining the ruggedness of highland scenery with the sheltered tidal loch 90 miles from the open sea.

The Castle is the home of the Duke and Duchess of Argyll. Its fairytale exterior belies the grandeur of its gracious interior. The building was designed by Roger Morris and decorated by Robert Mylne, the clerk of works being William Adam, father of Robert and John, who did much of the laying out of the present Royal Burgh, an unrivalled example of an early planned town.

Visitors may see the famous Armoury Hall containing some 1300 pieces, French tapestries made especially for the Castle, fine examples of Scottish, English and French furniture together with a wealth of other works of art including china, silver and family artifacts, all of which form a unique collection spanning the generations which are identified by a magnificent genealogical display in the Clan Room.

No photography. Guide books in French, Italian, Japanese and German translations.

Visitors may alight at the entrance. 2 wheelchair ramps to castle. All main public rooms suitable but two long flights of stairs to the smaller rooms upstairs. WCs.

Seats up to 50. Menus available on request. Groups book in advance. Tel: 01786 813317.

Available for up to 100 people at no additional cost. Groups please book. Tour time: 1 hr.

100 cars. Separate coach park close to Castle

£1.50 per child. A guide can be provided. Areas of interest include a nature walk.

Guide dogs only.

OPENING TIMES

1 April - 8 October

April, May, June, September & October:
Mon -Thur & Sats:
10am - 1pm & 2 - 5.45pm
Fris: Closed
Suns: 1 - 5.45pm.

July & August
Daily: 10am - 5.45pm
(including Friday)
Suns: 1 - 5.45pm.

Last admissions
12.30 & 5pm.

WINTER
Closed.

ADMISSION

House only

Adult	£4.50
Child (under 16yrs)	£2.50
OAP/Student	£3.50
Family (2+2)	£12.00
Groups (20+)	20% discount

ACHAMORE GARDENS

Tel: 01583 505254/505267

Isle of Gigha, Argyll PA41 7AD

Owner: Mr and Mrs Derek Holt **Contact:** Mr William Howden

Gardens only open. Sub-tropical gardens created by Sir James Horlick who bought Gigha in 1944.

Location: OS Ref. NR650 500. Off the Mull of Kintyre. Ferry from Tayinloan.

Opening Times: Dawn until dusk every day.

Admission: Adult £2, Child £1.

ANGUS'S GARDEN

Tel: 01866 822381 **Fax:** 01866 822652

Barguillean, Taynuilt, Argyll, West Highlands PA35 1HY

Owner: Mr Sam MacDonald **Contact:** Mr Sam MacDonald

Garden of peace, tranquillity and reconciliation.

Location: OS Ref. NM999 298.

Opening Times: All year: daily, 9am - 5pm.

Admission: £2.

ARDENCRAIG GARDENS

Tel: 01700 504225 **Fax:** 01700 504225

Ardencraig, Rothesay, Isle of Bute, West Highlands PA20 9BP

Owner: Argyll and Bute Council **Contact:** Allan Macdonald

Walled garden, greenhouses, avaries.

Location: OS Ref. NS105 645. 2m from Rothesay.

Opening Times: May - Sept: Mon - Fri, 10am - 4.30pm, Sats & Suns, 1 - 4.30pm.

ARDKINGLAS ESTATE

CAIRNDOW, ARGYLL PA26 8BH

Owner: *S J Noble* ***Contact:*** *The Estate Manager*

Tel: 01499 600261 **Fax:** 01499 600241 **e-mail:** Ardkinglas@btinternet.com

Ardkinglas House, a superb neo-baronial house near the head of Loch Fyne was built by Robert Lorimer in 1907. Although not open to the public, the house is available for corporate days or as a film location. The Woodland Gardens, which are open to the public, are part of a designed landscape and are of outstanding horticultural and scenic significance. The Gardens include at least five champion trees.

Location: OS Ref. NN179 106. Head of Loch Fyne, just off the A83 at Cairndow, 10m W of Arrochar. About 1hr from Glasgow.

Opening Times: Woodland Garden & woodland trails: All year: dawn - dusk. Tree Shop: All year: daily.

Admission: Garden: Adult £2.

Partially suitable. By arrangement. Limited In grounds, on leads.

ARDUAINE GARDEN

Harvey Wood

ARDUAINE, BY OBAN, ARGYLL PA34 4XQ

Owner: *The National Trust for Scotland* ***Contact:*** *Maurice Wilkins*

Tel/Fax: 01852 200366

A haven of tranquillity nestling on the west coast, Arduaine Garden is most spectacular in the late spring and early summer when the rhododendrons and azaleas are at their glorious best. With informal perennial borders giving a delightful display of colour throughout the season, the garden offers pleasant surroundings for a relaxing walk through the woodland garden to the coastal viewpoint, or simply an opportunity to sit and enjoy the peaceful atmosphere of the water garden.

Location: OS Ref. NM798 105. On A816, 20m S of Oban and 17m N of Lochgilphead.

Opening Times: All year: daily, 9.30am - sunset.

Admission: Adult £2.50, Conc. £1.70. Groups: Adult £2. Child/School £1.

By arrangement. Guide dogs only.

ARGYLL'S LODGING 

See page 450 for full page entry.

AUCHINDRAIN TOWNSHIP

Tel: 01499 500235

Auchindrain, Inveraray, Argyll PA32 8XN

Owner: Auchindrain Trust **Contact:** John McDonald

Open-air museum of an original West Highland township.

Location: OS Ref. NN050 050. On A83, 6m SW of Inveraray.

Opening Times: Please contact for details.

Admission: Please contact for details.

BALLOCH CASTLE COUNTRY PARK

Tel: 01389 758216 **Fax:** 01389 720922

Balloch, Dunbartonshire G83 8LX

Contact: Loch Lomond Park Authority Ranger Service

A 200 acre country park on the banks of Loch Lomond.

Location: OS Ref. NS390 830. SE shore of Loch Lomond, off A82 for Balloch or A811 for Stirling.

Opening Times: Visitor Centre: Easter - Oct: daily, 10am - 5.30pm. Country Park: All year: dawn - dusk.

Admission: Free for both Visitor Centre and Country Park.

BANNOCKBURN HERITAGE CENTRE

Tel: 01786 812664
Fax: 01786 810892

Glasgow Road, Stirling FK7 0LJ

Owner: The National Trust for Scotland **Contact:** Judith Fairley

In 1314 from this battlefield the Scots 'sent them homeward to think again', when Edward II's English army was soundly defeated by King Robert the Bruce. Inside the Heritage Centre there is a life-size statue of William Wallace, Bruce on his throne, a display enriched with replicas, vignettes of Scottish life and a panorama of historical characters.

Location: OS Ref. NS810 910. Off M80 & M9/J9, 2m S of Stirling.

Opening Times: Site: All year: daily. Heritage Centre shop & café: 1 - 31 Mar and 1 Nov - 23 Dec: daily, 11am - 4.30pm. 1 Apr - 31 Oct: daily, 10am - 5.30pm (last audio-visual show 1/2 hr before closing).

Admission: Adult £2.50, Conc. £1.70. Groups: Adult £2, Child/School £1.

 In grounds, on leads. 

BONAWE IRON FURNACE

Tel: 01866 822432

Taynuilt, Argyll

Owner: Historic Scotland **Contact:** The Custodian

Founded in 1753 by Cumbrian iron masters this is the most complete remaining charcoal fuelled ironworks in Britain. Displays show how iron was once made here.

Location: OS Ref. NN005 310. By the village of Taynuilt off the A85.

Opening Times: 1 Apr - 30 Sept: daily, 9.30am - 6.30pm, last ticket 6pm.

Admission: Adult £2.50, Child £1, Conc. £1.90.

CASTLE CAMPBELL

Tel: 01259 742408

Dollar Glen, Central District

Owner: The National Trust for Scotland **Contact:** Historic Scotland

Known as 'Castle Gloom' this spectacularly sited 15th century fortress was the lowland stronghold of the Campbells. Stunning views from the parapet walk.

Location: OS Ref. NS961 993. At head of Dollar Glen, 10m E of Stirling on the A91.

Opening Times: 1 Apr - 30 Sept: daily, 9.30am - 6.30pm, last ticket 6pm. 1 Oct - 31 Mar: Mon - Sat, 9.30am - 4.30pm (closed Thurs pm & Fris all day) Suns, 2 - 4.30pm, last ticket 4pm.

Admission: Adult £2.50, Child £1, Conc. £1.90.

CASTLE STALKER

Tel: 01883 622768 **Fax:** 01883 626238

Portnacroish, Appin, Argyll PA38 4BA

Owner: Mrs M Allward **Contact:** Messrs R & A Allward

Early 15th century tower house and ancient seat of the Stewarts of Appin. Picturesquely set on a rocky islet approx 400 yds off the mainland on the shore of Loch Linnhe. Reputed to have been used by James IV as a hunting lodge. Garrisoned by Government troops during the 1745 rising. Restored from a ruin by the late Lt Col Stewart Allward following acquisition in 1965 and now retained by his family.

Location: OS Ref. NM930 480. Approx. 20m N of Oban on the A828. On islet 1/4 m off-shore.

Opening Times: Apr - Sept for 25 days. Telephone for details. Times variable depending on tides and weather.

Admission: Adult £6, Child £3.

Not suitable for coach parties. Not suitable.

DOUNE CASTLE

Tel: 01786 841742

Doune

Owner: Earl of Moray (leased to Historic Scotland) **Contact:** The Custodian

A formidable 14th century courtyard castle, built for the Regent Albany. The striking keep-gatehouse combines domestic quarters including the splendid Lord's Hall with its carved oak screen, musicians' gallery and double fireplace.

Location: OS Ref. NN720 020. In Doune, 8m S of Callendar on the A84.

Opening Times: 1 Apr - 30 Sept: daily, 9.30am - 6.30pm. 1 Oct - 31 Mar: Mon - Wed & Sats, 9.30am - 4.30pm, Thurs, 9.30am - 12 noon, Fris, closed, Suns, 2 - 4.30pm, last admission 1/2 hr before closing.

Admission: Adult £2.50, Child £1, Conc. £1.90.

DUART CASTLE

ISLE OF MULL, ARGYLL PA64 6AP

Owner/Contact: *Sir Lachlan Maclean Bt*

Tel: 01680 812309 or 01577 830311 **e-mail:** duartguide@isle-of-mull.demon.co.uk

Duart Castle has been a Maclean stronghold since the 12th century. The keep was built by Lachlan Lubanach, 5th Chief, in 1360. Burnt by the English in 1758, the castle was restored in 1912 and today is still the home of the Chief of the Clan Maclean. It has a spectacular position overlooking the Sound of Mull.

Location: OS Ref. NM750 350. Off A849 on the east point of the Isle of Mull.

Opening Times: 1 May - 15 Oct: 10.30am - 6pm.

Admission: Adult £3.50, Child £1.75, Conc. £3, Family £8.75.

Not suitable. By arrangement. In grounds, on leads.

DUMBARTON CASTLE

Tel: 01389 732167

Dumbarton, Strathclyde

Owner: Historic Scotland **Contact:** The Custodian

Location: OS Ref. NS401 744. In Dumbarton on the A82.

Opening Times: 1 Apr - 30 Sept: daily, 9.30am - 6.30pm, last ticket 6pm. 1 Oct - 31 Mar: Mon - Wed & Sats, 9.30am - 4.30pm, Thurs, 9.30am - 12 noon, Fris closed, Suns, 2 - 4.30pm, last ticket 4pm.

Admission: Adult £2, Child 75p, Conc £1.50.

DUNBLANE CATHEDRAL

Tel: 01786 823388

Dunblane

Owner: Historic Scotland **Contact:** The Custodian

One of Scotland's noblest medieval churches. The lower part of the tower is Romanesque but the larger part of the building is of the 13th century. It was restored in 1889 - 93 by Sir Rowand Anderson.

Location: OS Ref. NN782 015. In Dunblane.

Opening Times: All year.

Admission: Free.

Historic Scotland.

Kilchurn Castle, West Highlands.

The Hill House, West Highlands.

DUNSTAFFNAGE CASTLE 

Crown Copyright

BY OBAN, ARGYLL PA37 1PZ

Owner: *Historic Scotland* ***Contact:*** *The Steward*

Tel: 01631 562465

A very fine 13th century castle built on a rock with a great curtain wall. The castle's colourful history stretches across the Wars of Independence to the 1745 rising. The castle was briefly the prison of Flora Macdonald. Marvellous views from the top of the curtain wall. Close by are the remains of a chapel with beautiful architectural detail.

Location: OS49 NM882 344. By Loch Etive, 3½ m from Oban on the A85.

Opening Times: Apr - Sept: daily, 9.30am - 6.30pm, last ticket ½ hr before closing. Oct - Mar: Mon - Sat, 9.30am - 4.30pm; Suns, 2 - 4.30pm.

Admission: Adult £2, Child 75p, Conc. £1.50. 10% discount for groups (10+).

Partially suitable. By arrangement. 
Free pre-booked school visits. In grounds, on leads.

GLENCOE

Tel: 01855 811307/811729 (during closed season) **Fax:** 01855 811772

Ballachulish, Argyll PA39 4HX

Owner: The National Trust for Scotland **Contact:** Derrick Warner

This is a breathtaking, dramatic glen with jagged peaks incised on either side by cascading water. In 1692 many of the MacDonald clan were massacred by soldiers of King William's army, to whom they had given hospitality. Wildlife abounds and herds of red deer, wildcat and golden eagle enjoy this wilderness area.

Location: OS Ref. NN100 590. Off A82, 17m S of Fort William.

Opening Times: Site: All year, daily. Visitor Centre, shop & snack bar: 1 Mar - 30 Apr & 1 Sept - 31 Oct: daily, 10am - 5pm; 1 May - 31 Aug: daily, 9.30am - 5.30pm (last admission 30 mins before closing).

Admission: Adult 50p, Conc. 30p (includes parking).

Ground floor suitable. WC.  Guide dogs only. 

THE HILL HOUSE

Tel: 01436 673900 **Fax:** 01436 674685

Upper Colquhoun Street, Helensburgh G84 9AJ

Owner: The National Trust for Scotland **Contact:** Mrs Anne Ellis

Certainly the finest domestic creation of the famous Scottish architect and artist, Charles Rennie Mackintosh. He set this 20th century masterpiece high on a hillside overlooking the Firth of Clyde. Mackintosh also designed furniture, fittings and decorative schemes to complement the house, and suggested a layout for the garden which has been renovated by the Trust.

Location: OS Ref. NS300 820. Off B832, between A82 & A814, 23m NW of Glasgow.

Opening Times: 1 Apr - 31 Oct: daily, 1.30 - 5.30pm (last admission 5pm). Tearoom: 1.30 - 4.30pm. Increasing visitor numbers are placing great strain on the structure of The Hill House, which was designed for domestic purposes. Access may be restricted at peak times and at the discretion of the Property Manager.

Admission: Adult £6, Conc. £4. Groups must book.

INVERARAY CASTLE

See page 451 for full page entry.

INVERARAY JAIL

Tel: 01499 302381 **Fax:** 01499 302195

Church Square, Inveraray, Argyll PA32 8TX

Owner: Visitor Centres Ltd **Contact:** J Linley

A living 19th century prison! Uniformed prisoners and warders, life-like figures, imaginative exhibitions, sounds, smells and trials in progress, bring the 1820 courtroom and former county prison back to life. See the 'In Prison Today' exhibition.

Location: OS Ref. NN100 090. Church Square, Inveraray, Argyll.

Opening Times: Apr - Oct: 9.30am - 6pm, last adm. 5pm. Nov - Mar: 10am - 5pm, last adm. 4pm.

Admission: Adult £4.75, Child £2.30, OAP £3, Family £12.95. Groups (10+): £3.80, OAP £2.50 (from 1 Apr 2000).

KILCHURN CASTLE

Tel: 01786 431323

Loch Awe, Dalmally, Argyll

Owner: Historic Scotland **Contact:** The Custodian

A square tower, built by Sir Colin Campbell of Glenorchy c1550, it was much enlarged in 1693 to give the building, now a ruin, its present picturesque outline. Spectacular views of Loch Awe.

Location: OS Ref. NN133 276. At the NE end of Loch Awe, 2½ m W of Dalmally.

Opening Times: Ferry service operates in the summer. Tel: 01838 200440 for times.

Admission: Adult £4, Child £2, Conc.£3, Family £10.

MOUNT STUART HOUSE & GARDENS

ISLE OF BUTE PA20 9LR

Owner: *The Mount Stuart Trust* ***Contact:*** *The Administrator*

Tel: 01700 503877 **Fax:** 01700 505313 **e-mail:** contactus@mountstuart.com

Spectacular High Victorian Gothic house, ancestral home of the Marquesses of Bute. Splendid interiors, art collection and architectural detail. Set in 300 acres of stunning woodlands, mature pinetum, arboretum and exotic gardens. Countryside Ranger Service. Scottish Tourism Oscar winner.

Location: OS Ref. NS100 600. 5m S of Rothesay Pierhead, local bus service to house. Frequent ferry service from Wemyss Bay, Renfrewshire & Colintraive, Argyll. 1 hr from Glasgow Airport.

Opening Times: Easter - Sept: daily (closed Tues & Thurs). House: 11am - 4.30pm. Gardens: 10am - 5pm.

Admission: House & Gardens: Adult £6, Child £2.50, Family £15, Season £15. Gardens: Adult £3.50, Child £2, Family £9. Conc. & group rates given. Pre-booked guided tours available.

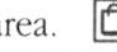 Picnic area.    By arrangement. 

Open all Year Index
PAGE 52

ROTHESAY CASTLE

Tel: 01700 502691

Rothesay, Isle of Bute

Owner: Historic Scotland **Contact:** The Custodian

A favourite residence of the Stuart Kings, this is a wonderful example of a 13th century circular castle of enclosure with 16th century forework containing the Great Hall. Attacked by Vikings in its earlier days.

Location: OS Ref. NS088 646. In Rothesay, Isle of Bute. Ferry from Wemyss Bay on the A78.

Opening Times: 1 Apr - 30 Sept: daily, 9.30am - 6.30pm, last ticket 6pm. 1 Oct - 31 Mar: Mon - Wed & Sats, 9.30am - 4.30pm, Thurs 9.30am - 12 noon, Fris closed, Suns, 2 - 4.30pm, last ticket 4pm.

Admission: Adult £2, Child 75p, Conc. £1.50.

ST BLANE'S CHURCH

Tel: 0131 668 8800

Kingarth, Isle of Bute

Owner: Historic Scotland

This 12th century Romanesque chapel stands on the site of a 12th century Celtic monastery.

Location: OS Ref. NS090 570. At the S end of the Isle of Bute.

Opening Times: All year: daily.

Admission: Free.

STIRLING CASTLE

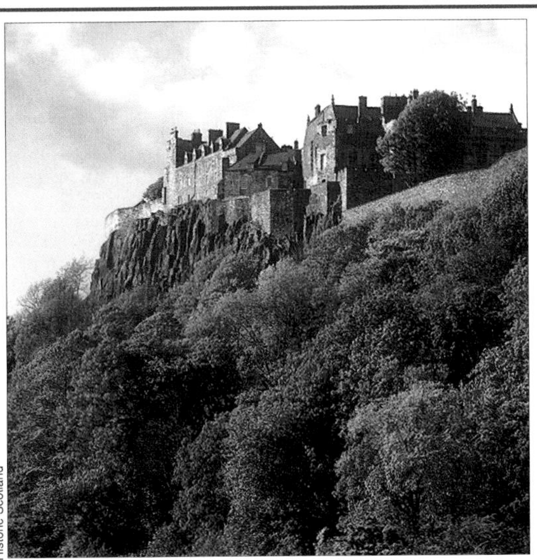

Historic Scotland

CASTLE WYND, STIRLING FK8 1EJ

Owner: *Historic Scotland* ***Contact:*** *Jon MacNeil*

Tel: 01786 450000 **Fax:** 01786 464678

Stirling Castle has played a key role in Scottish history, dominating the North–South and East–West routes through Scotland. The battles of Stirling Bridge and Bannockburn were fought in its shadow and Mary Queen of Scots lived here as a child. Marvellous Renaissance architecture and restored Great Hall.

Location: OS Ref. NS790 941. At the top of Castle Wynd in Stirling.

Opening Times: Apr - Sept: 9.30am - 6pm. Oct - Mar: 9.30am - 5pm, last ticket 45 mins before closing.

Admission: Adult £6, Child £1.50, Conc. £4.50. 10% discount for groups (10+). Free booked school visits, except July & August.

Picnic area. Joint ticket with Argyll's Lodging. Private hire. Partially suitable. WC. Licensed. Guide dogs.

Historic Scotland

Historic Scotland

TOROSAY CASTLE & GARDENS

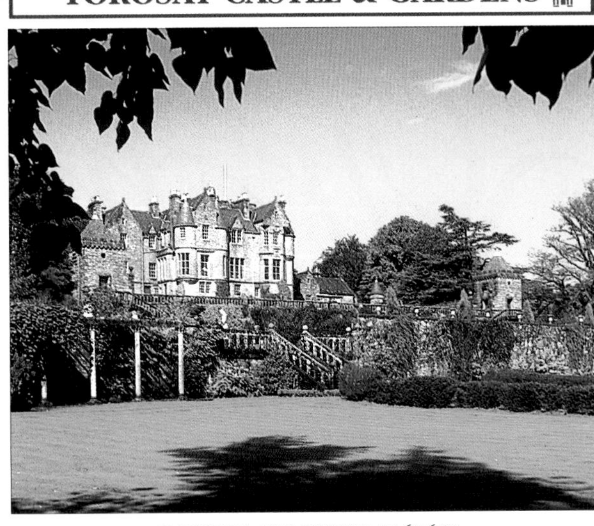

CRAIGNURE, ISLE OF MULL PA65 6AY

Owner/Contact: *Mr Chris James*

Tel: 01680 812421 **Fax:** 01680 812470 **e-mail:** torosay@aol.com

Torosay Castle and Gardens set on the magnificent Island of Mull, was completed in 1858 by the eminent architect David Bryce in the Scottish baronial style, and is surrounded by 12 acres of spectacular gardens which offer an exciting contrast between formal terraces, impressive statue walk and informal woodland, also rhododendron collection, alpine, walled, bog and oriental gardens. The house offers family history, portraits, scrapbooks and antiques in an informal and relaxed atmosphere.

Location: OS Ref. NM730 350. 1½ m SE of Craignure by A849.

Opening Times: House: Easter - mid-Oct: daily, 10.30am - 5.30pm, last admission 5pm. Gardens: All year: daily, 9am - 7pm or daylight hours in winter.

Admission: Adult £4.50, Child £1.50, Conc. £3.50. Groups: Adult £3.50, Child £1, Conc. £3.50.

Grounds suitable. WC. In grounds, on leads.

YOUNGER BOTANIC GARDEN BENMORE

Tel: 01369 706261
Fax: 01369 706369

Dunoon, Argyll PA23 8QU

Contact: The Curator

A botanical paradise. Enter the magnificent avenue of giant redwoods and follow trails through the Formal Garden and hillside woodlands with its spectacular outlook over the Holy Loch and the Eachaig Valley.

Location: OS Ref. NS150 850. 7m N of Dunoon on A815.

Opening Times: 1 Mar - 31 Oct: daily, 9.30am - 6pm.

Admission: Adult £3, Child £1, Conc. £2.50, Family £7. Group discounts available.

Historic Scotland

Stirling Castle Heads, West Highlands.

Grampian Highlands

Bennachie.

Aberdeen and Grampian Tourist Board.

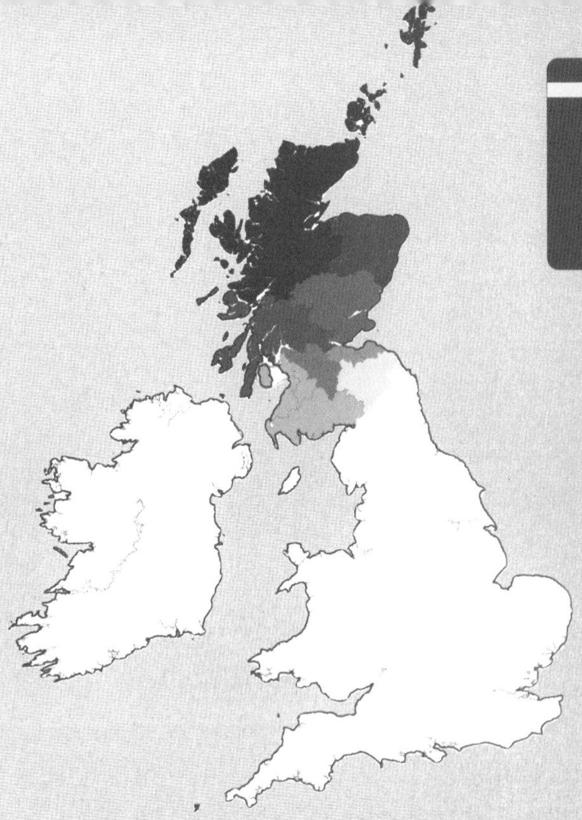

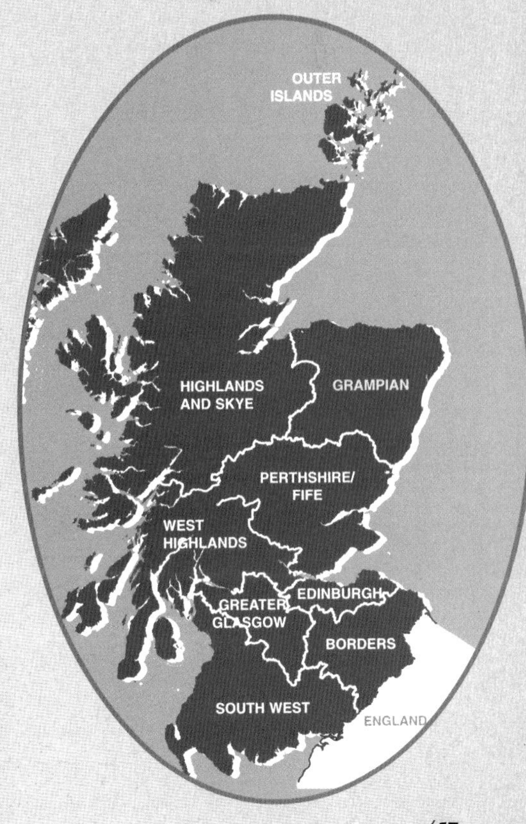

DUFF HOUSE
Banff

DUFF HOUSE is one of the most imposing and palatial houses in Scotland, with a strong classical façade and a grand staircase leading to the main entrance. It remained in the hands of the Duffs, Dukes of Fife, until 1906 when the family presented the estate to Banff and Macduff, consigning its contents to the saleroom.

Since then it has had a colourful history as an hotel, sanatorium and prisoner-of-war camp, before being taken into the care of Historic Scotland in 1956. After a comprehensive programme of structural repairs and extensive conservation and restoration, Duff House opened to the public as an outstation of the National Galleries of Scotland in April 1995.

Set in acres of parkland, by the banks of the River Deveron, Duff House is one of the glories of the North East. Designed by William Adam for William Duff (1st Earl Fife), it is dramatically sited next to the Royal Burgh of Banff and the fishing port of Macduff and is a splendid example of Scottish baroque architecture.

Drawn from the rich holdings of the National Galleries, highlights of the picture display include El Greco's *St Jerome in Penitence*, J G Cuyp's *Dutch Family Group* and Allan Ramsay's magnificent full length portrait of Elizabeth Cunyngham has been transformed by recent cleaning, revealing a wonderfully subtle range of colours.

CONTACT

The Chamberlain
Duff House
Banff
AB45 3SX

Tel: 01261 818181

Fax: 01261 818900

LOCATION

OS Ref. NT691 634

Banff. 47m NE of Aberdeen on A947.

CONFERENCE/FUNCTION	
ROOM	MAX CAPACITY
Long Gallery	100
Vestibule	65
Dining Room Salon	80
North Drawing Room	40

Audio-visual room, baby changing facilities, playground, assault course, woodland walks. Croquet and French boules equipment available for hire.

Special functions, corporate hospitality, conferences.

Access & parking, lift to gallery floor, wheelchairs. WC.

Tearoom serving light lunches. Open: 11am - 4pm.

Car and coach parking free, 4 coach spaces, coaches to book.

Schools admitted free, teachers' pack, education suite, teachers encouraged to pre-visit free.

Open all year.

OPENING TIMES

SUMMER

1 April - 31 October
Daily: 11am - 5pm.

WINTER

1 November - 31 March
Thur - Sun
11am - 4pm.

ADMISSION

Adult	£3.00
Conc	£2.00
Family	£7.00
Groups (10+)	£2.00

Free admission to shop, tearoom, grounds and woodland walks.

Free wedding photography permitted in grounds. Wedding photography permitted in vestibule for fee of £50.

ARBUTHNOTT HOUSE

Tel: 01561 361226 **Fax:** 01561 320476

Arbuthnott, Laurencekirk AB30 1PA **e-mail:** keith@arbuth.u-net.com

Owner: The Viscount of Arbuthnott **Contact:** The Master of Arbuthnott

Arbuthnott family home for 800 years with formal 17th century walled garden on unusually steep south facing slope. Well maintained grass terraces, herbaceous borders, shrubs and greenhouses.

Location: OS Ref. NO796 751. Off B967 between A90 and A92, 25m S of Aberdeen.

Opening Times: House: 23/24 & 30 Apr, 1 & 28/29 May, 9/10 Jul, 27/28 Aug. Guided tours: 2 - 5pm. Garden: All year: 9am - 5pm.

Admission: House: £3 Garden: £2.

Ground floor suitable. Obligatory.

BALFLUIG CASTLE

Tel: 0171 624 3200

Alford, Aberdeenshire AB33 8EJ

Owner/Contact: Mark Tennant of Balfluig

Small 16th century tower house in farmland, restored in 1967.

Location: OS Ref. NJ586 151. Alford, Aberdeenshire.

Opening Times: By written appointment to M I Tennant Esq, 30 Abbey Gardens, London NW8 9AT. Occasionally let by the week for holidays. Scottish Tourist Board ***.

Not suitable. 1 single, 4 double.

BALMORAL CASTLE (GROUNDS & EXHIBITIONS)

Tel: 013397 42334/42335 **Fax:** 013397 42271

Balmoral, Ballater, Aberdeenshire AB35 5TB **e-mail:** info@balmoral-castle.co.uk

Owner: Her Majesty The Queen **Contact:** Captain J R Wilson

Holiday home of the Royal Family, bought by Prince Albert in 1852. Grounds, gardens and exhibition of paintings and works of art in the ballroom.

Location: OS Ref. NO256 951. Off A93 between Ballater and Braemar. 50m W of Aberdeen.

Opening Times: 17 Apr - 31 Jul: daily, 10am - 5pm.

Admission: Adult £4, Child (5-16yrs) £1, OAP £3.

BALVENIE CASTLE

Tel: 01340 820121

Dufftown

Owner: Historic Scotland **Contact:** The Custodian

Picturesque ruins of 13th century moated stronghold originally owned by the Comyns. Visited by Edward I in 1304 and by Mary Queen of Scots in 1562. Occupied by Cumberland in 1746.

Location: OS Ref. NJ326 408. At Dufftown on A941.

Opening Times: 1 Apr - 30 Sept: daily, 9.30am - 6.30pm, last ticket 6pm.

Admission: Adult £1.20, Child 50p, Conc. 90p.

J Henderson.

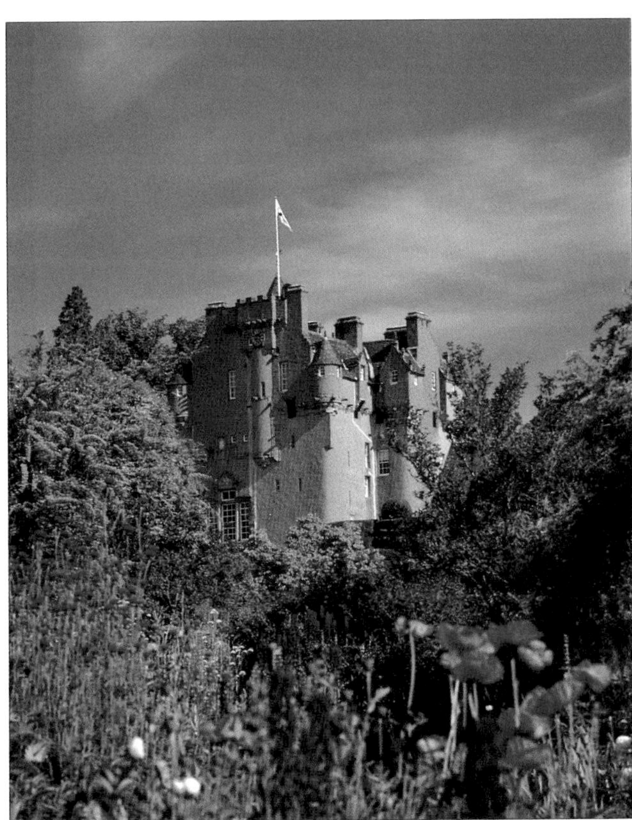

Crathes Castle, Grampian Highlands.

BRAEMAR CASTLE

BRAEMAR, ABERDEENSHIRE AB35 5XR

Owner: *Capt A A C Farquharson of Invercauld* ***Contact:*** *Bruce & Carrol McCudden*

Tel/Fax: 013397 41219 **e-mail:** invercauld@freenet.com

Braemar Castle has been the ancestral home of the Clan Farquharson for over 200 years. The 'Black' Colonel of Inverey, the enemy clan leader, attacked and burned the castle in 1689 and after being rebuilt was garrisoned by Hanoverian troops for some 60 years after the 1745 Jacobite rebellion. In some of the rooms you can see the 'graffiti' of the English soldiers. Nowadays, the castle is peaceful, and this family home attracts thousands of visitors each year to see the impressive selection of furnished rooms covering decades of the Farquharson history. A massive iron yett leads you to the pit dungeon, which was a gruesome place in years gone by.

Location: OS Ref. NO156 924. 1/2 m NE of Braemar on A93.

Opening Times: Easter Fri - end Oct: Sat - Thur (plus Fris in Jul & Aug), 10am - 6pm (last entry 5.30pm).

Admission: Adult £3, Child £1, Conc. £2.50.

Picnic area.  Not suitable. By arrangement.

In grounds on leads.

BRODIE CASTLE

FORRES, MORAY IV36 0TE

Owner: *The National Trust for Scotland* ***Contact:*** *Dr Stephanie Blackden*

Tel: 01309 641371 **Fax:** 01309 641600

This imposing Castle stands in rich Morayshire parkland. The lime harled building is a typical 'Z' plan tower house with ornate corbelled battlements and bartizans, with 17th & 19th century additions. The interior has unusual plaster ceilings, a major art collection, porcelain and fine furniture. There is a woodland walk by a large pond with access to wildlife observation hides. In springtime the grounds are carpeted with many varieties of daffodils for which Brodie Castle is rightly famous.

Location: OS Ref. NH980 577. Off A96 4 1/2 m W of Forres and 24m E of Inverness.

Opening Times: Castle & Shop: 1 Apr - 30 Sept: Mon - Sat, 11am - 5.30pm, Suns, 1.30 - 5.30pm; weekends in Oct, Sats, 11am - 5.30pm, Suns, 1.30 - 5.30pm (last admission 4.30pm). Tearoom closes at 4.30pm. Other times by appointment. Grounds: All year: daily, 9.30am - sunset.

Admission: Adult £5, Conc. £3.50. Groups: Adult £4, Child/Schools £1. Grounds only: £1 honesty box.

 In grounds, on leads. 

CANDACRAIG GARDEN & GALLERY

Tel: 01975 651226 **Fax:** 01975 651391

Candacraig Gardens, Strathdon AB36 8XT

Owner/Contact: Harry Young

1820s B listed walled display garden, art gallery and specialist plant nursery. Wedding ceremonies conducted in beautiful Victorian Gothic marriage room.

Location: OS Ref. NJ339 110. On A944 1½ m SW of Strathdon, 20m from Alford.

Opening Times: 1 May - 30 Sept: daily, 10am - 6pm.

Admission: Donation box. Pre-arranged groups: Adult £1, Child Free.

CASTLE FRASER & GARDEN

SAUCHEN, INVERURIE AB51 7LD

Owner: *The National Trust for Scotland* ***Contact:*** *Eric Wilkinson*

Tel: 01330 833463

Over 400 years of history could be told if the stout walls of Castle Fraser could speak. Begun in 1575 by the 6th Laird, Michael Fraser, the two low wings contribute to the scale and magnificence of the towers rising above them, combining to make this the largest and most elaborate of the Scottish castles built on the 'Z' plan. The stunning simplicity of the Great Hall, which occupies the entire first floor of the main block, with its striking fireplace, almost 3 metres wide, immediately creates for the visitor the atmosphere of past centuries.

Location: OS Ref. NJ723 125. Off A944, 4m N of Dunecht & 16m W of Aberdeen.

Opening Times: Castle: 21 Apr - 31 May & 1 - 30 Sept: daily, 1.30 - 5.30pm. 1 Jun - 31 Aug: daily, 11am - 5.30pm; weekends in Oct, 1.30 - 5.30pm (last admission 4.45pm). Shop & Tearoom open at 12.30pm when Castle opens at 1.30pm. Garden: All year: daily, 9.30am - 6pm. Grounds: All year: daily, 9.30am - sunset.

Admission: Castle, Garden & Grounds: Adult £5, Conc. £3.50. Groups: Adult £4. Child/School £1. Garden & grounds only: Adult £2, Conc. £1.30, Groups: Adult £1.60, Child/School £1. Car Park: All year: £1.

CORGARFF CASTLE

Tel: 013398 83635

Strathdon

Owner: Historic Scotland **Contact:** The Custodian

A 16th century tower house converted into a barracks for Hanoverian troops in 1748. Its last military use was to control the smuggling of illicit whisky between 1827 and 1831. Still complete and with star-shaped fortification.

Location: OS Ref. NJ255 086. 8m W of Strathdon on A939. 14m NW of Ballater.

Opening Times: 1 Apr - 30 Sept: daily, 9.30am - 6.30pm. 1 Oct - 31 Mar: Sats, 9.30am - 4.30pm. Suns, 2 - 4.30pm, last admission ½ hr before closing.

Admission: Adult £2.50, Child £1, Conc. £1.90.

CRAIGSTON CASTLE

Tel: 01888 551228/551640

Turriff, Aberdeenshire AB53 5PX

Owner: William Pratesi Urquhart **Contact:** Mrs Fiona Morrison

Built in 1607 to John Urquhart Tutor of Cromarty's individualistic plan. An arch and ornate sculptured balcony joins two towers, one noticeably wider than the other, to accommodate the Laird's private apartments. The largely unchanged interior, still lived in by the Urquhart family, includes carved portraits of the Scottish Kings and much else.

Location: OS Ref. NJ762 550. On B9105, 4½ m NE of Turrif.

Opening Times: 18 Jun - 3 Jul: daily (closed Mons & Tues), 10am - 4pm. 27 Aug - 11 Sept: daily (closed Mons & Tues), 10am - 4pm. Also groups throughout the year by appointment.

Admission: Adult £3.50, Child £1, OAP £2.50, Student £1.50.

Not suitable. Obligatory.  In grounds on leads. 

CRATHES CASTLE

Harvey Wood

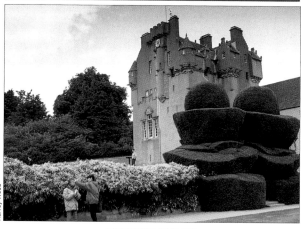

BANCHORY AB31 3QJ

Owner: *The National Trust for Scotland* ***Contact:*** *The Property Administrator*

Tel: 01330 844525 **Fax:** 01330 844797

Fairytale-like turrets, gargoyles of fantastic design, superb painted ceilings and the ancient Horn of Leys given in 1323 to Alexander Burnett by King Robert the Bruce, are just a few of the exciting features at this most picturesque castle. The building of the castle began in 1553 and took 40 years to complete. Just over 300 years later, Sir James and Lady Burnett began developing the walled garden and created not just one but eight superb gardens which now provide a riot of colour throughout the summer.

Location: OS Ref. NO733 969. On A93, 3m E of Banchory and 15m W of Aberdeen.

Opening Times: Castle, Visitor Centre, shop & restaurant: 1 Apr - 30 Sept: daily, 10.30am - 5.30pm. 1 - 31 Oct: daily, 10.30am - 4.30pm (last admission to Castle 45mins before closing). Other times by appointment only. Garden & Grounds: All year: daily, 9am - sunset. Castle admission is by timed ticket.

Admission: Combined ticket: Adult £6, Conc. £4. Group: Adult £4.80, Child/School £1. Car park: £1. Castle or Walled Garden only: Adult £4, Conc. £2.50.

Licensed. Limited.

CRUICKSHANK BOTANIC GARDEN

Tel: 01224 272704 **Fax:** 01224 272703

St Machar Drive, Aberdeen AB24 3UU

Owner: University of Aberdeen **Contact:** R B Rutherford

Extensive collection of shrubs, herbaceous and alpine plants and trees. Rock and water gardens.

Location: OS Ref. NJ938 084. In old Aberdeen.

Opening Times: All year: Mon - Fri, 9am - 4.30pm. May - Sept: Sats & Suns, 2 - 5pm.

Admission: Free.

DALLAS DHU DISTILLERY

Tel: 01309 676548

Forres

Owner: Historic Scotland **Contact:** The Custodian

A completely preserved time capsule of the distiller's craft. Wander at will through this fine old Victorian distillery then enjoy a dram. Visitor centre, shop and audio-visual theatre.

Location: OS Ref. NJ035 566. 1m S of Forres off the A940.

Opening Times: 1 Apr - 30 Sept: daily, 9.30am - 6.30pm, last ticket 6pm. 1 Oct - 31 Mar: Mon - Sat, 9.30am - 4.30pm, Suns, 2 - 4.30pm, last ticket 4pm. Closed Thurs pm and Fris in winter.

Admission: Adult £3, Child £1, Conc. £2.30.

Drum Castle, Grampian Highlands.

DELGATIE CASTLE

TURRIFF, ABERDEENSHIRE AB53 5TD

Owner: *Delgatie Castle Trust* ***Contact:*** *Mrs Joan Johnson*

Tel/Fax: 01888 563479
e-mail: jjohnson@delgatie.castle.freeserve.co.uk

11th century castle which has largely remained in the Hay family for the last 650 years and is now officially the Clan Hay centre. Mary Queen of Scots stayed here in 1562. Her bed-chamber is on view. Painted ceilings dated 1592 and 1597. Widest turnpike stair of its kind in Scotland. Lake and woodland walks.

Location: OS Ref. NJ754 506. Off A947 Aberdeen to Banff Road.

Opening Times: 2 Apr - 25 Oct: 10am - 5pm.

Admission: Adult £2.50, Child/OAP £1.50.

Ground floor suitable. WC. Home-baking. By arrangement. Guide dogs only.

DUNNOTTAR CASTLE

Tel: 01569 762173

The Lodge, Stonehaven AB39 2TL **Contact:** P McKenzie

Spectacular ruin. Impregnable fortress to the Earls Marischals of Scotland.

Location: OS Ref. NO881 839. Just off A92. 1½ m SE of Stonehaven.

Opening Times: Easter - Oct: Mon - Sat, 9am - 6pm. Suns, 2 - 5pm. Nov - Easter: Mon - Fri, 9am - sunset. Closed weekends when clocks change. Last admission: 30 mins before closing.

Admission: Adult £3, Child £1.

DUTHIE PARK & WINTER GARDENS

Tel: 01224 585310 **Fax:** 01224 210532

Polmuir Road, Aberdeen, Grampian Highlands AB11 7TH

Owner: Aberdeen City Council **Contact:** Colin Stuart

45 acres of parkland and gardens. Glasshouses.

Location: OS Ref. NJ97 044. Just N of River Dee, 1m S of city centre.

Opening Times: All year: daily from 9.30pm.

Admission: Free.

ELGIN CATHEDRAL

Tel: 01343 547171

Elgin

Owner: Historic Scotland **Contact:** The Custodian

When entire this was perhaps the most beautiful of Scottish cathedrals, known as the Lantern of the North. 13th century, much modified after almost being destroyed in 1390 by Alexander Stewart, the infamous 'Wolf of Badenoch'. The octagonal chapterhouse is the finest in Scotland. You can see the Bishop's home at Spynie Palace, 2m north of the town.

Location: OS Ref. NJ223 630. In Elgin on the A96.

Opening Times: 1 Apr - 30 Sept: daily, 9.30am - 6.30pm, last ticket 6pm. 1 Oct - 31 Mar: Mon - Sat, 9.30am - 4.30pm, Suns, 2 - 4.30pm, last ticket 4pm. Closed Thurs pm & Fris in winter.

Admission: Adult £2.50, Child £1, Conc. £1.90. Joint entry ticket with Spynie Palace: Adult £3, Child £1.20, Conc. £2.25.

FASQUE

Tel: 01561 340202 / 340569 **Fax:** 01561 340325

Fettercairn, Kincardineshire AB30 1DJ

Owner: Charles Gladstone **Contact:** The Administrator

Example of a Victorian 'upstairs - downstairs' stately home.

Location: OS Ref. NO648 755. On the B974, 1m N of Fettercairn, 4m from A90. Aberdeen/ Dundee 35m.

Opening Times: 1 May - 30 Sept: daily, 11am - 5.30pm. Groups by arrangement any time.

Admission: Adult £4, Child £1.50, Conc. £3.

DRUM CASTLE

Tel: 01330 811204

Drumoak, by Banchory AB31 3EY

Owner: The National Trust for Scotland **Contact:** The Property Manager

The combination over the years of a 13th century square tower, a very fine Jacobean mansion house and the additions of the Victorian lairds make Drum Castle unique among Scottish castles. Owned for 653 years by one family, the Irvines, every stone and every room is steeped in history. Superb furniture and paintings provide a visual feast for visitors. In the 16th century chapel, the stained glass windows, the font copied from the Saxon one in Winchester Cathedral and the Augsburg silver Madonna, all add immense interest for visitors.

Location: OS Ref. NJ796 004. Off A93, 3m W of Peterculter and 10m W of Aberdeen.

Opening Times: Castle: 21 Apr - 31 May & 1 - 30 Sept: daily, 1.30 - 5.30pm. 1 Jun - 31 Aug: daily, 11am - 5.30pm; weekends in Oct: 1.30 - 5.30pm (last admission 4.45pm). Garden: same dates, daily, 10am - 6pm. Grounds: All year, daily, 9.30am - sunset.

Admission: Castle, Garden & Grounds: Adult £5, Conc. £3.50. Groups: Adult £4, Child/ School £1. Garden & Grounds: Adult £2, Conc. £1.30. Groups: Adult £1.60, Child/Conc. £1. Car park £1.

DRUMMUIR CASTLE

Tel: 01542 810332 **Fax:** 01542 810302

Drummuir, by Keith, Banffshire AB55 5JE

Owner: The Gordon-Duff Family **Contact:** Liz Robson

Castellated Victorian Gothic-style castle built in 1847 by Admiral Duff. 60ft high lantern tower with fine plasterwork. Family portraits, interesting artefacts and other paintings. Organic walled garden and plant sales.

Location: OS Ref. NO881 839. Midway between Keith (5m) and Dufftown, off the B9014.

Opening Times: 26/27 Aug, 2/3 & 6 - 27 Sept: Tours at 2pm & 3pm.

Admission: Adult £2, Child £1.50. Pre-arranged groups: Adult £2, Child £1.50.

  Obligatory. P In grounds on leads.

DUFF HOUSE

See page 458 for full page entry.

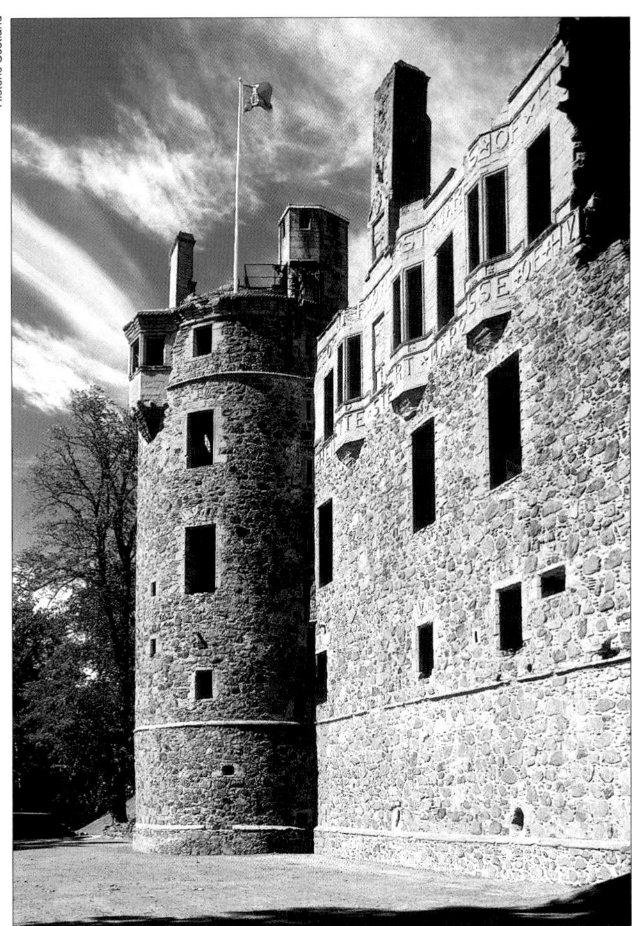

Historic Scotland

Huntly Castle, Grampian Highlands.

FYVIE CASTLE

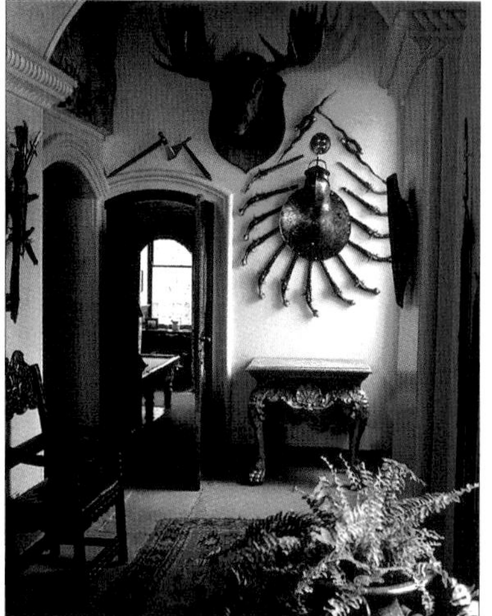

TURRIFF, ABERDEENSHIRE AB53 8JS

Owner: *The National Trust for Scotland* ***Contact:*** *The Property Manager*

Tel: 01651 891266 **Fax:** 01651 891107

The south front of this magnificent building employs a plethora of crow-stepped gables, turrets, sculpted dormers and finials in the form of musicians, to create a marvellous façade. The five towers of the castle bear witness to the five families who have owned it. Fyvie Castle boasts the finest wheel stair in Scotland and there is a superb collection of arms and armour and paintings, including works by Batoni, Raeburn, Romney, Gainsborough, Opie and Hoppner.

Location: OS Ref. NJ763 393. Off A947, 8m SE of Turriff, and 25m N of Aberdeen.

Opening Times: Castle: 21 Apr - 31 May and 1 - 30 Sept: daily, 1.30 - 5.30pm; 1 Jun - 31 Aug: daily, 11am - 5.30pm; weekends in Oct: 1.30 - 5.30pm (last admission 4.45pm). Tearoom & Shop: open at 12.30pm when Castle opens at 1.30pm. Grounds: All year, daily, 9.30am - sunset.

Admission: Adult £6, Conc. £4. Groups: Adult £4.80, Child/School £1.

HADDO HOUSE

TARVES, ELLON, ABERDEENSHIRE AB41 0ER

Owner: *The National Trust for Scotland* ***Contact:*** *Craig Ferguson*

Tel: 01651 851440 **Fax:** 01651 851888

This appealing house was designed by William Adam in 1731 for William, 2nd Earl of Aberdeen. Much of the splendid interior is 'Adam Revival' carried out about 1880 for John, 7th Earl and 1st Marquess of Aberdeen and his Countess, Ishbel. It is arguably the most elegant house in the north east, a classic English-style stately home transplanted to Scotland. Features of the house include the Italianate sweeping twin staircases at the front of the house, the atmospheric library and the subtlety of the great curving corridor.

Location: OS Ref. NJ868 348. Off B999, 4m N of Pitmedden, 10m NW of Ellon.

Opening Times: House: 21 Apr - 30 Sept: daily, 1.30 - 5.30pm; weekends in Oct: 1.30 - 5.30pm (last admission 4.45pm). Generally guided tours Mon - Sat. Shop & Tearoom: Weekends in Mar, Apr & Oct: 11am - 5.30pm; 1 May - 30 Sept: daily, 11am - 5.30pm. Garden & Country Park: All year: daily, 9.30am - sunset. Some rooms may be closed due to family occupation.

Admission: Adult £5, Conc. £3.50. Groups: Adult £4, Child/School £1.

HUNTLY CASTLE

Tel: 01466 793191

Huntly

Owner: Historic Scotland **Contact:** The Custodian

Known also as Strathbogie Castle, this glorious ruin stands in a beautiful setting on the banks of the River Deveron. Famed for its fine heraldic sculpture and inscribed stone friezes.

Location: OS Ref. NJ532 407. In Huntly on the A96. N side of the town.

Opening Times: 1 Apr - 30 Sept: daily, 9.30am - 6.30pm, last ticket 6pm. 1 Oct - 31 Mar: Mon - Sat, 9.30am - 4.30pm, Suns, 2 - 4.30pm, last ticket 4pm. Closed Thur pm & Fris in winter.

Admission: Adult £2.50, Child £1, Conc £1.90.

KILDRUMMY CASTLE

Tel: 01975 571331

Alford, Aberdeenshire

Owner: Historic Scotland **Contact:** The Custodian

Though ruined, the best example in Scotland of a 13th century castle with a curtain wall, four round towers, hall and chapel of that date. The seat of the Earls of Mar, it was dismantled after the first Jacobite rising in 1715.

Location: OS Ref. NJ455 164. 10m W of Alford on the A97. 16m SSW of Huntley.

Opening Times: 1 Apr - 30 Sept: daily, 9.30am - 6.30pm, last ticket 6pm.

Admission: Adult £2, Child 75p, Conc. £1.50.

KILDRUMMY CASTLE GARDEN

Tel: 01975 571203 / 571277

Kildrummy, Aberdeenshire **Contact:** Alastair J Laing

Ancient quarry, shrub and alpine gardens renowned for their interest and variety. Water gardens below ruined castle.

Location: OS Ref. NJ455 164. On A97 off A944 10m SW of Alford. 16m SSW of Huntley.

Opening Times: Apr - Oct: daily, 10am - 5pm.

Admission: Adult £2, Child free.

LEITH HALL

Tel: 01464 831216 **Fax:** 01464 831594

Huntly, Aberdeenshire AB54 4NQ

Owner: The National Trust for Scotland **Contact:** The Property Manager

This mansion house is built around a courtyard and was the home of the Leith family for almost 400 years. With an enviable family record of military service over the centuries, the house contains a unique collection of military memorabilia displayed in an exhibition *'For Crown and Country'*. The graciously furnished rooms are a delight to wander through and present a fine impression of the lifestyle of the Leith family.

Location: OS Ref. NJ541 298. B9002, 1m W of Kennethmont, 7m S of Huntley.

Opening Times: House & tearoom: 21 Apr - 30 Sept: daily, 1.30 - 5.30pm; weekends in Oct: 1.30 - 5.30pm (last admission 4.45pm). Garden & Grounds: All year, daily, 9.30am - sunset.

Admission: Adult £6, Conc. £4. Groups: Adult £4.80, Child/School £1. Gardens & grounds: Adult £2, Conc. £1.30. Groups: Adult £1.60, Child/School £1.

Partially suitable. WC.

MONYMUSK WALLED GARDEN

Tel: 01467 651543

Home Farm, Monymusk, Aberdeen AB51 7HL

Owner/Contact: Mrs E Whyte

Mainly herbaceous plants in walled garden setting.

Location: OS Ref. NJ692 152. N side of B993, $^1/_2$ m E of Monymusk village.

Opening Times: Nov - Mar: Mons, Weds, Fris & Sats, 10am - 3pm, Suns, 12 noon - 3pm. Apr - Oct: Mon - Sat, 10am - 5pm, Suns, 12 noon - 5pm.

Admission: Donations welcome.

Leith Hall, Grampian Highlands.

PITMEDDEN GARDEN 

Doug Westland

ELLON, ABERDEENSHIRE AB41 0PD

Owner: *The National Trust for Scotland* ***Contact:*** *The Property Manager*

Tel: 01651 842352 **Fax:** 01651 843188

The centrepiece of this property is the Great Garden which was originally laid out in 1675 by Sir Alexander Seton, 1st Baronet of Pitmedden. The elaborate designs, inspired by the garden at the Palace of Holyroodhouse in Edinburgh, have been painstakingly recreated for the enjoyment of visitors. The 100 acre estate contains the very fine Museum of Farming Life, which presents a vivid picture of the lives and times of bygone days when the horse was the power in front of the plough and farm machinery was less complicated than it is today.

Location: OS Ref. NJ885 280. On A920 1m W of Pitmedden village and 14m N of Aberdeen.

Opening Times: Garden, Visitor Centre, museum, tearoom, grounds and other facilities: 1 May - 30 Sept: daily, 10am - 5.30pm, last admission 5pm.

Admission: Adult: £4, Conc. £3. Groups: Adult £3.20, Child/School £1.

PROVOST SKENE'S HOUSE

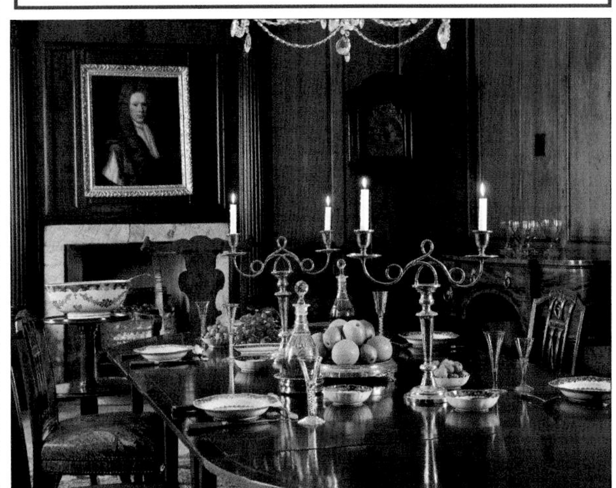

45 GUEST ROW, OFF BROAD STREET, ABERDEEN AB10 1AS

Owner: *Aberdeen City Council* ***Contact:*** *Christine Rew*

Tel: 01224 641086 **Fax:** 01224 632133

Built in the 16th century, Provost Skene's House is one of Aberdeen's few remaining examples of early Burgh architecture. Splendid room settings include a suite of Georgian rooms, an Edwardian nursery, magnificent 17th century plaster ceilings and wood panelling. Costume gallery features changing displays of historic dress. The painted gallery houses the most important cycle of religious painting in North East Scotland.

Location: OS Ref. NJ943 064. Aberdeen city centre, off Broad Street.

Opening Times: All year: Mon - Sat, 10am - 5pm, Suns, 1 - 4pm (closed 25/26/31 Dec & 1/2 Jan).

Admission: Adult £2.50, Conc. £1.50, Family £6, Child (under 5yrs) Free. Groups (10+): 10% discount.

No photography in house. Small functions. Not suitable. By arrangement. Nearby. Guide dogs only. 

PLUSCARDEN ABBEY

Tel: 01343 890257 **Fax:** 01343 890258

Nr Elgin, Moray IV30 8UA **Contact:** Father Giles

Valliscaulian, founded 1230.

Location: OS Ref. NJ142 576. On a minor road 6m SW of Elgin. Follow B9010 for first mile.

Opening Times: All year: 4.45am - 8.30pm. Shop open 8.30am - 5pm.

Admission: Free.

Brodie Castle, Grampian Highlands.

ST MACHAR'S CATHEDRAL TRANSEPTS

Tel: 0131 668 8800

Old Aberdeen

Owner: Historic Scotland

The nave and towers of the Cathedral remain in use as a church, and the ruined transepts are in care. In the south transept is the fine altar tomb of Bishop Dunbar (1514 - 32).

Location: OS Ref. NJ939 088. In old Aberdeen. 1/2 m N of King's College.

Admission: Free.

SPYNIE PALACE

Tel: 01343 546358

Elgin

Owner: Historic Scotland **Contact:** The Custodian

Spynie Palace was the residence of the Bishops of Moray from the 14th century to 1686. The site is dominated by the massive tower built by Bishop David Stewart (1461-77) and affords spectacular views across Spynie Loch.

Location: OS Ref. NJ231 659. 2m N of Elgin off the A941.

Opening Times: 1 Apr - 30 Sept: daily, 9.30am - 6.30pm. 1 Oct - 31 Mar: Sats, 9.30am - 4.30pm, Suns, 2 - 4.30pm. Last ticket 30 mins before closing.

Admission: Adult £1.80, Child 75p, Conc. £1.30. Joint entry ticket with Elgin Cathedral: Adult £3, Child £1.20, Conc. £2.25.

TOLQUHON CASTLE

Tel: 01651 851286

Aberdeenshire

Owner: Historic Scotland **Contact:** The Custodian

Tolquhon was built for the Forbes family. The early 15th century tower was enlarged between 1584 and 1589 with a large mansion around the courtyard. Noted for its highly ornamented gatehouse and pleasance.

Location: OS Ref. NJ874 286. 15m N of Aberdeen on the A920. 6m N of Ellon.

Opening Times: 1 Apr - 30 Sept: daily, 9.30am - 6.30pm. 1 Oct - 31 Mar: Sats, 9.30am - 4.30pm, Suns, 2 - 4.30pm. Last ticket 30 mins before closing.

Admission: Adult £1.80, Child 75p, Conc. £1.30.

The Highlands & Skye

Loch Maree, Wester Ross.

The Highlands of Scotland Tourist Board.

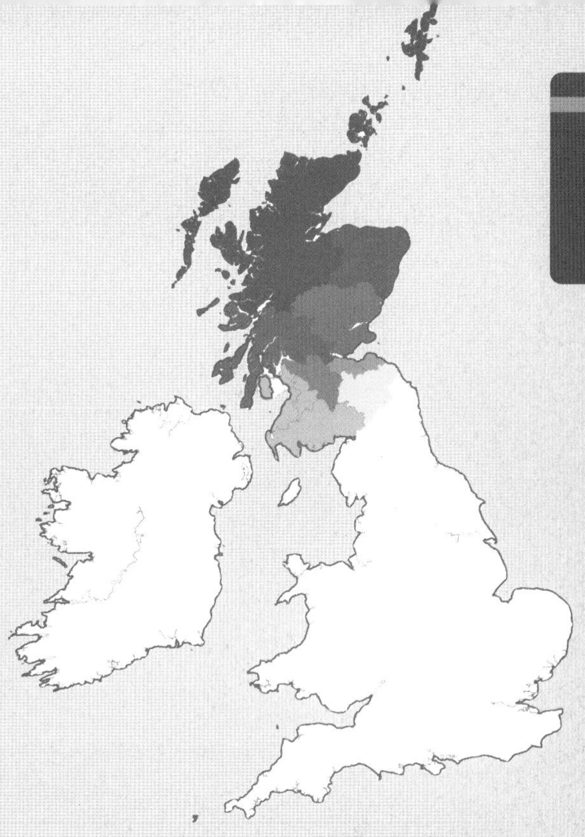

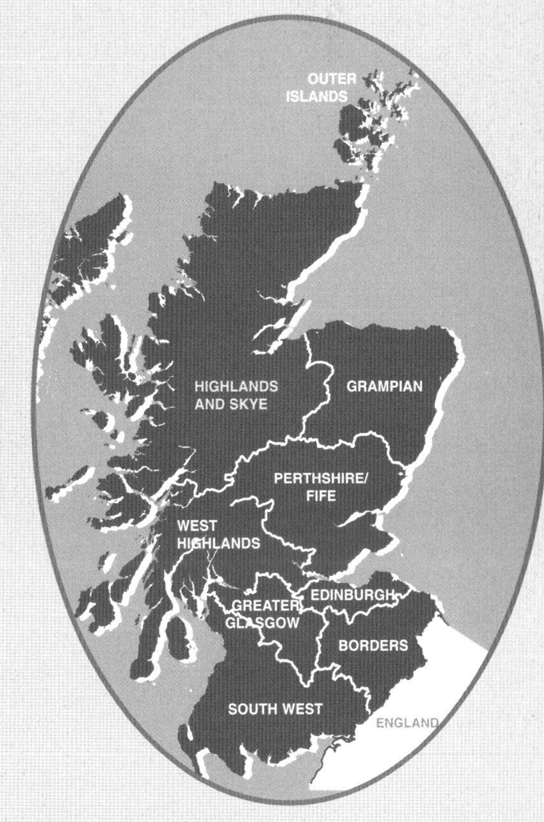

CAWDOR CASTLE
Nairn

This splendid romantic castle dating from the late 14th century was built as a private fortress by the Thanes of Cawdor, and remains the home of the Cawdor family to this day. The ancient medieval tower was built around the legendary holly tree.

Although the house has evolved over 600 years, later additions mainly of the 17th century were all built in the Scottish vernacular style with slated roofs over walls and crow-stepped gables of mellow local stone. This style gives Cawdor a strong sense of unity, and the massive, severe exterior belies an intimate interior that gives the place a surprisingly personal, friendly atmosphere.

Good furniture, fine portraits and pictures, interesting objects and outstanding tapestries are arranged to please the family rather than to echo fashion or impress. Memories of Shakespeare's *Macbeth* give Cawdor an elusive, evocative quality that delights visitors.

GARDENS

The flower garden also has a family feel to it, where plants are chosen out of affection rather than affectation. This is a lovely spot between spring and late summer. The walled garden has been restored with a holly maze, paradise garden, knot garden and thistle garden. The wild garden beside its stream leads into beautiful trails through a spectacular mature mixed woodland, through which paths are helpfully marked and colour-coded.

9 hole golf course, putting green, golf clubs for hire, Conferences, whisky tasting, musical entertainments, specialised garden visits. No photography, video taping or tripods inside.

Gift, book and wool shops.

Lunches, sherry or champagne receptions.

Visitors may alight at the entrance. WC. Only ground floor accessible.

Licensed buttery, May-Oct, groups should book.

250 cars and 25 coaches. Two weeks' notice for group catering, coach drivers/couriers free.

£2.50 per child. Room notes, quiz and answer sheet can be provided. Ranger service and nature trails.

Guide dogs only.

Owner: The Dowager Countess Cawdor

CONTACT

The Secretary
Cawdor Castle
Nairn
Scotland
IV12 5RD

Tel: 01667 404615

Fax: 01667 404674

e-mail: cawdor.castle@btinternet.com

LOCATION

OS Ref. NH850 500

From Edinburgh A9, 3½ hrs, Inverness 20 mins, Nairn 10 mins. Main road: A9, 14m.

Rail: Nairn Station 5m.

Bus: Inverness to Nairn bus route 200 yds.

Taxi: Nairn Taxis 01667 455342.

Air: Inverness Airport 5m.

CONFERENCE/FUNCTION

ROOM	SIZE	MAX CAPACITY
Cawdor Hall		40

OPENING TIMES

SUMMER

1 May - 8 October
Daily: 10am - 5.30pm.

Last admission 5pm.

WINTER

9 October - 30 April
Closed.

ADMISSION

SUMMER

House & Garden

Adult	£5.60
Child (5-15yrs)	£3.00
OAP/Student	£4.60
Family (2+5)	£16.50

Groups (20+)

Adult	£5.10
Child (5-15yrs)	£2.50
OAP/Student	£4.60

Garden only

Per person	£2.90

SPECIAL EVENTS

- **JUN 3 - 4:**
Special Gardens Weekend: Guided tours of gardens and Cawdor Big Wood.

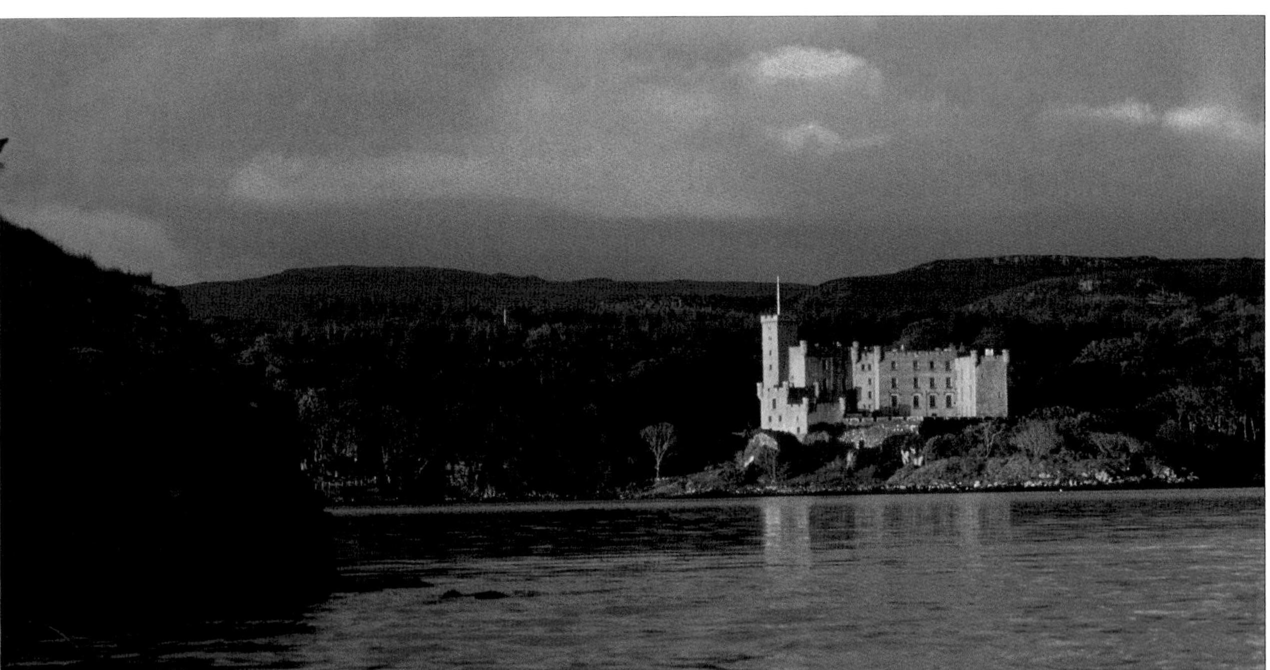

Owner: John Macleod of Macleod

CONTACT

The Administrator
Dunvegan Castle
Isle of Skye
Scotland
IV55 8WF

Tel: 01470 521206

Fax: 01470 521205

Seal Tel: 01470 521500

e-mail: info@dunvegancastle.com

LOCATION

OS Ref. NG250 480

1m N of village. NW corner of Skye.

From Inverness A82 to Invermoriston, A887 to Kyle of Lochalsh 82m. From Fort William A82 to Invergarry, A87 to Kyle of Lochalsh 76m.

Kyle of Lochalsh to Dunvegan 45m via Skye Bridge (toll).

Ferry: To the Isle of Skye, 'roll-on, roll-off', 30 minute crossing.

Rail: Inverness to Kyle of Lochalsh 3 - 4 trains per day - 45m.

Bus: Portree 25m, Kyle of Lochalsh 45m.

DUNVEGAN CASTLE
Isle of Skye

DUNVEGAN is unique. It is the only Great House in the Western Isles of Scotland to have retained its family and its roof. It is the oldest home in the whole of Scotland continuously inhabited by the same family – the Chiefs of the Clan Macleod. A Castle placed on a rock by the sea - the curtain wall is dated before 1200 AD – its superb location recalls the Norse Empire of the Vikings, the ancestors of the Chiefs.

Dunvegan's continuing importance as a custodian of the Clan spirit is epitomised by the famous Fairy Flag, whose origins are shrouded in mystery but whose ability to protect both Chief and Clan is unquestioned. To enter Dunvegan is to arrive at a place whose history combines with legend to make a living reality.

GARDENS

The gardens and grounds extend over some ten acres of woodland walks, peaceful formal lawns and a water garden dominated by two spectacular natural waterfalls. The temperate climate aids in producing a fine show of rhododendrons and azaleas, the chief glory of the garden in spring. One is always aware of the proximity of the sea and many garden walks finish at the Castle Jetty, from where traditional boats make regular trips to view the delightful Seal Colony.

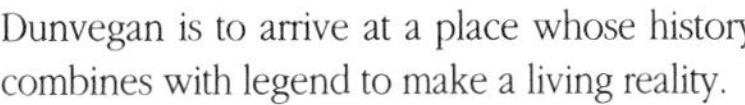

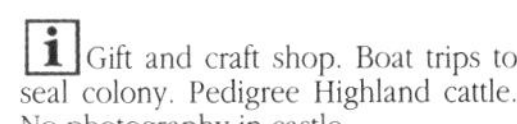

Gift and craft shop. Boat trips to seal colony. Pedigree Highland cattle. No photography in castle.

Visitors may alight at entrance. WC.

Licensed restaurant, (cap. 70) special rates for groups, menus upon request. Tel: 01470 521310. Open late peak season for evening meals.

By appointment in English or Gaelic at no extra charge. If requested owner may meet groups, tour time 45mins.

120 cars and 10 coaches. Do not attempt to take passengers to Castle Jetty (long walk). If possible please book. Seal boat trip dependent upon weather.

Welcome by arrangement. Guide available on request.

In grounds only, on lead.

4 self-catering units, 3 of which sleep 6 and 1 of which sleeps 7.

OPENING TIMES

SUMMER

20 March - 31 October
Daily: 10am - 5.30pm.
Last admission 5pm.

WINTER

November - March
Daily: 11am - 4pm.
Last admission 3.30pm.

Closed Christmas Day, Boxing Day, New Year's Day and 2 January.

ADMISSION

SUMMER

Castle & Gardens

Adult	£5.50
Child* (5 -15yrs)	£3.00
Conc.	£4.80
Family (2+3)	£15.00
Groups (10+)	£5.00

Gardens only

Adult	£3.80
Child* (5 -15yrs)	£2.00

Seal Boats

Adult	£4.00
Child* (5 -15yrs)	£2.50

*Child under 5yrs Free.

WINTER

11am - 4pm.
No boat trips.

ARMADALE CASTLE GARDENS & MUSEUM OF THE ISLES

Armadale, Isle of Skye IV45 8RS **Tel:** 01471 844305 **Fax:** 01471 844275

Owner: Clan Donald Lands Trust **Contact:** Flora MacLean - Visitor Services Manager

Part of Armadale Castle houses a visitor centre and the 'Museum of the Isles' telling the story of the Highlands and Islands.

Location: OS Ref. NG630 020. 1m N of the Mallaig - Armadale ferry terminal.

Opening Times: Apr - Oct: daily, 9.30am - 5.30pm.

Admission: Adult £3.85, Child/Conc./Groups £2.60.

BALLINDALLOCH CASTLE

GRANTOWN-ON-SPEY, BANFFSHIRE AB37 9AX

Owner: *Mr & Mrs Russell* ***Contact:*** *Mrs Clare Russell*

Tel: 01807 500206 **Fax:** 01807 500210

Ballindalloch is a much loved family home and one of the few castles lived in continuously by its original owners, the Macpherson-Grants, since 1546. Filled with family memorabilia and a magnificent collection of 17th century Spanish paintings, it is home to the famous breed of Aberdeen Angus cattle. Beautiful rock and rose garden, river walks.

Location: OS Ref. NJ178 366. 14m NE of Grantown-on-Spey on A95, 22m S of Elgin on A95.

Opening Times: Good Fri - 30 Sept: 10.30am - 5pm.

Admission: House & Grounds: Adult £5.20, Child (5-16) £2.50, Conc. £4.50, Family (2+3) £13. Grounds only: Adult £2, Child £1. Groups: (20+) Adult £4.50, Child £2.

Ground floor & grounds. WC. Audio-visual.

In grounds, on leads in dog walking area.

CAWDOR CASTLE

See page 466 for full page entry.

CROMARTY COURTHOUSE

Tel: 01381 600418 **Fax:** 01381 600408

Church Street, Cromarty IV11 8XA **Contact:** David Alston

18th century town courthouse, visitor centre and museum.

Location: OS Ref. NH790 680. 25m N of Inverness.

Opening Times: Apr - Oct: 10am - 5pm. Nov, Dec & Mar: 12 noon - 4pm.

Admission: Adult £3, Conc. £2.

CULLODEN

Tel: 01463 790607 **Fax:** 01463 794294

Culloden Moor, Inverness IV1 2ED

Owner: The National Trust for Scotland **Contact:** Ross Mackenzie

No name in Scottish history evokes more emotion than that of Culloden, the bleak moor which in 1746 saw the hopes of the young Prince Charles Edward Stuart crushed, and the end of the Jacobite Rising, the 'Forty-Five'. The Prince's forces, greatly outnumbered by those of the brutal Duke of Cumberland, nevertheless went into battle with a courage which has passed into legend.

Location: OS Ref. NH745 450. On B9006, 5m E of Inverness.

Opening Times: Site: All year: daily. Visitor Centre & Shop: 1 Feb - 31 Mar & 1 Nov - 31 Dec (except 24 - 26 Dec): daily, 10am - 4pm. 1 Apr - 31 Oct: daily, 9am - 6pm (last admission to exhibition area 30 mins before closing). Restaurant & audio-visual show: closes 30 mins earlier.

Admission: Visitor Centre & Old Leanach Cottage: Adult £3.50, Conc. £2.50. Groups: Adult £2.80, Child/School £1.

Visitor centre. Audio-visual. In dog walking area only.

DOCHFOUR GARDENS

Tel: 01463 861218 **Fax:** 01463 861366

Dochgarroch, Inverness IV3 6JY

Owner: Dochfour Estate **Contact:** Miss J Taylor

Victorian terraced garden near Inverness with panoramic views over Loch Dochfour. Magnificent specimen trees, naturalised daffodils, rhododendrons, water garden, yew topiary.

Location: OS Ref. NH620 610. 6m SW of Inverness on A82 to Fort William.

Opening Times: Gardens: Apr - Sept, Mon - Fri, 10am - 5pm. House not open.

Admission: Garden walk - £1.50.

THE DOUNE OF ROTHIEMURCHUS

Tel: 01479 812345

By Aviemore, PH22 1QH

Owner: J P Grant of Rothiemurchus **Contact:** Rothiemurchus Visitor Centre

The family home of the Grants of Rothiemurchus was nearly lost as a ruin and has been under an ambitious repair programme since 1975. This exciting project may be visited on selected Mondays throughout the year. Book with the Visitor Centre for a longer 2hr 'Highland Lady' tour which explores the haunts of Elizabeth Grant of Rothiemurchus, born 1797, author of *Memoirs of a Highland Lady*, who vividly described the Doune and its surroundings from the memories of her childhood.

Location: OS Ref. NH900 100. 2m S of Aviemore on E bank of Spey river.

Opening Times: House: selected Mons. Grounds: May - Aug: Mon, 10am - 12.30pm & 2 - 4.30pm, also 1st Mon in the month during winter.

Admission: House £5. Grounds only: £1. Booking essential.

Visitor Centre. Obligatory. Limited. In grounds, on leads.

DUNROBIN CASTLE

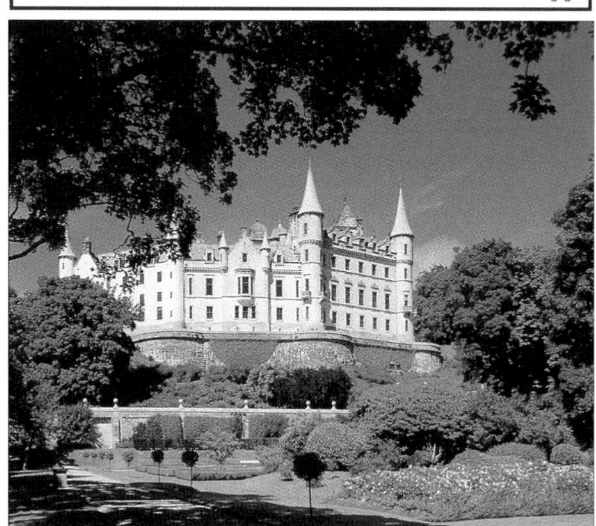

GOLSPIE, SUTHERLAND KW10 6SF

Owner: *The Sutherland Trust* ***Contact:*** *Keith Jones, Curator*

Tel: 01408 633177 **Fax:** 01408 634081

Dates from the 13th century with additions in the 17th, 18th and 19th centuries. Wonderful furniture, paintings, library, ceremonial robes and memorabilia. Victorian museum in grounds with a fascinating collection including Pictish stones. Set in fine woodlands overlooking the sea. Magnificent formal gardens, one of few remaining French/Scottish formal parterres. Falconry display.

Location: OS Ref. NC850 010. 50m N of Inverness on A9. 1m NE of Golspie.

Opening Times: 1 Apr - 31 May & 1 - 15 Oct: Mon - Sat, 10.30am - 4.30pm. Suns, 12 noon - 4.30pm. 1 Jun - 30 Sept: Mon - Sat, 10.30am - 5.30pm. Suns, 12 noon - 5.30pm (Jul & Aug: Suns, opens at 10.30am).

Admission: Adult £5.50, Child/Conc. £4. Groups: Adult £5, Child/Conc £4. Family (2+2) £16.

By arrangement. 

DUNVEGAN CASTLE

See page 467 for full page entry.

EILEAN DONAN CASTLE

Tel: 01599 555202

Dornie, Kyle of Lochalsh, Wester IV40 8DX **Contact:** The Administrator

Location: OS Ref. NG880 260. On A87 8m E of Skye Bridge.

Opening Times: Daily, 10am - 5.30pm

Admission: Contact for details.

FORT GEORGE

Historic Scotland

ARDERSIER BY INVERNESS IV1 2TD

Owner: *Historic Scotland* ***Contact:*** *Tommy Simpson*

Tel: 01667 462777 **Fax:** 01667 462698

Built following the Battle of Culloden to subdue the Highlands, Fort George never saw a shot fired in anger. One of the most outstanding artillery fortifications in Europe with reconstructed barrack room displays. The Queen's Own Highlanders' Museum.

Location: OS Ref. NH762 567. 11m NE of Inverness off the A96 by Ardersier.

Opening Times: Apr - Sept: daily, 9.30am - 6.30pm. Oct - Mar: Mon - Sat, 9.30am - 4.30pm; Suns, 2 - 4.30pm. Last ticket sold 45 mins before closing.

Admission: Summer: Adult £4, Child £1.50, Conc. £3. Winter: Adult £3.50, Child £1.20, Conc. £2.60. 10% discount for groups (10+).

Picnic tables. Private evening hire. Wheelchairs available. WCs. In summer. Free if pre-booked. In grounds, on leads.

GLENFINNAN

Tel/Fax: 01397 722250

Inverness-shire PH37 4LT

Owner: The National Trust for Scotland **Contact:** Mrs Lillias Grant

The monument, situated on the scenic road to the Isles, is set amid superb Highland scenery at the head of Loch Shiel. It was erected in 1815 in tribute to the clansmen who fought and died in the Jacobite cause. Prince Charles Edward Stuart's standard was raised near here in 1745. Despite its inspired beginnings, the campaign came to a grim conclusion on the Culloden battlefield in 1746.

Location: OS Ref. NM906 805. On A830, 18m W of Fort William, Lochaber.

Opening Times: Site: All year: daily. Visitor Centre, shop & snack bar: 1 Apr - 18 May and 1 Sept - 31 Oct: daily, 10am - 5pm. 19 May - 31 Aug: daily, 9.30am - 6pm. Glenfinnan Games: 19 August.

Admission: Adult £1.50, Conc. £1 (includes parking).

Visitor centre. Grounds suitable. WC. In grounds, on leads.

HUGH MILLER'S COTTAGE

Tel: 01381 600245

Cromarty IV11 8XA

Owner: The National Trust for Scotland **Contact:** Ms Frieda Gostwick

Furnished thatched cottage of c1698, birthplace of eminent geologist and writer Hugh Miller. Exhibition and video.

Location: OS Ref. NH790 680. Via Kessock Bridge & A832, in Cromarty, 22m NE of Inverness.

Opening Times: 1 May - 30 Sept: Mon - Sat, 11am - 1pm & 2 - 5pm. Suns, 2 - 5pm.

Admission: Adult £2.50, Conc. £1.70. Groups: Adult £2, Child/School £1.

Not suitable. Public parking at shore. Guide dogs only.

INVEREWE GARDEN

POOLEWE, ROSS & CROMARTY IV22 2LQ

Owner: *The National Trust for Scotland* ***Contact:*** *Keith Gordon*

Tel: 01445 781200 **Fax:** 01445 781497

Where in Scotland will you see the tallest Australian gum trees in Britain, sweetly scented Chinese rhododendrons, exotic trees from Chile and Blue Nile lilies from South Africa, all growing on a latitude more northerly than Moscow? The answer is Inverewe. Although you are in a remote corner of Wester Ross, you are also in a sheltered garden, blessed by the North Atlantic Drift. In a spectacular lochside setting among pinewoods, Osgood Mackenzie's Victorian dreams have produced a glorious 50 acre mecca for garden lovers.

Location: OS Ref. NG860 820. On A832, by Poolewe, 6m NE of Gairloch, Highland.

Opening Times: Garden: 15 Mar - 31 Oct: daily, 9.30am - 9pm. 1 Nov - 14 Mar: daily, 9.30am - 5pm. Visitor Centre & shop: 15 Mar - 31 Oct: daily, 9.30am - 5.30pm. Restaurant: 10am - 5pm. Guided garden walks: 15 Apr - 15 Sept: Mon - Fri at 1.30pm.

Admission: Adult £5, Conc. £3.50. Groups: Adult £4, Child/School £1.

Visitor centre. Grounds suitable. WC. Licensed. No shade for dogs. Guide dogs only.

URQUHART CASTLE

Tel: 01456 450551

Drumnadrochit, Loch Ness

Owner: Historic Scotland **Contact:** The Custodian

The remains of one of the largest castles in Scotland dominate a rocky promontory on Loch Ness. Most of the existing buildings date from the 16th century. A popular viewpoint for monster spotting.

Location: OS Ref. NH531 286. On Loch Ness, 1$^1/_2$ m S of Drumnadrochit on A82.

Opening Times: 1 Apr - 30 Sept: daily, 9.30am - 6.30pm, last ticket 5.45pm. 1 Oct - 31 Mar: daily, 9.30am - 4.30pm, last ticket 3.45pm.

Admission: Adult £3.80, Child £1.20, Conc. £2.80.

Fort George, Highlands & Skye.

Outer Islands

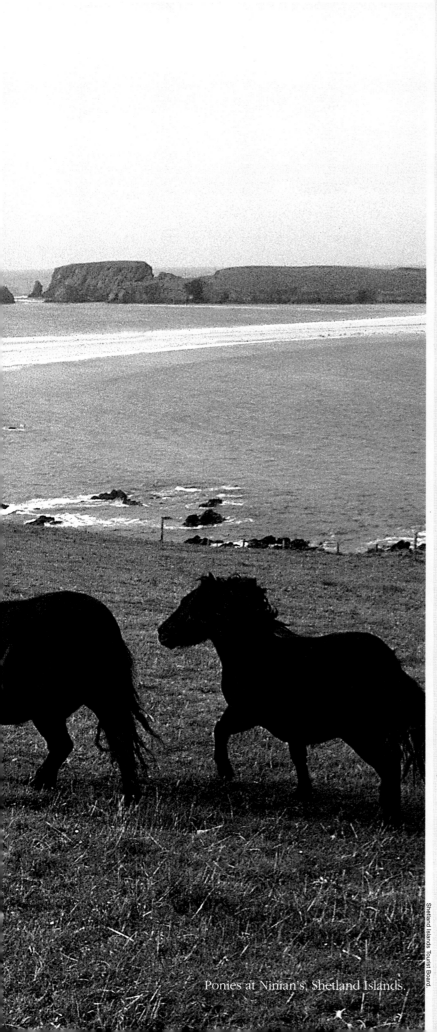

Ponies at Ninian's, Shetland Islands.

Shetland Islands Tourist Board.

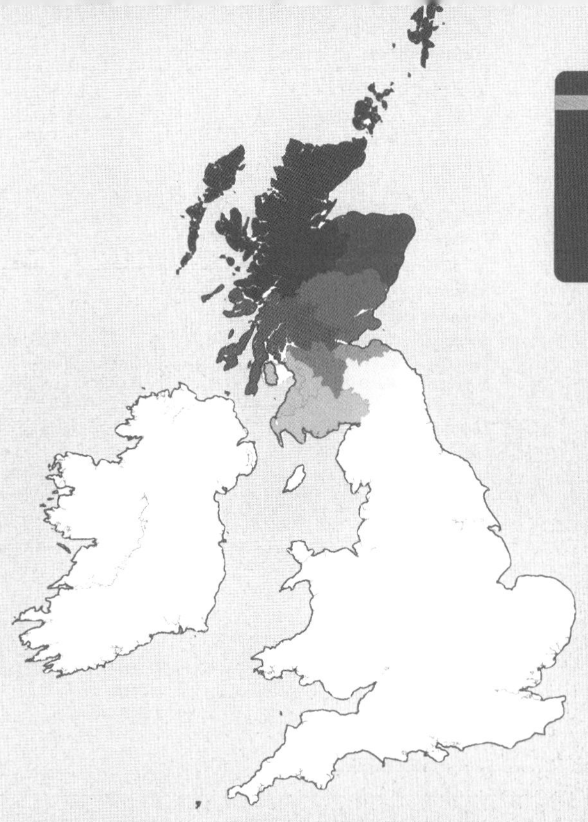

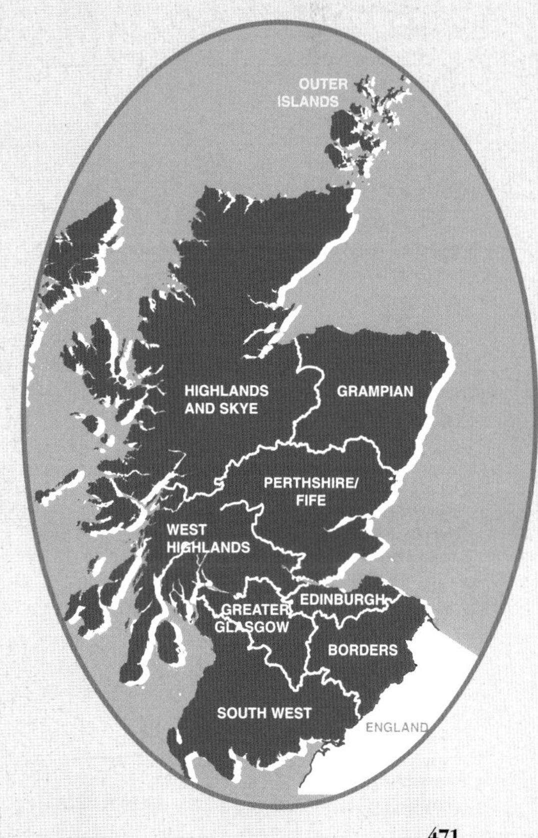

BALFOUR CASTLE

Tel: 01856 711282 **Fax:** 01856 711283

Shapinsay, Orkney Islands KW17 2DY **e-mail:** balfourcastle@btinternet.com

Owner/Contact: Mrs Lidderdale

Built in 1848.

Location: OS Ref. HY475 164 on Shapinsay Island, 3 1/2 m NNE of Kirkwall.

Opening Times: Mid-May – mid-Sept: Weds, 2.30 - 5.30pm.

Admission: £14 including boat fare, guided tour of castle and gardens and afternoon tea.

BISHOP'S & EARL'S PALACES

Tel: 01856 875461

Kirkwall, Orkney

Owner: Historic Scotland **Contact:** The Custodian

The Bishop's Palace is a 12th century hall-house with a round tower built by Bishop Reid in 1541-48. The adjacent Earl's Palace built in 1607 has been described as the most mature and accomplished piece of Renaissance architecture left in Scotland.

Location: Bishop's Palace: OS Ref. HY447 108. Earl's Palace: OS Ref. HY448 108. In Kirkwall on A960.

Opening Times: 1 Apr - 30 Sept: daily, 9.30am - 6.30pm, last ticket 6pm.

Admission: Adult £2, Child 75p, Conc. £1.50. Joint entry ticket available for all the Orkney monuments: Adult £10, Child £3, Conc. £7.50.

BLACK HOUSE

Tel: 01851 710395

Arnol, Isle of Lewis

Owner: Historic Scotland **Contact:** The Custodian

A traditional Lewis thatched house, fully furnished, complete with attached barn, byre and stock-yard. A peat fire burns in the open hearth. New visitor centre open and restored 1920s croft house.

Location: OS Ref. NB320 500. In Arnol village, 11m NW of Stornoway on A858.

Opening Times: 1 Apr - 30 Sept: Mon - Sat, 9.30am - 6.30pm, last ticket 6pm. 1 Oct - 31 Mar: Mon - Thur & Sat, 9.30am - 4.30pm, last ticket 4pm.

Admission: Adult £2.50, Child £1, Conc. £1.90.

BROCH OF GURNESS

Tel: 01831 579478

Aikerness, Orkney

Owner: Historic Scotland **Contact:** The Custodian

Protected by three lines of ditch and rampart, the base of the broch is surrounded by a warren of Iron Age buildings.

Location: OS Ref. HY383 268. At Aikerness, about 14m NW of Kirkwall on A966.

Opening Times: 1 Apr - 30 Sept: daily, 9.30am - 6.30pm, last ticket 6pm.

Admission: Adult £2.50, Child £1, Conc. £1.90. Joint entry ticket available for all Orkney monuments: Adult £10, Child £3, Conc. £7.50.

CALANAIS STANDING STONES

Tel: 01851 621422

Calanais, Stornoway, Lewis, Outer Islands

Owner: Historic Scotland

A cross-shaped setting of standing stones, unique in Scotland.

Location: OS Ref. NB213 330. 12m W of Stornaway off A859.

Opening Times: Visitor Centre: All year: daily, 10am - 7pm (4pm in winter). Closed Suns.

Admission: Adult £1.50, Child 50p, Conc. £1. Access to stones is Free.

CARRICK HOUSE

Tel: 01857 622260

Carrick, Eday, Orkney KW17 2AB

Owner: Mr & Mrs Joy **Contact:** Mrs Rosemary Joy

17th century house of 3 storeys, built by John Stewart, Lord Kinclaven Earl of Carrick younger brother of Patrick, 2nd Earl of Orkney in 1633.

Location: OS Ref. NT227 773. N of island of Eday on minor roads W of B9063 just W of the shore of Calf Sound. Regular ferry service.

Opening Times: Mid-Jun - mid-Sept: Sun afternoons. Other times by arrangement.

Admission: Adult £2, Child £1.

JARLSHOF PREHISTORIC & NORSE SETTLEMENT

Tel: 01950 460112

Shetland

Owner: Historic Scotland **Contact:** The Custodian

Over 3 acres of remains spanning 3,000 years from the Stone Age. Oval-shaped Bronze Age houses, Iron Age broch and wheel houses. Viking long houses, medieval farmstead and 16th century laird's house.

Location: OS Ref. HY401 096. At Sumburgh Head, 22m S of Lerwick on the A970.

Opening Times: 1 Apr - 30 Sept: daily, 9.30am - 6.30pm. Last adm. 1/2 hr before closing.

Admission: Adult £2.50, Child £1, Conc. £1.90.

KIESSIMUL CASTLE

Tel: 01871 810449

Castlebray, Isle of Barra, Western Isles HF9 5XD

Owner/Contact: Ian Allen MacNeil of Barra

Home of the Chief of the MacNeil clan. Dating from the 13th century, the castle has been restored to its 17th century condition.

Location: OS Ref. NL670 990. Just S of Castlebay on Barra, by boat S of A888 in Castlebay.

Opening Times: Apr - Sept: Mon Wed & Sat, 2 - 5pm wind and tide permitting. Please telephone to check.

Admission: Boat and entrance to castle: Adult £3, Child 50p.

MAES HOWE

Tel: 01856 761606

Orkney

Owner: Historic Scotland **Contact:** The Custodian

This world-famous tomb was built in Neolithic times, before 2700 BC. The large mound covers a stone-built passage and a burial chamber with cells in the walls. Runic inscriptions tell of how it was plundered of its treasures by Vikings.

Location: OS Ref. NY318 128. 9m W of Kirkwall on the A965.

Opening Times: 1 Apr - 30 Sept: daily, 9.30am - 6.30pm. 1 Oct - 31 Mar: daily, 9.30am - 5pm except Thurs pm, Fris and Suns am.

Admission: Adult £2.50, Child £1, Conc. £1.90. Joint entry ticket available for all Orkney monuments: Adult £10, Child £3, Conc. £7.50. Admission, shop and refreshments at nearby Tormiston Mill.

RING OF BRODGAR STONE CIRCLE & HENGE

Tel: 0131 668 8800

Stromness, Orkney

Owner: Historic Scotland **Contact:** The Custodian

A magnificent circle of upright stones with an enclosing ditch spanned by causeways. Of late Neolithic date.

Location: OS Ref. HY294 134. 5m NE of Stromness.

Opening Times: Any reasonable time.

Admission: Free.

ST MAGNUS CATHEDRAL

Tel: 01856 874894

Broad Street, Kirkwall, Orkney

Owner: Orkney Islands Council **Contact:** Mr J Rousay

Location: OS Ref. HY449 108. Centre of Kirkwall.

Opening Times: 1 Apr - end Sept: Mon - Sat, 9am - 6pm, Suns, 2 - 6pm. 1 Oct - end Mar: Mon - Sat, 9am - 1pm & 2 - 5pm.

Admission: Free.

SKARA BRAE & SKAILL HOUSE

Historic Scotland

SANDWICK, ORKNEY

Owner: *Historic Scotland/Major M R S Macrae* ***Contact:*** *The Steward*

Tel: 01856 841815

Skara Brae is one of the best preserved groups of Stone Age houses in Western Europe. Built before the Pyramids, the houses contain stone furniture, hearths and drains. New visitor centre and replica house with joint admission with Skaill House – 17th century home of the Laird who excavated Skara Brae.

Location: OS6 HY231 188. 19m NW of Kirkwall on the B9056.

Opening Times: Apr - Sept: daily, 9.30am - 6.30pm. Oct - Mar: Mon - Sat, 9.30am - 4.30pm, Suns, 2 - 4.30pm.

Admission: Apr - Sept: Adult £4.50, Child £1.30, Conc. £3.30. Oct - Mar: Adult £3.50, Child £1.20, Conc. £2.60. 10% discount for groups (10+). Joint ticket with other Orkney sites available.

Visitor centre. Partially suitable. WCs. Licensed. Free school visits when booked. Guide dogs only.

TANKERNESS HOUSE

Tel: 01856 873191 **Fax:** 01856 874615

Broad Street, Kirkwall, Orkney

Owner: Orkney Islands Council **Contact:** Bryce S Wilson

A fine vernacular 16th century town house contains Museum of Orkney.

Location: OS Ref. HY446 109. In Kirkwall opposite W end of cathedral.

Opening Times: All year: Mon - Sat, 10.30am - 12.30pm and 1.30 - 5pm, Suns, 2 - 5pm. Apr - Sept: 10.30am - 5pm.

Admission: Free.

WALES

Wales Tourist Board.

The Elan Valley Criag-Goch Reservoir

Wales

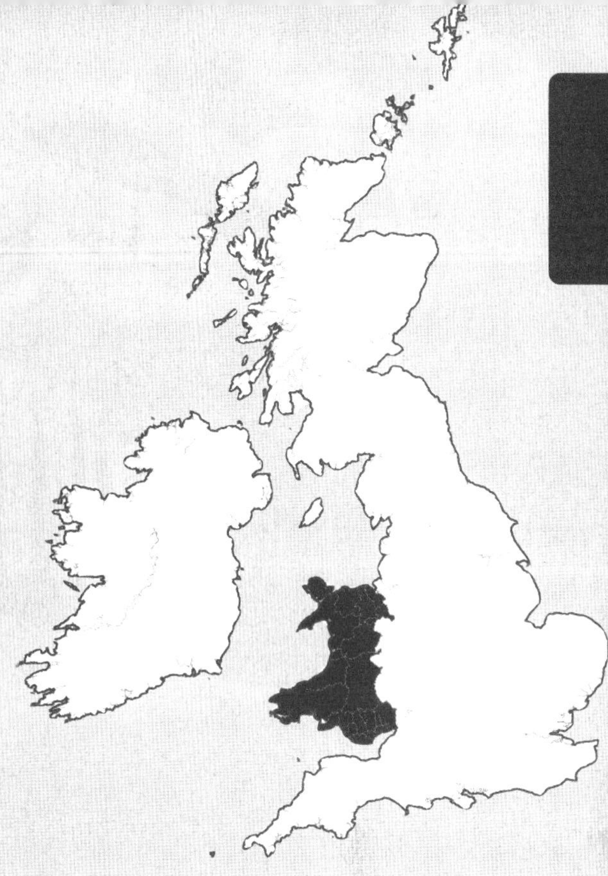

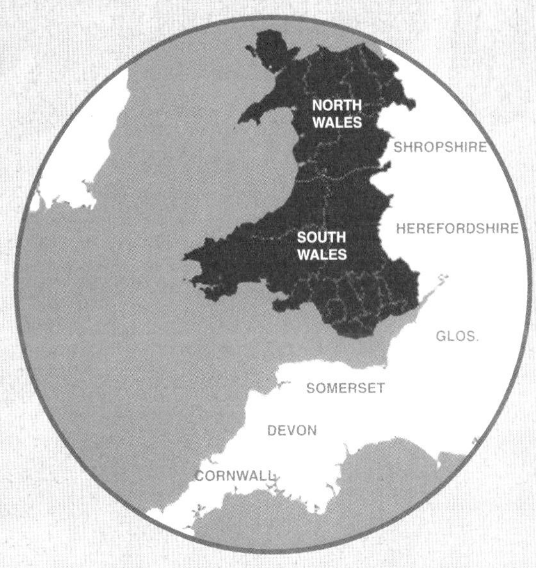

Conway, North Wales.

Featuring…

Plas Mawr

In a town sprinkled with a wealth of magnificent medieval historic houses, Plas Mawr, or the 'Great Hall' as its name unashamedly announces, is one of the grandest and most ambitious houses ever raised in a Welsh historic town.

Nestling between narrow streets in the heart of Conwy, this tall, lime-rendered building constructed between 1576-85 reflects the wealth and influence of its owner, the merchant Robert Wynn, and stands today as an architectural gem – the finest surviving town house of the Elizabethan era to be found anywhere in Britain.

Placed into the care of the State by Lord Mostyn in 1993, Plas Mawr has undergone a complete conservation programme. This highly sympathetic restoration was undertaken by Cadw: Welsh Historic Monuments, on behalf of the Secretary of State for Wales. The result provides a unique opportunity for the visitor to understand the workings of a great 16th century household.

Every gentleman, like Robert Wynn, needed servants to run his household and his estates. Wandering around Plas Mawr, you can glimpse into the lives of the 20 servants that would have worked in the house. The gatehouse has a suite of rooms, which would have been used by Wynn's steward, to run his master's finances and rural estates. The kitchen on the ground floor would have been run by a cook, perhaps two to three undercooks, and a boy to turn the spits on the rack.

Guests to the house would have been protected from this daily hustle and bustle and instead led by liveried servants to the first floor of the house. Here they reached the Great Chamber, which acted as the ceremonial pivot of a late 16th and 17th century household. In this magnificent receiving room Wynn would have entertained his equals or betters. Here the decorated plasterwork, which is one of the glories of Plas Mawr, has the garter and royal arms given prominence over the fireplace with the Wynn arms relegated to the ceiling and frieze. By contrast, in the hall and private bedchambers, the Wynn arms are displayed on the overmantels, and the royal badges and other emblems restricted to subservient positions.

Everything about Plas Mawr, the plaster detailing with full coats of arms and other emblems, the specially made items of furniture and silver plate that would have adorned the rooms, is a celebration of Robert Wynn and his new found status in society. It reflects the importance of the new entrepreneurial merchant and professional classes in Elizabethan society.

Visiting Plas Mawr today, it is hard to believe that over the last three hundred years, it was let out for a multiplicity of uses. Rooms were subdivided, stairs inserted, and new layers of paint added, yet no major part of the building was lost. Cadw have enabled this wonderful building to regain its integrity so that it may be appreciated and enjoyed by future generations.

For full details of this property see page 483.

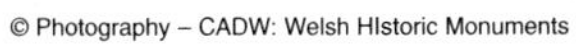

ABERCONWY HOUSE

Tel: 01492 592246

Castle Street, Conwy LL32 8AY

Owner: The National Trust **Contact:** The Custodian

Dating from the 14th century, this is the only medieval merchant's house in Conwy to have survived the turbulent history of this walled town for nearly six centuries. Furnished rooms and an audio-visual presentation show daily life from different periods in its history.

Location: OS Ref. SH781 775. At junction of Castle Street and High Street.

Opening Times: 29 Mar - 30 Oct: daily except Tues, 11am - 5pm. Last adm. 30mins before close.

Admission: Adult £2, Child £1, Family (2+2) £5. Pre-booked groups (15+) £1.80. National Trust members Free.

No indoor photography. Open all year. By arrangement. In town car parks only. Guide dogs only.

BEAUMARIS CASTLE

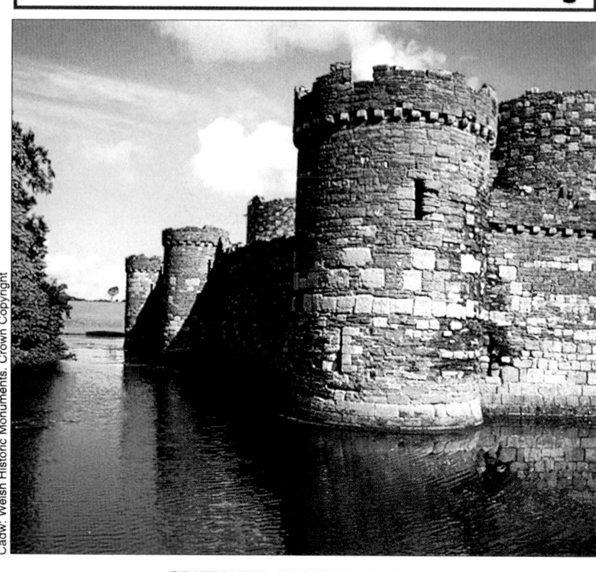

Cadw: Welsh Historic Monuments. Crown Copyright

BEAUMARIS, ANGLESEY LL58 8AP

***Owner:** In the care of Cadw* ***Contact:** The Administrator*

Tel: 01248 810361

The most technically perfect medieval castle in Britain, standing midway between Caernarfon and Conwy, commanding the old ferry crossing to Anglesey. A World Heritage Listed Site.

Location: OS Ref. SH608 762. 5m NE of Menai Bridge (A5) by A545. 7m from Bangor.

Opening Times: 29 Mar - 21 May: 9.30am - 5pm. 22 May - 3 Oct: 9.30am - 6pm. 4 - 31 Oct: 9.30am - 5pm. 1 Nov - 28 Mar: Mon - Sat, 9.30am - 4pm, Suns, 11am - 4pm. Closed 24 - 26 Dec & 1 Jan.

Admission: Adult £2.20, Child/Conc. £1.70, Family £6.10.

   Guide dogs only.

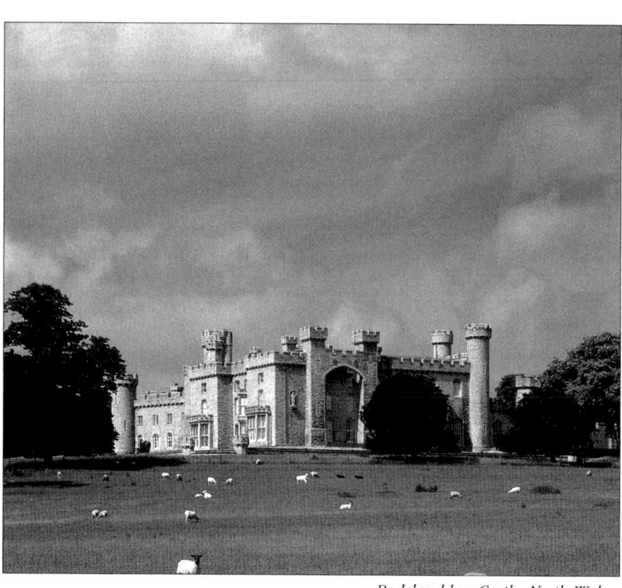

Bodelwyddan Castle, North Wales.

BODELWYDDAN CASTLE

BODELWYDDAN, DENBIGHSHIRE LL18 5YA

***Owner:** Denbighshire County Council* ***Contact:** Piers Norbury*

Tel: 01745 584060 **Fax:** 01745 584563

This magnificently restored Victorian mansion set in rolling parkland, displays extensive collections from the National Portrait Gallery, furniture from the Victoria and Albert Museum and John Gibson sculpture from the Royal Academy. There are exhibitions of Victorian Amusements and Inventions and a programme of temporary exhibitions takes place throughout the year.

Location: OS Ref. SH999 749. Follow signs off A55 expressway. 2m W of St Asaph, opposite Marble Church.

Opening Times: Apr - Oct: daily except Fri, 11am - 5pm. Nov - Mar: daily except Mon & Fri, 11am - 4pm. Last admission on site 1hr before closing. Note: minimum opening times - please telephone for further details.

Admission: Adult £4.30, Child (under 16yrs) £2.50 (under 5yrs Free),Conc. £3.80, Family (2+2) £10. Group: Adult £3.70, Child (under 16yrs) £2.15, Conc. £3.25. Season Ticket: Adult £12.60, Child/Student/Disabled £8.40, OAP/UB40 £10.50, Family (2+2) £27.30.

Partially suitable. WCs. By arrangement.  Guide dogs only.

BODNANT GARDEN

TAL-Y-CAFN, COLWYN BAY LL28 5RE

***Owner:** The National Trust* ***Contact:** General Manager & Head Gardener*

Tel: 01492 650460 **Fax:** 01492 650448

Bodnant Garden is one of the finest gardens in the country not only for its magnificent collections of rhododendrons, camellias and magnolias but also for its idyllic setting above the River Conwy with extensive views of the Snowdonia range. Visit in early Spring and be rewarded by the sight of masses of golden daffodils and other spring bulbs, as well as the beautiful blooms of the magnolias, camellias and flowering cherries. The spectacular rhododendrons and azaleas will delight from mid-April until late May, whilst the famous original Laburnum Arch is an overwhelming mass of yellow bloom from mid-May to mid-June. The herbaceous borders, roses, hydrangeas, clematis and water lilies flower from the middle of June until September. This 32-ha garden has many interesting features including the Lily Terrace, pergola, Canal Terrace, Pin Mill and the Dell Garden.

Location: OS Ref. SH801 723. 8 miles S of Llandudno and Colwyn Bay, off A470. Signposted from A55.

Opening Times: 18 Mar - 31 Oct: daily, 10am - 5pm.

Admission: Adult £5, Child £2.50. Groups (20+) £4.50. Refreshment Pavilion: Daily from 11am (Entrance fee does not have to be paid for the Pavilion).

 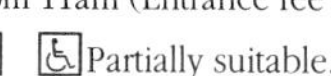   

BODRHYDDAN 

RHUDDLAN, CLWYD LL18 5SB

Owner/Contact: *Colonel The Lord Langford OBE DL*

Tel: 01745 590414

The home of Lord Langford and his family, Bodrhyddan is basically a 17th century house with 19th century additions by the famous architect, William Eden Nesfield, although traces of an earlier building exist. The house has been in the hands of the same family since it was built over 500 years ago. There are notable pieces of armour, pictures, period furniture, a 3,000 year old mummy, a formal parterre, a woodland garden and attractive picnic areas. Bodrhyddan is a Grade I listing, making it one of few in Wales to remain in private hands.

Location: OS Ref. SJ045 788. On the A5151 midway between Dyserth and Rhuddlan, 4m SE of Rhyl.

Opening Times: Jun - Sept inclusive: Tues & Thurs, 2 - 5.30pm.

Admission: House & Gardens: Adult £4, Child £2. Gardens only: Adult £2, Child £1.

Receptions by special arrangement.  Partially suitable. Obligatory.

BRYN BRAS CASTLE

Tel/Fax: 01286 870210

Llanrug, Caernarfon, Gwynedd LL55 4RE

Owner: Mr & Mrs N E Gray-Parry **Contact:** Marita Gray-Parry

Built in the Neo-Romanesque style in 1830, on an earlier structure and probably designed by Thomas Hopper. Elegantly romantic family home with fine stained-glass, panelling, interesting ceilings and richly carved furniture. The castle stands in the beautiful Snowdonian range and the extensive gardens include herbaceous borders, walled knot garden, woodland walks, stream and pools, 1/4 m mountain walk with superb views of Snowdon, Anglesey and the sea. Picnic area.

Location: OS Ref. SH543 625. 1/2 m off A4086 at Llanrug, 4 1/2 m E of Caernarfon.

Opening Times: Only for groups by prior appointment.

Admission: By arrangement. No young children please.

 Self-catering apartments for twos within castle. 

CAERNARFON CASTLE

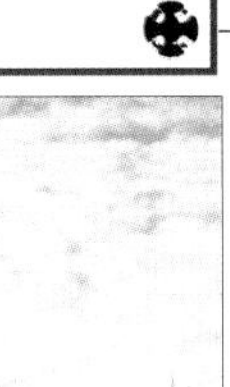

CASTLE DITCH, CAERNARFON LL55 2AY

Owner: *In the care of Cadw* ***Contact:*** *The Administrator*

Tel: 01286 677617

The most famous, and perhaps the most impressive castle in Wales. Taking nearly 50 years to build, it proved the costliest of Edward I's castles. A World Heritage Listed Site.

Location: OS Ref. SH477 626. In Caernarfon, just W of town centre.

Opening Times: 29 Mar - 21 May: 9.30am - 5pm. 22 May - 3 Oct: 9.30am - 6pm. 4 - 31 Oct: 9.30am - 5pm. 1 Nov - 28 Mar: Mon - Sat, 9.30am - 4pm, Suns, 11am - 4pm.

Admission: Adult £4.20, Child/Conc. £3.20, Family £11.60.

P Guide dogs only. 

Bodelwyddan Castle, The Ladies' Drawing Room, North Wales.

North Wales

CHIRK CASTLE 

National Trust Photographic Library: Matthew Antrobus

CHIRK LL14 5AF

Owner: *The National Trust* ***Contact:*** *The Property Manager*

Tel: 01691 777701 **Fax:** 01691 774706

700 year old Chirk Castle, a magnificent marcher fortress, commands fine views over the surrounding countryside. Rectangular with a massive drum tower at each corner, the castle has beautiful formal gardens with clipped yews, roses and a variety of flowering shrubs. The dramatic dungeon is a reminder of the castle's turbulent history, whilst later occupants have left elegant state rooms, furniture, tapestries and portraits. The castle was sold for five thousand pounds to Sir Thomas Myddelton in 1595, and his descendants continue to live in part of the castle today.

Location: OS Ref. SJ269 380. 8m S of Wrexham off A483, 2m from Chirk village.

Opening Times: 29 Mar - 29 Oct: daily (except Mons & Tues) & BH Mons. Castle: Mar - Sept: 12 noon - 5pm. Oct: 12 noon - 4pm. Last admission 1/2 hr before close. Garden: Mar - Sept: 11am - 6pm. Oct: 11am - 5pm. Last admission 1hr before closing.

Admission: Adult £5, Child £2.50, Family (2+3) £12.50. Pre-booked groups (15+) £4. Garden only: Adults £2.80, Child £1.40.

No indoor photography. Licensed. By arrangement. Guide dogs only.

CONWY CASTLE

Cadw: Welsh Historic Monuments. Crown Copyright

CONWY LL32 8AY

Owner: *In the care of Cadw* ***Contact:*** *The Administrator*

Tel: 01492 592358

Taken together the castle and town walls are the most impressive of the fortresses built by Edward I, and remain the finest and most impressive in Britain. A World Heritage Listed Site.

Location: OS Ref. SH783 774. Conwy by A55 or B5106.

Opening Times: 29 Mar - 21 May: 9.30am - 5pm. 22 May - 3 Oct: 9.30am - 6pm. 4 - 31 Oct: 9.30am - 5pm. 1 - Nov - 28 Mar: Mon - Sat, 9.30am - 4pm, Suns, 11am - 4pm. Closed 24 - 26 Dec & 1 Jan.

Admission: Adult £3.50, Child/OAP £2.50, Family £9.50.

By arrangement. Guide dogs only. 

COCHWILLAN OLD HALL

Tel: 01248 364608

Talybont, Bangor, Gwynedd LL57 3AZ

Owner: R C H Douglas Pennant **Contact:** Mrs P Scanlan

A fine example of medieval architecture with the present house dating from about 1450. It was probably built by William Gryffydd who fought for Henry VII at Bosworth. Once owned in the 17th century by John Williams who became Archbishop of York. The house was restored from a barn in 1971.

Location: OS Ref. SH606 695. 3$^1/_2$ m SE of Bangor. 1m SE of Talybont off A55.

Opening Times: By appointment.

Admission: Please telephone for details.

Criccieth Castle, North Wales.

CRICCIETH CASTLE

Tel: 01766 522227

Castle Street, Criccieth, Gwynedd LL52 0DP

Contact: The Administrator

Overlooking Cardigan Bay, Criccieth Castle is the most striking of the fortresses built by the native Welsh Princes. Its inner defences dominated by a powerful twin-towered gatehouse.

Location: OS Ref. SH500 378. A497 to Criccieth from Porthmadog or Pwllheli.

Opening Times: 29 Mar - 26 Sept: 10am - 6pm.

Admission: Adult £2.20, Child/Conc. £1.70, Family £6.10.

Guide dogs only.

CYMER ABBEY

Tel: 01341 422854

Dolgellau, Gwynedd

Owner: In the care of Cadw **Contact:** The Administrator

The modest little Abbey at Cymer, with its simple church, stands amid remote and beautiful countryside. Situated near the head of the Mawddach estuary.

Location: OS Ref. SH722 195. 2m NW of Dolgellau on A470.

Opening Times: 6 Apr - 31 Oct: 9.30am - 6pm. 1 Nov - 5 Apr: 9.30am - 4pm. Closed 24 - 26 Dec & 1 Jan.

Admission: Adult £1.20, Conc. 70p, Family £3.10.

Limited.

DENBIGH CASTLE

Tel: 01745 813385

Denbigh, Clwyd

Owner: In the care of Cadw **Contact:** The Administrator

Crowning the summit of a prominent outcrop dominating the Vale of Clwyd, the principal feature of this spectacular site is the great gatehouse dating back to the 11th century. Some of the walls can still be walked by visitors.

Location: OS Ref. SJ052 658. Denbigh via A525 or B5382.

Opening Times: Early Apr - late Oct: Mon - Fri, 10am - 5.30pm. Sats & Suns, 9.30am - 5.30pm. Winter: open site.

Admission: Castle: Adult £2, Child/Conc. £1.50, Family £5.50.

DOLWYDDELAN CASTLE

Tel: 01690 750366

Blaenau Ffestiniog, Gwynedd

Owner: In the care of Cadw **Contact:** The Administrator

Standing proudly on a ridge, this stern building remains remarkably intact and visitors cannot fail to be impressed with the great solitary square tower, built by Llewelyn the Great in the early 13th century.

Location: OS Ref. SH722 522. A470(T) Blaenau Ffestiniog to Betws-y-Coed, 1m W of Dolwyddelan.

Opening Times: Early Apr - late Oct: daily, 9.30am - 6.30pm. Late Oct - late Mar: Mon - Sat, 9.30am - 4pm, Suns, 11am - 4pm. Closed 25 Dec.

Admission: Adult £2, Child/Conc. £1.50, Family £5.50.

ERDDIG

National Trust Photographic Library: Rupert Truman

Nr WREXHAM LL13 0YT

Owner: The National Trust *Contact: The Property Manager*

Tel: 01978 355314 **Fax:** 01978 313333 **Info Line:** 01938 557019

One of the most fascinating houses in Britain, not least because of the unusually close relationship that existed between the family of the house and their servants. The beautiful and evocative range of outbuildings includes kitchen, laundry, bakehouse, stables, sawmill, smithy and joiner's shop, while the stunning state rooms display most of their original 18th & 19th century furniture and furnishings, including some exquisite Chinese wallpaper. The large walled garden has been restored to its 18th century format design with Victorian parterre and yew walk, and also contains the National Ivy Collection. There is an extensive park with woodland walks.

Location: OS Ref. SJ326 482. 2m S of Wrexham.

Opening Times: 25 Mar - 1 Nov: daily except Thurs & Fris, open Good Fri. House: 12 noon - 5pm. Garden: 11am - 6pm (10am - 6pm during Jul & Aug). From 1 Oct: House: 12 noon - 4pm, Garden: 11am - 5pm. Last admission 1 hr before closing.

Admission: All-inclusive ticket: Adult £6, Child £3, Family (2+3) £15. Pre-booked group (15+) £5. Below stairs (including outbuildings & Garden): Adult £4, Child £2, Family (2+3) £10, Pre-booked groups (15+) £3.20. NT members Free.

Partially suitable. WCs. Licensed. AV presentation.  Guide dogs only.

GWYDIR CASTLE

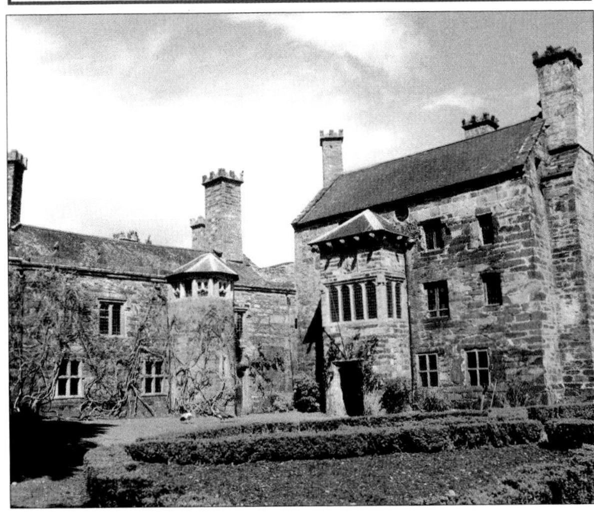

LLANRWST, GWYNEDD

Owner/Contact: Mr & Mrs Welford

Tel/Fax: 01492 641687

Gwydir Castle is situated in the beautiful Conwy Valley and is set within a Grade I listed, 10 acre garden. Built by the illustrious Wynn family c1500, Gwydir is a fine example of a Tudor courtyard house, incorporating re-used medieval material from the dissolved Abbey of Maenan. Further additions date from c1600 and c1826. The important 1640s panelled Dining Room has now been reinstated, following its repatriation from the New York Metropolitan Museum.

Location: OS Ref. SH795 610. ½ m W of Llanrwst on A5106.

Opening Times: 1 Mar - 31 Oct: daily, 10am - 5pm. Limited openings at other times. Occasional weddings on Sats.

Admission: Adult £3, Child £1.50. Group discount 10%.

Partially suitable. By arrangement. By arrangement. 2 doubles.

GYRN CASTLE

Tel/Fax: 01745 853500

Llanasa, Holywell, Flintshire CH8 9BG

Owner/Contact: Sir Geoffrey Bates BT

Dating, in part, from 1700, castellated 1820. Large picture gallery, panelled entrance hall. Pleasant woodland walks and fantastic views to the River Mersey and the Lake District.

Location: OS Ref. SJ111 815. 26m W of Chester, off A55, 4½ m SE of Prestatyn.

Opening Times: All year by appointment.

Admission: £4. Discount for groups.

Grounds suitable. By arrangement. Obligatory. Limited for coaches. On leads.

FFERM

Tel/Fax: 01352 770217

Pontblyddyn, Mold, Flintshire

Owner/Contact: Dr M Jones-Mortimer

17th century farmhouse. Viewing is limited to 7 persons at any one time. Prior booking is recommended. No toilets or refreshments.

Location: OS Ref. SJ279 603. Access from A541 in Pontblyddyn, 3½ m SE of Mold.

Opening Times: 2nd Wed in every month, 2 - 5pm. Pre-booking is recommended.

Admission: £4.

GLANSEVERN HALL GARDENS

Tel: 01686 640200 **Fax:** 01686 640829

Berriew, Welshpool, Powys SY21 8AH

Owner: Mr G and Miss M Thomas **Contact:** Mr & Mrs R N Thomas

A classic Greek revival house romantically positioned on banks of River Severn. Over 18 acres of mature gardens notable for variety of unusual tree species. Also much new planting. Lakeside and woodland walks, water and rock gardens, grotto, walled rose garden.

Location: OS Ref. SJ195 001. On A483, 5m S of Welshpool, 1m SE of Berriew.

Opening Times: May - Sept: Fris, Sats and BH Mons, 12 noon - 6pm. Groups by appointment on other days.

Admission: Adult £2, Child (under 16) Free.

   Grounds suitable.    In grounds, on leads.

Gyrn Castle, North Wales.

North Wales

HARLECH CASTLE

Cadw: Welsh Historic Monuments. Crown Copyright

HARLECH LL46 2YH

Owner: *In the care of Cadw* ***Contact:*** *The Administrator*

Tel: 01766 780552

Set on a towering rock above Tremadog Bay, this seemingly impregnable fortress is the most dramatically sited of all the castles of Edward I. A World Heritage Listed Site.

Location: OS Ref. SH581 312. Harlech, Gwynedd on A496 coast road.

Opening Times: 29 Mar - 21 May: 9.30 - 5pm. 22 May - 3 Oct: 9.30am - 6pm. 4 - 31 Oct: 9.30am - 5pm. 1 Nov - 28 Mar: Mon - Sat, 9.30am - 4pm, Suns, 11am - 4pm. Closed 24 - 26 Dec & 1 Jan.

Admission: Adult £3, Child/OAP £2, Family £8.

  Guide dogs only. 

PENRHYN CASTLE

National Trust Photographic Library: Matthew Antrobus

BANGOR LL57 4HN

Owner: *The National Trust* ***Contact:*** *The Property Manager*

Tel: 01248 353084

This dramatic neo-Norman castle sits between Snowdonia and the Menai Strait and was built by Thomas Hopper between 1820 and 1845 for the wealthy Pennant family, who made their fortune from the local slate quarries. The extraordinarily grand staircase and extravagant stone carving of the interior create an almost cathedral-like atmosphere. The castle contains fascinating Norman furniture, panelling and plasterwork all designed by Hopper, and houses an outstanding collection of paintings by the old masters. There is also an industrial railway museum, a countryside exhibition, a Victorian terraced walled garden and an extensive tree and shrub collection, as well as attractive walks in the grounds.

Location: OS Ref. SH602 720. 1m E of Bangor, at Llandegai on A5122.

Opening Times: 22 Mar - 5 Nov: daily except Tues. Castle: 12 noon - 5pm (Jul & Aug: 11am - 5pm). Grounds & exhibitions: 11am - 5pm (Jul & Aug: 10am - 5.30pm). Last audio tour 4pm. Last admission 4.30pm.

Admission: All inclusive ticket: Adult £5, Child £2.50, Family (2+2) £12.50. Pre-booked groups (15+) £4. Garden & Stableblock Exhibitions only: Adult £3.50, Child £2. Audio tour: additional £1 including NT members. NT members Free.

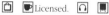

 Licensed.  

HARTSHEATH

Tel/Fax: 01352 770217

Pontblyddyn, Mold, Flintshire

Owner/Contact: Dr M Jones-Mortimer

18th and 19th century house set in parkland. Viewing is limited to 7 persons at any one time. Prior booking is recommended. No toilets or refreshments.

Location: OS Ref. SJ287 602. Access from A5104, 3½ m SE of Mold between Pontblyddyn and Penyffordd.

Opening Times: 1st, 3rd & 5th Wed in every month, 2 - 5pm.

Admission: £4.

ISCOYD PARK

Nr Whitchurch, Shropshire SY13 3AT

Owner/Contact: Mr P C Godsal

18th century Grade II* listed redbrick house in park.

Location: OS Ref. SJ504 421. 2m W of Whitchurch on A525.

Opening Times: By written appointment only.

PLAS BRONDANW GARDENS

Tel: 01766 770228

Plas Brondanw, Llanfrothen, Gwynedd LL48 6SW

Italianate gardens with topiary.

Owner: Trustees of the Second Portmeirion Foundation

Location: OS Ref. SH618 423. 3m N of Penrhyndeudraeth off A4085, on Croesor Road.

Opening Times: All year: daily 9am - 5pm.

Admission: Adult £1.50, Child 25p, Group £1 (if pre-booked).

Wales Torist Board.

Llyn Peninsula, North Wales.

PLAS MAWR

Cadw: Welsh Historic Monuments. Crown Copyright

HIGH STREET, CONWY LL32 8EF

Owner: *In the care of Cadw* ***Contact:*** *The Administrator*

Tel: 01492 580167

The best preserved Elizabethan town house in Britain, the house reflects the status of its builder Robert Wynn. A fascinating and unique place allowing visitors to sample the lives of the Tudor gentry and their servants, Plas Mawr is famous for the quality and quantity of its decorative plasterwork.

Location: OS Ref. SH779 777. Conwy by A55 or B5106.

Opening Times: 29 Mar - 21 May: 9.30am - 5pm. 22 May - 5 Sept: 9.30am - 6pm. 6 Sept - 3 Oct: 9.30am - 5pm. 3 - 31 Oct: 9.30am - 4pm. Closed on Mons except BHs.

Admission: Adult £4, Child/OAP £3, Family £11.

Limited. Guide dogs only.

PLAS NEWYDD

National Trust Photographic Library: Nick Meers

LLANFAIRPWLL, ANGLESEY LL61 6DQ

Owner: *The National Trust* ***Contact:*** *The Property Manager*

Tel: 01248 714795 **Fax:** 01248 713673 **e-mail:** ppnmsn@smtp.ntrust.org.uk

Set amidst breathtaking beautiful scenery and with spectacular views of Snowdonia. Fine spring garden and Australasian arboretum with an understorey of shrubs and wildflowers. Summer terrace, and , later, massed hydrangeas and Autumn colour. A woodland walk gives access to a marine walk on the Menai Strait. Rhododendron garden open April - early June only. Elegant 18th century house by James Wyatt, famous for its association with Rex Whistler whose largest painting is here. Military museum contains relics of 1st Marquess of Anglesey and Battle of Waterloo. A historic cruise, a boat trip on the Menai Strait operates from the property weather and tides permitting (additional charge).

Location: OS Ref. SH521 696. 2m S of Llanfairpwll and A5.

Opening Times: 1 Apr - 1 Nov: Sat - Wed. House: 12 noon - 5pm. Garden: 11am - 5.30pm. Last admission 1/2 hr before closing.

Admission: House & Garden: Adult £4.50, Child £2.25 (under 5s Free), Family (2+3) £11. Groups (15+) £3.70. Garden only: Adult £2.50, Child £1.25.

No indoor photography. Partially suitable. WCs. Licensed. Award winning. By arrangement.

PLAS PENHELIG

Tel: 01654 767676 **Fax:** 01654 767783

Aberdovey, Gwynedd LL35 0NA

Owner: The Richardson Family **Contact:** David Richardson

Edwardian house. 7 acres of gardens with azaleas, rhododendrons and spring flowers. Formal walled garden.

Location: OS Ref. SN622 961. 1/2 m E of Aberdyfi on the A493 coast road. 10m W of Machynlleth.

Opening Times: 1 Apr - 31 Oct: Wed - Sun, 10.30am - 5.30pm.

Admission: Adult £1.50, Child 50p.

PLAS YN RHIW

Tel/Fax: 01758 780219

Rhiw, Pwllheli LL53 8AB

Owner: The National Trust **Contact:** The Custodian

A small manor house, with garden and woodlands, overlooking the west shore of Porth Neigwl (Hell's Mouth Bay) on the Llyn Peninsula. The house is part medieval, with Tudor and Georgian additions, and the ornamental gardens have flowering trees and shrubs, divided by box hedges and grass paths, rising behind to the snowdrop wood.

Location: OS Ref. SH237 282. 12m SW of Pwllheli, 3m S of the B4413 to Aberdaron. No access for coaches.

Opening Times: 30 Mar - 15 May: daily except Tues & Weds. 17 May - 1 Oct: daily except Tues, 12 noon - 5pm.

Admission: Adult £3.20, Child £1.60, Family (2+2) £8. Guided tour for pre-booked groups additional £1.40 (including NT members).

Partially suitable. WCs. By arrangement. Limited. Guide dogs only.

PORTMEIRION

Tel: 01766 770000 **Fax:** 01766 771331

Portmeirion, Gwynedd LL48 6ET **e-mail:** info@portmeirion-village.com

Owner: The Portmeirion Foundation **Contact:** Mr R Llywelyn

Portmeirion was built by Clough Williams-Ellis as an 'unashamedly romantic' village resort. All the houses form part of the hotel with rooms and suites within comfortable walking distance from the main building on the quayside. The curvilinear dining room overlooking the estuary serves fresh local produce in elegant surroundings.

Location: OS Ref. SH590 371. Off A487 at Minffordd between Penrhyndeudraeth and Porthmadog.

Opening Times: All year (except Christmas Day): daily, 9.30am - 5.30pm.

Admission: Adult £4.50, Child £2.25, OAP £3.60, Family (2+2) £11.

Conference facilities. Partially suitable. Licensed. 40 double. Ensuite.

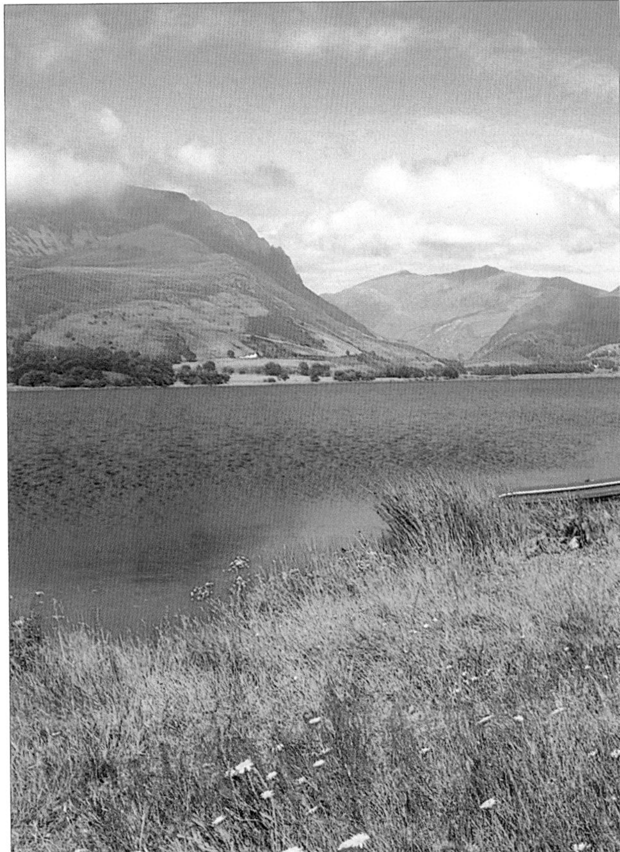

Wales Toruist Board.

Snowdonia, North Wales.

POWIS CASTLE & GARDEN

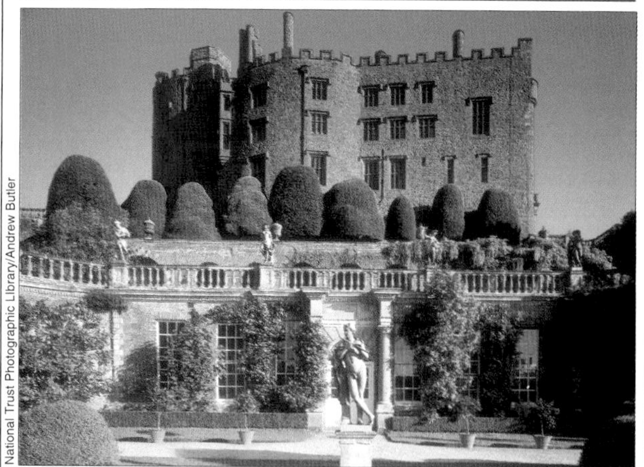

National Trust Photographic Library/Andrew Butler

Nr WELSHPOOL SY21 8RF

Owner: *The National Trust* ***Contact:*** *The Property Office*

Tel: 01938 554338 **Fax:** 01938 554336

The world-famous garden, overhung with enormous clipped yew trees, shelters rare and tender plants in colourful herbaceous borders. Laid out under the influence of Italian and French styles, the garden retains its original lead statues and, an orangery on the terraces. Perched on a rock above the garden terraces, the medieval castle contains one of the finest collections of paintings and furniture in Wales.

Location: OS Ref. SJ195 001. 1m W of Welshpool, 1m SE of Berriew, car access on A483.

Opening Times: Castle & Museum: 1 Apr - 29 Oct: daily except Mons & Tues (Jul & Aug: daily except Mons), but open BH Mons, 1 - 5pm. Garden: 11am - 6pm. Shop & Tearoom: Also open Nov - 17 Dec, Fri - Sun.

Admission: All inclusive: Adult £7.50, Child £3.75, Family £18.75. Groups: (15+ booked): £6.50. Garden only: Adult £5, Child £2.50, Family £12.50. Groups (15+ booked): £4. No groups rates on Suns or BH Mons. NT members Free.

No indoor photography. Licensed. Limited for coaches. Guide dogs only.

RHUDDLAN CASTLE

Tel: 01745 590777

Castle Gate, Castle Street, Rhuddlan LL18 5AD

Owner: In the care of Cadw **Contact:** The Administrator

Guarding the ancient ford of the River Clwyd, Rhuddlan was the strongest of Edward I's castles in North-East Wales. Linked to the sea by an astonishing deep water channel nearly 3 miles long, it still proclaims the innovative genius of its architect.

Location: OS Ref. SJ025 779. SW end of Rhuddlan via A525 or A547.

Opening Times: May - Sept: daily, 10am - 5pm.

Admission: Adult £2, Child/OAP £1.50, Family £5.50.

Guide dogs only.

The National Trust Photographic Library. Andreas Von Einsiedel.

Powis Castle Gallery, North Wales.

RUG CHAPEL & LLANGAR CHURCH

Tel: 01490 412025

c/o Coronation Cottage, Rug, Corwen LL21 9BT

Owner: In the care of Cadw **Contact:** The Administrator

Prettily set in a wooded landscape, Rug Chapel's exterior gives little hint of the wonders within. Nearby the attractive medieval Llangar Church still retains its charming early Georgian furnishings.

Location: Rug Chapel: OS Ref. SJ065 439. Off A494, 1m N of Corwen. Llangar Church: OS Ref. SJ064 423. Off B4401, 1m S of Corwen (obtain key at Rug).

Opening Times: Rug Chapel: 1 May - 26 Sept:10am - 2pm & 3 - 5pm. Closed Sun & Mon except BHs. Llangar Church: Interior access between 2 - 3pm through the Custodian at Rug Chapel. Both sites closed 27 Sept - 30 Apr.

Admission: Adult £2, Child/Conc. £1.50, Family £5.50.

By arrangement.

ST ASAPH CATHEDRAL

Tel: 01745 583597

St Asaph, Denbighshire LL17 0RL **Contact:** The Dean

Britain's smallest ancient cathedral founded in 560AD by Kentigern, a religious community enclosed in a 'llan', hence Llanelwy. Present building dates from 13th century. Post reformation period, close association with the translators of the Welsh Prayer Book and Bible. A copy of the William Morgan Bible of 1588 can be seen. The Translators' Memorial, erected in 1888, stands outside. Within, a 17th century Spanish Madonna in ivory, stained glass, an exhibit of literary treasures, the only recumbent effigy, from 1268 - 93, an iron chest (1738) and four painted angels in the choir roof are just some of the things of interest. Housing an original Hill organ and home to the International North Wales Music Festival yearly, in September.

Location: OS Ref. SJ039 743. In St Asaph, S of A55.

Opening Times: Summer: 7.30am - 6pm. Winter: 7.30am - dusk. Sun services: 8am, 11am, 3.30pm.

Ground floor suitable. Guide dogs only. 

TOWER

Tel: 01352 700220

Nercwys, Mold, Flintshire CH7 4ED

Owner/Contact: Charles Wynne-Eyton

This Grade I listed building is steeped in Welsh history and bears witness to the continuous warfare of the time. A fascinating place to visit or for overnight stays.

Location: OS Ref. SJ240 620. 1m S of Mold.

Opening Times: Summer: BHs plus most of May. Please telephone for exact dates and times. Groups welcome at other times by appointment.

Admission: Adult £3, Child £2.

TREWERN HALL

Tel: 01938 570243

Trewern, Welshpool, Powys SY21 8DT

Owner: Chapman Family **Contact:** Mrs Margaret Chapman

Trewern Hall is a Grade II* listed building standing in the Severn Valley. It has been described as 'one of the most handsome timber-framed houses surviving in the area'. The porch contains a beam inscribed RF1610, though it seems likely that parts of the house are earlier. The property has been in the ownership of the Chapman family since 1918.

Location: OS Ref. SJ269 113. Off A458 Welshpool - Shrewsbury Road, 4m from Welshpool.

Opening Times: Last week in Apr. May: Mon - Fri, 2 - 5pm.

Admission: Adult £2, Child/Conc. £1. (1999 prices).

Not suitable. No parking.

VALLE CRUCIS ABBEY

Tel: 01978 860326

Llangollen, Clwyd

Owner: In the care of Cadw **Contact:** The Administrator

Set in a beautiful valley location, Valle Crucis Abbey is the best preserved medieval monastery in North Wales, enhanced by the only surviving monastic fish pond in Wales.

Location: OS Ref. SJ205 442. B5103 from A5, 2m NW of Llangollen, or A542 from Ruthin.

Opening Times: 1 May - 26 Sept: 10am - 5pm.

Admission: Adult £2, Child/Conc. £1.50. Family £5.50.

WERN ISAF

Tel: 01248 680437

Penmaen Park, Llanfairfechan LL33 0RN

Owner/Contact: Mrs P J Phillips

This Arts and Crafts house was built in 1900 by the architect H L North as his family home and it contains much of the original furniture and William Morris fabrics. It is situated in a woodland garden and is at its best in the Spring. It has extensive views over the Menai Straits and Conwy Bay. One of the most exceptional houses of its date and style in Wales.

Location: OS Ref. SH685 752.

Opening Times: Mar: daily, 11am - 4pm. Please telephone for details.

Owner: The National Botanic Garden of Wales

CONTACT

Ian R Ball
Middleton Hall
Llanarthne
Carmarthenshire
SA32 8HG

Tel: 01558 668768

Tel: 01558 667134

Fax: 01558 667 138

e-mail: ian@gardenofwales.org.uk

LOCATION

OS159 Ref. SN518 175

1/2 m off A48(M4), 4 1/2 m NW Cross Hands, 7m SE Carmarthen. Cardiff 1hr, London 3 1/2 hrs.

Rail: Carmarthen 7m, Llanelli 14m, Llandeilo/Ffairfach 7m. Bus links.

CONFERENCE/FUNCTION		
ROOM	SIZE	MAX CAPACITY
Please telephone for availability.		

THE NATIONAL BOTANIC GARDEN OF WALES
LLANARTHNE

THE NATIONAL BOTANIC GARDEN OF WALES is the first national botanic garden to be created in the United Kingdom for more than two hundred years.

Set in the 18th century parkland of the former Middleton Hall, on the edge of the Towy Valley, the Garden of Wales commands spectacular views over the surrounding Carmarthenshire countryside. This is an area rich in history and culture, famed for its gentle beauty.

The Garden's creation is dedicated to horticulture, science, education and leisure driven by the vision of a 21st century centre of international botanical significance. The centre-piece is the Great Glasshouse, designed by Sir Norman Foster and Partners, which houses plants from the mediterranean ecosystems of the world within a landscape which uses innovative design to incorporate cliff faces and water walls.

The Great Glasshouse is surrounded by a necklace of lakes, a 220 metre long herbaceous Broadwalk with a rill and fountains, ancient woodland walks, a Water Discovery Centre, Lifelong Learning Centre and Middleton Square with its revolving threatre, café, restaurant and shops.

Visitors will be able to view the creation of the Double Walled Garden and areas of habitat dedicated to the woods and moorlands of the world.

OPENING TIMES

Public Opening Spring 2000: please phone for details.

April - May: Advanced group bookings only.

June, July & August: 10am - 7pm.

September - October: 10am - 5.30pm.

November - December: 10am - 4.30pm.

Last admission 1hr prior to closing. Closed Christmas Day.

ADMISSION

Adult	£6.50
Child/Student	£3.00
Conc.	£5.00
Family	£16.00
Groups	
Adult	£5.00
Child	£2.00
Conc.	£4.00

Group tickets must be booked at least 21 days in advance of your visit.

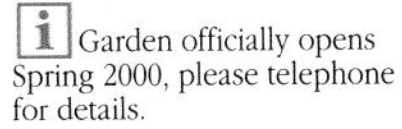
Garden officially opens Spring 2000, please telephone for details.

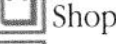
Shop.

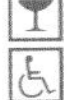

By arrangement.

Audio tours.

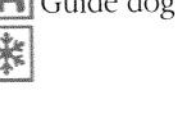
Ample.

Guide dogs only.

SPECIAL EVENTS

Please telephone for a schedule.

South Wales

ABERDULAIS FALLS

Tel: 01639 636674

Aberdulais, Vale of Neath SA10 8EU

Owner: The National Trust **Contact:** The Property Warden

For over 300 years this famous waterfall has provided the energy to drive the wheels of industry, from the first manufacture of copper in 1584 to present day remains of the tinplate works. It has also been visited by famous artists such as J M W Turner in 1796. The site today houses a unique hydro-electrical scheme which has been developed to harness the waters of the Dulais river.

Location: OS Ref. SS772 995. On A4109, 3m NE of Neath. 4m from M4/J43, then A465.

Opening Times: 1 - 26 Mar: Sats & Suns only, 11am - 4pm. 27 Mar - 31 Oct: daily. Apr - Oct: Mon - Fri, 10am - 5pm, Sats, Suns & BHs, 11am - 6pm.

Admission: Adult £2.80, Child £1.40, Family £7. Pre-booked Groups (15+): Adult £2.20, Child £1.10. National Trust members Free.

Light refreshments (summer only) Limited. 

BLAENAVON IRONWORKS

Tel: 01495 792615

Nr Brecon Beacons National Park, Blaenavon, Gwent

Owner: In the care of Cadw **Contact:** The Administrator

The famous ironworks at Blaenavon were a milestone in the history of the Industrial Revolution. Visitors can view much of the ongoing conservation work as well as 'Stack Square' - a rare survival of housing built for pioneer ironworkers.

Location: OS Ref. SO248 092. Via A4043 follow signs to Big Pit Mining Museum and Blaenavon Ironworks. Abergavenny 8m. Pontypool 8m. From carpark, cross road, then path to entrance gate.

Opening Times: Easter - end Sept: 10am - 4pm. For opening times outside this period call the above number or 029 2050 0200.

Admission: Adult £1.50, Child/Conc. £1, Family £4.

Partially suitable. By arrangement. Guide dogs only.

CAE HIR GARDENS

Tel: 01570 470839

Cae Hir, Cribyn, Lampeter, Cardiganshire SA48 7NG

Owner/Contact: Mr W Akkermans

This transformed 19th century smallholding offers a succession of pleasant surprises and shows a quite different approach to gardening.

Location: OS Ref. SN521 520. W on A482 from Lampeter, after 5m turn S on B4337. Cae Hir is 2m on left.

Opening Times: Daily, excluding Mons (open BH Mons), 1 - 6pm.

Admission: Adult £2.50, Child 50p, OAP £2. Groups: (20+) £2.

CAERLEON ROMAN BATHS & AMPHITHEATRE

Tel: 01633 422518

High Street, Caerleon NP6 1AE

Owner: In the care of Cadw **Contact:** The Administrator

Caerleon is the most varied and fascinating Roman site in Britain – incorporating fortress and baths, well-preserved amphitheatre and a row of barrack blocks, the only examples currently visible in Europe.

Location: OS Ref. ST340 905. 4m ENE of Newport by B4596 to Caerleon, M4/J25.

Opening Times: 29 Mar - 31 Oct: 9.30am - 5.15pm. 1 Nov - 28 Mar: Mon - Sat, 9.30am - 5pm, Suns, 12 noon - 4pm. Closed 24 - 26 Dec & 1 Jan.

Admission: Adult £2, Child/Conc. £1.50, Family £5.50.

  Guide dogs only.

Patrick Lane.

Cresselly, South Wales.

CAERPHILLY CASTLE 

Cadw: Welsh Historic Monuments. Crown Copyright

CAERPHILLY CF8 1JL

Owner: *In the care of Cadw* ***Contact:*** *The Administrator*

Tel: 029 2088 3143

Often threatened, never taken, this vastly impressive castle is much the biggest in Wales. 'Red Gilbert' de Clare, Anglo-Norman Lord of Glamorgan, flooded a valley to create the 30 acre lake, setting his fortress on 3 artificial islands. Famous for its leaning tower, its fortifications are scarcely rivalled in Europe.

Location: OS Ref. ST156 871. Centre of Caerphilly, A468 from Newport, A470, A469 from Cardiff.

Opening Times: 29 Mar - 21 May: 9.30am - 5pm. 22 May - 3 Oct: 9.30am - 6pm. 4 - 31 Oct: 9.30am - 5pm. 1 Nov - 28 Mar: Mon - Sat, 9.30am - 4pm, Suns, 11am - 4pm. Closed 24 - 26 Dec & 1 Jan.

Admission: Adult £2.50, Child/Conc. £2, Family £7.

Limited. Guide dogs only.

CARDIFF CASTLE

Tel: 029 2087 8100 **Fax:** 029 2023 1417

Castle Street, Cardiff CF10 3RB

Owner: City and County of Cardiff **Contact:** Mrs Jean Brown

2000 years of history, including Roman Walls, Norman Keep and Victorian interiors.

Location: OS Ref. ST181 765. Cardiff city centre, signposted from M4.

Opening Times: 1 Mar - 30 Oct: daily, 9.30am - 6pm. Nov - Feb: daily, 9.30am - 4.30pm. Closed Christmas and New Year.

Admission: Adult £5, Child/OAP £3.

CAREW CASTLE & TIDAL MILL

Tel/Fax: 01646 651782

Tenby, Pembrokeshire SA70 8SL

Owner: Pembrokeshire Coast National Park **Contact:** Mr G M Candler

A magnificent Norman castle which later became an Elizabethan country house. Royal links with Henry Tudor and the setting for the Great Tournament of 1507. The Mill is one of only four restored tidal mills in Britain. Introductory slide programme, automatic 'talking points' and special exhibition on *'The Story of Milling'*.

Location: OS Ref. SN046 037. 1/2 m N of A477, 5m E of Pembroke.

Opening Times: Easter - end Oct: daily, 10am - 5pm.

Admission: Adult £2.65, Child/OAP £1.70, Family £7 (prices under review).

Partially suitable. WC. By arrangement. In grounds on leads.

CARREG CENNEN CASTLE

Tel: 01558 822291

Tir-y-Castell Farm, Llandeilo

Contact: The Administrator

Spectacularly crowning a remote crag 300 feet above the River Cennen, the castle is unmatched as a wildly romantic fortress sought out by artists and visitors alike. The climb from Rare Breeds Farm is rewarded by breathtaking views and the chance to explore intriguing caves beneath.

Location: OS Ref. SN668 190. Minor roads from A483(T) to Trapp village. 5m SE of A40 at Llandeilo.

Opening Times: early Apr - late Oct: 9.30am - 7.30pm. Late Oct - late Mar: 9.30am - dusk.

Admission: Adult £2.50, Child/Conc. £2, Family £7.

CASTELL COCH 

Cadw: Welsh Historic Monuments. Crown Copyright

TONGWYNLAIS, CARDIFF CF4 7JS

Owner: *In the care of Cadw* ***Contact:*** *The Administrator*

Tel: 029 2081 0101

A fairytale castle in the woods, Castell Coch embodies a glorious Victorian dream of the Middle Ages. Designed by William Burges as a country retreat for the 3rd Lord Bute, every room and furnishing is brilliantly eccentric, including paintings of Aesop's fables on the drawing room walls.

Location: OS Ref. ST131 826. M4/J32, A470 then signposted. 5m NW of Cardiff city centre.

Opening Times: 29 Mar - 21 May: 9.30am - 5pm. 22 May - 3 Oct: 9.30am - 6pm. 4 - 31 Oct: 9.30am - 5pm. 1 Nov - 28 Mar: Mon - Sat, 9.30am - 4pm, Suns, 11am - 4pm. Closed 24 - 26 Dec & 1 Jan. Teashop: Summer: daily. Winter: weekends.

Admission: Adult £2.50, Child/Conc. £2, Family £7.

Guide dogs only.

CHEPSTOW CASTLE

Tel: 01248 624065

Chepstow, Gwent

Owner: In the care of Cadw **Contact:** The Administrator

This mighty fortress has guarded the route from England to South Wales for more than nine centuries. So powerful was this castle that it continued in use until 1690, being finally adapted for cannon and musket after an epic civil war siege. This huge, complex, grandiosely sited castle deserves a lengthy visit.

Location: OS Ref. ST533 941. Chepstow via A465, B4235 or A48. $1^1/_2$ m N of M4/J22.

Opening Times: 29 Mar - 21 May: 9.30am - 5pm. 22 May - 3 Oct: 9.30am - 6pm. 4 - 31 Oct: 9.30am - 5pm. 1 Nov - 28 Mar: Mon - Sat: 9.30am - 4pm, Suns, 11am - 4pm. Closed 24 - 26 Dec & 1 Jan.

Admission: Adult £3, Child/OAP £2, Family £8.

Partially suitable. Guide dogs only.

CILGERRAN CASTLE

Tel: 01239 615007

Cardigan, Dyfed

Owner: In the care of Cadw **Contact:** The Administrator

Perched high up on a rugged spur above the River Teifi, Cilgerran Castle is one of the most spectacularly sited fortresses in Wales. It dates from the 11th - 13th centuries.

Location: OS Ref. SN195 431. Main roads to Cilgerran from A478 and A484. $3^1/_2$ m SSE of Cardigan.

Opening Times: Late Mar - late Oct: 9.30am - 6.30pm. Late Oct - late Mar: 9.30am - 4pm.

Admission: Adult £2, Child/OAP £1.50, Family £5.50.

Open all Year Index PAGE 52

CLYNE GARDENS

Tel: 01792 401737

Mill Lane, Blackpill, Swansea SA3 5BD

Owner: City and County of Swansea **Contact:** Julie Bowen

50 acre spring garden, large rhododendron collection, 4 national collections, extensive bog garden, native woodland.

Location: OS Ref. SS614 906. S side of Mill Lane, 500yds W of A4067 Mumbles Road, 3m SW of Swansea.

Opening Times: All year: daily.

Admission: Free.

COLBY WOODLAND GARDEN

Tel: 01834 811885 / 01558 822800

Amroth, Narbeth, Pembrokeshire SA67 8PP

Owner: The National Trust **Contact:** The Centre Manager

An attractive woodland garden. There are walks through secluded valleys along open woodland pathways. Nearby is the coastal resort of Amroth.

Location: OS Ref. SN155 080. $^1/_2$ m inland from Amroth beside Carmarthen Bay. Signs from A477.

Opening Times: 1 Apr - 4 Nov: daily, 10am - 5pm. Walled Garden: 1 Apr - 31 Oct: 11am - 5pm.

Admission: Adult £2.80, Child £1.40, Family £7. Groups: by arrangement (15+): Adult £2.30, Child £1.15. National Trust members Free.

CRESSELLY

Fax: 01646 687045

Kilgetty, Pembrokeshire SA68 0SP

Owner/Contact: H D R Harrison-Allen Esq MFH

Home of the Allen family for 250 years. The house is of 1770 with matching wings of 1869 and contains good plasterwork and fittings of both periods. The Allens are of particular interest for their close association with the Wedgwood family of Etruria and a long tradition of foxhunting. Bed & Breakfast (dinner by arrangement). Wedding receptions and functions in house or marquee in gardens from 20 - 300 persons. Dinners and private or corporate events in historic dining room or panelled billiard room.

Location: OS Ref. SN065 065. In the Pembrokeshire National Park, W of the A4075 between Canaston Bridge and Carew in Cresselly village.

Opening Times: 28 days between May & Sept. Please write or fax for details.

Admission: Adult £3.50, no children under 12.

Ground floor only. Obligatory. Coaches by arrangement.

2 double en-suite, 1 twin, 1 single (children by arrangement).

CYFARTHFA CASTLE MUSEUM

Tel: 01685 723112

Brecon Road, Merthyr Tydfil, Mid Glamorgan CF47 8RE

Owner: Merthyr Tydfil County Borough Council **Contact:** Mrs Claire Dovey-Evans

Castle originates from 1824/1825, now a museum and school.

Location: OS Ref. S0041 074. NE side of A470 to Brecon, $^1/_2$ m NW of town centre.

Opening Times: 1 Apr - 1 Oct: Mon - Sun, 10am - 5.30pm. Winter: Tue - Fri, 10am - 4pm, Sat & Sun, 12 noon - 4pm.

Admission: Adult £1.80, Child/OAP £1.

Conference facilities. By appointment.

Guide dogs only.

DINEFWR PARK

Tel: 01558 823902

Llandeilo SA19 6RT

Owner: The National Trust **Contact:** The Property Manager

A deeply historic site with particular connections to the medieval Princes of Wales. An 18th century part 'naturalistic', part designed landscape parkland, with deer herd and White Park cattle, surrounds a Victorian gothic mansion. Access to Dinefwr Castle (Cadw).

Location: OS Ref. SN615 225. On outskirts of Llandeilo. M4 from Swansea to Pont Abraham. A48 to Cross Hands and A476 to Llandeilo. Entrance by police station.

Opening Times: House, Garden, Deer Park: 1 Apr - 29 Oct: daily except Tues & Weds, 11am - 5pm. Parkland: All year: 11am - 5pm (Nov - Mar: daily during daylight hours).

Admission: House & Park: Adult £3, Child £1.50, Family £7.50. Groups: (pre-booked 15+) £2.40. Park only (charges apply between 1 Apr - 29 Oct): Adult £2, Child £1, Family £5. National Trust members Free.

By arrangement. Limited for coaches.

In grounds on leads.

THE DINGLE

Tel: 01437 764370

Crundale, Haverfordwest, Pembrokeshire SA62 4DJ

Owner/Contact: Mrs J Jones

18th century country gentleman's home, surrounded by gardens. Gardens only open.

Location: OS Ref. SM973 175. 2m NE of Haverfordwest 600yds SE of B4329.

Opening Times: Mar - Oct: Wed - Sun inclusive, 10am - 6pm.

Admission: Adult £1, Child 50p.

DYFFRYN GARDENS

Tel: 029 2059 3328 Fax: 029 2059 1966

St Nicholas, Cardiff CF5 6SU

Owner: The Vale of Glamorgan Council **Contact:** G Donovan

Grade I listed Edwardian garden. 55 acres of landscaped gardens, beautiful at all times of year. Numerous small theme gardens, arboretum and extensive lawns.

Location: OS Ref. ST095 723. 3m NW of Barry, J33/M4. 1½ m S of St Nicholas on A48.

Opening Times: Summer: daily, 10am - 8pm. Winter: daily, 10am - 5pm

Admission: Adult £3. Please telephone for details of concessions and tours.

FONMON CASTLE

RHOOSE, BARRY, SOUTH GLAMORGAN CF62 3ZN

Owner: *Sir Brooke Boothby Bt* ***Contact:*** *Sophie Katzi*

Tel: 01446 710206 **Fax:** 01446 711687

Occupied as a home since the 13th century, this medieval castle has the most stunning Georgian interiors and is surrounded by extensive gardens. Available for weddings, concerts, corporate entertainment and multi-activity days.

Location: OS Ref. ST047 681. 15m W of Cardiff, 1m W of Cardiff airport.

Opening Times: 1 Apr - 30 Sept: Tues & Weds, 2 - 5pm (last tour 4pm). Other times by appointment. Groups: by appointment.

Admission: Adult £4, Child Free. Groups: Adult £3, Child Free.

Conferences. By arrangement (up to 120). Partially suitable. WC. Guide dogs only. 

Patrick Lane.

Dyffryn Gardens, South Wales.

THE JUDGE'S LODGING

BROAD STREET, PRESTEIGNE, POWYS LD8 2AD

Owner: *Powys County Council* ***Contact:*** *Gabrielle Rivers*

Tel: 01544 260650 **Fax:** 01544 260652

This stunningly restored Judge's Lodging captures the 'upstairs, downstairs' heyday of a most unusual Victorian household - by gaslight, lamp and candle. An 'eavesdropping' audio tour features actor Robert Hardy - A Victorian Revelation. Interpret Britain Award winner 1998 and Britain's 'Local Museum of the Year', *The Good Guide to Britain 1999.*

Location: OS Ref. SO314 644. In town centre, off A44 and A4113. Easy reach from Herefordshire and mid-Wales.

Opening Times: 1 Mar - 31 Oct: 10am - 6pm. Winter opening times may vary, please telephone for details. Bookings by arrangement accepted all year.

Admission: Adult £3.50, Child/Conc. £2.50. Groups (10-50): Adult £2.75, Child/Conc. £2.

Partially suitable (access via lift). In town. Guide dogs only.

KIDWELLY CASTLE

Tel: 01554 890104

Kidwelly, West Glamorgan SA17 5BG

Owner: In the care of Cadw **Contact:** The Administrator

A chronicle in stone of medieval fortress technology this strong and splendid castle developed during more than three centuries of Anglo-Welsh warfare. The half-moon shape stems from the original 12th century stockaded fortress, defended by the River Gwendraeth on one side and a deep crescent-shaped ditch on the other.

Location: OS Ref. SN409 070. Kidwelly via A484. Kidwelly Rail Station 1m.

Opening Times: 29 Mar - 21 May: 9.30am - 5pm. 22 May - 3 Oct: 9.30am - 6pm. 4 - 31 Oct: 9.30am - 5pm. 1 Nov - 28 Mar: Mon - Sat, 9.30am - 4pm, Suns, 11am - 4pm. Closed 24 - 26 Dec & 1 Jan.

Admission: Adult £2.20, Child/OAP £1.70, Family £6.10.

By arrangement. Guide dogs only.

LAMPHEY BISHOP'S PALACE

Tel: 01646 672224

Lamphey, Dyfed

Owner: In the care of Cadw **Contact:** The Administrator

Lamphey marks the place of the spectacular Bishop's Palace but it reached its height of greatness under Bishop Henry de Gower who raised the new Great Hall. Today the ruins of this comfortable retreat reflect the power enjoyed by the medieval bishops.

Location: OS Ref. SN018 009. A4139 from Pembroke or Tenby. N of village (A4139).

Opening Times: Daily, 10am - 5pm. Closed 25 Dec.

Admission: Adult £2, Child/Conc. £1.50, Family £5.50.

LAUGHARNE CASTLE

Tel: 01994 427906

King Street, Laugharne SA33 4SA

Owner: In the care of Cadw **Contact:** The Administrator

Picturesque Laugharne Castle stands on a low ridge overlooking the wide Taf estuary, one of a string of fortresses controlling the ancient route along the South Wales coast.

Location: OS Ref. SN303 107. 4m S of A48 at St Clears via A4066.

Opening Times: May - Sept: daily, 10am - 5pm.

Admission: Adult £2, Child/Conc. £1.50, Family £5.50.

Guide dogs only.

South Wales

LLANCAIACH FAWR MANOR

Tel: 01443 412248 **Fax:** 01443 412688

Nelson, Treharris CF46 6ER

Owner: Caerphilly County Borough Council **Contact:** The Administrator

Tudor fortified manor dating from 1530 with Stuart additions.

Location: OS Ref. ST114 967. S side of B4254, 1m N of A472 at Nelson.

Opening Times: All year: Tue - Fri, 10am - 5pm. Sats, 10am - 6pm. Oct - Mar: Suns, 12 noon - 6pm. Rest of year: 10am - 6pm. Closed Christmas week.

Admission: Adult £4.50, Child/Conc. £3, Family £12.

LLANDAFF CATHEDRAL

Tel: 029 2056 4554

Llandaff, Cardiff, Glamorgan CF5 2YF

Contact: The Administrator

Oldest cathedral in the British Isles. Epstein's *'Christ in Majesty'* and Rosetti's *'Seed of David'*.

Location: OS Ref. ST155 781. 2½ m NW of city centre, ¼ m W of A48 ring road.

Opening Times: Daily: 7am - 7pm. Sun services: 8am, 9am, 11am, 12.15pm (Holy Eucharist), 3.30pm Choral Evensong and 6.30pm Parish Evensong. Weekday service: Evensong 6pm, Weds 5.30pm.

Admission: Donation.

MARGAM PARK

Tel: 01639 881635 **Fax:** 01639 895897

Port Talbot, Glamorgan SA13 2TJ

Owner: Neathport Talbot County Borough Council **Contact:** Mr Ray Butt

Margam Orangery is the largest of its kind in Britain. Castle and Abbey ruins, 850 acres of parkland and forest, with waymarked signs.

Location: OS Ref. SS804 865. NE side of A48, 1m SE of M4/J38, 4m SE of Port Talbot.

Opening Times: Summer: daily, 10am - 5pm, last entry 4pm. Winter: Wed - Sun, 10am - 5pm, last entry 3pm.

Admission: Adult £3.75, Child £2.75.

MUSEUM OF WELSH LIFE

Tel: 029 2057 3500 **Fax:** 029 2057 3490

St Fagans, Cardiff CF5 6XB **e-mail:** post.awc@btconnect.com

St Fagans Castle, a 16th century building built within the walls of a 13th century castle.

Location: OS Ref. ST118 772. 4m W of city centre, 1½m N of A48, 2m S of M4/J33 off A4232.

Opening Times: All year: daily, 10am - 5pm.

Admission: Summer: Adult £5.50, Child £3.20, Conc. £3.90, Family (2+2) £14. Winter: Adult £4.50 Child/Conc. £2.65, Family (2+2) £10.25.

OXWICH CASTLE

Tel: 01792 390359

c/o Oxwich Castle Farm, Oxwich SA3 1NG

Owner: In the care of Cadw **Contact:** The Administrator

Beautifully sited in the lovely Gower peninsula, Oxwich Castle is a striking testament to the pride and ambitions of the Mansel dynasty of Welsh gentry.

Location: OS159 Ref. SS497 864. A4118, 11m SW of Swansea, in Oxwich village.

Opening Times: May - Sept: daily, 10am - 5pm.

Admission: Adult £2, Child/OAP £1.50, Family £5.50.

Guide dogs only.

PEMBROKE CASTLE

Tel: 01646 681510 **Fax:** 01646 622260

Pembroke, Dyfed SA71 4LA

Owner: Trustees of Pembroke Castle **Contact:** I B Ramsden

Early 13th century Norman castle with circular great tower or keep. The tower stands 75 ft high and dominates the castle. Birthplace of Henry VII. Interpretative exhibition of the Earls of Pembroke. Pembroke Yeomanry Exhibition. Introductory video.

Location: OS Ref. SM983 016. W end of the main street in Pembroke.

Opening Times: 1 Apr - 30 Sept: daily, 9.30am - 6pm. Mar & Oct: daily, 10am - 5pm. Nov - Feb: daily, 10am - 4pm. Closed Christmas Day, Boxing Day and New Year's Day.

Admission: Adult £3, Child/Conc. £2. Groups (20+): Adult £2.60, OAP £1.70.

   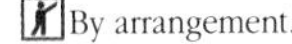 

Summer only. By arrangement. In grounds on leads.

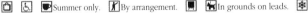

Website Index PAGE 46

PENHOW CASTLE

Nr NEWPORT, GWENT NP6 3AD

Owner: *Stephen Weeks Esq* ***Contact:*** *The Administrator*

Tel: 01633 400800 **Fax:** 01633 400990 **e-mail:** admin@penhowcastle.com

Wales' oldest lived-in Castle, the first home in Britain of the Seymour family. Now lovingly restored by the present owner, visitors explore the varied period rooms from battlements to kitchens. Discover the Norman bedchamber, 15th century Great Hall with minstrels' gallery, elegant panelled Carolean dining room, guided by the acclaimed 'Time Machine' audio tours included in the admission; also in French and German. Penhow holds 8 awards for careful restoration and imaginative interpretation. Exciting children's tours and school visits.

Location: OS Ref. ST423 908. Midway between Chepstow and Newport on the A48. Use M4/J24.

Opening Times: Summer: Good Fri - 30 Sept: Wed - Sun & BHs. Aug: daily, 10am - 5.15pm (last adm.) Winter: Weds, 10am - 4pm. Selected Suns, 1 - 4pm. Evening Candlelit Tours all year by arrangement. Christmas Tours: 15 Nov - 5 Jan.

Admission: Adult £3.60, Child £2.30, Family (2+2) £9.50. Groups: by arrangement all year, 10% discount for 20+.

Not suitable. By arrangement. Limited.  Guide dogs only. 1 double.

PENPERGWM LODGE

Tel/Fax: 01873 840208

Abergavenny, Gwent

Owner/Contact: Mrs Catriona Boyle

3 acre terraced garden including rose and vine walks.

Location: OS Ref. SO335 104. ¼ m N of B4598 to Usk, 3m SE of Abergavenny.

Opening Times: Mar - Oct: Thur - Sun, 2 - 6pm.

Admission: Adult £2, Child Free.

Patrick Lane.

Treowen, South Wales.

South Wales

PICTON CASTLE

HAVERFORDWEST, PEMBROKESHIRE SA62 4AS

Owner: *Picton Castle Trust* ***Contact:*** *Mr D Pryse Lloyd*

Tel/Fax: 01437 751326 **e-mail:** pct@pictoncastle.freeserve.co.uk

Built in the 13th century by Sir John Wogan, his direct descendants still use the castle as their family home, carrying the family name of Philipps. Retaining its external appearance, the castle was remodelled inside, above the undercroft in the 1750s and extended around 1800. The woodland and walled gardens cover 40 acres and are part of The Royal Horticultural Society access scheme for beautiful gardens. There is a unique collection of rhododendrons and azaleas, mature trees, unusual shrubs, wild flowers and a large collection of herbs as featured on television. The Picton Gallery is used for nationally acclaimed exhibitions. Events include spring and autumn plant sales.

Location: OS Ref. SN011 135. 4m E of Haverfordwest, 2m S of A40.

Opening Times: Castle: Apr - Sept. Closed Mon & Sat except BHs, open all other afternoons for guided tours. Garden & Gallery: Apr - Oct: Tue - Sun, 10.30am - 5pm.

Admission: Castle, Garden & Gallery: Adult £4, Child £1, OAP £3.50. Garden & Gallery: Adult £2.75, Child £1, OAP £2.50. Groups (20+): reduced prices by prior arrangement.

Art gallery. Conferences. No indoor photography. Licensed. Obligatory for castle. In grounds, on leads.

RAGLAN CASTLE

Tel: 01291 690228

Raglan NP5 2BT

Owner: In the care of Cadw **Contact:** The Administrator

Undoubtedly the finest late medieval fortress-palace in Britain, it was begun in the 1430s by Sir William ap Thomas who built the mighty 'Yellow Tower'. His son William Lord Herbert added a palatial mansion defended by a gatehouse and many towered walls. The high quality is still obvious today.

Location: OS Ref. SO415 084. Raglan, NE of Raglan village off A40 (eastbound) and sign-posted.

Opening Times: 29 Mar - 21 May: 9.30am - 5pm. 22 May - 3 Oct: 9.30am - 6pm. 4 - 31 Oct: 9.30am - 5pm. 1 Nov - 28 Mar: Mon - Sat, 9.30am - 4pm, Suns, 11am - 4pm. Closed 24 - 26 Dec & 1 Jan.

Admission: Adult £2.40, Child/Conc. £1.90, Family £6.70.

Guide dogs only.

ST DAVIDS BISHOP'S PALACE

Tel: 01437 720517

St Davids, SA62 6PE

Owner: In the care of Cadw **Contact:** The Administrator

The city of St Davids boasts not only one of Britain's finest cathedrals but also the most impressive medieval palace in Wales. Built in the elaborate 'decorated' style of gothic architecture, the palace is lavishly encrusted with fine carving.

Location: OS Ref. SM750 254. A487 to St Davids, minor road past the Cathedral.

Opening Times: 29 Mar - 21 May: 9.30am - 5pm. 22 May - 3 Oct: 9.30am - 6pm. 4 - 31 Oct: 9.30am - 5pm. 1 Nov - 28 Mar, Mon - Sat, 9.30am - 4pm, Suns, 12 noon - 2pm. Closed 24 - 26 Dec & 1 Jan.

Admission: Adult £2, Child/Conc. £1.50, Family £5.50.

Guide dogs only.

ST DAVIDS CATHEDRAL

Tel: 01437 720691 **Fax:** 01437 721885

St Davids, Dyfed SA62 6QW **Contact:** Mr R G Tarr

St Davids is Britain's smallest city by Royal Charter, March 1994. Premier cathedral of church in Wales. Over eight centuries old. Many unique and 'odd' features.

Location: OS Ref. SM751 254. 5-10 mins walk from car/coach parks: signs for pedestrians.

Opening Times: Daily: 7.30am - 6.30pm. Suns: 12.30 - 5.30pm, may be closed for services in progress. Sun services: 8am, 9.30am, 11.15am & 6pm. Weekday services: 7.30am, 8am & 6pm. Weds extra service: 10am.

Admission: Donations. Guided tours (Adult £3, Child £1.20) must be booked in advance.

STRATA FLORIDA ABBEY

Tel: 01974 831261

Ystrad Meurig, Pontrhydfendigaid SY25 6BT

Owner: In the care of Cadw **Contact:** The Administrator

Remotely set in the green, kite-haunted Teifi Valley with the lonely Cambrian mountains as a backdrop, the ruined abbey has a wonderful doorway with Celtic spiral motifs and preserves a wealth of beautiful medieval tiles.

Location: OS Ref. SN746 658. Minor road from Pontrhydfendigaid 1½m SE of Aberystwyth by the B4340.

Opening Times: 1 May - 26 Sept: daily, 10am - 5pm. Winter: open site.

Admission: Adult £2, Child/Conc. £1.50, Family £5.50.

 Guide dogs only.

TINTERN ABBEY

Tel: 01291 689251

Tintern NP6 6SE

Owner: In the care of Cadw **Contact:** The Administrator

Tintern is the best preserved abbey in Wales and ranks among Britain's most beautiful historic sites. Elaborately decorated in 'gothic' architecture style this church stands almost complete to roof level. Turner sketched and painted here, while Wordsworth drew inspiration from the surroundings.

Location: OS Ref. SO533 000. Tintern via A466, from M4/J22. Chepstow 6m.

Opening Times: 29 Mar - 21 May: 9.30am - 5pm. 22 May - 3 Oct: 9.30am - 6pm. 4 - 31 Oct 9.30am - 5pm. 1 Nov - 28 Mar: Mon - Sat, 9.30am - 4pm, Suns, 11am - 4pm. Closed 24 - 26 Dec & 1 Jan.

Admission: Adult £2.40, Child/Conc. £1.90, Family £6.70.

Guide dogs only.

TREDEGAR HOUSE & PARK

NEWPORT, SOUTH WALES NP1 9YW

Owner: *Newport County Borough Council* ***Contact:*** *Sarah Freeman*

Tel: 01633 815880 **Fax:** 01633 815895

South Wales' finest country house, ancestral home of the Morgan family. Parts of a medieval house remain, but Tredegar owes its reputation to lavish rebuilding in the 17th century. Visitors have a lively and entertaining tour through 30 rooms, including glittering State Rooms and 'below stairs'. Set in 90 acres of parkland with formal gardens. Winner of Best Public Park and Garden in Great Britain 1997. Craft workshops.

Location: OS Ref. ST290 852. M4/J28 signposted. From London 2½ hrs, from Cardiff 20 mins. 2m SW of Newport town centre.

Opening Times: Easter - Sept: Wed - Sun & BHs, 11am - 4pm. Evening tours by appointment. Oct: Sat & Sun, 11am - 4pm. Nov - Mar: Groups only by appointment.

Admission: Adult £3.95, Child £2, Conc. £3. Groups: Adult £3.50, Conc. £2.50. £1 car parking charge (1999 prices).

Conferences. No photography in house. Partially suitable. WC. Obligatory. In grounds, on leads. Tel. for details.

TREOWEN

Tel/Fax: 01600 712031

Wonastow, Nr Monmouth NP5 4DL **e-mail:** john.wheelock@virgin.net

Owner: R A & J P Wheelock **Contact:** John Wheelock

Early 17th century mansion built to double pile plan with magnificent well-stair to four storeys.

Location: OS Ref. SO461 111. 3m WSW of Monmouth.

Opening Times: May, Jun, Aug & Sept: Fris. Also Sat & Sun on 6/7, 13/14 & 20/21 May and 16/17 & 23/24 Sept: 10am - 4pm.

Admission: £4. £2.50 if appointment made. Groups by appointment only.

Entire house let, self-catering. Sleeps 22+.

The Gower Peninsula. Wales Tourist Board.

TRETOWER COURT & CASTLE

Tel: 01874 730279

Tretower, Crickhowell NP8 2RF

Owner: In the care of Cadw **Contact:** The Administrator

A fine fortress and an outstanding medieval manor house, Tretower Court and Castle range around a galleried courtyard, now further enhanced by a beautiful recreated medieval garden.

Location: OS Ref. SO187 212. Signposted in Tretower Village, off A479, 3m NW of Crickhowell.

Opening Times: 1 - 28 Mar: 10am - 4pm. 29 Mar - 21 May: 10am - 5pm. 22 May - 3 Oct: 10am - 6pm. 4 - 31 Oct: 10am - 5pm.

Admission: Adult £2.20, Child/Conc. £1.70, Family £6.10.

Guide dogs only.

TUDOR MERCHANT'S HOUSE

Tel: 01834 842279

Quay Hill, Tenby SA70 7BX

Owner: The National Trust **Contact:** The Custodian

A late 15th century town house, characteristic of the building tradition of south west Wales. The ground-floor chimney at the rear of the house is a fine vernacular example, and the original scarfed roof-trusses survive. The remains of early frescoes can be seen on three interior walls. Access to small herb garden, weather permitting. Furniture and fittings re-create the atmosphere from the time when a Tudor family was in residence.

Location: OS Ref. SN135 004. Tenby. W of alley from NE corner of town centre square.

Opening Times: 1 Apr - 30 Sept: daily except Weds, 10am - 5pm; Suns, 1 - 5pm. 1 Oct - 4 Nov: daily except Weds & Sats, 10am - 3pm; Suns, 12 noon - 3pm.

Admission: Adult £1.80, Child 90p. Groups: Adult £1.40, Child 70p. NT members Free.

No indoor photography. No parking. Guide dogs only.

USK CASTLE

Tel: 01291 672563

Usk, Monmouthshire NP15 1SD

Owner/Contact: J H L Humphreys

Romantic, ruined castle overlooking the picturesque town of Usk. Inner and outer baileys, towers and earthwork defences. Surrounded by enchanting gardens (open under NGS) incorporating The Castle House, the former medieval gatehouse lived in by owner.

Location: OS Ref. SO376 011. Off Monmouth Road in Usk, opposite fire station.

Opening Times: Castle ruins: daily, 11am - 5pm. Groups by appointment. Gardens & Castle House: by prior arrangement.

Admission: Castle ruins: Adult £2, Child Free. Gardens & Castle House: Adult £5, Child £2.

Partially suitable. By arrangement. Limited.

In grounds, on leads. 

WEOBLEY CASTLE

Tel: 01792 390012

Weobley Castle Farm, Llanrhidian SA3 1HB

Owner: In the care of Cadw **Contact:** The Administrator

Perched above the wild northern coast of the beautiful Gower peninsula, Weobley Castle was the home of the Knightly de Bere family. Its rooms include a fine hall and private chamber as well as numerous 'garderobes' or toilets and an early Tudor porch block.

Location: OS Ref. SN477 928. B4271 or B4295 to Llanrhidian Village, then minor road for $1^{1}/_{2}$ m.

Opening Times: For details of opening hours please telephone 029 2050 0200.

Admission: Adult £2, Child/Conc. £1.50, Family £5.50.

Guide dogs only.

WHITE CASTLE

Tel: 01600 780380

Llantillio Crossenny, Gwent

Owner: In the care of Cadw **Contact:** The Administrator

With its high walls and round towers reflected in the still waters of its moat, White Castle is the ideal medieval fortress. It was rebuilt in the mid-13th century by the future King Edward I to counter a threat from Prince Llywelyn the Last.

Location: OS Ref. SO380 167. By minor road 2m NW from B4233 at A7 Llantilio Crossenny. 8m ENE of Abergavenny.

Opening Times: 1 May - 26 Sept: 10am - 5pm. Winter: Closed.

Admission: Adult £2, Conc. £1.50, Family £5.50.

Wales Tourist Board.

Tintern Abbey, South Wales.

IRELAND

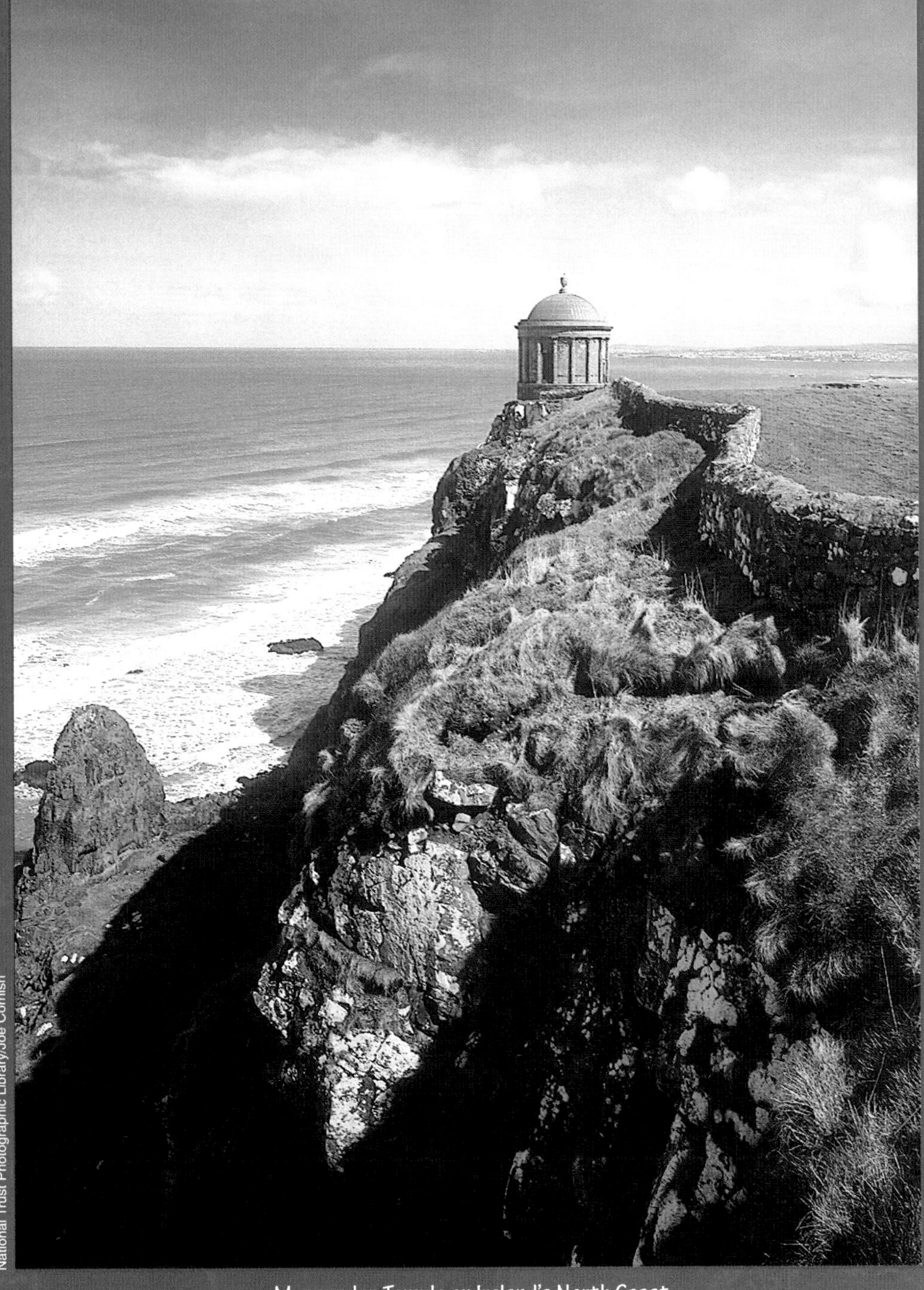

National Trust Photographic Library/Joe Cornish

Mussenden Temple on Ireland's North Coast

Ireland

ANNES GROVE GARDENS

Tel: +353 22 26145

Castletownroche, Co Cork

Owner/Contact: Mr P Annesley

The gardens around the 18th century house contain magnolias, eucryphias and hoherias of unusual size. Winding paths and riverside walks.

Location: 1.6 km N of Castletownroche.

Opening Times: 17 Mar - 30 Sept: Mon - Sat, 10am - 5pm; Suns, 1 - 6pm. Other times by arrangement.

Admission: Adult £3, Child £1.50, Conc. £2.

ANTRIM CASTLE GARDENS

Tel: 028 9442 8000 **Fax:** 028 9446 0360

Randalstown Road, Antrim BT41 4LH

Owner: Antrim Borough Council **Contact:** Gary Shaw

Situated adjacent to Antrim Town, the Sixmilewater River and Lough Neagh's shore, these recently restored, 17th century Anglo-Dutch water gardens are maintained in a manner authentic to the period. The gardens comprise of ornamental canals, round pond, ancient motte and a parterre garden planted with 17th century plants - many with culinary or medicinal uses. An interpretative display introducing the history of the gardens and the process of their restoration, along with a scale model of former Antrim Castle is located in the reception of Clotworthy Arts Centre - a major regional art gallery and theatre music venue.

Location: Outside Antrim town centre off A26 on A6.

Opening Times: All year: Mon - Fri, 9.30am - 9.30pm (dusk if earlier). Sats, 10am - 5pm. July & Aug: also open Suns, 2 - 5pm.

Admission: Free. Charge for guided group tours (by arrangement only).

ARDGILLAN CASTLE GARDEN

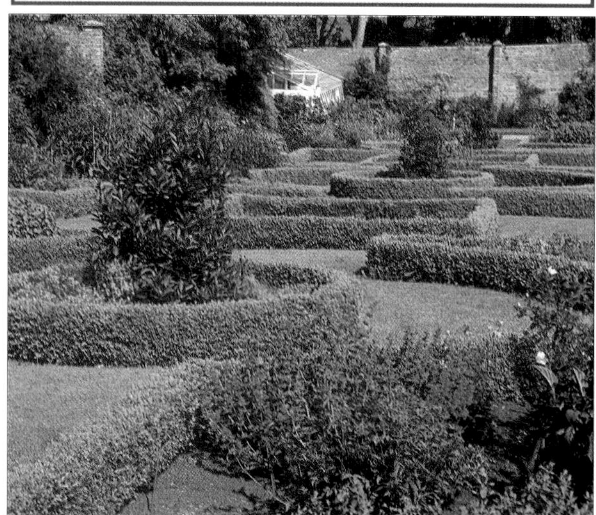

BALBRIGGAN, Co DUBLIN

Owner: *Fingal County Council* ***Contact:*** *Brenda Kenny*

Tel: +353 1 849 2212 **Fax:** +353 1 849 2786

"Flúirse talamh is mara" – Rich in land and sea – part of the Fingal Region of North County Dublin crest and nowhere more true than in Ardgillan Demesne. 194 acres of parkland and gardens surround this early 18th century house.

Location: 30km N of Dublin, off the N1.

Opening Times: All year: Jul & Aug: daily. 1 Apr - end May & Sept: Tue - Sun & Public Hols, 11am - 6pm. 1 Oct - 31 Mar: Tue - Sun & Public Hols, 11am - 4.30pm. Closed 23 Dec - 1 Jan.

Admission: Castle by guided tour only: Adult £3, Conc. £2, Family £6.50. Groups: (10+) £2.

No photography.

Castle: Obligatory. Gardens: Thurs in Jun/Jul/Aug at 3pm.

In grounds, on leads.

Open all Year Index PAGE 52

ARDRESS

Tel: 028 3885 1236

64 Ardress Road, Portadown, Co Armagh BT62 1SQ

Owner: The National Trust **Contact:** The Administrator

Originally a 17th century farmhouse, the main front and garden façades were added in the 18th century by the owner-architect George Ensor. The house contains some particularly fine neo-classical plasterwork as well as good furniture and pictures. There is a display of farm implements and livestock in the farmyard, an attractive garden and woodland walks.

Location: 7m from Portadown on Moy road B28, 5m from Moy, 3m from Loughgall intersection 13 on M1, 9m from Armagh.

Opening Times: Apr, May & Sept: Sats & Suns & BHs, 2 - 6pm; Easter (21-25 Apr): daily 2 - 6pm; Jun - end Aug: daily except Tues, 2 - 6pm.

Admission: Adult £2.70, Child £1.35, Family £6.75. Groups £2. Groups outside regular opening times £3.

Ground floor suitable. WC. Obligatory.

THE ARGORY

Tel: 028 8778 4753 **Fax:** 028 8778 9598

Moy, Dungannon, Co Tyrone BT71 6NA **e-mail:** uagest@smtp.ntrust.org.uk

Owner: The National Trust **Contact:** The Property Manager

Set in over 130ha of woodland overlooking the Blackwater River, the house dates from 1820 and remains substantially unchanged since the turn of the century. Fascinating furniture and contents, including an 1824 Bishop's barrel organ. Imposing stableyard with a coach house and carriages, harness room, laundry and acetylene gas plant. Also an interesting sundial garden and extensive walks.

Location: 4m from Moy, 3m from M1/J13 or J14.

Opening Times: Easter (21 - 26 Apr): daily. Apr, May & Sept: Sats, Suns & BHs. Jun - Aug: daily except Tues, 2 - 6pm (open 1 - 6pm on all BHs). Last tour 5.15pm.

Admission: Adult £3, Child £1.50, Family £8. Groups £2.50. Groups outside regular opening times £3.30. Estate: £1.50 per car. Coaches must book.

Ground floor suitable. WC. Obligatory.

BALLINLOUGH CASTLE GARDENS

Tel: +353 46 33135 **Fax:** +353 46 33331

Ballinlough Castle, Clonmellon, Co Westmeath

Owner: Sir John & Lady Nugent **Contact:** Sir John Nugent

Set in the lakeland county of Westmeath the gardens comprise of herbaceous borders, roses, fruit and much more.

Location: On N52 half-way between Clonmellon and Delvin. Signed from Athboy.

Opening Times: 1 May - 30 Sept: Tue - Sat, 11am - 6pm. Suns & BHs, 2 - 6pm.

Admission: £4, Child 12 - 16yrs £1.50, Child (under 12yrs) Free. Groups (20+): £3.

BALLYWALTER PARK

Tel: 028 4275 8264 **Fax:** 028 4275 8818

Nr Newtownards, Co Down BT22 2PP **e-mail:** enquiries@dunleath-estates.co.uk

Owner: Lord & Lady Dunleath **Contact:** The Secretary, The Estate Office

Victorian mansion, situated in 40 acres of landscaped grounds, built in the mid-19th century by Charles Lanyon, with Edwardian additions by W J Fennell. Currently undergoing major restoration works. Self-catered (4 star) listed gatelodge overlooking beach available for holiday lets (sleeps four).

Location: 1km S of Ballywalter village.

Opening Times: Please telephone for access, due to major restoration work.

Admission: House or Gardens: Adult £4, Child/Conc. £3. House and gardens: Adult £7, Conc. £5.50. Groups (Max. 50): Adult £4, Child/Conc. £2.

No photography indoors. Pick-your-own, Jun - Aug. Obligatory. 

NT Photographic Library, Andreas Von Einsiedel.

Ardress House, Ireland.

BANTRY HOUSE & GARDENS

BANTRY, Co CORK

Owner/Contact: *Mr & Mrs Egerton Shelswell-White*

Tel: +353 27 50047 **Fax:** +353 27 50795

Overlooking Bantry Bay, with views to the Cork-Kerry mountains, the house and gardens enjoy one of the most spectacular views in Ireland. Bantry House, home to the White family since 1739, is one of the finest stately homes in Ireland, containing a unique collection of tapestries, furniture, carpets and art treasures, collected mainly by the 2nd Earl in the 19th century. The magnificent gardens and grounds (under restoration) are home to many sub-tropical plants and shrubs – reflecting the best European design and style. Other features within the 45 acre grounds include the renowned 100-stepped 'stairway to the sky', the Italian Garden and the largest wisteria circle in the country. Bantry House and Gardens is a member of the Houses, Castles and Gardens of Ireland Scheme.

Location: E outskirts of Bantry town on the main Cork - Killarney coast road (N71).

Opening Times: 17 Mar - end Oct: daily, 9am - 5pm (last admission).

Admission: House & Gardens: Adult £6, Child Free, OAP £4.50, Student £4. Groups (min 20): £4, Child Free. Gardens only: Adult £2, Child Free, Conc. £2.

Partially suitable. In grounds, on leads. 8 doubles.

BARONS COURT

Tel: 028 816 61683 **Fax:** 028 816 62059

Newtownstewart, Omagh, Co Tyrone BT78 4EZ

Owner: Mount Castle Trust **Contact:** The Agent

The home of the Duke and Duchess of Abercorn, Barons Court was built in the late 18th century and subsequently extensively remodelled by William and Richard Morrison (1819 - 1841), Sir Albert Richardson (1947-49) and David Hicks (1975-76).

Location: 5km SW of Newtownstewart.

Opening Times: By appointment only.

Admission: Adult £4.50, Conc. £3. Groups max. 50.

 Partially suitable. WCs. By arrangement. 

BENVARDEN GARDEN

Tel: 028 2074 1331 **Fax:** 028 2074 1955

Dervock, Ballymoney, Co Antrim

Owner/Contact: Mr H J Montgomery

Beautiful walled gardens with woodland walks on the banks of the River Bush.

Location: 10km from Giants' Causeway on B67 Coleraine - Ballycastle road, then follow brown tourist signs.

Opening Times: 1 Jun - 31 Aug: daily (except Mons), 1.30 - 5pm. Other times by arrangement.

Admission: Adult £2.50, Child £1. Group rates on request.

Small museum. By arrangement.

Admission prices for properties in Northern Ireland are given in £ Sterling.

Admission prices for properties in the Republic of Ireland are given in Irish Punt.

BIRR CASTLE DEMESNE

Tel: +353 509 20336 **Fax:** +353 509 21583

Birr, Co Offaly **e-mail:** info@birrcastle.com

Contact: A Parsons

Discover the largest telescope for over 70 years; constructed here at Birr Castle in the 1840s by the 3rd Earl of Rosse. The telescope looks and moves just as it did over 150 years ago. Magnificent award-winning gardens which feature collections of rare trees, imaginative planting, the tallest box hedges in the world, beautiful landscapes with lake, rivers and waterfalls. At the science centre discover many pioneering achievements of the Parsons family and of other great Irish scientists in the fields of astronomy, photography, engineering, botany and horticulture.

Location: In town of Birr. 130km from Dublin; 90km from Shannon via Limerick.

Opening Times: Garden: All year: 9am - 6pm or dusk if earlier. Science Centre: Oct - Mar, by appointment for groups during weekdays.

Admission: Adult £5, Child £2.50, Conc. £3.50, Family (2+2) £12. Groups (20+): Adult £4, Child £2.50, Conc. £3.

Partially suitable. WC. By arrangement. Limited for coaches. In grounds, on leads.

BLARNEY CASTLE

Tel: +353 21 385252 **Fax:** +353 21 381215

Co Cork **e-mail:** info@blarneyc.iol.ie

Owner: Sir Richard La T Colthurst Bart **Contact:** Mervyn Johnston Esq

Site of the Blarney Stone.

Location: 5m from Cork city, off N20.

Opening Times: May & Sept: Mon - Sat, 9am - 6pm; Suns, 9.30am - 5.30pm. Jun - Aug: Mon - Sat, 9am - 7pm; Suns, 9.30am - 5.30pm, Oct - Apr: Mon - Sat, 9am - 5pm or sundown; Suns, 9.30am - sundown. Closed 24 - 25 Dec.

Admission: Adult £3.50, Child £1, Student/OAP £2.50.

CASTLE COOLE

Tel: 028 6632 2690 **Fax:** 028 6632 5665

Enniskillen, Co Fermanagh BT74 6JX **e-mail:** ucasco@smtp.ntrust.org.uk

Owner: The National Trust **Contact:** The Property Manager

This very fine neo-classical late 18th century house with colonnaded wings was designed by James Wyatt. It contains original decoration and furniture dating from before 1830, and is set in a landscaped parkland with mature oak woodland. State bedroom prepared for George IV in 1821. Exterior attractions include servants' tunnel, stables and nature display room in Grand Yard.

Location: 1/2 m SE of Enniskillen on A4, Belfast - Enniskillen road.

Opening Times: Easter (21 - 25 Apr): daily. Apr, May & Sept: Sats & Suns. Jun - Aug: daily (except Thurs), 1 - 6pm. Last tour 5.15pm. Grounds open daily during daylight hours.

Admission: Adult £3, Child £1.30, Family £8. Groups £2.50. Groups after hours £3.50. Estate: £2 per car.

Partially suitable. WC. In grounds, on leads.

CASTLE LESLIE

Tel: +353 47 88109 **Fax:** +353 47 88256

Glaslough, Co Monaghan **e-mail:** ultan@castle-leslie.ie

Owner/Contact: Samantha Leslie

The present castle was built in 1878. Contains Italian and Spanish furniture, tapestries and carpets. The family home of the Leslies.

Location: 6 km N of Monaghan at Glaslough village.

Opening Times: Open for accommodation and dining throughout the year.

CASTLE WARD

Tel: 028 4488 1204 **Fax:** 028 4488 1729

Strangford, Downpatrick, Co Down BT30 7LS **e-mail:** cwest@smtp.ntrust.org.uk

Owner: The National Trust **Contact:** The Property Manager

A fascinating 18th century mansion built in two completely different styles, Palladian Classic on one side and gothick on the other, in a breathtaking setting on the shores of Strangford Lough. Other attractions include a Victorian Laundry and Pastime Centre where dressing-up and games are on offer, as well as a working cornmill. The 285ha estate hosts Strangford Lough Wildlife Centre with audio-visual shows and Strangford Lough Sailing Club. There are many beautiful walks and equestrian trails through gardens, parkland and lough shore which is home to a vast variety of wildlife and flora.

Location: 1m W of Strangford village on A25 Downpatrick - Strangford road.

Opening Times: House & Gardens: Easter (21 - 30 Apr) May/Sept/Oct, Sats & Suns. Jun - Aug: daily (except Thurs), 1 - 5pm. Gardens: daily, dawn - dusk.

Admission: Adult £2.60, Child £1.30, Family £6.50. Groups £2 (after hours £3). Estate: £3.50 per car. £1 when house and other facilities closed.

Ground floor & grounds suitable. Obligatory. In grounds, on leads. Caravan park, holiday cottages, basecamp.

CLONALIS HOUSE

Tel: +353 907 20014

Castlerea, Co Rosscommon

Owner: P O'Conor Nash Esq

Ancestral home of the O'Conors of Connaught, descendants of the last High Kings of Ireland.

Location: W of Castlerea town on N60.

Opening Times: 1 Jun - 15 Sept: daily (except Suns), 11am - 5pm. Open all year to groups by arrangement.

Admission: Adult £3.50, Child £2, Conc. £2.50.

CRATLOE WOODS HOUSE

Tel: +353 61 327028 **Fax:** +353 61 327031

Cratloe, Co Clare

Owner/Contact: Mr & Mrs G Brickenden

House dates from the 17th century and is the only example of the Irish longhouse which is still a home.

Location: 8 km from Limerick and 16 km from Shannon airport on N7 westbound carriageway. Enter at Red Gate Lodge.

Opening Times: 1 Jun - mid Sept: Mon - Sat, 2 - 6pm. Open other times by arrangement.

Admission: Adult £3, Child £1.50, Conc. £2.50. Special rate for guided tour in morning with lunch, for groups of 20 - 40.

CROM ESTATE

Tel/Fax: 028 6773 8118/6773 8174

Newtownbutler, Co Fermanagh

e-mail: cromw@smtp.ntrust.org.uk

Owner: The National Trust

Contact: The Property Manager

One of the most important nature conservation sites owned by The National Trust.

Location: 5 km W of Newtownbutler.

Opening Times: 1 Apr - end Sept: Mon - Sat, 10am - 6pm; Suns, 12 noon - 6pm.

Admission: £3 per car or boat. Group rates available.

CURRAGHMORE

Tel: +353 51 387 101

Portlaw, Co Waterford

Owner: Lord Waterford

Contact: Katherine Hefferman

Magnificent home of the Marquis of Waterford and his ancestors since 1170.

Location: 14m from Waterford. 8m from Kilmacthomas.

Opening Times: House: Jan, May & Jun: Mon - Fri, 9am - 1pm. House, Grounds & Shell House may also be viewed by appointment: all year, Mon - Fri.

Admission: House £4. Grounds & Shell House: £3

DERRYMORE HOUSE

Tel: 028 3083 8361

Bassbrook, Newry, Co Amagh BT35 7EF

Owner: The National Trust

A late 18th century thatched cottage, built by Isaac Corry, who represented Newry in the Irish House of Commons for 30 years from 1776.

Location: Off the Newry - Camlough road at Bessbrook, 1½ m from Newry.

Opening Times: Easter, May - end Aug: Thur, Fri & Sat, 2 - 5.30pm.

Admission: Adult £2, Child 90p, Family £4.50. Groups: £1.30.

DRIMNAGH CASTLE

Tel: +353 450 2530

Longmile Road, Drimnagh, Dublin 12

Medieval castle with a flooded moat and boasts a barrel-vaulted undercroft.

Location: 5 km SW of Dublin. Buses: 18, 56, 77.

Opening Times: 1 Apr - 1 Oct: Wed, Sat & Sun, 12 noon - 5pm. 1 Oct - 31 Mar: Suns only, 2 - 5pm. Last tour 4.15pm.

Admission: Adult £1.50, Student/OAP £1, Child 50p.

Admission prices for properties in Northern Ireland are given in £ Sterling.

Admission prices for properties in the Republic of Ireland are given in Irish Punt.

NT Photogrpahic Library. Andreas Von Einsiedel.

Castle Ward, Ireland.

DUBLIN WRITERS MUSEUM

Tel: +353 1 8722077 **Fax:** +353 1 8722231

18 Parnell Square, Dublin 1

Owner: Dublin Tourism Enterprises

Contact: Eilish Rafferty

Situated in a very fine 18th century mansion in the north city centre, the museum features the lives and works of Dublin's literary celebrities over the past 300 years. Swift, Sheridan, Shaw, Wilde, Yeats, Joyce and Beckett are among those represented through their books, letters, portraits and personal items.

Location: City Centre, N of O'Connell Street.

Opening Times: Jan - Dec: Mon - Sat, 10am - 5pm. Suns & BHs, 11am - 5pm. Jun - Aug: late opening Mon - Fri, 10am - 6pm.

Admission: Adult £3.10, Child (3-11yrs) £1.45, Conc. £2.60, Family £8.50.

 By arrangement. 

DUNKATHEL

Tel: +353 21 821014 **Fax:** +353 21 821023

Glanmire, Co Cork

Owner: The Russell Family

Contact: Mr John Russell

House dates from around 1790. Contains splendid bifurcated staircase of Bath stone.

Location: 5 km from Cork off N25.

Opening Times: By appointment only.

Admission: Adult £2, Child £1, Conc. £1.50. Special group rate.

FERNHILL

Tel: +353 1 295 6000

Sandyford, Co. Dublin

Owner/Contact: Mrs Sally Walker

200 year old garden for all seasons. Fine trees, rare shrubs and Victorian kitchen garden.

Location: On the NE slope of the Three Rock mountain, 11 km S of the city centre on the Enniskerry Road. 6 km inland from Dun Laoghaire.

Opening Times: 1 Mar - 30 Sept: Tue - Sat & BH Mons, 11am - 5pm; Suns, 2 - 6pm.

Admission: Adult £3, Child £1, Conc. £2. Groups: £2.50.

FLORENCE COURT

Tel: 028 6634 8249 **Fax:** 028 6634 8873

Enniskillen, Co Fermanagh BT92 1DB **e-mail:** ufcest@smtp.ntrust.org.uk

Owner: The National Trust **Contact:** The Property Manager

One of the most important houses in Ulster, built in the mid-18th century by John Cole, father of 1st Earl of Enniskillen. Contents include fine rococo plasterwork and good examples of 18th century furniture. There are pleasure grounds with an ice house and water-powered sawmill, plus walled garden and fine views over surrounding mountains.

Location: 8m SW of Enniskillen via A4 Sligo road and A32 Swanlinbar road.

Opening Times: Easter (21 - 25 Apr): daily, 1 - 6pm. Apr, May & Sept: Sats, Suns, BH only. Jun - Aug: daily (except Tues), 1 - 6pm. Last adm. 5.15pm. Grounds: Apr - Sept: 10am - 7pm, Oct - Mar: 10am - 4pm. Closed 25 Dec.

Admission: House: Adult £3, Child £1.50, Family £8. Groups: £2.50. Groups outside opening hours £3.50. Estate: £2 per car.

Ground floor suitable. WC. Obligatory. In grounds, on leads.

THE FRY MODEL RAILWAY

Tel: +353 1 846 3779 **Fax:** +353 1 846 3723

Malahide Castle Demesne, Malahide, Co Dublin

Owner: Dublin Tourism Enterprises **Contact:** John Dunne

The Fry Model Railway is a unique collection of handmade models of Irish trains from the beginning of travel to modern times.

Location: 10m N of Dublin.

Opening Times: Apr - Sept (Closed Fris, Apr/May & Sept): Mon - Sat, 10am - 5pm, Suns & BHs 2 - 6pm. Oct - Mar: Sat, Sun & BHs, 2 - 5pm. Closed 1 - 2pm daily all year.

Admission: Adult £2.90, Child (3-11yrs) £1.70, Conc. £2.20, Family (2+4) £7.95.

GLIN CASTLE

Tel: +353 68 34173 **Fax:** +353 68 34364

Glin, Co Limerick **e-mail:** knight@iol.ie

Owner: The Knight of Glin **Contact:** Bob Duff

Glin Castle, one of Ireland's most historic properties and home to the FitzGerald family, hereditary Knights of Glin. The castle, with its superb interiors, decorative plasterwork and collections of Irish furniture and paintings stands on the banks of the River Shannon.

Location: Co Limerick.

Opening Times: 1 May - 30 Jun: daily, 10am - 12 noon & 2 - 4pm.

Admission: Adult £3, Child/Conc. £2.

Castle rentals & overnight accommodation.

GRAY'S PRINTING PRESS

Tel: 028 7188 4094

49 Main Street, Strabane, Co Tyrone BT82 8AU

Owner: The National Trust **Contact:** The Administrator

An 18th century printing press, shop and stationers. It may be here that John Dunlap, the printer of the American Declaration of Independence, and James Wilson, grandfather of President Woodrow Wilson, learned their trade. There is a collection of 19th century hand-printing machines. Strabane District Council has a local history museum/exhibition area in the former stationer's shop.

Location: Strabane centre.

Opening Times: Apr - Sept: Tue - Sat (other times by arrangement), 2 - 5pm.

Admission: Adult £2, Child 90p, Family £4.50. Group £1.30.

Florence Court, Ireland.

Ireland

HEZLETT HOUSE

Tel: 028 7084 8567 **e-mail:** uncwaw@smtp.ntrust.org.uk

107 Sea Road, Castlerock, Coleraine, Co Londonderry BT51 4TW

Owner: The National Trust **Contact:** The Administrator

A 17th century thatched house, with an interesting cruck truss roof construction. Furnished in late-Victorian style. Small museum of farm implements.

Location: 5m W of Coleraine on Coleraine - Downhill coast road, A2.

Opening Times: Easter (21 - 25 Apr): daily. Apr, May & Sept: Sats, Suns & BH only. Jun - Aug: daily except Tues, 12 noon - 5pm. Groups must book in advance.

Admission: Adult £1.80, Child 90p, Family £4.50. Groups £1.30 (outside hours £2).

Ground floor suitable. Obligatory. In grounds, on leads.

HILTON PARK

Tel: +353 47 56007 **Fax:** +353 47 56033

Hilton Park, Clones, Co Monaghan

Owner/Contact: Mr John Madden

Lakeside pleasure grounds, herb garden, parterre and herbaceous border in rolling parkland.

Location: 3m due S of Clones on L46, Ballyhaise Rd.

Opening Times: May - Sept: daily 2 - 6pm.

Admission: Adult £2.50.

THE IRISH MUSEUM OF MODERN ART

Tel: + 353 1 612 9900 **Fax:** +353 1 612 9999

Royal Hospital, Military Rd, Kilmainham, Dublin 8

Owner: Irish Museum of Modern Art **Contact:** Rowena Neville

The Irish Museum of Modern Art opened in 1991 in the magnificently restored Royal Hospital building and grounds, which include a formal garden, meadow and medieval burial grounds as well as a series of other historic buildings. The museum presents, through its permanent collection and temporary exhibitions, an exciting and innovative range of Irish and international art of the 20th century, alongside strong education and community, national and artists' residency programmes.

Location: Near Heuston Station, 2km from city centre.

Opening Times: Tue - Sat, 10am - 5.30pm. Suns, 12 noon - 5.30pm. Guided tours: Weds & Fris at 2.30pm, Suns at 12.15pm. Other times by appointment.

Admission: Free.

No inside photography.    

On leads in grounds.

JAMES JOYCE MUSEUM

Tel/Fax: +353 1 280 9265

Joyce Tower, Sandycove, Co Dublin

Owner: Dublin Tourism Enterprises **Contact:** Robert Nicholson

A martello tower containing a museum devoted to the life and works of James Joyce.

Location: Dun Laoghaire, 8m S of Dublin.

Opening Times: Apr - Oct: Mon - Sat, 10am - 5pm. Closed 1 - 2pm. Suns & BHs, 2 - 6pm.

Admission: Adult £2.70, Child (3 - 11yrs) £1.40, Conc. £2.20, Family £7.95. Group rates on request.

By arrangement.

JAPANESE GARDENS

Tel: +353 45 521617 **Fax:** +353 45 522964

Tully, Kildare Town, Co Kildare **e-mail:** stud@irish-national-stud.ie

Owner: Irish National Stud **Contact:** Pat Mullarkey Esq

Created 1906 - 1910.

Location: 1m from Kildare Town. 30m from Dublin off M/N7.

Opening Times: 12 Feb - 12 Nov: daily 9.30am - 6pm.

Admission: Adult £6, Child (under 12yrs) £3, Conc. £4.50, Family (2+4) £14. One ticket includes National Stud and Japanese Garden & St Fiachra's Garden.

KILLYLEAGH CASTLE

Tel/Fax: 028 4482 8261

Killyleagh, Downpatrick, Co Down BT30 9QA

Owner/Contact: Lt Col D Rowan-Hamilton

Oldest occupied castle in Ireland. Self-catering towers available to sleep 4-15. Swimming pool and tennis court available. Access to garden.

Location: At the end of the High Street.

Opening Times: By arrangement. Groups (30-50): by appointment.

Admission: Adult £3.50, Child £2. Groups: Adult £2.50, Child £1.50.

No photography in house. Wedding receptions. Not suitable. Obligatory.

KING HOUSE

Tel: +353 79 63242 **Fax:** +353 79 63243

Boyle, Co Roscommon **e-mail:** kinghouse-boyle@hotmail.com

Owner: Roscommon County Council **Contact:** The Administrator

Four-storey Georgian mansion dating from the early 18th century.

Location: In the centre of Boyle.

Opening Times: Apr - Oct: daily. Late October: weekends, 10am - 6pm. Last admission 5pm.

Admission: Adult £3, Child £2, Conc. £2.50, Family (2+4) £8. Group rates on request.

KYLEMORE ABBEY

CONNEMARA, CO GALWAY

Owner: *Benedictine Nuns* ***Contact:*** *Sister Magdalena OSB*

Tel: +353 95 41146 **Fax:** +353 95 41145 **e-mail:** enquiries@kylemoreabbey.ie

Set in the heart of the Connemara mountains. Kylemore is a premier tourist attraction, international girls' boarding school, a magnificent gothic church, superb restaurant and one of the finest craft shops in Ireland. Victorian Walled Garden opened Easter 1999, currently undergoing restoration. The walls stretch for up to half a mile to enclose: the kitchen garden, flower or pleasure garden, gardener's cottage, bothy and the glass (hot) house complex. The Benedictine Nuns at Kylemore continue to restore the estate and open it to the education and enjoyment of all who visit.

Location: Between Reccess & Letterfrack, West of Ireland.

Opening Times: Abbey Visit (Abbey reception rooms, lake walk, video & exhibition: All year (closed Good Fri & Christmas week). Shop & Restaurant: 17 Mar - Nov, (closed Good Fri). Garden Visit (Walled Garden, wilderness walk, Tea House, shop & exhibition): Easter - October.

Admission: Abbey: Adult £3.30, Conc. £2.30, Family £7. Groups: Adult £2. Gardens: Adult £3.30, Conc. £2.30, Family £7. Groups: Adult £2.25. Joint tickets available.

Ground floor & grounds suitable. WC.  

LISNAVAGH GARDENS

Tel: +353 503 61104 **Fax:** +353 503 61148

Lisnavagh, Rathvilly, Co Carlow, Ireland

Owner/Contact: Lord and Lady Rathdonnell

Ten acres of outstanding trees and shrubs, mixed borders, rock garden and cruciform yew walk, with panoramic views of the Wicklow Hills and Mount Leinster.

Location: Situated 2m S of Rathvilly. Signposted.

Opening Times: May - July: Suns, 2 - 6pm. Other times by appointment.

Admission: Adult £3, Child £1.50.

LISSADELL HOUSE

Tel: +353 71 63150 **Fax:** +353 71 66906

Drumcliffe, Co Sligo

House built in the 1830s by Sir Robert Gore-Booth, and still the family home.

Location: 13km NW of Sligo.

Opening Times: 1 Jun - mid Sept: (except Suns), 10.30am - 12.30pm & 2 - 4.30pm. Last admission 12.15pm & 4.15pm. Guided tours.

Admission: Adult £3, Child £1.50. Group: (20+) £2.50.

Irish Museum of Modern Art.

LODGE PARK WALLED GARDENS & STEAM MUSEUM

STRAFFAN, CO KILDARE

Owner: *Mr R Guinness*

Tel: +353 1 6273155 **Fax:** +353 1 6273477

Lodge Park Walled Garden with brick lined north wall of 18th century origin is a plantsman's delight. From the axis of the long walk it features garden rooms extending to a long rosarie. The Steam Museum building incorporates the roof, windows and other architectural features taken from the c1865 Great Southern & Western Railway Church of St Jude (attributed to the architect Sancton Wood) Inchicore, Dublin. Taken down in 1988 it was rebuilt here, under the consultant architect Mr Percy Le Clerc, and opened by the President of Ireland in 1992 as the Steam Museum. The Richard Guinness model hall displays his collection of historic prototype locomotive models. The Power Hall displays restored stationary engines working in steam. Interactive area for educational use. Memorabilia gallery.

Location: 16m from Dublin, signposted off the N7 road at Kill junction traffic lights.

Opening Times: Apr - May: Suns & BHs, 2.30 - 5.15pm. Jun - Aug: Tue - Sun & BHs, 2 - 5.45pm. Sept: Suns & BHs 2.30 - 5.15pm.

Admission: Adult £3, Conc. £2. Groups (10+) less 10%. Garden only: £2. Tech Student + card Free.

   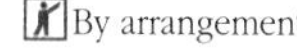By arrangement.  

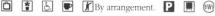

MALAHIDE CASTLE

MALAHIDE, Co DUBLIN

Owner: *Fingal County Council* ***Contact:*** *Maria Morgan*

Tel: +353 1 846 2184 **Fax:** +353 1 846 2537

Home of the Talbot family from 1185 until 1973, the castle is magnificently restored with beautiful period furniture together with an extensive collection of Irish portrait paintings. The castle has changed very little in 800 years and it and the surrounding parklands retain a unique sense of the history.

Location: 10m N of Dublin city.

Opening Times: Apr - Oct: Mon - Sat, 10am - 5pm. Suns & BHs 11am - 6pm. . Nov - Mar: Mon - Fri, 10am - 5pm. Sat, Sun & BH, 2 - 5pm. Closed 12.45 - 2pm daily. Closed for tours 12.45 - 2pm daily.

Admission: Adult £3.15, Child £1.75, Conc. £2.65, Family £8.75.

Duchas The Heritage Service.

Donegal Castle, Ireland.

MOUNT STEWART

Tel: 028 4278 8387 **Fax:** 028 4278 8487

Newtownards, Co Down BT22 2AD

Owner: The National Trust **Contact:** The Property Manager

Fascinating 18th century house with 19th century additions, where Lord Castlereagh grew up. Gardens largely created by Edith, wife of 7th Marquess of Londonderry, with an unrivalled collection of plants, colourful parterres and magnificent vistas. The Temple of the Winds, James 'Athenian' Stuart's banqueting hall of 1785 overlooks Strangford Lough.

Location: 15m SE of Belfast on A20, 5m SE of Newtownards.

Opening Times: House: 21 - 30 Apr: daily 1 - 6pm. Apr & Oct: Sats & Suns & BH Mons 1- 6pm, May - Sept: daily, except Tues, 1 - 6pm, guided tours only, last tour 5pm. **Garden:** Mar: Suns only, 2 - 5pm. St Patrick's Day: Fri 11am - 6pm. Apr & Oct: daily, 11am - 6pm. Temple of the Winds: Apr - Oct: Sats/Suns, 2 - 5pm, by appointment at other times.

Admission: House, Garden & Temple: Adult £3.50, Child £1.75, Family £8.75. Group £3 (after hours £6). Garden only: Adult £3, Child £1.50, Family £7.50. Group £2.50 (after hours £6). Temple of the Winds only: Adult £1, Child 50p. Groups 80p.

MUSSENDEN TEMPLE

Tel/Fax: 028 7084 8728

Castlerock, Co. Londonderry

The Temple is part of the landscaped estate laid out in the 18 century. Woodland glen and cliff top walks.

Location: 1m W of Castlerock.

Opening Times: July & Aug: 12 noon - 6pm. Groups by arrangement.

Admission: Grounds open free.

Admission prices for properties in Northern Ireland are given in £ Sterling.

Admission prices for properties in the Republic of Ireland are given in Irish Punt.

Ireland

NEWBRIDGE HOUSE

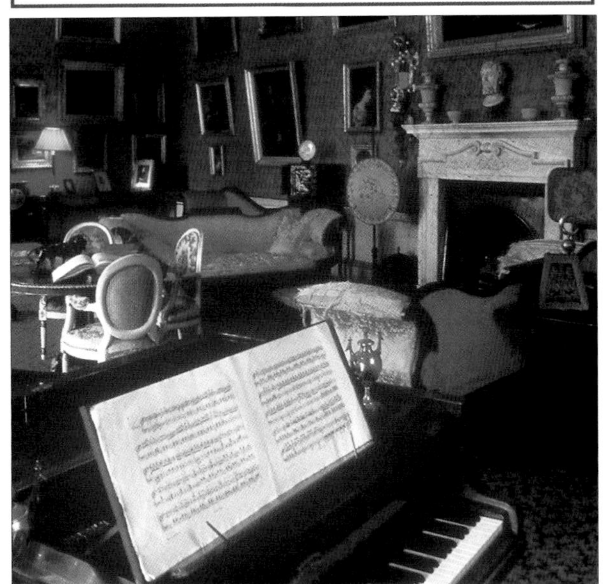

DONABATE, Co DUBLIN

Owner: *Fingal County Council* ***Contact:*** *Brigid Dunne*

Tel: +353 1 843 6534 **Fax:** +353 1 846 2537

This delightful 18th century manor is set in 350 acres of parkland 12 miles north of Dublin City. It boasts one of the finest Georgian interiors in Ireland. Each room open to the public has its own style of antique and original furniture – indeed the house appears much as it did 150 years ago.

Location: 12m N of Dublin City.

Opening Times: Apr - Sept: Tue - Sat, 10am - 5pm, Suns & BHs, 2 - 6pm (closed Mons). Closed 1 - 2pm daily. Oct - Mar: Sat, Sun & BHs, 2 - 5pm.

Admission: Adult £3, Child £1.65, Conc. £2.60, Family £8.25.

POWERSCOURT ESTATE

ENNISKERRY, CO WICKLOW

Owner: *The Slazenger Family* ***Contact:*** *The Estate office*

Tel: +353 1 204 6000 **Fax:** +353 1 286 3561 **e-mail:** gardens@powerscourt.ie

One of the world's great gardens, situated in the foothills of the Wicklow Mountains. It is a sublime blend of formal gardens, sweeping terraces, statuary and ornamental lakes together with secret hollows, rambling walks, walled gardens and over 200 varieties of trees and shrubs. (Powerscourt House incorporates an exhibition on the history of the estate, a terrace café overlooking the gardens and speciality shops.) 5km from the gardens is Powerscourt Waterfall, the highest in Ireland.

Location: 12m S of Dublin City centre, off N11 adjacent to Enniskerry village.

Opening Times: 1 Mar - 31 Oct: daily, 9.30am - 5.30pm. 1 Nov - 28 Feb: daily, 9.30am - dusk. Closed 25/26 Dec.

Admission: House Exhibition & Gardens: Adult £5, Child £3, Conc. £4.50. Groups: Adult £4.50, Child £2.70, Conc. £4. Special winter prices for groups (20+).

 Partially suitable. WCs. Guide dogs only.

5 double. En-suite available.

NEWMAN HOUSE

Tel: +353 1 706 7422 **Fax:** +353 1 706 7211

85/86 St Stephen's Green, Dublin

Owner: University College, Dublin **Contact:** Ruth Ferguson, Curator

Two Georgian houses containing examples of Dublin's finest 18th century plasterwork.

Location: Central Dublin.

Opening Times: Guided tours only. Contact for details of 2000 opening dates and times.

Admission: Adult £3, Conc. £2.

NUMBER TWENTY-NINE

Tel: +353 1 702 6165 **Fax:** +353 1 702 7796

Fitzwilliam Street Lower, Dublin 2

Owner: Electricity Supply Board & National Museum of Ireland **Contact:** K Burns

Restored middle-class house of the late 18th century.

Location: Merrion Square, central Dublin.

Opening Times: Contact for details of 2000 opening dates and times.

Admission: Adult £2.50, Conc. £1. (1999 prices).

PALM HOUSE BOTANIC GARDENS

Tel: 028 9032 4902

Belfast City

Owner: Belfast City Council **Contact:** Mr Reg Maxwell

Built by Richard Turner who later built the Great Palm House at Kew.

Location: Between Botanic Avenue & Stranmillis Road, South Belfast.

Opening Times: Palm House & Tropical Ravine: Apr - Sept: Mon - Fri, 10am - 12 noon & 1 - 5pm; Sats & Suns, 1 - 5pm. Oct - Mar: Mon - Fri, 10am - 12 noon & 1 - 4pm; Sats & Suns, 1 - 4pm. BHs as Sats & Suns. Park: 8am - sunset.

Admission: Free.

PATTERSON'S SPADE MILL

Tel/Fax: 028 9443 3619

Templepatrick, Co Antrim BT39 0AP

Owner: The National Trust

The last surviving water-driven spade mill in Ireland.

Location: Templepatrick.

Opening Times: Apr/end May & Sept: w/ends & BHs: daily, 2 - 6pm. Jun - Aug: daily, except Tues 2 - 6pm.

Admission: Adult £3, Child £1.25, Family £6.25, Groups £1.75.

POWERSCOURT TOWN HOUSE

Tel: +353 1 679 4144 **Fax:** +353 1 671 7505

South William St, Dublin 2

Owner: Clarendon Properties

Built for the 4th Viscount Powerscourt between 1771 and 1774.

Location: Central Dublin.

Opening Times: All year: daily, 9am - 6pm.

Admission: Free.

Chris Hill.

Springhill, Ireland.

RAM HOUSE GARDEN

Tel/Fax: +353 402 37238

Ram House, Coolgreany, Gorey, Co Wexford

Owner: Godfrey & Lolo Stevens **Contact:** Mrs Lolo Stevens

A two acre romantic scented garden. There are gravel and woodland areas, terraces, pergola and gazebo, immaculate lawns, mixed borders in soft colours, ponds, lavish planting around a little stream and over 70 varieties of clematis. Videos of garden on rainy days.

Location: In Coolgreany village, 3km off N11 between Arklow and Gorey.

Opening Times: May - Aug: Fri - Sun & BHs, 2.30 - 6pm. Other times and groups by appointment.

Admission: Adult £3, Child £2.

Garden plan & plant list. Not suitable. Limited. Guide dogs only.

RIVERSTOWN HOUSE

Tel: +353 21 821205

Glanmire, Co Cork

Owner: Mr & Mrs D Dooley **Contact:** Mrs D Dooley

Georgian House. Plasterwork by Lafrancini Bros.

Location: 6km from Cork City on old Cork/Dublin Rd.

Opening Times: May - mid Sept: Wed - Sat, 2 - 6pm. Other times by appointment.

Admission: £3.

ROTHE HOUSE

Tel/Fax: +353 56 22893

Parliament St, Kilkenny

Owner: Kilkenny Archaeological Society **Contact:** Mary Flood

Built 1594. Various exhibitions. Also houses the County Genealogical Research Service.

Location: Parliament Street, in Kilkenny City.

Opening Times: All year: Mon - Sat, 10.30am - 5pm. Suns, 3 - 5pm.

Admission: Adult £2, Child £1, Conc. £1.50. Groups (20+): Adult £1.50.

ROWALLANE GARDEN

Tel: 028 9751 0131 **Fax:** 028 9751 1242

Saintfield, Ballynahinch, Co Down BT24 7LH

Owner: The National Trust **Contact:** The Property Manager

A unique tree and shrub garden, containing many exotic species from around the world. There are spectacular displays of azaleas and rhododendrons and a notable rock garden with primulas, alpines and heathers. The walled garden has mixed borders which include the National Collection of Penstemons. There are also several areas managed as wildflower meadows.

Location: 11m SE of Belfast, 1m S of Saintfield, W of the A7 Downpatrick road.

Opening Times: 1 Apr - Oct: daily, weekdays 10.30am - 6pm, Weekends 2 - 6pm. Nov - Mar 2000: daily except Sat & Sun, 10.30am - 5pm. Closed 25, 26 Dec & 1 Jan.

Admission: Easter - Oct: Adult £3, Child £1.25, Family £6.25, Groups £1.75 (after hours £3). Nov '99 - Mar 2000: Adult £1.40, Child 70p. Groups 80p

Grounds suitable. WC. 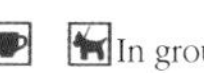 In grounds, on leads. 

RUSSBOROUGH

Tel: + 353 45 865239 **Fax:** +353 45 865054

Blessington, Co Wicklow **Contact:** The Administrator

A beautifully maintained 18th century house housing the Beit collection, fine furniture, tapestries, carpets, porcelain, silver and bronzes.

Location: 30km from Dublin on N81. 3km S of Blessington.

Opening Times: From Easter Sun, Apr & Oct: Sun & BHs, 10.30am - 5.30pm. May - Sept: daily, 10.30am - 5.30pm.

Admission: Main rooms: Adult £4, Conc. £3, Child £2. Upstairs: £2.50

SEAFORDE GARDENS

Tel: 028 44811 225 **Fax:** 028 44811 370

Seaforde, Co Down BT30 8PG

Owner/Contact: Patrick Forde

18th century walled garden and adjoining pleasure grounds, containing many rare and beautiful trees and shrubs; many of them tender. There are huge rhododendrons and the National Collection of Eucryphias. The oldest maze in Ireland is in the centre of the walled garden, which can be viewed from the Mogul Tower. The tropical butterfly house contains hundreds of beautiful highly coloured butterflies; also a collection of parrots, insects and reptiles. The nursery garden contains many interesting plants for sale.

Location: 20m S of Belfast on the main road to Newcastle.

Opening Times: Easter - end Sept: Mon - Sat, 10am - 5pm; Suns, 1 - 6pm. Oct - Mar: 10am - 5pm.

      By arrangement.   

SHAW BIRTHPLACE

Tel: + 353 1 4750854 **Fax:** +353 1 8722231

33 Synge Street, Dublin 8

Owner: Dublin Tourism Enterprises **Contact:** Eilish Rafferty

The first home of the Shaw family and the renowned playwright, George Bernard Shaw, has been restored to its Victorian elegance and charm. It has the appearance that the family has gone out for the afternoon. The neat terraced house is as much a celebration of Victorian Dublin domestic life as of the home of one of Dublin's Nobel Laureates for Literature.

Location: 10 mins from City centre.

Opening Times: May - Oct: Mon - Sat, 10am - 5pm, Suns & BHs 11am - 5pm. Closed 1 - 2pm.

Admission: Adult £2.70, Child £1.40, Conc. £2.20, Family £7.95.

By arrangement.

SPRINGHILL

Tel/Fax: 028 8674 8210

20 Springhill Road, Moneymore, Magherafelt, Co Londonderry BT45 7NQ

Owner: The National Trust **Contact:** The Property Manager

17th century 'Planter' house with 18th and 19th century additions. Springhill was the home of ten generations of a family which arrived from Ayrshire in the 17th century and the house contains family furniture, a refurbished nursery, paintings, ornaments, curios and 18th century hand-blocked wallpaper. Outbuildings house an extensive costume collection and there are walled gardens and woodland walks.

Location: 1m from Moneymore on B18.

Opening Times: Easter (21 - 25 Apr): daily. Apr, May, Jun & Sept: Sats, Suns and BH only, 2 - 6pm. Jun - Aug: daily except Thurs, 2 - 6pm. Open daily in Jun for booked tours.

Admission: Adult £2.75, Child £1.35, Family £6.50, Group £2 (outside hours £3.50).

 Partially suitable. WC.  In grounds, on leads.

STROKESTOWN PARK HOUSE

Tel: +353 78 33013 **Fax:** +353 78 33712

Strokestown, Co Roscommon

Owner: Westward Group **Contact:** Declan Jones

The Palladian-style house is complete with its original contents. Houses the National Famine Museum.

Location: 114 km from Dublin on N5.

Opening Times: 1 Apr - 31 Oct: daily, 11.30am - 5.30pm. Tours, other times by appointment.

Admission: £3.25 for one attraction. £6 for 2 attractions. £8.50 for 3 attractions.

THE TALBOT BOTANIC GARDENS

MALAHIDE DEMESNE, MALAHIDE, CO DUBLIN

Owner: *Fingal County Council*

Tel: +353 1 872 7777 **Fax:** +353 1 8727530

Botanical garden containing over 4,000 species of non-ericaceous plants with a comprehensive collection of southern hemisphere plants, many rare and unusual. The gardens now extend to 9ha including a Walled Garden of 1.6ha, which includes many tender shrub borders, alpine yard, pond and 7 glasshouses.

Location: 13km NE of Dublin City.

Opening Times: 1 May - 30 Sept: daily, 2 - 5pm. Guided tours: Weds, 2pm or by appointment.

Admission: Adult £2, Child/OAP Free. Groups (10+) £1.50. Guided tours of walled garden £2 (1999 prices).

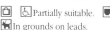

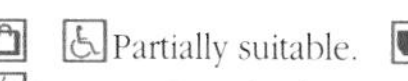 Partially suitable.  Licensed. By arrangement. In grounds on leads.

Ireland

TULLYNALLY CASTLE & GARDENS

Tel: +353 44 61159 **Fax:** +353 44 61856

Castlepollard, Co. Westmeath

Owner: Thomas & Valerie Pakenham **Contact:** Valerie Pakenham

Romantic woodland and walled gardens laid out in the early 19th century, with follies, grotto and ornamental lakes. The present owners have added a Chinese garden complete with pagoda and a Tibetan garden of waterfalls and streams, and a local sculptor has carved fantastic shapes from existing trees. The Gothick Revival castle forms a splendid backdrop.

Location: 1m from Castlepollard on Granard Road off N52, or N4 via Mullingar.

Opening Times: Gardens: 1 May - 31 Aug: 2 - 6pm. Castle: 15 Jun - 30 Jul:, 2 - 6pm. Open to groups at other times by appointment. Tearoom: daily, 2 - 6pm.

Admission: Castle & Gardens: Adult £4.50, Child £2.50. Groups: Adult £4. Gardens only: Adult £3, Child £1.

  Obligatory. 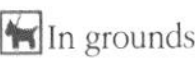In grounds, on leads. 

WELLBROOK BEETLING MILL

Tel: 028 8674 8210/8675

20 Wellbrook Road, Corkhill, Cookstown, Co. Tyrone BT80 9RY

Owner: The National Trust **Contact:** The Administrator

A hammer mill powered by water for beetling, the final process in linen manufacture. Original machinery is in working order. The mill is situated in an attractive glen, with wooded walks along the Ballinderry River and by the mill race.

Location: 4m W of Cookstown, 1/2 m off Cookstown - Omagh road, from Cookstown turn right at Kildress Parish Church or follow Orritor Road A53 to avoid town centre.

Opening Times: Easter (21 - 25 Apr): daily, 2 - 6pm. Apr, May, Jun & Sept: Sats, Suns & BHs only, 2 - 6pm. Jul & Aug: daily except Tues, 2 - 6pm.

Admission: Adult £2, Child £1, Family £5. Group £1.50 (outside hours £2.50).

Admission prices for properties in Northern Ireland are given in £ Sterling. Admission prices for properties in the Republic of Ireland are given in Irish Punt.

Dúchas – The Heritage Service

- Ardfert Cathedral
- Athenry Castle
- Aughnanure Castle
- Ballyhack Castle
- Barryscourt Castle
- Boyle Abbey
- Brú na Boinne Visitor Centre
- Cahir Castle
- The Casino
- Castletown House
- Charles Fort
- Clonmacnoise
- Derrynane House
- Desmond Castle (French Prison)
- Desmond Hall
- Donegal Castle
- Dunguaire Castle
- Dún Aonghusa
- Dwyer McAllister Cottage
- Emo Court
- Ennis Friary
- Fota Arboretum & Gardens
- Glebe House & Gallery
- Glendalough Visitor Centre
- Glenveagh Castle & Gardens
- Heywood Gardens
- Ilnacullin, Garinish Island
- JFK Arboretum
- Jerpoint Abbey
- Kilkenny Castle
- Kilmacurragh
- Kilmainham Gaol
- Lusk Heritage Centre
- Muckross House & Garden
- National Botanic Gardens
- Newmills Corn & Flax Mills
- Old Mellifont Abbey
- Ormond Castle
- Parke's Castle
- Pearse's Cottage
- Portumna Castle & Gardens
- Rathfarnham Castle
- Rock of Cashel
- Roscrea Heritage (Castle & Damer House)
- Ross Castle
- St Audeon's Church
- St Mary's Church
- Scattery Island Centre
- Sligo Abbey
- Swiss Cottage
- Tintern Abbey

For information on sites under the care of Dúchas please contact:

The Education and Visitor Service, 51 St Stephen's Green, Dublin 2, Ireland.
TEL: +353 1 661 3111 FAX: +353 1 661 6764
E-MAIL: info@heritageireland.ie
WEBSITE: www.heritageireland.ie

Duchas The Heritage Service.

The Casino, Marino, Ireland.

Opening Arrangements at Properties grant-aided by English Heritage

ENGLISH HERITAGE

23 Savile Row, London W1X 1AB

I am delighted to introduce our new list of opening arrangements at properties grant-aided by English Heritage. Some of these properties are already familiar friends; others may be less so. A few may even be unknown to many of us. Yet, large or small, they all share one essential characteristic – their outstanding architectural or historic importance.

Those who own or manage these buildings bear an enormous responsibility for the upkeep of the national heritage, a responsibility English Heritage is proud to help through the provision of grants for building repair. The heritage they conserve is the inheritance of us all and, in return for this assistance, owners agree to open their properties to the public.

The extent of public access varies from one property to another. The building's size, nature and function are all taken into account. Some buildings, such as town halls, museums or railway stations, are regularly open by virtue of their use. These are generally excluded from this access list, as are properties which we have grant-aided that are owned by the National Trust. For some other properties, especially those which are family homes, access may need to be arranged in a way which also recognises the needs of the building or of those who live in it. Usually this will mean opening 'by appointment' or on an agreed number of days each year. This is made clear by each entry.

In most cases access to a building which is grant-aided lasts for ten years from the date of the final grant payment. For grants over £100,000 the condition is extended for a further ten years. Those properties on the list which are marked with an asterisk are included on a voluntary basis following the expiry of their formal access obligation.

I hope that you will enjoy visiting these properties as much as we have enjoyed helping their owners to conserve them.

Jocelyn Stevens

Sir Jocelyn Stevens CVO
Chairman, English Heritage

BEDFORDSHIRE

WOBURN ABBEY OS Ref: SP965 325
Woburn MK43 0TP
Grant recipient/Owner: The Trustees of the Bedford Estates
Access Contact: Mr William Lash **Tel:** 01525 290666
Opening: **See page 62.** Wheelchairs in the Abbey by prior arrangement (maximum 8 per party). Access for wheelchair users to most areas
P800 £Yes Yes Guide dogs allowed

BERKSHIRE

WELFORD PARK OS Ref: SU409 731
Welford, Newbury RG20 8HU
Grant recipient/Owner: Mr J H L Puxley
Access Contact: Mr J H L Puxley **Tel:** 01488 608691
Opening: 29 May; 1 June – 26 June inclusive, and 28 August from 2.30pm to 5pm. House by prior arrangement. Grounds (free) suitable for wheelchair users
P40 £Yes Yes (no WC) Guide dogs allowed

BUCKINGHAMSHIRE

ABBEY FARMHOUSE OS Ref: SP896 012
Church Street, Great Missenden HP16 0AZ
Grant recipient/Owner: Mr N F Pearce
Access Contact: Mr N F Pearce **Tel:** 01494 862767
Opening: By prior arrangement (written appointments preferred). Access for wheelchair users to the ground floor only. There is a resident dog
P2 £No Yes (no WC) Guide dogs allowed

CHICHELEY HALL OS Ref: SP906 458
Newport Pagnell MK16 9JJ
Grant recipient/Owner: The Trustees of Mrs Nutting
Access Contact: Mrs Valerie Child **Tel:** 01234 391252
Opening: By prior written arrangement. Access for wheelchair users to the ground floor only
P60 £Yes Yes Guide dogs allowed

CHILTON HOUSE OS Ref: SP687 116
Chilton, Aylesbury HP18 9LR
Grant recipient/Owner: Chilton House Ltd
Access Contact: Lady Aubrey-Fletcher **Tel:** 01844 265200
Opening: By prior arrangement any day between 11am and 5pm
P £No Yes Guide dogs allowed

MARKET HOUSE OS Ref: SP807 035
Market Square, Princes Risborough HA27 0AS
Grant recipient/Owner: Princes Risborough Town Council
Access Contact: Mr D J Phillips **Tel:** 01844 273934
Opening: By prior arrangement on weekdays (telephone or written application). Short term parking (10 spaces) in High Street, public car park within 100 yards (next to parish church)
P £No No

WINSLOW HALL OS Ref: SP772 275
Winslow, Buckingham MK18 3HL
Grant recipient/Owner: Sir Edward Tomkins
Access Contact: Sir Edward Tomkins **Tel:** 01296 712323
Opening: All Bank Holiday weekends except Christmas/New Year from 2.30pm to 5.30pm; Wednesdays and Thursdays in July/August from 2.30pm to 5.30pm. Other times by prior arrangement. Additional street parking
P15 £Yes No Guide dogs allowed

CAMBRIDGESHIRE

BUCKDEN TOWERS OS Ref: TL193 677
High Street, Buckden PE18 9TA
Grant recipient/Owner: Claretian Missionaries
Access Contact: Mr John Huff **Tel:** 01480 810344
Opening: Visitors welcome. Tea shop open Saturday and Sunday afternoons in summer
P50 £No Yes Guide dogs allowed

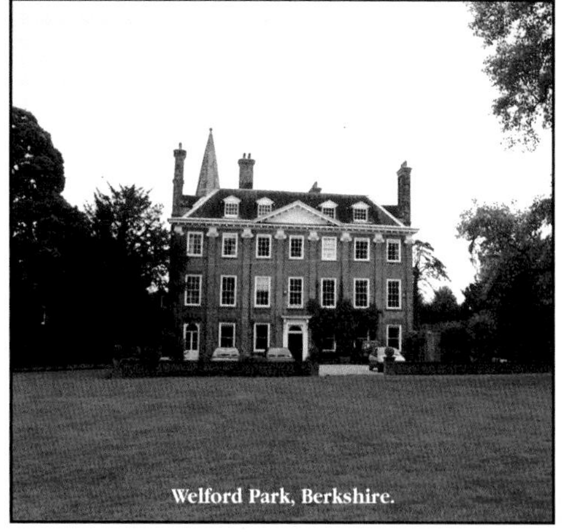
Welford Park, Berkshire.

ELTON HALL OS Ref: TL091 930
Elton, Peterborough PE8 6SH
Grant recipient/Owner: Mr William Proby
Access Contact: Joan Beard **Tel:** 01832 280468
Opening: **See page 228.** Access for wheelchair users, and guide dogs, to the Gardens only
P £Yes Yes (no WC)

HALL FARMHOUSE OS Ref: TL007 972
Hall Yard, Kings Cliffe, Peterborough PE8 6XG
Grant recipient/Owner: Mr J A R Grove
Access Contact: Mr J A R Grove **Tel:** 01780 470748
Opening: By prior arrangement
P3 £No No Guide dogs allowed

KIMBOLTON CASTLE OS Ref: TL101 676
Kimbolton, Huntingdon PE18 0EA
Grant recipient/Owner: The Governors of Kimbolton School
Access Contact: Mr J Mcleod **Tel:** 01480 862220
Opening: Guided tours: Easter Sunday and Monday; Spring Bank Holiday Sunday and Monday; last Sunday in July; Sundays in August and August Bank Holiday Monday, from 2pm to 6pm
P £Yes No Guide dogs allowed

THE MANOR OS Ref: TL290 706
Hemingford Grey, Huntingdon PE18 9BN
Grant recipient/Owner: Mr P S Boston
Access Contact: Mrs Diana Boston **Tel:** 01480 463134
Opening: **See page 230.** Parking provided at the house for disabled visitors, other visitors may park in the High Street
P £Yes No Guide dogs allowed

NEWNHAM COLLEGE OS Ref: TL442 578
Sidgwick Avenue, Cambridge CB3 9DF
Grant recipient/Owner: The Principal & Fellows of Newnham College
Access Contact: Mrs Carolyn Cocke **Tel:** 01223 335785
Opening: Access to the grounds without appointment in daylight hours except during the College's closed periods (25 August – 4 September and 22 December – 2 January 2001). Access to the grant-aided buildings by prior written arrangement with the Domestic Bursar
P0 £No Yes Guide dogs allowed

SACREWELL WATERMILL OS Ref: TF079 003
Sacrewell,Thornhaugh, Peterborough PE8 6HJ
Grant recipient/Owner: The William Scott Abbott Trust
Access Contact: Mr M Armitage **Tel:** 01780 782254
Opening: Daily (except Christmas Day, Boxing Day and New Year's Day) from 9.30am to 4pm in winter, 9.30am to 5pm in summer. Wheelchair access to the ground floor only
P300 £Yes Yes Guide dogs allowed

THORPE HALL OS Ref: TL170 986
Sue Ryder Home, Longthorpe, Peterborough PE3 6LW
Grant recipient/Owner: The Sue Ryder Foundation
Access Contact: Mrs P Bartlett **Tel:** 01733 330060
Opening: By prior arrangement in the afternoon only
P £No Yes Guide dogs allowed

CHESHIRE

BRAMALL HALL OS Ref: SJ886 863
Bramhall Park, Stockport SK7 3NX
Grant recipient/Owner: Stockport MBC
Access Contact: Ms Caroline Egan **Tel:** 0161 485 3708
Opening: Good Friday – end of September: Monday to Saturday from 1pm to 5pm, Sundays and Bank Holidays from 11am to 5pm; October – 1 January: Tuesday to Saturday from 1pm to 4pm, Sundays and Bank Holidays from 11am to 4pm; 2 January – Easter: weekends only from 1pm to 4pm. No wheelchair access to the first floor
P60 £Yes Yes Guide dogs allowed

CAPESTHORNE HALL OS Ref: SJ840 727
Macclesfield SK11 9JY
Grant recipient/Owner: Mr William Arthur Bromley-Davenport
Access Contact: Mrs Gwyneth Jones **Tel:** 01625 861221
Opening: **See page 369.** Access for wheelchair users to the ground floor of the Hall, the Butler's Pantry and the Gardens (compacted paths with some gravel)
P2000 £Yes Yes Guide dogs allowed

CHESTER TOWN HALL OS Ref: SJ404 665
Northgate Street, Chester CH1 2HS
Grant recipient/Owner: Chester City Council
Access Contact: Ms Rebecca Pinfold **Tel:** 01244 402320
Opening: Monday to Friday from 8.30am to 7pm. Saturdays by prior arrangement. Please telephone for details of Open Day. Parking in Princess Street
P £No Yes Guide dogs allowed

THE FERNERY OS Ref: SJ745 815
Tatton Park, Knutsford WA16 6QN
Grant recipient/Owner: Cheshire County Council
Access Contact: Mr A J Pellatt **Tel:** 01625 534400
Opening: 1 April – 31 October: Park: daily from 10.30am to 6pm; Gardens: Tuesday to Sunday and Bank Holidays from 10.30am to 5pm (Fernery closes 4pm); Mansion: Tuesday to Sunday and Bank Holidays from 12 noon to 4pm (2 – 31 October: Saturday and Sunday only). 1 November – 31 March 2001: Park: Tuesday to Sunday from 11am- 4pm; Gardens: Tuesday to Sunday from 11am to 4pm (Fernery closes 3pm); Mansion closed except for special openings. Partial access for wheelchair users
P1000 £Yes Yes Guide dogs allowed

HIGHFIELDS OS Ref: SJ674 410
Audlem, nr. Crewe CW3 0DT
Grant recipient/Owner: Mr J B Baker
Access Contact: Mrs Susan Baker **Tel:** 01630 655479
Opening: By prior arrangement, confirmed in writing
P20 £Yes No

LIGHTSHAW HALL FARM OS Ref: SJ615 994
Lightshaw Lane, Golborne, Warrington WA3 3UJ
Grant recipient/Owner: Mrs J Hewitt
Access Contact: Mrs J Hewitt **Tel:** 01942 717429
Opening: All year by prior telephone arrangement. Access for wheelchair users to the ground floor only
P20 £No Yes (no WC) Guide dogs allowed

MACCLESFIELD MUSEUMS AND HERITAGE CENTRE OS Ref: SJ917 734
Roe Street, Macclesfield SK11 6UT
Grant recipient/Owner: Macclesfield Museums Trust
Access Contact: Ms Barbara Arthur **Tel:** 01625 613210
Opening: Monday to Saturday from 11am to 5pm. Sunday from 1pm to 5pm
P0 £Yes Yes Guide dogs allowed

RODE HALL OS Ref: SJ819 573
Church Lane, Scholar Green ST7 3QP
Grant recipient/Owner: Sir Richard Baker Wilbraham Bt
Tel: 01270 873237
Opening: **See page 375.** Access to the Hall is possible for wheelchair users, but the Garden is unsuitable due to gravel paths. Unlimited parking on grass
P £Yes Yes (no WC) Guide dogs allowed

ST NICHOLAS CHAPEL OS Ref: SJ540 515
Cholmondeley Castle, Cholmondeley, Malpas SY14 8AH
Grant recipient/Owner: The Cholmondeley Estate
Access Contact: Mrs Penny Pritchard **Tel:** 01829 720383
Opening: 2 April – 28 September, (closed Good Friday): Wednesdays, Thursdays, Sundays and Bank Holidays from 11.30am to 5pm
P £Yes Yes Guide dogs allowed

WATERGATE HOUSE OS Ref: SJ402 662
85 Watergate Street, Chester CH1 2LF
Grant recipient/Owner: Ferry Homes Ltd
Access Contact: Miss Hayley Wynne **Tel:** 01352 713353
Opening: By prior telephone appointment from 9am to 11am or 3pm to 6pm
P0 £No No Guide dogs allowed

CORNWALL

CAERHAYS CASTLE GARDENS OS Ref: SW972 415
Gorran, St Austell PL26 6LY
Grant recipient/Owner: Mr F J Williams
Access Contact: Miss A B Mayes **Tel:** 01872 501144
Opening: Gardens: 13 March – 19 May: Monday to Friday from 10am to 4pm plus charity openings on Easter Sunday, 2 April and 1 May. House: 20 March – 28 April: Monday to Friday from 2pm to 4pm
PAmple £Yes Partial access All dogs on leads

THE CHAPEL OS Ref: SX382 563
Erth Barton, Saltash PL12 4QY
Grant recipient/Owner: Sir Richard Carew Pole Bt
Access Contact: Mr G Bentinck **Tel:** 01752 842127
Opening: By prior arrangement by telephone/fax (01752 842127) or letter. No coaches
P6 £No No

GODOLPHIN HOUSE OS Ref: SW602 318
Godolphin Cross, Helston TR13 9RE
Grant recipient/Owner: Mrs S E Schofield
Access Contact: Mrs S E Schofield **Tel:** 01736 762409
Opening: May – June: Thursdays from 2pm to 5pm; July – September: Tuesdays and Thursdays from 2pm to 5pm; August: Tuesdays from 2pm to 5 pm, Thursdays from 10am to 1pm and 2pm to 5pm. Bank Holiday Mondays (except Christmas). Parties and groups all year round by prior arrangement (please telephone and confirm in writing). Limited access for wheelchair users (downstairs only)
P50 £Yes Yes Guide dogs allowed

MOUNT EDGCUMBE HOUSE AND COUNTRY PARK OS Ref: SX452 527
Cremyll, Torpoint PL10 1HZ
Grant recipient/Owner: Mount Edgcumbe Country Park
Access Contact: The Manager **Tel:** 01752 822236
Opening: Country Park (with listed structures) open all year from dawn to dusk. House: 1 April – 1 October: Wednesday to Sunday and Bank Holidays from 11am to 4.30pm
P80 £Yes Yes Guide dogs allowed

PRIDEAUX PLACE OS Ref: SW913 756
Padstow PL28 8RP
Grant recipient/Owner: Mr Peter Prideaux-Brune
Access Contact: Mr Peter Prideaux-Brune **Tel:** 01841 532411
Opening: **See page 183.**
P40 £Yes Yes (no WC) Guide dogs allowed

SOUTHGATE ARCH OS Ref: SX330 847
Southgate Street, Launceston
Grant recipient/Owner: Launceston Town Council
Access Contact: Mr P J Freestone **Tel:** 01566 773693
Opening: 1 April – 25 December: Mondays, Tuesdays, Wednesdays, Fridays and Saturdays from 10am to 4.30pm (contact GWYNNGALA, lessees, 01566 777051)
P0 £No No Guide dogs allowed

TREGITHEW OS Ref: SW752 247
Manaccan, Helston TR12 6HX
Grant recipient/Owner: Mrs B Faull
Access Contact: Mrs B Faull **Tel:** 01326 231382
Opening: By prior written arrangement between June and September
P2 £No No

TREWITHEN HOUSE OS Ref: SW914 476
Grampound Road, Truro TR2 4DD
Grant recipient/Owner: Mr A M J Galsworthy
Access Contact: Mrs G Cates **Tel:** 01726 883647
Opening: **See page 187.** Limited access for wheelchair users
P100 £Yes Yes Guide dogs allowed

CUMBRIA

BRANTWOOD OS Ref: SD312 958
Coniston LA21 8AD
Grant recipient/Owner: The Brantwood Education Trust Ltd
Access Contact: Mr Howard Hull **Tel:** 01539 41396
Opening: 15 March – 15 November: from 11am to 5.30pm. Winter: Wednesday to Sunday from 11am to 4.30pm. Daily in the school holidays (except Christmas Day and Boxing Day)
P50 £Yes Yes Guide dogs allowed

CASTLETOWN HOUSE OS Ref: NY346 622
Rockcliffe, Carlisle CA6 4BN *
Grant recipient/Owner: Mr G H Mounsey-Heysham
Access Contact: Mr G H Mounsey-Heysham **Tel:** 01228 674205
Opening: By prior written arrangement
P £Yes No Guide dogs allowed

THE COOP HOUSE OS Ref: NY397 717
Netherby, nr. Carlisle.
Grant recipient/Owner: The Landmark Trust
Opening: Available for letting throughout the year. Open to the general public by prior written arrangement with the Landmark Trust, Shottesbrooke, Maidenhead, Berkshire SL6 3SW
P0 £No No Guide dogs allowed

HOLKER HALL OS Ref: SD359 773
Cark-in-Cartmel, Grange-over-Sands LA11 7PH
Grant recipient/Owner: Holker Estates Company Ltd
Access Contact: Mr D P R Knight **Tel:** 015395 58313
Opening: **See page 378.**
P £Yes Yes Guide dogs allowed

LEVENS HALL OS Ref: SD495 851
Kendal LA8 0PD
Grant recipient/Owner: Mr C H Bagot
Access Contact: Mr P E Milner **Tel:** 015395 60321
Opening: **See page 379.** House unsuitable for wheelchair users because of stairs and narrow doorways but all other facilities are accessible
P80 £Yes Yes Guide dogs allowed

MUNCASTER CASTLE OS Ref: SD103 965
Ravenglass CA18 1RQ
Grant recipient/Owner: Mrs P R Gordon-Duff-Pennington
Access Contact: Mr Peter Frost-Pennington **Tel:** 01229 717614
Opening: **See page 380.** Access for wheelchair users to the ground floor of the Castle only but other attractions/facilities are accessible. The hilly nature of the site can cause access difficulties so please ask for further information on arrival
P150 £Yes Yes Guide dogs allowed

BARN AT ORTHWAITE HALL OS Ref: NY252 341
Uldale, Carlisle CA5 1HL
Grant recipient/Owner: Mrs S Hope
Access Contact: Mr Jonathan Hope **Tel:** 016973 71344
Opening: At any time
P £No No Guide dogs allowed

COUNTY DURHAM

DURHAM CASTLE OS Ref: NZ274 424
Palace Green, Durham DH1 3RW
Grant recipient/Owner: University of Durham
Access Contact: The Porter **Tel:** 0191 374 3800
Opening: Easter – end of September: guided tours daily from 10am to 4pm; 1 October – Easter Monday: Wednesdays, Fridays, Saturdays and Sundays (afternoons only). Access for wheelchair users to courtyard. Parking in city car parks
P400 £Yes Yes (no WC) Guide dogs allowed

GATES & RAILINGS AT TANFIELD HALL OS Ref: NZ188 555
Tanfield DH9 9PX
Grant recipient/Owner: Mr D V Brewis
Access Contact: Mr D V Brewis **Tel:** 01207 234048
Opening: Daily from 9am to 5pm (fully accessible from the main road)
P0 £No Yes (no WC) Guide dogs allowed

RABY CASTLE OS Ref: NZ129 218
PO Box 50, Staindrop, Darlington DL2 3AY
Grant recipient/Owner: Lord Barnard TD
Access Contact: Mr David Hall **Tel:** 01833 660202
Opening: **See page 329.**
P500 £Yes No Guide dogs allowed

ROKEBY HALL OS Ref: NZ082 142
Barnard Castle DL12 9RZ
Grant recipient/Owner: The Trustees of Mortham Estates
Access Contact: Mr W H T Salvin **Tel:** 01833 690100
Opening: May Bank Holiday Monday and Spring Bank Holiday (Monday/Tuesday) then Mondays and Tuesdays until 2nd Tuesday in September from 2pm to 5pm (last admission 4.30pm). Access for wheelchair users to the ground floor only
P15 £Yes Yes (no WC)

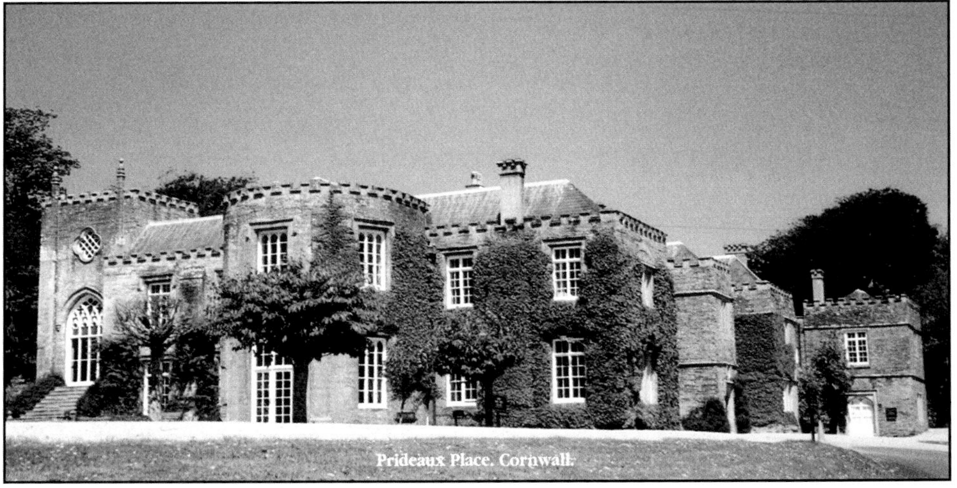
Prideaux Place, Cornwall.

SHERBURN HOSPITAL OS Ref: NZ308 415
Sherburn House, Durham DH1 2SE*
Grant recipient/Owner: The Governors of Sherburn Hospital
Access Contact: Mr Stephen Paul Black **Tel:** 0191 372 2551
Opening: By prior arrangement to the Chapel. Grounds always open
P20 £No Yes Guide dogs allowed

DERBYSHIRE

PADLEY CHAPEL & MARTYRS' SHRINE OS Ref: SK250 790
Upper Padley, Grindleford S32
Grant recipient/Owner: The Trustees of the Diocese of Hallam
Access Contact: Mrs Barbara M Smith **Tel:** 01433 651048
Opening: 30 April – end of September: Sunday and Wednesday afternoons from 2pm to 4pm. Other times by appointment. Accessible for wheelchair users by prior arrangement
P Nearby £No Yes (no WC) Guide dogs allowed

DEVON

BICKLEIGH CASTLE OS Ref: SS936 068
nr. Tiverton EX16 8RP
Grant recipient/Owner: Mr M J Boxall
Access Contact: Mr M J Boxall **Tel:** 01884 855363
Opening: See page 189. As much access as feasible for wheelchair users and people with guide dogs
P60 £Yes Yes (no WC) Guide dogs allowed

BOWRINGSLEIGH OS Ref: SX718 445
Kingsbridge TQ7 3LL
Grant recipient/Owner: Mr M C Manisty
Access Contact: Mr M C Manisty **Tel:** 01548 852014
Opening: By prior written appointment
P20 £No No

THE DEVON & EXETER INSTITUTION OS Ref: SX922 926
7 Cathedral Close, Exeter EX1 1EZ
Grant recipient/Owner: The Devon & Exeter Institution
Access Contact: Mrs M M Rowe **Tel:** 01392 274727
Opening: Open to members Monday to Friday from 9am to 5pm. Open to visitors on application. Closed for a week at Easter and Christmas
P0 £No Yes Guide dogs allowed

DUNKESWELL ABBEY OS Ref: ST143 107
nr. Honiton EX14 ORP
Grant recipient/Owner: Dunkeswell Abbey Preservation Fund
Access Contact: The Rev N J Wall **Tel:** 01404 891243
Opening: Always open. Roadside parking
P £No Yes (no WC) Guide dogs allowed

EASTLEIGH MANOR OS Ref: SS488 280
Eastleigh, Bideford EX39 4PA
Grant recipient/Owner: Mr D Grigg
Access Contact: Mr D Grigg **Tel:** 01271 860418
Opening: By prior written appointment
P0 £No No

ELIZABETHAN GATEHOUSE OS Ref: SS557 299
Tawstock Court, Tawstock, Barnstaple EX31 3HY
Grant recipient/Owner: The Governors of St Michael's School
Access Contact: Mrs S M Bennett **Tel:** 01271 343242
Opening: Easter – August during daylight hours
P2 £No No Guide dogs allowed

ENDSLEIGH HOUSE OS Ref: SX391 786
Milton Abbot, Tavistock PL19 0PQ
Grant recipient/Owner: The Endsleigh Fishing Club Ltd
Access Contact: Mr D Bradbury **Tel:** 01822 870248
Opening: April – September: Friday to Tuesday from 11am to 5pm; Wednesdays and Thursdays by prior arrangement
P20 £Yes Yes Guide dogs allowed

GREAT POTHERIDGE OS Ref: SS515 146
Merton, Okehampton EX20 3DN*
Grant recipient/Owner: Clinton Devon Estates
Access Contact: Mr G Smart
Opening: By prior written appointment
P £No No Guide dogs allowed

HIGHER THORNHAM OS Ref: SS735 182
Romansleigh, South Molton EX36 4JS
Grant recipient/Owner: Mr S W Chudley
Access Contact: Mr S W Chudley
Opening: 1 May – end of September: by prior written arrangement on Monday or Friday from 2pm to 4.30pm. No dogs please, and children to be accompanied by an adult. No photography
P0 £Yes No

THE OLD MANOR OS Ref: SY068 996
Talaton, Exeter EX5 2RQ
Grant recipient/Owner: Mr A S Dixon
Access Contact: Mr A S Dixon **Tel:** 01404 822485
Opening: By prior written appointment. The exterior of the building is accessible for wheelchair users but changes of level within present access difficulties
P3 £No Yes Guide dogs allowed

SAND OS Ref: SY146 925
Sidbury, Sidmouth EX10 0QN
Grant recipient/Owner: Lt-Col P V Huyshe
Access Contact: Lt-Col P V Huyshe **Tel:** 01395 597230
Opening: See page 195. Partial access for wheelchair users
P75 £Yes Yes (no WC) Guide dogs allowed

TOWN HOUSE OS Ref: SY134 984
Gittisham, Honiton EX14 0AJ
Grant recipient/Owner: Mr R J T Marker
Access Contact: Mr Andrew Hill
Opening: By prior written arrangement. Closed Easter and Christmas
P4 £No No Guide dogs allowed

YARDE FARMHOUSE OS Ref: SX718 400
Malborough, Kingsbridge TQ7 3BY
Grant recipient/Owner: Mr John Ayre
Access Contact: Mr John Ayre **Tel:** 01548 842367
Opening: Easter – mid-September: Sundays from 11am to 5pm. Coaches by prior written arrangement any other day. Access for wheelchair users to the first floor and garden
P10 £Yes Yes (no WC) Guide dogs allowed

Forde Abbey, Dorset.

THE PRIEST'S HOUSE OS Ref: ST057 190
Holcombe Rogus
Grant recipient/Owner: The Landmark Trust
Opening: Available for letting throughout the year. Open to the general public by prior written arrangement with the Landmark Trust, Shottesbrooke, Maidenhead, Berkshire SL6 3SW
P0 £No No Guide dogs allowed

ST LAWRENCE CHAPEL OS Ref: SX755 700
St Lawrence Lane, Ashburton TQ13 7DD *
Grant recipient/Owner: Dartmoor National Park Authority
Access Contact: Mrs Ruth Westall **Tel:** 01364 653414
Opening: Late May Bank Holiday – end of September: Tuesdays, Thursdays, Fridays and Saturdays from 2pm to 4.30pm. Heritage Open Days. Other times by arrangement
P0 £No No Guide dogs allowed

DORSET

FORDE ABBEY OS Ref: ST358 041
Chard TA20 4LU
Grant recipient/Owner: The Trustees of the Roper Settlement
Access Contact: Mrs Clay **Tel:** 01460 220231
Opening: See page 199. Access for wheelchair users and guide dogs to the garden only
P500 £Yes Yes Guide dogs allowed

HAMLET MALT HOUSE OS Ref: ST600 087
Hamlet, nr. Sherborne DT9 6NY
Grant recipient/Owner: Mr A Pope
Access Contact: Mr A Pope **Tel:** 01935 872325
Opening: Open all year for tours by prior arrangement
P0 £Yes No

NASH FARM OS Ref: SY375 989
Marshwood, Bridport DT6 5QL*
Grant recipient/Owner: The late Major J S Robertson
Access Contact: Miss Anne Robertson **Tel:** 01297 678273
Opening: By prior written arrangement (afternoons preferred)
P 3 £ No ♿ No Guide dogs allowed

PLACE MILL OS Ref: SZ159 925
Town Quay, Christchurch
Grant recipient/Owner: Christchurch Borough Council
Access Contact: Ms Ann Simon **Tel:** 01202 495127
Opening: Easter, Sundays and Bank Holidays until mid-May; then daily until the end of September, from 10am to 5pm. Guide dogs on the ground floor only
P 94 £ No ♿ No Guide dogs allowed

WOODSFORD CASTLE OS Ref: SY758 902
nr. Dorchester
Grant recipient/Owner: The Landmark Trust
Opening: Available for letting throughout the year. Open to the general public by prior written arrangement with the Landmark Trust, Shottesbrooke, Maidenhead, Berkshire SL6 3SW
P 0 £ No ♿ No Guide dogs allowed

ESSEX

BARN AT GREAT PRIORY FARM OS Ref: TL736 258
Panfield, Braintree CM7 5BQ
Grant recipient/Owner: Miss Lucy Tabor
Access Contact: Miss Lucy Tabor **Tel:** 01376 550944
Opening: By arrangement by telephone
P 20 £ No ♿ Yes (no WC) Guide dogs allowed

CRESSING TEMPLE OS Ref: TL798 188
Witham Road, nr. Braintree CM7 8PD
Grant recipient/Owner: Mr A L Cullen
Access Contact: Mrs L Rosewarne **Tel:** 01376 584903
Opening: March – October: Sundays from 10.30am to 5.30pm. Also May – September: Wednesdays, Thursdays and Fridays from from 10.30am to 5.30pm
P 150 £ Yes ♿ Yes Guide dogs allowed

GRANGE FARM BARNS OS Ref: TL653 213
Little Dunmow CM6 3HY
Grant recipient/Owner: Mr John Kirby
Access Contact: Mr John Kirby **Tel:** 01371 820205
Opening: By arrangement by telephone
P 6 £ No ♿ No Guide dogs allowed

HARWICH REDOUBT FORT OS Ref: TM262 322
Behind 29 Main Road, Harwich CO12 3LT
Grant recipient/Owner: The Harwich Society
Access Contact: Mr A Rutter **Tel:** 01255 503429
Opening: 1 May – 31 August: daily from 10am to 5pm. Rest of year: Sundays only from 10pm to 4pm
P 0 £ Yes ♿ No Guide dogs allowed

HORHAM HALL OS Ref: TL588 294
Thaxted CM6 2NN*
Grant recipient/Owner: Mr Michael Ward-Thomas
Access Contact: Mr Michael Ward-Thomas **Tel:** 01371 830389
Opening: By prior arrangement
P 70 £ Yes ♿ No Guide dogs allowed

HYLANDS HOUSE OS Ref: TL681 054
Hylands Park, London Road, Widford, Chelmsford CM2 8WQ
Grant recipient/Owner: Chelmsford Borough Council
Access Contact: Ms Linda Pittom **Tel:** 01245 606396
Opening: **See page 233.**
P 50 £ Yes ♿ Yes Guide dogs allowed

JOHN WEBB'S WINDMILL OS Ref: TL609 309
Fishmarket Sreet, Thaxted
Grant recipient/Owner: Mr M Arman
Access Contact: Mr L A Farren **Tel:** 01371 830285
Opening: May – September: Saturdays, Sundays and Bank Holidays from 2pm to 6pm. Conducted parties at other times by prior arrangement. Access for wheelchair users to the ground floor only. Parking in Thaxted
P £ Yes ♿ Yes (no WC) Guide dogs allowed

RAYNE HALL OS Ref: 733 229
Rayne, Braintree CM7 5BT
Grant recipient/Owner: Mr R J Pertwee
Access Contact: Mr R J Pertwee
Opening: By prior written arrangement
P 10 £ Yes ♿ Yes (no WC) Guide dogs allowed

ROYAL CORINTHIAN YACHT CLUB OS Ref: TQ947 956
The Quay, Burnham-on-Crouch CMO 8AX
Grant recipient/Owner: Royal Corinthian Yacht Club
Access Contact: Ms Margaret Pollard **Tel:** 01621 782105
Opening: By prior arrangement by telephone or in writing
P £ No ♿ No Guide dogs allowed

STANSTED WINDMILL OS Ref: TL510 248
Millside CM24 8BL
Grant recipient/Owner: Stansted Mountfichet Council
Access Contact: Mrs D P Honour **Tel:** 01279 813160
Opening: April – October: 1st Sunday in the month from 2pm to 6pm. Also Bank Holiday Sundays and Mondays and every Sunday in August. Parties by prior arrangement. For school groups contact Mrs Minshull (01279 812230). Children must be accompanied. Small souvenir shop
P 6 £ Yes ♿ No

STOCK WINDMILL OS Ref: TQ698 988
Mill Lane, Stock, Ingatestone
Grant recipient/Owner: Essex County Council
Access Contact: Mr M Hoyle **Tel:** 01621 828162
Opening: April – October: 2nd Sunday of each month from 2pm to 5pm, plus any reasonable time by arrangement for guided visits (admission charged). Access for wheelchair users to the exterior only on grass
P 6 £ For guided groups ♿ Yes (no WC)

THORRINGTON TIDE MILL OS Ref: TM083 194
Brightlingsea Road, Thorrington, Colchester
Grant recipient/Owner: Essex County Council
Access Contact: Mr M Hoyle **Tel:** 01621 828162
Opening: March – September: last Sunday of each month and Bank Holiday Mondays from 2pm to 5pm , plus guided group visits at other times by arrangement (admission charged). Access for wheelchair users to the exterior only down a steep slope
P 8 £ For guided groups ♿ Yes (no WC)

UPMINSTER WINDMILL OS Ref: TQ560 865
St Mary's Lane, Upminster RM14 2QH
Grant recipient/Owner: London Borough of Havering
Access Contact: Mr George Saddington **Tel:** 01708 772374
Opening: April – September: weekend openings once a month: 22/23 April, 13/14 May, 17/18 June, 15/16 July, 19/20 August, and 16/17 September. Group and individual visits throughout the year by prior arrangement
P 20 £ No ♿ Yes (no WC) Guide dogs allowed

GLOUCESTERSHIRE

ABBEY GATEHOUSE OS Ref: SO891 235
Tewkesbury
Grant recipient/Owner: The Landmark Trust
Opening: Available for letting throughout the year. Open to the general public by prior written arrangement with the Landmark Trust, Shottesbrooke, Maidenhead, Berkshire SL6 3SW
P 0 £ No ♿ No Guide dogs allowed

ACTON COURT OS Ref: ST676 842
Latteridge Road, Iron Acton BS17 1TJ
Grant recipient/Owner: Rosehill Corporation
Access Contact: Mr Bryan Hale **Tel:** 01454 228224
Opening: May – September: please telephone for details in the New Year
P 30 £ To be decided ♿ No

BERKELEY CASTLE OS Ref: ST685 990
Berkeley GL13 9BQ
Grant recipient/Owner: Mr R J Berkeley
Access Contact: Mr D Attwood **Tel:** 01453 810332
Opening: **See page 264.**
P 150 £ Yes ♿ No Guide dogs allowed

CHAVENAGE OS Ref: ST872 952
Tetbury GL8 8XP
Grant recipient/Owner: The Trustees of the Chavenage Settlement
Access Contact: Miss Caroline Lowsley-Williams **Tel:** 01666 502329
Opening: **See page 265.** Limited access for wheelchair users (ground floor only)
P 40 £ Yes ♿ Yes Guide dogs allowed

EAST BANQUETING HOUSE OS Ref: SP153 393
Chipping Campden
Grant recipient/Owner: The Landmark Trust
Opening: Available for letting throughout the year. Open to the general public by prior written arrangement with the Landmark Trust, Shottesbrooke, Maidenhead, Berkshire SL6 3SW
P 0 £ No ♿ No Guide dogs allowed

EBLEY MILL OS Ref: SO825 046
Westward Road, Stroud GL5 4UB
Grant recipient/Owner: Stroud District Council
Access Contact: Mr D Marshall **Tel:** 01453 754277
Opening: Open to the public from 8.45am to 5pm Monday to Thursday and from 8.45am to 4.30pm on Fridays excluding Bank Holidays. Tours may be arranged by (telephone) appointment
P 30 £ No ♿ Yes Guide dogs allowed

Hylands House, Essex.

Patrick Lane.

GREAT HOUSE FARM OS Ref: SO832 278
Hasfield GL19 4LQ
Grant recipient/Owner: The Hasfield Estate Trust
Access Contact: Mr D Banwell **Tel:** 01452 780206
Opening: By prior appointment to the interior from 1 April – end of September
P6 £No No Guide dogs allowed

PAINSWICK ROCOCO GARDEN OS Ref: SO864 106
The Stables, Painswick House, Painswick GL6 6TH
Grant recipient/Owner: Lord Dickinson
Access Contact: Mr P R Moir **Tel:** 01452 813204
Opening: See page 271. Groups by arrangement. Access is possible for wheelchair users but not easy
P80 £Yes Yes Guide dogs allowed

ST MARY MAGDALENE CHAPEL OS Ref: SO843 190
Hillfield Gardens, London Road, Gloucester
Grant recipient/Owner: Gloucester Historic Buildings Trust Ltd
Access Contact: Mr Malcolm J Watkins **Tel:** 01452 396620
Opening: By prior arrangement. Also Heritage Open Day in September (to be confirmed)
P0 £No Yes Guide dogs allowed

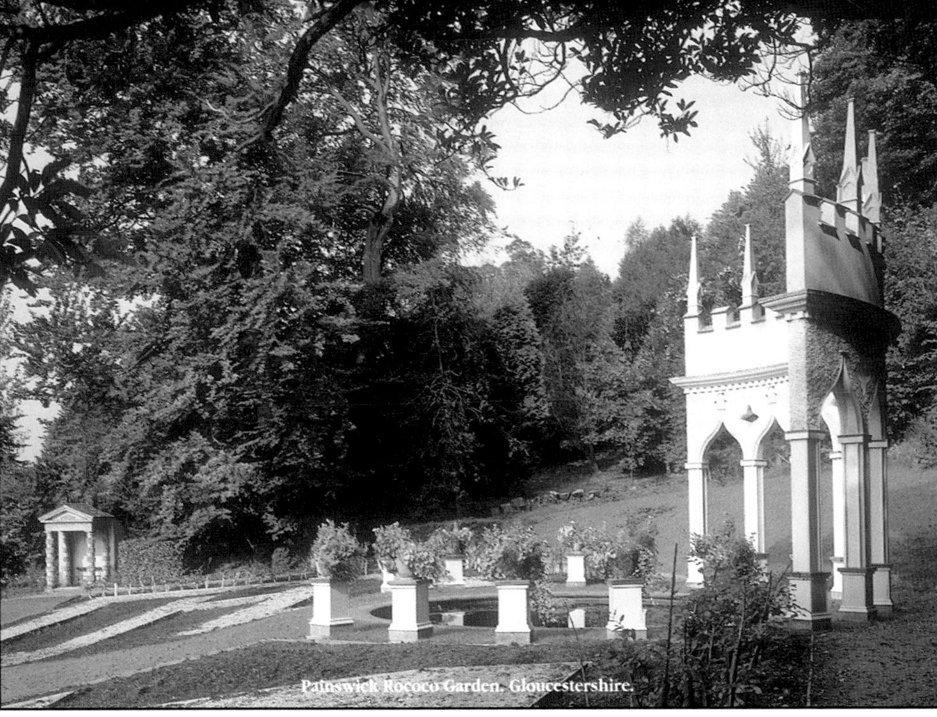
Painswick Rococo Garden, Gloucestershire.

STANLEY MILL OS Ref: SO813 043
Kings Stanley, Stonehouse GL10 3HQ
Grant recipient/Owner: Mr Peter Griffiths
Access Contact: Mr Mark Griffiths
Opening: By prior written appointment
P £No No

THE TEMPLE OS Ref: ST738 974
Stancombe Park, Dursley GL11 6AU
Grant recipient/Owner: Mr N D Barlow
Access Contact: Mrs G T Barlow **Tel:** 01453 542815
Opening: June – October
P50 £Yes No Guide dogs allowed

WICK COURT OS Ref: SO736 105
Overton Lane, Arlingham GL2 7JJ
Grant recipient/Owner: Farms for City Children
Access Contact: Ms Heather Tarplee **Tel:** 01452 741023
Opening: By appointment (please telephone first)
P20 £Yes Yes Guide dogs allowed

HAMPSHIRE

AVINGTON PARK OS Ref: SU534 324
Winchester S021 1DB *
Grant recipient/Owner: The late Colonel J B Hickson
Access Contact: Mrs Sarah Bullen **Tel:** 01962 779260
Opening: See page 78.
P50 £Yes Yes Guide dogs allowed

BREAMORE HOUSE AND MUSEUM OS Ref: SU152 191
nr. Fordingbridge SP6 2DF
Grant recipient/Owner: Sir Edward Hulse Bt
Access Contact: Sir Edward Hulse Bt **Tel:** 01725 512233
Opening: See page 78. Partial access for wheelchair users excluding first floor
P600 £Yes Partial Guide dogs allowed

THE DEANERY OS Ref: SU484 292
The Close, Winchester SO23 9LS
Grant recipient/Owner: The Dean and Chapter of Winchester Cathedral
Access Contact: Mrs Judy George
Opening: By prior written appointment with Mrs Judy George, The Cathedral Office, 1 The Close, Winchester S023 9LS
P0 £Yes No

FARNBOROUGH HILL OS Ref: SU871 546
Farnborough GU14 8AT
Grant recipient/Owner: The Farnborough Hill Trust
Access Contact: Mr J D Henwood **Tel:** 01252 545197
Opening: Spring Bank Holiday; Mondays, Wednesdays and Fridays in August. Guided tours at 2.15pm, 3.15pm and 4.15pm each day
P50 £No No Guide dogs allowed

HALL FARM OS Ref: SU665 392
Bentworth, Alton GU34 5JU
Grant recipient/Owner: Mr A C Brooking
Access Contact: Mrs M C Brooking **Tel:** 01420 564010
Opening: By prior arrangement by telephone or letter. Difficult access for wheelchair users
P30 £No No Guide dogs allowed

HIGHCLERE CASTLE AND PARK OS Ref: SU445 587
Highclere, nr. Newbury RG20 9RN
Grant recipient/Owner: The Earl of Carnarvon & Lord Porchester
Access Contact: H W Dean & Son **Tel:** 01223 351421
Opening: See page 76. Partial access for wheelchair users (no lift to first floor). Access enquiries may also be made to the Castle direct on 01635 253210. Unlimited parking
P £Yes Yes Guide dogs allowed

HOME FARM TITHE BARN OS Ref: SU152 191
Breamore, nr. Fordingbridge SP6 2DD
Grant recipient/Owner: Breamore Ancient Buildings Conservation Trust
Access Contact: Mr Michael Hulse **Tel:** 01725 512858
Opening: Weekdays by prior arrangement (telephone or written)
P10 £No Yes (no WC) Guide dogs allowed

HOUGHTON LODGE OS Ref: SU344 332
Stockbridge S020 6LQ
Grant recipient/Owner: Captain M W Busk
Access Contact: Captain M W Busk **Tel:** 01264 810502
Opening: See page 80.
P £Yes Yes Guide dogs allowed

NEW THEATRE ROYAL OS Ref: SZ638 999
Guildhall Walk, Portsmouth P01 2DD
Grant recipient/Owner: New Theatre Royal
Access Contact: Mr Gareth Vaughan **Tel:** 01705 646477
Opening: Whenever there is a performance and at other times by prior arrangement (for tours contact Fiona Cole). Wheelchair access to stalls only
P0 £Yes Yes Guide dogs allowed

ST AGATHA'S CHURCH OS Ref: SZ638 999
Market Way, Portsmouth
Grant recipient/Owner: St Agatha's Trust
Access Contact: Mr J D Maunder
Opening: October - May: Saturdays and Sundays from 10am to 2pm; June - September: Saturdays, Sundays and Wednesdays, from 10am to 3pm. Other times by prior arrangement
P £No Yes (no WC) Guide dogs allowed

WOODGREEN VILLAGE HALL OS Ref: SU171 176
Hale Road, Woodgreen, Fordingbridge SP6 2BQ
Grant recipient/Owner: Woodgreen Village Hall Committee
Access Contact: Mrs Angela Sales **Tel:** 01725 512288
Opening: Anytime when the hall is not in use but advisable to book first (contact Mrs Sales, or Mrs Windel on 01725 512529)
P20 £Yes Yes Guide dogs allowed

HEREFORDSHIRE

CHANDOS MANOR OS Ref: SO643 345
Rushall, Ledbury HR8 2PA
Grant recipient/Owner: Mr Richard White
Access Contact: Mr Richard White **Tel:** 01531 660208
Opening: Easter – September: 1st Sunday in each month by prior appointment
P12 £Yes No Guide dogs allowed

CHAPEL FARM OS Ref: SO394 684
Wigmore, nr. Leominster HR6 9UQ
Grant recipient/Owner: Mr M Pollitt
Access Contact: Mr M Pollitt
Opening: May – September: Mondays (except Bank Holidays) from 2pm to 4.30pm by prior written application giving home address and telephone number. Maximum 2 persons per visit. No children under 16 and no animals, please
P £No No

COLLEGE OF THE VICARS CHORAL OS Ref: SO511 397
The Cathedral Close, Hereford HR1 2NG
Grant recipient/Owner: The Dean and Chapter of Hereford Cathedral
Access Contact: Andrew Eames **Tel:** 01432 359880
Opening: Sundays (except Palm Sunday, Easter Day and Christmas Day) from 11am to 12.30pm and on other days by arrangement with the Chapter Clerk (written appointments not necessary)
P0 £No Yes (no WC) Guide dogs allowed

LANGSTONE COURT OS Ref: SO534 221
Llangarron, Ross-on-Wye HR9 6NR *
Grant recipient/Owner: Mr R M C Jones
Access Contact: Mr R M C Jones **Tel:** 01989 770254
Opening: 20 May – 31 August: Wednesdays and Thursdays and Spring and Summer Bank Holidays from 11am to 3pm
P20 (no coaches) £No No Guide dogs allowed

LION ASSEMBLY ROOMS OS Ref: SO495 590
Lion Yard, Broad Street, Leominster
Grant recipient/Owner: Leominster Properties Ltd
Access Contact: Mr Chris Sansom **Tel:** 01568 612874
Opening: Events most days and evenings. Contact Allan Ray, Leominster Farm Supplies, Broad Street, Leominster (01568 612277) for details. Out of hours a key can be obtained from Mr Chris Sansom. Car park open evenings and weekends
P £No ♿Yes Guide dogs allowed

THE PAINTED ROOM OS Ref: SO711 377
Town Council Offices, Church Street, Ledbury HR8 1DH
Grant recipient/Owner: Ledbury Town Council
Access Contact: Mrs J McQuaid **Tel:** 01531 632306
Opening: Easter – end of September: Monday to Friday from 11am to 3pm, also June – September: Saturdays and Sundays from 2pm to 5pm. Rest of year: Mondays, Tuesdays, Wednesdays and Fridays from 11am to 2pm. Town centre car parks nearby
P £No ♿No Guide dogs allowed

HERTFORDSHIRE

ASHRIDGE OS Ref: SP994 123
Berkhamsted HP4 1NS
Grant recipient/Owner: The Ashridge (Bonar Law Memorial) Trust
Access Contact: Mr T G Harvey **Tel:** 01442 841040
Opening: Gardens: Easter – end of September: Saturdays, Sundays and Bank Holidays from 2pm to 6pm. House: Easter Monday, May and Spring Bank Holidays and 31 July – 1 September (except Saturdays) from 2.30pm to 5pm. At other times by prior arrangement by telephone, fax (01442 841002) or letter
P300 £Yes ♿Yes Guide dogs allowed

DUCKLAKE HOUSE OS Ref: TL266 395
Springhead, Ashwell, Baldock SG7 5LL
Grant recipient/Owner: Mr P W H Saxton
Access Contact: Mr P W H Saxton
Opening: By prior written arrangement
P £No ♿No

HOMEWOOD OS Ref: TL245 205
Park Lane, Knebworth SG3 6PP
Grant recipient/Owner: Mr Stephen Pollock-Hill
Access Contact: Mr Stephen Pollock-Hill
Opening: By prior written arrangement at least 2 weeks in advance as the property is managed as a 'bed and breakfast'. Closed 20 December – 2 January. Access for wheelchair users to the ground floor only
P10 £No ♿Yes (no WC) Guide dogs allowed

KNEBWORTH HOUSE OS Ref: TL230 208
Knebworth, nr. Stevenage SG3 6PY
Grant recipient/Owner: Knebworth House Education & Preservation Trust
Access Contact: Miss Jacky Wilson **Tel:** 01438 812661
Opening: **See page 85.** Wheelchair access to the House restricted to the ground floor
P £Yes ♿Yes Guide dogs allowed

REDBOURNBURY MILL OS Ref: TL118 108
Redbournbury Lane, Redbourn Road, St Albans AL3 6RS
Grant recipient/Owner: Mr J T James
Access Contact: Mr J T James **Tel:** 01582 792874
Opening: 21 March – 3 October: Sundays from 2.30pm to 5pm plus Easter, late May and August Bank Holidays. National Mills Weekend, Heritage Weekend and New Year's Day open all day. Special events throughout the year. Private parties by prior arrangement. Wheelchair access to the ground floor only. Light refreshments and cream teas, milling demonstrations and organic flour and bread for sale
P30 £Yes ♿Yes (no WC)

SCOTT'S GROTTO OS Ref: TL355 137
Scott's Road, Ware SG12 9JQ
Grant recipient/Owner: Mr D L R Perman
Access Contact: Mrs Janet Watson **Tel:** 01920 464131
Opening: 1 April (or Good Friday if earlier) – end of September: Saturdays and Bank Holidays from 2pm to 4.30pm. Please bring a torch. Donation requested from adults
P0 £No ♿No Guide dogs allowed

SHIRE HALL OS Ref: TL326 127
Fore Street, Hertford
Grant recipient/Owner: Hertfordshire County Council
Access Contact: Mrs S Swain **Tel:** 01992 555613
Opening: Shire Hall is a working Court House from Monday to Friday (9am to 4.30pm) and not normally open to the public. Visitors can be accommodated by prior arrangement. There is a small step at the entrance but an internal lift
P0 £No ♿Yes (no WC) Guide dogs allowed

TORILLA OS Ref: TL205 077
11 Wilkins Green Lane, Nast Hyde, Hatfield AL10 9RT
Grant recipient/Owner: Mr Alan Charlton
Access Contact: Mr Alan Charlton
Opening: By written appointment only
P5 £Yes ♿No

KENT

CHIDDINGSTONE CASTLE OS Ref: TQ497 452
Chiddingstone, nr. Edenbridge TN8 7AD
Grant recipient/Owner: The Trustees of Denys Eyre Bower Bequest
Access Contact: The Custodian **Tel:** 01892 870347
Opening: **See page 94/95.** Wheelchair access to the ground floor only
P50 £Yes ♿Yes Guide dogs allowed

COMBE BANK SCHOOL OS Ref: TQ481 557
Sundridge, Sevenoaks TN14 6AE*
Grant recipient/Owner: The Governors of Combe Bank School
Access Contact: Mr H V C Phillips **Tel:** 01959 562918
Opening: By prior arrangement by telephone or letter
P £No ♿Yes (no WC) Guide dogs allowed

EASTBRIDGE HOSPITAL OS Ref: TR148 579
25 High Street, Canterbury, Kent CT1 2BD
Grant recipient/Owner: Eastbridge Hospital
Access Contact: Mrs Elizabeth Newby **Tel:** 01227 471688
Opening: Monday to Saturday from 10am to 4.45pm (excluding Good Friday, Christmas Day and other occasional Church Festival days)
P0 £Yes ♿No Guide dogs allowed

THE DAIRY OS Ref: TQ683 689
Cobham Hall, Cobham DA12 3BL
Grant recipient/Owner: The Cobham Hall Heritage Trust
Access Contact: Mr N G Powell **Tel:** 01474 823371
Opening: Easter – end August: Hall open Wednesdays and Sundays from 2pm to 5pm (last tour 4.30pm). Wheelchair access to the ground floor only. Self-guided tour of Gardens and Parkland (historical/conservation tour by prior arrangement). Special events. Telephone 01474 823371 to confirm opening times. Groups on other days by arrangement.
P100 £Yes ♿Yes (no WC) Guide dogs allowed

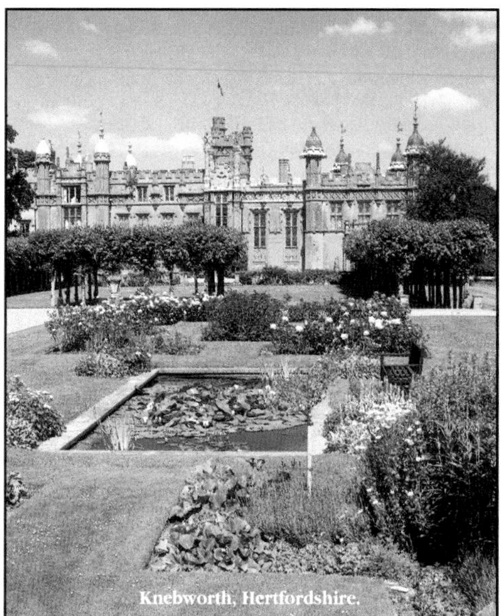
Knebworth, Hertfordshire.

FINCHCOCKS OS Ref: TQ700 365
Goudhurst TN17 1HH
Grant recipient/Owner: Mr Richard Burnett
Access Contact: Mrs Katrina Burnett **Tel:** 01580 211702
Opening: **See page 99.**
P100 £Yes ♿Yes Guide dogs allowed

THE FOORD ALMSHOUSES OS Ref: TQ736 672
Priestfields, Rochester ME1 3AF
Grant recipient/Owner: The Trustees of the Foord Almshouses
Access Contact: Mr David Hubbard **Tel:** 01634 844138
Opening: By prior arrangement (telephone or written). Partial access for wheelchair users
P £Yes ♿No

GOTHIC BATH HOUSE OS Ref: TQ490 725
112 North Cray Road, Bexley DA5 3NA
Grant recipient/Owner: Mrs Frances Chu
Access Contact: Mrs Frances Chu **Tel:** 01322 554894
Opening: Open day: 19 September (free admission). At other times by prior arrangement
P3 £Yes ♿No Guide dogs allowed

HERNE WINDMILL OS Ref: TR185 665
Mill Lane, Herne Bay CT6 7DR
Grant recipient/Owner: Kent County Council
Access Contact: Mr Ken Cole **Tel:** 01227 361326
Opening: National Mills Day from 11am to 5pm. Easter – end of September: Sundays and Bank Holidays from 2pm to 5pm; July/August: Thursdays 2pm to 5pm. Partial access for wheelchair users and guide dogs
P12 £Yes ♿Yes (no WC) Guide dogs allowed

LITTLEBOURNE TITHE BARN OS Ref: TR210 578
Church Road, Littlebourne, nr. Canterbury CT3 1TU
Grant recipient/Owner: Canterbury City Council
Access Contact: Canterbury City Conservation Section **Tel:** 01227 862190
Opening: Heritage Open Days and by arrangement
P15 £No ♿Yes Guide dogs allowed

NURSTEAD COURT OS Ref: TQ640 685
Nurstead Church Lane, Meopham, nr. Gravesend DA13 9AD
Grant recipient/Owner: Mrs S M H Edmeades-Stearns
Access Contact: Mrs S M H Edmeades-Stearns **Tel:** 01474 812121
Opening: Every Wednesday and Thursday in September and 4/5 October from 2pm to 5pm. By prior arrangement (telephone or written) all year
P30 £Yes ♿Yes (no WC) Guide dogs allowed

THE PROSPECT TOWER OS Ref: TQ986 564
Belmont Park, Faversham
Grant recipient/Owner: The Landmark Trust
Opening: Available for letting throughout the year. Open to the general public by prior written arrangement with the Landmark Trust, Shottesbrooke, Maidenhead, Berkshire SL6 3SW
P0 £No ♿No Guide dogs allowed

THE ROPER GATEWAY OS Ref: TR144 583
Adjacent to 33 St Dunstan's Street, Canterbury
Grant recipient/Owner: Canterbury City Council
Access Contact: Canterbury City Conservation Section **Tel:** 01227 862190
Opening: For visiting details contact the Secretary in the Conservation Section, Canterbury City Council
P0 £No ♿Yes (no WC) Guide dogs allowed

SQUERRYES COURT OS Ref: TQ440 535
Westerham TN16 1SJ
Grant recipient/Owner: Mr J Warde
Access Contact: Mr J Warde **Tel:** 01959 562345
Opening: **See page 109.**
P £Yes ♿No Guide dogs allowed

LANCASHIRE

THE 1830 WAREHOUSE OS Ref: SJ832 977
Liverpool Road, Castlefield, Manchester M3 4FP
Grant recipient/Owner: The Museum of Science and Industry in Manchester
Access Contact: Ms Kathryn Morgan **Tel:** 0161 832 2244
Opening: All buildings open daily from 10am to 5pm (except 24/25/26 December)
P Limited £ Yes ♿ Yes Guide dogs allowed

THE ALBION WAREHOUSE OS Ref: SJ937 987
Penny Meadow, Ashton-under-Lyne
Grant recipient/Owner: G A Armstrong Ltd
Opening: All year except Christmas Day and New Year's Day
P 80 £ No ♿ No Guide dogs allowed

ASHTON MEMORIAL OS Ref: SD489 613
Williamson Park, Lancaster LA1 1UX
Grant recipient/Owner: Lancaster City Council
Access Contact: Mrs Elaine Charlton **Tel:** 01524 33318
Opening: 1 April – end of September from 10am to 5pm. October – end of March from 11am to 4pm (Saturday/Sunday from 10am to 4pm). Closed Christmas Day, Boxing Day, and 1 January. Admission charge relates to the Tropical Butterfly House, the Mini Beast Cave, the Bird Enclosure, Gardens and the Ashton Memorial Viewing Gallery but admission to the ground floor of the Memorial is free
P 120 £ Yes ♿ Yes Guide dogs allowed

ASTLEY HALL MUSEUM & ART GALLERY OS Ref: SD574 183
Astley Park, Chorley PR7 1NP
Grant recipient/Owner: Chorley Borough Council
Access Contact: Mr Nigel Wright **Tel:** 01257 515555
Opening: 1 April – 31 October: Tuesday to Sunday from 12 noon to 5pm plus Bank Holiday Mondays; November – March: weekends only. Access for wheelchair users to the ground floor only
P 100 £ Yes ♿ Yes (no WC) Guide dogs

BROWSHOLME HALL OS Ref: SD683 452
nr.Clitheroe BB7 3DE*
Grant recipient/Owner: Mr R R Parker
Access Contact: Mr R R Parker **Tel:** 01254 826719
Opening: Arrangements for 2000 not yet confirmed. Please telephone for further details
P 30 £ Yes ♿ Yes Guide dogs allowed

ELM WOOD COUNTY PRIMARY SCHOOL OS Ref: SD870 057
Elm Street, Middleton M24 2EG
Grant recipient/Owner: Rochdale MBC
Access Contact: Mr A J Torr **Tel:** 0161 287 0607
Opening: By prior arrangement with the Headteacher, Monday to Friday during term-time between 9am and 5pm. Street parking
P £ Yes ♿ Yes Guide dogs allowed

HEATON HALL OS Ref: SD834 044
Heaton Park, Prestwich M25 5SW
Grant recipient/Owner: Manchester City Council
Access Contact: Ms Ruth Shrigley **Tel:** 0161 234 1459
Opening: Easter – 29 October: Wednesdays to Sundays and Bank Holiday Mondays from 10am to 5.30pm. Access for wheelchair users to a substantial part of the building
P 50 £ No ♿ Yes Guide dogs allowed

HOGHTON TOWER OS Ref: SD622 264
Hoghton, Preston PR5 0SH
Grant recipient/Owner: The Hoghton Tower Preservation Trust
Access Contact: Mr John Graver **Tel:** 01254 852986
Opening: **See page 387.**
P 250 £ Yes ♿ No Guide dogs allowed

LANCASTER MARITIME MUSEUM OS Ref:SD476 621
Custom House, St George's Quay, Lancaster LA1 1RB
Grant recipient/Owner: Lancaster City Council
Access Contact: Dr Nigel Dalziel **Tel:** 01524 64637
Opening: Daily (except Christmas and New Year). Easter – October inclusive from 11am to 5pm; November – Easter from 12.30pm to 4pm. No admission charge for local ratepayers
P 30 £ Yes ♿ Yes Guide dogs allowed

LEIGHTON HALL OS Ref: SD494 744
Carnforth LA5 9ST
Grant recipient/Owner: Mr R Reynolds
Access Contact: Mr R Reynolds **Tel:** 01524 734474
Opening: **See page 386.**
P 100 £ Yes ♿ Yes Guide dogs allowed

LIVERPOOL ROAD STATION, OS Ref: SJ832 977
Liverpool Road, Castlefield, Manchester M3 4FP
Grant recipient/Owner: The Museum of Science and Industry in Manchester
Access Contact: Ms Kathryn Morgan **Tel:** 0161 832 2244
Opening: All buildings open daily from 10am to 5pm (except 24/25/26 December)
P Limited £ Yes ♿ Yes Guide dogs allowed

MANCHESTER JEWISH MUSEUM OS Ref: SJ844 999
190 Cheetham Hill Road, Manchester M8 8LW
Grant recipient/Owner: The Trustees of Manchester Jewish Museum
Access Contact: Mr Don Rainger **Tel:** 0161 834 9879
Opening: All year: Monday to Thursday from 10.30am to 4pm; Sundays from 10.30am to 5pm. Closed 1/2/3/January, 20/26/27 April, 1/9/15/22 October, 24/25/26 December. Early closing (1pm) 19 April and 8 October. Group visits must be booked in advance. Access for wheelchair users to the ground floor only. On street parking immediately outside the museum
P £ Yes ♿ Yes (no WC) Guide dogs allowed

MANCHESTER LAW LIBRARY OS Ref: SJ840 981
14 Kennedy Street, Manchester M2 4BY
Grant recipient/Owner: Manchester Incorporated Law Library Society
Access Contact: Mrs Julia Bragg **Tel:** 0161 236 6312
Opening: By prior appointment by telephone or in writing
P 0 £ No ♿ No Guide dogs allowed

MARTHOLME OS Ref: SD753 338
Martholme Lane, Great Harwood, Blackburn BB6 7UJ
Grant recipient/Owner: Mr T H Codling
Access Contact: Miss P M Codling **Tel:** 01254 886463
Opening: Evenings and weekends by prior written appointment. Access to the ground floor only for wheelchair users. Guide dogs with prior notice
P 12 £ Yes ♿ Yes (no WC) Guide dogs allowed

STONYHURST COLLEGE OS Ref: SD690 391
Stonyhurst, Clitheroe BB7 9PZ
Grant recipient/Owner: Stonyhurst College
Access Contact: Miss Frances Ahearne **Tel:** 01254 826345
Opening: House: 17 July – 28 August, daily (except Friday), plus August Bank Holiday Monday, from 1pm to 5pm. Gardens: 1 July – 28 August, daily (except Friday), plus August Bank Holiday Monday, from 1pm to 5pm. Limited access for wheelchair users but assistance will be made available if contacted in advance. Coach parties by prior arrangement
P 200 £ Yes ♿ Yes Guide dogs allowed

TURTON TOWER OS Ref: SD733 153
Chapeltown Rd, Turton, Bolton BL7 0HG
Grant recipient/Owner: Lancashire County Museum Service
Access Contact: Mr M Robinson-Dowland **Tel:** 01204 852203
Opening: February and November: Sundays from 1pm to 4pm; March and October: Saturday to Wednesday from 1pm to 4pm; April: Saturday to Wednesday from 2pm to 5pm; May – September: Saturday and Sunday from 1pm to 5pm, Monday to Thursday from 10am – 12 noon and from 1pm to 5pm. Additional parking for 2 coaches. Access for wheelchair users to the ground floor, tea room and shop
P 55 £ Yes ♿ Yes Guide dogs allowed

LEICESTERSHIRE

LAUNDE ABBEY CHAPEL OS Ref: SK797 044
East Norton, Leicester LE7 9XB
Grant recipient/Owner: Launde Abbey
Access Contact: The Rev Graham Johnson **Tel:** 01572 717254
Opening: Easter Monday; May Bank Holidays; Mondays in June, July and August; Saturdays in August, from 10am to 5pm
P 200 £ No ♿ Yes (no WC) Guide dogs allowed

THE OLD RECTORY OS Ref: SK601 151
Cossington LE7 4UU
Grant recipient/Owner: Mrs V Jones
Access Contact: Mrs V Jones
Opening: By written arrangement
P 6 £ No ♿ No Guide dogs allowed

STANFORD HALL, OS Ref: SP587 793
Lutterworth LE17 6DH
Grant recipient/Owner: Lady Braye
Access Contact: Lt-Col E H L Aubrey-Fletcher **Tel:** 01788 860250
Opening: **See page 279.** Partial access for wheelchair users
P 1500 £ Yes ♿ Yes Guide dogs allowed

Stanford Hall, Leicestershire.

LINCOLNSHIRE

2-2A EXCHEQUERGATE OS Ref: SK978 718
Lincoln LN2 1PZ
Grant recipient/Owner: The Dean and Chapter of Lincoln Cathedral
Access Contact: Mr Gerald Burbidge **Tel:** 01522 527637
Opening: By prior written arrangement with the Clerk of Works, Lincoln Cathedral, 28 Eastgate, Lincoln LN2 4AA
P 0 £ No ♿ No

3-3A VICARS COURT OS Ref: SK978 718
Lincoln LN2 1PT
Grant recipient/Owner: The Dean and Chapter of Lincoln Cathedral
Access Contact: Mr Gerald Burbidge **Tel:** 01522 527637
Opening: By prior written arrangement with the Clerk of Works, Lincoln Cathedral, 28 Eastgate, Lincoln LN2 4AA
P 0 £ No ♿ No

3, 3A AND 4 POTTERGATE OS Ref: SK978 718
Lincoln LN2 1PH
Grant recipient/Owner: The Dean and Chapter of Lincoln Cathedral
Access Contact: Mr Gerald Burbidge **Tel:** 01522 527637
Opening: By prior written arrangement with the Clerk of Works, Lincoln Cathedral, 28 Eastgate, Lincoln LN2 4AA
P 0 £ No ♿ No Guide dogs

4-4A VICARS COURT OS Ref: SK978 718
Lincoln LN2 1PT
Grant recipient/Owner: The Dean and Chapter of Lincoln Cathedral
Access Contact: Mr Gerald Burbidge **Tel:** 01522 527637
Opening: By prior written arrangement with the Clerk of Works, Lincoln Cathedral, 28 Eastgate, Lincoln LN2 4AA
P 0 £ No ♿ No Guide dogs

12 EASTGATE OS Ref: SK978 718
Lincoln LN2 1QG
Grant recipient/Owner: The Dean and Chapter of Lincoln Cathedral
Access Contact: Mr Gerald Burbidge **Tel:** 01522 527 637
Opening: By prior written arrangement with the Clerk of Works, Lincoln Cathedral, 28 Eastgate, Lincoln LN2 4AA
P 0 £ No ♿ No Guide dogs

12 MINSTER YARD OS Ref: SK978 718
Lincoln LN2 1PJ
Grant recipient/Owner: The Dean and Chapter of Lincoln Cathedral
Access Contact: Mr Gerald Burbidge **Tel:** 01522 527637
Opening: By prior written arrangement with the Clerk of Works, Lincoln Cathedral, 28 Eastgate, Lincoln LN22 4AA
P0 £No No

13-13A MINSTER YARD OS Ref:SK978 718
Lincoln LN2 1PW
Grant recipient/Owner: The Dean and Chapter of Lincoln Cathedral
Access Contact: Mr Gerald Burbidge **Tel:** 01522 527637
Opening: By prior written arrangement with the Clerk of Works, Lincoln Cathedral, 28 Eastgate, Lincoln LN2 4AA
P0 £No No

17 MINSTER YARD OS Ref: SK978 718
Lincoln LN2 1PX
Grant recipient/Owner: The Dean and Chapter of Lincoln Cathedral
Access Contact: Mr Gerald Burbidge **Tel:** 01522 527637
Opening: By prior written arrangement with the Clerk of Works, Lincoln Cathedral, 28 Eastgate, Lincoln LN2 4AA
P0 £No No

18-18A MINSTER YARD OS Ref: SK978 718
Lincoln LN2 1PX
Grant recipient/Owner: The Dean and Chapter of Lincoln Cathedral
Access Contact: Mr Gerald Burbidge **Tel:** 01522 527637
Opening: By prior written arrangement with the Clerk of Works, Lincoln Cathedral, 28 Eastgate, Lincoln LN2 4AA
P0 £No No

22 MINSTER YARD OS Ref: SK978 718
Lincoln LN2 1PX
Grant recipient/Owner: The Dean and Chapter of Lincoln Cathedral
Access Contact: Mr Gerald Burbidge **Tel:** 01522 527637
Opening: By prior written arrangement with the Clerk of Works, Lincoln Cathedral, 28 Eastgate, Lincoln LN2 4AA
P0 £No No

BURGHLEY HOUSE OS Ref:TF048 062
Stamford PE9 3JY
Grant recipient/Owner: The Burghley House Preservation Trust
Access Contact: Mr Jon Culverhouse **Tel:** 01780 752451
Opening: See page 236. Partially accessible for wheelchair users
P500 £Yes Yes Guide dogs allowed

ELSHAM CHALK BARN OS Ref:TA050 135
Elsham Wolds Industrial Estate, Elsham DN18
Grant recipient/Owner: The Buildings at Risk Trust
Access Contact: Mr David Williams **Tel:** 01724 843533
Opening: By prior written arrangement made at least two weeks in advance with the Principal Keeper, North Lincolnshire Museum, Oswald Road, Scunthorpe DN15 7BD
P3 £No No

FYDELL HOUSE OS Ref:TF327 437
South Street, Boston PE21 6HU
Grant recipient/Owner: The Boston Preservation Trust Ltd
Access Contact: Ms Christine Wright **Tel:** 01205 351520
Opening: Open throughout the year, excluding Bank Holidays, but during term time access to rooms is limited. Weekend appointments for parties can be arranged. Public car park nearby
P0 £No Yes Guide dogs allowed

GUY'S HEAD LIGHTHOUSE OS Ref:TF491 258
Sutton Bridge PE12 9PJ*
Grant recipient/Owner: Mr Simon Normanton
Access Contact: Mr Simon Normanton **Tel:** 01406 351522
Opening: External viewing by prior appointment
P5 £No Yes (no WC) Guide dogs allowed

HEGGY'S COTTAGE OS Ref:TF105 254
Hall Road, Haconby, nr. Bourne PE10 0UY
Grant recipient/Owner: Mrs J F Atkinson
Access Contact: Mrs J F Atkinson **Tel:** 01778 570318
Opening: By prior written arrangement with Mrs J F Atkinson, Haconby Hall, nr. Bourne PE10 0UY
P1 £No No

THE HOUSE OF CORRECTION OS Ref:TF074 334
Folkingham
Grant recipient/Owner: The Landmark Trust
Opening: Available for letting throughout the year. Open to the general public by prior written arrangement with the Landmark Trust, Shottesbrooke, Maidenhead, Berkshire SL6 3SW
P0 £No No Guide dogs allowed

MAUD FOSTER WINDMILL OS Ref:TF333 447
Boston PE21 9EG
Grant recipient/Owner: Mr T E Waterfield
Access Contact: Mr James Waterfield **Tel:** 01205 352188
Opening: All year: Wednesdays and Saturdays from 11am to 5pm, Sundays from 1pm to 5pm, Thursdays and Fridays in July/August from 11am to 5pm, Bank Holidays from 10am to 5pm. Closed Christmas and New Year
P16 £Yes No

MOUNT PLEASANT WINDMILL OS Ref: SK939 995
Kirton-in-Lindsey DN21 4NH
Grant recipient/Owner: Mr P J White
Access Contact: Mr Patrick White **Tel:** 01652 640177
Opening: All year round: Saturdays, Sundays and Bank Holidays from 10am to 5pm, Fridays from 11am to 4pm . Closed Christmas Day and Boxing Day. Also open weekdays in August – please ring. Groups at any time by arrangement. Access for wheelchair users and visitors with guide dogs to the ground floor of the Mill. Bakery and tea room
P30 £Yes Yes Guide dogs allowed

WALTHAM WINDMILL OS Ref:TA260 034
Brigsley Road, Waltham, Grimsby DN37 0JZ
Grant recipient/Owner: Waltham Windmill Trust
Access Contact: Mrs M A Stennett **Tel:** 01472 822236
Opening: Easter – September: Saturdays and Sundays and Bank Holiday Mondays from 10am to 4pm. Group visits can be arranged by contacting Mrs Diana Le-Core (01472 752122 or fax, 01472 316788)
P30 £Yes Yes Guide dogs allowed

LONDON

BRUCE CASTLE OS Ref:TQ335 906
Lordship Lane N17 8NU
Grant recipient/Owner: London Borough of Haringey
Access Contact: Ms Lynn Flavell **Tel:** 0181 808 8772
Opening: Wednesday to Sunday from 1pm to 5pm plus Easter Monday, May Day, late May Bank Holiday and August Bank Holiday (closed Good Friday, Christmas Day, Boxing Day and New Year's Day). Groups at other times by prior arrangement
P15 £No Yes Guide dogs allowed

COLLEGE OF ARMS OS Ref:TQ320 810
Queen Victoria Street EC4V 4BT
Grant recipient/Owner: College of Arms
Access Contact: Officer in Waiting **Tel:** 0171 248 2762
Opening: Earl Marshal's Court only: all year (except Public Holidays and State and special occasions), Monday to Friday from 10am to 4pm. Group visits (up to 10) by prior arrangement. Record Room open for tours (groups of up to 20) by prior arrangement with the Officer in Waiting
P0 £No No Guide dogs allowed

HIGHGATE CEMETERY OS Ref:TQ285 873
Swain's Lane N6 6PJ
Grant recipient/Owner: Friends of Highgate Cemetery Ltd
Access Contact: Mrs J A Pateman **Tel:** 0181 340 1834
Opening: Eastern Cemetery: 1 April – 31 October from 10am (11am weekends) to 5pm, 1 November - 31 March from 10am (11am weekends) to 4pm. Western Cemetery: guided tours only, weekdays at noon, 2pm, 4pm (3pm in winter) and at weekends on the hour from 11am to 4pm (3pm in winter). No weekday tours in December, January or February. Special tours for groups of 10 or more by prior appointment please send large sae. Access for wheelchair users to Eastern Cemetery only. Guide dogs allowed under special conditions
P0 £Yes Yes (no WC) Guide dogs allowed

THE HOUSE MILL OS Ref:TQ383 828
The Miller's House, Three Mill Lane, Bromley-by-Bow E3 3DU
Grant recipient/Owner: River Lea Tidal Mill Trust
Access Contact: Mr William Hill **Tel:** 0181 472 2829
Opening: National Mills Weekend then Sundays to the end of October. 1st Sunday in each month from 11am to 4pm, other Sundays from 2pm to 4pm. Group visits by arrangement
P £Yes Yes Guide dogs allowed

PRENDERGAST SCHOOL MURALS OS Ref:TQ373 753
Hilly Fields, Adelaide Avenue SE4 1LE
Grant recipient/Owner: The Governors of Prendergast School
Access Contact: Miss E Pienaar **Tel:** 0181 690 2978
Opening: By prior written arrangement during term time and school hours
P0 £No Yes Guide dogs allowed

ROYAL GEOGRAPHICAL SOCIETY OS Ref:TQ268 796
1 Kensington Gore SW7 2AR
Grant recipient/Owner: Royal Geographical Society
Access Contact: Ms Denise Prior **Tel:** 0171 591 3090
Opening: Weekdays (except Bank Holidays) from 10am to 5pm. Map Room from 11am to 5pm. Limited parking by prior arrangement subject to availability (contact the House Manager's Office on 0171 591 3090)
PLimited £No Yes Guide dogs allowed

ST PANCRAS CHAMBERS OS Ref:TQ302 829
Euston Road NW1 2QP
Grant recipient/Owner: London & Continental Stations & Property Ltd
Access Contact: Mrs Lynda Nolan **Tel:** 0171 304 3900
Opening: Front entrance and former ground floor coffee lounge open each weekday from 11.30am to 3.30pm without charge. For guided group tours of the remainder of the building contact 0171 304 3900. Tours involve climbing several flights of stairs and there are no working lifts or other facilities for the disabled
P0 £Yes No

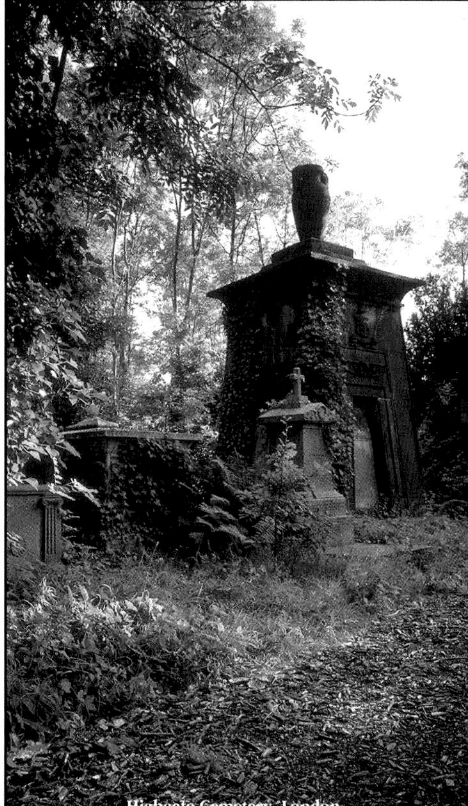
Highgate Cemetery, London.

THE TRAVELLERS CLUB OS Ref: TQ295 803
106 Pall Mall SW1Y 5EP
Grant recipient/Owner: The Travellers Club
Access Contact: Mr Nigel Sharpe **Tel:** 0171 930 8688
Opening: By prior arrangement, Monday to Friday from 10am to 12 noon. Closed Bank Holidays, August and Christmas
P 0 £ Yes ♿ No Guide dogs allowed

WALPOLE'S HOUSE OS Ref: TQ158 722
Strawberry Hill, Waldegrave Road, Twickenham TW1 4SX
Grant recipient/Owner: St Mary's, Strawberry Hill
Access Contact: Conference Officer **Tel:** 0181 240 4114
Opening: **See page 138.**
P £ Yes ♿ No Guide dogs allowed

MERSEYSIDE

BLUECOAT CHAMBERS OS Ref: SJ347 903
School Lane, Liverpool L1 3BX
Grant recipient/Owner: Bluecoat Arts Centre Ltd
Access Contact: Mr A Hurley **Tel:** 0151 709 5297
Opening: All year round except Bank and Public Holidays
P £ No ♿ Yes Guide dogs allowed

THE CONVENT CONSERVATORY OS Ref: SJ400 930
Convent of Mercy, Broughton Hall, Yew Tree Lane, West Derby, Liverpool L12 9HH
Grant recipient/Owner: The Institute of Our Lady of Mercy
Access Contact: The Sister Superior
Opening: By written appointment only, Monday to Saturday between 10am and 4pm. No access on Sundays, Religious Holidays and Bank Holidays. Access for wheelchair users and people with guide dogs by prior arrangement
P 4 £ No ♿ Yes Guide dogs allowed

THE TURNER MEMORIAL HOME OF REST OS Ref: SJ365 877
Dingle Lane, Liverpool L8 9RN
Grant recipient/Owner: The Trustees of the Turner Memorial Home of Rest
Access Contact: Mrs Alison Charlesworth **Tel:** 0151 727 4177
Opening: By prior arrangement
P 10 £ No ♿ Yes Guide dogs allowed

NEWCASTLE-UPON-TYNE

21-23 LEAZES TERRACE OS Ref: NZ244 647
Newcastle-upon-Tyne NE1 4LY
Grant recipient/Owner: University of Newcastle-upon-Tyne
Access Contact: Mr I Gibson **Tel:** 0191 222 6000
Opening: The repaired decorative stonework at the north west corner of the building is viewable at any time without access to the building. Access to the interior (now converted into bedsitters for postgraduate students) is restricted to Room 21F, retained in near original condition by agreement with English Heritage. Visits by prior written arrangement with Mr Gibson of the Estates Office, University of Newcastle, 7 Park Terrace, Newcastle-upon-Tyne NE1 7RU
P 0 £ No ♿ No

NORFOLK

BILLINGFORD CORNMILL OS Ref: TM165 786
Scole
Grant recipient/Owner: The Norfolk Windmills Trust
Access Contact: Miss A L Jaques **Tel:** 01603 222705
Opening: Arrangements for 2000 not yet confirmed. Please contact the Trust for further information
P 2 £ Yes ♿ No

CHURCHMAN HOUSE OS Ref: TG226 086
71 Bethel Street, Norwich NR2 1NR
Grant recipient/Owner: Norwich City Council
Access Contact: The Superintendent Registrar **Tel:** 01603 767600
Opening: By prior appointment normally on Tuesday or Thursday afternoons. All appointments are subject to there being no marriages arranged. Telephone appointments are acceptable
P 0 £ No ♿ Yes Guide dogs allowed

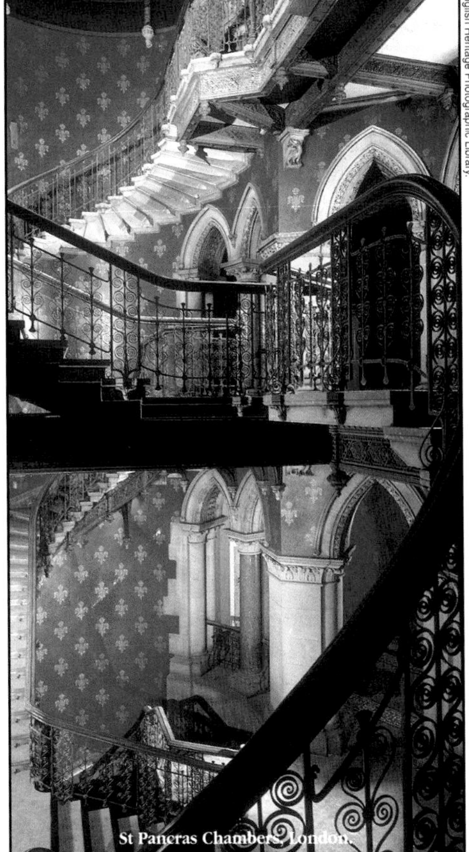
English Heritage Photographic Library
St Pancras Chambers, London.

CLEY MILL OS Ref: TG044 440
Cley-next-the-Sea, Holt NR25 7RP
Grant recipient/Owner: Mr C Blount
Access Contact: Mr Jeremy Bolam **Tel:** 01263 740209
Opening: Easter – end of September, from 2pm to 5pm
P 0 £ Yes ♿ No

CUSTOM HOUSE OS Ref: TF617 200
Purfleet Quay, King's Lynn PE30 1HP
Grant recipient/Owner: King's Lynn and West Norfolk Council
Access Contact: Mr Tim Hall **Tel:** 01553 774297
Opening: Easter – end of October: Monday to Saturday from 9.15am to 5pm, Sunday from 10am to 4pm. November – Easter: daily from 10.30am to 4pm. Public car parks. Access for wheelchair users to all ground floor displays
P £ No ♿ Yes (no WC) Guide dogs allowed

DAIRY FARM BARN OS Ref: TM220 992
Shotesham Park, Newton Flotman
Grant recipient/Owner: The Norfolk Historic Buildings Trust
Access Contact: Mr John Nott **Tel:** 01508 470113
Opening: All year by prior appointment. No cars during harvest
P 2 £ No ♿ Yes (no WC) Guide dogs allowed

GOWTHORPE MANOR OS Ref: TG208 023
Swardeston, Norwich NR14 8DS
Grant recipient/Owner: Mrs D M Watkinson
Access Contact: Mr D M Watkinson **Tel:** 01508 570216
Opening: By prior arrangement on Mondays and occasionally at other mutually convenient times eg an evening group
P 15 £ No ♿ No Guide dogs allowed

THE GRANGE OS Ref: TM212 796
Brockdish, Diss IP21 4JE
Grant recipient/Owner: Professor E Murphy
Access Contact: Professor E Murphy
Opening: By prior written arrangement at weekends only. Donation requested
P 4 £ No ♿ No

HALES HALL BARN OS Ref: TM370 960
Loddon NR14 6QW
Grant recipient/Owner: Mr Terence Read
Access Contact: Mr Terence Read **Tel:** 01508 548395
Opening: All year: Tuesday to Saturday from 10am to 5pm (or dusk if earlier). Also Easter – October: Sunday afternoons and Bank Holiday Mondays from 11am to 4pm. Closed 25 December – 5 January and Good Friday. Garden included in admission charge
P 40 £ Yes ♿ Yes (no WC) Guide dogs allowed

OLD BUCKENHAM CORNMILL OS Ref: TM063 910
Green Lane, Old Buckenham
Grant recipient/Owner: The Norfolk Windmills Trust
Access Contact: Miss A L Jaques **Tel:** 01603 222708
Opening: May – September: 2nd Sunday in each month from 2pm to 5pm. Organised parties at other times by prior arrangement
P 6 £ Yes ♿ No

ST BENET'S LEVEL MILL OS Ref: TG399 157
Ludham
Grant recipient/Owner: Crown Estates Commissioners
Access Contact: Mr D L Ritchie **Tel:** 01692 678232
Opening: 2nd Sunday in May and 1st Sunday in August. Visits at other times by prior arrangement. Limited provision for guide dogs. All enquiries during office hours should be directed to the Agents, Carter Jonas, 6-8 Hills Road, Cambridge CB2 1NH (01223 368771)
P 0 £ No ♿ No Guide dogs allowed, see above.

THORNAGE HALL DOVECOTE OS Ref: TG048 363
Thornage Hall, Thornage, Holt NR25 7QH
Grant recipient/Owner: Camphill Communities East Anglia
Access Contact: Ms A Gimelli **Tel:** 01263 860305
Opening: Open day of village fête and 1st Sunday in September from 2pm to 5pm. At other times by written appointment
P 500 £ No ♿ No Guide dogs allowed

NORTHAMPTONSHIRE

THE COURTEENHALL 1672 FOUNDATION OS Ref: SP762 532
The Old School House, Courteenhall, Northampton NN7 2QD
Grant recipient/Owner: Sir Hereward Wake Bt MC DL
Access Contact: Sir Hereward Wake Bt MC DL
Opening: By prior written arrangement
P 6 £ Yes ♿ Yes (no WC) Guide dogs allowed

LAXTON HALL OS Ref: SP960 970
Corby NN17 3AU
Grant recipient/Owner: PBF Housing Association Ltd
Access Contact: Reverend Sister Gratia **Tel:** 0171 359 8863
Opening: By prior written arrangement with the PBF Housing Association (2 Devonia Road, London N1 8JJ) in the early afternoon of the first Monday of each month (except during Religious Festivals)
P 10 £ No ♿ No

NUNNERY COTTAGES OS Ref: SP813 815
1/2 The Maltings, Desborough Road, Rothwell NN14 6JZ
Grant recipient/Owner: Rothwell Preservation Trust
Access Contact: Mrs C E Mackay
Opening: By prior written arrangement with Mrs C E Mackay, Secretary to the Rothwell Preservation Trust, 23 High Street, Rothwell NN14 6AD
P 0 £ No ♿ No

THE PREBENDAL MANOR HOUSE OS Ref: TL063 962
Nassington, nr. Peterborough PE8 6QG
Grant recipient/Owner: Mrs Jane Baile
Access Contact: Mrs Jane Baile
Opening: **See page 290.** Partial access for wheelchair users
P 14 £ Yes ♿ Yes (no WC) Guide dogs allowed

ROCKINGHAM CASTLE OS Ref: SP867 913
Market Harborough LE16 8TH
Grant recipient/Owner: Commander L M M Saunders Watson
Access Contact: Mr Michael Tebbutt **Tel:** 01536 770240
Opening: **See page 286.** Partial access for wheelchair users
P £ Yes ♿ Yes (no WC) Guide dogs allowed

NORTHUMBERLAND

BAMBURGH CASTLE
OS Ref: NU184 351

Bamburgh NE69

Grant recipient/Owner: The Trustees of Lord Armstrong Deceased

Access Contact: Mr R Bewley **Tel:** 01668 214515

Opening: **See page 333.** Partial access for wheelchair users

P100 £Yes Yes Guide dogs allowed

THE BARN
OS Ref: NY802 653

High Meadows Cottage, Whitshields, Bardon Mill NE47 7BN

Grant recipient/Owner: Mr D W Collinson

Access Contact: Dr M Crick **Tel:** 07771 996838

Opening: By prior arrangement by telephone. Access for wheelchair users not without difficulty

P4 £No Yes (no WC) Guide dogs allowed

BRINKBURN MILL
OS Ref: NZ116 984

Rothbury

Grant recipient/Owner: The Landmark Trust

Opening: Available for letting throughout the year. Open to the general public by prior written arrangement with the Landmark Trust, Shottesbrooke, Maidenhead, Berkshire SL6 3SW

P0 £No No Guide dogs allowed

CAUSEWAY HOUSE
OS Ref: NY770 645

nr. Bardon Mill

Grant recipient/Owner: The Landmark Trust

Opening: Available for letting throughout the year. Open to the gneral public by prior written arrangement with the Landmark Trust, Shottesbrooke, Maidenhead, Berkshire SL6 3SW

P0 £No No Guide dogs allowed

CHILLINGHAM CASTLE
OS Ref: NU062 258

Chillingham NE66 5NJ

Grant recipient/Owner: Sir Humphry Wakefield Bt

Access Contact: Mr A S dec Courtenay-Wellum **Tel:** 01668 215359

Opening: **See page 334.** Limited access for wheelchair users (different levels, steep and spiral staircases)

P £Yes Yes (no WC) Guide dogs allowed

Chillingham Castle, Northumberland.

HIGH STAWARD FARM
OS Ref: NY806 592

Langley-on-Tyne, Hexham NE47 5NS

Grant recipient/Owner: Mr R J Coulson

Access Contact: Mr R J Coulson **Tel:** 01434 683619

Opening: By prior appointment

P2 £No No

LAMBLEY VIADUCT
OS Ref:NY660 590

Lambley, Tynedale

Grant recipient/Owner: British Rail Property Board

Access Contact: Mr David Flush **Tel:** 01434 382045

Opening: Open at all times as part of South Tyne Trail between Featherstone Park and Alston. Partial wheelchair access from Coanwood End

P30 £No Yes (no WC) Guide dogs allowed

MOOT HALL
OS Ref:NY936 642

Market Place, Hexham NE46 3NH

Grant recipient/Owner: Tynedale District Council

Access Contact: Ms Janet Goodridge **Tel:** 01434 652351

Opening: Mondays, Tuesdays, Thursdays and Fridays from 10am to 12.30pm and from 1.30pm to 3pm. Closed Christmas to New Year

P0 £No No Guide dogs allowed

NETHERWITTON HALL
OS Ref: NZ102 906

Morpeth NE61 4NW

Grant recipient/Owner: Mr J H T Trevelyan

Access Contact: Mr J C R Trevelyan

Opening: By prior written arrangement. Limited access for wheelchair users

P50 £Yes Yes (no WC) Guide dogs allowed

THE TOWN HALL
OS Ref: NT998 528

Marygate, Berwick-upon-Tweed TD15 1BN

Grant recipient/Owner: Berwick-upon-Tweed Corporation (Freemen) Trustees

Access Contact: Mr J Q Allan **Tel:** 01289 330900

Opening: Easter – end of September: Monday to Friday, twice daily at 10.30am and 2pm and at other times by arrangement

P0 £Yes No Guide dogs allowed

NOTTINGHAMSHIRE

CARLTON HALL
OS Ref: SK799 640

Carlton-on-Trent, Newark NG23 6LP *

Grant recipient/Owner: Lt-Col G E Vere-Laurie

Access Contact: Lt-Col G E Vere-Laurie **Tel:** 01636 821421

Opening: By prior arrangement

P50 £Yes Yes (no WC) Guide dogs allowed

THE RESIDENCE
OS Ref: SK703 537

Church Street, Southwell NG25 0HP

Grant recipient/Owner: The Provost of Southwell Minster

Opening: By prior written arrangement with the Provost's Secretary, Trebeck Hall, Bishop's Drive, Southwell NG25 0JP

P0 £No No

OXFORDSHIRE

ALL SOULS COLLEGE
OS Ref: SP517 064

High Street, Oxford OX1 4AL

Grant recipient/Owner: All Souls College

Access Contact: Mr Paul Hunt **Tel:** 01865 279379

Opening: All year (except August): Monday to Friday from 2pm to 4pm. Parties over 6 in number must book in advance

P0 £No Yes (no WC) Guide dogs allowed

BLENHEIM PALACE AND PARK
OS Ref: SP441 161

Woodstock OX20 1PX

Grant recipient/Owner: The Duke of Marlborough

Access Contact: Mr N Day **Tel:** 01993 811325

Opening: **See pages 140 & 141.** High Lodge may be visited by prior written arrangement with the Estate Office.

P £Yes Yes Guide dogs allowed

BROUGHTON CASTLE
OS Ref: SP418 382

Banbury OX15 5EB

Grant recipient/Owner: Lord Saye

Access Contact: Lord Saye **Tel:** 01295 262624

Opening: **See page 142.**

P150 £Yes Yes Guide dogs allowed

CLATTERCOTE PRIORY FARM
OS Ref: SP458 492

Claydon, Banbury OX17 1QB

Grant recipient/Owner: Mr Adrian Taylor

Access Contact: Mr Adrian Taylor **Tel:** 01295 690476

Opening: By prior written arrangement

P4 £No No Guide dogs allowed

THE COTTAGE
OS Ref: SU555 863

Aston Tirrold OX11 9DQ

Grant recipient/Owner: Mr B C Bateman

Access Contact: Mr B C Bateman

Opening: By prior written appointment

P £No No Guide dogs allowed

POPE'S TOWER AND CHAPEL
OS Ref:SP416 056

The Manor House, Stanton Harcourt, Witney OX8 1RJ

Grant recipient/Owner: The Hon. Mrs Gascoigne

Access Contact: The Hon. Mrs Gascoigne **Tel:** 01865 881928

Opening: 23/24/30 April; 1/11/14/25/28/29 May; 8/11/22/25 June; 6/9/20/23 July; 3/6/17/20/24/27/28 August; 7/10/21/24 September from 2pm to 6pm. Group visits by prior arrangement

P15 £Yes Yes Guide dogs allowed

Broughton Castle, Oxfordshire.

SHOTOVER HOUSE
OS Ref:SP584 066

Wheatley OX9 1QS

Grant recipient/Owner: Sir John Miller

Access Contact: Sir John Miller **Tel:** 01865 872450

Opening: Access to the William Kent Temple, William Kent Obelisk and the Gothic Temple, which lie close to public rights of way, is available at all times. There is parking space for a few cars by the Gothic Temple and other arrangements can be made if visitors telephone in advance (as above, or 01865 874095 - Mrs Price)

P £No Yes (no WC) Guide dogs allowed

STONOR CHAPEL
OS Ref: SU743 893

Stonor Park, Henley-on-Thames RG9 6HF

Grant recipient/Owner: Lord Camoys

Access Contact: Lisa Severn **Tel:** 01491 638587

Opening: 2 April – 24 September: Sundays and Bank Holiday Mondays; July/August: Sundays and Wednesdays; Saturdays 27 May and 26 August, from 2pm to 5.30pm (last admission 5pm) Pre-booked groups welcome Tuesday to Thursday. Open for Mass: 10.30am every Sunday

P100 £Yes No

SWALCLIFFE TITHE BARN
OS Ref: SP378 378

Shipston Road, Swalcliffe, nr. Banbury

Grant recipient/Owner: The Oxfordshire Building Trust Ltd

Access Contact: Mr Martin Brown **Tel:** 01993 814114

Opening: Easter – end of October: Sundays and Bank Holidays from 2pm to 5pm. At other times by prior appointment (contact 01295 788278)

P10 £No Yes Guide dogs allowed

TUDOR HOUSE
OS Ref: SU530 885

East Hagbourne OX11 9LR

Grant recipient/Owner: Mr I C Barfoot

Access Contact: Mr I C Barfoot **Tel:** 01235 818968

Opening: By prior arrangement. Street parking

P £No No Guide dogs allowed

SHROPSHIRE

BLODWELL SUMMERHOUSE
OS Ref: SJ262 228

Blodwell Hall, Llanyblodwell, Oswestry SY10 8LT

Grant recipient/Owner: The Trustees of the Bradford Estate

Access Contact: Mr R J Taylor **Tel:** 01691 831531

Opening: By prior arrangement

P2 £No No Guide dogs allowed

BROMFIELD PRIORY GATEHOUSE OS Ref: SO480 770
nr. Ludlow
Grant recipient/Owner: The Landmark Trust
Opening: Available for letting throughout the year. Open to the general public by prior written arrangement with the Landmark Trust, Shottesbrooke, Maidenhead, Berkshire SL6 3SW
P0 £No ♿No Guide dogs allowed

DETTON HALL OS Ref: SO666 796
Neen Savage, Cleobury Mortimer, Kidderminster DY14 8LW
Grant recipient/Owner: Mr E C Ratcliff
Access Contact: Mr E C Ratcliff **Tel:** 01299 270387
Opening: By prior arrangement. Limited access for wheelchair users (a few steps)
P10 £Yes ♿Yes (no WC) Guide dogs allowed

HAWKSTONE HALL OS Ref: SJ581 299
Marchamley, Shrewsbury SY4 5LG
Grant recipient/Owner: The Rector and Trustees of Hawkstone Hall
Access Contact: The Guest Mistress **Tel:** 01630 685242
Opening: Spring Bank Holiday Monday and from 5 – 31 August from 2pm to 5pm
P £Yes ♿Yes (no WC) Guide dogs allowed

LANGLEY GATEHOUSE OS Ref: SJ537 001
Acton Burnell
Grant recipient/Owner: The Landmark Trust
Opening: Available for letting throughout the year. Open to the general public by prior written arrangement with the Landmark Trust, Shottesbrooke, Maidenhead, Berkshire SL6 3SW
P0 £No ♿No Guide dogs allowed

LUDFORD HOUSE OS Ref: SO513 741
Ludlow SY8 1PJ
Grant recipient/Owner: Mr D F A Nicholson
Access Contact: Mr D F A Nicholson **Tel:** 01584 872542
Opening: By prior written arrangement. Limited parking
P £Yes ♿No

PIMHILL DOVECOTE OS Ref: SJ492 210
Lea Hall, Harmer Hill, Shrewsbury SY4 3DY *
Grant recipient/Owner: Mr Richard Mayall
Access Contact: Mrs Ginny Whittaker **Tel:** 01939 290342
Opening: By prior written arrangement
P10 £No ♿No

PORCH HOUSE OS Ref: SO324 890
Bishop's Castle SY9 5BE
Grant recipient/Owner: Mrs J McColl
Access Contact: Mrs J McColl
Opening: Visits by prior written arrangement
P0 £No ♿No Guide dogs allowed

ST WINIFRED'S WELL OS Ref: SJ323 244
Woolston, nr. Oswestry
Grant recipient/Owner: The Landmark Trust
Opening: Available for letting throughout the year. Open to the general public by prior written arrangement with the Landmark Trust, Shottesbrooke, Maidenhead, Berkshire SL6 3SW
P0 £No ♿No Guide dogs allowed

THE TOWN HALL OS Ref: SO324 890
High Street, Bishop's Castle SY9 5BG
Grant recipient/Owner: Bishop's Castle Town Council
Access Contact: Mrs M M Griffiths **Tel:** 01588 638610
Opening: 11 January and every 4th Tuesday evening thereafter i.e. 8 February, 7 March, 4 April, 2/30 May, 27 June, 25 July, 22 August, 19 September, 17 October, 14 November and 12 December, by arrangement with the Town Clerk (written appointments not necessary)
P0 £No ♿No Guide dogs allowed

WESTON PARK OS Ref: SJ808 107
Weston under Lizard, Shifnal TF11 8LE
Grant recipient/Owner: The Weston Park Foundation
Access Contact: Mr Colin Sweeney **Tel:** 01952 850207
Opening: **See page 296.**
P £Yes ♿Yes Guide dogs allowed

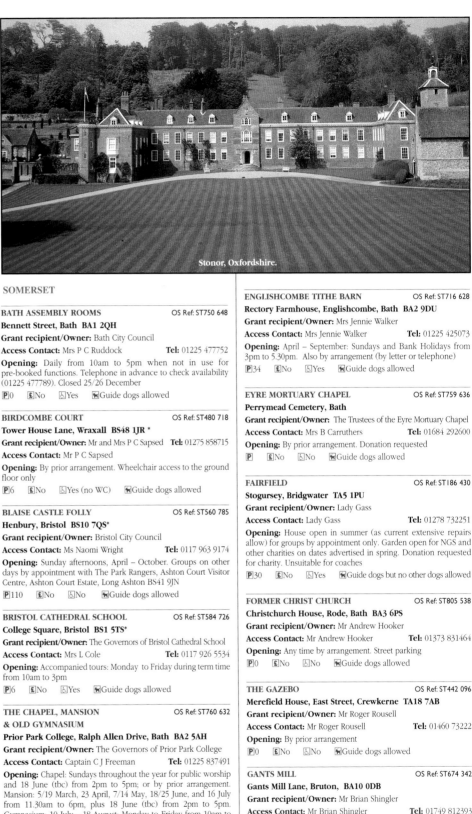

Stonor, Oxfordshire.

SOMERSET

BATH ASSEMBLY ROOMS OS Ref: ST750 648
Bennett Street, Bath BA1 2QH
Grant recipient/Owner: Bath City Council
Access Contact: Mrs P C Ruddock **Tel:** 01225 477752
Opening: Daily from 10am to 5pm when not in use for pre-booked functions. Telephone in advance to check availability (01225 477789). Closed 25/26 December
P0 £No ♿Yes Guide dogs allowed

BIRDCOMBE COURT OS Ref: ST480 718
Tower House Lane, Wraxall BS48 1JR *
Grant recipient/Owner: Mr and Mrs P C Sapsed **Tel:** 01275 858715
Access Contact: Mr P C Sapsed
Opening: By prior arrangement. Wheelchair access to the ground floor only
P6 £No ♿Yes (no WC) Guide dogs allowed

BLAISE CASTLE FOLLY OS Ref: ST560 785
Henbury, Bristol BS10 7QS*
Grant recipient/Owner: Bristol City Council
Access Contact: Ms Naomi Wright **Tel:** 0117 963 9174
Opening: Sunday afternoons, April – October. Groups on other days by appointment with The Park Rangers, Ashton Court Visitor Centre, Ashton Court Estate, Long Ashton BS41 9JN
P110 £No ♿No Guide dogs allowed

BRISTOL CATHEDRAL SCHOOL OS Ref: ST584 726
College Square, Bristol BS1 5TS*
Grant recipient/Owner: The Governors of Bristol Cathedral School
Access Contact: Mrs L Cole **Tel:** 0117 926 5534
Opening: Accompanied tours: Monday to Friday during term time from 10am to 3pm
P6 £No ♿Yes Guide dogs allowed

THE CHAPEL, MANSION & OLD GYMNASIUM OS Ref: ST760 632
Prior Park College, Ralph Allen Drive, Bath BA2 5AH
Grant recipient/Owner: The Governors of Prior Park College
Access Contact: Captain C J Freeman **Tel:** 01225 837491
Opening: Chapel: Sundays throughout the year for public worship and 18 June (tbc) from 2pm to 5pm; or by prior arrangement. Mansion: 5/19 March, 23 April, 7/14 May, 18/25 June, and 16 July from 11.30am to 6pm, plus 18 June (tbc) from 2pm to 5pm. Gymnasium: 10 July – 18 August: Monday to Friday from 10am to 4pm but please telephone in advance
P50 £Yes ♿Limited (no WC) Guide dogs allowed

COLSTON'S ALMSHOUSE OS Ref: ST585 733
St Michael's Hill, Bristol BS2 8DY
Grant recipient/Owner: The Trustees of the Society of Merchant Venturers
Access Contact: Mr Nigel Guzek **Tel:** 0117 973 8058
Opening: By prior arrangement with the Warden, Merchant's Hall, Bristol BS8 3NH.
P0 £No ♿No Guide dogs allowed

ENGLISHCOMBE TITHE BARN OS Ref: ST716 628
Rectory Farmhouse, Englishcombe, Bath BA2 9DU
Grant recipient/Owner: Mrs Jennie Walker
Access Contact: Mrs Jennie Walker **Tel:** 01225 425073
Opening: April – September: Sundays and Bank Holidays from 3pm to 5.30pm. Also by arrangement (by letter or telephone)
P34 £No ♿Yes Guide dogs allowed

EYRE MORTUARY CHAPEL OS Ref: ST759 636
Perrymead Cemetery, Bath
Grant recipient/Owner: The Trustees of the Eyre Mortuary Chapel
Access Contact: Mrs B Carruthers **Tel:** 01684 292600
Opening: By prior arrangement. Donation requested
P £No ♿No Guide dogs allowed

FAIRFIELD OS Ref: ST186 430
Stogursey, Bridgwater TA5 1PU
Grant recipient/Owner: Lady Gass
Access Contact: Lady Gass **Tel:** 01278 732251
Opening: House open in summer (as current extensive repairs allow) for groups by appointment only. Garden open for NGS and other charities on dates advertised in spring. Donation requested for charity. Unsuitable for coaches
P30 £No ♿Yes Guide dogs but no other dogs allowed

FORMER CHRIST CHURCH OS Ref: ST805 538
Christchurch House, Rode, Bath BA3 6PS
Grant recipient/Owner: Mr Andrew Hooker
Access Contact: Mr Andrew Hooker **Tel:** 01373 831464
Opening: Any time by arrangement. Street parking
P0 £No ♿No Guide dogs allowed

THE GAZEBO OS Ref: ST442 096
Merefield House, East Street, Crewkerne TA18 7AB
Grant recipient/Owner: Mr Roger Rousell
Access Contact: Mr Roger Rousell **Tel:** 01460 73222
Opening: By prior arrangement
P0 £No ♿No Guide dogs allowed

GANTS MILL OS Ref: ST674 342
Gants Mill Lane, Bruton, BA10 0DB
Grant recipient/Owner: Mr Brian Shingler
Access Contact: Mr Brian Shingler **Tel:** 01749 812393
Opening: Easter – end of September: Thursdays and Bank Holiday Mondays from 2pm to 5pm. Also groups by prior arrangement
P0 £Yes ♿No Guide dogs allowed

GURNEY MANOR OS Ref: ST264 394
Cannington
Grant recipient/Owner: The Landmark Trust
Opening: Available for letting throughout the year. Open to the general public by prior written arrangement with the Landmark Trust, Shottesbrooke, Maidenhead, Berkshire SL6 3SW
P0 £No ♿No Guide dogs allowed

HESTERCOMBE GARDENS OS Ref: ST241 287
Cheddon Fitzpaine, Taunton TA2 8LG
Grant recipient/Owner: Somerset County Council
Access Contact: Mrs J Manning **Tel:** 01823 413923
Opening: See page 210.
P100 £Yes Yes Guide dogs allowed

LANCIN FARM OS Ref: ST285 080
Wambrook, nr. Chard TA20 3EG
Grant recipient/Owner: Mr S J Smith
Access Contact: Mr S J Smith **Tel:** 01460 62290
Opening: Monday and Thursday afternoons (except May and August) from 2pm to 5pm. Please ring in advance
P0 £No No

THE OLD STATION OS Ref: ST596 724
Temple Meads, Bristol BS1 6QH
Grant recipient/Owner: The Empire Museum Ltd
Access Contact: Ms Holly Bown **Tel:** 0117 925 4980
Opening: From Easter 2000. Further details in the New Year
P25 £No Yes Guide dogs allowed

ORCHARD WYNDHAM OS Ref: ST072 400
Williton TA4 4HH
Grant recipient/Owner: The Wyndham Estate
Access Contact: Wyndham Estate Office **Tel:** 01984 632309
Opening: 3 – 31 August: Thursdays and Fridays from 2pm to 5pm; Bank Holiday Monday from 11am to 5pm. Last tour 4pm. Other days by written appointment. Wheelchair access to the Gardens only
P £Yes Yes (no WC) Guide dogs allowed

PENNILESS PORCH OS Ref: ST552 458
Market Place, Wells BA5 2RB
Grant recipient/Owner: The Dean and Chapter of Wells Cathedral
Access Contact: Caroe & Partners **Tel:** 01749 677561
Opening: Access to the interior by prior arrangement
P0 £No No

ROBIN HOOD'S HUT OS Ref: ST253 338
Halswell Park, Goathurst TA5 2DH
Grant recipient/Owner: The Somerset Building Preservation Trust Ltd
Access Contact: Mr D R Miller **Tel:** 01460 52604
Opening: Access to the exterior of the building and umbrello available at all times. Interior by arrangement with the Somerset Building Preservation Trust (as above) or The Landmark Trust, Shottesbrooke, Maidenhead, Berkshire SL6 3SW. One mile walk with stiles
P0 £No No Guide dogs allowed

ROWLANDS MILL OS Ref: ST344 163
Rowlands, Ilminster TA19 9LE
Grant recipient/Owner: Mr P G H Speke
Access Contact: Mr P G H Speke **Tel:** 01460 52623
Opening: 10am to 4pm on any Friday by prior written appointment
P7 £Yes No Guide dogs allowed

TEMPLE OF HARMONY OS Ref: ST253 338
Goathurst, nr. Bridgwater
Grant recipient/Owner: The Halswell Park Trust
Access Contact: Mr H M Humphreys **Tel:** 01823 443955
Opening: 1 June - 30 September: Saturdays and Sundays from 2pm to 5pm plus Easter Weekend and May Day Bank Holiday. Any other day by prior arrangement
P4 £Yes No Guide dogs allowed

WELLS OLD ALMSHOUSES OS Ref: ST550 455
Chamberlain Street, Wells
Grant recipient/Owner: Wells Old Almshouses Trust
Access Contact: Mr Adrian I'Anson **Tel:** 01749 341210
Opening: Heritage Day. At other times by prior written arrangement with the Secretary, Wells Old Almshouses Trust, 66 Portway, Wells, Somerset BA5 2BP telephone (daytime) as above or 01749 677499 (evenings)
P0 £No Yes Guide dogs allowed

WESTONZOYLAND PUMPING STATION OS Ref: ST350 345
Hoopers Lane, Westonzoyland, nr. Bridgwater
Grant recipient/Owner: Westonzoyland Engine Trust
Access Contact: Mrs Beryl Eaton **Tel:** 01823 275795
Opening: Static: Sundays all year from 2pm to 5pm, Thursdays in June, July and August from 2pm to 8pm. In Steam: 1st Sunday of each month from April to October, Bank Holiday Sundays and Mondays (except Christmas Day and Boxing Day) from 2pm to 5pm; also New Year's Day from 2pm to 5pm
P30 £Yes Yes (no WC) Guide dogs allowed

STAFFORDSHIRE

10 THE CLOSE OS Ref: SK116 097
Lichfield WS13 7LD
Grant recipient/Owner: The Dean and Chapter of Lichfield Cathedral
Access Contact: Mr Robert Sharpe **Tel:** 01543 306201
Opening: By prior written arrangement
P0 £No No

CHILLINGTON HALL OS Ref: SJ864 067
Codsall Wood, nr. Wolverhampton WV8 1RE *
Grant recipient/Owner: The late Mr P R de L Giffard
Access Contact: Mr J W Giffard **Tel:** 01902 850236
Opening: See page 304. Limited access for wheelchair users
P £Yes Yes (no WC) Guide dogs allowed

CLAYMILLS PUMPING STATION OS Ref: SK260 260
The Sewage Works, Meadow Lane, Burton-on-Trent
Grant recipient/Owner: Severn Trent Water Ltd
Access Contact: Mr Roy Barratt **Tel:** 01283 534960
Opening: Static viewing with free guided tours every Saturday (no charge). 1/2 January (Millennium Steaming); 23/24 April; (Easter Steaming); 13/14 May (non-steaming Model Weekend); 28/29 May (Whitsun Steaming); 24/25 June (Stretham Centenary Celebration); 27/28 August (August Bank Holiday Steaming); 23/24 September (Burton Festival Steaming); 21/22 October (October Steaming). Access for wheelchair users to the boiler house, workshop, blacksmith's forge and office, but not to the engine house
P £Yes Yes

INGESTRE HALL OS Ref: SJ976 247
Ingestre, Stafford ST18 0RF *
Grant recipient/Owner: Ingestre Hall Residential Arts Centre
Access Contact: Ms Jacqueline Blake **Tel:** 01889 270225
Opening: Strictly by prior written arrangement, Monday to Friday only. Access for wheelchair users by one entrance
P75 £Yes Yes (no WC) Guide dogs allowed

INGESTRE PAVILION OS Ref: SJ979 229
Tixall, nr. Stafford
Grant recipient/Owner: The Landmark Trust
Opening: Available for letting throughout the year. Open to the general public by prior written arrangement with the Landmark Trust, Shottesbrooke, Maidenhead, Berkshire SL6 3SW
P0 £No No Guide dogs allowed

SUFFOLK

BUTTRUM'S MILL OS Ref: TM275 487
Burkitt Road, Woodbridge IP12 4JJ
Grant recipient/Owner: Suffolk County Council
Access Contact: Mr M Barnard **Tel:** 01473 583352
Opening: May - September: Saturdays, Sundays and Bank Holidays from 2pm to 6pm. Guide dogs permitted on the ground floor only
P12 £Yes No Guide dogs allowed

ELMS FARM OS Ref: TM103 654
Old Station Road, Mendlesham IP14 5RS
Grant recipient/Owner: Mrs Pamela Gilmour
Access Contact: Mrs Pamela Gilmour
Opening: By written appointment
P10 £No No

SAXHAM HALL OS Ref: TL791 627
Great Saxham, Bury St Edmunds IP29 5JW
Grant recipient/Owner: Colonel David Gordon-Lennox
Access Contact: Colonel David Gordon-Lennox
Opening: Interested groups and organisations by prior written appointment
P £No No

SOMERLEYTON HALL AND GARDENS OS Ref: TM493 977
Somerleyton, Lowestoft NR32 5QQ
Grant recipient/Owner: The Rt Hon Lord Somerleyton GCVO
Access Contact: Mr Ian Pollard **Tel:** 01502 730224
Opening: See page 252.
P £Yes Yes Guide dogs allowed

Somerleyton Hall, Suffolk.

ST CLEMENT'S CHURCH OS Ref: TM169 443
Star Lane, Ipswich IP4 1LW
Grant recipient/Owner: The Ipswich Historic Churches Trust
Access Contact: Mr J S Hall **Tel:** 01473 232300
Opening: By arrangement during office hours. Visits outside office hours may also be possible on a very occasional basis
P0 £No Yes (no WC) Guide dogs allowed

WOODBRIDGE LODGE OS Ref: TM330 529
Rendlesham, nr. Woodbridge, IP12 2RA
Grant recipient/Owner: Dr C P Cooper
Access Contact: Dr C P Cooper **Tel:** 01394 460642
Opening: Exterior only, by prior arrangement (preferably in writing)
P3 £No No

SURREY

CARSHALTON WATER TOWER OS Ref: TQ275 644
West Street, Carshalton
Grant recipient/Owner: The Carshalton Water Tower Trust
Access Contact: Mrs Julia Gertz **Tel:** 020 8647 0984
Opening: 1st Sunday in April - last Sunday in September from 2.30pm to 5pm. Also local and National Heritage Days. Private tours by prior appointment by telephone or in writing to 136 West Street, Carshalton, Surrey SM5 2NR. Parking available by prior arrangement
P £Yes Yes Guide dogs allowed

CLAREMONT HOUSE OS Ref: TQ136 634
Claremont Drive, Esher KT10 9LY
Grant recipient/Owner: Claremont Fan Court Foundation Ltd
Access Contact: Mrs C Bradley **Tel:** 01372 467841
Opening: Guided tours: 5/6 February, 4/5 March, 1/2 April, 6/7 May, 3/4 June, 2 July, 5/6 August, 2/3 September, 7/8 October and 4/5 November, from 2pm to 5pm (last tour 4.30pm): Party bookings on other days by prior arrangement. Very limited access for wheelchair users
P100 £Yes Yes (no WC) Guide dogs allowed

FARNHAM CASTLE OS Ref: SY839 474
Farnham, GU9 0AG
Grant recipient/Owner: The Centre for International Briefing
Access Contact: Reception **Tel:** 01252 721194
Opening: Wednesdays from 2pm to 4pm. Guided tours only and groups by prior written arrangement
P60 £Yes No Guide dogs allowed

GODDARDS OS Ref: TQ120 450
Abinger Common, Dorking, RH5 6TH
Grant recipient/Owner: The Landmark Trust
Access Contact: Mrs Baker **Tel:** 01306 730871
Opening: Available for letting throughout the year. Open to the general public by appointment only on Wednesday afternoons from the Wednesday after Easter until the last Wednesday in October from 2pm to 6pm. Visitors have access to part of the garden and house only
PMust be booked £Yes No

THE HOSPITAL OF THE BLESSED TRINITY OS Ref:TQ001 496
Abbot's Hospital, High Street, Guildford GU1 3AJ
Grant recipient/Owner: The Hospital of the Blessed Trinity
Access Contact: Mr John W Moss **Tel:** 01483 562670
Opening: Easter – 31 October: Monday to Saturday from 10.30 am to 5pm (courtyard open to casual visitors). Guided tours by arrangement with the Town Guides (01483 569794). Special interest tours by arrangement with the Master (01483 562670). Please notify if intending to use a wheelchair
P 0 £ No Yes (no WC) Guide dogs allowed

THE LOVEKYN CHAPEL OS Ref:TQ185 694
Kingston Grammar School, 70 London Road, Kingston-upon-Thames KT2 6PY
Grant recipient/Owner: The Governors of Kingston Grammar School
Access Contact: Mr A Howard-Harwood **Tel:** 0181 939 8825
Opening: By prior arrangement (preferably in writing as this is an active school building in term time). Public car park nearby
P £ No Yes Guide dogs allowed

THE MUSEUM OF FARNHAM OS Ref: SU835 465
Willmer House, 38 West Street, Farnham GU9 7DX
Grant recipient/Owner: Waverley Borough Council
Access Contact: Mrs Anne Jones **Tel:** 01252 715094
Opening: Tuesday – Saturday from 10am to 5pm. Access for wheelchair users to the ground floor and garden only
P 0 £ No Yes Guide dogs allowed

THE OLD MILL OS Ref:TQ320 460
Outwood Common, nr. Redhill RH1 5PW
Grant recipient/Owner: Mrs Sheila Thomas
Access Contact: Mrs Sheila Thomas **Tel:** 01342 843644
Opening: Easter – October: Sundays and Bank Holidays from 2pm to 6pm. Booked parties by arrangement. Access for wheelchair users to the ground floor only
P 20 £ Yes Yes Guide dogs allowed

THE OLD PALACE SCHOOL OS Ref:TQ320 654
Old Palace Road, Croydon CRO 1AX
Grant recipient/Owner: The Whitgift Foundation
Access Contact: The Bursar **Tel:** 0181 688 2414
Opening: Guided tours: 10 – 15 April; 29 May – 3 June; 10 – 15 July; 17 – 22 July. Doors open 1.45pm (last tour 2.15pm). No unaccompanied visits. Unsuitable for wheelchairs
P 0 £ Yes No

OXENFORD GRANGE FARM OS Ref: SU932 431
Milford Road, Elstead, Godalming GU8 6LA
Grant recipient/Owner: Mr C F Baker
Access Contact: Mr A C Baker **Tel:** 01252 702109
Opening: 1 – 24 December: daily, from 9am to 5pm. At all other times by prior written arrangement
P £ No Yes (no WC) Guide dogs allowed

PAINSHILL PARK OS Ref:TQ099 605
Portsmouth Road, Cobham KT11 1JE
Grant recipient/Owner: The Painshill Park Trust Ltd
Access Contact: Mrs Harriet Richards **Tel:** 01932 868113
Opening: See page 152.
P £ Yes Yes Guide dogs allowed

RED HOUSE OS Ref: SU968 445
Frith Hill Road, Godalming GU71 2DZ
Grant recipient/Owner: ßMr H A Laws
Access Contact: Mrs S Laws
Opening: By prior written appointment in June, July and September (excluding Wednesdays, Thursdays and Sundays). Additional street parking
P 2 £ No No

ST MARY'S HOMES OS Ref:TQ357 515
Church Lane, Godstone RH9 8BW
Grant recipient/Owner: The Trustees of St Mary's Homes
Access Contact: Mr Paul Madsen **Tel:** 01883 742385
Opening: The grounds and chapel open at all reasonable times. No school parties by request
P 0 £ No Yes (no WC) Guide dogs allowed

Painshill Landscape Garden, Surrey.

SUSSEX

BRICKWALL HOUSE OS Ref:TQ831 241
Northiam, Rye TN31 6NL
Grant recipient/Owner: The Frewen Educational Trust
Access Contact: Mr Peter Mold **Tel:** 01797 253388
Opening: All Bank Holidays between April and October plus Wednesday afternoons in the school holidays. Please telephone for details
P 40 £ Yes Yes Guide dogs allowed

GLYNDE PLACE OS Ref:TQ457 093
Glynde, nr. Lewes BN8 6SX
Grant recipient/Owner: Viscount Hampden
Access Contact: Viscount Hampden **Tel:** 01273 858224
Opening: See page 166.
P 150 £ Yes No

GREAT DIXTER HOUSE AND GARDENS OS Ref:TQ817 251
Northiam, nr. Rye TN31 6PH
Grant recipient/Owner: Mr Christopher Lloyd
Access Contact: Ms Elaine Francis **Tel:** 01797 252878
Opening: See page 167. Partial access for wheelchair users
P 100 £ Yes Yes Guide dogs allowed

HAMMERWOOD PARK OS Ref:TQ442 390
nr. East Grinstead RH19 3QE
Grant recipient/Owner: Mr David Pinnegar
Access Contact: Mr David Pinnegar **Tel:** 01342 850594
Opening: See page 167.
P £ Yes Yes Guide dogs allowed

HIORNE TOWER OS Ref:TQ013 081
Arundel Park, Arundel BN18 9AB
Grant recipient/Owner: The Earl of Arundel and Surrey
Access Contact: Mr M C G Baxter **Tel:** 01903 883400
Opening: Arundel Park is open to the public daily (except 24 March). Access to the interior of the Hiorne Tower by prior arrangement with the Estate Office. Partial access for wheelchair users
P 0 £ No Yes (no WC) Guide dogs allowed

POLEGATE WINDMILL OS Ref:TQ582 041
Park Croft, Polegate BN26 5LB
Grant recipient/Owner: The Eastbourne Civic Society
Access Contact: Mr Lawrence Stevens **Tel:** 01323 734496
Opening: Easter Sunday to the end of October: Sundays, Bank Holidays, Wednesdays in August from 2pm to 5pm (last admission). Special events. Group bookings at other times (contact 01323 506795). Access for wheelchair users and visitors with guide dogs to the ground floor only
P 10 £ Yes Yes Guide dogs allowed

THE ROYAL PAVILION OS Ref:TQ313 043
Brighton BN1 1EE
Grant recipient/Owner: Brighton and Hove Council
Access Contact: Ms Cara Bowen **Tel:** 01273 292810
Opening: See page 160. Car parking for disabled visitors is available in the grounds by prior arrangement
P 0 £ Yes Yes Guide dogs allowed

SACKVILLE COLLEGE OS Ref:TQ397 380
East Grinstead RH19 3AZ
Grant recipient/Owner: The Warden and Trustees of Sackville College
Access Contact: Mr David Russell **Tel:** 01342 326561
Opening: 1 May. June, July and August: Wednesday to Sunday from 2pm to 5pm. Groups welcome April – October by prior arrangement
P 8 £ Yes Yes

THE SHELL HOUSE OS Ref: SU888 088
Goodwood House, Chichester PO18 0PX
Grant recipient/Owner: The Goodwood Estate Company Ltd
Access Contact: Ms Kathryn Bellamy **Tel:** 01243 755048
Opening: By prior written arrangement
P £ Yes No Guide dogs allowed

SHIPLEY WINDMILL OS Ref:TQ144 218
Shipley, nr. Horsham RH13 8PL
Grant recipient/Owner: The Shipley Windmill Charitable Trust
Access Contact: Ms Penny Murray **Tel:** 01243 777642
Opening: April – October: 1st and 3rd Sundays in each month and Bank Holiday Mondays. National Mills Day, Shipley Festival (May) and Horsham and District Arts Fanfare (June)
P 10 £ Yes No

THE VICTORY HALL OS Ref:TQ307 307
Stockcroft Road, Balcombe, Haywards Heath RH17 6HP*
Grant recipient/Owner: The Victory Hall Management Committee
Access Contact: Mrs J M Dutton **Tel:** 01444 811366
Opening: Murals on view to the public at all times when the hall is in use for village hall functions and otherwise by prior arrangement with the steward or members of the management committee. Unlimited parking in Stockcroft Road
P £ No Yes Guide dogs allowed

WARWICKSHIRE

THE BATH HOUSE OS Ref: SP285 533
Walton, Stratford-upon-Avon
Grant recipient/Owner: The Landmark Trust
Opening: Available for letting throughout the year. Open to the general public by prior written arrangement with the Landmark Trust, Shottesbrooke, Maidenhead, Berkshire SL6 3SW
P0 £No No Guide dogs allowed

LORD LEYCESTER HOSPITAL OS Ref: SP280 648
High Street, Warwick CV34 4BH
Grant recipient/Owner: The Governors of Lord Leycester Hospital
Access Contact: Captain D I Rhodes **Tel:** 01926 491422
Opening: Tuesday to Sunday from 10am to 4pm (winter), 10am to 5pm (summer) plus Bank Holiday Mondays. Closed Good Friday and Christmas Day. Limited access for wheelchair users (ground floor only)
P15 £Yes Yes (no WC) Guide dogs allowed

RAGLEY HALL OS Ref: SP073 555
Alcester B49 5NJ
Grant recipient/Owner: The Marquess of Hertford
Access Contact: Mr G Timms **Tel:** 01789 762090
Opening: **See page 310.**
P £Yes Yes Guide dogs allowed

ST JAMES CHURCH OS Ref: SP223 840
Packington Park, Meriden, nr. Coventry CV7 7HF
Grant recipient/Owner: St James Great Packington Trust
Access Contact: The Estate Office **Tel:** 01676 522020
Opening: By telephone arrangement with the Estate Office during office hours or Lord Guernsey at other times (01676 522274). Access for wheelchair users if accompanied (two small steps and a very heavy door)
P10 £No Yes (no WC) Guide dogs allowed

ST PETER'S AND ST PAUL'S CHURCH OS Ref: SP315 394
The Presbytery, Friars Lane, Lower Brailes OX15 5HU
Grant recipient/Owner: St Philip's Presbytery
Access Contact: The Rev A Sims
Opening: Chapel open daily from 9am to 6pm
P30 £No No Guide dogs allowed

WEST MIDLANDS

BRATCH PUMPING STATION OS Ref: SO866 938
Bratch Lane, Wombourne, Wolverhampton
Grant recipient/Owner: Severn Trent Water Ltd
Access Contact: Mr David Throup **Tel:** 0121 722 4563
Opening: Opening arrangements to be finalised when negotiations to establish a charitable trust to manage the building have been concluded. Partial access for wheelchair users (excluding the engine room)
P200 £Yes Yes Guide dogs allowed

WILTSHIRE

THE CLOISTERS OS Ref: ST800 589
Iford Manor, Bradford-on-Avon BA15 2BA
Grant recipient/Owner: Mrs E Cartwright-Hignett
Access Contact: Mrs E Cartwright-Hignett **Tel:** 01225 862364
Opening: **See page 221.** Please note that the House is not open to the public at any time
P £Yes No Guide dogs allowed

FONTHILL UNDERGROUND BATH HOUSE OS Ref: ST935 330
c/o The Estate Office, Fonthill Bishop, Salisbury SP3 5SH
Grant recipient/Owner: Lord Margadale
Access Contact: The Resident Agent **Tel:** 01747 820246
Opening: By prior written arrangement with the Estate Office in spring and summer (1 March – 31 July inclusive)
P0 £Yes No

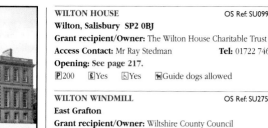

Ragley Hall, Warwickshire.

LYDIARD PARK OS Ref: SU104 848
Lydiard Tregoze, Swindon SN5 9PA
Grant recipient/Owner: Swindon Borough Council
Access Contact: Mrs Sarah Finch-Crisp **Tel:** 01793 770401
Opening: **See page 219.**
P400 £Yes Yes Guide dogs allowed

THE OLD BISHOP'S PALACE OS Ref: SU144 294
Salisbury Cathedral School, 1 The Close, Salisbury SP1 2EQ
Grant recipient/Owner: Salisbury Diocesan Board of Finance
Access Contact: Lt-Col A J Craigie **Tel:** 01722 555300
Opening: Guided tours in July and August on dates to be confirmed. Please telephone for details in the spring
P0 £Yes No

ST JOHN'S COURTHOUSE OS Ref: ST935 869
St John's Street, Malmesbury
Grant recipient/Owner: The Warden and Freemen of Malmesbury
Access Contact: Mr Oliver Pike **Tel:** 01666 823338
Opening: Visits by prior arrangement
P0 £No Yes (no WC) Guide dogs allowed

WILTON HOUSE OS Ref: SU099 311
Wilton, Salisbury SP2 0BJ
Grant recipient/Owner: The Wilton House Charitable Trust
Access Contact: Mr Ray Stedman **Tel:** 01722 746720
Opening: **See page 217.**
P200 £Yes Yes Guide dogs allowed

WILTON WINDMILL OS Ref: SU275 616
East Grafton
Grant recipient/Owner: Wiltshire County Council
Access Contact: Mr John Talbot **Tel:** 01672 870072
Opening: Guided tours of interior: Easter - end of September on Sundays and Bank Holidays from 2pm to 5pm. Access to the exterior available at all times free of charge. Access for wheelchair users to the site but not to the interior of the building
P8 £Yes Yes (no WC) Guide dogs allowed

WORCESTERSHIRE

THE CONSERVATORY OS Ref: SO641 766
Hopton Court, Cleobury Mortimer, Kidderminster DY14 0EF
Grant recipient/Owner: Mr C R D Woodward
Access Contact: Mr Christopher Woodward **Tel:** 01299 270734
Opening: The conservatory is open four days a year without appointment, at other times by prior arrangement
P150 £Yes Yes Guide dogs allowed

EDGAR TOWER OS Ref: SO852 545
Worcester
Grant recipient/Owner: The Dean and Chapter of Worcester Cathedral
Access Contact: The Cathedral Steward **Tel:** 01905 28854
Opening: Access to the interior is available in the school holidays by prior written arrangement with the Cathedral Steward, 10a College Green, Worcester WR1 2LH. Visits to the Tower are demanding due to a steep and narrow stairway
P0 £No No

Lydiard Park, Wiltshire.

SARUM COLLEGE OS Ref: SU144 296
19 The Close, Salisbury SP1 2EE
Grant recipient/Owner: Sarum College
Access Contact: Mrs Linda Cooper **Tel:** 01722 424800
Opening: Residential accommodation throughout the year. Visitor access without prior arrangement during term time
P37 £No Yes Guide dogs allowed

TOTTENHAM HOUSE OS Ref: SU250 640
Savernake Forest, Marlborough
Grant recipient/Owner: The Trustees of the Savernake Estate
Access Contact: The Earl of Cardigan **Tel:** 01672 512161
Opening: By prior arrangement on most days. A large flight of steps to the front door inhibits wheelchair access
P30 £No No Guide dogs allowed

MALVERN COLLEGE OS Ref: SO778 452
College Road, Malvern WR14 3DF*
Grant recipient/Owner: The Governors of Malvern College
Access Contact: The Bursar **Tel:** 01684 581500
Opening: Access to the exterior of the Main Building, Chapel and Memorial Library every Saturday (except Easter Saturday) from 9am to 5pm. Interior of the Main Building by prior written appointment
P £No Yes Guide dogs allowed

THE OLD PALACE OS Ref:SO849 546
Deansway, Worcester WR1 2JE
Grant recipient/Owner: Worcester Diocesan Board of Finance
Access Contact: Mrs J Dowling **Tel:** 01905 20537
Opening: Monday to Thursday from 9am to 5pm, Fridays from 9am to 4.30pm. Limited access for wheelchair users (ground floor and exterior/garden)
P0 £No Yes (no WC) Guide dogs allowed

ORKSHIRE

CKWORTH SCHOOL OS Ref: SE441 172
ontefract WF7 7LT
rant recipient/Owner: The Committee of Ackworth School
ccess Contact: Mr Christopher P Jones
pening: By prior written arrangement
P40 £No No Guide dogs allowed

EAMSLEY HOSPITAL OS Ref:SE080 530
r. Skipton
rant recipient/Owner: The Landmark Trust
pening: Available for letting throughout the year. Open to the eneral public by prior written arrangement with the Landmark rust, Shottesbrooke, Maidenhead, Berkshire SL6 3SW
P0 £No No Guide dogs allowed

IRTHWAITE HALL OS Ref: SE300 104
Iuddersfield Road, Dalton, Barnsley S75 5JS *
rant recipient/Owner: Mr Martin Shepherd.
ccess Contact: Mr Martin Shepherd **Tel:** 01226 383500
pening: By prior appointment at any time
P6 £No Yes (no WC) Guide dogs allowed

URTON AGNES HALL OS Ref:TA103 633
riffield YO25 4NB
rant recipient/Owner: Burton Agnes Hall Preservation Trust Ltd
ccess Contact: Mrs Susan Cunliffe-Lister **Tel:** 01262 490324
pening: **See page 352.** Access for wheelchair users to the round floor and gardens
P150 £Yes Yes Guide dogs allowed

CALVERLEY OLD HALL OS Ref: SE208 372
Calverley, nr. Leeds
Grant recipient/Owner: The Landmark Trust
Opening: Available for letting throughout the year. Open to the general public by prior written arrangement with the Landmark Trust, Shottesbrooke, Maidenhead, Berkshire SL6 3SW
P0 £No No Guide dogs allowed

CASTLE HOWARD OS Ref: SE716 701
York YO60 7DA
Grant recipient/Owner: The Hon. Simon Howard
Access Contact: Mr D N Peake **Tel:** 01653 648444
Opening: **See page 341.** Partial access for wheelchair users
P £Yes Yes Guide dogs allowed

CAWOOD CASTLE OS Ref: SE574 376
nr. Selby
Grant recipient/Owner: The Landmark Trust
Opening: Available for letting throughout year. Open to the general public by prior written arrangement with the Landmark Trust, Shottesbrooke, Maidenhead, Berkshire SL6 3SW
P0 £No No Guide dogs allowed

THE CHURCH OF ST PAULINUS OS Ref: NZ173 010
Brough Park, Richmond DL10 7PJ
Grant recipient/Owner: Mr Greville Worthington
Access Contact: Mr Greville Worthington **Tel:** 01748 812127
Opening: By prior arrangement
P2 £No No Guide dogs allowed

THE CROSSLEY PAVILION OS Ref: SE085 248
The People's Park, King Cross Road, Halifax
Grant recipient/Owner: Calderdale MBC
Access Contact: Mr Dominic Clarke **Tel:** 01422 359454
Opening: Dawn to dusk (as Park). Access through grille to view statue of Sir Francis Crossley by prior arrangement. Street parking
P £No Yes (no WC) Guide dogs allowed

THE DOVECOTE OS Ref: NZ172 124
Forcett Hall, Forcett, Richmond DL11 7SB
Grant recipient/Owner: Richmondshire Preservation Trust
Access Contact: Mrs P E Heathcote **Tel:** 01325 718226
Opening: By prior arrangement
P0 £No No

DUNCOMBE PARK OS Ref: SE604 830
Helmsley, York YO62 5EB
Grant recipient/Owner: Lord Feversham
Access Contact: The Agent **Tel:** 01439 770213
Opening: **See page 354.** Partial access for wheelchair users. For group and school visits contact the Estate Office
P £Yes Limited Guide dogs allowed

THE GAZEBO OS Ref: SE084 291
Holdsworth House, Holdsworth, Halifax HX2 9TG
Grant recipient/Owner: The Cavalier Country Club
Access Contact: Mr Peter Phillips **Tel:** 01422 240024
Opening: Hotel open throughout the year (excluding Christmas)
P40 £No Yes (no WC) Guide dogs allowed

FARNLEY HALL OS Ref: SE215 474
Farnley, nr. Otley LS21 2QF
Grant recipient/Owner: Mr G N Le G Horton-Fawkes
Access Contact: Mr G N Le G Horton-Fawkes
Opening: By prior written arrangement. Owners generally available to conduct tour on informal basis
P £Yes No

LEDSTON HALL OS Ref: SE437 289
Hall Lane, Ledston, Castleford WF10 2BB
Grant recipient/Owner: Mr G H H Wheler
Access Contact: Mr J F T Hare **Tel:** 01423 523423
Opening: May – August: Monday to Friday from 9am to 4pm
P £No Yes (no WC) Guide dogs allowed

THE LINDLEY MURRAY SUMMERHOUSE OS Ref: SE593 510
The Mount School, Dalton Terrace, York YO24 4DD
Grant recipient/Owner: The Mount School
Access Contact: Ms Anne Bolton **Tel:** 01904 667506
Opening: By prior arrangement Monday to Friday throughout the year (apart from Bank Holidays) from 9am to 4.30pm
P3 £No Yes Guide dogs allowed

MARLBOROUGH HALL OS Ref: SE093 254
Crossley Street, Halifax HX1 1VG
Grant recipient/Owner: Halifax and District YMCA
Access Contact: Mr C F Love **Tel:** 01422 353626
Opening: Daily from 10am to 4pm (except Bank Holidays and weekends)
P0 £No Yes Guide dogs allowed

MARKENFIELD HALL OS Ref: SE294 672
Ripon HG4 3AD*
Grant recipient/Owner: Lady Grantley
Access Contact: Mrs C M Wardroper **Tel:** 01609 780306
Opening: Parties by prior written appointment with Strutt & Parker, Thornfield Business Park, Standard Way, Northallerton DL6 2XQ. Partial access for wheelchair users
P8 £Yes Yes (no WC) Guide dogs allowed

MERCHANT TAYLORS HALL OS Ref: SE606 521
Aldwark, York YO1 2BX
Grant recipient/Owner: The Company of Merchant Taylors
Access Contact: Mrs Audrey Lambert **Tel:** 01904 632967
Opening: May – September: Tuesdays from 10am to 4pm. At other times by prior arrangement
P0 £No Yes Guide dogs allowed

THE MUSEUM OF SOUTH YORKSHIRE LIFE OS Ref: SE547 039
Cusworth Hall, Cusworth Lane, Doncaster DN5 7TU
Grant recipient/Owner: Doncaster MBC
Access Contact: Mr F Carpenter **Tel:** 01302 782342
Opening: Monday to Friday from 10am to 5pm, Saturdays from 11am to 5pm, Sundays from 1pm to 5pm. Early closing (4pm) in December and January. Closed Christmas Day, Boxing Day and Good Friday. Access for wheelchair users to the ground floor only
P £No Yes Guide dogs allowed

NORTON CONYERS HALL OS Ref: SE670 795
nr. Ripon HG4 5EQ
Grant recipient/Owner: Sir James Graham Bt
Access Contact: Sir James Graham Bt **Tel:** 01765 640333
Opening: Easter Sunday and Monday plus other Bank Holiday Sundays and Mondays; Sundays from 7 May – 3 September; daily from 3 – 8 July. House open from 2pm to 5pm, Garden (no admission charge but donations welcome) from 11.30am to 5pm. Limited access for wheelchair users
P60 £Yes Yes Guide dogs allowed

OLD GRAMMAR SCHOOL MUSEUM OS Ref:TA099 285
South Church Side, Hull
Grant recipient/Owner: Hull City Museums
Access Contact: Mr D A Northmore **Tel:** 01482 613902
Opening: Saturdays from 10am to 5pm, Sundays from 1.30pm to 4.30pm. Monday to Friday during school holidays from 10am to 5pm. School groups by arrangement Monday to Friday during term time
P0 £No Yes Guide dogs allowed

THE PIGSTY OS Ref: NZ950 055
Robin Hood's Bay
Grant recipient/Owner: The Landmark Trust
Opening: Available for letting throughout the year. Open to the general public by prior written arrangement with the Landmark Trust, Shottesbrooke, Maidenhead, Berkshire SL6 3SW
P0 £No No Guide dogs allowed

THE ROUNDHOUSE OS Ref: SE288 333
Roundhouse Business Park, Wellington Bridge, Wellington Road, Leeds LS12 1DR
Grant recipient/Owner: Wellbridge Properties Ltd
Access Contact: Mr J D Miller **Tel:** 0113 2435964
Opening: By prior written arrangement with the occupiers, Leeds Commercials, as the property is a working garage
P30 £No Yes Guide dogs allowed

SCAMPSTON HALL OS Ref: SE865 755
Scampston, Malton YO17 8NG
Grant recipient/Owner: Sir Charles Legard Bt
Access Contact: Sir Charles Legard Bt **Tel:** 01944 758224
Opening: 21 May – 4 June and 23 July – 6 August (closed Saturdays) from 1.30pm to 5pm. Private parties at other times by prior arrangement
P50 £Yes No Guide dogs allowed

SIR WILLIAM TURNER'S HOSPITAL OS Ref: NZ594 215
Kirkleatham TS10 4QT
Grant recipient/Owner: The Trustees of Sir William Turner's Hospital
Access Contact: The Clerk to the Trustees **Tel:** 01642 482828
Opening: Daily from 9.30am to 6pm (except Christmas Day, Boxing Day and New Year's Day). Tours of the almshouses and chapel by prior arrangement. Guide dogs not permitted in the chapel. Parking for coaches in the museum car park nearby
P25 £No Yes (no WC) Guide dogs allowed

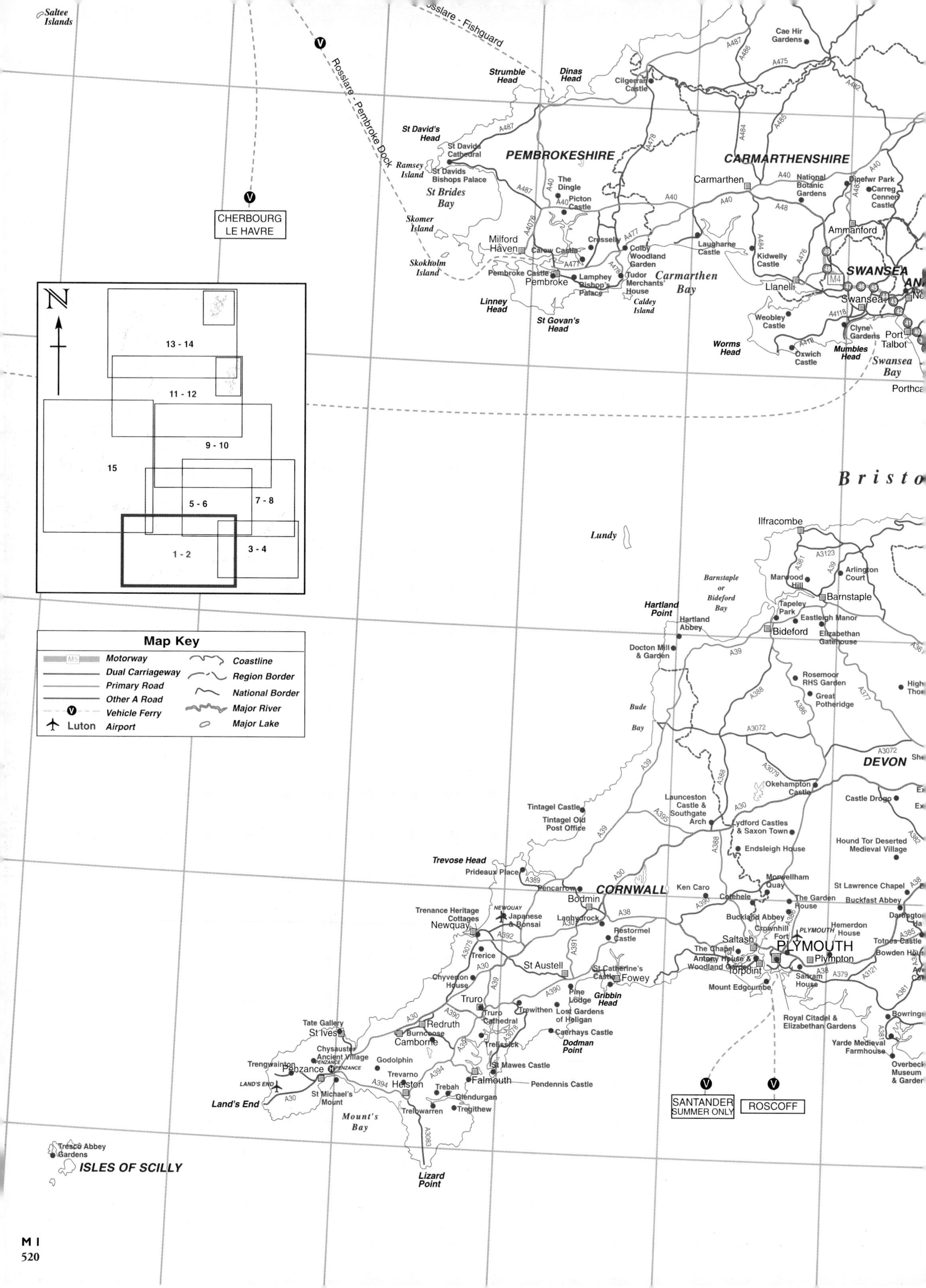

Saltee Islands
Rosslare - Fishguard
Rosslare - Pembroke Dock
CHERBOURG
LE HAVRE
Strumble Head
Dinas Head
Cilgerran Castle
Cae Hir Gardens
St David's Head
St Davids Cathedral
PEMBROKESHIRE
CARMARTHENSHIRE
Ramsey Island
St Davids Bishops Palace
St Brides Bay
The Dingle
Picton Castle
Carmarthen
National Botanic Gardens
Dinefwr Park
Carreg Cennen Castle
Skomer Island
Milford Haven
Carew Castle
Cresselly
Colby Woodland Garden
Laugharne Castle
Kidwelly Castle
Ammanford
Skokholm Island
Pembroke Castle
Pembroke
Lamphey Bishop's Palace
Tudor Merchants' House
Carmarthen Bay
Caldey Island
SWANSEA
Llanelli
Swansea
Linney Head
St Govan's Head
Weobley Castle
Worms Head
Oxwich Castle
Clyne Gardens
Mumbles Head
Port Talbot
Swansea Bay
Porthca
Bristo
13 - 14
11 - 12
9 - 10
15
5 - 6
7 - 8
1 - 2
3 - 4
Map Key
Motorway
Dual Carriageway
Primary Road
Other A Road
Vehicle Ferry
Luton Airport
Coastline
Region Border
National Border
Major River
Major Lake
Lundy
Ilfracombe
Arlington Court
Marwood Hill
Barnstaple or Bideford Bay
Barnstaple
Hartland Point
Hartland Abbey
Tapeley Park
Eastleigh Manor
Bideford
Elizabethan Gatehouse
Docton Mill & Garden
Rosemoor RHS Garden
Great Potheridge
Bude Bay
DEVON
Okehampton Castle
Castle Drogo
Launceston Castle & Southgate Arch
Lydford Castles & Saxon Town
Tintagel Castle
Tintagel Old Post Office
Hound Tor Deserted Medieval Village
Endsleigh House
Trevose Head
Prideaux Place
Morwellham Quay
St Lawrence Chapel
Pencarrow
CORNWALL
Ken Caro
Cotehele
The Garden House
Buckfast Abbey
Bodmin
Trenance Heritage Cottages
Newquay
Japanese & Bonsai
Lanhydrock
Restormel Castle
Buckland Abbey
Crownhill Fort
Hemerdon House
Saltash
PLYMOUTH
Plympton
The Chapel
Antony House & Woodland Garden
Torpoint
Saltram House
Trerice
St Austell
St Catherine's Castle
Fowey
Mount Edgcumbe
Chyverton House
Truro
Pine Lodge
Gribbin Head
Trewithen
Lost Gardens of Heligan
Truro Cathedral
Royal Citadel & Elizabethan Gardens
Tate Gallery
St Ives
Redruth
Burncoose
Camborne
Caerhays Castle
Dodman Point
Trelissick
Yarde Medieval Farmhouse
Chysauster Ancient Village
Godolphin
St Mawes Castle
Trengwainton
Penzance
Trevarno
Falmouth
Pendennis Castle
Helston
Trebah
Glendurgan
Trelowarren
Tregithew
St Michael's Mount
Land's End
Mount's Bay
SANTANDER SUMMER ONLY
ROSCOFF
Tresco Abbey Gardens
ISLES OF SCILLY
Lizard Point

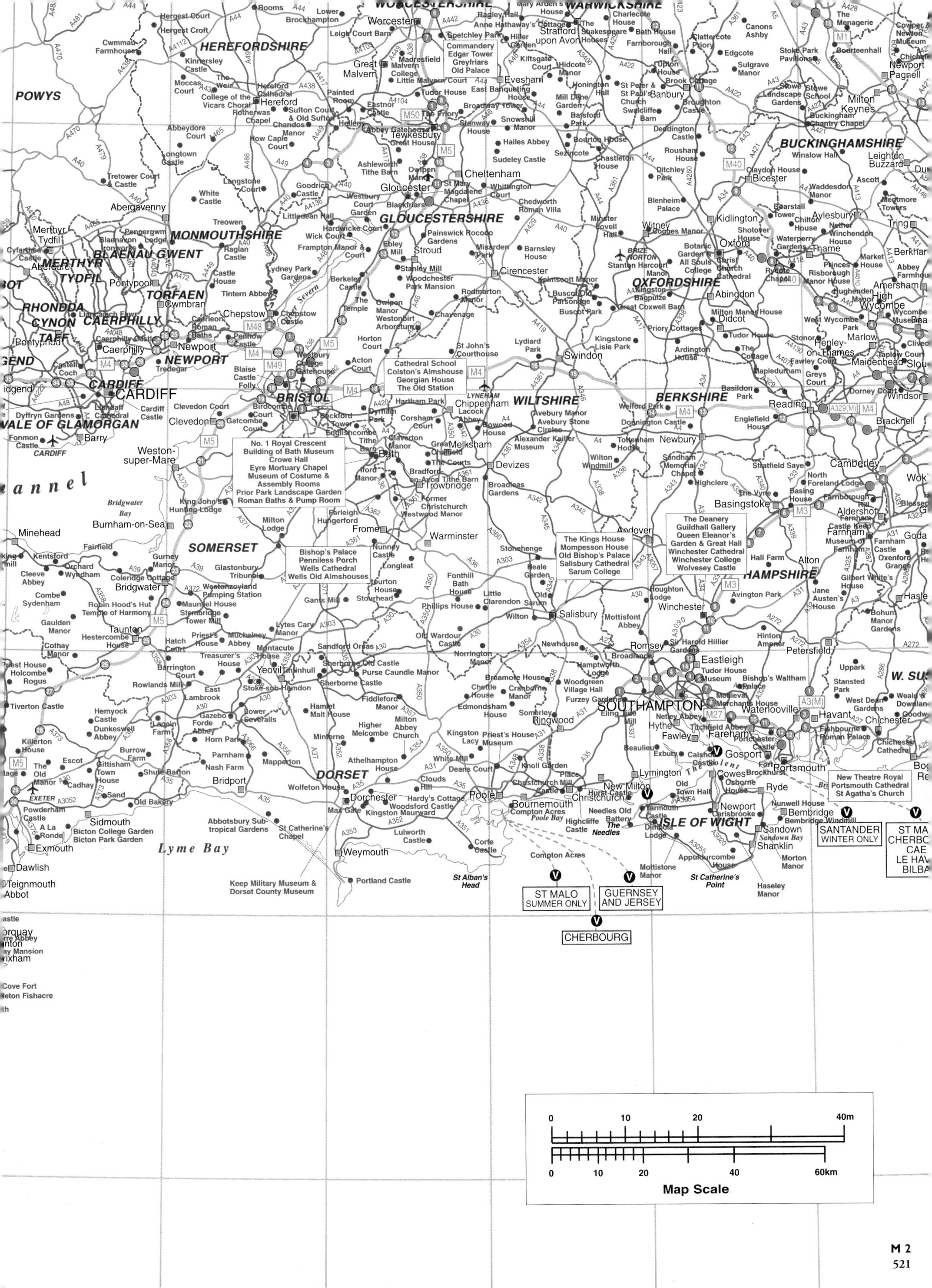

WORCESTERSHIRE
WARWICKSHIRE
HEREFORDSHIRE
POWYS
BUCKINGHAMSHIRE
GLOUCESTERSHIRE
MONMOUTHSHIRE
BLAENAU GWENT
MERTHYR TYDFIL
TORFAEN
RHONDDA CYNON TAFF
CAERPHILLY
NEWPORT
CARDIFF
VALE OF GLAMORGAN
OXFORDSHIRE
WILTSHIRE
BERKSHIRE
SOMERSET
HAMPSHIRE
DORSET
ISLE OF WIGHT
W. SUSSEX
Worcester
Hereford
Great Malvern
Tewkesbury
Cheltenham
Gloucester
Stratford upon Avon
Evesham
Banbury
Milton Keynes
Bicester
Oxford
Abingdon
Didcot
Witney
Aylesbury
High Wycombe
Henley-on-Thames
Maidenhead
Windsor
Reading
Bracknell
Newbury
Camberley
Basingstoke
Aldershot
Farnham
Alton
Winchester
Andover
Salisbury
Swindon
Chippenham
Melksham
Devizes
Trowbridge
Bath
Bristol
Frome
Warminster
Chepstow
Newport
Caerphilly
Cardiff
Barry
Abergavenny
Pontypool
Cwmbran
Clevedon
Weston-super-Mare
Burnham-on-Sea
Minehead
Bridgwater
Taunton
Yeovil
Dorchester
Weymouth
Bridport
Poole
Bournemouth
Christchurch
Ringwood
Lymington
Southampton
Eastleigh
Romsey
Fareham
Gosport
Portsmouth
Havant
Chichester
Petersfield
Waterlooville
Newport
Ryde
Sandown
Shanklin
Sidmouth
Exmouth
Dawlish
Teignmouth
Lyme Bay
Bristol Channel
No. 1 Royal Crescent
Building of Bath Museum
Crowe Hall
Eyre Mortuary Chapel
Museum of Costume & Assembly Rooms
Prior Park Landscape Garden
Roman Baths & Pump Room
Cathedral School
Colston's Almshouse
Georgian House
The Old Station
Bishop's Palace
Penniless Porch
Wells Cathedral
Wells Old Almshouses
The Kings House
Mompesson House
Old Bishop's Palace
Salisbury Cathedral
Sarum College
The Deanery
Guildhall Gallery
Queen Eleanor's Garden & Great Hall
Winchester Cathedral
Winchester College
Wolvesey Castle
Commandery
Edgar Tower
Greyfriars
Old Palace
New Theatre Royal
Portsmouth Cathedral
St Agatha's Church
ST MALO SUMMER ONLY
GUERNSEY AND JERSEY
CHERBOURG
SANTANDER WINTER ONLY
Map Scale
0
10
20
40m
0
10
20
40
60km

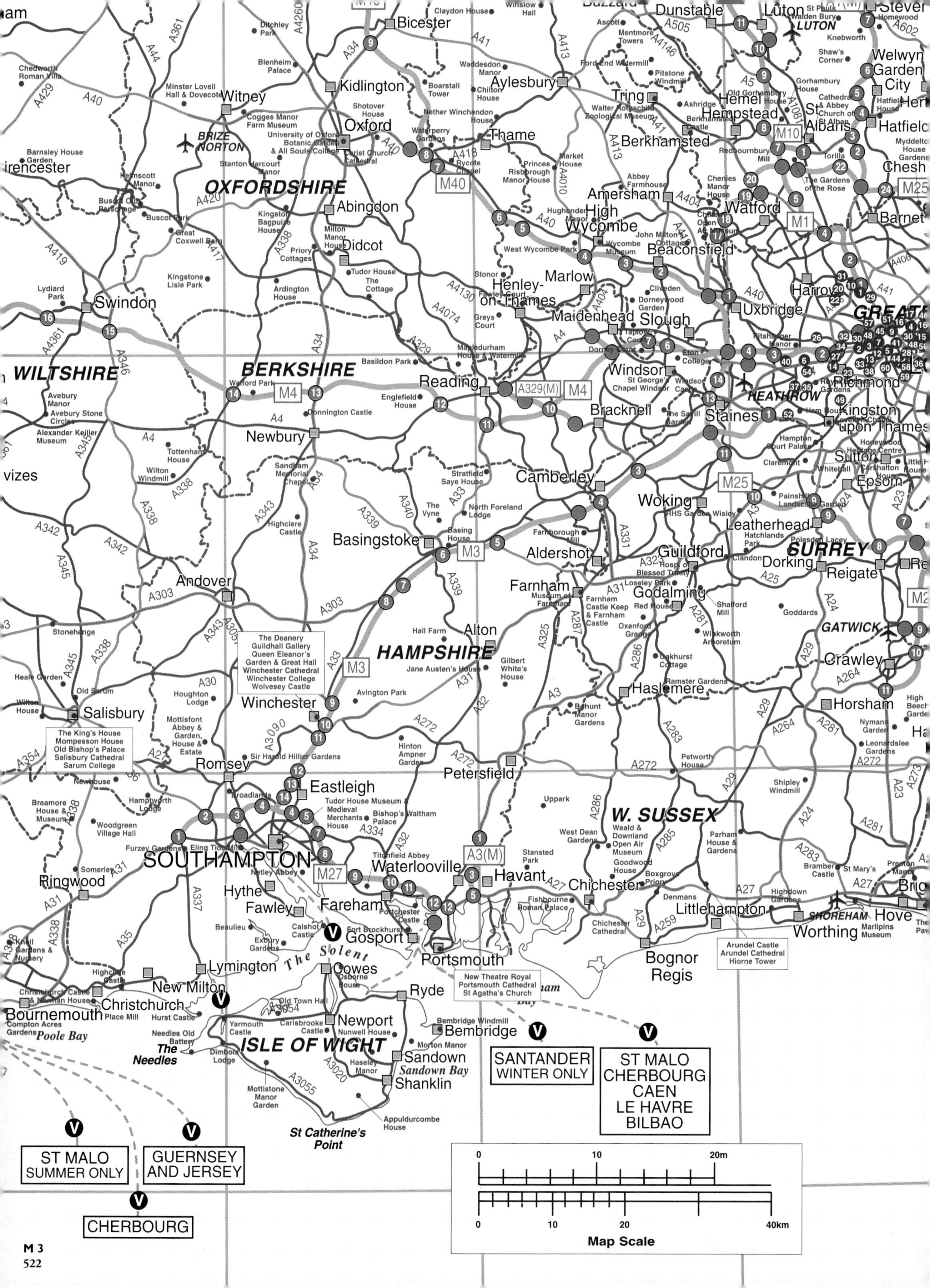
OXFORDSHIRE
BERKSHIRE
WILTSHIRE
HAMPSHIRE
SURREY
W. SUSSEX
ISLE OF WIGHT
GREATER
Bicester
Claydon House
Winslow Hall
Dunstable
Luton
LUTON
Stevenage
Ditchley Park
Ascott
Mentmore Towers
Knebworth
Blenheim Palace
Waddesdon Manor
Ford End Watermill
Pitstone Windmill
Shaw's Corner
Welwyn Garden City
Chedworth Roman Villa
Minster Lovell Hall & Dovecote
Witney
Kidlington
Boarstall Tower
Chilton House
Aylesbury
Tring
Hemel Hempstead
Old Gorhambury House
Gorhambury House
Cathedral & Abbey Church of St Alban
St Albans
Hatfield House
Hatfield
Myddelton House Gardens
Shotover House
Nether Winchendon House
Walter Rothschild Zoological Museum
Ashridge
Berkhamsted Castle
Berkhamsted
Cogges Manor Farm Museum
University of Oxford Botanic Garden & All Souls College
Oxford
Christ Church Cathedral
Waterperry Gardens
Thame
Rycote Chapel
Princes Risborough Manor House
Market House
Redbournbury Mill
Torilla
Cheshunt
The Gardens of the Rose
BRIZE NORTON
Barnsley House Garden
Cirencester
Stanton Harcourt Manor
Kelmscott Manor
Buscot Old Parsonage
Buscot Park
Great Coxwell Barn
Abingdon
Kingston Bagpuize House
Milton Manor House
Didcot
Priory Cottages
Tudor House
The Cottage
Ardington House
Abbey Farmhouse
Amersham
Chenies Manor House
Watford
Barnet
Hughenden Manor
High Wycombe
West Wycombe Park
Wycombe Museum
John Milton's Cottage
Chiltern Open Air Museum
Beaconsfield
Stonor
Henley-on-Thames
Fawley Court
Marlow
Cliveden
Dorneywood Garden
Maidenhead
Slough
Taplow Court
Dorney Court
Eton College
Uxbridge
Harrow
Kingstone Lisle Park
Lydiard Park
Swindon
Greys Court
Mapledurham House & Watermill
Basildon Park
Pitshanger Manor
Windsor
St George's Chapel Windsor
Windsor Castle
HEATHROW
Richmond
Reading
Englefield House
Bracknell
The Savill Garden
Staines
Ham House
Kingston upon Thames
Hampton Court Palace
Honeywood Heritage Centre
Sutton
Claremont
Whitehall
Carshalton House
Little Holland House
Epsom
Wellford Park
Avebury Manor
Avebury Stone Circles
Donnington Castle
Newbury
Alexander Keiller Museum
Tottenham House
Wilton Windmill
Sandham Memorial Chapel
Stratfield Saye House
Camberley
Woking
RHS Garden Wisley
Painshill Landscape Garden
Leatherhead
Hatchlands Park
Polesden Lacey
Devizes
Highclere Castle
The Vyne
North Foreland Lodge
Basing House
Basingstoke
Farnborough Mill
Aldershot
Guildford
Hosp. of Blessed Trinity
Clandon
Dorking
Reigate
Andover
Farnham
Museum of Farnham
Farnham Castle Keep & Farnham Castle
Loseley Park
Godalming
Red House
Shalford Mill
Goddards
Stonehenge
Hall Farm
Alton
Oxenford Grange
Winkworth Arboretum
GATWICK
The Deanery
Guildhall Gallery
Queen Eleanor's Garden & Great Hall
Winchester Cathedral
Winchester College
Wolvesey Castle
Jane Austen's House
Gilbert White's House
Oakhurst Cottage
Crawley
Heale Garden
Old Sarum
Houghton Lodge
Avington Park
Ramster Gardens
Haslemere
Wilton House
Salisbury
Winchester
Behunt Manor Gardens
Horsham
High Beeches Gardens
The King's House
Mompesson House
Old Bishop's Palace
Salisbury Cathedral
Sarum College
Mottisfont Abbey & Garden, House & Estate
Hinton Ampner Garden
Nymans Garden
Leonardslee Gardens
Sir Harold Hillier Gardens
Romsey
Petersfield
Petworth House
Newhouse
Eastleigh
Uppark
Shipley Windmill
Breamore House & Museum
Hamptworth Lodge
Broadlands
Tudor House Museum & Medieval Merchants House
Bishop's Waltham Palace
Woodgreen Village Hall
West Dean Gardens
Weald & Downland Open Air Museum
Parham House & Gardens
Furzey Gardens
Eling Tide Mill
SOUTHAMPTON
Titchfield Abbey
Stansted Park
Goodwood House
Boxgrove Priory
Bramber Castle
St Mary's
Preston Manor
Somerley
Netley Abbey
Waterlooville
Havant
Chichester
Brighton
Ringwood
Hythe
Fawley
Fareham
Portchester Castle
Fishbourne Roman Palace
Denmans
Highdown Gardens
Littlehampton
SHOREHAM
Hove
Worthing
Marlipins Museum
Beaulieu
Calshot Castle
Fort Brockhurst
Gosport
Chichester Cathedral
Bognor Regis
Arundel Castle
Arundel Cathedral
Hiorne Tower
Knoll Gardens & Nursery
Exbury Gardens
The Solent
Portsmouth
Highcliffe Castle
Lymington
Cowes
Osborne House
New Theatre Royal
Portsmouth Cathedral
St Agatha's Church
Christchurch Castle & Norman House
New Milton
Christchurch
Ryde
Old Town Hall
Bournemouth
Place Mill
Hurst Castle
Newport
Compton Acres Gardens
Poole Bay
Yarmouth Castle
Carisbrooke Castle
Nunwell House
Bembridge Windmill
Bembridge
Needles Old Battery
The Needles
Dimbola Lodge
Morton Manor
Sandown
Haseley Manor
Sandown Bay
Shanklin
Mottistone Manor Garden
Appuldurcombe House
St Catherine's Point
SANTANDER
WINTER ONLY
ST MALO
CHERBOURG
CAEN
LE HAVRE
BILBAO
ST MALO
SUMMER ONLY
GUERNSEY
AND JERSEY
CHERBOURG
M40
M4
A329(M)
M25
M1
M10
M3
M27
A3(M)
0
10
20m
0
10
20
40km
Map Scale

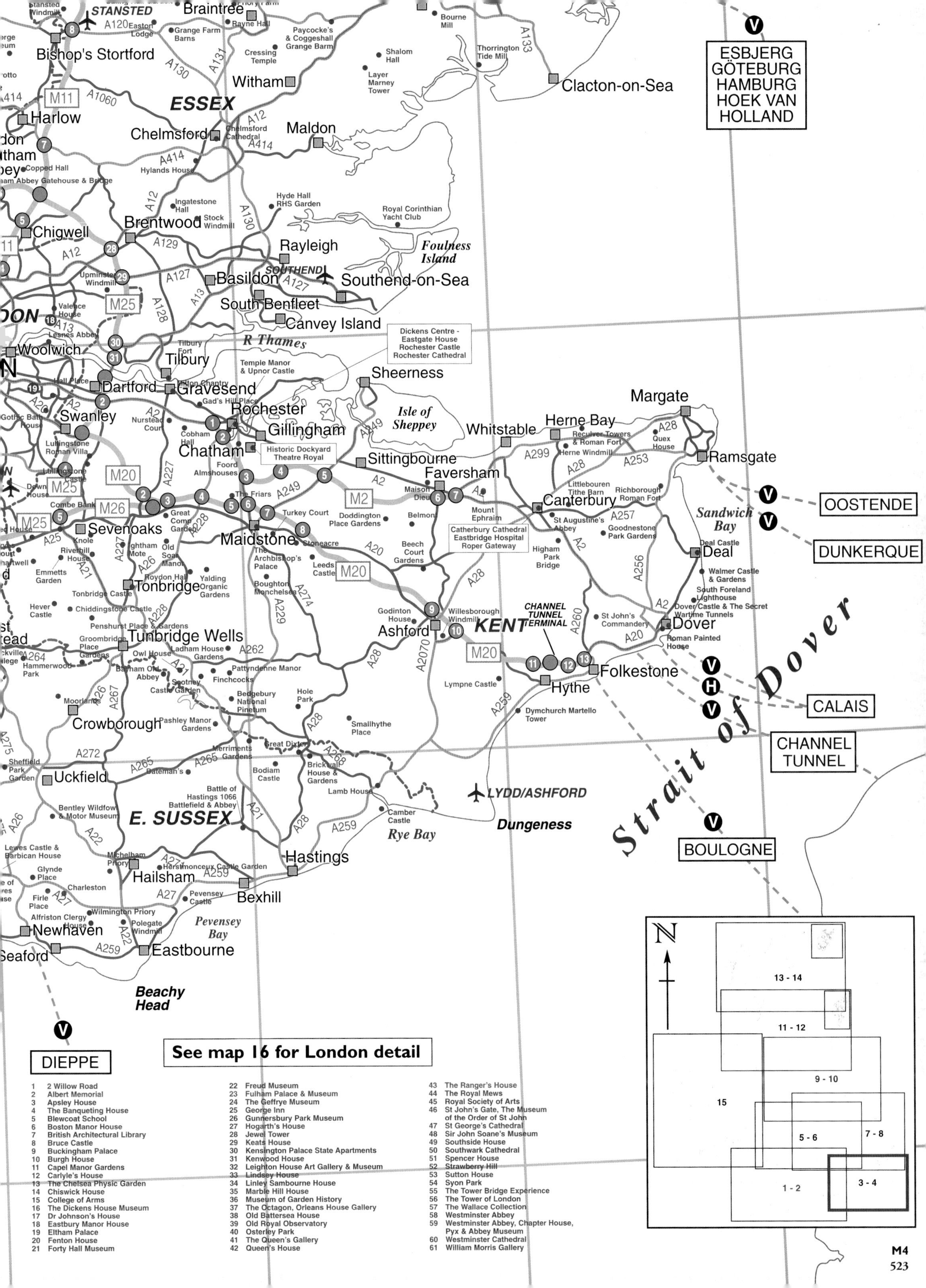
STANSTED
Braintree
Bishop's Stortford
ESSEX
Witham
Clacton-on-Sea
ESBJERG
GÖTEBORG
HAMBURG
HOEK VAN
HOLLAND
Harlow
Chelmsford
Maldon
Chigwell
Brentwood
Rayleigh
Foulness Island
SOUTHEND
Southend-on-Sea
Basildon
South Benfleet
Canvey Island
R Thames
Dickens Centre - Eastgate House
Rochester Castle
Rochester Cathedral
Woolwich
Tilbury
Sheerness
Isle of Sheppey
Dartford
Gravesend
Margate
Herne Bay
Whitstable
Rochester
Gillingham
Swanley
Chatham
Historic Dockyard
Theatre Royal
Ramsgate
Sittingbourne
Faversham
Canterbury
OOSTENDE
Sandwich Bay
DUNKERQUE
Catherbury Cathedral
Eastbridge Hospital
Roper Gateway
Sevenoaks
Maidstone
Deal
Tonbridge
CHANNEL TUNNEL TERMINAL
KENT
Dover
Ashford
Tunbridge Wells
Folkestone
Hythe
CALAIS
Crowborough
CHANNEL TUNNEL
Strait of Dover
Uckfield
LYDD/ASHFORD
Dungeness
E. SUSSEX
Rye Bay
BOULOGNE
Hastings
Hailsham
Bexhill
Pevensey Bay
Newhaven
Eastbourne
Seaford
Beachy Head
DIEPPE
See map 16 for London detail
1 2 Willow Road
2 Albert Memorial
3 Apsley House
4 The Banqueting House
5 Blewcoat School
6 Boston Manor House
7 British Architectural Library
8 Bruce Castle
9 Buckingham Palace
10 Burgh House
11 Capel Manor Gardens
12 Carlyle's House
13 The Chelsea Physic Garden
14 Chiswick House
15 College of Arms
16 The Dickens House Museum
17 Dr Johnson's House
18 Eastbury Manor House
19 Eltham Palace
20 Fenton House
21 Forty Hall Museum
22 Freud Museum
23 Fulham Palace & Museum
24 The Geffrye Museum
25 George Inn
26 Gunnersbury Park Museum
27 Hogarth's House
28 Jewel Tower
29 Keats House
30 Kensington Palace State Apartments
31 Kenwood House
32 Leighton House Art Gallery & Museum
33 Lindsey House
34 Linley Sambourne House
35 Marble Hill House
36 Museum of Garden History
37 The Octagon, Orleans House Gallery
38 Old Battersea House
39 Old Royal Observatory
40 Osterley Park
41 The Queen's Gallery
42 Queen's House
43 The Ranger's House
44 The Royal Mews
45 Royal Society of Arts
46 St John's Gate, The Museum of the Order of St John
47 St George's Cathedral
48 Sir John Soane's Museum
49 Southside House
50 Southwark Cathedral
51 Spencer House
52 Strawberry Hill
53 Sutton House
54 Syon Park
55 The Tower Bridge Experience
56 The Tower of London
57 The Wallace Collection
58 Westminster Abbey
59 Westminster Abbey, Chapter House, Pyx & Abbey Museum
60 Westminster Cathedral
61 William Morris Gallery
N
13 - 14
11 - 12
9 - 10
15
5 - 6
7 - 8
1 - 2
3 - 4

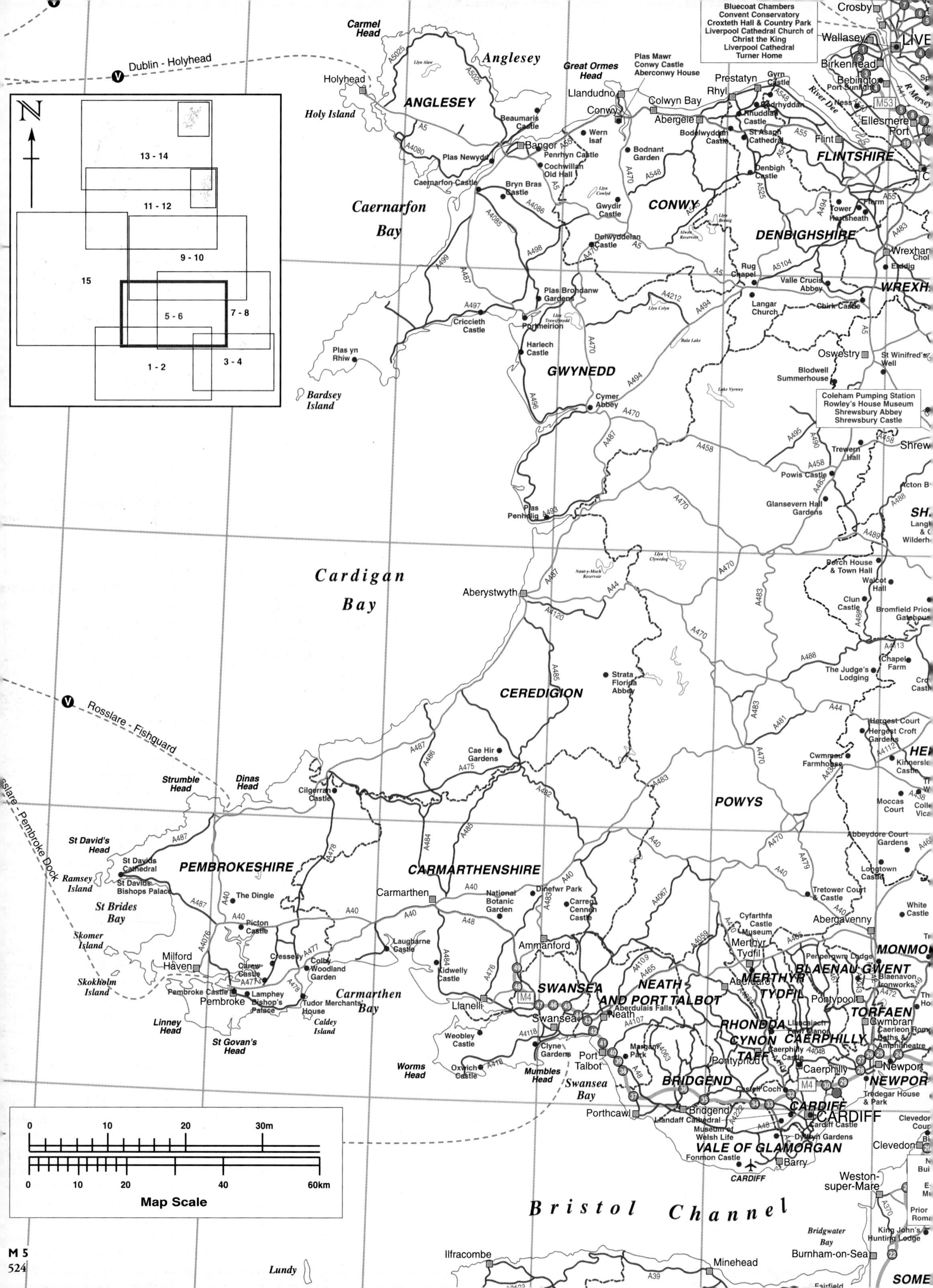

Bluecoat Chambers
Convent Conservatory
Croxteth Hall & Country Park
Liverpool Cathedral Church of Christ the King
Liverpool Cathedral
Turner Home
Crosby
Wallasey
Birkenhead
Bebington
Port Sunlight
Ness
Ellesmere Port
Flint
FLINTSHIRE
Carmel Head
Dublin - Holyhead
Anglesey
Holyhead
ANGLESEY
Holy Island
Beaumaris Castle
Great Ormes Head
Plas Mawr
Conwy Castle
Aberconwy House
Llandudno
Conwy
Colwyn Bay
Prestatyn
Rhyl
Gyrn Castle
Bodrhyddan
Rhuddlan Castle
Abergele
Bodelwyddan Castle
St Asaph Cathedral
Bangor
Wern Isaf
Penrhyn Castle
Plas Newydd
Bodnant Garden
Cochwillan Old Hall
Caernarfon Castle
Bryn Bras Castle
Gwydir Castle
CONWY
Denbigh Castle
Tower
Hartsheath
Caernarfon
Bay
DENBIGHSHIRE
Dolwyddelan Castle
Wrexham
Erddig
Rug Chapel
Valle Crucis Abbey
WREXHAM
Plas Brondanw Gardens
Langar Church
Chirk Castle
Criccieth Castle
Portmeirion
Harlech Castle
Oswestry
St Winifred's Well
Plas yn Rhiw
GWYNEDD
Blodwell Summerhouse
Bardsey Island
Cymer Abbey
Coleham Pumping Station
Rowley's House Museum
Shrewsbury Abbey
Shrewsbury Castle
Trewern Hall
Powis Castle
Glansevern Hall Gardens
Plas Penhelig
Cardigan
Bay
Aberystwyth
Porch House & Town Hall
Walcot Hall
Clun Castle
Bromfield Priory Gatehouse
Chapel Farm
The Judge's Lodging
Strata Florida Abbey
CEREDIGION
Hergest Court
Hergest Croft Gardens
Rosslare - Fishguard
Cae Hir Gardens
Cwmmau Farmhouse
Kinnersley Castle
Strumble Head
Dinas Head
Cilgerran Castle
POWYS
Moccas Court
Abbeydore Court Gardens
St David's Head
St Davids Cathedral
St Davids Bishops Palace
PEMBROKESHIRE
CARMARTHENSHIRE
Longtown Castle
Ramsey Island
The Dingle
Dinefwr Park
Carmarthen
National Botanic Garden
Carreg Cennen Castle
Tretower Court & Castle
White Castle
St Brides Bay
Picton Castle
Cyfarthfa Castle Museum
Abergavenny
Skomer Island
Laugharne Castle
Ammanford
Merthyr Tydfil
Penpergwm Lodge
MONMOUTHSHIRE
Milford Haven
Cresselly
Colby Woodland Garden
Kidwelly Castle
BLAENAU GWENT
Blaenavon Ironworks
Skokholm Island
Carew Castle
SWANSEA
NEATH AND PORT TALBOT
MERTHYR TYDFIL
Pontypool
Pembroke Castle
Pembroke
Lamphey Bishop's Palace
Tudor Merchants' House
Carmarthen Bay
Llanelli
Aberdare
Aberdulais Falls
Neath
Swansea
TORFAEN
Cwmbran
Caerleon Roman Baths & Amphitheatre
Linney Head
Caldey Island
RHONDDA CYNON TAFF
Llancaiach Fawr Manor
CAERPHILLY
St Govan's Head
Weobley Castle
Clyne Gardens
Port Talbot
Margam Park
Pontypridd
Caerphilly Castle
Caerphilly
Newport
Worms Head
Oxwich Castle
Mumbles Head
Swansea Bay
BRIDGEND
Castell Coch
NEWPORT
Tredegar House & Park
Porthcawl
Bridgend
CARDIFF
Llandaff Cathedral
Cardiff Castle
Museum of Welsh Life
Dyffryn Gardens
VALE OF GLAMORGAN
Fonmon Castle
Barry
Clevedon
Clevedon Court
Weston-super-Mare
Bristol Channel
Bridgwater Bay
Burnham-on-Sea
King John's Hunting Lodge
Ilfracombe
Lundy
Minehead
SOMERSET
13 - 14
11 - 12
9 - 10
15
5 - 6
7 - 8
1 - 2
3 - 4
N
0
10
20
30m
0
10
20
40
60km
Map Scale

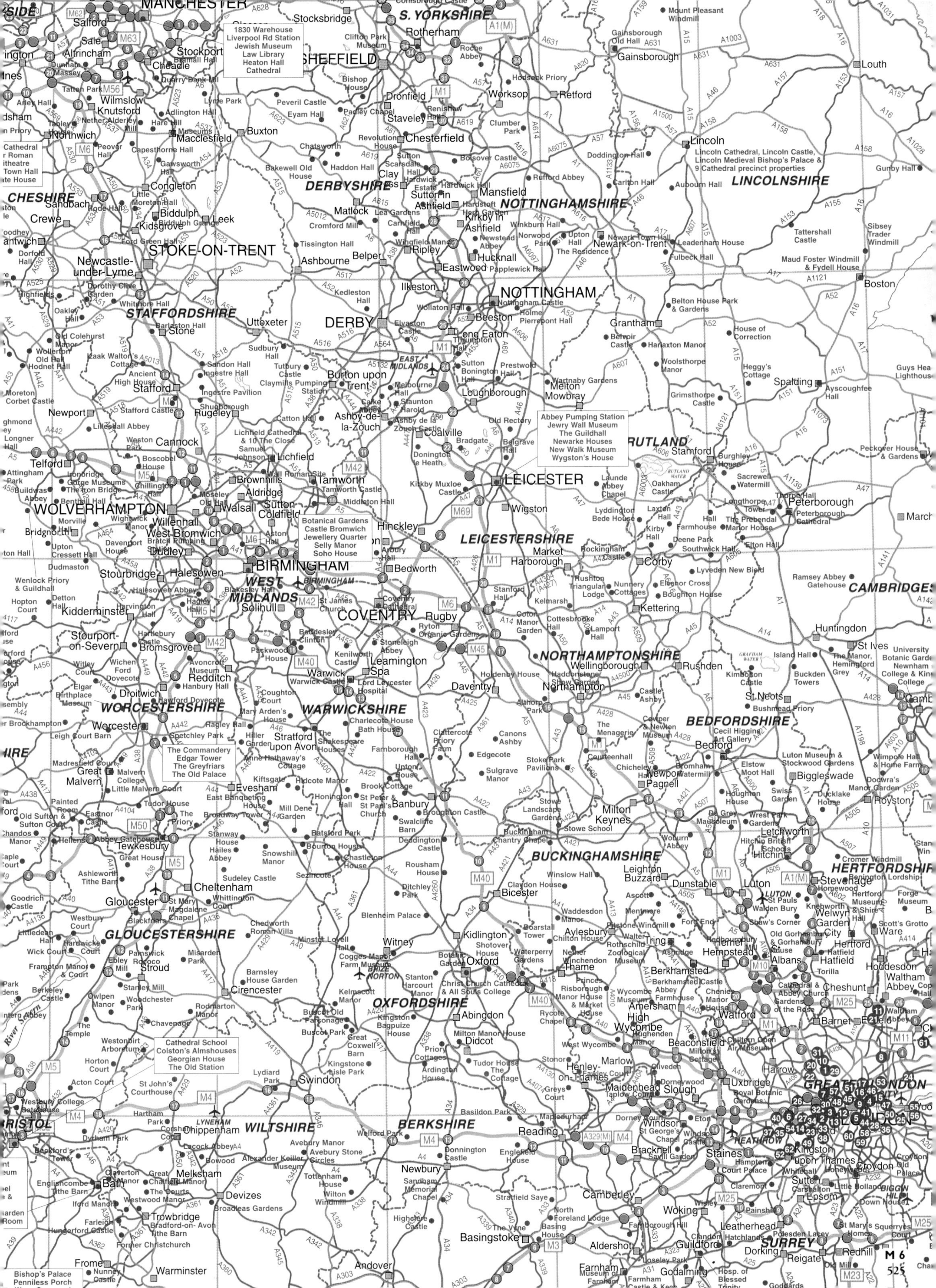

MANCHESTER
Salford
Sale
Altrincham
Stockport
Cheadle
1830 Warehouse
Liverpool Rd Station
Jewish Museum
Law Library
Heaton Hall
Cathedral
Stocksbridge
S. YORKSHIRE
Rotherham
SHEFFIELD
Clifton Park Museum
Roche Abbey
Mount Pleasant Windmill
Gainsborough Old Hall
Gainsborough
Louth
Tatton Park
Wilmslow
Knutsford
Quarry Bank Mill
Lyme Park
Bishop House
Dronfield
Hodsock Priory
Worksop
Retford
Peveril Castle
Eyam Hall
Padley Chapel
Staveley
Renishaw Hall
Clumber Park
Arley Hall
Tabley House
Nether Alderley Mill
Adlington Hall
Hare Hill
Northwich
Museums
Macclesfield
Buxton
Chatsworth
Revolution House
Chesterfield
Lincoln
Lincoln Cathedral, Lincoln Castle,
Lincoln Medieval Bishop's Palace &
9 Cathedral precinct properties
Doddington Hall
Gunby Hall
Peover Hall
Capesthorne Hall
Gawsworth Hall
Bakewell Old House
Haddon Hall
Sutton Scarsdale Hall
Hardwick Estate
Hardwick Hall
Bolsover Castle
Rufford Abbey
Carlton Hall
Auborn Hall
LINCOLNSHIRE
Congleton
CHESHIRE
Sandbach
Crewe
Little Moreton Hall
Rode Hall
Biddulph
Biddulph Grange
Leek
Kidsgrove
DERBYSHIRE
Matlock
Lea Gardens
Cromford Mill
Sutton in Ashfield
Hardstoft Herb Garden
Mansfield
NOTTINGHAMSHIRE
Kirkby in Ashfield
Carnfield Hall
Winkburn Hall
Norwood Park
Upton Hall
The Residence
Newark Town Hall
Newark-on-Trent
Leadenham House
Tattershall Castle
Sibsey Trader Windmill
Ford Green Hall
STOKE-ON-TRENT
Newcastle-under-Lyme
Tissington Hall
Ashbourne
Belper
Wingfield Manor
Ripley
Newstead Abbey
Hucknall
Papplewick Hall
Eastwood
Fulbeck Hall
Maud Foster Windmill
& Fydell House
Boston
Dorothy Clive Garden
Whitmore Hall
Kedleston Hall
Ilkeston
NOTTINGHAM
Nottingham Castle
Wollaton Hall
Beeston
Holme Pierrepont Hall
Belton House Park & Gardens
STAFFORDSHIRE
Oakley Hall
Barlaston Hall
Stone
Uttoxeter
DERBY
Elvaston Castle
Long Eaton
Thrumpton Hall
Grantham
Belvoir Castle
Harlaxton Manor
House of Correction
Old Colehurst Manor
Wollerton Old Hall
Hodnet Hall
Izaak Walton's Cottage
Sandon Hall
Ingestre Hall
Sudbury Hall
Tutbury Castle
Burton upon Trent
EAST MIDLANDS
Sutton Bonington Hall
Prestwold Hall
Woolsthorpe Manor
Heggy's Cottage
Spalding
Ayscoughfee Hall
Guys Head Lighthouse
Ancient High House
Stafford
Claymills Pumping Station
Melbourne Hall
Loughborough
Wartnaby Gardens
Melton Mowbray
Moreton Corbet Castle
Newport
Ingestre Pavilion
Shugborough Hall
Rugeley
Stafford Castle
Calke Abbey
Staunton Harold
Ashby-de-la-Zouch
Ashby de la Zouch Castle
Grimsthorpe Castle
Lilleshall Abbey
Catton Hall
Coalville
Old Rectory
Abbey Pumping Station
Jewry Wall Museum
The Guildhall
Newarke Houses
New Walk Museum
Wygston's House
RUTLAND
Stamford
Burghley House
Peckover House & Gardens
Weston Park
Cannock
Lichfield Cathedral
& 10 The Close
Samuel Johnson
Lichfield
Bradgate
Belgrave Hall
Donington le Heath
Telford
Attingham Park
Ironbridge Gorge Museums
The Iron Bridge
Boscobel House
Chillington Hall
Brownhills
Wall Roman Site
Tamworth
Tamworth Castle
Kirkby Muxloe Castle
LEICESTER
Launde Abbey
Chapel
Oakham Castle
Sacrewell Watermill
Buildwas Abbey
Benthall Hall
WOLVERHAMPTON
Moseley Old Hall
Aldridge
Walsall
Sutton Coldfield
Middleton Hall
Wigston
Lyddington Bede House
Laxton Hall
Longthorpe Tower
Thorpe Hall
Peterborough
Peterborough Cathedral
The Prebendal Manor House
March
Morville Hall
Bridgnorth
Wightwick Manor
Willenhall
West Bromwich
Botanical Gardens
Castle Bromwich
Jewellery Quarter
Selly Manor
Soho House
Hinckley
LEICESTERSHIRE
Kirby Hall
Deene Park
Farmhouse
Elton Hall
Upton Cressett Hall
Davenport House
Bratch Pumping
Dudley
Aston Hall
Arbury Hall
Market Harborough
Rockingham Castle
Southwick Hall
Corby
Dudmaston
Stourbridge
Halesowen
BIRMINGHAM
Bedworth
Lyveden New Bield
Ramsey Abbey Gatehouse
CAMBRIDGESHIRE
Wenlock Priory
& Guildhall
WEST MIDLANDS
Halesowen Abbey
Blakesley Hall
BIRMINGHAM
Rushton Triangular Lodge
Nunnery Cottages
Eleanor Cross
Boughton House
Hopton Court
Detton Hall
Kidderminster
Harvington Hall
Hagley Hall
Solihull
St James Church
Coventry Cathedral
COVENTRY
Rugby
Stanford Hall
Kelmarsh
Cottesbrooke Hall
Kettering
Stourport-on-Severn
Hartlebury Castle
Bromsgrove
Baddesley Clinton
Ryton Organic Gardens
Coton Manor Garden
Lamport Hall
Huntingdon
St Ives
Island Hall
The Manor, Hemingford Grey
University Botanic Garden
Newnham College & King's College
Packwood House
Stoneleigh Abbey
Kenilworth Castle
Leamington Spa
NORTHAMPTONSHIRE
Wellingborough
Rushden
Kimbolton Castle
Buckden Towers
Witley Court
Wichen Ford Dovecote
Avoncroft Museum
Redditch
Hanbury Hall
Warwick
Warwick Castle
Lord Leycester Hospital
Holdenby House
Haddonstone Show Gardens
Daventry
Northampton
Castle Ashby
St Neots
Bushmead Priory
Elgar Birthplace Museum
Droitwich
Hawford Dovecote
Coughton Court
WORCESTERSHIRE
Mary Arden's House
WARWICKSHIRE
Charlecote House
Althorp Park
The Menagerie
Cowper & Newton Museum
BEDFORDSHIRE
Cecil Higgins Art Gallery
Brockhampton
Worcester
Ragley Hall
Leigh Court Barn
Spetchley Park
Hiller Garden
Stratford upon Avon
The Shakespeare Houses
Bath House
Clattercote Priory Farm
Canons Ashby
Bedford
The Commandery
Edgar Tower
The Greyfriars
The Old Palace
Anne Hathaway's Cottage
Farnborough Hall
Edgcote
Courteenhall
Luton Museum &
Stockwood Gardens
Wimpole Hall
& Home Farm
Madresfield Court
Great Malvern
Malvern College
Little Malvern Court
Kiftsgate
Hidcote Manor
Upton House
Sulgrave Manor
Stoke Park Pavilions
Chicheley
Bromham Watermill
Newport Pagnell
Elstow Moot Hall
Biggleswade
Evesham
Brook Cottage
Swiss Garden
Dodwra's Manor Garden
Royston
Painted Room
Old Sufton & Sufton Court
Eastnor Castle
Tudor House
The Priory
East Banqueting House
Broadway Tower
Mill Dene Garden
Honington Hall
St Peter & St Paul's Church
Banbury
Broughton Castle
Swalcliffe Barn
Stowe Landscape Gardens
Stowe School
Milton Keynes
Houghton House
De Grey Mausoleum
Wrest Park Gardens
Ducklake House
Letchworth
Hellens
Abbey Gatehouse
Tewkesbury
Stanway House
Hailes Abbey
Batsford Park
Bourton House
Deddington Castle
Buckingham Chantry Chapel
Woburn Abbey
Hitchin British Schools
Hitchin
Cromer Windmill
Great House
Snowshill Manor
Chastleton House
Rousham House
BUCKINGHAMSHIRE
Leighton Buzzard
Benington Lordship
HERTFORDSHIRE
Ashleworth Tithe Barn
Sudeley Castle
Sezincote
Winslow Hall
Dunstable
Luton
LUTON
Stevenage
Homewood
Cheltenham
Whittington Court
Ditchley Park
Claydon House
Bicester
Ascott
Mentmore
St Pauls Walden Bury
Hertford Museum
Forge Museum
Goodrich Castle
Gloucester
St Mary Magdalene Chapel
Blackfriars
Westbury Court
Blenheim Palace
Waddesdon Manor
Fort End
Knebworth House
Welwyn Garden City
Shaw's Corner
Scott's Grotto
Ware
GLOUCESTERSHIRE
Chedworth Roman Villa
Minster Lovell Hall
Witney
Kidlington
Boarstall Tower
Aylesbury
Chilton House
Pitstone Windmill
Walter Rothschild Zoological Museum
Tring
Hemel Hempstead
Old Gorhambury House
Hertford
Hatfield
Hoddesdon
Littledean Hall
Hardwicke Court
Wick Court
Painswick Rococo Garden
Misarden Park
Cogges Manor Farm Museum
Botanic Garden
Shotover House
Waterperry Gardens
Oxford
Nether Winchendon House
Thame
Ashridge
Berkhamsted
Berkhamsted Castle
St Albans
Hatfield
Torilla
Frampton Manor & Court
Ebley Mill
Stroud
Barnsley House Garden
BRIZE NORTON
Stanton Harcourt Manor
Christ Church Cathedral
& All Souls College
Princes Risborough Manor House
Waltham Abbey
Berkeley Castle
Stanley Mill
Owlpen Manor
Woodchester Park
Cirencester
Kelmscott Manor
OXFORDSHIRE
Wycombe Museum
Chenies Manor House
Cathedral & Abbey Church
Gardens of the Rose
Cheshunt
Rodmarton Manor
Buscot Old Parsonage
Kingston Bagpuize House
Abingdon
Rycote Chapel
Hughenden Manor
Amersham
High Wycombe
Watford
Barnet
Enfield
Nether Lypiatt Manor
Chavenage
Buscot Park
Great Coxwell Barn
Milton Manor House
Didcot
West Wycombe
Beaconsfield
Chiltern Open Air Museum
Milton's Cottage
The Temple
Westonbirt Arboretum
Cathedral School
Colston's Almshouses
Georgian House
The Old Station
Horton Court
Kingstone Lisle Park
Priory Cottages
Ardington House
Tudor House
The Cottage
Stonor
Henley-on-Thames
Marlow
Cliveden
Dorneywood
Harrow
GREATER LONDON
Acton Court
St John's Courthouse
Lydiard Park
Swindon
Greys Court
Maidenhead
Taplow Court
Slough
Uxbridge
Royal Botanic Gardens
Westbury College
Gatehouse
BRISTOL
Hartham Park
Corsham Court
Chippenham
LYNEHAM
WILTSHIRE
BERKSHIRE
Basildon Park
Mapledurham
Reading
Dorney Court
Windsor
St George's Chapel
Windsor Castle
Eton
HEATHROW
Dyrham Park
Lacock Abbey
Bowood
Avebury Manor
Avebury Stone Circles
Alexander Keiller Museum
Welford Park
Donnington Castle
Englefield House
Bracknell
Savill Garden
Staines
Hampton Court Palace
Kingston upon Thames
Croydon
Croydon Old Palace
Beckford's Tower
Claverton Manor
Great Chalfield Manor
Melksham
Tottenham House
Newbury
Englishcombe Tithe Barn
Bath
The Courts
Westwood Manor
Devizes
Broadleas Gardens
Wilton Windmill
Sandham Memorial Chapel
Stratfield Saye
Camberley
Whitehall
Sutton
Carshalton House
Little Holland House
BIGGIN HILL
Down House
Iford Manor
Farleigh Hungerford Castle
Trowbridge
Bradford-on-Avon Tithe Barn
Highclere Castle
North Foreland Lodge
Woking
Epsom
The Vyne
Basing House
Farnborough Hill
Painshill
Leatherhead
St Mary's Homes
Squerryes Court
Former Christchurch
Basingstoke
Aldershot
Clandon
Hatchlands
Polesden Lacey
SURREY
Frome
Nunney Castle
Warminster
Andover
Farnham
Farnham Castle & Keep
Loseley Park
Guildford
Godalming
Hosp. of Blessed Trinity
Dorking
Reigate
Redhill
Old Mill
Goddards
Bishop's Palace
Penniless Porch
M6
M62
M63
M56
M1
A1(M)
M42
M54
M6
M69
M5
M50
M40
M45
M4
M3
M25
M23
M10
M11
A329(M)
River Severn

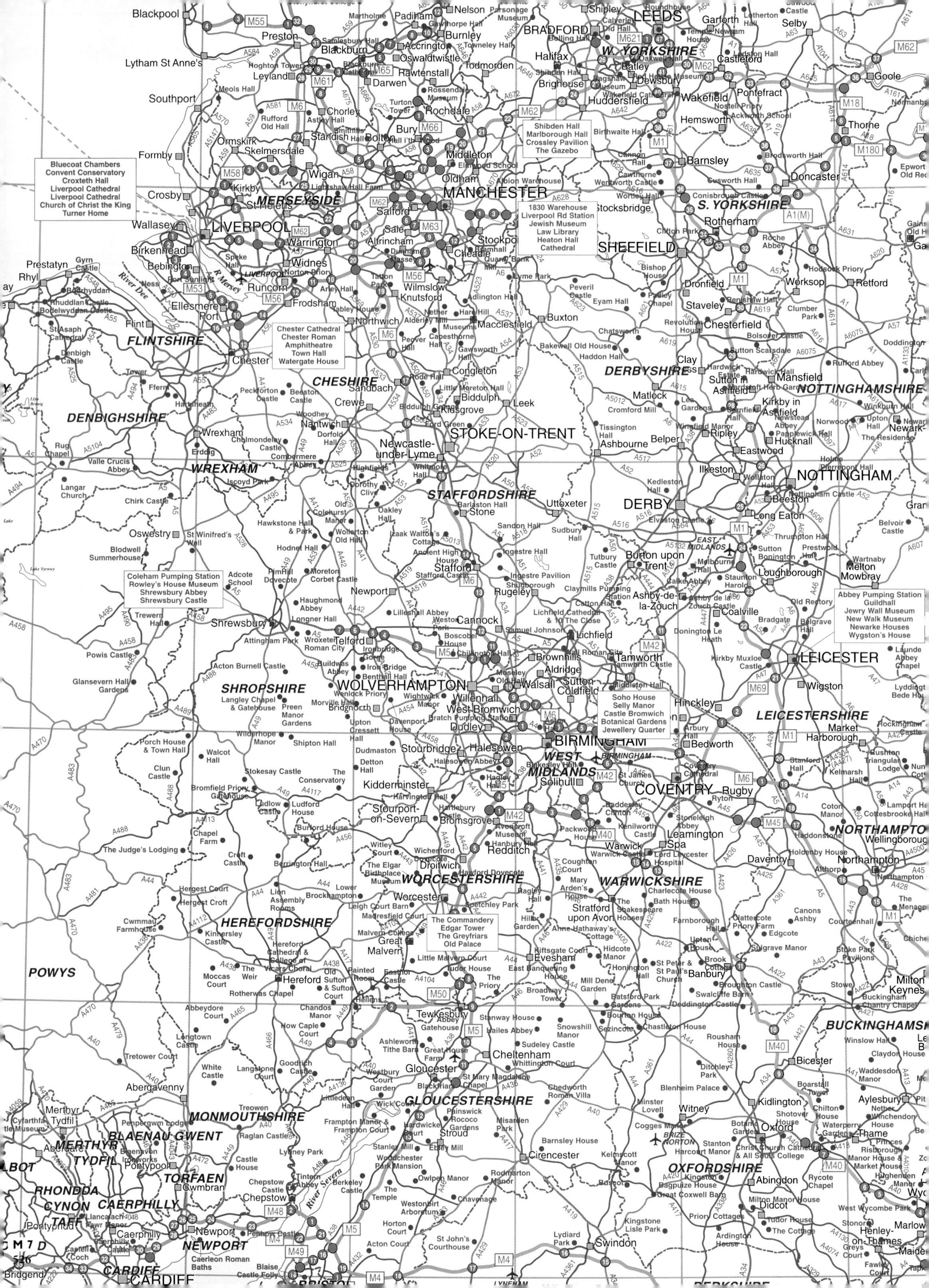

Blackpool
Preston
Lytham St Anne's
Southport
Formby
Crosby
Wallasey
Birkenhead
Bebington
Prestatyn
Rhyl
Flint
St Asaph
Denbigh Castle
Rhuddlan Castle
Bodelwyddan Castle
Gyrn Castle
Bluecoat Chambers
Convent Conservatory
Croxteth Hall
Liverpool Cathedral
Liverpool Cathedral
Church of Christ the King
Turner Home
LIVERPOOL
MERSEYSIDE
Ormskirk
Skelmersdale
Kirkby
St Helens
Wigan
Standish
Chorley
Leyland
Hoghton Tower
Blackburn
Samlesbury Hall
Martholme
Padiham
Nelson
Burnley
Accrington
Oswaldtwistle
Rawtenstall
Darwen
Towneley Hall
Gawthorpe Hall
Todmorden
Rochdale
Rossendale Museum
Turton Tower
Bury
Bolton
Smithills Hall
Hall i' th' Wood
Middleton
Oldham
Ellenrood School
Astley Hall
Rufford Old Hall
Meols Hall
Lightshaw Hall Farm
Salford
MANCHESTER
Sale
Altrincham
Dunham Massey
Stockport
Cheadle
Bramhall
Quarry Bank Mill
Lyme Park
Warrington
Widnes
Runcorn
Speke Hall
Port Sunlight
Norton Priory
Frodsham
Ellesmere Port
Ness
River Dee
R Mersey
Arley Hall
Tatton Park
Wilmslow
Knutsford
Adlington Hall
Tabley House
Northwich
Nether Alderley Mill
Hare Hill
Macclesfield
Museums
Capesthorne Hall
Peover Hall
Gawsworth Hall
Chester
Chester Cathedral
Chester Roman Amphitheatre
Town Hall
Watergate House
CHESHIRE
FLINTSHIRE
DENBIGHSHIRE
Tower
Ffern
Hartsheath
Peckforton Castle
Beeston Castle
Sandbach
Crewe
Rode Hall
Congleton
Little Moreton Hall
Biddulph
Biddulph Grange
Kidsgrove
Leek
Woodhey
Nantwich
Dorfold Hall
Wrexham
Erddig
Cholmondeley Castle
Combermere Abbey
Rug Chapel
Valle Crucis Abbey
WREXHAM
Langar Church
Chirk Castle
Iscoyd Park
Ford Green
Newcastle-under-Lyme
STOKE-ON-TRENT
Whitmore Hall
Highfields
Dorothy Clive
Oakley Hall
Old Colehurst Manor
STAFFORDSHIRE
Barlaston Hall
Stone
Sandon Hall
Uttoxeter
Hawkstone Hall & Park
Wollerton Old Hall
Izaak Walton's Cottage
Oswestry
St Winifred's Well
Blodwell Summerhouse
Lake Vyrnwy
Hodnet Hall
Ancient High House
Stafford
Stafford Castle
Ingestre Hall
Ingestre Pavilion
Shugborough
Rugeley
Coleham Pumping Station
Rowley's House Museum
Shrewsbury Abbey
Shrewsbury Castle
Adcote School
Pimhill Dovecote
Moreton Corbet Castle
Newport
Haughmond Abbey
Longner Hall
Lilleshall Abbey
Weston Park
Cannock
Boscobel House
Trewern Hall
Shrewsbury
Attingham Park
Wroxeter Roman City
Telford
Ironbridge Gorge
Iron Bridge
Benthall Hall
Buildwas Abbey
Powis Castle
Acton Burnell Castle
Glansevern Hall Gardens
SHROPSHIRE
Langley Chapel & Gatehouse
Preen Manor Gardens
Wenlock Priory
Morville Hall
Bridgnorth
WOLVERHAMPTON
Wightwick Manor
Willenhall
West Bromwich
Moseley Old Hall
Walsall
Brownhills
Aldridge
Sutton Coldfield
Lichfield
Lichfield Cathedral & 10 The Close
Samuel Johnson
Hall Roman Site
Tamworth
Tamworth Castle
Middleton Hall
Chillington Hall
Upton Cressett Hall
Davenport House
Dudley
Bratch Pumping Station
Wilderhope Manor
Shipton Hall
Dudmaston
Stourbridge
Halesowen
Halesowen Abbey
BIRMINGHAM
WEST MIDLANDS
Soho House
Selly Manor
Castle Bromwich
Botanical Gardens
Jewellery Quarter
Porch House & Town Hall
Walcot Hall
Clun Castle
Stokesay Castle
The Conservatory
Detton Hall
Kidderminster
Harvington Hall
Hagley Hall
Blakesley Hall
Solihull
St James Church
COVENTRY
Coventry Cathedral
Bromfield Priory Gatehouse
Ludlow Castle
Ludford House
Stourport-on-Severn
Hartlebury Castle
Bromsgrove
Avoncroft Museum
Baddesley Clinton
Kenilworth Castle
Packwood House
Stoneleigh Abbey
Leamington Spa
Warwick
Warwick Castle
Lord Leycester Hospital
Chapel Farm
Burford House
The Judge's Lodging
Croft Castle
Berrington Hall
Witley Court
The Elgar Birthplace Museum
Wichenford Dovecote
Droitwich
Hanbury Hall
Redditch
Hawford Dovecote
WORCESTERSHIRE
WARWICKSHIRE
Coughton Court
Mary Arden's House
Charlecote House
Bath House
Hergest Court
Hergest Croft
Lion Assembly Rooms
Lower Brockhampton
Worcester
Leigh Court Barn
Spetchley Park
Ragley Hall
Stratford upon Avon
The Shakespeare Houses
Anne Hathaway's Cottage
Hill Garden
Madresfield Court
The Commandery
Edgar Tower
The Greyfriars
Old Palace
Malvern College
Great Malvern
Cwmmau Farmhouse
Kinnersley Castle
HEREFORDSHIRE
Hereford Cathedral & College of Vicars Choral
Hereford
The Weir
Moccas Court
Rotherwas Chapel
POWYS
Old Sufton & Sufton Court
Painted Room
Eastnor Castle
Little Malvern Court
Tudor House
The Priory
Kiftsgate Court
Evesham
East Banqueting House
Hidcote Manor
Honington Hall
Mill Dene Garden
Broadway Tower
Abbeydore Court
Chandos Manor
Tewkesbury Abbey
Gatehouse
Stanway House
Hailes Abbey
Snowshill Manor
Batsford Park
Bourton House
Sezincote
Chastleton House
Longtown Castle
How Caple Court
Ashleworth Tithe Barn
Great House Farm
Cheltenham
Sudeley Castle
Whittington Court
Tretower Court
White Castle
Langstone Court
Goodrich Castle
Gloucester
Westbury Court Garden
Blackfriars
St Mary Magdalene Chapel
Chedworth Roman Villa
Abergavenny
MONMOUTHSHIRE
Treowen
Littledean Hall
Wick Court
GLOUCESTERSHIRE
Painswick Rococo Gardens
Frampton Manor & Frampton Court
Hardwicke Court
Stroud
Misarden Park
Merthyr Tydfil
Cyfarthfa Museum
MERTHYR TYDFIL
BLAENAU GWENT
Raglan Castle
Penpergwm Lodge
Bedwellty House
Blaenavon Ironworks
Pontypool
TORFAEN
Cwmbran
Castle House
Lydney Park
Stanley Mill
Ebley Mill
Woodchester Park Mansion
Owlpen Manor
Cirencester
Barnsley House
Rodmarton Manor
Tintern Abbey
Chepstow Castle
Chepstow
Berkeley Castle
The Temple
River Severn
Westonbirt Arboretum
Chavenage
RHONDDA CYNON TAFF
CAERPHILLY
Pontypridd
Llancaiach Fawr Manor
Caerphilly Castle
Newport
Penhow Castle
NEWPORT
Horton Court
St John's Courthouse
Acton Court
Caerleon Roman Baths
Blaise Castle Folly
Castell Coch
CARDIFF
Bridgend
BRISTOL
Lydiard Park
Swindon
Kelmscott Manor
Buscot
Shibden Hall
Marlborough Hall
Crossley Pavilion
The Gazebo
Halifax
BRADFORD
Bolling Hall
Shipley
Calverley Old Hall
LEEDS
Roundhay House
Garforth
Temple Newsam House
Lotherton Hall
Selby
W. YORKSHIRE
Oakwell Hall
Batley
Dewsbury
Red House Museum
Brighouse
Huddersfield
Wakefield Cathedral
Wakefield
Castleford
Ledston Hall
Pontefract
Nostell Priory
Ackworth School
Hemsworth
Birthwaite Hall
Barnsley
Cannon Hall
Cawthorne
Wentworth Castle
Wortley Hall
Stocksbridge
1830 Warehouse
Liverpool Rd Station
Jewish Museum
Law Library
Heaton Hall
Cathedral
SHEFFIELD
Conisbrough Castle
S. YORKSHIRE
Cusworth Hall
Doncaster
Brodsworth Hall
Goole
Thorne
Epworth Old Rectory
Rotherham
Clifton Park
Roche Abbey
Hodsock Priory
Worksop
Retford
Bishop House
Dronfield
Padley Chapel
Renishaw Hall
Staveley
Clumber Park
Peveril Castle
Eyam Hall
Buxton
Chatsworth
Revolution House
Chesterfield
Bolsover Castle
Bakewell Old House
Haddon Hall
Sutton Scarsdale
Hardwick Estate
Hardwick Hall
DERBYSHIRE
Clay Cross
Sutton in Ashfield
Hardstoft Herb Garden
Mansfield
Rufford Abbey
NOTTINGHAMSHIRE
Matlock
Lea Gardens
Cromford Mill
Kirkby in Ashfield
Newstead Abbey
Papplewick Hall
Hucknall
Norwood Park
Upton Hall
The Residence
Newark
Winkburn Hall
Tissington Hall
Ashbourne
Belper
Wingfield Manor
Ripley
Eastwood
Holme Pierrepont Hall
NOTTINGHAM
Nottingham Castle
Wollaton Hall
Ilkeston
Beeston
Kedleston Hall
DERBY
Long Eaton
Elvaston Castle
Belvoir Castle
Sudbury Hall
Tutbury Castle
Burton upon Trent
EAST MIDLANDS
Thrumpton Hall
Sutton Bonington Hall
Prestwold Hall
Wartnaby
Melton Mowbray
Loughborough
Melbourne Hall
Calke Abbey
Staunton Harold
Claymills Pumping Station
Catton Hall
Ashby-de-la-Zouch
Ashby de la Zouch Castle
Coalville
Old Rectory
Bradgate
Belgrave Hall
Abbey Pumping Station
Guildhall
Jewry Wall Museum
New Walk Museum
Newarke Houses
Wygston's House
Donington Le Heath
Kirkby Muxloe Castle
LEICESTER
Launde Abbey Chapel
Lyddington Bede House
Wigston
Hinckley
Arbury Hall
Bedworth
LEICESTERSHIRE
Market Harborough
Rockingham Castle
Stanford Hall
Rushton Triangular Lodge
Kelmarsh Hall
Rugby
Ryton
Coton Manor
Lamport Hall
Cottesbrooke Hall
NORTHAMPTONSHIRE
Wellingborough
Haddonstone
Holdenby House
Althorp
Daventry
Northampton
Northampton Cathedral
The Menagerie
Courteenhall
Canons Ashby
Olattercote Priory Farm
Edgcote
Farnborough Hall
Upton House
Sulgrave Manor
Stoke Park Pavilions
Broughton Castle
Banbury
St Peter & St Paul's Church
Swalcliffe Barn
Deddington Castle
Stowe
Milton Keynes
Buckingham Chantry Chapel
BUCKINGHAMSHIRE
Rousham House
Winslow Hall
Claydon House
Bicester
Ditchley Park
Blenheim Palace
Waddesdon Manor
Aylesbury
Boarstall Tower
Kidlington
Minster Lovell
Witney
Cogges Manor
Shotover House
Chilton House
Nether Winchendon House
Waterperry Gardens
Thame
Oxford
Botanic Garden
BRIZE NORTON
Stanton Harcourt Manor
Christ Church Cathedral & All Souls College
Princes Risborough Manor House & Market House
Hughenden Manor
OXFORDSHIRE
Kingston Bagpuize House
Abingdon
Rycote Chapel
Great Coxwell Barn
Milton Manor House
Didcot
West Wycombe Park
Tudor House
The Cottage
Priory Cottages
Ardington House
Kingstone Lisle Park
Stonor
Henley-on-Thames
Greys Court
Marlow
Fawley Court
Maidenhead
BERKSHIRE

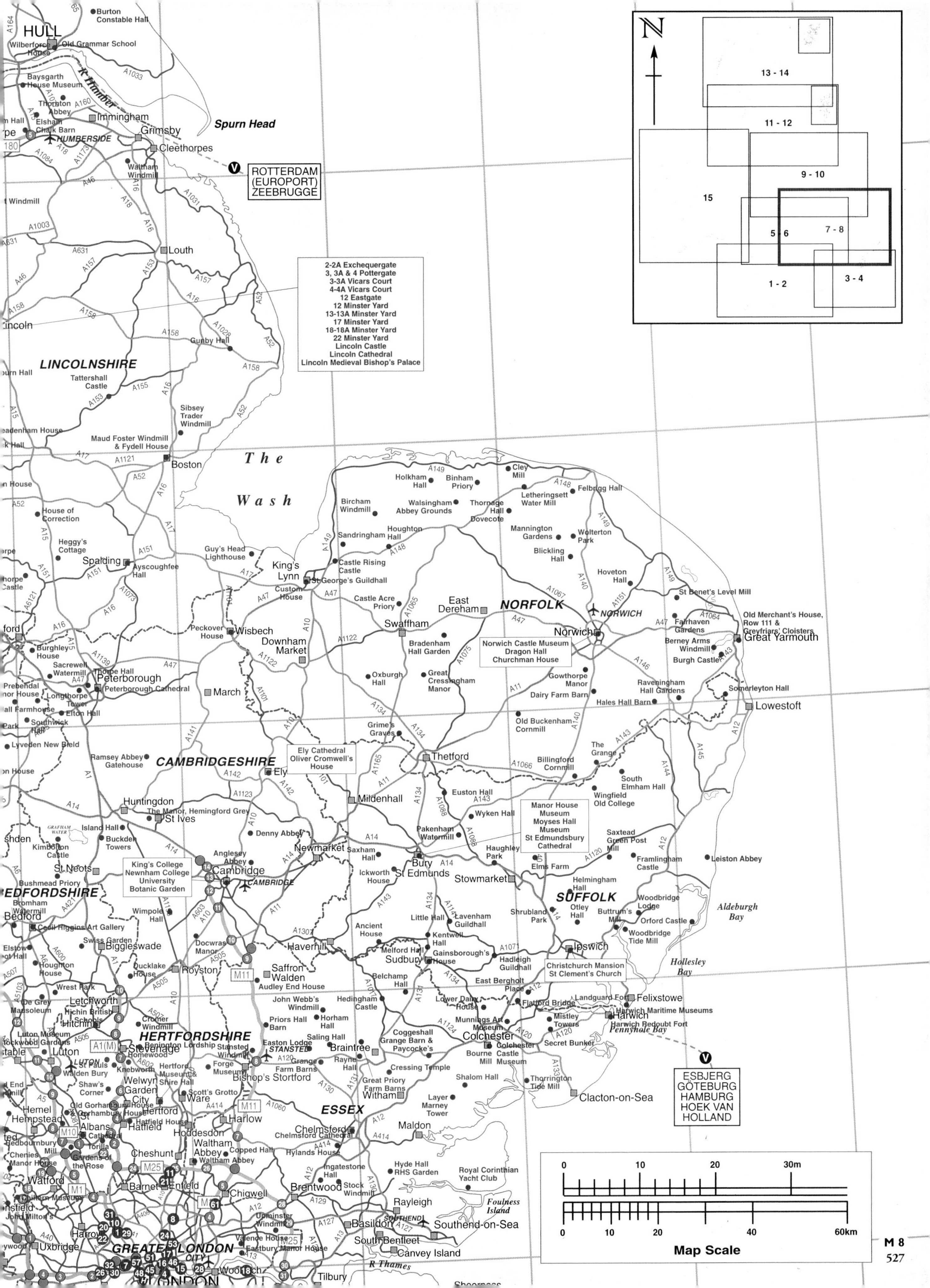
HULL
Burton Constable Hall
Wilberforce House
Old Grammar School
Baysgarth House Museum
Thornton Abbey
Elsham Hall
Chalk Barn
HUMBERSIDE
Immingham
Grimsby
Cleethorpes
Spurn Head
R Humber
ROTTERDAM (EUROPORT) ZEEBRUGGE
Waltham Windmill
Louth
2-2A Exchequergate
3, 3A & 4 Pottergate
3-3A Vicars Court
4-4A Vicars Court
12 Eastgate
12 Minster Yard
13-13A Minster Yard
17 Minster Yard
18-18A Minster Yard
22 Minster Yard
Lincoln Castle
Lincoln Cathedral
Lincoln Medieval Bishop's Palace
Lincoln
Gunby Hall
LINCOLNSHIRE
Tattershall Castle
Sibsey Trader Windmill
Maud Foster Windmill & Fydell House
Boston
The Wash
House of Correction
Heggy's Cottage
Spalding
Ayscoughfee Hall
Guy's Head Lighthouse
King's Lynn
St George's Guildhall
Custom House
Castle Rising Castle
Sandringham
Houghton Hall
Bircham Windmill
Walsingham Abbey Grounds
Holkham Hall
Binham Priory
Cley Mill
Letheringsett Water Mill
Felbrigg Hall
Thornage Hall Dovecote
Mannington Gardens
Wolterton Park
Blickling Hall
Hoveton Hall
St Benet's Level Mill
Castle Acre Priory
Swaffham
East Dereham
NORFOLK
NORWICH
Norwich
Norwich Castle Museum
Dragon Hall
Churchman House
Fairhaven Gardens
Old Merchant's House, Row 111 & Greyfriars' Cloisters
Great Yarmouth
Berney Arms Windmill
Burgh Castle
Bradenham Hall Garden
Oxburgh Hall
Great Cressingham Manor
Gowthorpe Manor
Dairy Farm Barn
Raveningham Hall Gardens
Hales Hall Barn
Somerleyton Hall
Lowestoft
Peckover House
Wisbech
Downham Market
Burghley House
Sacrewell Watermill
Thorpe Hall
Peterborough
Peterborough Cathedral
Prebendal Manor House
Longthorpe Tower
Elton Hall
Southwick Hall
Lyveden New Bield
March
Old Buckenham Cornmill
Grime's Graves
Ely Cathedral
Oliver Cromwell's House
Thetford
The Grange
Billingford Cornmill
South Elmham Hall
Ramsey Abbey Gatehouse
CAMBRIDGESHIRE
Ely
Mildenhall
Euston Hall
Wingfield Old College
Huntingdon
The Manor, Hemingford Grey
St Ives
Island Hall
Buckden Towers
Wyken Hall
Manor House Museum
Moyses Hall Museum
St Edmundsbury Cathedral
Denny Abbey
Pakenham Watermill
Saxtead Green Post Mill
Kimbolton Castle
St Neots
Anglesey Abbey
Newmarket
Saxham Hall
Bury St Edmunds
Haughley Park
Elms Farm
Framlingham Castle
Leiston Abbey
King's College
Newnham College
University Botanic Garden
Cambridge
CAMBRIDGE
Ickworth House
Stowmarket
Helmingham Hall
Bushmead Priory
BEDFORDSHIRE
Bromham Watermill
Bedford
SUFFOLK
Woodbridge Lodge
Otley Hall
Buttrum's Mill
Orford Castle
Aldeburgh Bay
Woodbridge Tide Mill
Wimpole Hall
Little Hall
Lavenham Guildhall
Shrubland Park
Cecil Higgins Art Gallery
Swiss Garden
Biggleswade
Docwra's Manor
Ancient House
Kentwell Hall
Haverhill
Melford Hall
Gainsborough's House
Sudbury
Hadleigh Guildhall
Ipswich
Christchurch Mansion
St Clement's Church
Hollesley Bay
Elstow
Houghton House
Ducklake House
Royston
Saffron Walden
Audley End House
Belchamp Hall
East Bergholt Place
Flatford Bridge
Landguard Fort
Felixstowe
Harwich Maritime Museums
Harwich
Harwich Redoubt Fort
Pennyhole Bay
Wrest Park
Letchworth
Hitchin British Schools
Hitchin
De Grey Mausoleum
John Webb's Windmill
Hedingham Castle
Lower Dairy House
Mistley Towers
Munnings Art Museum
Priors Hall Barn
Horham Hall
Cromer Windmill
HERTFORDSHIRE
Luton Museum
Wrockwood Gardens
Luton
LUTON
Stevenage
Benington Lordship
Stansted Windmill
STANSTED
Easton Lodge
Saling Hall
Coggeshall Grange Barn & Paycocke's
Braintree
Colchester
Colchester Castle Museum
Bourne Mill
Secret Bunker
ESBJERG GÖTEBURG HAMBURG HOEK VAN HOLLAND
St Paul's Walden Bury
Knebworth
Hertford Museum & Shire Hall
Forge Museum
Bishop's Stortford
Grange Farm Barns
Rayne Hall
Cressing Temple
Great Priory Farm Barns
Witham
Shalom Hall
Thorrington Tide Mill
Clacton-on-Sea
Welwyn Garden City
Shaw's Corner
Scott's Grotto
Ware
Hertford
Harlow
ESSEX
Layer Marney Tower
Hemel Hempstead
Old Gorhambury House
Gorhambury House
St Albans Cathedral
Hatfield House
Hatfield
Hoddesdon
Chelmsford
Chelmsford Cathedral
Maldon
Bedbourbury Mill
Chenies Manor House
Gardens of the Rose
Cheshunt
Waltham Abbey
Waltham Abbey
Copped Hall
Hylands House
Hyde Hall RHS Garden
Royal Corinthian Yacht Club
Watford
Barnet
Enfield
Ingatestone Hall
Brentwood
Stock Windmill
Chiltern Museum
Chigwell
Rayleigh
Foulness Island
John Milton's
Harrow
Upminster Windmill
Basildon
SOUTHEND
Southend-on-Sea
Uxbridge
GREATER LONDON
CITY
Valence House
Eastbury Manor House
South Benfleet
Canvey Island
R Thames
LONDON
Woolwich
Tilbury
Sheerness
13 - 14
11 - 12
9 - 10
15
5 6
7 - 8
1 - 2
3 - 4
0 10 20 30m
0 10 20 40 60km
Map Scale

EAST AYRSHIRE
Ayr
Burns Cottage
Culzean Castle
Crossraguel Abbey
Blairquhan Castle
Souter Johnnie's Cottage
Craig
SOUTH AYRSHIRE
Bargany Gardens
Drumlanrig Castle
Craigdarroch House
BORDERS
Jedburgh Abbey & Mary Queen of Scot's House
Drumlanrig Tower
Ferniehurst Castle
Craigieburn Woodland Garden
DUMFRIES AND GALLOWAY
Hermitage Castle
NORTHUMBE
Cragside
Herterton House
Wallington
Capheaton Hall
Belsay H
Gilnockie Tower
Dumfries
Rammerscales
Carlyle's Birthplace
Caerlaverock Castle
Coop House
Chipchase Castle
Chesters Roman Fort
Hadrian's Wall
Housesteads Roman Fort
Museum
Lanercost Priory
Vindolanda
High Meadows Cottage Barn
Hexham Moot Hall
Sweetheart Abbey
Shambellie
New Abbey Corn Mill
Threave Castle
Threave Garden
Castletown House
CARLISLE
Naworth Castle
Lambley Rail Viaduct
Causeway House
Corbridge Roman Site
High Staward Farm
Castle Kennedy Gardens
Glenwhan
Stranraer
Stranraer Castle
Glenluce Abbey
Cardoness Castle
MacLellan's Castle
Broughton House
Dundrennan Abbey
Carlisle
Carlisle Castle & Carlisle Cathedral
21-23 Leazes Terrace
Bessie Surtees House
Castle Garth
Cathedral Church of St Nicholas
Ardwell Gardens
Luce Bay
Logan Botanic Garden
Galloway House Gardens
Whithorn Priory
Solway Firth
Orthwaite Hall
Weardale Museum
Workington Hall & Helena Thompson Museum
Workington
Wordsworth House
Mirehouse
Hutton-in-the-Forest
Penrith
Penrith Castle
Acorn Bank
Dalemain
Brougham Castle
Appleby-in-Westmorland
Appleby Castle
Whitehaven
Bowes Museum
Barnard Castle
Egglestone Abbey
Brough Castle
Dove Cottage & Wordsworth Museum
CUMBRIA
Rydal Mount & Gardens
Hardknott Roman Fort
Stagshaw Garden
Townend
Muncaster Water Mill
Beatrix Potter Gallery
Steam Yacht Gondola
Holehird
Muncaster Castle
Abbot Hall Art Gallery
Hill Top
Kendal
Brantwood
Stott Park Bobbin Mill
Sizergh Castle
Levens Hall
Bolton Castle
Ulverston
Holker Hall
Furness Abbey
Leighton Hall
Warton Old Rectory
White Scar Cave
Barrow-in-Furness
Morecambe
Parcevall Hall
Isle of Walney
Heysham
Lancaster
Ashton Memorial & Maritime Museum
Knaresborough & Mother Ship
ISLE OF MAN
Douglas
Fleetwood
Skipton
Skipton Castle
Broughton Hall
Browsholme Hall
LANCASHIRE
Clitheroe
Stonyhurst College
Gawthorpe Hall
Martholme
Padiham
Colne
Nelson
Keighley
Brontë Parsonage Museum
Towneley Hall
Burnley
Blackpool
Preston
Samlesbury Hall
Blackburn
Accrington
Oswaldtwistle
Blackburn Cathedral
Rawtenstall
Todmorden
Lytham St Anne's
Hoghton Tower
Leyland
Darwen
Turton Tower
Rossendale Museum
Southport
Meols Hall
Rufford Old Hall
Chorley
Astley Hall
Smithills Hall
Hall i'th' Wood
Rochdale
Ormskirk
Skelmersdale
Standish
Bolton
Bury
Middleton
Formby
Wigan
Elm Wood School
Oldham
MANCHESTE
Bluecoat Chambers
Convent Conservatory
Croxteth Hall
Liverpool Cathedral
Liverpool Cathedral
Church of Christ the King
Turner Home
Crosby
Kirkby
MERSEYSIDE
St Helens
Lightshaw Hall Farm
Salford
Wallasey
LIVERPOOL
Warrington
Sale
Altrincham
Stockport
Bramhall
Birkenhead
Speke Hall
Dunham Massey
Cheadle
Widnes
Bebington
Port Sunlight
LIVERPOOL
Runcorn
Arley Hall
Tatton Park
Wilmslow
Knutsford
Norton Priory
Frodsham
Tabley House
Nether Alderley Mill
Adlington Hall
Hare Hill
Ellesmere Port
Northwich
Capesthorne Hall
Museums
Macclesfield
Gawsworth Hall
Peover Hall
Chester Cathedral
Chester Roman Amphitheatre
Town Hall
Watergate House
Chester
Rode Hall
Congleton
Little Moreton Hall
Biddulph
Leek
Beeston Castle
CHESHIRE
Sandbach
Crewe
Peckforton Castle
Biddulph
Kidsgrove
Ford Green
STOKE-ON-T
Woodhay
Nantwich
Newcastle-under-Lyme
Cholmondeley Castle
Dorfold Hall
Wrexham
Erddig
WREXHAM
Valle Crucis Abbey
Highfields
DENBIGHSHIRE
Tower
Hartsheath
Efenechtyd
Flint
FLINTSHIRE
River Dee
Ness
R Mersey
St Asaph Cathedral
Denbigh Castle
Rhuddlan Castle
Bodelwyddan Castle
Bodrhyddan
Gyrn Castle
Prestatyn
Rhyl
Colwyn Bay
Abergele
Llandudno
Great Ormes Head
Conwy
Aberconwy House
Conwy Castle
Plas Mawr
Bodnant Garden
Gwydir Castle
CONWY
Dolwyddelan Castle
Carmel Head
Anglesey
ANGLESEY
Holyhead
Holy Island
Beaumaris Castle
Wern Isaf
Bangor
Penrhyn Castle
Cochwillan Old Hall
Plas Newydd
Bryn Bras Castle
Caernarfon Castle
Caernarfon Bay
0 10 20 40m
0 10 20 40 60km
Map Scale

Dunstanburgh Castle
Howick Hall Gardens
Alnmouth Bay
Warkworth Hermitage
Warkworth Castle
Druridge Bay
Blyth
Seaton Delaval Hall
Tynemouth Priory & Castle
Whitley Bay
Arbeia Roman Fort
Tynemouth
South Shields
NEWCASTLE UPON TYNE
Jarrow
Souter Lighthouse
SUNDERLAND
Washington
Washington Old Hall
Houghton le Spring
Bede's World Museum & St Paul's Monastery
BERGEN STAVANGER
GÖTEBORG SUMMER ONLY
HAMBURG SUMMER ONLY
AMSTERDAM SUMMER ONLY
Crook Hall
Durham Cathedral
Durham Castle
Durham
Sherburn Hospital
Peterlee
Hartlepool
Hartlepoole Bay
Tees Bay
Billingham
Redcar
Auckland Castle & Deer House
Stockton-on-Tees
Middlesbrough
Turner's Hospital
Ormesby Hall
Darlington
TEESSIDE
Whitby
Whitby Abbey
The Pigsty
Robin Hood's Bay
Danby Watermill
Easby Abbey
Mount Grace Priory
Kiplin Hall
Northallerton
Ryedale Folk Museum
Scarborough Castle
Scarborough
Rievaulx Terrace & Temples & Rievaulx Abbey
Sion Hill Hall
Thorp Perrow Arboretum
Duncombe Park
Helmsley Walled Garden & Castle
Pickering Castle
Filey Bay
Byland Abbey
Shandy Hall
Nunnington Hall
Ampleforth College Junior School
Scampston Hall
Norton Conyers
Newburgh Priory
Hovingham Hall
Castle Howard
Ripon
Newby Hall
Flamborough Head
Sewerby Hall
Bridlington
Bridlington Bay
Burton Agnes Hall & Manor House
Aldborough Roman Town
Markenfield Hall
Kirkham Priory
Sutton Park
Sledmere House
Beningbrough Hall
Knaresborough
Harrogate
Brockfield Park
EAST RIDING OF YORKSHIRE
York
Spofforth Castle
Farnley Hall
Harewood House
Stockeld Park
Acorn Cottage
LEEDS & BRADFORD
Tadcaster
Clifford's Tower
Fairfax House
Merchant Adventurers' Hall
Merchant Taylors Hall
Lindley Murray Summerhouse
St William's College
Treasurer's House
York Minster
Beverley
Burton Constable Hall
Bramham Park
Roundhouse
LEEDS
Lingy Beeches
Garforth
Cawood Castle
Selby
Temple Newsam
HULL
The Old Grammar School & Wilberforce House
W. YORKSHIRE
Ledston Hall
Castleford
Batley
Dewsbury
Goole
Pontefract
Wakefield
Nostell Priory
Ackworth School
Thornton Abbey
Baysgarth House Museum
Normanby Hall
Humber
Elsham Hall
Elsham Chalk Barn
Immingham
Hemsworth
Thorne
Scunthorpe
HUMBERSIDE
Grimsby
Spurn Head
Cleethorpes
Barnsley
Brodsworth Hall
Epworth Old Rectory
ROTTERDAM (EUROPORT) ZEEBRUGGE
Doncaster
Cusworth Hall
Waltham Windmill
S. YORKSHIRE
Conisbrough Castle
Mount Pleasant Windmill
Clifton Park Museum
Rotherham
Gainsborough Old Hall
SHEFFIELD
Roche Abbey
Gainsborough
Louth
Bishop House
Hodsock Priory
Dronfield
Worksop
Retford
2-2A Exchequergate
3, 3A & 4 Pottergate
3-3A Vicars Court
4-4A Vicars Court
12 Eastgate
12 Minster Yard
13-13A Minster Yard
17 Minster Yard
18-18A Minster Yard
22 Minster Yard
Lincoln Castle
Lincoln Cathedral
Lincoln Medieval Bishop's Palace
Renishaw Hall
Staveley
Clumber Park
Revolution House
Chesterfield
Lincoln
Sutton Scarsdale Hall
Bolsover Castle
Doddington Hall
Gunby Hall
Hardwick Estate
Rufford Abbey
Carlton Hall
Aubourn Hall
LINCOLNSHIRE
DERBYSHIRE
Hardwick Hall & Old Hall
Mansfield
Sutton in Ashfield
Winkburn Hall
NOTTINGHAMSHIRE
Tattershall Castle
Matlock
Cromford Mill
Kirkby in Ashfield
Norwood
Upton Hall
Sibsey Trader Windmill
Newstead Abbey
Newark Townhall
Newark-on-Trent
Leadenham House
Ripley
Tissington Hall
Hucknall
Maud Foster Windmill & Fydell House
Ashbourne
Belper
Fulbeck Hall
Eastwood
Papplewick Hall
Ilkeston
NOTTINGHAM
Boston
The
Cley Mill
N
13 - 14
11 - 12
9 - 10
15
5 - 6
7 - 8
1 - 2
3 - 4

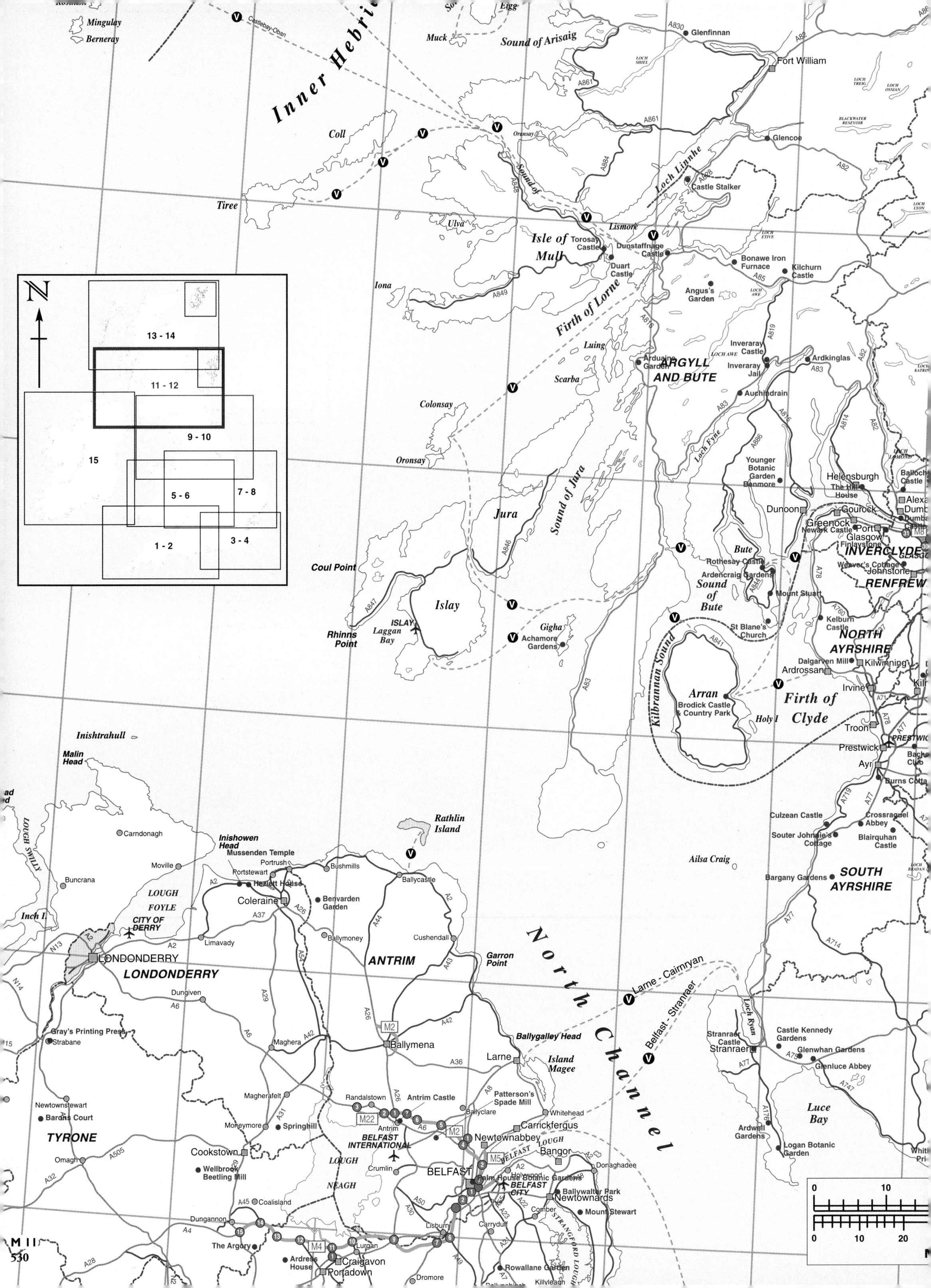
Mingulay
Berneray
Castlebay-Oban
Inner Hebrides
Muck
Eggs
Sound of Arisaig
Glenfinnan
Fort William
Loch Shiel
Loch Treig
Loch Ossian
Blackwater Reservoir
Coll
Oransay
Glencoe
Tiree
Sound of Mull
Loch Linnhe
Castle Stalker
Loch Lyon
Ulva
Lismore
Loch Etive
Isle of Mull
Torosay Castle
Dunstaffnage Castle
Duart Castle
Bonawe Iron Furnace
Kilchurn Castle
Iona
Firth of Lorne
Angus's Garden
Loch Awe
Luing
Inveraray Castle
Ardkinglas
Arduaine Garden
ARGYLL AND BUTE
Inveraray Jail
Scarba
Auchindrain
Colonsay
Loch Fyne
Loch Lomond
Oronsay
Younger Botanic Garden Benmore
Helensburgh
The Hill House
Balloch Castle
Dunoon
Jura
Sound of Jura
Greenock
Gourock
Newark Castle
Port Glasgow
Finlaystone
INVERCLYDE
Bute
Rothesay Castle
Ardencraig Gardens
Weaver's Cottage
Johnstone
RENFREW
Coul Point
Sound of Bute
Mount Stuart
Islay
ISLAY
Laggan Bay
Rhinns Point
Gigha
Achamore Gardens
St Blane's Church
Kelburn Castle
NORTH AYRSHIRE
Kilbrannan Sound
Dalgarven Mill
Kilwinning
Ardrossan
Irvine
Arran
Brodick Castle & Country Park
Holy I
Firth of Clyde
Troon
Prestwick
Ayr
Burns Cottage
Inishtrahull
Malin Head
Rathlin Island
Culzean Castle
Crossraguel Abbey
Souter Johnnie's Cottage
Blairquhan Castle
Lough Swilly
Carndonagh
Inishowen Head
Mussenden Temple
Ailsa Craig
Moville
Portrush
Portstewart
Bushmills
Buncrana
Hezlett House
Ballycastle
Bargany Gardens
SOUTH AYRSHIRE
LOUGH FOYLE
Coleraine
Benvarden Garden
Inch I.
CITY OF DERRY
Limavady
Ballymoney
Cushendall
North Channel
LONDONDERRY
ANTRIM
Garron Point
Larne - Cairnryan
Dungiven
Belfast - Stranraer
Loch Ryan
Gray's Printing Press
Strabane
Maghera
Ballymena
Ballygalley Head
Stranraer Castle
Stranraer
Castle Kennedy Gardens
Glenwhan Gardens
Larne
Island Magee
Glenluce Abbey
Magherafelt
Randalstown
Antrim Castle
Patterson's Spade Mill
Newtownstewart
Barons Court
Antrim
Ballyclare
Whitehead
Luce Bay
Ardwell Gardens
Moneymore
Springhill
TYRONE
BELFAST INTERNATIONAL
Carrickfergus
Newtownabbey
Logan Botanic Garden
Cookstown
Lough Neagh
Bangor
Omagh
Crumlin
BELFAST
Belfast Lough
Donaghadee
Wellbrook Beetling Mill
Holywood
Palm House Botanic Gardens
BELFAST CITY
Ballywalter Park
Newtownards
Coalisland
Comber
Mount Stewart
Dungannon
Lisburn
Carryduff
Strangford Lough
The Argory
Lurgan
Craigavon
Ardress House
Portadown
Rowallane Garden
Dromore
Killyleagh

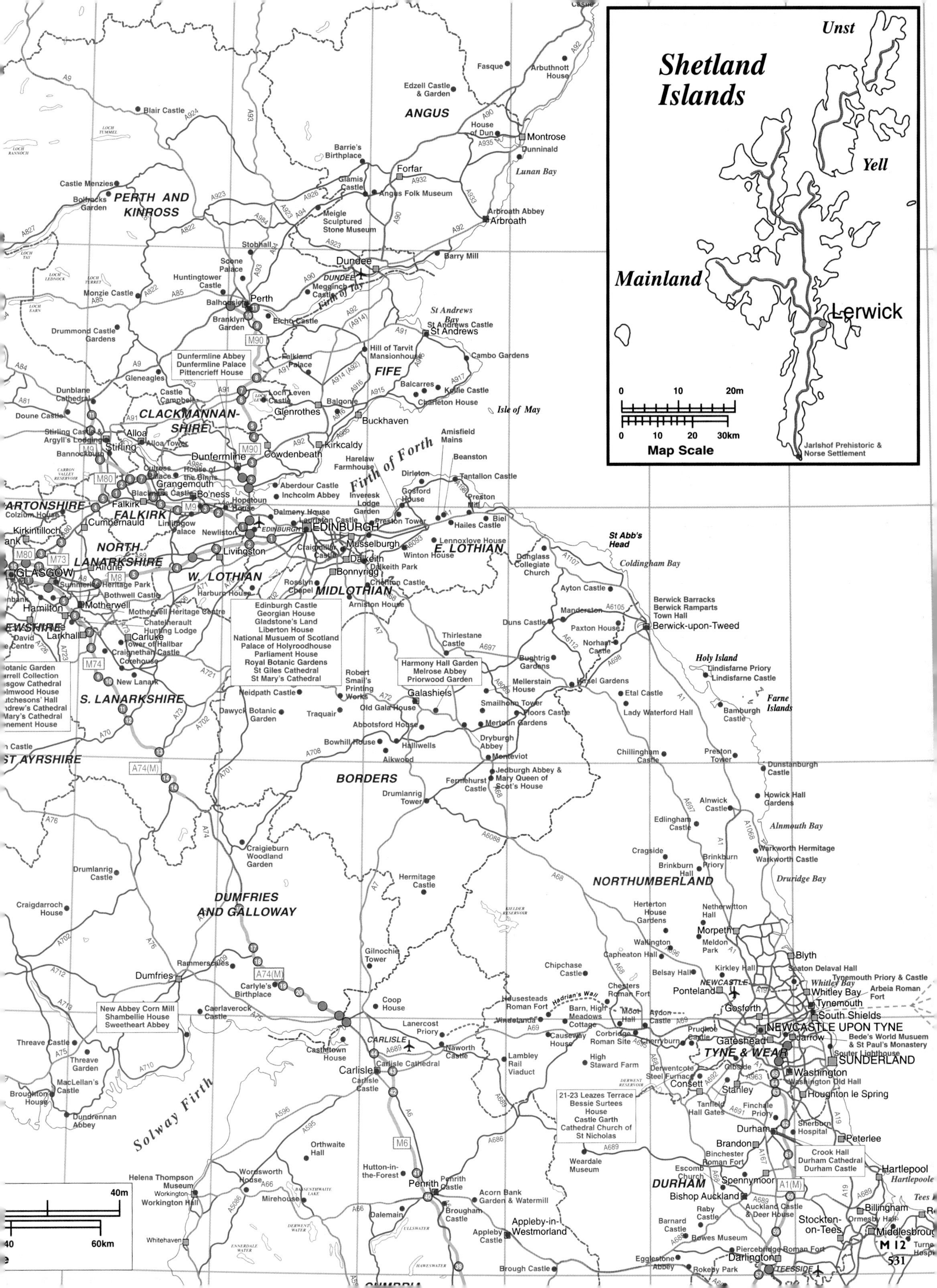

Shetland Islands
Unst
Yell
Mainland
Lerwick
Jarlshof Prehistoric & Norse Settlement
0 10 20m
0 10 20 30km
Map Scale
Fasque
Arbuthnott House
Edzell Castle & Garden
ANGUS
House of Dun
Montrose
Dunninald
Lunan Bay
Barrie's Birthplace
Forfar
Glamis Castle
Angus Folk Museum
Meigle Sculptured Stone Museum
Arbroath Abbey
Arbroath
Barry Mill
Blair Castle
Castle Menzies
Bolfracks Garden
PERTH AND KINROSS
Stobhall
Scone Palace
Huntingtower Castle
Monzie Castle
Dundee
Megginch Castle
Firth of Tay
Perth
Balhousie
Branklyn Garden
Elcho Castle
Drummond Castle Gardens
St Andrews Bay
St Andrews Castle
St Andrews
Hill of Tarvit Mansionhouse
Cambo Gardens
Dunfermline Abbey
Dunfermline Palace
Pittencrieff House
Falkland Palace
FIFE
Gleneagles
Dunblane Cathedral
Castle Campbell
Loch Leven Castle
Glenrothes
Balgonie
Balcarres
Kellie Castle
Charleton House
Isle of May
Buckhaven
Doune Castle
CLACKMANNAN-SHIRE
Alloa
Alloa Tower
Stirling Castle & Argyll's Lodging
Stirling
Bannockburn
Kirkcaldy
Cowdenbeath
Dunfermline
Amisfield Mains
Beanston
Harelaw Farmhouse
Firth of Forth
Dirleton
Tantallon Castle
Culross Palace
House of the Binns
Grangemouth
Bo'ness
Hopetoun House
Aberdour Castle
Inchcolm Abbey
Inveresk Lodge Garden
Gosford House
Preston Mill
Blackness Castle
Falkirk
FALKIRK
Cumbernauld
Linlithgow Palace
Newliston
Dalmeny House
Lauriston Castle
EDINBURGH
Preston Tower
Hailes Castle
Biel
Lennoxlove House
Winton House
E. LOTHIAN
St Abb's Head
Coldingham Bay
Dunglass Collegiate Church
Colzium House
Kirkintilloch
NORTH LANARKSHIRE
Livingston
Craigmillar Castle
Musselburgh
Dalkeith
Dalkeith Park
Bonnyrigg
GLASGOW
Airdrie
Summerlee Heritage Park
W. LOTHIAN
Rosslyn Chapel
MIDLOTHIAN
Crichton Castle
Arniston House
Bothwell Castle
Harburn House
Hamilton
Motherwell
Motherwell Heritage Centre
Chatelherault Hunting Lodge
Larkhall
Carluke
Tower of Hallbar
Craignethan Castle
Corehouse
New Lanark
Edinburgh Castle
Georgian House
Gladstone's Land
Liberton House
National Museum of Scotland
Palace of Holyroodhouse
Parliament House
Royal Botanic Gardens
St Giles Cathedral
St Mary's Cathedral
Ayton Castle
Berwick Barracks
Berwick Ramparts
Town Hall
Berwick-upon-Tweed
Manderston
Duns Castle
Paxton House
Norham Castle
Thirlestane Castle
Bughtrig Gardens
Holy Island
Lindisfarne Priory
Lindisfarne Castle
Harmony Hall Garden
Melrose Abbey
Priorwood Garden
Mellerstain House
Hirsel Gardens
Etal Castle
Farne Islands
Robert Smail's Printing Works
Neidpath Castle
Galashiels
Smailholm Tower
Floors Castle
Lady Waterford Hall
Bamburgh Castle
S. LANARKSHIRE
Dawyck Botanic Garden
Traquair
Old Gala House
Abbotsford House
Mertoun Gardens
Bowhill House
Halliwells
Dryburgh Abbey
Chillingham Castle
Preston Tower
Dunstanburgh Castle
AYRSHIRE
Aikwood
Monteviot
BORDERS
Ferniehurst Castle
Jedburgh Abbey & Mary Queen of Scot's House
Drumlanrig Tower
Howick Hall Gardens
Alnwick Castle
Alnmouth Bay
Edlingham Castle
Craigieburn Woodland Garden
Cragside
Brinkburn Priory
Warkworth Hermitage
Warkworth Castle
Drumlanrig Castle
Hermitage Castle
NORTHUMBERLAND
Druridge Bay
Craigdarroch House
DUMFRIES AND GALLOWAY
Herterton House Gardens
Netherwitton Hall
Morpeth
Meldon Park
Wallington
Gilnochie Tower
Capheaton Hall
Blyth
Chipchase Castle
Kirkley Hall
Seaton Delaval Hall
Belsay Hall
Tynemouth Priory & Castle
Whitley Bay
Arbeia Roman Fort
Dumfries
Rammerscales
Carlyle's Birthplace
Chesters Roman Fort
NEWCASTLE
Ponteland
Whitley Bay
Tynemouth
Hadrian's Wall
Housesteads Roman Fort
Vindolanda
Barn, High Meadows Cottage
Moot Hall
Aydon Castle
Gosforth
South Shields
Coop House
New Abbey Corn Mill
Shambellie House
Sweetheart Abbey
Caerlaverock Castle
Lanercost Priory
CARLISLE
Naworth Castle
Causeway House
Corbridge Roman Site
Cherryburn
Prudhoe Castle
NEWCASTLE UPON TYNE
Gateshead
Jarrow
Bede's World Museum & St Paul's Monastery
Souter Lighthouse
SUNDERLAND
Threave Castle
Threave Garden
Castletown House
Carlisle
Carlisle Cathedral
Carlisle Castle
Lambley Rail Viaduct
High Staward Farm
TYNE & WEAR
Derwentcote Steel Furnace
Gibside
Consett
Washington
Washington Old Hall
Stanley
Houghton le Spring
MacLellan's Castle
Broughton House
Solway Firth
Dundrennan Abbey
21-23 Leazes Terrace
Bessie Surtees House
Castle Garth
Cathedral Church of St Nicholas
Tanfield Hall Gates
Finchale Priory
Durham
Sherburn Hospital
Peterlee
Orthwaite Hall
Brandon
Binchester Roman Fort
Crook Hall
Durham Cathedral
Durham Castle
Hartlepool
Helena Thompson Museum
Workington
Workington Hall
Wordsworth House
Hutton-in-the-Forest
Penrith
Penrith Castle
Weardale Museum
Escomb Church
DURHAM
Spennymoor
Bishop Auckland
Auckland Castle & Deer House
Billingham
Mirehouse
Dalemain
Brougham Castle
Acorn Bank Garden & Watermill
Appleby-in-Westmorland
Appleby Castle
Raby Castle
Barnard Castle
Bowes Museum
Stockton-on-Tees
Ormesby Hall
Middlesbrough
Whitehaven
Piercebridge Roman Fort
Darlington
Egglestone Abbey
Rokeby Park
TEESSIDE
Brough Castle
40m
60km
M 12
531

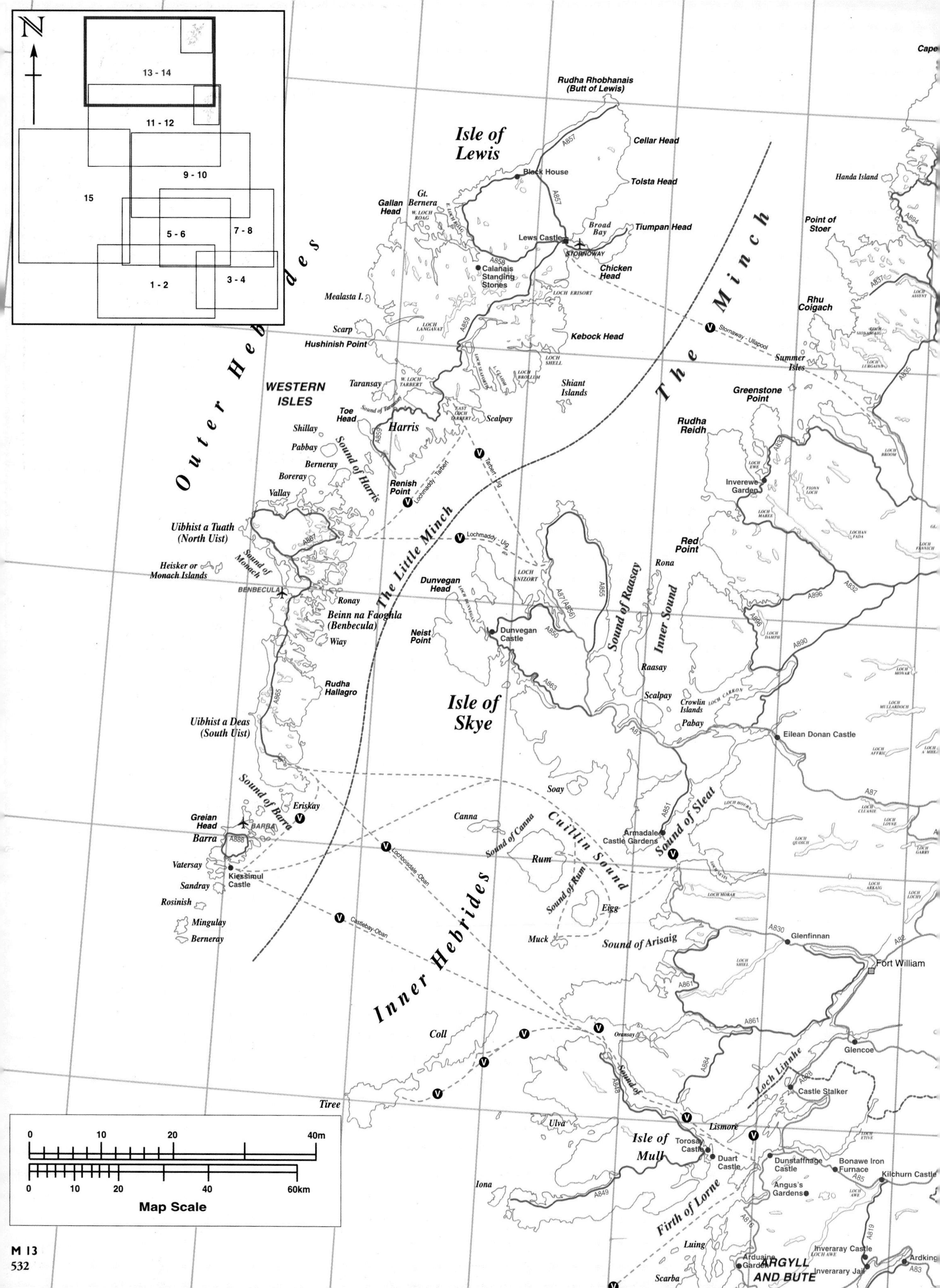

13 - 14
11 - 12
9 - 10
15
5 - 6
7 - 8
1 - 2
3 - 4
Rudha Rhobhanais (Butt of Lewis)
Isle of Lewis
Cellar Head
Black House
Tolsta Head
Gt. Bernera
Gallan Head
Broad Bay
Tiumpan Head
Lews Castle
STORNOWAY
Chicken Head
Calanais Standing Stones
Mealasta I.
LOCH ERISORT
Scarp
Hushinish Point
Kebock Head
LOCH SHELL
Taransay
Shiant Islands
WESTERN ISLES
Toe Head
Sound of Taransay
Scalpay
Harris
Shillay
Pabbay
Berneray
Boreray
Sound of Harris
Renish Point
Lochmaddy - Tarbert
Tarbert - Uig
Vallay
Uibhist a Tuath (North Uist)
Lochmaddy - Uig
Sound of Monach
Heisker or Monach Islands
BENBECULA
Ronay
Beinn na Faoghla (Benbecula)
Wiay
Rudha Hallagro
Uibhist a Deas (South Uist)
Sound of Barra
Eriskay
Greian Head
BARRA
Barra
Vatersay
Kiessimul Castle
Sandray
Rosinish
Mingulay
Berneray
Outer Hebrides
The Little Minch
The Minch
Stornaway - Ullapool
Dunvegan Head
LOCH SNIZORT
Neist Point
Dunvegan Castle
Isle of Skye
Sound of Raasay
Inner Sound
Rona
Raasay
Scalpay
Crowlin Islands
LOCH CARRON
Pabay
Soay
Canna
Sound of Canna
Cuillin Sound
Rum
Sound of Rum
Eigg
Muck
Sound of Sleat
Armadale Castle Gardens
Lochboisdale - Oban
Castlebay - Oban
Sound of Arisaig
Inner Hebrides
Coll
Tiree
Oransay
Ulva
Isle of Mull
Torosay Castle
Duart Castle
Iona
Sound of Mull
Lismore
Firth of Lorne
Luing
Scarba
Arduaine Garden
ARGYLL AND BUTE
Cape
Handa Island
Point of Stoer
Rhu Coigach
Summer Isles
Greenstone Point
Rudha Reidh
Inverewe Garden
Red Point
Eilean Donan Castle
LOCH HOURN
LOCH MORAR
LOCH SHIEL
Glenfinnan
Fort William
Glencoe
Loch Linnhe
Castle Stalker
Dunstaffnage Castle
Bonawe Iron Furnace
Kilchurn Castle
Angus's Gardens
Inveraray Castle
Inveraray Jail
Ardkinglas
A857
A858
A859
A865
A867
A888
A87
A850
A855
A863
A851
A830
A861
A82
A849
A848
A884
A828
A85
A816
A819
A83
A835
A832
A896
A890
A894
A837
0
10
20
40m
0
10
20
40
60km
Map Scale

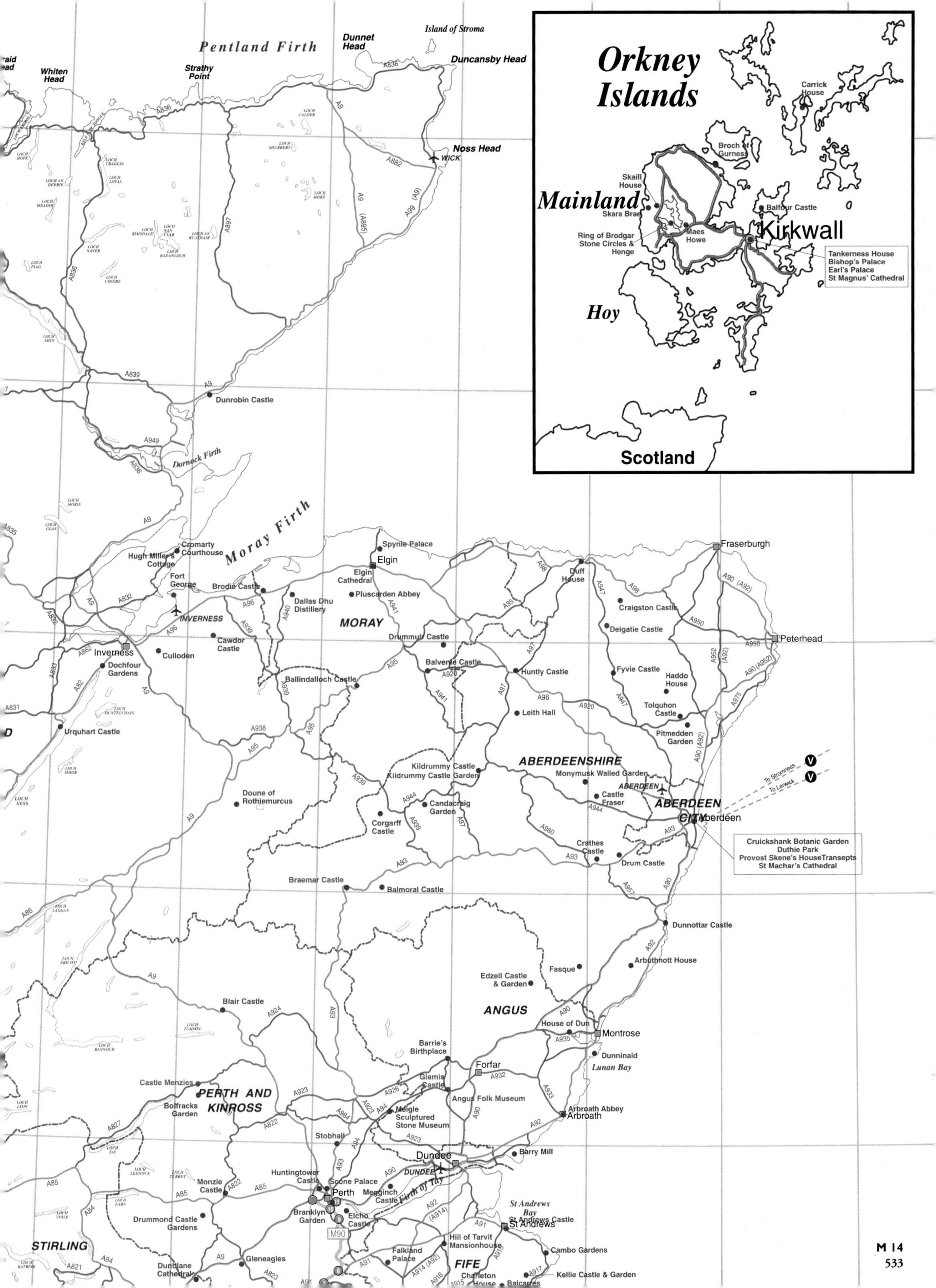
Orkney Islands
Mainland
Hoy
Scotland
Kirkwall
Carrick House
Broch of Gurness
Skaill House
Skara Brae
Balfour Castle
Maes Howe
Ring of Brodgar Stone Circles & Henge
Tankerness House
Bishop's Palace
Earl's Palace
St Magnus' Cathedral
Island of Stroma
Pentland Firth
Dunnet Head
Duncansby Head
Whiten Head
Strathy Point
Noss Head
WICK
Dunrobin Castle
Dornock Firth
Moray Firth
Cromarty Courthouse
Hugh Miller's Cottage
Fort George
Brodie Castle
INVERNESS
Inverness
Culloden
Cawdor Castle
Dochfour Gardens
Urquhart Castle
Spynie Palace
Elgin
Elgin Cathedral
Pluscarden Abbey
Dallas Dhu Distillery
MORAY
Drummuir Castle
Balvenie Castle
Ballindalloch Castle
Huntly Castle
Leith Hall
Fraserburgh
Duff House
Craigston Castle
Delgatie Castle
Peterhead
Fyvie Castle
Haddo House
Tolquhon Castle
Pitmedden Garden
ABERDEENSHIRE
Kildrummy Castle
Kildrummy Castle Garden
Monymusk Walled Garden
Castle Fraser
ABERDEEN
ABERDEEN CITY
Aberdeen
To Stromness
To Lerwick
Cruickshank Botanic Garden
Duthie Park
Provost Skene's HouseTransepts
St Machar's Cathedral
Doune of Rothiemurcus
Candacraig Garden
Corgarff Castle
Crathes Castle
Drum Castle
Braemar Castle
Balmoral Castle
Dunnottar Castle
Arbuthnott House
Fasque
Edzell Castle & Garden
ANGUS
Blair Castle
House of Dun
Montrose
Dunninald
Lunan Bay
Barrie's Birthplace
Forfar
Glamis Castle
Angus Folk Museum
Castle Menzies
PERTH AND KINROSS
Bolfracks Garden
Meigle Sculptured Stone Museum
Arbroath Abbey
Arbroath
Stobhall
Barry Mill
Dundee
DUNDEE
Huntingtower Castle
Scone Palace
Perth
Megginch Castle
Firth of Tay
Monzie Castle
Branklyn Garden
Elcho Castle
St Andrews Bay
St Andrews Castle
St Andrews
Drummond Castle Gardens
Hill of Tarvit Mansionhouse
Cambo Gardens
STIRLING
Gleneagles
Dunblane Cathedral
Falkland Palace
FIFE
Charleton House
Balcarres
Kellie Castle & Garden

N
13 - 14
11 - 12
9 - 10
15
5 - 6
7 - 8
1 - 2
3 - 4
Achamore Gardens
Mussenden Temple
Hezlett House
Benvarden Garden
Glenveagh Castle & Glebe House & Gallery
Newmills Corn & Flax Mills
LONDONDERRY
ANTRIM
DONEGAL
Gray's Printing Press
Donegal Castle
Baronscourt
Antrim Castle Gardens
Patterson's Spade Mill
Springhill
TYRONE
Wellbrook Beetling Mill
BELFAST
Palm House Botanic Gardens
Ballywalter
Mount Stewart
Donegal Bay
Lissadell House
Parke's Castle
Sligo Abbey
The Argory
Ardress
Rowallane Garden
Killyleagh Castle
Castle Ward
FERMANAGH
Castle Coole
Florence Court
Castle Leslie
DOWN
Seaforde Gardens
SLIGO
MAYO
Crom
MONAGHAN
ARMAGH
Hilton Park
Derrymore House
Boyle Abbey
King House
LEITRIM
ROSCOMMON
Colonalls House
CAVAN
Strokestown Park House
LONGFORD
LOUTH
Kylemore Abbey
GALWAY
Tullynally Castle
Ballinlouch Castle
Old Mellifont Abbey
Brú Na Boinne
WESTMEATH
MEATH
Pearce's Cottage
Aughanure Castle
Athenry Castle
Ardgillan Castle & Castle Garden
Lusk Heritage Centre
Newbridge House
DUBLIN
Malahide Castle, Fry Model Railway
Talbot Botanic Gardens
Clonmacnoise
KILDARE
Galway Bay
Dún Aonghusa
Lodge Park
Dunguaire Castle
OFFALY
Fernhill
James Joyce Museum
Powerscourt Estate
Casino
Castletown
Drimnagh Castle
Dublin's Writers Museum
Irish Museum of Modern A
Kilmainham Gaol
National Botanic Gardens
Newman House
Number Twenty-Nine
Powerscourt Town House
Rathfarnham Castle
St Audeon's Church
St Mary's Abbey
Shaw Birthplace
Portumna Castle
Birr Castle Demesne
Emo Court
Japanese Garden
Russborough
CLARE
Damer House & Roscrea Castle
LAOIS
Glendalough
Ennis Friary
Heywood Gardens
WICKLOW
Kilmacurragh
Cratloe Woods House
Lisnavagh
Dwyer McAllister Cottage
Scattery Island Centre
LIMERICK
TIPPERARY
CARLOW
Ram House Garden
Glin Castle
Rothe House & Kilkenny Castle
Ardfert Cathedral
Desmond Hall
Rock of Cashel
Cahir Castle & Swiss Cottage
Jerpoint Abbey
KILKENNY
WEXFORD
Ormond Castle
JFK Arboretum
WATERFORD
Curraghmore
Anne's Grove Gardens
Tintern Abbey
Dingle Bay
Ross Castle
KERRY
Muckross House
Ballyhack Castle
CORK
Riverstown House
Blarney Castle
Dunkathel
Barryscourt Castle & Fota Arboretum
Derrynane House
Kenmare River
Ilnacullin
Bantry House
Bantry Bay
Charles Fort & Desmond Castle
Timoleague Castle Gardens
St Davids Cathedral & St Davids Bishops Palace
CHERBOURG LE HAVRE
ST MALO SUMMER ONLY
ROSCOFF
CHERBOURG SUMMER ONLY
LE HAVRE SUMMER ONLY
Cork - Swansea
Rosslare - Pembroke
0 10 20 40 60m
0 10 20 40 60 80 90km
Map Scale

London Detail

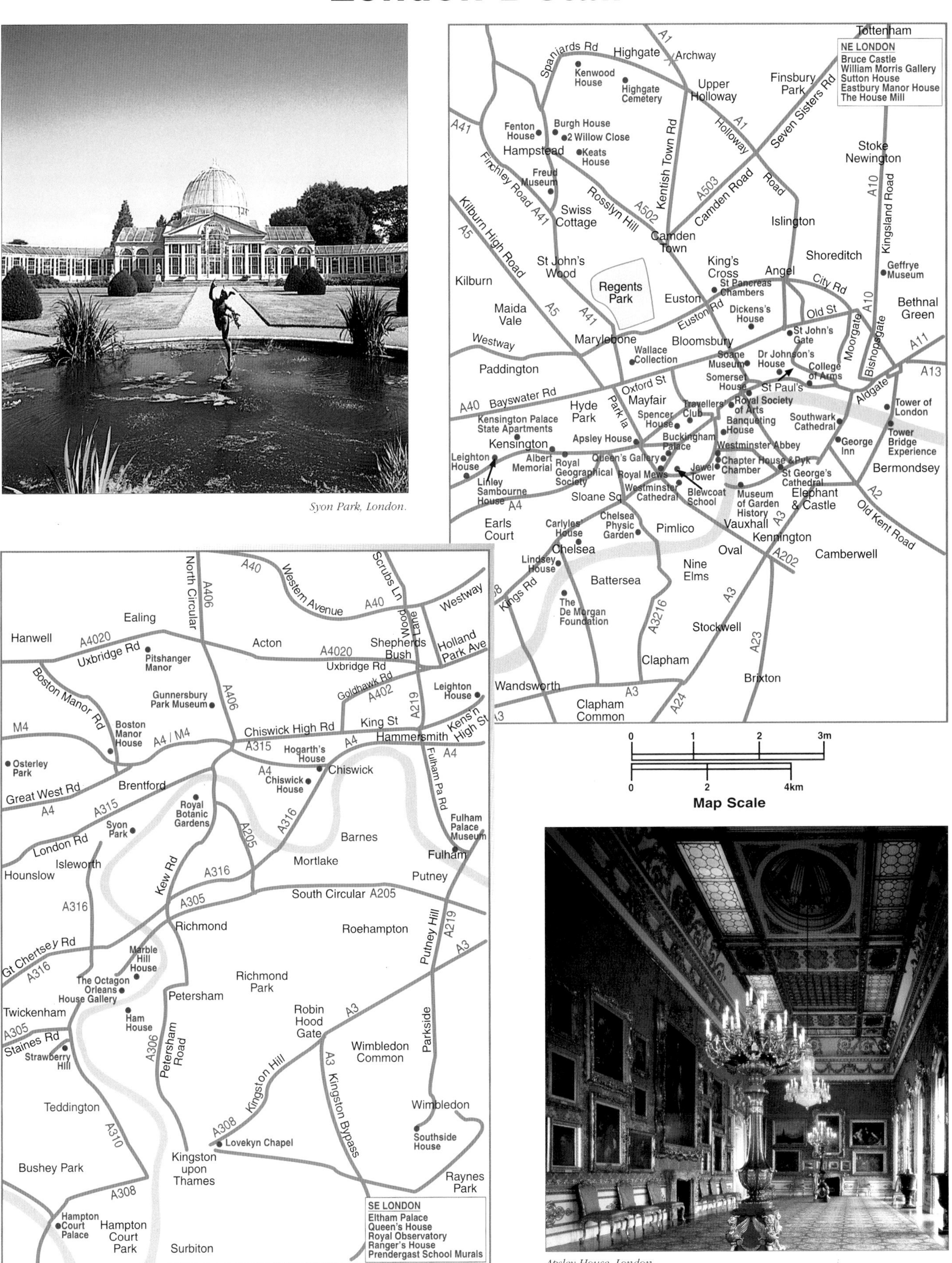

Syon Park, London.

Tottenham, Highgate, Archway, Upper Holloway, Finsbury Park, Spaniards Rd, Kenwood House, Highgate Cemetery, Stoke Newington, A1, A41, Fenton House, Burgh House, 2 Willow Close, Hampstead, Keats House, Freud Museum, Kentish Town Rd, Holloway, A1, A503, Seven Sisters Rd, Road, Kingsland Road, A10, Kilburn High Road, Finchley Road A41, Rosslyn Hill, A502, Camden Road, Islington, Shoreditch, Geffrye Museum, Bethnal Green, A5, Swiss Cottage, St John's Wood, Camden Town, King's Cross, Angel, City Rd, A10, Kilburn, Regents Park, Euston, St Pancras Chambers, Old St, St John's Gate, Moorgate, Bishopsgate, A11, A13, Maida Vale, A5, Euston Rd, Dickens's House, Dr Johnson's House, College of Arms, Aldgate, Tower of London, Westway, Marylebone, Bloomsbury, Soane Museum, St Paul's, Southwark Cathedral, George Inn, Tower Bridge Experience, Bermondsey, Paddington, Wallace Collection, Somerset House, Royal Society of Arts, Banqueting House, Westminster Abbey, Chapter House & Pyx Chamber, St George's Cathedral, Elephant & Castle, Old Kent Road, A202, A40, Bayswater Rd, Oxford St, Mayfair, Travellers' Club, Spencer House, Buckingham Palace, Jewel Tower, St George's Cathedral, Hyde Park, Park la, Apsley House, Queen's Gallery, Royal Mews, Westminster Cathedral, Blewcoat School, Museum of Garden History, Kennington, Camberwell, Kensington Palace State Apartments, Kensington, Royal Geographical Society, Sloane Sq, Pimlico, Vauxhall, Leighton House, Albert Memorial, Linley Sambourne House, A4, Earls Court, Carlyle's House, Chelsea Physic Garden, Chelsea, Lindsey House, Battersea, Nine Elms, Oval, A3, A3216, Stockwell, A23, Brixton, A24, Clapham, Wandsworth, Clapham Common, The De Morgan Foundation

Map Scale

0 — 1 — 2 — 3m

0 — 2 — 4km

A40, Western Avenue, North Circular, Scrubs Ln, Wood Lane, Westway, A40, A406, Ealing, Acton, A4020, Shepherds Bush, Holland Park Ave, Hanwell, A4020, Uxbridge Rd, Pitshanger Manor, Uxbridge Rd, Goldhawk Rd, A402, Leighton House, Wandsworth, Boston Manor Rd, Gunnersbury Park Museum, A406, Kens'n High St, A219, Boston Manor House, Chiswick High Rd, King St, Hammersmith, A4, Osterley Park, A4/M4, A315, Hogarth's House, Chiswick, Fulham Pa Rd, M4, Brentford, A4, Chiswick House, Fulham, Great West Rd, A4, A315, Royal Botanic Gardens, A316, Barnes, Fulham Palace Museum, London Rd, Syon Park, A205, Mortlake, Putney, Hounslow, Isleworth, Kew Rd, A316, South Circular A205, Roehampton, A219, A316, Richmond, Putney Hill, Gt Chertsey Rd, A316, A305, Richmond Park, A3, Marble Hill House, Robin Hood Gate, A3, Parkside, The Octagon, Orleans House Gallery, Petersham, Wimbledon Common, Twickenham, A305, Ham House, Petersham Road, A306, Kingston Hill, A3 Kingston Bypass, Staines Rd, Strawberry Hill, Teddington, A310, A308, Lovekyn Chapel, Kingston upon Thames, Wimbledon, Southside House, Bushey Park, A308, Surbiton, Raynes Park, Hampton Court Palace, Hampton Court Park

Apsley House, London.

Mount Stewart House, the Hall. National Trust Photographic Library/Peter Aprahamian

A

B

C

D

E

F

N

O

P

Q

R

S